BLOND'S

ENCYCLOPAEDIA OF EDUCATION

Blond's
ENCYCLOPAEDIA
OF EDUCATION

edited by Edward Blishen

BLOND EDUCATIONAL

First published 1969
by Blond Educational Ltd
56 Doughty Street
London WC1

© Blond Educational Ltd 1969

Printed in Great Britain by W. & G. Baird Ltd., Belfast.

Introduction

LIKE education itself, this book has a complex of aims. It sprang, in the first place, from our observation that there existed no single-volume work of reference covering the whole field of education, and from our feeling that such a work was desperately needed. It is needed by the young teacher and educationist especially, but also by their busy senior colleagues, by parents, and by all who wish to satisfy their curiosity about the educational scene but shrink (as they may well do) from trying to make their unguided way through the wilderness of the professional literature. Our first aim, then, was to pack into this volume as much information as it would hold about educational administration, teaching methods, legislation and reports, examinations, teaching aids, the primary schools, the secondary schools, further and higher education, the history and philosophy of education, and the scores of other topics into which education divides itself. We have tried to keep in mind the innumerable sorts of reader we might have: the young teacher wishing to know about the teaching of English or geography, or anxious for information about some professional issue; the layman wanting to check a newspaper reference to the Thorne scheme, or to zoning; the reader who wants to know about the whole area of further education—or who discovers that this is the field into which he is drawn by cross-reference when he consults the volume for information about regional colleges.

But as we went along we became aware of many subsidiary aims. Education, like other professional subjects, tends to produce its own ingrown jargon, a sort of mumbling to which the ear of the specialist has become attuned but which leaves other readers wondering what exactly is being said to them. We have tried, with the sympathetic help of our contributors, to keep this obscurer kind of educational language out of our pages. We have endeavoured, at the same time, to make this volume not only a readable guide to the past and the amazingly busy present of education, but a guide also to further reading and reference. We have aimed at being brisk and terse without being superficial; but in the book-lists that follow many of the articles we have tried to help the reader who, having read what we have to tell him, wishes to dig deeper into a subject.

Above all, however, two aims have emerged that have excited the editor, the contributors and all those others who have worked on the preparation of this encyclopaedia. The first of these aims is an effect of the turbulent quality of education today: it is in a state of constant growth, and this has demanded that we be as up-to-date as the needs of book-making would allow. The final form of many contributions has been left until the very last moment so that articles shall be as little stale as possible. The world of education now revolves so fast that we must be left behind, here and there; but we have aimed very carefully to limit the extent to which this must happen, and hope, by reasonably frequent revisions, to keep this encyclopaedia constantly close to the current state of things. The second of these aims arose directly out of the very enterprise of compiling such a volume as this. It has become a commonplace to lament the isolation of one part of the educational scene from another. The teacher shut in his classroom, and immensely busy there, tends not to know what is happening in subjects other than his own; the primary school knows too little about the secondary school; the schools altogether know too little about the world of further education. Too few have access to the latest research, the newest thinking. As this encyclopaedia grew we saw that we were, within the covers of a single volume, bringing together many of these uncommunicating parts of education: we were giving them a common platform. The aim of uniting the fragments of the educational enterprise within a single work of reference was certainly where we began: but the excitement of doing this is something we could not have guessed at until we actually set to work. We hope indeed that this volume will prove not simply a convenient handbook, but a means of bringing about contact between educational workers too often out of earshot of one another, and between them and the community they serve.

I thank Michael Holt, Lecturer in Mathematics, University of London Goldsmiths' College, for his permission to reproduce in the article on the new mathematics a glossary of symbols that first appeared in his book *What is the New Maths?* (Anthony Blond, 1967); and the Managing Editor of *Education* for his permission to reproduce in abridged form, as Appendix 2, a list and description of colleges of education that first appeared in the *Education Committees Year Book* 1967–68 (Councils and Education Press Ltd).

I am more indebted than I can easily express to many contributors whose help went well beyond what was strictly required by the contract between us; and to members of the publishing staff, whose sympathetic support was combined with readiness to question any obscurity to which my educationist's ear had become insensitive.

EB

Key to Contributors' Initials

For information about the contributors, see List of Contributors
at the end of this volume

DGOA	D. G. O. Ayerst	LAC	Lois A. Child
GEA	G. E. Allen	MC	Maisie Cobby
KA	Professor K. Austwick	NC	Nadine K. Cammish
NSA	N. S. Asbridge	AD	Alec Dickson
RA	Rene Adams	ADu	Anthony Dunk
WHGA	Professor W. H. G. Armytage	CD	Dr Charles Duddington
AJB	Instructor Rear Admiral A. J. Bellamy	HD	Professor Harry Davies
		JAD	Dr John Downing
BRB	Professor Bernard R. Blishen	JAMD	Joan A. M. Davis
CRB	C. R. Burrows	JCD	J. C. Dancy
DB	Donald Burrows	LJD	L. J. Drew
DBo	Derek Bowskill	RFD	R. F. Dearden
DBr	Derek Bryan	TJHD	Colonel T. J. H. Davies
EB	Edward Blishen	WD	W. Davies
FB	Frank Barraclough	WJD	W. J. Dickson
GB	Geoffrey Beaghen	HLE	H. L. Elvin
GBo	George Bott	JE	Joseph Edmundson
JB	J. Benjamin	RE	Reese Edwards
MB	Michael Brawne	RPAE	R. P. A. Edwards
MCMB	M. C. M. Binks	BF	Professor Boris Ford
NB	Nicholas Bagnall	HF	H. Fairhurst
RDB	Dr R. D. Bramwell	JF	J. Fairbairn
SAB	Dr S. A. Bridges	KEF	K. E. Foster
SB	Sydney Bolt	RF	Professor Ronald Fletcher
SEB	Dr S. E. Barnes	SF	Stanley Foster
BWC	B. W. Canning	SHF	S. H. Fisher
DEC	David E. Clark	BG	Brian Groombridge
HATC	H. A. T. Child	CJG	C. J. Gill
JBC	Dr Jeanette B. Coltham	DEMG	D. E. M. Gardner

A*

IG	Ivan Gray	PCJL	P. C. J. Likeman
NG	Nigel Grant	RL	Dr Royston Lambert
RG	Ronald Gulliford	SL	Dr Sonya Leff
RJG	Dr R. J. Goldman	AM	Angus Maude, MP
WAG	W. A. Grandage	AMo	Alan Morton
APH	A. P. Higgins	DEM	D. E. Mumford
DH	Professor Denys Hinton	DJM	D. J. Merriman
DJH	Derek J. Holroyde	DMcL	Donald McLean
DLH	D. L. Howard	EM	Edwin Mason
EH	Ernest W. Hawley	EMu	Elizabeth Mugridge
EJH	E. J. Hodges	JEM	John E. Merritt
GAH	G. A. Hicks	JM	Joyce Mpanga
GH	Geoffrey Herbert	MM	Margaret Miles
HH	Harold Haywood	PM	Philippa Macliesh
HWH	Dr H. W. Howes	RFM	Richard F. Morgan
JH	Dr James Hemming	TJM	T. J. McElligott
JHey	J. Heywood	TWM	T. W. Melluish
LMH	L. M. Harrod	WM	W. Murray
MHa	Melville Hardiment	YM	Yvonne Millwood
MHi	Michael Hirst	GWEN	Wing Commander G. W. E.
MTH	M. T. Haskew		Newby
PGHH	Philip G. H. Hopkins	OWN	O. W. Newport
RAH	R. A. Harrison	PSN	P. S. Noble
CJ	Charity James	ADCP	A. D. C. Peterson
DJJ	D. J. Johnston	DSP	Derek S. Pugh
FJ	Fred Jarvis	EMP	Elizabeth M. Pepperell
JAJ	Jack A. Jones	EP	Edwin Packer
JMJ	Mark James	HP	Hugh Pierce
NSJ	Dr N. S. Junankar	HPl	Henry Pluckrose
WJ	Walter James	JBP	John B. Prizeman
AK	Anthony Kamm	JCP	J. C. Poulton
HRK	H. Raymond King	LP	Leslie Paul
JK	James Kenyon	VP	Violet Philpott
SK	Professor Sumie Kobayashi	AJR	Dr A. J. Richmond
ZEK	Professor Z. E. Kurzweil	FR	F. Rubin
EL	Eric Linfield	GR	Geoffrey Richardson
HL	Harold Levy	JMR	Joan M. Russell
HLo	Helen Lowenthal	JRo	John Robinson
ILML	I. L. M. Long	KR	K. V. Russell
JAL	Professor J. A. Lauwerys	NLR	Neill L. Ransom
JALl	John Anthony Llewellyn	PER	P. E. Richmond
LJL	Professor L. J. Lewis	PR-J	P. Richards-Jones
LL	Leonie Lichtenstein	WBR	Dr W. Bonney Rust

WGAR	Dr W. G. A. Rudd	PEV	Professor P. E. Vernon
WKR	W. Kenneth Richmond	FW	Frank Worthington
BS	Professor Brian Simon	GLW	G. L. Williams
CHS	Ald. C. H. Sheill	IWW	Dr Iolowyn Williams
FS	Frances Stevens	JCW	J. C. Walters
GS	Geoffrey Summerfield	JDW	J. D. Williams
HS	H. T. Swain	JEW	John E. Watson
JCS	J. C. Stone	JHW	J. Helen Wheeler
LAS	L. A. Smith	JW	Joseph Weltman
LS	L. Syson	JWa	Jack Walton
MS	Michael Segal	KLW	K. L. Woodland
MSm	Baroness Mary Smirnoff	KSW	Keith S. Wheeler
RIS	R. Irvine Smith	MW	Dr Mary D. Wilson
ALT	A. L. Tibawi	SJW	S. J. Willis
JWT	Professor J. W. Tibble	SW	Shirley Williams, MP
NT	Nicholas Tucker		

A

A level This means General Certificate of Education (GCE), Advanced Level. In 1951 it replaced Higher School Certificate and was intended 'to provide a reasonable test in the subject for pupils who have taken it as a specialist subject for two years of sixth-form study' (1st SSEC report, 1947). The examination was made a subject examination (*q.v.*), subsidiary level was abolished and scholarship papers (now called special papers) were created 'with ample choice of questions not necessarily covering a substantially wider field of study than those in the Advanced papers, to give specially gifted pupils an opportunity for showing distinctive merit and promise'. In 1952, 40,482 candidates took A level papers: in 1964 the number was 87,787, reflecting the growth in importance of A level.

The matriculation and selection of university candidates has come to depend on A level performance, and industry, commerce and the professions prefer A to O level. This examination has become the objective of most sixth formers; they will normally take two or three subjects and receive a highly specialised education. This narrow specialisation and the nature of subject syllabuses has been much criticised. Indeed A level suffers, to a lesser degree, from some of the weaknesses of O level (*q.v.*): much work is done solely to be examined. A level is neither an accurate prognostication of university success nor a measure of an appropriate education for a sixth former.

Attempts at curriculum reform (*q.v.*) are, however, including A level within their scope, and the Schools Council is encouraging a re-examination of syllabuses. Their Working Paper No. 5, *Sixth-form Curriculum and Examinations* (HMSO, 1966) makes suggestions which would involve a considerable reform of A level, and the establishment of major and minor subjects, with time devoted to unexamined general studies. This would imply a possible return to subsidiary level.

See also **GCE**

HD

AAA *See* **Athletic Association, Amateur**

ABC *See* **Curriculum, Agreement to Broaden the**

Aberdare Report (1881) Terms of reference: to enquire into the condition of intermediate and higher education in Wales and to recommend measures for improving and supplementing available facilities.

The Report, which preceded the Welsh Intermediate Education Act 1889, concluded that the existing endowed grammar schools, which provided 2,846 places (of which 1,540 were taken up), were entirely inadequate for the population of about 1,500,000. It recommended that the schools be reconstituted to serve a wider section of the population, and governed by their representatives. It also recommended that there should

1

be less Anglican influence in schools serving a basically nonconformist population.

In higher education, the Report recommended the setting up of two more university colleges, which led to the foundation of the University College of South Wales and Monmouthshire at Cardiff (1883) and the University College of North Wales at Bangor (1884).

See also **Wales, Education in**

Ability, Theory of It is now thought that ability, defined roughly as the power to perform some more or less skilled act, is a generalised rather than a specific attribute in any one individual. That is to say, if an individual has any special aptitude, it is highly probable that he has a good measure of potential in other fields too, although perhaps not to the same extent. The idea of a general factor of intelligence was first put forward in the 1920s by an American psychologist, Professor Spearman. He called it 'g' (*q.v.*), rather than attempt to describe such a factor in words. Since then there have been many attempts to discover some of the more specific abilities with the aid of aptitude tests, and so far one of the clearest to have emerged is special ability, found in relatively few people. Other psychologists claim to have found number, reasoning, fluency, rote memory and verbal comprehension abilities, although it is still not clear how much these may be due to innate potential, and how much to cultural background and level of aspiration (*q.v.*).

FURTHER READING
P. E. Vernon. *The Measurement of Abilities*, Univ. of London Press, 1956.

NT

Absence from school *See* **School attendance**

Academic dress The costume worn on official occasions by members of a university, academic dress consists of gown, hood and cap. The undergraduate gown in most universities is black, but in some Scottish universities it is scarlet. Graduates commonly wear a long black gown, the hood being black with a coloured lining or edging (though at Oxford and Cambridge and several other universities, the hood has a trimming of white fur). Doctors have two forms of gown, for 'un-dress' and 'full dress' occasions. The first is black, with a coloured lining; the second is scarlet, faced with silk in a colour which indicates the faculty in which the doctorate was awarded. The doctor's hood is scarlet, with a coloured lining of silk. The headgear for lower degrees is usually a mortarboard, but for doctors it consists of a flat, brimmed cap of black velvet.

Academic freedom With academic freedom, as with such other freedoms as those of speech, worship and assembly, there are always two aspects to be considered: what it is that somebody wants or might want to do, and in what ways that desire might be impeded by others. Questions of academic freedom arise, therefore, when the desire to teach, study, research, publish and engage in associated activities is impeded. At a personal level, someone may be refused an appointment on irrelevant grounds of politics, race, religion or unorthodoxy, or restricted in the interpretation of what is proper to his function.

More widespread in their consequences, however, are restrictions on the academic freedom of institutions, usually by governments. It may be that a government wishes to suppress sources of criticism of itself, or to make the policies of academic institutions more closely reflect public policy. Numbers and categories of students admitted, the proportion of time spent on teaching rather than research, and the shape of future developments, are examples of possible areas of conflict.

In all such cases it is important to distinguish the formal powers available to government from what actually happens; for an apparent rigour of control may in fact not be exercised, while freedom which is formally greater may be accompanied by considerable indirect interference. The practical problem may therefore be said to be that of insulating proper academic pursuits from irrelevant pressures, while at the same time avoiding the abuse of public funds and ensuring a certain responsiveness to public policies.

RFD

Accidents, Royal Society for the Prevention of (RoSPA) The Society was founded in 1916. Its Safety Education Division is concerned with the pre-school child and the whole school-age range. It is interested in all aspects of accident prevention: on the roads, in the home, in school workshops and laboratories, on land, in and on water and at outdoor pursuit centres. Over 90% of LEAs subscribe to its Education Safety Service and over 30,000 copies of its journal, *Safety Education*, are distributed to schools each term.

Terminal House, 52 Grosvenor Gdns, London, SW1.

Accidents in schools
Accidents to pupils Legal liability to compensate pupils hurt in school or school activity would depend on whether or not it could be established that their injuries were a direct result of negligence on the part of the staff or the proprietor of the school. (In the case of the duty of care of the staff, see under **Law and the teacher.**) The proprietor of the school has a general duty of care under the Occupiers' Liability Act 1957, and in the case of an LEA, the Schools Amending Regulations 1965 provide that 'The premises of the school shall be kept in a proper state of repair, cleanliness and

hygiene and adequate arrangements shall be made for the health and safety of the pupils and staff in the case of danger from fire and other causes.'

The practical step on the occurrence of an accident will, of course, be the administration of first aid, and it is recommended in the Ministry of Education Pamphlet No. 13 *Safety Precautions in Schools* that all teachers should have a simple working knowledge of first aid and that it is very desirable that some members of the staff should have first aid qualifications. Skilled medical attention should also be secured with the minimum of delay in proper cases. In an emergency, it is probable that a teacher acting *in loco parentis* could give the necessary consent to an operation to a pupil. However, arrangements should be made for the contacting of parents in an emergency. The first duty of the school authorities is to the child, and the notification of the parents of an accident should not in any way delay the securing of proper medical attention.[1]

From a practical point of view, the important thing is to prevent accidents, and very useful guidance can be obtained from the DES publication *Safety Precautions in Schools* and the Administrative Memoranda of the Department relating to industrial safety and the Education Service.

When an accident occurs in a school, details should be entered in the appropriate form issued by the employing authority. In addition to this, if the circumstances of the accident give rise to the possibility that a teacher in the school might in some way be involved, that teacher should immediately contact his or her professional association.

Accidents to members of the staff The entitlement of the staff to compensation would depend on the existence of negligence on the part of the employing authority, its servants or agents. Apart from this, if the accident was sustained in the course of a teacher's employment, there would *prima facie* be an entitlement to industrial injury benefit under the provisions of the National Insurance (Industrial Injuries) Act 1946, and steps should be taken to register the injury as an industrial accident. In addition, the teacher should notify his or her professional association.

REFERENCE
1. Felgate v. Middlesex County Council per Cassels J. Unreported.

HP

Accountancy, Qualification in The minimum entry requirements of the various professional bodies concerned with accountancy are five or six GCE O level passes, which must include English and mathematics. The usual time taken to qualify is five years, and preparation for examinations must be combined with experience in an accountant's office. Graduates in any subject may become qualified after a period of employment with an accountant (the period varying between three and five years according to the quality and nature of the degree), together with part-time preparation for the professional examinations.

Institute of Chartered Accountants in England and Wales, City House, 56–66 Goswell Rd, London, EC1.

Accumulation A higher degree is said to have been achieved by accumulation when it and a lower degree in the same faculty are awarded at the same time.

Achievement test A standardised test used to assess knowledge and skill in any subject. An Achievement Quotient (AQ) is expressed as a percentile ratio of the achievement age to the chronological age.

Acland, A. H. D. (1847–1926) Appointed Vice-President of the Committee of Council on Education in 1892, Acland was the author of Circular 321 which set out certain building and sanitary conditions to which grant-earning schools must conform. He caused the leaving age for children at elementary schools to be raised to 12, and that for deaf and blind children to 16. His was the decision to appoint the Bryce Commission (*q.v.*) 'to consider what are the best methods of establishing a well-organised system of secondary education in England.' Acland also devoted himself to the encouragement of further education in evening schools, personally drafting the syllabus on the duties of a citizen, and securing that grants were given to the evening schools not on a basis of results but on the number of hours of instruction that were given.

Action research The simplest form of this kind of research is practised by the teacher trying out an idea in the classroom. The same technique is used at a more sophisticated level when a method is tried with pupils in a 'laboratory classroom' with the aim of determining how far it speeds up the learning process and contributes to understanding.

Activity A term used to describe a mode of learning in which the total area to be covered, as well as the ultimate objectives, may be less easily foreseen than in the case of a project (*q.v.*). Making, doing, moving about, were all somewhat over-emphasised in the early use of an activity: in many cases mental activity was not clearly seen as an activity.

Ad eundem degree A term meaning that a graduate of one university is admitted to the same degree in another university (from the Latin *ad eundem*— 'to the same').

Adams, Sir John (1857–1934) First professor of education in the University of London, and director of the London Day Training College from 1902 until

4

1922, Adams published in 1897 his book *The Herbartian Psychology Applied to Education*, a review of the ideas of Herbart (*q.v.*) that was welcoming but critical. In pressing the new claims of educational psychology, Adams wrote: 'Verbs of teaching govern two accusatives—the master taught John Latin. He must know Latin and he must know John. Not long ago it was considered enough for him to know Latin.'

Adaptive teaching machines *See* **Teaching machines; Programme, Extrinsic**

Aden and Southern Arabia, Education in 1965–6 statistics: 195 primary schools (enrolment 31,230); 38 intermediate schools (enrolment 8,878); 16 secondary schools (enrolment 7,099); two technical and vocational schools (enrolment 765); two teacher training colleges (enrolment 430). Population: approximately 1¼ million.

Adjustment to industry courses *See* **Leaving school**

Adler, Alfred (1870–1937) Alfred Adler was a Viennese psychiatrist and one-time colleague of Freud. He founded the school of individual psychology, which puts great emphasis upon the child's position in the family and the inferiority complex that can result from this, or from any organic or bodily indisposition. Such feelings of inferiority, common to almost every child at some point, can result either in over-compensation, as in the case of the small child who wants to be a great leader when he is a man, or else in a serious loss of confidence from which an individual may never recover. Treatment of very disturbed patients would involve their realising the reasons for their present 'life-style', and also its effects upon themselves and upon others. Such realisation can often bring about a change for the better, if this is done with the help and support of the psychiatrist.

Adler was also a pioneer both of child guidance clinics and of progressive education. Inspired by his ideas, an experimental school was founded in the poorest part of Vienna in 1931 where children were encouraged to work on individual projects and to share in school government. Teachers kept in close touch with psychiatrists treating any of their pupils, and classes were unstreamed to encourage a sense of community. A politically extremist government caused the school to close in 1934, although it was revived in 1946.

FURTHER READING
A. Adler. *What Life Should Mean to You*, Allen and Unwin, 1966.
Lewis Way. *Adler: An Introduction to hi· Psychology*, Penguin, 1956.

NT

Administration, Educational The public system of education in England and Wales is administered by LEAs. In the provinces the LEAs are the county and county borough councils; in the Greater London area they are the 20 London boroughs and the Inner London Education Authority. The public system of education was first created and developed by voluntary agencies, mainly the religious denominations. Progress was accelerated in the latter part of the 19th century by the creation of locally elected bodies, known as School Boards, with power to raise an education rate. School boards were succeeded in 1903 by LEAs which, in 1945, were restricted to county and county borough councils; London boroughs were added in 1965.

The political importance of the public system of education only painfully emerged, and it was not until the Education Act 1944 that the efforts of social reformers and local authorities for over a hundred years were recognised by the central government's assumption of responsibility for a national policy in education, and for the prescription of national standards to be executed and observed by LEAs under the control and direction of the Minister (now the Secretary of State) for Education. His powers and duties, and those of LEAs, are laid down by the law, which defines their obligations and their powers with respect to the public, parents, pupils, teachers, voluntary bodies, and the managers and governors of schools. The law also defines the rights and duties of these third parties.

The law gives the Secretary of State the power to enforce the national policy and the prescription of national standards in education by means of statutory directions, orders and instruments, by control of exchequer grants, and, in the last resort on application by him to the Courts, by mandamus. Subject to those qualifications, it is true to say that there are three main differences between the public system of education in England and Wales and that to be found in many other countries, namely: that here administration is decentralised; that here voluntary agencies play a prominent part; and that teachers here are free from official direction on methods of teaching and on curricula. Moreover, LEAs, voluntary bodies and teachers, mainly through their national organisations, play a prominent part in the formulation of national policy and are consulted by the Secretary of State on all matters of importance before he takes decisions.

LEAs build and own schools and colleges; maintain, supply and inspect their own establishments and voluntary schools; train, appoint and dismiss teachers and other staff; enforce school attendance; provide school meals and milk; supply a school health service; award scholarships; aid universities; regulate the employment of children and young persons; provide a youth service; and finance, with exchequer aid, all these and other ancillary services in education. They spend well over £1,400 m. a year on the running costs of the education services, and incur capital expenditure of about £160 m. a year for their development.

An LEA is required to appoint an education committee to which it may delegate all its powers relating to education, except the power to borrow money or to raise a rate. The extent to which LEAs delegate their powers to their education committees varies, but it is the education committee that is charged with the educational work of the LEA. To deal with the business of administration, it is necessary for the committee to appoint sub-committees for the different branches of the service; the sub-committees report to the education committee, whose meetings must be open to the public and the press.

In country areas administrative functions are also delegated to local divisional executives (q.v.), and schools generally have their managing and governing bodies.

At least a majority of every education committee must be members of the LEA, i.e. the elected members, councillors and aldermen. But the law also requires the appointment of co-opted members to every education committee. They must have educational experience and be acquainted with the educational conditions in the committee's area. Such a provision, permissive at the time when LEAs were created in 1903, became mandatory in 1945, and is most valuable. It enables the bodies with whom the education committee has to do daily business, e.g. voluntary schools and teachers, to be represented on the education committee and to take part in its discussions and voting. The presence of co-opted members greatly facilitates the local administration of the education service, even if that is not always fully appreciated by some councillors and aldermen who adhere to the view that only elected members should be allowed to serve.

A system of administration in which Parliament, the Secretary of State,

LEAs, their education committees and sub-committees, divisional executives, and managers and governors of schools, are all involved in the democratic control of education, is obviously complicated and time-consuming in reaching decisions and in executive action. The same goes for other local government services; that is why, time and again, the central government, which is responsible for the creation of the system and for its increasing complications, promotes elaborate inquiries with the object of reforming it. Three such inquiries are in process at the present time, the most important being the Royal Commission on Local Government, due to report in 1968.

In its evidence to the Royal Commission, the NUT recommended that head teachers should be regarded as full members of the governing bodies of schools, and that their power in matters of detailed administration should be increased. The NUT recommended also that an increase in the grant to voluntary aided schools should be accompanied by an increase of public control, through the LEA, which should either have more representatives on the governing body or should be able to apply greater safeguards in the matter of teachers' tenure of service.

A further recommendation was that, should single-purpose authorities be created for education, then some services not at present part of the education service should be so regarded.

A basic weakness in the present complicated system of the administration of the public system of education stems from the provisions made by Parliament in the Education Act 1944. In this day and age the central government must have the power to determine the national policy in education, and, because it is bound to cost a lot of money, must have the power to control both revenue and capital expenditure on it. Beyond that, it is only necessary that the Secretary of State should safeguard the interests of third parties,

and prescribe broadly the national standards to be observed in the administration of education. In fact, prescription in detail obtains, and minutiae are determined centrally. As a result, MPs deal with details formerly left to councillors, and the Secretary of State and his department determine matters formerly dealt with by the LEAs and their education committees. Perhaps only part of this change was made deliberately by Parliament in 1944, the rest inevitably following from the operation of Whitehall machinery, however good its intentions.

If it should prove possible to reform central government processes to eliminate the defects mentioned, thereby making local government more responsible and more interesting and attractive to its citizens, an essential condition may be the reform of local government itself. At present there are no fewer than 162 LEAs, the populations of whose areas range from as few as 18,000 to as many as three million, the majority having fewer than 200,000 people in their areas. The local dilemma can be stated quite simply. On the one hand there is the strong desire of civic leaders of small and medium-sized areas to control their own educational services; on the other hand there is an increasing demand for functional efficiency at local level, and for more specialised techniques in the administration and practical operation of local services, which only large authorities can supply economically.

Whether it is politically possible to resolve that clash of interests remains to be seen after the Royal Commission has reported. If it is decided to have many fewer LEAs, all sufficiently large, and with substantial financial resources to cope with the magnitude of their tasks, the result will be unsatisfactory unless the central government entrusts them with far wider powers than it now allows to LEAs. This would enable them in their turn to delegate more than rubber-stamping powers to bodies subordinate to them. Without a substantial change of that sort, local government cannot hope to appeal to a wider range of citizens to offer themselves for its service, and the old gibe that it attracts estate agents, speculative builders, landowners, lawyers, trade union officials and the retired, will persist.

FURTHER READING
P. H. J. H. Gosden. *The Development of Educational Administration in England and Wales,* Basil Blackwell, Oxford, 1966.
J. Stuart Maclure. *Educational Documents, England and Wales, 1816–1963,* Chapman and Hall, 1965.

FB

Admission to school *See* **Reception class**

Adolescence This is usually defined as the period between childhood and becoming an adult. It can be said to begin with puberty, and is thus associated with sexual maturation as well as with a general peak in mental and physical growth. All these physical changes happening at once can naturally be unsettling.

Socially, an adolescent often feels unattached either to the child or to the adult world, and this can lead to increased loyalty to a group of other adolescents, or to sudden enthusiasms for public figures such as pop singers or for political movements or religious ideals. This need to identify with something may be because the adolescent still feels socially insecure, and therefore needs the support of some group or movement. It is noticeable that adolescents seem to have more problems of adjustment in highly developed cultures where there is a long period between childhood and adulthood, often devoted to full-time study. In simpler societies, where young people at an early age take up their parents' way of life as a matter of course, typical adolescent frictions are harder to find.

Adolescence is also a time when a young person should start becoming interested in, and making relationships with, the opposite sex, although in early adolescence it sometimes appears that young people go through a slight and largely unconscious homosexual phase. Mentally, it is a time for increased powers of imagination, abstract thought and introspection, which can lead on to periods of mild depression and lethargy. It is a phase that some parents find very hard to deal with because unconsciously they may not wish their children to grow up and become independent, particularly if this involves increased criticism of the adult world around them. In this sense, some adolescent problems may be as much a result of older people's inability to deal with youngsters as of any problem posed solely by the adolescents themselves.

FURTHER READING
C. M. Fleming. *Adolescence,* Routledge and Kegan Paul, 1948.
James Hemming. *Problems of Adolescent Girls,* Heinemann, 1960.

NT

Adult education Adult education is inevitably the most compendious, heterogeneous and imprecise of all categories of educational provision. Unlike the others (primary schooling or higher education, for example), adult education does not cater for any particular academic level, it is provided by a large number of dissimilar agencies, and the age span it covers is exceptionally wide. In the UK today, adult education includes, at one extreme, classes with discreet titles, laid on by LEAs to teach adults to read or write (*See* **Adult illiteracy**), and at the other extreme, universities maintain the knowledge of graduate specialists at the peak of contemporary scholarship and research. Between these extremes it is possible to repair all kinds of educational deficiencies, due either to imperfections in schooling, to having left school too young, or to advances in knowledge itself. It is possible to undertake studies or pursue activities which, while they may be attempted in schools or colleges, make better sense to people with some experience of life—aspects of literature, political studies and history, parentcraft, for instance—or for which the need might not have made itself felt until adult life.

Until recently, most of its promoters identified 'adult education' with education for adults, which was non-vocational and did not lead to qualifications. This distinction is now breaking down at several points. Much adult education is expressly related to preparation for particular occupations, and there is a growing insistence from the public that it should be a route for recognised qualifications. Nevertheless, it cannot (yet) be equated with all education for adults. Even the definition of E. M. Hutchinson, Secretary of the National Institute of Adult Education (*q.v.*) while philosophically attractive, is more comprehensive in its scope than contemporary usage and practice: 'Adult education is the organised provision of learning situations to enable mature men and women to enlarge and interpret their own living experience.' At present, this provision takes five main forms, each tending to be associated with particular agencies offering distinctive programmes. There are many exceptions to all the generalisations that follow (especially in Scotland).

University-like education Provided mainly by long-term residential colleges, by university extra-mural departments (*q.v.*) and voluntary organisations working in association with universities, especially the Workers' Educational Association (*q.v.*). Birkbeck College, London (*q.v.*) offers degree courses for men and women who combine their studies with a full-time job, but, apart from mature intra-mural students, university adult education students are still not normally working for degrees. Some of them may be seeking vocational qualifications (e.g. in child care); others will be awarded diplomas (e.g.

in sociology, archaeology); but for the majority the study itself is its own reward. The subjects are those of the university curriculum, often adapted to take account of adult interests and needs; the level tends to be high; the style, especially as expressed in the tutor-class relationship, owes much to the Oxford tutorial tradition. The students are usually part-timers meeting once a week for terms or sessions of varying length. The eight long-term residential colleges in the UK accommodate over 500 students between them; there were 214,300 part-time students of university extra-mural departments and the WEA in 1965; in 1965–6 1,429 men and women (mature students (*q.v.*) rather than adult education students) were studying part-time at Birkbeck.

Secondary and further education for adults Provided mainly by LEAs and private correspondence colleges. People over 21 take part in all phases of further education, but there are two important points of growth: (1) An increasing demand for O and A level qualifications by adults, either for their own satisfaction or as means to vocational advancement. In the UK this is just beginning to happen; in the USA it is recognised and deliberately provided for as 'high school grade completion'; in Eastern Europe, it is called 'adult education at the secondary level' and is almost synonymous with what is meant there by 'adult education'. (2) The new occupations created by technological change lead to demands for adult training and retraining in such subjects as operational research, systems analysis, computer programming. While these new provisions are patently education for adults, it would as yet be unusual for the administrators responsible or for adult educationists to classify them as 'adult education'. In the UK as elsewhere, new types of provision are forcing their way through old and often

9

inappropriate concepts and institutional forms.

Education in activities and skills Classes in e.g. singing and acting, woodworking and flower arrangement, speaking French and keeping fit, are provided mainly by LEAs, some voluntary organisations with educational objectives and many others set up expressly to pursue specialised interests. These classes are the main part of what is often called non-vocational further education, through which LEAs discharge their responsibility (under the Education Act 1944) for 'leisure-time occupation, in such organised cultural training and recreative activities . . . for any persons over compulsory school age who are able and willing to profit by the facilities provided. . . .' Although more than half the students in all phases of further education provided by LEAs are over 21, the statistics do not distinguish mature men and women returning to further education after some experience of work or other adult responsibilities, and young people still preparing for their careers. It is estimated that there are some 1½ million participants in non-vocational further education in any year. There are thought to be about half a million who enrol for correspondence courses each year.

Social education There are several voluntary organisations which exist to promote active citizenship and to improve community life. They are themselves sociable organisations and running them is regarded as an integral and important part of their educational value. Chief among them are the National Federation of Women's Institutes, the National Union of Townswomen's Guilds, the National Council of Women, the National Association of Women's Clubs, the National Federation of Community Associations and the Guilds and other auxiliary organisations attached to the Co-operative Movement. The largest is the NFWI, with nearly 500,000 members.

Specialised education The four kinds of adult education listed so far are mostly organised by educational bodies, voluntary, statutory or independent. Organisations with other objectives also arrange educational programmes for the public or their own members. Thus education is a consciously fostered ingredient in the total activity of many social bodies (e.g. the YMCA), pressure groups (UNA, the National Federation of Consumer Groups, Oxfam and many others), religious institutions (e.g. the British Council of Churches, the Jewish Board of Deputies), industrial organisations (several trade unions, the Trades Union Congress, the Industrial Society and so on), and prisons.

Apart from the growing habit of co-operation between the agencies offering these five different kinds of education, there are three media of education which in a sense embrace them all: broadcasting, the so-called short-term residential colleges and educational centres. Broadcast adult education includes series on subjects similar to those taught by universities, colleges of further education, adult education institutes and the major voluntary bodies; similarly, the programmes of the short-term residential colleges and of (non-residential) educational centres (which may themselves be under various auspices—universities, the WEA, LEAs, voluntary bodies, or consortia representing all these) are likely to include seminars, courses or classes for which the university, the WEA, the LEA, a special interest organisation or the members themselves are responsible.

The long-standing involvement of the universities and of a number of major voluntary organisations in adult education is responsible for three of its characteristic virtues, which are gradually spreading into the other sectors: (1) a relationship of equality between teachers and taught (the mature experience of the students is valued along with the expertise of their tutors); (2) democratic organisation—not only do tutors plan syllabuses with students, but students also participate in programme planning and institutional management; (3) it is not surprising, therefore, that there has been a strong tradition urging the social responsibilities of adult education and of the people benefiting from it. The characteristic vices of British adult education are amateurism (organisers with other full-time jobs, recruiting tutors without training in educational method to conduct classes in makeshift premises for students whose work is not tested or evaluated), and separatism (many of the agencies involved have distrusted or simply ignored each other, so that scarce resources were wastefully deployed).

There are signs of progress—most agencies now believe training for adult education to be desirable; more LEAs are appointing full-time adult educationists; more agencies, often through ingenious interpretations of grant regulations, are building or converting premises designed for adults. Agencies and the professional associations involved are more ready to collaborate with each other than they were a few years ago. The characteristic virtues seem fortunately to be spreading while the vices are eroded. Demand for adult education, stimulated by the new dimensions of work and leisure among relatively prosperous people, consequently increases at a faster rate than the population itself.

ENROLMENTS BY STUDENTS OF 18 YEARS
OF AGE AND OVER

Year	LEAs (evening institute classes)			University extra-mural departments		
	M	W	T	M	W	T
	'000	'000	'000	'000	'000	'000
1961	208.6	488.3	696.9	46.9	54.2	101.1
1962	232.3	534.9	767.2	59.6	66.2	125.8
1963	236.4	560.1	796.5	57.8	63.1	120.9
1964	248.9	609.5	858.4	60.0	68.2	128.2
1965	291.3	689.4	980.9	63.2	72.0	135.2

Year	Workers' Educational Association			Short residential courses		
	M	W	T	M	W	T
	'000	'000	'000	'000	'000	'000
1961	29.2	44.2	73.4	17.4	19.0	36.4
1962	31.6	47.4	79.0	20.3	20.3	40.6
1963	31.9	47.0	78.9	20.9	20.2	41.1
1964	35.2	44.3	79.5	22.3	22.2	44.5
1965	34.1	45.0	79.1	21.5	23.1	44.6

M men; W women; T total.

In many phases of adult education women considerably outnumber men; in most, there is a strong tendency for participants to be drawn disproportionately from those sectors of the population in the higher socio-economic levels and with the most full-time education. The improved standards of endeavour and achievement owe much to the advocacy and research of the National Institute of Adult Education (q.v.) and of HM Inspectorate. They owe little to government initiative. Most post-war British governments have been indifferent or hostile to adult education (in marked contrast to those in the USA, Sweden, France, West Germany, the USSR and other nations). The imaginative but imprecise idea of an Open University (of the Air—q.v.) is virtually the sole sign at present of governmental enthusiasm for any aspect of adult education.

This indifference not only harms the development of adult education itself; it also inhibits planning for education as a lifelong process, thereby helping to put earlier phases of the education system under severe pressure, much of which is avoidable, and rendering quite impossible any re-organisation as fundamental as that implied in UNESCO's concept of Lifelong Integrated Education (q.v.).

It is still almost universal for British writers and speakers to equate 'education' with schools for children and colleges for adolescents and the young. The USA is familiar with the concept of 'continuing education'; the French now call it 'l'éducation permanente';

11

but meanwhile the narrowness of our child-biassed education encourages distorted educational policies and probably erects a barrier that prevents many adults from perceiving and satisfying their needs for education or re-education.

See also **Adult Education, National Institute of; Appendix 10**

FURTHER READING

J. F. C. Harrison. *Learning and Living, 1790–1960*, Routledge and Kegan Paul, 1961.
Thomas Kelly. *A History of Adult Education in Great Britain*, Liverpool Univ. Press, Liverpool, 1962.
Year Book of Adult Education, National Institute of Adult Education.
Periodical:
Adult Education (bi-monthly), National Institute of Adult Education.

BG

Adult Education, Association of Tutors in A national society for all who teach in the field of adult education whether as full-time or as part-time tutors. It also includes as full members administrators in extra-mural departments or in the Workers Educational Association, and tutors working in related fields under LEAs.

Gen. Sec.: A. J. Woolford, 1066 Green La., Temple Ewell, Dover.

Adult Education, European Bureau of The Bureau was set up in 1954. Its name should be taken literally; it is not a federation of European adult education agencies—it is a bureau, a clearing-house of information on their activities, and a service for Europeans engaged in the work, especially through stimulating developments and exchanging ideas. Despite modest resources, it has usefully focussed attention on the education and training of adult educationists by comparing projects in different countries, and it has explored the relevance of adult education (in its traditional north European identification with liberal education) to industrial change. For some of its recent enterprises the Bureau has had help from the Council of Europe, but it adheres to a geographical definition of Europe in its work, which would be harmed by partial political concepts of 'Europe'.

Apart from its occasional book-length reports, the Bureau regularly publishes *Notes and Studies* (four times a year) in English, French and German from its headquarters in the Netherlands, to keep professionals in touch with courses, conferences and relevant literature. It also publishes an annual calendar of residential short courses at which adults from more than one country can meet round a common interest or at which people from different countries can enlarge their knowledge of the European context of the particular countries in which the courses are held (*Meeting Europe*).

Hoflaan 22 (NH), Bergen, The Netherlands.

Adult Education, National Institute of (England and Wales) The NIAE, established in 1949 as the result of a merger between the National Foundation for Adult Education and the British Institute of Adult Education, exists primarily to provide backroom services for its corporate members, but in recent years it has been increasingly used by the general public as a point of reference. The heterogeneity of its aims and agencies makes adult education probably the only phase of education which requires such an institute. Its members include almost every LEA; the universities and adult colleges; voluntary organisations created expressly to provide educational opportunities for adults (such as the Workers' Educational Association, the Women's Institutes and Townswomen's Guilds), representatives of the educational branches of the Services, the Prison Department of the Home Office and other organisations not principally concerned with education (e.g. the British Council of Churches, the TUC and the Co-operative Union).

The NIAE is primarily (1) a medium of contact, consultation and co-operation between its members; (2) a source of information and ideas, especially through conferences and publications (including an annual directory of organisations, the professional journal *Adult Education* and the practical periodical *Teaching Adults*); (3) a centre for research and enquiry (a reference library on adult education is available to *bona-fide* students); (4) a channel of communication with the government; and (5) a point of international contact.

Twice a year the Institute publishes for the general public its *Calendar of Residential Short Courses*, a chronological listing of the programmes of the short-term residential colleges and others. Largely owing to lack of counselling facilities for adults elsewhere in the system, members of the public also seek the Institute's advice on the development of their careers and education, though the Institute was not set up for this function and is not at present geared to discharge it on any enlarged scale.

35 Queen Anne St, London, W1.

Adult Education, Universities Council for The UCAE was constituted in 1945 for the interchange of ideas and formulation of common policy on extra-mural education. It consists of two or more representatives from each of those universities and independent university colleges (at present 30 in number) which make formal provision for extra-mural work.

Adult education, Women in A remarkable feature of 20th-century adult education is the extent to which women participate in it. Women outnumber men in almost every type of adult education activity. In evening institutes there are roughly three women to every one man (in 1965 the actual numbers were 291,300 men, 689,400 women). Evening institutes provide many classes specifically for women—on aspects of housecraft, cookery, dressmaking and so on; but in general cultural courses which are open equally to men and women, women are still in the majority. Again taking the figures for 1965, total enrolments for university extra-mural classes were 63,200 men, 72,000 women. In Workers' Educational Association classes the difference was even greater: men numbered 34,000, women 45,000.

Two at least of the major women's organisations must also be included in any conspectus of adult education activity: the Women's Institutes have over 450,000 members; the Townswomen's Guilds over 200,000. The women's clubs affiliated to the National Association of Women's Clubs also have broad educational aims and there are other nation-wide organisations—Women's Co-operative Guilds, Young Women's Christian Association, National Council of Women, to name only a few—in which women are organising for themselves educational opportunities.

Desire for increased domestic competence is obviously one of the principal motives which bring women to the evening institutes. It might be argued that this is the equivalent of male vocational education, and that, to give a fair picture, other further education figures should be included.

Many women develop a strong desire for personal development, whether intellectual or artistic. Recent research has shown that the more education of this kind people have, the more they want. As more and more girls stay on at school, therefore, and go on to some kind of higher education, it seems likely that the proportion of women in these classes will increase still further. University extra-mural work originated as part of the movement for the higher education of women, and this movement towards equality has not yet lost its impetus.

The voluntary organisations, to which there is no male equivalent, are in one sense symptomatic of inequality. They can give a collective 'women's view', but they can also act as pressure groups and as instruments for promoting social awareness.

BG

Adult illiteracy Our society is run on the assumption that everyone can at least read 'Open this end' or 'Give way', and since every child in Britain is compelled to attend school for ten years, the assumption seems reasonable (apart from a tiny minority of ineducable children). Statistics are difficult to obtain and definitions of illiteracy disputable, but some experts believe that the proportion of children leaving schools unable to read and write is higher in Britain now than in 1939. Probably less than 5% of the population is absolutely illiterate, but semi-literacy is more widespread.

A brief reference on *Woman's Hour* (in 1966) to the possibility of introducing illiterate adults to suitable tutors drew about forty letters from women married to men whose illiteracy was blocking their promotion or preventing them from reading stories to their children. There are enough illiterate men and women in London to justify the regular provision of classes (tactfully advertised) at several adult education institutes, even though evening classes do not attract those illiterates (probably the majority) who are unwilling to reveal their predicament. (Evening classes for immigrant illiterates, for whom English is not the first language, tend to be well attended.) Cambridge House, the university settlement in South-East London, trains volunteers to teach adult illiterates privately, on a one-to-one basis. The 'students' are referred to Cambridge House from all over London by probation officers and other social workers and, as the grapevine spreads, by parents and spouses. At any one time, about 120 people are likely to be receiving lessons; some of these will stop prematurely, but of these 120, perhaps 40 will be 'discharged cured'. The volunteer tutors, mostly in their 20s or 50s, tend to be graduates (about a third), trained teachers (a third) and women (two-thirds).

BG

Adult learning If maturity and adulthood were synonymous, then to guide the learning experiences of adults would be easy. As persons they would be able to accept themselves for what they are without aggression or withdrawal, and accept others being different from them. They would have exchanged erratic, casual and shallow interests for deeper and more deeply sustained interests. To their learning they would bring a longer time perspective, not expecting all rewards to be immediate, and being able to digest frustration. They would be able to sustain in themselves unresolved differences of opinion and to be receptive to the unfamiliar and unattractive ideas of others. But because adults are not necessarily mature, much of their learning resembles the learning of children. In two respects, however, their learning is likely to be significantly different.

First, except in vocational studies, an adult's 'attendance' to a book, at a class, or on a course, is likely to be voluntary, and over an increasing range of subjects is unlikely to have the passing of an examination as its goal. Adult learning consequently depends upon people having a variety of goals satisfied, and the process of working towards these goals must in itself be satisfying. Students in adult classes or on adult courses want to learn to perform (paint, maintain their cars, speak a foreign language, etc.), or to make (coffee tables, eiderdowns, dresses, hats, etc.). Their motives may not be 'educational' or even social (they may want, for example, to save money), but their goals must be obtainable if learning is to continue. Persistence despite all the discouragements and difficulties that learning encounters cannot be engineered by the external reward of a diploma or a certificate but depends upon the extent to which the adults' basic psychological needs are satisfied, and those who organise adult learning situations must know what these needs are: acceptance, approval and praise from others, and an increase in their self-esteem. Organisers and tutors must try to avoid making people feel inferior or inadequate, breaking down tasks which would be too difficult for them. They should try to enable their students to progress and to receive praise and approval, and try to satisfy people's need for order and security by introducing new experiences cautiously and carefully, recognising that over-familiar, hackneyed material leads to boredom. Above all, perhaps, the organiser of adult learning attempts to satisfy people's need for some responsibility by helping them to assume more and more responsibility for selecting their own goals and for choosing the method by which to reach them.

The second respect in which adult learning is likely to be significantly different from child learning is that many of the subjects which an adult studies are those about which he has prior knowledge, some experience, and towards which he will have established attitudes. If the subject deals with any of the common and recurrent situations and objects in life (e.g. food, clothing, furnishings, recreation, human beings) adult students will, to some extent, be 'set in their ways'. The student in the cookery class, for instance, will not have an open mind towards the use of certain foods or to certain ways of preparing them for the table. And the student in a politics class is obviously likely to have difficulty with his prejudices.

The organiser of adult learning experiences will attempt to deal with this situation in two related ways designed to modify the adult student's attitudes.

1) He will seek to expose the adult learner to new information. In doing so he will try to ensure that the new information will not be seen to be too threatening lest it inhibits change. He will try to discover what his students want to be and want to do so that he can, if possible, show the new information as having instrumental value in helping them become and do what they want. And he will try in most instances to leave his students to draw their own conclusions from the new information, because they are more likely to resist the imperatives he derives from the information than the ones which they produce.

If the new information he presents is to be readily received, the person who presents it to adults or arranges that they be exposed to it must be regarded by them as trustworthy, attractive, and 'one of us'; he will avoid breaking promises, being slovenly and careless, and being remote from his students.

2) The teacher of adults who wants to modify his students' attitudes may use the adult class itself to modify the attitudes of the students who are its members. Much adult education is group-centred, not just because it is more economical to conduct it that way, but because without it, the modifying of students' attitudes would often be difficult and sometimes impossible to accomplish. For example, the mere provision of information about the virtues of offal has not persuaded many housewives to use it, nor has mere information about the nutritional values of cod liver oil and orange juice persuaded many mothers to feed it to their infants. But groups who have discussed this information and committed themselves to a decision, have changed significantly. So in the adult class student discussion and student decision will be encouraged in all those matters where fashion, taste and

inherited attitudes would otherwise inhibit learning.

WJ

Adult School Union, National This Union comprises some 18 county unions (each with its honorary secretary) and in all some 300 adult schools. The schools are old-established adult educational groups which seek, on the basis of friendship, to learn together and to enrich life through study, enhanced appreciation and social service. A vein of broad religious idealism runs through the work, which began in 1798 in Nottingham and throughout the 19th century owed a good deal to Quaker influence. The aim is a search for knowledge in an atmosphere of reverence, and the achievement of unified personal living.

The NASU issues annual study handbooks for its groups to work through. It also arranges summer schools, special lecture-schools (both non-residential and residential), overseas guided visits and a variety of other educational gatherings. There are a number of guest houses situated in ideal surroundings for holiday and educational courses. A monthly magazine, *One and All*, provides information and topical articles on a wide range of subjects and gives news of the school-groups and county unions. An international committee arranges visits abroad and sponsors special projects of international service for both young and old. Young people's activities are arranged to suit the tastes and needs of younger members.

Local groups meet once a week or even fortnightly, usually on hired premises, their own premises, or in members' homes. There is no professional teaching service, but skills of chairmanship and leadership are always valued when available. The movement is entirely self-supporting, though a number of charitable trusts make modest contributions to the maintenance of the national office, the area

lecture services, and general extension work.

Drayton Hse, Gordon St, London, WC1.

Adult schools Adult schools are groups of men and women who meet with the aim of learning together. As a rule there is no regular professional teaching: the schools mostly take the form of study circles which follow a curriculum outlined in the annual *Study Handbook*, published by the National Adult School Union (*q.v.*), which also publishes a magazine, *One and All*. Emphasis is laid on the relation of religion to the social problems of the day. The movement has a long history: the schools first spread rapidly in the early years of the 19th century, when the aim was principally to teach the poor to read and write, the most accessible book for the purpose being the Bible. The standard history is G. C. Martin's *The Adult School Movement* (1924).

Adults, Residential courses for *Long-term* Men and women who have not been to a university have an opportunity of studying under similar conditions in the long-term residential colleges for adults. There are eight of these colleges in Britain: their aims and auspices differ, but all offer courses which last one or two years, often leading to a university diploma. Conditions of entry vary, but a number of scholarships are available each year and students are eligible for grants from their local authority. The colleges are Coleg Harlech, Harlech; Co-operative College, Loughborough; Fircroft College, Birmingham (for men only); Hillcroft College, Surbiton (women only); Newbattle Abbey, Dalkeith; Plater Hall, Oxford; Ruskin College, Oxford; Woodbroke College, Birmingham.

Short-term A new development in adult education since the second world war is the foundation of a number of colleges (currently about 30) which offer courses lasting anything from a weekend to a fortnight. Many of these colleges are directly sponsored by LEAs, some by voluntary organisations and some by universities. The subjects offered vary very widely (though some colleges specialise); most courses are open to anyone without qualifications and fees are often surprisingly modest. A complete list of courses, with dates and prices, is published twice a year by the National Institute of Adult Education, 35 Queen Anne St, London, W1.

BG

Adventure holidays *See* **Youth hostelling**

Adventure Playground Association, London Set up in 1962, the Association aims to raise money for existing adventure playgrounds in London; to assist groups that wish to open new playgrounds; and to promote and publicise the concept of the adventure playground. The chairman, Lady Allen of Hurtwood, is founder of the adventure playground movement in the UK. A major object of the LAPA is to establish the status of adventure playground leaders as part of the Youth Service or the educational system.

Sec.: Hon. Mrs Viney, 4 Lansdowne Rd, London, W11.

Adventure playgrounds An adventure playground has been defined as 'one where most of the site can be used by children for games of their own invention; where a variety of tools and materials are provided, and where children can rely on the backing of a capable and friendly adult . . .'[1]

Introduced to this country by Lady Allen of Hurtwood and pioneered by voluntary bodies operating on temporary sites, the idea of the adventure playground led to a number of experimental projects in the 1950s, grant-aided by LEAs and such bodies as the National Playing Fields Association and the Nuffield Foundation.

The efforts of the children themselves proved that constructive play is both desirable and practical. Den building, previously a prohibited activity, was developed by children into increasingly imitative and responsible patterns of social play: houses, shops, police stations, hospitals and fire departments.

The success of the early experiments attracted the interest of LEAs and, as more money became available for this kind of work, play huts were introduced into the various schemes. As a result, many playgrounds began to o erate throughout the whole year.

Adventure playgrounds do not provide a structured programme of activities. Tools and scrap materials of all kinds are introduced, and the children are free to pursue their own particular interests under the unobtrusive guidance of the play leader. While the outdoor opportunities remain adventurous, and often controversial, the provision of play huts has enabled children to develop a wide range of art and craft skills, from painting and pottery to cooking, sewing and editing their own magazines. The opportunities provided through the medium of play have led the children to other fields of activity: cleaning windows and redecorating rooms for old people, sawing logs, and carrying out minor maintenance tasks of many kinds.

The social and educational value of this approach to play is now being increasingly recognised, and many LEAs throughout the country are either establishing schemes of their own or are more generously grant-aiding local voluntary groups.

REFERENCE
1. Mary Nicholson. *Notes on Adventure Playgrounds*, National Playing Fields Association, 1954.

FURTHER READING
Lady Allen of Hurtwood. *Adventure Playgrounds*, National Playing Fields Association, 1965.

Joe Benjamin. *In Search of Adventure*, National Council of Social Service, 1966.
H. S. Turner. *Something Extraordinary*, Michael Joseph, 1961.

JB

Adviser A specialist appointed to advise an LEA and its teachers on the teaching and organisation of a subject or stage of education.

Advisory Centre for Education Founded in 1960, with Dr Michael Young as its chairman and Brian Jackson as its director, ACE aims to disseminate information on education to parents, teachers and students and anyone interested in education. Its journal *Where* is published six times a year. Members may use the ACE Advisory Service, which covers a wide range of educational topics. ACE also publishes books, runs residential courses, and conducts educational experiments.

57 Russell St, Cambridge.

Advisory teachers Peripatetic advisers who, under some LEAs, work beside teachers in the classroom.

Aegrotat A certificate of illness produced by an examination candidate (from the Latin meaning 'he is ill'). By the use of the term is indicated the examiners' view that, although the candidate was absent from the whole of the exam, he has nevertheless been deemed to have passed.

Afghanistan, Education in Education is compulsory where places are available. Secondary schools exist only in Kabul and capitals of the provinces. 1965/6 statistics: 2,086 primary schools (enrolment 403,285). There are two universities at Kabul (enrolment 3,384) and Nangrahar (enrolment 70).

The country's population in 1966 was nearly 16 million.

Africa, East, Education in Kenya, Uganda and Tanzania have national systems of elementary and secondary education, with some institutions of higher education. University education, formerly controlled by the East African Common Services Organisation, is now in the hands of the East African Community, formed in December 1967. The British colonial past has made for similarities in the educational systems of each country, and in the problems which they face.

Kenya, with an area of 582,644 sq. km., has a population of 9·6 million and a population density of 17 per sq. km. Tanzania, with an area of 939,701 sq. km. and a population of 10·8 million, has a population density of 12 per sq. km. Uganda has an area of 236,036 sq. km., a population of 7·7 million, and a population density of 33 per sq. km. Over 45% of the population in each country is under 15 years of age, and the population growth is at the rate of about 2·5%. Wealth is not evenly distributed, and a large section of the community is economically unproductive. The pattern of settlement, and social conditions, make it necessary that secondary education should be conducted in boarding schools.

Before independence, African education was pioneered by missionaries. Their main aim was to convert Africans to Christianity and as soon as possible to produce the manpower necessary to make their parishes self-sufficient. Every other aim in education was subordinate to this one.

The Kenyan government was the first to establish, in 1911, a department of education together with a system of grants in aid to the voluntary agencies that ran schools. With this acceptance of financial responsibility came government control of the policy and standard of education. The government of Tanganyika (the mainland of what is now Tanzania) and Uganda followed with the same policy in 1925 after the Phelps Stokes Commission of 1922. Because of this policy, most of the outstanding schools in East Africa are mission-owned.

Education was provided separately and unequally for the different racial groups that lived in East Africa. For instance, in Kenya (which offers the clearest example of this arrangement) there were Europeans, Asians, Arabs and Africans. The Europeans went to government, grant-aided and private schools, where the content of education was that of similar schools in the UK. For higher education, they went either to South Africa or the UK. The Asians provided their own education, helped by the government grants in aid, and with further assistance from the Aga Khan's Ismaili community. African education was run by missionaries and other religious agencies, and was therefore arranged on denominational lines. Arrangements in Uganda and Tanganyika were similar, except that in these countries there was no secondary education for Europeans, who had to go to Kenya for it. European secondary education was finally established in Tanganyika in 1954. Arabs and Somalis in Tanganyika attended African schools. Compulsory education was found only in Kenya, and then only for Europeans between seven and 15 and Asians of the same age-group living in Nairobi, Kisumu and Mombasa. This discriminatory law was repealed in 1963.

It can be said, therefore, that until independence there were in East Africa several systems of education; they were racial and provided different facilities, goals, standards, curricula and examinations. Even the government grants did not follow a common pattern. The educational structure was similar. In each country on the eve of independence, elementary education covered a period of eight years; with the important difference that in Uganda children who dropped out after the first elementary stage had received six years of schooling, as against four years in the other two countries. For Europeans, secondary education was automatic. For the rest, the secondary entrance examinations filtered out only the fittest few for the places available. Even with the greatly increased number of places offered today, the three countries can provide secondary education only for 10% of their primary school leavers. The limiting factors are the scarcity of secondary school teachers, the absence of money for expansion and the fear that the economy might not grow fast enough to absorb all secondary school leavers.

Today, education has been integrated, so far as both race and religion are concerned, to produce a single system for each nation. Elementary education has been reduced to seven years throughout East Africa. The teaching of English begins much earlier in the primary school than it used to; and about 60% of the children of primary school age are in schools. The aim is to make elementary education universal by 1980.

Secondary education lasts for six years. The syllabuses followed are agreed on by the East Africans and the Cambridge Local Examination Syndicate, which is the examining body. Forms I to IV lead to the Cambridge School Certificate or GCE O level. Forms V and VI exist only in a few selected secondary schools, and the work of these forms leads to Higher School Certificate or GCE A level. The East African Examination Board will soon take over the functions of the examining body. Secondary education has been widened to include more technical and commercial education at separate institutions or in the existing secondary schools. Since 1963 secondary education has been free in Tanzania for those able to gain places.

In the field of higher education, Makerere University College at Kampala, Uganda, was founded in 1922 and has been awarding London University external degrees since 1953. This was the only college in British East and Central Africa until 1963, when the

University of East Africa was formed with three constituent colleges. All have faculties of arts and science. The University College of Nairobi offers engineering, art and architecture, veterinary science, education and special professional studies such as business studies and domestic science. The University College of Dar-es-Salaam offers law, while Makerere has faculties of medicine, agriculture, fine art, social science, law, education. Since East Africa is not a federation, the time will clearly arrive when each university college will become a national university.

Teacher training was formerly organised largely by voluntary agencies, but the East African governments now take a more direct responsibility. There are today roughly three levels of teacher training. Primary school teachers must train for four years after completing primary education, or for two years after O level. To meet the demand for secondary teachers, there is three years' training for those with a better O level certificate, or two years after A level; teachers so trained are qualified to teach the lower classes in secondary schools. Other classes are in the hands of graduate teachers. Under a Teachers for East Africa scheme originally intended for American graduates, British and Commonwealth graduates are trained for a year at Makerere and then teach in one of the three countries for two years. Each university college has an institute of education for teacher education.

Adult education is outside the educational system and is the concern of the Ministry of Community Development in each country. The extra-mural department of each university college makes arrangements for university and pre-university courses for adults. Many mature students qualify through such courses.

JM

Africa, North, Education in Beneath the façade of national states in North Africa, the essential and deeper link between the countries and peoples from Cairo to Rabat is not really the European notion of nationalism but the bonds of Islam and the Arabic language, first forged in the seventh century AD, while nationalism in the European sense is barely half a century old. Islam has always been not only a religious faith but also a way of life, a civilisation and a culture. In addition to its rich literature, Arabic became the repository and the vehicle of propagating the Islamic heritage. The alliance between Islam and Arabic is a fundamental fact of Arab life to which nationalism itself had to be adjusted. There can scarcely be real Arab nationalism or true Arab education without Islam.

Muslim education in the classical age was predominantly religious. In the countries here discussed, as elsewhere in Arab lands, its handmaid was always Arabic. This classical education survives to this day in primary schools known locally under different names, but more prominently in higher schools, the most famous of which are the Qarawiyyin at Fez, the Zaitunah in Tunis and the Azhar in Cairo. While the first two remained until recently parochial, the third has developed into a full-scale university for the whole Muslim world. It is reputed to be the oldest in the world.

The introduction of education on European lines began in Egypt in the first half of the 19th century. New schools were established parallel to the traditional schools. The aim was military not academic—to produce army officers. The move was initiated by a governor who established himself as semi-independent ruler acknowledging the suzerainty of the Ottoman sultan. The traditional schools were left alone; they were affected only indirectly when they were combed for suitable recruits as pupils, teachers, or eventually as scholars to be sent for further training to Europe.

This form of educational modernisation was carried out by a Muslim ruler, but another form was imposed almost simultaneously by a Christian power as a result of conquest. In 1830 France pounced on Algeria, then acknowledging the suzerainty of the Ottoman sultan. In the field of education French was imposed as a language and as a medium of instruction, almost always at the expense of Arabic. The curriculum was radically changed, not so much for the development of Islamic and Arabic culture, as for forcing French civilisation and culture on the inhabitants.

In 1881 France forced a protectorate on Tunisia and in 1912 also on Morocco. In both countries a milder educational policy than in Algeria was followed, because of the difference in political status between protected states and a conquered country whose territory was incorporated in metropolitan France. But there was no essential difference in the practical application of the French educational policy and its overriding aim of promoting French language and culture.

After occupying Egypt in 1882, Britain followed no comparable aim of 'anglicising' the young generation through education. But even English writers have been very critical of the British record, and of the neglect to develop either the modern state system or to promote the modernisation of the traditional schools. They expected the schools to aim only at the production of junior government officials in annual numbers that could be absorbed. The British were, however, more tactful than the French in managing, or rather omitting to manage, religious affairs including schools and foundations.

In 1912 Italy attacked the territory now known as the Kingdom of Libya and began a long war of conquest of a country that was a province of the Ottoman Empire. But even when peace with Italy was signed, the fight was continued by a religio-political order whose members were carefully educated and initiated in a chain of traditional schools. When finally fascist Italy subjugated the country, it followed on the whole a policy similar to that adopted by France in Algeria, both in administration and education.

With the emergence of completely independent national states, first in Egypt and finally in Algeria, educational reconstruction and expansion was one of the main concerns of the national governments. They had, however, to accept or seek to overcome, among others, two major difficulties: the incorporation of the traditional religious schools in the national modern system, and the 'decolonisation' of the modern schools, particularly as regards curricula and language of instruction. The second problem was found harder to tackle in the former French spheres of influence, which demonstrates how determined was the French effort. There is now little trace of the English influence in Egypt, and the Italian influence in Libya was obliterated by the British military authorities.

The character of the present education in the national states is professedly Arab nationalist, but beneath this veneer the Muslim character and the Arab cultural heritage, itself very profoundly Muslim, are unmistakable. Though several of its modern aspects were inspired or imposed by Europe, there is now so wide a disillusionment with Europe that henceforth Arab education in North Africa may look for inspiration either inward or eastward, to its roots.

ALT

Africa, Portuguese, Education in
Angola In 1963 there were 2,019 primary schools (enrolment 104,213); 74 secondary schools (enrolment 9,554); 32 technical schools (enrolment 5,003); eight ecclesiastical colleges (enrolment 610). In 1965 there were altogether 3,023 schools (enrolment 258,431). The

University at Caixas Postais had 500 students. Angola had a population of nearly 5 million in 1965.

Mozambique In 1962 there were 4,172 primary schools (enrolment 452,880); 63 secondary and technical schools (enrolment 12,088); two teacher training colleges. The University of Mozambique at Lourenco Marques had 603 students. Total population was approximately 6¾ million in 1962.

Cape Verde 1963 statistics list 135 primary schools (enrolment 16,992); two secondary schools (enrolment 1,076); two technical schools (enrolment 440). Population: approximately 220,000 (1963).

Portuguese Guinea In 1963 there were 13 primary schools (enrolment 2,058); one secondary school (enrolment 744); one technical school (enrolment 498). Population in 1963 was approximately 550,000.

São Tomé and Príncipe Islands In 1962–3 there were 30 primary schools (enrolment 4,952); one secondary school (enrolment 583); one technical school (enrolment 91). Population in 1963 was nearly 60,000.

Africa, West, Education in The education systems of the West African countries are based upon foundations laid by the Christian missionaries, gradually modified by increasing state control and now treated as a state responsibility in which the voluntary agencies continue to participate. In all countries the governments have accepted the main recommendations of the UNESCO-sponsored Addis Ababa conference (1961), namely that by 1980 there shall be universal primary education, secondary school provision for 23% and university provision for approximately 2% of the appropriate age groups, and that the development of education should be planned in relation to plans for socio-economic development.

Progress in reaching the primary school target is on the whole satisfactory, but the development of secondary education is not so. The rate of development of higher education is marred by the imbalance between the humanities compared with the sciences and technology, despite appreciation of the importance to economic development of a satisfactory supply of scientists and technologists. This imbalance is in part due to the inadequacies of secondary education arising from the shortage of qualified teachers of science and mathematics.

This latter failure is part of a general failure to provide adequate teacher training facilities and to the 'bridge-occupation' status of the teaching profession, resulting in continuing loss of the abler and better educated teachers to administration, industry, trade and other more prestigious forms of employment.

Whilst the planning and administration of education are now entirely in the hands of the local governments, these governments are still very dependent upon expatriate teachers and specialists in secondary and higher education.

With political independence there has been a considerable pressure to modify the curriculum in the interests of local values, attitudes and environmental needs. In Franco-phonic West Africa, much of this curriculum revision has been carried out under the aegis of the Institut Pédagogique Africain et Malagache (Paris). In Anglo-phonic West Africa, curriculum reform is stimulated and assisted by the Centre for Curriculum Renewal and Educational Development Overseas (CREDO) and the Educational Development Centre (Boston, Mass.).

One of the more important educational issues is that of language. Except in the elementary levels of instruction, where indigenous languages are used as the medium of instruction, the newly independent countries continue to use the language of the former metropolitan power. Sékou Touré, at the Fifth Congress of the Parti Démocratique de Guinée in 1959, recognised this dependence on the French whilst indicating the national aspiration to be pursued: 'In using French we consider the language must be used in making young people aware of what is African first of all.'

The most urgent problem shared by all the countries is that of relating primary education to vocational training. For a large proportion of the primary school leavers, farming is likely to be the only way of making a living. Efforts to provide vocational training, even when linked with land resettlement projects, are, however, proving very expensive and not very satisfactory. Linked with this weakness is the failure at the secondary school level to attract sufficient numbers of pupils to skill-training appropriate to middle-level manpower requirements and opportunities. There are signs that secondary school pupils are beginning to become more realistic in their job aspirations.

The development of university education since 1945 has been pursued with great vigour and has been generously financed by local governments and external aid. In Franco-phonic West Africa the new universities are linked directly with a university in the former metropolitan power, i.e. Louvanium University, Congo, with Louvain University, Belgium. In Anglo-phonic West Africa the university colleges were directly linked with the University of London in special relationship, except the Fourah Bay College, Sierra Leone, which has an older affiliation with Durham University, and the University of Nigeria, Nsukka, and University College, Njala, which are supported by special contractual relations with individual American universities. In addition, the Anglo-phonic universities have been assisted through the Inter-University Council for Higher Education Overseas (q.v.). In the early

stages the new universities were patterned closely upon the metropolitan universities, but increasingly they are seeking to relate their organisation, research and teaching to the interests and service of the societies they serve.

In all the countries special efforts have been made to provide adult education through literacy classes and extension services and some attempts have been made to use sound radio and television for this purpose.

Faith in the efficacy of education as a means of promoting socio-economic development is great and is reflected in the high proportion of national budgets given to education and in the readiness to accept external aid to further particular educational projects. Despite disappointments and setbacks, the pressure for expanding and improving the provision of education is unlikely to diminish.

FURTHER READING

UNESCO. *Conference of African States on the Development of Education in Africa, held in Addis Ababa, May 15–25, 1961,* UNESCO, Paris, 1961.

UNESCO-IIEP. *New Educational Media in Action,* Vols II and III, UNESCO, 1967.

Abdou Moumouni. *Education in Africa,* André Deutsch, 1968.

J. T. Saunders and M. Dowuona. *The West African Intellectual Community,* Ibadan University Press, 1962.

John C. de Wilde *et al. Experiences with Agricultural Development in Tropical Africa,* Johns Hopkins Press, Baltimore, 1967.

LJL

Africa Centre The Centre, which provides facilities for meetings and a club with international membership, exists to study African problems and needs from a Christian viewpoint.

Hinsley Hse, 38 King St, London, WC2.

African Institute, International The Institute was founded in 1926 under the chairmanship of Lord Lugard in order to promote the serious study of the peoples of tropical Africa, their languages, cultures and social life.

The Institute sponsors research in tropical African countries, and organises research seminars and other meetings on various aspects of African social studies. It maintains a small reference library and an extensive classified bibliographical card index of Africanist literature.

Publications: *Africa* and *African Abstracts* (quarterlies), *Ethnographic Survey of Africa*, *Africa Bibliography*, *Handbook of African Languages*, monographs on African peoples and cultures, etc.

St Dunstan's Chambers, 10–11 Fetter La., London, EC4.

Agraphia *See* **Aphasia**

Agreed syllabus By the provision of the Education Act 1944, religious instruction in state-aided schools must be given in accordance with an agreed non-denominational syllabus.

See also **Religion in schools**

Agreement of service This is the phrase used in England and Wales to describe the written agreement between an LEA, or the governors of a school, and a teacher. Under the Primary and Secondary Schools Regulations of the DES, such an agreement must exist, and it must set out the conditions under which the teaching appointment is held. The phrase used in Scotland is 'Conditions of Service'.

Agricultural colleges *See* **Appendix 3**

Agricultural Education Staffs of Local Authorities, Association of The AAES exists to further the interests of agricultural education, particularly at the farming level, and to safeguard and improve the professional and economic status of its members. Its membership largely consists of those teaching in the county agricultural colleges. It is represented on most of the national bodies concerned with agricultural education, including examinations boards and the Industrial Training Board for Agriculture, Horticulture

and Forestry. It examines closely those aspects of national policy affecting agricultural education. Regional meetings are held periodically, when topics of current interest are discussed; also an annual conference, devoted partly to business and partly to educational matters.

Institute of Agriculture, Moulton, Northampton.

Agricultural Research Council The Council was set up under Royal Charter in 1931, and is under the Secretary of State for Education and Science.

Cunard Bld., 15 Regent St, London, SW1.

Agriculture, Association of The Association is an independent voluntary charity, working in the fields of general and adult education. Its publications and lectures provide unbiased information on farming and the land. Teaching aids are provided such as a farm study scheme of representative British and Commonwealth farms; a handbook and coloured map on types of farming in Britain; a bibliography and advisory service on the use of agriculture in education including farm visits.

Gen. Sec.: Miss Joan Bostock, 78 Buckingham Ga., London, SW1.

Agriculture, Qualification in At present full-time agricultural education in Britain is available at three levels, university, college and institute, leading to degrees (three to four years), diplomas (two years) and certificates (one year) respectively. Nationally recognised qualifications are available at both diploma (NDA) and certificate (NCA) level. Part-time education is also available, leading to qualifications awarded by such bodies as the City and Guilds of London Institute.

Since the second world war a number of government committees have examined various aspects of agricultural education. The most recent of these was the Pilkington Committee 1966, whose report is likely to lead to fundamental changes in the structure of agricultural education. Although required to report on education at diploma level, the Committee ranged more widely to indicate how this should fit into the overall picture of agricultural and technical education. The Pilkington Committee recommended that the NDA and college diplomas be replaced by an Ordinary National Diploma (OND) and a Higher National Diploma (HND). The OND will probably be at a somewhat lower level than the present NDA and will be particularly suited to those seeking responsible positions in farming, whereas the HND will be nearer pass degree standard, providing for careers in advisory and experimental work and in the ancillary industries. The report also recommends a further development of specialised short courses suitable for workers already employed in farming and an Ordinary National Certificate (ONC) for students undertaking part-time courses. A result of the report is that the distinction between colleges and institutes will become blurred; already many farm institutes have taken the name 'college'.

With such changes taking place it is difficult to be precise about the structure of agricultural education in a few years' time; but the following developments can be envisaged: technical colleges and local centres providing part-time courses in preparation for ONC, City and Guilds and similar qualifications; county colleges or institutes offering NCA and OND courses and specialised short courses for farm workers; agricultural colleges offering OND, HND, post-diploma and specialised courses; universities awarding degrees in agriculture and its related sciences.

It is characteristic of farming that the farmer and his men must be skilled in a variety of tasks, involving the handling of machinery and livestock; training in husbandry, therefore, must be linked to technical instruction, emphasising the need for practical training on the farm. At present, this is mainly provided for by a three-year apprenticeship scheme and the 12–18 months pre-entry farming required for all types of full-time courses. Many feel that these arrangements are far from satisfactory as there is often too little control over the breadth or quality of the practical training given. An industrial training board for agriculture has recently been established, and one of its tasks will be to organise and supervise practical training on selected farms.

Perhaps the greatest problem in agricultural education is to equate it to the needs of the industry, and in doing this to avoid the danger of assuming that agriculture is similar to urban industry. For example, the clear distinction between executive, administrator, manager, foreman and worker, typical of most industries, seldom exists in farming; in many cases the farmer fulfils all the first three or four of these functions himself and must be able to undertake most jobs on the farm as well. Further, the ratio of employers to employees is high compared with other industries, the farming business being essentially still a family one. Whether or not agricultural education succeeds in training the right people in ways best suited to their calling or inheritance will largely depend on how well appreciated is the character of the industry it seeks to serve, both now and in the future.

FURTHER READING

Report of the Advisory Committee on Agricultural Education, HMSO, 1966.

Full-time Education in England and Wales: List 185, DES and Ministry of Agriculture.

See also **Appendix 3**

SJW

Aided Grammar Schools, National Association of Governing Bodies of The Association has a membership of about 120 schools in England and Wales, including those affiliated to the national body through membership of London and Roman Catholic organisations.

In order to ensure greater understanding and support for aided schools, full amalgamation between the National and London Associations is planned for the near future.

The Association exists to encourage co-operation between its members, to preserve the status of aided grammar schools and to uphold their rights and privileges, to collect and disseminate information, and to assist members in negotiations with LEAs and the DES.

Hon. Sec.: Dr L. John Stroud, King Edward School, Southampton.

Aided school A voluntary school whose managers are responsible for repairs to the exterior of the building and for the capital cost of such alterations as are required by the LEA to bring the premises up to the standards of the Building Regulations (*see* **Standards for School Premises Regulations 1959**). Expenditure on improvement and repair of the external fabric is eligible for a 75% grant from the Exchequer. All running costs of the school are met by the LEA. The managers have powers to appoint and dismiss staff and to determine the nature of the religious education given by the school. The LEA appoints one-third of the managing body.

Aides, Teachers' The Plowden Report suggested that trained teachers' aides in the ratio of one full-time aide to 60–80 children (two infant classes) and one to 120–160 children (four junior classes) should be employed in primary schools, except in educational priority areas, and should be supervised by qualified teachers; the purpose of these aides being to provide the teachers with help within the classroom. The Report recommended that the conditions of service of aides should be regulated by LEAs, but discretion in the matter of their duties should be left to head teachers. A national scheme for employing such aides should be coupled with an assurance that objectives in teacher-pupil ratios would not be adversely affected.

AIESEC (Association Internationale des Etudiants en Sciences Economiques et Commerciales) An international organisation with 38 member countries, AIESEC arranges exchanges between business and economics students attending its member schools who wish to undergo training in commercial or government enterprises.

British National Executive, Clare Market, London, WC2. International Secretariat, 28 Ave Pictet-de-Rochemont, Geneva, Switzerland.

Aims of education Attempts to formulate and specify the aims of education are apt to founder unless the way in which education can have aims is first clarified. For education is not related to its aims as training is to its objectives, or as some useful means may be to a quite separately specifiable end; nor is education the sole function of a school, so that there can be no simple identification of the aims of education with all the goals of a school.

Education is the process by which the general values of a culture are transmitted. To formulate its aims, therefore, will not be to indicate the social utilities and proficiencies which it contingently makes possible, but rather to set out what are regarded as the general values of that culture. These might include regard for the varieties of empirical truth, aesthetic taste, moral goodness, and religious or political belief. Plainly there is room for argument here both as to which things ought properly to be valued and as to what order of priority, if any, ought to obtain between them in given circumstances: whence the debate about aims.

There are three ways in which these points are commonly missed. First, education may be regarded as being 'for life' or 'for leisure'. The false implication here is that life and leisure are somehow instrumentally served by education, much as travel is by railways, whereas the function of education is rather to provide that transformation of outlook and understanding which is itself the condition of our conceiving life and leisure in any worthy form.

Secondly, from the requirement that education should not be useless it may falsely be concluded that social utility ought to determine what is included in it. The consequence of this is not simply to distort the concept of education, but ultimately to fail by the very criterion of social utility itself.

Thirdly, it may falsely be supposed that aims of education can be formulated purely in terms characterising educational processes, such as 'growth', 'the development of potentialities', 'the cultivation of interests' and so on. Yet worthwhile growth, desirable development and cultivation cannot be characterised in a way which provides clear procedural guidance without at some point appealing to the general values mentioned above.

Finally, it may be said that the various stages of formal education do not have separate and absolutely distinct aims, but rather mark stages which are administratively convenient and developmentally significant in the long process of transmitting general values.

See also **Philosophy of education**
RFD

Air Training Corps The objects of the ATC are to encourage among young men an interest in aviation; to train them to serve in the armed forces; and to give them training in adventure, sport and other activities calculated to develop them into good leaders and citizens.

The ATC was formed in 1941 and is organised into wings and squadrons under the control of the Commandant who is based at HQ Air Cadets, RAF White Waltham, Maidenhead, Berks. Activities include flying, gliding, shooting and all kinds of sports. Camps are held annually at RAF stations.

See also **Cadet Force, Combined**

Albania, Education in Education between the ages of six and 13 is nominally compulsory, but not all areas have sufficient school places available. 1965/6 statistics: 428 kindergartens (enrolment 24,987); 3,404 primary schools (enrolment 392,511); 51 secondary schools (enrolment 23,991); eight higher education institutions including the University of Tirana with 7,548 students.

The population of the country in 1966 was nearly 2 million.

Albemarle Report (1960) Terms of reference: to review the contribution which the youth service of England and Wales can make in assisting young people to play their part in the life of the community, in the light of the changing social and industrial conditions and of current trends in other branches of the education service; and to advise how best value can be obtained for the money spent. The report defined the age range covered by the youth service as 14 to 20, and called for a ten-year plan, including a building programme, to help to expand it. It also called for a Youth Service Development Council to direct this expansion, and for a recruitment programme for youth leaders, which resulted in the setting up of an emergency training college at Leicester, and the negotiation of an agreed scale of salaries for youth leaders.

The Committee laid down three main aims for youth service: association, training and challenge. They rejected some of the more ideological claims for the basis of the service, and denied that this basis was principally educational or directed towards moral reform, emphasising that the youth service must speak to young people through their own terminology.

See also **Youth service**

Alexander, Sir William (b. 1905) General Secretary of the Association of Education Committees for England, Wales, Northern Ireland, the Isle of Man and the Channel Isles since 1945, Sir William Alexander was Director of Education, Sheffield, 1939–44 and is joint secretary to the management panel of the Burnham Committees and Associated Committees for the Negotiation of Teachers' Salaries. He is the author of *The Educational Needs of Democracy, A Parent's Guide to the Education Act* (1944) and *Education in England* (1953).

Algebra Algebra is a generalised arithmetic written in a concise notation which was developed to reveal clearly relationships between numbers and simplify the rules of manipulation, e.g. laws of arithmetic (*q.v.*). It deals mainly with equations, which are mathematical statements containing an equality (=), such as '$2x + 3 = 7$', and the set of numbers which replace x to make the statement true is the solution set, *viz*, 2.

If arithmetic processes are understood some generalised problems can be discussed in the primary school, using diagrams. In the secondary school, formal notation is introduced as required so that there is facility in translating from English into 'algebra' and back. Recognition of pattern is essential to creative mathematics, and algebraic notation is helpful if the child is confident in its use.

FURTHER READING
W. W. Sawyer. *Vision in Elementary Mathematics*, Pelican, 1966.

JCW

Algebra, Abstract Whereas ordinary algebra (*q.v.*) deals with numbers, abstract algebra considers sets whose members may be undefined, together with one or more operations. The combinations of pairs of members produces another set of elements which, if it has certain properties, is said to be a group, ring or field. The set of even and odd numbers under addition form a group. The rational numbers (*see* **Number**) under addition and multiplication are a field, i.e. all the operations of arithmetic can be carried out.

The subject figures mainly in experimental syllabuses such as the School Mathematics Project and Midlands Mathematical Experiment (*q.v.*). By using the symmetries of the square, etc., groups can be introduced to secondary children.

JCW

Algeria, Education in 1966 statistics (enrolments only): state schools 828,118; French cultural schools 91,512; private schools 17,672; three universities at Algiers, Constantine and Oran (enrolments 6,888). 2,000 students study abroad.

The country's population in 1966 was approximately 12 million.

All-age schools An all-age school is a maintained school (*q.v.*) for pupils of all ages between five or seven and the end of compulsory school life. This was the original form of organisation of English elementary education, persisting from the time before compulsory education when the number of pupils in their 'teens was small. By the time of the Hadow Reports, 1926–33 (*q.v.*) most towns had separate infant schools for children aged from five to seven so that the town all-age school had a seven to 14 age range, while in the country the typical age range was five to 14. Hadow recommended a break at the age of 11, thus providing three separate schools in towns—infants to seven, juniors to 11, and seniors to 14; and in the country two schools—juniors-with-infants to 11, and seniors from 11 to 14. He recommended this three-fold division because it corresponded with a difference in educational methods and provision which he considered appropriate to children at these various stages of development. The break at 11 was, however, partially determined by the fact that, with the minimum leaving age as low as 14, a higher age of transfer would make the senior school course too short and the school itself too small to be satisfactory.

Progress in re-organisation was slow. The Hadow scheme was proposed in 1926. Fifty-nine per cent of all 13-year-olds were still in all-age schools in 1933, and 36% in 1949. The raising of the minimum school leaving age to 15 had made the provision in all-age schools for seniors even more clearly inadequate, and there was pressure to complete re-organisation. During the next six years nearly all town all-age schools were closed. The 12% of 13-year-olds who were still in all-age schools in 1955 were nearly all country children. In the next ten years re-organisation was rapid in country districts, and by 1965 only 1% of all 13-year-olds were in all-age schools.

Among independent schools there are a larger number of schools, especially girls' schools, which provide for both primary and secondary education in the same school.

DGOA

All-through schools *See* **Comprehensive Schools, National Foundation for Educational Research Report on**

Allotments and Gardens Society, National Established for the purpose of securing the organisation of allotment gardens and to encourage the formation of horticultural village produce and social welfare societies throughout England and Wales, the Society aims to secure improved legislation and the promotion of horticultural education. It is the world's largest horticultural

society and has a membership of some 3,000 garden organisations and some 250 local authorities.

22 High St, Flitwick, Bedford.

Publications: *Annual Report, Gardeners' Companion* (annual), *Garden* (monthly).

Allowances, Special responsibility These are payments for teachers who carry out duties additional to the ordinary appointment as a class teacher. They comprise payments for graded posts (*q.v.*), heads of departments (*q.v.*), senior masters and mistresses, deputy heads (*q.v.*). In the main they are paid to full-time teachers appointed specifically to one or other of these posts, and are permanent. Exceptions to this are teachers who are not attached to the staff of a particular school but who are considered to undertake responsibilities equivalent to those of the permanent staff holding a responsibility which justifies the additional payment. The only case of duplication occurs where a head of department may also be a deputy head teacher.

SEB

Amateur Athletic Association *See* **Athletic Association, Amateur**

Ancillary services Ancillary services maintained by LEAs are as follows:

School Health Service LEAs are required to undertake the medical inspection of school children at appropriate ages and deal with minor ailments, provide dental inspection and treatment, and enforce cleanliness. For this service, the equivalent of nearly 7,000 full-time doctors, dentists, nurses and auxiliaries are employed by LEAs in England and Wales.

School Meals and Milk Service The provision of a school meals service is an obligation of LEAs, and in England and Wales meals are now supplied at all except about 200 of the 30,000 maintained schools. About 4½ million children (two in every three) take school dinners. The service costs over

£90 million a year, of which only £34 million is charged direct to the parents, the rest being met by the LEAs, whose expenditure has previously been reimbursed by the exchequer, but is now to be aided by the new general rates support grant. The charge to parents for a school meal for their children remained at 1s a head from 1957 to 1968, when it rose to 1s 6d a head. About 7% of meals are supplied free to children of poor parents. Free school milk is supplied and is taken by over 81% of children in maintained schools. Non-maintained schools are included in this scheme, and nearly 80% of the children at such schools as have accepted the provision take free school milk. The annual cost of supplying children with one-third of a pint on school days is over £12 million in England and Wales. The expenditure of LEAs on school milk has previously been reimbursed by the exchequer, but is now to be aided by a rates support grant.

Youth Employment Service This service is provided by most LEAs, but in some rural counties and small county boroughs, whose school children amount only to about 15% of all children in maintained schools, the LEAs concerned have left it to the Ministry of Labour to provide the service for their areas.

The Youth Employment Service deals with school-leavers from the age of 15 until 18 (or later if they stay at school beyond that age), provides careers guidance, helps to place them in employment, provides a follow-up service, and deals with the payment of unemployment benefit. About 1,300 youth employment officers are engaged in the service. A specific grant of 75% of their net administrative expenses, approved by the Minister of Labour, is paid to LEAs by the exchequer.

FB

Anderson Report (1960) This Report, on grants to students, recommended that students admitted to first degrees at universities should receive awards from public funds provided they had two A level passes or the equivalent; that parental contributions should be abolished; and that State Scholarships should be replaced with a single national system of awards.

Animals, Royal Society for the Prevention of Cruelty to The Royal Society for the Prevention of Cruelty to Animals exists to promote kindness to animals, which it does principally by the employment of 240 inspectors, the maintenance of nearly 200 clinics, animal welfare centres and mobile units (at which needy people may have free veterinary treatment for their animals) and by the employment of a corps of school lecturers.

Founded in 1824 and made 'Royal' by Queen Victoria in 1840, the Society early began educational work with the publication of pamphlets and posters, to which films have now been added.

105 Jermyn St, London, SW1.

Anna Westmacott Fund Formerly administered by the Teachers' Guild, this has a small annual income from which non-recurrent grants can be made 'for the benefit of women teachers in high schools and other schools for the higher education of girls, in cases of illness or overwork, or for needful relaxation, such teachers being persons whose private means are not adequate for making due provision for such cases.'

Applications should be addressed to the Trustees at Gordon Hse, 29 Gordon Sq., London, WC1.

Annan Report (1963): 'The Teaching of Russian' The Annan Committee, set up in 1962 under Mr Noel Annan, was asked to 'investigate the possibility of improving and extending the teaching of Russian in schools and establishments of further education in the UK, and to make recommendations.' Its report concluded that, despite the importance of the USSR in the international scene, 'only a handful' of boys and girls were studying Russian at school. In 1961, for example, as against 154,000 candidates offering French at GCE O level, only 1,027 offered Russian. The Committee recommended that the study of Russian should be raised to the level that German had reached in many schools; that there should be an increase in the number of Russian language teachers; and that, to help to bring this about, one-year courses in Russian should be provided for language teachers willing to add Russian to their repertoire.

Anson By-Law In 1903 LEAs were required, by an order framed by Sir William Anson, Parliamentary Secretary to the Board of Education, to adopt a by-law that permitted the withdrawal of children from a provided school at such time as religious instruction was given, so that they might receive such instruction in some other place.

Anthropological Institute of Great Britain and Ireland, Royal The Institute is concerned with all aspects of the science of man. Its membership, which is open to all those interested in this subject, is international. Special terms are available for those under 26. The library (48,000 books and more than 500 periodicals) offers a postal borrowing service for all members in the UK as well as reading room facilities.

Publications: *Man* (quarterly), *Proceedings of the Royal Anthropological Institute* (annually), *Index to Current Periodicals* (quarterly), occasional papers.

Hon. Sec., 21 Bedford Sq., London, WC1.

Aphasia This is a condition resulting from brain damage, which can lead to speech disorder or lack of ability to understand speech. The term is sometimes used to describe agraphia, the inability to write words, and dyslexia (*q.v.*).

Apprenticeship An apprentice is a learner of a craft or trade who enters into an agreement with an employer to work for him for a number of years during which time he receives instruction in the trade. This is the basis of the system which has persisted with variations from the 12th century until the present day. It was not instituted primarily to train the young or to produce satisfactory standards of workmanship, but to control entry into a particular trade and thus provide a buttress against unemployment through limiting the number of competitors.

In England the system was first operated by the merchant guilds whose members were allowed to take one apprentice in addition to their own sons, the apprentice living under the same roof as his master though not necessarily being treated as one of the family. After the Black Death in 1349 these guilds were gradually superseded by the craft guilds whose restrictive policies caused the various crafts to become associated with certain families. After completing his training an apprentice would work as a journeyman for another master and later set up as a master craftsman.

The system came under statutory control in the reign of Elizabeth I when the Statute of Artificers, 1563, fixed seven years as the period for apprenticeship for all trades, and restricted entry to the sons of persons who held freehold to the value of 40 shillings. The usual age for entering into an apprenticeship was 12, the document signed being known as the 'indentures' from the custom of tearing it in two and giving the contracting parties one-half each. If a dispute arose over terms the two halves were brought together, and if their indented edges matched the document was held to be genuine. A fee was payable by the boy's parents when the indentures were signed; on the master's side it was customary to pay the apprentice a small amount of pocket money towards the end of the term of service.

With the coming of the industrial revolution the importance of trained workers lessened, excepting those in the engineering industry, craftsmen being replaced by factory operatives. Apprentices were little more than semi-skilled child slaves whose indentures restricted their ability to seek other employment. The first of the Factory Acts, the Health and Morals of Apprentices Act 1802, aimed at improving their conditions and was also a landmark in the development of state education in England. Limited in scope, it applied only to apprentices in cotton and woollen mills, regulating their working hours to 12 a day and forbidding night work. Employers had to provide them with instruction in reading, writing or arithmetic during the first four years of indentures. Unfortunately the Act had little effect. The government failed to increase the factory inspectorate sufficiently to ensure that the statute was complied with, and as an abundance of child labour was available many employers abandoned the apprenticeship system. State control of apprenticeship lapsed in 1814 when the Elizabethan Statute of Artificers was repealed.

In the second half of the 19th century when the skilled trades began to organise themselves into unions they adopted the apprenticeship system as a means of protecting the economic position of members. The unions were strong enough to insist that admission to skilled trades be limited to those who had served a five- to seven-year apprenticeship, the number of apprentices to be an agreed ratio of the number of adult union members. As the scheme was primarily for the benefit of the trade-unionists little thought was given to the training of the apprentices, which did not conform to any agreed syllabus of instruction. An apprentice learned by watching skilled men at work and by practising under supervision when allowed to do so; a great deal of time was spent in trivial tasks such as running errands.

In the 20th century changes in the industrial process lessened the demand for skilled workers once again, and apprenticeship declined accordingly. But during the second world war it was realised that a lack of trained workers would adversely affect the UK's economic well-being in the post-war period. A joint consultative committee of the British Employers' Confederation and the Trades Union Congress issued a report in 1942 as a result of which schemes of training for young people were introduced into many industries. Generally uniform in character, they made apprenticeship a five-year period between the ages of 16 and 21, with rates of pay increasing yearly in proportion to the adult worker's wage. The employer undertook to allow the apprentice to attend day release classes on one day a week without loss of pay. Thus apprenticeship changed its character; no longer a form of cheap labour, it became quite a costly undertaking by an employer. The schemes were adopted in the main by big employers as the small ones had neither the financial resources nor the full range of manufacturing operations needed for training the apprentice. But the weakness of earlier forms of the system still persisted; the apprentice was not guaranteed that he would receive instruction from skilled craftsmen and was therefore left to 'pick up' what practical knowledge he could. At the end of the apprenticeship period he was recognised automatically as a skilled man without having to pass any examination aimed at measuring his theoretical and practical knowledge.

In 1958 the Carr Committee reported on the training and recruitment of young workers. The report resulted in the passing of the Industrial Training

Act 1964. There are now more than a hundred training schemes in existence, and they are concerned with nearly all industries and workers outside the Departments of Government. The Ministry of Labour has been active in promoting the training of young workers; in 1960 it established training centres for them at which full-time instruction is given for one year. This is aimed at helping the smaller firms unable to bear the cost of the normal apprenticeship schemes. The Ministry has also introduced a scheme whereby youngsters can receive training allowances if they have to live away from home in order to learn a trade. In the UK there were in 1965 some 209,000 boy and 4,600 girl apprentices; of the latter 1,400 were in the clothing industry.

Other industrialised countries such as the USA, West Germany, Belgium, the Netherlands and France have apprenticeship schemes, usually of shorter duration than the British model and containing an examination to test competence at the end of the training period.

FURTHER READING

John Hilton. *Report of an Enquiry into Apprenticeship and Training for the Skilled Occupations in Great Britain and Northern Ireland* 1925–26, Ministry of Labour, HMSO.

Kate Liepmann. *Apprenticeship*, Routledge and Kegan Paul, 1960.

Gertrude Williams. *Recruitment to Skilled Trades*, Routledge and Kegan Paul, 1957.

EP

Apprenticeships, Commercial *See* **Industrial education**

Apprenticeships, Craft *See* **Industrial education**

Approved schools These are boarding schools approved by the Children's Department of the Home Office for the treatment of young delinquents, or children regarded by the courts as 'in need of care and protection'. Children under 10 may be committed to approved schools only in exceptional circumstances; no youngster may be detained in one after his 19th birthday. Once sent, children normally remain for three years or until they have reached the age of 15, whichever is the longer. Boys and girls may be released on licence by the school managers at any time after one year, or earlier if the Home Office agrees. They are subject to supervision by an aftercare agent (representing the school managers) throughout the licence period, i.e. for three years minus the time they were held in the school; and for a further three years after the licence has expired. Supervision is terminated automatically at the age of 21, if not before. Managers can readmit a child to the school for completion of a full three years, if they think this desirable, at any point during the licence period. Boys and girls may be recalled for a further stay of six months, even after the expiry of the licence, so long as detention does not go beyond the age of 19.

Few approved schools hold more than 100 children; none is co-educational. In 1966, of 123 schools, 32 were run by national voluntary societies, 60 by ad hoc local committees of managers, and the remainder by local authorities. There were 7,000 boys in 90 schools, and 1,000 girls in 33 schools. 10% of the boys and 64% of the girls were not criminal offenders: broken homes and early sexual experience were common. The voluntary approved schools receive nearly 100% of their income from public funds, and like the others are subject to Home Office inspection. There is considerable variation in the way the institutions are managed; lack of educational or sociological knowledge on the part of many managers has been commented upon, and closer control by the Home Office—which can withdraw the certificate of approval from an undesirable school—has been urged.

A government White Paper *The Child, the Family and the Young Offender*

(1965) proposed that approved schools for older teenagers should be merged with the Borstal system under direct Home Office management, and that those taking 10- to 16-year-olds should be transferred to local authorities. Confirmation of this change by the Home Secretary was expected in 1967.

On committal, youngsters go to a classifying school from which they are allocated to a suitable institution. The typical approved school is organised on a house system. Housemasters (rarely qualified as teachers or social workers) are the principal agents in training, but few schools have attracted well-qualified men to these posts, which offer salaries well below the Burnham Scales. Firm discipline is a main element in approved school training. Outward obedience to regulations—or lack of it—is accompanied by various rewards and punishments; the notion that children's behaviour is motivated principally by external incentives is implicitly accepted; the close personal relationship between staff and children which could have therapeutic value is generally considered undesirable. Hence approved school staff tend toward stiffness and detachment toward their charges, who learn to show little spontaneity. Except in the few approved schools where affection between adult and adolescent is regarded favourably, boys and girls tend to see the staff as punitive figures.

Some formal education is offered to children under 15. By no means all have a full day's schooling comparable with that of an LEA secondary school. While some approved schools have special facilities for intelligent youngsters, most are lacking in intellectual, emotional or social stimulus commensurate with the children's needs. Teachers (who receive a special schools allowance in addition to the Burnham salary) are usually expected to undertake supervisory duties in the evenings and at weekends; their relationship with housemasters often requires skilful handling by the managers. It is from among teachers, rather than housemasters, that headmasters of these schools are usually recruited.

Of boys leaving approved schools in 1961, 60% were reconvicted within three years. Closed blocks, i.e. maximum security buildings, have been erected at some selected approved schools in an attempt to deal with the persistent problem of absconding. They are separately staffed and are expected to have a deterrent effect, though their negative approach to the instability and emotional anxiety of escapees has not proved successful.

FURTHER READING
John Gittins. *Approved School Boys*, HMSO, 1952.
Gordon Rose. *Schools for Young Offenders*, Tavistock Press, 1967.

DLH

Approved schools, Salaries of instructors in

Qualified. Instructors with recognised qualifications entitling them to be paid on the qualified teachers' scale who are employed in approved schools, are paid in accordance with the salary scales set out in the Scales of Salaries for Teachers in Primary and Secondary Schools, England and Wales (*see* **Burnham Scales**) together with an addition of £215 which is also carried beyond the maximum of the scale.

Substantially but not fully qualified—exceptional cases. Salary Scale £930 × £30(2) × £50 × £60(3) × £50(7) × £60—£1,630.

Substantially but not fully qualified. Salary scale £800 × £30(4)—£920.

If further increments beyond the maximum are recommended by the managers and approved by the Secretary of State, the instructors progress by increments of £30(3) and £35(4) to a maximum of £1,150.

In regard to the definition of the above categories of staff the intention of the Joint Negotiating Committee is that the description 'substantially but not fully qualified', as applied to instructors, should indicate possession of a suitable formal qualification awarded after the successful completion of a recognised course of study (and/or training) which falls short of one entitling the instructor to 'fully qualified' status (and therefore to payment on the Burnham Scale with the approved school addition). The acceptability of the qualification(s) held in each case is decided by the Home Office.

SEB

Approved schools, Salaries of teachers in Salaries of teachers in approved schools are based upon those of teachers in primary and secondary schools. However, account is taken of the special difficulty of the work, and so every qualified teacher receives an additional £215 to the salary otherwise calculated under the Burnham Primary and Secondary Schools Report. Where unqualified teachers and temporary teachers are employed on a full-time basis the corresponding addition is £155. The system of allowances for additional responsibility in respect of class teachers is different from the Burnham Main Report. These teachers are referred to as senior assistants, principal teachers, instructors etc. and reference should be made to the individual headings. Headmasters and headmistresses, deputy headmasters and deputy headmistresses have consolidated scales of salary. These are as follows:

HEADMASTERS AND HEADMISTRESSES

Group	Certified accom. (£)	Salary scale (£)
I	Up to 17	Increments of 60 to 2,535
II	18 to 51	2,320 + 75 (4) = 2,620
III	52 to 102	2,430 + 75 (4) = 2,730
IV	103 to 171	2,580 + 75 (4) = 2,880
V	172 to 257	2,710 + 75 (4) = 3,010
VI	258 to 360	2,915 + 75 (4) = 3,215

DEPUTY HEADMASTERS
AND DEPUTY HEADMISTRESSES

Group	Certified accom.	Salary scale
I	Up to 17	1,480/2,180
II	18 to 51	1,530/2,230
III	52 to 102	1,615/2,315
IV	103 to 171	1,700/2,400
V	172 to 257	1,800/2,500
VI	258 to 360	1,930/2,630

These scales comprise 14 annual increments of £30 (2) + £50 + £60 (3) + £50 (7) + £60.

Deputy heads who are qualified teachers Where applicable, the amounts in respect of university degrees, other recognised qualifications and extra training provided for in the 'Scales of salaries for teachers in primary and secondary schools, England and Wales' are payable in addition to the scale salary.

SEB

Approved Schools and Remand Homes, Joint Negotiating Committee for This Committee follows the pattern of other negotiating committees in that it consists of two panels —one of employers' representatives and the other of the staffs. On the employers' side, the County Councils Association and the Association of Municipal Corporations each send three representatives, together with five representatives of the Association of Managers of Approved Schools. The staff are represented by six persons appointed by the NUT, three by the Association of Headmasters, Headmistresses and Matrons of Approved Schools, three by the National Association of Approved Schools Staffs and two by the National Association of Remand Home Superintendents and Matrons. The chairman of the Committee is drawn from the Committee itself, a representative from the employers' side alternating annually with a representative from the staff side. In the case of the employers, the secretary is not a member of the Committee, but on the staff side the joint secretary is drawn from the NUT's representation.

The Committee is not concerned merely with salary negotiations but with conditions of service generally. These are of course complicated by the fact that the Committee is concerned with residential institutions. Thus, meal charges for members of the family and guests of the person appointed to the approved school form a feature of the overall salary settlement. In addition, however, arrangements for sick leave, allowances for the use of motor cars and other matters which may occur from time to time would be examined and dealt with either by the Committee as a whole or by the joint secretaries on the Committee's behalf. Thus, persons engaged in this branch of the education service receive through their school correspondence information from time to time set out in circular form from the joint secretaries. There are no specific arrangements for regular meetings but these are convened to meet particular needs.

SEB

Aptitude test A test, usually of an objective kind, that is used to assess a person's innate capacity to carry out particular tasks.

Arbitration The art of settling disputes between two parties, usually by reference to some independent person or body of persons, has been a long-established practice in industry. In the educational world, however, the use of arbitration has been very limited. This is because both sides of the appropriate negotiating committee have sought to reach agreement. The compulsion of reaching an agreement has rendered arbitration in the main unnecessary and perhaps even undesirable.

The earliest example of arbitration was in 1925 when failure to reach agreement by the two sides of the Burnham Committee (*q.v.*) was referred to Lord Burnham, the chairman, for a settlement. This followed financial difficulties after the first world war. A voluntary abatement of 5% was in operation during the financial years 1923/24 and 1924/25. Consequently teachers never enjoyed the full benefit of the standard scales. On the other hand the offer of the abatement, and its extension to the following year, probably saved the principle of national bargaining, saved the standard scales, and saved thousands of teachers a larger reduction. But the abatement was not enough. Demands for a 15% reduction of the standard scales were successfully resisted. Eventually the panels agreed to arbitration on the standard scales in full rather than suffer a reduction.

Lord Burnham accepted a unanimous invitation to act as arbitrator, and ten representatives of each panel were present during the proceedings, which occupied ten days during December 1924 and January 1925. The LEAs' panel put up a strong plea for a substantial reduction of the scales. The teachers' panel pressed for the payment of the scales in full. During the proceedings the Burnham Committee agreed to higher scales being allocated in three areas and referred nine disputed cases to the arbitrator. Compromises were reached, and thus the original Burnham recommendations were never fully implemented. It was not until the 1944 Education Act that it became possible to apply the Burnham scales mandatorily. Before then, any arbitration (apart from Lord Burnham's) which took place was of a local character and restricted to those areas where the employing authority refused to undertake the payment of the Burnham recommendations. No authority sought to exceed it.

The post-second world war period has experienced some dozen salary settlements to date, the last in 1967. Most of these settlements were reached without the need for arbitration in the full sense: namely, the two sides of the

Committee were able to agree in general terms. In 1952, however, when there was a dispute concerning the size of a salary improvement during the currency of the 1951 Report, the device of a panel of advisers was used, and a special flat-rate addition of £40 for men and £32 for women was secured. In 1953 there was a dispute concerning the size of the London allowance (q.v.), when the device of a panel of advisers was again used. They were given the following terms of reference:

1) (a) Whether there should be or should not be a London allowance; (b) what should be the area covered by the London allowance.

2) (a) Whether there should be any provincial allowance or allowances; (b) if so, what should be the nature of the areas to which such allowance or allowances should apply.

The following recommendations resulted (see also **London allowance**):

1) (a) That there should be a London allowance; (b) that the area covered by the London allowance should be the City of London and the Metropolitan Police District.

2) That there should be no provincial allowance.

In 1963 the Burnham agreement was fundamentally a set of scales which were imposed by the Minister of Education although adopted by the Burnham Committee. With this Report, however, there was foreshadowed a change in the structure of the Burnham Committee, giving government representation on the management panel. This change caused teachers to take the view that as the Minister (now Secretary of State) was to be represented in this way he could not be judge and jury at one and the same time. It was therefore decided that arbitration machinery should be built into Burnham Committee procedure, and this is now covered by The Remuneration of Teachers Act.

The Arbitration tribunal was established by the Minister of Labour who nominated the chairman himself and the other two members by selecting a name from lists submitted by the management and teachers' panels of the Burnham Committee respectively. Under the Remuneration of Teachers Act the Secretary of State is required to accept the recommendations of arbitrators except when each House of Parliament resolves that national economic circumstances require that effect should not be given to the recommendations.

In negotiations for the 1965 Report the two sides failed to reach agreement and so recourse to arbitration was in fact made before the actual machinery was completed, for some delay occurred in setting up the tribunal pending the appointment of the chairman and the representative on the one hand for the employers and on the other for the teachers.

The whole structure of the salary scales was submitted to the arbitrators for their decision. The teachers disliked the management proposals not only in amount but in content; for example, they resisted the introduction of consolidated scales for head teachers, particularly in regard to the new groupings suggested by the management panel. In the event, however, the arbitrators decided in favour of almost the whole of the management panel's recommendations, the only concessions to the teachers' viewpoint being a slight increase in the minimum of the scale and the retention of a qualifications payment which the management panel wished to reduce in order to bring it into line with a corresponding payment for other qualifications.

The negotiations for the 1967 salary scales took place against a background of government incomes policy which, starting with a complete freeze of existing salaries, thawed only very slightly during the period when negotiations were taking place. Indeed, the second stage was known as a 'period of severe restraint'. It was not surprising therefore that the management panel reflected the central government attitude by making only very limited concessions to the teachers. Since, however, the government had promised a better deal for education, the teachers' side of the Burnham Committee felt that more negotiation should have taken place, and, ultimately, again pressed the issue to arbitration. A number of modest improvements were made in the salary scales and two points were referred back to the Working Party of the Burnham Committee to effect a settlement, or, if they could not agree, a reference back to the arbitrators could be made by either side. On one question the teachers secured a complete victory. This was in relation to salaries which might be adversely affected by the reorganisation or closure of schools. From 1 July 1967 the arbitrators ruled that no teacher could suffer a diminution in current or prospective salary (*see also* **Safeguarding**).

It is always a matter of conjecture whether recourse to arbitration produces a better agreement than may be secured by persisting in establishing a negotiated settlement. The fact that machinery is available may cause the management side of the committee to break off their offer at a lower point than they would be prepared to concede, believing that the arbitrators may award something which, although this may be greater than the offer reached when negotiations broke down, would nevertheless be less than the amount the teachers were prepared to settle for by negotiation. In other words it is possible for the authorities rather than the teachers to gain from arbitration. National economic events, however, in recent years have tended to curb the freedom of arbitrators and indeed to condition what they may do on the merits of the cases put before them. In the case of the Burnham Committee an arbitral award can be rejected by the Secretary of State even though he has to secure the permission of Parliament to do so.

SEB

Archaeology, Council for British The Council seeks to safeguard all kinds of archaeological material, including ancient monuments, historic buildings and antiquities. It promotes research by means of conferences and publications, and provides guidance and information to students, teachers and members of the public. Its periodicals include an *Annual Report*, the *Archaeological Bibliography* and the *Calendar of Excavations*, listing sites where volunteers are required.

The Council was formed in 1944 as the co-ordinating body for British archaeology, and its membership includes societies, museums and universities.

Sec.: Miss Beatrice de Cardi, BA, FSA, 8 St Andrew's Pl., Regent's Park, London, NW1.

Archery The practice of archery was once compulsory for all able-bodied men; today it is a rapidly growing recreation among adults of all ages and also in secondary schools throughout the country. It is also one of the permissible sports in the Duke of Edinburgh's Award Scheme (*q.v.*).

Since the bow and arrow form a lethal weapon, the most strict supervision during archery sessions is required both with adults and younger people.

Competition Rules can be obtained from the Grand National Archery Society, Marley, Kennington, Ashford, Kent. In Scotland the controlling body is the Scottish Archery Association, 41 Hunter Cres., Troon, Ayrshire.

JE

Architectural Association Founded in 1847 to 'promote and afford facilities for the study of architecture'. There are 350 full-time students studying at the Association School of Architecture, and some 50 in post-graduate departments. The Association organises meetings, lectures, symposia and visits for its 4,000 members, most of whom are practising architects.

34–36 Bedford Sq., London, WC1.

Architecture, Qualification in
Architectural education is a good illustration of the interaction of theory and practice. It is concerned as much with the understanding of principles as with their application, and most courses bring together the two activities at each stage of the learning process.

Entry to the architectural profession and the conduct of its members are governed by the Architects Registration Act, which makes it illegal for anyone to practise whose name is not on the Register of Architects. This Act set up a Registration Council which has powers to recognise for admission to the Register the qualifying examinations of various bodies. In the past, the main route into the profession was via the examinations of the Royal Institute of British Architects, a professional body to which most architects belong. More recently, however, an increasing number of schools have become recognised both by the Architects Registration Council of the UK and by the RIBA, and their examinations provide entry into the Register and to membership of the RIBA itself.

This swing towards full-time education, providing greater breadth of courses and scope for a wide range of studies, is now almost complete. Some of the recognised schools are in universities and some in colleges of art and technology. The university schools award their own degree and most of the college schools make diploma awards. Some of the latter are in institutions which may well become polytechnics and these may in future be able to award degrees through the Council for National Academic Awards (*q.v.*).

Most full-time courses last five years.

In addition, many require students to do one year of practical training in an approved office, often after the third year of the undergraduate course. A minimum of two years practical training is required before full professional qualifications, and one of these must be taken after graduation.

Although the majority of those entering architecture courses intend to qualify professionally, the study of architecture is a part of higher education and academic standards both for entry and for performance are considered accordingly. There are many links with other disciplines, and these call for breadth of interest and of experience in sixth-form studies.

There is no simple yardstick for entry qualifications. The minimum requirement is five GCE subjects, with two passes at A level. Some schools require more A level passes and some specify certain subjects (maths and physics being the most common). But most are influenced also by other factors, including performance at an interview. Almost invariably a sense of purpose and an interest in other people are qualities which are sought.

Many teachers in schools are themselves practising architects. There are, however, growing opportunities for combining academic work with research and for interchange between teaching and practice. Postgraduate work is increasing and this too will develop links with other disciplines and other professions.

Some graduate architects read for higher degrees in order to become specialists, and town planning has attracted many of these. There are several schools of planning at the same centres as schools of architecture, often with faculty ties and practising joint activities. Similar ties are growing with other departments such as building, engineering and social science.

Powerful forces are at work in architectural education, and the architectural profession has a long tradition of concern for the education of its members. More recently it has given great encouragement to the growth of a Society of Architectural and Associated Technicians, a group formed to look after the interests of those working in the technical fields of architecture and building.

FURTHER READING

Booklets published by the RIBA (66 Portland Place, London, W1): *Schools of Architecture Recognised by the RIBA; Becoming an Architect; A Career as an Architectural Technician.*

See also **Appendix 7**

DH

Architecture, Schools of *See* **Appendix 7**

Archives, National Register of *See* **Record Association, British**

Area colleges *See* **Further education in England and Wales**

Area Training Organisation An ATO is a regional organisation, in most cases part of a university, that is responsible for supervising the training of teachers in the region. Most commonly it is an institute of education, but sometimes is a school of education. The first ATOs in England and Wales were established in 1945, and there are now 18 of them. Represented on the governing body of each ATO are the universities, the colleges of education and the LEAs, and the assessor is appointed by the DES. It is the ATO that examines candidates for a teacher's first qualification; the award of such a qualification is subject to the approval of the DES. ATOs are charged also with responsibility for in-service training, and also engage in educational research.

See also **Teacher education in England and Wales** *and* **In-service training of teachers**

Argentina, Education in The state system provides free compulsory education from six to 14 years, covering the whole primary stage (six to 12) and one year of the secondary stage (13–17/19). Secondary education consists of a three-year general studies course followed by specialised courses for teacher training, and in commercial, technical, professional and agricultural subjects as well as the arts and the baccalaureat. In 1965, enrolments in pre-primary schools (non-compulsory) were 146,741; in primary schools (including independent and state) 3,279,290; in secondary schools 789,071; in universities and institutes of higher education 243,303. There are nine national universities, three provincial and 11 private universities, and a number of national, provincial and private institutes of higher education. University courses last from three to six years, and post-graduate studies one or two years.

The population of the country was approximately $22\frac{1}{4}$ million in 1965.

Argyll Report (1867) The Argyll Commission inquired into the whole range of Scottish schooling. Its findings in the matter of elementary education resembled those of the Newcastle Commission (*q.v.*) in England. It discovered that of 4,451 schools in rural districts, only 1,133 were parish schools; the others were private schools, most of them hopelessly inadequate. The Report recommended that the Education Department should take the parish schools under its control and should, where necessary, provide state-aided schools. The Report found the state of secondary education to be generally satisfactory, but there was great unevenness between schools in the matter of curriculum. The founding of district or supplementary schools was recommended, together with a system of scholarships enabling pupils to pass to such schools from the elementary schools and on to the universities.

Aristotle (384–322 BC) Aristotle's main works relating to education are *Ethics* and *Politics*. Aristotle argued that all activities have good as their end, and that the final end is happiness. The activities in which happiness consists will be those which best exemplify man's nature, his characteristic being the exercise of reason.

The activities of reason are of two kinds: theoretical, such as studying metaphysics and the sciences; and practical, such as being just, liberal, courageous and temperate. The theoretical are regarded as the finest. Politics, war, business and the practical arts serve to secure the leisure in which to engage in fine activities, while education serves to introduce man to them. Character must first be formed, which requires the control of feeling and desire in such ways as will become habitual and a pleasure, while later on instruction is needed in theoretical activities. Professional skills and all menial tasks are unbefitting in a gentleman, and should be left to slaves, women and others whose social function it is to serve.

See also **Philosophy of education**
RFD

Arithmetic Numbers can be combined to produce another number by means of binary operations of addition and multiplication with their inverses, subtraction and division, according to the 'laws of arithmetic'.

(1) Commutativity — interchanging two numbers gives an equivalent result: $a+b=b+a$, $a \times b = b \times a$.

(2) Associativity—the order of operations is immaterial: $2+(3+4)=(2+3)+4$, $2 \times (6 \times 3)=(2 \times 6) \times 3$ (bracketed operation first).

(3) Distributivity — addition and multiplication can only be combined thus: $6 \times (2+3)=(6 \times 2)+(6 \times 3)$.

All methods of computation must comply with these laws.

The theory of numbers (Greek—*Arithmetike*) is a difficult and elegant branch of mathematics which considers the properties of prime, triangular, perfect numbers, etc.

Counting, ordering, addition and subtraction with materials is begun in the infants school, together with measuring. Four operations with number and money, with an introduction to fractions, decimals and ratio form suitable study for juniors. If ideas are understood, speed and accuracy with standard rules come easily to upper juniors. At the secondary stage comes the extension of number systems, laws of arithmetic, indices and logarithms.

JCW

Army, Education in The function of the Royal Army Educational Corps (RAEC) is to carry out the system of education and resettlement approved by the Army Department, to advise commanders on its organisation and actively to instruct or supervise instruction in all military units and educational establishments.

In greater detail, the responsibilities of the RAEC involve the provision of facilities for officer education at all levels, including an education scheme for junior officers, staff/promotion candidates, specialist courses for officers of the technical arms and specific courses for senior officers. Facilities must be provided for the education of the soldier, and these include remedial education, courses for Army Certificates of Education, educational classes and activities covering a wide range of demands, such as resettlement and personal advancement. The education of apprentices and junior soldiers leads to Army Certificates of Education and to appropriate civilian examinations, such as GCE O and A levels and Ordinary National Certificates. Facilities are provided for language training, both for military purposes and to promote good relations with inhabitants of countries in which the Army serves. The teaching of English to overseas personnel is also involved.

The RAEC is responsible in addition for the education of dependants (i.e. of children overseas and of wives and children over school age at home and overseas); for a resettlement information and advice service for personnel about to leave the service; and for the provision of resettlement training facilities together with liaison with the Ministry of Labour and other job-finding agencies; for the control and administration of the Army's library service, which provides books of every kind to the Army throughout the world; for the provision of news and information services to the Army, with current affairs training for all ranks and an orientation service for those units proceeding to foreign stations; and for participation in the field of methodology (limited at present) so far as it affects Army training and, in particular, technical training.

See also **Army Units, Junior; Forces, Teaching in the**

TJHD

Army apprentice schools *See* **Army Units, Junior**

Army Education, Institute of Established in 1946: the executive organisation of the Directorate of Army Education in the Ministry of Defence. The Commandant of the Institute is responsible for the organisation of army educational syllabuses and examinations, for the staffing of Army children's schools overseas, and for the supply of publications, text books and library books to Army libraries and education centres. The Institute is also responsible for giving specialist advice to service personnel on educational facilities for themselves and their children and on resettlement. Correspondence courses are provided for all three services, and specialised sections provide language training facilities for the Army and publish information on international affairs. Lecturers are provided for overseas stations. There is also a Research and Inspectorate Department which carries out specialist

work for the Director of Army Education.

The Institute is located in the grounds of Eltham Palace. The Palace is the Headquarters Mess of the Royal Army Educational Corps and is the venue for courses and conferences.

Court Rd, Eltham, London, SE9.

Army Units, Junior These units provide opportunity for entry to the Army after school leaving and before entry to adult service is possible. A range of junior units caters for those able to undertake apprenticeships, leadership training and trade training and also provides openings for junior infantry and musicians.

All Apprentice Colleges, Junior Leaders Regiments, Junior Tradesmen's Regiments, the Junior Infantrymen's Battalion and Junior Soldiers Wings of infantry depots are run similarly to boarding schools.

In addition to trade and leadership training there is a generous provision of education to support this training and to permit junior soldiers to study for the educational qualifications necessary for promotion. The curriculum is appropriately rounded off with military training, PE, sports and games.

Arnold, Matthew (1822-88) The eldest son of Dr Thomas Arnold (*q.v.*), Matthew Arnold as a young man had a brief experience of teaching at his old school, Rugby, but his involvement in education appears to have been accidental; it followed the procurement for him by Lord Lansdowne in 1851 of an inspectorship of schools. He gave himself indefatigably to his duties though his chief interest and, of course, his eminent skill was in poetry and literary criticism.

In his official work he was most happy when travelling abroad to inspect foreign schools and universities: from these travels emerged his books *Popular Education in France* (1861),

A French Eton (1864), *Schools and Universities on the Continent* (1868). He felt very strongly that the schools of France and the universities of Germany demonstrated that high academic standards could accompany modern studies, and that the study of modern languages was of importance. He supported the campaign for a national educational system and for compulsory training of teachers. He was opposed to Lowe's Revised Code (*q.v.*), and it seemed at one time that this would lead to his resignation as an inspector. In *Culture and Anarchy* he set down his vision of the unifying quality of a national system of education. Such a system must provide the 'Barbarians' (the public schoolboys) with a more liberal curriculum and more sensitive and intelligent teaching; it must offer the 'Philistines' (the middle class) the broad humanities as well as the narrow sciences; and must provide the 'Populace' (the working class) with literature, which to Arnold was 'the greatest power available in education'.

Arnold, Thomas (1795-1842) Great reforming headmaster of Rugby (1828-42). Though less of an innovator than is commonly supposed, he gave his reforms importance by the personal qualities he brought to them. He introduced into the normal timetable such modern subjects as French and mathematics, encouraged wide-ranging inquiry as well as purely syntactical consideration of a text, and used his sixth form to strengthen the discipline and moral tone of the school.

Art, Colleges and schools of There are about 200 art establishments which are recognised by the Ministry of Education. Of these, 36 are colleges of art which offer courses approved by the National Council for Diplomas in Art and Design (*q.v.*). There are six art schools attached to universities (London (2), Oxford, Reading, Durham and Aberystwyth).
See also **Appendixes 5** *and* **6**

Art, Society for Education through The Society's aim is to further the teaching of art in primary, secondary and further education in the UK.
29 Gt James St, London, WC1.
Publication: *Athene* (twice annually).

Art colleges with courses leading to the Diploma in Art and Design *See* **Appendix 6**

Art and Design, Diplomas in These are awarded to students who have completed courses at approved colleges of art. The separate subjects for which diplomas are awarded are painting, sculpture, silversmithing, industrial design (engineering), furniture, ceramics, interior design, crafts (wood, metal and ceramics), theatre, woven and printed textiles, fashion and embroidery. At present 36 colleges offer approved courses in one or more of these subjects. The courses and awards are supervised by the National Council for Diplomas in Art and Design (*q.v.*).

In May 1967 a memorandum (No. 16/67) issued by the DES announced the decision of the Secretary of State to pause in the development of further courses for the Diploma. He would not definitely be prepared to approve proposals for new courses in the graphic design, three-dimensional design and textiles/fashion areas of study to begin in the session 1968–9.
See also **Appendix 6**

Art and Design, National Council for Diplomas in The Council was set up in March 1961 as an independent body under the chairmanship of Sir John Summerson to supervise courses leading to the awarding of Diplomas in Art and Design (*q.v.*).
16 Park Cres., London, W1.

Art in education Two figures have dominated new thinking about the place of art in general education in the UK. Marion Richardson (d. 1947) introduced into the classroom at

43

Dudley High School in 1912 methods which combined the disciplined learning of craftmanship with a freedom of expression quite new to school art of the time. Recognition of her work by Roger Fry, the exhibitions at the Omega workshops of the art by her pupils and her subsequent employment in the training of teachers firmly established the revolution on which present-day attitudes are based. The second figure, Herbert Read (d. 1968) continually championed the cause of individuality, in art as in living, and of creative work as a means by which the individual may grow as a free-thinking, mature personality. Read saw creativity as a compensatory process through which the individual may reconcile primitive and selfish instinctual urges with the inhibitions implicit in social grouping.

All forms of creative expression have their origins in man's need to digest experience and learn from it. They help him assimilate something of the confused miscellany of occurrences which make up his life and find in them some form of order which will relate them to each other and to his self. They are methods of studying internal reactions to outside events, of giving them meaning and of reconciling the often contradictory demands of the primitive individual and sophisticated group member which every person in fact is. The process of actually making something, whether poetry, music or visual art, serves to concentrate all the faculties of understanding on the matter to be understood.

The educational value for the artist stems from this total involvement—intellectually, intuitively and physically—with his subject matter whilst he constructs his work of art. For him it is the process he is engaged in which is important and the change this brings about in him. Through art he seeks understanding and in doing so he creates a by-product which is the work of art. The work of art is important as

the agent of change and it has a communicative potential for others, but for the artist it must be always subordinate to the understanding that making it has brought about. The practice of art is a dynamic form of meditation.

In some ways creative work in art resembles dreaming, its deeper significance often concealed beneath an imagery open to more literal and superficial interpretation. Any understanding it promotes may be absorbed at a deeper than conscious level, through intuition more than intellect. In Western man intuition has been allowed so nearly to atrophy that its value is barely recognised, and intellectual understanding has become almost the only essential for belief. The reduced awareness resulting from this has caused much of the bewilderment felt by rational-minded people faced with modern art idioms.

Despite some recent developments in the teaching of other subjects, our educational system is still based predominantly on the development of the intellect and on verbal communication. Less attention is paid to encouraging emotional growth. The exercise of intuition through creative work is seen by many as a move towards a more balanced approach which will seek to educate the whole man, emotional as well as intellectual.

Although the artist and subject are usually referred to as separate, the subject being outside the artist—something he can see—it would be more appropriate to consider them together, as parts of the same entity. For the artist may perceive the world only from within his own unique personality, arriving at meaning by subjectively interpreting information received through his senses. The nature of this interpretation will depend on associations of past experience evoked by the matter seen. This experience is often of so long ago that it exists only in unconscious memory and is recognised only as feeling. If the artist's reactions to his subject are direct and honest, that is to say original rather than conditioned to conventional attitudes, the meaning he gives them will be largely personal to him.

What the artist will understand from his studies will be the effect of the subject-matter on him, how he reacts to it, what changes are brought about through his exposure to it. Total subject-matter becomes his experience when concentrating on what is commonly thought of as 'the subject'—and to that extent it *is* him, artist-with-subject.

The composite activity of making art combines emotional reactions, some of which may be perceived unconsciously, and intellectual processes which may be induced, with the physical activity of making the image. All the faculties are used simultaneously to help bring about the growth which is the true aim of art.

Of course the work of art does not function only for its maker. Looking at art provides another form of visual experience, and this is as much open to personal interpretation as the artist's view of his subject. The viewer measures the excellence of the created image according to associations it, in its turn, evokes in him and the meaning he puts on them. Since viewers, like artists, are individual in their reactions and bound to make subjective judgements, 'beauty' and 'ugliness' are ambivalent terms with personal rather than general significance.

Art teachers no longer set out to inculcate a shared conception of aesthetic beauty. The variety of response any visual experience may call up makes a standard measure of worth impossible. At extremes one man's beauty may constitute another man's ugliness, and there are all shades of difference between. Art teaching has become very much a process of helping the student or pupil to find methods of contacting what is unique and personal in his experience, what constitutes reality for him and perhaps, sometimes, only for him. Some aspects of this reality may not be pleasant and the imagery they induce may be disturbing. Not all art will comfort the spectator.

The probing of original experience will give rise to new visual concepts. However, these may well share certain stylistic similarities which mark them as the symbolic language of groups. This has been the case always with the art of societies, where groups of people living together have developed certain common characteristics of behaviour and outlook. We are no different today, for we share an environment and a very powerful cultural climate, and from these come the pressures and collective attitudes which influence aspects of visual form. But at this point in evolution, and whilst recognising aspects of living which are shared, the artist in the West has set himself the task of expressing particularly what is unique and individual in his response to life. The teacher of art will recognise this, and the infinite variations possible in approaching art despite any tendencies which are shared. Art teaching will no longer aim just to familiarize the pupils with a commonly accepted visual symbology. Emphasis will shift from the work of art as end product, to the artist and what he gains from making it. Pupils will not, say, learn how to make pictures for their own sakes. Teaching will be concerned more with the analysis of experience through an imagery shaped by responses originating in the individual and personal to him. The pupil will be learning how to use art for his own education rather than as a means of communicating already known data to a viewer. What is communicated as a result may be something of his own experience, but equally the painting may provoke quite different reactions in the viewer and provide him with further experience for which the painting was only the catalyst. One of the principal tasks of the art teacher may well be to free the pupil from conventional and stereotyped attitudes in order that he may invent an art which is entirely suitable to himself.

It is not likely that any one person will share fully the emotional experience of another. If the pupil or student is honestly engaged with his own reactions it will not be possible for the teacher to show him what form the imagery through which he considers them should take. With this realisation the teacher no longer sees himself as arbiter of aesthetic taste and an authority able to dispense expertise in how-to-do-it lessons. He has become more of a partner with his pupil in exploration, a fellow searcher.

Aesthetic problems are today seen as emanating from the individual, inseparably tied to personality, and capable of as many solutions as there are artists. This has necessitated a change to a studio climate related more to original research than a steady progress towards predictable results. The teacher sets the tone of experiment, provides the stimulating environment and instructs in craftsmanship and technique where these are necessary. The pupil makes the experiments and draws his own inferences from them. The teacher offers beginnings, points of departure from which the pupil will decide his own direction for development.

The pupil will also invent the imagery, determined by his own feeling. He must be encouraged to find himself rather than to try to be what he is not. He should not, for instance, be expected to draw in the Renaissance manner before he may explore ideas of his own. Neither should he be expected to reproduce the reactions of his teacher, who will be a different personality and a different age. He should be encouraged to be his age, and to be of his age.

All artists, whether professional or in primary school, are at their own levels engaged in what is essentially the same pursuit. They are advancing their own education through the use of visual media. Art is used as a means of study; and the artist is not so much, say, learning how to paint, as learning through painting. For the professional, the practice of art will provide his principal means of seeking understanding. For the amateur, including most pupils in schools of general education, it will take its place as a subject among others through which he may learn. For all, creativity whether expressed through visual art or another subject will advance understanding of both spiritual and material worlds and the relationship between them.

In helping the pupil to discern the truly original reaction and to acquire the means of expressing this in his own way, the teacher himself will require sensitivity and imagination and the ability to encourage and inspire without dominating his pupil's imagination. He must be able to sense what kind of subject-matter will induce creative activity, and at what time for the pupil. He must be able to provide the technical knowledge when it is needed—and he must recognise the moment when he should not interfere. He will guide his pupil through work which will help him to develop perception and sensibility, and give him confidence when making aesthetic decisions. The teacher will lead experimental work to familiarise the pupil with the vocabulary of line, shape, tone and colour from which he may develop his own language of expression. He will provide for observational work of all kinds, and inventive and imaginative exercise. A considerable portion of any syllabus will be given to craft, including designing and working in the new materials of technology which are so much a part of life today.

The purely expressive function of art, self-motivated and self-centred as it may be, is very closely related to the more socially-oriented work of the designer. All art involves rational deductive thinking and planning as well as intuitive feeling, for the artist must decide on the materials and physical structure of his image as well as its aesthetic form. It must hold together. In the designer's work there is greater emphasis on decisions which depend on reason and deduction and which guide that part of the designing which prepares the object to fulfil its function. But there comes a time when the artifact will work, although there is still room for the designer to manoeuvre. He will then make his aesthetic choices as to proportion, shape, colour, surface treatment and other formal relationships, and he will depend for success in these upon his imagination and sensibility.

The rational, analytical thinking processes involved in designing may be learned comparatively quickly by an intelligent student. The ability to make the aesthetic choices which are the expressive aspects of designing depends upon a sense of form, and it is unlikely that this can be learned. It must be developed and allowed to grow through the exercise of perception and sensibility over a prolonged period of time. Art teachers recognise that 'design appreciation' and 'art appreciation' are best developed through practical work backed by discussion and analytical enquiry. Lecture and discussion alone can go only a very small part of the way towards helping pupils to develop the personal taste in design which is vital to expressive form. The ability to conceive original ideas in visual design will come through practice in designing—in all forms of art and craft, providing that at the same time there is some help for the pupils as far as possible to become consciously aware of the processes involved.

There is some movement in secondary schools towards more closely relating the work of technical departments of study and art, and providing an integrated form of art and design education. This will constitute a decided advance on any system where the art pupil indulges only in expressive work which he sees as irrelevant to practical living, and the handicraft pupil learns only the techniques of making without knowing how to design what he makes.

Art and education will never reach a point of arrival, where they can rest. Since the artist is concerned with the expression of original thought and feeling and since his reactions to experience must be linked inseparably with the continually evolving climate of thought and feeling in contemporary society, the practice of art and the form it takes will change continually too. It follows that methods of teaching art must keep pace.

FURTHER READING
Pamphlets on aspects of art and education, loan collection of slides available from the Secretary, Society for Education through Art, Morley College, Westminster Bridge Rd, London, SE1. Pamphlets on equipment and materials available from Gen. Sec., National Society for Art Education, 37a East St, Havant, Hants.
Anton Ehrenzweig. *The Hidden Order of Art*, Weidenfeld and Nicolson, 1967.
Gyorgy Kepes. *Education of Vision*, Studio Vista, 1965.
Victor Lowenfeld. *Creative and Mental Growth*, Collier Macmillan, 1965.
Sybil Marshall. *Experiment in Education*, Cambridge Univ. Press, 1966.
Herbert Read. *Education through Art*, Faber, 1961.
Marion Richardson. *Art and the Child*, Univ. of London Press, 1964.
Journal
Athene (three times a year). Society for Education through Art.
See also **Appendix 15**

GB

Art Education, National Advisory Council on Terms of reference: to advise the Secretary of State on all aspects of art education in establishments of further education. This body provides the DES with periodical reports.

Chairman: Sir William Coldstream, CBE.

Art Education, National Society for See **Art in education** (*Further reading*)

Art galleries and museums, Selected list of See **Appendix 15**

Art training centres Many local authorities and colleges, in co-operation with local industry, have set up art training centres to organise courses designed for local needs. Here the standards required for entry are not so stringent as those required by the Diploma in Art and Design courses. The provision of these courses is, according to the 1962 report of the National Advisory Council on Art Education, 'primarily a matter for local initiative and organisation'. Most centres award their own diplomas.

Arts, Royal Society of The Royal Society for the Encouragement of Arts, Manufactures and Commerce (membership 7,200), founded in 1754, covers the fine and applied arts and the sciences. Its chief educational activities include the arrangement of many lectures on these subjects (published in a monthly *Journal*), the encouragement of industrial design through a large annual competition for students, and the organisation of national examinations on all aspects of business studies, including modern languages. The Society works closely with the central and local education authorities and with the teachers' organisations, and pays particular regard to teaching techniques and the needs of the present day. It also holds examinations for teachers of shorthand, typewriting and office practice, and for proficiency in English as a second language.

John Adam St, Adelphi, London, WC2.

Arts Council of Great Britain Created under Royal Charter in 1946, the Arts Council was set up by King George VI to develop 'a greater knowledge, understanding and practice of the fine arts exclusively, and in particular to increase the accessibility of the fine arts to the public throughout Our Realm, to improve the standard of execution of the fine arts and to advise and co-operate with Our Government Departments, local authorities and other bodies on any matters concerned directly or indirectly with these objects.'

The 16 members are appointed by the Secretary of State for Education and Science after consultation with the Secretaries of State for Scotland and Wales. There are four unpaid advisory panels of experts in music, drama, the visual arts and literature. Although the terms of reference cover the whole field of the arts, in practice the Council limits its activities to music, opera, ballet, drama, literature, painting and sculpture. It works chiefly by subsidising suitably constituted independent bodies connected with the promotion and performance of the arts; though it is prepared, where no organisation exists, itself to promote the required activity.

England: 105 Piccadilly, London, W1. Scotland: 11 Rothesay Terrace, Edinburgh, 3. Wales: Holst Hse, Museum Pl., Cardiff.

Arts and Crafts, Colleges of See **Appendix 5**

Ascham, Roger (1515–68) A brilliant classical scholar, mathematician, musician and penman, Ascham taught Greek at Cambridge; wrote a celebrated treatise on archery, which he dedicated to Henry VIII; and was for a time tutor to Princess Elizabeth, later Elizabeth I. He spent the years from 1563 until his death writing *The Scholemaster*. The origin of the book was an occasion when Ascham dined at Windsor with Sir William Cecil. The conversation turned to the news that a number of scholars had fled from Eton for fear of a flogging, and Ascham spoke strongly against corporal punishment. So impressed were the other guests by his argument that they urged him to write a practical treatise on education.

The first book of *The Scholemaster*, besides containing many reminiscences, expresses Ascham's extremely liberal outlook on education; he believed that a child should be drawn to learning by gentle methods and not driven to it by didactic bullying. A main preoccupation of the second book (he died before he could complete the work) is with Ascham's own method of teaching Latin, which consisted of requiring a student to translate from Latin into English, and then back into Latin.

Ashby Report (1954): The Organisation and Finance of Adult Education Terms of reference: to review the present system by which the extra-mural departments of the universities, the WEA and the other responsible bodies provide local facilities for adult education, with special reference to the conditions under which the facilities are organised and are aided by grant from public funds; and to make recommendations.

The Committee recommended that the ceilings for grants should be discarded, and that limits on salaries for full-time tutors should be abandoned. In most other respects it found the system satisfactory, although it suggested that the control exercised by the Ministry over some aspects should be more flexible.

See also **A d u l t e d u c a t i o n ; Responsible bodies**

ASLIB Founded in 1924 as the Association of Special Libraries and Information Bureaux, ASLIB aims to promote the growth of specialised libraries and information agencies, especially those concerned with research in science, technology and the social sciences, and to develop the study of documentation and information control. It organises short courses in abstracting, classification and indexing and related topics, and individual courses for scientists taking over the administration of industrial information services. It provides advice and training in computer systems of information control and in library operating techniques generally. In addition, ASLIB organises conferences, publishes journals, operates an information service and maintains a library of the world's literature on documentation.

3 Belgrave Sq., London, SW1.

Aspiration, Level of It frequently appears that pupils who have already experienced success in their work will approach new tasks with confidence, setting themselves reasonable and realistic goals. In this sense, their levels of aspiration are suitable and helpful to them. Pupils who have frequently failed, however, often approach new tasks without real confidence. They may set themselves unrealistically high goals which they are therefore bound to fail, thus justifying their own feelings about themselves, but usually they are over-cautious and consequently set themselves tasks well below their real potential. Pupils who in this sense have poor levels of aspiration can best be helped by support, encouragement and praise in the early stages, and the setting of tasks well within their reach until they have the confidence to tackle something more demanding.

NT

Assemblies, School *See* **Religious assemblies**

Assistant, Foreign A term used to describe a student or graduate who, as part of an exchange scheme arranged between the DES and the education ministry in the assistant's own country, spends a year in a British secondary school helping to teach his native tongue.

Assistant Masters' Association The Association, founded in 1891, represents assistant masters in public and other independent schools, direct grant grammar schools and in all types of maintained secondary schools. Two of its most important objects, as defined in the memorandum of association, are: to promote the cause of education generally; and to protect and improve the status and further the legitimate professional interests of teachers.

The AMA is a constituent member of the Joint Four Secondary Associations of FIPESO. It has representatives on the Burnham Committee and the Schools Council and on all important educational bodies. It is actively concerned with the GCE and CSE examinations and their organisation. Great importance is attached to its educational as well as its professional work, and the Association has published memoranda on the teaching of English, history, geography, modern languages, classics, mathematics and science, and reports on teaching in comprehensive schools. Its journal, *The AMA*, is published eight times a year.

Gordon House, 29 Gordon Sq., London, WC1.

Association, Laws of Aristotle and many others since have noticed how one idea, event or emotion becomes associated with another when presented together in space or time. Such associations may be anything from noticing the link between lightning and thunder, to learning a list of French nouns with their English equivalents. If the association took place recently, was reasonably vivid and has frequently been noticed since, then it stands a good chance of being remembered on another occasion. From this, and with many refinements, a theory of learning was evolved explaining everything in terms of forming associations that go on to activate other associations in a vast chain of knowledge. Although it is now no longer thought that these rules do govern our mental processes in quite this way, they can still make useful guides to certain aspects of teaching and revision.

NT

Association football The modern version, derived from ball games played in English public schools in the early 19th century, has spread all over the world. In state schools in the UK soccer is still the most widely played of all outdoor, winter team games, although in recent years in some parts of the country rugby football has tended to take its place or run parallel with it.

Though some competitive football is played at the top of the primary school, it is in the secondary schools that the game is highly organised at all levels, including the international, by bodies (such as the English Schools Football Association) run by voluntary officials. Many outstanding schoolboy footballers 'discovered' in these competitions have gone on to reach international class in both the amateur and professional game.

Coaching facilities and schemes now widely available throughout Great Britain have done much to improve technique at all levels; today the young footballer is taught basic skills and tactics, whereas in the past these were all too often acquired incidentally, and only those with an innate flair for the game achieved outstanding success.

English Schools Football Association: S. E. Tye, 126 Boston Manor Rd, Brentford, Middlesex.

Football Association, 22 Lancaster Gate, London, W2.

FURTHER READING
The FA Guide to Coaching and Training, Heinemann, 1967.
FA Handbook. Annual.
Modern Soccer—The Skills in Play, Educational Productions, 1966.
Playing Fields and Hard Surface Areas, HMSO, 1965.
Skilful Soccer for Young Players, Educational Productions, 1966.

JE

Association of Special Libraries and Information Bureaus *See* **ASLIB**

Astronomical Association, British The Association's aims are to assist and organise all astronomical observers, to circulate current astronomical information, and to encourage popular interest in astronomy. Schools, universities and colleges may be affiliated (as are some 200 at present) at a minimum annual fee equal to one member's subscription. A library and collections of astronomical instruments, slides and film strips are available to members.
303 Bath Rd, Hounslow West, Middlesex.

Publications: *Journal* (six times annually); *Handbook* (annually)—both included in subscription; *Memoirs* (occasional); *Circulars* (occasional notifications of special events, such as the discovery of a comet or new star, posted on payment of a small additional subscription). Other publications (pamphlets) are available.

Astronomical Society, Royal Founded in 1820 with the aim of encouraging and promoting astronomy, the RAS was one of the first learned societies to be formed for the study of a specific science. Its main functions are to publish the results of astronomical and geophysical research, to maintain as complete a library as possible of astronomical literature and to hold meetings, in London and other cities, at which astronomical and geophysical matters can be discussed. Membership is open to any person interested in astronomy whose application is acceptable to the Society; academic or professional qualifications are not demanded.

Junior membership (for those under the age of 25) is generally intended for students undergoing a course of study.
Burlington Hse, London, W1.

Astronomy in schools Until recently serious educational thinking about astronomy had been restricted to university courses. Astronomy, as such, very seldom amounted to more in secondary education than a brief look at the solar system and possibly some elementary dynamics, part of the physics course.

A great change is now occurring that perhaps had its origin with the first earth-orbiting satellite in 1957, the year when the 'space age' is generally reckoned to have begun. Young people are becoming more and more space-minded, with the result that astronomy has caught educational attention and is beginning to be more seriously taught at the earlier stages. In 1965 it was introduced as a GCE O level subject by the Council of Examiners for the University of London. The examination has settled down and shows every sign of success. In the first year, 1965, the number of candidates was 36; this increased to 60 in 1966 and 117 in 1967. These figures are significant in that they show a general trend towards specialising in the subject in its own right, instead of treating it piecemeal as in the past.

In May 1966 the London Schools' Planetarium, the first of its kind in the UK, was opened at Wandsworth Comprehensive School in SW London. The Planetarium is open to all schools in the London area, from primary upwards, and also to colleges of education.

The astronomical section of the Nuffield physics course adopts an approach that is perhaps not so pragmatic as the O level course but is certainly designed to help a student to understand the theories on which astronomy is founded.

FURTHER READING
P. F. Burns. *First Steps in Astronomy*, Ginn, 1962.
Patrick Moore. *The Solar System*, Methuen, 1959. *The New Look of the Universe*, Zenith Books, 1966.
W. Schroeder. *Practical Astronomy*, Werner Laurie, 1961.
Stars at a Glance, Geo. Philip and Sons, 1961.

Film strips
The Solar System, C. A. Ronan, Foundation Film Library, 572/G2.

The Stellar Universe, E. A. Beet, Foundation Film Library, 573/G3.
Periodical
Space (monthly). PR-J

Athletic Association, Amateur
Founded in 1880 to co-ordinate and govern amateur athletics in England and Wales, the AAA was incorporated in 1948 as a non-profit company and is assisted by the DES, which makes substantial annual grants towards the salaries of AAA national coaches. The main work of these coaches is to conduct courses for teachers, athletes and all other persons who wish to qualify by examination as AAA coaches. DES grants also assist in the administration of the AAA and in the provision of equipment.

The AAA consists of clubs and associations affiliated to the Midland, Northern, Southern and Welsh Associations, and certain national associations affiliated direct. Affiliation is open to all clubs and associations whose membership is restricted to amateur athletes, to schools and to youth organisations through application to the appropriate area association.

26 Park Cres., London, W1.

Athletics Athletics (basically running, jumping and throwing) has been organised as a sport for at least 3,000 years; there are records of the Olympic Games of 776 BC, but the Games were banned by the Roman Emperor Theodosius in 394 AD and not revived again until 1896 in Athens.

About the middle of the 19th century, the army, the civil service and the universities of Oxford and Cambridge instituted meetings and began an era of modern athletics in the UK. The Amateur Athletic Association (AAA) was formed in 1880 to govern the sport. Women began to compete in the early 1920s, formed their own governing body, and were admitted to the Olympic Games in 1928.

Over the last 20 years there has developed a far more scientific approach to both methods of training and coaching and the study of techniques—particularly in the field events (jumping and throwing)—largely as a result of the excellent coaching schemes organised by the AAA through their national coaches. These schemes have had an enormous effect on athletics in schools, many teachers having qualified under them as honorary coaches and passed on their knowledge to their pupils. Today many boys and girls of 14–15 years of age are producing athletic performances that 20 years ago would have been considered excellent if achieved by athletes five or six years older.

In schools, the sport is organised by the Schools Athletic Association, which has local and county associations to arrange coaching and athletic meetings, all of which lead to the national annual athletic meeting (held in different parts of the country in different years) at which, it is said, more athletes compete than in the Olympic Games. Many of these outstanding young athletes go on to adult competition and ultimately take part in international events.

Amateur Athletic Association, 36–39 Park Cres., London, W1.

Women's Amateur Athletic Association: Miss M. Hartman, 41 Hayward Court, Levehurst Way, Clapham, SW4.

Schools' Athletic Association: Mr. Foyston, 16 Cavendish Rd, Hull, Yorks.

FURTHER READING
AAA Coaching Handbooks.
AAA Handbook (for rules and equipment specifications).
H. G. Dyson. *The Mechanics of Athletics*, Univ. of London Press, 1963.
H. G. Dyson and J. Edmundson. *Athletics for Schools*, Univ. of London Press, 1964.
See also **Athletic Association, Amateur**

JE

Atlantic College An international sixth-form college founded in 1962 at St Donats, Glamorgan. In 1964 it received grants of £50,000 from the British government, £45,000 from the West German government and a further £45,000 from the Ford Foundation. The number of pupils is expected to rise to about 300.

The curriculum of Atlantic College is strongly influenced by the ideas of Dr Kurt Hahn (*q.v.*) and, as at Gordonstoun and the Outward Bound Schools, lays stress on fitness, endurance and public service. Mountaineering and sea-going, and rescue work both in the mountains and at sea, play a large part. At the same time, very high academic standards are set. While English is the language in which most subjects are taught, students study their own national history and literature in their own languages.

Atlantic Information Centre for Teachers Administered by an international governing body, the Centre exists to assist teachers of current international affairs in the secondary schools of Western Europe and North America by providing for its subscribers documentation on international problems and information on teaching methods, material, audio-visual aids and current educational exchanges and conferences. Three times a year it publishes *The World and the School*, a review containing material for current affairs lessons and discussion, articles on geography and socio-economic issues, bibliographies, a chronology of world events and notes on relevant developments within the teaching world. The Centre sponsors biennial Atlantic Education Study Conferences and also, from time to time, international summer schools and seminars for teachers of current affairs and related social sciences.

23-25 Abbey Hse, 8 Victoria St, London, SW1.

Attendance centres Non-residential establishments to which magistrates may sentence boys between 10 and 21, on conviction for offences which carry a penalty of imprisonment when committed by adults.

Courts may order attendance *during normal leisure hours* for not less than 12 hours in all (unless the offender is under 14 and 12 hours is thought excessive in his particular case), and each visit usually lasts for two hours on a Saturday afternoon. Thus sentences of 24 hours (the maximum) can involve forfeiture of 12 otherwise free afternoons. Objects are to deprive the youngster of free time; to provide strenuous physical activity, instructional lectures and employment in handicrafts instead. Offenders are not subject to supervision at work or at home, or to after-care.

Attendance centres are a Home Office responsibility, centrally financed. Junior establishments (for those between 10 and 17) are staffed by local police forces and conducted, usually, on police premises or in LEA schools. Approximately 50 were open in 1967. There were two senior centres, taking boys between 17 and 21, and directly administered by the Home Office (Prison Department), staffed by prison officers. No centre for girls has yet been opened.

An advantage of the treatment is that normal relationships and responsibilities can be continued while the offender is punished, as they cannot be if he is committed to a detention centre instead. There are doubts as to the therapeutic value of attendance centres, and in particular regarding their effect upon youngsters' attitudes to the police: no other penal method is applied directly by policemen in this country.

The centres were introduced by the Criminal Justice Act 1948; the first opened in 1950. Suggestions that they would encourage drifting youngsters to continue organised recreational activity on completion of sentence have not so far proved generally valid. It appears that young people do not associate the centres closely with their own notions of acceptable recreation.

c

FURTHER READING
Committee on Children and Young Persons Report, HMSO, 1950.
F. H. McClintock. *Attendance Centres*, Macmillan, 1961.
The Treatment of Young Offenders, HMSO, 1959.

DLH

Attention Although human beings can do two or more things at once, most of us can really concentrate on only one thing at a time; whatever else we may be doing will probably be fairly automatic behaviour. If we continually switch our attention between two demanding tasks, probably neither will be done as well as if we had concentrated entirely upon one. Inattention may be caused by immaturity, mental handicap or lack of intelligence, but the usual explanation is that the subject matter has become boring. We will willingly pay attention to something that really interests us, and also cannot help noticing something which is extra-vivid, unusual in contrast to its background, or in any other way forces itself upon our attention. Furthermore, it is almost impossible not to pay attention to something we are used to observing: for example, an architect often cannot help noticing the buildings around him even if he is on holiday and wants to think of something else. If our consciousness is heightened in any way, perhaps by drugs, excitement or fear, then we may become extra-attentive to things that previously may have seemed unimportant to us.

See also **Boredom**

NT

Audile Any person who is better able to learn through the ear than through the eye is said to be audile.

Audio-lingual courses *See* **Modern languages, Teaching of**

Audio-visual Aids in Eucation, National Committee for Established by the Ministry of Education in 1946 to meet the needs of LEAs, teachers and other educationists in the promotion, production and distribution of audio-visual aids, the Committee is responsible for determining policy at national level, and promoting the use of audio-visual methods. It is assisted by the Central Committee of Teachers' Visual Aids Groups, and the Central Committee of Organisers of Audio-Visual Aids in Education.

The NCAVAE organises national and regional conferences and exhibitions, and provides a reference library, an extensive permanent display of equipment and training facilities at the National Audio-Visual Aids Centre, Paxton Place, Gipsy Rd, London, SE27.

Publications: *Visual Education* and *Visual Education National Information Service for Schools* (*VENISS*).

33 Queen Anne St, London, W1.

See also **Visual Aids, Educational Foundation for**

Australia, Education in Disregard for education as a factor for social and economic advancement went along with Australia's egalitarian frontier philosophy until the last decade or so. Now an educational revolution has taken place. It is accepted that advanced education for all is essential in a democratic society based on technology and developing a unique culture of its own. Social classes like the 'squattocracy' have almost ceased to be influential. Today the élite are those with good university degrees or technical diplomas. As a result, the enrolments in fourth, fifth and sixth forms of secondary schools have increased dramatically and the number of students in Australian universities grew from 31,000 in 1955 to 95,000 in 1967 (out of a total population of 12 million).

Systems of education vary from state to state, but there is a general pattern. The vast majority of children attend public (i.e. state) schools, but there are also independent and church schools of very much the same type as those in the UK. The administration of public schools is a state matter, but the federal government provides funds for universities and technical education and for science laboratories and equipment in both state and private sectors of education. It also offers a generous number of scholarships without a means test to cover students' fees in secondary and tertiary institutions. There is a continual agitation for state aid to Catholic schools.

DMcL

Austria, Education in State education in Austria was reorganised under the School Organisation Act of 1962. Schools are classified according to the education given, i.e. as providing a general, technical, vocational, or teacher training education, and also according to the level at which education is given, i.e. compulsory schools, intermediate schools, secondary schools and academies and other higher institutions. Compulsory education, free in state schools, covers an eight-year period from six to 14 years, and this primary schooling is followed by courses stressing vocational training.

There are universities at Vienna, Graz, Innsbruck and Salzburg, and important technical institutions at Vienna and Graz. In 1965/66 there were 5,331 primary schools with an enrolment of 794,387; 556 secondary vocational schools (enrolment 291,777); 31 teacher training schools (enrolment 2,484); and 15 higher education centres including universities (enrolment 52,169).

The country's population was approximately 7¼ million in 1966.

Austrian Institute Set up in 1956 by the Austrian Ministry of Education to promote cultural relations between Great Britain and Austria.

28 Rutland Ga., London, SW7.

Authority, Part III Abolished by the Education Act 1944, the Part III Authorities (commonly the smaller municipal authorities) were LEAs responsible within their areas only for elementary education.

Autistic children Autistic children (from *auto*—self) are those who at an early age seem to remain unaware of their environment and fail to establish relationships with people. It is not known whether autism is due to a failure in the emotional life—a form of infantile psychosis—or is the consequence of abnormal visual and auditory perception. It is usually accompanied by severe educational retardation, often by absence of speech. Recently special education has been provided in hospital units and in classes and schools established by LEAs and voluntary bodies. A Society for Autistic Children was established in 1962 (1a Golders Green Rd, London, NW11).

FURTHER READING
Mildred Creak. 'Schizophrenic Syndrome in Childhood', *Developmental Medicine and Child Neurology*, October 1964.
J. K. Wing. *Early Childhood Autism*, Pergamon Press, 1967.
L. Wing. *Autistic Children*, National Association of Mental Health, 1964.

See also **Special education**

MW

Autistic Children, National Society for Founded in 1962 on the initiative of parents of autistic children (of whom there are at least 5,000 in England and Wales), the Society soon drew into its membership many professionally interested people. Its aims are to provide and promote the education of autistic children, to help the parents of such children and to encourage research. It offers an advisory service for parents, intended to assist them with educational or hospital placement, and a service of information for those who are professionally concerned. It also publishes literature on the management and education of these children. Membership is open to parents whose children have been diagnosed as autistic, aphasic or non-communicating, and to doctors, teachers, social workers and others interested in this problem.

The Society School for Autistic Children, opened in London in 1965, is a pilot scheme to demonstrate the effectiveness of remedial education as a means of helping these children, and to provide material for educational research.

1A, Golders Green Rd, London, NW11.

Auto-tutor *See* **Programmed learning; Teaching machines**

Auxiliaries *See* **Teacher estimates and teacher shortage**

Average ability, Pupils of Perhaps the best attempt to define this term, and 'pupils of less than average ability', is contained in the Newsom Report (*q.v.*) which comments on the latter phrase thus: 'If those words have any precise meaning at all, they must refer to at least half the children in the country.'

The Report was unhappy about the emotional overtones in the phrases. It identified 'average' pupils as commonly the largest group in a secondary modern school; and asserted that 'a test score which even 14 years ago [prior to 1963, the date of the Report] would have been good enough to put boys or girls well into the above-average category, would today put them firmly into the below-average group,' as 'the standard indicated by "average" is rising all the time.'

B

BACIE *See* **Commercial and Industrial Education, British Association for**

Backward Children, Guild of Teachers of The parent body of the College of Special Education (*q.v.*), the Guild has as its main object the promotion of the educational welfare of all backward, severely subnormal, educationally subnormal and retarded children. Over the past decade, it has established an authoritative voice in this field, contributing significantly to greater knowledge of the problems involved and encouraging more progressive treatment of backward children.

It has a membership of approximately 1,500 teachers, lecturers, educational psychologists and others specialising in this field. Patrons include Sir Cyril Burt, Professor M. M. Lewis and Professor Sir Fred Schonell.

Registered Office: National Book League, 7 Albemarle St, London, W1.

Backwardness Pupils are considered backward if their educational attainments fall markedly below those of their age group. There are many causes — intellectual, emotional, physical and environmental — which interact. Low intelligence is obviously important; but the limited verbal and cultural background which is readily seen as a factor in educational backwardness is now believed to contribute in some measure to intellectual backwardness. Teaching the backward therefore aims at more than 3R work.

It aims at compensating for deprivations, improving thinking and language, and interpreting experience.

Emotional factors are often important. Children may be unsettled by unhappy home situations or unable to adjust to other children and adults. Maladjustment usually results in some degree of backwardness; backwardness itself brings a sense of failure and eventually, if not treated, an unwillingness to try.

Physical ailments are common: slight defects of vision and hearing; clumsiness in large or fine movements. Some children are continuously below par in health, resulting in absences as well as reduced energy for learning.

The most severely backward need to be referred to the school health or psychological service for examination, with a view to placement in a special school or class for educationally subnormal pupils. Special schools cater for children with IQs in the range 55–75 and aim to ensure successful adjustment to social and working life after leaving school at 16. The aims are, therefore, personal and social, with 3R attainments seen as means not ends. It is estimated that about 1% of the school population needs this type of education; over 40,000 pupils are in special ESN schools.

There is a larger group of backward children, at least 10% of the school population, whose backwardness is associated with below-average intelligence and a combination of unfavourable environmental, physical and

57

emotional circumstances. Ideally, they need: (a) smaller classes taught by experienced trained teachers; (b) a curriculum in which emphasis is given to social and practical attainments; and (c) methods which are highly motivating and carefully planned.

Although not academically inclined, their educational diet should not be sparse. They need all that can be offered in imaginative and creative experience, in the development of oral and written expression, in help towards an understanding of their human and natural environment. When taught well, by teachers who understand them, the morale and atmosphere of the class can be high.

A third group consists of children who are of average or above average ability (IQ 90+). Their failure to learn may be general or specific to, for example, reading or arithmetic. Every effort should be made to identify the cause of the difficulty and to provide appropriate remedial teaching.

The extent of backwardness in schools in this country is a serious problem. Earlier detection of backwardness is needed. Some remediable backwardness can be prevented by timely help at the end of the infant school and the beginning of the junior school. Special school provision in most areas is adequate, but more special classes in ordinary schools are necessary as well as more coherent planning of curriculum in backwardness departments in secondary schools.

See also **Special education**

RG

Bacon, Francis (Lord Verulam, 1561–1626) Of enormous influence on educational thought in the 17th century, Bacon urged that knowledge was a means by which man gained power over his environment (he attacked the universities for failing to provide opportunity for experimental science); that such knowledge could be acquired only if preconceived ideas were set aside and

natural fact submitted to inductive analysis; and that there must be some attempt to classify the branches of learning and to separate what was already established from what was still in need of inquiry.

Badminton This indoor court game derives its name from the Duke of Beaufort's house at Badminton, Glos., where it was first devised and played in the 1860s. The game is played by four players (doubles) or by two (singles). The doubles court measures 44 ft by 20 ft; the singles court is 3 ft narrower. Players use light-weight rackets (about 5½ oz) to hit a feathered shuttle weighing about 1/5 oz over a net, the top of which is 5 ft from the ground.

An extremely fast and energetic game, played by many athletes not only for enjoyment but also for its value in training for other sports, badminton has also become a popular 'high pressure' game in secondary schools, colleges and universities throughout the UK.

Players from many countries compete in the All-England championships held in March each year in London. In the UK the game is controlled by the Badminton Association of England; internationally the governing body is the International Badminton Federation, founded in 1934.

Badminton Association of England: 6 Southampton Pl., London, WC1.

FURTHER READING
Badminton, Know the Game Series, Educational Productions, 1950.

JE

Ballet, Teaching of In some quarter of the UK's general educational schools (mostly girls') ballet is taught as higher physical training at all ages, one period per week being the typical allocation per class. The aim is to give basic discipline and understanding of expressive movements in co-ordination with body and music.

All pupils must undergo a physical examination before entering a professional ballet school. Between eight and ten years of age is the ideal time to commence training. Pupils must from the start undergo a high degree of discipline which may prove physically and mentally exhausting for some time until the pupil is attuned to the daily routine. About two periods per day is the average amount of time given to ballet, usually at the beginning and near the end of the daily timetable. Other arts in connection with ballet, e.g. modern and folk dance, drama, notation, music and art will usually be encouraged.

The Associated Examining Board is preparing a scheme for ballet as a GCE subject. At present no formal qualifications may be obtained at general educational schools. For teaching, a Diploma or Associateship of the ISTD (Imperial Society of Teachers of Dancing) or RAD (Royal Academy of Dance) is required. These qualifications usually require two or three years' full-time training.

Ballet is also taught in some drama schools, for physical co-ordination and use of stage space, gestures, etc. It is also an asset to any persons who are training for modelling, ice-skating, and general good poise in every-day life.

MSm

Bank Education Service Bank Education Service was set up by the eleven Clearing Banks to inform young people about banking, to give them an understanding of the part played by banks in a modern society, and to explain banking services in an interesting and practical way. It is not concerned with the training of bank staffs or recruitment.

The Service provides speakers, experienced men drawn from the banks, to visit schools and talk about the part played by the banks in business and family affairs. In addition, publications are available to assist schools in their own treatment of the economic and financial aspects of national and international life.

The publications available include visual aids and booklets explaining such subjects as the history of banking, banking services, the cheque system, overseas trade, balance of payments, decimal coinage and the history of money. There is no charge for any of the services provided.

Copies of publications and details of arrangements for a visit by one of the speakers can be obtained from the Secretary, Bank Education Service, 10 Lombard St, London, EC3.

Barbados, Education in 1965 statistics: 118 primary schools (enrolment 43,695); 16 secondary schools (enrolment 10,909); one technical school (enrolment 545); one teacher training college (enrolment 146); one theological college (enrolment 23); University of the West Indies (enrolment 226).

The island's population in 1965 was approximately a quarter of a million.

Barlow Report (1946): Report of the Committee on Scientific Manpower Terms of reference: to consider the policies which should govern the use and development of scientific manpower and resources during 1946–56, and to submit a report on broad lines at an early date so as to facilitate planning in fields dependent on the use of scientific manpower. Chairman: Sir Alan Barlow.

The main recommendation of the Committee was that the universities should be expanded so as to double the output of scientists, though not at the expense of the humanities. A finding was that only about one in five boys and girls with intelligence equal to that of the top 50% of university students had any chance of entering the universities. From this the Committee concluded that university numbers could be doubled and standards raised at the

59

same time. In fact the number of students climbed from around 50,000 in 1938/9 to over 100,000 in 1958/9.

Barnardo, Thomas John (1845–1905) Born in Dublin, Barnardo became an evangelist during his 'teens and, to prepare himself for missionary work, trained as a doctor. Appalled by the numbers of homeless children, he turned his thoughts from missionary work overseas to the problem of destitute boys and girls at home.

The first Dr Barnardo's Home was opened in Stepney in 1870; three years later he founded a home for girls in Essex. With the support of philanthropists (including Lord Shaftesbury) and of public contributions, Barnardo set up schools in which boys were prepared for the navy and the merchant service, a technical school and other homes. By the time of his death, the number of children rescued by him from destitution was more than 60,000.

See also **Dr Barnardo's**

Basic salary This is the salary scale which a teacher is entitled to receive on account of his training, qualifications and experience. It takes account of the fact that the minimum period of training is three years; thus any recognised additional training, which must be in complete years after the age of 18, earns additional increments up to a maximum of three. Teachers who are graduates or who possess qualifications recognised by the Burnham Report as graduate equivalents receive an additional £100 as a part of their basic scale and those who possess a first or second class ('good honours') Degree receive a further £120 per annum incorporated in their basic scale. There is also provision for a merit payment for those who satisfy the requirements of the Burnham Report in respect of certain additional qualifications: for example, a graduate who also possesses a Post-Graduate Certificate or Diploma in Education receives the merit payment of £50 provided the additional diploma has not formed part of the teacher's qualifications. A further example where the merit payment would apply would be a non-graduate teacher who has successfully passed a special one-year course of advanced study or has achieved a similar result in respect of handicapped children. The basic salary scale is featured in all Burnham Reports and in the Salary Scales for Teachers in Approved Schools and Remand Homes, but there is no exact parallel in the other Salary Reports.

The current basic scales (the merit payment of £50 being added where applicable) for qualified assistant teachers are as follows:

Incremental point	Group I Non-graduates £	Group II Graduates (other than good honours graduates) £	Group III Good honours graduates £
0	800	900	1,020
1	830	930	1,050
2	860	960	1,080
3	910	1,010	1,130
4	970	1,070	1,190
5	1,030	1,130	1,250
6	1,090	1,190	1,310
7	1,140	1,240	1,360
8	1,190	1,290	1,410
9	1,240	1,340	1,460
10	1,290	1,390	1,510
11	1,340	1,440	1,560
12	1,390	1,490	1,610
13	1,440	1,540	1,660
14	1,500	1,600	1,720

SEB

Basketball This was devised as an indoor winter team game by a YMCA official at Springfield, Mass., USA. It was not very popular in this country until after the second world war, but has since developed enormously in schools, where it is played competitively, and is also used as a training for major sports and recreations. It is also played by girls and women as a faster alternative to netball. Now played in most countries of the world, it has reached Olympic Games status, and is said to be watched by more spectators than any other game.

Basketball courts, approximately 80 ft x 45 ft, can be put down on any hard surface, such as wood, asphalt, concrete or shale.

Amateur Basketball Association of England and Wales: K. K. Mitchell, Dept of Physical Education, The University, Leeds 2.

English Schools Basketball Association: P. Deadman, Morrison Boys Secondary School, Rose La., Liverpool.

FURTHER READING
Handbook of the Amateur Basketball Association.
B. Jagger. *Basketball Coaching and Playing,* Faber, 1964.

JE

Basketball Association, English Schools' The Association fosters the playing of basketball in primary and secondary schools by organising courses, national competitions and international games. Membership is open to local school basketball associations based in LEA areas; also to individual schools where there is no local association.

Sec.: Philip G. Deadman, 239 Menlove Ave, Woolton, Liverpool, 25.

Publication: Annual Handbook.

BBC Education Officers Recruited from people with substantial professional educational experience, these Education Officers are appointed jointly by the BBC and the School Broadcasting Council. Their work provides these bodies with a continuous diagnosis of educational opportunities and reports on educational broadcasts; through liaison with the educational world they ensure an appropriate provision of broadcasts and facilitate their use in schools, colleges and other centres.

There were 22 BBC Education Officers in 1968, of whom 17 were responsible for divisional areas in the UK, one specialised in primary educa-

tion, one in science education and three in further education.

BBC educational broadcasting The BBC is required by its charter to provide a service of 'information, education and entertainment'. Its policy has always been that its educational responsibility should be carried out mainly through its programmes as a whole, since it is through the whole range of offered programmes that the educative influence of broadcasting is felt throughout the community. Within this general responsibility, the BBC has in addition since its earliest years provided regular series of educational programmes for people of all ages beyond school-age.

Broadcasts to schools began in April 1924, when the initials 'BBC' stood for 'British Broadcasting Company' and within 18 months of the start of daily broadcasting by the Company. The service of school broadcasting has grown steadily over the years and has responded both to external pressures, such as the war, and to a succession of new educational challenges, such as secondary education for all and the great increase in the number of young people staying longer at school.

The BBC's service of television broadcasts to schools began in 1957 with four series for secondary schools, devoted to science, geography, current affairs and careers, following a detailed pilot study by closed-circuit in a selected area. Now, in the late-60s, there are about 60 radio series and 20 television series for schools each term of the school year; these amount together to 1,007 hours of transmission time during the year. They cover almost every area of the school curriculum and all stages of development, from music and stories for infant groups to careers series and talks for sixth forms. Most of the series are supported by illustrated pupils' pamphlets and nearly all of them also by notes for the teachers. Radio has in recent years

61

developed 'radiovision', i.e. broadcasts accompanied by filmstrips. Radio series are used by about 30,000 schools and television series by about 13,500 schools (most of the latter using both media), out of a total of approximately 37,000 schools in the country.

The general policy for school broadcasting and the scope and purpose of each series is laid down by the School Broadcasting Council for the United Kingdom, a body on which teachers, LEAs, the DES and other educational organisations are represented. (There are separate school broadcasting councils for Scotland and Wales.) The Council's four sub-committees, made up largely of members of the teaching profession, and organised to be responsible for programmes at the various levels of education, meet regularly to review the educational effectiveness of each series and to recommend changes if necessary. The Council has its own permanent staff and a team of 22 full-time education officers in various parts of the country (*see* **BBC education officers**). A system of surveys and reports from schools provides data on the basis of which the School Broadcasting Council can formulate policy. It also enables the BBC to keep in touch with the classroom. The broadcasts themselves are produced by two specialist BBC departments (radio and television).

Educational broadcasts for adults began in 1927. They were supported in 1928 by a joint report of the BBC and the British Institute of Adult Education (as it then was), and for many years were designed mainly for listening groups, who discussed questions raised in the broadcasts. They were succeeded at the end of the war by the forces educational broadcasts and in the early 1950s by a new policy of further education broadcasting (following a detailed study of the whole field), by which programmes in series would be addressed mainly to listeners in their own homes, where the pro-

grammes would be heard by a much larger number of people. These series were mainly studies in depth in the arts and sciences, in history and public affairs, in social and industrial studies, and a growing range of language-teaching courses.

The address to home audiences has continued to be the broad mainstream of further education broadcasting; but a number of important developments have taken place during the mid-60s. The first of these was the introduction in October 1963 of six television series of adult education, which initiated a new phase in further education broadcasting, in response to a government White Paper following the Report of the Pilkington Committee on Broadcasting. Almost at the same time there was a substantial increase in the hours devoted to radio further education, which was given an hour each day, except Sunday, with the overall title of 'Study Session' (now 'Study on Three'). 1964 saw the introduction of further education in the new television channel, BBC 2.

Within three years the service had grown to some 20 radio series and 11 or 12 television series running concurrently at any time of the year. Many of these series are supported by illustrated booklets, gramophone records and other aids to further study, such as reading lists and notes for tutors of discussion groups. Two other significant developments in recent years have been the organisation of discussion groups in connection with these series and the increasing number of series designed for sharply defined professional and vocational groups, e.g. primary and secondary teachers, social workers, industrial management, technicians and technical students, doctors and farmers.

This provision is prepared with the guidance and advice of the Further Education Advisory Council, with its three programme committees, and is produced by two specialist departments, one for radio and one for television. It has the support in enquiry and liaison of the education officers, intensive work being done by a small team specialising in further education.

The whole of the BBC's educational output is under the charge of a Controller of Educational Broadcasting. Account is taken in its planning of ITA educational broadcasts, so as to avoid undesirable duplication. Links are also established with the growing number of closed-circuit educational television systems in various parts of the country. Developments in recent years such as large area closed-circuit ETV systems, the Open University and local radio stations have all produced important implications for educational broadcasting; but they are seen as opportunities for co-operation and not as forms of competition.

BBC educational producers Producers of broadcasts in radio and television are responsible for the planning and execution of series of programmes. In school broadcasting they work to a brief supplied by the School Broadcasting Council and are responsible for the content of the programmes, the selection of speakers, and, in the case of television, for the preparation of film illustration and various other visual elements. Most of these producers have professional educational experience.

In adult education producers have roughly the same responsibilities but prepare their programmes to conform to the suggestions of the Further Education Advisory Council.

In 1968 the BBC had some 43 producers in radio and 43 in television, working exclusively in the field of educational broadcasting.

JRo

Beale, Dorothea (1831-1906) and **Buss, F. M. (1827-94)** Miss Beale and Miss Buss, both early students of Queen's College, Harley Street, were pioneers in the movement to establish secondary education for girls. Miss Buss founded the North London Collegiate School in 1850, and Miss Beale founded Cheltenham Ladies' College in 1858.

See also **Girls, Education of**

BEd (Bachelor of Education) The Robbins Report, 1963 (*q.v.*) included among its recommendations the proposal that to the normal three-year courses for teachers should be added, for suitable students, four-year courses leading both to a degree and to professional qualification. The aim should be to achieve by the 1970s a large increase in the number of students taking four-year courses.

By the end of 1967 all universities maintaining an institute or school of education had, in consultation with the colleges of education in their areas, completed arrangements for these new four-year BEd courses. In the areas for which Keele, Leeds, Reading, Sheffield and Sussex are responsible, the first awards were to be made in 1968; elsewhere in 1969.

The conditions under which students are to be selected and registered vary from university to university, as does the composition of the courses themselves and the classification of the degree. In most areas the qualifying requirements are those normally expected by the universities involved (that is, a certain number of GCE passes or their equivalent), but provision may be made for exceptions. The normal process is for students to be chosen and recommended by their college of education, and for this recommendation to depend on satisfactory results in the third-year certificate examinations of the colleges. Nearly everywhere, students will be based on their colleges throughout the four years of the course, but the need to economise on teaching resources may require some inter-collegiate teaching, transfers from college to college, or the attendance of students at university lectures. Some universities are offering BEd with honours; others are not. Forecasts suggest that the big increase in four-year courses hoped for will not quickly be achieved, and that by 1968–9 fewer than one in ten of students in the year group will be proceeding to a fourth year and the degree course.

No details have yet been announced of arrangements for BEd courses to be taken by serving teachers.

Behaviour problems This term generally refers to children who continually annoy and disturb parents, teachers and sometimes other children too. Such children tend to get noticed and more often referred to agencies such as child guidance clinics than the timid introverted children who may be as seriously maladjusted, but whose symptoms are less obvious and have less nuisance value.

Belgium, Education in School attendance is compulsory and free from six to 15, but most Belgian children enter nursery school at the age of three and continue their education until they are 16 or 18. A feature of the state system is the notion of neutrality of education embodied in the School Pact 1963, which was signed by the three national parties, and which aims at objectivity in expounding facts and ideas and respect for the religious and philosophical convictions of the pupils. Children may attend according to their parents' wishes the courses of non-confessional moral instruction as well as Catholic, Protestant or Jewish courses.

As a principle, teaching is done in the language of the region; French in the Walloon country, Dutch in the Flemish district, German in the East district, and in the Brussels district teaching is done in the mother tongue of the pupil.

Belgium has four universities at Brussels, Liège, Ghent and Louvain (Catholic).

Enrolments for the academic year 1965/66: nursery schools (three to six) 440,000; primary schools (six to 12) 967,124; secondary schools (12 to 18) 329,150; universities (18 to 23) 42,441; technical institutes (18 to 23) 318,242. The population of the country in 1966 was approximately 10 million.

Bell, Andrew (1753–1832) With Joseph Lancaster (*q.v.*), one of the chief English advocates of the 'monitorial system'. 'Give me 24 pupils today,' he said, 'and I will give you 24 teachers tomorrow.' Bell first used older pupils to teach their juniors when he was superintendent of the Madras Male Orphan Asylum. He also superintended the work of the National Society.

Beloe Report Appointed in 1960 by the Secondary School Examinations Council, a committee under R. Beloe found that for many pupils in secondary school the GCE O level examination was unsuitable. It recommended that a new examination, at a lower level and on a subject basis, should be instituted, and that regional authorities should be set up with responsibility for this new examination.
See also **CSE**

Bentham, Jeremy (1748–1832) Bentham's ideas on education flow directly from his philosophy of utilitarianism. This philosophy was based on the belief that pain and pleasure are the great determinants of human behaviour—'It is for them alone to point out what we ought to do'—and that any human act is invariably motivated by self-interest. This led Bentham to urge not only that there should be universal elementary education but that it should reinforce those sanctions that are likely to make a person subordinate his own happiness to that of the whole community. Secondary education, in his view, ought to be 'chrestomathic'—that is, all the teaching, in middle-class day schools, should be directed towards a useful social end (the classics should be taught only to those going into the learned professions) and should cover the whole spectrum of human knowledge and performance.

Berne Convention The International Copyright Union established by the Berne Convention of 1886 includes in its membership most of the principal countries of the world, with the important exceptions of the USA (*see* **Copyright Convention, Universal**), the USSR, China and some of the South American republics. The basic principle of the Convention is that the work of a national of any member country enjoys in other member countries the protection granted under their domestic copyright laws; so does the work of a national of a non-member country if that work is first, or simultaneously, published in a member country. These rights are acquired automatically without formalities such as registration or deposit of copies. The term of copyright protection is the life of the author and 50 years after his death.

The Convention was revised in 1896 (Paris), 1908 (Berlin), 1928 (Rome) and 1948 (Brussels), each revision extending the protection and making it more comprehensive as new technical developments produced new media. It was revised again in Stockholm in 1967, and, under pressure from the developing countries, with their vast needs for cheap copyright material for educational purposes, a Protocol Regarding Developing Countries was included in the Berne Convention Stockholm Act 1967. This allows such countries to shorten the term of copyright protection to 25 years from the author's death; to appropriate copyright works for 'teaching, study and research in all fields of education', paying the proprietor what they choose in blocked currency; and to grant non-exclusive licences for the publication of copy-

right works for 'educational and cultural purposes', and for the publication of translations, subject in both cases to 'a just compensation' in blocked currency. Copies of books published under such licences may be exported to other developing countries.

The Protocol may not, however, be used in respect of copyright works, the country of origin of which has not agreed to it in advance. Owing largely to pressure from the Publishers Association and the Society of Authors, both independently and through their membership of the British Copyright Council, the UK had not, at November 1968, signed the Stockholm Act. Unless, therefore, HM Government does so, the Protocol cannot be applied to British books.

PM

Bernstein, Basil (b. 1925) Formerly a teacher and now a reader in the sociology of education in the University of London, Basil Bernstein has made a particular study of the sociology of language and its effects upon the educational prospects and performances of different types of children. He has distinguished two quite different speech systems: the elaborate code, characterised by verbal explicitness, varied syntax and the potential to express individual and abstract thoughts; and the restricted code, where a low level of vocabulary and syntax is used which is suitable only to express thoughts and ideas at a simplified and condensed level.

Children born in the middle class may be expected to possess both codes of language for use whenever appropriate, but a child born in some sections of the manual working class may be limited to the use and knowledge of the restricted code only. If the latter is to be a success at school, with its predominantly middle-class outlook and language, he will have to acquire at some time an understanding and even mastery of the elaborate code.

Many pupils can make the change from their home background, but there are others who will find it too hard, and Dr Bernstein has argued for greater sensitivity on the part of the teacher to the cultural and cognitive demands made on certain pupils. He has also laid great importance upon education facilities and advice for parents before children start full-time school, so that there may be some broadening of outlook and extension of vocabulary in these very formative years.

FURTHER READING
B. Bernstein. 'Language and Social Class', *British Journal of Sociology*, 1960. 'A Socio-linguistic Approach to Social Learning', *Survey of the Social Sciences*, Penguin, 1965.

NT

Beth ha-Midrash This is a room attached to a synagogue, or a synagogue itself, where Jewish religious texts are studied.

Bible Reading Association, International *See* **Christian Education Council, National**

Bible societies These societies exist to translate and distribute the scriptures and to further the reading and understanding of the Christian scriptures among adults and children. The largest, founded in 1804, is the British and Foreign Bible Society (*q.v.*).

Systematic Bible reading is encouraged by the Bible Reading Fellowship, 148 Buckingham Palace Rd, London, SW1; the International Bible Reading Association, Robert Denholm Hse, Nutfield, Redhill, Surrey; and the Scripture Union, 5 Wigmore St, London, W1.

Bible Societies, United A fellowship of 35 Bible societies working in 120 countries, responsible for 95% of all Scriptures distributed in Africa, Asia and Latin America. Since the Bible Society movement began 160 years ago,

its aim has been to make the Scriptures available for all at a price all can afford. Some part of the Bible has been translated into 1,250 languages, and translation continues. Current emphasis is on providing Scriptures for new readers — schoolchildren, students, new literates — and on producing attractive Scripture editions in modern translations.

101 Queen Victoria St, London. Gen. Sec.: Dr. Olivier Béguin.

Bible Society, British and Foreign Founded in 1804, the object of the Society is the wider circulation of the Scriptures, without note or comment, in vernacular languages. Inter-denominational, it engages with the united Bible societies of the world in translating, publishing and distributing the Scriptures. In 1966 the combined Bible societies distributed 77 million copies; the number of languages exceeded 1,200.

With a traditional policy of selling at prices suited to local needs and not for profit, the Society averages a loss of 50% on sales. This is made up by voluntary subscriptions, mainly in the UK, Australia, Canada, New Zealand and South Africa. It has an annual budget of over £1 million. Its charitable nature is recognised by a Royal Charter.

146 Queen Victoria St, London, EC4.

Bilateral school A secondary school which combines two types of school: e.g. a grammar-technical or technical-modern school.

Binary system of higher education *See* **Universities, English; Technical education**

Binet, Alfred (1857–1911) Alfred Binet was a French psychologist working in Paris who developed the first widely used intelligence test. In collaboration with a colleague, Dr T. Simon, he devised some tests in 1905 as a more scientific way of separating subnormal children who needed special education from children who appeared backward through lack of cultural stimulation but who had the potential for intelligent behaviour. Some of Binet's original tests, standardised by L. M. Terman of Stanford University in 1916 and revised since, still survive in the Stanford-Binet Test, which continues to be widely used by educational psychologists, especially when working with younger children.

See also **Intelligence tests**

FURTHER READING
George Miller. *Psychology, The Science of Mental Life*, Penguin, 1966.

NT

Biology, Institute of Founded in 1950, the Institute exists to advance the knowledge of biology and to promote the professional standing, efficiency and usefulness of biologists. Its educational activities include: publication of *The Journal of Biological Education*: a scheme for granting the qualification MIBiol by examination; responsibility, with the DES, for the Higher National Certificate in Applied Biology; sponsorship, jointly with the Royal Society, of the Biological Education Committee which exists to improve the teaching of biology in schools, universities and colleges; branch meetings which help teachers to keep up-to-date in biological matters.

41 Queen's Ga., London, SW7.

Biology, Teaching of Biology is taught in most secondary schools today. In sixth forms botany and zoology are taught separately, but below sixth form level the two subjects are usually combined. Biology may be taken at O level, either as a separate subject or combined with chemistry and physics as general science.

Biology is satisfactory to teach, for children are naturally interested if it is presented as a living subject and not as a mere catalogue of long words to be learnt. Furthermore, it is essentially a practical subject, students learning as much from their own observations in laboratory and field as they do from text-books. Here the good teacher can play an important part in stimulating interest, and in suggesting how further experiments or observations may be able to elucidate problems that arise. Thus guided, the student can be encouraged to teach himself.

Work in the field plays an essential part in the teaching of biology, particularly botany, for though animal life is often difficult to follow in the field, plants are all around for everyone to see. In sixth-form work for A level, formal plant ecology plays an important part, but there is no reason why it should be confined to the sixth form. Middle school pupils take a keen interest in working out quadrants and transects, if the principles that underlie the methods being used are first carefully explained to them. Even juniors can carry out simple ecological techniques if handled by a good teacher.

In field work, as with practical work generally, the taking of full and accurate notes is essential if the students are to reap all possible benefit from their work. A notebook and pencil are essential equipment for every student in the field, and a ruler for measuring the heights of plants.

It might be thought that city schools are poorly placed for carrying out field work, but an extraordinary amount of useful work can be done in a local park, and bird watching can be attempted anywhere.

Besides pure biology, applied biology comes into the syllabus in many schools. It is included in hygiene and domestic science, agriculture and rural science, and the preliminary training of girls who intend to take up nursing.

CD

Bipartism This term is sometimes used to describe the selective secondary school system in England and Wales, rather than the term 'tripartism' (*q.v.*), since the technical schools, which form the third part of the system, are negligible in number: there are roughly seventeen secondary modern schools and six grammar schools to every one technical school.

Birds, Royal Society for the Protection of The RSPB is concerned with the protection and conservation of wild birds. Its work includes the establishment of nature reserves (at present there are 28 in Great Britain), research into toxic chemicals and oil pollution and education of the public.

In its educational programme, the RSPB hires films, runs courses, publishes leaflets, runs competitions for schools, advises teachers, and runs the Young Ornithologists' Club (*see below*). Educational aids available include 16-mm. colour films, bird-song records, identification wall charts, field notebooks and various booklets on the care and study of wild birds.

The Young Ornithologists' Club The club is for all children (in both primary and secondary schools) interested in birds or wanting to learn about them. A choice of individual, family or group membership (for schools and clubs) is offered.

The YOC publishes an informative magazine, *Bird Life*, runs bird study courses and visits to reserves, has a network of adults throughout the country to take members on local field outings and organises national projects and surveys suitable for school children.

The Education Officer, The Lodge, Sandy, Beds.

Birkbeck, Dr George (1776–1841) As Professor of Natural Philosophy and Chemistry in the Andersonian Institution in Glasgow (to which he was appointed in 1799), Birkbeck visited the workshops where apparatus for his classes was being made, and was greatly impressed by the mechanics' interest in

their work. He invited them to attend a special class and met with an extraordinary response: over 500 turned up to the fourth meeting of the class. In London, where he went in 1804 to practise as a physician, Birkbeck was one of the founders of the London Mechanics' Institute (1823). Birkbeck College (*q.v.*), which began by providing instruction in economics and the physical sciences and later added literary studies and art, sprang from the work of such institutes.

Birkbeck College A constituent college of the University of London since 1920, distinguished for the fact that many of its undergraduates, though reading for an internal degree, are following their own occupations and attend lectures part-time. The College offers first-degree courses in arts and sciences, and a variety of advanced courses. In 1966/67 there were nearly 2,000 students, about half of them working as undergraduates (although many of them already have degrees). The report (1967) of an Academic Advisory Committee on Birkbeck College concludes that as demand for university courses from mature students will continue to increase, only persons in full-time employment should be enrolled as undergraduates (i.e. school leavers should be excluded) and that both curricula and timetables need to be still more flexible.

The College was originally founded in 1823 as the London Mechanics' Institute (*see* **Mechanics' institutes**) and is now named after the first president, Dr George Birkbeck.

BG

Birmingham Education League The League was set up in 1869 to press for free, compulsory and non-sectarian education, and played a large part in the discussions that led to the 1870 Education Act (*q.v.*). Joseph Chamberlain was its vice-chairman.

Biserial 'r' *See* **Correlation**

Blackboard *See* **Chalkboard; Visual aids**

Blind, National College of Teachers of the *See* **Blind children, Teaching of**

Blind, National Library for the Provides a library service for the blind and partially sighted. There is both a bulk and individual loan service to teachers and pupils.

35 Gt Smith St, London, SW1.
Publication: *Braille Library Bulletin* (six times annually).

Blind, Royal National Institute for the Founded in 1868 to supply services best provided on a national rather than a local or regional basis, the Institute makes available Braille publications, apparatus and talking books, and has built up a library for students. It also concerns itself with rehabilitation, and with the provision of specialised training and employment services, hostels and holiday homes. Its contribution to special education includes the establishment of a parents' counselling service, six residential nurseries, two grammar schools, two schools for children with handicaps additional to blindness, and a vocational guidance and assessment centre.

224/6/8 Great Portland St, London, W1.

Blind children, Teaching of Pupils are 'educationally blind' if they require education by methods not involving the use of sight. In Britain this is the rarest category of handicap. Numbers have been steadily falling since 1925, apart from a temporary increase due to retrolental fibroplasia in babies born between 1948 and 1954. There is, however, an increase in the proportion of blind children with additional handicaps.

Blind children are usually educated in boarding schools, some maintained by LEAs but the majority by voluntary bodies with financial support from public funds. The maximum size of a class in a school for the blind is 15. Blind children can with special permission be educated in ordinary schools. Teachers of the blind must have obtained additional qualifications–either by a one-year university course or by passing the diploma examination of the College of Teachers of the Blind— within three years of taking up work in a recognised school for the blind.

The possibility of educating blind people was recognised early in the history of special education (*q.v.*), but little success was achieved until the 18th century when Valentin Haüy, of Paris, used Roman letters heavily printed on wax to enable the blind to read by touch. In 1829 Louis Braille, who had been blinded in childhood, perfected a system of six embossed dots which could be used in different combinations to represent letters of the alphabet. The dots can be produced by means of a special frame and stylus, thus enabling the pupil to write as well as read. The Braille system was not adopted in Britain until 1872, but its use in the education of blind children is now universal. In recent years machines resembling typewriters have been developed which enable children to write Braille less laboriously. A Braille shorthand machine is also available, and 'talking books' for advanced students.

Nursery schools are available for blind children from the age of two, and a parent guidance hostel has been established by the Royal National Institute for the Blind. Schools have been established for blind children with additional handicaps, and for those of high academic ability aiming at university entrance. Others with a technical bent can receive training from the age of 16 in commercial subjects, music, piano-tuning, telephony, brush- and basket-making or capstan lathe operating. A residential assessment centre provides vocational guidance and work experience.

Voluntary societies have a long and honourable tradition in the education of blind children.

National College of Teachers of the Blind, The School for the Blind, Westbury-on-Trym, Bristol. Journal: *The Teacher of the Blind*. Quarterly.

Royal National Institute for the Blind, 224 Gt Portland St, London, W1.

FURTHER READING
Directory of Agencies for the Blind, Royal National Institute for the Blind.

MW

Blind and Deaf Children Act (1893) Giving the school boards power to provide special schools for blind and deaf children, this Act was part of a move towards regular medical supervision and specialised treatment which began in 1890 with the appointment of a medical officer by the London school board.

See also **School Medical Service**

Block practice In teacher training, practice in the schools for continuous periods of up to a term is called block practice.

Block release *See* **Further education in England and Wales**

Board of Education Constituted in 1899 by Act of Parliament to superintend education in England and Wales, the Board of Education consisted of a president, the principal Secretaries of State, the First Commissioner of the Treasury and the Chancellor of the Exchequer. It was a combination of three existing government departments: the Committee of the Privy Council on Education, established in 1839 by Order in Council as a grant-awarding body for elementary schools, and presided over and spoken for, after 1856, by a vice-president; the Science and Art Department, established at South Kensington in 1856 to disburse parliamentary grants for the encouragement of science and art teaching; and the

Charity Commission established in 1853 (*see* **Charity Commissioners**).

The Board had powers additional to those of its three forebears, notably the right to inspect secondary schools and, up to 1919, responsibility for grants to universities and the promotion of physical education. After the Public Libraries Act 1919, it was the approving body for schemes for public libraries. But above all it had a consultative committee whose reports, even when not officially mandatory, acquired the status of an official writ. Indeed, successive chairmen of this committee, like A. H. D. Acland, Sir Henry Hadow and Sir Will Spens, were even better known than the presidents.

The Board issued regulations, some of which had to be presented to Parliament, and suggestions to teachers and managers. Its work was annually reviewed during the debate on the estimates. In 1944 it was upgraded to the Ministry of Education, and in 1964 merged with the Ministry of Science to become the Department of Education and Science.

WHGA

Board of Education Act (1899) This established the Board of Education following the recommendations of the Bryce Report (*q.v.*). It merged the old Education Department and the Science and Art Department under a president. The Charity Commission, which controlled the endowed schools, was also gradually merged. A consultative council was set up, and a register of teachers started.

Board of studies The senior teachers of any university subject are constituted into a committee, known as the Board of Studies, which is responsible for the syllabus in that subject, for the admission of students and for other related matters.

Boarding school education Education away from home, in a residential community of children, goes back beyond civilised society. It still exists in primitive cultures as part of the process of initiation to manhood. In the ancient world it was used for the training of the élite in Sparta. Our present (English) system derives from the medieval practice of the sons of nobility being educated in the households of others. Residential schools (Winchester and Eton) followed, multiplied in the 16th century and again in the 19th century when they took their present closed character, social structure and goals. In England, boarding has always been associated with the governing élite. In other contemporary countries where residential education is used for absolutely more children than the number boarding in the UK, e.g. the Soviet Union and Israel, it is not associated with the training of an élite and takes different, less closed forms.

Just over 2% of the school children of England and Wales are boarders: 161,000 children in all. Of these 137,000 are in independent schools. Only 12,000 boarders are in LEA-maintained schools and another 11,000 in direct grant schools. Of the independent boarders about a third are in boys' public schools and another quarter in associated preparatory schools. Girls tend to board less than boys (53,000 girls to 108,000 boys). Altogether 1,780 schools provide boarding places— 145 LEA schools, 73 direct grant ones, and 1,562 independent ones (479 of which are officially unrecognised).

The boarder at an independent school tends to be educated throughout outside the state system of education. Entering prep school (from the pre-prep or primary school) at eight, he transfers to his public or secondary school at 13 and leaves that between 16 and 18. Most public and many independent schools are outside urban areas, and the boy lives in a closed society, returning home for 12 weeks in the year only, in holidays. In its length of stay, and removal from the home, this traditional English boarding pattern differs from that of other countries or state boarding schools where the length of stay is shorter and varied and the boarder's life is more integrated with that of his home and locality.

English boarding schools place great stress on extra-academic development, e.g. moral and religious qualities, social and managerial competence. To this end, the typical school is organised by a hierarchy in which the senior boys have very considerable authority. Some few 'progressive' schools stand outside this tradition: co-educational in composition, they try to remove external pressures and regulations and enlarge individual freedom of choice and behaviour, in the hope that their own distinct extra-academic goals will voluntarily be internalised. Interestingly, most 'progressive' schools are residential (*see* **Progressive education**).

The problems of boarding education arise from: the closed nature of schools, their one-sex nature, rural setting and the inflexibility of the system which ordains boarding from eight to 18 or nothing. Changes in family relationships and the decline of the nursery, together with the rise of an adolescent culture, are pushing boarding schools towards allowing greater contact with home and parents, reducing control and compulsion over pupils, diminishing the hierarchy (fagging) and brutality (beating), permitting contact with the other sex and experimenting with flexible patterns of boarding (e.g. weekly boarding).

There is much controversy on the effects of boarding. Whatever benefits there might be derive from the stable environment, close staff-pupil relations and the stimulating possibilities of being in an educational environment more continuously than the day child. The defects derive from the removal from the family and ordinary society (in sex, age), from limitation of choice, privacy and from incessant routine.

The future of boarding education will be decided by the solution of two problems: How to make it less exclusive, less the training ground for the élite; and how to make it less opposed in style and pattern to day school and family life.

RL

Bolivia, Education in Free education, from six to 16 years, is nominally compulsory but lack of schools prevents implementation of the statute. Of a 1966 estimate of 1,055,800 children in this age range, 658,860 were thought to be enrolled. All illiterates, between 15 to 50 years, are compelled to attend literacy classes. In 1964 there were 495,083 primary schoolchildren and 71,404 secondary schoolchildren, 46 technical colleges had an enrolment of 6,655, and 15 teacher training colleges 4,951. Universities are at La Paz, Santa Cruz, Sucre, Oruro, Potosí, Tarija and Cochabamba.

The country's population in 1965 was approximately 4¼ million.

Book agencies The sale of books direct to pupils and students in schools and colleges presents many problems: selection, supply, staffing, legal difficulties. The size of the school will partly determine the number of books likely to be sold, but certain essentials of success suggest themselves: a centrally situated room of ample dimensions to house and display the books; someone reliable, probably a member of staff, to control ordering and accounting; effective and continuous publicity; plans to buttress sales after first enthusiasms have cooled.

The simplest solution (and one that copes with the legal situation) is to start a bookshop or sales point under the Publishers Association Book Agency Scheme. Local booksellers will usually supply and maintain stock; they may even be willing to consider help with staffing the school shop at selected times. Books must be sold at standard retail prices but normally some discount is allowed to the school—about 10% is a reasonable figure. Some booksellers prefer instead to offer books on sale or return or favourable credit facilities. Such agencies are granted for the sale of books for recreational reading to individual buyers and not for class or library use.

Once a bookseller has agreed to co-operate and terms of operation have been discussed and settled, application should be made to the Publishers' Association (19 Bedford Sq., London, WC1) for the granting of a book agency.

GBo

Book Development Council Ltd Established in 1965 by the principal exporting members of the Publishers Association, the BDC now has 73 publishers as its subscribing members. It acts as a co-operative to assist British publishers in their export function, and also serves as a clearing house for those in the UK willing to give assistance in the field of book production and distribution to bodies outside the UK who ask for such assistance.

London office: 7 Albemarle St, London W1; Services Centre: c/o Book Centre Ltd, North Circular Rd, Neasden, London, NW10.

Borderline children *See* **Ineducable children**

Boredom This occurs primarily when we are working at a task, often a monotonous one, or when we are merely existing at a level that does not hold our interest. In school, signs of boredom amongst pupils are often mistaken for dreaminess or sheer perversity. Boredom is an inconsistent feeling since it can suddenly disappear when an individual discovers a new interest in something he has become bored with; on other occasions, a well-loved task may soon feel tedious. With younger or backward pupils, with shorter spans of concentration, there is a greater risk of boredom, especially with more demanding work. The teacher can sometimes avoid this by splitting such periods into shorter units, interspersed with other more relaxing activities.

See also **Attention**

NT

Borstal A system of residential training for young offenders between 15 and 21 years of age at the time of conviction. Borstals are administered by the Prison Department of the Home Office (England and Wales) and by the Scottish Home Department. The sentence of borstal training has a maximum length of four years. It is divided into two parts, a period of up to two years in a borstal institution being followed by two years or less 'on licence', i.e. at liberty under the supervision of an after-care associate (who is usually a probation officer). The length of stay in the institution, never less than six months, is determined in practice by the governor, advised by an Institution Board comprised of senior members of staff; the governor may be given positive direction from the Prison Department on this matter in certain cases. Responsiveness to training is the first consideration in fixing the date of discharge on licence; the progress of each individual is regularly reviewed. Approximately two months before release young people in borstal are allowed five days home leave in which to make plans for resettlement together with the aftercare associate concerned. At any stage before the two-year aftercare period has elapsed, those who do not appear to have settled adequately may be required to spend a further short period in custody at a borstal recall centre.

The system takes its name from the village of Borstal, Kent, where the first institution of this kind was established under the Prevention of Crime Act 1908. Experiments on similar lines had been conducted there since 1902 and

at Bedford Prison since 1900. From the beginning, borstal training has concentrated upon changing the attitudes of young offenders, rather than on punishment, although secure custody is considered important, particularly in the closed institutions, which consist for the most part of converted prisons. In 1965 there were in England and Wales 12 closed borstals and 11 open borstals for boys, the latter being hutted camps or large houses, usually in remote countryside. There were four institutions for girls, three closed and one open. The borstal population figures were in 1965:

	Boys	Girls
Closed borstals	2,967	123
Open borstals	1,685	26
Total in borstals	4,652	149

The sentence of borstal training may be imposed only by Sessional Courts, Assizes or the Court of Criminal Appeal. On sentence, offenders are sent initially to Borstal Allocation Centres at Wormwood Scrubs, London; Strangeways, Manchester (for boys); or Bullwood Hall, Essex (for girls). Offenders are then transferred to the institution whose regime is thought most suitable in the light of their medical and psychological history, intellectual capacity, vocational training requirements and criminal record.

There is considerable variation both in the training facilities offered by different borstals and the degree of individual treatment young people in them receive. In all boys' institutions there are some vocational training courses, taught by civilian instructors (i.e. not prison officers) working toward UEI and City and Guilds trade qualifications. Other educational activities are the responsibility of a tutor organiser nominally on the staff of the LEA but under the direction of the governor. The tutor organiser's appointment is often part-time, but in large borstals (200 or more boys) a full-time tutor organiser may be assisted by one or more full-time teachers. In all borstals, educational activities are largely confined to evening classes. All employ a number of part-time teachers on an evening institute basis. They are paid by the LEA, which is reimbursed in turn by the Prison Department. There is strict Treasury control of funds for educational purposes; provision of equipment and books is poor by comparison with further education establishments under sole control of local authorities. Boys and girls in borstals may have opportunities to prepare for a wide range of GCE and other examinations, but tuition facilities vary widely. From some borstals youngsters are permitted to attend part-time courses at technical colleges.

Borstals are organised on a house system, each house normally accommodating between 40 and 60 boys and in the charge of a housemaster with the rank of assistant governor. With the exception of the tutor organiser and teachers, the staff (including vocational training instructors) are employed by the Prison Department of the Home Office or its equivalent in Scotland. Most are liable to transfer between borstals and prisons.

It is now rare for first offenders to be sentenced to borstal training. Most boys have previously been on probation, at an approved school or in a detention centre, and show some criminal sophistication. Restriction upon the sentencing of people under 21 to terms of imprisonment has made borstal training increasingly a sentence of last resort in the 15 to 21 age group.

FURTHER READING
L. W. Fox. *The English Prison and Borstal Systems*, Routledge and Kegan Paul, 1952.
T. C. N. Gibbens. *Psychiatric Studies of Borstal Lads*, Oxford Univ. Press, 1963.
Home Office. *Annual Reports of the Prison Department. Prisons and Borstals*, HMSO, 1960.
R. Hood. *Borstal Reassessed*, Heinemann, 1966.
A. G. Rose. *Five Hundred Borstal Boys*, Blackwell, Oxford, 1954.

S. K. Ruck. *Paterson on Prisons*, Muller, 1951.

DLH

Botanical Society of the British Isles The leading national body devoted to the study of the classification and distribution of the flowering plants and ferns of the British Isles. Its 1,700 members include large numbers of amateur as well as professional botanists. The Society is descended from the Botanical Society of London, founded in 1836, and was reconstituted under its present name after the second world war. Its activities include the holding of field and indoor meetings, exhibitions and conferences, besides the issuing of scientific journals and reports. A panel of specialists answers queries from members on a wide range of botanical topics and assists with the naming of particularly difficult groups.

A Junior Activities Committee organises field and occasional indoor meetings for botanists of school age in different parts of the country; and local schools are notified of these accordingly. Special week-long field meetings on the continent have also been held for junior members (under 21) in past years.

Hon. Gen. Sec.: D. E. Allen, c/o Department of Botany, British Museum (Natural History), Cromwell Rd, London, SW7.

Botswana, Education in 1965 statistics: 247 primary schools (enrolment 66,061); nine secondary schools (enrolment 1,325); two teacher training colleges (enrolment 268). Students studying abroad 125.

Total population in 1964: approximately half a million.

Boxing Modern boxing is a direct descendant from the old, bare-knuckle prize fighting in which rounds ended only when a fighter went down on the ground and the contest was not won until, after a knockdown, one fighter failed to be ready to resume the contest within 30 seconds. In 1867 the Marquess of Queensberry and J. G. Chambers drew up a set of rules for the sport and these have since formed the basis of boxing.

Professional boxing in this country is now controlled by the British Boxing Board of Control, amateur boxing by the Amateur Boxing Association and boxing in schools by the Schools Amateur Boxing Association.

In recent years many attempts have been made by certain members of Parliament and some quite eminent medical authorities to ban the sport altogether, particularly for young people, on the grounds that continued blows on the head can cause serious damage to the brain. Those who advocate the continuance of the sport deny this and say that strict rules prevent any serious or permanent injury. Nevertheless, there are signs that the anti-boxing advocates are gaining ground and that, with the increase in the number of other sports now available, boxing is losing some of its previous popularity.

Very strict control of schools' boxing is maintained by the SABA which, among other things, stipulates a close season during the summer, limits the number of bouts permitted during a year, and pays particular attention to the fair matching of opponents.

Amateur Boxing Association, 69 Victoria St, London, SW1.

Schools Amateur Boxing Association: A. J. P. Martin, 'Medina', Marlow Bottom La., Marlow, Bucks.

FURTHER READING
Boxing for all, SABA.
J. Edmundson. *Handbook for Sports Organisers*, Evans, 1960.
Handbook of the Schools Amateur Boxing Association.
Instructors' Guide and Amateur Boxers' Textbook, ABA.
Referees' and Judges' Manual, ABA.

JE

Boyle, Rt Hon Sir Edward (b. 1923) Parliamentary Secretary to the Ministry of Education from 1957 to 1959, Sir Edward Boyle became Minister in 1960. On the reorganisation of the Ministry in 1964, and its redesignation as the DES, he became Minister of State, holding that post until the change of government in the autumn of that year.

Boys' Brigade Founded in 1883 by Sir William Smith and claiming to be the oldest voluntary uniformed organisation for boys, the Brigade has as its object—'The advancement of Christ's Kingdom among boys, and the promotion of habits of obedience, reverence, discipline, self-respect, and all that tends towards a true Christian manliness.' Based on the twin pillars of religion and discipline, the Brigade in the UK consists of 2,948 Companies of boys between the ages of eight and 18. In addition there are 1,545 Companies in 64 countries overseas. Each Company is connected with a church or other Christian body. Drill is used as a means of banding the boys together and of training them in discipline and self-respect, but bands, club rooms, athletics, swimming, arts and crafts, wayfaring, life saving, gymnastics, first aid and summer camps are extensively carried on.

Sec.: Ian G. Neilson, DFC, TD, BL, Brigade Hse, Parsons Green, London, SW6.

Boys' Clubs, National Association of The administrative organisation for some 2,000 boys' clubs all over the country, with a total membership of 160,000 boys. Its purpose is to provide opportunities and encouragement for boys to develop themselves physically, mentally and spiritually, through the boys' club environment. In sport, probably 100,000 boys' club members are gaining skill and experience. Adventure activities form part of the Association's regular programme: canoeing, rock-climbing, sailing, sub-aqua swimming. Local arts festivals are held by

75

at least 30 boys' clubs each year, and include painting, handicrafts, sculpture, photography, drama and music.
17 Bedford Sq., London, WC1.

Boys' Clubs of Wales This organisation aims to educate boys through their leisure-time activities in such a way as to develop their physical, mental and spiritual capacities towards individual maturity and make them capable of social contribution and self-improvement. Membership is open to boys aged 11-20. The organisation provides boys' clubs in Wales and organises courses and competitions.
Gen. Sec.: G. H. Stokes, 26 High St, Cardiff, Glamorgan.

Braille *See* **Blind children, Teaching of**

Brain-injured children Brain-injured children may receive special educational treatment as physically handicapped (e.g. cerebrally palsied), maladjusted, or educationally subnormal children, according to the effect of the disability on the child's learning capacity or behaviour. Recently attention has been drawn to a group of children of normal general intelligence whose educational retardation may be due to 'minimal cerebral dysfunction'. Such children require remedial education which can be supplied within an ordinary school, a remedial class, or a child guidance clinic.
FURTHER READING
A. H. Strauss and L. Lehtinen. *Psychopathology and Education of Brain-Injured Children*, 2 vols, Grune and Stratton, New York, 1947.
MW

Branching programme (*see also* **Programmed learning**) A technique of programming, popularised by Norman Crowder, in which the learner is presented with units of information and then tested with multiple-choice questions. Wrong answers are treated according to their merits and the nature

of the error explained. Under this system different individuals are allowed to follow different routes in order to arrive at the same direction — hence the term 'branching'. Crowder himself refers to the technique as 'intrinsic' programming because the remedial treatment and material are written into the programme.

Brass Band Association, National School The Association was formed in 1952 to encourage the development of brass groups in schools, with the view that a brass band provides the readiest means of obtaining rapid and musically satisfactory results from young instrumentalists. It set out not only to raise the standard of performance of school bands but also to grapple with the difficulty that, at the time of its foundation, there was an almost total absence of good music suitable for young bands.

The Association has held lectures, demonstrations and courses in many parts of the country, on both a local and national basis, and a considerable amount of original music and of arrangements of classics has been produced for it. Local festivals and inter-school visits have been arranged, and a national festival is held each year. This concludes with a concert by massed bands under a distinguished guest conductor. A panel of experts is available to give advice on any aspect of teaching brass in schools.

The executive committee consists of practising teachers, and has the support and help of an advisory council of eminent musicians representing every aspect of school and instrumental music.
Sec.: E. Charles Sweby, 2 Gray's Close, Barton-le-Clay, Bedford.

Brazil, Education in Primary education is free and compulsory for a four-year period in urban areas and a three-year period in rural areas, but in some parts of the hinterland education is rudimentary or non-existent. According to the 1960 census 53.5% of the population over the age of five was literate. Secondary education is split into a four-year junior and a four-year senior course. In 1964 these were 124,946 primary schools (enrolment 10,217,324); 9,196 secondary schools (enrolment 2,154,430); 1,829 commercial colleges (enrolment 288,351); 356 industrial colleges (enrolment 79,230); 1,811 teacher-training colleges (enrolment 220,272 students); 1,224 higher education colleges and institutes including 45 universities (enrolment 155,781). Of the universities 10 are Roman Catholic foundations, 11 other foundations, and 24 state established.

The country's population was approximately 80 million in 1964.

Breakdown pensions (or disablement allowance) After 10 years of recognised and/or contributory service, a breakdown pension or disablement allowance is claimable where permanent incapacity on medical grounds is established to the satisfaction of the Secretary of State. Application for this particular benefit should be made on Form 18 Pen.—obtainable from the DES—within the prescribed time. The prescribed time within which a teacher must have been employed in contributory service before the date on which he applies for a breakdown pension is six months immediately preceding the application, or such longer period as the Secretary of State may allow in any case where he is satisfied that there is sufficient cause for the application not having been made within six months. A continuous period of absence on sick leave not exceeding 12 months (18 months in the case of pulmonary tuberculosis) and with not less than half pay will be treated by the Secretary of State as contributory service. In this case the period of six months mentioned above will therefore commence from the date the teacher's period of contributory sick leave ended.

Under the Act of 1925 the Secretary of State has power, provided the teacher is less than 60 years old, to suspend a pension granted on the grounds of permanent incapacity until a further direction has been given, or to cease payment where he is satisfied that the teacher has ceased to be so incapacitated. For this purpose the Secretary of State will require the teacher concerned to undergo a medical examination by the Department's local doctor.

The Secretary of State has power, however, to grant subsequently a fresh superannuation allowance on the teacher attaining the age of 60—the period of incapacity being treated as qualifying service.

The breakdown pension and lump sum are calculated in the same way as that for the retiring pension, but where the teacher has rendered 10 years but less than 20 years of service the benefits will be based on 20 years, the additional years being added to the commencement of the teacher's actual service. If the teacher cannot complete 20 years of service by the time he attains the age of 65, the breakdown pension benefits will be calculated on the number of years which could have been rendered by that age.

In the case of a teacher who has been contributing under the modified scheme of superannuation the breakdown pension will be the unreduced pension. But on the teacher becoming qualified for the National Insurance pension at 60 in the case of a woman, 65 in the case of a man, the breakdown pension will be reduced according to the scale of reduction operating under the modified scheme.

SEB

Brinsley, John (1585–1665) Headmaster of Ashby-de-la-Zouch School in Leicestershire, and author of *Ludus Literarius, The Grammar School* (1612), which gives a rich picture of the life of a grammar school of the period. In it

Brinsley stressed the importance of the teaching of English on the grounds that it is the language most widely used both in speech and writing; that the good use of it ought to be regarded as 'a chief part of the honour of our nation'; and that very few of those taught in the school went on to take up learned professions. He was opposed to the great strictness of the schoolmasters of his time, and impatient with their ignorance, and was much concerned with the physical welfare of his pupils.

British Association of Commercial and Industrial Education *See* **BACIE**

British Council The Council was founded in 1934, and granted a Royal Charter in 1940. It aims at the promotion of a wider knowledge of Britain and the English language abroad, and the development of closer cultural relations with other countries.

In recent years, it has increasingly concentrated on educational work, particularly in the developing countries of Asia and Africa, to which about four-fifths of its work is devoted. In its work of promoting English language teaching, the Council's main task is to advise and assist educational authorities overseas, particularly in the training of teachers. It is becoming increasingly concerned with advising on science teaching in schools. It promotes educational and other exchanges with overseas countries, primarily by sponsoring visits in both directions, but also by recruiting British teachers for service overseas, and the award of scholarships and bursaries.

The Council runs, or assists, about 200 libraries overseas, and presents overseas the best in the arts in Britain. It maintains centres in Britain to provide welfare and other services for overseas students and professional visitors.

65 Davies St, London, W1.

British Drama League *See* **Drama League, British**

British Film Institute *See* **Film Institute, British**

British Honduras, Education in 1966 statistics: two state primary schools, 137 grant-aided primary and 21 private primary schools (total enrolment 25,268); 16 secondary schools (enrolment 2,122); state technical high school (enrolment 115); teacher training college (enrolment 157).

The country's population was approximately 114,000 in 1966.

British Sociological Association *See* **Sociological Association, British**

British Standards Institution *See* **Standards Institution, British**

British Volunteer Programme *See* **Voluntary Societies Committee on Service Overseas**

Brougham, Lord (1778–1868) A powerful early advocate of state education, Brougham persuaded Parliament to appoint a Select Committee on the Education of the Lower Orders, and in 1818 secured the appointment of a commission to inquire into the misuse of educational charities (an Act rendered virtually ineffective by amendments in the House of Lords). He introduced, but was obliged to withdraw, the Education Bill of 1820. In 1825 he published his pamphlet *Observations on the Education of the People*, which led to the founding of the Society for the Diffusion of Useful Knowledge. He was a strong supporter of the establishment of Mechanics' Institutes (*q.v.*).

Bryce Report (1895): Royal Commission on Secondary Education Terms of reference: to consider what were the best methods for establishing a well organised system of secondary education in England, taking into account existing deficiencies and local sources of revenue for endowments or otherwise which were available or

might be made available for this purpose, and to make recommendations accordingly. Chairman: James Bryce. The commission recommended that a central authority should be set up for secondary education, under a Minister of Education. This led to the establishment of the Board of Education, which took over the work of the Charity Commission in 1899. The Report also recommended that an educational council should be set up to assist the Minister, and that local authorities for secondary education should be set up, of which the majority should be chosen by the counties and county boroughs, with powers to supply, maintain and aid schools. The Report made it clear that secondary education could no longer be treated as a separate part of the whole system.
See also **Board of education**

Building Bulletins Published from time to time by the DES and available from HMSO, the Bulletins, usually extensively illustrated, vary from studies of new developments both in the UK and abroad (e.g. No. 19 *The Story of Clasp* or No. 18 *Schools in the USA*) to guides to specific questions of school design and building (e.g. No. 9 *Colour in School Buildings* or No. 25 *Secondary School Design: Sixth Form and Staff*).

Building Code, DES *See* **Major (building) works; Minor (building) works; Standards for School Premises Regulations, 1959**

Building industry, Qualifications for posts in For positions in the building industry at administrative, managerial or technical levels, a candidate with four or five GCE O level passes (including English, mathematics and at least one science subject) may study part-time or full-time at a technical college for the Ordinary or Higher National Certificate or Ordinary or National Diploma in Building; this must be combined with

four or five years experience as an articled pupil in a building firm. Alternative qualifications include a degree in a building subject, or two years practical experience combined with a Diploma in Technology (Building).

Institute of Builders, 48 Bedford Sq., London, WC1.

Building projects *See* **Major (building) works; Minor (building) works**

Bulgaria, Education in Education is free and compulsory between the ages of seven and 16 years. Although in 1946 there was a 23% illiteracy rate, the government was able in 1966 to declare it officially eliminated. In 1965/6 there were 7,719 kindergartens (enrolment 351,918); 3,057 elementary schools (enrolment 1,117,482); 2,477 primary schools (enrolment 577,398); 238 secondary schools (enrolment 102,078); 566 technical and vocational schools (enrolment 197,654); 35 higher education institutes (enrolment 98,394). There are 115 research institutes, and the University of Sofia had an enrolment in 1963 of 13,500. National minorities such as the Turks and Armenians have schools and teacher training colleges.

The population of the country was approximately $8\frac{1}{4}$ million in 1965.

Bulge The name given to the post-war increase in the birth-rate. It was at first thought that the bulge would be temporary, but it is now clear that the birth-rate for some time to come will remain higher than it was before the war.

Burgh schools A term, no longer used, which described the long-established grammar schools in Scottish burghs (i.e. towns with a charter).

Burma, Education in Education is free where it is available. The educational system was reorganised in 1966

79

and all private schools were taken over by the state. In 1965/6 there were 13,903 primary schools (enrolment 1,886,335); 858 middle schools (enrolment 369,603); 605 high schools (enrolment 501,424); 22 institutes (enrolment 6,708); two universities (enrolment 24,482). Burmese is the official language but English is a compulsory second language in secondary schools.

The population of the country was approximately 25 million in 1966.

Burnham Committees Originally the Burnham Committee was described as the Standing Joint Committee on the Salaries of Elementary School Teachers, but like most committees of a national character it later adopted the name of its chairman, Lord Burnham. It first met in 1919. Previously, there had been an unhappy era of area scales, with the result that the purpose of the new Committee was 'to secure the orderly and progressive solution of the salary problem in public elementary schools by agreement on a national basis'. The original scales were recommendations only, but they made a considerable step forward by replacing over 300 individual sets of local authority scales by the recommendation that there should be only four. The highest of these applied in the London area (Scale IV); Scale III applied to major provincial towns (e.g. Birmingham); Scale II to smaller provincial towns (e.g. Winchester); and Scale I to rural areas.

Unfortunately, post-war financial difficulties caused the original scales not to be implemented anywhere, but they were somewhat reduced by Lord Burnham's award which became operative on 1 April 1925 (see **Arbitration**). While the majority of areas adopted the appropriate scale for their teachers, disputes occurred between teachers and their employers, usually over the actual grade which should be used. The outcome of these disputes was that in the Education Act 1944 (Section 89) there was provision for the implementation of scales which would be produced by a realigned Burnham Committee after the second world war. Parallel to the Elementary Committee there were set up in 1920 separate committees for secondary teachers and for teachers in technical institutes. To match the educational reforms of the 1944 Act, however, it was necessary to bring the Elementary Committee and the Secondary Committee into one. The word 'Elementary' had been dropped, and so the new Committee was formed to produce scales for teachers in primary and secondary schools. As, however, the Education Act 1944 had recast the system into primary, secondary and further education, and generally the needs for students over the age of 18 are different from those below that age, it was necessary to set up a Further Education Burnham Committee to take the place of the former Technical Committee.

The third Burnham Committee produces the scales of salaries for the teaching staff of farming institutes and for teachers of agricultural (including horticultural) subjects. There are thus three Burnham Committees where the scales are mandatory, and these are popularly known as the Main Committee (primary and secondary schools), the Further Education Committee and the Farm Institutes Committee. In all these cases the Secretary of State issues an order to LEAs to pay the scales prescribed.

Further Education Committee The Further Education Committee has a function similar to that of the Main Committee in that its efforts are entirely devoted to formulating new salary scales whenever the two sides agree to carry out this purpose. In practice, however, it has always met after the Main Committee, because in fact what is settled there has repercussions throughout the education service. In particular, the basic scales for primary- and secondary-school teachers re-appear in the Further Education and Farm Institute Reports as the Scales for Assistant Lecturers.

But for the rest, the needs of the further education service are different. The scales agreed (or arbitrated) are designed to meet the special needs of the service which include work of university standard. The constitution and procedures of the Further Education Committee match those of the other two committees. In size, it is about half that of the main committee, the management panel having 15 members against 13 for the teachers' panel. The additional two resulted from the addition of Department of Education and Science representatives to the management side when the Remuneration of Teachers Act was introduced. Otherwise, the same organisations representing local authorities in the other committees supply representatives to the Further Education Committee, but in different numbers and proportions. On the teachers' side the Association of Teachers in Technical Institutions supply eight members, the Association of Principals of Technical Institutions and the National Society for Art Education two each and the National Federation of Continuative Teachers one.

Controlled by the Remuneration of Teachers Act, the two sides of the Committee come to terms with the salary problems of teachers in this sector and attempt to reach agreement. If this succeeds, the Secretary of State issues his statutory order to give effect to the decisions. If agreement is not reached, arbitration is available in the same way and with the same procedures as mentioned for the other two committees. In 1967, no agreement was reached and the machinery of arbitration was used. The outcome produced minor improvements on the management offer in a very few appointments. The main factor which influenced the arbitrators towards doing this was that work of university standard is carried out in a number of technical colleges, and, in order that recruitment to them should not suffer, there was a need to pay salaries more closely related to similar appointments in universities.

Farm Institutes Committee This committee consists of a management panel and a teachers' panel, the former being composed of representatives of the County Councils Association, the Association of Education Committees, the Welsh Joint Education Committee and the DES. The teachers' panel is composed of representatives of the Association of Agricultural Education Staffs of Local Authorities and of the Association of Teachers in Technical Institutions.

Its function is to establish scales of salaries for the teaching staff of farm institutes and for teachers of agricultural (including horticultural) subjects. Because of its close connection with the other two Burnham Committees, the scales of salaries prescribed are influenced by what happens in these other Committees, not only in relation to amount but in date and length of operation.

There are other Committees closely related to these three where the mandatory position does not exist. These produce scales of salaries for the teaching staff of colleges of education (usually referred to as the Pelham Committee—*q.v.*); salary scales and service conditions for inspectors, organisers and advisory officers of LEAs (usually referred to as the Soulbury Committee —*q.v.*); the Joint Negotiating Committee for Youth Leaders and Community Centre Wardens (*q.v.*); the Joint Negotiating Committee for Approved Schools and Remand Homes (*q.v.*).

SEB

Burnham Scales These are the Scales of Salaries which are officially prepared by the Secretary of State for Education and Science under Sections 2 and 4 of the Remuneration of Teachers Act 1965, but which are consequential upon the deliberations in the Burnham Committees (*q.v.*), either through agreement or by recourse to arbitration. There are three Burnham Committees, the main one producing scales of salaries for teachers in primary and secondary schools. There is a corresponding document for teachers in establishments for further education maintained by LEAs, and the third is for the teaching staff of farm institutes and for teachers of agricultural (including horticultural) subjects in England and Wales.

All these reports are very detailed. Their purpose is to take account of the length of training, the qualifications and the additional responsibility carried by teachers who are entitled to be remunerated under the scales. The main details are set out elsewhere in this volume under the appropriate heading, e.g. **Basic salary, Consolidated scales, Heads of department,** etc. Although these three salary reports are the only strictly Burnham Reports and have legal force, there are other scales of salary produced by the appropriate negotiating committees which depend upon settlement in the main committee, i.e. Committee for Teachers in Primary and Secondary Schools. These, too, are dealt with in this volume under their appropriate heading, e.g. the scales of salary negotiated for teachers in colleges of education are dealt with by the Pelham Committee (*q.v.*).

SEB

Burt, Sir Cyril (b. 1883) In 1913 Cyril Burt, already a promising lecturer in psychology, was appointed educational psychologist by the London County Council, the first appointment of its type anywhere. In it, he was asked to examine and report on ESN, gifted and delinquent children as well as to carry out surveys and study psychological aspects of problems that might arise in the Council's schools from time to time. From this experience Burt developed and standardised intelligence and attainment tests that are still basically in use today. He also published pioneering works on delinquency and backwardness in children, which in each case revolutionised future research by linking these states with environmental conditions such as poverty or defective home discipline, rather than always with inheritance or even individual perversity, still used as easy explanations of 'badness' in human beings.

Burt's findings were always based on sound research and statistical evidence, although he never lost sight of the personal aspect of the people he was writing about. At one time he antedated future work with delinquent gangs in America by himself becoming accepted as a member of a criminal gang in Soho, with the personal nickname of 'Charlie the Parson'. In 1931 he resigned from the LCC on being appointed professor of psychology in the University of London. Perhaps more than anyone else he has succeeded in getting educational psychology accepted as a reliable and essential tool both in teacher training and in schools as practised by the now growing number of educational psychologists (*q.v.*).

FURTHER READING
C. Burt. *The Backward Child*, Univ. of London Press, 1937. *The Young Delinquent*, Univ. of London Press, 1925.

NT

Burundi, Education in Education is free. 1965 statistics: 147,329 children in primary schools, 2,469 in secondary schools, 1,359 in vocational schools and 1,829 in teacher training colleges. The University College at Bujumbura has 253 students. 345 students are at foreign universities. Total population: approximately 3¼ million.

Busby, Dr Richard (1606–95) Headmaster of Westminster School for 57 years, Busby (who taught Dryden, Locke and Wren) was noted for the violence of his flogging and for his sense of the dignity of a headmaster; he refused to remove his hat in the presence of Charles II, on a visit to the school, on the grounds that it was not fitting for him to take off his hat for anyone in the presence of his pupils.

Business education Education for business covers a wide range of studies, from shorthand and typewriting to post-graduate qualifications. The entire pattern has been reshaped since the publication of the McMeeking Report, 1959, which recommended provision of education for business on the same level and in the same comprehensive pattern as that provided for technology. The report resulted in greatly extended activity by the then Ministry of Education which introduced the following pattern of studies:

Certificate in Office Studies A two-year course intended for school leavers aged 16 who enter general or special clerical occupations and who have not the four GCE O level passes required for admission to the Ordinary National Certificate or Diploma courses. The Certificate is based on an assumption that day-release from employment for one day a week will be granted by employers.

The course includes English and general studies, and clerical duties. Two further subjects must be studied, but the Certificate is awarded to candidates achieving passes in the two compulsory subjects and one other. Candidates with four passes at credit level may be admitted to an ONC or OND course. A pass may be equated with GCE O level.

Ordinary National Certificate (ONC) in Business Studies In 1960 this replaced the former Ordinary National Certificate in Commerce. The two-year course can be taken either as an evening course or on day-release. Minimum admission standard is four subjects at GCE O level.

Courses usually consist of four subjects, often economics, general principles of law, accountancy and English: economics is compulsory. Other options are available beyond the three mentioned. The standard of pass is about GCE A level. Candidates gaining credit passes (50%) may obtain exemption on a subject-for-subject basis from the intermediate examination of many professional bodies, e.g. Chartered Institute of Secretaries.

Ordinary National Diploma (OND) in Business Studies This is the equivalent of the ONC but requires full-time study for two years; courses are available in colleges of commerce and some technical colleges. Five subjects (including economics) must be studied in each year. The standard of pass is slightly higher than for the ONC. The same exemptions are granted as for ONC from intermediate professional examinations.

Higher National Certificate (HNC) in Business Studies A two-year, part-time day or evening course; courses are available in polytechnics, colleges of commerce and some technical colleges. Admission standard is two GCE A level passes in appropriate subjects, e.g. economics or law, or a pass in the ONC or OND.

Applied economics is a compulsory subject in each year of the course and two further subjects must be studied each year. The standard of pass is intended to be at or near a pass degree in the subjects studied.

Higher National Diploma (HND) in Business Studies The full-time study equivalent of the HNC; courses are available in polytechnics and colleges of commerce. Minimum admission standard is one GCE A level subject (plus appropriate O levels) or a pass in the ONC or OND. Five subjects, including applied economics, must be studied in each year of the course. The standard of pass is a little above that of the HNC.

The HND may also be obtained on a 'sandwich' basis: i.e. six months of each year spent in study, the remaining six months in supervised work experience. The minimum overall period in these circumstances is three years.

Degree qualifications Beyond the above awards, which are supervised by the DES, the Council for National Academic Awards instituted in 1963 awards, degrees or diplomas to students in forms of education other than the universities. The subjects cover a wide variety of technologies but incorporate degrees in business studies as recommended by the Crick Report (1964). Only a small number of polytechnic and technical colleges offer such degrees at present, but their number is likely to grow rapidly.

Entrance qualifications are two passes at A level plus appropriate O level passes, or a good pass in the ONC or OND.

Post-graduate qualifications These are now concentrated in the two major business schools set up in Manchester and London in 1965 following the Franks Report (1963). The two schools are modelled on American post-graduate business colleges and offer either a one or two-year post-graduate or post-professional qualifications. The two schools also offer short intensive courses for practising managers and businessmen.

A second major field of study is provided by the Diploma in Management Studies (post-graduate or post-professional qualification studies). The minimum age of commencement is 23 in order to ensure that some practical business experience will precede management studies. The course may be completed by various combinations of full-time and part-time study ranging

from a minimum of six months full-time study to three years part-time study. Such courses are offered in the major technical colleges or polytechnics.

Professional examinations A wide spectrum of business studies continues under the aegis of many professional institutions which offer their own examination. These include accountants, bankers, company secretaries, insurance employees and statisticians. Courses are available in colleges of commerce and some technical colleges.

In principle there is a general move towards acceptance by professional bodies of the ONC or OND as exempting (by credit pass) from appropriate subjects of the professional intermediate examination.

Secretarial studies The progressive development of audiotyping and photocopying in offices has somewhat reduced the need for the shorthand typist. The secretary, however, continues to be in great demand and is developing towards a more highly qualified type of person capable of acting as a personal assistant.

Qualifications are offered by the Royal Society of Arts and the London Chamber of Commerce. Courses are available in many secondary schools, in colleges of commerce and in many technical colleges.

FURTHER READING
BACIE Journal (quarterly), British Association for Commercial and Industrial Education, 16 Park Cres., London, W1.
See also **BACIE**

WBR

Business schools The Franks Report (1963) recommended the setting up of two major business schools in the UK. An appeal to industry for financial aid brought in substantial sums and schools were opened in Manchester and London in 1965. Each school is intended to provide mainly post-graduate or post-experience courses, as well as short booster courses for practising managers.

The Manchester school established a one-year full-time post-graduate course. The London school offers a two-year course. Both schools leaned heavily on American experience when establishing the new courses.

Business Studies, Higher National Diploma in This award was introduced in 1962, and covers either three years' sandwich or two years' full-time study. It is designed to provide a combination of general and specialised education for business for young people of 18 or over who already hold the Ordinary National Certificate or Diploma, or who have at least one A level pass. The fact that the diploma course is full-time or sandwich permits a wider range of study than in the certificate course, and the final standard approaches that of a university pass degree. Some 40 colleges offer the courses at present.

Business Studies, Ordinary National Diploma in This award was introduced for the first time in 1961 as a full-time alternative to the Ordinary National Certificate in Business Studies. The two-year course, during which it is possible to study various subjects at a deeper level than during a part-time certificate course, seems to have a strong attraction for girls, who form more than three-quarters of the student body, largely because it enables them to learn shorthand and typing at the same time as they follow the Diploma course. About 190 colleges offer the Diploma courses at present.

Butler, Dr Samuel (1774–1839) Headmaster of Shrewsbury, great classical scholar and grandfather of the author of *The Way of All Flesh*, Dr Butler is also memorable for having had to endure, for 37 years, a condition of bitter stalemate in his relations with his second master, Jeudwine, a poor scholar and wretched disciplinarian who refused to allow Dr Butler any control whatever over the lower school.

Butler Act 1944 *See* **Education Act 1944**

Butler of Saffron Walden, Baron (R. A. Butler) (b. 1902) Now Master of Trinity College, Cambridge, since 1965, Lord Butler was Minister of Education between 1941 and 1945 and was responsible for the Education Act 1944 (*q.v.*).

Buying-in of previous employment of value to teaching for pension purposes A period of other employment (up to a maximum of 10 years) prior to entering the teaching profession and which, in the view of the Secretary of State, provides experience of direct value to the teacher in the post he holds may be treated as contributory service on payment of additional contributions according to tables prepared by the Government Actuary, but not for the purpose of making up the appropriate service-minimum to establish eligibility for pension benefits. Teaching service before entry into contributory teaching service, war service or national service which is not already treated as contributory service will not be accepted under the 'buying-in' rules.

A teacher in contributory service who wishes to 'buy-in' a period of previous employment must make application to the Secretary of State within 18 months of entry into contributory service. The Rules are limited to teachers who, on first entry into contributory service, were 21 years of age or over, but under the age of 50.

The additional contributions may be paid either as periodical payments (Method I) or in a lump sum (Method II). Under Method I the contributions will be payable from the first day of the month in which the Secretary of State's decision is given, for all periods of contributory service up to the teacher's sixtieth birthday, or earlier breakdown or death, and will normally be deducted from salary. Liability for contributions continues for one year

D

during a break in service. Payment under Method I is limited to an amount which, together with the basic contribution of 6%, does not exceed 15% of salary. The capital value of any excess will be paid by a lump sum or instalments of lump sum. This method is adopted to satisfy tax requirements permitting the periodical payments to qualify for tax relief. Tax relief cannot be given for the lump sum payment or instalments of lump sum.

Under Method II the lump sum payment will be made direct to the Department of Education and Science and will not qualify for tax relief.

Any balance of contributions repaid to a teacher will include the whole of any additional contributions paid under the Teachers Superannuation (Previous Employment) Rules 1957, whether by Method I or Method II with compound interest at 3% per annum. If a teacher paying contributions under Method I fails to discharge his liability, or has a break in service of more than a year, his additional contributions will similarly be returned to him with compound interest and the period of previous employment will cease to reckon as contributory service.

The form in which application should be made and the actuarial tables in regard to 'buying-in' of a period of previous employment are contained in the Schedules to the 1957 Rules, copies of which can be obtained from HM Stationery Office.

SEB

C

Cadet Force, Army The aim of the ACF is to train and inspire the nation's youth to 'serve their Queen and country' by developing character, powers of leadership, soldierly and civic qualities, and arousing interest in the Army. There are 1,492 units of the ACF in the UK; 166 of these are school units and open only to pupils in these schools. The rest are open to all boys between 13 and 18 years of age. Activities include drill, weapon training, map reading, fieldcraft, shooting and camps and courses at Army establishments. Assistance from the Army includes accommodation, equipment, uniform and financial grants.

Gen. Sec.: W. F. L. Newcombe, Army Cadet Force Association, 58 Buckingham Gate, London, SW1.

Publications: *The Cadet Journal and Gazette* (monthly).

Cadet Force, Combined Founded in 1860, this organisation became the Junior Division of the Officers' Training Corps in 1908 and developed into the Combined Cadet Force in 1948. There are currently CCF contingents in 290 independent and maintained schools. Membership is confined to pupils in these schools.

The broad function of the CCF within the schools is to provide the framework of a disciplined organisation, through which there may be developed within boys qualities of endurance, resourcefulness, self-reliance, leadership and responsibility, and a sense of public service, in the belief that these things are of value in civil as well as in Service life. In addition the CCF gives a background knowledge of Service methods and conditions, and assists and encourages boys with a special interest in a Service career to become officers in the Regular, Territorial and Reserve Forces.

Contingents may have three Service Sections—RN, Army and RAF, or one or two of these. There is a wide field of activities both at schools and camps, expeditions and holiday courses. Contingents receive help in equipment and training from the Services.

Sec.: W. F. L. Newcombe, Combined Cadet Force Association, 58 Buckingham Gate, London, SW1.

Calculus Calculus was invented to solve physical problems involving the rate of change of one variable with respect to another, e.g. the decay of a radioactive substance varies with the amount of substance present. A clear understanding of a function (or mapping) as the association of two variables and their graphical representation is essential. Discussion of non-terminating processes, e.g. continued bisection of a line, leads to the intuitive idea of a limit, as a value of a function which is approached as near as is desired, but never reached.

A geometrical instance of a limit is that of a tangent to a curve at a point A, as the limiting position of chords through A and another point in the curve B, as B becomes closer to A. The gradient of a tangent to a curve may be calculated, if the function of the curve is known, by a technique called *differentiation*. An allied problem is to compute the area bounded by a curve to any degree of accuracy, which can be solved by *integration*.

Though areas were studied by the Greeks, and differentiation was invented by Newton and Leibnitz in the 17th century, the order is usually reversed in school courses. Integration is often introduced as the inverse of differentiation, i.e. finding a function (indefinite integral) whose derivative is a given function. The indefinite integral can then be related to the area 'under' a curve (definite integral). Calculus is a powerful tool whose applications are numerous, especially in physics.

FURTHER READING
Mathematical Association. *Teaching of Analysis in Sixth Forms*, Bell, 1963.
E. A. Maxwell. *Analytical Calculus for School and University*, Vol. I, Cambridge Univ. Press, 1954.
W. J. Reichmann. *Calculus Explained*, Methuen, 1964.
O. Toeplitz. *Calculus: A Genetic Approach*, Univ. of Chicago Press, Chicago, Ill., 1963.

JCW

Caldecott Community A day-nursery for children of working mothers was established by Edith Rendel in St Pancras in 1908 to alleviate the evils of baby-minding. Three years later, when the time came for these children to leave the day nursery, an adjoining nursery school was established by Leila Rendel and Phyllis Potter. This was not only one of the first nursery schools in England, but it included a parents' club, a clothing club and a community centre which took its name from the reproduction of Randolph Caldecott's illustrations that hung round the walls.

The Community later extended its scope to include children of broken homes, including adolescents, in its care. From 1932 onwards, under Leila Rendel and Ethel Davis, it also pro-vided a firm family base for such children attending local secondary schools.

An experimental reception and observation centre for deprived children was established after the war when the Community moved to Mersham-le-Hatch, Kent (the Kent County Council assumed responsibility for this in 1951), and later a further experimental venture for the remedial teaching of educationally retarded children.

Today children come to the Community through child guidance clinics or children's committees of local authorities.

FURTHER READING
Kellmer Pringle and B. Sutcliffe. *Remedial Education—An Experiment*, University of Birmingham, Institute of Education, Birmingham, 1960.
Leila Rendel. *The Caldecott Community: A Survey of Forty-Eight Years*, Mersham-le-Hatch, Ashford, 1960.

WHGA

Cambodia, Education in State education is steadily expanding and slowly taking over from the Buddhist monks who have traditionally had responsibility for education. In 1965 there were 4,011 primary schools (700,811 enrolments); 194 secondary schools (81,223 enrolments); 11 technical colleges (3,814 students); four arts colleges (2,014 students); and the Royal University at Phnom-Penh with seven faculties and 3,858 students. The country's population was approximately $6\frac{1}{4}$ million in 1965.

Cambrian Educational Society Set up as a crisis group in 1846 by Hugh Owen, an expatriate Welshman in London, the Cambrian Educational Society must be seen in the context of the vigorous Anglican school building campaign in North Wales after 1832. Reinforced by the establishment of St David's College, Lampeter, and training colleges, the church was so successful that by 1843 its schools were serving 320,000 of the 396,000 population.

In 1843 the Home Secretary had introduced a scheme for educating children working in factories which seemed so liable to direct them to Anglican schools that throughout England and Wales nonconformists began to reinforce their own schools in protest. Since there were only two of these—run by the British and Foreign Schools Society—in the whole of North Wales, Hugh Owen called for a national campaign to start more non-denominational schools. In response, the British and Foreign Schools Society sent a special agent to North Wales, whose efforts produced 38 new schools in the next three years. The resultant teacher shortage led Owen to advise the Welsh to send young men to the Society's training college, and to start the Cambrian Educational Society.

When in 1847 Parliament sent special commissioners to inquire into the state of Welsh elementary education and especially the existing facilities for learning English, another uproar ensued. The commissioners' strictures on the ignorance and immorality of the Welsh were widely interpreted as the prelude to an Anglican coup. It took all Owen's skill, as secretary of the Cambrian Educational Society, to secure another 50 non-denominational schools by 1852; by 1870 there were 300, including some in South Wales.

In 1854 Owen and his associates had a scheme for a Queen's College for Wales, but the Crimean War intervened and he turned his energies to founding Bangor Normal College.

As well as the Cambrian Educational Society Owen helped to found a revived Cymmrodorion and a reformed Eisteddfod: both these he tried unsuccessfully to infuse with the spirit of the National Association of Social Science.

See also **Wales, Education in**

WHGA

Cambridgeshire village colleges See **Village colleges**

CAME (Conference of Allied Ministers of Education) See **UNESCO**

Cameroon, Education in Education is free in state schools but the number of places is inadequate. Protestant and Catholic schools are numerous. Technical education is chiefly in E. Cameroon. 1965–6 statistics: 4,066 primary schools (enrolment 716,411); 114 secondary schools (enrolment 28,169); 47 technical schools (enrolment 8,931). There is a university at Yaoundé (266 students); and 1,274 higher education students study abroad. Population: approximately $5\frac{1}{4}$ million.

Campaign for Education 1963 See **Educational Advance, Council for**

Camping From a school's point of view, camping can be divided into four main categories: fixed or standing camps, lightweight camping, cycle camping and canoe or boat camping.

Many authorities have permanent camps (or camping sites with all hygienic conveniences) to which parties from schools go for short periods during the spring and summer months. Whilst there they undertake for part of the time certain projects in subjects such as nature study, geography, local history and architecture, the remaining time being devoted to recreation.

In lightweight camping all the equipment needed, including the tent, is carried on the back, and short, even one-night, stops are made either at recognised camping sites or other convenient spots. Knowledge of the techniques of this type of camping is indispensable for candidates for the Duke of Edinburgh's Award (q.v.).

Cycle camping is similar, the journey being made by, and equipment carried on, a bicycle.

In many schools where canoeing is an activity within the PE curriculum, it has become usual for parties to undertake canoeing expeditions during vacation periods on the waterways both of this country and of the Continent.

Advice on all aspects of camping can be obtained by becoming a member of the Camping Club of Great Britain and Ireland, 11 Lower Grosvenor Pl., London, SW1.

FURTHER READING
Boating (*Know the Game* Series), Educational Productions, 1960.
Camping (*Know the Game* Series), Educational Productions, 1963.
Camping and Education, HMSO, 1961.

JE

Canada, Education in Like that of any other society, formal education in Canada reflects social structural divisions and value differences. These divisions are based on constitutional, economic, religious, ethnic and cultural differences. The British North America Act 1867 allocated educational authority to the provincial rather than the federal government, so that today each of the ten Canadian provinces has its own educational system with responsibility for organisation, curriculum, standards and financing. Each system is divided into three levels, elementary, secondary (including various technical levels), and university. Generally speaking, elementary education embraces the first eight years of schooling, and secondary education the next four or five years; both of these are financed largely by local taxes and provincial government grants. University education includes all those years from the end of the secondary level to the completion of a university degree, and is financed mainly through provincial government grants, plus student fees and federal government grants. School attendance, which is compulsory up to 15 or 16 years of age, is encouraged by the federal government which makes the payment of its family allowances dependent upon regular school attendance.

At the elementary school level in most provinces there exists a division between Catholic education, in which religious values are an obvious element in the curriculum, and Protestant education in which there is less emphasis on religious values.

The most significant ethnic and cultural division in Canada is that between the French and English groups. The Quebec Act 1774 gave to the French the right to their own language, religion and civil law as well as their own educational system. On the basis of these rights the French–Canadian people of the province of Quebec, which includes the majority of the French-speaking population, have built an educational system based on traditional, humanitarian and spiritual values rather than the scientific, individualistic values of English-speaking Canada. This French–Canadian educational system is now being rapidly reorganised in order to meet the requirements of an advanced industrial order.

In some areas various ethnic groups, seeking to nurture values derived from a culture left behind by their immigrant members, have organised schools in which their language and cultural traditions are taught. These schools are financially supported by the ethnic group and, unlike the elementary schools, attendance is not compulsory.

At the elementary and secondary levels there exist a number of schools which are fundamentally supported by private rather than public funds. These schools are usually attended by pupils coming from families able to afford substantial fees. This reflects the economic divisions in Canada, as well as a lingering belief in elitism and privilege, a facet of Canadian culture which has its roots in Canada's former economic, political and cultural dependence on Britain.

Economic differences between the geographic regions of Canada are also reflected in the distribution of educational facilities throughout these regions, with the economically disadvantaged unable to provide the educational resources necessary for the realisation of the abilities of the population.

These divisions within the Canadian educational system and the pressures for change generated by a changing social order have resulted in a debate about the organisation, content and purposes of education at all levels. This has led to a close scrutiny of the prospects for equality of educational opportunity so that human potential can be more fully realised.

BRB

Canford Summer School of Music
See **Mills Music Limited**

Canning House Canning House, the headquarters in London of the Hispanic and Luso-Brazilian Councils, was founded in 1943 for 'the advancement of knowledge in the British Commonwealth and in the countries of Latin America, Spain and Portugal, of the culture, languages, history and economies' of the countries concerned and the promotion of closer relations between them. Much of the Councils' work is concerned with economic and international relations, but they also do a great deal in the educational field and have the only public lending library in the UK devoted to books concerned with Spain, Portugal and Latin America.
2 Belgrave Sq., London, SW1.

Canoeing Canoeing, a most popular post-war activity in many secondary schools throughout the UK, owes its origin as a sport to John MacGregor who in 1865 devised and built the first 'Rob Roy' canoe.

Impetus was given to the development of canoeing in schools by the advent of construction 'kits' of prefabricated parts which enabled school clubs and individuals to produce craft at a relatively low cost, and by the proximity to most schools of suitable rivers, canals, lakes and flooded gravel pits. From simple beginnings on local waters many school canoe clubs have ventured farther afield, and continental canoe expeditions are increasing.

The most popular canoes for schools are single-seaters and two-seaters, or rigid canoes of plywood or canvas stretched over a wooden frame and painted.

Competitively, canoe races in specially designed kayaks and Canadian canoes form part of many regattas, and canoe racing is an Olympic sport. Apart from pure racing, *experienced* canoeists take part in slalom competitions over zig-zag marked courses, in fast moving water, and wild water racing down mountain rivers with hazards such as rocks and rapids.

British Canoe Union, 26 Park Cres., London, W1.
Journal: *Canoeing in Britain*. Quarterly.

FURTHER READING
Boating, Know the Game Series, Educational Productions, 1960.

JE

Cantor, Georg (1845–1918) Russian-born German mathematician, Professor of Mathematics at Halle, Cantor worked out an arithmetic of the infinite that resulted in the theory of sets for irrational numbers (*see* **Sets**). His major work, written between 1895 and 1897, was entitled *Contributions to the Founding of a Theory of Transfinite Numbers*.

Care committee *See* **School care service**

Careers advisory officer Careers advisory officers (CAOs) are employed by the Youth Employment Service (the great majority by LEAs rather than the Ministry of Labour). The CAO is responsible for careers and education advice for older pupils, usually those at school or technical college taking GCE courses who will go on to further or higher education courses either before or after obtaining employment. Many schools that excluded the YEO now welcome the CAO. In the majority of cases he is a graduate, often with experience of teaching or youth employment work. His intitial salary is generally higher than that of the new YEO.

Most LEAs now employ one or two CAOs and although they have existed for several years their numbers have increased rapidly since the publication of the Albemarle Report on the Youth Employment Service in 1965 (*q.v.*). It is impossible to estimate their number since they have no professional association separate from their YEO colleagues and their very title varies from one LEA to another—Careers Advisory Officer, Careers Officer, Vocational Guidance Officer, etc.

Careers guidance Young people today grow up in a working world of extraordinary complexity. Some are bombarded with irrelevant information, others have none at all. As a result many choose jobs with which they are dissatisfied, and cause themselves frustration and their employers expense. Careers guidance aims to minimise, though it never expects to eliminate, both frustration and expense.

Secondary schools are in an ideal position to give careers guidance. They know their pupils well, and are in a position to compare pupils; they are also staffed in such a way as to make it possible for every school to have at least one member of the staff specialising in the subject. They can maintain close links with the Youth Employment Service, and use its wide knowledge of occupations and opportunities in the area.

Since 1960 there has been a rapid increase in interest in careers guidance in this country. This is shown by the courses organised by the DES, by the DES's excellent and popular pamphlet *Careers Guidance and the Schools,* by the increasing time devoted to careers topics by the BBC and ITV, and by the successful independent foundation of the Careers Research and Advisory Centre (*q.v.*).

The prerequisite for guidance is for pupils to be informed. To this end the school should provide, easily accessible to all pupils, a careers library. This should contain information on the widest possible variety of occupations and further educational opportunities, pitched so as to provide for all levels of ability within the school. This information will need to be brought to the attention of pupils by as many means as can be devised. Ordinary lessons, extra-curricular discussion groups, sound and TV broadcasts, film shows, parents' evenings, careers conventions, visits to places of work, and actual work experience, are some of the many ways in which this can be attempted.

While pupils need access to information on different careers, they must also be guided in the general questions connected with entering employment. Topics such as the differences between school and work, applying for a job, interviews, National Insurance, money, etc, are all part of the guidance the school should provide, though it may not in fact be part of the careers staff's programme.

But careers guidance is essentially concerned with encouraging the young person to make his or her informed individual choice. Therefore the object will be to encourage the pupil to assess him- or herself just as much as the career in which he or she is interested. In the last resort this cannot be done in the class unit. In many instances, of course, it will not be achieved at all—objective self-assessment is not one of young people's most common attributes. If either teacher or Youth Employment Officer is successful in his object, it will most probably be by individual interview.

Individual interviews are time-consuming and require considerable expertise to be effective. It is unlikely that a successful guidance system in this country will be established unless a conscious policy decision is taken to afford it.

See also **Youth Employment Service**

JMJ

Careers Guidance Adviser The first appointment to this post (believed to be the first of its kind in the country) was made by the ILEA in 1967. The Adviser acts as a link between careers teachers in ILEA schools and specialist advisers within the Youth Employment Service. The Adviser, with the status of an Inspector, is responsible for the maintenance of standards of vocational guidance in the schools and in the ILEA's own careers offices.

Careers Research and Advisory Centre CRAC provides a link between education and employment. Its publications and services are designed to meet the needs of teachers in secondary schools, colleges and universities and those professionally engaged in advising young people in their educational and occupational decisions. Services include a wide range of publications, conferences, training courses and seminars. The CRAC Higher Education Information Unit publishes 46 *Guides* to the content and treatment of degree courses in universities in the UK, runs six study courses for those concerned with advising students on university admissions, and answers questions on degree problems. Recurrent questions are dealt with in the Unit's publication *Degree Questions*.

The CRAC Education and Occupational Library and Information Unit maintains a unique reference library in Cambridge which contains about 20,000 documents and publications. In collaboration with the Central Youth Employment Executive the Library has published a system for classification of educational and occupational information. It also provides and services a card index service for careers libraries.

Other CRAC publications include: *Students in Transition, CRAC CBI Yearbook of Education and Training Opportunities* (Vols 1 and 2, 1967, 1968), *Beyond a Degree, Handbook of Recruitment Literature, Middle School Choice, Interests and Occupations, CRAC Journal.*

Bateman St, Cambridge.
See also the end of this volume.

Careers teacher Most British secondary schools now have on their staffs at least one member defined as 'careers teacher'. In large schools there will probably be a careers team. Much of the careers teacher's work is outlined elsewhere in this volume (*see* **Careers guidance**). In order to do this work effectively the careers teacher will obviously have to spend a good deal of time making contacts with local employers, keeping his own records of the progress and career aspirations of pupils, liaising with, and providing documentation for, the Youth Employment Service (*q.v.*), as well as coping with his own teaching load. All these occupations point to the careers teacher's need of some permanent base or office. Office work will indeed take up a considerable part of his time, and he will welcome clerical help if he is lucky enough to get it.

There is at the moment no special training available for this work beyond the DES short courses. Industrial experience may be helpful, and the Confederation of British Industry and the Schools Council in 1965 sponsored a scheme for 'work experience' for teachers. Certain skills such as clerical facility, counselling, and interview techniques will obviously be useful, but ability to get on with colleagues is vital, since it is often the careers teacher who is responsible for the collation of information about a pupil.

See also **School leaving age, Raising the**

FURTHER READING
Choice of Careers Pamphlets, Central Youth Employment Executive, HMSO.
Department of Education and Science. *Careers Guidance in Schools*, HMSO, 1965.

Schools Council Working Paper, No. 7, HMSO, 1966.
D. E. Wheatley (Ed.). *Industry and Careers*, Iliffe, 1961.

JMJ

Carnegie, Andrew (1835–1918) A Scot who emigrated with his father in 1848 from Dunfermline to Pittsburgh, Carnegie made a vast fortune from iron and steel, and made benefactions during his lifetime of over £70 million; these established public libraries in many places in the USA and Britain, and included gifts to Scottish and American universities.

Carnegie Dunfermline Trust Established in 1903 for social, recreational and cultural purposes in Andrew Carnegie's birthplace of Dunfermline, Scotland. The income from the original capital (£750,000) is used for maintaining Pittencrieff Park and for the benefit of inhabitants of the town and other philanthropic schemes. Past activities include establishment of school medical and treatment schemes, public baths and community institutes, foundation of Dunfermline College of PE, establishment of youth centres, playing fields, museums, public halls, etc.

Present capital (exclusive of properties now owned or those donated to local authorities) is £1¼ million. The income (£60,000) is applied to the maintenance of Pittencrieff Park (including aviary, tea house, music pavilion), Pittencrieff House Museum, Music Institute, Youth Centre, Craft School, the promotion of a Festival of Music and the Arts and the making of grants to clubs, schools and other local organisations.

Sec.: F. Mann, MA, LLB, Abbey Park Hse, Dunfermline.

Carnegie Hero Fund Trust Established by Andrew Carnegie in 1908 with a capital of £250,000 to make provision for those injured or the families of those killed in attempting to save life in peaceful pursuits. Present capital is £625,000; annual income (£30,000) is used for monthly allowances ranging (depending on circumstances) up to £30 per month and for special grants in cases of illness, educational needs of children, etc.

Sec.: F. Mann, MA, LLB, Abbey Park Hse, Dunfermline.

Carnegie Trust for the Universities of Scotland Set up in 1901 by Andrew Carnegie to assist Scottish students with class fees and to foster the improvement and expansion of the Scottish universities in science, medicine, history, economics, English literature, modern languages and technical or commercial subjects.

Since fees are now in general met out of public funds, the Trust's current activities are concentrated on assisting the universities by allocations for capital purposes, the award of postgraduate fellowships and scholarships, and grants for research, equipment and publication.

Sec.: T. Erskine Wright, MA, The Merchants' Hall, 22 Hanover St, Edinburgh, 2.

Carnegie United Kingdom Trust Established in 1913, the Trust exists to promote the well-being of the people of the UK by charitable methods.

Comely Park Hse, Dunfermline, Fife.

Caroline Haslett Memorial Trust *See* **Electrical Association for Women**

Carr Report (1958) *See* **Apprenticeship**

Carr-Saunders Report (1949): Report of the Special Committee on Education for Commerce Terms of reference: to consider the provision which should be made for education for commerce and for the professions relating to it, and the respective contri-

94

butions to be made thereto by universities and by colleges and departments of commerce in England and Wales. Chairman: Sir Alexander M. Carr-Saunders.

The report made many recommendations for improving the quality and quantity of commercial education, but at the time the emphasis was on industry's requirements for facilities for further education in technology and science, and it was not until the McMeeking Report (*q.v.*) was published 10 years later that 'business studies' were introduced.

See also **Business education**

CASE *See* **State Education, Confederation for the Advancement of (CASE)**

Case history When investigating the medical, social or personal difficulties of an individual, it is useful to have a record of the important episodes in his past history relating to his particular problem. Thus in a child guidance clinic dealing with personal problems, parents may be asked to describe the so-called 'milestones' of their child's life; for example, his birth, physical development, weaning and toilet training, as difficulties around such areas can give a clue to the parents' attitudes and the present disorder. Other possibly disturbing experiences, such as the child's reaction to maternal separation, hospitalisation, parental disharmony or the arrival of a sibling, will also be investigated. All this will be written up by the social worker into a case history, with a view to putting the present problem into perspective.

NT

Catchment areas *See* **Zoning**

Catechetical Centre, National *See* **Catholic public schools**

Catholic colleges of education St Mary's College was founded in 1850 by the Catholic Education Council at Brook Green, Hammersmith, and transferred in 1925 to Strawberry Hill, Horace Walpole's famous home. It is run by the Vincentian Order, and has over 1,100 students, of whom in 1966 160 were women. The De la Salle College at Hopwood Hall, Manchester, is the only surviving men's college on its own campus.

Among women's colleges are Digby Stewart (formerly St Charles), Roehampton (run by the Order of the Sacred Heart), Coloma, and Maria Assumpta, all in the London area; Cavendish Square provides a one-year course for graduates. These colleges come under the aegis of the University of London Institute of Education, whose visitors they receive.

Outside the London area are the College of the Immaculate Conception, Southampton; Endsleigh, Hull; Our Lady's, Mount Pleasant, Liverpool; St Mary's, Fenham, Newcastle; St Paul's, Rugby; and Sedgley Park College, Manchester. These are conducted by some of the better known religious orders connected with education and all are expanding rapidly with the assistance of government grants.

Among the new colleges, Christ's, Liverpool, and All Saints and Trinity, Leeds, lead the field. The former is mixed and the two latter are for women and men respectively on the same site, and run many joint courses. Planned for the near future are Mary Ward College, Nottingham (for women), and Newman College, Birmingham (for men).

All colleges have clerical or religious principals, except Trinity and Newman where laymen have recently been appointed.

Various courses are offered at these colleges, and full details may be obtained from the Catholic Education Council handbook, as well as from brochures issued by colleges. In addition, each college gives Religious

95

Teaching Certificates authorising students to teach in Catholic schools.

CHS

Catholic education Before the first state schools were built following the Act of 1870, there were already in existence 350 Catholic 'poor' schools catering for 100,000 children. Today there are over 2,900 Catholic schools of various types, attended by over 777,000 children. It was the Balfour Act 1902 which incorporated the 'non-provided' schools, as they were called, in the national system; but subsequently attempts were made to overthrow this settlement. The 1944 Act firmly established the 'voluntary' schools, as they are now termed.

These schools largely conform to the national pattern, are aided by the LEAs and until 1966 were assisted by a government grant of 75% towards the church authorities' costs of maintenance. New legislation in 1966 has resulted in a grant of 80% towards the managers' and governors' costs, both in regard to new buildings (primary and secondary) and day-to-day maintenance. As we are on the threshold of secondary reorganisation, with all the financial implications of such a change, this reform is well-timed.

Apart from the voluntary schools, there are also other types of Catholic schools: 56 direct grant (helped by grants direct from the DES), 574 independent schools (subsisting entirely on fees) and 22 special schools for handicapped children of several types.

The development of education in Catholic schools is controlled within the dioceses by Schools Commissions, set up by the bishops, who negotiate with both LEAs and the DES. As an advisory body to them all the Hierarchy early established an organisation now known as the Catholic Education Council, with Archbishop Beck as its present chairman. This Council undertakes negotiations with the DES, advises managers (of primary schools)

and governors (of secondary schools) as well as the diocesan commissioners, and issues a handbook every two years called *Catholic Education* giving all the relevant facts of the Catholic system, and periodic bulletins and manuals of guidance to all concerned in operating the schools.

Apart from problems of administration—and the finding of even 20% of the cost of new schools will present a problem to the bishops—two topics are occupying the attention of all concerned with Catholic schools. The reorganisation of secondary education is the concern not merely of administrators but also of teachers. The distribution of the Catholic population is not at all uniform throughout the country and, whereas it may be comparatively simple to set up comprehensive schools of one sort or another for, say, the Catholic children of London, it is quite another thing to consider the future of Catholic secondary education in Cumberland, for instance, where Catholics are more scattered. Then, too, in making arrangements anywhere, the position of religious orders, who hitherto have been in charge of Catholic secondary schools, must be taken into account, together with the demands of Catholic lay teachers who are very much concerned with their future role.

The other matter of moment discussed wherever the question of Catholic education is raised is the revolution in methods of religious teaching. New thinking has been going on for some years but this has been accelerated by the Vatican Council decrees, and today courses and conferences everywhere are filled to overflowing by teachers anxious to be brought up to date. Directing it all is the new National Catechetical Centre set up by the Hierarchy in 1966.

A Catholic Teachers' Federation was formed in 1907 and organises teachers of all grades in local associations or guilds throughout the country. It publishes a house magazine, *The Catholic Teacher*, and also, in co-operation with the principals of colleges, the bi-monthly journal *Catholic Education Today*.

CHS

Catholic Education Council for England and Wales The representative body for Roman Catholics in educational matters, established by the Catholic bishops of England and Wales. Members are nominated by dioceses and Catholic organisations concerned with education.

The Council acts for the Catholic body in educational questions of a national character. Its secretariat provides an advisory service for managers and governors of Catholic schools throughout the country and for Catholics generally; it has available specialist legal, financial and statistical advisers and maintains a building office to deal with certain specialised questions arising in school-building.

41 Cromwell Rd, London, SW7.

Catholic Emancipation Act (1829) This Act removed discrimination against Roman Catholic teachers and schools. Shortly afterwards, some of the most famous Roman Catholic schools were founded, such as Mount St Mary's (1842), Ratcliffe College (1847), the Oratory School (1859) and Beaumont (1861).

Catholic Handicapped Children's Fellowship Primarily concerned with the spiritual welfare of handicapped children, the Fellowship engages in activities that cover not only welfare work but also holidays, clubs and an advisory service. The religious education of handicapped children receives close attention, and to this end close liaison is established with educational bodies.

Gen. Sec.: John P. Williams, 42 Portland St, Hereford.

Catholic Institute for International Relations *See* **Overseas Aid and Development, Voluntary Committee on**

Catholic Poor Schools Committee A forerunner of this committee was the Society for the Instruction of Children of Catholic Indigent Parents founded in London in 1764; another was the Catholic Institute, formed in 1845 to promote the education of the Roman Catholic poor, which ascertained that there were about 250 schools, many not deserving the title. In 1847 the Institute was dissolved by order of the bishops and its funds transferred to a Catholic Poor Schools Committee, a body of priests and laymen eligible for government grants. Allotted an HMI in 1849, and another in 1851, the Committee spent until 1851 in correspondence over the exact duties of school managers. It also started a periodical *The Catholic School*, and approved a visiting teacher of pedagogy in 1849. By 1856 there were 430 schools, by 1860 743 schools, mainly in Lancashire and Middlesex, and the Catholics claimed that their share of the school population was 1:18.

From 1853 until 1890 its secretary was T. W. Allies, formerly a Protestant clergyman, who set up the Women's training College at Liverpool and worked for a Catholic university. He wanted a national Catholic trust fund pool, to be available for localities where difficulties were greatest. In 1905 the Catholic Education Council absorbed the Catholic Poor Schools Committee and the Catholic Secondary Education Council (founded in 1904). It consisted of members of the diocesan school associations and the conference of Catholic colleges. The Council is recognised by the government as representing the interests of Catholics in education matters.

WHGA

Catholic public schools These date back to the beginning of the 19th

97

century, although it can be justly claimed that the origins of the system go back to pre-Reformation days when Eton, for example, was an ecclesiastical establishment. Among the earliest foundations are Ampleforth and Downside, both in the hands of the Benedictine Order, and Stoneyhurst, a Jesuit college. Others almost equally long-established are Ratcliffe College, Leicester, run by the Rosminian Fathers, and the Oratory School at Edgbaston, a college established by the Fathers of the Oratory, of whom Cardinal Newman was the most distinguished member. Other colleges for boys are St. Benedict's, Ealing, and Douai, both Benedictine colleges; Mount St. Mary's, Sheffield, another Jesuit school; the Josephite college of St George's, Weybridge; and Prior Park, a Christian Brothers college.

It is more difficult to name the girls' establishments, as the definition of a girls' public school is vague. Those convents which seem to qualify are Farnborough Hill; Holy Child, Edgbaston; Sacred Heart, Woldingham; St Joseph's, Reading; Mayfield Convent; St Mary's, Ascot; St Mary's, Shaftesbury; Upton Hall Convent, Wirral.

CHS

Catholic Student Union Formed in 1967 by an amalgamation of various Catholic student organisations. Membership is not restricted to Catholic students.

15 Carlisle St, Soho Sq., London, W1.

Publications: *CSU News* (twice termly); *News Bulletin*; other occasional publications.

Catholic Students International Chaplaincy This is one of many organisations trying to cope with the great influx of students of all kinds who flock to England from all over the world. Its aim is to assist them to make their mode of life one which is a help

rather than a hindrance to their studies. Though the Chaplaincy deals mainly with Catholics, neither accommodation nor social facilities is restricted; both are open to all. The hostel at Manchester (St Augustine's Overseas Students Hostel, 2 Anson Rd, Victoria Park—capacity 36) and the one in North London (16 Portland Rise, London, N4—capacity 200) are concerned with providing students with accommodation and the normal amenities of hostels.

The hostel at 41 Holland Park, London, W1—capacity 17—is at the same time the national centre and headquarters of the various national societies and the venue for their meetings and functions. These societies are composed of students from all over London, living either in hostels or in private accommodation; the national societies merge to form what is called OSCO (England)—Overseas Students Co-Ordination—which, together with similar organisations in other European countries, forms OSCO (International).

Catholic Teachers Federation of England and Wales Founded in 1907 to ensure the incorporation of Roman Catholic schools in the education system. Its principal aims are the furtherance of Catholic education and the interchange of thought among Catholic teachers. It stands for parental choice, the provision of Catholic school places for all Catholic children and the availability of posts in Catholic schools for all suitably qualified Catholic teachers.

Its present activities include the organisation of conferences and courses on educational topics, the publication of text books and memoranda, and assistance to its 90 local associations in arranging activities for both teachers and children, such as retreats, pilgrimages and displays. The Federation is represented on the Catholic Education Council, the National Catechetical Centre, the National Lay Apostolate and other bodies. It is a member of the World Union of Catholic Teachers or UMEC.

Its publications include the *Catholic Teacher*, a quarterly house magazine, and, in conjunction with the principals of colleges, the *Catholic Teachers Journal*, a subscription magazine issued bi-monthly.

Hon. Sec.: Ald. C. H. Sheill, 12 Queens Rd, London, NW4.

Catholic Young Men's Society of Great Britain

Founded in 1849, the Society exists today mainly to train Catholic laymen of all ages for religious and social work in the 330 parishes in which it is established. Its annual training programmes, based on the *Decree on the Laity* promulgated at the Second Vatican Council (Rome, 1963–65) and set out in the Society's *Bulletin*, are designed to be adapted to local conditions. Weekend courses at St Dominic Savio House, Bollington, and elsewhere, provide specialist training.

Gen. Sec., Brownlow Hill, Liverpool, 3.

Catholic Youth Service Council

Founded in 1962, the Council aims to make a Catholic contribution to youth service. Membership is open to young people aged 14–21. Facilities include clubs and leadership training centres.

41 Cromwell Rd, London, SW7. Publication: *Bulletin* (quarterly).

CATs *See* Colleges of Advanced Technology

Central Advisory Councils

There are two Central Advisory Councils for Education, one for England and one for Wales. These were set up in 1944 to advise the Minister of Education, now the Secretary of State, on matters referred to them by him. The membership of the Councils changes for each reference made to them. The latest report from the Council for England is the Plowden Report on primary education (*q.v.*).

Central African Republic, Education in

In 1965 there were 65 kindergartens, 2,100 elementary schools, 140 secondary schools, 40 technical schools, and 17 vocational schools, with a total enrolment of about 130,000 pupils. About 300 students from the Republic are following higher education studies abroad.

The country's population was approximately 1¼ million in 1965.

Central Office of Information

The Publications Division (H) supplies a guide to material and information about the Commonwealth available to schools, including pictures, films and filmstrips, posters, maps and exhibitions. Some publications, including an illustrated magazine *Commonwealth Today*, are available free to secondary schools. Teachers can request to be put on mailing lists for free publications concerned with international and economic affairs.

Hercules Rd, Westminster Bridge Rd, London, SE1.

Central Register and Clearing House Ltd

The function of this private, non-profit making, limited company is to help candidates who wish to train as teachers to gain admission to a college of education, and to avoid duplication of applications. Procedures for application and a list of colleges in England and Wales are detailed in the annual information booklet (*MWI*) which is issued to all schools, technical colleges and other advisers of candidates, and also to the candidates themselves with their forms, at the moment of application. The correspondence section of the Clearing House deals with written enquiries from candidates, before or during their time of application, and another section forwards forms of candidates, not accepted by colleges of their choice, to other colleges with suitable vacancies.

The company also provides annual statistics about the numbers of people

99

who apply to train, with details of unplaced candidates, numbers who withdraw, and the quality of accepted students.

151 Gower St, London, WC1.

Central schools School boards (*q.v.*) in large towns soon discovered that their best pupils needed further teaching and so in 1876, at Sheffield, it was proposed to establish 'a central school, to which advanced scholars from the elementary schools of the town are to be promoted', and where the specific subjects of the Revised Code (*q.v.*) were taught as well as 'other subjects, said to bear on the industries of the district'. This became a higher grade school (*q.v.*). In 1902 when these became municipal grammar schools, they left a gap in the large towns where the elementary schools were left without 'tops'. So London (1911) and Manchester (1912) started central schools just before the first world war. Afterwards other authorities established selective and non-selective central schools, admitting pupils at 11 and providing a four-year course. 'Scholarships' were also offered.

They were the precursors of the secondary modern school.

See also **Higher grade schools**

WHGA

Central Society of Education *See* **Education, Central Society of**

Central Training Council The Council was set up under the Ministry of Labour after the Industrial Training Act 1964. On it are representatives of the trade unions, the employers, the nationalised industries, the chairmen of the industrial training boards, and a variety of educational and training interests.

See also **Industrial education**

Certificate of Secondary Education *See* **CSE**

Ceylon, Education in Education is compulsory and free between the ages of six and 14 years, and about 80% of this age group were in school in 1962. In 1965/6 there were 9,552 primary and secondary schools (enrolment 1,656,191); 24 teacher training colleges (enrolment 5,550 students); eight special higher education establishments (enrolment 960 students). There are three universities: the University of Ceylon at Peradeniya has eight faculties and 10,723 students, Vidyalankara University at Colombo has 1,995 students, and Vidyodaya University at Nugegoda 2,030 students—the last two being Buddhist foundations. The Higher Education Act 1966 established a National Council of Higher Education, which co-ordinates the activities of the universities and higher education institutes. Administratively Ceylon is divided into 24 education districts.

The island's population was approximately 10½ million in 1963.

Chalkboard Formerly, because of its colour, this was called the blackboard. Blackboards continue in ubiquitous use: teachers and pupils write, calculate and draw on them with chalks of various colours, though white is the most universally used. There is, however, increasing use of chalkboards of other colours. In the 30s research established that white surfaces written on in blue characters were more easily read than blackboards, though they were more costly. Further developments in the 60s are leading to a smoother-surfaced white board chemically treated to enable the writer to use felt pens of different colours. These developments lead to a cleaner atmosphere with no dust on teachers' and children's clothes.

See also **Visual aids**

Change of residence, Effects on schooling of Anxiety in moving from familiar to unfamiliar situations and in having to make appropriate adjustments in knowledge, feeling and behaviour is an unavoidable aspect of human life. It is bound to be more intensely felt during early years when a child is ill-equipped for and vulnerable to the world and society.

One of the most important transitions from the familiar to the unfamiliar is the move from home, family and neighbourhood to a school. The child (in the context of all the kaleidoscopic uncertainties and diffidences of his experience) has become deeply attached to, and to some extent at ease within, a particular social situation—the known physical characteristics of his home, yard, street, and the known personal qualities of his close family and neighbours. Suddenly, whether he likes it or not, these familiar figures leave him alone in a larger, unknown, and more complicated situation in which everyone else seems more at home than he does, and to which he has no orientation at all beyond the immediate, confused awareness of what is around him in the classroom: the smell of chalk, the authoritative voice of the teacher, an elbow nudging him at the desk. Inevitably, time must elapse before orientation and adjustment are achieved, and meanwhile the child must suffer some anxiety.

Children obviously differ in the degree of severity of the anxiety they undergo. Some are reasonably happy and at ease after a few days. Others experience an uncontrollable intensity of misery and, at the worst, can become pathologically distressed. They reject school absolutely, sometimes locking themselves in their bedroom in violent panic, sometimes not outwardly showing any intensity of feeling but manifesting pathological symptoms—sore throats, headaches, bilious attacks, bedwetting, etc. These pathological extremes—intensifications of the normal experience of anxiety—are now referred to as 'school-phobia' (q.v.).

A change in residence also confronts the child with a situation of unfamiliar-ity and necessary adjustment and reawakens old anxieties (and patterns of response to them). It may also stimulate new anxieties. The child's progress in school work proper may be temporarily set back by these fears. The change of home and neighbourhood brings its own unfamiliarities, and the new school is an added strangeness. Most children are resilient and, with understanding at home and at school, adapt quickly and well. But those who experience great anxiety can encounter much insecurity and misery.

Extreme pathological conditions clearly may benefit from the help of a clinical psychologist, but a good deal short of this some things seem obvious. It must help if parents and teachers alike are able to understand the situation, entering into the mind of the child, sensing what the situation is like for him, acting in such a way as to link home and school satisfactorily. This will help the re-orientation to take place as painlessly as possible, and parents and teachers should be sensitive to the anxieties of the child in order to give the support whereby his confidence can grow quickly and effectively. Quite ordinary things are important, such as trying to introduce the child to the school, to his teacher, etc., before he has actually to attend, so that the school situation is not totally new to him, and totally unexpected. But great care has to be exercised in all this, since too great an appearance of concern may intensify the child's anxieties, and perhaps even engender dimensions of anxiety which might not otherwise have been there. Normally, the child will quickly want to dispense with any overt and obvious parental support, indeed will want to keep it at a distance, as soon as his adaptations are made.

See also **Home and school**

FURTHER READING
J. H. Kahn and J. P. Nursten. *Unwillingly to School*, Pergamon Press, 1964.

RF

Chaplaincies' Advisory Committee *See* **Church of England Board of Education**

Character training It has been said that while the public schools taught leadership, the humbler elementary schools were teaching their pupils 'followership'. Be that as it may, character training is a goal almost every school has always aimed at, although the type of character in mind may differ and the methods of training may range from beatings and house-points to voluntary lessons or learning left-wing tenets in Socialist Sunday Schools. Psychological evidence seems to suggest that it may be more genuinely constructive to encourage a pupil rather than make him too aware of his own deficiencies, and that, whatever the importance given to an external system of values, pupils are still apt to follow the example of character set consciously or unconsciously by a teacher whom they like and respect.

NT

Charities, Educational The Charities Act 1960 defines a charity as an institution established for charitable purposes—which is not quite as circular as it seems—and the word 'institution' is defined as including 'any trust or undertaking'. The law of charity is part of the law of trusts and in this field the law is concerned with purposes rather than institutions. The first criterion to be fulfilled for a purpose to be charitable in law is that it must be for the public benefit.

An Act of Parliament in 1601, known to lawyers as the Statute of Elizabeth the First, listed ten purposes regarded by the law as charitable. In 1891 the House of Lords, for the sake of convenience, compressed these ten into four categories, one of which was 'the advancement of education'.

The advancement of education comprises three main activities. First, there is the teaching of specified subjects which may cover a wide field—even 'the arts of personal contact, or social intercourse' will do—but the subject must be for the public benefit and the teaching of the programme of a particular party has been held not to be charitable. Secondly, there is the education of special classes or sections of the public, even the inhabitants of a small parish will do, but the education provided must not be restricted to persons who stand in some private relationship to the benefactor—such as members of his family or employees of his firm. Finally, there is the provision and support of educational institutions—universities, colleges and schools—and such incidental matters as scholarships, prize funds and buildings for such institutions. This heading of charity includes everything from a gift to provide an annual school treat to the endowment of the most expensive and exclusive school in the country, since an educational trust may be charitable in law although there is no element of poverty in the beneficiaries, and a well-endowed school may comprise a hundred or more distinct and separate charities.

An example of the borderland between the educational and charitable on the one hand and the uncharitable on the other is research. Research for its own sake is not charitable; but it qualifies if it educates, either directly (by benefiting the researcher) or indirectly (for example where it is intended to add eventually to the sum of knowledge).

As mentioned above, the purposes of an institution or gift, if they are to be legally charitable, must not only fall within one of the four categories enunciated in 1891; they must also be for the public benefit. This involves two elements: the purposes must be beneficial; and they must benefit the public. The latter, which has been mentioned in the context of the education of special classes of the public, does not involve the proposition that what is good for Eton is good for the nation; what it means is that the purpose must not be *private* benefit. So far as the former is concerned, the Court will ordinarily assume that that which is expressed to be for educational purposes will be beneficial; but if its beneficial character is called in question the Court will admit evidence and decide the issue as a question of fact. In a recent case the Court heard evidence that the contents of a museum bequeathed by the testator contained what one Lord Justice of Appeal described as a 'mass of junk' and, accepting that evidence, held that the bequest was not for the benefit of the public and accordingly not charitable in law.

Two rather technical legal privileges are enjoyed by all charitable gifts, including of course those for the advancement of education. First is exemption from a rule of law known as the rule against perpetuities, which, very broadly speaking, prevents property being tied up in the same hands indefinitely. Secondly, the preservation of the gift even when its original object could no longer be carried out— a prize for Greek verse, for example, does not come to an end if the school at which it is awarded gives up classics, but may (under a procedure referred to below) be awarded instead for some other subject. These are liberating privileges, enabling donors to avoid some of the more onerous restrictions of a rigid system of law, and until fairly recently the Courts generally looked kindly on gifts that were intended to be charitable. The substantial practical privilege of charities is however unquestionably exemption from tax of practically all kinds, the most recent being the selective employment tax, and relief from rates. There is now accordingly a strong counterbalancing public interest—it is in general the taxpayer at large who suffers most if the validity of a doubtful gift is upheld —and the recent tendency has been

for the Courts to take a sterner line. The tendency too has been for the line to be taken at a higher level, largely because the Commissioners of Inland Revenue are in a better position to take cases to the Court of Appeal and the House of Lords than any private litigant, however affluent.

Charitable trusts, particularly those for the advancement of religion, have been known, and regulated by Act of Parliament, from very early times; for instance, there was an Act of Henry VIII relating to assurances and trusts of land to the use of parish churches, chapels etc. They were regulated and protected by the old Court of Chancery and they are still subject to the supervisory jurisdiction of the Chancery Division of the High Court. Since the turn of the century this jurisdiction has also been exercised in relation to educational charities (other than those— mainly the universities old and new— exempted by statute) by the DES and its predecessors, the Board of Education and the Ministry of Education. In the exercise of this jurisdiction the Department makes schemes for the variation of the trusts of gifts and endowments which have become impossible of performance and controls by Order the sale, leasing and mortgaging of land owned by charities.

Finally, the law relating to charities is extremely complex for two reasons. First, because the Statutory definition of purposes which are charitable goes back to 1601 when conditions of life were vastly different from what they are today. Secondly, because the Courts, particularly during the last hundred years, have had to decide whether purposes, which were not contemplated in 1601, were within the spirit or intention of that Act. Inevitably there have been many decisions of the Court over the years which have conflicted with each other or have been reconciled only by tortuous or hairsplitting argument.

Charity Commissioners From 1597 and 1601, the power to deal with abuses in endowments, especially those for education, was vested in Commissioners for Charitable Uses. But appointment was for specific charities, and long expensive suits in the Court of Chancery had to be endured by petitioners against abuse of an endowment. So in 1853 the Charity Commission was constituted. Consisting of three salaried Commissioners and an MP, it was empowered on the applications of trustees to frame new schemes for submission to Parliament. Seven years later it acquired judicial powers analogous to those of Chancery.

Prevented from dealing with endowments yielding more than £50 a year, it was severely criticised by the Taunton Commission in 1867, and as a result its powers over endowed schools were given to a new body, the Endowed Schools Commission, consisting of three members. This had power to initiate new schemes without waiting for applications from trustees, but was fenced off from the great public schools and the elementary schools and from endowments less than 50 years old. So effectively did the commission execute its mandate that the Headmasters' Conference was called into existence as a protest body. In 1873 when the Commission came to an end its powers reverted once more to the Charity Commissioners. This time the Charity Commission worked effectively and by 1893 had reorganised 668 schemes out of 1,262 endowments. In the following year it was estimated that all educational endowments within its scope would be covered by new schemes within nine years.

In 1899 the Charity Commission handed over to the newly constituted Board of Education its responsibilities and powers over educational trusts and endowments.

WHGA

Charity Organisation Society See Physically handicapped pupils

Charity schools movement See Christian Knowledge, Society for Promoting

Chemical Society A society for chemistry masters. Its numerous publications include a *Journal* and *Quarterly Review*, and cover-to-cover translations of Russian journals.
Burlington House, London, W1.

Chemistry, Society for Analytical The Society's aim is to encourage, assist and extend the knowledge and study of analytical chemistry and of all questions relating to the analysis, nature and composition of natural and manufactured materials by promoting lectures, demonstrations, discussions and conferences and by publishing journals, reports and books. Membership is general to those interested in analytical chemistry.
9–10 Savile Row, London, W1.
Publications (monthly): *The Analyst*; *Analytical Abstracts*; *Proceedings of the Society for Analytical Chemistry*.

Chemistry, Teaching of Chemistry has been defined as the study of matter and its interactions. Matter consists of a relatively few elements, many quite simple compounds and many extremely complex ones. Reactions between substances are governed by a small number of variables, primarily the concentrations and proportions of the reactants, the solvent or phase in which the reaction occurs, the temperature, pressure and electrical conditions, and the time for which the reaction is allowed to proceed, all of which may be readily controlled, often independently of one another. This adds up to an infinite variety of chemical 'facts' (or verifiable experimental observations)—which is both the joy and despair of the subject.
Most chemistry courses begin by building up an understanding of matter

as comprised of unique, discrete substances, which is then broadened to include the quantitative nature of chemical composition and reaction. Traditionally, courses have then followed the historical lead to the atomic theory, but newer courses tend to short-circuit this argument and accept more modern physical evidence for the theory so as to progress to the modern chemist's preoccupation with the interpretation of chemical behaviour in atomic, molecular, ionic, structural, kinetic, energetic and electrical terms. As a contribution to general education in a scientific context, chemistry has the following particular merits. Many of the facts of the subject are easily redetermined, using simple techniques. The teacher may limit the materials and the reaction variables chosen for study as he wishes, opening up an enormous field for exploration and discovery; the practical techniques themselves may be chosen to suit the student's developing skills. Chemistry provides extensive opportunities for logical reasoning not only of a mathematical but also of a non-mathematical nature. The number of patterns of behaviour, models and theoretical studies which may be developed from observation and refined from stage to stage is a feature of chemistry. At each stage the student should be able to interpret experimental data in terms of the pattern or model and to predict experimental behaviour, and in the ease with which such predictions may be put to the experimental test chemistry is unequalled. Teaching should emphasise that the prediction that fails is not a disaster but rather a starting point for further scientific work. One danger is that models and theories may be so persuasively presented that they become more real in the student's mind than the experimental facts by which they stand or fall. The CBA programme is one modern course that boldly accepts the challenge that this danger presents.[1]

In consciously directing attention away from the most fascinating chemical materials that surround us—living materials, modern synthetics, etc.—to more tractable simple compounds, chemistry becomes rather a sophisticated subject and one important source of interest is lost, but as a compensation it becomes possible to acquire a greater understanding of a limited field. The delight and educational value of the heuristic approach, with its stress on experience and discovery in the limited context of early chemical endeavour, is most apparent in the papers of J. Bradley.[2] The Nuffield O level chemistry programme[3] attempts to relate the teaching to the modern chemist's interest in patterns and models without yielding the essential element of exploration, speculation and discovery. Important contributions to the modernising of specialist courses have come from America,[1,4] Britain,[5] Australia[6] and Europe.[7] The ultimate aim is to maintain the student's curiosity and originality despite the diversity of the subject and its extensive theoretical structure.

REFERENCES

1. *Chemical Bond Approach Project*, McGraw-Hill, New York, 1963.
2. J. Bradley. 'Chemistry V: Water', 'Chemistry IV: Air and Fire', *School Science Review*, June 1966.
3. Nuffield Foundation Science Teaching Project. *Chemistry O Level*, Longmans/Penguin, 1966.
4. *CHEM Study Project*, W. H. Freeman, 1963.
5. Science Masters' Association and Association of Women Science Teachers. *Science and Education Report: Chemistry for Grammar Schools*, John Murray.
6. *Approach to Chemistry*, Univ. of New South Wales, annually from 1961.
7. OECD, Paris. *New Thinking in School Chemistry*, 1961. *Chemistry Today*, 1963. *School Chemistry—Trends in Reform*, 1964.

IWW

Chess Chess experienced a period of great popularity after the second world war, and the interest inevitably invaded schools. Almost all secondary schools now have chess clubs, and some primary schools also. The British Chess

Federation, which controls all chess in the country, gives every encouragement to the development of the game, organising inter-school competitions through its local units and supporting school associations where a number of schools wish to form one. The London grammar schools have long had such an association, and the Welsh schools; and an English Primary Schools Association held its first congress in 1967, to which nine groups in Yorkshire, Lancashire and the Midlands sent representative teams.

A national schools tournament was started in 1957. It was sponsored by the *Sunday Times* and managed by the BCF, and has a simple handicapping system enabling the local primary school to compete on level terms with Manchester Grammar or Eton or the largest comprehensive. Its entry is now approaching 1,000, and it has to be organised in preliminary zonal competitions covering Great Britain and Northern Ireland before the main national tournament and the London final. Any school team required to travel more than 25 miles may opt to play by telephone.

During the Easter and Christmas holidays thousands of boys (and a few girls) play in the numerous local and regional congresses which are organised for them. London, Manchester, Plymouth, Gloucester, Huddersfield and numerous other centres have several hundred players in their congresses; the largest, for a week at Liverpool, has over 1,400, a third of them from primary schools, playing in sections ranging from the Merseyside Open (Under 18) Championship down to the Merseyside Infants. A few primary congresses are held; they are very local, with 60–100 boys and girls.

Few girls continue chess in the secondary schools, where it is virtually a boys' game. Many of the older boys are good enough to play in adult chess, and often do so with distinction.

KLW

Chief education officer Before the Education Act 1944, LEAs were not required to appoint a chief education officer, though they did so, normally designating him 'director of education'. The 1944 Act made such an appointment obligatory and, for the first time, required LEAs to submit to the Minister a short list of candidates for the post, with particulars of their qualifications and previous experience, and gave the Minister the right to veto anyone on the list. A chief education officer, who is the head of the LEA's education department, is normally recruited from candidates with wide experience in LEA administration and previous experience of teaching.

Child Care, Advisory Council for In the Children Act of 1948, passed after the findings of the Curtis Report (*q.v.*), two Advisory Councils for Child Care were set up, one for England and Wales and the other for Scotland. Under the Act each local authority was also required to appoint a Children's Committee, each with a Childrens' Officer.

Child Care, Central Training Council in See **Home Office Children's Department**

Child Care, Home Office Certificate in See **Children's Department**

Child Care, National Bureau for Co-operation in Founded in 1963 with the aim of contributing to the building up of an accepted body of knowledge on the welfare, education and treatment of children, normal or handicapped, whether living with their own families or receiving some form of substitute care. Membership is composed of local authorities providing health, education and children's services, professional associations and voluntary organisations concerned with children, university departments, colleges of education and other educational institutes, and individuals.

Adam House, 1 Fitzroy Sq., London, W1.

Publication: *Newsletter* (four times annually); reports on the results of the Bureau's surveys.

Child-centred education This phrase represents the practice of building education round the needs and interests of the child himself, based on a study of his natural development. As a philosophy it might be thought to have begun with Rousseau (*q.v.*), and to have included since Froebel, Pestalozzi and Montessori (*qq.v.*).

Child development Interest in the study of child development was first aroused with the challenge of the commonly held idea that children were in need of 'conversion' and that education consisted in breaking their will in order to form their minds. Educationists such as Rousseau, Pestalozzi and Froebel made a valuable contribution to our knowledge of children, even though their work was primarily based on observation and deduction rather than on what we would today consider systematic study.

The scientific study of the living child began with Darwin, but the foundation of modern child psychology was laid with the publication in 1882 of Preyer's *The Mind of the Child*. After that, in quick succession, a number of records appeared describing the development of individual children. Other important early books were James Sully's *Studies of Childhood* (1903) and Granville Stanley Hall's *Aspects of Child Life and Education* (a study of the child's mind soon after entering school at the age of six; 1912). These earlier methods of studying children have continued: Baldwin, Stern, Valentine and later Piaget have all made studies of their own children.

The nursery school movement, particularly in America, gave a considerable impetus to observational and also experimental studies of young children, including team work by psychologists (clinical and experimental), teachers, doctors, physiologists, biologists and sociologists. Since the beginning of the century a considerable amount of experimental work has taken place, particularly in the USA, but also in Austria and the UK. In the USA particularly there have been available all the resources of apparatus and laboratories, and fully trained research workers have been freed from other responsibilities to devote themselves entirely to this work. By the publications of the Society for Research in Child Development, founded in 1930, the results became widely known. Gesell (*q.v.*) and others following him have created developmental scales illustrating the sequence of development in many aspects of a child's life. Methods of testing children popularised by the pioneer work of Binet (*q.v.*) have been applied to younger children, and we now have norms of development for comparing individual children from the earliest months. Longitudinal studies of the same children over very long periods have also been undertaken and are still going on.

The work of Piaget in Geneva is contributing further knowledge of the young child's ways of thinking and forming conceptions of the world. In this country the work of Susan Isaacs threw light on many aspects of young children's learning, thinking and feeling when in a nursery school, where they were closely observed and recorded, rather than in an experimental situation.

Valuable knowledge about child-development has been contributed by clinical studies, especially by child analysts such as Melanie Klein and Anna Freud.

In England the National Foundation for Educational Research (*q.v.*) was founded in December 1945, and this has led to research into and surveys of children in the school situation and much testing of children's attainments under various conditions. Another recent influence is from the field of anthropology, which has aroused interest in the psychological effects of different methods of child-rearing. While experimental studies of children still go on, other studies are concerned with the impact upon children of their family, social and school setting, and with their relations to their peers.

DEMG

Child Development Study, National (1958 Cohort) Sponsored by the Institute of Child Health, University of London, the National Birthday Trust Fund, the National Bureau for Co-operation in Child Care, and the National Foundation for Educational Research, the project is a major longitudinal study of child development. The study is based partly on information collected in 1958, when a national peri-natal inquiry was carried out on a sample of 17,000 children, whose subsequent all-round development is now being investigated.

On the consultative committee, chaired by Sir Lionel Russell, are represented LEAs and voluntary bodies concerned with child development, together with representatives of the DES, the Home Office, the Ministry of Health, the Scottish Education Department and the Scottish Home and Health Departments.

Directors: Professor Neville Butler and Dr M. L. Kellmer Pringle, Adam Hse, 1 Fitzroy Sq., London, W1.

Child guidance Anyone who comes into regular contact with children, from parents to park-keepers, offers some sort of child guidance from time to time. In a technical sense, however, the phrase is normally taken to refer to the clinical diagnosis and treatment of anything from mildly disturbed to seriously maladjusted children, along with the active involvement of their parents or guardians. Although it is the child who is nominally referred, the real problem very often lies with the parents, and in some cases it may be the whole family who will be treated, if this is possible.

Such diagnosis and treatment is usually carried out in a child guidance clinic or hospital psychiatric unit, and the full team consists of a psychiatrist, an educational psychologist, a social worker and possibly a psychotherapist. Generally the social worker will take a case-history from the parents, and the educational psychologist may assess the child's intelligence and keep in touch with the school situation. The psychiatrist will generally diagnose the problem, both from the reports of his colleagues and from a diagnostic interview with the child and possibly with the parents too. After this, the psychiatrist may continue to treat the child himself, or else delegate the case to one of his colleagues. The treatment that follows varies from clinic to clinic, but is generally designed to give patients and their parents insight into their problems, and to help in tackling them more successfully in the future. It may last a long time, or it may be necessary to see the patient only for a few more sessions, according to the seriousness of the problem and its accessibility to treatment.

Children can be referred to child guidance by family doctors, by educational psychologists working in the school psychological service, and from various other sources including, in some clinics with an 'open door' policy, the parents themselves. In 1965 approximately 57,000 children in England and Wales were receiving child guidance, and they were served by the full-time equivalents of 110 psychiatrists, 324 educational psychologists and 160 psychiatric social workers. The first child guidance clinic, in the sense that it would be recognised today, was the East London Child Guidance Clinic, opened in 1927 by the Jewish Health Organisation.

See also **Psychologist, Educational; Maladjusted pupils**

FURTHER READING

Report of the Committee on Maladjusted Children, HMSO, 1955. *Psychologists in Education Services*, HMSO, 1968.

NT

Child Poverty Action Group The Group is concerned with the problem of poverty among families in Britain, and in particular, with the effects of material deprivation on children. It has drawn attention to the educational handicaps of children from families where the income is low in relation to family size, and has put forward detailed proposals for improved family allowances and other social benefits. It has also pressed for better publicity for existing benefits such as educational maintenance allowances and free school meals, which many families fail to claim.

The Group publishes a quarterly journal, *Poverty*, obtainable from bookshops and sent free to members (minimum annual subscription £1).

1 Macklin St, Drury La., London, WC2.

Child psychiatrist A child psychiatrist is a doctor of medicine who practises psychiatry with children and almost certainly also with adults. He will probably have extra qualifications in psychiatry, but at the moment this is still not considered essential. He may work in a general hospital with a psychiatric unit or in a child guidance clinic.

Child Study Association, British *See* **Psychology, Educational**

Children, National Society for the Prevention of Cruelty to Founded in 1884 to help children in their own homes, and parents with problems affecting their children. There is a staff of over 300 Inspectors and Women Visitors throughout England, Wales and Northern Ireland, and 50,000 voluntary workers.

Publications: *Child's Guardian* (quarterly). *Blue Bird Magazine* (twice annually).

1 Riding House St., London, W1.

Children Act 1908 Known at the time as the 'Children's Charter', this Act introduced special children's courts, instituted remand homes and industrial or reformatory schools for young offenders, made it illegal for young people under 16 to smoke, and provided legislation for the prevention of cruelty to children.

Children Act 1948 This Act laid upon the councils of counties and county boroughs in England and Wales, and of counties and burghs in Scotland, the duty of caring for children under 17 without parents or guardians, abandoned or lost children, and those whose parents are unable to provide for them. Under the Act, each local authority was required to appoint a Children's Committee and a Children's Officer.

Children and Young Persons Acts 1933 and 1938 These Acts, defining children as persons under 14 years of age and young persons as those between 14 and 17, gave the courts the power to remove from their homes children who had broken the law, or were out of control or in need of care and protection. They also established that no child under the age of eight could be charged with an offence; and that young offenders could either be sent to an approved school (*q.v.*) or committed to the care of a fit person willing to receive them. Local authorities were recognised as fit persons for this end.

Children's centre Among the recommendations of the Plowden Report (*q.v.*) was the proposal that expanded nursery education should be made available for children between the ages of three and five in 'nursery groups' of 20 places. Two or three such groups, it was suggested, might make one unit, to be called a 'nursery centre'; or the

109

groups might be combined with day nurseries or clinics in 'children's centres'.

See also **Nursery schools**

Children's Day Nurseries, National Society of *See* **Day nurseries**

Children's Department This is the department of a County or County Borough Council set up as required by the Children Act 1948. It is headed by a Children's Officer responsible to the Children's Committee of the Council and assisted by a number of Child Care Officers.

Local authority Children's Departments 'receive into care' people under 17 in their areas who are 'deprived of a normal home life', when there is no reasonable alternative course to be taken. Deprivation of normal home life may include circumstances arising from committal of one or both parents to hospital or the desertion or death of parents or guardians, or their failure for any reason to feed, shelter and clothe the child adequately. The Children's Officer must see that reports made to his department about any child suffering neglect or ill-treatment are investigated and, if appropriate, acted upon.

Child Care Officers (normally expected to complete a two-year course of training leading to the Home Office Certificate in Child Care) visit private homes as necessary; they visit foster-homes regularly to see that youngsters in them are being looked after properly and to give advice and support to the foster-parents, and call frequently at children's homes maintained by the Children's Department or by voluntary bodies. They supervise adoptions, and are usually responsible for the main recommendations to the courts in this connection. Calling upon potential foster-parents and adoptive parents and advising as to their suitability is an important part of the work. Their

attention may be drawn, by voluntary or statutory agencies, to situations where incipient family breakdown may have ill-effects on children of the marriage. Thus Child Care Officers often take the role of marriage counsellor and general adviser to anxious parents on the control and upbringing of children. Since the Children and Young Persons Act, 1963, increasing emphasis has been put on such preventive work.

Children may be committed to the care of the local authority by the courts, as 'in need of care and protection'. They are boarded out with foster-parents rather than held in children's homes whenever this is desirable (as it is deemed to be in most cases) if acceptable substitute parents are available. Any private arrangements made by any parent to have his child fostered by others must be notified to the Children's Department. If necessary, the Department can forbid foster parents to go on looking after a child; in the case of children directly in local authority care, it can remove a youngster from the substitute home immediately if this seems desirable.

Parents whose children are placed in a home or hostel, or with foster-parents, by the Children's Department, must be kept informed of their child's welfare; in most cases, they may visit the child when they want, and bring him home again at any time. In unusual circumstances, the Department may take over full parental responsibility. Normally this requires a Fit Person Order to be made by the court. Parents are then forbidden from visiting or removing their child without permission.

There were 69,157 children in the care of local authorities in 1966. The total has risen steadily since 1959, but the number of cases dealt with annually is constant if taken as a percentage of the population under 18 years old.

In recent years, child care officers have shared in the supervision of children released 'on licence' from approved schools.

FURTHER READING

K. Brill and R. Thomas. *Children in Homes*, Gollancz, 1964.
D. V. Donnison. *The Neglected Child and the Social Services*, Manchester Univ. Press, Manchester, 1954.
Jean S. Heywood. *Children in Care*, Routledge and Kegan Paul, 1959.
Margaret Kornitzer. *Child Adoption in the Modern World*, Putnam, 1952.

DLH

Children's Home, National The National Children's Home was founded in Lambeth in 1869 by Dr Thomas Bowman Stephenson, a young Methodist minister, as a voluntary agency to provide shelter and care for 'homeless boys in the streets of London.' It grew steadily to provide services for a wide variety of boys and girls in all parts of the UK. Today it gives care and help to more than 3,000 children each year. Its 45 establishments throughout England, Scotland and Wales include children's homes for boys and girls needing residential care; residential nurseries for babies under two years old; four nursery schools; two special units for disturbed children; two residential schools for physically handicapped children; three residential schools for backward children; three junior approved schools (two for boys, one for girls), and a staff training college for residential workers. It also provides an adoption society arranging 250 legalised adoptions each year; foster care for children of all ages; case investigation and home visitation; family aid (preventive and rehabilitative), after-care planning, advice and support, and co-operation and consultation with other voluntary agencies, local authorities and government departments.

85 Highbury Pk, London, N5.

Children's literature No-one has bettered the dictum of C. S. Lewis, 'I am inclined to set it up as a canon that a children's story which is enjoyed only by children is a bad children's book'. The more enjoyable a children's book is to adults as well as children, the longer will it remain in favour. And the better the book, the more also will it stand the test of being read aloud.

The freshest of early 20th-century writers to children today is E. Nesbit, who knew children so well that her characters will remain real until children themselves change their characteristics. Stories peopled entirely with fantasy characters, and whose secret of success is to present the illusion of reality rather than reality itself, have the greatest chance of survival. So children today revel in Kenneth Grahame's *The Wind in the Willows* (1908), Hugh Lofting's Dr Dolittle stories (the first appeared in 1922), A. A. Milne's *Winnie the Pooh* (1926), J. R. R. Tolkien's *The Hobbit* (1927), and Walter de la Mare's incomparable poetry in verse and prose.

The consciousness of children's literature as an art form, serving a definite purpose in a child's development, came in the early 1930s, and was marked in particular by Geoffrey Trease's *Bows against the Barons* (1934), Arthur Ransome's *Swallows and Amazons* (1930), and Erich Kästner's *Emil and the Detectives* (1931), the prototypes respectively of the modern children's historical novel, the holiday adventure and the detective story. Publishers at this time became more aware of the possibilities of good literature for children, and in 1936 the Library Association instituted the Carnegie Medal, awarded annually for a distinguished contribution to children's literature.

Among the other books of this period which are still as highly thought of by adults as they are popular with children are Joyce Lankester Brisley's Milly-Molly-Mandy stories (the first was published in 1928), Cwynedd Rae's *All Mary* (1931), P. L. Travers' *Mary Poppins* (1934), Noel Streatfeild's *Ballet Shoes* (1936), Barbara Euphan Todd's

Worzel Gummidge (1936), Kate Seredy's *The Good Master* (1937) and Ursula Moray Williams' *Adventures of the Little Wooden Horse* (1938).

Non-fiction was slower to develop. Landmarks before the second world war were *Arthur Mee's Encyclopaedia* and the *Wonder Books*, in which are the origins of the successful integration of text and illustration which marks the best of this genre today.

The post-war years saw standards of production, design and illustration rise to match visual techniques in other fields of communication. As educational methods developed, so the books which children enjoyed could be more thought-provoking than before. Several writers of fantasy have used this licence to the full. The adventure stories of C. S. Lewis are set in another, allegorical world. Lucy Boston fuses reality with an atmosphere of a different place and time. Mary Norton's feeling for life in miniature is superior even to Tolkien's. Alan Garner uses scholarship and local lore to bring wide-ranging elements to his stories. Philippa Pearce's *Tom's Midnight Garden* (1958) is a time fantasy which leaves the reader fully satisfied but eager to discuss the book with teacher or friends.

Geoffrey Trease's later historical adventure stories are rousing, scrupulously accurate and as popular as ever. But another kind of historical novel has developed, the two leading exponents of which have been Rosemary Sutcliff and Henry Treece, whose main purpose is to evoke a situation and the atmosphere of a whole way of life.

The writer who has most consistently made demands on his readers is William Mayne, whose fantasies and adventure stories show a particularly skilled ear for sound and dialogue. Stories of everyday life which depend entirely on plot and situation are often ephemeral because they are contemporary, but Paul Berna's *A Hundred Million Francs*

(1957) is comparable to *Emil and the Detectives*, and Philip Turner has brought humour and characterisation to the holiday adventure story.

The growth of literacy has created new demands, and publishers have responded, often with books in series, so that they can be easily recognised and more economically produced and marketed—unsophisticated novels for older girls' fiction to encourage reluctant juniors and to start off younger children who were reading by themselves at an earlier age than before. Backward readers were diagnosed, and a literature provided. A new milieu in fiction was required too, corresponding to the background of children who were attending secondary modern schools.

Leaving aside *Little Black Sambo* (1899), the fore-runners of the modern picture book for children were Jean de Brunhoff's *Babar* (1934) and Edward Ardizzone's *Little Tim and the Brave Sea Captain* (1936). In the immediate post-war years this field was dominated by American productions, but Brian Wildsmith with his *ABC* (1962) and *The Lion and the Rat* (1963) proved conclusively that children of all backgrounds appreciate good art as much as strict representation.

The very number of books available presents vast problems of selection, which are greatly increased with non-fiction. The awareness of technological advances through TV and the press has made children eager and able to understand scientific principles more readily than some of their teachers. Again, it is an accepted principle of education that children should be encouraged to discover things for themselves and to use as many different books as possible in the process. Hence the proliferation of information books.

It was a further educational development that opened up the market for paperbacks for children. The book that is produced in a sufficiently hard-wearing form for the school or public library is outside the buying capacity of a child. The encouragement from teachers for children to build up their own personal libraries has made the children's paperback a viable proposition.

The growth of literacy is directly responsible for the wide provision of children's literature today. From 1,300 new children's books published in 1939 to over 2,500 a year in the 1960s represents an increase in range and quality as well as in numbers. There are more than twice as many publishers seriously involved in this field than there were in 1950.

FURTHER READING

Children's Literature: A Guide to Reference Sources, Washington, Library of Congress, 1967.

Marcus Crouch. *Treasure Seekers and Borrowers*, Library Association, 1962.

F. J. Harvey Darton. *Children's Books in England*, Cambridge Univ. Press, 2nd ed. 1958.

Department of Education and Science. *The Use of Books*, HMSO, 1964.

Margery Fisher. *Intent upon Reading* (a critical appraisal of modern fiction for children), Brockhampton Press, revised ed. 1964.

Bettina Hurlimann. *Three Centuries of Children's Books in Europe*, Oxford Univ. Press, 1967.

Antony Kamm and Boswell Taylor. *Books and the Teacher*, Univ. of London Press, 1966.

Cornelia Meigs. *A Critical History of Children's Literature*, Macmillan, New York, 1954.

John Rowe Townsend. *Written for Children*, Garnet Miller, 1965.

Geoffrey Trease. *Tales Out Of School* (a survey of children's fiction), Heinemann, revised ed. 1964.

Periodicals

Children's Book News. 6 issues a year.
Growing Point. 9 issues a year.
The Junior Bookshelf. 6 issues a year.
The School Librarian. 3 issues a year.
Organisations regularly publishing booklists: National Book League, 7 Albemarle St, London, W1. School Library Association, Premier Hse, Southampton Row, London, WC1.

See also **Paperbacks in schools; Libraries, school; Fiction, Teaching of; Poetry, Teaching of**

AK

Children's Officers, Association of

Set up after the passing of the Children Act 1948 (*q.v.*), the Association aims to further the welfare of children deprived of a normal home life and to encourage and assist in the preservation of the family. Of its members, 99% are children's officers.

Members meet on a regional basis at roughly quarterly intervals, and there is an annual conference to which local authority representatives are commissioned to talk on subjects of current interest. The Association has given evidence to every relevant commission and committee since its inception, the most recent being the Seebohm Committee, which is in being to recommend means by which a new personal service department might be set up.

5 Polebarn Gdns, Polebarn Rd, Trowbridge, Wilts.

Children's Theatre Association, British

Founded by Michael Pugh in 1959 to provide a meeting place for theatre directors, writers and teachers involved in presenting theatre to children, the Association holds an annual conference, usually in London, organises exhibitions and play-writing competitions and produces directories, bibliographies and papers. It publishes enquiries (such as *Repertory Theatres and Young People* and *A Theatre for Children*).

The Association was enlarged to become a Commonwealth organisation in 1961, and in 1964 it launched the International Association of Theatres for Children and Young People, which pursues similar activities throughout the world.

Details of membership from Miss Anne Cossentine, 28 Blackmoor Rd., Wellington, Somerset.

Children's Welfare, Council for

Open to anyone interested in children, the Council has launched and been associated with a number of investigations and projects: among them studies of the impact of television on children, of problem families, of the effects of selection at 11-plus, of the need for a family service and a family court, and on the care of pre-school children. Its most recent inquiry has been into children's play needs and opportunities. The Council is a pressure group that concerns itself with the needs of children, especially in relation to the problems created by the present state of continual social change.

183–189 Finchley Rd, London, NW3.

Periodical: *Our Children*.

Children's and Young Persons' (Harmful Publications) Act (1955) *See* **Comics**

Chile, Education in State education is free and, where possible, compulsory from the age of seven to 15 years. In 1964 the numbers of pupils in educational establishments were: kindergarten 44,053; primary 1,435,807; secondary 218,661; technical and vocational 104,685; universities 43,141. There are eight universities, of which six are state and two Catholic, at Santiago (three), Valparaíso (two), Antofagasta, Concepción and Valdivia. The literacy rate is 75% of the population, but in cities this is probably 90%.

The population of the country was approximately 8½ million in 1965.

China, Education in China's educational task is not only the biggest in the world but it is complicated by the country's unique historical and cultural heritage. For twenty centuries or more the traditional educational system had produced an élite of scholar-bureaucrats, skilled in the use of a beautiful but very difficult script, who ruled China in accordance with the feudal-Confucian code. But the overwhelming majority of people had no access to education at all.

By the end of the 19th century, traditional education, having failed

utterly to protect the country against the brutal military, political and economic inroads of the West, was completely discredited, and in 1906 it received its death-blow when the official examinations ceased to be based on the Confucian classics. Western-style education was introduced, for its utilitarian value rather than for any intrinsic merits. Western textbooks were modified superficially, or not at all, and were often used in their original language. Thus, particularly in Protestant missionary schools and colleges, English largely supplanted Chinese as the medium of instruction.

In the first half of the 20th century, as China gradually struggled, through revolution, civil war and Japanese invasion, towards the independence finally achieved in 1949 under Communist leadership, modern education developed only slowly and often in a way irrelevant to the country's real needs. Only when social change started on a nation-wide scale after the establishment of the People's Republic in 1949 did schooling become the rule rather than the exception. In this generation China is being transformed from an essentially feudal agricultural society into a modern socialist and industrialised society. Millions of formerly illiterate peasants are now working in industry, sometimes as skilled technicians. Individual peasants have become members of rural people's communes, in which farming techniques are gradually being improved. Scientific methods have been introduced, often through the study of politics, and applied to agriculture even by illiterates. Experimentation and invention on a mass scale have produced remarkable results.

Whereas education used to be regarded as the only possible way of escaping from a life of grinding toil into the privileged class of those who did no manual labour, the tradition that the scholar does not soil his hands is now thoroughly discredited.

The beginnings of today's education can be traced back to the 1920s and 30s, when the Chinese revolution led by Mao Tse-tung was based in the countryside, and the gap between intellectuals and manual workers was for the first time beginning to be narrowed. In 1949 the People's Government inherited the high illiteracy rate and the more or less westernised educational system of the old society. But it was also able to draw on the accumulated experience of over twenty years administration of areas in which the main educational effort had been that of the people themselves.

The resulting educational system has been a mixture. The regular system of six-year primary schools has been continued and extended, but spare-time primary schools and literacy classes have been widely organised in both town and country for adults, and in the cities, universal primary education has been generally achieved. Full-time secondary education for six years has been possible for only about one in ten of primary school leavers; for the rural majority, many 'part-farm, part-study' schools have been set up, most of the study being done in the relatively slack farming seasons.

At secondary and college level, all students and young teachers have spent an increasing amount of time working on the land and in factories, consciously aiming to integrate themselves with workers and peasants, mentally as well as physically. By the end of 1965 a million secondary school leavers and college graduates had gone back to settle permanently in the villages, where their skills are helping to redress the balance between town and country.

From 1949 to 1958 primary school enrolment increased from 23 million to 86 million (out of a total population of over 700 million), secondary from less than 2 million to about 10 million (not including spare-time schools), and higher education from 155,000 to 660,000. No statistics are available for the very widespread and popular nursery schools. Illiteracy, generally estimated at 80–85% before 1949, has been cut dramatically. The difficulty of mastering the Chinese script in adult life makes the achievement of anything like universal literacy impossible in one generation, but the majority of those under fifty, including all young people, are literate.

Despite all the progress, old ways die hard. In mid-1966, during the early stages of the Cultural Revolution, a more thorough-going organisation of the whole educational system was initiated by the students themselves. Among their grievances were: the length of time taken by education, from primary school to college; the unsuitable nature of an over-academic curriculum for a country building socialism; and unfair discrimination against children from worker and peasant families.

The suspension of all formal secondary and higher education from the summer of 1966 demonstrated, more clearly than anything else could have done, the primacy of politics in China. Millions of young people travelled about the country for months at a time. Many outside observers have freely prophesied disastrous setbacks for China as a result, but it would be wiser to wait and see: in the course of the great upheaval of 1966–7 the young people may have learned more about their country than in a dozen years of formal schooling.

Among policies likely to be adopted in the reorganisation are a great reduction in written examinations in general, the introduction of 'open book' examinations in particular, and the selection of students for higher education on the basis of service to the community rather than of academic prowess. While it would be premature to attempt to forecast in detail the lines of the new system that will emerge, some things are certain: 'productive labour' will have a permanent place in the curriculum, of which sciences will constitute a major part; and politics will continue to be in command.

FURTHER READING
Stewart Fraser. *Chinese Communist Education: Records of the First Decade*, Vanderbilt Univ. Press, Nashville, Tennessee, 1965.
C. H. G. Oldham. 'Science and Education in China', *Bulletin of Atomic Scientists*, Chicago, Ill., June 1966.
Journals
China Reconstructs (monthly), Peking.
Peking Review (weekly), Peking. Especially Nos. 26 and 30, 1966.

DBr

China, Nationalist (Taiwan), Education in Elementary education is free and compulsory between the ages of six and 12 years, and in this age-group about 97% attend classes. In 1965/6 there were 553 pre-school groups (enrolment 78,620); 2,114 primary schools (enrolment 2,243,503); 546 secondary schools (enrolment 661,961); 1,140 vocational schools (80,972 students); 56 higher education institutes including 10 universities (enrolment 85,346 students). The National Taiwan University at Taipei is the largest university with 9,426 students.

The island's population was approximately 13 million in 1966.

Chinese, Teaching of *See* **Modern Languages, Committee on Research and Development in**

Choice of Employment Act *See* **Education Act (1910)**

Choir schools Several Anglican cathedral, collegiate chapel and a few parish church foundations of England, Scotland and Wales maintain schools to provide boy choristers for singing their daily choral services. Some of these choir schools are of very old foundation; others were founded, or re-founded, in the 19th century. Most are independent preparatory schools, though some constitute the junior departments of larger public schools

and at least one is a voluntary aided grammar school. Most accept both day boys and boarders at eight or nine years.

The smaller choir schools include those where every boy is a singer, while larger schools can allow only a minority to sing with the choir at any one time. Musical tradition and training are of a high standard, although care is taken that other subjects are not neglected because of choristers' duties.

Choristers receive some remission of fees, and may become eligible for special scholarships to a public school. There is a Choir Schools' Association (Hon. Sec.: the Rev. Duncan Thomson, The Cathedral Choir School, Ripon, Yorks).

DB

Christian Alliance of Women and Girls A missionary society for all ages. It provides residential hostels for business women and women students, holiday houses for families, and clubs for all ages and often for both sexes.
16 Dartmouth St, London, SW1.
Publication: *You and I* (quarterly).

Christian Association, Welsh Executive Committee of the Young Men's *See* **Responsible bodies**

Christian Association of Great Britain, Young Women's The Association, founded in 1855, aims to advance the Christian religion among women and young people of either sex, to advance their education, and to promote any other charitable purposes for their benefit. Associate membership is open to all over the age of 11; full membership to all over 16 who accept the Christian commitment. As well as providing accommodation (including hostels for girls over 16 working or studying away from home and transit accommodation for school parties), the Association organises youth clubs, pre-school groups further education, day release schemes and industrial training and a holiday and travel service.

Gen. Sec.: Miss Evelyn Joynt, National Offices, Hampden Hse, 2 Weymouth St, London, W1.

Publication: *The Blue Triangle* (three times annually).

Christian Associations Inc., National Council of Young Men's The YMCA is a spiritual movement which exists for the purposes of uniting young men and boys in the service of Jesus Christ, of helping them in the development and training of their powers of body, mind and spirit during the whole period in which character is being formed, and of enabling them to take their share in the service of God and their fellow-men.

The movement, which is interdenominational, was founded in London in 1844, and is now active in more than 70 countries of the world, with an international headquarters in Geneva. The National Council of England and Wales appoints an Education Committee. In recent years the Committee has particularly concerned itself with young people in industry and commerce. It has established four residential centres with courses varying from one to eight weeks' duration, which are chiefly concerned with the transition period from school to work, though one centre runs courses for managers. It has also appointed six full-time and some part-time tutors who work with groups of young people on industrial sites. The most recent project has been concerned with young operatives. There are more than 300 local associations, which are autonomous, and many of which organise a variety of educational activities, including work with schoolleavers.

Education Sec.: G. F. Palmer, 112 Great Russell St, London, WC1.

Christian Education, Institute of *See* **Christian Education Movement**

Christian Education Council, National The NCEC (formerly the National Sunday School Union) is a charitable organisation which aims to further the work of Christian and religious education within the Church and in the day school. Its main field of publishing is in this sphere, including books for children, books for young people and their leaders, and books, audio-visual aids and general teaching requisites for teachers.

Within the NCEC is the International Bible Reading Association, which publishes booklets of dated daily Bible readings for children and adults.

Robert Denholm Hse, Nutfield, Redhill, Surrey.

Christian Education Fellowship A section of the Graduates' Fellowship of the Inter-Varsity Fellowship, the Fellowship forms a loosely-knit Christian Union within the teaching profession. Among its aims is the encouragement of its members to make the fullest use of their professional training and abilities in the development of a Christian approach to educational issues. In study groups and in day conferences held in London and a number of provincial centres in recent years the CEF has sought to apply Christian insights and biblical doctrines of man to current problems. Discussion on similar lines has taken place in the CEF section of the quarterly journal *The Christian Graduate.* For teachers of religious education the Fellowship has held an Easter vacation course for the past 25 years, and the teachers are also helped by a detailed book review service and an advisory service on textbooks and syllabuses.

The Fellowship co-operates with the Inter-School Christian Fellowship and the Teachers' Prayer Fellowship in sponsoring residential weekend conferences in a number of centres in the early autumn, when the interests of all three societies are served.

Sec.: G. Landretti, 39 Bedford Sq., London, WC1.

E

Christian Education Movement The CEM is the result of a merger in 1965 between what was known as the Institute of Christian Education and the Student Christian Movement in schools. The concern of the CEM is to further Christian belief and action amongst boys and girls at school, and to draw into common service teachers and others interested. Its work for pupils includes the organising of day conferences, residential conferences, adventure and specialist interest holidays, international work camps; for teachers it runs courses and an extensive advisory service and publishes material.

The Movement works closely with Community Service Volunteers for school-leavers. Membership is interdenominational and internationally it is related to the World Student Christian Federation.

Journal: *Learning for Living*.

Annandale, North End Rd, London, NW11.

Christian Endeavour Union of Great Britain and Ireland Founded in 1881 in the USA by the Rev. Francis E. Clarke to assist the growth of Christian character among young people of his church by consistent teaching of Biblical matters and the endorsement of a covenant. The movement was introduced to the UK under the aegis of the National Sunday School Union, and the Union was formed in 1896. Its activities include weekly devotional meetings for children and young people, who are graded by age. An annual convention is held in the spring, and there are local conventions and young people's weekend house-parties, with holiday homes at 19 centres and occasional tours at home and abroad.

31 Lampton Rd, Hounslow, Middlesex.

Christian Fellowship, Inter-School This organisation promotes the growth of voluntary Christian societies in secondary schools and the Christian faith generally, and encourages social concern among groups and individuals. Membership is open to teachers and pupils in secondary schools. The ISCF arranges leadership training for senior pupils, academic courses for sixth-formers, social service work projects for pupils over 16, recreational camps and sailing cruises for secondary pupils of all ages, and termly discussion groups for teachers and training groups for pupils in 150 main centres in England and Wales.

47 Marylebone La., London, W1.

Publications: *Spectrum* (jointly with other Societies; termly); *Viewpoint* (quarterly).

Christian Knowledge, Society for Promoting The SPCK was founded in 1698 to carry out that purpose through education and literature, both in the UK and overseas. It is the oldest Anglican missionary society and publisher. It co-ordinated and directed the 18th-century Charity Schools movement, and was the main provider of schoolbooks for the educational expansion of the next century. Its wide range of publications in English have always been complemented by its foreign-language publishing, including some 200 Prayer Book translations. It has developed the use of visual aids. As an overseas missionary society it has disbursed vast sums in educational grants, but being the author, in 1960, of a comprehensive literature plan for the Anglican Communion, it now concentrates mainly on helping overseas churches to conduct their own literature operations. A chain of 60 home and overseas bookshops, of which those in India and East Africa have become autonomous, is geared to the Society's purposes and closely involved in educational developments overseas.

Holy Trinity Church, Marylebone Rd, London, W1.

Christian Students, Young YCS is an international organisation of students for students who accept responsibility in their own field for their own education, training themselves under Christian principles to co-operate with all those engaged in their education. They seek to take genuine student initiatives in the field of education through self-programming groups who look for concrete action in the community. This involves work on student structures and attitudes through training sessions and programmes of action based on local needs, which include careers and further education advice, accommodation, voluntary service and whatever may be of interest to the cultural, physical and spiritual development of students throughout the world.
57 Chalton St, Euston, NW1.

Christian Unions *See* **Inter-Varsity Fellowship of Evangelical Unions**

Christians and Jews, Council of Founded in 1942 for the promotion of mutual understanding and goodwill between Jewish and Christian communities, and between all the various racial and religious groups in the UK. Among facilities provided for schools are the arrangement of national and international conferences, lectures and visual aid demonstrations.
41 Cadogan Gdns, London, SW3.
Publication: *Common Ground* (quarterly).

Church Army Training College Recently re-housed in new premises at Blackheath, London, the College exists to train selected men and women as evangelists to work in all departments of the Church Army. An up-to-date three-year course is given, which includes a study of Biblical knowledge, Anglican worship and practice, psychology, and a study of contemporary social conditions. This is accompanied by a great deal of contact with social service personnel in units of all kinds, and strengthened by a variety of practical projects involving the whole student body.
Vanbrugh Park, London, SE3.

Church Colleges of Education, Council of *See* **Church of England Board of Education**

Church of England Board of Education The Board is charged by the Church of England National Assembly to be concerned with all the work of the Church in education. This work is carried out through the following constituent councils and committees:
(1) The Council of the Church Colleges of Education. The Church has 27 colleges (two belonging to the Church in Wales) with 13,000 students. £4¼ million has been spent by the Church since the war on modernising and expanding colleges.
(2) The Schools Council advises the Board on policy in relation to Church schools, co-ordinates the work of the dioceses in schools, and is concerned with religious education in all schools.
(3) The Church of England Youth Council (*q.v.*).
(4) The Children's Council promotes the religious education of children under the age of 14, and organises training for voluntary teachers in Sunday schools and leaders in junior clubs. It produces a wide range of publications, and fosters relationships with many different bodies concerned with children's needs. Its study centre provides courses in the content of religious education. Every diocese has a religious education adviser concerned with the religious education of children in church and school.
(5) The Adult Committee encourages the development of new methods of adult religious education, including the application of group techniques, the supply of suitable materials, and an advisory service.
(6) The Chaplaincies Advisory Committee fosters the development of

Anglican chaplaincies in universities and colleges and makes grants from central funds for this purpose.

Church House, Dean's Yard, Westminster, London, SW1.

Church of England Board of Education, the Church in Wales Council for Education, and the Free Church Federal Council, Central Joint Education Policy Committee of the

Formed in 1959, this body aims to help implement, without recourse to public enquiry and controversy, those sections of the Education Acts concerned with denominational schools and religious instruction in county schools. It is recognised by the DES as the authoritative channel for negotiation in such matters. The Chairman is the Bishop of London and the Secretaries, Canon Eric Wild (Church of England) and Rev. H. Bramwell Howard (Free Church Federal Council).

Church of England Youth Council

The Council is a constituent council of the Church Assembly Board of Education, and promotes the education of all young people between the ages of 14 and 25 years, irrespective of any religious affiliation and none.

Through its staff, the Council is concerned with the training of clergy in specialist posts in youth service, the training of leaders in partnership with statutory and voluntary bodies, the training of young people with some commitment to the Church and open provision for those who have no attachment. The implementation of the Newsom Report and the raising of the school-leaving age are special concerns in relation to school, youth service and community.

The Council's work is increasingly ecumenical in character through the World and British Councils of Churches. Nationally and regionally the Council operates in close partnership with the DES, the LEAs and the

national voluntary organisations, while in the 43 C of E dioceses it works through 75 diocesan youth officers.

35 Great Peter St, London, SW1.

Church Lads' Brigade

The object of the Brigade for over 75 years has been 'to extend the Kingdom of Christ among lads'. In pursuit of this object there are spiritual, recreational, social and educational activities designed to meet the needs of boys.

The method of operation is to form companies in parishes, and normally these would employ such military symbols and organisation as are useful in promoting the object. Besides stressing the value of a disciplined, responsible way of life in accordance with the teaching of the Church, CLB activities include such games, sports and other things as can help towards securing that end. These include canoeing, fencing, judo, national competitions and the use of many new badges, as well as the Duke of Edinburgh's Award. Boys from the ages of eight to 21 may join. The Brigade is subdivided into young boys, Junior Training and Senior Corps.

Gen. Sec.: Major H. S. Forbes, MBE, MC, 58 Gloucester Pl., London, W1.

Church Schoolmasters, Association of British

Following a successful protest against a minute of 1852 giving the clergy the right to dismiss a schoolmaster in a national school, a militant breakaway group of the Metropolitan Church Schoolmasters, together with provincial groups in Birmingham, Liverpool and Manchester, in 1853 formed the General Associated Body of Church Schoolmasters in England and Wales at a conference in London of 400 members representing 18 associations. In 1855 the Association survived a crisis over the exclusion of clergy, and membership grew slowly to 660. Later that year it increased to 1,200 as a result of the Association's agitation against the Revised Code (*q.v.*). It later carried out an inquiry into the financial effects of the Code and with other associations promoted a movement to establish a teachers' registration council, analagous to one set up for doctors.

Remodelled in 1866 as the General Association of Church Schoolmasters, it participated with other bodies in 1868 in forming a teachers' political pressure group, the London Association of Schoolmasters. The role which these two bodies took in forming the first National Union of Elementary Teachers is best reflected in the fact that J. J. Graves, secretary of the ABCS in 1857–63 and 1866–9, became first president, and William Lawson, secretary of the London Association of Schoolmasters, first secretary of the NUET, later the NUT.

FURTHER READING
Asher Tropp. *The School Teachers*, Heinemann, 1957.
WHGA

Circuit training A method of high-pressure exercising by tackling a 'circuit' of individually prescribed activities, circuit training aims at the progressive development of muscular and circulo-respiratory fitness. It owes much of its present popularity with adolescent and adult sportsmen to the experimental work done in the Dept of PE, Leeds University, by R. E. Morgan and G. T. Adamson, and to their book *Circuit Training* (Bell, 1957). In this the authors state that circuit training was not 'designed as a comprehensive gymnastic system nor as a form of recreative activity, though experience has proved that it has considerable appeal to young men and boys, many of whom show little enthusiasm for ordinary forms of physical training'.

The method's three main characteristics are: (a) that it endeavours to produce muscular and circulo-respiratory fitness; (b) that it applies the 'overloading' principles (*see* **Weight train-**

ing); (c) that by devising a circuit of consecutively numbered exercises or activities, round which each performer moves while doing an individually prepared schedule of work or 'repetitions' to a strict time allowance, it allows large numbers of performers to exercise at the same time.

Whereas exercises in weight training are done at almost maximal level, which means that short bouts of intense activity must be followed by periods of rest, in circuit training activities are done at sub-maximal levels for relatively long periods, which makes a continuous demand upon the heart and lungs and has a cumulative effect upon the development of stamina.

This would seem at first sight to rule out circuit training except for those already fit; but such is not the case since, though each person is fully extended on his individual circuit, he is not asked to do anything beyond his capability.
JE

Circular 10/65 *See* **Comprehensive schools**

Circulars *See* **Regulations, Statutory**

Circulating school A type of elementary school founded in 18th-century Wales, with a peripatetic staff.

Cités Universitaires The first of these was begun in the south of Paris between the wars. It consists of a number of buildings of different sizes and styles set in appropriate gardens. These serve as hostels and provide reasonably priced accommodation for a number of male and female students. During vacations cheap accommodation and meals are available to foreign students. Most French university cities have now followed the example of Paris.

City and Guilds of London Institute The aim of the Institute is the advancement of technical and scientific education as a service to the individual, to industry and to the nation. The Institute was founded in 1878 and in 1900 was granted a royal charter as an educational association for the advancement and application of 'all such branches of Science and the Fine Arts as benefit or are of use to . . . productive and technical industries especially and to commerce and industry generally'.

The Institute's technical examinations are intended for the great majority of industrial workers whose studies are in part-time classes held in their local technical college as a supplement to industrial experience. The Institute's purpose in offering examinations has always been, and still remains, to promote the establishment of courses of study, to set nationally recognised standards of attainment and provide machinery whereby industries can develop and adopt, on a national basis, schemes of further education which are integral components of apprenticeship and training schemes.

The system of technical examinations has developed vigorously and ranges over some 250 subjects which provide for the needs of operatives, craftsmen and technicians in industries such as agriculture, building, catering, chemicals, clothing and footwear, electrical engineering, furniture, food trades, mechanical engineering, metal manufacture, mining and quarrying, paper and printing, retail distribution, shipbuilding, textiles and vehicles, together with a range of artistic crafts, domestic subjects, important certificates for teachers engaged in further education and handicrafts and a number of general courses for intending technicians.
76 Portland Pl., London, W1.

Civic Trust This was founded in 1957 as an independent body supported by voluntary contributions. Its object is to improve the appearance of town and country, and it has initiated hundreds of schemes to brighten and tidy up streets all over Britain. With the help of volunteers, it has removed many eyesores which marred the countryside; has moved over 650 semi-mature trees into London as part of a wider campaign; by conferences and reports, focuses attention on current problems of planning and architecture. Its films are seen in all parts of the world. It makes awards for good development of all kinds. At the request of local authorities, it prepares appraisals of urban planning problems, and offers advice and support to over 500 local amenity societies. Regional Trusts are now in being for the North West, the North East, Wales and Scotland.

Walter Hse, Bedford St, London, WC2.

Civic Trust for the North West: Director: Graham Ashworth, Century Hse, St Peter's Sq., Manchester 2. Civic Trust for the North East: Director: Nevil Whitaker, 26 Sutton St, Durham. Civic Trust for Wales: Director: Stanley Hall-Cox, 46 The Parade, Cardiff. Civic Trust for Scotland: Director: Maurice Lindsay, 183 West George St, Glasgow, C2.

Civics *See* **General studies; Liberal studies; Social sciences, Teaching of**

Civil Service Council for Further Education *See* **Further Education, Civil Service Council for**

Claparède, Edouard (1873–1940) A Swiss doctor and psychologist, drawn into the educational field when he was asked for advice on the teaching of backward and abnormal children in Geneva, Claparède urged the importance of adapting education to the individual pupil. A school should be fitted to children as their shoes are fitted to their feet (his own term was *l'école sur mesure*—the 'school to measure'). His work, *The Psychology of the*

Child and Experimental Pedagogy (1905), was influential in the general ferment of educational experiment that marked the early years of this century. Claparède was a founder of the Institut J. J. Rousseau in Geneva.

Clarendon Report (1864) (Royal Commission) Terms of reference: to enquire into the nature and application of the endowments, funds and revenues belonging to or received by certain named colleges, schools and foundations; to enquire into the administration of these colleges, schools and foundations, and into their system and course of studies, as well as into the methods, subjects and extent of the instruction given to their students. The schools named were Eton, Winchester, Charterhouse, St Pauls', Merchant Taylors', Harrow, Rugby and Shrewsbury. The Commission prepared detailed reports on each of the eight schools, and recommended some revisions of their statutes. It affirmed that classics should continue to be the basis of the courses but recommended a broadening of the curriculum so that each boy should learn mathematics, one modern language, science, and drawing or music. It also recommended that specialisation should be allowed during the last few years, and that some classic subjects could be dropped to this end.

Clarke, Sir Fred (1880–1952) Director of the Institute of Education of London University from 1937, and first chairman of the English Advisory Council, Sir Fred Clarke had pioneer views on the relevance of sociology to educational thought.

FURTHER READING
Sir Fred Clarke. *Education and Social Change*, Sheldon Press, 1947. *Freedom in the Educative Society*, Univ. of London Press, 1947.

CLASP The Consortium of Local Authorities Special Programme was formed in 1957 by a number of local authorities co-operating voluntarily to sponsor and control a method of building for their specific needs. The system is based on the educational requirements of schools, university and other local authority buildings, and consists mainly of factory-made components that can be assembled rapidly and in a wide variety of ways. By mechanisation and bulk production the quality and economy of the buildings are comparatively increased to give maximum possible value. The present annual building programme is £17m., carried out by the 18 members of the Consortium.

A characteristic of the buildings is that they can be used safely during mining subsidence. This is achieved by making them light in weight and flexible in construction.

All parts of the system have been designed either by a group of development architects or in collaboration with manufacturers to rigid cost controls. The system is gradually being improved and modified to meet changing user needs, national co-ordination of dimensions and standards. Maintenance costs are not greater than in traditional or other forms of building.

The current Mark IV consists of a pin-jointed steel frame of $4\frac{1}{2}$ in. square tube stanchions with lattice beams supported on precast concrete bases.

Horizontal planning flexibility There is a basic module of 4 in. for all dimensions. Planning grid is 1 ft and structural grid 3 ft x 3 ft. External walls may change direction at any 3 ft grid position from stanchions spaced at 6 ft or 12 ft centres.

Vertical flexibility Room heights are: single and up to 4 storeys, 8 ft and 10 ft; high single storey, 12 ft, 14 ft, 16 ft, 18 ft, with 20 ft and 22 ft special. Floor and roof thicknesses are normally 2 ft total, but for long span girders of 48 ft, 54 ft and 60 ft they are 4 ft deep. Ground floor changes of level can be 2 ft or 4 ft. Window-sill and transom heights are 2 ft, 2 ft 8 in., 3 ft 4 in. and 6 ft 8 in. above floor level.

External walls consist of (a) timber windows, delivered glazed and painted; (b) tiles in various patterns, textures and colours; (c) boarding; (d) concrete panels in various colours and textures. Internal partitions are $6\frac{1}{4}$ in. thick and can be planned at 1 ft positions. They have either half-hour or one-hour fire resistance and 35 db. or 45 db. sound reduction properties. Finishes are mainly plasterboard, but impact and water-resistant qualities are available. Ground floor finishes are variable to suit requirements; upper floor finish is sheet rubber with a foam underlay, on timber decks units. Ceilings are suspended to conceal services and are either plasterboard or a mineral fibre board with a one-hour fire resistance. Internal screens are 2 in.-thick stove enamelled steel frames, pre-glazed. Staircases fit between walls at 9 ft centres. Internal doors are either polished hardwood or painted softwood. For schools, the furniture is in a range of standard mobile table and cupboard units. Heating is by recirculated warm air from cabinets thermostatically controlled.

The quality of CLASP architecture depends, as in all buildings, on the sensitivity and understanding of the architect using the system.

JCS

Class teaching A long-established educational arrangement has been the teaching of classes of children by single teachers. In early days in the English system classes of between 70 and 100 pupils were fairly common, as they still are in some developing countries today. Methods adopted by teachers confronted by these large numbers always seem to have placed a first insistence on control or discipline. Simultaneous drill movements were expected from pupils, and close supervision of these drills was an important part of the teacher's work. From this

arrangement came the generalised analogy that the speed of a caravan was the speed of the slowest camel. The subject matter taught in large classes tended to be a readily acceptable minimum.

This arrangement persisted despite the belief of idealists that the aim of education is the development to the maximum of each pupil's potentialities. This aim became easier, although it remains difficult, when the supply of teachers and of school buildings combined to reduce the size of classes: in many cases today classes remain overlarge even by recommended standards.

The reduced size of classes led to the removal of the teacher's dais and gradually to the introduction of comfortable and movable classroom furniture. Class teaching persists as a very important means of conducting educational affairs. It is particularly valuable in introducing new skills and new data and in correcting common errors and misconceptions. It is of undisputed value in offering common aesthetic pleasure and affords an acceptable opportunity for children to identify themselves as members of a unit smaller than the whole school. It has resilience as an organisational unit, though it also, though decreasingly, permits the survival of certain obsolescent methods of teaching.

Class teaching is now conducted as a rule by much less formal techniques than formerly and is indeed frequently amended into a series of 'group' activities or methods.

See also **Group methods**

DJ

Classes, Size of In state primary schools roughly one child in four is in a class of 30 or fewer children. One child in six is in a class of over 40. The classes of over 40 are certainly too large. They would be done away with at once if there were sufficient teachers to go round. Many of the classes under 30 are in small schools and contain children of several different ages. They require as much skill to teach effectively as much bigger classes confined to children of the same age, so that, where this still is lacking, there is no educational advantage, but possibly a handicap, to a child who attends one of these very small classes. They are always extravagant to staff, but in sparsely populated districts there is no alternative. The opinion of teachers is clearly in favour of a maximum size of 30, but the fact that nearly half primary school-children are in classes of over 35 means that this objective will take a long time to secure. Independent primary schools have the advantage of much smaller classes, about half the size of those in state schools on an average, which many parents feel outweighs the fact that more of their teachers are untrained.

Secondary school forms, as classes in these schools are termed, are smaller. Roughly every other child in a state secondary school is in a form of 30 pupils or less; one in five is in a form of 25 or less. Only 2% are in forms of over 40. This looks like favouritism towards secondary as opposed to primary schools, and no doubt before 1944 what we now call grammar schools ranked higher than what were described as elementary. Part of the difference is, then, inherited. But part is determined by other factors. The smaller secondary forms are on the whole those made up of older children. Many first-year and second-year forms are in fact 35 or so in number, and the Plowden report considered that there was no case for a different size of class in junior and lower secondary schools. But from the third year on, boys and girls are offered an increasing variety of choice between subjects so that, unless the school itself is to be very large, some of the teaching units for certain subjects are bound to be relatively small. In some subjects, too, safety considerations have suggested that only half forms should be taught

together, and the schools have been planned on this assumption. In the sixth form, teaching groups also need to be smaller: 20 is an uncomfortably large maximum. Secondary school work is, therefore, marked by a gradual reduction in the size of the teaching units so that a better comparison between primary and secondary staffing is given by teacher/pupil ratio than by size of class. There is roughly one teacher to every 29 primary pupils, one to every 19 secondary pupils.

DGOA

Classical Association The Association, founded in 1903, aims at encouraging public interest in the classics, maintaining their rightful position in education and giving scholars and teachers opportunities to meet for the discussion of common problems. It has a world-wide membership of 4,000, and in Gt Britain has 29 branches which provide programmes of varied interest. The Association organises reading competitions in Latin and Greek for schools all over the country.

Hon. Secs: T. W. Melluish, 32 Poplar Walk, Herne Hill, London, SE24; Professor B. R. Rees, University College, Cardiff.

Journals: *The Classical Quarterly*, *The Classical Review*, *Greece and Rome*, *The Proceedings of the Classical Association*.

Classical Teachers, Joint Association of *See* **Classics, Teaching of**

Classics, Teaching of The full classical syllabus in schools is generally taken to include the learning of Latin and Greek with a view to studying the masterpieces written by ancient authors in those tongues, and the history, literature, thought and civilisation of the Greeks and Romans. Schools, according to their capacity, arrange for pupils to be taught appropriate parts or the whole of this course. Beginning in the first or second year, Latin is taught to all, or selected,

E*

pupils, until a four- or five-year course is completed. During this time Greek may be added for selected pupils. Then, in the 6th form, the full classical course of Latin, Greek and ancient history may be taken by specialists, while others on the arts side may take Latin as a supporting subject to other humane studies. At the university, classics is pursued to degree standard.

The teaching of Latin goes back to antiquity, beginning as a training in rhetoric, and developing as a training in the Latin language, since this was the only medium in which a scholar could address his European contemporaries. The linguistic side was stressed, and it was not until later that Virgil and Horace, Livy and Tacitus were studied for their literary eminence. The arid learning of grammatical forms by rote and the poor quality of teaching sometimes brought Latin into disrepute. Yet although Latin has had its detractors in the past, it has had its stout champions too—so that in spite of the advent of new subjects in the syllabus, and the foundation of municipal grammar schools, avowedly for the purpose of teaching science, classics has never wholly lost its place as a very worthwhile subject of study.

The traditional method, developed during the 18th and 19th centuries in the public schools, presupposes a lengthy course and an ample allowance of time. Accidence and syntax are learnt slowly and systematically from grammars and textbooks. The pupil is only gradually, and after long preparation, introduced to the reading of Latin authors. There is much stress on translating English into Latin sentences, and little reference to the life of the Greeks and Romans themselves. The slow and tedious pace of this course, and its meagre results in terms of literature read, caused much criticism, even though for those who had the patience to pursue it to the end 'the grand old fortifying curriculum' seemed to bring ample rewards.

Perhaps the first real breakthrough came when in 1907 Lodge published a Latin vocabulary based on a systematic study of word frequency. Textbooks thereafter confined themselves to the limits of this word list. Dissatisfaction with traditional teaching then led Dr W. H. D. Rouse of the Perse School, Cambridge, to propound the direct method, which he himself used with brilliant success. Harking back to earlier times, he used Latin as a spoken tongue, and all instruction was given in that medium. Most of the work was oral, and translation into English was largely abandoned. Imitation, repetition, association and induction were used to give the pupils a lively sense that they were learning a living language. Authors were read much faster as translation was replaced by question and answer, and oral exegesis from the teacher. Dr Rouse founded an Association for the Reform of Latin Teaching, which still gives demonstrations of this method. If the direct method is less widespread than it should be, this is possibly because it demands very unusual teachers.

The word order method (1929), advocated by Mason, Gray and Appleton in connection with their book *Latin For Today*, placed emphasis on the reading of a whole Latin sentence before attempting to translate. Comprehension of reading matter took priority over syntax, and copious provision of synthetic Latin, and then simplified Latin authors, with numerous illustrations, supplied a large background of classical history and mythology. For those who had time for it the method marked a distinct advance.

Today, although educational reorganisation threatens a further retrenchment of the time allowance, some fresh and interesting work is being vigorously pursued. Oral Latin, reading competitions, gramophone recordings all figure largely in new methods. *Acta Diurna*, a termly Latin newspaper, reveals a wholly new outlook. Archaeology has increasing adherents; theatrical productions of classical plays flourish; more books about classical times are being produced than ever before. The Classical Association, Association for the Reform of Latin Teaching, the Orbilian Society, the Joint Association of Classical Teachers, all foster the classical interest. Classical teaching may take on a new look, but he would be a rash man who would predict its disappearance.

FURTHER READING
Incorporated Association of Assistant Masters. *The Teaching of Classics*, Cambridge Univ. Press, 2nd ed. 1961.
D. J. Morton. *Classics and the Reorganisation of Secondary Schools*, JACT Pamphlet No. 2, Joint Association of Classical Teachers.
Suggestions for the Teaching of Classics, Ministry of Education Pamphlet No. 37, HMSO, 1959.

TWM

Classifying schools These are schools associated with approved schools but having the responsibility of making a close investigation of the child sent to the school in order to determine which approved school would suit his needs best. The salary scale for the warden of a classifying school is £2,320 × £75(4) to £2,620: for a deputy warden the scale is £1,530 × £30(2) × £50 × £60(3) × £50(7) × £60 to £2,230.

Certain staff of classifying schools, associated training schools and special units also receive additional allowances to the salaries otherwise determined and these are as follows: senior assistants £160, principals of schools with special units £400, and other principals £320.

Classrooms The traditional method of educating children was conceived in terms of the teacher teaching and the child listening. The rectangular classroom was the result of the need to contain, as economically as possible, this structured situation of children, seated in symmetrical rows, facing teacher and blackboard. In the 19th and early 20th centuries the windows of the classroom were built high in the walls to prevent the children from window-gazing. Today, classroom design is undergoing a process of slow change, and there has been research on such environmental factors as heating and lighting. Government control of school planning has influenced design; for example, the present building regulations for schools demand that a 2% daylight factor be provided on the surface of any desk. This has resulted in wall-to-wall and sill-to-ceiling glazing in some schools.

Since in the past teachers have rarely been consulted when school plans were drawn up, classroom design is often at variance with teaching needs. Frequently those classrooms with extensive window areas have insufficient wall space for the display of children's work, which in consequence may sometimes be stuck on the windows themselves. Architects in the main are briefed by local authorities in building, not teaching, terms; i.e. they are told how many pupils a school is to accommodate and how many classrooms must be provided, without mention of the teaching methods to be employed and the resultant activities that will take place in and around the building. An encouraging feature of school design in the second half of the 20th century has been the impetus given to good planning by the DES through the publication of its building bulletins, which emphasise the need for relating buildings to teaching methods.

As schools are built to last, teachers have to adapt existing classrooms to new teaching methods. In general the movement, more noticeable in primary than in secondary schools, has been away from the passivity of teacher teaching and children listening, to child participation in the learning process by activity, either alone or as a member of a small group. Where this has taken place in the classroom of traditional shape and size, group activities have to be carried on in various corners of the room and also outside its walls—in the corridors, cloakrooms, hall, playground and school field. But where regard has been paid to modern teaching techniques, stemming from a deeper understanding of the ways in which children learn and grow, the distinction between teaching and non-teaching areas has disappeared.

There has been a tendency (1) for two or three small classrooms to be built as a cluster with its own cloakroom and lavatory accommodation housing some hundred children of the same yearly intake; (2) for space to be utilised intensively so that it serves two or more purposes during the day. In many recently-built schools the rigidity of the conventional classroom has been abandoned altogether, particularly in primary schools. Partly inspired by the need for strict cost control, architects have planned for a number of small groups rather than for classes of 40 pupils. Areas of space, rather than classrooms, have been provided in which children can move around and do things, with water available at low sinks, small low-level cupboards for storing children's work and books, wall boards and containers and work benches. The result has been schools built on an open plan system (*see* **Open Plan**) with only partial division between groups, not classroom walls.

A show-place of this type is the Eveline Lowe Primary School, in SE London, built on an open-plan arrangement of inter-related spaces, connected with veranda space out-of-doors, which permits a very flexible organisation. Although pupil groups of 40 were envisaged, the organisation allows for experiments with groups of 60 and 30, and, for many purposes, much smaller units. These smaller groups, whose number and size are continually changing, allow for free movement of individual children between groups. At the same time there are quiet areas and clearly defined spaces in which 30 or 40 children can gather with one teacher when required.

In modern schools so designed, attention has been paid to the provision of screens and partitions for the simple and temporary division of space, and to acoustics and the control of noise. In secondary schools the provision of bulky and expensive equipment, language laboratories and the like, and specialist teaching, has meant greater movement within the school so that the classroom is no longer the focal point of class activity; the social needs of older children are now being given consideration by the provision of junior common rooms in place of classrooms. With the coming of team teaching to the UK (now widely used in the USA), further changes in classroom design are inevitable since this method must still further break down the concept of one teacher to one room.

See also **School buildings**

FURTHER READING
Ministry of Education/DES. *Building Bulletins*, 1955 onwards.
Pilkington Research Unit, Department of Building Science, Liverpool University. *The Primary School: An Environment in Education*, 1967.

EP

CLAW Founded in 1963, CLAW (Consortium, Local Authorities, Wales) aims to gain the advantage of bulk tendering by joint orders for certain elements in buildings that are required for education and other social services except housing. CLAW, unlike some other similar consortiums, is not at the moment committed to any one building system. Members are Anglesey, Breconshire, Cardiff, Cardiganshire, Carmarthenshire, Glamorgan, Merthyr Tydfil, Monmouthshire, Newport and Swansea.

Clean Air, National Society for
The objects of the Society are to promote clean air in the UK by creating

an informed public opinion on the dangers of all forms of atmospheric pollution.

Established in 1899 (originally as the Coal Smoke Abatement Society), the Society is a voluntary body, deriving its support from members' subscriptions. It publishes *Smokeless Air*, its quarterly journal, the Clean Air Year Book, annual conference proceedings and clean air pamphlets, booklets and leaflets of educational value. Various services are available to members, including information and advice, library facilities and a publicity advisory service.

Field Hse, Breams Bldgs, London, EC4.

Cleaning staff, School *See* **Schoolkeeping**

Closed-Circuit Television Association, National Educational Formed in 1968, the Association represents the interests of educational institutions that systematically employ closed-circuit television for teaching purposes. Experience is shared, views exchanged on common problems, and information co-ordinated. An aim is to establish proper standards, both educational and technical, as well as to promote a high quality of production and to encourage new methods and materials.

Chairman: D. J. G. Holroyde, Director of Television, Leeds University.

Closed-circuit television in education A major development in educational communication in Britain, which began to assume significant proportions in the early 1960s. It owes its origins to: (1) the limited extent to which broadcast television services could meet the wide and increasing national needs in education; (2) the shortage of schools teaching staff and the rapid increase of student numbers in higher education; (3) the development of transistorised television studio cameras and other equipment which makes its purchase and use feasible in educational institutions; (4) the need to improve the quality of much teaching at all levels; (5) the realisation that to achieve full effectiveness, teaching programmes must be devised and used by teachers within a total educational environment.

The first closed-circuit television service for schools was started in Glasgow in the summer of 1965, and began with regular teaching programmes in mathematics and French. Similar developments followed in Plymouth, Edinburgh, Hull, Liverpool and the ILEA; the ILEA plans to serve 1,300 educational institutions.

About 35 colleges of education were using closed-circuit television by the end of 1968, some for direct teaching, others for the observation of classroom situations to enable student teachers to gain new insights and experiences into teaching techniques and problems. Colleges at Hull, York, Durham, Huddersfield, Coventry, Cardiff, Twickenham, Leicester, Goldsmiths' (London), Avery Hill (London), Jordanhill (Glasgow) and Notre Dame (Glasgow), are among those using CCTV. Experimental educational uses of television were also developed at Bolton College of Technical Training, Garnett College and in colleges of further education in Hertfordshire.

In universities, television was first used in medical schools for the observation of surgical treatment, demonstration of teaching material in anatomy, physiology, pharmacology, biochemistry, etc, and in diagnostic radiology.

The first university television studio was set up at Leeds in 1963 by the School of English; the first comprehensive central television services for all university teaching were instituted at the Universities of Leeds and Glasgow (1965) and Sussex (1966). Other universities using television as a visual aid or as a regular medium of teaching for departmental use include Strathclyde (mathematics and physics),

Liverpool, Heriot-Watt, Nottingham, Surrey, East Anglia, Hull, York, Brunel, Cambridge (zoology), Birmingham (anatomy) and Manchester. Others use simple CCTV systems for microscopy and research work.

Since CCTV services use cable distribution systems it is possible for them to plan up to eight or more simultaneous channels, enabling eventually all teaching material to be given systematic repeat showings for classroom or student viewing at most suitable times. All CCTV systems in Britain use 625-line standards and most use vidicon camera channels. A full university or LEA service employs professional technical and production staff, but all the learning programmes are presented by teachers. Many Universities and colleges also have mobile units to enable material to be collected away from the institution, or to take recorded material to outlying classes. Average cost of installation of CCTV in a college of education is £10–15,000; in a university, £50–£100,000; in an LEA studio centre, £250,000.

Most CCTV operations involve use of videotape recording equipment to enable (a) experimental work to be played back for evaluation; (b) recorded material to be repeated as often and as frequently as needed, and (c) teaching staff to improve existing teaching methods, through viewing their own teaching techniques.

CCTV permits close liaison over planning and utilisation of teaching programmes between teaching staff; facility for immediate and sustained 'feed-back' from learning audiences; introduction of visual elements into teaching material which is not otherwise available; much clearer and closer views of demonstration material in teaching, e.g. laboratory experiments, specimens, working models. CCTV is also of significant teaching value in observing human situations, e.g. consultations between patient and doctor/dentist/psychiatrist. It can be used in language laboratories, for the relay of lectures to overflow audiences, for combining different visual resources in presenting lectures (e.g. animated diagrams, graphic or photographic or cinematographic inserts, superimpositions or dramatised sequences), or for relaying pictures into lecture theatres from otherwise inaccessible sources, e.g. cloud chambers, electron microscopes, engineering workshops.

Uses of CCTV being planned or investigated include: exchange of recorded teaching material between universities or other educational institutions; rationalisation of teaching resources; stimulation of new curriculum development and overcoming shortages of specialised teaching staff in some subjects. These new services are complementary to the provision of series of educational programmes by broadcasting authorities and are almost invariably being used for direct teaching to meet quite specific educational objectives. It is likely that the next five years will see a dramatic increase in the use of television by universities and other educational bodies. It is increasingly recognised as having the potential to improve both the quantity and quality of teaching.

A National Educational Closed-Circuit Television Association was formed in 1967, with about 80 educational institutions as members. There are also several inter-university working parties on television co-operation.

The University of Sussex plans close links with the colleges of education and of technology at Brighton, and with some local schools, thus providing inter-relationship between different levels of teaching. Training courses for teachers in the educational uses of CCTV are available in Leeds, London (Goldsmiths' College), Glasgow, Plymouth, Coventry and Bolton. The University of Leeds is also the main centre for research into the impact and effectiveness of educational television, with particular emphasis on the contribution of television, as a means of educational communication, to the learning situation. Most universities are now planning a central television service with which will be associated all other teaching media, e.g. film and overhead projection facilities, audio systems, programmed learning, etc, thus following a pattern already established in many North American universities, where the uses of television and other developments in educational technology are well organised.

FURTHER READING
Audio-Visual Aids in Higher Scientific Education. HMSO, London, 1965.
Closed-Circuit Television in Education in Great Britain. National Committee for Audio-Visual Aids in Education, London, 1965.
Educational Television and Radio in Britain. BBC, London, 1966.
Television in the University of Leeds. National Committee for Audio-Visual Aids in Education, 1966.
Roderick MacLean. *Television in Education,* Methuen Modern Teaching Series, 1968.
DJH

Clothing, LEAs' power to provide for schoolchildren *See* **Legal rights and obligations of parents**

Clustering and clusters Group-work is an essential feature of IDE (interdisciplinary enquiry, *q.v.*) and the other three parts of the fourfold curriculum devised by the Goldsmiths' College Curriculum Laboratory. To emphasise that the new curriculum involves pupils collaborating in small groups, this form of grouping has been called *clustering.*

Clustering involves task-orientated grouping, task-differentiated grouping, and friendship grouping. It is a process which occurs naturally when teachers create conditions in which the sharing of interests and collaborative learning can take place; and because of the nature of interest, collaboration and learning, clustering is also a process of change.

Theoretical considerations and the observations of teachers who have experienced working with groups of pupils in the way IDE makes possible combine to favour the view that pupils collaborate effectively when they cluster in groups composed of no more than seven.

Within the cluster individual and shared enquiries and *making* (*q.v.*) proceed; and learning is also shared, as dialogue between the members of the group proceeds continuously. The teachers in this group-dynamic situation are seen to be working with each cluster in turn, tackling individual problems, showing how individuals can receive assistance from their workmates, guiding the collaborative venture, and often bringing the various clusters together to share experiences and to help to move the undertaking to a new phase.

The cluster is the basic unit of the collaborative school which operates the fourfold curriculum. It replaces the concept of the class or set. It resembles the *focus group* (*q.v.*), the basic unit in which teachers collaborate.

FURTHER READING
Charity James. *Live Now; Live Later,* Collins, 1968.
L. A. Smith (Ed.). *Ideas No. 1,* Goldsmiths' College Curriculum Laboratory, 1967.
LAS

Cockerton Judgement This was a test case brought before the High Court to establish the legality or otherwise of school boards in dealing with secondary education. The ruling was made that the boards' expenditure on secondary education was illegal, and the result was the rapid passage of the Education Act 1902 through Parliament to ensure the legal future of secondary education.

A district auditor, T. B. Cockerton (acting on the instructions of Dr Garnett, secretary of the Technical Education Board), charged the members of the school board concerned with the North London (Camden) School of

131

Art with some of the expenditure on the school, on the grounds that the education provided was not elementary and was therefore outside their brief. The board took the matter to the High Court, and after a year of legal battle judgement was given against the school boards, making immediate new legislation necessary to legalise any form of state or rate-supported secondary education.

See also **Education Act 1902; Morant, Sir Robert**

Code Committee As described in *Hansard* of 8 August 1881, the Code Committee, established by A. J. Mundella, consisted of the permanent secretary, two of his assistants and three HMIs, with four other HMIs from large towns called in for consultation. This machinery for revision of the codes ensured that changes were discussed. Changes were pressed upon the Committee by the Code Reform Association amongst others under its energetic secretary Sonnenschein. The Code Committee was the forerunner of the Consultative Committee (established in 1902) and the present Schools Council for the Curriculum and Examinations.

WHGA

Codes of grants Since 1839 the Committee of Council had issued its Minutes regulating its relations with schools, and in 1858 they were consolidated and published as a parliamentary paper. These were digested and recast as a code of regulations, published in 1860. From henceforth this code was laid annually before the House of Commons, and, after a month, unless criticised, acquired the force of law.

As the result of the Newcastle Commission's Report of 1861 (*q.v.*), this code was revised and published to accommodate its proposal that grants to schools should depend on the attendance and performance of pupils in the basic skills of reading, writing and arithmetic—oracy, literacy and numeracy. The Revised Code (1862) was launched on a sea of protests and came into effect in 1863, as 'a spur to improvement', in the words of the Vice-President generally associated with it, Robert Lowe.

As finally amended after much debate, the Revised Code made available grants of 4s per pupil (or 6s 6d for pupils under six) for general merit and attendance, and 2s 8d per pupil for passes in reading, writing and arithmetic respectively. It also instituted six standards (*q.v.*), to replace the existing four age groups.

Subsequent codes illustrate the slow broadening of the curriculum of elementary schools. The 1871 Code abolished the old Standard I and added a new Standard VI. Attendance grants for infants were raised to 8s (or 10s if taught separately) and for older children to 6s while grants for passes in the three Rs were raised to 4s and further grants were made available in Standards IV-VI of 3s for passes in each of not more than two 'specific' subjects: geography, history, grammar, algebra, geometry, natural philosophy, physical geography, natural science, political economy, languages or any other subject approved by the HMI. These grants could not exceed 15s per scholar in average attendance, nor, cumulatively, the total income of the school from fees, subscriptions and rates.

The 1875 Code introduced 'class' subjects, like grammar, geography, history and needlework, capable of being taught above Standard I; 'good' passes could earn 4s per scholar and 'fair' passes 2s. This was accompanied by a reduction to 3s for a pass in one of the three Rs, and a raise of the grant for a pass in the 'specific' subject to 4s. The total grant each scholar could earn in average attendance was raised to 17s 6d.

As modified in the 1882 Code, grants were not reckoned individually but on the average attendance at school (to diminish the temptation to forge the registers), and special 'merit' grants were given for infant schools as a whole. The 1893 Code encouraged evening schools by recognising the attendance of students over 21 as grant earners, and abolishing the requirement that they should pass in elementary subjects.

WHGA

Co-education A book published in 1927 began with a definition of a 'co-educational or mixed school' as one which admitted boys and girls on equal terms, or more fully, as one 'in which boys and girls are educated together, usually in the same classes, and are allowed some freedom of association both within and without school hours'. The author distinguished between a school so organised and a 'dual school' in which boys and girls shared a building and even acknowledged the same head, but otherwise led quite separate existences.

Co-education became an issue only when society thought of providing some kind of liberal as opposed to vocational education for all girls. Educators from the humanists of the Renaissance onwards had advocated the education of girls, but in England only the few had any formal schooling until the Act of 1876 made their attendance at school compulsory. After that, girls accompanied their brothers to the village schools, but in urban areas they usually attended schools or departments of their own.

Meanwhile, in the second half of the 19th century, Miss Beale at Cheltenham, Miss Buss at the North London Collegiate School and Miss Davies, founder of Girton, were pioneering the cause of higher education for girls. Though they had no thought of advocating co-education, their work contributed to its ultimate widespread acceptance, for they showed that girls could equal, if not exceed, their brothers in the mastery of a cur-

riculum designed for boys. In this way they proved the feasibility of educating boys and girls together even at post-primary levels. The Balfour Act 1902 promoted this development by providing for the first time a national scheme of secondary education, in which some of what had formerly been mixed higher-grade elementary schools now became co-educational secondary schools.

In 1923 the Board of Education published the *Report of the Consultative Committee on Differentiation of the Curriculum for Boys and Girls Respectively in the Secondary School*. In spite of the tenor of this report the president of the Incorporated Association of Head Masters (IAHM) claimed only four years after its appearance that 'one of the most striking developments in day school education in recent years (had been) the growth of the mixed secondary schools'. By that time co-education had certainly become a much-debated issue, for it was of a piece with changing social circumstances. Women had taken men's places in factory and field during the war years, and were less committed than they had ever been before to becoming permanently housewives and mothers. They had won new standing in society—as witness, for example, the Representation of the People Act 1928, by which they gained the same right to vote as their menfolk. These and associated changes conferred greater freedom for men and women to work and to play together. Something of this ferment evidently informed the debate on co-education which occupied a prominent place in the educational literature of the decade spanning the 20s and 30s.

Some parents and educators were strongly opposed to the spread of co-education. One of their chief objections to it was the supposed 'moral' danger inherent in it. No-one complained that little boys and little girls should be educated together. Again, no-one complained that young men and young women should use the same lecture theatres and laboratories in the universities. But many people thought then that to educate boys and girls of secondary age together might cause them to suffer emotional disturbances which would interfere with their studies. For their part co-educationists argued that to segregate the sexes in educational institutions was as unnatural and probably as unhealthy as to segregate them in everyday life. Accordingly they maintained that the best way of helping adolescent boys and girls to adjust to their new-found powers and interests was to provide for them to work side by side intellectually as well as socially.

The second objection to co-education canvassed at this time was that boys needed a curriculum different from that provided for girls. The curricula—so it was said—had to take account of the different roles which the sexes would play as adults. The boy would become practical bread-winner and master; the girl, gentle mother and housewife. Again, those opposed to co-education argued that differences of interests between boys and girls could be satisfied only by providing different curricula for them. While co-educationists accepted that boys and girls might have different interests, they argued that no substantial differences in ability distinguished the one from the other, and that they could therefore quite properly share the bulk of any acceptable curriculum.

Many single-sex schools still remain in the UK, but opposition to co-education as a theory is now no longer subject for debate. To this extent practice in the UK has fallen into line with what has always been commonly accepted in Protestant Europe and North America. The introduction of a comprehensive system of secondary education in England must mean that co-education will be even more widely practised in the future.

Systems of education in the UK have undergone radical alterations since the debate concerning co-education was at its liveliest. Consequently statistics for, say, 1925, are not comparable with those of 1965. However, authorities would generally agree that these last 40 years have witnessed an accelerating trend towards co-education at all stages. The last issue of *Statistics of Education*[1] shows 30,927 (or almost 90%) of a total of 34,614 maintained schools or departments for children of compulsory school age as mixed. Schools and departments in the UK, other than nursery schools, whether maintained, direct-grant or independent, now number 38,777, and of these 32,858 or 85% are mixed.

See also **Curriculum differentiation; Girls, Education of**

REFERENCE
1. Department of Education and Science, *Statistics of Education*, Part I, HMSO, 1966.

FURTHER READING
B. A. Howard. *The Mixed School*, Univ. of London Press, 1928.
J. H. Newsom. *The Education of Girls*, Faber, 1948.
R. Snell (pseud. L. B. Pekin). *Co-education in its Historical and Theoretical Setting*, Longmans, Toronto, 1939.
Alice Woods. *Educational Experiments in England*, Methuen, 1920.

RDB

Coefficient of correlation The extent of the relationship between any two sets of variables—a child's IQ and his marks in an exam form an example—is expressed by a number, the coefficient of correlation. Where there is absolutely no relation between the two sets, the coefficient is 0. An inverse relationship is expressed by a coefficient of -1.00. Where the sets relate completely, the coefficient is $+1.00$.

Cognition This term covers the factor common to all types of knowing, such as awareness of feelings, relationships, ideas and the process of imagining, judging, reasoning, remembering or

COLLEGES OF ADVANCED TECHNOLOGY

understanding. It contrasts with *con-ation*, which describes all types of feeling. Nowadays, cognition is thought to be most effective with pupils if they understand all aspects of a learning situation, not merely how to arrive at the correct answer without much understanding of the processes involved.

Coherence subjects Proposed as a means of adapting the sixth-form curriculum to modern needs, 'coherence subjects' would be taken by all sixth-formers and would be taught and examined at GCE Complementary or C level. The proposal is fully described by Michael Hutchinson and Christopher Young in their book *Educating the Intelligent* (1962), where they suggest that all pupils would take the Development of Scientific Thought as a coherence subject. Science specialists would also choose a coherence subject from English or history, and a third which would be a modern language. The arts specialist would choose his second coherence subject from English, history or modern languages, the subject selected being different from his choice of specialist subjects; the third coherence subject in his case being either mathematics or statistics. Hutchinson and Young emphasise that, if coherence courses were adopted, entirely new syllabuses (drawn up, they suggest, by joint panels of school and university teachers) would be required.
See also **Half-subjects**

Coldstream Reports Reports of the National Advisory Council on Art Education (*q.v.*) under the chairmanship of Sir William Coldstream.

Colet, John (1467-1515) The foremost English humanist of his time, and a leader of the English Reformation, Colet, when Dean of St. Paul's, founded and endowed St Paul's School, being assisted in this by Erasmus. Colet was one of the great educational pioneers— believing in kindliness of teaching in a period when much teaching was harsh, in the encouragement of original thought and individual intelligence at a time when learning by rote was normal. He wrote, with Lily, the first headmaster of St Paul's, a Latin grammar which, revised by Erasmus, had a long life in the schools and became the 'Eton Latin Grammar'.

College-based students *See* **Further education in England and Wales**

College of Handicraft Founded in 1924 by the Institute of Handicraft Teachers, the College exists to set a standard for the teaching of craftwork equal to the educational importance of the subject; to organise courses at which teachers can improve their skill and knowledge in crafts and teaching techniques; and to establish advanced teaching qualifications in craft education. Summer schools are held annually at St John's College, York and Goldsmiths' College, London. Tutorial courses and examinations are conducted for qualified teachers wishing to become Members (M.Coll.H.) or Fellows (F.Coll.H.) of the College.
Registrar: D. C. Fuller, F.Coll.H., Long Riston, Hull, Yorks.

Colleges of advanced technology During the 1950s much concern was expressed at Britain's failure to produce sufficient highly qualified scientific and technical manpower not only for research but for manufacturing and design. A campaign developed for the introduction of special courses for the full-time education and training of technologists for industry to replace traditional day-release courses from which so many industrial engineers came. It was held that day-release courses were inadequate for the education of technologists but not technicians. Many believed that it was possible to offer a qualification equivalent to a university degree but different. With the aid of this different qualification it was hoped technical colleges doing high-level work would be able to shake off the restraints placed on them by having to operate courses for internal and external degrees of the University of London and national certificates and diplomas. There would be a new freedom to experiment. The history of these pressures is best illustrated by the reports of the Barlow and Percy Committees (*qq.v.*). Detailed analyses have been written by Cotgrove and Payne (see *Further reading*).

Some 10 years elapsed before the government responded to pressures to raise the status of some of the technical colleges. Plans were announced in a White Paper on Technical Education published in 1956 for the creation of a limited number of Colleges of Advanced Technology (CATs). These were to do only advanced work (beyond that done at school) and research. They were developed from 10 technical colleges already doing considerable degree or equivalent teaching. They were to encourage full-time and sandwich education and to shed as many of their part-time courses as possible. By 1967 these 10 colleges, as a result of recommendations of the Robbins Committee on Higher Education, had achieved university status. From their inception until June 1961 the CATs were managed by LEAs. From that date they were given a new constitution, receiving their grants direct from the Ministry of Education. Staff were represented on the new Boards of Governors necessitated by this reorganisation.

At about the same time as the CATs were initiated, the government established the National Council for Technological Awards with powers to create and administer new qualifications equivalent to first and second university degrees. The NCTA initiated the qualification of Diploma in Technology

(Dip Tech), equivalent to an honours degree, and the Membership of the College of Technologists (MCT) for a post-graduate qualification based on research done jointly by college and industry. The Diploma in Technology was characterised by compulsory integrated industrial training, liberal studies and extensive projects during the latter part of the students' training. All courses for the Dip Tech were sandwich-structured in one form or another.

Some believed this award should have been made available only to the CATs. Had this been so, the story of their development might have been different and a nearer parallel between the English and German systems might have emerged. In fact any technical college with suitable facilities (NCTA requirements for staff standards and physical facilities were high and its inspections rigorous) could make application to run a course for the Dip Tech, and some did. So the CATs had to compete with some regional technical colleges for students and industrial training places. Indeed, industrialists were more concerned with the qualifications offered than the level of the institution which offered them. Complaints such as those made by the Electrical and Electronic Manufacturers Joint Education Board were not directed at educational institutions but at the content of the Dip Tech or the administration of sandwich courses.

Minimum entry qualifications to Dip Tech courses were similar to those for universities. But a good Ordinary National Certificate (and other alternatives) were acceptable, many students entering courses via these alternative routes. Nevertheless, over half the students had A level GCE qualifications. The search for such students brought the CATs into competition with the universities. Various researches had shown that able sixth-formers were not wanting to enter university departments of technology, let alone those in the CATs. Another research showed that school-teachers ranked the CATs between universities and technical colleges; it also showed them to prefer thick to thin sandwich courses (defined below), which they associated with vocational education—an extension of the image of day release. Status considerations blinded many to the developments taking place in the CATs. It is easy to see why CATs able to offer internal degrees of the University of London were not prepared to give up this facility and support whole-heartedly the new Dip Tech scheme.

The three London CATs continued to offer both full and part-time courses for internal degrees of the University of London. Chelsea, for example, with some 700 students pursuing full-time university courses in 1962, gave very little support to Dip Tech schemes. Eventually Chelsea became a constitu-ent college of the University of London. The courses offered at Chelsea were mainly in the applied sciences. More recently this college has established a centre for the study of science educa-tion.

Battersea (now the University of Surrey at Guildford) offered various courses in engineering, thus balancing the science tendencies at Chelsea. Battersea also had a department of Hotel Management and Catering which continues and sponsors the first-ever chair in hotel management. Unlike Chelsea, Battersea gave much more support to Dip Tech schemes. Although sandwich courses of the 'thin' type (six months in industry followed by six months in college repeated over four years, were offered by some depart-ments) Battersea was noted for its support of the two-one-one 'thick' scheme (two academic years in college followed by a year in industry and completed by an academic year in college). The development of this 'thick' structure inspired much of the contro-versy over the spacing of sandwich courses.

The City of London Northampton College (now City University) was the first of the CATs to offer 'end-on' sandwich courses. With such arrange-ments the College is open most of the year (48 weeks) for tuition. When the students are in industry on one course they are replaced by other students for a six-month college period. This enables firms to fill their training places throughout the year. North-ampton CAT, with the support of the oil companies, pioneered a Dip Tech course in instrumentation and control.

Significant support for Dip Tech schemes came from the CATs in the provinces. Birmingham (now the Uni-versity of Aston) pioneered the Dip Tech scheme with the support of the General Electric Company. Among the schemes introduced at Birmingham were applied mathematics, applied physics and applied chemistry. With similar support from the colleges at Bradford, Brunel and Salford, the idea of inte-grated training in applied science subjects other than engineering was developed. Bristol (now the University of Bath) and Brunel initiated sandwich schemes in biology. Some of the earliest courses in cybernetics were run at Loughborough, the only residential CAT.

Bristol made an important modifica-tion to the 'thin' sandwich structure. The number of periods in industry was reduced to three so that the final period in college could be lengthened. The Welsh CAT (University of Wales Institute of Science and Technology) also included the Welsh schools of Architecture, Navigation and Pharm-acy. It found difficulty in getting local support for sandwich schemes, but nevertheless found it worth-while to introduce a pattern of one year in industry followed by one year in college, six months in industry, one year in college, six months in industry and a final academic year. This arrangement retains the academic terms and gives industry students for training through-out the year.

Two factors preventing development in the CATs were a shortage of staff and the inability to establish strong research schools. Up to 1963, CAT staff were paid the same salaries as those in the technical colleges. The chief difference lay in the number of senior posts allocated to the CATs. They did not have professional appointments. In all, the universities were in a better position to compete for staff. The MCT did not get off the ground. It had little or no prestige and its regulations were restrictive. Students with Diplomas in Technology could opt to read for higher external degrees or even join (as some did) university departments. Although new syllabuses were developed within Dip Tech schemes, there was only limited scope for new ideas. The only means open to the CATs to throw off these restrictions was actively to pursue demands for university status. Their case found favour in many and diverse quarters. Many persons and institutions recommended this path to the Committee on Higher Education, which itself supported the view. All CATs have now achieved university status. It is as yet too early to comment on recent developments in these institutions other than to note considerable interest in the social and behavioural sciences which is in keeping with their technological traditions.

See also **Technology, Diploma in**

FURTHER READING
S. Cotgrove. *Technical Education and Social Change*, Allen and Unwin, 1958.
G. L. Payne. *Britain's Scientific and Technological Manpower*, Oxford Univ. Press, 1960.

JHey

Colleges of arts and crafts *See* **Appendix 5**

Colleges of education *See* **Appendix 2**

Colleges of education, Admission to Candidates for admission to colleges of education should write individually to the colleges, listed in *A Compendium of Teacher Training Courses in England and Wales* (List 172) published by HMSO. The application forms of the colleges will then be sent to them, together with cards to be sent to the Central Register and Clearing House (*q.v.*), which will then supply its own forms. On these forms, candidates must name two preferences among the colleges, with a selection of four colleges for their third choice. The papers of candidates not accepted by either of their first two preferences are sent on to any of the other four; if a candidate is still not accepted, his papers are sent on to other colleges with suitable vacancies.

Candidates should be 18 on or before 1 October in the year in which training would commence (or 1 February in the case of the few colleges that begin their course in January). The process of selection continues right up to the start of the course. At least five passes at GCE O level, or three O levels and one A level in another subject are necessary; or two O levels and two A levels in other subjects; or three A levels if candidates can show that they have kept up other subjects after they were 16. A Grade 1 pass in CSE is accepted as an alternative to a GCE O level pass. A pass in English language is usually expected, and students who intend to take primary school courses will stand a better chance of acceptance if they have at least an O level pass in mathematics. In general, candidates with one or more A level passes have an advantage over those who lack them; but in their selection colleges take note of personality, range of interests and general suitability for teaching as well as of a candidate's academic record.

Colleges of music, drama and dancing *See* **Appendix 4**

Colombia, Education in Public education is free but not compulsory. About 60% of the population is literate. In 1964 there were 1,104 nursery schools with 45,190 pupils; 23,611 primary schools with 2,213,423 pupils; 1,295 secondary schools with 228,646 pupils; 736 technical institutes with 97,834 pupils; 960 higher education colleges with 114,836 students. Of the higher education colleges, 15 are designated as public universities and 13 as private universities.

The population of the country was approximately 17¾ million in 1965.

Colour factor The Colour Factor Set is a model used for the development of number concepts and arithmetic operations, and was conceived by Seton Pollock in 1961. The set consists of lengths of wood of 1 cm. square cross-section, starting at 1 cm. long and increasing, in steps of 1 cm., up to 12 cm. long. Each rod is therefore a 'model' of one of the numbers 1 to 12. The rods are not scored at centimetre intervals, since each rod represents a number as an entity in its own right and not simply as a collection of units.

The unit rod is coloured white, and the three primary colours red, blue and yellow are treated as analogues for the three smallest primes in their function as *factors* operating upon the unit. Thus a 2 rod is pale red, a 3 rod is pale blue and a 5 rod is yellow. Since $6 = 1 \times 2 \times 3$, a 6 rod is coloured a mixture of pale red and pale blue (i.e. lilac); and since $8 = 1 \times 2 \times 2 \times 2$, an 8 rod is coloured a triple power of red (i.e. maroon). Seven and 11 having no factors, these rods are coloured shades of grey.

Leaflets can be obtained from the Colour-Factor Advisory Service, 72 London St, Reading, Berks.

WD

Coloured immigrant children The situation of coloured immigrant children in schools in the UK can be understood only against the background of the total immigrant situation and the way it has changed. Although the total estimated number of immigrants in England and Wales was stated in the 1966 Sample Census to be 942,310, some consider the true total to be well over a million. Of a total population in England and Wales of 47 million the estimated numbers of coloured immigrants amount to less than 2%; yet over 80% are concentrated in urban areas, with more than half of them in Britain's largest cities. For example, 310,000 are shown by the 1966 Sample Census to be living in Greater London (total population 7·7 million) and 82,000 in the West Midland conurbation (total population 2·4 million).

In some cities the immigrant concentration is as high as 8% and in particular neighbourhoods 50% or more. In 1966 in total the immigrants numbered 268,000 from the Caribbean, 232,000 from India, 73,000 from Pakistan, and some 147,000 from Africa and Cyprus. In addition 'white' Commonwealth immigrants numbered over 155,000 and Southern Irish almost 700,000.

The chief reasons behind immigration seem to have been poverty and lack of opportunity in the home country, the availability of jobs in the UK and the active recruitment of foreign workers by some industries here. The main arrival began in the early 1950s, rising from an estimated 42,000 in 1955 to an estimated 136,000 in 1961. The number arriving before the Commonwealth Immigration Act (1962) rose sharply in anticipation of the controls, which regulated entry of those wishing to work by determining the number of Ministry of Labour vouchers allowed. Although the Act restricted immigration to some degree, this was counterbalanced by an increase in the women and children accompanying or joining the head of family, particularly among the West Indians. A high proportion of Indians and Pakistanis are bringing their children, which appears to indicate that they plan to settle here. A later Act (1965) restricted the number of vouchers to 8,500 a year, of which

1,000 are reserved for Malta. Since 1965 the annual number of vouchers actually taken up has been 5,000 or less; 4,978 Commonwealth voucher-holders were admitted in 1967.

Most immigrants are young and the birthrate has been estimated to be 25 per 1,000 — above the UK average of 18 per 1,000. This birthrate seems to be higher among the less educated. The Five-Year Survey of Race Relations estimated at the end of 1964 that there were about 250,000 immigrant children in England, many born here and many others immigrating after their parents. The term 'immigrant' will soon be outmoded since many of the children will be second and third-generation British born.

The immigrants' immediate need on arrival is to find accommodation, and this tends to be in areas already in desperate need of additional housing for their normal populations. The schools in such areas are often short-staffed, overcrowded and have inadequate buildings, and any influx accentuates these difficulties. Because the immigrants are easily identified by colour they appear to be accused by some of the host population as the cause of these difficulties, although it is noteworthy that in many areas the influx of Irish has been greater than that of coloured immigrants.

The Commonwealth Immigrants Advisory Council, set up by the 1962 Act to advise the Home Secretary on matters affecting immigrants and to examine the powers of the local authorities to deal with their welfare, made four reports, including one on the education of Commonwealth immigrants and another on immigrant school leavers. It also established a National Committee for Commonwealth Immigrants, with a paid advisory officer to collect and circulate information to local authorities on how best to improve relations between immigrants and the community. A new National Committee for Commonwealth Immigrants was set up in 1965, headed by the Archbishop of Canterbury. In 1968 the Race Relations Bill proposed the creation of a Community Relations Committee to replace the NCCI.

During the last decade immigrant children have been entering schools in the Greater London region and in Midland and Northern cities in increasing numbers. In 1956 it was estimated that 8,000 pupils in London schools were of overseas origin; by 1964 the figure had risen to 38,000. The rate of increase has made the task of integration more difficult. In areas of high immigration density, immigrant children can form large percentages in some schools. For example, in Birmingham, although the average proportion of immigrant children is only 5% of the children in all maintained schools, there are 22 primary schools with between 16% and 70% of coloured immigrant children. This may cause racial tension, since parents fear their children will be affected by alleged lower standards of the immigrant children as the latter increase in numbers.

LEAs have tried in several ways to meet the problems of this sudden influx into schools already overcrowded and understaffed. The Ministry of Education Pamphlet No. 43 (1963) discussed the schools' problems, advising flexibility in cultural matters and outlining some administrative procedures in teaching the children. These recommendations were not based on research, and could not have been, since research evidence was not available.

Most schools do not separate immigrant from English children at the primary stage, although they may have special teaching in the secondary schools for one hour a day. Immigrant children are not being segregated but they are often in the C streams or remedial classes apparently simply because of their language problems. Tapper and Stopes (1963) point out that about half the immigrants in one secondary school are placed in the D stream each year. However, there is a tendency for them to move upward as their English improves. Arithmetic is reported to be a favourite subject; immigrant children are well represented among maths and science prize-winners. Bolton attempted to evaluate, by non-linguistic tests which they were aware were not culture-free, the ability levels of pupils they thought might profit from a grammar school education. These revealed an IQ range from 76 to 131.

LEAs making special provision for children who do not speak English have classes organised in different ways. In Birmingham, specialist visiting teachers are employed. They visit 15 specialist classes who meet in one school and pupils are drawn from three schools. Other smaller groups are visited three times a week within the schools. The children participate with English children in the main part of the school. Bradford has been distributing its non-English-speaking Asians to full-time language tuition centres. Since 1963 Southall has been dispersing immigrants to schools outside the children's locality by school bus, whenever the local school has more than a certain percentage of immigrant pupils. Of its 20 schools, 14 have reception classes where children remain from 12 to 15 months, each class having a welfare assistant. Manchester has appointed part-time teachers in its junior schools, the children being withdrawn from their normal classes for short periods of intensive instruction in English and number work each day. Yet in Nottingham, with a large immigrant population, 27 out of 113 primary schools with more than 10% immigrant children cater for linguistic needs by using group methods within normal classes. The ILEA has several centres where a special staff member teaches non-English-speakers from secondary schools. Many other London secondary schools have their own special arrangements to meet the widely different needs of their immigrant pupils. The primary schools cater for their immigrants with the help of off-quota teachers.

Huddersfield channels all its immigrant school children (2·8%) into a school with a special English department, where they are taught conversation, reading and writing in several stages, joining the rest of the school for subjects such as PT and needlework. When sufficiently well-established they join the appropriate school near their homes. This technique has been adopted by other boroughs. However, in 1964 Huddersfield found it necessary to establish another special English department in a secondary school and, as the number of immigrant children has increased, it has established special English classes in other schools.

Whether or not a quota of non-English-speaking children should be established in each school or class is a controversial issue, and there is no guidance as yet from research. Special arrangements for language teaching, for example, should perhaps be geared to the proportions of non-English-speaking children in the area, and it is recommended by some that the children should not be isolated too long from English-speaking classmates.

Common-sense would support the recommendation of the DES (Circular 7/65) that the proportion of immigrant children taught in any one school should not be unduly high. However, fixing a particular proportion will not of itself solve the problem. Research in the USA suggests that integration will depend much on staff attitudes, the programmes of a school and attitudes in the wider community outside. The danger of fixed proportions and enforced dispersal is that they may be seen as colour discrimination.

Specific problems of the education of coloured immigrant children are: problems in determining ability levels; linguistic difficulties; cultural factors affecting the education of immigrant

141

children; social education in a multi-racial society. (From the demographic figures quoted earlier it is clear that Britain is already a multi-racial society. This is not apparent in rural areas nor in most urban areas of Wales and Scotland, but it is very evident in the large cities and industrial areas of England.) These educational problems, and the measures taken to overcome them, cannot be isolated from larger social issues. We are faced with a multi-dimensional problem, not with a narrowly-based school problem. In a sense, the plight of coloured immigrant children is essentially the plight of the indigenous socially disadvantaged children in slum and problem areas, with the added dimensions of language difficulties and colour prejudice to overcome. This cannot be separated from questions of housing, health, facilities for pre-school and after-school activities, youth employment and many other factors.

Many surveys indicate that of the three ethnic groups now settling in Britain — Indian, Pakistani and West Indian — it is the last which appears to illustrate our difficulties most vividly. Linguistically, they seem to have an advantage over the other two groups, but it is their partial mastery of English, and their use of dialect, that appears to be a major barrier to educational motivation and achievement. This question is currently being investigated at the University of Birmingham. West Indians also seem to be more susceptible to the weather, in terms of health; they also pose difficulties for the host community because of the high incidence of broken families of children or varied parentage. Much work needs to be done on the varied family structure of immigrants, since it is evident that authoritarian or other climates within the family affect attitudes to education.

There is an urgent need for objective information and for an assessment of the many factors in the situation. A simple measure would be to provide a continuous pooling of information by LEAs with numbers of immigrants resident in their areas. To some extent this is being done through national committees and the Schools Council, but much more is required. Some LEAs keep very full records, but others resist keeping records which indicate ethnic group or country of origin, on the grounds that this will foster racial prejudice. This basic information must be available if research is to be done; it will not foster prejudice, but will provide data that will help schools to become better instruments of education for tolerance.

A further example of the need for research springs from the way in which the policy of a one-third dispersal of coloured immigrant children was initiated without the full implications being perceived. If such a policy is rigidly enforced, and if immigrants tend to congregate in certain areas, then more and more schools will have to transport some children to other areas. It has been found that schools in predominantly 'coloured' areas were often not being used to capacity, since there were not enough 'white' pupils to make up the necessary two-thirds proportion. The logic of this situation is that these schools will die, gradually shrinking in size, with more and more immigrant children going by bus to distant schools. Alternative policies would be to disregard the dispersal policy and have many almost totally 'coloured' schools; to transport 'white' children into these areas, as is done in New York but in the face of great opposition; and by a carefully planned municipal re-housing policy to balance the 'white' population which might otherwise move away.

The assessment of abilities of coloured immigrant children also requires systematic investigation. While there is a culturally induced backwardness among these groups, it might be worthwhile to think of potential rather than of problems, and that, although retarded in an English educational sense, these children are *above average* compared with their peers in their country of origin, simply because their parents possess the means and initiative to emigrate. The testing of immigrant children is currently being investigated by the National Foundation for Educational Research.

Some clarification of aims in education for the coloured immigrant is needed. Integration—meaning that the incoming group adapts itself to permanent membership of the host society in certain areas including education, and is accepted by that society as an entity differing in religion, culture and family patterns — should be the minimum aim. These children need a sufficient mastery of English to make full use of the British educational system and, through social studies, should be helped to understand British culture. It seems vital to explore how best both British and immigrants can be helped to understand immigrant cultures, religions and ethnic identity as enriching contributions within the British culture.

FURTHER READING
C. Bibby. *Race, Prejudice and Education*, Heinemann, 1959.
T. Burgin and P. Edson. *Spring Grove: An Experiment in the Education of Immigrant Children*, Oxford Univ. Press, 1966.
J. Derrick. *Immigrant Children: Teaching of English Report*, Univ. of Leeds Institute of Education, unpublished report.
Education of Commonwealth Immigrants in British Schools (Commonwealth Immigrants Advisory Council Second Report), HMSO, Cmd 2266, 1964.
Memorandum on Immigrant Children in London Schools, Pegg for London Head Teachers' Association, 1965.

RJG

Combined system The former system by which teachers were confined to giving secular instruction, while ministers of various denominations came into the schools to give religious instruction.

Comenius, John Amos (1592-c.1670) A Moravian, Comenius was spurred in his thinking by the poor quality of his own education. Having himself been taught with inadequate textbooks and by the dreary memorisation of grammatical rules, he wrote a Latin textbook designed to make learning both pleasanter and more effective. It had a European success, being not only a rational aid to learning but also an elementary encyclopaedia of knowledge. From methods of education he turned to a consideration of its content, using the term *pansophia* for that acquisition of universal knowledge which he believed to be not only the proper aim of education but also a means of uniting men in a single brotherhood.

In 1641 he was invited by the English Parliament to come to England, where he hoped he might establish a pansophic college and found a system of schools that would provide education for all the children of England. The scheme foundered in the political upheaval leading to the Civil War, and Comenius went to Sweden to write textbooks for the Swedish schools.

After six years there, he returned to Poland and, in an interlude from his duties as senior bishop of the Moravian Church, set up a school intended to be fully pansophic; this scheme, too, failed, largely because the teachers were reluctant to follow Comenius' ideas. When war broke out between the Poles and the Swedes, Comenius was forced to flee, and many of his manuscripts were lost.

Among his works were the *Orbis Pictus*, the first school textbook with pictures, and the *Didactica Magne*, in which he set out his principal ideas. Comenius is an important figure in the movement away from harshness and toward gentleness and affection in teaching; away from the narrow to the wide curriculum; and towards a trained profession, the rooting of education in sense experience, and an understanding of the value of reasonable physical conditions in schooling.

Comics The first really successful comic strips in this country, Alfred Harmsworth's *Comic Cuts* ('Amusing Without Being Vulgar') and *Chips*, founded in 1890, were aimed deliberately at wooing children away from Penny Dreadfuls, and to a certain extent this aim was successful. Nevertheless, comics have always had a bad reputation with most educationists, and, where not seen as actually offensive, have been regarded as trivial, time-wasting and a tempting escape from the struggle with reading difficulties. Children, however, were not put off, almost whatever the penalties, and famous comic characters gradually became accepted as part of a new folk lore—in the case of such figures as Weary Willie and Tired Tim, as part of the language itself.

The attack against comics redoubled after the last war, when Britain became flooded with American horror comics, some quite sadistic and curiously reminiscent of Victorian penny dreadfuls and 'bloods', although of course the stories in this case were conveyed in garish pictures. In 1955 the Children's and Young Persons' (Harmful Publications) Act was passed by Parliament, enacting that books or magazines 'which consist wholly or mainly of stories told in pictures portraying (1) commission of crime; (2) acts of violence or cruelty; (3) incidents of a repulsive or horrible nature . . . in such a way that the work as a whole tends to corrupt a child or young person into whose hands it might fall', should be banned for the next ten years.

Meanwhile publishers were beginning to experiment with the comic as a means of education as well as entertainment, and there are now several educational comics covering subjects ranging from general knowledge to specific histories of recent events through a mixture of pictures and prose. Other publishers who tried to mix pure entertainment with self-education in the same comic were less successful.

Today many of the older comics are extinct, killed off perhaps by television and increasing youthful sophistication; but those that remain, notably the *Beano* and *Dandy*, seem to be flourishing. Other new comics have been founded to exploit post-war phenomena such as wide-spread television, pop music and, of course, the increased and more lucrative teenage market. Educationists still do not look kindly upon the 'love' comics adolescent girls now read or the brand of sex and violence in some American publications that seems to be creeping back again largely for the young male audience.

Yet with younger children, many primary schools do not now set out to discourage comic reading, especially during school breaks in wet weather, and at this age level comics still retain their almost universal readership, and do not appear to have any deleterious effect upon a child's education, providing that he reads books as well. Indeed, the very feeling of ownership and pleasure that comics can provide at this early age possibly leads many children on to take a more general interest in the whole field of reading provided the opportunity is there. In this sense comics may sometimes do a far more useful job than teachers or parents in the past would ever have imagined possible.

FURTHER READING
George Perry and Alan Aldridge. *The Penguin Book of Comics*, Penguin Books, 1967.

NT

Commerce Degree Bureau, University of London The Bureau provides courses of study by correspondence in preparation for Parts I and II of the BSc (Economics) Examination

(Revised Regulations). The Part I course covers the compulsory and nine alternative subjects and tuition is offered in six special subjects of the Part II examination. The courses are under the direct supervision of Professors and Readers in the Faculty of Economics in the University of London, assisted by a staff of tutors, most of whom are also university teachers. If intelligently and conscientiously followed over an adequate period, the courses cover the requirements of the examinations, and no supplementary tuition should be necessary except in foreign languages, in which oral practice is essential; but some students may find attendance at a class in e.g. economics helpful if opportunity for discussion is provided.

A lending library service is available within the British Isles to students paying a composition fee and following the Bureau's course of study.

Senate Hse, London, WC1.

Commercial and Industrial Education, British Association for The only voluntary non-profit-making organisation specialising in all aspects of commercial and industrial training in the UK, BACIE exists to promote the better education and training of employees at all levels in industry and commerce. Membership includes industrial and commercial firms, the nationalised industries, government departments, industrial training boards, LEAs, universities, technical and commercial colleges, trade associations and trade unions, as well as many overseas members. Eleven regional groups cater for local needs.

Having pooled and collected information for nearly 50 years, BACIE puts its experience at the disposal of members through a quarterly journal and a news bulletin published seven times a year, together with other publications; through its information department; through courses designed for education and training officers and others working in further education; and through national and regional conferences and exhibitions.

16 Park Crescent, Regents Park, London, W1.

Committee of Council on Education Set up by Order in Council in 1839 to superintend the grants made by the government for the provision of schools and training colleges, this special department of the Privy Council was replaced in 1856 by the Education Department (*q.v.*).

Common day school The term used to describe a former type of private elementary school attended by poorer children and charging specially low fees.

Common Entrance 'Common Entrance' is the short title of the Common Examination for Entrance to Public Schools, taken normally at 13-plus. It is the qualifying examination for entry to Headmasters' Conference schools and to many other independent boys' schools, and is regulated by a Board of Managers drawn from the Headmasters' Conference and the Incorporated Association of Preparatory Schools (*qq.v.*). Although set by examiners appointed by the Board, the papers are marked by the candidates' own schools. The examination takes place three times a year—in February, June and November; and may be taken a second time if a candidate is still under the age limit of 14 and has the permission of his headmaster.

The examination normally covers English, scripture (Roman Catholic schools do not require this), geography, history, maths, French and Latin. There are more advanced papers, which are not compulsory, in maths, French and Latin, which help the public schools to place boys in suitable classes or sets when they arrive.

See also **Preparatory schools** *and* **Public schools**

Commonwealth Education Liaison Unit This unit was set up in 1960, following the First Commonwealth Education Conference, to collect information from governments about the progress of educational plans and schemes. It issues an annual report.

Commonwealth Friendship, Victoria League for The Victoria League was founded in 1901 to promote friendship between Britain and the peoples of the Commonwealth.

It does this, first, by providing a centre at its London headquarters, Victoria League House, where visitors from all parts of the Commonwealth can meet English members and take part in a varied programme of entertainment—morning coffee parties, luncheon lectures, evening at-homes, outings, bridge, etc. An active Younger Members' Group caters specially for the interests of those between 18 and 30.

Secondly, through its 75 branches, the League arranges hospitality for Commonwealth visitors in the homes of English members, either on day or week-end visits.

There are reciprocal, autonomous Victoria Leagues in Scotland, Australia, New Zealand, Africa, the West Indies and other parts of the Commonwealth.

Victoria League Hse, 38 Chesham Pl., London, SW1.

Commonwealth Institute The Commonwealth Institute is a statutory, grant-aided organisation, founded originally in 1887 as the Imperial Institute to commemorate the Golden Jubilee of Queen Victoria. The Institute moved to its present modern building in 1962. Its income is derived principally from the governments of the UK and all the other Commonwealth countries. In the UK, parliamentary responsibility for the Institute rests with the Secretary of State for Commonwealth Affairs.

The Institute's primary function is to provide in its exhibition galleries, open free to the public, a visual survey of the peoples of the Commonwealth and their environment. Altogether there are some 60,000 square feet, on three floors, devoted to individual displays for each of the Commonwealth countries and their dependencies. Apart from their appeal to the general visitor, these galleries, specially designed with this purpose in mind, provide an excellent teaching aid and the Institute has been in the forefront with the development of techniques applicable to museum and gallery teaching. Many tens of thousands of schoolchildren and students, in organised parties, receive lessons from either their own teachers or the Institute's own professional teaching staff. Important adjuncts to the exhibition galleries are a cinema, seating 450, which shows regular programmes of Commonwealth documentary films, and an art gallery with temporary exhibitions of painting and sculpture by Commonwealth artists. In addition, the Institute maintains a library, a schools information service, a loan service of teaching aids and a publications centre, organises conferences in colleges and lectures in schools throughout the UK and circulates travelling exhibitions which tour provincial towns. An autonomous Scottish branch of the Institute at 8 Rutland Sq., Edinburgh provides educational aids for schools and colleges in Scotland.

Education Officer: Mrs J. Russell. Kensington High St, London, W8.

Commonwealth Society, Royal The Society's headquarters are in London, but there are local branches at Bath, Bournemouth, Bristol, Cambridge, Liverpool, Oxford, Hove and Edinburgh. There are ordinary, family and junior subscriptions, the rate varying according to the area. At the London headquarters, full club facilities are provided, together with a Commonwealth library (containing

more than 350,000 items), an assembly hall, and an information bureau. The bureau publishes papers on life in most countries of the Commonwealth, and provides a loan service of visual aids. Northumberland Ave, London, WC2.
Publication: *Commonwealth Journal.*

Commonwealth Universities, Association of Founded in 1913 and incorporated by royal charter, the Association holds quinquennial congresses of the universities of the Commonwealth and other meetings in intervening years; it publishes the *Commonwealth Universities Yearbook*, the *Compendium of University Entrance Requirements* and other books giving factual information about universities and about access to them; it acts as a general information centre on universities in the UK and other Commonwealth countries; and provides an advisory service for the filling of university teaching staff appointments overseas. It also supplies the secretariat for the Committee of Vice-Chancellors and Principals of the Universities of the United Kingdom, for the Commonwealth Scholarship Commission in the United Kingdom, for the Marshall Aid Commemoration Commission, and for the Kennedy Memorial Trust.

General office: 36 Gordon Sq., London, WC1; branch office: Marlborough House, Pall Mall, London, SW1 (for Commonwealth scholarships and appointments).

Communication Research Centre *see* **Nuffield Foundation**

Communist education It is axiomatic that educational systems sustain and support the political and economic systems which sustain and support them. Communist education is clearly designed by philosophical analysis, social purpose, educational research at great depth and continuous experiment to support the communist way of life. The system has been most efficiently worked out in the USSR and some excellent theorists are also found in the German Democratic Republic. Every communist state has its own gloss on fundamental principles; common elements are clearly recognised in all countries in Eastern Europe. Less time has been spent in the study of the systems in Cuba, Albania, and China. Indeed it is not yet clear exactly what shape the new Chinese educational system will take (*see* **China, Education in**).

Visitors to the USSR and to Eastern Europe generally must quickly appreciate that there are two fundamental and complementary parts of the school system of education. The first is the provision through an agreed common curriculum of certain established syllabuses spread over ten years of schooling; the second is the provision through the pioneer movement of additional extra-curricular opportunities, some of which may be found in the school curriculum in some non-communist countries. While school attendance is compulsory, membership of the pioneer movement, including over 95% of all children over the age of nine, is voluntary and ostensibly secured by election of existing members.

Communist educational systems include a generous provision of pre-school facilities. Since men and women are deemed to be economically and politically equal, and since adequate maternity leave is offered, factories or 'enterprises', collective farms, trade union branches, local residents' groups, and local health authorities are expected to provide crèches, kindergartens and nursery schools. A very high proportion of all children in communist countries attend such pre-school institutions. While the authorities are interested in securing the speedy return of the mother to productive activity, it is also true that magnificent care is lavished on all children and that immense strides have been made in devising kinds of social education.

Formal education begins for all boys and girls on the first day of the school year after they have reached the age of seven. Provision is made for 10 years of schooling. The first four years are 'elementary' or primary, and teachers are general practitioners. The remaining six years are secondary, and teachers are specialists. Most lessons are more formally arranged than in the UK or USA; much homework is set each evening in preparation for the next day's lessons, all normally of 45 minutes duration. Homework sustains parental interest, which is much drawn upon in communist schools. Rote learning persists, and lessons are based on centrally produced and approved text-books. Pupils are normally required to complete each year's course, or they may have to repeat a year. A special feature of the Russian system has been the remarkable growth of boarding schools, attended by pupils from Monday morning to Saturday evening.

All communist systems have first proceeded to eradicate illiteracy. This has sometimes demanded the creation of an alphabet for nomadic peoples without previous literate traditions. Mathematics teaching and the development of scientific interests are also areas of great success. Mathematics 'Olympics' are held annually to encourage promising young mathematicians.

The dignity of work as a socially desirable human activity is positively taught through polytechnicalisation. Attempts have been made to permeate the whole curriculum with a polytechnical approach: e.g. examples in mathematics are clearly related to industry and industrial development. Efforts are also made to give every pupil, in the last four years at school, real-life experience in factories and on collective farms. One school session per week is spent in a factory or on a collective farm. This approach is being modified somewhat in Russia; in East Germany some excellently detailed syllabuses in wood and metal work, in electrotechnics, and in animal husbandry and agriculture have been prepared.

An important change in communist education is the slight tendency to provide some element of curricular choice for older pupils. All pupils continue with the study of Marxist-Leninism as well as the main body of the common curriculum.

The costs of education are high in communist countries, and the teaching profession is especially honoured and relatively well paid. Higher education normally lasts for five years in universities and in many institutes of university status. After five years, students receive a diploma and may proceed by two further stages to the degree of doctor. A great deal of part-time higher education is provided, the most notable feature being the provision of correspondence tuition facilities. Much technical provision is available at an intermediate level; most employees are expected to obtain the necessary diploma for their work.

See also **China, Education in** *and* **USSR, Education in**

DJJ

Community Associations, National Federation of The NFCA is the recognised national body for community associations. Under its conditions of membership, a community association is defined as a voluntary association of organisations and residents in a given neighbourhood whose objects are to provide facilities for physical and mental training and recreation and social and intellectual development, and to foster a community spirit for the achievement of these and other such purposes as may by law be deemed to be charitable. An association is also required, under this definition, to establish, maintain and manage a community centre for activities promoted by the NFCA and its constituent members. An association is non-party in politics and non-sectarian in religion. By 1966, 372 community associations were full members of the NFCA.

The work of the NFCA is assisted by funds provided by the DES and the National Council of Social Service. 26 Bedford Sq., London, WC1.

Community centre wardens' scales
The salary scale for a qualified community Centre warden is £895 × £50(9) × £55(1)—£1,400. The scale assumes an age of entry of about 23 and new entrants should be placed at a suitable point having regard to age and previous experience.

Additions for longer training and/or higher qualifications and posts of responsibility. The provisions for additional payments shall apply on a similar basis as for qualified youth leaders, i.e. £100 per annum in respect of longer training and/or higher qualifications and £115 to £475 per annum for posts carrying greater responsibility and in excess of £475 in exceptional cases. Because of the wide range of responsibilities undertaken in some cases by community centre wardens, it is recognised that a more extensive and flexible use may be required of the provisions for additions for posts carrying greater responsibility.

Salary scales for unqualified community centre wardens. £690 × £30(1) × £35(5)—£895.

The conditions of service, London Area payment, remuneration of residential duties by emoluments, interpretation, incremental date, transfer from unqualified scale to qualified scale, are the same for community centre wardens as for youth leaders (*see* **Youth leader scales**).

SEB

Community colleges *See* **Village colleges**

Community school The Plowden Report (*q.v.*) recommended that community schools should be developed in all areas, but especially in educational priority areas (*q.v.*). Such schools were defined in the Report as those 'open beyond the ordinary school hours for the use of children, their parents and, exceptionally, for other members of the community.' For a discussion of the Plowden Committee's view that progress towards such use of schools was slow in the UK, and faster in other countries, and of ways in which the community can be given greater use of the schools (which 'represent an immense capital investment which has been provided by the community'), see Chapter 4 of the Report (*Children and their Primary Schools*, I).

Community service and schools
Community service by young people in Britain can be said to have evolved round about 1961–2, taking shape first, for diverse reasons, in a handful of independent schools. It began as an attempt to counterbalance the intense pursuit of academic ambition, as an alternative to the corps or to fund-raising for charities and as a growing expression of social awareness amongst young people themselves. Elsewhere, as the tradition whereby many old-established schools supported a youth club in the poorer area of some city was felt to be no longer relevant, it seemed more practical to seek opportunities of service in the immediate vicinity of a school. With the approach of the raising of the school leaving age, some are now advocating a year of community service as a fundamentally educative alternative to continued classroom work for those who clearly can get no more from formal schooling.

In the early years it tended to be a nucleus of senior pupils who undertook community service, either in their leisure time or in preference to games or the corps—at all events as an out-of-class activity. New patterns of social

149

F

action were pioneered: for example, tandems were used to give blind children the pleasure of cycling; schoolboys took on the task of shaving patients in a geriatric ward on the way to school. Meals on Wheels' were extended to cover the week-ends. Of this period in the movement L. C. Taylor of Sevenoaks School said: 'Community service can be regarded as having arrived in a school when it is just as natural to let the community service group out of class at midday to tackle a job as it is to let the First Eleven off for an away match, or to keep food late for them as it is for a returning team.'

With the publication of the Newsom Report (paragraphs 196 and 200 of which specifically urged the involvement of early leavers in community service projects) the pendulum began to swing in the opposite direction. At worst, community service was seized upon as 'something to keep the fourth years busy', while the more intelligent were excused from participation lest it interfered with their classroom work. There was sometimes a poverty of imagination when it came to actual projects, gardening seeming to predominate. But a growing number of schools have welcomed the opportunity to open their pupils' eyes to social problems and to involve them in action on behalf of others. The really significant difference between community service as initiated in the early 1960s amongst sixth-formers, and what is happening now with younger pupils in secondary moderns and comprehensives, is that whereas the service was formerly undertaken outside classroom hours, it is now increasingly part of the timetable. Some argue that this does damage to the voluntary principle; others (having in mind particularly children from backgrounds with little tradition of public service) believe that this exposure to situations of human need and learning to give

constitute too vital an experience to be treated as an optional extra.

Examples of work now being done include the devising, by county secondary school girls at Walkden, near Manchester, of mechanisms to waken the deaf (blasts of warm air secured by linking alarm clocks and hair dryers), and of a contrivance that sounds an alarm if a baby is snatched from a perambulator. (These activities are known in the school as 'feminine science'.) Other volunteers have approached elderly people and asked them to allow immigrant children to visit them and practise their English; they have then asked Asian boys and girls if they would agree to visit the lonely. On meeting, each party has been convinced that it is of service to the other. To give them a sense of being needed, some approved school heads are involving their young people in community service, so that they discover they can help others in worse trouble than their own.

The Schools Council's *Working Paper on Community Service and the Curriculum* (1968) examines some of the factors that have to be considered when social service is made part of the curriculum. Should responsibility be vested in an individual teacher, or in a team? What physical provision (e.g. a separate telephone) is required? How can parental opposition ('I'm not having my girl going into houses in that street' or 'This is not what I send my boy to school for') be overcome? How can the lack of commitment in most liberal studies courses, the superficiality of so many observation visits, be transformed into personal or group involvement? What is required of the teacher or head when a class has undertaken a survey and, on the basis of what it has discovered, demands action against some authority for neglecting the needs of some section of the community?

Charitable work in the neighbourhood or for overseas causes will be unreal in a school containing immigrants if out of school there is virtually no contact between white and coloured pupils. Then there must be gradation in the forms of service undertaken. What is applicable to 14-year-olds should deepen into patterns of service relevant to the greater capacity and understanding of 17-year-olds.

New insights into history, English, geography and religious knowledge, no less than science, music and PE, are required if what is studied under the school roof is to connect with social needs and community service. Thus study of possession by spirits as described in the scriptures, of Lear's madness, of 17th-century attitudes to witchcraft, might lead to the establishment of a club for retarded youth, or the holding of debates in the convalescent ward of a psychiatric hospital in which patients recovering from their illness can participate. Biblical references to solitude, 19th-century ideas of penal reform. a comparison of the extended family unit and the role of the elders in African and Asian society with our own current treatment of the aged, might merge into a study of loneliness and perhaps the 'adoption' of a day centre for the old. Or research might be undertaken into life jackets, involving the examination of the buoyancy material in the science laboratory, testing of equipment in the baths, correspondence with manufacturers, the Board of Trade and the Royal Navy.

It is sometimes difficult for county secondary schools in areas where the children disperse to the four points of the compass when school is finished—and also for boarding schools in country settings—to decide how and whom they can help. The difficulty is solved by bringing social problems into the schools. Dunmow County Secondary School, for example, has invited Sikh boys from Southall to be their guests; Ludlow Grammar School

has shared a home-made 'Outward Bound' course with boys from a Staffordshire approved school. It is schools in the new towns—lacking both the old people to help (through imbalance of population) and derelict accommodation to redecorate—which have to be particularly alert for new situations of need, sometimes working for the young rather than for the old, and recognising that apathy and boredom can be problems as acute as poverty and deprivation. Elsewhere there is a need to blur the distinction between social service and constructional projects, e.g. canal reclamation, the clearance of industrial dereliction, the improvement of the local environment. Such work can involve hundreds rather than dozens.

If young people are to give, the adult community must be ready to receive. Nearly all schools encounter difficulty in persuading statutory authorities and voluntary bodies to accept their service. Even where a hospital has agreed, the matron's welcome may not have communicated itself to individual ward staff: an attitude of 'So it's you we have to find work for' can result in children being given domestic chores that prevent face-to-face contact with the patients they wish to help. To meet this problem, many organisations have emerged during the last few years, most of them based on local initiative and local resources: Sheffield's Youth Action, Young Volunteers of Merseyside, Manchester's Youth and Community Service, Cardiff's Voluntary Community Service, Birmingham's Young Volunteers, Youth Enterprise in Scotland, and many more. In addition, International Voluntary Service, Toc H and the Christian Education Movement provide opportunities both at home and abroad. The Young Volunteer Force Foundation—set up by the government in November, 1967, in the face of considerable controversy —aims to help local authorities establish clearing-houses based on the experience of Task Force in London. Community Service Volunteers, which places school leavers and other young people in full-time projects in the UK, also has an advisory service for schools seeking local opportunities (28 Commercial St, London, E1).

FURTHER READING
Lawrence Bailey. *Youth to the Rescue*, Arthur James, 1967.
Sidney Bunt. *Voluntary Service by Young People*, Association of Jewish Youth, 1965.
Christian Education Movement. *Focus on Service*, 1965. *Practical Service by Groups*.
Community Service Volunteers. *Service in Your Neighbourhood*, 1966. *Community Service and the Curriculum* (on behalf of the Schools Council), 1968. Other papers on work by volunteers in mental health, delinquency, practical projects, etc.
Alec and Mora Dickson. *Count Us In: A Community Service Handbook*, Dobson, 1967. *In Classroom or Community?*, Unitarian Youth Department, 1968. *One Million Hours for Britain*, The Scouter, May/June, 1968. *School in the Round*, Ward Lock, 1968 (a series of booklets relating community service to the curriculum).
George Eustace. *Young Volunteers in Hospitals*, National Association of Leagues of Hospital Friends, 1968.
Richard Hauser. *A New Approach to the Educationally Unsuccessful in Secondary Modern Schools. Prevention of Social Inadequacy*. Also other papers on social education from the Centre for Group Studies, Friends Hall, Barnet Grove, London, E2.
Neil Paterson. *Experiments in Education at Sevenoaks* (chapter on voluntary service), Constable, 1965.
Schools Council. Working Paper No. 11: *Society and the Young School Leaver*, 1967. Working Paper No. 17: *Community Service and the Curriculum* (prepared by CSV), HMSO, 1968.

AD

Community Service Volunteers

This organisation offers young people the opportunity to give full-time service away from home for four months or longer in return for their board, lodging and £2 per week pocket money. It offers an advisory service for teachers including visual aids, speakers and various handbooks on community service, both as a part-time activity and as an integral part of the school curriculum.
28 Commercial St, London, E1.
Publication: *Ideas* (once a term).

Comparative education Comparative education is that branch of the theory of education concerned with the analysis and interpretation of educational practices and policies in different countries and cultures. The starting-point is the collection and classification of information, both descriptive and quantitative, about schools and teaching. The aim goes further: it is to explain why things are as they are. The hope is to provide a body of principles which will guide policy-makers by predicting possible outcomes of the measures they propose. Comparative education is not normative: it does not prescribe rules for the good conduct of schools and teaching. It does not lay down what should be done: it tries instead to understand what is done and why, taking into account ideology as well as socio-economic background and racial, national and religious prejudices.

The name was first used by Marc-Antoine Jullien of Paris who in 1817 proposed the establishment of an office for the collection and dissemination of information about education. The idea, however, of studying the manner in which other people bring up their children, in order to copy what is valuable, is much older. Plato explained how some of the institutions of Sparta could be adapted to the needs—as he saw them—of Athens. Many such examples could be given. In 1641 Comenius came to London to advise the English about the establishment of a national system of education. Peter the Great desired to transplant Western culture to Russia and for this purpose sent Russians abroad to study schools and brought foreigners to Russia. During the 19th century Victor Cousin, who became Minister of Education in

France, the Americans Henry Barnard and Horace Mann, and the Englishman Matthew Arnold examined the systems of continental Europe, particularly of Russia, studying carefully what was being done with the intention of copying promising practices and developments. All these were administrators, men of action who wished, in a practical way, to understand better their own systems and to improve them. Yet they were also convinced that it was possible to discover general principles about the operation of education through a study of foreign systems.

Michael Sadler, in charge of the Department of Special Inquiries and Reports (1895-1903) in the Department of Education, may perhaps be considered the founder of the study of comparative education in England because, although primarily interested in the establishment of a sound system of secondary education, he displayed more direct concern with theory than most of his predecessors. Like them he frequently used history as the tool for explaining why institutions are what they are: the French *lycée* differs from the English grammar school because it grew and developed in a different way and under other influences. He was also, however, much concerned with social interpretations. To him, educational systems were almost living, evolving things constantly reshaped by religious, political, ideological pressures and clashes. They had an organic nature: therefore it was exceedingly difficult to transplant parts of them elsewhere. Sadler gave a new orientation to comparative studies.

The subject was not taught systematically in universities until the beginning of the present century when I. L. Kandel taught in Manchester (1905); Sandiford and Monroe in the USA (1905); F. Clarke in Southampton (1905), Cape Town (1912), McGill and later London (1932); N. Hans in London (1930); F. Schneider in Austria. All these pioneers relied on historical analysis but in addition developed views of their own. Hans, for example, thought it possible to identify factors or determinants which affect education in the various systems of the world in a more or less permanent way. He thus discussed the influence of language, race, social class and religion as well as ideologies like humanism, socialism and communism.

Since World War II, interest in comparative education has greatly increased. The reasons are obvious: more travel by teachers and administrators; more international conferences; the establishment of organisations like UNESCO, OECD, the Council of Europe, the Pan-American Union, etc.; the problems posed by the enormous expansion of education both in industrialised and newly independent countries. In consequence, it is now taught in many universities and colleges of education and is beginning to form a part of the training given to intending teachers.

An example of one such course will indicate the present scope of the subject at the elementary level. The topics dealt with include a discussion of the methods to be applied and of the contributions of sociology, history and demography; the influence of language situations with particular reference to Belgium, the USSR, India and Ceylon; possible policies in multilingual countries; the influence of religion; policies in multilingual countries; the influence of religion; policies protecting the rights of minorities; state and church in France, Canada, the USA and the UK; social class and educational structures, e.g. in France, England and Germany; the trend towards comprehensive education in the USA, the USSR and Sweden; the racial factor as it operates in Brazil, South Africa, the USA and New Zealand; education and social change; the forces which lead to change in industrialised countries; the reform of school systems; the pool of talent and the extensions of education; education and economic development in newly independent countries; ways in which schools promote social advance and material property, and analysis of examples, e.g. Mexico and Peru; comparative analysis of industrial progress and its relation to education in England, Denmark and Japan; the educational problems of industrialised societies and their relation to technological change; causes and consequences of the education explosion; a detailed study of the five educational systems which have the most widespread influence in the modern world: the American, Soviet, British, French and German.

Courses of this kind can be pursued at a more specialised and advanced level, leading up to the MA degree. Beyond comes the stage of independent research, i.e. the MPhil and PhD degrees. The theses presented deal with topics such as studies of the effects of racial policy in various countries; the consequences and contributions of missionary education; method of financing higher education; problems of recruitment and training of teachers; the trends towards greater equality of educational opportunity in various countries. Evidently almost any educational problem can be studied and investigated in detail with the aid of the comparative method. A brilliant example is the study of problems of admission to higher education conducted by F. Bowles for UNESCO and the International Association of Universities (1964).

Outside the universities, public authorities display increasing awareness of the contribution which comparative study can make. An example is the report of the Robbins Committee on higher education in England and Wales. A special volume describes the visits made and the lessons learned by members who went to the USA, the USSR and continental Europe. Unfortunately, lack of professional expertise hampered them greatly, so that this instance should perhaps be related to the journeys undertaken a century earlier by Matthew Arnold *et al.*, rather than to modern comparative studies. OECD also attempts to compare the achievements of member states, the amounts they spend on education, etc.

Two international organisations have made important contributions to the growth of comparative education. UNESCO gathers and publishes large collections of data: its four *World Handbooks* are a mine of information, while its general reports are a substantial resource. The International Office of Education (Geneva) publishes annually reports from the authorities of over a hundred countries, describing progress made, as well as studies on particular problems such as the extension of primary education and the training of teachers. Mention should also be made of the *World Year Book of Education*, published for the University of London and Columbia University, New York. This presents, each year, an international symposium centred on the discussion of a particular theme, e.g. the reform of education, the social position of teachers, guidance and counselling, the curriculum of secondary schools, higher education, the gifted child, teacher training, the education explosion, examination problems of church and state, etc.

There are two societies which exist to promote comparative studies: the Comparative Education Society (chiefly USA) which publishes a quarterly review, and the Comparative Education Society in Europe which publishes accounts of its biennial conferences, e.g. on the determinants of educational policy, general education, reform of higher education. Since about 1950 comparative education has given birth to two related subsidiary disciplines: the economics of education and educational planning. The former endeavours to treat education as an economic enterprise, studying costs and returns and investment. The second is an attempt to draw together all the threads, economic, social and administrative, which determine the course of educational development, in the hope that such development can be accelerated by the avoidance of waste, overlaps and fruitless experiment. It is receiving strong support both from international organisations and national governments, whose hopes are increasingly focused on the contribution which education can make to technological and economic growth.

There is little doubt that the study of education, at an international level, using the comparative method of analysis and interpretation, will grow vigorously in the coming years. The subject is well attuned to the scientific spirit of the age and can give to policymakers the counsel and advice, free of ideological preconceptions, which they need in a period when demand for schooling grows at an explosive rate. The chief need now is for a strengthening of the theoretical component, so that waste can be avoided and direction given to effort.

FURTHER READING
G. Z. F. Bereday. *Comparative Method in Education*, Holt, Rinehart and Winston, New York, 1964.
Nicholas Hans. *Comparative Education*, Routledge and Kegan Paul, 1958.
Brian Holmes. *Problems in Education*, Routledge and Kegan Paul, 1965.
E. J. King. *World Perspectives in Education*, Methuen, 1962.
V. Mallinson. *Introduction to the Study of Comparative Education*, Heinemann, 1960.
World Year Book of Education, Evans Bros, London; Harcourt, Brace, New York.
See also UNESCO

JAL

Complex This describes an impulse, idea or remembered experience that becomes highly charged with emotion, and continues to influence the individual, sometimes unconsciously, in a way that may seem highly irrational. For example, if an individual is suffering from a guilt complex, perhaps from something disturbing to him in the past that he has now suppressed in his memory, he may continue to feel guilty about numerous and quite innocuous aspects of his present life. Although it may be tempting for all of us to try to analyse other people's complexes, it is probably a task best left alone or to the attentions of a psychiatrist.

FURTHER READING
S. Freud. *The Psychopathology of Everyday Life*, Penguin, 1939.

NT

Comprehension This means the intelligent grasp of the situation at hand. Comprehension tests are standard parts of many intelligence tests, including the Stanford–Binet. They are thought to favour the articulate child from a good cultural background rather more than would be the case with a non-verbal test item, such as short-term memory for different numbers.

Comprehensive schools The comprehensive school was first officially defined, in a Ministry of Education circular in 1947, as 'one which is intended to cater for *all* the secondary education of *all* the children in a given area, without an organisation in three sides' (Circular 144, 16 June 1947). Such a school was intended, therefore, to cater for an age range of from 11 to 18, and it is this single-tier type which has remained the classic model of the comprehensive school. In June 1965, the DES issued Circular 10/65 which required all LEAs to submit plans for the reorganisation of secondary education in their areas on comprehensive lines. Owing largely to the need to fit the reorganised system into existing school buildings, a number of alternative patterns were suggested, some of them involving two-tier systems. Circular 10/65, however, remains an historic document, since it presaged a fundamental reconstruction of secondary education involving the abolition of selection at 11-plus and the development of the single secondary school in place of the tripartite system of separate grammar, technical and modern secondary schools inherited from the past.

The idea of the 'common' school dates back to proposals made by the Chartists (e.g. William Lovett) and by radical politicians (e.g. Richard Cobden) in the 1840s, and indeed further back to the plans put forward by Comenius and others in the 17th century. Thus the famous puritan schoolmaster John Brinsley referred to the rural grammar school as 'the common country school' in the early 17th century and, with the exception of the paupers, these were attended by all classes.

In recent times the idea was taken up by organisations of the labour movement and teachers. Following the first world war a movement for the unification of post-primary education developed in several European countries, and the demand for the *Einheitsschule* in Germany and the *école unique* in France was paralleled in Britain. In the late 1920s, organisations representing both elementary and secondary school teachers (the NUT and the Association of Assistant Masters in Secondary Schools) proposed the establishment of the single secondary school (or 'multibias' school as it was then called) as a reaction against the proposals for differentiated types of post-primary school recommended in the report of the consultative committee to the Board of Education *The Education of the Adolescent*, known as the Hadow Report (*q.v.*), which was published in 1926. In the 1930s and especially the early 1940s the TUC, the Labour and Communist Parties and other organisations pressed for the establishment of the 'multilateral' (many-sided) school, as it now came to be called; and significantly in 1935 the Education Committee of the London County Council declared that the single school should be the model for the future development of secondary education in London.

Until the passage of the Education Act 1944, however, it was not legally or administratively possible to set up the single school, since elementary and secondary education, although covering a similar age range after 11, were administered under different statutory provisions and different codes of regulations. By defining all education for children over 11 (except that given in all-age schools) as secondary, the Act overcame this obstacle; nor did the Act lay down any specific organisational form for secondary education, the relevant clause merely stating that it was the duty of local authorities to provide secondary education according to the ages, abilities and aptitudes of the pupils. LEAs had the task of drawing up development plans under the Act and an analysis of one third of these, made in 1947, showed that a quarter of the authorities were proposing to include some comprehensive schools in their provision. Many of these authorities were not, however, able to carry out such plans, which involved new buildings, owing to financial stringency in the next two decades.

Although the Labour Party, committed by successive conference resolutions to the comprehensive school, won power in 1945 and remained in office until 1951, the Labour government preferred to reinforce the tripartite system of three separate types of secondary school proposed by the Consultative Committee in 1938 in its report entitled *Secondary Education*, known as the Spens Report (*q.v.*) and in the Norwood Report (*q.v.*), *Curriculum and Examinations in Secondary Schools*, published in 1941. However a few LEAs were able to bring comprehensive schools into being, the most important of these being Anglesey, the Isle of Man, West Riding, Coventry and London. In 1952 the Anglesey County Council was able to abolish the 11-plus examination, the population now being served by four fully comprehensive schools taking all children aged 11 to 18. In 1947 the London County Council published the *London School Plan* which proposed the building of 103 single-tier comprehensive schools, the first of these to be brought into operation being Kidbrooke school in 1954. The first two Coventry schools of this type were also opened in that year (Woodlands and Caludon Castle). Both London and Coventry were able to make progress because new building had been made absolutely necessary as a result of severe bombing during the second world war.

In the 1950s, however, progress was slow, owing partly to continuing economies in education and partly to the policy of the Conservative Party which was, in general, opposed to this development, restricting it to sparsely populated rural areas and new housing estates. In the early 1960s, however, a powerful swing to comprehensive education developed among LEAs: many, such as Liverpool, Manchester and Bradford, now proposed to make a short-term transition to the comprehensive school using existing buildings, and based either on the grouping of schools to make a single viable unit or on the two-tier system already pioneered by the Leicestershire County Council in 1957. It was this movement that culminated in Circular 10/65, issued eight months after the Labour Party's return to office.

Although some 200 comprehensive schools of various sizes had by this time been brought into being (with from 220 pupils at Windermere to 2,200 at Birmingham), the bulk of the new purpose-built schools at London, Coventry and elsewhere were planned for between 1,000 and 2,000 pupils.

The term 'comprehensive', which became generally accepted after the second world war, implies a common school not rigidly structured into different 'sides' (grammar, technical and modern) but having a flexible inner organisation, able to offer its pupils a wide variety of courses. In these schools the pupils generally follow a common curriculum between the ages of 11 and 14 (sometimes 13), after which a number of different paths are open to them, the choice being made as a result of careful educational guidance at the age of 14. These courses (or 'biases') include academic, commercial, technical and craft or other components. There is, however, no one method of organising a comprehensive school; the internal academic organisation differs from school to school, though having common factors. Schools also differ in the extent to which they are streamed or setted, varying again from the strict division of children into 'ability' streams to complete non-streaming throughout the school.

Comprehensive schools differ also in their internal social organisation. Large schools are broken down into smaller units in one of three different ways. In Coventry all children are allocated to 'houses' of about 180 children, to which a housemaster and about eight staff are attached; these houses have a separate physical existence and act as a home base and centre for their members. Some comprehensive schools (for instance Sheldon Heath in Birmingham) are divided horizontally into lower, middle and upper schools, each with its own head and buildings; others operate on a year-group basis, with certain members of staff responsible for a year group as a whole. In many cases, tutorial groups consisting of some 20 pupils and one tutor are formed.

Circular 10/65 (and the parallel Circular No. 600 issued in October 1965 by the Scottish Education Department) favoured the single tier 11 to 18 school as educationally the most effective type; LEAs were, however, permitted to put forward plans for other forms of organisation: a two-tier system with a break at 13 or 14, or a

157

F*

system based on sixth-form colleges catering for the 16 to 18 age range, preceded by comprehensive schools from 11 to 16. Another method involves the development of 'middle' schools (eight to 12 or nine to 13), legally acceptable since the passage of the Education Act 1964.

Circular 10/65 permitted reorganisation on the basis of providing two parallel schools for pupils over the age of 13, with different educational facilities and leaving ages, the decision as to which school the child will attend being made through 'guided parental choice'. This latter scheme was defined in the Circular as being acceptable only as an 'interim' measure, and has little to do with comprehensive education.

In 1968 a movement developed for the introduction of a new Education Act to make the provision of comprehensive education obligatory on local authorities.

See also **End-on comprehensive schools; Leicestershire Plan schools; School bases; Secondary education, Selection for; Two-tier comprehensive schools**

BS

Comprehensive Schools, National Foundation for Educational Research Report on This was the first of a series of reports on secondary reorganisation which the National Foundation for Educational Research was asked to prepare for the DES. A survey of the comprehensive schools of England and Wales, it was published in 1967. By the NFER's definition there were 385 schools in England and Wales that could be considered comprehensive, and 331 replied to the Foundation's questionnaire. Of these, 81 were within the ILEA, 136 in English county areas, 110 in English county boroughs, and 54 in Wales. When the survey began in September 1965 222 of these schools were fully comprehensive, and 182 covered the age range from 11 to 18. The schools varied in size from 400 to more than 2,000, rather more than half having fewer than 1,000 pupils. There were 262 co-educational comprehensive schools.

In order to establish the character of the schools' intake, the Foundation made inquiries about three groups of ability: the top 20% (Group X), the middle 60% (Group Y) and the lowest 20% (Group Z). The report concluded that the all-through schools (11–18) had a 'markedly lower percentage' of Group X pupils than other schools with 11-plus intakes; and that the more urban the authority, the lower seemed the intake of pupils in this group. Thirteen of the schools felt they had fewer than 5% of the Group X pupils in their area, 74 schools had 5% or less, and 179 less than 16%. Among these all-through schools, 103 competed directly for their intake with grammar schools. Seventy schools were taking at least 5% fewer top-ability pupils than the general situation in their area would suggest they should be taking.

On the other hand, some 20% of the schools were taking a higher proportion of Group Z than might be expected in their localities. But over a quarter of the schools were receiving fewer than 16% of Group Z pupils.

In the view of the compilers of the report, the most significant figures were those for the intake of Group Y pupils—that is, the middle 60%. More pupils in this group than might have been expected from reference to the local situation were being received by 117 of the schools. The report suggested a relationship between this finding and the fact that some parental occupations —especially in the professional and clerical groups—were under-represented in the comprehensive schools covered by the survey.

In an attempt to weigh the justice of the criticism that in large schools children remain unknown to the staff or the headmaster, the report inquired into forms of grouping within the schools. It established that grouping by houses was a feature of 299 schools; in 113 there were tutor groups (more common in large schools than small ones); and 60 were divided into lower, middle and upper schools (a form of organisation more common in boys' than in girls' schools).

On the staffs of these comprehensive schools there were very slightly more non-graduates than graduates; of the latter, 80% had received professional training. There were four men non-graduates to every three men graduates; but three women non-graduates to every two women graduates.

Comprehensive Schools Committee A national non-political organisation founded in 1965 to promote the extension of the comprehensive principle throughout secondary education, the Committee regularly compiles and publishes factual information about the progress of reorganisation throughout the country, summaries of findings from research projects involving comprehensive schools, and reading lists. It operates a speakers service and an information service for those interested in knowing more about comprehensive schools.

Membership of CSC does not necessarily imply commitment to the comprehensive principle, but the wish to be kept informed. Members come from 95% of the LEAs of England and Wales, also from Scotland, Ireland, Germany, France, Israel and the Scandinavian countries. They include educators, researchers and teachers.

In 1967 an advisory panel of the Committee was set up, under the chairmanship of Professor Brian Simon, to help teachers to carry out research into techniques and problems of comprehensive schooling. CSC members seeking advice should write to the Research Advisory Panel at 123 Portland Road, London, W11.

Journal: *Comprehensive Education*. 209 Belsize Rd, London, NW6.

Compulsory attendance *See* **School attendance**

Computer education The rapid growth in the use of computing equipment over the past two decades has given a great responsibility to educational resources. The personnel requirements of industry and commerce fall, broadly, into a need for equipment designers, specialist programmers, application programmers and problem analysts. The greatest demand is for analysts, particularly in business and management applications. In the past, most of the training has been accomplished through manufacturers' short courses and experience within user establishments, and only recently has formal education in computer science developed to any extent.

Studies in computer science will usually include fundamental aspects of computer equipment, programming (from machine code to problem-oriented languages), information structures and systems analysis. Supporting studies will include mathematics, numerical methods, statistics and, in some courses, business and management studies. Specialist applications will be studied in one or more of such topics as numerical analysis, commercial data processing, management science and operations research.

Opportunities now exist for schools and colleges to teach computing fundamentals through the City and Guilds Courses (CG 319, 320) and at A level through, for example, the Associated Examining Board.

Many colleges of technology offer post A level courses in mathematics, statistics and computing either as HNC (part-time) or HND (full-time or sandwich), under the general direction of a joint committee set up by the DES. The usual entry requirement to such a course is at least A level in mathematics. Similar courses are being offered in business studies with computing.

Many universities offer undergraduate and postgraduate courses in computer science; these generally being with considerable mathematical and numerical bias. Few universities offer undergraduate courses leading to the requirements of business and management application.

There are, currently, six colleges of technology (polytechnics-designate) at Brighton, Hatfield, Leicester, Middlesbrough (Constantine College), Staffordshire and Wolverhampton, offering four-year sandwich courses in computer science leading to a CNAA degree (honours or ordinary). These courses deal with computing fundamentals in the early years, later options concentrating on either scientific or business and management applications. The usual entrance qualification is at least two A level passes, and two of the colleges (Middlesbrough and Stafford) encourage applications from students with A level passes in arts subjects, providing they have shown reasonable mathematical aptitude to at least O level.

The Education Division of the British Computer Society, in addition to articles in the regular publications, publishes special reports and summaries of educational opportunities available at all levels. In the near future, the Society will be setting Part I and II examinations (approximately equivalent to honours degree standard) leading towards professional qualification and full membership of the Society.

The National Computing Centre, in conjunction with the British Computer Society, supports special six-week courses in systems analysis at many colleges throughout the country, in an attempt to satisfy the immediate needs of business and commerce.

There is a growing awareness throughout the educational system of the need for fundamental education in computing and more specific training in some spheres of activity, and it is gradually being appreciated that the logical thought necessary in computer studies provides a worthwhile academic discipline in its own right.

FURTHER READING

Careers with Computers, British Computer Society, 1966.

Computer Courses, 1967, British Computer Society, 1967.

Computer Education (Report of an Interdepartmental Working Party), HMSO, 1967.

The Computer Bulletin Vol. II No. 1, British Computer Society, June 1967.

On Course (Quarterly Journal of Education for Industry and Commerce), DES.

JALl

Computer Society, British Set up in 1957, the Society exists to promote knowledge of the development of computing machinery and related techniques.

23 Dorset Sq., London, NW1.

Computing Computing is often synonymous with mechanical arithmetic, i.e. a means of processing numbers to obtain an equivalent number in a standard form, e.g. $2 \times 3 + 6 \rightarrow 12$. Universal methods (algorithms) have been devised, such as the decomposition method for subtraction, based on the laws of arithmetic ($q.v.$).

Initially, computing should be carried out with counters, fingers, structural apparatus, abacus, etc., recording only the answers. Children should devise their own methods of recording intermediate steps, discussion of which gives a clue to a child's understanding. Calculating machines such as Napier's Bones, nomograms, slide rules made and studied by children, underline the variety of methods and the interrelations of mathematics.

Computing also involves the simulation of complex and lengthy calculations by electronic circuits at high speed in a digital or analogue computer. The idea of a computer is given by a flow diagram, which can be prepared for simple situations by secondary children. It is excellent training in careful thinking.

JCW

Conation *See* **Cognition**

Concentric method A method of teaching in which the same area of learning in a subject is covered in each year of the course, but in increasing depth from year to year.

Concept formation A baby is not born with the knowledge that great danes and dachshunds are both dogs, or chickens and sparrows both birds. Indeed, one object alone may not be recognised by a baby on some occasions, if it is presented to him at a different angle from that at which he is accustomed to seeing it. Soon, however, he should develop a mental picture of a substance, for example milk, which he will recognise as the same whether it be in a bottle, a cup, or spilt on the floor. Sometimes the pictorial images a young child is capable of having are astonishingly vivid, so that in some cases a picture he has only just seen can be remembered in great detail.

As he grows older, however, he will find language rather than imagery the most useful way of forming concepts that will stand for categories of concrete objects or events. Even so, abstract concepts (for example, 'faith, hope and charity') will usually remain difficult for children to appreciate thoroughly until they approach secondary school; and it is now thought that abstract mathematical concepts have often in the past been introduced to children too early. The emphasis in junior mathematics is now far more upon the concrete and practical aspects. In this, as in many other fields, the ideas of Piaget (*q.v.*) have fundamentally changed our notions on the development of conceptualisation in children.

FURTHER READING
J. Piaget. *The Child's Conception of Numbers*, Routledge and Kegan Paul, 1952. *The Child's Conception of the World*, Routledge and Kegan Paul, 1929.

NT

Concurrent course A course of teacher training in which academic and professional studies are followed at the same time.

Conditioning While working on the digestive processes of dogs, Pavlov had noticed that sometimes a dog would begin to salivate merely on seeing the man who fed him, even if the man was not bringing food at that moment. This, Pavlov realised, was a conditioned reflex: the dog had learned to associate a quite different stimulus (the man) with the food itself. Later, he tried ringing a bell before food was about to be presented, and once again the dog salivated before he had even seen the food.

This discovery, simple though it may look, was to be the corner-stone for Pavlov's vast work and theories on learning through conditioned reflexes. There were many other aspects to be inquired into: the best time intervals for learning between conditioned stimulus and response; how animals distinguish between different stimuli; how a conditioned reflex can be unlearned; how this sort of learning can be transferred to different situations; and from all this, how conditioned reflexes are represented in the physiology of the brain. Since then, there have been schools of thought that see the conditioned reflex as the basis for all human behaviour, and some psychiatrists use a form of conditioning in attempts to cure bed-wetting, or to rid the patient of various neurotic symptoms or tendencies. In education, conditioning theory has contributed particularly to the development of programmed learning and teaching machines.

FURTHER READING
E. R. Hilgard and D. G. Marquis. *Conditioning and Learning*, Appleton–Century–Crofts, New York, 1961.
I. Pavlov. *Conditioned Reflexes*, Oxford Univ. Press, 1927.

NT

Conditions of service *See* **Agreement of service**

Confederation of British Industry *See* **Industry, Confederation of British**

Congo, Democratic Republic of, Education in In 1964/5 there were 6,973 primary schools (enrolment 1,592,225); 486 secondary schools (enrolment 92,069); 101 vocational schools (enrolment 17,334); 13 higher education establishments (enrolment 1,734). There are three universities: Université Lovanium de Kinshasa (Catholic: 1,600 students); Université Officielle du Congo at Lubumbashi (640 students); and the Université Libre du Congo at Kinshasa (210 students).

The country's population was approximately 16 million in 1965.

Congo, Republic of (Brazzaville), Education in All schools are run by the state. In 1964/5 there were 847 schools (enrolment 187,190); 50 secondary schools (enrolment 13,030); 33 technical schools (enrolment 2,893). About 65% of the children attend school, but there is no provision for higher education. Technical and university education are available in France for selected students.

The country's population was approximately one million in 1965.

Congregation In some universities the general assembly of senior members of the universities, who have powers to confer degrees and make regulations, is called 'congregation'.

Conscientious objection to RI *See* **Legal rights and obligations of** parents; Law and the teacher; Religion in schools

Conservative National Advisory Committee on Education The purpose of the Committee is to advise the Conservative Party on policy matters relating to education and the teaching profession.

Members of the Committee represent all those engaged in education in a professional capacity in schools, colleges and universities and those engaged in educational administration.

Local committees were formed as early as 1925, and the national committee in 1933. The name has recently been changed from 'The Conservative and Unionist Teachers' Association' in order to embrace all those interested in education, and not only teachers in schools.

The Committee prepares reports on all aspects of education and has given written and oral evidence to the Robbins and Plowden Committees. It has also submitted its recommendations to the Commission on Public Schools.

See also **Conservative Party and education**

Conservative Party and education Political controversy about education is nearly always concerned with the organisation of the nation's schools, rather than with what is taught in them. To Conservatives, this seems to be putting the cart before the horse. Conservatives hold that institutions are important only as means for getting things done, and that the important thing is to decide what you want done.

If there is a distinctively Conservative attitude towards the content of education, it is to be found in a belief in the development of the individual child in and for himself rather than an emphasis on his education in and for society. Men have to live together in societies, but education is much more than adaptation to social living. Society is itself imperfect, and the task should be to prepare individuals to look at it critically and wish to improve it; conformism is not enough.

A good education must provide three things: individuality and independence; an appreciation of quality, in people and in things; and a sense of responsibility towards others. It is impossible to develop the individual personality without discovering what qualities and talents are latent in it. Similarly, it is no good developing a spirit of independence unless the individual is qualified and trained to *be* independent; this means more than providing the educational equipment to earn a living.

All these things require that the qualities and talents of individual children should be identified and developed to the full. And this means *selection*, in some form or other; not just the segregation of the most able and intelligent, but the provision of the best and most suitable education for every child. We are very far from achieving this, and it will cost a great deal of money to achieve it. But Conservatives believe that the indiscriminate mixing of all children in non-selective schools, for the whole of their school careers, cannot bring out the best in them.

The comprehensive school may be the best, or even the only efficient, form of secondary school in a particular area; but Conservatives are wholly opposed to the imposition of uniform patterns of school organisation on local authorities for ideological reasons. This is to put a theoretical concept of society above the interests of individuals. Again, Conservatives oppose the abolition of good grammar schools of adequate size and the creation of artificial units with no geographical cohesion.

Unlike the Labour Party, which is opposed to them for reasons of doctrine, the Conservative Party strongly supports the direct grant grammar schools, which provide a bridge between the independent and maintained sectors of education and a wide social spread among their pupils. Conservatives would like to see the list opened to more schools. They believe that the independent schools should be allowed to compete with other schools on their merits—neither artificially subsidised nor dictatorially abolished. If the taxpayers and ratepayers cannot or will not provide a first-class education for all, then to abolish private provision for parents who are prepared to pay must result in a lowering of the total quality of education.

Conservatives believe, then, in variety and quality, not in uniformity of education; above all, in education for the child, not for an ideological view of society.

AM

Consolidated scales These are scales which represent the payment of salary to the person appointed to a post irrespective of his training and qualifications. As a rule previous experience is taken into account in placing a teacher on the starting point of a consolidated scale although usually the maximum cannot be exceeded.

Consolidated scales for head teachers of primary and secondary schools were introduced into the Burnham Report in 1965. Previous experience in units of five years was taken into account in giving one increment up to the maximum of the scale. A special provision was also given in that Report which in individual cases could enable a teacher to exceed the maximum of the scale if it was necessary to do this to secure an improvement in salary of not less than £150 per annum. In 1967, the corresponding arrangement ensured that no head teacher had a salary increase of less than £100 per annum. In each case the figure chosen is the amount by which the maximum of the basic scale was improved.

The method used for the smaller schools is different from the rest. A teacher appointed to the headship of a

Group O school (up to 40) receives a promotion increment of £210 and then proceeds by an annual increment of £50 to a maximum of £1,710. In the case of a Group I school (41–100) the promotion increment is £260, the annual increment £50 and the maximum £1,820.

The remainder of the scales are truly consolidated in the sense that no-one can receive less than the prescribed minimum nor can exceed the prescribed maximum save in exceptional circumstances. The current scales are set out below:

Salaries of qualified head teachers

PRIMARY AND SECONDARY SCHOOLS
OTHER THAN SPECIAL SCHOOLS

Group	Review Av. or unit total	Min. (£)	Annual Incre- ment (£)	Max. (£)
2	101–200	1,770	50(3)	1,920
3	201–300	1,845	60(3)	2,025
4	301–500	1,945	60(4)	2,185
5	501–700	2,070	75(4)	2,370
6	701–1,000	2,285	75(4)	2,585
7	1,001–1,300	2,500	75(4)	2,800
8	1,301–1,800	2,710	75(4)	3,010
9	1,801–2,400	2,955	75(4)	3,255
10	2,401–3,300	3,165	75(4)	3,465
11	3,301–4,600	3,380	75(4)	3,680
12	4,601–6,000	3,595	100(3)	3,895
13	over 6,000	3,810	100(3)	4,110

A superintendent of a nursery school is classed as a head teacher for salary purposes.

SPECIAL SCHOOLS

Group	Review Av. or unit total	Min. (£)	Annual Incre- ment (£)	Max. (£)
1(S)	Up to 60	See para. 2(b), Part B, Appx. II, Burnham Report	50	1,960
2(S)	61–180	1,860	50(4)	2,060
3(S)	181–360	1,945	60(4)	2,185
4(S)	361–600	2,105	60(4)	2,345
5(S)	601–900	2,265	60(4)	2,505
6(S)	901–1,260	2,420	75(4)	2,720
7(S)	1,261–1,620	2,580	75(4)	2,880

In a case where the Unit Total (S) of a special school exceeds 1,620 the LEA shall determine a head teacher scale appropriately related to the scale for Group 7 (S).

SEB

Consortium of Local Authorities Special Programme *See* **CLASP**

Constructed response At each step in a programme the learner is an active participant, i.e. he or she is required to answer a question or to do something. In the case of a linear programme, where normally there is only one acceptable answer, he or she is given sufficient information to enable him or her to arrive at it, and is said to make a 'constructed response'. By contrast, in working through a branching programme the learner selects an answer from a given set of alternatives.

Construction Industry Training Board Set up under the 1964 Industrial Training Act in order to encourage training throughout the Construction Industry, the Board levies some 56,000 firms at 1% of their annual payroll and provides a generous range of grants to companies sending personnel on approved courses of further education and training. Details are published in CITB's *Grant Scheme* 1967/68.

The Librarian, Radnor Hse, London Rd, Norbury, SW16.

Constructive Education Project *See* **Educational Research in England and Wales, National Foundation for**

Consultation The practice of consultation between administrators and/or elected representatives and the teaching profession is highly developed in England and Wales and embraces consideration both of educational policy and administrative detail. While there may be some fields in which the practice could be more fully developed, in general teachers in this country are much more fully consulted than their colleagues in other countries. The subject is best considered first in national and then in local terms.

National level At national level consultation is an established practice, and it works in the main through the representatives of the teachers' professional associations on the national bodies that are concerned with matters involving teachers' interests. Various kinds can be distinguished.

(1) *Salary negotiations.* This is negotiation rather than consultation, and it is carried out through the Burnham Committee (*q.v.*).

(2) *Central Advisory Council.* This is the body, reconstituted under successive chairmen, which has produced such documents as the Crowther, Newsom and Plowden Reports. The Council is asked to advise the Secretary of State on broad educational principles and possible major reforms. It includes no representatives, as such, of the teachers' or indeed of any other organisations, but consists of a number of individuals chosen, presumably, for their personal capacity and experience in education or related fields. The function of the teachers' associations here is to present expert evidence, written and oral, to the Council which may have to take into consideration factors of general, as well as special educational importance. The Council usually attaches considerable weight to the views submitted by the teachers' organisations.

(3) *Advisory Bodies such as the National Advisory Council for the Training and Supply of Teachers.* On this and similar bodies, membership is very largely by representatives of the interests involved. For instance, the NACTST includes representatives of the teachers in schools and colleges, through their professional associations; of the local authorities, and their education committees and chief officers, through their associations; universities and institutes of education, etc. They have the assist-

ance of Ministry assessors and secretariat, but powers of decision lie with the nominated members.

Decisions of these bodies (usually in the shape of recommendations to the Minister) 'emerge' from the process of debate, persuasion and compromise, and occasionally from the formal confrontation of power expressed in votes. The matters dealt with are of deep concern to all those involved in education, but there is no permanent and clear-cut division of interest, no 'two sides of the table' as there normally is over salary matters. This system works well provided that there is a broad basis of agreement and that there are generally accepted common aims among the members and no permanent lines of cleavage. This is generally the case, so on many questions the committee is united, though occasionally there are conflicting views on means and emergency measures. It should be noted, too, that in strict legal theory a consultative committee of this kind does not usually exercise direct power, although it is a convention of the constitution that a Minister does not lightly reject the advice proferred.

(4) Nationally, also, there is a *Joint Negotiation Committee of Teachers and Authorities* on which bodies like the National Union of Teachers are represented, and which deals with conditions of tenure of teachers, sick pay conditions and maternity leave recommendations. The recommendations of the Joint Committee have been adopted by the vast majority of authorities in England and Wales. This body, unlike those mentioned above, does not involve the Secretary of State for Education or his officials; it is moreover a negotiating rather than a consultative body.

(5) *The Schools Council for the Curriculum and Examinations.* This body was set up in 1964 to keep under review curricula, teaching methods and examinations in primary and secondary

schools, including aspects of school organisation so far as they affect the curriculum. Its establishment is regarded as one of the most important educational developments since the passing of the Education Act of 1944. The teachers' organisations are strongly represented on the Schools Council and are thereby able to play an important part in such matters as curriculum and examination developments.

The various modes of consultation listed above are relatively formal, in that they involve specific bodies with defined terms of reference. In addition, however, there is at national level continuous informal consultation which plays a valuable part in the shaping of opinion and events. The National Union of Teachers, for example, meets the Association of Education Committees from time to time on a semiformal basis, but in addition, the officers, officials and members of the executive of the union are constantly meeting elected members of the LEAs and their officials, and officials of the DES, on many different bodies. Thus, they get to know each other's minds and informal exchanges can often play a very useful part in preparing the way for more formal consultation, and in shaping policies. Continuous contact between the respective officials in routine matters of 'casework' also provides a basis for consultation over matters of a more general nature.

Local level At local level the situation is more complex. The principle of consultation is very widely recognised but the form and reality vary greatly.

It is the practice of some chief education officers, for example, to call together a group of head-teachers, entirely of their own choosing, and after presenting proposals to them for their observations and discussion, to claim on this basis that they have 'consulted the teachers'. There are not many, however, who would accept this as a genuine form of consultation. Consultation should involve represen-

tation, which means that a teacher, before he can claim to speak for, still less to commit, his colleagues, must have been chosen by them by democratic processes which give all those whom he represents an opportunity to have a voice in his selection.

The machinery of consultation at local level varies in formality and effectiveness. The most common methods are as follows.

County and county borough councils are obliged to co-opt on to their education committee persons having knowledge and experience of education at various levels. Authorities vary in the way in which they interpret this requirement, but there is no legal impediment to the co-option on to the education committee of teachers in the service of the authority, nor to their exercising the full powers and responsibilities of other members, elected and co-opted, subject only to the statutory limitations as to pecuniary interest that apply to all. It is generally recognised that serving teachers have a contribution of particular value to make and this is conceded by most local authorities, who do include teacher representatives on their education committees. A teacher representative, as the name implies, is one nominated by the teachers themselves and responsible to them. Some local authorities accept the nominees of the biggest teachers' organisations for the position of teacher representative; others prefer to see a direct election carried out among all teachers in their area.

In some areas consultative or advisory committees have been established, either between teachers alone, or jointly with the LEA. They may, in some cases, be able to perform a useful additional service, but generally they would not be regarded as a substitute for direct representation on the education committee. Indeed, in as much as they may be regarded as substitutes for such representation, they diminish the authority and effectiveness of the teacher representative and may actually weaken the teachers' case.

Many LEAs and chief education officers keep closely in touch with the officers of the county or county borough associations of the teachers' organisations for their area. This kind of contact is often of great value, for the officers of a teachers' association are particularly well placed to interpret the views and attitudes of their members to the administration and to take back to their members the views of the administrators or the local authorities' elected representatives. Consultation of this kind may often be a matter of two people getting to know each other's minds, but it can make an important contribution to harmonious relations between teachers and their employers, and can make more formal consultations issuing in action easier and more effective.

FJ

Consultative Committee The forerunner of the Central Advisory Councils (*q.v.*), by which it was replaced under the Education Act 1944, the Consultative Committee was established under the Board of Education Act of 1899 to give the Board advice on specific matters referred to it.

Consumer Council An independent, grant-aided body set up by the government in March 1963, the council provides booklets, wall-charts, films and filmstrips on aspects of consumer education. It also maintains a list of interested teachers who are informed of publications as they appear. A lecture service is provided on a regional or area basis. The Council is ready to arrange and co-operate in conferences attended by several schools, but cannot accept individual speaking engagements.

Booklets already published, free for classroom use if requested on a school's official notepaper, include: *About Shopping*, *About Buying Furniture*, *About Buying*

Toys, *About Buying Food and Drink*, *About Buying School Uniforms*, *About Credit*. A reference booklet for teachers, *Information for Consumer Education*, is available from HMSO.

Journal: *Focus*. Monthly.

Education Officer: 3 Cornwall Terrace, London, NW1.

Consumer education Yesterday's shoppers have become today's consumers. Consumers need to be educated, since they are expected to identify their needs clearly, assess the various goods and services available after the study of comparative information, and then make a logical selection based on their own needs and not in mere response to pressures from manufacturer or retailer. They must know their rights in law and be able to stand up for them when necessary.

Shopping becomes more difficult with the growth in the number of goods and services available. Outside pressures to buy become increasingly more sophisticated and harder to resist. It is only in the schools that tomorrow's consumers will learn to become more discriminating in their shopping habits, more knowledgeable of their rights and responsibilities, than their parents often are. And it is most important that consumer education should reach those who need it most—those in the lower income groups.

Examination boards are recognising the need to train children to look carefully at the goods and services on offer and to assess them in terms of their own needs. At O level, A level and particularly in CSE, a broad knowledge of consumer guidance and protection is required in a number of subjects. Thus, the West Yorkshire Examining Board calls for a knowledge of forms of credit sale, hire purchase, protection of consumers, consumers' organisations, the British Standards Institution and chambers of commerce. The Southern University Joint Board in domestic subjects at O level asks for a knowledge of consumer advisory services. The Joint Matriculation Board A level housecraft paper sets a question on consumer protection. The South West Examinations Board ends the regulations section of a domestic science paper with this sentence: 'It is hoped that during these studies candidates will become aware of pressures from the commercial world, of the need to possess a sense of discrimination, and of the services available to the community.'

Some suggestions follow as to ways of introducing a consumer emphasis in various subjects.

Geography. A local survey of shops, dividing them into types, mapping their distribution: national and local expenditure patterns.

History. History of shops and shopping; tracing the development of products; the law and the consumer.

English. Examination of advertising brochures and sales literature—and weighing up claims made; use of words in such literature.

Art. Good and bad design; labels and wrapping papers; pictorial aspects of advertising.

Mathematics. Personal budgeting; hire purchase and other means of having now and paying later; savings; bargain and special offers; evaluating special credit offers.

Homecraft. Standards of goods, their quality and quantity; buying a house; properties of new materials; careless labelling and informative labelling; family expenditure.

Civics. Consumer protection departments and Citizens' Advice Bureaux; weights and measures inspectors; public health inspectors.

FURTHER READING
Booklets available from the Consumer Council, 3 Cornwall Terrace, London, NW1: *About Shopping; About Buying Toys; About Buying Food and Drink; About Buying Furniture; About Credit; Buying a House?; Teltag Informative Labelling Scheme.*
Consumer Council. *Information for Consumer Education*, HMSO, 1965.

Consumers' Association. *Which? In Secondary Schools: Maths and Science*, 1967.
Michael Marland. *Looking at Advertising*, Chatto and Windus, 1967.

YM

Consumers' Association Started in 1956, the CA is an independent, non-profit-making organisation whose aim is to help people shop discriminately by giving them factual, independent and objective information about consumer goods and services. In its monthly magazine *Which?*, it publishes the results of comparative tests on consumer goods (all bought anonymously in the shops), and investigations into consumer services.

Consumers' Association is financed entirely by subscriptions to *Which?* and the sales of other publications including Raymond Postgate's *Good Food Guide, The Law for Consumers, The Legal Side of Buying a House*, etc. A book of teaching notes based on *Which?* reports, *Which? In Secondary Schools: Maths and Science*, was published in 1967. Consumers' Association also provides speakers on consumer protection and allied topics for meetings.

14 Buckingham St, London, WC2.

Continuation schools First originating in 1855 when evening schools became recipients of government grants, continuation schools were considered by the Newcastle Commission 1861 as enabling those who left school at 11 to continue their education. The Education Act 1870 limited continuation schools to pupils between the ages of 12 and 18; this was raised by the 1876 code to 21. But with the emergence of the higher grade schools (*q.v.*) numbers declined from 73,375 students in 1870 to 26,009 in 1886. As the Cross Commission realised, they had to march with the times and offer opportunities for entry into higher courses, as well as more recreation. The Commission was anxious that continuation schools should have freedom to adapt to local conditions. Indeed, the Cross

Commission was deeply impressed with the value of evening continuation schools, and hoped they would become educational centres in their own right. Here the influence of the Recreative Evening Schools Association, especially of its leading spokesman, the Rev. J. B. Paton of Nottingham, was obvious.

Compulsory attendance at continuation schools was canvassed by Michael Sadler in *Continuation Schools in England and Elsewhere*, a question which the Royal Commission on the Poor Laws (1908), the Consultative Committee on Continuation Schools (1909) and the Inter-Departmental Committee on Partial Exemption from School, teased out.

Following the recommendations of the departmental committee on juvenile employment, the Fisher Act 1918 made provision for compulsory attendance for 320 hours a year at day continuation schools for these leaving school at 14, up to the age of 16. Later the obligation was extended to 18. But the Geddes Axe 1921 (*q.v.*) enabled most employers and local authorities to abandon the scheme, and by 1939 only 13 firms and one local authority, Rugby, had a day continuation school.
See also **Trade schools**

FURTHER READING
P. I. Kitchen. *From Learning to Earning* (The story of the Rugby day continuation school), Faber and Faber, 1944.
Michael Sadler. *Continuation Schools in England and Elsewhere*, Manchester Univ. Press, Manchester, 1908.
WHGA

Continuative Teachers' Associations, National Federation of A federation of associations of teachers engaged in further education, the NFCTA has as its major aim to assist the development of further education as an integral part of the national education service. Founded in 1920 and granted representation on the Burnham Further Education Committee in 1922, it is the only association of teachers wholly concerned with the interests of the part-time teacher in establishments for further education.
Hon. Gen. Sec.: W. Ifor Davies, 44 Trinity Church Sq., London, SE1.

Contributory service The normal contribution by a teacher for the benefits under the Teachers' Superannuation Scheme is 6% of current gross salary throughout the teaching career. This is supplemented by a contribution of $8\frac{1}{2}\%$ of that salary payable by the teacher's employers. If any future actuarial enquiry reveals deficiencies in the superannuation account, the cost will fall upon the employers in the form of increased contributions. An example of this occurred in the five-year period ending 31 March 1961, when an actuarial deficiency of £148 million was declared, and this is being met by an extra $2\frac{1}{2}\%$ contribution from the local authorities for 40 years from that date, making their contribution $8\frac{1}{2}\%$ while for the teachers the contribution is pegged at 6%.

Those who entered the teaching profession after 5 July 1948 are subject to what is called 'the modified scheme'. The contribution is calculated as 6% of salary, but with a reduction of £5 18s a year in the case of a woman and £4 16s in the case of a man, which is shared equally between the teacher and employer. Thus the reduction of contribution for a woman teacher will be £2 19s a year and £2 8s for a man. These reductions enable slight reductions to be made in the teacher's pension when the national retirement pension becomes payable.

Contributions are not payable on any service in excess of 45 years for calculating the annual pension. Where a teacher suffers a reduction in salary while continuing to be employed, or upon being re-employed, in contributory service he may, with the approval of the Secretary of State, elect to pay contributions on the salary at which he was last employed before the reduction, and thus receive a pension based on that salary.

Under regulations made in 1967, 'contributory service' in future will be known as 'reckonable service'.

SEB

Controlled schools These are voluntary schools for which the LEA is financially responsible. In aided schools (*q.v.*) the authority appoints one-third of the managers; in controlled schools it appoints two-thirds. The Agreed Syllabus (*q.v.*) is followed in controlled schools, but parents may opt for not more than two periods of denominational instruction each week, and teachers (called 'reserved teachers', *q.v.*) may be appointed for this purpose.

Convergent thinking This is a term made popular by the psychologist Dr Liam Hudson,[1] and describes the type of thinking which excels in close reasoning, and thus in conventional intelligence tests, but associated with little power of imagination. The converse to this type of thinking is described by Dr Hudson as 'divergent' (*q.v.*). In a study of older pupils with high IQ scores, Dr Hudson found that 'convergers' tended to have rather conventional responses, liked to be discreet or even to hide their feelings, and often felt uneasy on open-ended questions where there was no obvious answer; a typical example is 'How many uses can you think of for a brick?' Convergers often chose to specialise in the physical sciences, perhaps because the impersonal certainties of these subjects tended to appeal to them. However, there seems some evidence that the very convergent thinker does not make the best scientist (*see* **Creativity**).

REFERENCE
1. Liam Hudson. *Contrary Imaginations*, Methuen, 1966; Penguin, 1967.

Cookery Emphasis in the teaching of cookery is laid on the practical applica-tion of a knowledge of simple nutrition, and on the development of an ability to prepare and serve family meals to suit all occasions and income groups. Consideration is given to changed eating habits, to the value of modern food products and appliances used in the preparation of food at home. Some study is made of feeding problems nationally and internationally, e.g. malnutrition, dental caries, obesity.

See also **Home Management (Housecraft), Teaching of**

Co-operative Education Association, National The National Co-operative Education Association is composed of 481 co-operative societies with a total of over 12 million members.

In each of the eight sections of the Co-operative Union in Great Britain a sectional Education Council is selected representing the committees responsible for education in the local societies and the auxiliary organisations. From each section representatives are appointed to form the national Education Executive which directs the work of the Education Department of the Co-operative Union and has a staff of officers at national headquarters and in the various sections.

The Education Department offers a comprehensive range of services and advice to societies and students, and the variety of educational activities is very wide indeed—in staff education and training, in adult education in all its forms, and in youth work. The service of the Education Department of the Union has the following main elements: (a) provision of syllabuses, examinations, and awards; (b) guidance and material, including many publications, for local classes and groups; (c) system of correspondence courses; (d) a programme of short residential courses; (e) development at the Co-operative College of long-term and short intensive residential courses; (f) direction and material for the Co-operative Youth Movement.

Information from Chief Education Officer, Stanford Hall, Loughborough, Leics.

Copyright Act (1956) The 1956 Act provides that copyright shall subsist in every original literary, dramatic and musical work if *either* it was first published in the UK *or* the author is a British subject or other 'qualified person'. The period of protection for works published during the author's lifetime lasts until 50 years from the end of the calendar year in which he died. For a published work of joint authorship, the period runs from the end of the calendar year of the death of the author who dies last. Works not published during the author's lifetime are protected until publication and for 50 years thereafter. The author automatically acquires this protection as soon as the work is written (a letter is protected as a literary work), subject to certain provisions covering cases where the author is employed under a contract of service or apprenticeship. Protection is also given to artistic works (defined to include photographs), sound recordings, films, TV and sound broadcasts and to the typographical arrangement of published editions of works.

The acts restricted by copyright in a literary, dramatic or musical work are: reproducing the work in any material form; publishing the work; performing the work in public; broadcasting the work; causing the work to be transmitted to subscribers to a diffusion service; and making an adaptation of the work (this includes making a dramatisation, translation or 'picturised' version). The doing of any of these in relation to a substantial part of a work is an infringement, but the term 'substantial part' is not defined. Individual decisions have, however, established that length is not the only test, e.g. four lines from Kipling's 32-line poem *If* have been held to amount to a substantial part.

Greater latitude is allowed when the quotation is made for purposes of criticism or review of the work from which the quotation is taken, or of another work, and is accompanied by acknowledgement to the author. In this connection the Society of Authors and the Publishers Association have jointly expressed the view that objection could not normally be taken to the quotation in a book or article, for purposes of review or criticism, of the following:

Prose: A single extract up to 400 words, or a series of extracts (with comments interposed) up to a total of 800 words but of which no one extract exceeds 300 words.

Poetry: An extract or extracts up to a total of 40 lines, but in no case exceeding one quarter of any poem.

There is no copyright in an idea or in the bare bones of a plot. To succeed in an action for infringement of copyright, the plaintiff would have to show that the combination or series of dramatic events in the allegedly infringing work had been taken from the like situations in the plaintiff's work. Proceedings have failed because it has been held that incidents common to two works were stock incidents or revolved around stock characters common to many works. Also, as copyright is not a monopoly, it is a good defence if a later author can prove that he had no knowledge of an earlier author's work.

It should also be noted that, provided certain stringent conditions are complied with, it is not an infringement to include a single short passage from a copyright work in a collection mainly consisting of out-of-copyright works and intended for use in schools.

Under further provisions for the use of copyright material in schools, copyright cannot be infringed by the reason that a work is reproduced or adapted (1) in the course of instruction, whether at a school or elsewhere, where the reproduction or adaptation is made by a teacher or pupil otherwise than by the use of duplicating process, or (2) as part of the questions to be answered in an examination or in an answer to such a question. 'Duplicating process' includes virtually any kind of process involving the use of an appliance for reproducing multiple copies. It does not refer to the writing of a single copy by hand. Performances 'in class, or otherwise in the presence of an audience . . . in the course of the activities of a school, by a person who is a teacher in, or pupil in attendance at, the school' are not performances in public if the audience is limited to teachers, pupils or others 'directly connected with the activities of the school', but this does not include parents or guardians of pupils.

The right of libraries of various kinds and of individuals to make photocopies (including micro-photocopies) is widely misinterpreted. The pamphlet entitled *Photocopying and the Law* issued jointly by the Society of Authors and the Publishers Association clarifies the position.

FURTHER READING

Copinger and Skone James on Copyright, Sweet and Maxwell, 10th ed.

PM

Copyright Convention, Universal The Universal Copyright Convention (UCC) was signed in Geneva in 1952 and at February 1968 had over 50 members including the UK and the USA, which is not a member country of the Berne Convention. The familiar copyright notice ©, followed by the name of the copyright owner and the year of first publication, is that prescribed by the UCC and it is particularly important that this notice should appear on British books, since thereby they secure protection in the USA.

The UCC is supplementary to the Berne Convention and provides a lower standard of protection—the duration of this is covered by the law of the country in which protection is claimed, but must in no case be less

than 25 years from the death of the author or, in countries where under existing legislation the term of protection runs from the date of publication, 25 years from first publication. Countries which belong to both Conventions are bound in their relations with each other by the Berne Convention.

PM

Copyright Council, British The British Copyright Council (29–33 Berners St, W1) was formed in 1953 by the Performing Right Society, the Society of Authors, and half a dozen other organisations representing copyright-owners. Its purposes are to defend and foster the true principles of copyright and their acceptance throughout the world, to bring together bodies representing all who are interested in the protection of copyright and to keep watch on any legal or social changes which may require an amendment of the law.

The Council's first major task was to make representations to the government on behalf of copyright owners before and during the passage of the Copyright Act 1956. It has since advised numerous Commonwealth and foreign governments on their copyright legislation.

In 1965 the Council was reconstituted in order to broaden the basis of its work and extend its membership. Sir Alan Herbert became chairman. Since then the Council has been concerned with the prevention of unauthorised use of copyright works by pirate radio stations; representations concerning the revision of the Berne Convention at Stockholm in 1967 (*see* **Berne Convention**); and the study of the many copyright problems presented by technical developments in the computer age.

PM

Corporal punishment At common law, a teacher may administer reasonable corporal punishment for a school offence, and provided the punishment is not inflicted 'to gratify passion or rage or with an instrument which is unfitted for the purpose and dangerous to life and limb and that it is not excessive in nature or degree or protracted beyond the pupil's power of endurance'[1] it will afford the teacher a good defence in any action for assault which might be brought. Caning on the hand is a recognised method of punishment, but a blow on the head cannot be so regarded.[2] Corporal punishment of girls also is not unlawful, although possibly not desirable. It is, however, inadvisable for a man to administer corporal punishment to a girl.

It is important, however, for a teacher to pay due regard to the Domestic Regulations of his employing authority which, under the powers conferred by Section 23 of the Education Act 1944, has the control of the secular instruction of county and voluntary schools and also of any rules laid down by the head teacher of the school who, under the Rules of Management and Articles of Government, is invariably responsible for the internal organisation, management and discipline of the school. The LEA or school regulations might limit the class of teachers who can administer corporal punishment in a particular school to the head teacher, his deputy, and possibly also certain senior members of the staff. If a teacher administers corporal punishment in breach of the LEA or school regulations, even though it is otherwise reasonable, he or she could place his or her tenure in jeopardy.

Each school must have a punishment book which should record all cases of corporal punishment and the head teacher is responsible for its completeness and accuracy.

REFERENCES
1. R. v. Hopley, 1860, 2 FLF 202 per Cockburn CJ.
2. Ryan v. Fildes, 1938, 3 AER.
See also **Discipline**

HP

Correlation The degree of correspondence between two measures of the same individuals is known as the correlation coefficient, often symbolised by r. This ranges from $+1.0$ for perfect agreement, through 0.0 for no agreement, to -1.0 for complete reversal. For example, there is a close resemblance between the marks of a class of junior pupils in English and arithmetic, though also some exceptions, and the correlation coefficient is usually about 0.80. However, age often gives small negative correlations with school attainment, since many of the younger children in a class are brighter than the older ones. Correlations are usually calculated by the product-moment or Pearson–Bravais method, though there are several other techniques appropriate to particular types of data, such as rank order coefficients, biserial r (for correlating test scores etc with a Pass–Fail criterion), tetrachoric r (for correlating two dichotomous measures). The investigation of correlations plays an important part in studies of the reliability of examinations, or in using intelligence or other tests for predicting educational or vocational suitability.
See also **Intelligence tests**

PEV

Correspondence courses The minimal correspondence course might be defined as organised provision for instruction through the post. In fact, printed material may be supported by photographs, records, tape, radio and TV; the postal contact may be supplemented by occasional lectures, tutorial meetings and short residential courses. Correspondence education is well developed and integrated with the rest of the education system in Australia, Japan, Sweden, the Soviet Union and other countries. In the UK a few notorious examples of malpractice, and the almost wholly commercial organisation, have tended to give correspondence courses a bad reputation in educational circles. Yet they are clearly meeting a demand neglected by other forms of education. It has been estimated that about half-a-million correspondence students enrol each year in Britain alone, and many more from overseas enrol with British colleges. About a quarter of the British students are seeking some kind of professional qualification; others are studying for civil service and local government examinations; others are trying to gain A or O level certificates, external university degrees, technical awards.

Attempts to regulate and register correspondence schools have so far not succeeded. The unofficial Gurr Committee recommended (1966) that a council of accreditation, on which the colleges could be represented, should inspect their work. The National Extension College and other non-commercial colleges would prefer inspection by the DES or a completely independent body, but the DES has decided to adopt the Gurr Committee's scheme.

BG

Correspondence courses in schools
An experiment in the use of correspondence courses by schools, in which pupils from 80 independent and state schools took part, was reported on in 1967 by the National Extension College (*q.v.*), which sponsored the experiment. It was found that these courses could be of use to boys and girls who were out of step with their form-mates or, having persistently failed at a subject, needed a change of teaching method. The experience of learning in a rather more independent manner than by normal teaching was judged in some cases to put boys and girls on their way towards a sixth-form attitude to work. These courses were also described as 'an interesting stage between traditional methods and programming'. It was pointed out that a wider choice of subjects could be offered than a normal school timetable could provide. In

certain cases, however, there might arise the problem of motivating a pupil in an unfamiliar learning situation.

On the basis of the experiment, the NEC plans to operate a national service which will enable a pupil to enter for GCE subjects of his choice where a teacher has fallen ill or one cannot be appointed. Schools will be able to join the scheme in order to add new subjects to their timetables.

FURTHER READING
Correspondence Courses in Schools, National Extension College, Shaftesbury Rd, Cambridge.

Costa Rica, Education in All state education is free, and elementary education from seven to 12 years is compulsory. There is a high rate of literacy, among the best in South America. Since 1944 English has been taught in all secondary schools. In 1965 there were 2,050 primary schools with 276,921 pupils; 85 secondary schools with 41,118 pupils; 36 technical and vocational schools with 7,013 pupils; five higher education institutes with 8,634 students; the University of San José with 5,824 students.

The population of the country was approximately 1½ million in 1965.

Costs of education The study of educational costs and expenditure is one of the most important branches of educational economics. Analyses of educational costs are an important prerequisite of any investigation of educational efficiency. In addition they are required by administrators and educational planners for estimating the real resources devoted to the various branches of education, for comparing the expenditure of different educational institutions and different regions of the country, for assessing the feasibility of educational plans and forecasts and as a basis for teachers' salary negotiations.

A major issue in the analysis of educational costs from an economic viewpoint is whether or not to include in these costs an estimate of the income foregone by students during the time that they are in school. Clearly a nation which has as much as a quarter of its potential labour force in school is losing a considerable amount of possible economic output, and an important factor influencing individual decisions about whether to undertake post-compulsory education is the loss of earnings in relation to the anticipated subsequent benefits.

The cost of education in the UK Expenditure on public education in real terms (measured at 1948 prices) rose from £100 million in 1920 to £300 million in 1955.[1] During the same period private educational expenditure rose from £13 million at 1948 prices to £22 million.

In the UK in 1964 public expenditure devoted to each of the main branches of education and the amounts devoted to teachers' salaries and other current capital expenditure were as follows:

PUBLIC EXPENDITURE ON EDUCATION IN THE UK, 1964–5 (*£ million*)

	Teachers' salaries	Other current expenditure	Capital expenditure
Primary	219.0	111.6	48.2
Secondary	248.7	168.0	88.5
Further	83.6	93.2	41.0
Universities	50.8	82.2	61.3
Miscellaneous	28.5	152.2	24.3
Total	630.6	607.2	263.3

REFERENCE
1. John Vaizey (*see below*).

FURTHER READING
D. Blot and M. Debauvais. 'Les Dépenses d'Education dans le Monde: Une Analyse Statistique', *Tiers Monde*, Paris, April–June 1965, pp. 443–63.
John Vaizey. *The Costs of Education*, Allen and Unwin, 1958.
See also **School finance; Economics of education**

GLW

Costs per place Statistics on the cost per student place are of fundamental importance to educational policy-makers, yet few are beset with more conceptual or practical difficulties. In principle, it should be possible to arrive at figures of cost per place by dividing the number of students in any branch of education by the expenditure. In practice the problem is far more complex.

One of the best short analyses of cost per place in the UK is contained in the Robbins Report[1]. It is shown that educational expenditures in any year can be grouped under four headings: teaching and research, loan charges, student maintenance and capital expenditure. However, only the first and third of these are directly related to the current number of students. Loan charges are a reflection of past capital expenditure, and capital expenditure is governed not by the number of students in a particular year but by the future expected increase in students and the number of old buildings that need replacement. Other problems are created by part-time students, since in general it costs more to educate a full-time student. A further difficulty is that it is often desirable to estimate costs per student place according to different curricula (a medical student costs much more to keep at university than a history student) but current financing and administrative arrangements often make this impossible, particularly in secondary education. It may also be mentioned that student maintenance presents special problems in that only an arbitrary part of these costs are a charge to public funds. Finally, it may be remarked that there are noticeable regional disparities, particularly in capital costs.

Table 1 below shows the average current cost per full-time student in each of the main branches of public education in the UK, and Table 2 gives an estimate of the average capital costs of providing a new student place in each of these main branches in England and Wales.

Table 1

CURRENT COSTS PER FULL-TIME
STUDENT: UK, 1964–5
(Public education only)

	Teaching costs (£)	Premises costs (£)
Primary	43·4	22·1
Secondary	77·1	51·7
Further education	147·3	164·2
Universities	333·3	539·4

Table 2

ESTIMATED COST OF PROVIDING A
NEW STUDENT PLACE: ENGLAND AND
WALES, 1964–5
(Public education only)

	£
Primary	230
Secondary	435
Universities:	
Arts	1,500
Pure science	3,400
Applied science	4,800

REFERENCE

1. *Report of the Committee on Higher Education* (Cmnd. 2154–IV, Appendix IV), London, 1963, pp. 99–116.

See also **Costs of education**

GLW

Counselling *See* **Guidance and counselling**

County college The Education Act 1944 gave LEAs the duty of providing county colleges for the part-time education of boys and girls who after the age of 16 did not attend a secondary school or an institution of higher education. Each young person concerned was to receive a notice directing him or her to attend such a college for a minimum of 330 hours a year. This provision of the Act is as yet unimplemented.

County Councils in Scotland, Association of Founded in 1894, and representative of the 33 county councils in Scotland, the Association has three main functions: first, to protect the interests, rights and privileges of member councils, especially where these may be affected by legislation or proposed legislation, public or private; secondly, to supervise and take any necessary action regarding the functions, powers and duties of members; and thirdly, to disseminate information on matters of importance and interest to members.

In Scotland the county councils are education authorities, with the exception of Kinross and Nairn, which are combined for education with Perth and Moray respectively. The Association has a general interest in all Scottish educational matters and is the channel of communication through which government departments consult local authorities in regard to matters of general educational interest.

3 Forres St, Edinburgh, 3.

County schools These are schools that are built, maintained and staffed by LEAs, the full cost of which is met from public funds.

County secondary schools *See* **Secondary modern schools**

Covenanters' Educational Trust Founded in 1946 by Sidney James Perry, the Trust provides grants to promising students in the UK and the Commonwealth unable to obtain adequate financial support from other sources. The Trust also assists teachers to study teaching conditions and methods overseas. To the end of 1967, £85,705 had been distributed for the benefit of 637 young people. In the period 1964–7 grants towards training in teaching and medicine were the most numerous, followed by engineering and the arts.

Cowper-Temple Clause Section 14 (2) of the Education Act 1870 which declares that 'no religious catechism or religious formulary, which is distinctive of any particular denomination, shall be taught' in the board schools set up under that Act, was designed by W. F. Cowper-Temple,

MP for South Hampshire, to allay sectarian suspicion that these schools would fall under clerical influence. When Disraeli described it as 'inventing and establishing a new sacerdotal class . . . which will in the future exercise an extraordinary influence upon the history of England and upon the conduct of Englishmen', he was right. For the principle was reaffirmed in 1902 and, with modifications, in 1944.

CRAC *See* **Careers Research and Advisory Centre**

Craft Education, Institute of The new name given in 1967 to the Institute of Handicraft Teachers (*q.v.*).

Crafts Centre of Great Britain The Centre exists to sell and exhibit the best of British craftsmanship. Schools may visit exhibitions free of charge.
43 Eastham St, London, WC2.

Craik, Sir Henry (1846–1927) First secretary of the Scottish Education Department (1885), Craik introduced the new Code of 1886 which abolished examinations in the three Rs for classes below Standard 3, and enlarged the curriculum of the elementary schools. In 1890 he abolished individual examinations (relics of payment by results) in the senior classes of maintained schools. In 1893 he secured free elementary education in Scotland between the ages of three and 15. He set up a secondary education committee in each county and in the five largest towns to distribute grants made under the Education and Local Taxation Act. In 1888 he gave a firm sense of direction to secondary education in Scotland by instituting the Leaving Certificate Examination. Craik also reformed scientific and technical education, set up a system of higher-grade schools, secured the raising of the school leaving-age to 14, and began reforms in the training of teachers.

Creaming This metaphor is usually applied to those highly selective schools which by their record and reputation attract the ablest pupils from a wide area, leaving the 'skimmed milk' to be shared among the other schools providing a comparable curriculum. The practice is much more common with boys' schools than with girls', though it is not confined to them. Manchester Grammar School, a direct grant school (*q.v.*), and Dulwich College, an independent school, are typical examples of schools which have this reputation. Both serve highly developed communities in which there is a great deal of academic talent, and both attract pupils from a considerable distance. Most English conurbations have at least one such school.

The practice is attacked on egalitarian grounds; it is defended on the ground that the schools which attract this very talented intake do so because they achieve standards of scholarship which it is in the national interest to maintain. A reliable judgement must take into account the fate of those who just fail or just succeed in securing admission. There is reason to think that the best pupils in the more ordinary grammar schools in these conurbations do better academically than they would have done if they had just secured admission to the 'creaming' school. Much will also depend on how extensive the creaming is.

The metaphor is also sometimes applied to the practice in certain schools, usually but not exclusively boys' schools, of selecting the ablest pupils at an early age for a special, shortened general course so that they may have longer to devote to advanced work. Creaming as between schools and and within a school is closely connected with the competitive nature of the entry to higher education in England.

DGOA

Creative writing *See* **Writing**

Creativity Recently there has been much interest in the detection and measurement of creativity: in this sense meaning flexibility, originality and sensitivity in response to ideas or situations. This cannot be measured by conventional methods of intelligence testing, and in the USA open-ended tests that emphasise divergent thinking (*q.v.*) have come to be called 'tests of creativity.' Getzels and Jackson, two University of Chicago psychologists, conducted an intensive study in 1962 on high IQ pupils (HIQ), and highly creative pupils (HC), in a middle-class school in a Chicago suburb. They found that both groups were doing equally well at school subjects, although teachers tended to prefer the HIQ pupils. This may have been because these pupils tended to be studious and serious in their outlook, whereas the HC pupils tended to be more unpredictable, and often shared a type of rebellious humour. The study has been repeated since in different parts of the country with similar results.

Dr Liam Hudson (*see* **Convergent thinking**) has questioned the idea that conspicuous success in answering open-ended tests necessarily means the presence of 'creativity'. He finds that really creative people do not tend to produce noticeably original answers but rather a quantity of the more usual ones. He prefers to think that really creative scientists should be capable of some divergent thinking, just as the creative artist should be able to manage some convergent thinking too. In both sciences and arts, however, creativity seems to flourish more in a permissive than an authoritarian school atmosphere.

FURTHER READING
J. W. Getzels and P. W. Jackson. *Creativity and Intelligence*, Wiley, New York, 1962. Liam Hudson. *Contrary Imaginations*, Methuen, 1966.

NT

Crèche The term originally used for 'day nursery', and still used to describe a few such nurseries pioneered by the church at the end of the 19th century in days of casual labour with no sickness and unemployment benefit or widows' pensions. An example is the Kingsway Crèche founded in 1887 by the West London Mission and still run by a voluntary committee. Originally, 30 children from 0 to 5 years were cared for by three voluntary workers called sisters. The crèche was open for 12 hours a day, and it rescued children who were found alone in attics or basements or tied to table legs.

See also **Day nurseries**

CREDIF (**Centre de Recherche et d'Etude pour la Diffusion du Français**) A centre for research into linguistics and language teaching. I organises French language courses fo foreigners in France, and trains staf in audio-visual teaching methods. It two well-known audio-visual method for teaching French are *Bonjour Lin* for children, and *Voix et Images d France* for adults.

8 Rue Jean Calvin, Paris, 5.

Crick Report (1964) *See* **Busines education**

Cricket Games using a form of ba and a ball have been played in mos countries of the world for many cen turies, but the game of cricket as w know it to-day traditionally had it origin over 250 years ago when player from the village of Hambledon i Hampshire played against teams fror the counties of Surrey and Kent. Th first laws of the game were drawn up i 1774; these have changed considerabl over the years, yet the modern game basically the same as that played o village greens of long ago.

Administration of the game is un usual, differing from most other inter national sports in that there is n official governing body; it is ruled by th MCC (Marylebone Cricket Club), wit headquarters at Lord's Cricket Groun in London, whose pronouncements on the rules and conduct of the game are accepted almost without question.

In secondary schools, colleges and universities, cricket is still regarded as the major summer game for boys and men, though in fact today probably far greater numbers take part in other sports such as tennis and swimming.

In English schools the game is organised to a very high standard by the English Schools' Cricket Association through regional, county and local associations run by schoolmasters acting in an honorary capacity. The associations arrange matches at all levels and many of the excellent schoolboy cricketers produced and 'discovered' over the years have gone on to play first-class cricket for their counties and for England. A recent outstanding event was a very successful tour of India in 1965 by a schoolboy team from the London Schools Cricket Association.

English Schools' Cricket Association: C. R. Hansford, 11 Coombe Rise, Findon, Worthing, Sussex.

FURTHER READING
The Laws of Cricket (*Know the Game* Series), Educational Productions.
R. S. Rait Kerr. *Cricket Umpiring and Scoring*, Phoenix Sports Book, 1957.
The MCC Cricket Coaching Book.
JE

Cricket Association, English Schools' The principal aims of the Association are the mental, moral and physical development of schoolboys through the medium of cricket, to raise the standard of schoolboy cricket and to facilitate the playing of matches. Organised on county basis, its membership has risen from 13 schools at its foundation in 1948 to its present 52. It is administered in two sections: senior, including any boy on a school register; juniors, for boys under 16 on 1 September of the current year. Two residential coaching courses for boys are held annually. The senior teams play an annual match at Lord's against public schools and one against Welsh schools, either at home or away. They have also played international matches against Indian and South African schools. The juniors play in an annual series of inter-regional matches, followed by matches for a fully representative side.

Hon. Sec.: C. R. Hansford, 11 Coombe Rise, Findon Valley, Worthing, Sussex.

Publications: *English Schools Cricket Association Handbook* and *Cricket Spotlight.* Annual.

Crippled children *See* **Physically handicapped pupils** *and* **Spastic children**

Criterion frame (*see also* **Frame**) A special-purpose or test frame which the programmer inserts, either to ascertain whether the learner has understood the previous sequence, or to determine whether the learner needs to go through the sequence which follows.

Cross Report (1888) (Royal Commission) Terms of reference: to enquire into the working of the Elementary Education Acts, England and Wales. Recommendations from this report were incorporated into legislation in 1897 and 1902.

The commission was set up after complaints by the Roman Catholics about the effects and administration of the Education Act 1870. It was constituted from members drawn from a very wide field, with the result that very few conclusions were unanimous.

The majority found that, within certain limitations, the demand for school places had been met. They did not think that the entry qualifications for teacher training should be too high, in case this should exclude those with a 'natural aptitude', and they called for more women to be trained as teachers. Where they disagreed with the minority report, drawn up separately by eight members of the commission, was in the use of pupil teachers, who, it was thought, should continue. The minority report described the pupil teacher system as 'the weakest part of our educational machinery,' and deplored a recommendation to lower the commencing age of pupil teachers to 13. The majority considered that the HMIs should report on the moral training and conditions of schools; the minority thought this was impossible.

Both sides agreed that payment by results should cease, and that a new system of payments should be worked out. Although this report revealed many possible improvements in the state of education, it did not go very far in solving the denominational issues which had caused it to be set up.

See also **Education Act (1897); Education Act (1902)**

Crowther Report (1959) Terms of reference: to enquire into the education of boys and girls between the ages of 15 and 18. Chairman: Sir Geoffrey Crowther.

The report recommended that the school leaving age should be raised to 16 by 1968, to be followed soon by the setting up of county colleges for all children up to the age of 17 not receiving full-time education. It also recommended that the number of sandwich courses available should be increased, and that more time should be allotted for all courses, which should follow a more coherent national plan than at present.

The report backed up its findings with statistical evidence that a great deal of talent was still not being developed and trained, and that there were clearly defined differences of opportunity at different social levels. It recommended less specialisation in the sixth form, and the introduction of a general element into all specialised training.

See also **Specialisation**

Crystal Palace National Recreation Centre Largely financed by the GLC and excellently administered by the Central Council of Physical Recreation (*q.v.*), the Centre was opened in 1964. Though magnificent in conception and providing some of the finest multi-sport facilities in the country, it is unfortunately situated (SE London) and is not easy of access by public transport. It has however overcome its initial difficulties by its attractive up-to-date opportunities for competition and coaching at all levels in most sports.

First-class hostel accommodation is provided for residential coaching courses and conferences organised for national sports associations, youth organisations and private bodies. There are also facilities for school activities on a regular basis, and for members of the general public who, on payment of a fee, become 'authorised users'.

The Centre is used for competition at national and international level in such sports as athletics, association football, badminton, netball, swimming, trampolining, judo, lawn tennis and table tennis.

CSE The Certificate of Secondary Education originated in a report of the Beloe Committee 1960, which had been appointed to enquire into all external examinations except GCE. Increasingly, secondary school pupils had been taking various external examinations organised by bodies over which the Ministry of Education had no control. The Beloe Report recommended that a new CSE examination should be started, to be taken at 16, and that only CSE or GCE should be taken by secondary pupils. Assuming that the top 20% of the intelligence range took GCE, the next 20% (mostly in secondary modern schools) would take CSE together with some of the next 20% who might take a few subjects. Teachers in the schools were to control the examination, which was to be organised by regional examination boards (eventually 14 were set up).

In 1963 a number of experiments began, and the Secondary Schools Examinations Council issued the first Examination Bulletin. Many subject panels were set up regionally to determine syllabuses, and in 1965 and 1966 CSE began to operate. New methods of assessment have been tried, including field and course work, oral work and objective tests. The examination can be completely external (mode 1); or schools may offer subject syllabuses to be accepted by the board (mode 2); or, in addition to this, schools may set and mark their own examinations under external moderation (mode 3). Subjects are marked on a five-point scale: grade 1 is equal to grade 5 (pass mark) of O level, and grade 4 is the level to be expected of a 16-year-old of average ability. Universities and professional bodies have almost all come to recognise CSE qualifications. The strength of the new examination lies in teacher control and the strong element of research which has been built into it.

The Schools Council pamphlet, *Examining at 16+* (HMSO 1966) discusses problems arising from the existence, side by side, of CSE and GCE.

See also **Beloe Report; Examinations; Secondary modern schools**

HD

Cuba, Education in Education is free and compulsory from age six to 14 years. In 1962 a system of student teaching was introduced into primary schools as part of in-service teacher training. Efforts to remove illiteracy have been intensified in recent years and in 1964 illiteracy was officially declared to have been eliminated. In 1964/65 primary school enrolments numbered 1,280,664; secondary 137,745; technical 29,844; vocational 10,706; teacher training 25,000; adult education classes 10,706; universities (three) 26,934.

The population of the country was approximately 7¾ million in 1966.

Cuisenaire Cuisenaire rods consist of a set of coloured, wooden rods of square cross-section used for demonstrating operations on numbers in a concrete manner. There are ten lengths, from one to ten centimetres, each identified by a colour. Each rod represents a number, the choice depending on the computation involved. Abstract operations can be interpreted as physical actions: for example, addition involves putting rods end to end; equivalence involves matching lengths side by side.

FURTHER READING

J. C. Cattegno. *Numbers in Colour*, Educational Explorers, 1963.

JCW

Culture Epoch Theory Originating in the work of the French philosopher Etienne Bonnot de Condillac (1714-80), the Culture Epoch Theory rested on the view that the best form of learning for children was one that followed the stages through which mankind has passed. From this it was deduced that at each stage of a child's development he should work with the products of the corresponding cultural period in human history.

Curriculum Defined in the Spens Report (1938) as 'in the strict sense a statement or programme of courses of teaching and instruction'. A wider definition might be 'all the experience which a pupil has under the guidance of the school'.

By 1900, the primary school curriculum had hardly developed beyond the 3 Rs — a limited training in the tool subjects for the children of the poor. Change came slowly, influenced by Froebel, Montessori, Margaret McMillan, and in 1904 the Elementary Code made a bid for reform. In 1931, the Board of Education's Report on Primary Schools contained the famous sentence 'the curriculum should be thought of in terms of activity and experience rather than of knowledge

181

G

to be acquired and facts to be stored.' Since then, the infant school has been transformed and change has gone far in the junior school. Much greater knowledge of how children learn has made a child-centred curriculum possible, and new methods of teaching reading and number have helped. School life has included many different experiences, artistic and physical as well as intellectual, and experiments are taking place in the teaching of languages and science.

Until the Hadow Report (1926), secondary education meant what we now call grammar school education, academic and theoretical, aimed at the more intelligent children and increasingly dominated by external examinations. In some areas, central or junior technical schools allowed a second selection of pupils, but most children remained in higher elementary or senior schools, with a narrow curriculum which paid little attention to the needs of the growing child. The Hadow and Spens Reports emphasised the need for, and the 1944 Education Act established, secondary education for all. Following the Spens Report this was usually organised in grammar and secondary modern schools, with technical high schools in a few areas.

The curriculum of the secondary modern schools (*q.v.*) has been largely based on the orthodox subjects which are found in the grammar school (English, a language, history, geography, scripture, science, mathematics, PE) though often with a greater emphasis on art, music and practical subjects. The Newsom Report (1963) drew attention to the failure of this curriculum to excite the interest of many pupils and so helped to provoke an interest in curriculum reform (*q.v.*). Technical education has had little part to play. Secondary education has changed very slowly, and the spread of external examinations into the secondary modern school has been another conservative influence.   HD

Curriculum, Agreement to Broaden the (ABC) Initiated by a group of headmasters of maintained and independent schools in June 1961. They were concerned with 'the growing pressure on their schools towards premature and excessive specialisation'. They invited other schools to pledge themselves (a) to provide a broad curriculum so that a choice of arts and science subjects was open to those staying in the sixth form; (b) to ensure that at least one-third of a sixth-former's time should be devoted to non-specialist subjects. 360 schools promised to operate this scheme not later than September 1963 and 269 declared themselves in sympathy but unable to start so soon. The result was a great impetus to the cause of general studies (*q.v.*), and the General Studies Association (*q.v.*) took over from ABC.

Curriculum differentiation This term is perhaps most commonly applied to the adjustment of curricula to the different needs, interests and supposed abilities of boys and girls. In 1923 the Board of Education published a report of a Consultative Committee (see *Further reading* below) on this subject. This and other sources suggest that curriculum-makers should consider, first, the different adult domestic roles for which boys and girls would need preparation. Boys might therefore take woodwork and metalwork, while girls would practise needlework, domestic science and mothercraft Again, curriculum-makers might need to consider different vocational possibilities likely to be open to boys and girls leaving school. With these in mind, boys might take technical drawing or accounting, while girls learned shorthand and typewriting.

Further, the supposed different interests of boys and girls might properly influence curricula. Commonly, boys are expected to show more interest than girls in mechanical and mathematical subjects, while girls will generally be more interested than boys in humanities and languages.

Finally, syllabuses in physical education leading to adult interests and leisure-time pursuits are likely to be different for boys and girls. Boys may be coached in football and cricket, girls in netball, hockey and tennis. Concern to cater for these differences should not obscure the fact that boys and girls, or young men and young women, commonly share the bulk of the curricula offered in educational institutions at all levels in the UK.

The term *curriculum differentiation* may be used, though less usually, in two other contexts. It may mean the adjustment of curricula to suit children of different abilities and capacities. An academically more demanding curriculum may be proposed for those who are quicker at their books; some slower-learning children of the same age must follow special remedial courses. Again, some children recognised as gifted in, say, art or music, may with profit follow specially-designed curricula. The ultimate in this form of *curriculum differentiation* would be 'individualised programmes' —as they are now called—or individual assignments, as proposed by Helen Parkhurst in the Dalton (Laboratory) Plan. The second and more marginal use of the term *curriculum differentiation* refers to the division of a 'subject' into more specialised 'subjects'. 'Nature', as a concern of the primary school, becomes biology—if not botany and zoology—physics and chemistry in the secondary school.

See also **Co-education; Dalton Plan; Girls, Education of**

FURTHER READING

Board of Education. *Report of the Consultative Committee on Differentiation of the Curriculum for Boys and Girls Respectively in the Secondary Schools*, 1923.

J. B. Henry (Ed.). *National Society for the Study of Education 61st Year Book*, Part 1: *Individualising Instruction*, NSSE, Chicago, Ill., 1962.

Helen Parkhurst. *Education on the Dalton Plan*, Bell, 1922.

RDB

Curriculum reform This refers to efforts to reform secondary school curricula in this country, arising from a widely felt discontent. The Newsom Report (1963) pointed out the unreality and irrelevance of much work done with children in the lower half of the intelligence range: others felt that the same criticism could be levelled at the static examination-ridden curriculum of the other half of the pupils. The pupil-centred curriculum in the best primary schools has been contrasted with the domination of the academic subject in most secondary schools. The proposed raising of the school leaving age has drawn particular attention to the need for new thinking. A similar discontent in the USA, dramatised by the Russian sputnik, started projects for the reform of physics (1956), mathematics and the other sciences and had a considerable effect in this country. Other incentives to change include discontent with individual subject syllabuses which fail to meet the needs of children at this time, the neglect of applied science in spite of the needs of society, and the slowness with which the schools are using a great variety of mechanical aids and programmed learning.

The absence in this country of any central body which could supervise the curriculum has long been a problem. A cautious move in this direction, and one which was mistrusted by teachers, came with the establishment of the Curriculum Study Group by the Min. of Ed. in 1962. (Before this, the Nuffield Foundation had entered the field with projects to reform science (with the Association for Science Education), mathematics (in primary and secondary schools) and languages.) Its work has not only produced new syllabuses and teaching methods, but, by the use of schools and teachers for experiment, has done a great deal to arouse a wider enthusiasm for curriculum reform. Side by side with Nuffield, various mathematical projects have developed, chiefly the School Mathematics Project (*q.v.*) (1961) centred on Southampton University and the Midlands Mathematical Experiment (1964): modern mathematics has entered the schools and O level papers (with A level to follow) are now set on the new syllabuses by a number of boards.

In 1964, the Schools Council was set up to supervise the curriculum and examinations, with the Curriculum Study Group in an advisory capacity. The Council stimulates development and enquiry through many agencies and is taking over from Nuffield the curriculum projects which it initiated. Progress has followed in other subjects. Scripture is undergoing changes as a result of the work of Goldman, Loukes and others. The National Association for the Teaching of English, supported by the SSEC report on the examining of English language, 1964, is tackling English. The emergence of cross-disciplinary studies, social, environmental and scientific, in schools and colleges of education is a sign of the times. Experiments in many schools along the lines recommended by the Newsom Report are making good progress. Other important developments include the rise of General Studies (*q.v.*) in sixth forms, and proposals for the reform of the sixth form curriculum by the Schools Council (*q.v. under* **A level**). Reform is at last on the way.

HD

Curtis Report (1945) Appointed to advise on ways in which children might be brought up in conditions that would compensate them for the lack of a normal home life, the Curtis Report (named after the chairman, Dame Myra Curtis) recommended the setting up of two Advisory Councils for Child Care, one for England and Wales and one for Scotland, together with the

establishment by each LEA of a Children's Committee and a Children's Officer.

Cyprus, Education in Elementary education is free and compulsory between the ages of six and 12 years. Secondary and technical education for the 13 to 18 year age group are fee-paying. About 70% of elementary pupils go forward to the secondary stage. In 1964/5 there were 773 elementary schools (88,000 enrolments); 66 secondary and 12 technical schools (38,000 enrolments). There are two teacher training colleges (one for Greeks, one for Turks) and six evening institutes specialising in foreign languages which have an enrolment of 4,100 students. The island also possesses a school for delinquents, a nurses' training school, a forestry college and one private higher education institute. Illiteracy is largely confined to older people, especially to women over 60 years of age.

The island's population (approximately 80% Greek and 18% Turkish) was about half-a-million in 1965.

Czechoslovakia, Education in Education is compulsory and free from the age of six to 15 years, after which pupils may continue voluntarily at secondary, vocational or apprentice training schools for a further three years; about 40% do this. Passing a matriculation examination enables students from these secondary schools to study at a technical institute or university. In 1965/66 there were 11,330 primary schools with an enrolment of 2,221,160 pupils; 374 secondary schools (enrolment 112,928); 645 technical and teacher training colleges (enrolment 297,654); 38 institutes of higher education, including five universities (enrolment 144,990). The universities are at Prague, Bratislava, Brno, Olomouc and Kolice.

The population of the country was approximately 14¼ million in 1966.

D

Dahomey, Education in In 1965/6 there were 761 primary schools (enrolment 130,774); 50 secondary schools (enrolment 11,295); 11 technical schools (enrolment 232); one teacher training college (enrolment 71). Some students go to France for higher education.
The country's population was approximately 2¼ million in 1966.

Dainton Report (1968) This report of the Council for Scientific Policy, under the chairmanship of Dr F. S. Dainton (*Enquiry into the Flow of Candidates in Science and Technology into Higher Education*) appeared in March 1968, and pointed to a notable swing away from science and technology in England and Wales. Between 1962 and 1965, the Council discovered, 4,000 science places were vacant in universities. It was likely that the numbers of sixth-formers studying science would fall from 40,000 in 1964 to 31,500 in 1971, with a rise in those not studying science from 54,500 to 76,000. It was established that universities have tended to accept, in science and technology, candidates whose A level grades were lower than those applying for places in arts and social sciences. In the colleges of education, entrants with A level science fell from 16% in 1961 to 13% in 1963. There had been a strong decline in the numbers of O level candidates in science among boys; girls showed very little interest.
The situation in Scotland was healthier, and worthy of imitation in those respects that gave it an edge over England and Wales. Its secondary courses were more broadly based, new syllabuses in mathematics and science were more quickly adopted, and Scottish students were helped by the four-year courses at university and by the opportunity given to students to change their minds about their major interests.

A similar swing from science and technology had been detected in Australia, West Germany and the Netherlands, but it had not occurred in the USA or France. It was found that French secondary schools laid a stress on science, and nearly 75% of all French pupils followed courses with a science bias in the first year of the *baccalauréat*. The percentage in the UK at a comparable point of the examination system was 42%.

Science subjects increased in popularity from the mid-1940s to the late 1950s, and the swing was possibly due to the intense competition that arose during that period, and to a growing feeling that science, engineering and technology were remote from larger human and social concerns. Significantly, biology, medicine and the social sciences, all dealing with people and society, were free from the decline.

The Council proposed that sixth-form studies should be broadened, that irrevocable choices should be left as late as possible, and that all pupils should study mathematics throughout the whole of their school lives, with special emphasis on the application of mathematics to the sciences; that science teaching should be made more attractive, and that there should be a system of incentives to attract more well-qualified science graduates to teaching; that the universities might help by rethinking their entrance requirements in the light of the need for a broader spectrum of sixth-form studies, and should attempt to draw students as yet uncommitted into science and technology; that employers should make careers in these fields more attractive to the young; that there should be more research into the ways in which careers were chosen, and into the effects of specialisation on manpower.

Dalton plan A teaching method devised to enable pupils to proceed at their own pace, using resource material, particularly in libraries, to complete agreed and planned assignments of work. Great forward planning was demanded from all teachers when the Dalton plan was fully used. Modifications of the Dalton plan are currently in much more general use than is a fully Daltonised curriculum.

Dame schools Run, as their name implies, by women, who taught children to read for 2d or 3d a week, dame schools have been immortalised in Shenstone's *The Schoolmistress* (1737) and Crabbe's *The Borough* (1783). They have figured in many autobiographies since, notably that of William Lovett (1876). Though no adequate statistical survey of their incidence is extant, they seem to have been widely diffused as basic institutions for primary education up to 1870 and in many cases beyond. The Newcastle Report (*q.v.*) described them as 'often so small that the children cannot stand in a semi-circle round the teacher', but 'closely packed as birds in a nest, and tumbling over each other like puppies in a kennel'. 'That deeply seated foible . . . the passion for the genteel or the supposedly

genteel', as one HMI remarked in 1873, 'kept them alive'. Associated with them were horn books: boards on which the alphabet or other letters had been written and covered with transparent horn as a preservative.

WHGA

Dance in education Dance has played an increasingly important part in education in Great Britain in this century. At the beginning of the century dance was included in the curriculum in some girls' schools, taking the form of English country dancing or European national dance styles. In some schools Greek dance and eurhythmics were introduced.

In 1938 Rudolf Laban, who had already established a reputation in Europe as an innovator of free dance, escaped from Nazi Germany and settled in England. His ideas were already known here through artists and teachers who had studied in Germany, and were able to take root at a time when the educational climate was propitious. Laban's philosophy stemmed from his concern with the deep implications of movement as a means of human expression and with its importance in everyday living and behaviour. He saw movement as an activity not only concerned with the functioning of the body but springing from thinking and feeling: as a process involving the mental, emotional and spiritual, as well as the physical aspects of human personality. He thought it important that people should have opportunities to practise movement as an educative and re creative experience because of it power to enrich the personality.

As a result of his investigations into movement both from a scientific point of view and also as an art form Laban formulated movement concept which have formed the basis of dance in education in Great Britain.

Considerable progress has been made in the last 30 years. Some school continue to teach folk dance, and there has been pressure to introduce classical ballet technique. However, the outstanding development has been in modern educational dance. Laban's pupil and collaborator, Lisa Ullmann, established the Art of Movement Studio in England and trains many of those who introduce dance into schools and colleges. All colleges of education now include the subject in their professional courses of training; a number provide opportunities for specialisation in dance as a part of PE; an increasing number of colleges offer courses, at principal and subsidiary level, in dance as a study in its own right. A number of vacation and in-service courses for teachers have been established. In consequence an increasing number of schools are introducing dance into the curriculum.

The aims of dance in education are to foster the child's natural tendency to engage in dance-like activity; to encourage him, through lively action, to explore and understand his personal capacity for movement; to aid his mastery of the rhythms and patterns which he invents; and to provide opportunities for him to use this movement vocabulary creatively in dance. Because of its power to enrich the child's inner life, dance may be seen as a means of education in its deepest sense.

In dance education, the child may gain experience in several inter-related aspects. He becomes aware of the range of bodily action which he can employ; he experiences degrees of energy and variations of time which contribute to his feeling for rhythm and dynamic action; he increases his awareness of the space in which he moves and of the pathways and shapes he traces in it. Individual exploration, mastery and invention go hand in hand with group dances which demand a sensitive awareness towards others.

Movement themes appropriate to the child's stage of development are used. The simple dance plays of the younger children form the basis for the structured dances of the secondary child. Dances may be unaccompanied, the rhythms deriving from the action; they may be accompanied by voice, sound or percussion; music may serve as a stimulus or accompaniment. Themes may be dynamic, spatial, abstract, dramatic, lyrical or humorous. The essential element is the development of movement ideas into the artistic expression of the dance. Laban in *Modern Educational Dance* sums up the aim thus: 'It is not artistic perfection or the creation and performing of sensational dances which is aimed at, but the beneficial effect of the creative activity of dancing on the personality of the pupil.'

FURTHER READING
Diana Jordan. *Childhood and Movement*, Blackwell, Oxford, 1966.
Rudolf Laban. *Modern Educational Dance*, Macdonald and Evans, 1948. *The Mastery of Movement*, Macdonald and Evans, revised by Lisa Ullmann, 1960. *Choreutics* (Ed. Lisa Ullmann), Macdonald and Evans, 1966.
Rudolf Laban and F. C. Lawrence. *Effort*, Macdonald and Evans, 1947.
Valerie Preston. *A Handbook to Modern Educational Dance*, Macdonald and Evans, 1963.
Joan Russell. *Modern Dance in Education*, Macdonald and Evans, 1965. *Dance in the Primary School*, Macdonald and Evans, 1965.

JMR

Davies, Emily (1830–1921) Pioneer with Miss A. J. Clough (first principal of Newnham College, Cambridge) of higher education for women, Miss Davies founded, in 1869 at Hitchin, the college that later, on moving to Cambridge, became Girton College.
See also **Women, Higher education for**

Dawes, Richard (1793–1867) A remarkable educationist and far ahead of his time, Dawes became interested in schooling when in 1836 he was appointed vicar of King's Samborne, in Hampshire, a large village plunged in economic and social depression. Many put their children to work in the fields. Dawes set out to establish a school that would provide for all the village children. It was self-supporting and had a staff of eight (six being pupil-teachers). The syllabus included geography, history, science, mathematics, the physical sciences, and music, and much of the teaching was by an early form of the project method. The children did homework and owned their own books. An account of the work at King's Samborne was given by Matthew Arnold in evidence before the Newcastle Commission (*q.v.*). In 1850 Dawes was appointed Dean of Hereford, and there continued his work in the field of secondary education.

Day, Thomas (1748–89) Disciple of Rousseau and friend of the Edgeworths (*see* **Edgeworth, Maria**), Day adopted two little girls and attempted, by rearing them according to the pure Rousseauist doctrine (they were protected from the common womanly vanities and subjected to a startling process of 'hardening'), to turn either into a fit bride for himself. The experiment was a failure. Day's *Sandford and Merton* is a classic account of advanced late 18th-century views on child-rearing.

Day continuation schools Under the Education Act 1918, pupils leaving school at 14 were required to attend a day continuation school for 320 hours each year, and LEAs were to submit to the Board of Education schemes for the step-by-step establishment of a system of such schools. Like the similar provision for the setting up of county colleges under the 1944 Act, this provision of the Act was not realised. *See also* **Further education**

Day nurseries These exist primarily to serve a social need. The term is used mainly to mean Local Health Authority nurseries, but recently hospital day

nurseries have been established[1] to help hospital staff recruitment.

In December 1965, of the 2,612 day nurseries in England for which the Ministry of Health was the responsible central department,[2] 448 were LHA nurseries, 56 were factory nurseries, and 2,108 private nurseries (unspecified). LHA nurseries had approved places for 21,396 with an average daily attendance of 16,470; factory nurseries had 2,098 places.[3]

The first day nurseries were voluntary. The National Society of Children's Day Nurseries was founded in 1906, and this raised standards. To encourage working mothers, wartime day nurseries sprang up rapidly in the early 1940s, using converted houses or specially designed pre-fabricated buildings. In 1946 the 100% Exchequer grant ceased, and in 1952 LHAs were empowered to make an economic charge instead of merely charging for meals. This resulted in a marked decrease in day nursery demand and patchy provision throughout the country, with considerable local variation in conditions and charges. A typical charge at present would be 7s a day, scaled down where necessary. There are now non-priority cases, mostly the children of nurses and teachers, and in such cases 10s—12s 6d a day is a typical charge.[4] It is well established that priority is given to families with illness, with only one parent, or with an illegitimate child. Increasing numbers of staff are NNEB-trained.[5]

Day nurseries are normally open from 7.30 or 8 am to 6 or 6.30 pm, and ordinarily close only for public holidays.

See also **Nursery assistants; Crèche**

REFERENCES
1. Ministry of Health circular, June 1966
2. Note, however, the Plowden Report 1967, Vol. 1, para. 343, viii: 'The education of children over three should be the responsibility of education rather than health departments.'
3. *Ibid.*, page 110, table 5.

4. In the circular on hospital day nurseries (1966) the Minister leaves the charge open but says that it should not normally be less than 5s a day (2s 6d a half day).

5. National Nursery Examination Board.

JHW

Day release *See* **Further education in England and Wales**

Day training colleges *See* **Teacher education in England and Wales**

Daydreaming Pre-school children can often be heard talking loudly to themselves or to imaginary friends. Later, this sort of dialogue and fantasy is turned into silent daydreaming, kept for odd moments of boredom or inactivity. A child (or adult) who daydreams excessively, however, may be using it as an easy but ultimately harmful escape from facing up to ordinary realities and relationships and, if this is so, may need some help in his personal adjustment.

Attempts to give this help by ridicule or brisk commonsense, however, may only succeed in driving the child further into his dream world. It is better for parents to respect the validity of daydreams to the child, and even enter into them if required. At the same time, though, they should very tactfully make available to the child situations such as play groups, casual street gangs, or friends invited home, which may help him to form real relationships that should ultimately prove more satisfying.

NT

Deaf Children's Society, National The NDCS is an organisation of deaf children's parents with the co-operation of medical, educational and welfare experts and of the ministers and local authorities. The Society is devoted to the whole emotional and social development of the deaf child. It promotes and ensures for these lonely children the maximum benefits and happiness from their home environment, educational facilities and the co-operation of the general public. There are 37 regional associations in England, Scotland, Wales and Northern Ireland.

31 Gloucester Pl, London, W1.

Deaf and partially hearing children Children born totally deaf will lack 'naturally acquired speech or language'.[1] They must therefore be taught mainly by methods independent of hearing. Other children, who hear only sounds of high intensity or who have a 'selective' hearing loss (e.g. for sounds of high frequency), may acquire speech only slowly or imperfectly. These 'partially hearing' children also require education by special methods— particularly auditory training to enable them to make the best use of their residual hearing. It is now generally the practice to separate deaf and partially hearing children for educational purposes: the latter can often be partially integrated with normally speaking children in special units attached to ordinary schools. The number of deaf and partially hearing children receiving special education in England and Wales is approximately 5,000, i.e. an incidence of considerably less than 1 in 1,000. Classes are limited to ten, and teachers are required to have additional training either by a university one-year course for qualified teachers or by passing the diploma examination of the College of Teachers of the Deaf.

Ever since the 18th century there has been lively controversy between exponents of the two different methods of teaching the deaf, the oral method and the finger-spelling or signing method. The oral method is now the one preferred in the UK. Children are taught to speak by watching and feeling the organs of speech and to follow speech by a combination of lip-reading and sound. Advances in electronics during the 20th century have produced

189

G*

greatly improved individual hearing aids, loop systems and amplifiers, so that children who would previously have been classified as totally deaf now receive some sound feedback which improves the intonation of their artificially acquired speech. There remain, however, some profoundly deaf children who cannot acquire intelligible speech; for them the use of a combined method with some finger-spelling is at present being reconsidered. Partially hearing children must be taught by the oral method, while deaf/blind children can use only finger-spelling interpreted by touch.

Other important advances during this century have followed on the realisation that training in auditory discrimination and speech must begin in the pre-school period. Nursery education is available from the age of two, and home teachers give advice to parents. Early diagnosis, especially the important differentiation from mental sub-normality, has improved so that few profoundly deaf children escape detection before school age. The identification of partially hearing children has been helped by the increasing use of pure tone audiometry: in 1963 half the LEAs in England and Wales were screening all new entrants to school by this means.[2]

Deaf children have great difficulty in acquiring the language of abstract thought and therefore are less likely than blind children to proceed to higher education. Selective secondary schools are available however for those who show high academic ability. The handicap is also a difficult one to accept emotionally, and because of communication difficulties personal relationships can easily be disturbed. Schools have been opened for deaf children with additional handicaps, the most recent being one for maladjusted deaf children.

Guidance and services for deaf children are provided by two voluntary societies: the Royal National Institute for the Deaf, 105 Gower St, London, WC1, and the National Deaf Children's Society, 31 Gloucester Pl., London W1.

REFERENCES
1. *The Handicapped Pupils and Special Schools Regulations*, HMSO, 1962.
2. *The Health of the School Child*, 1962–3, HMSO.

FURTHER READING
A. W. G. Ewing (ed.) *The Modern Educational Treatment of Deafness*, Manchester Univ. Press, Manchester, 1958.
M. Sheridan. *The Child's Hearing for Speech*, Methuen, 1948.

MW

Death gratuity After service amounting in the aggregate to five years of recognised and/or contributory service, the Secretary of State will pay to the legal personal representatives in the case of a teacher who dies while in contributory service, or (subject to such conditions as appear equitable to the Secretary of State) within 12 months of ceasing to be employed in such service, a death gratuity of (1) an amount not exceeding the average salary of the teacher's last three years of service, or (2) an amount equal to the lump sum which might have been granted had the teacher at the date of death become, by reason of ill-health, permanently incapable of serving efficiently as a teacher, or (3) the balance of his contributions at 3% compound interest, whichever is the greatest.

If a teacher dies after receiving the lump sum and pension instalments then, if the aggregate amount received is less than the average salary, the Secretary of State will pay to the legal personal representatives a supplementary death gratuity not exceeding the difference between the average salary and the aggregate amount actually received.

SEB

Decimal currency The government's decision to bring the UK into line with other countries by introducing, in February 1971, a system of decimal currency based on the £ and the new penny was announced in a White Paper (Cmnd 3164) in December 1966.

The decision to retain 'the familiar £' was based on the argument that it would be against 'the economic logic of history' to base the new currency on a unit of 10s: that is, to change to a major unit that had only half the value of the present £. If the 10s unit were adopted, there would be great difficulty in finding a generally acceptable name for the new major unit. It was also argued that a £ system would make it easier to translate from £ s d to decimals, that the £ unit would remain a 'familiar point of reference' and that under a 10s system many people might find difficulty in removing the £ from their minds as the standard of value. A 10s system would be cheaper to introduce in the case of slot-machines, but a £ system would reduce conversion costs for many business machines and also the costs of conversion of many non-machine methods of accountancy. Finally, there was a strong international case for retaining the £ as 'a symbol known throughout the commercial centres of the world'.

Under the new system, the £ will be divided into 100 pennies, which during the period of transition from one currency to another will be known as 'new pennies'. The three coins smallest in value (the new halfpenny, new penny and two new pence) will be of bronze, plain-edged; the five new penny and 10 new penny pieces are of cupro-nickel, milled-edged, and equal in size and weight to the present 1s and 2s pieces; the 50 new penny piece will be of another metal to be announced later. There will be no change in the denominations, specifications and designs of the present £1, £5 and £10 banknotes.

February has been chosen as the month for the changeover because February is the slackest time of the year for banks, retailers and transport undertakings. On a day to be appointed in that month the new system will be adopted by banks, most government departments and many non-governmental organisations. A long preparatory period is necessary, coupled with a short transition period, because 'a clean, nation-wide, overnight switch from £ s d to decimal working' is not practicable. Dual price labels will be used in shops, and conversion tables will be available. The Decimal Currency Board (appointed at the time of the White Paper) is investigating all possible means of publicising the change, and has in mind particularly the problems of school-children, the old and those who handle small amounts of cash throughout the working day.

The changeover will require the minting of some 9,000 million decimal coins and the conversion of $2\frac{1}{2}$ million business machines and the same number of slot-machines.

Decroly, Dr Ovide (1871–1932) By profession a doctor, Decroly began to be interested in education when he worked in a school for abnormal children. Later he provided a home for defectives (from which developed the Institute for Abnormal Children in Uccle, in Decroly's native Belgium). Finding that, in a home-like environment, he was obtaining better results from his children than were obtained in ordinary schools, Decroly sought—from 1907, when he opened a school for normal children known as the Hermitage—to apply his methods to the teaching of the non-defective. The essence of these methods was that the classroom should be used as a workshop, in which each child was free to follow his own interests within the framework of a careful analysis of children's needs: there being, in Decroly's view, four such needs—of food, shelter, defence and work. One of these needs formed a centre of interest for the work of each year. The teachers followed a systematic pattern of guidance: observation, association and expression.

Defence mechanism Sigmund Freud, the founder of psychoanalysis, believed that we have various ways of protecting ourselves from the anxiety caused by our own internal conflicts, and these he termed defence mechanisms. For example, an individual may repress altogether a memory which might seriously disturb him, or he may project the cause of his anxiety onto someone else rather than himself, such as the paranoid personality who feels he is being persecuted by others. Another individual may stick at a certain stage of his development, because of his fear of change and the unknown, or he may even attempt to retreat by behaving like a much younger person. This type of regression is often found with children who, when faced with a crisis, such as a sudden fright or even the birth of a new brother or sister, may themselves behave like babies and demand extra love and attention until they feel more secure again.

NT

Deferred annuity Teachers who contributed under the Elementary School Teachers (Superannuation) Act 1898 could, on attaining the age of 65, be entitled to such an annuity as their contributions under that Act might purchase. Application for the annuity was made to the Pensions Branch of the Department of Education and Science a month or two prior to the teachers' reaching the age of 65. Only certificated teachers were eligible to participate in this scheme.

Degree The main university award for the successful completion of a course of study is a degree. The first or Bachelor's degree is awarded at the end of the undergraduate course; this is either a classified or pass degree. For postgraduate studies there is a range of higher degrees: the Master's (though in Scotland this is still an undergraduate award), the higher Bachelor's degrees in some universities, and then the Doctor's.

London alone offers external degrees to students not in residence and studying elsewhere, either on their own or through correspondence courses or in other colleges of higher education.

Honorary degrees are conferred, not for completing a course, but as a university's way of recognising academic or public eminence.

Degree, Classified A Bachelor's degree is awarded as a result of the Finals examinations. It may be taken with honours, when the candidates are classified into grades: these are commonly First, Two-one, Two-two, Third (at Oxford they are First, Second, Third, Fourth). A First is a mark of considerable academic brilliance.

In theory the standard of classes, and especially of the First, is common to all subjects and all universities; this common standard is maintained by the system of external examiners. In fact there is a 'pecking order', which Oxford and Cambridge believe they head.

Degree, External *See* **Degree, First; Degree, Higher**

Degree, First The university award for the successful completion of an undergraduate course of study examined in Finals is a first or Bachelor's degree; and it can be either a classified or a pass degree (*qq.v.*). At Oxford, Cambridge and some of the new universities, the only first degree is a BA (Bachelor of Arts); but at other universities there is also a BSc (Bachelor of Science). For some first courses which are shorter than a degree course, a diploma is awarded. And, such is the confusion of terms, there are a number of specialised Bachelor's degrees for graduate courses of study (e.g. BLitt, BMus, BPhil).

Honours or classified degrees are commonly taken in a single subject (some 130 subjects are listed for all the universities). But in many universities it is possible to take two subjects (joint honours) or more rarely three (e.g. PPE at Oxford). The pass degree, on the other hand, is usually taken in a number of subjects, and is therefore sometimes called a 'general' degree: but erroneously, for in some universities it is possible, if difficult, to take a general degree with honours.

London alone offers an external degree for part-time study.

Degree, Higher After graduating, a student may proceed to various kinds of postgraduate study for a higher degree—if he is good enough and can obtain a grant or funds. The first of these is the Master's degree of Arts or of Science (MA, MSc). Formerly a modest research degree, it is now fairly generally a fourth-year course of further study, often including a dissertation. Oxford and Cambridge BAs do not study for the MA but may, after a period of years, purchase it from their university. (At the four older Scots universities, the MA is the first honours degree in arts.) In addition, many universities award other higher degrees, with a bewildering variety of titles, for a period of further study in a specialist field.

Then there are the higher degrees which are awarded for research and study in an approved topic leading to a thesis, normally for a full-time period of two or three years. All universities offer the PhD (at Oxford, Sussex and York, DPhil); and some also offer the MPhil or other degree for a research thesis of less ambitious scope. Universities have their own complex regulations for candidates for a higher degree who have graduated in another university, or who wish to undertake their period of study and research part-time or residing elsewhere. London alone offers an external degree.

Degree, Honours *See* **Degree, Classified**

Degree, Pass A Bachelor's degree is awarded as a result of the Finals examinations. It may be a classified honours degree (*q.v.*), or it may be a pass (or ordinary) degree. In a number of universities, candidates who fail to reach honours standard may be awarded a pass. But more commonly, candidates read throughout the course either for an honours or a pass degree and thus sit different examinations. The pass degree is taken in a number of subjects, seldom related to each other.

Delicate children The first special schools for delicate children, established in Germany in 1904 and in London in 1907, were called 'open air' schools because they provided food, rest and fresh air for pupils suffering mainly from tuberculosis and malnutrition. In 1945 the 'delicate' were listed as a separate category of handicapped children with the definition: 'Pupils not falling under any other category who by reason of impaired physical condition need a change of environment, or cannot, without risk to their health or educational development, be educated under the normal regime of ordinary schools.' There is no clear dividing line between delicate and physically handicapped children, but in the main the former are children whose impaired physical condition is not permanent. The schools today provide for a wide variety of conditions, but by far the largest group are respiratory conditions, especially asthma, and debility. Diabetic children do not usually attend special schools but can be accommodated in hostels from which they attend ordinary school. In these hostels they learn to manage their diet and insulin injections.

The environment of the school for delicate children today has been found suitable for children with mild emotional disturbance and/or educational retardation. The newest schools are normally heated and ventilated, but the provision of meals (breakfast, dinner and tea), nursing care, and rest is still considered important. Class size is usually well below the official maximum of 30. Delicate pupils remain in the special school only until they have recovered their health, but remedial education is now considered as important as physical care.

Invalid Children's Aid Association: 4 Palace Ga., London, W8.

FURTHER READING
The Handicapped Pupil and Special School Regulations, HMSO, 1962.
D. G. Pritchard. Education and the Handicapped, Routledge and Kegan Paul, 1963.

WM

Delinquency It is now thought that almost all children go through something of a delinquent stage, and that for most young people their first appearance in a juvenile court will also be their last. With persistent delinquency, however, where the crime is usually theft, there is often an association with emotional instability, defective home discipline, backwardness at school, and in some cases a family history of vice or crime. Not surprisingly, the greatest incidence of delinquency is generally found in depressed and over-crowded areas with low communal standards and suffering from lack of facilities and opportunities for young people. In such areas, it is arguable that quite serious delinquency may be a matter of social conformity as much as anything else. Dr John Bowlby has suggested another possible factor: some of the most persistently delinquent adolescents, who tend also to be emotionally maladjusted, may still be reacting against traumatic separation from home and parents during the first years of life. Other researchers have noticed the lack of a stable and understanding father in the lives of many persistent young offenders.

FURTHER READING
J. Bowlby. Maternal Care and Mental Health, World Health Organisation, Geneva, 1952.
C. Burt. The Young Delinquent, Univ. of London Press, 1925.
J. B. Mays. Growing up in the City, Univ. of Liverpool Press, 1954.

NT

Denmark (including Greenland and Faroes), Education in Education is free and compulsory between the ages of seven and 14 years (the primary stage), and secondary education after 14 years is free, as is most of higher education. In 1966 there were 2,836 primary schools, with an enrolment of 531,982; 101 secondary schools, with an enrolment of 27,571. Of these schools, 302 were privately owned. There were in 1966–67 Folk High Schools, 30 agricultural schools and 35 schools for home economics, with a total enrolment of 14,302; 21 nautical schools and colleges of marine engineering, with an enrolment of 1,573; 71 technical, vocational and apprenticeship schools, with an enrolment of 79,633; 187 commercial colleges, with an enrolment of 60,376; 32 teacher training colleges, with an enrolment of 20,482; and universities at Copenhagen (enrolment 16,874), Aarhus (enrolment 5,926) and Odense (enrolment 183).

The population of the country was approximately 4¾ million in 1966.

See also **Scandinavia, Education in**

Dental service, School See **School dental officer**

Dentistry, Qualification in The course of training in dentistry, leading to a degree or licence in dental surgery (BDS or LDS), is five or six years long and must be taken at a university dental school. Students having GCE A level passes in chemistry, physics and biology or zoology are granted exemption from the first year of the course.

General Dental Council, 37 Wimpole St, London, W1.

Department of Education and Science *See* **Education and Science, Department of**

Department of Scientific and Industrial Research *See* **Scientific and Industrial Research, Department of**

Depth psychology Some psychologists, impressed by the work of Freud and later psychoanalysts, feel that the reason and cure for certain serious individual neuroses must lie in an exploration of the childhood memories and unconscious feelings of the patients concerned. Techniques for doing this differ, although projection tests (*see* **Personality tests**) are now becoming increasingly popular. Amateur psychologists are often tempted to make their own interpretations of themselves or the people around them, and it is usually this over-enthusiastic response that has often caused ridicule in the past, rather than the work of responsible psychologists themselves.

NT

Deputy heads Local authorities are required under the Burnham Report to establish posts of deputy head teachers in all schools above a given size. The requirement is mandatory from Group 3 upwards, that is to say, in any school where there are 201 pupils or more. There is discretion available to local authorities to establish these posts in smaller schools if they so wish. Indeed, there is a requirement that in a primary school in Group 2 (unit total 101–200) where there are both infant and junior children the mandatory provision applies.

Deputy heads are not paid a consolidated salary but receive an allowance for their duties in addition to the salary otherwise payable to them as qualified teachers. The amount of the allowance varies according to the size of school, the smallest being £145 in a Group 3

school (unit total 201–300) and the highest £1,055 for a Group 13 school (unit total over 6,000).

These allowances are almost universally applied but there is provision in the Report enabling an LEA in the special circumstances of a particular case of a deputy head teacher, having regard to the duties and responsibilities involved, to pay a higher allowance if it deems such an improvement to be necessary.

SEB

Design Centre Opened in 1956, the Centre houses a permanent but constantly changing exhibition of modern British goods in current production, everything shown having been selected by committees of the Council of Industrial Design (*q.v.*) for qualities of design, which include functional efficiency, good workmanship, appropriate use of materials and good appearance.

28 Haymarket, London, SW1.

Detention The teacher is entitled to detain pupils for a reasonable period by way of punishment for disobedience unless it is for disobedience of an order which the teacher has no power to give. There is no maximum period laid down in law for the detention of pupils, the sole test being that of reasonableness, taking into consideration the circumstances of the case. It is important in this case, as in the case of corporal punishment, to have due regard to the regulations of the employing authority, and to the rules of the school.

See also **Discipline**

HP

Detention centres Penal institutions administered by the Prison Department of the Home Office, and established under the Criminal Justice Act 1948, which also abolished the sentence of corporal punishment and limited the courts' powers to commit people under 21 to prison. Detention centres were justified politically as an alternative to birching or imprisonment for youngsters; the first was opened in 1952, at a time of anxiety about an apparent rise in juvenile delinquency. Its purpose was described as giving a 'short, sharp shock' to young criminals. Nineteen centres were in operation in 1965, and more were planned to open in the following three years. Deterrence has been presented officially as the first aim of detention centres.

Junior centres take youngsters between 14 and 17; senior centres those over 17 but under 21. Adults may not be committed to them. Inmates experience a physically demanding routine with emphasis upon instant obedience to orders and smart appearance. In recent years a social worker has been appointed in most centres, but the large number of young people passing through each institution annually, and the authoritarian regime, make effective casework difficult.

The minimum sentence is three months; the maximum six months. Consecutive sentences may be awarded. All criminal courts, including magistrates' courts, have powers to commit youngsters to the centres. They are widely used by magistrates, who have consistently demanded more detention centre places since 1952.

The centres are regionalised, each serving a group of courts. There is no system by which offenders needing particular types of treatment are sent to detention centres offering facilities appropriate to them. The 'short, sharp shock', now a little blunted at some centres, is thus indiscriminately applied.

Educational activities are provided in the evenings by tutor organisers nominally employed by LEAs but responsible to the warden (i.e. governor) of each centre. Classes tend to be very formal and narrow in range. Financial provision for education is meagre. HM Inspectors of Education have the right to visit classes and comment upon them.

Since 1965 youngsters released from detention centres have been subject to compulsory aftercare under probation officers' supervision. More than 50% of those discharged are reconvicted within three years. Detention centres have been described variously as the most retrograde step in modern British penal policy and as a welcome method of keeping juveniles out of prison. There can be no doubt that they offer adolescents an experience of rigid authoritarianism unusual elsewhere in Britain.

FURTHER READING
Anne B. Dunlop and Sarah McCabe. *Young Men in Detention Centres*, Routledge and Kegan Paul, 1965.
M. Grunhut. 'Juvenile Delinquents under Punitive Detention', *British Journal of Delinquency*, Vol. 5, 1955.　　DLH

Development centres Perhaps the decisive origin of the recent movement to establish local centres where teachers might meet to discuss curriculum development lies in the work that has been done in connection with Schools Council or Nuffield Foundation projects (*q.v.*) and with the new Certificate of Secondary Education. Such work has given many teachers the experience of working together on new curricula for new purposes and of experimenting with syllabuses and teaching methods. However—and although centres have been set up in a number of areas—the form they might ideally take has still to be determined. It seems unlikely for some time to come that LEAs will be able to think in terms of special buildings. Meanwhile, there is considerable discussion of the aims of such centres (meeting in whatever accommodation is available) and of ways in which they might be organised.

An important spur to this discussion has come from the Schools Council itself, which has suggested that a standard pattern for centres throughout the country is 'neither desirable nor necessary'. LEAs should give such encouragement as they can, together with practical help where required in the form of accommodation, apparatus and secretarial assistance. There should be consultation between LEAs and teachers, and support should be given by universities and colleges of education. There should be interplay between national projects and local ones, but the local centres should be free to pursue ends that particularly concern them.

The first function of a development centre is to concentrate local interest and to provide opportunities for the hammering out and thorough testing of new ideas. Centres will also act as testing grounds for new methods suggested by national projects, and as channels through which the results of research and experiment in curriculum development can as quickly and informedly as possible be fed to the mass of teachers. In particular, reports on work in progress on national projects can be passed on, through the local centres, by the few who are able to attend courses such as those laid on by the Schools Council to familiarise teachers with national development work.

The Schools Council's view is that the motive power for this 'should come primarily from local groups of teachers accessible one to another'; and that there must be freely accepted and close collaboration between all concerned—teachers, LEAs, universities, colleges of education and others—with 'no hierarchy of initiative or control'.

See also **Curriculum reform** *and* **In-service training of teachers**

FURTHER READING
Curriculum Development: Teachers' Groups and Centres, Schools Council Working Paper No. 10, HMSO, 1967.

Deviation quotient *See* **Norm**

Devonshire Report (1872–5): Report of the Royal Commission on Scientific Instruction and the Advancement of Science Terms of reference: to enquire into scientific instruction and the advancement of science; to enquire what aid was desired from grants voted by Parliament or from endowments belonging to universities and colleges in Great Britain and Ireland; and whether such aid could be rendered more effectively. Chairman: the Duke of Devonshire.

The report made a detailed survey of scientific education at the universities and throughout higher education. It recommended that older children in the elementary schools should get more scientific education than was then available, and that training college programmes should be changed so that teachers were equipped to provide the instruction. It asked for more coordination between the Science and Art Department and the Education Department. There were also many recommendations for the reallocation of funds and the improvement of the status of the science teacher.

Dewey, John (1859–1952) Main works on education: *Democracy and Education, School and Society* and *Experience and Education.*

Dewey was in strong reaction against current conceptions both of human nature and society and of human knowledge, each of which had helped to shape the traditional system of schooling. This system assumed man to be self-interested, society properly to be divided between a narrowly trained labouring mass and a leisured few whose culture was merely ornamental, and knowledge to be a passively gained theoretical matter of books and ideas from the past rather than an instrumentally valuable matter of control over environment.

But social life, Dewey argued, involves a shared understanding of values, ideas, beliefs and practices, and education is an initiation into such life. Mind is not a ready-made collection of faculties externally related to things or institutions, but develops as natural impulses are selected and coordinated by our coming to share in a common life. The best form of society, democracy, is one in which there is a maximum of shared interest and social interaction, which is therefore without separation of distinct social classes, and which applies its knowledge to improving progressively its sources and means of satisfaction for the benefit of all.

Educational method must therefore centre round 'occupations': lifelike situations which permit social interaction and situational control, which spring from existing interests and which are sufficiently problematic to stimulate inquiry. Such inquiry should model itself on the scientific method of formulating a problem, putting up a hypothesis and then testing it. Its yield should be a continuous reconstruction of experience and growth in practical intelligence, with more and more connections seen and continuities opened up. Such a reconstruction and growth can have no aim beyond its own further development.

See also **Philosophy of education**

RFD

Diascope *See* **Visual aids**

Dickens Fellowship A literary society which aims to promote the enjoyment of, and assist in studies of, the life and works of Charles Dickens; to preserve places and objects associated with Dickens and his books and encourage others to do likewise; to support charitable objects in which he might have been interested (children, old people, etc.). The Dickens Fellowship was founded in 1902 and has over 60 branches in the UK and overseas. Journal: *The Dickensian*, published since 1905.

48 Doughty St (also Dickens House Museum and Library), London, WC1.

Dienes These multibase arithmetic blocks consist of a structured set of 'unit' cubes, 'longs,' 'flats' and 'blocks', providing experiences which help pupils to form the concept of place notation. (*See* **Mathematics, Teaching of.**) In the set 'base 4', the long is equal to 4 units, the flat to 4 longs, the block to 4 flats: that is, each is a power of 4. Varying bases emphasise properties common to all grouping and recording of numbers.

FURTHER READING

Z. P. Dienes. *Building up Mathematics*, Hutchinson, 1960.

Differentials In the teaching profession the term 'differentials' may be related to allowances payable in respect of additional qualifications and extra responsibility or to the unit total system which certainly has its impact on responsibility allowances. The former of these are dealt with elsewhere in this book under the appropriate headings, e.g. **Good honours degree allowance, Graded posts allowance,** and reference should be made to the specific heading for the qualifications and/or responsibilities involved. Here only the unit total system will be considered, which produces a pattern of school structure serving as the framework for the responsibility allowances for assistant teachers and the consolidated scale for head teachers.

At the present time the method used is to allocate the unit based upon the age of the child. Children below the age of 13 count as one unit (possibly $1\frac{1}{4}$ units after 1st April 1969). Those between the ages of 13 and 15 count as two, each pupil aged 15 and under 16 counts as four units, each pupil aged between 16 and 17 counts as six units and those over the age of 17 count as ten units. Since children in primary schools are all under the age of 13, the unit count and the number of children produce the same result. When the unit total has been ascertained, schools are placed in groups (*see* **Consolidated scales).** No attempt is made to alter the group placing of a school in the event of a casual change in the unit total; a review is made every three years when the group is established; the group placing remains the same until reviewed.

198

It should be noted that the escalation of units according to age for older pupils can have a very substantial impact upon the unit total and therefore the group of the school. Thus, a secondary school having say 600 pupils could have a unit total of more than 1,800. The result is that the secondary school would be placed in Group 9 whereas the primary school would be in Group 5. The impact on salaries is substantial. The salary of the head teacher would be greater by more than £885 per annum. The deputy head in the secondary school would receive about £380 a year more than his corresponding colleague in the primary school. In addition to this, the opportunities for the assistant staff in the secondary school for head of department posts and graded posts would be considerably greater.

The present system was introduced in 1956 after some eight years' experience of a unit total system where all children of statutory school-age counted as one unit. The change made in 1956, producing a count of two at the age of 13 instead of the age of 15, has caused resentment in the teaching profession and attempts are constantly being made to remedy the position.

In special schools the method of weighting is different. Each child is counted according to a handicap weighting irrespective of his age. The 'unit total' (S) is at present calculated on the following basis:

	For each pupil count
Delicate, educationally sub-normal children	4 units
Blind, partially sighted, epileptic, physically handicapped children	5 units
Deaf, partially hearing, maladjusted, and children suffering from speech defect	6 units

Children in a hospital school should count on the basis of the handicap in accordance with the weightings given above. Indeed, it should be emphasised that these handicap weightings apply to children rather than schools. Thus, if educationally sub-normal and physically handicapped children were in the same school, the counts would be four and five units respectively. Where a child has more than one handicap, the higher or highest handicap weighting is the one which is applied to the child.

These units were revised during the currency of the 1967 Burnham Report, having been referred to a sub-committee by the arbitrators.

SEB

Diocesan Purchasing Service The DPS provides an advisory service to schools, convent schools and all Catholic establishments desiring to purchase suitable equipment at the best prices. It is an official unit of the Roman Catholic Church, but assists other denominations on request. Established in 1962 with the purpose of introducing manufacturers and suppliers to diocesan buyers, the DPS now often acts as the buying agency drawing up purchasing schedules in conjunction with architects engaged on major projects. In obtaining better terms and services it can claim to have saved the Catholic Church something like £300,000 per annum. The same overall services are provided for the smallest school or unit; because of the DPS's negotiating power throughout the UK, the financial benefits to the large buyer apply also to small units.

Showrooms at 16 Holland Villas Rd, London, W14 contain a wide range of exhibits; visitors from schools are welcomed at any time.

Direct grant schools Direct grant schools occupy a somewhat anomalous position midway between the independent schools and the state schools in England and Wales (and in Scotland too, where the regulations are broadly the same). Each of these schools has its own governing body and is financed partly from endowments and fees and

199

partly from a per capita grant directly from the DES (or the Scottish Education Department.) Thus it does not come under the control of the LEA. In return for the grant, however, the school is required to make available a certain number of places for the use of the LEA which pays the fees of pupils allocated to them. Under the 1959 Direct Grant Regulations the proportion of 'free places' must not be less than 25% of the previous year's intake of the school, and only by the special agreement of the governors can the proportion exceed 50%. The residuary places are paid for by the parents, provided that the pupils concerned have reached the standards of attainment and levels of ability set by the school.

Apart from a few technical schools, the vast majority of direct grant schools are grammar schools (there are about 180 in England and Wales). Almost without exception they enjoy a reputation for high standards of scholarship. Many of them are represented on the Headmasters' Conference (*q.v.*) and vie in status and prestige with the leading public schools. Size of classes and teacher-pupil ratios tend to be more favourable to academic success than in the state-maintained schools: indeed, the performance of direct grant schools at GCE O and A level and in the Oxford and Cambridge open scholarship examinations is held to be superior to that of the independent schools and the state grammar schools.

For this reason, there is a strong body of opinion which urges the need for the retention of the direct grant schools. Equally strong is the criticism that their existence serves to perpetuate the class distinction which has bedevilled English secondary education from its beginnings. A third view is that these schools may offer a solution of the problem of integrating the independent sector within the statutory system. The government's decision to adopt the comprehensive principle in the reorganisation of secondary schools raises a number of fundamental issues which are bound to affect the future status and function of the direct grant schools—issues which remain to be decided.

WKR

Direct method *See* **Modern languages, Teaching of**

Director of Education *See* **Chief Education Officer**

Disablement allowances *See* **Breakdown pensions**

Discipline 'Discipline' is certainly one of the most dangerous words in a teacher's vocabulary. This is so even in the most difficult teaching circumstances—in, say, a poorly staffed down-at-heel secondary modern in a dilapidated part of a city, where children come to school with no sense of excitement about education, with little feeling that their own future is likely to be enriched by their schooling, and with a powerful impression that the teacher is an enemy and an alien. Even here, where the word 'discipline' is most likely to leap into a teacher's mind as a description of the sanctions by which he or she might hope to master recalcitrant children—even here it seems probable that an undue focus on the word used in this sense may take the teacher further from and not closer to a solution of his problems. A more useful attitude, even in desperate circumstances, may be to think in terms of relationship rather than of discipline.

The impact of the teacher on the children, and vice versa—which is what is at stake—is clearly a matter of relationship. Every relationship in life, it is true, has its discipline. In the home, reasonable relationships between parents and children rest on a discipline. But when we have said that, we realise how odd it is to use, in describing the subtle and complex framework of rules spoken and unspoken that gives shape to family relationships, a word so loaded as 'discipline'. The relationship has from its earliest days a network of purposes, and it is these purposes that underlie and give rise to family discipline. It is because the family wants to get on with its tasks, and with its general purpose of being a family with a coherent and tolerable way of life, that the necessary techniques evolve. In a good family, the rules seem incidental, since behind them is always seen to lie the sensible intention of creating a form of family life reasonably satisfying and convenient and profitable to all the members of the family.

The relationship between a teacher and the children he teaches must, whatever the circumstances, strive to be just such a relationship as is found in good families. And just as in families, the essence of good order in the relationship lies in the sense of a common purpose. The teacher faced with what he sees as 'disciplinary problems' may find, however luxurious it at first appears, that he is well-advised to re-define his difficulties, and to see them as difficulties of relationship, and primarily as a problem of creating with his children a shared sense of purpose. Leaving aside the immemorial and unalterable difficulties of the case— that the best-adjusted of children at times find the school situation irksome, their high spirits difficult to control— a teacher's task anywhere, if he wishes to bring order to his classroom, is to establish a feeling that what is done there is on the whole purposeful and relevant and well worth doing. Where 'discipline' is generally bad, his task will be harder. But it still remains his task, and the quest for 'good discipline' must still involve him in attempting to reach these ends. There is no means of achieving real order worth having, other than by convincing the children, if necessary against severe odds, that schooling is meaningful.

Obvious peremptory sanctions do not achieve this end. The cane, and most obvious punishments and sanctions, do not achieve it. They may, in the hands of a resolute teacher (rarely in those of a desperate one), bring about a sterile orderliness; but it *will* be sterile, since the real problems of the classroom will sulk beneath it, unresolved. Nevertheless, once he has begun to think like this, a teacher may well consider his task in terms of 'discipline', but in a broader and less frantic sense than is commonly given to the word.

Knowing that order will result only if he makes the work of the classroom significant and interesting, the teacher must still ask himself what the techniques are that foster this end, and what the habits are that tend against it. Here is a field of inquiry which every teacher must embark upon for himself. He will have to ask himself such questions as: What part in the pattern of the children's day is played by any particular lesson I take? What sort of background have the children come from? Where are they going next? Is the physical environment of my classroom, in so far as I have power over it, a good or bad one? What sort of impression do I myself create? Are the things I do in the classroom clearly done? Do I create an atmosphere of expectation and alertness, or of boredom or uncertainty or reluctance? Do I seem to think well of the children, and expect well of them, or do I give the opposite impression? Is what I am doing today linked to what I did yesterday and to what we shall do tomorrow? Have I taught myself to be sufficiently at home in the classroom to give full play to my powers and qualities? Can I, quite naturally, be light-hearted, dramatic, solemn, quizzical, or simply interested, and so fill the classroom with a lively natural sequence of moods, or am I confined to one note, as teachers too often are?

In the answers to questions of this kind, rather than in a desperate search for sanctions, may lie the teacher's hope of achieving 'discipline' where it is absent. It is true that in many situations this may leave him wondering what to do about the behaviour of particular children who, for reasons beyond his single control, are so disaffected that they create serious problems in the classroom. No one, within the limits of such punishment as teachers are allowed to give, has the right to lay down the law as to what a teacher should do in such circumstances. He has a clear duty towards the rest of his children. He cannot tolerate anarchy even if brought about by a particular problem of behaviour that may be, by him alone, insoluble. In many cases the roots of such disturbed conduct lie outside the school, in the social or family condition of the child. Too often, it must be said, a school fails to recognise that such problems, likely to occur anywhere, need the combined attention of the whole staff, and where necessary or useful the co-operation of outside agencies, and ought not to be left to individual teachers to attempt to solve, each in his own way. The real disciplinary difficulties of some schools might easily be traced to a handful of special cases which should be the responsibility of the entire staff, pooling at once their wisdom and their firm intention to do everything their ingenuity suggests to reconcile a disturbed child (always an unhappy one) to his schooling. In the meantime, in schools where there is no sense of the importance of such a shared and determined approach to special problems, a teacher must do what he can. Resort to the obvious sanctions may damp the situation down, but will not cure it.

No teacher needs telling what sanctions are available to him. Most of them are venerable, from the giving of lines (which ruin a child's handwriting) to beating on the hands (which, since the hands are primary educational tools, seems the most perverse

as also one of the most cruel of all school punishments). Resort to such sanctions, in the search for 'discipline', seems likely to continue for some time. But successful experiments in some areas and under some authorities of teaching without corporal punishment, such straws in the wind as the strong suggestion by the Plowden Committee that corporal punishment be legally excluded from the school, together with the slow but certain disappearance of the view that the teacher's attitudes to his children must of necessity be severe and defensive, are bound to carry us further and further from the stage at which it is thought profitable to consider 'discipline' as a separate problem, rather than as an incidental facet of the whole conduct of teaching and learning. Quite certainly the major reasons for the persistence of the older view lie in the inadequacy of our educational provision, which leaves so many children still able to feel that schooling is not of obvious profit to them; the rift between the essential outlook of the schools, which must be disinterested, and the outlook of much of the world outside them, which lays the stress elsewhere; and imperfections in teacher training, which fails to foster the personality of some teachers in such a way that they are capable of the subtle exercise in relationships that is at the core of teaching—and that, in almost any circumstances whatever, where it is worked through successfully, makes talk of 'discipline' irrelevant.

FURTHER READING
Richard Farley. *Secondary Modern Discipline*, Black, 1960.
ILEA. *Punishment in Schools*, 1966.
C. W. Valentine. *The Difficult Child and the Problem of Discipline*, Methuen, 1950.

EB

Discussion techniques These were given a great boost by the adult education activities planned and conducted for members of the British armed forces during World War II. The raising of the school leaving age in 1945 and the return of teachers to schools, together with the recruitment of some 37,000 emergency-trained teachers, gave a fillip to the use of discussion techniques in schools. This was progressively lost with the extension of public examinations to all kinds of secondary schools. The techniques may regain importance with the further raising of the school leaving age in the 1970s.

Meanwhile, with older students discussion is an important device. It demands initial preparation and the acquisition of a general body of data. In sophisticated forms, small sub-groups discuss specific facets of the data, each sub-group ultimately reporting its discussion to the parent group.

DJJ

Dissenting academies After the Act of Uniformity 1662, nearly 2,000 dissenting rectors and vicars lost their livings, by refusing to conform; one of their first resources was to teach. Those who had been tutors at Oxford and Cambridge offered an education of a more advanced kind than others. Until the Toleration Act these were furtive and migratory. After that, especially when helped by funds, they became institutionalised and by the 18th century acquired, with trustees and subscribers, a standing and position in the intellectual world which has led to them being compared to universities. H. P. Roberts (1930) has listed those in Wales, and Dr McLachlan in *English Education under the Test Acts* (1931) has described 72 of these academies, while Dr Ashley Smith in *The Birth of Modern Education* (1954) has considered their curricula and their tutors.

Pupils at these academies were by no means all dissenters, nor were they all preparing for the dissenting ministry. On the contrary, the value of a knowledge of mathematics (for surveying and navigation), medicine and law was well appreciated and indeed prevented

several of them from being subjected to persecution as nurseries of schism after the Schism Act 1714. Ironically, it was as an 'arsenal in which subversive doctrines and arguments were forged' that Burke later castigated one of their leading academies—Hackney.

Perhaps the most outstanding academy was Warrington, which lasted from 1757 to 1783. Former students at dissenting academies include three archbishops, two bishops, two Lord Chancellors, a Master of the Rolls, a Lord Chief Justice, several professors, Daniel Defoe, William Hazlitt, T. R. Malthus, the scientists Dr Joseph Priestley, Dr Price and Dr Southwood Smith, the social reformers Thomas Percival and John Howard, the technologist Dr J. A. Roebuck, and the great ironmaster John Wilkinson.

From the time of the Napoleonic wars the academies were restricted to the training of clergy.

FURTHER READING
I. Parker. *Dissenting Academies*, Cambridge University Press, 1914.
H. McLachlan. *English Education under the Test Acts*, Manchester University Press, Manchester, 1931. *Warrington Academy: its History and Influence*, Manchester University Press, Manchester, 1943.
J. W. A. Smith. *The Birth of Modern Education*, Independent Press, 1954.

WHGA

Dissenting schools The penal clauses of the Acts of Conformity that forced some clergy to train youths forced others to take in boys. Later a movement began for endowing such schools. One at Gravel Lane in London was founded in 1687 and, during the 18th century, about 60 similar schools were endowed, educating about 2,000 children.

The Schism Act 1714 was aimed directly at non conformist tutors and schoolmasters and limited their scope. But in 1779, non conformists were released from the obligation to subscribe to the articles of religion before teaching; this enabled them to enter grammar schools in towns. Yet for long afterwards a number of specifically nonconformist private academies persisted, as Matthew Arnold's fictional Dr Archimedes Silverpump, PhD in *Friendship's Garland* (1871) shows.

WHGA

Divergent thinking For some time it has been felt that conventional intelligence tests may not do justice to a type of thinking loosely defined as 'divergent', which excels in lively imagination or unusual or bizarre ideas rather than in deductive logic and conventional responses, as found in 'convergent' thinking (*q.v.*). Divergent thinkers often have extremely valuable and original ideas, and one way of trying to spot them on intelligence tests is to include various open-ended questions where there is no obvious right or wrong answer, and the candidate is given the chance to write as much as he likes in a direction he chooses for himself. (A typical open-ended question of this sort might be: 'How many uses can you think of for a brick?') Dr Liam Hudson has suggested[1] that 'divergers' in the UK have tended to specialise in arts rather than sciences, perhaps because they prefer to study personal rather than impersonal problems.

REFERENCE
1. Liam Hudson. *Contrary Imaginations*, Methuen, 1966; Penguin, 1967.

Divisional executives Under the Education Act 1902, and subsequently until 1945, county councils were the LEAs for higher education in their areas, and for elementary education too, except in numerous non-county boroughs and urban districts whose size entitled them to be LEAs themselves for elementary education only. These elementary education LEAs survived ministerial attempts to abolish them until they disappeared under the Education Act 1944, whereupon the county councils became the sole LEAs throughout their areas, for primary,

secondary and further education. An attempt, however, by the Minister, immediately before the preparation of the 1944 Bill, to console the elementary education LEAs, about to be dispossessed, by proposing that they should have district sub-committees of their county education committee, was strongly opposed.

Instead, therefore, the Education Act 1944 created a new type of public body for education, a Divisional Executive, and required county LEAs to prepare schemes of divisional administration for their areas. These statutory schemes were subject to the Minister's approval, and they provided that some of the executive functions of the county LEA should be delegated to divisional executives, with respect to primary and secondary education in the divisions of the county. The nature of such functions was indicated by the Minister in *Circular 5*, 1944.[1] Divisional executives, however, are required to work under the financial control of their county LEA, and, to avoid inconsistency of administration within a county, to observe the county's regulations prescribed for the whole county. Some other educational functions are also retained by the county LEA.

It has been said that favourable comment on the system of divisional executives seems to be based on its theoretical possibilities rather than on its practical achievements. Nevertheless, though complicated, and involving additional administrative expense, the system serves the purpose of giving local public representatives the opportunity to exercise some local educational functions of a not insignificant kind, to that extent mitigating or avoiding local frustrations.

Twenty-one rural and sparsely populated counties have no divisional executives. The other 37 counties have some 180 divisional executives between them, of which some were created in districts which previously had no LEA for elementary education. Thirty-two of the divisions are known as 'excepted districts'. Normally they are county districts with a population of 60,000 or more, or which had 7,000 or more pupils in their elementary schools in 1939. In an excepted district, the divisional executive is the council of the district itself. Other divisional executives are composite bodies, consisting of public representatives of the county and the county districts concerned, and co-opted members. The council of an excepted district normally exercises rather wider powers than the average divisional executive. It also prepares its own scheme of divisional administration for submission for the Minister's approval, the district thereby being excepted from the county's scheme, hence the term 'excepted district'.

REFERENCE
1. G. Taylor and J. B. Saunders. *The New Law of Education*, Butterworth, 1965.
See also **Administration, Educational**

FB

Divisional Executives for Education, National Association of The Association was formed in 1946 as a consequence of the administrative arrangements established by the Education Act 1944. That Act made the county councils the LEAs, but directed that they should establish bodies responsible for primary and secondary education, acting through schemes of delegation. These schemes were made by the county authorities, except in the case of the larger towns which were empowered to frame their own schemes. Divisional executives (there were originally approximately 200 of them) undertook the local day to day administration of the education service. In 1946 they established the National Association to act as a centre for information, advice and research, to make submissions to the DES, local authority associations and other bodies, and to organise annual conferences.

Education Offices, Walpole Rd, Gosport, Hants.

Dog Spotters' Club A junior organisation run by the National Canine Defence League, the Club aims to encourage children to take a genuine and permanent interest in canine welfare. Supplies of Dog Spotters' forms and of wall charts are sent to teachers on request.
10 Seymour St, Portman Sq., London, W1.

Domestic science *See* **Home economics**

Domestic Science, Association of Teachers of The Association's aims are to foster and advance the teaching of domestic science, to safeguard and raise the status of teachers of the subject, to promote the exchange of opinions among them, to communicate resolutions and suggestions to the DES, LEAs and other organisations, and to give members legal aid and advice.
Hamilton Hse, Bidborough St, London, WC1.

Dominican Republic, Education in Education is free at the primary stage and, when places are available, compulsory between the ages of seven and 14. 1964–5 statistics: 4,901 primary schools (enrolment 517,769); 395 intermediate and secondary schools (enrolment 52,998); 205 technical and evening institutes (enrolment 28,440); five teacher training colleges (enrolment 432). Two universities: state maintained at Santo Domingo (5,503 students), Catholic at Santiago de los Caballeros (700). Population: approximately 3¾ million.

Don Derived from the Spanish title (which in English was applied by transference to any distinguished man, leader or adept), the term 'don' as a description of a head, fellow or tutor of a college in an English university dates from the mid-17th century. Though it should properly retain this narrow application, the term is now popularly used to refer to anyone who teaches in a university.

Drama Advisers, National Association of The National Association of Drama Advisers was formed in 1961 to provide an organisation for members to unite and discuss the promotion of desirable policies for the development of speech and drama. Membership was at first limited to full-time drama advisers, but has recently been opened to area drama tutors and teacher-advisers. The Association, besides fostering the interest of its members, has promoted courses for teachers both locally and nationally, has recently published a booklet *The Design of Drama Spaces in Secondary Schools*, and has representatives on several bodies in the fields of speech, drama and education.

Hon. Sec.: Mrs Margaret Birkett, County Offices, Westholme, Leicester St, Westgate, Sleaford, Lincs.

Drama Association, Educational Founded in 1943, the EDA is dedicated to the development of child drama based on the principles and methods of Peter Slade, Drama Adviser to Birmingham, and permanent director of the EDA since 1947. Groups are trained by Peter Slade in children's theatre, adult theatre and dance.

Catering for an international membership, EDA also provides short courses on child drama, a summer school on 'Drama in Education', a magazine *Creative Drama*, and a loan service of photographs and films of child drama, dance and theatre. It publishes pamphlets and plays, and assists Peter Slade in a course organised by the Birmingham Education Committee and leading to a Child Drama Certificate, the first of its kind in the world.

Drama Centre, Reaside School, Rea St South, Birmingham, 5.

Drama Associations, Standing Conference of Membership is open to LEA bodies and institutions for dramatic education in England and Wales. SCDA promotes amateur dramatic activity from primary school age upwards.

26 Bedford Sq., London, WC1.

Publications: *Newsletter*; occasional papers.

Drama Board An examining board for amateur drama. It issues Certificates of Association to successful candidates.

Gen. Sec.: Leo Baker, 26 Bedford Sq., London, WC1.

Drama in education The position of drama in education has changed radically in the past 20 years. Although there are still those who consider its function to be completely satisfied by the annual performance of a text of literary merit behind the confines of a poorly equipped mock proscenium stage, the general body of opinion is moving towards an understanding of the need for a more flexible creative approach fully integrated into the curriculum.

Drama in education encourages the imaginative communication of significant experience between children at their own level, and accepts that this should be an expression of the personality of the child and not an impression of the personality of the teacher, who is much more a catalyst for personal and group relationships than he is a director of theatre.

Drama begins in the world of the child's imagination, very often in absorbed personal activity. After this, the child should find himself in a permissive atmosphere which encourages him to express his experience. As the experiences of the world of the spirit grow richer, and as he grows in his ability to express them, then he will wish, and should be encouraged, to share and communicate them. This development from inner experience, through personal expression, to full communication appears to be a cornerstone of modern educational drama.

Drama should offer to children a stimulating, exciting situation which promotes and improves their language flow and general speech ability; offers them an opportunity to examine the emotional and spiritual factors in their lives and to learn to use them fully and control them sensitively; encourages them to extend and control the potential of their own speech and movement—the potential of their personality in action. There are many life situations which clearly tell children who they are and what they must expect to become. Drama is the pre-eminent activity which should encourage the child, in the safe-keeping of the teacher, to put out new antennae of self and discover *for himself* who he would like to be and who he might be able to become. In brief, drama should offer a really deep and practical exercise in growing up and getting on with others.

Educational or creative drama sets out to engage the imagination of the child and to stimulate expression and communication through movement, dramatic dance, voice and speech. Much drama work is divided as follows, in this order: (a) individual, (b) pairs, (c) groups and (d) class. The children are learning to share ideas and action, and this involves discipline and self-control and helps to foster a sensitivity towards the ideas and moods of others.

If drama is to be satisfactorily taught, proper equipment must be provided, and children must be able to move about freely in a space which is acoustically insulated, so that they will not disturb the rest of the school and outside noise will not destroy their concentration.

The basis of drama in education is improvisation—spontaneous, imaginative activity involving movement and speech. The free-wheeling, unselfconscious dynamic of the world of the spirit that exists in the playground is harnessed and channelled to provide experiences which are exploited in depth in school. It is this depth of experience which short-circuits the slow learning process in life and crystallises and makes clear the human condition in the child's terms. In drama the child learns how to play upon his own personality, much in the way a violinist plays his violin. The paradox is that, though self-consciousness is a barrier to expressive work, a main aim in drama is to help the child reach a proper consciousness of self.

Inhibitions, a lack of absorption and concentration cause most of the difficulties. To overcome this many teachers use movement work as a way into improvisation. Unfortunately, this 'way-in' has often remained the exclusive activity of the drama lesson or has led to a false division between movement, drama and speech, just as an equally false division has sometimes been encouraged between drama and theatre. Conscious dramatic activity begins with the understanding that different circumstances need different behaviour. Each of us, in fact, presents a different persona under varying conditions and to different people. This is acting. It is this acting that is involved in the drama lesson. It means learning to be sensitive to one's own proper needs as well as to those of others; learning that giving is only fruitful if someone wishes to take, learning to accept from others quickly, readily and completely. The natural leader must play out the part of the subordinate to gain a fuller concept of leadership; the natural subordinate must learn, by accepting and taking leadership, the responsibility that lies on him, who apparently rejects it. Educational drama begins with the reality of personal relationships in the school.

A proper integration with other subjects, especially the expressive ones, seems to be desirable—a free flow between dancing, painting, sculpting, music-making, reading and writing.

Drama would appear to be a most useful catalyst in promoting an approach to block and team teaching. The 'creative workshop' is an essential if there is to be any real carry-over in the minds of children.

Many teachers use music and percussion to help stimulate movement; more are beginning to use them to stimulate voice and speech work. A more recent feature is the use of directional lighting, together with blocks, ramps and steps, curtains and drapes in a blacked-out free space. The darker spaces allow the more inhibited to progress happily, secure in their retreat, but cut off by no physical barrier; entry to the light is easy and immediate. The lighting itself encourages an understanding of colour and form. The handling of technical equipment by the children in an expressive way should help to marry the two cultures. The creation of a *genius loci* by electric and electronic aids does much on its own account to release children's imaginations. Not only can the self be transported, but it can be done so demonstrably into a world of mystery and magic through technical aids.

If the drama lesson has used these aids at intervals throughout the child's life, the connection between drama and theatre will be seen as a natural one with no major step to be taken at any one point—save the first, where the child may need to be positively encouraged to give active, physical reality to the world of the imagination and the spirit.

There should be a free movement from absorbed experience to its physical expression. This is a very personal development and difficult to assess. In drama the process can work in reverse order. The execution of a simple movement task works kinaesthetically, and the imagination is engaged as a result of the activity. In one approach imagination leads to action; in the other action leads to imagination. Both are appropriate, but require different standards of assessment.

The general progression would appear to be: creative play in the infant range; improvisation in the junior; polished improvisation in the lower secondary and complete plays in the upper secondary. The work seems to develop best when reference is made at all stages, with different biases, to all aspects of the work: so that at the extremes, the sixth form is still engaging in creative play movement and improvisation and the infants are trying to find out how many different ways they (not the teacher) can say 'Mummy, I want to go to the fair'—a study of text.

A complementary activity to the drama arranged within the curriculum is a visit from a children's theatre company. The more progressive of these companies are relating their performances, which often involve complete audience participation from beginning to end, directly to the work in schools, even to the extent of staying after the performance and undertaking follow-up work with children and staff. The work of Brian Way at the Theatre Centre has been invaluable in this field.

There has been a considerable expansion in drama with young people—out-of-school, in youth clubs and in youth drama groups. Many areas have now established youth drama groups which have very strong connections with the local secondary schools. This method of bridging a gap or forming a link seems very fruitful. It also ensures that the young people's work is not plucked out of its proper environment and brought together on a county or national basis for an otherwise unnecessary performance potentially harmful to theatre and young people alike.

Throughout the whole range of drama in education there is a concerted effort to prevent compartmentalising. The past haphazard arrangement has not been fruitful, and there should be the possibility of a continuing development from primary school to adult theatre. To this end some LEAs are providing theatre workshops or drama centres to which come school children, youth groups, teachers, students and amateurs. This mixing and integrating in a full-time centre seems a wholly admirable idea, and it is hoped the idea will be taken up by more authorities. In 1966 there were more than 70 colleges of education with drama departments, numerous drama schools and a number of universities operating various schemes of drama training. If drama in education is to take its rightful place in the next decade, attention must be paid to the fact that there is a need for some re-organisation and regularisation if the recruitment of actors for the theatre and drama teachers for schools is not to be a haphazard one. Out of this regularisation might come an opportunity for the actor/teacher. The more the barriers are taken down between drama and theatre, amateur and professional, the greater the need for competent all-rounders in classroom, children's theatre, youth drama groups, dramatic societies and theatre workshops will be seen to be. It is to these actor-teachers that drama in education must look.

FURTHER READING

A. F. Alington. *Drama and Education*, Blackwell, 1961.
Rose Bruford. *Speech and Drama*, Methuen, 1963.
E. J. Burton. *Drama in Schools: Approaches, Methods and Activities*, Herbert Jenkins, 1955.
Alan Garrard and John Wiles. *Leap to Life—An Experiment in Youth Drama*, Chatto and Windus, 1957.
Bertram Joseph. *Acting Shakespeare*, Routledge and Kegan Paul, 1960.
Peter Slade. *An Introduction to Child Drama*, Univ. of London Press, 1958.
Building Bulletin No. 30: Drama and Music, HMSO.
The Design of Drama Spaces in Secondary Schools, National Association of Drama Advisers/Strand Electric.

DBo

Drama League, British Supported by an annual grant from the DES, the training department of the League specialises in training leaders in the amateur theatre. Summer schools and courses are provided for producers, actors, students and teachers.

9–10 Fitzroy Sq., London, W1.

Dr Barnardo's The aim of Dr Barnardo's is to care for children in need, and in doing so, to give them a knowledge and understanding of the Christian faith. This national child care society was founded in 1866 by Thomas John Barnardo, a young Irish medical student who planned to be a missionary in China on completing his studies at the London Hospital.

While helping with the terrible epidemic of Asiatic cholera which swept London in 1866, Barnardo discovered great poverty and neglect among the children of the East End. With a group of friends he started a school in a donkey stable in Stepney, and from this has grown the vast child care organisation which now cares for over 8,000 children in the British Isles, Australia and Kenya.

Booklets and films about the work of Dr Barnardo's are available from the Information Department, Dr Barnardo's, Stepney Causeway, London, E1.

Dressmaking *See* **Needlecraft, Teaching of**

Driving, Teaching of, in schools It may be said that three basic requirements are necessary in a safe driver: good powers of concentration, observation and imagination, and these qualities can, to a very large extent, be developed by a qualified driving instructor. Over the already-formed character of an adult learner-driver, however, the instructor has very little control. Thus it is beginning to be realised that a firm foundation for a safe driving temperament should be laid before the learner-driver reaches the age of 17, when he may drive a vehicle on the public roads.

There are two primary sources of instruction for young people at school:

the Royal Automobile Club and the Automobile Association.

The RAC course The RAC instituted a standard course of instruction for use in schools in 1962, and about 400 schools have now embarked on this course. The syllabus is designed to train students to a standard of driving proficiency higher than that required for the Ministry of Transport driving test; it includes two subjects not covered by the Ministry test—a driver's responsibilities and breakdown routine.

Students begin in the classroom with seven periods of theoretical instruction before progressing to two periods of practical instruction on a car within school or private grounds. There follow 30 hours of group driving tuition when three students having reached 17 years of age are given instructions in a dual-control vehicle on the public roads, learning from each other's mistakes while each in turn gets a minimum of ten hours instruction at the wheel. The usual age for commencing the 'Junior Driver' course is 16, when the law already allows the student to be a partial road user. The course is designed to instruct young drivers in three main fields: a driver's responsibilities; driving proficiency; breakdown routine. The instruction is carried out by RAC Registered Instructors or other authorised persons.

The AA scheme Another major research project into the teaching of motoring and roadcraft in schools began in the autumn of 1968, sponsored by the Automobile Association and the Company of Veteran Motorists, and supported like the RAC course by the DES, the Ministry of Transport, and the Road Research Laboratory. The project is mounted in Lancashire with support from the LEAs and police in the area.

Seven grammar schools are taking part, and 600 sixth-formers from these schools have been divided into two groups. One of the groups receives driving instruction at school, and the later driving record of the young people concerned is assessed by a research team from the University of Salford and compared with the performance of members of the other group. The study of motoring in depth is part of the curricula of the seven schools, and includes tuition, by a teacher specially appointed, in traffic rules and their enforcement; the causes of accidents; the history, economics and mechanics of the motor car; road traffic vehicle engineering; the characteristics of drivers and traffic citizenship. There is also, for the 300 sixth-formers in this first group, driving instruction given in dual control cars, skid pan training and a driving test of Ministry of Transport standard. It is hoped that the results of the project, intended to cover four years, will establish a blueprint for the future use of all senior schools.

WAG

Drugs During the years 1959–67 the number of addicts to dangerous drugs (see below under *The Law* for definition) known to the Home Office rose from 454 to 1,729. The number of addicts to amphetamines and other drugs is unknown although the *British Journal of Addiction* (November 1965) estimates the total at 400,000. The proportion of young people under 20 who are addicted to dangerous drugs is increasing.

ADDICTS TO DANGEROUS DRUGS
AGED UNDER 21 KNOWN TO HOME
OFFICE, 1959–66

'60	'61	'62	'63	'64	'65	'66	'67
1	2	3	17	40	145	329	359

Various terms are in current use. *Drug addiction* is a state of periodic or chronic intoxication produced by the repeated consumption of a drug (natural or synthetic). Its characteristics, according to the 1961 Report of the Interdepartmental Committee on Drug Addiction, include an overpowering desire or need (compulsion) to continue taking the drug and to obtain it by any means; a tendency to increase the dose, though some patients may remain indefinitely on a stationary dose; a psychological and physical dependence on the effects of the drug; the appearance of a characteristic abstinence syndrome in a subject from whom the drug is withdrawn; an effect detrimental to the individual and to society.

Drug habituation is a condition resulting from the repeated consumption of a drug. The characteristics of this condition include a desire (but not a compulsion) to continue taking the drug for the sense of improved well-being which it engenders; little or no tendency to increase the dose; some degree of psychological dependence on the effect of the drug, but absence of physical dependence and hence of abstinence syndrome; detrimental effects, if any, primarily on the individual.

The World Health Organisation Expert Committee (1964) recommended that the term *drug dependence* should replace the terms *drug addiction* and *drug habituation*. *Drug dependence* is defined as 'a state arising from repeated administration of a drug on a periodic or continual basis'. In each case the type of drug used must be stated: thus, for example, there is drug dependence of the morphine type and drug dependence of the amphetamine type.

Repeated use of some drugs causes *physical dependence*. The body learns to live with the drug, which must be taken to prevent withdrawal symptoms occurring. *Psychic dependence* is when a person feels unable to function normally without a drug, which enables an escape to be made from problems and frustrations.

No section of the community is immune from the risk of drug dependence. Three factors need to be present to cause drug dependence: a basic personality weakness, a crisis, and the availability of a drug.

Drugs of abuse: Narcotics, e.g. opium, opium derivatives (morphine, heroin, codeine), synthetic opiates (meperidine, methadone). *Nicknames:* Heroin—H, Horse, Harry, etc. *Effects:* Drowsiness, sleep, reduction in physical activity. Side effects may include nausea, vomiting, constipation, itching, flushing, constriction of the pupils. Anxiety, restlessness, lack of sexual interest, absence of menstruation. *Dependence:* Physical; psychic.

Stimulants, e.g. (a) amphetamines (benzedrine, dexedrine, methedrine), ephedrine, phenmetrazine (preludin). *Nicknames:* Benny, bombers, pep pills, dixies. *Effects:* Stimulates the central nervous system. Increases alertness, produces excitability, feeling of well-being, talkativeness, drunken appearance. *Dependence:* Psychic. Physical dependence occurs only when taken with barbiturate in a combined tablet. (b) Cocaine. *Nicknames:* C, Charlie, Coke, girl, snow. *Effects:* Excitability, talkativeness, reduction in feeling of fatigue. Feeling of euphoria, anxiety, fear, hallucinations. Dilates pupils, increases heartbeat and blood pressure. *Dependence:* Strong psychic.

Sedatives, e.g. barbiturates (amytal, luminal, nembutal, phenobarbitone, seconal, soneryl), other sleeping tablets and alcohol. *Nicknames:* Yellow terrors, goof balls, sleepers. *Effects:* Slurred speech, staggering gait, reactions sluggish, irritable, antagonistic, impression of euphoria. *Dependence:* Principally psychic, slight physical.

Hallucinogens, e.g. (a) LSD 25, mescalin, dimethyltryptamine psilocybin. *Nicknames:* Acid, sugar, sugar lumps. *Effects:* Weird distortion of time, perspective, colour, movement, sound. Insight and revelations may produce emotional reaction. Vivid hallucinations. *Dependence:* Psychic, almost no physical. (b) Cannabis. *Nicknames:* Marijuana, ganga, dagga, grass, charas, hash, hashish, hemp, kif, mary-jane, pot, rope, tea, weed. *Effects:* Feeling of euphoria, exaltation, dreamy sensation, distortion of sense of time, distance, vision, hearing. Panic and fear may be experienced. Dizziness, dry mouth, diarrhoea, nausea, vomiting, hunger for sweets. *Dependence:* Psychic, almost no physical.

Different drugs produce different effects, depending on dose and frequency of administration. Detection of drug use by observation is very difficult, and without urine tests evidence of drugtaking is difficult to obtain. Certain patterns of behaviour are suspicious and the teacher should be conscious of these. Many young people who use drugs do so at the weekend, so uncharacteristic behaviour may occur at the beginning of the week and frequent Monday absences may be significant. Extra tiredness or sleepiness after the weekend, lack of interest and willingness to co-operate in pupils who are normally amenable and co-operative, irritability, depression, lack of concentration, secretiveness and untrustworthiness may all be pointers to drug-taking.

Evidence of drug use amongst children should be reported by a teacher to the head-teacher who is responsible for informing the School Medical Officer of Health. If drugs are found the Chief Education Officer should be immediately informed as it may be necessary to report the matter to the police.

The law In the UK four acts of parliament embody legislation in respect of drugs. The Dangerous Drugs Act 1965 together with the Dangerous Drugs (2) Regulations 1964 makes the unauthorised possession of opium, morphine, heroin, cocaine, cannabis and other specified drugs illegal. The Dangerous Drugs Act 1967 requires that all addicts to dangerous drugs must be notified to the Home Office and prohibits doctors from prescribing heroin and cocaine for addicts unless under licence. The supplying of these drugs will be limited to the staff of treatment centres set up by the Ministry of Health. The Drugs (Prevention of Misuse) Act 1964 makes unauthorised possession or importation of scheduled drugs an offence. The Pharmacy and Poisons Act 1933 and the Poisons Rules 1964, 1965 permit authorised sellers of poisons to dispense Schedule IV drugs to patients with prescriptions. Barbiturates, some amphetamines and other sedatives are in Schedule IV.

Treatment The Addiction Unit at All Saint's Hospital, Birmingham, which was established in 1964, is one of the pioneer organisations in this country. The criterion for cure suggested by the World Health Organisation is when an addict has abstained from drugs for five years. There are two standard methods of treatment of physical dependence—the gradual and abrupt withdrawal of the drug. Gradual withdrawal permits the patient to take the drug under medical supervision in reduced quantities over a period of time. This method is costly, time-consuming and not very successful in curing patients.

The abrupt withdrawal of the drug (referred to as 'going cold turkey') is used in most institutions. Without the drug the addict is bad-tempered, restless and irritable. He yawns, sneezes, has watery eyes, hoarseness of voice and muscular weakness develops. Chills, hot flushes, vomiting, diarrhoea are experienced as muscles twitch and painful muscle cramps occur. There is inability to sleep, together with severe tremors. The patient may become hysterical or delirious. Sometimes death occurs, but where withdrawal is successful the problem remains of supporting and rehabilitating the addict.

Education All schools should include information about drugs in their health education programme. Teachers have a vital role in preventing the development of drug abuse. Material should be presented factually without moralising or preaching. The infant school presents an early opportunity for teachers to assist children to be aware of the dangers of taking pills, tablets or medicines in mistake for sweets. In the junior school references might be made to questions of health and illness, the use of medicines for prevention and cure of disease, the dangers of improper use, the effects of drug abuse on health and behaviour, techniques of refusing drugs when offered them, the effect of dependence on future life. In the secondary school, consideration could be given to the history of the use of drugs, to types of drugs, drug abuse, problems of drug abuse in different countries, the law relating to drugs, the effects of drugs on personality and behaviour, methods by which people are introduced to drugs, techniques of refusing drugs, the treatment of drug dependence, and the social effects of drug-taking.

FURTHER READING

Drug Addiction, Report of the Interdepartmental Committee, HMSO, 1961.
Drug Addiction, Second Report of the Inter-departmental Committee, HMSO, 1965.
E. Harms (Ed.). *Drug Addiction in Youth*, Pergamon, 1964.
J. Larner and R. Tefferteller. *The Addict in the Street*, Penguin, 1966.
P. Laurie. *Drugs*, Penguin, 1967. *The Teenage Revolution*, Blond, 1965.
K. Leech and B. Jordan. *Drugs for Young People: their Use and Misuse*, Religious Education Press, Oxford, 1967.
R. E. L. Masters and J. Houston. *The Varieties of Psychedelic Experience*, Blond, 1967.
S. O'Callaghan. *The Drug Traffic*, Blond, 1967.
E. M. Schur. *Narcotic Addiction in Britain and America*, Tavistock, 1963.

KR

Dual System This took shape in England and Wales in 1870 when the rate-aided secular and undenominational board schools were established to fill up the gaps in the existing system of religious grant-aided voluntary schools (*See* **National Society**). When the 1902 Act replaced school boards by LEAs the voluntary schools (in spite of opposition by the non-conformists) obtained rate-aid, and Welsh local authorities, who were tardy in providing that aid, were officially told that the Board of Education would deduct the amount due from its grant to the local authority and pay it to the managers.

Attempts to overturn the Dual System in 1906 failed when Augustine Birrell's Bill was withdrawn. So was another presented two years later by Reginald McKenna.

The recommendations of the Hadow Committee in 1926 stimulated a re-organisation of all-age schools. Three years later the Board offered 50% grants to provide separate secondary schools. When these grants were withdrawn in 1931 the problem of the all-age country church schools became acute. To solve it, the Education Act 1936 made provision for LEAs to make 50-75% grants for building senior schools to prepare for the raising of the school-leaving age to 15 by September 1939. These schools were to be known as 'special agreement schools', and were to offer both denominational teaching by LEA-appointed 'denominational' teachers, as well as non-denominational teaching on 'agreed syllabus' lines.

These agreed syllabuses, the first of which, the Cambridgeshire, was published in 1924, certainly did much to cool down Anglican and such free church opposition as remained to state education, so advocacy of the voluntary case, essential in the Dual System, was increasingly taken over by the Roman Catholics, who resisted the NUT's objection to denominational schools with 'closed' headships, clergy 'right of entry' and 'tests for teachers'. When the voluntary schools were offered three futures by the 1944 Act— to become 'aided' (and obtain 50% of their costs from the government), to become 'controlled' (and obtain 100%), or to be 'special agreement' schools under the 1936 Act—the Catholics unanimously chose to be 'aided'.

H

Further pressure on secondary school building in post-war years raised the percentage of the costs obtained from government grants to 75% (by the Education Act 1959) and 80% (by a further Act of 1966).

See also **Anglicans and education; Free Churches in education; Catholic education**

WHGA

Duke of Edinburgh's Award The Duke of Edinburgh first offered his Awards in 1956 to boys between 15 and 18 years of age. The aim was 'to help the young generation, first to discover their talents and then to use them, particularly in the service of others.' In 1958 the scheme was extended to include girls.

Today the scheme is available for the use of organisations catering for boys and girls between 14 and 20. It can also be taken up by individuals who do not belong to any youth organisation or club.

There are three Awards: the Bronze Stage Award for those between 14 and 17, the Silver Award (15 to 18) and the Gold Stage Award (16 to 20). Any boy or girl over 14 years of age can enter the scheme by obtaining a Record Book (price 5s) from any of the user organisations; he or she then, in consultation with adults running the scheme locally, chooses activities from each of the four sections and sets out to reach the required standard in each activity.

Three sections are common to boys and girls: Service, which calls for training in subjects such as first aid, life-saving, youth leadership and home nursing; Pursuits and Interests, calling for perseverance and sustained effort in drama, woodwork, judo, fencing, dressmaking, sailing and music, etc.; Expeditions, involving journeying in small groups, on horseback or cycle or by canoe or small boat. A fourth section, for boys, is Fitness, in which they are required to reach fixed standards in athletics, swimming or physical efficiency; Design for Living is aimed at helping girls to become well-groomed, poised, good home-makers with organising ability and skill.

Duke of Edinburgh's Award Office, 2 Old Queen St, London, SW1; 10 Palmerston Pl., Edinburgh 12; 9 Cathedral Rd, Cardiff; 49 Malone Rd, Belfast.

JE

Dullness See **Ineducable children**

Dunce's Act Under the Education Act 1876 (q.v.), conditions were laid down for the employment of children between the ages of 10 and 14; it was made illegal to employ such children unless they had a certificate which showed they had passed Standard IV in the three Rs, or had made 250 attendances at school for each of five years. This provision led to the Act being known as the Dunce's Act.

Dyslexia In 1878 the phrase 'word-blindness' was first coined by a German neurologist to describe the condition of patients of normal intelligence, education and vision who were unable to read or spell simple words. Since then many different words have been used to describe this phenomenon, the latest being 'dyslexia'. Dyslexic children are often of good intelligence; but for some reason that no-one understands they seem confused between left and right, are prone to mirror-writing (q.v.), and have enormous difficulty in reading and spelling. They frequently become very muddled about the correct order of letters in front of them in even quite simple words.

There is still controversy over the relative importance of neurological or psychological disturbance as a cause of dyslexic symptoms. Most authorities however, would agree that there is such a thing as dyslexia in the sense of some sort of minimal brain dysfunction, but that we should be very careful of diagnosing it while there are other more obvious factors, such as a broken educational record, backwardness or some sort of maladjustment capable of producing the same effect. Genuine dyslexia seems to be at its worst between 6–12 years, and occasionally improves of its own accord during the early teens. There is now a Word Blind Centre for dyslexic children in London, set up by the Invalid Children's Aid Association.

FURTHER READING

J. Money. *Reading Disability*, Johns Hopkins Press, Baltimore, Md, 1962.

M. Vernon. *Backwardness in Reading*, Cambridge Univ. Press, 1957.

NT

E

Early Childhood Education, World Organisation for Founded in 1948, this organisation (known as OMEP, from its international title: Organisation Mondiale pour l'Education Pre-Scolaire) exists to promote greater understanding of children under eight years of age, and to share between different countries the experience and knowledge gained through the study of young children during their formative years. OMEP is an international, non-governmental educational organisation, and membership is open to any organisations and persons of any race, creed or nationality. World assemblies are held every two years. National committees have been established in 24 countries.

World president: Professor Ase Gruda Skard, Department of Child Psychology, Oslo University, Norway. UK National Committee: The Housing Centre, 13 Suffolk St, London, SW1.

'Early Leaving': Report of the Minister of Education's Central Advisory Council (1954) Chairman: Sir Samuel Gurney-Dixon. Terms of reference: 'to consider what factors influence the age at which boys and girls leave secondary schools which provide courses beyond the minimum school leaving age; to what extent it is desirable to increase the proportion of those who remain at school, in particular the proportion of those who remain at school roughly to the age of 19; and what steps should be taken to secure such an increase.' Producing figures,

the results of a survey, that showed that social class played a highly significant part in achievement at school, the Report urged that maintenance allowances for needy children staying on after 15 should be increased; that family allowances should be paid in respect of all children still at school; and that more grammar school places should be provided.

Earnings related benefits These were introduced into the National Insurance Scheme in 1966. Their purpose is to provide something more by way of income during periods of sickness or unemployment than has hitherto been possible through the flat-rate benefit. Where the income is less than £9 per week only the flat-rate benefit can be secured and there is no requirement to pay extra contribution. Over £9 per week, the earnings related supplement is one-third of the weekly earnings in the previous year, with a limit placed at £30 per week. Thus the greatest earnings related supplement is £7 per week, and this can be secured only by those who earn £30 per week or more. This benefit only begins to operate when an illness lasts more than 12 days. To pay for these benefits a contribution amounting to approximately ½% of salary between £9 and £30 per week is payable both by the employer and employee (the actual amount varies from 1d to 2s 1d per week).

It should be noted that in occupations such as teaching there is usually a good sick-pay scheme providing full pay for specified periods. Such pay, however, is reduced by the amount of benefit a teacher receives through National Insurance. Thus, unless a teacher suffers a long illness resulting in half pay or less from the Scheme, the chief benefits are those relating to unemployment and the long-term benefit of graduated pension.

SEB

East and West Friendship Council The Council exists to arrange for hospitality in British homes for non-European students from overseas. 101 Gower St, London, WC1.

Eccles, Lord (b. 1904) As Sir David Eccles, Minister of Education 1954–57 and 1959–62.

Economics, Teaching of Economics as a school subject has grown rapidly. Between 1956 and 1966 A level passes in economics and associated subjects rose by over 500%. Such a rise is attributable mainly to the introduction of economics at sixth-form level as a specialist subject. But the teaching of economics is not confined to sixth-form specialists: it is frequently included in general studies courses for sixth-formers and many schools now include it as an O level subject. Recently CSE (Certificate of Secondary Education) courses have been established which include economics.

This rapid development can be ascribed partly to the general interest in current affairs, but this is not the sole reason for teaching the subject. The aims of teaching economics are to provide knowledge about the environment in which men produce and trade goods and services (descriptive economics); and to find out whether there are any structures or patterns in such economic behaviour (analytical economics). This second aim is important because description by itself will not necessarily encourage logical thought about the subject and may leave

unquestioned the saying 'economics is common sense', which is a dangerously limited view of the subject. It follows that there is also a purely vocational reason for teaching economics, as groundwork for a business career.

Although economics has first established itself in the sixth form both at A level and as an extra O level, training of the ability to reason about economic problems should not be limited to sixth-formers. By careful choice of subject-matter and adoption of the 'developmental' approach, 14- and 15-year-old pupils who may not enter sixth forms can be taught to think about economics principles (e.g. division of labour can be initially demonstrated by the family group). Recent experiments, some based on American experience, have extended the teaching of economic ideas to younger children.

The basic idea of the developmental approach is that, *whatever the age of the pupils*, it is important that they all handle some concrete, often numerical, examples of economic principles, in order to develop the skill of abstract thought. Pupils will construct tables and draw diagrams from demand and supply data, showing how quantities of a good purchased and supplied will vary with price, and how cost varies with output. Owing to the complexity of real economic data, such exercises are usually from hypothetical examples, but able sixth-formers may manage to handle some real-world examples. Major industries (e.g. car manufacturing, steel, oil and electricity generation) and particular trades (e.g. grocery) can be studied in detail to provide examples of economies of scale, methods of competition, contribution to exports and imports. Pupils should be familiar with the most important economic indicators, e.g. the retail price index, index of wages, percentage of the working force unemployed, and the bank rate. Field work will assist in giving reality to economic concepts.

Visits to factories are an obvious example. Some schools combine geography and economics field studies.

Mathematical skills (e.g. the ability to draw and interpret a graph) required from pupils studying economics are no more than the normal for their age and ability, but at A level, above-average mathematical ability will permit quicker mastery of certain relationships. Economics is being increasingly used in sixth-form time-tables as a bridge subject, which can be combined either with arts or science subjects.

Testing of pupils' ability is done mainly by the traditional essay, but this can be complemented by individual or group projects, and more objective multiple choice questions are being introduced in examinations.

Economics is a 'circular' subject, with all its parts interrelated, so the order in which the topics of the syllabus are studied can vary greatly, but the basic concepts of opportunity cost underlying our economic choices, and price determination by supply and demand, will be met at all stages, and so an initial treatment of these must come early in the course. Other major topics at A level are: the factors of production (land, labour, capital, and the entrepreneur), population, industry (structure, finance, location), theories of monopoly and competition between firms, national income (measurement, distribution), trade unions, wage bargaining, money and banking, monetary policy, fiscal policy, inflation and deflation, the determination of the level of national income and employment, international trade (theory of comparative costs, structure of balance of payments, finance of trade), state control of industry (nationalisation, restrictive practices legislation), economic growth and planning. In O level courses most of these topics are studied, but for non-examined work, both in the sixth form and below, it is beneficial to con-centrate on a few topics, which may be particularly relevant at the time.

FURTHER READING
N. Lee (Ed.). *Teaching Economics*, Economics Association.

GH

Economics Association Founded in 1947, the Association has 1,142 members, most of them lecturers and teachers of economics. Its aims are to promote the study of economics and to provide an organisation for the exchange of views and experience on methods of teaching the subject. Book lists, film lists and information on careers are issued at regular intervals, together with handbooks and pamphlets on teaching problems and film strips.

President: Sir Arnold Plant. Vice-President: Rt Hon. Michael Stewart, MP. Chairman: J. L. O. Ciano. Hon. Sec.: R. F. R. Phillips, 110 Banstead Rd South, Sutton, Surrey.

Economics of education Many of the great economists of the past two centuries, including men with such diverse political and analytical views as Adam Smith, Karl Marx and Alfred Marshall, have been aware of the economic importance of education. It is, however, only since the mid-50s that the economics of education has become an established and rapidly growing branch of economic studies. The reasons for this rapid development are essentially twofold: on the one hand, it has become increasingly clear to economists that 'human capital' is at least as important a component of economic growth as physical capital; on the other, the rapid expansion of national resources devoted to education has led economists and educational administrators to seek methods of ensuring efficient utilisation of these resources.

Education as an investment in human capital
Since the second world war economists working on problems of economic

development have made a number of major statistical discoveries which have resulted in a wide recognition of the investment element in education. Roughly speaking, this means that the allocation of economic resources to education, as well as being a good thing in its own right—the consumption element—also makes an important contribution to subsequent economic growth. These statistical discoveries can be summarised under four headings:

(1.) Rich nations appear to have more and better educated people than poor nations. The same results are found if a single nation is studied at different periods in its history.

(2.) It is not possible to explain satisfactorily the economic growth of any nation in terms of capital accumulation and labour force growth only. There is a third or residual factor which many economists have associated with education. As much as half the economic growth of some countries has been attributed to this third factor.

(3.) Comparisons of the lifetime earnings of people with different levels of educational attainment have revealed that the rate of return on educational expenditure has in the past varied between about 10% and 30% (where education is provided free by the state, the rate of return *to the individual* who stays on at school can, of course, be much higher than this).

(4.) Structural changes in the economy as development proceeds cause a relative increase in the need for qualified manpower (doctors, engineers, etc.) and a relative decline in the need for less qualified manpower (unskilled manual workers, farm labourers, etc.).

All of these statistical findings are subject to severe reservations. However, they all point in the same direction and there is little doubt that any country, rich or poor, which wishes to secure continuing economic growth must devote considerable attention to its educational system.

Efficient resource utilisation in education The rapid expansion of educational expenditure in most countries, both as a result of the investment approach mentioned above and the growing demand by individuals for the social, cultural, and economic benefits of education, has led to a growing interest in educational efficiency. Overall measures of educational productivity are difficult to take because of the lack of suitable definitions and measures of educational output and because the process of transforming the inputs of pupils, teachers, buildings, equipment, etc. into outputs of educated people is extremely complex.

Nevertheless, a vast amount of work is being undertaken with a view to ensuring that the subjects taught and the content of curricula are in accordance with economic and social needs, that drop-out of students from uncompleted courses is minimised, that teachers and classrooms are utilised efficiently and that the size of classes is economically efficient in relation to the age of pupils and the subject being taught. Recently work has started to assess the economic advantages of new teaching aids such as programmed learning, teaching machines and television.

FURTHER READING

G. Beneviste. *The Economics of the New Educational Media*, International Institute of Educational Planning, Paris, 1965.

C. S. Benson. *The Economics of Public Education*, Houghton Mifflin, New York, 1961.

M. Blaug. *Economics of Education* (selected annotated bibliography), Pergamon, 1966. *The Rate of Return on Investment in Education in Great Britain*, Manchester, 1965.

W. G. Bowen. 'Assessing the Economic Contribution of Education: An Appraisal of Alternative Approaches', *Report of the Committee on Higher Education (Robbins Report)*, Cmnd. 2154–IV, Appendix IV, HMSO, 1963.

F. Harbison and C. A. Myers. *Education, Manpower and Economic Growth*, McGraw-Hill, New York, 1964.

H. F. Parnes (ed.). *Planning Education for Economic and Social Development*, OECD, Paris, 1963.
T. W. Schultz. 'Investment in Human Capital', *American Economic Review*, Stanford, Calif., March 1967.
John Vaizey. *The Economics of Education*, Faber and Faber, London, 1962.
OECD. *Economic Aspects of Higher Education*, Paris, 1964. *The Residual Factor and Economic Growth*, Paris, 1965. *Handbook of Statistical Needs for Educational Investment Planning*, Paris, 1966.
UNESCO. *Economic and Social Aspects of Educational Planning*, Paris, 1964.

GLW

Ecuador, Education in Education is free and compulsory only where school places are available. In 1962 a five-year plan was instituted to provide an additional 850,000 school places, and in 1965 plans for the establishment of an adult education authority were drawn up to organise the work of 1,300 literacy centres. 1965–6 statistics: 131 kindergartens (14,184 enrolments); 6,992 primary schools (813,677 enrolments); 252 secondary schools (61,975 enrolments); 220 technical schools (40,126 enrolments); 39 teacher training colleges (13,260 enrolments); 5 higher education institutes (318 enrolments); 7 universities (13,827 enrolments). The population of the country was approximately 5 million in 1966.

Edgeworth, Maria (1767-1849) Maria was the second child of R. L. Edgeworth, a utilitarian who (like his friend Thomas Day, *q.v.*) determined to put into practice the educational ideas of Rousseau (*q.v.*). Edgeworth conducted the experiment of bringing up his elder son on the pattern set out in Rousseau's *Emile*. The boy was dressed unconventionally, and was subjected to experiences designed to make him unafraid and indifferent to privation: 'He had all the virtues', Edgeworth wrote, 'of a child bred in the hut of a savage, and all the knowledge of THINGS which could be well acquired at an early age by a boy bred in civilised society. . . .' The experiment

was nevertheless not a success. Edgeworth persisted in his educational experimentation, however, the raw material being provided by the large family that resulted from his four marriages. Maria, novelist and writer of children's books, collaborated with him in the writing of *Practical Education*, a summary of the conclusions that Edgeworth and his family had reached after a quarter of a century of educational experience in the home.

Many of the Edgeworths' ideas have become commonplaces of progressive thinking on education—for example, they stressed the importance of toys (and thought it important that a child should not hesitate to destroy them); they argued that a child's attention to teaching can be secured only if the teaching is clear, does not try to achieve too much at once, and is interlarded with periods for physical exercise. They believed that the study of geography and history should be rooted in the contemporary world, and mathematics in concrete experience and not in abstractions. Experimental science should be approached through a consideration of everyday phenomena (a starting point for chemistry, for example, might lie in the study of butter-making).

The Edgeworths differed from Rousseau in suggesting that learning to read is an important early acquisition, and in being sceptical about the value of play as a teaching method. They followed Plato in regarding imaginative literature as over-stimulating to the emotions (they were strongly in favour of emotional restraint), and they were doubtful of the educational value of poetry ('vague and . . . exaggerated description'). They believed oral English was the best basis for written English, and that conversational usage was the best approach to grammar.

Education, Central Society of Set up in 1836 under the presidency of

Lord Denman, the Central Society existed to bring about an improvement in education by secular means. It urged that the cause of education could be fostered by offering definite civil advantages to those who had been educated, and by imposing disadvantages on those who had not. It attacked the voluntary system, contending that it had 'not only not worked well, but worked nearly as ill as any system . . . could'. Its reports were sharply critical of the working of the National and British schools, pointing in particular to the fear shown by these schools of imparting secular knowledge.

Education Act 1876 This Act established school attendance committees in districts where no school boards had been created. It was introduced by Lord Sandon, and violently opposed by the church, which saw it as a measure to force dissenters to attend available schools. But Sandon, together with the opposition, forced the bill through, although it was weakened and gave the committees only the power to make laws enforcing school attendance, without compelling them to do so. Compulsion came in 1880.
See also **School boards**

Education Act 1880 This Act, introduced by A. J. Mundella, made school attendance up to the age of 10 compulsory, compelling all school boards and school attendance committees to introduce bye-laws immediately. At 10 a child could obtain an educational certificate entitling him to leave, but if he had registered too few attendances he had to go on to 13. Employers of children between 10 and 13 who did not have the educational certificate became liable to a penalty.
See also **School boards**

Education Act 1889 This Act empowered county councils to levy a penny rate for technical education.

A bill was originally introduced in 1887 allowing LEAs to decide whether or not they would have technical education, but this was dropped because of political complications. But in 1888 the Local Government Act was passed by which county councils were empowered to direct sections of education.

Education Act 1897 This Act allocated extra finance to voluntary schools (£615,000) and to board schools (£514,000), but failed to clear up the confusion as to who should distribute the money, or to eradicate the overlapping of the various educational provisions as recommended by the Bryce Commission (*q.v.*).

Education Act 1902 This, the first really comprehensive Education Act, rationalised the various recommendations of preceding reports already implemented, and introduced a sense of coherence into the education system.

The Act laid the foundations of the control of the LEA over education in its area, and limited the supervisory powers of the Board of Education. Although the Board of Education could inspect school activities closely, it had no power to enforce a certain rate of progress. The Act was a step towards the unification of the education system, and led to the setting up of county secondary schools and teacher training colleges. Expenditure was initially limited to a twopenny rate.

Education Act 1906 This Act provided for school meals, and gave the LEAs the authority to provide these and the necessary premises. This was the result of the findings of the Interdepartmental Committee on Physical Deterioration, which established that many children were underfed. LEAs were empowered to pay for these meals from the rates, where they could not obtain finance from voluntary associations.

H*

Education Act 1907 This Act empowered the LEAs to provide medical treatment for schoolchildren. It was introduced as a result of the work of Margaret McMillan, who had been working for a long time to establish a series of health centres to inspect and treat schoolchildren. Medical treatment, or provision for it, became compulsory 11 years later.

See also **School Medical Service**

Education Act 1910 This Act, also known as the Choice of Employment Act, empowered the LEAs to establish juvenile employment bureaux to advise boys and girls under 17 on their choice of career.

Education Act 1918 Also known as the Fisher Act, this changed the structure of the finance of education, by providing block Treasury grants to cover part of the costs being met by the rates. Fifty-seven existing grant schemes were simplified to two—elementary and higher education. Elementary education was aided on the same basis as grants laid down in 1917, calculated at 36s per child, plus three-fifths of the teachers' salaries, plus one-third of all other educational expenditure, and minus the product of a sevenpenny rate. Higher education was paid for at a flat rate of 50%. The whole scheme was devised to encourage the local authorities to spend more on education.

Education Act 1936 This Act raised the school leaving age to 15 with effect from 1939, but implementation was prevented by the war. There had already been an attempt to introduce such a measure in 1931, but the voluntary schools said that they could not meet the costs. Between 1931 and 1936 they were assured that they would receive grants to cover up to 75% of the cost, and this provision was incorporated into the Act.

Education Act 1944 Having as its purpose 'to reform the law relating to education in England and Wales,' the 1944 Education Act (sometimes known as the Butler Act, after Mr R. A. (now Lord) Butler, the Minister responsible) introduced radical changes in the law relating to education. It replaced the former Board of Education by a Ministry, and created a Minister whose duty it was to direct national policy and ensure that it was carried out by local authorities. The Minister had power to apply compulsion to a backward authority.

The number of LEAs was reduced from 315 to 146 by making the county and county borough councils the local authorities for education. (*See* **Administration, Educational.**) The Act set up Central Advisory Councils (one for England and one for Wales) having greater power than the Consultative Committee (*q.v.*) which they replaced in that they could of their own initiative advise the Minister on matters of educational theory and practice. (Since the passing of the Act they have been largely occupied with inquiries on which the Minister has asked their advice.)

Education was reorganised in three stages: primary (for pupils up to 12), secondary (for pupils over 12 and under 19) and further (for pupils over the school leaving age). The compulsory school leaving age was raised to 15—though this provision of the Act was not implemented until 1947. Universal free secondary education was introduced, and all fees were abolished in maintained schools. Education was to be in accordance with 'the age, ability and aptitude of the pupil'. It was a parent's obligation to see that this was carried out in the case of his own children; though this did not mean that school attendance was compulsory, since any parent with the requisite knowledge and skill might instruct his own children or engage a a private tutor to do so. Denominational schools were absorbed into the state system under the title of 'aided' or 'controlled' schools. Religious education and a daily act of worship were made obligatory in every school, but parents retained the right of withdrawal, and no teacher was compelled to give religious instruction.

From a date to be specified there was to be compulsory registration and inspection of independent schools: a provision not implemented until 1957. LEAs were made responsible for medical inspection and free medical and dental treatment of schoolchildren, for the provision of milk, meals and other refreshments and, in case of need, for clothing, board and lodging, and also for the special education of children under handicap (*see* **Special education**). LEAs were authorised to pay fees for pupils at fee-paying schools, to pay maintenance grants for children in maintained schools and to grant scholarships and awards for further and higher education. It was also made their duty to provide for leisure-time occupation in organised cultural training and recreational activities, to provide nursery schools where necessary and to establish county colleges for the part-time education of boys and girls who after the age of 16 did not attend a secondary school or an institution of higher education (the last two provisions have not yet been implemented). Finally, the LEAs were required to pay teachers according to Burnham scales (*q.v.*), and equal pay was introduced.

The 1944 Act has been followed by a number of amending Acts: the Education Consolidating Act 1946; the Education (Miscellaneous Provisions) Act 1953, which revised the conditions governing payment of grants towards the building of new aided schools on new building estates, and gave assistance to voluntary schools in their building programmes in such areas; the Education Acts 1959, 1962 and 1964 (*qq.v.*); and the Remuneration of Teachers Act 1963 (*q.v.*).

Education Act 1959 This Act was intended primarily to encourage the voluntary schools to increase their programmes. They were given a 75% grant, instead of the previous 50%, to provide secondary schools for pupils from their own primary schools. To ensure the necessary number of teachers for this expansion, the grant to the voluntary teacher training colleges was raised from 25% to 75%.

Education Act 1962 This Act revised arrangements for grants to students (*q.v.*) and also changed the law relating to the school leaving age. Instead of three school leaving dates each year, two dates only were fixed: at the end of the Easter term, for those born between September and February inclusive; and at the end of the summer term for the rest.

Education Act 1964 This Act gave LEAs the power to vary the age of transfer from primary to secondary schools and also to pay maintenance grants in respect of 15-year-old pupils in special schools.

Education Act 1967 This Act made provision for the increase of grants to certain educational institutions (e.g. aided and special agreement schools); extended the power to require LEAs to defray the expenses of establishing controlled schools; and made provision for loans in respect of capital expenditure for colleges of education.

Education of the adolescent *See* **Hadow Report**

Education authorities *See* **Administration, Educational**

Education Bill 1833 Introduced into the House of Commons by J. A. Roebuck, this Bill would have obliged every child in Great Britain and Ireland between the ages of six and 12, not receiving sufficient education elsewhere, to attend a national school regularly. Three types of school were proposed: infant, industrial, and a teacher training school. The cost was to be met by taxation, by fees where parents could afford them, and by the use of existing educational endowments. The Bill was abandoned, but a grant of £20,000 was voted 'in aid of Private Subscriptions for the Erection of School Houses, for the Education of the Children of the Poorer Classes in Great Britain.'

Education committees *See* **Administration, Educational; Consultation**

Education Committees, Association of Consisting of education committees of the LEAs in England, Wales, Northern Ireland, the Isle of Man and the Channel Islands, the AEC has as its objects: to act as a medium of communication between the committees and the DES or other government departments on questions connected with the statutory powers or duties of the education committees or their LEAs; to consider and take action in respect of any proposed legislation or administrative procedure that affects or is likely to affect the powers and duties of the authorities and their committees; to promote and encourage interchange of opinion on questions regarding the provision and administration of education and the law relating to it; and generally to take such action as may be deemed advisable for the general good in any matters that relate to the provision, administration or law of education.

Secretary: Sir William Alexander, 1 Devonshire Place, London, W1.

Education Correspondents Group Founded in 1961 by a committee of ournalists convened by Roy Nash, Education Correspondent of the *Daily Mail*, the Group aims to create a focal point for journalists concerned with education and to develop increasing contacts with people and institutions in education. Like other journalists' groups, concerned with such spheres as industry, politics and science, it exists as a supplementary aid to the flow and exchange of information. It does not attempt to usurp the news-gathering role of the individual correspondent.

Membership is open to all journalists who devote the whole, or a substantial part, of their professional time to the subject of education. It had at March 1968 nearly 50 members who were correspondents representing the national and London evening newspapers, periodicals and the BBC.

Hon. Sec.: Peter Newell, *Education*, 10 Queen Anne St, London, W1.

Education Department Set up in 1856 to replace the Committee of Council on Education (*q.v.*), the Department was until 1899, with the Department of Arts and Science, the central instrument of educational administration. It was itself replaced by the Board of Education.

Education (Miscellaneous Provisions) Act 1948 This Act authorised the promotion of able children from junior to secondary school six months earlier than the accepted age of 11.

Education (Miscellaneous Provisions) Act 1953 This Act revised the conditions governing the payment of grants for the building of new aided schools on new building estates, and gave assistance to voluntary schools in their building programmes in such areas.

Education (Northern Ireland) Act 1947 This Act accomplished for education in Northern Ireland what the Education Act 1944 did for education in England and Wales. It established general rulings in the same terms, and allowed for the particular circumstances of Northern Ireland.

See also **Ireland, Northern, Education in**

Education (Provision of Meals) Act 1906 *See* **Morant, Sir Robert**

Education and Research, Federal Trust for The Federal Trust, founded in 1945, promotes education and research in the principles of international relations, international justice and supranational government: it organises and/or sponsors conferences, seminars, courses, discussion groups, etc.
12A Maddox St, London, W1. Director: Diarmid McLaughlin. Sec.: Miss P. M. David.

Education and Science, Department of The Department of Education and Science is a direct successor to the Board of Education (*q.v.*) which came into being in 1900 with the object of placing all matters relating to education in England and Wales under a central authority. Between 1856 and 1900 these functions had been shared between the Education Department (itself successor to the original body, a Committee of the Privy Council, set up in 1839 with responsibility mainly for elementary education) and five other authorities for secondary education, including the Charity Commission and the Science and Art Department.

Following the Education Act 1944 the Board's functions became those of the Ministry of Education. On 1 April 1964 the functions of the Minister and of the Minister for Science, and those of the Lord President relating to universities, were merged in one Department under the overall responsibility of the Secretary of State for Education and Science. (For his powers and duties see **Secretary of State for Education and Science.**) Later responsibilities covered government expenditure and policy for the arts, including the national museums and galleries, and, with the advice of the Sports Council, matters relating to sport in the UK. The Department, of which the

Secretary of State is the political head, has its headquarters in Curzon St, London, W1 and is staffed by civil servants, whose appointments are not dependent on political considerations. Their work is organised in branches concerned with schools, further education, teachers and kindred subjects in England and Wales, universities in Great Britain, and civil science. Specialist branches for health, buildings, planning and statistics, law and information are available to provide professional advice for all branches. The Department's responsibilities in Wales are looked after by the Education Office for Wales, whose headquarters is in Cardiff.

The Department does not run any schools or technical colleges, or engage any teachers, or prescribe any textbooks or curricula, but it does:

Set minimum standards of educational provision; control the rate, distribution, nature and cost of educational building; control teacher training and supply and determine the principles governing teacher qualification; administer a superannuation scheme for teachers; arrange for the incorporation of estimates of local education expenditure in provision for rate support grant; support financially by direct grant a limited number of educational institutions; support some research at all levels within the educational system, through the National Foundation for Educational Research (*q.v.*), university departments and other bodies; settle disputes, for example, between a parent and an LEA, or between an LEA and the managers of a school. Control under the Education Acts is exercised and guidance given by means of regulations, orders and circular letters, and by pamphlets and handbooks.

Schools The Department's functions relating to primary and secondary education are carried out by the Schools Branch. Territorial teams keep in daily contact with the LEAs in a particular region, maintaining a detailed picture of local provision and practice. Much of their work is concerned with the provision of schools, LEAs' programmes for building projects being considered in the light of information available, supplemented by the LEAs and HM Inspectors. The teams are also responsible for seeing that the statutory requirements are followed when schools are to be opened or closed, and for handling cases of individual pupils referred to the Secretary of State for decision.

The Special Services Branch is concerned with the basic and further education of handicapped pupils in special schools, institutions or classes provided by LEAs and voluntary bodies, or elsewhere; promotion of the school meals service and milk in schools scheme.

Teachers Teachers are the direct concern of several branches. The Teachers' Branch I is responsible for policy on the long-term demand for and supply of teachers and for administering the teacher quota scheme (*q.v.*). It advises on policy relating to teachers' qualifications, conditions of service, salaries and pensions.

The Teachers' Branch II is responsible for all aspects of teacher training and deals with the LEAs, the universities and the voluntary bodies which provide such training. Territorial teams cover all the establishments belonging to the area training organisations (most of which are based on a university) and deal with their building programmes and other plans to expand the number of students in training. Other teams deal with matters of curricula, the government of colleges of education, recruitment and admissions, technical teacher training and courses of further training for serving teachers.

The Teachers' Salaries and Qualification Branch is responsible for determining the status of qualified and other teachers, for teachers' promotion and medical requirements, and for the application of the Reports relating to teachers' salaries.

A Pensions Branch deals with the administration of the teachers' superannuation Acts.

Further education Two branches deal with further education (other than the universities and colleges of education). The Further Education I Branch falls into four divisions. The first is responsible for higher education and concerns itself principally with the establishment and development of centres of higher education, the approval of advanced courses, the public relations of further education and liaison with the Council for National Academic Awards (*q.v.*). The second division deals with general policy on vocational education for operatives, craftsmen and technicians, with the issues arising from the Industrial Training Act (*q.v.*) and with engineering and construction education. It also deals with examinations, particularly those for national certificates and diplomas. The third division is responsible for vocational education in all subjects except engineering and construction. The fourth division handles the further education building programmes, services the National Advisory Council on Education for Industry and Commerce and deals with the National Colleges and other direct-grant establishments. This division also deals with the provision of computers, the use of audio-visual aids in technical colleges and further education for overseas students.

The Further Education II Branch has three divisions. The first is concerned with adult education; with the provision made by LEAs in further education establishments (mainly evening institutes); with the Department's responsibilities under the Public Libraries and Museums Act 1964; and also with art education, the national music colleges and the Royal Academy of Dramatic Art. The second division deals with the youth service. The third, with the advice of the Sports Council, is concerned with amateur sport and physical recreation facilities and handles the government's general relations with professional sport.

The universities The DES is responsible for the universities and college vote, on which the main Exchequer grants to the universities of the whole of Great Britain are borne. These grants are allocated to individual universities by the University Grants Committee (*q.v.*). The Universities Branch is therefore mainly concerned with broad questions of finance and policy in the light of the universities' total grant needs, and with the overall development of the system in relation to national requirements. It is also responsible for policy relating to financial support for students in England and Wales.

Civil science The DES has responsibilities for civil science throughout Great Britain, and finances the five research councils (Science Research Council, Medical Research Council, Agricultural Research Council, Natural Environment Research Council and Social Science Research Council). A grant-in-aid is also made to the Royal Society and the British Museum (Natural History). The Council for Scientific Policy has been appointed to advise on long-term policy issues and the distribution of resources among the Councils.

The General Science Branch provides the secretariat for both the Council for Scientific Policy and, with the Ministry of Technology, for the Committee on Manpower Resources for Science and Technology, and provides the main link between the DES and the Research Councils.

For international scientific relations and for scientific information the DES's responsibilities are dealt with by the International Science and Scientific Information Branch.

General services Other specialised branches of the DES include the Architects and Building Branch, with responsibility for building policies and procedures and the scrutiny and approval of educational building projects, other than university projects; the Finance Branch, which controls and plans educational expenditure; and the Planning Branch, which is concerned with the quantitative implications of long-term educational developments in terms of money, manpower and other scarce resources, as well as with the DES's statistical service, its educational research programme and local government questions. There is also a Legal Branch and an Arts, Intelligence and External Relations Branch (the term 'Intelligence' covering the Department's interests in the development of audio-visual aids in education, the use of broadcasting, TV and the library).

See also **Inspectorate, Her Majesty's**

Education (Scotland) Act 1946 This Act accomplished for Scottish education what the 1944 Act had done for education in England and Wales. It laid down firm rulings on primary and secondary education and on junior colleges. It also established the general principle that pupils were to be educated in accordance with the wishes of their parents.

See also **Scotland, Education in**

Education (Scotland) Acts 1872, 1883, 1901, 1908 *See* **Scotland, Education in**

Education Shop Set up by the Advisory Centre for Education (*q.v.*) in a Co-operative Society store in Ipswich in 1965, the Education Shop stemmed from the belief of ACE that parents needed advice and information and were not having their needs satisfied by existing sources. They also believed that research has shown that a parent's interest in his child's educational welfare is a vital factor in the child's success at school, and that parents' ignorance or diffidence regarding a child's education tends to be traceable to lack of education in the parents themselves.

Ipswich was chosen for the experiment because, though it had a large working-class population, it was not a one-class town. It drew in people from a nearby rural area, had a sympathetic education committee and the Co-operative Society had, in its nature, an interest in education together with foundations in the working class.

The Education Shop, opened by Sir John Newsom, consisted of a small exhibition of general information on education, together with a counter staffed by advisers from the ACE postal advisory service. During the week it was open, its services were sought by 250 visitors, two out of five being manual workers and clerical and shop workers. Though most questions came from parents, there were some from adults and schoolchildren anxious for advice or information about their own educational problems. Questions on careers and further education topped the list, with questions on schools following, and after these questions relating to details of schoolwork. Interest in health and behaviour problems was little. The organisers felt the Shop was too small, hard to find and lacking in privacy, but that it had 'tapped a positive need.'

Education Welfare Officers' National Association This professional organisation provides full trade union negotiating machinery, legal aid and professional training.

Hon. Sec.: James Midgley, 4 Wythburn St, Salford 6, Lancs.

Publication: *Education Welfare Officer* (bi-monthly).

Education Writers' Section of the Writers' Guild of Great Britain Formed in 1966 to represent corpor-

ately those members of the Guild writing for education in all media, the Section aims to improve the writer's status in films, radio and TV; and to establish contact between all contributors to educational programmes and common ground for discussion of such subjects as the improvement and furtherance of programmes' content and production.

The Guild is to negotiate national agreements for educational writers with all main producers of these programmes. These agreements will establish the principle that commercial companies and the BBC should budget a higher proportion of money and backing for programmes.

There is a standing committee of the Guild consisting of full-time professional writers in the field of education, some of whom are teachers.

Educational TV programme producers are attached to the committee as specialist advisors and as full members of the committee. The general secretary of the Writers' Guild of Great Britain is always in attendance, and educational forums, open to non-members, are held at regular intervals throughout the year. To become associated with the Education Section writers are obliged to become members of the Guild as a whole.

7 Harley St, London, W1.

Educational Advance, Council for The Council is an affiliation of nearly 70 national bodies, including educational bodies, organisations of parents and churches, women's organisations, professional organisations, trade unions, and the main teachers' organisations. Its aim is to work for the improvement and expansion of the education system, and to provide a meeting ground and platform for opinion outside the state organisations. The Council arose out of the successful 1963 Campaign for Education.

Sec.: Fred Jarvis, MA, Hamilton Hse, Mabledon Pl., London, WC1.

Educational Advisory Council, Independent Television Authority
The Council was established in accordance with the Television Act 1964. It is assisted by two educational committees—one for schools and the other for adult and further education—and is the central source of advice on educational policy matters for the whole of the ITV system. In association with the Schools Committee, the Council guides the Authority in the twin tasks of ensuring that programmes conform to the needs and practices of the schools, and that the programmes as a whole represent a reasonable spread between the requirements of different subject fields, educational levels and types of school. Close and continuous consultation with the educational world in different areas of the country is also maintained through the committees of nominated representatives directly advising those companies which produce school programmes.
See also **ITA educational television**

Educational Centres Association
The ECA is the only national body representing the idea of the centre in adult education. The centre, in this context, is thought of not simply as a building, but as a community of people brought together. In the ECA's view, the mark of an effective centre is that it provides sufficient accommodation primarily for adult use to give it a physical identity; that there is a warden or principal responsible for at least its educational programme, with a tutorial staff involved in the centre's well-being; that it provides a programme covering a wide range of subjects and interest; that members take a responsible part in day-to-day management; and that social and corporate activity emerges naturally from the centre's existence as a community.
The ECA is aided by the DES and is recognised by all major bodies in adult education. Among the services it provides are conferences and study groups, practical assistance and advice on the various aspects of centre development, and financial help with experimental educational projects. Membership is open to bona fide centres whose main characteristics are those defined by the ECA's constitution, or that are aiming to acquire such characteristics; and also to educational organisations and individuals in sympathy with the Association's objects.
Hon. Sec.: Ray Lamb, Greenleaf Rd, Walthamstow, London, E17.

Educational cruises Introduced by the British India Steam Navigation Co. in 1961, most educational cruises are operated by three of that company's converted troopships, carrying over 50,000 passengers each year. Cruises take from 11 to 21 days; ports in the Mediterranean or in Scandinavia are visited, though the area covered continues to expand. For many spring and autumn cruises, passengers travel by air to join or leave the ship at base ports such as Venice, Genoa and Malta. A particular age-group is catered for on some cruises. Ships are often chartered by one or more LEAs. Opportunities for parties of mixed nationalities are developing.
Educational cruises are worthy of a prominent place in a modern system of education, since they provide excellent opportunities for learning by experience and for short periods of residential education. The ship's director of education and his assistants organise a time-table while the ship is at sea, making use of such facilities as an assembly hall for religious services, lectures and films, classrooms for project work and compiling records, and sports facilities for deck games and swimming. Shore excursions are arranged, preceded by lectures on ports of call, with some time allowed for individual sight-seeing under the guidance of party-leaders. Visits to the bridge, the engine room and the catering department are also arranged.

Pupils are accommodated in dormitories. Facilities include a reading room, library, recreation room, launderette and dark-room. Pupils are encouraged to take part in and organise evening activities such as quizzes, sketch clubs and dances.

The shipping company is advised on educational matters by a committee consisting mainly of directors of education and inspectors of schools.

LS

Educational Development Association Over half a century old, the EDA devotes itself to the introduction and development in schools of subjects and teaching methods involving the use of hand and eye. It works through branches, summer schools (five in Britain and one in the USA), an examination board, a magazine, and its direct members.

Gen. Sec.: P. R. Worth, 60 Loxley Rd, Stratford-upon-Avon, Warwickshire.

Educational Equipment Association Founded in 1932, the Association exists to provide a means whereby the educational activities of members may find expression and be adequately represented and safeguarded; to represent the views of members and to co-operate with the promoters of educational exhibitions and others in order to ensure the success of such exhibitions; to maintain close contact with the secretariats of educational associations and organisations, so that matters of common interest might be discussed; and to aid and co-operate with other organisations having similar interests. The Association actively promotes and supports national, regional, county and teacher exhibitions and, with a membership of 150 firms, provides a service for all concerned with teaching by establishing a link between supplier and user. It helps to ensure that the equipment available matches the demand and that the latest developments are brought to the notice of teachers and others.

Hon. Sec.: J. W. Grove, 10 Queen Anne St, London, SW1.

See also **Appendix 13**

Educational Films of Scotland This Committee was established by the Secretary of State for Scotland in 1948, under the title Scottish Joint Production Committee, to advise on visual material for Scottish schools and to arrange for its production. The present title was adopted in 1956.

By April 1967 the Committee had produced over 130 16-mm. films, 10 8-mm. film loops, eight filmstrips and 30 sets of art transparencies. Production programmes are based on recommendations by panels of teachers representing infant, primary and secondary schools, and financed from grants received from the Scottish Education Department.

16–17 Woodside Terrace, Glasgow, C3.

Educational Group of the Publishers' Association The Group serves the widespread and varying interests of educational publishers at home and abroad. Its 156 members in 1966 included 70 full members (who publish textbooks) and 86 affiliate members (who publish mainly other books of use to schools). The Group meets three or four times a year and its executive committee about twice as often.

Its principal activities are: dealing centrally with government, official and educational bodies of all types; gathering, preparing and disseminating information and statistics; handling questions of copyright and other legal or official matters; arranging book exhibitions; and making recommendations to members in connection with publishing problems or practices. These recommendations are not mandatory.

Sec.: P. C. L. Phelan, 19 Bedford Sq., London, WC1.

See also **Appendix 12**

Educational Interchange Council (Incorporated) Founded in 1947 to promote and assist educational visits and exchanges of all kinds, it is especially concerned with experimental projects with countries where normal educational and cultural contacts have been made difficult by economic, political and other factors.

In addition to exchanges of teachers, students and senior pupils, the Council arranges study visits to and from Britain for youth leaders and social workers, young people engaged in industry and commerce, and a large number of other professional and specialised groups.

The Council is a composite body, its membership consisting of the principal organisations concerned with educational and cultural matters, together with individuals prominent in these fields and in public affairs.

43 Russell Sq., London, WC1.

Educational journals *See* **Appendix 14**

Educational opportunity To some extent it has always been thought (by those few who have thought about education at all in times past) that opportunities for education and instruction should be given to all those in society who wanted it and could benefit from it. By and large, however, the resources of education have been differentially allocated among sections of the community in accordance with the social roles they were to fulfil—the priestly officials of ancient Egypt, the professional middle classes of mid-19th century Britain, etc.—and, of course, according to their ability to provide it for their own children by private means. During the past 150–200 years, however, with the expansion of industrial productivity and the sum of social wealth, the extension of political citizenship and pressures towards 'egalitarianism', it has become possible, and thought to be socially just, that government should provide educational opportunities for all children in society (according to their level of ability and their needs) as an essential social service. 'State' education of a compulsory nature has come to be a general provision in modern industrial societies, and it has been gradually extended from elementary education for all to secondary education for all, and now to higher education of various kinds for all who prove their capacity for it.

The principle underlying this public provision is that in order to maximise the well-being and happiness of both individuals and society alike it is essential that educational resources should be allocated to all in accordance with their individual qualities and potentialities, and not in accordance with the wealth and status of their forbears, which are irrelevant and arbitrary factors in this connection.

It is important to note too that this principle does not take any crude measure of 'social need' or 'social function' as its basis, but is sensitive to particular conditions of need among individuals and seeks to offer appropriate educational opportunity. For example, appropriate educational opportunities have been extended to mentally defective and sub-normal children who may never 'justify' public expenditure in terms of their subsequent 'economic' contribution to society. Children who suffer grave disadvantages are thus equipped as far as is possible to live happy, fulfilled and socially useful lives.

However (*see* **Social class and education; Home and school; Family size, Education and**) the attempt publicly to provide appropriate educational opportunity encounters considerable difficulties—since it is well-nigh impossible to measure the conditions of need and ability of children independently of the very personal and social inequalities beyond which one is trying to probe. Perhaps the future improvement in our ability to maximise educational opportunity for individuals lies essentially in this: in improving our methods of assessing conditions of need and ability beyond the possibly obscuring façade of social and economic differences, and improving our knowledge of the kinds of educational provisions which are most appropriate to these assessments.

RF

Educational Planning, Institute for See **UNESCO**

Educational priority areas The Plowden Report recommended that certain areas should be designated by the Secretary of State for Education as 'education priority areas' (EPAs), i.e. having a high incidence of educational deprivation and therefore being in need of special provision. The topic is fully discussed, and criteria for the designation of EPAs suggested, in Chapter 5 of the Report. The Secretary of State has said, in answer to requests for a detailed analysis of the EPAs in which it is proposed to spend £3 million for the rebuilding of schools, that he does not have it in mind formally to designate such areas. The schools concerned, he said, were situated in the areas of the following LEAs: Barking, Birmingham, Blackburn, Bolton, Bradford, Bristol, Cheshire, Darlington, Derbyshire, Doncaster, Dudley, Essex, Haringey, ILEA, Leicester, Lincolnshire (Kesteven), Liverpool, Manchester, Middlesbrough, Newcastle-upon-Tyne, Newham, Nottingham, Salford, Shropshire, Sheffield, South Shields, Stoke-on-Trent, Walsall, Waltham Forest, Warrington, Wolverhampton.

In the summer of 1967, in its report on the implications of Plowden for London, the ILEA expressed unease about attaching 'some kind of label of social deprivation' to children in schools in such areas, and suggested that the designation of whole areas might lead to the inclusion of schools that were not in special need.

See also **Primary education; Plowden Report**

Educational publishing Nearly all the educational books used in British schools are published by the 150 members of the Educational Group of the Publishers Association (*q.v.*). These books range from simple 'readers', costing a shilling or two, to sets of encyclopaedias. Many publishers also produce programmes, tapes, loop-films, records, and other audio-visual aid materials.

About 70 firms publish textbooks for school use, the other 80 largely confining their educational publishing to books, both fiction and non-fiction, for school and class libraries, or to reference works.

The total number of titles published annually by all members of the PA, including the 150 members of the Educational Group, now exceeds 25,000, including 5,000 reprints or new editions. Of this total, about 2,000 titles p.a. are textbooks, and 2,500 are children's books. The annual turnover of all publishers in the UK now exceeds £100m., of which nearly half is from overseas sales. Many of the educational books are specially written and produced for overseas use.

Authors Virtually all textbooks are written by teachers or lecturers. Supplementary books are often written by professional writers, sometimes in collaboration with teachers.

Writing a textbook, or a series of textbooks, is not a task to be undertaken lightly. Some series may require years of work, by both author and publisher, before publication can be achieved. But anyone who has an idea for a new textbook, or has prepared a manuscript, is certain of a ready hearing.

Authors of educational books generally receive a royalty expressed as a percentage of the published price. Books for the primary school — which often require substantial illustration schemes — may carry a lower rate of royalty than books for secondary schools. 10% is an average royalty rate, but this may be lower, especially on the first edition; or higher, according to the kind of book and the costs. Manuscripts are sometimes purchased outright by publishers, but this is seldom to be recommended.

Substantial incomes are earned by a handful of textbook writers, but the majority of authors earn modest sums. Indeed, many writers of textbooks do not aim, primarily, to earn large sums: they look upon their books as an extension of their teaching. Not infrequently, the publisher shares this ideal by publishing books from which he expects little, if any, profit, but which merit publication for the value of their contribution to education.

Production The creation of a new book is a lengthy, complicated operation involving the time and skills of many people apart from the publisher and the author. A few books can be produced quickly, especially if they are not illustrated; but even in ideal circumstances, three to six months would be required for production. Nine to twelve months would be more normal for educational books, and those with major illustration schemes would take longer.

Not every printer is equipped to print books, and the specialist book printers in the UK have to devote much of their resources to reprints, including the enormous quantities required for export. This inevitably slows down the production of many new books.

Costs Once a publisher has accepted a manuscript for publication he begins to spend money, as all production costs are borne by him. A new series of four or five textbooks could require an investment of £20,000 or more. Costs in 1966 of a typical first edition of 15,000 copies of an illustrated textbook of 256 pages Crown Octavo (7½ in. x 5 in.) amounted to:

	£
typesetting	560
illustration costs	
including block-making	785
paper	825
printing	520
binding	1,145
TOTAL	£3,835

These figures do not include the publisher's overheads — premises, staff, rates and taxes, office equipment, and so on; nor do they include the royalty which the author receives for each copy sold.

It will be seen that the actual printing costs are modest compared with other charges. Because of the high initiation charges and the extremely competitive pricing structure of textbooks, the publisher is unlikely to make any real profit on the first edition; his hope is that the demand will justify reprints which do not carry heavy initial cost of type-setting and illustrations, and so will be more rewarding.

Sizes of editions vary. It is seldom possible to print economically fewer than 7,500 copies of any new textbook; the first printing number may well exceed 10,000 copies. If colour printing is involved, even larger numbers are essential if the cost per copy, and consequently the published price, is not to be excessive; excessive, that is, for the relatively small sums available to schools for their book purchases.

Distribution Unlike publishers in most other countries of the world, the educational publisher in Britain has no guarantee that publication will be followed by widespread purchases: the teacher has freedom to choose from all available books the particular ones that suit his own, and his pupils', needs.

There are three principal ways in which educational books in Britain reach the schools: by direct purchase by an LEA; through a particular contractor nominated by the local authority; or by purchase by the school concerned from a bookshop. Of these, the second method is the most widely used. Discounts allowed on school textbooks are lower than those given on 'net' or 'trade' books, largely because textbooks are usually purchased in bulk. The average discount is 20% of the published price, and this the contractor generally shares with the buying authority.

Publishers have accepted in principle that with the added attractiveness of some school books these are now worthy of a place on booksellers' shelves, but the usual educational discount is certainly insufficient to allow stocks to be held. A practice has therefore grown up among booksellers to increase the price of such books so that a margin of up to $33\frac{1}{3}\%$ is in fact obtained. Some publishers have already agreed to inserting a notice in their catalogues to the effect that the prices quoted are the ones usually acceptable for bulk orders but that customers wishing to buy single copies from booksellers' shelves must expect to pay more.

Before ordering the teacher needs to make a choice from books available. To assist him, all educational publishers are willing to send 'inspection' copies of books suitable for class use. The terms on which they are sent vary from publisher to publisher, but it is normal to allow a period of three weeks or more before the copies are either returned to the publisher, purchased, or retained gratis under certain conditions.

In addition to press advertising and the distribution of catalogues or prospectuses, educational publishers employ representatives to call on schools or colleges to show and discuss their firms' publications. Educational representatives are not permitted to sell books, and their activities are regulated by a strict code of conduct.

Educational publishers exhibit books at some 120 exhibitions a year in the UK, ranging from the big exhibitions at such annual events as the NUT and EIS conferences, to small specialist meetings. These exhibitions are sometimes arranged in collaboration with the National Book League (q.v.). Some selected organisations receive free copies for permanent display. College of education textbook libraries may purchase single copies of school textbooks direct from publishers at half-price.

In these ways, among others, publishers try to enable as many teachers as possible to become aware of the range of educational books so that the right choice can be made.

Careers in publishing Many former teachers work in educational publishing, both in the UK and abroad; and the boards of many publishers include the names of eminent educationists. Often these appointments are of an editorial nature, and it is probably in the editorial departments that there are to be found the most interesting and worthwhile opportunities.

For school-leavers, there are openings in production, publicity, and accounts departments for both boys and girls. Art and design appointments generally call for appropriate art college training. Graduates are likely to be more interested in editorial openings, although they would be wise not to insist on this, especially at first. Experience of selling books, for example, can be salutary; and with greater emphasis on international publishing and selling, a career on the sales side can be both stimulating and rewarding.

A few of the larger firms operate trainee schemes, catering for either school-leavers or graduates. Courses in book production can be studied on day release or at special courses arranged by the PA. There are good openings for girls with secretarial training. Although most publishers have offices in London, educational publishers are to be found in Edinburgh, Exeter, Glasgow, Huddersfield, Leeds, and other cities.

FURTHER READING
Kamm, Anthony and Taylor, Boswell. *Books and the Teacher*. University of London Press, London, 1966.
Unwin, Philip. *Book Publishing as a Career*, Hamish Hamilton, London, 1965.
Unwin, Sir Stanley. *The Truth About Publishing*, Allen and Unwin, London, revised ed. 1960.
See also **Appendix 12**

SF

Educational Puppetry Association
Aims to present and develop the full educational possibilities of puppetry as a creative and dramatic activity with important emotional and social values; to encourage experimental work in the education of retarded, subnormal and maladjusted children, and in adult rehabilitation; to exchange ideas and information with similar organisations in other countries.

Formed in 1943, from the schools section of the British Puppet and Model Theatre Guild, the Association provides amenities and activities including a library service; evening and vacation courses; headquarters open to visitors on Monday evenings during term; magazine and newsletters. Instructional leaflets and puppet books are available from the sales section.
23a Southampton Place, London, WC1.

Educational reconstruction White Paper issued by Mr R. A. (later Lord) Butler in 1943, forecasting the contents of the Education Act 1944 (*q.v.*).

Educational research This may be defined as the process whereby information relevant to the decisions involved in the improvement of educational practices is obtained. The aim is usually to collect and organise this information as *systematically* and *objectively* as possible.

Content The domain of educational research, difficult to define precisely, can be classified approximately. The following are some of the classes of research that fall within this domain; examples of research topics are given in each case. (1) *The learner*. What is the best way to describe his abilities? What is the most efficient way of selecting pupils for any particular kind of education? (2) *The teacher*. Which kinds of teacher-training are best for which kinds of teaching task? How effective is in-service training? (3) *Teaching content*. Should a second language be taught in primary schools? To what extent should 'modern mathematics' replace traditional topics? (4) *Teaching methods*. Should a phonetic alphabet be used? Should instruction be automated? (5) *School organisation*. How should classes be structured? How big should classes be? (6) *Teaching circumstances*. What is the best architecture for schools or design for desks?

There are certainly other ways of categorising educational research but this classification may indicate some of the topics with which educational research concerns itself.

Instruments The main instruments by which the researcher obtains information are the following:
(1) *Instruments of assessment* (mainly tests, attitude scales and questionnaires). These constitute objective means of registering particular aspects of educational situations, of rendering such situations comparable, and, if necessary, of effecting quantification.
(2) *Instruments of analysis* (mainly descriptive and inferential statistics). Procedures exist for demonstrating the important features of the raw information that is collected, and for drawing conclusions from it. Information is usually summarised in terms of general tendencies, and relationship is usually assessed in terms of probabilities.
(3) *Instruments of control*. In certain kinds of research it is necessary to

ensure that prescribed conditions obtain. There are no standard instruments for this purpose. Textbooks, for example, can be used as a means of controlling learning content; special learning materials (e.g. the abacus) can control manner of learning; use of the film can ensure that the dimension of time, as well as that of content, is controlled; programmed instructional devices can control very closely the precise sequence in which the learner acquires information.

Kinds of research Educational research can be classified in terms of the degree to which it involves the manipulation of the learning situation. Four classes of research can be identified:

(1) *Inspection of data amassed for purposes other than that of research.* For example, the relation between GCE results and degree results may be established from past records. How accurately can GCE results indicate how successful a student will be in his degree course?

(2) *The survey.* A step further along the dimension of manipulation would be to collect information for analysis from a particular standpoint. In this case the investigator determines what information is collected in the first place. For example, the possible effect of teaching conditions, such as size of class, on academic attainment might be investigated. Data would be collected (perhaps by testing pupils) only if it was relevant to the subject of the survey, and only from a sample of learning situations that represented fairly those situations within the field of the survey.

(3) *The experiment.* Even with the selectivity that the survey affords, existing conditions cannot always be found that will provide a full answer to questions arising. Sometimes such conditions must be contrived. For example, in assessing a new method of teaching reading, it might first be introduced into schools of certain kinds. Where, as in this case, the investigator

actually arranges conditions for the convenience of his study, he can be said to be experimenting. This kind of investigation often involves considerable control and manipulation of relevant circumstances.

(4) *Basic research.* In the kinds of research outlined above, manipulation of situations is limited, for a real learning situation is being investigated—that is, a situation likely to occur in the ordinary course of educational events. Also, findings might be generalised to cover other situations held to be of a similar kind. In basic research, however, problems are investigated that may not relate directly to a real situation, and findings might be relevant to educational practice only indirectly. In basic research the interest might be only in an isolated aspect of the educational situation, or in a situation prescribed by a theoretical framework which mediates between investigation and practice. Frequently, basic research is seen as belonging primarily to disciplines other than education, and may arise out of interests other than educational. Examples of such research are investigations of Piaget's theory of conceptual development, or experiments on rats in order to establish principles of learning.

Implementation of research findings The information produced by research takes various forms and, correspondingly, so does its application. Below are some of the ways in which this information becomes available for application:

(1) *Direct availability.* Where a research finding is directly relevant to a specific educational practice, its implementation may be a simple matter. For example, if it were found that young children's handwriting developed more readily when they practised on squared paper, the indication would be clear that squared paper should be used in schools.

(2) *Availability through general principles.* In many cases research findings are formulated as general principles,

whose scope of application is not immediately apparent. For example, distributed learning is more effective than massed learning—but not for all kinds of material. Insightful learning may be more effective than rote learning for certain kinds of material, but not at all intelligence levels. It could be said that such principles usually refer to tendencies, and that a certain amount of interpretation and qualification may be needed before they can be applied to specific educational problems.

(3) *Availability through theories.* The differences between theories and general principles are too complex for explanation here. Suffice it to say that sometimes research findings are used to support suppositions whose implications are by no means a direct consequence of the truth of these findings. For example, certain behaviours of children brought up in orphanages might support a Freudian theory of early development. This theory might then be used for drawing conclusions about other kinds of behaviour of children who have been brought up in an entirely different environment.

(4) *Availability through teaching devices.* Just as theories and principles can embody and thereby communicate research findings, so can teaching devices. Of these, the devices used for programmed instruction are particularly significant because (a) a programme can be carefully planned and empirically adjusted to conform to research findings—in fact, the very process of constructing and validating a programme could be described as educational research; (b) programmed instruction permits the kind of tight control over the learning situation that is necessary for the implementation of research findings; (c) programmes are replicable and thus can facilitate generalisation of research findings.

The manner in which educationists actually utilise research findings is extremely varied. As the form in which the information is made available becomes less specific, so the utilisation of this information tends to become less easy to define. It may not be difficult to see the effect on educational decision-making of a finding concerning the advisability of using squared paper—but frequently the results of research affect practice less tangibly. In some cases (as in that of the researches into discovery-learning) results may exercise great influence by adding a bias to the general climate of opinion.

Experimental innovation In most cases, change in educational practice does not consist merely, or even primarily, in the implementation of the findings of educational research. Usually, *a priori* reasoning suggests a change—for example, the introduction of 'modern mathematics' into the curriculum, or the use of desk calculators in teaching mathematics—which is then tried out to see whether it is viable. However, it can be said that, partially and indirectly, such innovations do derive from educational research, for the reasoning that gives rise to them is likely to be influenced by a prevailing intellectual climate, which in turn may be influenced by research findings. It can also be said that these experimental innovations actually constitute educational research, for although they tend not to involve any formal and objective evaluation, they usually incorporate an evaluative element: a practice is tried out to see whether it is practicable, and if it proves not to be, it might be abandoned or modified; this test of practicability would constitute an assessment.

JDW

Educational Research Board Set up in 1967 by the Social Science Research Council, the ERB has as its aims the development of ways in which research findings can affect actual practice in schools; the stimulation of the supply and training of educational researchers; and the examination of the structure of research in education.

Educational Research in England and Wales, National Foundation for The functions of the NFER are to encourage, organise, co-ordinate and carry out educational research, its primary concern being the study and resolution of such practical problems as arise within the public system of education and are amenable to scientific investigation.

A number of projects concerned with primary school education are currently in progress. These include researches on the teaching of arithmetic, with special reference to structural methods; a series of projects on reading; and one on the teaching of French in primary schools. A project concerned with the effects of 'streaming' and similar practices in primary schools was begun in 1962. This involves a large-scale survey and intensive studies.

Research on secondary education includes projects concerned with technical education and with problems relating to the aims and organisation of secondary schools. A study of guidance in secondary technical education is nearing completion, a project to explore the influence of school on children's attitudes and behaviour (the Constructive Education Project) is now in its second year, and a study of the aims and organisation of comprehensive schools was begun at the end of 1965.

In the field of further education, a project concerned with the relative effectiveness of block and day release systems is in its concluding phases, and a study of the adjustment problems of overseas students, with special reference to the learning of English, has been finished.

An important new feature of the NFER's research programme is the Examinations and Tests Research Unit set up with financial assistance from the DES and the Schools Council.

Director: W. D. Wall, BA, PhD, The Mere, Upton Park, Slough, Bucks.

Publications: *Educational Research* (thrice yearly), *Technical Education Abstracts* (quarterly), a series of Research Reports and an Occasional Publication series.

See also **Educational research**

Educational Technology, National Council for The formation of this council was announced in March 1967, its purpose being to advise bodies engaged in education, industrial training and the services on the most appropriate and economical use of audio-visual aids and media. Guidance will be given, on the educational side, at all levels from primary schools to universities. The Council has been set up jointly by the DES, the Secretary of State for Scotland and the Ministries of Defence, Labour and Technology. In its advisory capacity, it will survey the work being done in educational technology and will attempt to improve co-ordination and to encourage research and development projects. The Council will also collect and make available information about experiences in the use of existing aids and about new developments.

The Chairman is Dr Brynmor Jones, who was Chairman of the Committee on Audio-Visual Aids in Higher Scientific Education which in 1965 recommended the setting-up of a national centre to provide information and guidance on the availability and use of audio-visual aids and media. Part of the work of the Council will be to advise the Secretaries of State as to the ultimate need of such a centre and the form it should take.

Educational Visits and Exchanges, Central Bureau for Government-financed and controlled by a board of trustees representative of the various sections of the education service, the Central Bureau provides a service of information, advice and assistance on all aspects of travel abroad for educational purposes, both by schools and youth groups and by individuals. It administers school and associated-class linkings with foreign schools, leading to the exchange of correspondence, tape recordings and other material, individual and group exchanges and visits. Arrangements are made for the term-time exchange of individual senior pupils with schools in France, and, under the aegis of the Joint Committee for Language Study Holidays in Europe, for language-study courses using group and private family accommodation. The Bureau advises teachers and youth leaders on group visits abroad; issues annual publications for individual pupils and young people, listing a wide range of opportunities; recruits direct for a number of projects; advises on individual exchanges, and arranges the placing of young people over 18 as *Moniteurs* in children's summer camps abroad, and as junior language assistants in schools in France and Germany.

The Bureau has assumed responsibility for administering the schemes for exchanging language assistants between England and Wales and the co-operating European countries, and the interchange of teachers between England and Wales and countries other than the USA and the Commonwealth.

91 Victoria St, London, SW1.

Educational and Vocational Guidance, International Association for
The Association promotes contacts between individuals and organisations in the field of educational and vocational guidance; organises international congresses, seminars and study tours; promotes vocational training for staff and grants scholarships for study purposes.

Gen. Sec.: Jacques Schiltz, 86 Ave du X Septembre, Luxembourg.

Publications: *Information Bulletin* (once or twice annually); reports of congresses.

Educational Writers Group This Group of the Society of Authors was established in 1964 to advise members individually on their publishing, broadcasting and television problems; to study the educational market at home and overseas; to watch developments in teaching as they affect the educational writer; and to hold meetings where experience can be pooled, surveys presented, and all matters of mutual interest discussed. Publishers, agents, broadcasting authorities and others concerned with the production of educational material have welcomed the existence of the group and shown a keen desire to co-operate in negotiations with its officers and members.

The annual subscription (£5.5.0d.) to the Society of Authors covers membership of all its groups and subscription to *The Author*. Election to membership of the group is at the discretion of its executive committee.

84 Drayton Gardens, London, SW10.

Educationally subnormal children
'Educationally subnormal pupils, that is to say pupils who by reason of limited ability or other conditions resulting in educational retardation, require some specialized form of education wholly or partly in substitution for the education normally given in ordinary schools': this is the definition of 'educationally subnormal' (ESN) which appeared for the first time in 1945 (*Handicapped Pupils and School Health Regulations 1945*). Children backward enough to require special education had previously been described as mentally defective, which emphasized their difference from other children. In 1953 it was estimated that about 10% of the school population require some special treatment, though it is unlikely that more than 2% will attend special schools. Boarding schools are available in rural areas and in urban areas for pupils whose home circumstances adversely affect their ability to learn.

Backward children who remain in ordinary schools are correctly described as educationally subnormal, but it is common to refer to them as 'slow learning'. They may attend special classes, full or part-time, which are variously called remedial (*q.v.*), opportunity or progress classes. Other children receive tuition in small groups for part of the day, especially those of normal general intelligence who have a specific learning difficulty, e.g. in reading. Classes for ESN children have a maximum of 20 per class.

Before the Education Act 1944 children attending special schools were usually in the IQ range 50–70, but the current definition, being based on purely educational criteria, makes it possible to admit children of higher IQ, say 70–85, who are retarded for other reasons such as cultural deprivation, emotional disturbance, or brain injury. The population of the ESN school is, therefore, a heterogeneous one. In some areas, immigration has added to the complexity of the problem. (*See* **Coloured immigrant children.**

Early experimenters in the education of mentally handicapped children, such as Itard and Séguin, concentrated on sense training—or what would now be more properly considered perceptual training. Useful apparatus was devised by Séguin, and later Montessori, to aid learning. In the 20th century, methods usually resemble the activity methods used in primary schools. The essentials are a modified curriculum, lavish use of visual aids and concrete materials, learning through experience, and step-by-step grading of the pupil's work to ensure that the pupil's achievement and self-esteem are enhanced by frequent success.

Children leaving ESN schools can reasonably expect to succeed in employment, though their success will depend partly on personality factors and partly on the availability of unskilled or semi-skilled work. Children who have been excluded as 'unsuitable

for education in school' become the responsibility of the health authorities. A suggestion is being considered that the DES rather than the Ministry of Health should be responsible for severely subnormal children.

Teachers for special education are usually recruited from qualified experienced teachers in ordinary schools and receive an additional salary allowance. Some take additional training in institutes of education. There is not yet a sufficient number of advanced courses to train all the teachers required for this very large group of handicapped children. Accordingly, this extra qualification is not yet compulsory.

FURTHER READING
Handicapped Pupils and School Health Regulations 1945, HMSO, revised 1953, 1959, 1962.
Mental Health Act 1959, HMSO.
Special Educational Treatment, Ministry of Education Pamphlet No. 5, HMSO, 1953.
A. E. Tansley and R. Guillford. *The Education of Slow Learning Children*, Routledge and Kegan Paul, 1960.
See also **Backwardness; Special education**

MW

Edwina Mountbatten Awards to Commonwealth Students *See* **Sir Ernest Cassel Educational Trust**

El Salvador, Education in In 1929 the state took over control of all schools. Education is free and compulsory where places are available. 1965 statistics: 2,663 primary schools (enrolment 360,810); 639 secondary schools (enrolment 51,452); eight technical colleges (enrolment 2,326); one university (enrolment 3,900 students). The country's population was approximately 3 million in 1965.

Electrical Association for Women The EAW is an independent voluntary women's organisation whose object is domestic electrical education on a formal and informal basis. The Association has a headquarters in London and over 250 branches throughout England, Scotland and Wales, and each branch draws up a programme of electrical demonstrations, visits, films and practical classes, covering the main applications of electricity in the home. From time to time, surveys are conducted to obtain the user's point-of-view on the design and problems of electrical equipment. The Association is also represented on several committees of the British Standards Institution and on the British Electrical Approvals Board and works closely with the BSI and other bodies in connection with the national labelling scheme of the Consumer Council.

The EAW arranges courses of instruction in domestic electricity, issues a wide range of publications, and is the examining body issuing certificates and diplomas in electrical housecraft, the demonstrators' and teachers' and home electricity certificates for adults and for students in both boys' and girls' schools.

The EAW administers the Caroline Haslett Memorial Trust which awards scholarships to girls intending to make a career in the electrical industry and other ad hoc awards.

25 Foubert's Pl., London, W1.

Elementary Education Act (1870) Introduced by W. E. Forster, vice-president in charge of the Education Department, formed by Gladstone in 1868.

This Act steered a middle course between the radical and the religious bodies who wanted to reform the education system. It guaranteed on the one hand the right of withdrawal from religious instruction on grounds of conscience, in all public elementary schools including those run by the churches. On the other hand it stated that in any schools established after the Act, and paid for out of local rates, no particular denomination should be allowed to predominate.

The Act stated that school boards should be set up by the Education Department where there was a shortage of schools; the members should be elected directly, and should be empowered to raise money from the rates to finance themselves. The idea of compulsory attendance from five to 13 was left to local decision, and the enforcement to local bye-laws. Voluntary schools were to receive a 50% grant from the Education Department, but building grants were discontinued.

See also **School boards**

Elementary Education (Blind and Deaf Children) Act 1893 This Act empowered school boards to provide education for blind and deaf children.

See also **Special education**

Elementary schools *See* **Free elementary schools**

Eleven-plus The origins of the classification '11-plus' are to be found in the Hadow Report, *The Education of the Adolescent*, of 1926. Fixing on 11-plus as the age of transition from primary to secondary schooling, the Report observed: 'There is a tide which begins to rise in the veins of youth at the age of 11 or 12. It is called by the name of adolescence. If that tide can be taken at the flood, and a new voyage begun in the strength and along the flow of its current, we think that it will move on to fortune'. This was a poetic and even slightly mystical attempt to justify a conclusion behind which lay administrative convenience rather than a sound view of the development of children; given a leaving-age of 14, a break was necessary at 11 if there was to be a post-primary course of any substance.

The same thinking is found in the Spens Report of 1938 (*q.v.*), which considered 'the organisation and inter-relation of schools . . . which provide education for pupils beyond the age of 11-plus'. The Spens Report rejected the notion of multilateral schools; concluded that grammar schools and modern schools should be separate institutions; and discussed secondary education in terms of three types— grammar, technical and modern. However, since it recognised that mistakes in selection might be made at 11-plus, it recommended that the curriculum of grammar and technical schools should be similar for the first two years, in order to make changes at 13 possible.

The Norwood Report of 1943 (*q.v.*) agreed with this division of secondary education into three distinct types, and supported the idea that 11-plus should be the age of transition. The difficulties of making a sound selection at that age were acknowledged, and the Report laid stress on the importance of well-kept school record cards as a means of supporting the selection procedures. The Norwood Report also rejected the notion that multilateral schools might be better than separate types of secondary school: it contended that the word 'multilateral', as used by witnesses it had heard, was a word of vague and varying connotation.

Under Section 3 of the Education Act 1944, secondary education was defined as that suited to pupils who had attained the age of 10 years and six months and whom it was deemed expedient to educate with older children. In this definition lay an unquestioned acceptance of the recommendation of the Hadow Report.

During the years that followed the passing of the 1944 Act, anxiety about selection at 11-plus grew up in many quarters. Parents felt it; many educationists and others, for educational, psychological and social reasons, worked together to undermine confidence in the rational and equitable character of selection at 11-plus. The Government's White Paper of 1958, *Secondary Education for All: A New Drive*, supported a very wide definition of selection, contending that since children differed from one another they needed courses that would nourish their individual abilities and aptitudes; but the White Paper came down firmly against the idea that children's educational fate could fitly be determined by selection tests at 11-plus. The government asserted that it was not prepared to impose a uniform type of secondary education on the whole country, but stated that it welcomed experiments in comprehensive schooling. Such schooling, it thought, was most suitable in rural districts where population was scattered, and also in industrial areas where there were new housing estates and no established schools.

Though the conflict of views for a long time seemed to follow a clear political division—that is, the Conservative Party was in favour of selection at 11-plus and the Labour Party opposed it—this simple pattern was breaking down by the end of the 1950s. There was much talk, in quarters where formerly there had been straightforward support for selection, of the need for 'overlap' between the types of secondary schooling. By the time of the issue of the famous Circular 10/65 (*q.v.*), which required LEAs to submit schemes of comprehensive secondary schooling, the division of views no longer followed clear political lines; and indeed many LEAs had already attempted to replace the original selection procedures with subtler variations of one kind or another.

See also **Selection procedures for secondary education; Comprehensive schools**

Elitism Elitism in education is the belief that the educational resources and efforts of a community should be used to educate to the highest level a small proportion of children possessing the greatest abilities and potentialities. Usually it entails also the idea and practice that this minority should be segregated for instruction from the less able majority so that their qualitatively different education can proceed at the pace and to the limits appropriate to their abilities. In this way they are not held back by the necessity of teaching to the lowest common denominator of the majority. This idea of segregation is now changing.

In general, both theoretically and practically, with regard both to the social allocation of resources and educational theory, British education has concentrated upon the education of its élite, and has thought segregation to be necessary and proper to this end. The public schools and universities have catered predominantly for the children of the upper and the professional middle classes. State education for 'the masses' has always been considered of a lower order, and, indeed, is still thought to be so. In many respects—the smaller size of classes, the higher qualifications of teaching staff, the possession of a many-dimensioned and well-established background of tradition, etc.—the schools for the privileged are thought to offer an education superior to that provided by the state for the majority of children. Only recently, since the second world war, has the marked emphasis arisen in some educational theory and practice that, though the education of élites is undoubtedly important, it should take place within the context of education shared by all children. Élites have after all to live in, to understand and to serve society at large, and it is difficult to see how this can be achieved if from early years they are segregated from the vast majority of their fellows and the varieties of family and social background from which they come.

Elitism, therefore, has taken different forms. Lord James of Rusholme, for example, has argued and consistently maintained that the education of élites is essentially related to the achievement of necessary and effective leadership in society. Professor H. Rée has held similar views, but now maintains that élites should be educated in the 'comprehensive' context mentioned above.

An élitist prescription in education of an altogether different kind is given by F. Musgrove. He argues that since in our modern bureaucratic society professional élites have to be 'migratory'—experiencing continual geographical, occupational and social mobility—they should be appropriately educated for the continuous adjustment which this entails. Their attachments to local communities and local personal ties should be purposely disrupted and weakened by their education. Factors which are obstacles to movement, change and adaptation should be eliminated, and this will make for success and effectiveness in their later social roles, and will also minimise the anxiety of their adult experience.

FURTHER READING
E. James. *Education and Leadership*, Harrap, 1951.
F. Musgrove. *The Migratory Elite*, Heinemann, 1963.
H. Rée. *The Essential Grammar School*, Harrap, 1956.

RF

Ellis, William (1800–81) Economist, tireless businessman who took no holiday at all for 30 years, Ellis was drawn in such leisure as he had to teaching—and especially to the teaching of political economy, which he believed to be of great importance to children. Encouraged by his success in 1846 with a conversation class on economic subjects conducted in a British school, he went on to form a class of schoolmasters, and in 1848 founded the first Birkbeck school. By 1852, at his own expense, he had founded five such schools.

ELYOT, SIR THOMAS (1490?-1546)

Elyot, Sir Thomas (1490?-1546) In

1531 Elyot wrote his *Boke called the Governour*, dedicated to Henry VIII and dealing with the education of statesmen. The author's own statement of his purpose was 'to instruct men in such virtues as shall be expedient for them, which shall have authority in a weal public, and to educate those youths that hereafter may be deemed worthy to be governors.' He argued that individuals differ from one another in their ability, and that the education of 'those youths' should acknowledge such differences. The teaching of the classical languages should start at seven or before, and no women should be involved in a boy's education after this age. Greek was of first importance, but when a boy reached adolescence the classics should be buttressed with history, geography, logic, rhetoric and philosophy. The teacher should regard himself as a moral exemplar as well as an instructor.

Elyot also struck a note that has often been struck since in educational writing and argument and is to be heard today, when he claimed that the status of the teacher ought to be raised, and that an obvious means of raising it was to increase the teacher's salary.

Embroidery *See* Needlecraft, Teaching of

Emergency training scheme To

help to counter the desperate shortage of teachers following the second world war, the emergency training scheme, designed to recruit men and women teachers from the ranks of those who had done national service, was launched in 1943. Emergency trainees had a single intensive year of training, and were obliged afterwards to provide evidence of having followed a course of directed reading and study. The scheme, which came to an end in October 1951, provided some 35,000 teachers, of whom 23,000 were men. There were 124,000 applicants for

places in the colleges; 54,000 were accepted. The history of the scheme was described in the pamphlet *Challenge and Response* (HMSO, 1950).

Employment of Children Act 1903

Under this Act local authorities were empowered to fix a minimum age at which children could be employed outside school hours, and the maximum number of hours of such employment per day and per week.

Employment of schoolchildren

Under the provisions of the Children and Young Persons Act 1933, as amended by the Children and Young Persons Act 1963, no child can be employed until he or she has attained the age which is two years below the current compulsory school age. A child cannot be employed during school hours and no leave of absence can be given to him or her for that purpose. Neither can the child be employed before 7 o'clock in the morning or after 7 o'clock at night, or for more than two hours a day during term time or for more than two hours on a Sunday. These provisions apply even though the child receives no wages, it being sufficient that he or she assists in a trade or occupation carried on for profit. Under the provisions of Section 19 of the Children and Young Persons Act 1933, local authorities are empowered to make bye-laws for the employment of persons under the age of 18. There are also provisions restricting children taking part in entertainments or theatrical performances except on licences granted by local authorities. Apart from the provisions of the Children and Young Persons Act, an LEA under the provisions of Section 59 of the Education Act 1944 may prohibit the employment of a child who, in this context, is a person of compulsory school age, if it appears that he or she is being employed in a manner prejudicial to his or her health or which might make him or her unfit to obtain the full benefit of the education provided for him or her.

HP

Employment and Training Act 1948 This Act gave a basis on which the Ministry of Labour was able to establish in industrial areas 13 training centres offering courses of up to six months for obtaining skills, and also courses for apprentice training and re-training.

End-on comprehensive schools One method of bringing comprehensive education into being is the development of end-on comprehensive schools, that is, some form of two-tier system with automatic transfer from one tier to the next. This system differs from those ('interim') systems which involve the provision of two parallel types of school over the age of 13, the decision as to the direction any pupils will take being determined by 'guided parental choice', as in the case of Doncaster and some other authorities.

End-on systems being established include a variety of schemes, usually involving some form of middle school. The characteristic of the end-on system is that entry from one stage to the next is either automatic or open to all pupils without exception; that is, it involves no form of academic or social selection.

See also **Comprehensive schools**

Endowed Schools Commission (1869) The Commission was set up following the publication of the Taunton Commission Report (*q.v.*) on the public schools. The three commissioners were given the power to revise endowed schools over 50 years old—excluding the nine big public schools (Eton, Winchester, Westminster, Charterhouse, St Paul's, Merchant Taylor's, Harrow, Rugby, Shrewsbury). During a term of three and a half years they established for 235 schools schemes creating popular governing bodies and

introducing courses in science and modern languages. Special provision was also made for the education of girls.

Endowments Described by Burke as 'the usual fruit of a late penitence' and by Adam Smith as 'necessarily soporific', endowments were the very stuff of English schools and colleges. Indispensable accounts of these have been given in several studies by W. K. Jordan, in 1959, 1960 and 1961, of which perhaps the best is *Philanthropy in England 1460–1660* (1959). He estimates that it cost £500 to endow a grammar school and £1,000 to endow a good one. The donors he described were anxious to secure the Protestant reformation and insisted on the teaching of the holy languages—Latin, Greek and Hebrew.

Efforts to break the dominant hold which Greek and Latin acquired in the grammar school culminated in the appointment of a Royal Commission in 1819 which in its 20-year survey examined 28,480 endowments yielding £1,209,395 annually. During its marathon sessions, it did not consider the universities or the six large public schools. Its reports prompted a select committee to recommend in 1835 that a permanent board should superintend charities. In the case of grammar schools an Act of Parliament in 1840 allowed governors and trustees to apply discretion in the matter of compulsory Latin and Greek. In 1842 it was found that there were 2,194 endowed non-classical schools, 905 founded between 1660 and 1730, and 72 re-endowed between 1660 and 1730.

In 1849 yet another Royal Commission reported that no satisfactory remedy for abuses had yet been fashioned, and they too urged the appointment of a permanent superintending board.

Such a board was finally constituted in 1853 as the Charity Commission (*q.v.*). It consisted of three salaried

J

members and an MP and was empowered to remodel trusts on the application of trustees and submit them for Parliamentary approval. By 1860 it also acquired judicial powers.

But by this time a major ground swell was flooding through the educational system in the shape of four major commissions of enquiry. Of the four, three, those on Oxford and Cambridge (1850–2), the Newcastle Commission on elementary schools (1858–61) and the Clarendon Commission on the nine great public schools (1861–4), concerned themselves incidentally with the matter of endowments. The fourth and last (1864–7) on the endowed schools, known as the Taunton Commission, found that of 820 schools with a net income of £195,184 (plus exhibitions to the annual value of £14,264), 198 were elementary schools with an income of £8,762 and exhibitions worth £17. They also found that the Charity Commission had frequently failed to carry out reforms in educational trusts in the face of strong local opposition, that many endowments ran contrary to the founders' intention, that many trustees continued in perpetuity, and that the distribution of endowments could be described as chaotic (*Report* I, 112). To remedy this the Taunton Commission recommended that the Charity Commission should be enlarged and supplemented by an educational committee, and, helped by a number of district commissioners and provincial authorities, it should be given the supervision of all secondary schools.

Though elementary schools continued to profit from endowments after 1870—their income from these sources rising from £50,516 in 1871 to £148,000 by 1881—the real flow of endowments in the last quarter of the 19th century was to higher education. Here most impressive continuous private administration of private and corporate funds for education is afforded by the City Companies of London. Having earlier assumed responsibility for schools like St Pauls, Merchant Taylors', Tonbridge, Aldenham, Mercers', Grocers', Bancrofts, Haberdashers Aske's, Dame Owen's, Coopers' (Stepney), Stationers' (Hornsey), Collier's (Horsham), Oundle (Northants), Sutton Valence and many others, these companies turned, after 1873, to foster technical education in London and the provinces. The civic university colleges owed much to them individually, while corporately they founded the City and Guilds of London Institute for the Advancement of Technical Education. Concomitantly the wealth of London charitable endowments, as revealed by the Northumberland Commission in 1880, was applied to the establishment of polytechnics.

But endowments could not cope with the steadily increasing cost of scientific education and, in spite of the generosity of South African millionaires towards Imperial College in 1907, heavy government expenditure in the first world war, followed by the Geddes Axe (*q.v.*), led to American aid being invoked. The Rockefeller Foundation provided substantial sums for the University of London, and libraries at Oxford and Cambridge, while further help from the Ford Foundation in the 1960s has made possible the foundation of Wolfson College, Oxford. The foundation represents a more flexible type of endowment. The Peabody Educational Fund of $2 million, set up in 1867 to aid education in the south, was the first real foundation, though the Smithson bequest in 1829 of half a million dollars 'for the increase and diffusion of knowledge among men' had adumbrated the idea. By 1964 the total assets of these American foundations were estimated at $12 million, of which the biggest holdings were those established by Carnegie, Rockefeller and Ford. In the past, foundations assisted the secularisation of American education. Today they are trying to seek out 'germinal ideas', to 'push at the growing edges of knowledge' and 'catalyse interdisciplinary reactions'. In many cases they have been able to move faster than governments. The foundation idea has caught on in this country with the Leverhulme trust and the Nuffield, Gulbenkian, and Wolfson foundations.

FURTHER READING
Robert S. Morison. 'Foundations and Universities', *Daedalus*, XCIII, 1109–1141, Cambridge, Mass., 1964.
WHGA

Engineering, Qualification in The field of engineering is immensely complex, but some general truths apply to the training and education of engineers. Entry is possible, at craft level, from 15 upwards; an apprenticeship in most cases lasts five years, leading to ONC, HNC, City and Guilds or other qualifications (*See* **Further education in England and Wales**). The second level is that of technician; many examining bodies award qualifications at this level, including the City and Guilds of London Institute, and the ONC itself is a technician's qualification. For qualification at the third level, that of technologist, there are various types of courses, some full-time and some sandwich, from university degree courses to college diploma courses that are recognised as exempting a candidate from the examinations of professional institutions. There are also HND sandwich courses that commonly last three years and must be followed by further study of specific subjects; and in Scotland, full-time four-year courses that lead to the Associateship of a Scottish Central Institution. In some cases, the HNC confers part exemption from the examinations of professional institutions.
See also **Technical education**

Engineering Industries Group Apprenticeship Scheme *See* **Industrial education**

Engineering Industry Training Board Set up as a result of the Industrial Training Act 1964 (*q.v.*), the Board set up the first school for its own use in 1967 when the Leeds Training Centre was opened. As well as providing training, the Centre will occupy itself with research into training and training methods.

English, Examining of The traditional way of examining English is to make a distinction between literature and language, and then to further subdivide language into such components as précis, comprehension, essay, etc. Such distinctions and sub-divisions are slowly being abandoned in favour of a more unified paper. Hitherto, the intentions and methods of the examination have dominated the teaching of the subject so that, by a backwash or undertow effect, the curriculum has been so devised as to embrace all aspects of the examined skills, often repetitively. A further characteristic of this situation has been that whatever could not be examined has not been included in the curriculum. For example, since few examinations included an oral test, little or no attention has been paid to oral skills such as attentive efficient listening and clear expressiveness.

As a result of the introduction of the CSE examination and of Mode 3 in particular, not only may teachers in secondary schools determine the content of the examination (ensuring that it examines what the pupils have learnt rather than determining what they shall learn), but also the means of assessment can be built more comfortably and more realistically around the actual school work of the pupil. The effect of Mode 3 is to obviate the practice of writing against the clock and also the hit-or-miss fortuitousness of a now-or-never examination; the total performance of the pupil over an extended period of time can be considered when evaluating his competence. This is not to deny that the influence of cramping illiberal exams such as those of the Union of Educational Institutions (UEI) and Royal Society of Arts (RSA) does not survive; but their influence is mercifully on the wane.

Similar changes are taking place in the O level paper of the GCE, but both O and A level papers still rely far too heavily on both memorisation and a limiting and limited slickness in writing to order.

GS

English, National Association for the Teaching of *See* **NATE**

English, Oral Hitherto, oral work—conversation, discussion and so on—has been squeezed out of the syllabus by a disproportionate stress on written English. Pupils learned to master the formal complexities of paragraph structure and yet remained inarticulate. At a time of increasing social mobility, this anomaly is now receiving some attention, since one of the conditions of comfortable social mobility is the mastery not only of a non-standard dialect but also of the standard dialect.

Many linguists suggest that it is not the function of the teacher to disapprove of and drive out the non-standard dialect, but to give his pupils access to the standard dialect. The English teacher need not give his pupils speech-training or elocution, but much of the time given to English in the time-table will be devoted to conversation and discussion, and these will both precede and follow the exercise of other skills. Many CSE examinations now have an oral section; its purpose is not to penalise deviations from the standard dialect but to reward the pupil whose speech is clear, vivid, lively and well controlled, and who can listen attentively and sustain an argument in conversation.

The admission of oral skills into the examination should serve to ensure that due recognition is given to one of the most important talents of man, his gift of speech.

GS

English, Teaching of This has changed considerably over the past 20 years or so, in response to a new attitude to the pupil, who is increasingly regarded and respected as a *maker* rather than assessed as an embryonic clerk, retarded essayist, or third-rate belletrist. Like many other revolutions, it seems to have started at the bottom; secondary teachers have followed in the wake of their primary colleagues.

For some time now, the best primary schools have been places where the child's exploratory inquiring attitude to the world has been used as the centre of the learning situation; the emphasis has been less on the teacher as instructor and more on the child as learner. Unhelpful distinctions between geography and history, biology and English, have been rejected in favour of a more empirical recognition that the child is constantly making connections for himself, and that in almost every minute of the day he is engaged in the exercise and, implicitly, the improvement of his command of his mother tongue. Emphases have changed radically, so that more time is found for dramatic improvisation, for making up stories, for conversation, and for a wide range of first-hand experiences, on which children may report back to their friends and teachers.

Such a *modus operandi* is inevitably quite unlike a curriculum dominated by the scrappy diet of the textbook, whereby the child is made to handle bits and pieces of language as if they were things outside himself, like nuts and bolts, which he could usefully and profitably manipulate without any degree of personal involvement. Flexibility is necessarily an essential feature of the newer approach to English: although statistically the 40 children in a class may be of comparable ability—and we are learning to take such statistics with a pinch of scepticism—individuals need to work at their own pace and in accordance with their own immediately relevant needs. The class-teaching of such things as spelling by means of lists-of-words-to-be-memorised-and-tested is therefore abandoned and replaced by attention to the particular problems of each child.

Such an approach is certainly more strenuous and more taxing for the teacher, since it calls for a new degree of attentiveness, yet its rewards in terms of pupils' morale and the vivacity of their work are more than adequate compensation. The ethos of the classroom changes, so that it is felt to be no longer a place where pupils are talked at and respond by all doing the same work in exactly the same way, uniformly and impersonally; it becomes, instead, the context for activity which fluctuates and changes in pressure, direction and pace according to the predilections of the individual. The teacher meanwhile keeps a close eye on the performance of each child, nudging, coercing, guiding and correcting, as necessary.

As such an approach gains ground in the secondary school we can expect to see far more classrooms where the pupils are engaged in a great variety of jobs: writing novels, plays, short stories and radio-scripts; making films, with the exercising of all the language skills that such work involves; producing magazines and documentary programmes; preparing handbooks about their schools for visitors and parents; engaging in dramatic improvisations and mime; recording 'radio' programmes for broadcasting to the rest of the school or for exchanging with schools abroad; exploring the meanings of their own experience through writing autobiography and fiction; and engaging in talk—a never-ending conversation, purposeful, open, and increasingly adequate to their own personal and social needs.

Inevitably, those who resist this movement in the teaching of English make distinctions between a loose permissiveness on one hand and good rigorous intellectual discipline on the other. Yet such distinctions are tendentious and false. For it is in the *making* that the child best learns how to make, and it is in an increasingly inclusive and subtle exploration of his or her own self and of all that lies outside it, that he or she becomes most actively, searchingly and fruitfully engaged with language.

The stress in such work is less on the word than on what it is that the word is etching, fixing, celebrating or ordering; this does not involve us in an abandonment of the word but in a closer attention to language as behaviour and to the word of experience, of life, rather than to the broken abstracted word of the text-book. The pupil, in such a scheme of things, can bring his or her own self into the classroom, authentic and unashamed, instead of leaving it outside along with dropped aitches and muddy boots.

The objection is sometimes raised that the newer methods make excessive demands on the energies of the teacher. The answer lies partly in the proper provision of teaching and learning materials—tape-recorders, projectors, good classroom libraries, radio and television, and the use of such admirable broadcast programmes as *Listening and Writing* and *Picture Box*. But more fundamentally the answer lies in the children themselves, and in the fact that, given the congenial mode, they will provide energy and resourcefulness, imagination and enterprise, in abundance.

FURTHER READING
S. Bolt. *The Right Response*, Hutchinson, 1966.
A. B. Clegg (Ed.). *The Excitement of Writing*, Chatto and Windus, 1964.
J. W. P. Creber. *Sense and Sensitivity*, Univ. of London Press, 1965.
J. Cutforth. *English in the Primary School*, Blackwell and Mott, Oxford, 1952.

F. Flower. *Language and Education*, Longmans Green, 1966.

P. Gurrey. *Teaching the Mother Tongue in Secondary Schools*, Longmans Green, 1958.

D. Holbrook. *English for Maturity*, Cambridge Univ. Press, 1961. *English for the Rejected*, Cambridge Univ. Press, 1964.

B. Jackson (Ed.) *English Versus Examinations*, Chatto and Windus, 1965.

B. Jackson and Denys Thompson (Eds). *English in Education*, Chatto and Windus, 1962.

M. M. Lewis. *Language, Thought and Personality in Infancy and Childhood*, Harrap, 1963.

S. Marshall. *An Experiment in Education*, Cambridge Univ. Press, 1963.

G. Summerfield. *Topics in English*, Batsford, 1965.

J. H. Walsh. *Teaching English to Children of Eleven to Sixteen—An Account of Day-to-Day Practice*, Heinemann, 1965.

F. Whitehead. *The Disappearing Dais: A Study of the Principles and Practice of English Teaching*, Chatto and Windus, 1966.

See also **NATE; Fiction, Teaching of; Grammar, Teaching of; English, Oral; Poetry, Teaching of; Punctuation, Teaching of; Writing**

GS

English Association The aim of the Association is to promote knowledge and appreciation of the English language and of English literature, and to uphold standards in English writing and speech. It provides opportunities of co-operation among all those interested in English by furthering the recognition of English as essential in education, by discussing methods of English teaching, and by the holding of meetings and the forming of local branches at home and overseas.

8 Cromwell Pl., London, SW7.

English language schools Since 1946 there has been an immense increase, all over the world, in the number of people learning English, and an important part of this development has been the flow of foreign students into England to learn the language from English teachers and among English people.

Since 1957 the DES has extended the work of its inspectorate and, in conjunction with the British Council, has provided voluntary inspection to private schools engaged in teaching English as a foreign language. These inspections are thorough: they include observation of the work of all members of the staff, the study of teaching methods, a survey of premises and arrangements for students' accommodation and out-of-school activities. Schools which satisfy the inspectors are formally recognised as efficient.

At the beginning of 1967 there were 43 recognised schools of English, all, apart from one at Exeter, being in London, the home counties or the south coast resorts. The number of unrecognised schools is unknown, but is believed to be in the region of 250. The recognised schools vary from large day establishments with over 1,000 students to small residential schools with 40, and it is estimated that they are attended by no fewer than 30,000 students a year.

In 1960 the schools officially recognised as efficient formed the Association of Recognised English Language Schools which has its offices at 43 Russell Sq., London, WC1. The purpose of the Association is to enable member schools, while retaining their own individual characters, to exchange information and experience for their mutual benefit and thus to set an increasingly high standard, designed to improve generally the quality of service to the foreign student of English in the UK. The Association arranges frequent training courses for teachers in member schools. It is represented on the relevant Syllabus Committee of the Cambridge Local Examinations Syndicate and, in order to broaden the scope of examinations available to foreign students in England, has prepared an examination for its own Diploma in Spoken English. An ARELS scholarship scheme exists to bring to Britain teachers of English from abroad. This is financed by contributions from member schools, from outside bodies including the British Council and from individual subscribers. In the field of student welfare the Association's chief contribution has been the publication of a handbook, *A Foreign Student in Your Home*, designed to instruct hostesses on the kind of treatment a student guest from overseas should receive.

AMo

English Language Schools, Association of Recognised The functions of the Association are exchange of members' experience with a view to setting increasingly high standards of instruction and student welfare, cooperation in research into methods of teaching English as a foreign language and teacher training. Facilities provided for teachers in member schools include refresher courses and examination for the ARELS Diploma in Spoken English; an advisory service on courses is available to overseas students.

Gen. Sec.: Mrs. G. M. Smith, 43 Russell Sq., London, WC1.

Publications: *ARELS Year Book; Members' List* (with summer courses); *A Foreign Student in your Home* (handbook).

English Schools' Cricket Association *See* **Cricket Association, English Schools'**

English Schools' Swimming Association *See* **Swimming Association, English Schools'**

English Teaching Information Centre *See* **Language Teaching, Centre for Information on**

Entering behaviour A term used in programmed learning.
See also **Learning sets**

Environmental studies The development of environmental studies in colleges of education and schools arises out of the desire of many teachers to overcome the division of learning into the several subject disciplines, the condition being that this division is not in accordance with the way children learn. ('The craving for expansion, for activity, inherent in youth is disgusted by dry imposition of disciplined knowledge.'—A. N. Whitehead, *Aims of Education.*) Teachers also argue that the child's curiosity is fostered by using the local environment as a basis for exploring reality.

The term 'environment' includes the observable physical, biological, historical and social milieux in which man lives. As a method of enquiry, environmental studies is not an amalgam of diluted geography, biology, history and sociology, but a means of developing an attitude of mind alert to the interest of the environment as a whole. Thus the student ignores the traditional subject boundaries—although he may use their techniques in so far as they advance his line of enquiry. Environmental studies is therefore an educational method rather than an identifiable intellectual discipline. Indeed, many teachers also use the emotive impact of the environment upon their pupils as a stimulus for creative work. The approach is empirical, and relies for its driving force upon the innate desire of human beings to satisfy their curiosity according to their individual interest. Often this ability is stifled by conventional education, but it can be reawakened and nourished by fieldwork in the local area. This involves the student in real-life situations, and these fresh experiences encourage learning because the student enjoys the immediacy and purpose of the work.

The starting-point is therefore personal observation which leads the student to ask questions about the local environment and then to find out answers to them. This involves the investigation of topics discernible in the character of the locality. In this way the recognition, definition, investigation, and solution of problems is given the widest scope, ensuring that 'wholeness' is not destroyed. Typical examples of questions that can be asked are: Why is this windmill here? Why do these people live in this part of the town? Why should these plants grow here? Questions of this sort have a limited point of origin, yet they can lead out to the study of a wider topic according to the scope of the student's curiosity. Thus an environmental study of a church might begin by the student asking: Why was this built here? and then continue by making a study of the building materials used; tracing architectural history in the styles present; analysing local population changes by deciphering church records; enquiring into the role of the church in the local community, etc.

In the classroom, emphasis is placed on learning the methods for discovering information, as opposed to being supplied with it. This involves activities which range from identifying geological specimens to conducting sociological enquiries.

KSW

Environmental theories in education *See* **Nature/nurture**

Epidiascope *or* **Episcope** *See* **Visual aids**

Epilepsy Association, British This Association was founded in 1950 to fill gaps in the state and local authority services for epileptics. Over the last 15 years there has been a great expansion of these services, so that help and advice to individuals are more readily available from local sources. The need remains to improve public understanding of epilepsy and to encourage and assist research. Activities include lecture courses all over the country for social workers, teachers and welfare officers; talks to teacher training colleges and small groups of interested

people; meetings in the London area. The Association also produces leaflets, posters and a journal, and sponsors the making of films.

3/6 Alfred Pl., London, WC1.

Epileptics, National Society for The Society admits girls and boys over the age of 16 for vocational training courses in building, metalwork, leatherwork, basketry and carpentry; for girls there is instruction in domestic science, needlework, etc.

Chalfont Colony, Chalfont St Peter, Bucks.

EPTA (Expanded Programme of Technical Assistance) *See* **UNESCO**

Equal pay The Burnham Scales provide salaries for teachers; the same rates apply to both men and women. This has not always been so, and fierce battles have been fought in the past in an endeavour to secure equal pay. Its introduction is comparatively recent, for when a decision was taken by the government to implement equal pay in the civil service, the Burnham Committee followed suit for teachers and, following the pattern adopted in the civil service, introduced equal pay in stages by seven instalments over a period of six years. The first instalment came on 1 May 1955, with the result that full equal pay for men and women was not achieved until 1 April 1961. Since, however, pensions are calculated on the average salary over the last three contributory years of service, it was not until 1 April 1964 that a woman teacher could retire having a parity position in respect of her pension compared with that of her male colleague.

This is perhaps not the place to enter into an extended debate concerning the pros and cons of equal pay. Professionally and socially it is regarded as just. On professional grounds it certainly can be said that employers can no longer be tempted to engage women in jobs for the reason that their salary will be less as a result. In this respect it is a safeguard to the man's professional aspirations. Socially, equal pay is just in the sense that prices of commodities are not related to any sex differentiation. The argument that a man should have a bigger income because of greater social responsibilities is well known, but the social attitude to this is really demonstrated in the tax reliefs which a married man secures for dependants and the family allowances which the state provides. It may be argued that these are not yet adequate. All the same it should be observed that these responsibilities are experienced by married men in every occupation, and so a government determination of the tax reliefs given and the family benefits paid is perhaps the wisest course to adopt.

SEB

Esperantist Teachers, British Society of Founded in 1939, the society aims to foster the teaching of Esperanto as a means of education for international understanding. It gives guidance to teachers of Esperanto in connection with public examinations; issues publications (including the quarterly *The Esperantist Teacher*); holds courses for teachers.

Gen. Sec.: R. H. M. Markarian, 2 Hazel Grove, Hartwood Park, Chorley, Lancs.

Esperantist Teachers, International League of Founded in 1949, the League aims to stimulate education for international understanding through the teaching of Esperanto in schools, colleges and universities. It also seeks to encourage, through the medium of the international language, a frank interchange of ideas between teachers of all disciplines on matters of pedagogical interest. It has branches in 16 countries and representatives in most others. Through its contacts with other branches, the British section under-

takes to arrange individual or class links and exchanges, by way either of correspondence or visits. Delegates are elected and sent by national branches to an annual meeting and conference.

Publications: *Edukado Internacia*, concerned with problems of organisations and administration (from W. M. Goodes, 7 Osborne Close, Hornchurch, Essex); and *Kajeroj*, an international pedagogical review for which contributions are invited on esperantology and problems in teaching Esperanto, together with pedagogical articles translated into Esperanto and reviews of books and aids for teaching the language (from C. Quayle, 82 Mildenhall, Tamworth, Staffs).

British Branch Sec.: Raif Markarian, ERD, MA, FBEA, 2 Hazel Grove, Hartwood Park, Chorley, Lancs. International Sec.: Dr M. Dazzini, Via Palestro 36, Massa, Carrara, Italy.

Esperanto Association, British Founded in 1904 to promote the use of Esperanto in the UK the Association consists of individuals who sympathise with the idea of Esperanto and wish to help in its promotion. It has some 60 affiliated groups, active in their own localities, and 11 affiliated federations, which co-ordinate the activities of groups and individuals in several adjacent counties. It keeps in stock all important books in Esperanto, runs correspondence courses for those who cannot or do not wish to attend classes, holds an annual congress, organises competitions and conducts examinations.

140 Holland Park Ave, London, W11.

Esperanto Foundation, Norwich Jubilee Founded in 1966, this is a trust for the promotion of education in international understanding: travel grants are awarded and educational research carried out into methods of teaching Esperanto.

Sec.: Norman Williams, MA, BSc, Egerton Park Secondary School,

J*

Denton, Manchester. Educational Director: Raif Markarian, ERD, MA, The Grammar School, Chorley, Lancs.

Essay writing *See* **Writing**

Ethiopia, Education in From secondary level upwards the main language of instruction is English. Higher education is co-ordinated under the control of the Haile Selassie I university at Addis Ababa. 1963–4 statistics: 1,466 primary schools (338,361 enrolments); 55 secondary schools (11,927 enrolments); 21 special colleges (5,497 enrolments); 2 universities (1,626 enrolments). In addition there are 10,000 Ethiopian church schools scattered throughout the country with an unknown enrolment.

The population of the country was approximately 22½ million in 1965.

European Association of Teachers The aim of the Association is to promote closer contact and co-operation among teachers of all kinds in the European countries, on the basis of the belief that, as the countries of Europe move towards greater unity, education has a vital role to play in the process. The Association co-operates with the Council of Europe and other bodies working for European unity. Activities include the exchange of information and conferences, both national and international, for the discussion of common problems and interests. Founded in 1962, EAT now has eleven member nations.

Acting Hon. Sec. (UK Section): Barbara M. Hall, 32 Parkview Court, Fulham High St, London, SW6.

Evangelical Students, International Fellowships of *See* **Inter-Varsity Fellowship of Evangelical Unions**

Evening institutes These have been defined by H. J. Edwards as 'convenient lodging houses for awkward educational problems' (*The Evening Institute*, 1961). The evening institute under various guises has accommodated secondary, technical, liberal and recreational forms of education, but today is usually limited to adult education provided by the LEAs.

Traditionally the evening institute (or night school) affords to both men and women an opportunity of learning whatever it may be that they need or want to know after the day's work is over. Evening institutes are in fact classes and students rather than buildings; the classes themselves are often practical, rather than theoretical, and the bulk of the work is now in modern language instruction, in craft classes, music, painting, pottery, cookery and so on.

Evening institutes usually meet in school premises; most of the staff are part-time; about two-thirds of the students are women. As an increasing (though still small) number of LEAs are now providing separate premises and full-time staff for adult education, and others are fostering a more mature atmosphere even in the old settings, this old descriptive phrase seems now to be passing into history.

BG

Examination fees, Recognition for grant for *See* **Secondary modern schools**

Examinations Too often education seems to be an obstacle race—O levels, A levels, etc.—in which competition for paper qualifications increasingly tends to become an end in itself, not a means to an end. Teachers, likewise, often complain that examination requirements leave them too little room for manoeuvre, that they are tied hand and foot to a prescribed syllabus.

In this situation, inevitably, most discussions of the pros and cons lead only to a conclusion in which nothing is concluded: examinations are a necessary evil, apparently. On the positive side, however, examinations serve a number of purposes, among others

(1) in assessing the pupils' progress; (2) as a check on the teacher's efficiency as an instructor; (3) in showing pupils what they have learnt; (4) in providing a yardstick for comparing pupils, teachers and schools; (5) in serving as diagnostic and prognostic tests; (6) in providing guidance for directing pupils to special courses and future careers; (7) in acting as an incentive to serious study; (8) in certifying standards of attainment necessary for employment, higher education, etc; (9) in providing some measure of general educational background and intelligence.

The *validity* of an examination or test may be defined as the degree to which it measures what it is intended to measure. Its *reliability* may be defined as the consistency with which it does this. Conventional essay-type examinations are open to the criticism that they frequently fall short of both these criteria: there are wide discrepancies between the marks awarded to the same candidate by different examiners. Moreover, it has been shown that even the adjudication of experienced boards of examiners is no less liable to subjective bias—and that this applies to oral examinations as well as to written papers. Even so, the bulk of research evidence indicates that serious disagreements in assessment do not normally arise in carefully conducted public examinations. According to Vernon (*see below*), the average correlation between different examiners is as high as 0.80. At the same time it is conceded that many of the examination results obtained in schools are deplorably unreliable. Because of this, many teachers favour the use of so-called objective-type tests in which the candidate is posed a series of true/false or multiple choice questions. These, it is argued, eliminate the subjective element in marking and so reduce the margin of possible error. Against this, it is argued that objective-type tests provide too little scope for critical and original thinking and writing.

Latterly, a new and significant function of examinations has come to the fore. Briefly, this is to exhibit the teacher's objectives to his pupils so that the examination serves as a means of evaluating the course of instruction. Both in the field of curriculum reform and in programmed learning the philosophy of 'testing-as-you-go' is now generally accepted. Teaching, in other words, is seen as a dialogue, a two-way process of communication in which regular feedback from the pupils plays an essential part. To examine is to question; to measure is to appraise.

FURTHER READING
P. Hartog and E. C. Rhodes. *An Examination of Examinations*, Macmillan, 1935.
P. E. Vernon. *The Measurement of Abilities*, Univ. of London Press, 1955.
See also **Curriculum reform; GCE; CSE; Appendix 11**

WKR

Examinations, External External examinations are conducted by external examination bodies. In theory, effective teacher participation is possible through subjects committees and representation of teachers' associations on the governing body. In practice, external examination bodies have grown into large complex pieces of machinery and have built up a system upon which it is difficult to bring effective influence to bear. For a variety of reasons, external examinations (*e.g.* GCE, *q.v.*) have come to dominate the curriculum and syllabuses of English secondary schools. The schools themselves, in many cases, have come to accept this domination.

Examinations, Internal Internal examinations are conducted by a school, without the control of any outside body. They may vary between comparatively informal tests and the mock O level of the grammar school. Where the teacher tests work which he has decided is appropriate, by what seems to him a suitable method, an internal examination can be a valuable educational instrument. Attempts have been made particularly in the Norwood Report (1943) to replace external by internal examinations, but these have usually failed because an internal examination can rarely achieve more than a local currency.

Examinations, Teacher control of
Teacher control of examinations has been discussed and sought after throughout this century: in principle, if an examination is used as an educational instrument those who teach should also control the assessment. In this country, external examining bodies have normally had behind them the superior prestige of a university and the teacher has often felt inferior. The Northern Universities Board included teachers on its central committee (1910): more usual was the establishment of subject committees which contained many teachers. In 1914 the Board of Education established that teachers should be represented on examining bodies and have the right to submit their own syllabuses (a right not often used).

Gradually more teachers played an active part and were very largely used in the actual examining of School Certificate and O level. By 1960, however, the GCE bodies had become large rigid organisations and teacher control seemed as far away as ever. Even local school leaving examinations were not always under the complete control of the teacher. CSE (*q.v.*), partly as a result of dissatisfaction with this situation, was under teacher control from the very start: teachers form a majority on all committees and subject panels, though naturally much depends on the permanent officials.

See also **Examinations**

HD

Examinations and Tests Research Unit *See* **Educational Research in**

England and Wales, National Foundation for

Examining bodies *See* **Appendix 11**

Excepted district An excepted district is a municipal borough or urban district which was able to claim the right to be excepted from the division of its county, for educational purposes, which followed the requirements of the 1944 Education Act. An excepted district has the right, in consultation with the county, to prepare its own administrative scheme; and the local council constitutes the executive body.
See also **Divisional executives**

Exceptional difficulty, Schools of
One significant way in which the Plowden Report (*q.v.*) made an impact is that a new section has been written into the Burnham Report enabling the Secretary of State to designate certain schools as 'schools of exceptional difficulty.' It has long been realised that many children have an unequal opportunity because of the social conditions in which they live. That attempts should be made to even up this opportunity has been recognised by the many social services operating in these areas designed to improve life for the community. Health and welfare service are but two of many examples. Perhaps one way in which something more positive could be done is to ensure that the school provision does not reflect the deficiencies which may exist outside the school. For example, equipment in schools could be on a better level, the number of teachers increased and the size of classes reduced. The Burnham Report (1967) was therefore amended in March 1968 to enable local authorities to pay an additional £75 to each qualified teacher on the staff of schools designated as 'schools of exceptional difficulty.'

It will be necessary for the LEA to make application to the Secretary of State for a school to be recognised as one of 'exceptional difficulty,' and in making recommendations the authorities will be required to have regard to the following criteria: (1) The social and economic status of the parents of children at the school. (2) The absence of amenities in the homes of children attending the school. (3) The proportion of children in the school receiving free meals or belonging to families in receipt of supplementary benefits under the Ministry of Social Security Act 1966. (4) The proportion of children in the school with serious linguistic difficulties.

Each local authority will make its recommendations to the Secretary of State who then has to determine in the light of all the claims and the overall financial limitation which schools shall be so recognised. Recognition will be given for a temporary period (not exceeding three years) and if the school is then still regarded as being in the category of 'exceptional difficulty' an application to continue the classification must be made to the Secretary of State; in which case, if he approves, the additional payment to the teachers will continue. It is hoped that social conditions will improve in those areas where they are bad so that the schools that are classified in this way will be reduced in number and in time disappear altogether.

SEB

Exchange of teachers The idea of exchanging teachers with another country is so obviously sensible that it is at first sight surprising that so little is done about it. The total number of exchanges officially arranged is about 200 each year; the total number of teachers is about 300,000; the total number of schools is about 33,000. Clearly it is a rarity for a teacher to go on an exchange visit or for a school to have the experience of a visiting teacher from overseas. The exchange of teachers with the countries of the old Common-wealth was first seriously discussed at the Education Conference of 1907; it began in 1919. About 100 British teachers go each year to Canada, Australia or New Zealand. Rather fewer go to the USA; a handful go to European countries.

The limiting factors are many, but do not include a lack of good will. The primary one is language. It is no good exchanging teachers with countries where they cannot teach because they cannot understand. Any large development must be within the English-speaking world. This brings in at once two other difficulties—distance and differences in the cost of living. The high standard of living in North America and its high cost in sterling places an obvious limit on numbers. The great expense of travel to Australia and New Zealand is another serious obstacle. The total cost to the Exchequer in grants has run at about £60,000 a year, and may be roughly equated per teacher with the cost of a year's full-time education, though in this case it is in addition to the salary earned by the teacher for his full-time work.

There are also educational difficulties, apart from language, which spring from the different ways in which the educational systems of the English-speaking world have developed. Roughly speaking, North America has gone one way and Britain and the Australasian countries another. This adds to the value of exchanges with Canada and the United States from an in-service training point of view, but makes it more difficult for the visiting teacher in either country to play as effective a part in the work of the school as the teacher they are replacing. This is more apparent in secondary schools with their developed specialist teaching where some external examination work normally forms part of most teachers' loads. If a whole school time-table has to be re-made to absorb an exchange teacher efficiently there are obvious difficulties about employing one.

By no means all the Commonwealth teachers working in English schools, especially in the London area, are here under an exchange scheme. A good many Australian and New Zealand teachers come to this country partly or wholly for holiday and as valuable experience, and pay their way by teaching for a time in English schools. About a thousand English teachers go to the older Commonwealth countries each year so that there is probably a bigger indirect than direct exchange of teachers, though some of it is on a permanent instead of a temporary basis.

There is another type of overseas teaching open to English teachers which may be considered here. A certain number of English teachers go out to the newer Commonwealth countries for a period of service in the course of their career. By doing this they do not forfeit their position in the English education service and can and do come back to serve again in English schools. It is natural, however, that, in spite of promises, there should be some doubt whether a teacher who goes out to Africa does not sacrifice some chances of promotion at home. In recent years about 600 teachers a year have gone out on short-service contracts to the developing countries. For the time being this type of overseas experience is bound to be substantially a one-way traffic, though there is no reason why it should always remain so.

For a considerable time there have been students from overseas training in Britain to teach in their own countries. In one recent year there were about 1,300 students from developing countries training in England and Wales. A much smaller number of English students now undertake their professional training as teachers overseas and teach there for a fixed period before they return to this country.

A better known example of educational exchange at student level is the old-established scheme of foreign language 'assistants'. Each year between one and two thousand young men and women, mainly French and German, come to spend a year attached to English secondary schools. They come to help by giving conversation lessons to small groups—the conditions of their employment are strictly controlled—and to improve their own knowledge of English. A considerably smaller number of Englishmen go to Europe for a similar purpose. There has been a steady growth in the number of 'assistants' coming from and going to Europe. By no means all will eventually become teachers, though no doubt many will, and all help with teaching.

For obvious reasons the great majority of people taking advantage of one or other of the schemes described in this article are near the beginning of their career. The increasingly early age of marriage restricts the field. The financial implication of this is something that will have to be tackled if teacher interchange in the widest sense is to develop.

DGOA

Exhibition of 1851, Royal Commission for the The 1851 Commissioners were permanently incorporated to administer the Exhibition surplus in promoting 'the knowledge of science and art and their application in productive industry'. Since the establishment on their South Kensington estate of the various museums and colleges the Commissioners have promoted postgraduate scholarships as follows:

(1) Science Research Overseas Scholarships offered annually to the universities of the overseas Commonwealth and the Republics of Ireland and South Africa.

(2) Research Fellowships for advanced scientific research, offered annually to the universities of the UK.

(3) Rome Scholarships in the fine arts offered annually by the British School at Rome (office also at 1,

Lowther Gdns, Exhibition Rd, London, SW7).

1 Lowther Gdns, Exhibition Rd, London, SW7.

Exploring Society, British Schools Founded in 1932 by the late Surgeon Commander G. Murray Levick, RN (a member of Scott's last Antarctic Expedition), the Society organises arduous expeditions for young men (not necessarily schoolboys) between the ages of 16½ and 19 who must be physically fit, able to swim and keen on at least one subject worthy of exploration.

Expeditions take place annually during the summer holidays. Applications to join an expedition must be made by boys of British citizenship resident in the UK, in the autumn of the year prior to the expedition in which they wish to take part; an applicant must be between 16½ and 19 years of age at the time of the expedition and will be required to attend an interview before a selection committee. Cost per head of expeditions is roughly £150; scholarships are available for boys whose parents cannot afford total expenses.

2 Whitehall Crt, London, SW1.

Expulsion In considering the question of the right to expel a pupil from a maintained school, it is necessary to bear in mind that the LEA has a continuing duty under the Education Acts to provide education for all pupils in its area according to their ages, abilities and aptitudes. If, therefore, a child were to be removed from one school, the question of his continued education in a school would still remain, particularly if the child were of compulsory school age.

The governors and managers of a school, under the provisions of the rules of management and articles of government, generally have the overall control of the conduct of the school, and in exercise of this control, could require the removal of a pupil. As a matter of practice, this would be done only in consultation with the LEA which has the statutory duty of providing education for the pupil.

The head teacher, by virtue of his office (and this is normally stated in the rules of management and articles of government of the school), is responsible for the internal administration and discipline of the school. He would be entitled to take appropriate action in the case of misbehaviour and indiscipline of pupils. Where such misbehaviour or indiscipline was serious, he would be entitled to suspend a child from attendance at the school, but could not, acting on his own initiative, expel a child. On suspension, the head teacher would have to report his action to the managers or governors of the school, and he is usually required to do this forthwith under the provisions of the rules of management and articles of government. A suspension of a pupil would be considered by the managers or governors in consultation with the LEA, and the LEA would need to have regard to the provisions of the Schools Regulations 1959 which state: 'A pupil shall not be excluded from a school on other than reasonable grounds.'

The courts have upheld the right of a head teacher, supported by the governors and the LEA, to suspend a pupil from attendance where the pupil was sent to school wearing clothing which was prohibited under the school rules.[1] In this case, the child was not expelled but refused admission until she complied with the rules of the school. It would be quite proper for the managers or governors of a school, on the suspension of a pupil by the head teacher, to refuse re-admission until the pupil had complied with certain conditions with regard to future behaviour.

In the case of an independent school, the attendance of the pupil is a question of contract between the parents and the proprietor. It would be either an expressed or implied provision in such a contract that in appropriate cases, the head teacher of the school could require the removal of the child if his conduct was such that he could no longer be permitted to remain at the school.

REFERENCE

1. Spiers v. Warrington Corporation 1952, 2 AER, p. 1052.

HP

Extended day The suggestion was made in the Newsom Report, *Half Our Future (q.v.)*, and has been adopted by some schools, that in certain areas LEAs and schools might experiment with an extended day of three sessions. Two of these, in the morning and early afternoon, would correspond with the existing school day; the third session would be one in which 'a substantial number of pupils' remained on the premises either to pursue individual work or hobbies, or to take part in informal group activities. The Report met the obvious objection that this would be to strain further an already over-burdened teaching profession with the suggestion that leaders of such activities might be drawn from persons other than qualified teachers. Such an arrangement might, it was argued, 'effect a helpful interchange between the schools and the general community.'

Extension College, National The aim of the College is to provide educational facilities to students whose needs cannot be met by the existing educational system. Correspondence tuition is provided and also face-to-face teaching at day and weekend study sessions. Some courses are linked with BBC and ITV study programmes.

Level of study ranges from beginners' courses to university degrees and professional courses. A teacher's course is provided in modern mathematics (primary and secondary). Correspondence courses for schools are at $12\frac{1}{2}\%$ price reduction.

Shaftesbury Rd, Cambridge.

Publication: *Home Study* (quarterly).

Extra experience, Salary increments for Whilst the basic principle upon which the salary scales are erected is that normally entry should take place at the minimum and that increments are added to that annually through the teaching service up to the maximum of the salary scale, there are several ways in which salary increments can be secured in respect of experience outside the teaching profession.

In the first place experience gained prior to entry to a course of teacher training must be taken into account, provided there is not less than three years of experience after the age of 18. Where longer periods are involved, multiples of three to the nearest whole number would count for increments up to a maximum of 12 increments. Thus five years of pre-qualified experience which is counted on a one-for-three basis entitles the teacher to two increments. However, there is special provision that where part of such experience (other than teaching) gained after the age of 21 is deemed by the LEA to be of special value to the teacher in the performance of his particular duties, the LEA may allow the teacher one increment in respect of each year of experience which they approve for the purpose. Any experience so assessed is still subject to the overall limit of two increments.

As far as post-qualified experience is concerned, there is a wide range of service which is accepted on the basis of one increment for each year of service; but it is impossible to give the complete picture here. For details, Appendix II, Part C of the Burnham Report should be consulted.

The general pattern is that where teaching is undertaken in educational establishments of various kinds, whether in the UK or abroad, and where the standards are accepted by the DES as equivalent to those in LEA schools in the UK, such experience may rank for salary increments. Indeed, such service is not limited for increment purposes, and a person having sufficient recognised experience could secure the maximum of the salary scale. This does not apply, however, to time spent in industry or commerce or in professional or research work after the age of 21. Post-qualified experience of this kind likely to be of value to the teacher in the performance of his duties may be approved by the LEA at its discretion, and if approved shall be given incremental value up to a maximum of 12 increments.

SEB

Extra-mural departments, University *See* **University extra-mural work**

Extra training/study/research, Increments in teachers' salary for Normally the period of full-time training to become a qualified teacher is three years. Again, normally, the starting salary would be the minimum on the basic scale. However, one, two or three increments are paid by the salary scale for teachers who have, after the age of 18, undertaken and satisfactorily completed four, five or six years respectively of full-time study, training or research, excluding any period spent in repetition. 'The age of 18' is acceptable provided the teacher concerned reached that age during the first term of the course.

These increments are mandatory provided the conditions are satisfied. Thus, for example, a teacher who entered a college of education at the age of 19 for a three-year course having previously satisfactorily completed one year of full-time study in the sixth form of a grammar school would, on qualifying, be regarded as a teacher with four years of training and would enter the salary scale one point up from the minimum. Further, an authority has discretion to pay an additional one or two increments where study, training or research has exceeded six years. Increments that are secured through

extra training do not extend beyond the maximum of the scale.

SEB

Extraneous duties This is a generic term covering a very wide range of extra-curricular activities undertaken in the teaching profession. Unlike industrial posts it is usually the case that a professional appointment involves no set hours, for the professional is required to devote such time as may be necessary to achieving a desired end. Educationally, where schools are concerned, there are specified times when a school is open and closed, but for many years practitioners in this country have taken for granted that education is a continuing process and that much is necessary outside the normal hours of classroom time.

Teachers play a major part in bringing up the rising generation. Enthusiasts have devoted much of what might otherwise have been called their leisure time to developing school sport—football, cricket, swimming, netball, hockey, etc.—and to drama, music, philately, photography, etc., all of which require much organisation quite apart from the classroom timetable. These are, of course, voluntary activities for which there is no payment in the salary scale.

SEB

Extraneous duty allowance Where teachers are appointed in residential establishments (e.g. approved schools and remand homes) there is an obvious need for regular duty to be performed in addition to that of the normal teaching duties. For this reason it is usual to regard the hours of primary duty as being between 9 am and 5 pm during which the teaching timetable will be carried out. From 5 pm until bed time and from rising until 9 am and at weekends there are many calls upon the staff and these are classified as extraneous duties. The work is shared on a rota basis and payment is made in proportion to the volume of the duty carried. At the present time the maximum amount a teacher can receive in this way is £320 per annum provided his tour of duty is for an average of not less than 15 hours per week over a 44-week year. The amount is reduced proportionately in respect of lesser duties, e.g. an average of 7½ hours would be paid £160, etc.

The work in which staff are engaged during the periods for which extraneous duty allowances are payable is either of a professional or a supervisory nature. Classes in the evenings may be held and hobbies pursued under the guidance of suitable staff. On the other hand, there would be periods of relaxation when, for example, a TV programme may be seen, but there is an obvious need for supervision.

SEB

F

Factor analysis Primarily factor analysis is a statistical technique for resolving a large number of variables or measurements into a few major dimensions or components. The correlations (*q.v.*) between all the measures are calculated and analysed to see how far they can be accounted for by one underlying component. Thus it has been held that all tests of intellectual abilities depend on the same g or general factor, plus s factors specific to each separate test. The influence of the first factor on the correlations is removed, and the remaining or residual correlations are studied to reveal further groupings. For example, all tests that involve understanding of words may correlate highly, yielding a v or verbal factor; those involving number an n factor, and so on.

However, there are many variations in the techniques of finding and interpreting factors, and consequently some conflict between the views and conclusions of different factor analysts. Generally British workers stress the importance of g or general intelligence in all abilities, while recognising subsidiary specialised abilities or group factors. American psychologists stress the diversity of abilities along different lines and attempt to measure large numbers of distinct factors, which they label with capital letters: V=Verbal, S=Spatial, M=Rote Memory, etc.

Factor analysis has many applications in education, when it is desired to explore the structure or grouping of variables: for example, how far are academic and technical abilities distinctive at various ages; can vocational or leisure interests be classified into a limited number of general types for use in giving guidance; can teachers assess many separate personality characteristics of their pupils, or do they mainly judge in terms of general good behaviour plus attainment; do different examiners or markers of the same papers fall into types who favour different kinds of answers?

See also **g**

PEV

Factory nurseries *See* **Day nurseries**

Factory schools Without an adequate system of schools to keep pace with the growing population, Acts like those of 1802 and 1819, requiring compulsory instruction of children working in factories, were never likely to be effective. Some employers, however, like David Dale and Robert Owen at New Lanark (*q.v.*), started schools for their employees. Institutions such as these and the school for the Tobacco Boys in Edinburgh (1820) were pioneers.

In 1833 another Factory Act made attendance at school a condition of employment, and provision was made for deducting school fees from children's wages. Four inspectors were appointed. From their reports emerges a vivid picture of the lengths to which some employers went in order not to provide a school. By 1843 factory schools were catering for 36% of the children in Yorkshire, south and east England, and for 46% in the four northern counties.

These reports stimulated further reforms, but in 1843 when the Home Secretary tried to arrange for factory children to attend voluntary schools, he evoked an outcry led by dissenters who suspected an Anglican plot.

The Factory Acts were not really effective until the 1870 Act provided board schools. Factory schools then changed their role, and better firms, like Mather and Plat, started 'continuation schools' (q.v.).

Today, as industry becomes more oligopolic, some industrial training centres have virtually become post-graduate schools.

FURTHER READING

Adam Henry Robson. *The Education of Children Engaged in Industry in England 1833–1876*, London, Kegan Paul, 1931.
G. Ward. 'The Education of Factory Child Workers', *Economic History*, III, London, 1935–7.

WHGA

Faculty of Teachers in Commerce Ltd. A national organisation for teachers of commercial subjects, the Faculty has 12 branches holding regular meetings, while regions hold conferences. The examinations section conducts papers in all commercial subjects at both student and teacher levels.

Probably the oldest subject-teachers' organisation in the country, the Faculty was founded in 1872 as 'the Phonetic Shorthand Writers' Association' and assumed its present title in 1916. Membership is open to those holding acceptable qualifications.

Quarterly journal: *Teacher in Commerce*.

Gen. Sec.: James Snowdon, 13 Stamford Pl., Sale, Cheshire.

Fading Also referred to as 'vanishing', fading is a term used in programmed learning. Once prompts (q.v.) have served their purpose in helping the learner to grasp a particular point or concept, they are gradually withdrawn and finally eliminated. The process whereby the intensity of the stimulus, i.e. the 'obviousness' of the prompt, is gradually reduced until it disappears, is known as fading.

Families Education Service, British An inter-services organisation sponsored by the Army Department of the Ministry of Defence, the BFES caters for the children of service personnel stationed in North-West Germany, Berlin and Belgium. It is responsible for 67 primary schools and nine comprehensive secondary schools, three of which are boarding schools.

Headquarters: HQ, BAOR, British Forces Post Office, 40.

Family Benefits Scheme *See* **Teacher's Family Benefits Scheme**

Family Caseworkers, Association of Founded in 1940, the Association aims to represent the views of its members, to maintain and raise standards, and to encourage further training. Members are professionally qualified social workers who have been supervised by an experienced family caseworker. Some small private funds are available to help intending family caseworkers to acquire professional training, where they cannot get funds from other sources.

Oxford Hse, Mape St, London, E2. Journal: *Social Work*. Quarterly.

Family Discussion Bureau *See* **Tavistock Institute of Human Relations**

Family grouping This is, more accurately, vertical grouping. It has been devised as an alternative to the arrangement of children strictly according to age, and is particularly used to describe an arrangement by which children are first admitted to school. Instead of entering a single class all together (traditionally called the 'reception' class) new entrants are attached to small groups of children of between five and seven years of age in a number of rooms. These small groups tend to reflect a 'family' grouping of children and they have led to the evolution of new techniques and methods for the earliest steps in learning at school.

Teachers who pioneered this method did so because they knew the extent to which slightly older children in a family teach their brothers and sisters. The method was also known to have important social, and so educational, results; it was devised to reduce the strain of entering school as a member of a completely new group or class within the community.

See also **Infant schools; Reception class**

DJJ

Family Psychiatry and Community Mental Health, Committee on *See* **Tavistock Institute of Human Relations**

Family size, Education and It is at present established by all available evidence that the average level of measured ability of children declines with each increase in completed family size. The average test scores of children from large families are lower than those of children from small families, and these differences are borne out in school performance. These facts were clearly demonstrated in the Scottish Mental Survey (which compared the measured ability of all 11-year-old Scottish children in 1932 with that of all the 11-year-olds in 1947) and has been confirmed in the more recent studies (which measured intelligence at the ages of eight and 11) undertaken by J. W. B. Douglas and his colleagues (1964).

These findings are therefore definite, but the factors involved are complicated and cannot yet be said to be explained. Some important points are as follows:

(1) This correlation does not mean that there is any intractable decline in the level of intelligence throughout society as a whole. With improved economic, material and environmental conditions, the average level of measured intelligence can be totally raised in new generations. Even so the correlation between family size and average measured ability (at this new, totally raised level) remains true.

(2) This correlation is true of all social classes and conditions: of middle-class families as well as of the poorer families of manual workers. There is no social level of which it is not true. Clearly, large families in working-class conditions frequently suffer from deprivation, ignorance, lack of parental encouragement, etc., and a lower average test score is not surprising. But large middle-class families do not suffer in these ways, and yet the correlation remains true for them also.

(3) The largest single factor which compensates for this condition is the interest and encouragement shown for the education of their children by parents. When children receive much encouragement from their parents, those from large families perform almost as well as those from small. Here, however, there is a class difference, since middle-class parents maintain such encouragement until they have as many as three or four children, whereas the encouragement shown by working-class parents appears to diminish with each additional child.

(4) Curiously, there appears to be a difference between the sexes. Family size does not seem to have a significant influence on the performance in intelligence tests of middle-class girls, whereas it does on that of middle-class boys.

(5) A very interesting fact is that the intelligence scores of children from large families do not deteriorate between the ages of eight and 11 years. In short, the influence of family size upon measured ability must be exerted during the earlier years of childhood.

Clearly these facts still await satisfactory explanation, but they are so definite that they must be taken into account in the theory and practice of education: both within the schools, in matters of teaching proper, and in the administrative formulation of educational policies.

FURTHER READING

M. L. Steckel. 'Intelligence and Birth Order in Family', *Journal of Social Psychology*, vol. i, p. 329, 1930.
J. W. B. Douglas. *The Home and the School*, MacGibbon & Kee, 1964.
J. Maxwell. *Social Implications of the* 1947 *Scottish Mental Survey*, Univ. of London Press, 1953. *The Level and Trend of National Intelligence*, Univ. of London Press, 1961.
Scottish Council for Research in Education. *The Trend of Scottish Intelligence*, Univ. of London Press, 1949.

See also **Home and school**

RF

Farm Institutes Committee *See* **Burnham Committees**

Farm institutes scales

Assistant Lecturers. The scales are: Group I £800–£1,500, Group II £900–£1,600, Group III £1,020–£1,720. Increments of £30(2), £50, £60(3), £50(7) and £60. (Group I are non-graduates, Group II graduates or degree equivalents, Group III honours graduates.)

Lecturers grade I

Group I £	Group II £	Group III £
935	1,035	1,155
965	1,065	1,185
995	1,095	1,215
1,045	1,145	1,265
1,105	1,205	1,325
1,165	1,265	1,385
1,225	1,325	1,445
1,275	1,375	1,495
1,325	1,425	1,545
1,375	1,475	1,595
1,425	1,525	1,645
1,475	1,575	1,695
1,525	1,625	1,745
1,575	1,675	1,795
1,635	1,735	1,855
1,665	1,765	1,885
1,695	1,795	1,915
1,735	1,835	1,955

Where a Lecturer Grade I has responsibilities of a supervisory or administrative nature which, in the opinion of the LEA, justify an allowance over and above the scale salary, the LEA may pay an allowance of £175 per annum.

Lecturers Grade II. £1,725–£2,280. Increments of £55(9) and £60.

Special allowances for lecturers. The authority may, in its discretion and after consultation with the Minister, make an additional payment of £130–£400 where a lecturer undertakes special responsibilities which in its judgment are not adequately recompensed by the lecturer's scale. Where the authority feels an allowance of £400 is not adequate, having regard to the particular responsibilities of the post, a higher allowance may be paid subject to agreement of Secretary of State.

Grading of posts. The grading of posts in the grades of assistant lecturer, lecturer Grade I and lecturer Grade II shall be determined by the LEA in agreement with the Minister. In considering the grading of posts the authority should regard assistant lecturer as being appropriate only for work of school standard, i.e. work not above the ordinary level of the GCE. For work above school standard, lecturer Grade I should be regarded as the appropriate basic scale. The Burnham Committee is aware that some of the extra-mural work in agricultural education is of school standard, but normally work in farm institutes is above school standard. The Committee considers, therefore, that normally it is not appropriate to have a fixed establishment of assistant lecturer posts for staff engaged in full-time teaching in farm institutes.

Vice-principals. A lecturer appointed as vice-principal is paid an allowance of not less than £210 or more than £500. An allowance may be granted to a lecturer who undertakes the duties and responsibilities of the vice-principal in the absence of the vice-principal, or pending the appointment of a new vice-principal. The amount of the allowance to be made in any particular case is left to the discretion of the authority, provided that the total remuneration in respect of the period shall not exceed that which would be payable to the lecturer if he/she were the vice-principal.

Principals. The rate of salary payable to principals under the 1965 Burnham Report has been increased thus:

Max. of present salary scale	Increase
Up to £2,750	£175
£2,751–£3,000	£190
£3,001–£3,250	£205
£3,251–£3,500	£220
Over £3,500	£235

An allowance may be granted to a teacher who takes charge of a farm institute in the absence of the principal, or pending the appointment of a new principal. The amount of the allowance to be made in any particular case is left to the discretion of the authority, provided that the total remuneration in respect of the period shall not exceed that which would be payable to the teacher if he/she were the principal.

Residential duties. Residential duties are to be remunerated by agreed emoluments or equivalent allowances additional to the remuneration otherwise payable under the Report.

SEB

Fatigue What is called mental fatigue is very often sheer boredom (*q.v.*), and it is well-known that interest in a task often seems to create new energy, even though the student may have been very tired before he approached the task. Some students seem to have greater powers of genuine concentration than others, but ultimately everyone has limits, and it is certainly a mistake to continue working after the optimal level of concentration has been passed, when exhaustion sets in and very little can be usefully achieved. Signs that the optimal level of concentration has been reached may be an increasing amount of errors plus a general feeling of irritability.

Fauna Preservation Society The Society is especially concerned with the conservation of species in danger of extinction. It works closely in conjunction with the International Union for Conservation of Nature, the International Council for Bird Preservation and the World Wildlife Fund. It brings to public notice the urgent need for the preservation of wild life, doing so through the press, radio and TV and by means of the Society's journal *Oryx*, published three times a year.

The Society also promotes ecological investigations on the spot into all problems of wildlife preservation and encourages the formation of national parks and reserves. It keeps governments informed about the need to protect wild animals, forms a focus in London for work on conservation and co-operates with similar organisations in other countries.

The Society holds regular meetings, gives lectures to other societies and to schools and lends films from its film library.

Hon. Sec.: R. S. R. Fitter, c/o The Zoological Society of London, Regent's Park, London, NW1.

Federal Trust for Education and Research *See* **Education and Research, Federal Trust for**

Federated Superannuation Scheme for Universities (FSSU) The FSSU is a contributory pension scheme for staffs of universities. This is not administered by the government and under Acts of Parliament, but through an insurance company.

Feeble-minded children *See* **Ineducable children**

267

Feedback A term borrowed from electrical engineering, widely and loosely used in programmed learning. Strictly, a device by means of which the effects of a process or system are used to control the process or system itself. More broadly, it denotes the two-way nature of communication and the ways in which continuous interchange of information between instructor and pupil affects the learning process.

See also **Programmed learning**

Feedback in learning Originally a technical term referring to a self-regulating device such as a thermostat in an electrical heating system. It is now often used to describe the knowledge of results a learner should have if he is to form effective learning patterns. Too often in the past, pupils were not told if they were right or wrong until well after they had forgotten the original question. As knowledge of success is perhaps the most potent positive reinforcement (*q.v.*) that there is, it is a pity not to use it as quickly as possible. On the other hand, if a child has made a mistake he should be shown the error of his ways immediately, so that the faulty learning pattern can be unlearned and disposed of with little delay. One obvious way of doing these things lies in the use of programmed learning, which provides instant 'feedback' (*q.v.*) after each item on the programme.

NT

Fellow The senior members of Oxford and Cambridge colleges are called Fellows, and they share the responsibilities and privileges of college power (and until 1871 the disadvantage of having to be single). They have rooms and dining rights in college, and they are paid for teaching the undergraduates, usually in supervisions or tutorials of one or two. In addition, most Fellows hold paid teaching posts in the university.

The Oxbridge Fellows are not easily tempted to move to other universities, and they are the envy of the many members of their own university who do not hold college fellowships, for whom new colleges (and pseudo-colleges) are now being formed.

Fencing The art of swordsmanship has been practised for many centuries by most nations. As long ago as the early 16th century, Henry VIII founded a governing body for fencing, known as the Corporation of Fencing Masters. In the UK today the sport is controlled by the Amateur Fencing Association, founded in 1902.

In modern fencing three weapons are used: the foil, épée and sabre. Men compete with all three, but girls and women fence only with the foil. Special clothing must be worn, and must be white to facilitate the spotting of hits during contests. At all times a special mask designed to protect the face *must* be worn.

The sport has become extremely popular in recent years, not only with adults but also in public and secondary schools, for it offers intensive exercise without undue cost, requires little space and few officials.

The AFA employs a national coach and runs special courses, mainly in the midlands, for schoolmasters wishing to train as amateur coaches or 'leaders'.

Amateur Fencing Association: 83 Perham Rd, London, W14.

FURTHER READING
R. Crosnier, *Fencing with the Epée*, Faber, 1958.
R. Crosnier, *Fencing with the Foil*, Faber, 1951.
R. Crosnier, *Fencing with the Sabre*, Faber, 1954.
Rules for Competitions, Amateur Fencing Association.

JE

Fiction, Teaching of As with drama and poetry, the teaching of fiction has moved away from teaching *about* literature towards a shared and guided experience of literature. In many primary schools, a time is set aside for the teacher to read a story to the class over a period of days or weeks; the range of good fiction now available for younger children is so wide that no teacher need have difficulty in whetting pupils' appetites and thus making adequate and varied provision for satisfying their needs.

In the past, the secondary pupil's enjoyment of fiction has often been stultified by the imposition of arduous and pointless essays in which the pupil was expected to offer paraphrases of the plot and detailed psychological analyses of the main characters. Such tasks are yielding to a much more informal and relevant discussion of the short story or the novel as an ordered body of experience which can be recreated imaginatively and drawn upon in discussing point of view, motive, presentation of character, action, and the relationships between these parts. A literary-critical approach involving fairly sophisticated literary evaluation is properly reserved for sixth-form work.

With changes in method have come changes in curriculum, so that, while the classics have not been expelled from school, more room is found for 20th-century fiction, especially the work of Lawrence, Hemingway and Orwell, much of whose writing appeals to the morally passionate adolescent.

As for the moral value of fiction, the debate continues and seems likely to prove interminable. On the one hand are those who claim that a properly guided experience of fiction can extend and refine the pupil's sensibility and awareness, while the opposing view is that fiction never modifies anyone's sensibility and cannot be expected to do so. The 'moral' case is perhaps not the most persuasive or useful argument for the inclusion of fiction in the English syllabus, even if it could be substantiated by anything more than a consensus of intuitions. The pleasures, absorptions and captivations of reading fiction may be regarded as their own justification.

GS

Field Studies Council The Council was founded in 1943 as the Council for the Promotion of Field Studies, with the aim of encouraging field work and research in all branches of knowledge whose essential subject matter is out-of-doors. The CPFS was the pioneer in taking school, university and adult students into the field, away from restrictions of desk and laboratory bench. By December 1955 (when the name was changed) four residential field centres had been established, each with a small scientific staff and laboratory and library facilities for about 50 students at a time, and the Council had a recognised and valued place in the sphere of further education.

In 1967–8 there were nine centres, distributed over England and Wales, in localities selected for the richness and variety of the opportunities offered for both general and specialised biological, geographical and geological studies. Organised courses, lasting mostly a week, are held from March to November; sixth-form courses predominate, but the centres also cater for colleges of education, undergraduates, teachers and amateur naturalists. A Scientific Director was appointed in 1967, and research is being increasingly fostered.

Membership is a condition of admission to any of the Council's centres. Members receive full programmes each November for the following year.

The centres administered by the Council are as follows: Dale Fort Field Centre, near Haverfordwest, Pembs.; Flatford Mill Field Centre, East Bergholt, Colchester, Essex; Juniper Hall Field Centre, Dorking, Surrey; Malham Tarn Field Centre, near Settle, Yorks.; Nettlecombe Court, The Leonard Wills Field Centre, Williton, Taunton, Somerset; Orielton Field Centre, Pembroke, Pembs.;

Preston Montford Field Centre, near Shrewsbury; Rhyd-y-Creuau, The Drapers' Field Centre, Betwys-y-Coed, Caerns.; Slapton Ley Field Centre, Slapton, Kingsbridge, Devon.

Sec.: R. S. Chapman, MA, FCA, 9 Devereux Court, Strand, London, WC2.

Journal: *Field Studies*. Annual.

Film in education

Movie film enables the teacher to use a combination of communication techniques (moving pictures, animated drawings and diagrams, maps, slow-motion and time-lapse photography, words, music, natural sound) to give his pupils knowledge and experiences which otherwise they would not have. Film can give them vicarious experience of life and work in any part of the world, enable them to observe most forms of animal and vegetable life, re-create historical events, demonstrate skills, etc. In the hands of a creative artist, moreover, film can also appeal to the imagination and engage the emotions. The film-maker draws on a wide variety of resources; film is vivid and concrete, and it can powerfully stimulate interest and focus attention; thus it is one of the most valuable of teaching aids. It is, however, an *aid*, and films can rarely be used effectively without careful preparation and follow-up. Moreover, where pupils can have direct experience (e.g. of scientific experiments or local geography), film is a poor substitute. Again, where still pictures are an adequate aid, the more expensive movie film is unnecessary.

The 16-mm. portable sound projector is becoming standard equipment in schools; 35-mm. movie film is rarely used. 16-mm. films are normally hired rather than bought, at prices from 1s to 3s per minute. Many 16-mm. free-loan films are also available; some of these are useful in school, though few are intended specifically for such use. For forward projection (essential for large audiences) darkness is necessary, but in the average classroom a translucent rear-projection screen is satisfactory in daylight and enables the teacher to face, and see, his class.

Short, silent 8-mm. cassette films are now used increasingly. These single-concept loop films, intended to teach one specific point, can be shown continuously as many times as necessary. The projector, with built-in rear-projection screen, is easily portable, needs no black-out, and is simple enough for a child to operate. Single-concept films are cheap enough (£2–£4) to buy rather than hire. The teacher who makes his own films, either for the normal or for the cassette projector, can do so more cheaply in 8-mm. than in 16-mm.

As well as being a teaching aid, film is also a subject of study in itself. (*See* **Screen education.**)

Still film is used in a projector, sometimes called a miniature diascope, which may take 2-in. x 2-in. slides, or a length of 35-mm. film (a film-strip), or both. A wide variety of film-strips and sets of slides is available at prices from 10s to £3. Some film-strips are intended to be accompanied by synchronised tape-recordings. The teacher can easily make his own aids—film-strip or, more easily, slides, with tape-recording if desirable. Slides are more convenient in use, but the weight and storage-space required are much greater than for equivalent material in film-strip form.

The Educational Foundation for Visual Aids (33 Queen St. London, W1) publishes a comprehensive catalogue listing educational film material (still and movie) from all sources.

See also **Visual aids**

APH

Film Foundation Ltd, Children's

The Foundation receives payments from the British Film Fund Agency and other organisations, which it applies for the production, promotion, organisation and distribution of cinematograph films specially suitable for showing at children's matinées and other performances given specially for children or for the entertainment of children and others in any part of the world. Membership is composed of representatives of the four film trade associations.

Sec.: W. G. R. Thom, 6–10 Gt Portland St, London, W1.

Publication: *Saturday Morning Cinema*, 1967.

Film Institute, British The Institute exists to encourage the development of the art of the film, to promote its use as a record of contemporary life and to foster its study and public appreciation. Similar purposes regarding TV are now included within its terms of reference. It maintains the National Film Archive, and houses an information department, a book library, a stills library and a film distribution library. As well as occasional pamphlets, it publishes *Sight and Sound* and *Monthly Film Bulletin*. The Institute is also responsible for operating the National Film Theatre. In the broadest sense the Institute is an educational organisation, but the more specifically teaching functions are handled by its Education Department.

The Education Department exists to promote the study of film and TV as art and entertainment within all branches of education. It provides lectures and courses, runs an advisory service for teachers, makes available special film teaching materials and publishes pamphlets and books on film teaching and general film topics.

Director: Stanley Reed; Education Officer: Paddy Whannel. 81 Dean St, London, W1.

Film Library, Central With its affiliated libraries in Scotland and Wales this is the agency for non-theatrical distribution of films produced or acquired by the Central Office of Information (which in 1946 succeeded to the Ministry of Information) for use in Britain.

The Library holds some 2,000 documentary and short films and a small selection of filmstrips. A hire charge is made for most films, but a number are available on free loan; filmstrips are normally on sale only. The CFL's borrowers include many educational establishments at all levels, from schools to universities. In addition to films on more general topics, in both national and international fields, the Library houses a large number of authoritative films of a specialised or instructional nature (on scientific, industrial, medical, vocational guidance and other topics) on which it is always prepared to advise.

Publications include a main catalogue and a catalogue *Films for Industry*.

Central Film Library, Government Building, Bromyard Avenue, Acton, London, W3; Scottish Central Film Library, 16-17 Woodside Terrace, Charing Cross, Glasgow, C3; Central Film Library of Wales, 42 Park Pl., Cardiff.

Film School, National The setting up of a National Film School in London was recommended in a report in mid-1966 from an independent committee to the Minister Responsible for the Arts. The committee was against the raising of any existing film school to the rank of a national school on the grounds that only a new and autonomous establishment could command 'the degree of national and international prestige which will attract to it the personnel and resources without which it cannot hope to achieve its aims.' It was recommended that the school should be directly accountable to the DES and, while having a principal and small permanent staff, much of its teaching should be done on a part-time basis by members of the film industry. Students should be between the ages of 20 and 28, and should be recruited as widely as possible; as many as 30% might come from abroad. The school should not duplicate the work of present institutions in the field of audio-visual education, but should work at a high professional level. The three-year course would be at post-graduate level.

FURTHER READING
National Film School, HMSO, 1966.

Film strips *See* **Film in education**

Film and Television, Society for Education in Formed in 1950 (as the Society of Film Teachers) this small but influential group of teachers and lecturers has developed the notion of classroom studies of the cinema and TV. The Society's journal *Screen Education* (five times a year) and its *Yearbook* maintain a regular flow of information about feature films, short films and extracts, and how these may be incorporated into school and college time-tables to promote serious study of the 20th-century art media. Study groups meet regularly, and occasional publications of special interest grow from these, e.g. *Young Film Makers, A Film Society Handbook*.

Gen. Sec.: 70 Old Compton St, London, W1.

Finland, Education in Education is compulsory and free between seven and 15. In 1964–5 there were 6,659 primary schools, with an enrolment of 565,407; 577 secondary schools, with an enrolment of 258,167; 653 secondary vocational schools, with an enrolment of 77,264; 14 higher education establishments, including universities, with an enrolment of 35,910. There are six universities.

The population of the country was approximately 4½ million in 1965.

Fire precautions in schools Fire precautions consist basically of two parts: those planned into the building and those taken by the occupants.

The first category is largely covered by the Ministry of Education's Building Bulletin No. 7 *Fire and the Design of Schools*[1]. This bulletin recommends standards required for local authority day schools and may also be used as a guide for other educational buildings. Plans for new buildings submitted for approval to the DES are expected to comply with these recommendations, which broadly cover four inter-related functions: means of escape, fire resistance, surface spread of flame and combustibility.

For adequate means of escape, the normal standard is the provision of two separate routes to the open air from the door or doors of every room on an upper floor. Escape through windows can be considered for ground floor rooms. Additional escape routes are required from all large spaces for assembly and dining. Escape routes may be protected and separated by self-closing smoke-stop doors so placed that smoke cannot block more than one route. In certain cases, rooms for up to 120 children may be permitted on the first floor of a two-storey building with only one staircase provided that additional precautions are taken to protect the escape route down that stair.

To ensure that fire does not spread quickly, the surface lining materials of walls and ceilings in various locations will have to comply with British Standard 476 classifications for surface spread of flame.

Combustible materials are permitted in construction of school buildings but their use is restricted according to the height of the building and additional requirements of the other functions.

The second category of fire precautions, those taken by the occupants, are even more important because they can nullify all the precautions planned in the first category. The need for great care is shown by the fact that fire brigades are called to about 900 fires in educational establishments in the UK every year and the number is tending to increase.

The duties of the occupants are set out in Pamphlet No. 53 *Safety at School*[2]. The most important of these duties are:

(1) To ensure that escape routes are never obstructed by loose furniture or locked doors while the building is in occupation.
(2) To hold periodic fire drills to evacuate the building.
(3) To understand the procedure for calling the fire brigade and put it into operation as soon as a fire is suspected.
(4) To check that self-closing smoke-stop doors are in working order and in an emergency are all closed immediately.
(5) Not to allow combustible rubbish to accumulate, particularly in stairways, stores and high fire risk rooms.
(6) To take great care with all temporary decorations and costumes.
(7) To ensure that teachers in laboratories, housecraft rooms, etc., are aware of the detailed precautions set out in *Safety at School*.
(8) To ask the fire brigade for advice, particularly on the type and siting of fire-fighting equipment.
(9) To check that all alterations to electrical and mechanical circuits are carried out only by competent persons.
(10) To consider what checks on security are necessary when the buildings are unoccupied at night and weekends.

REFERENCES
1. Ministry of Education Building Bulletin No. 7 *Fire and the Design of Schools*, HMSO, 3rd ed. 1961.
2. Department of Education and Science Pamphlet No. 53 *Safety at School*, HMSO, 1967.

KEF

First schools *See* **Junior schools**

Fisher, H. A. L. (1865-1940) President of the Board of Education, 1916–22, and responsible for the Education Act 1918 (sometimes known as the Fisher Act).

Fisher Act (1918) *See* **Education Act (1918)**

Fit Person Order *See* **Children's Department**

Fitch, Sir Joshua (1824-1903) Schoolmaster and later Principal of Borough Road Training College, Fitch was from 1863 an Inspector of Schools and played an important part in the development of the national system of education. Author of *Lectures on Teaching* (1881).

Flannelgraph *See* **Visual aids**

Flash card An aid used in the teaching of reading, a flash card has a word or phrase printed on it in large letters; it is shown briefly to a pupil as a means of increasing the power of recognition of words.

Fleming Report (1944): Report of the Committee on Public Schools Terms of reference: to consider means whereby the association between the public schools and the general education system of the country could be developed and extended; also to consider how far any measures recommended in the case of boys' public schools could be applied to comparable schools for girls. Chairman: Lord Fleming.

The Report was commissioned at the instigation of the public schools themselves, who were anxious after a wartime period of extreme financial difficulty not to be isolated from the general post-war surge of interest in education. The Report was part of the general inquiry that preceded the Education Act 1944. It suggested various schemes for integrating LEA pupils with those of the public schools and for replacing the direct grant system, but very few of its recommendations were ever implemented.

Flogging The extent to which the English inherited ideas of corporal punishment from the Romans can be seen in the fact that the instruments used had counterparts in those days: strap (*scutica*), cane or rod (*ferula*), cat (*flagellum*), switch or birch (*virga*). From organised Christianity came the idea of flagellation (of which flogging is a schoolboy abbreviation) as a means of penance used inside and outside monasteries. By the 15th century it became such a ritual in schools that, when degrees in grammar for schoolmasters were instituted, an incepting master received, not a book like masters of other faculties, but a 'palmer and a birch'.

Coloured by the punitive theology of the Protestant churches, which substituted pictures of vivid hells for the practice of excommunication, flogging survived the Reformation, and, to the gentle English botanist Turner, the birch still served 'for betynge of stubborne boyes'. Overcrowding and unpalatable curricula—Greek was often 'caned into' a boy—made punitive techniques often a matter of self-defence, and even enlightened 18th-century headmasters, like Valpy of Reading, used to flog. In 1775 Dr Johnson thought that 'there is now less flogging in our great schools than formerly, but then less is learned there; so that what the boys get at one end they lose at the other'.

The most celebrated exponent of punitive therapy was John Keate, headmaster of Eton 1809–34. On one day alone, 30 June 1832, he was said to have flogged 80 boys, and was cheered afterwards by them. His problem was of course that he had to contain 170 boys in one room—the upper school—and they used to pelt him with rotten eggs, smash up his desk and sing ribald songs in his presence.

Yet even in Keate's time, flogging was on the decline. The reasons are various: the increase of the economic rewards of education, the use of Bentham's 'place-capturing principle', the influence of competitive examinations, the increasing appeal of new subjects like science, history and modern languages, and the emergence of a professional spirit amongst teachers. By 1862 the Rev. C. H. Bromley could claim that 'enlightened teachers have discarded rod and ferrule'. Yet teachers, including those in board schools, retained corporal punishment as a last resort, and were supported in so doing by the law.

'By the law of England', ruled Lord Chief Justice Cockburn in R. v Hopley (1860), 'a parent or schoolmaster (who for this purpose represents the parent, and has the parental authority delegated to him), may for the purpose of correcting what is evil in the child, inflict moderate and reasonable corporal punishment—always, however, with this condition: that it is moderate and reasonable.' Mr Justice Charles in Gardner v Bygrave (1889) opined: 'When Parliament lays down a chart showing the particular region of the body to which corporal punishment in schools shall be confined, the court will take care that those limits are not overstepped. At present these is no such chart.' A civil servant, G. C. T. Bartley, in *Schools for the People* (1871), found flogging only in reform schools and training ships, and in the latter used 'but rarely'.

In 1871 the London School Board forbade pupil-teachers to inflict corporal punishment, and in 1874 they extended the prohibition to assistant teachers. This attitude spread, and since 1902 LEAs have forbidden irregular forms of punishment like boxing the ears or shaking. Some forbid caning for children under eight, and the use of any kind of corporal punishment by probationers, temporary or supply teachers, and in some cases all teachers without seven years service.

Perhaps the most explicit rulings permitting flogging are those laid down in the Home Office Approved School Rules 1933, Nos. 35 and 36, which stipulate not more than three strokes with an approved cane or tawse on each hand, or not more than six on the clothed posterior for boys under 15. In the case of girls, only those under 15 may be caned, and those only on the hand. In the case of both boys and girls such punishment must not be administered in the presence of other children. Prior approval of a medical officer must be obtained before such punishment is inflicted on those suffering from physical or mental disability.

FURTHER READING
Christopher Hibbert. *The Roots of Evil*, Penguin, 1966.
M. E. Highfield and Arthur Pinsent. *A Survey of Rewards and Punishments in Schools*, Newnes for National Foundation for Educational Research, 1952.
See also **Corporal punishment**
WHGA

Flow chart A term used in programmed learning, the flow chart is a kind of critical path analysis of the main concepts and the order in which they are to appear in the programme.

Focus group This term describes a small group of teachers collaborating among themselves and with students in conducting IDE (interdisciplinary enquiry, *q.v.*). The term was first introduced in the University of London Goldsmiths' College Curriculum Laboratory in 1966 to indicate specifically (in contrast to team-teaching, which is variously interpreted) a group of specialist teachers working as equals through whom a school focuses on the needs and interests of a 'division group' of some 60–150 pupils working in clusters' (*q.v.*) within a broad area of investigation, on diversified activities.[1]

The focus group operates in time blocks of up to 50% of the timetable and is supported by a peripheral group of teachers contributing occasionally to IDE or taking pupils for other studies.

The concept and practice of focus-grouping differs essentially from the range of techniques commonly employed in team-teaching, which may be seen as a means of economising and making more effective *instructional* effort. For instance, one specialist will give an exposition, using a variety of media, to a large group of children who will continue studies of the subject in classes under the supervision of other members of the team, who will be advised by the specialist. The aim is to achieve a degree of standardisation of what is taught. The strength of team-teaching is that students are not exposed to a confusing array of specialists, and a class-teacher has more contact with his class, while shared planning of work is possible. Its weakness is the second-handedness of the instructional treatment, since most of the teachers involved may be out of their depth and reliant, exactly as the pupils are, on notes and resources provided by the specialist.

In contrast, the primary purpose of the focus group is not to instruct or standardise, but to pool its expertise in helping children to learn through their own collaborative enquiries. Since ease of communication and common understanding of purposes matter supremely in such a group, its size is limited to five or six, supported by members of the peripheral group, where they are needed and where the timetable allows such a teacher to replace a member of the focus group at certain times. It parallels in size the clusters in which children are encouraged to work, each cluster having such contact with a teacher as it needs, but not full-time detailed supervision. (*See* **Clustering and clusters.**)

In supervising IDE each member of a focus group performs a trend-watching function, looking out for the common objectives agreed by the group as well as for his own specialist objectives. He acknowledges when students are outrunning his own expertise and directs them to more expert colleagues or resources. The close collaboration of the focus group facilitates rapid 'local agreements' on division of labour in the group.

Other functions of members of a focus group are (1) trendwatching for agreed group and individual behavioural objectives; (2) diagnosing specific remedial needs of each child; (3) spotting the emergence of the particular strengths of each child (so that all children may get both remedial treatment at the appropriate level and opportunity either alone or in like-minded groups to develop their strengths); (4) encouraging and maintaining a high level of communication within and between clusters—one teacher at least in a focus group should be especially concerned with helping those children to contribute who have, through social or other impediments, most difficulty in doing so.

A focus group could at times undertake the instructional team-teaching described above, but it would rarely do so. When an interdisciplinary enquiry is planned the group would normally begin with a vigorous common presentation of possible lines of enquiry, and a survey of resources provided. This might involve lectures, demonstrations and exhibitions, but thereafter it is desirable that enquiries should 'fan out' among clusters without duplication. Although there will certainly be times when particularly exciting work of a cluster should be presented to all to encourage more ideas in the whole division-group, the fanning-out should have a great variety of product. Minimum standards may certainly be aimed at, but there should be no 'standardisation' of product. This demands that all teachers in a focus group will be concerned to help children record their discoveries in communicable form, for immediate consumption or for exhibition. This keeps up the cross-communication which generates collective ferment among the clusters, and also allows, if photography or other graphic media are used, storage for later reference of a highly varied range of expression. Notes need not be preferred to poems, written to recorded speech, or words to music and dance. All kinds of 'making' (q.v.) can be encouraged, and some though not all of them can be recorded.

REFERENCE

1. Charity James. *Live Now; Live Later,* Collins, 1968; L. A. Smith (Ed.). *Ideas No. 1,* Goldsmiths' College Curriculum Laboratory, 1967.

EM

Folk Dance and Song Society, English Aims to encourage the performance and enjoyment of English folk music, song and dance. The EFDSS has grown from the union of two long-established organisations, one, founded in 1898, devoted to folk song; and the other, founded by Cecil Sharp in 1911, to preserve and encourage traditional music in its various forms, but especially folk dance. The two societies merged in 1932. There are over 10,000 individual subscribers and an organisation in every county. The London headquarters has dance halls, canteen, library, sound library, recording studio and offices.

Cecil Sharp House, 2 Regents Park Rd, London, NW1.

Folk-Lore Society The first of its kind, the Folk-Lore Society was founded in 1878 as a central organisation for those interested in the systematic comparative study of oral traditions and cultures. The primary object of the Society is publication, but meetings are held nine times a year in order to hear papers read and to discuss them. The Society's journal, *Folk-Lore,* contains papers by leading folklorists and articles of general folkloric interest.

There is an extensive library available to members, and the Central Register of Folk-Lore Research encourages and co-ordinates study of the subject. c/o University College London, Gower St, WC1.

Football *See* **Association football; Rugby football**

Football Association, English Schools *See* **Association football**

Forces, Teaching in the All three branches of the services have schools for the children of service families, the usual rule being that the service with the most children in any area has charge of the schools there. Of the three services the Army Children's Schools have the largest enrolment and, although there are minor variations, conditions in these schools will serve as an example of what may be found in RAF and Royal Navy Schools.

Basically there are two kinds of teacher in the schools. The first kind, recruited in the UK from teachers serving with LEAs, are termed 'UK-based teachers'. Technically these are temporary civil servants, and it is not the policy of the Crown to engage temporary civil servants for specified periods. But in practice engagements are offered for three years (two years in the Far East), and the Ministry of Defence likes to re-engage teachers for a second three-year tour and even for a third tour. Such teachers are under an obligation to give three months' notice, but the Ministry of Defence can terminate any appointment without notice at any time for inefficiency, neglect of duty, misconduct or on the grounds of physical unfitness.

All UK-based teachers are paid Burnham rates, plus the normal perquisites of civil servants living overseas: i.e. foreign service allowance, rent-free accommodation (or allowance), subsidised fuel and light, free passage of car overseas and return.

Competition for service teaching appointments is keen, with about three applicants for each vacancy. A condition of appointment is that the teacher should have had at least two years' experience in a British school, although this may be waived for teachers of infants.

The second category of teacher is recruited from among the dependants of servicemen serving overseas. These are termed locally-entered teachers. They must have a UK teaching qualification, and in general must be able to offer at least a year's service. They are paid according to local rates or Burnham scale, whichever is the less, and, unlike their UK-based colleagues, work to one month's notice.

In 1968 there were nearly 39,000 children in the Army's 119 schools overseas, with 1,929 teachers. The current teacher/pupil ratio in Army primary schools is 1:25 and in secondary schools 1:14, comparing favourably with the UK ratio of 1:28 in primary schools and 1:19 in secondary comprehensive schools. The Army encourages its soldiers to send their children of secondary age to boarding schools in Britain and provides generous allowances to make this possible. In consequence there are fewer children in secondary than in primary schools. In the spring of 1967 there were 12,677 in Army infants' schools, 16,821 in junior schools and 9,303 in secondary schools.

Although the secondary schools are comprehensive the 11-plus examination is retained in the primary schools as a guide to ability to LEAs in the UK should the parents of a child return to Britain. Pupils in the secondary schools sit for the GCE and the CSE. HM Inspectors from the DES are invited to inspect service schools, and do so more regularly than they inspect schools in Britain—although they have no statutory authority in service schools. Considerable latitude is allowed to head teachers; streaming or non-streaming, the introduction of new methods such as the i.t.a., Nuffield science and maths, French in primary schools, all being at the head teacher's discretion. The RAF has some 550 qualified teachers in 30 RAF schools, where 12,000 pupils are enrolled.

Teachers can also join the services by enlisting in the education branch of one of the three. Although there are slight variations, a description of the conditions of service in the education branch of the RAF gives a fair picture of conditions in all three. The teachers in this branch serve the educational needs of a force in which professional experts and skilled technicians predominate; their task is to furnish the educational component of flying and technical training and to provide facilities at home and overseas for general education of the men in the service and the development of their technical proficiency. So the education officer will find himself teaching such subjects as mathematics, mechanics, physics, electronics, engineering, history, geography and current affairs. A range of courses is covered, from an elementary level for the less skilled tradesmen to advanced courses of university standard for cadets at the RAF College or Technical College. Certain officers with high qualifications in engineering, science or mathematics may receive post-graduate training and may be selected subsequently as senior specialist teachers.

The work of an education officer in a training school in the RAF may be compared broadly with that of an assistant or lecturer in a technical college or institute of further education. There are two classes of commission: general list officers who have the prospect of a full career in the service, and supplementary list officers who serve for a shorter period, the length depending on the type of commission. The upper age limits are 30 for the general list and 39 for the supplementary list commissions. Qualifications demanded are a British degree, teaching certificate with mathematics or science as the principal subject, or Higher National Diploma or Certificate in engineering together with GCE O level in English language. Salaries are based on the credit system, credits being given (which raise the entrant above the minimum salary) for academic qualifications and professional experience. A man under 25, with no credits, would start as a Pilot Officer on £730 plus £296 marriage allowance and £130 ration allowance, a total of £1,156; after 12 years he would be receiving £1,964 (assuming he had not risen to Squadron Leader). The highest rank in the education branch is that of Air Vice Marshal, which carries basic pay of £4,581, marriage allowance £693, ration allowance £130, total £5,404 (1967 scale).

As equal pay for women has not yet permeated the services, the female entrant would receive £620 if she had no credits, or £748 after two years or if she qualified on entry for credits; after 12 years her pay would be £1,241, and the limit of her career would be the rank of Group Officer when after eight years she would receive £2,820 (1967 scale).

Inevitably Britain's withdrawal of her forces from the Far and Middle East, announced at the end of 1967, will lessen demand for teachers in service schools and in the education branches of the three services. Before this phased withdrawal began, teachers in service establishments were to be found in Aden, Singapore, Cyprus, Gibraltar, Ghana, the Arabian Gulf, Hong Kong, Australia, Norway, Malta, Germany, North Africa, Sarawak, the Levant and the USA.

EP

Form entry The number of classes admitted to a school each year. The size of a school is defined by the use of this term: for example, a two-form entry school will have an annual intake of between 60 and 80 pupils, divided into two forms.

See also **Size of schools**

Formosa, Education in *See* **China, Nationalist (Taiwan), Education in**

Forster, William Edward (1818-86) As Vice-president of the Committee of the Privy Council for Education, he was responsible for the passage of the Education Act 1870, which took the first step towards making education compulsory.

Foundation governors of schools *See* **Instrument and articles of government**

Foundation managers of schools *See* **Instrument and rules of management**

Frame A term used in programmed learning, borrowed from visual aids. It denotes the amount of information and instruction displayed during a single step in the sequence to the learner using a programmed text or a teaching machine. In linear programmes, a frame consists of little more than a sentence accompanied by a question; in branching programmes it may run to page-length, and is followed by a multiple-choice question (*q.v.*).

See also **Programmed learning**

France, Education in The French system of education is at present undergoing a radical transformation. Prior to 1939 the system was characterised by its highly centralised administration and its élitism. It was essentially a two-track system with the *lycée* and the *collège* catering for an able minority, geared to a classical academic curriculum, and the elementary schools providing a modicum of 'culture générale' for the great majority. This same dualism was reflected in the teaching

profession itself, graduate members holding the rank of 'professeur', non-graduates that of 'instituteur'.

From the 1920s onward there was growing dissatisfaction with the lack of educational opportunity for the many who failed to gain a place in the *lycée* or *collège* as well as with the high failure rates at the *baccalauréat* (leaving certificate examination) among the few who did. After the end of the second world war, this criticism culminated in the ambitious Langevin Plan which, though never formally adopted, has served as the blueprint for recent reforms. Briefly, these seek to replace the old vertical division between selective, academic and non-academic types of school by a horizontal division which envisages the continuous process of education for all pupils in a series of cycles.

From six to 11, all children attend the primary school and then proceed to a two-year diagnostic course (*cycle d'observation*) which is broadly the same for all. Selection is, in effect, deferred until the age of 13, and the allocation to different types of course is then decided on the basis of the pupil's record and on teachers' estimates. At this stage there are a number of options. Pupils who are able and willing can proceed to a 'long' course which may take the form of General Education (Classical or Modern) or Technical Education, at the end of which they are eligible as candidates for the *baccalauréat* examination. The latter now allows of a variety of options according to the type of course which has been followed. Less able pupils, roughly 50% of the age-group, take a 'short' course lasting three years, either of general or technical education or, in the case of those whose formal schooling is to end at 16, a terminal course.

The obvious difference between the old and new regimes is the dramatic expansion of technical education at all levels. This expansion is in a large measure due to the policies laid down by the Le Gorgeu Commission which is responsible to the Commissariat Général au Plan, the State Planning Authority. These policies are by no means fully implemented and the present position is best described as one of flux.

From the time of Condorcet, 'L'enseignement fonction d'état' has always been a guiding principle in French education. While some delegation of powers has been achieved, the system remains centralised, with no local unit of administration to compare with the English LEA or the American School Board. The country is divided into some twenty *académies*, each of which is a region and based on a university. The university's *recteur* is the Minister's representative in the region, responsible to him directly for secondary and higher education and indirectly for primary education.

Parallel with the statutory system France has a large number of independent, denominational (mostly RC) schools. This dual system is the cause of friction and controversy—'la question scolaire'—but since 1960 a compromise solution akin to that for 'aided' and 'controlled' schools in England has helped to make the religious issue less contentious than it was formerly.

The student rebellion in the spring of 1968, beginning in the Sorbonne and spreading to other university centres and also to the *lycées*, was expressive of enormous dissatisfactions with the quality, organisation and accessibility of education in France, and must certainly lead to far-reaching reforms.

WKR

Franks Commission (Oxford)
Appointed by the Hebdomadal Council of Oxford University in 1964, the Commission of Inquiry under Lord Franks, Provost of Worcester College, was required to report upon 'the part which Oxford plays now and should play in future in the system of higher

education in the UK, having regard to its position as both a national and an international university.'

The establishment of the Commission sprang from criticisms of the University embodied in the Robbins Report (*q.v.*), but the Commissioners stated that during the inquiry they had heard and read much which went far beyond the observations of the Robbins Committee. Many of their witnesses believed that radical changes were called for if Oxford was to continue to play its part as one of the great universities, not only of Britain but of the world.

The Report, issued in 1966, gives an account of the complaints made against Oxford. Its administration was less effective than that of most universities; the Robbins Report had spoken of 'slowness', and there was a lack of decision. The University seemed incapable of explaining what it was doing in a way that would make it possible to compare its performance with that of other universities. As an example, the University Grants Committee (*q.v.*) had found that Oxford was unable to present statistical and other information in the form generally adopted. There was force, said the Franks Report, in the charge that University and colleges were 'too self-satisfied to explain themselves'.

Again, it was complained that Oxford was a privileged place; that it courses were rigid and narrow; that its admission system did not allow it to draw on the full range of ability to be found in the variety of secondary schools throughout the country; that it gave less care, and devoted fewer resources, to post-graduate education than to the education of undergraduates. This last was a criticism that, when made from outside the University, came with special force at a time when the need for training after the first degree was increasing. Finally, the merits of Oxford's collegiate system were disputed, since it introduced an unjust distinction between those who shared in it fully and those without college attachments.

The Report stated the assumptions that underlay its recommendations. These were that Oxford was both tied, and given a special freedom, by her very large private endowment income (about 20% of the University's whole income); that Oxford must be encouraged to do those things for which it was best fitted by its past experience, making its individual contribution to learning and teaching; that, having the duties of an international university, it must exhibit research and teaching of distinction, not in one field alone but widely; that it must accept its responsibilities as a major established centre of learning in the British pattern of higher education; and that there must be a proper balance between teaching and research.

The first major recommendation of the Report concerned the administration of the University. The problem was to make it possible for 'the mind of Oxford' to be known, clearly and without delay. An alteration was proposed in the method by which the Vice-Chancellor was selected, and his tenure of office was to be lengthened. To secure and strengthen continuity of policy, the Hebdomadal Council should be supported by a new General Purposes Committee, in part chosen by the Vice-Chancellor. There would also be a new General Board responsible for the academic work of the University as a whole, together with a Council of Colleges. The existing faculty boards were to be thinned to five, in order to remedy 'the present fragmentation of academic studies'.

The Commission felt that as a result of such reforms as these 'the mind of the academic community will be made up where it is at present often only pieced together.' They believed that part-time academics were capable of efficient administration if they were well served by an adequate structure of officials. The University's ultimate legislative

body would continue to be Congregation, but proposals were made for giving it new life.

Criticising the colleges for a tendency to hold aloof from schemes proposed generally for the University, and for clinging to the privilege of dissenting from such schemes, the Report outlined a new college contributions system which would secure a minimum level of endowment for all colleges; this would raise the level of the weaker colleges without producing absolute equality. The Council of Colleges would have the task of determining common policies and practices, not as a means to uniformity but in order to create a framework within which variation might be preserved.

As to the size of the University, the Report proposed a planning figure of 13,000 for the total student population, to be attained during the 15 or 20 years following the issue of the Report. There should be a large increase in the number of postgraduates, and also in the number of undergraduates in science and social studies and of women undergraduates. The number of men reading arts must be held at its present figure or reduced.

On admission to the University, the Commission stated that in the long run it was in favour of a national university entrance examination; but meanwhile it had devised a scheme for a two-stream entry based on the fact that pupils advance in their secondary education at rates that differ from school to school. All closed scholarships and exhibitions should be abolished, and the number of open scholarships held by undergraduates in any college should not exceed 10% of the total number of undergraduates in the college.

The curriculum at the moment was artificially narrow, and there should be a selective and swift development in the fields of advanced technology. Postgraduate studies should be given parity with undergraduate studies.

The Report recommended that all permanent appointments to the University staff should be the joint concern of a college and the University, both having to agree on the appointment. Time should be given for research to all members of staff, and a maximum of teaching hours should be fixed. Oxford should, without delay, increase its staff until it reached at least the national average staff/student ratio.

Finally, believing that the tutorial was becoming debased, and was being widely used, not to enable a student 'to think and to argue on some selected topic before a critical and older person', but to cover the ground of a course, the Report recommended that undergraduates should each week write only one essay and as a rule attend only one tutorial. Other ways must be found of 'covering the ground'.

FURTHER READING
University of Oxford: Report of Commission of Inquiry, 2 vols, Oxford Univ. Press, 1966.

Free Church Federal Council The Free Church Federal Council acts on behalf of the Free Church denominations in educational concerns that are questions of policy or of legislation, in which matters it negotiates with the DES and with the other principal Church bodies, the Church of England Schools Council and the Catholic Education Council. For these purposes it has an education committee, which is a sub-committee of the executive, and an education policy committee. The latter meets with a corresponding group from the Church of England Schools Council in the Central Joint Education Policy Committee. The concern of the Free Churches in more general educational matters is pursued through the Education Department of the British Council of Churches where the Free Churches are separately represented.

Gen. Sec.: Dr A. R. Vine, MA, BSc, 27 Tavistock Sq., London, WC1.

See also **Free Churches in education.**

Free Churches in education The term 'free churches' is normally understood to mean those denominations in England and Wales which owe their origins to a break with the established church. The largest are the Baptists, Congregationalists, Presbyterians and Methodists, although there are 12 constituent members of the Free Church Federal Council. The Council is the channel of corporate free church judgment and action vis-à-vis the Anglican and Roman Communions and the state.

The free churches of England and Wales have traditionally supported the state school system, whereas the established church (*see* **Anglicans and education**) supports a dual system of voluntary aided and state schools. This divergence of opinions has caused much bitterness in the past but since 1944 relations have steadily improved. Free churchmen have come to respect the convictions held by Anglicans and Roman Catholics about the church's role in education. They agree it is equitable that, where a sufficient number of children of a given persuasion live in an area, there should be a school which conforms to that persuasion, provided this does not create a 'single school area'. They recognise that these schools should not be inferior to county schools and that it is reasonable that a proportion (recently raised by agreement to 80%) of public money should be spent on them.

Through the Central Joint Education Policy Committee the free churches have since 1959 regularly conferred with Anglicans on educational matters of common concern and there have been informal discussions with Roman Catholics, as a result of which an agreed basis has been found for recent legislation.

The free churches have always believed it to be part of their contribution to education to promote teacher-training, and Westhill College of Education is a foundation governed by a

282

consortium of the free churches. There are other denominational colleges, notably Westminster College, Oxford, and Southlands College, Wimbledon, both Methodist foundations. Each of the free churches has strong youth and education departments, and each is actively concerned with Sunday schools.

Headquarters of the Free Church Federal Council: 27 Tavistock Sq., London, WCI.

RJG

Free day *See* **Infant schools**

Free elementary schools Advocated by the National Education League in 1869, free elementary education sustained from rates was opposed in 1870 by those who realised that fees provided a third of the expenditure in elementary schools; by 1886–7 fees were bringing in nearly four times as much.

Fees were abolished in 1891 by Act of Parliament, which made a fee grant of 10s a year to take the place of fees paid for children aged five to 15.

See also **School fees**

Free writing *See* **Writing, Free**

French Guiana, Education in 1966 statistics (enrolments only): public primary 6,624, private primary 1,320, secondary 2,237, technical 530. Total population: approximately 35,000.

French in the primary school A Schools Council interim report on the pilot project sponsored by it and the Nuffield Foundation (*q.v.*), *French in the Primary School* (Working Paper No. 8), was published in 1967 and concluded generally that where French had been included in the primary school curriculum it had had a beneficial effect on the children's approach to other subjects.

The scheme, which will continue until September 1970, involves 6,000 eight-year-olds in 125 schools from 13 different areas. A Schools Council

survey, mentioned in the working paper, showed that about one in five primary schools included French in their syllabuses. The scheme seemed so far to be working well, but until the final assessment was made after its completion it was not possible to say whether the success might be partly explained by novelty. Reservations were felt by some teachers as to the wisdom of teaching French to the least able children; but the principle that children of all abilities should take part in the scheme will be maintained.

French Somaliland, Education in 1964 statistics: 26 primary schools (enrolment 4,186); three secondary schools (enrolment 446); five technical schools (enrolment 337). Total population: approximately 90,000.

Freud, Sigmund (1856-1939) Freud first trained as a doctor of medicine in Vienna, but it was his later experience as a neurologist, often in contact with profoundly neurotic patients, that led him on to his theory of psychoanalysis. Briefly, this form of understanding and treatment believes that emotion is more important than reason in governing human beings, and that many of our most basic and powerful emotions have their origin in early childhood and operate later at a level about which we are unconscious. Treatment, therefore, often consists in putting patients in touch with their basic emotions, and thus releasing the pressures that can build up in those cases when an individual is divided against himself.

Freud himself claimed never to have contributed anything directly to education, but the gradual spread of his ideas had a profound effect upon some schools, especially where infants and nursery children were concerned. Here the Freudian theory of ambivalence, in the sense that one individual can have violently conflicting feelings about another without these being fully or even partly realised, was recognised in the case of infants who often seem to feel a mixture broadly of love and hate towards their parents or teachers. When the negative side of this feeling is expressed as rage, destructiveness or even anxiety on the child's part, it is most important to understand these emotions and to try to canalise them perhaps into play or activity where aggression can be safely expressed. The alternative, where such feelings are regarded as wicked and to be suppressed, can in the long term be most harmful, whatever the short-term success in stifling them.

Such ideas understandably aroused a great deal of hostility from some parents and teachers, and there may have been some justification for this in the sense that early and over-enthusiastic followers of psychoanalysis perhaps advocated too much freedom for children to express their basic wishes, with the result sometimes that such children merely became anxious at the general lack of order and control in their lives. It was soon realised, however, that children do need a framework of order in which to grow, but one based on understanding and the need to express the total personality, albeit in ways that may have to become modified, or in psycho-analytic terms, sublimated, in order to become more or less acceptable to society. In this process, it is equally as important for the adult to realise some of his own conflicting feelings towards the child as it is for him to understand why the child will occasionally do or say things that the adult will find it hard but nevertheless important to accept.

With older children, who show less of their feelings at an immediate level, psychoanalysis has still been able to indicate some of the emotional roots to learning or behaviour difficulties. Disturbed or delinquent children in particular are now treated with far greater understanding, and their cure is seen more in terms of their own personality adjustment than in the need for punitive discipline. Such cures are not easy, and with children often involve the whole family situation as well; but if psychoanalysis has revealed some of the genuine complexities of many emotional problems, it has helped some child guidance clinics and schools for maladjusted pupils to pro-duce outstanding results with cases that would once have been written off as either incurable or generally un-worthy of any special effort.

Bearing in mind some of the faults of psychoanalysis, such as its dogmatism or occasional obscurity, it has neverthe-less provided a humane working guide to the dynamics of personality, and an explanation of particular human traits with an indication for their treatment that is unlikely to be superseded. It has also led to far more sympathy and flexibility in the way we now look upon children, especially when they are very young.

FURTHER READING
Ilse Hellman. 'Psychoanalysis and the Teacher', *Psychoanalysis and Contemporary Thought*, ed. John D. Sutherland, Hogarth Press, 1958.
Ernest Jones. *The Life and Work of Sigmund Freud*, Penguin Books, 1964.

NT

Friends Education Council The Council correlates the work of the Quaker schools, administers bursaries for pupils and students and links Quaker teachers and young people in all forms of education. A library, lesson notes, help with individual projects and talks are among facilities provided.

Friends Hse, Euston Rd, London, NW1.

Publications: *Bulletins* (occasionally).

Froebel, Friedrich (1782–1852) Main educational work: *The Education of Man*.

In Froebel's view, all things have an outer and an inner aspect and are symbols of a hidden spirit. Further-more, all things share a single inner unity because they manifest the single spirit of God. To know is to see through to this unity of spirit, a task greatly assisted by natural science and by mathematics. All things unfold towards their essential perfection through an inner law of development, much as a plant does. Where children are con-cerned, men conceitedly impose their own stunting and distorting ideas on the child's natural development.

To be in harmony with nature, education should ensure that all that a child does will self-actively spring from his present desires and interests. Play is at first the most perfect expression of this self-activity, especially when assisted by the materials and games devised for the kindergarten. Later, ordinary instruction may be given, but it must always allow for self-activity, observe the laws of development, and point through its variety to the inner unity of things.

Perhaps more than anyone else, Froebel and his energetic disciples have influenced the training of infant teachers and the curriculum and organi-sation of primary schools in this country today. Himself an architect-student turned teacher, Froebel rejected the idea of academic grind for young children and founded the kinder-garten—a nursery where pupils could learn through their own activity and play, great importance being given to nature work, constructive games and toys, music, drawing, handwork and stories. It was hoped that the teacher would provide the means and encour-agement, but not attempt to mould the child, as this would be to interfere with a process which should happen natu-rally.

Since Froebel's time, some of his original suggestions for games and handwork have of course been revised but many of his basic ideas are still highly relevant, such as his belief that the first few years of life are the really formative ones, and that parents should be encouraged to join in school activi-ties as much as possible. On the other hand, child development is now seen as a far more complicated story, and Froebel's vision of tranquil, uninter-rupted growth under the influence of a benign environment is no longer thought to be really adequate. Froebel's great service to children, however, was to see them as beings to be encouraged rather than repressed. This emphasis may have led to a few excesses, such as too much play when occasionally something a little more structured may be needed; but the fact that so many infants and juniors now look forward to the next day at school, often to the incredulity of their parents, has a lot to do with Froebel and the various societies all over the world—in this country the National Froebel Society—that carry on the message of his work.

FURTHER READING

Evelyn Lawrence (Ed.) *Friedrich Froebel and English Education*, Univ. of London Press, 1952.

RFD and NT

Froebel Foundation, National Oper-ating under a scheme approved by the DES, the Foundation acts as a centre of education: it organises conferences, courses, lectures and other activities, and publishes pamphlets and a house-magazine. The training of teachers concerned with children of five to 12, particularly in-service training, is a main interest.

The Foundation is also an examining body, and issues certificates and diplomas. Courses for the Froebel Teacher's Certificate A take one year of full-time study and two years part-time in the UK—three years in Eire. Seminars in preparation for the Trainer's Diploma, a qualification for work in training colleges, are held in London.

Membership is open to parents, teachers and others interested in the Foundation's work.

2 Manchester Sq., London, W1.

K*

Fulbright Exchange Programme Provides for the exchange of students, teachers, lecturers, research scholars and specialists between the USA and designated countries. The scheme is financed from the sale of US surplus properties left in certain countries at the end of the second world war. The object of the programme is to further international goodwill and understanding, and all forms of research and study are included.

Full-time education *See* **School attendance**

Full-time teaching service An appointment of a teacher by an LEA is normally regarded as a full-time appointment without definition of hours. In making its statistical return to the DES all an LEA is required to do, for the purposes of superannuation entitlement, is to state the number of teachers engaged on a full-time basis. This is the position in regard to primary and secondary schools.

In some branches the same may be true in respect of a wide range of further education posts, but where hourly engagements are involved it is clearly necessary to be more precise about the nature of the engagement. Thus, for these cases an average of 30 hours per week over a 36-week year (i.e. not less than 1,080 hours) would for the purposes of superannuation contributions and benefits constitute a full-time engagement. Part-time appointments were first made pensionable from 1 December 1967 by legislation making it possible under existing qualifying conditions to establish an entitlement to benefits, provided the part-time teacher is able to establish the equivalent of not less than ten years full-time service through part-time work, and has had at least a year's full-time pensionable service. SEB

Further Education, Civil Service Council for The Council is a national Whitley body under the aegis of the Civil Service National Whitley Council. It has headquarters in London and regional secretaries throughout the UK. Being concerned with all aspects of further education (other than job-training) for civil servants of all ages and grades, it promotes and publicises existing courses and facilities throughout the civil service and also provides an educational advisory service. In addition, it is responsible for arranging day-release facilities for many thousands of young civil servants under 18. These activities make it necessary for the Council to have very close links with LEAs, educational bodies of all types and government departments.

Treasury Chambers, Great George St, London, SW1.

Further Education, Regional Advisory Councils for These were established in 1946/47 to provide machinery for consultation by adjacent LEAs on the provision of further education in a region without undue overlap and duplication of courses (*see* **Further education**). The Councils cover 10 areas as follows:

Region 1. London and Home Counties Regional Advisory Council for Technological Education (Barking, Barnet, Bedfordshire, Bexley, Brent, Brighton, Bromley, Buckinghamshire, Canterbury, Croydon, Ealing, Eastbourne, Enfield, Essex, Haringey, Harrow, Hastings, Havering, Hertfordshire, Hillingdon, Hounslow, Inner London, Kent, Kingston-upon-Thames, Luton, Merton, Newham, Redbridge, Richmond-upon-Thames, Southend-on-Sea, Surrey, Sussex (East), Sussex (West), Sutton, Waltham Forest). Sec.: R. D. Jamieson, Tavistock Hse South, Tavistock Sq., London, WC1.

Region 2. Southern Regional Council for Further Education (Berkshire, Bournemouth, Dorset, Hampshire, Isle of Wight, Oxford, Oxfordshire, Portsmouth, Reading, Southampton, Sussex (West) and Wiltshire). Sec.: J. M. C. Philip, 9 Bath Rd, Reading.

Region 3. Regional Council for Further Education for the South-West (Bath, Bristol, Cornwall, Devon, Dorset, Exeter, Gloucester, Gloucestershire, Plymouth, Somerset, Wiltshire and Isles of Scilly; with Jersey and Guernsey as associate members). Sec.: S. Brook, 12 Lower Castle St, Bristol, 1.

Region 4. West Midlands Advisory Council for Further Education (Birmingham, Burton-upon-Trent, Coventry, Dudley, Herefordshire, Shropshire, Solihull, Staffordshire, Stoke-on-Trent, Walsall, Warley, Warwickshire, West Bromwich, Wolverhampton, Worcester and Worcestershire). Sec.: J. Lord, Pitman Bldgs, 161 Corporation St, Birmingham, 4.

Region 5. Regional Advisory Council for Further Education in the East Midlands (Derby, Derbyshire, Grimsby, Leicester, Leicestershire, Lincoln, Lincolnshire (Holland), Lincolnshire (Kesteven), Lincolnshire (Lindsey), Northampton, Northamptonshire, Nottingham, Nottinghamshire and Rutland). Sec.: W. C. Watterson, Robins Wood Hse, Robins Wood Rd, Aspley, Nottingham.

Region 6. East Anglian Advisory Council for Further Education (Bedfordshire, Cambridgeshire and Isle of Ely, Essex, Great Yarmouth, Hertfordshire, Huntingdon and Peterborough, Ipswich, Norfolk, Norwich, East and West Suffolk). Sec.: Dr F. Lincoln Ralphs, County Education Office, Stracey Rd, Norwich, Norfolk.

Region 7. Yorkshire Council for Further Education (Barnsley, Bradford, Dewsbury, Doncaster, Halifax, Huddersfield, Hull, Leeds, Lindsey, Middlesborough, Nottinghamshire, Rotherham, Sheffield, Wakefield, York, Yorkshire (East Riding), Yorkshire (North Riding), Yorkshire (West Riding) and York). Sec.: John Leese, Bowling Green Terrace, Jack La., Leeds, 11.

Region 8. Regional Advisory Council for Further Education in the North-West (Barrow-in-Furness, Birkenhead,

Blackburn, Blackpool, Bolton, Bootle, Burnley, Bury, Cheshire, Chester, Derbyshire (in part), Lancashire, Liverpool, Manchester, Oldham, Preston, Rochdale, St Helens, Salford, Southport, Stockport, Wallasey, Warrington, Westmorland (in part), West Riding (in part) and Wigan). Sec.: I. K. Jackson, Africa Hse, 54 Whitworth St, Manchester, 1.

Region 9. Northern Advisory Council for Further Education (Carlisle, Cumberland, Darlington, Durham, Gateshead, Middlesbrough, Newcastle-upon-Tyne, Northumberland, South Shields, Sunderland, Tynemouth, West Hartlepool, Yorkshire (North Riding) and Westmorland). Sec.: A. T. Morrison, 5 Grosvenor Villas, Grosvenor Rd, Newcastle-upon-Tyne, 2.

Region 10. Welsh Joint Education Committee (Anglesey, Breconshire, Caernarvonshire, Cardiff, Cardiganshire, Carmarthenshire, Denbighshire, Flintshire, Glamorgan, Merioneth, Merthyr Tydfil, Monmouthshire, Montgomeryshire, Newport, Pembrokeshire, Radnorshire and Swansea). Sec.: D. Andrew Davies, 30 Cathedral Rd, Cardiff.

Further Education Advisory Council *See* **BBC educational broadcasting**

Further Education Committee *See* **Burnham Committees**

Further education in England and Wales Further education is a general term used to describe full- or part-time education for those who have completed their secondary education. Further education includes technical, commercial and art education, higher education (i.e. academic or professional education for students over 18 with university entrance or equivalent qualifications) and adult education. However, higher education provided in universities, colleges of education and certain other specialist colleges, and adult education provided by 'responsible bodies' (like the WEA), are not normally regarded as part of the further education system.

Historical development Further education may be provided in establishments variously described as colleges of technology, technical colleges, polytechnics, colleges of commerce, schools or colleges of art, colleges of further education, or in evening institutes. Nearly all are maintained by LEAs who, however, receive grants towards the cost from the central government. Evening institutes, of which at present there are about 7,500, normally function in schools or premises used for other educational purposes in the daytime. The main provision of further education is in about 700 permanent colleges which differ greatly in size and character; the smallest may have only about a dozen or so full-time staff while the largest will employ between two and three hundred.

A large number of colleges have been established since 1945 to cope with the big increase in demand for technical education associated with industrial and commercial expansion since the war. One group of colleges, mainly in the north of England and the industrial midlands, however, is directly descended from mechanics institutes (*q.v.*) founded in the 18th and 19th centuries, while the origin of another group lies in the schools of art and science whose foundation was stimulated by the Great Exhibition of 1851. The City Parochial Charities Act 1883 provided the money with which most of the London polytechnics were started, while the Customs and Excise Act 1890, which allocated to technical education the compensation money originally intended for publicans deprived of their licences, provided sufficient funds for the foundation of over a hundred institutions, many of which subsequently faded out in the early 1900s.

Further education colleges Further education has grown up in an ad hoc fashion, largely in response to local needs, and only recently have attempts been made at systematisation and rationalisation. In certain areas, particularly in the north and the midlands, adjoining LEAs have at various times set up joint committees to advise on the best form of provision for further education in their areas. After the war the system was extended to the whole country and in 1946–7 ten regional advisory councils were formally established to provide machinery by which adjacent LEAs could consult together about further education provision in the region, to assess needs and to advise on measures designed to prevent unnecessary overlap and duplication of courses. All courses which require the approval of the DES must now be submitted first to the appropriate regional advisory council for approval.

In June 1956 the Ministry of Education issued Circular 305 defining four categories of colleges: (1) *colleges of advanced technology*, which would be concerned only with advanced courses (i.e. higher education), mainly in the fields of technology, science, management and business studies; (2) *regional colleges*, which though concerned mainly with advanced work might also have an appreciable volume of work at a lower level; (3) *area colleges*, providing some advanced courses, mainly of a part-time nature to suit particular needs of the area, but mainly concerned with less advanced work; (4) *local colleges*, providing mainly part-time courses and only up to the level of the Ordinary National Certificate (*see below*) or its equivalent.

In 1964 there were ten colleges of advanced technology and 25 regional colleges; the boundary between area and local colleges has never been precisely defined but between 100 and 150 of the 700 colleges concerned with further education fall within the definition of an area college.

Following the recommendations of the Robbins Report on Higher Education 1963 nine of the ten colleges of advanced technology (Northampton, Battersea and Brunel Colleges in London, and those at Birmingham, Bradford, Bristol, Cardiff, Loughborough and Salford) became independent universities, while Chelsea College was affiliated to London University. Further reorganisation was foreshadowed by the announcement in 1964 of the 'binary' system for higher education, envisaging the development of a higher education sector in the maintained system which would be similar in standard to the autonomous university sector, but different in character. In 1966 a White Paper announced a plan for the development of about 30 polytechnics based on existing regional and large area colleges, into which the majority of full-time advanced courses would eventually be concentrated.

Organisation of courses Further education before the second world war was mainly a part-time system conducted in the evenings for those in full-time employment. In the daytime colleges were mainly occupied by junior technical schools providing trade courses, usually of two years duration, and starting a year before the statutory school-leaving age. A few part-time courses were held in the day-time for students released by employers. The Education Act 1944 included a clause (the county college clause) making it compulsory for all young people under the age of 18 who left school to attend a further education college for at least one day each week.

Although this clause has never been implemented, there was a very rapid rise after 1945 in part-time day ('day release') courses for students released by employers on full wages to attend further education colleges, usually for one day, but occasionally for a half day, each week. In fields like engineering

and building, which employ indentured apprentices, the apprenticeship agreement normally includes a clause obliging the employer to allow day release up to the age of 18. By 1965, 680,000 students were attending part-time day courses. The junior technical schools which had hitherto occupied college premises during the day-time disappeared. Some courses were closed and some were absorbed into the secondary system in new technical high schools; for the remainder, the entry age was raised to 15 or 16, and the students, being above school-leaving age, came wholly into the province of further education.

Full-time courses of further education which were almost unknown before 1939 also developed rapidly after the war and by 1965 enrolled over 160,000 students. Most of these courses are 'end-on' to school, taking in students aged 15–19, but nearly one-fifth of the total enrolment in 1965 consisted of students over 21.

In the 50s another type of course, the 'sandwich' course, was developed, in which students spend a substantial part of each year, usually six months, in college and work for the remainder of the period in industry, where they receive appropriate training. Students may be either 'industry-based', in which case the firm by which they are employed maintains them during the period at college, or 'college-based', in which case the college recruits the student and makes arrangements for him to receive appropriate industrial or commercial training during the period he is away from college. The number of students in 'sandwich' courses grew very rapidly and reached over 17,000 by 1965; in addition there were several thousand sandwich course students in the universities based on the former colleges of advanced technology. Since about 1960 experiments have been made with 'block release' courses in which a student is released from employment for a period of several weeks at a time, instead of for one day each week. This arrangement avoids the weekly readjustment from the atmosphere of employment to that of college which can cause tensions, and greatly reduces time spent in travelling, but may leave the student out of contact with the college for considerable periods. Experiments on the relative value of day release and block release courses providing roughly the same total period of education each year have not yielded conclusive results. A considerable change-over from day release to block release has however already occurred.

With most day release courses the student is expected also to attend the college on one or two evenings each week. Courses for professional and technical qualifications provided in the evenings only, which once formed almost the only provision for further education (hence the term 'night-school') have greatly declined in importance and have largely disappeared from the technological field. It is only in the field of commerce and business, where day release has been slow to develop, that any significant proportion of evening courses continue. In their place many colleges have developed evening programmes of non-vocational adult education, particularly in languages.

Numbers of students

ENROLMENTS IN
FURTHER EDUCATION, 1965

Type of course	Total enrolment	For qualifications
Full-time	161,084	133,907
Short full-time	8,748	—
Sandwich	17,206	17,206
Part-time day and block release	679,761	546,563
Evening only	795,880	306,524
Total in all FE colleges	1,662,679	1,004,200
Total in evening institutes	1,252,913	24,504
Total students	2,915,592	1,028,704

Since on average the weekly attendance required is about 30 hours for a full-time or sandwich course, 8–10 hours for a part-time day course, and 2–3 hours for an evening course, the volume of work in the day-time greatly exceeds that in the evenings.

The table above shows that most day students and about 40% of the evening students in further education establishments are following courses leading to recognised qualifications. The remaining students may be following postgraduate or refresher courses, designed to familiarise them with recent developments, or general cultural or recreational courses in fields like art, literature, music, languages, domestic subjects or physical education.

Fields of work covered In the courses leading to recognised qualifications, over 70% of students in 1965 were preparing to enter, or were already employed in, manufacturing industries of all types, in the construction and extraction industries, in service industries and trades, in business, administration and commerce, and in the professions.

Engineering in its various forms is by far the most important single field for which courses are provided; over one-third of the total enrolments in 1965 were in engineering courses, and half the part-time day and two-thirds of the sandwich-course students were employed in engineering.

Courses for those intending to take up careers in art and design have long been established; although they only accounted for about 2% of the total enrolments in 1965. About 12% of the full-time students were studying for design qualifications.

A recent significant development has been the rapid growth of courses for the General Certificate of Education (*q.v.*) at both O and A level; GCE enrolments now account for about 20% of the million enrolments from students seeking recognised qualifications. O all full-time students in 1965 over one-quarter were studying solely for GCE subjects.

Levels of work In any particular field courses may be provided at more than one level. In engineering, for instance, three levels are distinguished—that of the technologist, the technician and the craftsman. These were defined in the White Paper *Technical Education* (1956) as follows:

Technologists. A technologist has the qualifications and experience required for membership of a professional institution. Most university graduates in engineering and other applied sciences, and a good proportion of holders of higher national diplomas or certificates or similar qualifications, become technologists. A technologist has studied the fundamental principles of his chosen technology and should be able to use his knowledge and experience to initiate practical developments. He is expected to accept a high degree of responsibility and in many cases to push forward the boundaries of knowledge in his own particular field.

Technicians. A technician is qualified by specialist technical education and practical training to work under the general direction of a technologist. Consequently, he will require a good knowledge of mathematics and science related to his own speciality. Examples of technicians in the factory are assistant designers and junior ranks of management on the shop floor.

Craftsmen. Craftsmen represent the skilled labour of manufacturing industry and account for more than one-third of its manpower. With the growing complexity of machines and the introduction of new materials it becomes all the more necessary for them to appreciate not only the how but the why of the work they do.

At each level courses are provided leading to appropriate recognised qualifications (a description of the qualifications is given under the heading *Examinations and examining bodies* below), the most important of which are the following:

Technologist level. A degree or graduateship of a professional institute (e.g. Grad IEE, Grad RIC, Grad Inst P, Grad RICS); a final qualification of a professional institute (e.g. accountant, banker, chartered secretary); a Diploma in Technology (now superseded by a CNAA degree) or Higher National Diploma.

Technician level. Higher and Ordinary National Certificate; Technician's Certificate of the City and Guilds of London Institute.

Craft level. Craft certificate of the City and Guilds of London Institute; certificate of the Royal Society of Arts; certificate of a regional examining union.

Examinations and examining bodies

Degrees. Until recently the only degree open to students in further education was the external degree of London University. In the 50s a National Council for Technological Awards (NCTA) was set up which was empowered to award a Diploma in Technology (the Dip Tech) to students successfully completing courses in various technological fields previously approved by the Council as being of honours degree standard. Most sandwich courses were designed to lead to this award.

Following the recommendations of the Robbins Committee this system was greatly extended and the Council for National Academic Awards (CNAA) was set up and empowered by Royal Charter to award degrees, including higher degrees, of the same standard and status as those of universities. The Council's field of work is not limited in any way. The CNAA, however, absorbed the NCTA and awarded CNAA degrees retrospectively to those who had qualified for the Dip Tech. Colleges wishing to run courses for a CNAA degree are required to submit the fullest particulars about the college, its staffing and general amenities, together with detailed syllabuses and proposed examination arrangements, including the appointment of external examiners responsible for maintaining standards. The Council's specialist sub-committees consider the proposals in detail and a panel of members visits the college and meets the staff concerned with the courses. Only if it is fully satisfied that the proposed course will be strictly comparable with a university degree course does the Council give its approval. Any approvals are periodically reviewed.

National diplomas and certificates. A diploma is normally awarded after a full-time or sandwich course, while a certificate is awarded after a part-time day or block release or (very occasionally nowadays) after an evening course. To run a diploma or certificate course a college must submit details of the course, syllabuses and examination arrangements to a joint committee, composed of representatives of the professional institutions in the field of work concerned, of the DES, and of further education teachers' organisations. If the joint committee approves the course (usually for a period of five years) examinations at the end of the course are set and marked by the college staff. Both examination papers and marked scripts must be submitted to an external assessor, appointed by the joint committee, who is responsible for ensuring that proper standards are maintained.

The Higher National Diploma (HND) is a course requiring at least one GCE A level pass, or its equivalent, for entry, and normally extends over two years as a full-time or three years as a sandwich course. Its level is comparable with a university pass or ordinary degree. Many professional institutions (e.g. the Institute of Electrical Engineering) accept the HND as meeting a substantial part of their academic requirements for membership. The Ordinary National Diploma (OND) is a full-time or sandwich

course, normally of two years' duration, requiring certain GCE O level passes for entry, and offering an alternative to GCE A level as a means of entry to the HND. The OND may also be accepted as a qualification to enter university and other courses of similar standard.

The Higher National Certificate (HNC) is a two-year part-time day or block release course, normally end-on to the Ordinary National Certificate or Diploma, and similar in standard to, but more restricted in coverage than, the equivalent HND. The HNC at one time was recognised as fulfilling certain academic requirements of the professional institutions, but this recognition is gradually being withdrawn and the HNC is coming to be regarded as a higher technician qualification. The ONC is also of two years' duration; entry to it usually requires four appropriate GCE O level passes or completion of a specific General (G) course.

Certificates of the City and Guilds of London Institute. The Institute conducts examinations, and awards certificates on syllabuses published by the Institute. Syllabuses are provided for courses covering a very wide industrial and commercial field at both technician and craft level. Over 200 different subjects are offered and the number is constantly increasing as new industrial and commercial needs develop. In devising syllabuses, the Institute is advised by committees which include appropriate representatives of industry and commerce, practising teachers, and other educational interests in the field covered.

City and Guilds certificates are normally designed for part-time day or block release courses, but may occasionally be taken in full-time courses. A typical pattern provides for a basic (formerly often called an intermediate) certificate at the end of a two-year course with an advanced (formerly called a final) certificate after a further two-year course. There are, however, many variations in the pattern and in some subjects further levels beyond advanced.

Regional examining unions and the Royal Society of Arts. There are five regional examining unions awarding certificates for craft and technicians' courses, on a pattern similar to that of the City and Guilds of London Institute. A certificate of a regional examining union may be accepted in lieu of the equivalent City and Guilds certificate. The Royal Society of Arts functions in some respects as a regional examining union for London and the home counties, but also provides examinations on a national scale, particularly in secretarial and commercial subjects, such as shorthand, typewriting and book-keeping.

Diploma in Art and Design. This is a degree-level qualification awarded at the end of a three-year full-time course, available at a limited number of recognised colleges. Entrants to the course must be over 18, have certain GCE qualifications and have successfully completed a preparatory course of at least one year at a school or college of art.

Nature of courses A large number of courses in further education, particularly those leading to national diplomas and certificates and City and Guilds certificates, are 'vocational'; this does not mean that the content is largely practical but that the subjects are selected for their relevance to a specific field of employment (this is equally true for instance of university courses in medical sciences, engineering and other technologies). Mathematics and science are the basic subjects of most technical courses, and economics and law of most commercial and business courses. The objective is to provide a background of theoretical knowledge which will have an application in a particular field of employment, and which will increase the student's understanding of basic principles and make him adaptable to change.

Some courses, particularly at craft level, include an element of workshop practice, but its object is not to teach practical skills but to provide laboratory experience of processes and materials. This technical education is often confused with industrial training which is concerned with the development of usable skills. Technical education has been defined as preparation for the unknown whereas industrial training is preparation for the known.

In Great Britain industrial training is the responsibility of industry and not of the educational system. It is usually given during the period when a part-time or sandwich-course student is working in industry; it may also be given in an uninterrupted period at the end of a degree or other full-time course of theoretical study. The rather haphazard nature of this training was long recognised as inefficient and unsatisfactory and led eventually to the passing of the Industrial Training Act in 1963 which provided for the setting up of training boards for all important industries. The boards are charged with the responsibility of devising appropriate training schemes for workers at all levels in their field; they have the power to raise a levy from all employers in the industry and to make grants to employers carrying out training schemes inspected and approved by the board.

Apart from subjects which have vocational relevance, most full-time and part-time further education courses now provide a considerable proportion of time for non-vocational liberal and general studies.

Comparisons with other countries The further education system in England and Wales differs considerably from that of other countries. Amongst its unusual characteristics are the following: (1) the wide range of subjects available at most colleges and the small use made of 'monotechnics' limited to one particular field; (2) the availability in a single college of courses at several different levels;

(3) the widespread use of sandwich and day-release courses enabling students to pursue their education while gaining practical experience in employment; (4) the sharp distinction between 'technical education' and 'industrial training'; (5) the overlap of the work of further education colleges with that of schools and universities, and of bodies responsible for adult education.

Further education associations The oldest and largest body is the Association of Technical Institutions, founded in 1895. Most colleges belong to this association; each is empowered on election to nominate three representatives who are normally the principal, the chief education officer of the authority maintaining the college, or one of his deputies, and the chairman or a member of the college governing body. The teachers' professional organisations are the Association of Principals of Technical Institutions and the Association of Teachers in Technical Institutions which is affiliated to the National Union of Teachers.

Teachers in further education Since most further education colleges are large they are normally organised under the principal (who may be assisted by a vice-principal) on a departmental basis. There are six grades of departmental headships; the grade depends on the size and academic responsibilities of the department. Other staff may be graded, depending on qualifications, experience, and academic and other responsibilities, as readers, principal lecturers, senior lecturers, lecturers or assistant lecturers.

For teaching at technologist or technician level, staff are normally required to have a degree, or a final professional or equivalent qualification, together with some relevant experience in industry, commerce or research. For teaching at craft level, City and Guilds qualifications together with industrial experience are usually appropriate. At one time it was unusual for staff to have

received formal pedagogical training, but there are now four colleges of education (technical) in London, Bolton, Huddersfield and Wolverhampton, which provide full-time pre-service or four-term 'sandwich' courses leading to a Certificate of Education, for those wishing to enter, or already teaching in, further education.

FURTHER READING

M. Argles. *South Kensington to Robbins*, Longmans, 1964.

Central Office of Information. *Technical Education in Britain*, HMSO, 1962.

Committee on Higher Education. *Higher Education* (Robbins Report), HMSO, 1963.

Stephen Cotgrove. *Technical Education and Social Change*, Allen and Unwin, 1958.

Department of Education and Science. *A Plan for Polytechnics and Other Colleges*, Cmnd. 3006, 1966. *Day Release* (Heniker-Heaton Report), HMSO, S.O. Code 27–370, 1964.

Ministry of Education. *Further Education*, HMSO, Pamphlet No. 8, 1947. *Technical Education*, HMSO, Cmnd. 9703, 1956. Reports of National Advisory Council on Art Education: *First Report*, HMSO, S.O. Code 27–344, 1960; *Vocational Courses in Colleges and Schools of Art*, HMSO, Code No. 27–354, 1962; *Post-Diploma Studies in Art and Design*, HMSO, Code No. 27–374, 1964. *Better Opportunities in Technical Education*, HMSO, Cmnd. 1254, 1961. *Forward from School*, HMSO, Code 27–351, 1962.

Ministry of Labour. *Industrial Training— Government Proposals*, HMSO, Cmnd. 1892.

See also **Appendixes 8, 9, 10, 11** (*Technical education*)

DEM

Further Education Officers in Scotland, Association of Membership is open to officials employed by LEAs in Scotland who are directly concerned with the provision of further education at a county or district level. ('Further Education' includes Youth Service, Community Service, adult education, day and evening further education classes and social and recreational activities).

The Association aims to provide a forum for the exchange of information and views between members, and between members and others; to act as an advisory and consultative body; to undertake research and experiment; to provide the means for corporate action on the conditions of service of all or some of its members (the Association is not a salary negotiating body); to promote further education and members' welfare.

Donald MacDonald, Further Education Section, County Buildings, Hamilton.

Further education scales

Assistant lecturers Group I £800–£1,500, Group II £900–£1,600, Group III £1,020–£1,720. Increments of £30(2), £50, £60(3), £50(7) and £60. (Group I are non-graduates, Group II graduates or degree equivalents, Group III honours graduates.)

Lecturers Grade I Group I £1,035–£1,735, Group II £1,135–£1,835, Group III £1,255–£1,955. Increments of £30(2), £50, £60(3), £50(7) and £60. Where a lecturer Grade I has responsibilities of a supervisory or administrative nature which, in the opinion of the LEA, justify an allowance over and above the scale salary, the LEA may pay an allowance of £175 per annum.

Lecturers Grade II £1,725–£2,280. Increments of £55 (9) and £60.

Senior Lecturers £2,280–£2,595. Increments of £60(2) and £65(3).

Principal lecturers £2,530–£2,770 (bar)–£3,250. Increments of £80(9). Posts with salaries beyond the bar may be established in departments of which the head is either Grade V or Grade VI if the principal lecturer is responsible for a significant amount of work of university level.

Readers £2,465–£3,250. Increments of £65(2), £80(5) and £85(3). The establishment of a post of Reader in an establishment where significant commissioned and sponsored research is undertaken will be subject to the approval of the Secretary of State. The salary scale will be any four consecutive points on the above as determined by the LEA.

Heads of department Grade I £2,100–£2,360; increments of £50(3) and £55(2). Grade II £2,360–£2,685; increments of £65(5). Grade III £2,620–£2,930; increments of £75(2) and £80(2). Grade IV £2,850–£3,170; increments of £80(4). Grade V £3,090–£3,440; increments of £85(2) and £90(2). Grade VI £3,350–£3,780; increments of £85(4) and £90.

Where the LEA or governing body of a college in Group 7 or above requires a head of department to exercise the function of co-ordination or supervision over other departments, thus acting as head of faculty, the head of department may be paid an addition to his salary as head of department of such amount as the authority may determine, not exceeding £300.

Vice-principals The allowance paid to vice-principals who are also heads of departments shall not exceed £500.

Full-time vice-principals (1 September 1967 to 31 March 1969)

Group	Range of min. salary (£)	Increments (£)	Range of max. salary (£)
1	1,785–1,945	60(3), 65(1)	2,030–2,190
2	1,960–2,125	60(3), 65(1)	2,205–2,370
3	2,140–2,305	60(3), 65(1)	2,385–2,550
4	2,320–2,485	60(3), 65(1)	2,565–2,730
5	2,500–2,665	60(3), 65(1)	2,745–2,910
6	2,685–2,850	80(2), 85(1)	2,930–3,095
7	2,870–3,035	80(2), 85(1)	3,115–3,280
8	3,055–3,300	80(2), 85(1), 90(1)	3,390–3,635
9	3,320–3,570	80(2), 85(1), 90(1)	3,655–3,905
10	3,590–3,835	80(2), 85(1), 90(1)	3,925–4,170
11	3,855–4,100	80(2), 85(1), 90(1)	4,190–4,435
12	Determined by the LEA in the light of these scales		

Principals (1 September 1967 to 31 March 1969)

Group	Range of min. salary (£)	Increments At discretion	Range o max. salary (£)
0			Not over 2,450
1	2,170–2,370	75(4)	2,470–2,670
2	2,390–2,590	75(4)	2,690–2,890
3	2,610–2,810	75(4)	2,910–3,110
4	2,830–3,030	75(4)	3,130–3,330
5	3,050–3,250	75(4)	3,350–3,550
6	3,275–3,475	100(3)	3,575–3,775
7	3,500–3,700	100(3)	3,800–4,000
8	3,725–4,025	100(4)	4,125–4,425
9	4,050–4,350	100(4)	4,450–4,750
10	4,375–4,675	100(4)	4,775–5,075
11	4,700–5,000	100(4)	5,100–5,400
12	Determined by the LEA in the light of these scales		

SEB

Further education in Scotland

There are some 80 further education centres that make local provision for further education in Scotland, providing part-time courses for those who have left school after only three or four years of secondary education, together with full-time pre-vocational and first-year apprenticeship courses. Courses include those leading to Certificates of the City and Guilds of London Institute, Craft Certificates, National Certificates and Diplomas, and Certificates of the Scottish Council for Commercial, Administrative and Professional Education. In some cases, courses lead to recognition by the professional institutions, and a few centres offer courses at degree level.

Regionally, further education is provided by 13 central institutions, which are advanced colleges that receive a grant direct from the Scottish Education Department or the Department of Agriculture and Fisheries for Scotland, and are administered by independent boards of governors. These institutions offer full-time and sandwich courses to students who have spent at least five years in a secondary school; the courses lead to the institutions' own associateships and diplomas or, in some cases, to degrees granted by the Council for National Academic Awards (q.v.). The central institutions include polytechnic institutions and specialised colleges of art, agriculture, music, textile technology, nautical subjects and domestic science.

Further Education Staff College

The Further Education Staff College was founded in 1963 as a residential centre offering a series of study-conferences, usually lasting one week, at which senior staff from establishments of further education can exchange information, ideas and experience with each other and with senior people from universities, industry, commerce, central and local government and other associated fields.

The College aims to increase the effectiveness of the process of education and training in all branches of further education and to improve its administration.

Coombe Lodge, Blagdon, near Bristol.

G

g Standing for 'general ability', g is a cipher (introduced by the psychologist C. E. Spearman) indicating that innate ability that is at work, in varying degrees, in all intellectual activity.

Gabon, Education in Education is provided in both state and mission schools, and state provision is steadily increasing. In 1965 there were 631 schools with an enrolment of 77,021 pupils, and about 88% of children are in attendance. There is no provision for higher education, but selected students continue their education in France.

The country's population was approximately half-a-million in 1965.

Galton, Francis (1822–1911) Led by his interest in the theory of evolution and the idea of hereditary genius, Francis Galton established an 'anthropometric laboratory' for the International Health Exhibition held in London during 1884. This aimed at the measurement of 'human form and faculty', and by collecting personal and physical data from parents and children, which might range from measuring height to assessing colour sense, Galton hoped to have enough material to analyse the spread of ability and its relation to purely physical data, such as the width of the skull. Although very few of his measuring techniques would be considered relevant today, at the time he was the first to advocate the scientific psychological study of individual children and its possible relevance to their future career. Galton was also an important pioneer in the development of statistical concepts and techniques.

FURTHER READING
Francis Galton. *Hereditary Genius*, Macmillan, New York, 1914.
George Miller. *Psychology. The Science of Mental Life*, Penguin, 1966.

NT

Gambia, Education in Education is provided through government and mission schools. 1965 statistics: 83 primary schools (enrolment 12,624); 17 secondary schools (enrolment 3,385); two vocational schools (enrolment 69); one teacher training college (enrolment 129). About half of the schools are in the area around Bathurst, the chief city.

The country's population was approximately 330,000 in 1965.

Games, Organised These words have appeared in the time-tables of primary and secondary schools for many years; but in some cases the games were far from organised.

Both the common lack of organisation and the paucity of games experience led to the report 'No good at games' being given quite erroneously on many children who in fact were no good only at one particular school game; they might well have been excellent at that game had there been organised coaching in skills and tactics, or excellent at some other field game or individual sport, if opportunities for these had been provided.

Happily this state of affairs is changing rapidly in most schools, and has already disappeared in many.

Education in schools being a continuous process from infant school to secondary school, and the whole being a preparation for a full adult life, it is logical that the simple games and practices in the lower stages should lead to more complex ones in the secondary schools and to full enjoyment and maturity of skill at some stage in post-school life.

In the teaching of games (and other athletic activities) in recent years, the skills of a particular game have been extracted and taught to those learning the game. Unfortunately, there were those who concentrated more on the teaching of the skills than on the complete game; the skills became ends in themselves and not means to an end. Today it is realised that skills should either be in games-form or returned to the context of the actual game at the earliest possible moment. For instance, it is of little value if a boy becomes expert at dribbling a football round obstacles in a playground if he cannot evince equal skill during an actual game of football.

Whilst the traditional major team games, such as association football, rugby, hockey, cricket and netball, are still popular in schools, the scope of activities has been increased widely in recent years to include almost every known game or recreation from table tennis to rowing, and from fencing to rock climbing, and this has also meant increased pleasure in participation by those for whom the traditional games were of little interest.

In secondary schools, with more and more pupils staying on for examination purposes, another trend, that of stressing 'high pressure' activities, is becoming evident. These activities (e.g. trampolining, circuit training, squash, volleyball and judo) are such that a considerable amount of physical activity can be compressed into a short

period of time and—in many cases—in limited space. The time element is of particular importance; while a boy is not prepared, say, to devote a whole afternoon to football, he may be willing to do half an hour's intensive physical activity and then return with a clear conscience to his academic work.

Parallel with this development is the long-term one of introducing activities, such as sailing, archery and riding, which can be continued in post-school life for many years; for it is realised that, with the advent of automation and the shortening of the working week, education for leisure is becoming most important. As a result of the work of the Central Council of Physical Recreation (q.v.), sports and recreations which in the past were too expensive for the average adult are now widely available at a reasonable cost, so that the seeds of active leisure sown in schools have every chance of reaching maturity.

See also **Physical education**

FURTHER READING
M. Dower. *Fourth Wave: The Challenge of Leisure*, Civic Trust, 1965.
P. C. McIntosh. *Sport in Society*, C. A. Watts, 1964.
Sport and the Community, CCPR, 1960.

JE

Gang In a technical sense, and as used by sociologists, this term implies something far more formal and cohesive than an ordinary 'group' (q.v.). According to American studies some delinquent gangs have a stable rather than a fluid membership, a recognised leader, an acknowledged hierarchy with specified roles, a name for the gang and/or nicknames for its members, and possibly even a uniform. It is doubtful whether gangs for young people, in this organised sense, have ever managed to last very long or indeed often existed in the UK. There are certainly groups, usually with one dominant personality as leader at one particular time, but the organisation tends to be informal and most of the members seem to be more or less of equal status, with the right to share in group decisions.

FURTHER READING

F. M. Thrasher. *The Gang*, Univ. of Chicago Press, Chicago, Ill., 1927.

W. F. Whyte. *Street Corner Society*, Univ. of Chicago Press, Chicago, Ill., 1943.

NT

Gaussian distribution *See* **Normal distribution**

GCE The General Certificate of Education is awarded on a subject basis at Ordinary, Advanced and Special levels. It is organised by eight examination boards (Oxford, Cambridge, Oxford and Cambridge, London, Northern Universities Joint Matriculation Board, Central Welsh, Southern Universities Joint Board, Associated Examining Board). There exists machinery, under the aegis of the Schools Council, which attempts to produce some uniformity of standards in the examinations. Passes in GCE are accepted by universities for matriculation and entry purposes, by the civil service and most professional bodies as entrance qualifications, and have therefore a national currency and an overriding importance in the educational system.

See also **Examinations; A level; O level; S level**

Geddes Axe The name applied to the swingeing recommendations (Committee on National Expenditure *Reports*, cmnd. 1581, 1582, 1589:1922) of a committee of business leaders appointed in 1921 under Sir Eric Geddes, a transport administrator who had earlier stated the intention: 'we will get everything out of her (Germany) that you can squeeze out of a lemon and a bit more.' Out of a total cut of £75 million in public administration, £18 million was to come from the education vote by excluding children under six from school, reducing teachers' salaries, shelving the raising of the school leaving age to 15, and stifling compulsory attendance at continuation schools

(*q.v.*). The baleful effects of Geddes Axe on education in the inter-war years cannot be over-emphasised.

WHGA

General Certificate of Education *See* **GCE**

General science *See* **Science, Teaching of**

General studies Sixth-formers spend most of their time at school studying two or three subjects to A level. This arrangement could in theory amount to a well-balanced curriculum, provided that subject-courses were properly designed and related to one another. In practice, however, this curriculum is widely criticised for failing to develop essential skills, interests and attitudes in sixth-formers, closing their minds to important areas of experience and knowledge, and alienating them from contemporaries. Pupils are shut into cultural boxes too early and too completely.

In an attempt to minimise the impoverishing effects of over-specialisation, most schools arrange non-specialist courses to run alongside the A level courses. Some schools go further in their battle against fragmentation, and regard their GS programmes as the core of the curriculum, common to the whole sixth form; GCE courses are grouped around this core, and viewed as 'excursions in depth'. At the other extreme are schools which pay lip-service to the idea of general education, providing one or two periods a week of propitiatory 'balancing studies' which no one takes seriously.

Schools are free to use what subject-matter and methods they please in GS, and experiments here give interesting evidence on the way teachers view the curriculum. They tend to adopt criteria for the selection of material and methods which are unusual in the selective school: they focus on the pupil rather than on the subject, asking questions about his needs as an individual. Courses tend to be related to the contemporary world—social and political issues, the impact of science and technology, problems of personal belief and behaviour, changing cultural patterns and values. Teachers are less concerned to transmit data—even though the data are in this case important and relevant—to memories already over-loaded by A level courses, than to help their pupils to develop interests and skills.

Teaching methods are often more adventurous than in specialist courses: they are more pupil-centred, more exploratory, often reminiscent of methods the pupils last encountered in their primary schools. GS is the place for trial and error: failure here has no disastrous consequences in terms of grades and careers. Schools can therefore experiment with team-teaching, the use of aids of various sorts, integrated studies which cut across traditional boundaries, 'new' subjects such as psychology, town planning or criminology, ambitious projects and surveys, and creative work in the arts, sciences and technologies.

GS is often criticised as being a palliative, supporting a system which is fundamentally unsound. But while waiting for reform, GS is a useful testing-ground for new ideas. It may also be helping generations of sixth-formers to make sense of their world, to widen their interests, and to grow.

See also **Curriculum, Agreement to Broaden the**

FURTHER READING
Back numbers of the *Bulletin of the General Studies Association* describe experiments and discuss problems. Obtainable from D. Burrell, Bulmershe College of Education, Woodley, Reading.

RIS

General Studies Association The central question which the GSA exists to discuss can be stated very simply: how can we best provide a general education in a school system which attaches so much importance to the specialised study of traditional academic subjects and to the passing of examinations in these subjects? Its first members were mainly sixth-form teachers, who arranged in 1962 to exchange information and ideas about the use of 'minority time' to counteract over-specialisation among A level candidates. Since then membership has spread to teachers of both younger and older students, and to teachers in other countries. The Association publishes between six and eight pamphlets a year, and arranges conferences, courses and summer schools for teachers and students. It works closely with subject associations and other bodies interested in curriculum reform. Its publications go to rather more than 2,000 teachers and other members.

Hon. Sec.: R. Irvine Smith, Department of Education, University of York. See also **Curriculum, Agreement to Broaden the; Specialisation**

Genius Men who have later proved themselves to be of exceptional ability often have not done particularly well at school or in college examinations. It has been suggested that one reason for this is that such people may have become so interested in one particular aspect of a subject that they quite neglected the other subjects required of them at the time. Some very able men were moderately unpopular with their teachers when young, perhaps because they were unwilling to have their attention directed elsewhere, and may have been thought of as very self-willed. This quality of intense interest and concentration in a subject has been noticed in geniuses from Archimedes onwards—in Archimedes' own case with tragic results. Some other men of genius did not give any sign of their exceptional talents until almost middle-aged.

Francis Galton (*q.v.*) studied the records of 400 eminent men, and found that a great many of them also had eminent relations. He concluded that genius runs in families and that types of genius, for example in medicine or law, can also be handed down from generation to generation. Although Galton minimised the effect of environment, particularly upon the choice of interest, he was probably right in thinking that exceptional ability can be inherited.

FURTHER READING
Liam Hudson. *Contrary Imaginations,* Methuen, 1966; Penguin, 1968.

NT

Geo-boards These are plywood, or similar boards (sometimes called nail-boards), on one face of which are set patterns of nails or pegs, the most common patterns being on a square lattice and around the circumference of a circle. With a geo-board and some coloured elastic bands, various plane rectilinear figures can be formed by simply stretching the bands over the nails. By using the geo-boards in this way children can obtain experience of shape, area and other geometrical properties.

Geographers, Institute of British A professional association founded in 1933 with the object of promoting the advancement of geography in Britain by means of regular meetings of professional geographers and the publication of research, the Institute now has over 1,000 members, largely drawn from universities and other institutes of higher education, research institutes and government departments. It holds an annual conference and publishes volumes of research papers and monographs.

Office and sales enquiries: 1 Kensington Gore, London, SW7. Hon. Sec.: Prof. W. Kirk, Dept of Geography, University of Leicester.

Geographical Association The Association exists to further the study and teaching of geography. It was founded in 1893 by a small group of teachers, and today has a membership of over 7,000, drawn from all levels. The Association has members in most countries overseas as well as in the UK, and various forms of membership are available — student, full, corporate, etc.

The Association publishes a quarterly journal, *Geography,* and many special handbooks. It maintains a large geographical library; organises courses and conferences; undertakes advisory and research work; promotes local branch activities; and is represented at a national level on educational and other committees.

343 Fulwood Rd, Sheffield, 10, Yorkshire.

Geographical fieldwork As a teaching method, geographical fieldwork derives from the work of the now defunct Le Play Society which carried out regional surveys by field investigation. These developed the techniques of the geographical analysis of the environment.

Geography teaching has emphasised too frequently the memorising of facts; only recently have geography teachers accepted fieldwork dependent upon active observation as a valid educational method. Several factors have caused this change—although fieldwork is not yet universally practised by schools. These factors include the educational movement away from learning solely from books to learning through activity; the work of numerous teachers disseminated through the medium of the Geographical Association (*q.v.*); the training of teachers in fieldwork techniques; the provision of residential field centres by the Field Studies Council and other institutions; and the inclusion of fieldwork in several examination syllabuses.

The late Professor S. W. Wooldridge states: 'the object of field teaching is to develop an eye for country.'[1] He also expresses the principles of geographical fieldwork thus: (1) The ground and not the map is the primary document; (2) it is the comparison of the ground with the map which is the essence of geographical fieldwork; (3) the order of working is thus from the ground to the map, and not vice versa; (4) the essential 'doing part' lies in making significant additions to the map.

Geographical fieldwork is therefore the investigation of landscape—rural or urban—by the direct observation of field data which can be mapped. This brings reality to geography teaching by first investigating the 'known' local scene. As Wooldridge argues: 'To make a thing real you must make it local . . . This involves developing the art of seeing and using accessible local ground as a laboratory for our teaching.' Such observations provide standards of reference that enhance the student's ability to visualise the geography of more distant places. Fieldwork engenders an appreciation of terrestrial space and time; trains for citizenship by inculcating a critical awareness of the human environment; and has a socialising value because 'pupils not only learn geography but can also learn life'.[2]

The basic fieldwork methods are: (1) Mapwork—using, adding to and making maps; (2) landscape analysis by field teaching; (3) land form investigations, e.g. a river study; (4) a traverse with transect across belts of changing landscape; (5) a land use survey; (6) a parish study; (7) a farm study; (8) an urban study.

In practice, fieldwork proceeds in three connected stages. First there is long-term organisation, and preparation with the class. Teachers must be knowledgeable about the area concerned. Secondly, field excursions beginning near the school develop outwards, in conjunction with the syllabus. Field instruction is not outdoor lecturing; investigations by the children must be related to their ability. Finally, as soon as possible after each excursion,

the class reports back and correlates observations. These can be recorded by various forms of display or by written accounts.

REFERENCES

1. *The Geographer as Scientist*, 1956.
2. G. M. Hickman. *Developments in Geography*, 1965.

FURTHER READING

M. Dilke (Ed.). *Field Studies for Schools*, Vols 1 and 2, Rivingtons, 1965.
K. S. Wheeler and M. Harding. *Geographical Fieldwork: A Handbook*, Blond Educational, 1965.

KSW

Geographical Society, Royal The Society was founded in 1830 for the advancement of geographical knowledge by linking all interested in geography in its widest interpretation. Today it makes grants to approved expeditions and acts as a liaison between British and foreign geographers in the organisation of expeditions, and by inviting distinguished foreign scientists to lecture. The library, which is open to members and research workers, contains about 100,000 books, and the map room, open to the public, has a collection of several hundred atlases and about 450,000 sheets of maps. The Society publishes the quarterly *Geographical Journal*, reproductions of early maps, research memoirs, and other publications of value to schools and universities.

In addition to ordinary membership, there is a special membership for schools and colleges of education. Lectures are held approximately once a week from October to June.

1 Kensington Gore, London, SW7.

Geography, Teaching of 'The primary function of the school geographer is to discover if relationships exist between the distribution of man's life and work, and the distribution of non-human conditions.'[1] Clearly geography involves the study of man (human geography) and what he produces (economic geography), together with that of landscape (physical and historical geography), of land forms (geomorphology), climate (climatology) and natural vegetation (bio-geography). Much information about the earth is recorded on maps; their study is essential to geographers (cartography).

Children up to the age of 16 years normally study all facets of geography in an areal framework (regional geography). The school syllabus is devised to include substantial areal cover of the world, with some reference to all branches of the subject as they arise within regions. For able children the physical setting of the earth with respect to the sun (part of mathematical geography) is included. In the 6th form the subject matter is separated into its various branches for systematic study in depth. Geography is taught when possible by the study of landscapes in the field. For class work in school, reality is provided by means of accurate and interesting data such as maps, pictures, sample studies, statistics and descriptive texts for analysis. In method, the field study approach of 'observe, record and interpret' is applied.

Field work is organised to enable children to study human and non-human conditions at first hand. Observation of the physical and cultural landscape develops an eye for a country, and offers real examples of human activity, land forms, physical processes, and weather, for comparison with those of other lands. The work may be organised for a single or double period, an afternoon or day excursion, or for longer. Children first observe. Their attention is drawn to relevant features by the provision of maps and duplicated questionnaires. They record what they see by written description, maps, transects, sections, field sketches and annotated diagrams. They then attempt explanation. Such explanation may be beyond their powers on observable evidence alone. Follow-up work in class provides further explanatory detail from other sources.

The interpretation of maps is another of geography's unique contributions to knowledge. The most commonly used maps are those of the atlas. Large-scale maps are nearest to reality; primary school children normally acquire familiarity with 50 and 25 in. Ordnance Survey maps of the school locality. At secondary level they use 6, 2½ and 1 in. Ordnance Survey maps. They are taught to find their way, give directions and plan routes; to interpret maps, analyse the distribution of features such as settlement and vegetation, to subdivide the area mapped into regions, to draw sections and transects. Home and foreign topographical maps are used to introduce regions the characteristics of which they exemplify. Children draw their own maps. This skill is difficult to acquire; it is learnt in progressive stages by first transferring information to a printed outline, then drawing simple maps of limited areas. More complex mapping skills develop progressively, with the inclusion in 6th form work of advanced cartographical exercises in plotting distributions.

The interpretation of pictures has developed with the availability of film-strips and colour transparencies. The attention of children is drawn to salient features by means of questions. These are concerned with land-forms, vegetation, people, their activities and response to climate. Pupils may annotate duplicated sketches of pictures, or devise sketches from them. Pictures can be mounted with relevant questions to form individual work cards, or a series of pictures on a topic, with appropriate exercises, can form an individual file. These are particularly useful for less able children, who complete the work at their own pace. Young children draw their own pictures to illustrate, or replace, words.

Sample study has developed from the field records of academic geographers. A sample study is a detailed study of a unit—a farm, parish, small town, mountain-side or factory—chosen particularly to show human response to environment, and to be typical of the major region concerned. The sample must first be located. If a map of it is available, study of this provides the second step, together with analysis of descriptive detail of landscape, and human activity in response to climate. The third step is generalisation. Pupils should realise that the particular conditions they have been studying are the general conditions of a larger area.

Statistics are not normally meant to be learnt, but are used as a yardstick for comparisons and contrasts. Figures for temperatures and rainfall of given stations may be graphed, and analysed to discover seasons, annual range of temperature, precipitation, distribution and type. Such statistics summarise climatic conditions. To understand them children need to know how averages are found; they should also be able to estimate rainfall and temperatures in and out of doors, and learn statistics appropriate for the climate of their locality. Additional descriptive material helps climate study. Other statistics commonly used include those for import and export, mineral, crop and industrial production, and land use. The least able children may find statistics incomprehensible.

The geography text-book should be appropriate to the mental level of the class. It should be interesting, accurate, up-to-date and illustrated with photographs integrated with the text. Additional material in the form of Ordnance Survey and foreign topographical map extracts, sample studies, descriptive passages, statistics and a range of exercises is useful. The text-book is a reference book for the child; its study should be planned to fit in with the syllabus, not to dominate it. In lessons, relevant parts of the text may be read silently, and oral or written questions asked about them. If the questions are logically ordered and full sentences written in answer, the result often takes the form of a well-ordered essay. Text-

books can be used to train children in note-taking, appropriate paragraphs being reduced to one or two short sentences which précis vital points. Text-book facts can be tabulated, illustrated, reproduced in diagram form or mapped by children.

It should be remembered that geographical study is being used as a means to education, as a vehicle of intellectual development and cultural enrichment. In general, all lessons have the broad aim of furthering the development of children as individuals and citizens. Within this broad aim there should be for every lesson a more specific aim, closely related to the subject matter it is proposed to cover. Most teachers would accept that telling is not teaching. It is not much of an educational process for children to have absorbed, by ear and memory, or by hand and writing, a series of facts about an area, however valuable by themselves and however logically set out.

A geography lesson should be, as often as possible, a process of discovery. The aims of most lessons should be so framed that children discover, or account for, some particular feature of the area or topic of study. Lessons must be adjusted to the age and ability of the class; aims of different degrees of complexity are possible. Simple aims for 11-year-olds might be 'To find out how a Danish farmer lives', 'To find out what life is like in the Sahara', 'To find out how farmers grow fruit in north-east Kent'; 15-year-olds could discover 'Why Denmark exports so much dairy produce', 'How man utilises the resources of the Sahara', and 'Account for land-use contrasts in south-east England'. The problem should be posed near the beginning of the lesson, generally by the use of introductory data which suggest it. Considerable skill is then needed to arrange the content of the lesson in the correct order, so that it is in clearly marked sections or steps. These steps should be presented so that each step, completed in reasonable time, follows on and is closely related to the previous one. Lack of a unifying link between one section and the next often leads to loss of sight of the aim, so that facts not essential to the purpose may be included, and the end of the lesson may bear little relation to its beginning. The final stage or section draws all the threads of the lesson together and presents the conclusion. The conclusion normally summarises the answer to the problem posed at the beginning of the lesson.

The lesson form described has a clear structure, an orderly arrangement of the material planned to form a coherent unit. The facts needed as the basis of the lesson are provided by the maps, pictures, sample studies, statistics and descriptions suggested. No geography lesson should be entirely oral. Oral work must be reinforced by a written record. Recording makes a change in activity, is useful for revision, and maintains interest. The teacher's broad summary should seldom be copied; copying involves little thought. Essays, transects, sketches, diagrams, maps, graphs and occasional notes are but some of the possibilities for recording which enrich geographical study.

See also **Geographical fieldwork**

REFERENCE
1. N. V. Scarfe. 'Geography as an autonomous discipline in the school curriculum', *Journal of Geography*, LXIII, 1964.

FURTHER READING
E. W. H. Briault and D. W. Shave. *Geography in and out of School*, Harrap, 1960.
M. S. Dilke (ed.). *The Purpose and Organisation of Field Studies*, Rivington, 1965.
O. Garnett. *Fundamentals in School Geography*, Harrap, 1960.
Geography and Education, Ministry of Education Pamphlet No. 39, HMSO, 1960.
M. Long (ed.). *Handbook for Geography Teachers*, Methuen, 1964.
M. Long and B. S. Robertson. *Teaching Geography*, Heinemann, 1966.
ILML

Geologists' Association The Association was founded in 1858 with the aim of providing facilities for the study of geology by those who, while not devoting their lives to its pursuit, took an active interest in its facts and teaching. There are now over 2,000 members, including both professional and amateur geologists and others interested in geology and allied sciences. The Association has published much original matter, and provides excellent facilities for students and amateurs to gain practical knowledge of the subject. To obtain the full benefits of membership, however, those without previous knowledge should undertake a course of study such as those made available by colleges of technology and university extra-mural departments.

The Association holds meetings for the reading of papers and delivery of lectures, organises museum demonstrations, publishes proceedings, pamphlets and guides and conducts field meetings. The latter range from whole-day or half-day week-end meetings, when places of geological interest within easy reach of London are visited, to longer visits to remoter parts of Great Britain and to Europe. The Association's library is incorporated with that of University College, London, and contains most of the standard geological works of reference. Over 500 geological maps are available for loan.

Sec.: Dr F. H. Moore, BSc, PhD, FGS, 278 Fir Tree Rd, Epsom, Surrey.

Geology, Teaching of Geology is a subject which is becoming increasingly popular in schools. Being a science, it provides an excellent training in the observation and collection of facts, in the combination of inductive with deductive reasoning, and in accuracy both of thought and language. Unlike most other sciences, its introduction into the school curriculum does not involve a large expenditure on laboratories and equipment.

In primary schools geology is rarely studied as a separate subject. More commonly, certain aspects of geology are introduced through the study of the home area, of a topic (viz. fossils, coal, water supply), or in connection with a school journey. In secondary schools the organisation of the teaching of geology is usually on a more systematic basis (the subject may be taken at CSE and GCE O and A levels). Much of this teaching is carried out within the separate 'compartments' of physical geology, mineralogy and petrology, palaeontology, stratigraphy and economic geology. More and more teachers are, however, integrating these various elements of the subject into a coherent whole, by linking all aspects of geology within the study of stratigraphy.

Geology is essentially an outdoor subject. The scale and form of features can be more easily understood in the field, and it is only there that a full appreciation of the three-dimensional aspect of geology can be made. Fieldwork is therefore an important part of geology teaching at all levels of education. All geology courses include day, or half-day, excursions arranged to enable pupils to gain a first-hand knowledge of selected areas. Some courses include rather longer excursions to areas whose geology contrasts markedly with that of the school area.

Teachers should attempt to re-create the field atmosphere of investigation within the classroom. Considerable reality can be achieved by the skilful use of teaching aids. Combinations of film, filmstrip, colour transparency, map, model and hand specimen can be used to enable pupils to observe, to record and to interpret in the way that they have been trained in the field.

In conclusion, it must be stressed that throughout the teaching of geology the emphasis should at all times be on the pupil's experience, both in subject matter and in the method of the science.

FURTHER READING

Geology in Primary and Secondary Modern Schools, Proceedings of the Geological Society of London, No. 1638, 1967.

T. N. George. 'Syllabus and Method in the Teaching of Geology', *Advancement of Science*, XX, 1964.

C. H. R. Halfyard. 'Why not Geology?' *Geography*, XLVIII, 1963.

ADu

Geometry, Teaching of Geometry is the study of the properties of space. The relationships between such elements as lines, points and area are expressed in the form of statements called theorems. Theorems may be linked in a chain of logical thinking, at the beginning of which is a small number of simple statements called axioms or postulates, from which all subsequent results derive.

The Mathematical Association (*q.v.*) has suggested that geometry should be taught in three stages. The first of these is the *experimental* stage. Geometrical facts and terminology are acquired by accurate drawings of simple figures, by measuring lengths and angles with applications to elementary surveying, by building geometrical solids and dissecting and fitting together plane shapes. Relationships are accepted intuitively as true, being obviously true in particular cases, or demonstrated by working models. This stage should never be a hurried one.

The second stage is the *deductive*. A small number of important theorems are assumed to be true and are used to deduce sets of other theorems. In solving problems there is great flexibility of method: e.g. working forwards and backwards, using analogy to a problem already solved, making use of plausible guesswork, constructions and so on. But finally the proof is to be in the form of a sequence of steps linked by logical reasoning. The standard of logical proof must be appropriate to the child's understanding—which is later, according to Piaget (*q.v.*), than is usually imagined.

The third stage is one of *systematisation*. This stage, in which a survey is made of the chain of theorems and axioms (usually those of Euclid), is often omitted or deferred.

A more modern treatment of the second stage is to assume the properties of distance-preserving transformations such as translation (sliding), rotation about a point, reflection in a line and the angle-preserving transformation of enlargement (similarity). Greater prominence is given, in this treatment of the stage, to axial and rotational geometry.

FURTHER READING
F. J. Budden and C. P. Wormell. *Mathematics Through Geometry*, Pergamon, 1964.
M. Jeger. *Transformation Geometry*, Allen and Unwin, 1966.
Mathematical Association. *The Teaching of Geometry in Schools*, Bell, 1929.
Midland Mathematics Experiment, Books 1–3, Harrap, 1963–67.
School Mathematics Project, Books 1 and 2, Cambridge Univ. Press, 1964–66.

JCW

German, Association of Teachers of Founded in 1958, the Association aims to assist teachers of German in their task; to provide a forum through which they may meet each other, members of the universities and educationists from abroad; to provide lectures in English and German on a a wide range of subjects of interest to teachers of German, with opportunities for discussion; and to carry out study and research. There are some 700 members, with branches in London, Leicester, Liverpool, Manchester, Northern Ireland, Nottingham and Reading; it is hoped to re-establish two branches based on the West Midlands and on Wales and the South-West.

Branches hold meetings about twice a term and issue regular bulletins.

1 Christ Church Terrace, London, SW3.
Journal: *Newsletter*. Six times annually.

German Democratic Republic and East Berlin, Education in Elementary and secondary schools were abolished in 1959, being replaced by general and polytechnic high schools. Education is compulsory between the ages of six and 16. Older pupils work outside the school one day a week. 1964/5 statistics: 18,806 infant schools (enrolment 962,388); 8,285 general polytechnics (enrolment 2,247,557); 303 specialist polytechnics (enrolment 81,097); 1,123 vocational schools (enrolment 387,100); 212 technical colleges (enrolment 128,719); 37 colleges of technology and seven universities (enrolment 111,580). The largest university is Humboldt University of Berlin with 14,000 students.

Total population in 1965: approximately 17 million.
See also **Communist education**

German Institute The Institute exists to promote cultural relations between Great Britain and West Germany.
51 Princes Gate, London, SW7.

Germany (West), Education in Each *Land* government in the German Federal Republic is responsible for its own education service. Berlin, Hamburg and Bremen, with their respective environs, are separate *Länder*. There is no Federal Minister of Education but close co-ordination is maintained in Bonn by a Standing Conference of Ministers of Education and by a number of related specialist committees.

The West German system has succeeded in eliminating the appalling propagandist features of the Nazi education service. It has also shaken off the sheer imitation of the educational systems of the three occupying powers, the USA, the UK and France. Friendly connections are maintained with other western systems and the popular, compulsory education system has achieved a national character with a return to the recognition of the value of high academic standards.

The education system tends to reflect the wealth, politics and religion of the people of a particular *Land*. Hessen and Lower Saxony, with stronger social democratic traditions, have slightly different developments from those of the overwhelmingly Catholic Bavaria. These differences extend to teacher training, most of the colleges in Catholic *Länder* being provided by the Church.

Children start school at six and are required by their *Land* statutes to remain until 14 or 15. German schools are generally morning schools and young children (and their teachers) spend fewer hours in school each day than do older children. The *Volksschule*, now described in many *Länder* as a primary school, may be followed by a *Mittelschule*, or intermediate school, and both may lead to a *Gymnasium* or high school. The *Gymnasium* course ends at the age of 19 or 20 with a final examination, called the *Abitur*, which, when successfully obtained, provides the right of entry to a university.

Hamburg, Bremen and West Berlin have established general schools in a kind of comprehensive system. These are schools which may be attended by pupils for their whole school life. There have also been experiments with whole day schools, *Tagesheimschulen*, but the school day starting at 8 a.m. and running through to 1 p.m. is traditionally well-based.

A significant feature of West German education is the magnificent provision of facilities for technical education. Every school leaver, almost without exception, is required to continue his education in some institution offering day-release opportunities. Employers are required to facilitate the attendance of their young employees. Every trade or profession has an institution offering approved courses. These institutions are known as *Berufschulen, Berufsfach-schulen* and *Fachschulen*, the last category providing courses similar to those found in technical colleges in the UK.

There are 18 universities in West Germany and a total of nine technical universities. This last figure is important, as the technical university was an early 19th-century German invention in higher education. A new status has also been accorded to colleges of education, which now fit into the provision of higher education in each *Land*.

German educators have been very prominent in encouraging international discussions of current educational problems. A magnificent setting for international conferences is the Congress Hall in West Berlin; the proceedings of these conferences have been published through the agency of the West Berlin Senate. A scenically attractive setting in the Hartz Mountains at Sonnenburg House has also fascinated progressive educationists from many countries. Sonnenburg Societies have sprung up in many countries.

Very serious attention is also paid to the service of youth; state, church and voluntary associations combine to bridge the gap between school and life.

DJJ

Gesell's norms Dr Arnold Gesell (1880–1961) was an American psychologist who, through systematic observation of infants and young children, was able to plot the sequence of normal mental and physical development in young human beings. Gesell also indicated the chronological ages when these developments can normally be expected, though he did not intend these to be taken too literally. It is, of course, unlikely that any child will be found to conform to these developmental norms in *every* case, and Gesell's work was intended to be more of a rough guide than an inflexible blueprint of normal development. Unfortunately, some parents still become upset when their child appears to deviate in any way, even though this may in itself be quite normal or merely indicative of a late developer. If, however, a child is consistently late or defective on nearly all the norms suggested by Gesell, then this may give an early warning of quite serious backwardness.

FURTHER READING

A. Gesell. *The First Five Years of Life*, Harper and Row, New York, 1940.

NT

Gestalt psychology Early psychologists tended to think of learning and perception in terms of a steady accumulation of useful associations, gathered together in some sort of chain of knowledge. Some German psychologists, however, believed that the brain has an inbuilt capacity to organise these thought-associations into meaningful patterns, which would somehow be more significant than the parts they contained. Hence the word *gestalt*, from the German word for 'configuration'. For example, without realising it we may try to organise a series of notes into a tune, rather than hear them merely as a series of notes. Most people have had the experience of trying to organise their thoughts or perceptions into something meaningful, rather as a detective pieces together a crime from the clues at his disposal. If we succeed in doing this, it may be due to a sudden flash of insight. This was described by the Gestalt school as the 'Aha!' experience, since its surprising suddenness is often one of its chief characteristics. Once again, this seemed to indicate some sort of inbuilt rather than learned organising function in the brain itself. Such insight into a problem can often occur only on the basis of groundwork and basic learning more in line with association theory and its 'laws' (*q.v.*).

FURTHER READING

R. S. Woodworth. *Contemporary Schools of Psychology*, Methuen, 1949.

NT

Ghana, Education in Primary, secondary and technical education is free and compulsory between the ages of six and 16. 1965/6 statistics: 10,212 primary and middle schools (enrolment 1,404,929); 105 secondary schools (enrolment 42,628); 11 technical schools (enrolment 6,671); 82 teacher training colleges (enrolment 14,000). The University of Ghana, the University of Science and Technology, and the University College have a total enrolment of 4,286. Total population: approximately $7\frac{3}{4}$ million.

Gifted children The Plowden Committee has recommended long-term research into the problems of educating gifted children, but so far there is no satisfactory definition of what constitutes giftedness. Some educators lay stress on the ability to score highly on an individual intelligence test such as the Stanford-Binet or the Wechsler Intelligence Scale. Others, while admitting that this is one form of giftedness, claim that creative or aesthetic ability is at least as important a form of giftedness. Others again lay stress on social giftedness. It would seem then that there are several forms of giftedness, and education should provide opportunities for their development.

Hitherto most effort seems to have been made to provide a favourable environment for children who can score highly on intelligence or achievement tests. Three different approaches have been favoured:

(1) *Special schools or selective education.* A few educators have advocated special schools for gifted children, but these have tended so far to be for those talented in music or ballet. In England the approach has been largely through the provision of selective secondary schools (grammar and technical schools) with selection at about 11 years. This approach is now less favoured, and advocates of comprehensive secondary education claim that comprehensive

L

schools will be able to cater for children with a variety of gifts. Some educators believe that adequate provision must be made in the primary schools.

(2) *Acceleration.* Children of high ability or outstanding achievement have been promoted to higher classes to work with children of their own mental development. This has often been successful, but acceleration has its limitations and must depend on the developmental age of the children. Excessive acceleration, especially about the stage of puberty, is likely to lead to social problems, which may be harmful ultimately to mental development.

(3) *Enrichment of the curriculum.* This approach has some advocates and might prove beneficial to all pupils. There are, however, some difficulties. For example, the enrichment required by some gifted children is such that a great deal of teacher-preparation is needed: such preparation requires time which the teacher of large classes cannot afford. There is also the danger that enrichment in the primary school may lead to anticipating some of the work to be undertaken eventually in the secondary school, thus causing or aggravating boredom later in a child's school career. In experimental work being carried out with gifted children at Brentwood College of Education in Essex, an attempt is being made to avoid this particular danger by basing the enrichment as far as possible on the areas that tend to lie between certain disciplines as, for example, art and mathematics, or art and dance. In these experimental groups gifted children have shown an ability to work at far higher levels than are normally possible in the ordinary primary school class of over 30 children.

Much research is being carried out at present on creativity (*q.v.*), which some educators regard as a form of giftedness which is independent, or largely independent, of intelligence expressed as an IQ. For example, Getzels and Jackson have tried to show that adolescents with high scores on creativity tests perform as satisfactorily in school as those with higher scores on IQ tests. Subsequently, Kogan and Wallach have tried to demonstrate that some children may be gifted in both intelligence and creativity, but that others may be gifted in one of those fields but not in the other. At Brentwood College of Education it has been found that children chosen through creativity tests have usually scored well above the average on intelligence tests. There is some evidence that some of our present school curricula tend to restrict or to discourage creativity (*cf.* Torrance, Hudson in *Further reading*) so that it may be true to state that many of our gifted children are not being provided with an environment likely to help them to develop their gifts.

Recent developments include the foundation of the National Association for Advancing the Education of Gifted Children, Neill's study of some fifty gifted children in the north of England, a grant to Liverpool University for research, conferences held by county authorities, the frequent appearance of this topic in refresher courses, and the publication of such books as *Gifted Children* by Branch and Cash, and *Contrary Imaginations* by Liam Hudson. These, with the recommendation in the Plowden Report, should inspire further research into the nature and distribution of giftedness and also into the effect of different environments, including both home and school, on the encouragement or discouragement of the development of various gifts.

FURTHER READING

Margaret Branch and Aubrey Cash. *Gifted Children*, Souvenir Press, 1966.
J. W. Getzels and P. W. Jackson. *Creativity and Intelligence*, Wiley, New York, 1962.
E. Hildreth. *Introduction to the Gifted*, McGraw-Hill, 1966.
Liam Hudson. *Contrary Imaginations*, Methuen, 1966; Penguin, 1968.
N. Kogan and M. A. Wallach. *Modes of Thinking in Young Children*, Holt, Rinehart and Winston, 1965.

E. P. Torrance. *Education and the Creative Potential,* Univ. of Minnesota Press, Minneapolis, Minn., 1963.

SAB

Gilchrist Educational Trust Founded by the will of Dr John Borthwick Gilchrist (who died in 1841), the Trust exists for the 'benefit, advancement and propagation of education and learning in every part of the world, as far as circumstances will permit.'
1 York St, London, W1.

Gilpin, William (1724-1804) Headmaster of Cheam school from 1752 till 1780, Gilpin had educational ideas much in advance of those common in his day. He dispensed with corporal punishment and gave the pupils a real measure of self-government through a jury that imposed fines on those who broke school rules. The money raised in this way was spent on sports equipment and books for the library. Each boy was given a plot in the school garden and was free to cultivate it as he wished, selling the produce to the school or outside it. These plots were actually owned by the boys, who were able when they left the school to bequeath them to others or to sell them. Gilpin attached the utmost importance to the teaching of English, although his methods of teaching the classics were also of an advanced kind; he thought it important that boys should be able as soon as possible to read Latin and Greek with enjoyment.

Girls, Education of In Western society the education of girls is often referred to as a problem, whereas the education of boys is taken for granted. The problem, so far as Britain is concerned, dates not from time immemorial but from the industrial revolution and the accompanying growth of urban life.

Formerly, girls learned from their mothers in the home the crafts of cooking, preserving, spinning, weaving, horticulture, bee-keeping, milking, dairying and so on. In educated families girls shared with boys cultural discussion, reading aloud and listening to sermons. When they married they took on the running of their homes; if they remained unmarried there would usually be a place for them in the homes of brother, sister or parents. In the new towns of the early 19th century, however, girls had no such opportunities. The girl-children of the poor worked outrageous hours in new factories; and those of the middle classes sat at home and learned accomplishments, such as piano playing, embroidery, singing, perhaps a little French which, it was thought, made them acceptable as wives; they were being educated to get husbands rather than to be good housewives. It was in these middle classes that the education of girls came to be seen as a problem.

The 19th century saw a great development of public school education for boys. Administrators and governors were needed for the expanding empire, the new professional civil service and growing commercial and industrial enterprises; for all of these, public schools educated boys. But for their sisters, there was nothing, neither the work nor the education, to fit them for work, except young ladies' seminaries such as Miss Pinkerton's in Thackeray's *Vanity Fair,* or the sad, heroic, ridiculous Victorian governess. Exceptions were those few fortunate and talented girls whose homes, particularly whose fathers and sometimes later whose husbands, shared with them their own learning, enthusiasm and experience. Among these were Elizabeth Fry, Elizabeth Barrett, Florence Nightingale, Dorothea Beale and others. There was also that extraordinary group of talented novelists (e.g. the Brontës and George Eliot) who rose above the limits of their narrow education but had to adopt men's names in order to get their works recognised.

The appointment of Miss Beale, herself a highly intelligent home-educated Victorian, to Cheltenham Ladies' College in 1858 and its subsequent transformation, and the foundation of the North London Collegiate School for day girls by Miss Buss in 1850, started a new era in the education of girls. Both schools set out to do for girls what the public schools did for their brothers.

The evidence given by women, including Miss Buss, Miss Beale and others, to the Taunton Commission (*q.v.*) in 1865 reveals the lack of any intellectual discipline in the accepted pattern of the day for girls' education. It is therefore not surprising that the schools influenced by these same women stressed the need for girls to experience the intellectual discipline of subjects like Latin and mathematics; thus they tended to model their curriculum on that of the boys. This tendency was enhanced by the fact that there was no positive replacement of the old useless accomplishments by genuine study of the domestic arts in addition to the much needed academic disciplines. Indeed it is only in the middle 20th century that cookery, dressmaking and homecraft have found acceptance as part of the education for all girls. Even so, many of the more academic schools still consider them soft options to be undertaken only by those not clever enough to do the full academic course.

The high schools of the Girls Public Day Schools' Trust (*q.v.*) were founded in the last quarter of the 19th century and were largely modelled on the North London Collegiate School. They provided sound education for middle-class girls, an education which was based on the classical tradition of boys' public schools and which made possible women's assault on the universities and professions at the end of the 19th century.

High schools in their turn provided the model for the new state secondary schools founded after the 1902 Act.

These schools charged small fees but were mainly open to talent as assessed in the examination first known as the scholarship and later as the 11-plus. The 1902 Act provided a link between the middle-class tradition and that of the working class for whom elementary schools had been founded in 1870, but the two traditions did not merge until the middle 20th century. To the new secondary schools (later known as grammar schools) with their middle-class traditions, modelled on the public schools and high schools and in many cases staffed by their products, came the bright children from the elementary schools.

In most of the elementary schools boys and girls were educated together; the 1902 Act did not advocate mixed secondary schools but it did provide equally for girls and boys, sometimes in mixed schools, sometimes in separate single-sex schools. These schools gave a good secondary education based on the classical and academic tradition of the public schools, but with slightly more emphasis on mathematics, science and modern languages. Some people wished they had followed the more realistic curriculum of modern technical schools developing in Germany. They did, however, add to the linguistic classical curriculum some practical work, and art, domestic science and woodwork soon came to be accepted as a necessary part of secondary education. The majority of both boys and girls, however, did not go to the new secondary schools but stayed on at their elementary schools.

By the end of the first quarter of the 20th century, girls appeared to have the same educational opportunities as boys at secondary level, but in higher education opportunity was less. More seriously, society still expected less of educated girls, and the idea prevailed that the higher education of women was an alternative to marriage and a useful device which enabled single women who had been unfortunate enough not to get husbands to earn their living. Society was conditioned to accept this pattern because the first half of the 20th century was a time when women greatly outnumbered men and when the economy was a depressed one which did not need and could not use all its potential trained manpower; there was no question, therefore, of seeking to fill skilled vacancies by recruiting more women.

The second half of the 20th century faces a different situation, and girls' education emerges as a problem again, and this time not just one for the middle classes. The change in the ratio of the sexes means that virtually all girls expect to marry; but they no longer see marriage as an alternative to paid work, and more girls than ever are now going on to higher education in order to be trained for a job. The problem now is not how to provide for middle-class girls who need an education as good as that of their brothers; i.e. it is not a problem for a minority but one for the whole of society. The problem is how best to educate girls who are going to marry, have children, run a home without domestic help, and do a job outside the home. It is impossible to answer this question by looking at the education of girls in isolation. The new-style partnership marriage, undertaken at a much younger age than marriages used to be, requires a new look at all secondary education, of boys as well as of girls.

These social changes have brought closer the two traditions of working-class and middle-class girls' education, and the 1944 Act which established secondary education for all encouraged this trend. After 1944 all girls (like boys) attended secondary schools: the majority secondary modern, a few comprehensive, and about one-fifth grammar (the former secondary schools now open only to the most able). The academic minority for whom the high schools and then the new secondary (1902) schools catered, began to lose their hold on the curriculum of girls' schools, and the post-1944 secondary schools tried to recognise women's modern role. The old established schools have moved away from the ugly uniforms, compulsory team games, the down-grading of domestic arts, competitive marking, and the exclusive attitude to society they had taken over from public and high schools. It is now recognised in nearly all girls' schools that the choice is no longer career *or* marriage, but which career *and* whom to marry. Thus a girl may actually study physics and dressmaking, or Latin and French cookery. Schools try to provide an education which enables the academic girl to study sciences, mathematics or languages, and at the same time not to lose sight of the fact that she will marry and have children and that any career she takes up will be interrupted.

Many secondary modern schools have organised imaginative courses for senior girls which recognise the complicated roles these pupils will have to play. The growing number of comprehensive schools, too, provide courses in homemaking, retail distribution, child care and so on, as well as still-needed academic courses for some. It is in modern and comprehensive schools, too, that vocational courses in catering, commerce and dressmaking have been developed in a context of general education. These courses were first developed in the early 20th century, mostly in trade schools, for girls from the elementary schools who had the skill and ambition to learn a trade. They were not incorporated in the 1902 secondary schools whose ethos denied the educational value of vocational studies.

The introduction of the CSE in 1965 has recognised the importance of the practical, vocational and oral work done in the schools, and new examining techniques are being evolved to assess it.

The DES Circular 10/65, which asked LEAs to reorganise secondary education on comprehensive lines, has accelerated the trend towards co-education and the consequent disappearance of the single-sex girls' school. It is arguable that a good co-educational school gives more opportunity to individual girls than does the separate girls' school. Through being educated with boys, taught by men as well as women, girls may be better able to cope with the choices and problems of management they are all going to be faced with. The possible disappearance of girls' schools will make a considerable difference to the career prospects in teaching for girls, as there is a tendency for headships and senior posts in mixed schools to go to men.

See also **Women, Higher education for**

MM

Girls' Brigade An international Christian (interdenominational) organisation for girls aged 5 to 18. There are about 1,500 branches. Activities include annual camps, Bible-study, cycling, rhythmic movement and music.

Brigade House, 8 Parsons Green, London, SW6.

Publication: *Monthly Magazine* (for girls); *Monthly Gazette* (for officers).

Girls' Public Day School Trust The largest organisation of direct grant grammar schools for girls in the UK, the pupils in its 23 schools numbering over 14,000.

26 Queen Anne's Ga., London, SW1.

Gittins Report on Primary Education in Wales (1968) The Central Advisory Council for Education (in Wales) was asked to consider all aspects of primary education. Many of its conclusions and recommendations resemble those of the Plowden Report (*q.v.*) on primary education in England —for example, on the need to establish educational priority areas (*q.v.*) and to employ teachers' aides, and on the stages into which primary education might be divided. Perhaps its three outstanding original recommendations relate to in-service training of teachers, religion and the teaching of the Welsh language.

On in-service training, the Central Advisory Council recommended that every teacher be allowed a period of secondment for such training, on full salary, on the basis of a week of study leave for each year served. All expenses should be paid, and there should be additions to salary where in-service training had been completed. An In-Service Training Council should be set up to evaluate the usefulness of various forms of training, and should partly be financed by the DES. A National In-Service Training Centre for Wales might be established, the Report suggests, with a core of permanent staff; it would offer courses of up to one term in length.

The Report takes a notably different view on religion from the Plowden Report. Religious education should continue to play an important part in Welsh primary schooling, but there could be a relaxation of the statutory clauses that make it compulsory. Discretion as to teaching and worship would then be left to the judgment of head teachers. Behind the Council's thinking on this matter lay the view that compulsory RI and worship make it more, not less, difficult to achieve the 'end in view', and that some teachers, not believers, feel bound to teach religion rather than impose extra burdens on their colleagues. The Report pointed out there had been voluntary RI in Wales before the 1944 Education Act introduced compulsion, and that this would undoubtedly continue if the protection of the Act were removed.

As to the teaching of Welsh, the Report was in favour of a fully bilingual education. Children should be taught in their mother tongue and be given opportunities to acquire the second language. There should be effective teaching of Welsh in all schools, and progressively the language should become a medium of instruction. Each LEA should set up bilingual schools. Other recommendations included the setting up of a universal system of nursery education from the age of three, 15% of full-time places being reserved for children with specific social or emotional needs. Dependent on this provision, a long-term plan was recommended leading to a single annual entry to the infants' school at an average age of five-and-a-half, with transfer to secondary education at 12½. The infants' school stage should cover three years. Selection exams should be abolished, or should be replaced by methods of allocating children between secondary schools that did not depend on testing. As part of the process, co-operation and communication between primary and secondary school teachers should be improved by joint in-service courses.

Schools should consider the losses and gains that come from basing classes on ability and attainment, and teachers should be helped to re-shape their approaches to teaching and specially to learn the techniques of group and individual work. There should be no streaming in the primary school, but grouping by age with room for vertical or family grouping. A declining or mobile rural population made it necessary, the Report felt, that area schools should be planned, with at least 60 pupils and three teachers, capable of being reached by each child within 45 minutes. These should be either two-tier schools for children between five and eight, leading to an area school from eight to 12, or all-through schools for children between five and 12. Various suggestions were made for strengthening the small rural schools and ensuring that there were connections between them and agencies providing social education, education for leisure and further education.

See also **Wales, Education in**

Gliding It is a measure of the present-day wider concepts of PE that gliding has become an acknowledged recreational activity in a number of secondary schools, technical colleges and colleges of education. The growth of the sport has been stimulated by voluntary organisations and by the British Gliding Association.

As the cost of a glider is prohibitive for most schools, tuition by qualified instructors is normally obtained through affiliation to clubs and bodies catering for the sport. These often run short and one-day courses. Initial instruction is given in two-seater gliders with a wing span of 50–60 ft, launched by a winch or tow car, or towed up by a light aeroplane. Most British gliders, immensely strong in the air, are made of wood and covered with ply and fabric, though some are now made of metal.

A basic leaflet, *Come Gliding*, obtainable from the BGA, contains a short article on learning to glide, a reading list and a map showing the location of British clubs. The BGA also publishes *Introduction to Gliding* for new members of clubs or students on one-day courses.

British Gliding Association, Artillery Mansions, 75 Victoria St, London, SW1.

Organisations dealing especially with young people: John Simpson, Leighton Park School (Gliding), c/o Lasham Gliding Centre, nr Alton, Hants. Air Scouts: Laurie Bittlestone, Scout Air Training Base, Lasham Airfield, nr Alton, Hants. Upward Bound Trust: Sec., A. Proctor, 120 Cowley Rd, Littlemore, Oxon. ATC: Wing Cdr M. Wight-Boycott, HQ Flying Training Command, RAF, White Waltham, nr Maidenhead, Berks.

JE

Godwin, William (1756–1836) Egalitarian, republican and atheist, Godwin in his *Enquiry concerning Political Justice* launched a massive attack on the notion of state control of education, believing that it could lead only to political indoctrination.

Goldsmiths' Company Founded in 1327, the Company makes grants for educational and other purposes, including fellowships in applied science, travelling fellowships for members of the academic staff of technological universities, university studentships for postgraduate study at African colleges and universities, and grants to enable (1) schoolmasters and -mistresses to travel abroad during periods of sabbatical leave, (2) undergraduates from British public schools to attend Commonwealth universities, and (3) undergraduates of certain London colleges to travel abroad during the long vacation.

Goldsmiths' Hall, Foster La., London, EC2.

Good honours degree allowance This is in addition to annual salary payable to graduates whose degrees are classified as good honours degrees, that is to say, they have secured a first or second class honours degree or have obtained a higher degree. At the present time the allowance is £120 per annum.

Some universities award honours degrees which are unclassified; graduates who obtain posts in the teaching profession possessing such a degree are dependent upon the discretion of the employing authority as to whether the good honours degree allowance is added to the annual salary.

Unlike degrees which are other than good honours degrees, there are only very limited opportunities for equivalents to qualify for the good honours payment. These are (1) a first class honours degree or a second class honours degree of the Council for National Academic Awards, or a higher degree of the Council obtained by examination or as a result of research work or post-graduate achievement; and (2) a diploma in technology with first class honours or with second class honours (or membership) of the College of Technologists, awarded by

the National Council for Technological Awards or the Council for National Academic Awards. It should also be noted that an honours degree of a Commonwealth university (other than in the UK) or a higher degree of such a university resulting from examination, research work or post-graduate achievement, would also qualify. This is provided that the standard of the degree is accepted by the DES as equal to that of a first or second class honours degree of a university in the UK.

SEB

Gordon Walker, Rt Hon Patrick Chrestien (b. 1907) Secretary of State for Education and Science, 1967-8.

Gould, Sir Ronald (b. 1904) General Secretary of the National Union of Teachers since 1947; first president of the World Confederation of Organisations of the Teaching Profession, 1952.

Governing Bodies of Aided Grammar Schools, National Association of See **Voluntary Aided Secondary Schools, Association of**

Governing Bodies of Public Schools, Association of Founded in 1941 the GBA has 239 schools in membership made up of 151 independent, 79 direct grant and nine other schools.

The objects of the GBA are the advancement of education; discussion of matters concerning policy and administration of schools; and consideration of the relation of such schools to general educational interests.

The principal matters which have engaged the attention of the GBA recently are the future of public schools, with particular reference to the Public Schools Commission; the position of direct grant schools in relation to comprehensive re-organisation; and the rating assessment of schools.

Sec.: Brigadier A. J. Knott, OBE, West Rood, West Hill, Harrow-on-the-Hill, Middlesex.

Governors, School *See* **Instrument and articles of government**

Graded posts These are appointments for assistant teachers where some additional responsibility is required and undertaken. There are no precise details laid down as to the nature of the work required. Where a teacher undertakes advanced work this may justify such a post, but there are often many other activities which contribute to the smooth and efficient running of a school which could justify such appointments. If, for example, the school has a library, then a member of staff may act as librarian in addition to his other normal classroom duties and this activity would clearly merit a graded post.

A limitation, however, is placed upon the number of appointments which can be made under this heading. In a small school where there are 300 children or less, there is no mandatory provision at all; but an LEA may at its discretion make an appointment in a school where the number of children is between 201 and 300. Above 300 each group of school is allocated a 'score' (*see* **Graded posts allowances**). The score allows some flexibility in the scale of the appointments, and at the present time there is a discretion where an LEA chooses to use it to denude some of the score for graded posts in order to apply it to Grade A and Grade B head of department allowances respectively.

SEB

Graded posts allowances In addition to the salaries otherwise payable to them, teachers holding graded posts are classified in three groups with a fixed payment as indicated below:

| Scale I £ 125 | Scale II £ 210 | Scale III £ 315 |

Schools are given a score according to size as follows:

Primary and secondary schools other than special schools

Group	4	5	6	7
Review average or unit total	301– 500	501– 700	701– 1,000	1,001– 1,300
Score	2	4	7	10

Group	8	9	10
Review average or unit total	1,301– 1,800	1,801– 2,400	2,401– 3,300
Score	15	21	30

Group	11	12	13
Review average or unit total	3,301– 4,600	4,601– 6,000	Over 6,000
Score	43	57	70

Special schools

Group	4(S)	5(S)	6(S)	7(S)
Review average or unit total	361– 600	601– 900	901– 1,260	1,261– 1,620
Score	2	4	6	8

The LEA may, at its discretion, establish a graded post on Scale I in a school or department in Group 3 (Unit Total 201–300) or Group 3(S) (Unit Total (S) 181–360) Also, where the unit total (S) of a special school

317

L*

exceeds 360 the LEA may, in its discretion, establish a graded post on Scale I additional to the posts established under the above provisions.

It is mandatory for the score for graded posts to be entirely used, but there is flexibility in the allocation of this score according to the grading considered to be appropriate. Thus, for example, a score of seven could be utilised by seven Scale I posts or say three Scale I and two Scale II posts, or two Scale I posts, one Scale II and one Scale III or such other arrangements as may be considered desirable to suit the needs of the school in regard to the responsibilities undertaken provided, by so doing, a score of seven is not exceeded.

SEB

Graduate allowance This is additional salary producing at the present time £100 per annum higher than the basic scale for non-graduates at every point of the scale. It places such graduates other than good honours graduates in the Group II scales set out in the Burnham Report.

Degrees, other than honorary degrees, awarded by the following bodies are accepted for the graduate allowance: (1) English, Welsh, Scottish and Irish universities; (2) St David's College, Lampeter; (3) the Council for National Academic Awards; (4) Commonwealth and other universities, provided the standard of the degree (or equivalent qualification otherwise described) approximates to that of an English university. Each case of such qualifications should be referred to the DES for decision unless the individual case of the teacher has already been considered for this purpose in consultation with the Department.

There are, however, many other qualifications that are equally accepted for this addition: qualifications in architecture, art, modern and other languages, music, various branches of engineering and technology, law quali-

fications, etc. The inclusion of such qualifications in the Burnham Report means that the Burnham Committee has been satisfied that the qualifications required for entry to the course, its length and the final award may be regarded on the same basis as a university degree for salary purposes. However, in many cases a teacher can secure this payment only if he satisfies all the requirements laid down in the Report, which may include professional experience of an acceptable level and for a stipulated period of time. For full details Appendix V of the Burnham Report should be consulted.

SEB

Graduate Teacher Training Registry The purpose of the Registry is to assist graduates, or undergraduates in the final year of their degree course, to gain admission to a course of professional training in England and Wales, in a university department of education, or in a college of education which provides a postgraduate course. The Registry deals with written and verbal enquiries from candidates, and provides details of available vacancies.

151 Gower St, London, WC1.

Graduate teachers The normal basis of entry to the teaching profession for graduates is the completion of a postgraduate year of study either in a university department of education or in a college of education. The year of study leads usually to the award of an education diploma or certificate of education of the university. Such teachers are usually referred to in the profession as trained graduate teachers; and it may be worthwhile noting that, in addition to receiving the graduate allowance, such teachers qualify for the merit payment (*q.v.*) under the Burnham Report.

At the present time university graduation is in itself accepted for granting qualified teacher status. Thus, graduates may enter the teaching

318

profession direct from taking their university degree, and if they do so they would receive the salary for qualified teachers together with the graduate allowance; but there would be no payment of the merit addition unless and until the teacher secured the education diploma or its equivalent referred to above. Graduates who secure a first or second class honours degree or a higher degree are entitled to the good honours degree allowance (*q.v.*); entitlement to the merit payment applies on the same basis as for other graduates.

SEB

Graduates, Supply of Pupils receiving a grammar school type of education, whether it is in a comprehensive school, a grammar school or an independent school, require to be taught at least for the greater part of their course by men or women who have themselves that standard of knowledge which is associated with a university degree in the subject which they are teaching. The abler boys and girls, especially as they grow older and if they are going on to higher education, need to be taught by men or women who are themselves able enough to have taken a good honours degree in their subject. The recruitment and the proper employment of men and women who fulfil these qualifications is both vitally necessary for the schools and a matter of great difficulty.

There are about 250 pupils in secondary schools to every science graduate; about 300 to every modern language graduate and about 450 to every mathematics graduate. Clearly there are not enough graduates to go round. A teacher of these subjects who had no sixth form work to do would be able to teach about 150 pupils a week; if he has sixth form work the number will be substantially less. Some concentration is necessary, and does in fact take place. In independent secondary schools there are about 172 pupils to every maths

graduate and about 100 to every science graduate. In grammar schools the corresponding figures are 206 and 112. For modern schools they are 2,400 and 1,000. If instead of separate schools we think of different programmes of work within one comprehensive school or system the terms of the problem are not really changed. There will barely be enough graduates, at least in these subjects, to teach all the boys and girls who in a selective system get teaching at this level. In fact there will not be enough to teach all those who are missed by a selective system at the age of 11 and discovered a little later in the comprehensive schools. There is both a recruitment and a deployment problem. The recruitment problem is at least in part a matter of the comparative rewards for particular types of qualification inside and outside the schools; the deployment problem is closely bound up with arguments about 'streaming' (*q.v.*).

If the proportions are taken out in terms not just of all teachers with certain qualifications to pupils, but of men and women teachers separately it is clear that the supply of women maths and science graduates is much worse than that of men. This has severe implications for the girls' schools in which a high proportion of all girls are educated. To some extent this disparity is perhaps a reflection of feminine antipathy to these subjects, but the loss through marriage is much more to blame.

There is an equally severe problem, and one that affects all subjects, with the supply of men and women of first-rate academic ability. They are not confined to those who hold first class honours degrees, but the supply of those who have such a degree provides a useful yard-stick. In the direct grant schools there is about one teacher with a 'first' to every 250 pupils, and in maintained grammar schools to every 300; but in modern schools there is only one to every 5,000. The terms of the recruitment and deployment problem are almost identical with that affecting the scarcity subjects. And the position is getting worse because the older teachers have a higher proportion of firsts among them. The Crowther Report pointed out that 'in 1950 we ploughed back into the school sector only 9% of the young men who got firsts. Numerically, they were insufficient to replace in due course the schoolmasters who had taught them. And the expansion of sixth forms means that a mere replacement rate is not enough.' Since then the great expansion of universities and of colleges of education has increased the academic competition for men and women with firsts, while the rapid introduction of comprehensive education has frightened some away from schools, while no doubt it has attracted others.

See also **Teacher estimates and teacher shortage**

DGOA

Grammar, Teaching of Nowhere is the teaching of English in a greater state of transition, with all the uncertainties that such a state involves, than in the teaching of grammar. The last ten years have seen a gradual abandonment of the traditional skills of analysis and parsing, derived from the structures of classical grammar, and the present position is characterised by considerable doubt as to (a) whether or not *any* grammar is required and (b) the kind of grammar that might *usefully* come to occupy a place in the English curriculum.

In the field of linguistics, expecially in the USA, new descriptive grammars have emerged, each with its own claims to coherence and comprehensiveness; but the question of when (i.e. at which stage in the pupils' education) a systematic study of grammar is either helpful or necessary is still wide open. Socio-linguistics seems to be teaching us that inadequacy in language depends on a complex interaction of numerous factors, social, intellectual, cognitive and affective (*see e.g.* **Bernstein, Basil**): we now begin to recognise the crucial role of conversation and other kinds of oral exchange in the growth of the pupils' language. But we are not yet able to say either '*This* is the most useful kind of work in grammar' or '*This* is the stage at which to introduce such and such an aspect of grammatical work'.

Teachers of English are in the position of having to await the results of the extensive collaboration now going on between linguisticians and teachers themselves: it is to be hoped, however, that teachers will be allowed to make the decisive choices. One also hopes that the needs, opinions and responses of pupils will be thoroughly canvassed—not only in terms of their ability to recognise, and be helped by recognising, a Gerundive Nominal of Purpose or a Nominal Infinitive of Obligation (to name two terms from a current text of Transformational Grammar), but also in terms of their morale and sense of purpose. The fear must always be that the old pedantry might be replaced by a new one.

FURTHER READING

J. R. Firth. *The Tongues of Men and Speech*, Oxford Univ. Press, 1964.

M. A. K. Halliday, A. McIntosh and P. D. Strevens. *The Linguistic Sciences and Language Teaching*, Longmans Green, 1964.

R. Quirk. *The Use of English*, Longmans Green, 1962.

R. H. Robins. *Ancient and Medieval Grammatic Theory in Europe*, Bell, 1951. *General Linguistics: An Introductory Survey*, Longmans Green, 1964.

B. Strang. *Modern English Structure*, Arnold, 1962.

GS

Grammar schools In the Christianisation of Saxon England, the founding of bishoprics was regularly associated with the founding of grammar schools designed to train candidates for the priesthood and the secular orders in the knowledge and use of Latin. There were also monastic schools. The rise of the medieval universities was accompanied by the rapid foundation of grammar schools. In the late middle ages such schools were often founded in association with chantries. Both religious and secular guilds founded grammar schools, and private benefactors continued to do so up to the end of the 18th century.

After the Reformation the closing of the monastic schools and, more important, the destruction of the chantries, meant the loss of a large number of schools. During the 17th century the boarding grammar schools (i.e. most of the 'public schools') became more sharply differentiated from the day schools, the majority of which entered on a long period of decline. The Taunton Commission (1864–7) (*q.v.*) found the endowed schools, with few exceptions, in a sad state of degeneration and numerically quite inadequate to the increase and redistribution of the country's population.

From the beginning, the grammar school educated children from the large middle area of society between the nobility and the lowest classes. At first all or most of the pupils were charged no teaching fees, though there might be certain extra payments. From the 16th century onwards there was an increasing proportion of fee-paying pupils, and a distinction was often made between them and the 'free scholars'. The curriculum of the early schools was predominantly concerned with the mastery of Latin. The revival of learning brought an increased study of Greek, a humanist approach to literature and—though the Tudor school regime was generally spartan—some promising experiments in dramatic and other techniques of teaching. The impulse did not last, however, and studies settled down to a formal grammar grind which persisted for centuries. As late as the 19th century, schools were tied by their foundation statutes to a classical curriculum, and some attempts to introduce modern studies were frustrated. Not until the revision of endowments in the 1870s by the Endowed Schools Commissioners, who succeeded in diverting some endowments for the foundation of girls' schools, was any significant provision made for the secondary education of girls (*see* **Girls, Education of**).

The Education Act 1902 established LEAs empowered (not compelled) to found and maintain secondary schools. Within the new system were some ancient schools whose endowments had dwindled, a few former private schools, former higher grade and elementary schools and pupil-teacher centres, and many newly-founded schools. Most were small single-sex schools. Fees were charged, but there was from the first a proportion of free places, and by 1938 nearly half the places in maintained secondary schools were free. At this point the different history of secondary education in Wales should be noted. By 1893 Wales possessed an integrated national educational system with primary, secondary and university levels linked by an extensive scholarship system that made advanced teaching available to all those capable of profiting from it.

The Education Act 1944 abolished fees in maintained schools of every kind, proclaimed 'secondary education for all' administered under a single code, and required, not merely empowered, local authorities to provide education at all stages in accordance with the 'age, ability and aptitude' of pupils in their area. It did not stipulate how this was to be done. The Norwood Report of 1943, however, had advocated a tripartite system of secondary schools (grammar, technical and modern), professing to find in it a general correspondence with three distinguishable psychological types; and most authorities adopted tripartite or bipartite schemes (technical schools were very much in the minority). Selection procedures were intended in theory to allocate children to the types of secondary education to which they were best suited. Unfortunately, the social and curricular prestige of the secondary grammar school, memories of the old 'scholarship' examinations, and the rivalry of primary schools combined to make the procedure competitive rather than distributive in function.

After the 1944 Act, the maintained grammar schools were anything but a homogeneous group. They varied in size from under 200 to nearly 1,000 pupils. They might be single-sex or co-educational. Some were former county secondary schools, some 'aided' or 'controlled' church schools, some former central or senior schools, some new establishments. In academic standards and tradition there was corresponding variety. Some schools had large sixth forms and an impressive record of university scholarships: others found it difficult to maintain a sixth form at all. Social composition also varied. Some schools were 'zoned'; others received their pupils (via the selection procedure) by the operation of a kind of competitive market. There were also important differences between the school which was the only grammar school serving a large and socially varied area, and that which was one of many maintained by a large city authority.

After 1902 a major curricular decision had been taken. Robert Morant, Permanent Secretary to the Board of Education, took as his model the older grammar schools, and the regulations issued for the guidance of the new schools prescribed a highly academic curriculum. The School Certificate examinations introduced in 1917 further encouraged narrowly academic and formal work and the pretence that the schools were, substantially, pre-university institutions. Some 30 years later the Spens Report criticised the false division between secondary and technical education and the overladen, subject-centred curriculum. The Norwood Report noted the dominance of public examinations. In 1950 the new GCE seemed to promise some freeing of the curriculum, but neither teachers nor public grasped its reforming principle. Except for the absence of subject-grouping, O and A levels were quickly assimilated to the old School and Higher School Certificates, and the abolition of the minimum age limit of 16 soon put an end to the pretence that this was to be normally a single broad-based examination taken at the end of a seven-year course. Misgivings about undue and premature specialisation—particularly characteristic of boys' schools—continued, however, and the Crowther Report of 1960 advocated a constructive use of sixth-form minority time and a balanced curriculum which should ensure that science students were literate and arts students 'numerate'. Since then the liberalising movements have grown, and have received particular encouragement from the Schools Council formed in 1964. (*See* **Curriculum, Agreement to Broaden the; General studies** *and* **Schools Council.**)

The post-war maintained grammar schools should in theory have been wholly satisfactory institutions. Fee-paying pupils had disappeared, ability was now the sole criterion of entry, and the grammar school population should therefore have been more democratically determined and more intellectually homogeneous than ever before. In fact, however, the schools faced many difficulties. They had in considerable numbers a new kind of pupil who understood and cared little for their assumptions. Parental anxiety, primary school rivalry and newspaper and other publicity combined to make '11-plus selection' an experience of tension and frustration for many children, while successive sociologists showed that children from more favoured socio-economic groups tended to do disproportionately well, and those from less favoured groups disproportionately badly, in academic education.

In 1966, responding to a demand from the DES, the majority of LEAs submitted schemes for comprehensive secondary education in their areas. The future of the direct grant or semi-independent schools is uncertain. Some authorities have refused to send any pupils to them unless they 'go fully comprehensive'. Other authorities propose to transfer selected pupils to them at a later age than 11. There is also a proposal to retain some ten to twenty of these schools as highly selective grammar schools educating the top 2% or 3% of the ability range.

The days of the maintained grammar schools appear to be numbered. Any assessment of them must therefore be retrospective. In the half-century of their history, many have grown from tiny schools working with dubious efficiency on a narrowly conceived curriculum, to dynamic societies with big sixth forms and impressive standards of scholarship. The grammar schools have educated wave after wave of 'first generation' children. At their worst they have been dully academic, timidly or arrogantly conventional, and a Procrustean bed to those who could not easily take their curriculum or ethos. At their frequent best they have been civilising and enlightening agencies; and they have achieved, through kindliness, respect for individuals, and the sense of a common purpose, a complex social integration. It is insufficiently recognised that they have also sometimes shown themselves pioneers in curricular innovation. One must hope that comprehensive schools will succeed in incapsulating the scholarship, the sensitivity and the good personal relations of the grammar school at its best.

FURTHER READING

J. A. Adamson. *A Short History of Education*, Cambridge Univ. Press, 1919.
W. H. G. Armytage. *Four Hundred Years of English Education*, Cambridge Univ. Press, 1964.

S. J. Curtis. *History of Education in Great Britain*, Univ. Tutorial Press, 1965.
S. J. Curtis and M. E. A. Boultwood. *An Introductory History of English Education since 1800*, Univ. Tutorial Press, 1966.
H. Davies. *Culture and the Grammar School*, Routledge and Kegan Paul, 1965.
J. W. B. Douglas. *The Home and the School*, McGibbon and Kee, 1964.
E. Floud, A. H. Halsey and F. M. Martin. *Social Class and Educational Opportunity*, Heinemann, 1956.
B. Jackson and D. Marsden. *Education and the Working Class*, Routledge and Kegan Paul, 1962.
T. L. Jarman. *Landmarks in the History of Education*, Cresset Press, 1951.
Frances Stevens. *The Living Tradition*, Hutchinson, 1962.

FS

Grammar Schools Act 1840 Governors of a grammar school were empowered under this Act to introduce into the curriculum any subjects that were not provided for in the original foundation of the school.

Grant, Block The notion that Treasury grants to LEAs, the amount of which was more or less based on the percentage of money spent by local authorities on education, should be replaced by a block grant covering all local services was embodied in a Treasury departmental committee report in 1911 (the Kempe Report, *q.v.*). The argument for the percentage system was that, since more spent locally meant more received from central funds, it encouraged LEAs to step up their spending on education. The counter-argument in favour of a block grant was that such a grant would level out inequalities of rate. The proposal was revived during the economy drives of the 1920s but met with strong opposition, partly on the ground that LEAs then had widely differing functions, some being responsible for elementary education only and others having responsibility also for higher education. The block grant system finally replaced the percentage grant system in 1959.

Grant, Capitation Capitation grants are paid by the Secretary of State to the proprietors of direct grant grammar schools. At present they amount to £52 a year for each pupil in the upper school, with an additional grant of £84 a year for each pupil in the sixth form. The detailed conditions which the schools must fulfil to receive the grants, and the definitions of the ages of the pupils mentioned above, are set out in the *Direct Grant School Regulations*, 1959 (Ministry of Education). The regulations have since been amended to take account of increased costs, and in 1968 the capitiaton grant was reduced by £20 to the £32 mentioned, as a government economy measure.

These capitation grants are the only main grants received by direct grant grammar schools from the exchequer. For the remainder of their finance, the schools have to rely on the fees they are allowed to charge, and on the income of such endowments as they may possess. In addition to allotting not less than 25% of the school places free of fee, school governors are required to remit fees, wholly or in part, to parents unable to pay them, according to an income test approved by the Minister. The amount of these remissions is reimbursed to the governors by the exchequer.

See also **Direct grant schools**

FB

Grant, Deficiency Under a percentage plan introduced in 1919, the principle was established that the state and the LEA should each pay half of the LEA's total expenditure on higher education. The LEA's income, which came mostly from fees, was first deducted, and half the remaining expenditure was met by a grant from the Board of Education called the deficiency grant. It was abolished by the National Economy Order of 1931.

Grants, General Introduced by the Local Government Act 1958, general grants changed the system of exchequer aid to local education authorities. Previously, for nearly 40 years, specific grants were made for education in the form of a percentage of the actual net expenditure of the individual LEA. Other factors took account of the different circumstances of authorities as regards their rateable resources and the proportion of school children to the population, so that, shortly before the system was abolished, the main education grant ranged between 42% and 65% of the net expenditure of individual LEAs. Specific percentage grants were retained for police and highway services, and separate housing grants were maintained. Otherwise, virtually all other local services were included in the general grant arrangements in 1959. In addition to education, these comprised local health services, child care and welfare of the old, fire services, and a variety of services involving minor expenditure. Education accounted for over 85% of the local expenditure concerned, the whole range of the other local services involved making up less than 15% of the local budget.

The essential virtue of the specific percentage grant was the automatic adjustment of exchequer aid to the actual expenditure of the individual LEA. So, as education loomed so large in the local expenditure, when the Conservative government, in proposing the change to general grants, declared that percentage grants acted 'as an indiscriminating incentive to further expenditure', they were strongly, but unsuccessfully, opposed by all educational interests.

The amount of the general grant is determined for all local authorities in the aggregate, and in advance of the period of expenditure to which it applies. The Minister of Housing and Local Government, with the consent of the Treasury, fixes the total grant, after consultation with the associations of local authorities, following a forecast of local authorities' expenditure for two years ahead. During the grant period, the Minister may increase the grant if he decides that unforeseen increases in costs, and salaries, are such that they ought not to fall entirely on local authorities.

The distribution of the global general grant to individual authorities is made on a prescribed basis, largely determined by the population and the number of children in the area. Other factors in a weighted formula of distribution include allowances for a high proportion of school children to population, the number of children under five years of age, and account is taken of the differing rateable resources of authorities.

In 1966–7, the relevant expenditure of all local authorities in England and Wales was £1,338m., of which £1,081m. was attributable to education. The general grant towards the former figure is £788m. Local authorities allocate the grant towards their general expenditure. They are not free to ignore prescribed standards of performance, as deduction of grant may be made. Provided they avoid that, they derive immediate benefit from economies in savings to the rates, just as they have to bear additional expenditure immediately on the rates alone if they progress at a faster pace than the average, as it is the average of all authorities' progress that determines increases in the general grant.

In practice, through the predominant control of central government over the major items of educational expenditure, such as teacher supply and salaries, and the school building programme, the general grant system has not realised many of the fears of its opponents, but in individual instances it has affected some items of development.

Although the Labour party had previously declared in favour of restoring percentage grants for education, in 1966, in the White Paper on *Local*

Government Finance (Cmd 2923), the government stated that there was 'no prospect of any major reform of local government finance within the present structure of local government'; and what the Royal Commission on Local Government will recommend awaits the event. Meanwhile, the Local Government Bill of 1966 proposes to continue general grants under the new designation of *rate support grants*, and to bring school milk and meals within their ambit. Some other changes in the formula and method of distribution of grant are to be made: in particular, the introduction of a 'domestic element' of grant, whereby it is intended to reduce by half the rate increases which householders would otherwise be called upon to bear in 1967 and successive years.

Local Government Act, 1958 by Seward and Forster (Butterworth, London, 1959) and *Equalisation and the Future of Local Goverrment Finance* by Lawrence Boyle examine and explain the problems involved in the grant system.

See also **Costs of education; School finance**

FB

Grants, LEA Apart from the wide range of grants which LEAs have the power, or in certain cases the duty, to make to pupils and students (*see* **Scholarships and other benefits**), LEAs have power to make grants to local authorities and voluntary bodies towards the establishment and maintenance of facilities for recreation and social and physical training, e.g. playing fields, swimming baths, and village halls. LEAs may also make grants towards universities.

Grants, Percentage *See* **Grants, General**

Grants, Rate support *See* **Grants, General**

Grants, Student *See* **Students, Grants for**

Grants-in-aid The term means grants by the exchequer in aid of local services. Beginning in 1833 the first grant-in-aid of education, of £20,000 a year, was made towards the building of schools by voluntary bodies, then the initiators and providers. Local government was brought in by the Elementary Education Act 1870, which created school boards, and today the county and county borough councils are the LEAs.

Between 1833 and 1945, public education changed from a voluntary service, with tenuous exchequer aid, to a locally administered national service with massive grants-in-aid. Corresponding changes have been made in the principles and practice of grants-in-aid, from near *laissez-faire* to the present system which is: (1) the promotion, or control, of local enterprise, by means of the amount of exchequer grant and the formula for its distribution; (2) the central prescription of the standards of services to be provided in the localities, accompanied by central government inspection and audit, as a condition of grant-aid; (3) the endeavour to equalise the rate burdens of different localities by means of the grant formula.

See also **Grants, General**

FB

Greece, Education in Education is free and compulsory between the ages of six and 15 years. In 1965–6 there were 10,791 public and private primary schools and 921 secondary schools, with a total enrolment of 213,479; 1,500 nursery schools, with an enrolment of 50,730; 27 public and private technical institutions, with an enrolment of 59,447; 14 teacher training colleges, with an enrolment of 2,949. There are two universities at Athens, one at Thessaloniki, and a new one planned at Patras.

The population of the country was approximately 8½ million in 1965.

Group methods These were devised as a reaction against, and in compensation for, class-teaching methods. Every teacher knew that in a large class it was possible to group the children into five or more groups according to their speed in learning new skills, in understanding new processes, or absorbing new data. The division of a class into groups was a conscious attempt by the teacher to pay more regard to individual differences: thus each group was made up of those pupils whose individual capacities most closely approximated to the national average for the group. Group methods were once in great favour as a means of allowing a whole class of children to practise their skill in reading aloud. Group methods are still used in the teaching of subjects like mathematics, since it is possible to grade exercises so as to provide reasonable challenge to the varying abilities of different groups of children. An essential condition of the use of group methods in class-teaching is that complete freedom must exist for promotion to higher groups when the requisite achievement warrants it. An ultimate refinement of group-methods is found in setting (*q.v.*).

See also **Class teaching**

DJJ

Group tests These tests may attempt to test anything from non-verbal intelligence to arithmetic attainment, and are usually administered by the teacher to a class of children. Such tests will be reliable only if they have been carefully standardised and validated on a wide scale with other children before the test is finally issued, and also if they are administered in strict accordance with the written instructions. Their chief virtue is that they can give the teacher a clear idea of the standing of his class in contrast to any other class of the same age and type in the country; this can be useful for checking standards or evaluating different techniques of teaching the same thing.

The danger of the group tests is that they are obviously more inaccurate than individual tests, where a personal approach is certainly more helpful and fair to certain pupils, and that one teacher may allow the test questions to direct his own syllabus more than they should.

Group tests are not as popular with teachers now as they were; but now that they are no longer used as methods of selection to the same extent that they were, they may return to favour as the useful tools they can be in appropriate circumstances.

FURTHER READING
P. E. Vernon. *The Measurement of Abilities*, Univ. of London Press, 1956.

NT

Groups Human beings, along with many other animals, seem to have a natural inclination to form social groups. Such groups may become formal and recognised (for example, the club or the family), or they may exist in a far looser sense, in such form as the casual group of friends or acquaintances, based perhaps on similarities of age, social background, past history, geographical proximity, or something even more random. Whatever the grouping, it is important to realise that its individual members can be extremely influenced by its expectations, mores and general frame of reference, and it is a mistake to see the individual in isolation from his many different group influences.

The study of these strong and occasionally conflicting forces, which can operate even in the most casual of groupings, is known as group psychology, and has been studied in situations ranging from experiences in concentration camps to interactions among a ship's crew. Group psychology is particularly applicable to the classroom situation.

FURTHER READING
C. M. Fleming. *The Social Psychology of Education*, Routledge and Kegan Paul, 1959.
W. J. H. Sprott. *Social Psychology*, Methuen, 1952.

NT

Grundy-tutor *See* **Programmed learning; Teaching machines**

Guatemala, Education in Elementary education is free and compulsory in urban areas, extending over a 10-year period of five years primary and five years secondary. There is a shortage of state schools, compensated for by numerous private establishments, and in 1966 a scheme costing $22 million was launched to provide an additional 1,000 teachers and to build new state schools. There are two public universities (the more important being San Carlos de Gautemala) and two colleges of arts. 1964 statistics: 3,084 rural primary schools (155,253 enrolments); 1,210 urban primary schools (245,817 enrolments); 280 secondary schools (44,104 enrolments); 19 technical schools (3,283 enrolments); 2 universities (7,547 enrolments).

The population of the country was approximately 4¾ million in 1966.

Guidance and counselling Most schools provide for differing abilities and interests by organising streams, sets, ability groups and optional courses; educational guidance helps a pupil to enter the most suitable course for his particular needs. Some pupils find the work too difficult and a transfer to another group, or a change in the teacher's approach, may meet the situation; others may fall behind because they are troubled by home circumstances or by a failure in their personal relations with friends or teachers, and for them counselling might be helpful. The counsellor tries to form a relationship in which a pupil can talk freely about what is troubling him; by observing the feeling associated with what is said the counsellor is often able to help him to clarify the question at issue and to move towards his own solution. Pupils who fall seriously behind others, or who have unusual behaviour difficulties, may be referred to an educational psychologist or to a psychiatrist at a child guidance clinic.

In secondary schools, educational decisions made earlier may narrow the range of vocational choices later, especially for those wishing to go on to universities, colleges of education or technical colleges. Some members of secondary school staffs are responsible for careers; they provide information on occupations and possible jobs and co-operate with youth employment officers, who help school-leavers to choose the work they wish to do and to find a job.

Large secondary schools in the future may have pupils across the whole range of ability; some will leave school for low-skilled employment, others will enter honours degree courses. To give relevant information and guidance to all will require a team approach from the school staff interested in careers work and youth employment officers, in co-operation with parents. The opportunities opening up in secondary, higher and further education, and in employment, will be unfamiliar to many parents; and parents and pupils will need help to understand these opportunities and to use them wisely.

In some countries, the USA in particular, counselling is a recognised service in schools: counsellors are appointed in a full-time or part-time capacity after a course of training. Their training includes psychology and the use of standardised tests and inventories, but counselling interviews are at the heart of their work. They help individuals to understand themselves— to have a realistic self-image—and to make decisions in the light of what is within their powers and range of opportunities.

Counsellors have been appointed in a few English schools; other schools are experimenting with the appointment of social workers to strengthen the relations between home and school. Teachers charged with the responsibility for giving guidance will need to know of factors in the home and social background that may be favourable or unfavourable to educational attainment. Emphasis is beginning to move from the cross-section of individual differences taken at 11-plus to individual development over a period of time, and educational and vocational guidance is coming to be regarded not solely as an activity to be undertaken at crisis points when decisions must be taken, but as a continuous process throughout school life. Cumulative school records on individual pupils will assume a greater importance. Counsellors might be expected to have some part in maintaining records and in the administration of tests of aptitude and ability, but their main contribution to guidance will be through the counselling interview.

FURTHER READING
M. P. Carter. *Home, School and Work*, Pergamon, 1962.
P. Halmos. *The Faith of the Counsellors*, Constable, 1965.
M. Reuchlin. *Pupil Guidance: Facts and Problems*, Council of Europe Council for Cultural Co-operation, Strasbourg, 1964.
C. R. Rogers. *Client-centred Therapy: its Current Practice, Implications and Theory*, Houghton Mifflin, Boston, Mass., 1951.
B. Steffire (ed.). *Theories of Counselling*, McGraw-Hill, New York, 1965.
C. G. Wrenn. *The Counsellor in a Changing World*, American Personal and Guidance Association, Washington, DC, 1962.
DES. *Careers Guidance in Schools*, HMSO, 1965.

CJG

Guinea, Education in Education is free. The number of primary, superior primary, secondary and vocational training schools is not available, but about 100,000 children are under instruction. Total population was approximately $3\frac{1}{2}$ million in 1964.

Gulbenkian Foundation, Calouste
The Foundation administers grants and
awards in the UK and the Commonwealth.
98 Portland Pl., London, W1.

Gurney-Dixon Report *See* 'Early
Leaving', etc.

Gurr Report In 1965 the Association
of British Correspondence Colleges and
Cleaver–Hume Ltd, a firm owning
several correspondence colleges, together set up a committee under the
chairmanship of Dr C. E. Gurr,
formerly the Chief Education Officer
of Middlesex, to prepare a scheme for
the establishment of a national ac-
crediting body for correspondence
colleges. The report of this committee,
known as the Gurr Report, was
published in May 1966. It contained
proposals for a code of conduct to which
all correspondence colleges in the UK
would have to adhere. The Secretary
of State for Education and Science
agreed to co-operate, but asked to be
allowed first to see the scheme in the
precise form in which it will be carried
into effect after the necessary legal
instruments are drafted. The scheme
was returned to the committee with
suggested amendments and, given the
committee's acceptance of these amendments, the Secretary of State was to
nominate the chairman and five
independent members of the accreditation council.
See also **Correspondence courses**

Guyana, Education in Education is
free between the ages of five and 16 and
compulsory from six to 14 years. In
1964 there were 377 primary schools
(enrolment 163,194); 39 secondary
schools (enrolment 14,431); and 13
state-aided secondary schools. Higher
education is provided for by 18
domestic science and handicraft
centres, three technical schools (enrolment 1,334), a teacher training centre

(enrolment 407), a technical institute
for apprentices and the University of
Georgetown. Literacy is estimated at
85% of the population.
The country's population was nearly
three-quarters of a million in 1965.
See also **West Indies, Education
in the**

Gymnasia PE involves far more than
the learning of skills, the techniques of
games and the repetition of formal
exercises. Movement is not only functional, but also expressive of attitudes
and feelings. In common with other
living creatures, man has his own
particular characteristics of movement
and individual patterns and rhythms;
PE teaches children how to co-ordinate
body and mind so that they may exploit these characteristics with imagination and ingenuity. In order that this
should be successfully done, the accommodation provided must be flexible.
A series of spaces of varying size may
provide accommodation that can be
used intensively and flexibly. One space
should be large enough to permit
activities by fairly big groups. It may
not be necessary to heat this space or
enclose it on all four sides. The remaining spaces may be much smaller,
but should enable equipment to be
erected for such activities as are performed at any particular time. Such
accommodation will prevent the waste of
floor space that frequently occurs when
an activity in the centre of a gymnasium
sterilises the surrounding area.
The standard school gymnasium designed primarily for formal gymnastics
measured 60 ft by 30 ft and was provided with wall bars along each side,
beams, ropes and vaulting apparatus,
consisting of a buck, horse and box.
Today the tendency is to enlarge the
available floor space and to dispense
with much of the fixed apparatus. This
change has been caused by the new
conception of PE, in which formal
gymnastics play a minor part and games
and wider activities play a major part.

A modern gymnasium, or, as some prefer to call it, 'sports hall', provides a large covered space, which can be divided by hanging netting. This gives scope for activities such as cricket training, long jumping, pole vaulting, athletic throwing events, climbing, badminton, judo, basketball, volleyball and coaching in most of the major ball games.

FURTHER READING
Indoor Sports and Social Recreation Spaces, Fixtures and Equipment (Architects' Journal Information Sheets, 23.9.64 to 14.10.64. Ref. SfB 85).
Secondary School Design, Physical Education (Building Bulletin No. 26, DES, HMSO).

JCP and JE

Gypsies, Education of The Plowden Report 1967 (*q.v.*) described the children of gypsies as 'probably the most severely deprived children in the country'. At the time of the Report, these children were calculated to number fewer than 4,000, but this number is likely to double in the next 20 years. Few go to school; and, being always on the move, they are quoted as an example of groups (others are children from canal boat families, and many from army and air force families) who would not be selected for special educational attention by the criteria laid down in the Report.

H

Hadow Report (1926): Report of the Consultative Committee of the Board of Education on the Education of the Adolescent Terms of reference: (1) To consider and report on the organisation, aim and curriculum of courses of study suitable for children remaining in full-time attendance at schools other than secondary schools up to the age of 15. Consideration was given on one hand to the provision of a good general education with a reasonable variety of curriculum for children of differing tastes and abilities; and on the other hand to the probable careers of pupils in commerce, industry and agriculture. (2) To advise as to the arrangements which should be made (a) for testing the attainments of the pupils at the end of their course; (b) for facilitating in suitable cases the transfer of individual pupils to secondary schools after the normal age of transition.

The Report recommended that there should be secondary education for all children, with a minimum school leaving age of 15. This meant that the original purely academic concept of secondary education was broadened.

Hadow Report (1931) *See* **Primary School Report (1931)**

Hahn, Kurt Gordonstoun, an English public school in Scotland, more re-nowned for its physical than for its intellectual activities, was founded in 1934 by Kurt Hahn, a German, of Jewish parentage, who later became a

Christian. He was born on 5 June 1886, attended the Wilhelms Gymnasium in Berlin and subsequently, with long interruptions caused by ill health following severe sunstroke, studied classics at the Universities of Oxford, Heidelberg, Freiburg and Göttingen.

In August 1914 he entered the German Foreign Office and became, in 1917, the Private Secretary of Prince Max von Baden. After Germany's defeat, Prince Max, accompanied by Hahn, returned to his ancestral home at Salem and sponsored Hahn's cherished ambition to establish in Germany a boarding school on English public school lines but based on the tenets of Plato's educational philosophy. The school soon acquired a reputation in Germany and beyond.

Hahn publicly opposed the Hitler regime and was imprisoned in a concentration camp in 1933. Freed by the personal intervention of Ramsay Macdonald he fled penniless to England. His colleagues at Salem, Dr Erich Meissner and N. Pares, did likewise.

In 1934 he started a new school at Doune (Perthshire) with three pupils but transferred in the same year to the Gordonstoun premises where he opened initially with 13 pupils. This event attracted several former pupils of Salem, including Prince Philip of Greece. In 1937, a preparatory school, Wester Elchies, was opened at Aberlour. At the outbreak of war, the school moved to Plas Dinam in mid-Wales.

After its return to Gordonstoun in 1945, the number of pupils in the school increased rapidly and additional premises had to be acquired at Altyre and elsewhere. Hahn received at this time considerable financial assistance from M. Anton Besse, an admirer of his work, who selected the school's French motto, 'Plus est en vous'.

Hahn owed much to Cecil Reddie and he introduced both at Salem and Gordonstoun many of Abbotsholme's features. He was elected a member of the Headmasters' Conference in 1944. As a headmaster he was impulsive and eccentric, concerned with principles not details. Nevertheless, he was the inspiration for the Moray Badge Scheme which later became the pattern for the Duke of Edinburgh's Award Scheme, the Outward Bound Schools, the Atlantic College and the Trevelyan Scholarships. The Doon School (India), Anavryta (Greece), Rannoch (Perthshire), Ibadan (Nigeria), are among those schools now organised along Gordonstoun lines.

Hahn, who never married, retired in 1953 and died in 1968.

See also **New schools movement**

FURTHER READING
A. Arnold Brown. *Unfolding Character— The Impact of Gordonstoun*, Routledge and Kegan Paul, 1962.
F. R. G. Chew. *Gordonstoun*, Univ. of Aberdeen, 1963.
Kurt Hahn. 'Education and Changes in our Social Structure', *British Association for Commercial and Industrial Education Journal*, XIV, 1, March 1960.
Hugh Heckstall-Smith. *Doubtful Schoolmaster*, Peter Davies, 1962.
A. J. C. Kerr. *Schools of Europe*, Bowes and Bowes, 1962.
Eric Meissner. *The Boy and his Needs*, Macdonald, 1956.
                                                RE

Haiti, Education in Education is free where available. 1965 enrolments: urban primary schools 143,144; rural primary schools 131,236; secondary schools 8,850; agricultural and industrial schools 4,177; Haiti University 1,822.

The country's population was approximately 4½ million in 1966.

Half-subjects 'Half-subjects' at GCE A level were proposed originally by Sir Desmond Lee, headmaster of Winchester, as a means of relieving present pressures on the sixth form and also of meeting the needs of the wide range of ability increasingly found in it. The scheme is fully described by Michael Hutchinson and Christopher Young in *Educating the Intelligent* (1962). Having proposed that present A level syllabuses should have their factual content reduced by 25%, Hutchinson and Young suggested that a half-subject should contain a half of the new content: that is, about three-eighths of the content of a present A level syllabus. A half-subject would be examined in the same way as full A levels after two years in the sixth, but would be taken at a new 'complementary' level, or C level, of GCE. For normal A level candidates, success in such a paper would count as a half-subject at A level: for others it would count as a pass at C level.

See also **Coherence subjects**

Halo effect If we are attempting to assess an individual either by interview or by our general impression of him, and if there is one thing about him that we particularly like, such as his quickness of thought or even facial expression, then we are very often tempted to allow this single good impression to colour estimation of all his other abilities. This effect of a single impression on the whole assessment is referred to as a 'halo effect'.

Of course, the halo can spread in the other way too; if the luckless interviewee has started off on the wrong foot, the examiner may become prejudiced against every aspect of him and be quite unjust without realising what is actually happening.

This effect can be guarded against by warning examiners about it and having a number of examiners who can pool their opinions so that any final impression should be slightly more objective than an individual one.

Handicapped children *See* **Special education**

Handicapped Children, Advisory Committee on Set up by the DES, the Committee advises the Secretary of State on such matters relating to children who require special educational treatment as he may submit to them or they may consider it necessary to investigate.

Handicapped school leavers *See* **Special education**

Handicraft Laymen, and teachers who are not specialists in practical school subjects, are often confused by the variety of names given to these subjects; but there is in fact a current convention by which 'handicraft' is the collective term for woodwork and metalwork (sometimes called 'heavy crafts'), and 'craft' is taken to denote 'light crafts' such as bookbinding, basketry, weaving, pottery, etc. The obvious links between handicraft, craft and art have always been recognised in principle and, to a varying extent, in practice. Handicraft students have often taken courses with an art component, and in schools the subjects have sometimes been organisationally unified in the same department; but their marriage has frequently been one in name only, and the increasing emphasis upon technological and scientific studies in relation to metalwork is sharpening the differences in emphasis between some handicraft studies and work in art and craft.

The history of handicraft in schools is one of development from simple woodwork, undertaken with makeshift equipment in classrooms, to the complex and advanced work sometimes attempted with excellent facilities in today's schools. Fairly full accounts of this process of development may be found elsewhere, but the principles, aims and objectives which have been formulated in relation to handicraft must be given some consideration here since they influence, to varying degrees, what is done in practice.

Solomon Barter and the other pioneers of 'manual training' introduced woodwork into the curriculum of elementary schools in the late 19th century. They believed that the overwhelming emphasis previously placed upon the development of the purely 'mental faculties' of children was mistaken, if not positively harmful. The neglect of the 'creative faculty' and the lack of attention to 'constructive aptitude' meant that education was unbalanced and incomplete. These innovators considered that practical work was conducive both to the physical and to the mental development of children. It was maintained, however, that the acquisition of practical skill was of great importance in its own right since most elementary school pupils were likely to become artisans. These general principles have been widened and elaborated over the years, but contemporary writers on the subject still find it convenient to classify the aims of handicraft teaching in a similar way.

In the available literature one may find references to the usefulness of handicraft as a medium through which children may develop such diverse personal and social attributes as good character, a sense of responsibility, self-reliance, initiative, self-respect, willingness to co-operate, good citizenship, aesthetic sensitivity, and a 'right attitude' to work. It has also been claimed that the study of handicraft can train the memory, be conducive to the development of the ability to think logically, help one to acquire a sense of judgement and the elements of good taste. Beneficial effects upon the powers of perseverance and 'neatness of mind' also find a mention. Reference is very frequently made to the therapeutic value of handicraft as a recreational activity through which one may find emotional satisfaction and mental and physical well-being. The actual practical skills acquired through the wide range of activities offered in school workshops are regarded as being intrinsically useful. They may also be thought to present opportunities for the discovery and nurture of vocational interests and aptitudes.

Consideration of this formidable catalogue may well cause one to conclude that handicraft education is nothing if not comprehensive in its aims and objectives. This proliferation of aims may have had a number of causes, but it is likely to be related to the fact that handicraft specialists have waged an unremitting struggle to attain higher status for the subject (and for themselves). This concern to prove the value of handicraft has led them to espouse some claims concerning its educational value which are of dubious validity and ought to be quietly dropped. A detailed discussion of the examples given above cannot be attempted here, but a number of them are readily recognisable as being based upon outdated or naïve psychological notions. In spite of these shortcomings, however, it must be recognised that handicraft teachers have for long been actively concerned not only with the teaching of practical skills but also with specific areas of the cognitive and affective development of children. Their attempts to formulate a general theory of their role and function in contemporary education have been admirable.

At the present time handicraft is part of a curriculum and a system of school organisation that is undergoing a process of reappraisal and reform. Older ideas concerning the nature of aptitudes and abilities (which provided the rationale for the tripartite system) are now largely discredited. Separatism in secondary education is being replaced by a comprehensive system, and streaming within schools is being modified or abandoned. Handicraft, until now, has generally been regarded as having a more important role to play in the education of children of average, and below average, intelligence, than in the education of the 'academically more able'. Handicraft teachers have been willing to acknowledge, or even to lay a claim to, this special function with children of lower ability, but they have bitterly resented the concomitant direction of gifted children towards predominantly academic courses. The current reappraisal of the curriculum, and the abandonment of streaming, make it important that both the nature and the role of handicraft should be re-examined. This process has, in fact, begun and the trend of some future developments is already apparent.

The long-fought battle to make the study of design an integral part of all handicraft courses is not yet won, but the position is much improved. The teaching of craft skills and techniques alone is now universally recognised to be insufficient. The recognition of the desirability of teaching design through craftwork does not, unfortunately, ensure that it is always attempted. Teachers find it difficult to teach design, and more research into design courses and teaching methods could be extremely useful, providing that constructive findings are passed on to teachers through easily available literature and in-service training courses.

The isolation of handicraft from other school subjects, and its limited relevance to life in a technological society, are points of criticism which are now becoming common. For a number of years handicraft teachers have been urged to broaden the scope of the subject by exploring areas of overlap with other disciplines, particularly science. This development is gaining ground and some innovators are advocating that workshops should be places in which the creative abilities of boys should be expressed through work on practical scientific projects. Page's report *Engineering Among the*

Schools[1] gathered together an impressive collection of evidence concerning experiments along these lines which have been taking place in a number of different schools. Strong official interest in such experiments may be inferred from the Schools Council support for further research by a team of investigators working at Loughborough College. The publication of Schools Council Curriculum Bulletin No. 2 *A School Approach to Technology* is likely to accelerate the process of curriculum change. Bulletin No. 2 suggested a number of topics suitable for study in schools. These included studies of metals, structures, prime movers, harmonic motion, calculating mechanisms and devices, the hovercraft, and the linear motor. All the topics require some study of physics and mathematics as well as the craft practice involved in the construction of the models. There is no reason why this kind of work should not be undertaken with pupils of all levels of ability. Such an approach has obvious motivational value for both the theoretical and practical aspects of the activity. A course along these lines is obviously relevant to general education for life in our society, and should provide pupils with the kind of experience which could lead to the development of vocational interests in a number of different fields.

It will not be easy to introduce into all schools the kind of applied science work that has been undertaken by the pioneers of such projects. Teachers will find a need to undertake courses of study and retraining to equip themselves for such work, and electronic apparatus must be provided for workshops as well as laboratories. Science teachers, too, will encounter new problems together with great opportunities.

The acceptance in principle and practice of this new aspect of creative practical work does not imply that all previous work in handicraft has been mistaken or unrewarding and should be abandoned, but applied science must in one sense represent a challenge to every other aspect of the normal handicraft syllabus. It is impossible to do everything: and if applied science work is to be given serious attention, less rewarding fields of work may have to be abandoned. At this stage it would be hazardous to predict the changes that may take place, but there is a possibility that the general field of handicraft may be divided into (a) areas of work which have a cultural and aesthetic value—such as silversmithing and cabinet making; and (b) constructional and metal-shaping techniques that are required for applied science projects and other activities related to boys' interests.

At present it seems permissible to include within a handicraft course any, or all, the processes that may be performed by a member of the multitude of different trades whose tools are provided in school workshops. An attempt to establish some criteria by which teachers can judge the relative values of the many different practical activities would be very worthwhile.

Handicraft in schools has traditionally been surrounded by a mystique which has effectively insulated the subject from outside interference. Very few research workers have paid attention to the subject—presumably through disinterest or because they have felt ill-equipped to investigate the difficult problems involved. Some descriptive works have already been mentioned: these have been extremely useful, but evaluation of the educational effects of handicraft must await more basic researches. One such project is being undertaken at the University of Leicester, but there is a need for a number of others. Teaching in many other disciplines has been profoundly affected by research findings (in some cases the changes have been revolutionary), and it is more than unfortunate that handicraft has been neglected in this way.

Fortunately the answers to many problems can be found by intelligent experimentation, and the observation of ongoing educational processes. This is just as well, since education cannot be suspended until all doubts over aims and methods have been resolved. Some of the problems of method in handicraft teaching are fundamental and unlikely to be solved by curriculum changes. A few of these problems are discussed in the articles on **Woodwork, Teaching of** and **Metalwork, Teaching of.**

REFERENCE

1. G. T. Page, *Engineering among the Schools*, Institution of Mechanical Engineers, 1965.

FURTHER READING

G. Blachford. *A History of Handicraft Teaching*, Christophers, 1962.

S. H. Glenister. *The Technique of Handicraft Teaching*, Harrap, 1953.

N. Porter. *A School Approach to Technology*, Schools Council Curriculum Bulletin No. 2, Schools Council, 1966.

FW

Handicraft, College of A statutory part of the Institute of Craft Education (formerly the Institute of Handicraft Teachers), the college is open to qualified teachers. Candidates pursue study courses in craft education and social and craft history, which lead to written examinations. Craftsmanship is assessed in the design and execution of a major piece in one of a number of crafts. The College organises summer vacation courses.

Long Riston, near Hull, Yorks.

Handicraft Teachers, Institute of Founded seventy years ago and now with 50 branches in the UK and an overseas branch, the Institute exists to raise the standard of craft teaching generally and to enhance craft subjects as a necessary and vital part of any educational programme; to promote the interchange of experience in craft education by conferences and meetings; to safeguard the welfare and security of members. Membership is open to all teachers responsible for, or interested in, the teaching of craftwork in any kind of school. Monthly journal: *Practical Education and School Crafts.*

Gen. Sec.: T. E. Atkinson, 'Hillside', Little Weighton, Hull, Yorkshire.

Handwriting Mastery of handwriting was a necessary component of the Renaissance 'whole man' and Queen Elizabeth I wrote an attractive script as a result of Ascham's instruction. Legibility is still a concern of schoolteachers (many of whom write illegibly) simply because they have to read their pupils' written work; but it is a matter about which a sense of proportion is particularly needful since for most people it is a means and not an end in itself. The test of a good hand is that it should be not merely handsome and legible but also fast to execute.

With the spread of cybernetics, tape, computers and other mechanical aids, it may well be that in the foreseeable future the use of a pen will be largely confined to the classroom, and that the main criteria for any hand will be restricted to speed and facility of acquisition in the primary years, and mere legibility and economy of effort subsequently. A fastidious minority will probably deplore such a state of things, but resistance to change is unrealistic: the response of some teachers to the arrival of the ball-point pen seemed more appropriate to the imminent collapse of civilisation.

GS

Hansard Society for Parliamentary Government Founded in 1944 by Sir Stephen King-Hall, the society is a non-national, non-party and non-profit-making educational body, with the aim of promoting the cause of parliamentary government throughout the world; educating people about the origins, practices and procedures of their own parliament, foreign parliaments and supra-national bodies of a quasi-parliamentary character; and, in general, informing and arousing the interest of the electorate and young people in all aspects of representative democratic institutions. The Society provides lectures and holds conferences for young people. Publications include the quarterly *Parliamentary Affairs*.

162 Buckingham Palace Rd, London, SW1.

Hawthorne effect When people are knowingly taking part in an experimental situation they usually, and often unconsciously, try extra-hard at whatever they are doing. Many educational experiments have suffered in this way, the well-meaning enthusiasm of the teachers taking part leading to magnificent results that will not be reproduced when people are working normally.

The term comes from experiments carried out in the Hawthorne works of the General Electric Company in Chicago between 1924 and 1927, when it was noticed that production went up owing, it was thought, to improvements in methods introduced by a research team then working in the factory. However, a 'tough-minded individual' suggested that all these improvements be taken away to see what would happen; to general surprise, output was then the highest ever recorded, owing purely to the atmosphere of experiment prevailing in the factory at the time.

One way to guard against Hawthorne effect is, of course, not to tell people that they are involved in an experiment; though this, too, has its difficulties.

FURTHER READING
J. A. C. Brown. *The Social Psychology of Industry*, Penguin, 1967.
NT

Head teacher allowance Before 1965 allowances were paid to persons appointed as head teachers according to the group of the school. These payments were added to the salary otherwise determined for the teacher

as an assistant teacher. Thus, the salary might consist of the following elements: basic scale (which might include increments for pre-qualified experience and increments for additional training), graduate addition or additions and the allowance for the responsibility as a head teacher. These arrangements have been superseded by the introduction of a consolidated scale (*q.v.*). However, it is still possible in exceptional cases, where the LEA at its discretion regards the responsibility carried by a particular head teacher to be greater than that normally undertaken by the head teacher of a similar school, to pay an additional allowance at any stage in the consolidated scale.

Head Teachers Association, London Membership of this professional organisation is drawn from head teachers of county or voluntary schools and principals of institutes maintained by the ILEA.

Gen. Sec.: W. J. P. Aggett, 19 Gloucester Crt, Swan St, London, SE1.

Publication: *The London Head Teacher*.

Head Teachers, National Association of Associations of head teachers existed in many parts of the country before the NAHT came into existence in 1897. The uniting of these associations in that year was inspired by the wish to ensure that views of head teachers on educational and professional matters were properly represented. Today the NAHT is the largest association of head teachers in England and Wales, representative of all types of school. Its main objects are to provide a ready means of communication between head teachers throughout the country; to give sympathetic and professional help to members in difficulty; to further the cause of education generally; and to uphold a high standard of professional conduct among head teachers. It is represented on the

337

Burnham Committee, the Schools Council and all the major educational organisations. It has played a leading role in urging the government to agree to the setting up of a teachers' general council, and is actively engaged in pressing for the resumption of meetings of the National Advisory Council for the Training and Supply of Teachers.

Gen. Sec.: R. J. Cook, 29a The Broadway, Crawley, Sussex.

Headmasters Ideally, the function of a headmaster is to lead and coordinate the affairs of the school which is placed in his charge, a task which calls for more than mere administrative ability. Maintaining good relations among his staff, between staff and pupils, and not least with parents, represents only one side of his duties. In addition, he must be intellectually and academically competent in the whole field of curricular studies, and is usually expected to excel in at least one of them. In the case of independent schools he is, in the last resort, responsible to his governors for everything that goes on in the school, in the case of state schools to his LEA.

Leaving aside 'political' appointments (which there is reason to believe are not exceptional), there are two main avenues to promotion for assistant teachers aspiring to a headship. One is by seniority and length of service: a criterion adopted by many big city LEAs. The other and quicker route is via service in schools which enjoy high reputations for academic success. Either way, the route is uncertain. For the ambitious young man, recognition is likely to come sooner if he places himself under the wing, and earns the backing, of someone who is himself a distinguished headmaster.

Long service as a principal teacher or deputy head certainly helps to give candidates some mastery of the routine skills that are needed. In general, however, the reliance on length of service must be judged a naïve basis in the selection of a headmaster: as

Shaw observed, a man who is a fool at twenty is likely to be three times as big a fool at sixty. Discipleship or tutelage under an able headmaster, similarly, is no guarantee that the candidate will himself possess the qualities that are needed.

As school organisation becomes increasingly complex it seems evident that something akin to management studies will have to be provided if amateurism is to be avoided. Keeping a finger on the pulse of the complex machine which the modern school is becoming calls for techniques which are not ordinarily acquired in the course of an assistant teacher's career.

WKR

Headmasters' Association Membership of this professional organisation is open to headmasters of public secondary schools in England, Wales and Northern Ireland. Among facilities for members are legal advice and trading discount schemes.

Sec.: H. E. Birkbeck, 29 Gordon Sq., London, WC1.

Publication: *HMA Review* (April, July and December).

Headmasters' Association of Scotland Membership of this professional association is open to headmasters of schools which present pupils for the higher grade of the Scottish Certificate of Education.

Hon. Sec.: R. W. Young, George Watson's College, Edinburgh.

Headmasters' Conference schools This is an association of most of the boys' public schools and direct grant schools, providing secondary education for boys over 13, in England, Scotland and Wales, Northern Ireland, the Irish Republic, and the Isle of Man. Applications for membership are considered by a committee. The main criteria are the scheme or other instrument under which the school is administered, taking into consideration particularly the degree of independence enjoyed by the governing body, the number of boys over 13 at the school, the proportionate size of the sixth form, and the amount of success in getting boys into university. Most of these schools are also members of the Association of Governing Bodies of Public Schools.

Sec.: F. L. Allan, 29 Gordon Sq., London, WC1.

Headmistresses Women heads of girls' secondary schools, boarding or day, are usually referred to as headmistresses, whereas heads of junior schools are often referred to as head teachers. The title 'headmistress' came into use with the establishment of secondary schools for middle-class girls in the 19th century, and the office acquired a recognised professional status when Miss Buss, first headmistress of the North London Collegiate School, called together 13 headmistresses and founded the Association of Headmistresses in 1874. The Association was incorporated in 1896, when its membership reached 166. The early members were mainly heads of independent and high schools, but they readily accepted into membership the heads of the new maintained secondary schools founded after the Education Act 1902. The heads of these schools now form the greater part of the membership.

After 1945 the Association opened membership to the heads of the newly recognised secondary schools, known as 'modern' schools, which had developed from the old senior elementary schools, but heads of 'modern' schools are still a minority of the membership. Headmistresses thus have a single professional association and the distinction between HMC schools (q.v.) and others well known in the boys' school world does not exist.

With the extension of co-educational schools there will be fewer posts for headmistresses, as authorities tend to appoint men to the headships of mixed schools. Until recently nearly all headmistresses were unmarried, but recent appointments show a move towards appointing married women.

The Association of Headmistresses joins with the Incorporated Association of Headmasters, the Association of Assistant Mistresses Incorporated, and the Incorporated Association of Assistant Masters to discuss matters mainly to do with grammar school education through a joint organisation known as the Joint Four (q.v.).

MM

Headmistresses, Association of See **Headmistresses**

Headmistresses of Preparatory Schools, Association of The AHMPS, affiliated to the Association of Headmistresses (q.v.) and offering membership to headmistresses of recognised preparatory schools, was founded in 1929 to provide such headmistresses with opportunities to discuss problems peculiar to preparatory schools, both amongst themselves and with headmistresses of senior schools to whom children go on for their secondary education. The Association is represented on the Girls' Common Entrance Board, and appoints delegates to the Boarding Schools' Association.

Sec.: Miss M. Macvicar, Rookesbury Park School, Wickham, Hants.

Heads of departments These are appointments for assistant teachers whose duty it is to organise and generally supervise the work done in a subject throughout the school. Although the majority of such posts are in secondary schools, appointments may be made at the discretion of the LEA in larger primary schools, i.e. schools with 301 children or more. Where such appointments are made, only Grade A or Grade B allowances can be paid (see below). In secondary schools in which advanced work is undertaken, i.e. work above GCE O level leading to the A level, the LEA is required to establish head of department posts, but the schools have control over the number of such posts. In other secondary schools, discretion is available in the smaller schools, but where a school has a unit total of 701 or more, there is a requirement to establish heads of departments. In special schools in which there are a substantial number of senior pupils, the LEA may establish posts of head of department Grade A of such number as the authority deems appropriate.

Although LEAs have discretion within the limits indicated above, the Burnham Report gives guidance on the following basis.

Normally in schools up to Group 5, Grade A only will be required. In schools in Group 6, Grade B will be used for the more important departments and Grade A for the less important. In schools in Group 7 or 8, Grade C will be used for the most important departments and Grades A and/or B for the others according to their size and importance. In schools in Group 9, Grade D will be used for the most important departments and the lower Grades for the others according to their size and importance. In Group 10 or above, Grade E will be used for the most important departments and the lower Grades for the others according to the load of work in each.

In determining the grading of an allowance for a post of head of department the LEA should have regard to the size of the department and its importance in the curriculum, to the number of teachers engaged and to the amount of advanced work, as defined in paragraph 1 above, undertaken. In the case of a subject department, however, the fact that only one teacher is engaged in teaching the subject or that there is no advanced work need not preclude the establishment of a post of head of department in that subject if the authority is satisfied that the circumstances in the school justify such establishment.

Posts of head of department may be established in other circumstances, for example, where a teacher is not attached to the staff of a particular school, but is responsible for a special centre, or where a school is organised in separate buildings and a teacher is in charge of a substantial annexe, although he does not take responsibility for a subject. In large schools of say 1,000 pupils or more where the school is organised in sections (for example—lower school, middle school) a teacher in charge of such a section may be appointed as a head of department. In all cases such as these it is for the authority to determine the appropriate grade of allowance, having regard to the responsibility involved in the particular post.

The current allowances which are added to the salaries otherwise payable are as follows: Grade A £210, Grade B £315, Grade C £445, Grade D £570, Grade E £700.

SEB

Health, Royal Society of Founded in 1876 to promote the health of the people, the RSH is the largest society of public health and other health workers in the world. Its scope and work is not confined to any one branch of health, but includes such aspects as architecture, building, estate management, food inspection, clean air, health hazards from atomic radiation, plumbing, health visiting, municipal engineering, pharmacy, and much else. The strength of the Society, now an international organisation, lies not only in the size of its membership (the overseas section being particularly strong in America), but in the creation of a world-wide body of general, as well specialised, knowledge which can be made widely known through the various media of expression available to the Society. Among the 34,000 members are members of public health committees members of the medical, engineering, architectural, veterinary, legal, dental, pharmaceutical, optical and other professions, and a large proportion of those in public health work under government departments and local authorities. There are also many members engaged in commerce, industry and private practice allied to the objects of the Society. A panel of technical consultants exists to assist members where possible, especially those living in remote parts of the world. The library contains 37,000 volumes. Various examinations are conducted by the Society.

90 Buckingham Palace Rd, London, SW1.

Health and Development of Children, National Survey of This is a unique and continuing survey directed by Dr J. W. B. Douglas, director of the Medical Research Council Unit at the London School of Economics, with the help of grants from foundations and government sources. Practical work started in 1946 when some 5,000 women who had borne a child in one week of March of that year were interviewed concerning the quality and quantity of ante-natal and maternity services. This formed the basis of the Survey's first report *Maternity in Great Britain* (see *Further reading* for this and other titles mentioned below).

By keeping in touch with the children and parents, the authors of the Survey are recording experience concerning health, growth, educational development and social change. Particular attention is being paid to individual and group differences in attitudes and behaviour and to the influence of environment. The book *Children Under Five* reported on the major types of illnesses suffered by the pre-school child, and *The Home and the School* dealt with the ability and attainment of the children of the Survey as they passed through primary school. Two volumes in preparation are concerned

with the secondary education of the children and the transition from school to work or higher education. More than 30 articles have also been published in educational journals on specific findings of the Survey.

FURTHER READING
J. W. B. Douglas. *The Home and the School*, MacGibbon and Kee, 1964.
J. W. B. Douglas and J. M. Blomfield. *Children under Five*, Allen and Unwin, 1958.
National Survey of Health and Development of Children. *Maternity in Great Britain*, Oxford Univ. Press, 1948.

EP

Health education In the Report by the DES Chief Medical Officer for the years 1964–5,[1] the proportion of school-children reported to be in an unsatisfactory condition was 0.38%, the lowest on record; this, it is suggested, is a reflection of the improved economic and social circumstances of many families. At the same time, however, improved conditions have also brought about an unwelcome increase in the number of fat children.

The report also points out how the pattern of the school health service has changed, the bulk of the work now being concerned with the investigation and supervision of children at school with emotional and behaviour difficulties, speech and language disorder, learning difficulties, epilepsy, respiratory disorders and physical handicaps.

In primary schools much health education teaching is incidental and is concentrated on the hygienic aspects of daily life, the provision of regular periods of exercise, and therapeutic and developmental play; but in secondary schools health problems are often more acute and demand direct teaching methods.

Guidance and sympathetic advice are needed by both boys and girls on the physiological and mental problems of an often turbulent adolescence, as well as on some of the social difficulties

341

M

experienced. The question of the extent to which sex education (*q.v.*) is the responsibility of the school is a controversial one, but more and more schools are now including this in the curriculum. Of lesser importance, but necessary in view of the increasing amount of obesity in children, is guidance in simple dietetics. This guidance should be directed not only at the young persons involved but also at their parents.

The question of smoking has also occupied much thought and time in recent years; and many authorities, stimulated by medical and government pressure, have produced anti-smoking propaganda and encouraged schools to include this in the health education time-table. In many cases this has produced encouraging results; but in some schools the anti-smoking drive has been most disappointing, mainly because of the lack of parental co-operation.

A far more sinister problem of relatively recent development in the upper forms of grammar schools, technical colleges, colleges of education and the universities is that of the growing incidence of drug-taking. In many cases students under examination pressure first yield to the temptation of taking stimulant drynamil tablets ('purple hearts') in gradually increasing amounts; and later some fall victims to pedlars (sometimes fellow-students) of highly dangerous drugs such as cocaine and heroin and become addicts, with all the medical and social problems that addiction produces. (*See* **Drugs.**)

There is little doubt that direct teaching on the dangers of drug addiction will have to occupy an increasing amount of time in the health education programme of the adolescent student. There is also little doubt that such teaching on drugs and on sex education cannot be really done effectively by untrained personnel, and that specialist teachers will have to be appointed who will work closely with psychiatrists and the specialised clinics provided by the school medical service.

See also **Drugs; School medical service; Smoking and school-children**

REFERENCE
1. *The Health of the School Child*, HMSO, 1966.

JE

Health Education, British Society for International Founded in 1962 to promote assistance for health education overseas and particularly in the developing countries, the Society gives priority to training in health education. Courses based on local problems are organised in developing countries to train local teaching staff in the best methods of training others. Fellowships for post-graduate training in health education are awarded to selected students, and international seminars are arranged for overseas students already in the UK.

85 Central Bldgs, 24 Southwark St, London, SE1.

Health Education, Central Council for The Central Council offers assistance to LEAs in the form of short courses for teachers and others; a four-day seminar for the discussion of the educational and medical aspects of the health of schoolchildren; an annual summer school; a library of books and periodicals; material on health education, including leaflets, films, filmstrips and posters; and advice on the planning of syllabuses and other aspects of health education.

Tavistock Hse North, Tavistock Sq., London, WC1.

Publications: *Health Education Journal* (four times a year), *Health Information Digest* (twice a year), *Better Health* (monthly).

Health Education, Scottish Council for The Council gives assistance on matters relating to health education to statutory and other bodies in Scotland, arranging meetings, conferences and films and providing literature free to local authorities. Apart from schools held during holidays for teachers and others, the Council organises intensive short courses for teachers-in-training, social workers and others specialising in health education or intending to do so.

16 York Pl., Edinburgh, 1.

Publications include *Teaching Health* and *Report on Health Education in Schools*.

Health and Morals of Apprentices Act (1802) This Act was introduced by Sir Robert Peel, to regulate the conditions under which children were working. Among its measures were moves to shorten the working day, to discontinue night work, to ensure separate sleeping apartments for males and females, and to lay down certain minimum standards of hygiene. Apprentices were to receive some instruction in reading, writing and arithmetic during their first four years. Two inspectors were appointed to see whether the Act was being implemented. The Act was the forerunner of the later, more comprehensive Factory Acts.

Health Visitors, Council for the Training of Established by the Health Visiting and Social Work (Training) Act 1962, the Council promotes the training of health visitors by providing facilities and approving courses, and by seeking to attract trainees. The Council also provides courses for further training, and undertakes, or assists, in research.

In 1966 there were in the UK a total of 31 courses providing health visitor training for state-registered nurses, and a further five courses which integrate nursing training and health visitor training. Most of these courses are held in universities and colleges of further education, but a few are run by local health authorities and two by professional bodies.

The Council awards a Health Visitor's Certificate to those successfully completing a course.

Clifton House, Euston Rd., London, NW1.

Heder (or **cheder:** pl. **hadarim** or **chadarim**) An elementary Jewish religious school.

Heniker-Heaton Report (Day Release), 1964 *See* **Further education in England and Wales**

Her Majesty's Inspectorate *See* **Inspectorate, Her Majesty's**

Her Majesty's Stationery Office The full educational catalogue of HMSO, which is responsible for government publications on all subjects, is available free on request, as are the following catalogues of UNESCO publications for which HMSO is the UK agents: *UNESCO Current List Catalogue, UNESCO Education Catalogue, UNESCO Libraries and Librarians Catalogue, UNESCO Scientific and Technical Publications Catalogue,* and *UNESCO Publications in the Social Sciences Catalogue.*

Publicity Section/P6B, Atlantic Hse, Holborn Viaduct, London, EC1.

Herbart, Johann Friedrich (1776–1841) Chiefly memorable for his attempt to formulate rules for the presentation and conduct of lessons (*see* **Herbartian Steps**), Herbart conducted courses in pedagogy at the University of Königsberg. His major work was *Outlines of Educational Doctrine*.

Herbartian steps These were originally conceived, and subsequently supported by disciples, as apparently obeying laws of mental activity. The Herbartian formula applied less well to the teaching of skills and to aesthetic appreciation. The acquisition of knowledge, the Herbartians held, should pass through four phases: Preparation, Presentation, Formulation and Application. Many followers of Herbart made

343

use of five steps and could quote Herbart in support: 'Instruction must care equally and in regular succession for clearness of every particular (Preparation and Presentation), for association of the manifold (Association), for coherent ordering of what is associated (Generalisation), and for a certain practice in progression through this order (Application).'

Heuristic method This is an approach to teaching long established and receiving fresh support in the modern use of 'discovery' methods in teaching the sciences. An element in heuristic methods is the creation of circumstances to enable the pupil to follow the experimental and rational processes of the original discoverer. Some opponents of this approach point out that it is time-wasting particularly with human knowledge growing at its present pace. They would, however, support the greater use of 'discovery' techniques, which suggests radically modifying the starting-point of the heuristic approach.

See also **Science, Teaching of**

DJJ

High schools *See* **Leicestershire Plan schools**

Higher class schools *See* **Scotland, Education in**

Higher Education, Unit for Economic and Statistical Studies on Created to undertake research on economic and statistical aspects of higher education, the Unit includes among its projects some concerned with methods of educational planning at national level; some inquiring into the relationship between educational provision and the needs of industry and the labour force; some related to the financing of higher education, and others to the working of institutions of higher education. Research is concerned wherever possible with other

countries as well as Britain—including both developing and advanced countries.

Apart from its research work, the Unit is also engaged in teaching and in organising seminars, and maintains contact with researchers and educational planners abroad.

Director: Professor C. A. Moser, London School of Economics and Political Science, Houghton St, Aldwych, London, WC2.

Higher Education Overseas, Inter-University Council for Established by the universities of the UK in 1946, the Council encourages co-operation, in so far as is mutually desired, between UK universities and universities in East, West and Central Africa; Botswana, Lesotho and Swaziland; the Sudan; the Caribbean; Hong Kong; Malaysia and Singapore; Malta; and certain other areas. The Council generally assists in the development of higher education in these countries.

The Council provides general consultative services, assists in staff recruitment, arranges overseas visits by university staff from the UK, assists in the development of libraries, and runs a small training programme for locally born university staff.

33 Bedford Pl., London, WC1.

Higher Education of Working Men Association to Promote the *See* **Workers' Educational Association**

Higher grade (higher elementary) schools The need for a 'higher' school to accommodate those pupils from the elementary schools who from their ability to learn and to teach might be considered as proper persons to be admitted to its higher advantages, was first appreciated by the National Society in 1838, but demands on its resources for training colleges prevented the Society from implementing the idea.

School boards, especially in large towns, found that 'higher' schools could earn grants from the Science and Art Departments, so higher grade schools were opened under their aegis in Sheffield and Nottingham, closely followed by Bradford, Manchester and other large towns. These schools were officially encouraged by A. J. Mundella, vice-president of the Committee of Council from 1880 to 1885, who regarded them as comparable to the newly-established intermediate schools in Wales. As providers of 'middle-class' education, they evoked the criticism of the high master of Manchester Grammar School, Dr Samuel Dill, since they undercut existing endowed schools.

At the turn of the century there were three higher grade schools in London and 60 in the provinces; most of them were well equipped to teach science. Embryonic versions also existed in the 'tops' of elementary schools, of which London alone had 60.

But the Cockerton Judgement (1900) showed that school boards had acted illegally in this and other ventures in higher education, so when these schools came under the LEAs in 1902, they became municipal secondary schools.
WHGA

Hispanic and Luso-Brazilian Councils See **Canning House**

Historical Association Founded in 1906 to promote the study of history in all its aspects. Membership is open to all, and the Association now has more than 11,000 members, including teachers in schools, universities and colleges of education, archivists, local historians, and many historians now working in other fields. There are over 90 branches in the UK and overseas.

The annual conference is usually held in April and at a different centre each year. The tours committee arranges visits to places of historical interest at home and abroad under expert leadership. Each summer a revision course is arranged at a university centre.

The Association has a library of 6,000 volumes available to members; and its journal, *History*, is published three times a year.

59a Kennington Park Rd, London, SE11.

Historiography of education How past societies tried to freeze the future, and how their successors tried to thaw their own times, makes the history of educational institutions a fascinating study and explains why it is often, and perhaps best, pursued through the history of particular schools or colleges. Its fascination is enhanced by the time-lag between intention and execution and effect of particular policies, a lag which some estimate to be more than a generation—thirty years. Unconsciously, many historians of education, as of other subjects, tend to present a story initiated by special pleading, enhancing readability at the expense of reliability. For memories of unfortunate episodes in the history of education have been exploited, especially in the 19th century, to exacerbate controversy. This is particularly true of the unfortunate assaults of the Act of Uniformity (*see* **Dissenting schools**).

The history of education really begins with the great unlocking science of the early 19th century, geology. Thus the geologist Karl von Raumer, professor of mineralogy and pedagogy at Erlangen, wrote a four-volume *Geschichte der Pädagogik* (1843–54). Other geologists, notably James Heywood of Great Britain, turned to educational history to uncover the assumptions and economies of schools and colleges.

As the state succeeded the church as the main providing agent, successive civil servants—like A. F. Leach, Michael Sadler and R. Fitzgibbon Young—who were involved in the preparation of policy papers, turned their attention to unravelling a past. Indeed, from his work as a member of the Charity Commission from the year

1884 to 1915, A. F. Leach was able to write the history of education for at least 18 counties in the *Victoria County History*, in addition to his *English Schools at the Reformation* and *Schools of Medieval England*. His conclusions have evoked debate from the time they were published until today; a study by Joan Simon correcting his views was published in 1966 (see *Further reading*). Michael Sadler, as Director of the Office of Special Inquiries and Reports and later professor of the History and Administration of Education at Manchester University, vice-chancellor of Leeds and master of an Oxford College, wrote in more popular vein. R. Fitzgibbon Young, as secretary of the Consultative Committee of the Board of Education (*q.v.*) wrote the historical introductions to, amongst others, the Hadow (1926) and Spens (1938) Reports, both still reliable and much used for those seeking perspectives on secondary education.

Interest in their own milieu led dons like J. Bass Mullinger and Hastings Rashdall to study intellectual history. Rashdall's classic, *The Universities of Europe in the Middle Ages* (1895), re-edited and revised by Sir Maurice Powicke and A. B. Emden, has long been a standard work. Histories of individual universities by D. A. Winstanley (Cambridge), Sir Charles Mallett (Oxford), H. Hale Bellot (University College, London) and A. W. Chapman (Sheffield) have been supplemented by histories of newer foundations.

Then too, the economic pacemaking of other countries stimulated inquiries into those countries' educational systems. Victor Cousin in France, Bulwer Lytton in England and James Pillans in Scotland, all pioneered in this field, and further prompted the question 'How did the British obtain their system?', or, as it was, their 'absence of system'. Their work was amplified by the early number of 'education departments' in the universities.

The first two Scottish professors of education, S. S. Laurie (Edinburgh) and J. M. D. Meiklejohn (Aberdeen), from their appointment in 1876, did much to provide a historical setting for their efforts, as did Oscar Browning at Cambridge. Of the heads of day training colleges established in 1890 at the civic university colleges, perhaps the most outstanding historians of education were Foster Watson of Aberystwyth, whose *English Grammar Schools to 1660* (1908) and *The Beginnings of the Teaching of Modern Subjects in England* (1909) are still standard texts. R. L. Archer of Bangor, W. H. Woodward of Liverpool, G. H. Turnbull of Sheffield, J. W. Adamson, F. A. Cavenagh, A. V. Judges and A. C. F. Beales of Kings College, London, H. C. Barnard of Reading, S. J. Curtis of Leeds and Brian Simon of Leicester have continued the tradition. Their writings reflect the change in historical emphasis over this century.

Today education is chiefly studied in its sociological, rather than its historical setting, and for all the protests of its exponents tends to be approached in rather too antiquarian a spirit. Recent works addressed to a more academic public seem to be divorcing the subject still more from the needs of teachers and administrators. For this, a collective inferiority complex on the part of educationists seems to have been partly responsible.

FURTHER READING

History of Education Journal, Ann Arbor, Mich., 1950.

Arthur Francis Leach. *English Schools at the Reformation, 1546–8*, Westminster, Constable & Co., 1896. *The Schools of Medieval England*, Methuen, 1915. *Victoria County Histories*, Oxford Univ. Press.

Hastings Rashdall. *The Universities of Europe in the Middle Ages* (eds Sir Maurice Powicke and A. B. Emden), Clarendon Press, Oxford, 1936.

Karl von Raumer. *Geschichte der Pädagogik*, 1843–54, Vols I and II (abridged) translated by L. W. Fitch and F. B. Perkins, 1959; Vol III translated by Henry Barnard, 1863; F. C. Brownell, New York.

Joan Simon. *Education and Society in Tudor England*, Cambridge. Univ. Press, 1966. Foster Watson. *The Beginnings of the Teaching of Modern Subjects in England*, Sir Isaac Pitman & Sons, 1909. *The English Grammar Schools to 1660: Their Curriculum and Practice*, Cambridge Univ. Press, 1908.

WHGA

History, Local, Standing Conference for This organisation encourages the study of local history and the provision of necessary services. Membership is composed of county local history committees of England and Wales and national organisations. SCLH reviews work done in local history and promotes selected activities, e.g. recording family portraits; it assists in the establishment of committees for the continuation of local history work within counties, and provides guidance for amateur historians.

26 Bedford Sq., London, WC1.

Publications: *The Local Historian* (quarterly); pamphlets, e.g. *Local History for Students, How to Read a Coat of Arms, A Medieval Farming Glossary: Latin and English*.

History, Teaching of Since man has always felt the need to look over his shoulder at the path he has followed, history exerts a special pull on his imagination. Unfortunately, as a subject in the school curriculum it easily becomes a mere worrisome array and burden of facts and incidents. Like other subjects it suffers, particularly in the secondary school, from isolation behind its subject barrier. It is perhaps best loved in the primary school, before its charms are smothered. It has even been suggested that it might be more sensible to omit it altogether from the curriculum for older pupils. But this is wildly negative, and we have, in spite of all the difficulties, to consider how the subject might be taught so that it inspires affection rather than revulsion.

In recent re-consideration of the aims of history teaching, it has been suggested

by some that greater interest can be created and the spirit of discovery drawn upon without radical change in traditional methods. Stimulating talk by the teacher, together with the use of improved textbooks and especially of the school library, can (it has been argued) transform the situation. Here and there this approach has led to reasonable results, but it is open to the criticism that it easily becomes stereotyped; that it is difficult for the best of teachers to be always interesting, and that with a mediocre teacher the results may be catastrophic.

More radical re-thinking ought perhaps to begin with a deeper examination of the needs of the pupil than has been common. In the past he has been thought of as the receptacle for a body of knowledge that educated society feels he should know, and perhaps be able to manipulate, before he leaves school. In history this has usually meant such a chronological arrangement of the syllabus that at the age of 16 the pupil will have 'done' the major historical periods. But the work of psychologists and sociologists has made us aware that it is important to select material for teaching that is appropriate to an age group and to the intellectual capacity of particular pupils. From this it follows that no successful history syllabus can be devised that does not take into account the pupils' ability to understand what is being imparted.

Not only must they be able to understand it: they must also find it relevant and of interest to them. This may well mean that a teacher with an honours degree in history will have sensitively to adapt his own understanding of the subject if, for example, he is to capture the real attention of a group of 15- or 16-year-old pupils, from a background alien to that of the teacher's, staying on at school for a further compulsory year.

The system of teaching by perpetual lecture, particularly common among teachers of history, has also to be reconsidered. The history teacher is

347

usually a combination of narrator and post-narrative inquisitor. Much more thought than is common has to be given to so structuring lessons that pupils themselves become more active. The formal classroom lesson, with desks in serried rows, ought more often to be replaced by a more flexible arrangement. The emphasis should be on individual learning and enquiry. Every opportunity should be seized to encourage the use of a variety of teaching aids. And in the enquiry situation books become more important—though not textbooks. History teachers taking over departments in new schools would be well advised to spend more of their requisition on individual books appropriate to the work they mean to undertake.

It may well be important, and certainly much current thinking among history teachers suggests that it is, to rescue history from its isolation from other subjects. Subject disciplines, with their boundaries defined by nice distinctions deriving from work in the universities, have small relevance to the needs of the younger secondary-school child. Even the sixth-former looking towards the university now finds that the straightforward honours course is disappearing, to be replaced by more complex courses involving associated —and sometimes contrasting—subjects. Of course, if the history teacher begins to think in terms of co-operating with his colleagues in geography, English and divinity, he may find himself faced with timetable problems. But the general movement now is away from formal class teaching and towards greater emphasis on individual learning, and teachers may be well-advised to think again about the single teaching period as the most desirable unit. Double periods certainly give greater opportunities for interesting work; and double periods blocked with related subjects enable teams of teachers to create varied timetables and to bring to their teaching an increased spontaneity.

Once this emphasis is given to the needs of the pupil, against a background of new teaching methods and forms of class organisation, the real nature of history teaching can be revalued. Its possible objectives might be set out as follows:

1. *Knowledge.* The pupil knows specific historical facts.

2. *Understanding.* The pupil develops and strengthens a sense of time and a sense of sympathy with the past; becomes familiar with certain historical concepts; understands and applies historical generalisations.

3. *Imagination.* The pupil is able to recapture the spirit of the past.

4. *Thinking skills.* The pupil demonstrates an ability to think critically; to distinguish between facts and opinions, between reliable and unreliable sources; to draw valid conclusions from data; to recognise assumptions underlying those conclusions; to recognise the limitations of the data.

5. *Technical skills.* The pupil is able to interpret photographs and maps and to use statistics; he has a knowledge of the techniques of classification; he is able to execute field sketches; he is able to use various audio-visual aids.

6. *Communication skills.* The pupil is able to present clear and accurate accounts or reports—written or oral.

7. *Adjustment.* The pupil is able to work co-operatively with others.

Each of these objectives can, of course, be usefully subjected to further examination: especially difficult ones like familiarisation with historical concepts and the ability to apply historical generalisations. In a recent publication, Professor Peel quotes the results of an investigation of pupils' understanding of social concepts that have historical significance.[1] A group of pupils between the ages of nine and 19 were asked to define, among others, the concept of king. Four categories of answer in ascending order of maturity were identified.

1. The King lives in a castle far away.
2. A king is somebody very important and a king is very rich, a famous man out of the royal family.
3. A king is a ruler of the country.
4. A person who may rule his country by himself, may rule it in co-ordination with advisers or a government, may simply be a figurehead.

Obviously it is extremely important that a teacher should be certain that there is no misunderstanding of the concepts he may be using, and that the age and ability of the pupil are taken into account when new historical concepts are being introduced.

Repetition helps, as obviously does co-operation, where possible, between departments so that they use concepts in the same way. Teachers themselves, with the help of experts, could make useful contributions to research and to the effectiveness of their own teaching by devising such tests as that quoted by Professor Peel to assess children's awareness, at different ages, of a variety of historical information.

The understanding and applying of historical generalisations is a particularly important objective for the history teacher. This is so because one of the disadvantages of history to the student lies in its lack of theorems, laws, or rules similar to those that obtain in the sciences. Especially in the secondary school, the pupil tends to regard the subject as a mass of facts that he has to remember and manipulate. Teachers are wary of formulating guide lines for their pupils; and indeed, fear of being political or of laying oneself open to accusations of unhistorical behaviour has meant that little thought has been given to the problem. Yet little real objectivity exists in the teaching of history. Teachers in secondary or higher education are more often than not quite subjective in their reading, writing and teaching. More open recognition of this fact would not only be refreshing —it might also enable new and exciting developments in teaching to take place.

W. H. Burston suggests that 'the process of teaching history involves generalisations and the use and understanding of abstract concepts much more than is commonly realised. Many of the concepts and laws of social science which are taken for granted by the historian have to be acquired by the pupil, if not as part of the process of learning history, at any rate as a necessary preliminary to its successful study.'[2] An example of a general law that he mentions ('Other things being equal, an increase in the amount of currency in a community or in its velocity of circulation will cause inflation and the rise of prices') suggests others: for instance, that rapid urban spread is indicative of industrial development; that political revolution often occurs when the form of government lags behind economic expansion; and that explosive international situations occur with the development of nationalism.

Particularly with older children in secondary schools, such historical generalisations as these, carefully thought out, could be the keys to pupil enquiry on a broad front. Intense and detailed work on a particular subject could be accompanied by wide sweeps across the world at different periods. No generalisation need be considered a law—only a guide to study.

From a consideration of aims and methods, one is led to the attempt to create a framework within which these can be realised and practised. Perhaps the most stimulating recent work on the history syllabus is that done by P. Carpenter.[3] He examines the traditional five-year chronological syllabus and stresses the sense of security that it gives to the teacher (a security that, it must be admitted, is sometimes accompanied by anxiety as teachers race against time to finish the Tudors or the 18th century before the end of term). With the great amount of information now available, problems of selection within such a syllabus become more difficult, and treatment is often scanty

349

and superficial. Pupils quickly lose interest, particularly in the middle forms of the secondary school, and develop a lively contempt for the periods they have to 'do'.

A teacher's syllabus in history is always a personal document, representative of the teacher's own interests and enthusiasms; this makes it easier for a teacher to dispense with any feeling of guilt when he resists the temptation to frame a traditional syllabus, but it also makes it necessary to suggest only general aims. The first aim might be to try to give the opportunity for intensive study of particular topics as well as more general sweeps over wider areas of time. Secondly: wherever possible, the teacher should emulate the good geographer and sample both vertically and horizontally. History teachers too often teach within the strict confines of the period their pupils are studying. An iron-age hut or a 19th-century revolution become really meaningful only if related to similar huts and revolutions from other periods or parts of the world. Thirdly, the teacher should not hesitate to import into the syllabus contributions from other subjects, such as sociology and geography. Fourthly, he should arrange for combined work with colleagues in other disciplines. Fifthly, he should not be afraid of dealing with the present time. Sixthly, local history is often relevant, and should be made part (though not the major part) of the teaching programme.

To sum up, it may be said that the general agreement among thoughtful history teachers today is that the teaching of the subject can be reinvigorated only if there is a really radical departure from methods that are time-worn but not time-honoured.

REFERENCES
1. W. H. Burston, *Studies in the Nature and Teaching of History*, London, 1967.
2. *Studies in the Nature and Teaching of History*.
3. P. Carpenter, *History Teaching: The Era Approach*, London, 1964.

FURTHER READING
H. Butterfield. *History and Human Relations*, Collins, 1951.
Louis Gottschalk (Ed.). *Generalisation in the Writing of History*, University of Chicago Press, 1963.
R. Symn-Crampton. 'Has History Any Use?' Cambridge Institute of Education *Bulletin*, II, 2, December, 1964.
W. H. Walsh. *Introduction to the Philosophy of History*, Hutchinson, revised ed. 1958.

JWa

History of education in England
The struggle to train an increasing population as law-abiding citizens with agricultural, military or sea-faring, and later industrial skills has been the perennial preoccupation of English governments. The regulation of supply for particular needs, the contest of creeds, and the need to secure social discipline complicate the story, but the history of English education virtually begins, as far as we are concerned, with the outpouring of endowments (*q.v.*) in the 16th and 17th centuries.

By 1600 there was a grammar school available for boys in every part of the country. Some withered away through abuse of their endowments and ceased to exist. As other centres of population grew up, a second wave of school founding began at the close of the 17th century, this time of parochial charity schools, dissenting schools (*q.v.*) and academies (*q.v.*). A third wave, of Sunday Schools in the rapidly developing industrial towns, began in the later 18th century. All were fostered by religious bodies, such as the SPCK or the Sunday School Union. Other religious organisations such as the Institution for Providing the Education of the Labouring and Manufacturing Classes of Society of Every Religious Persuasion (later the British and Foreign Schools Society), and the National Society for Educating the Poor in the Principles of the Established Church throughout England and Wales (*see* **Lancasterian system** and **National schools**) took shape in 1808 and 1811 respectively and, supplemented by the Home and Colonial Infant School Society (1836), the Wesleyan Education Committee (1840), the Congregational School Union (1843) and the Roman Catholic Poor School (1847), carried the burden of providing for the children of the poor by means of subscriptions and fees.

Helped after 1833 by grants from the government for schools and teachers' houses, their work was endorsed by the factory inspectors also appointed as a result of an Act in 1833 designed to prevent the undue exploitation of children. For their unfavourable reports on the factory schools (*q.v.*) of the time led the Home Secretary to propose educational clauses in a new Factory Bill in 1843 which revived Nonconformist fears of an Anglican take-over of their children and led to the drafting of the famous minutes of 1846 whereby the seven-year-old Committee of Council agreed to make maintenance grants to schools of all major religious denominations. This sectarian rivalry spread to grammar schools and a large number were founded at this time in large towns throughout the country.

The problem of endowments for education had also been preoccupying reformers. Following Lord Brougham's successful initiative in securing the appointment of a Royal Commission on Charities in 1818, successive legislation curbed and redeployed them (*see* **Charity Commissioners**). The educational doomsday books of the country's resources were mapped by four massive royal commissions on the universities (1850–2), the elementary schools (1859–61), the public schools (1861–4) and the endowed schools (1864–7). Their recommendations became the agenda of educational debate for the rest of the century.

Such debate simmered, and at times boiled, especially after school boards (*q.v.*) were established in 1870. The imposition of compulsion to attend elementary school in 1880 solved the problem of children working in factories, but it posed many more. For, all the children having been swept into schools, who and what to teach them became important as well as institutions to take them further (*see* **Pupil teacher centres, Central schools, Higher grade schools**). Before the 1870 Act 2,000,000 places were provided in grant-aided schools (of which only 55% were actually filled). Five years later there were places for 3,500,000, and to fill them the Sundon (1876) and the Mundella Acts (1880), by making attendance obligatory in both voluntary and board schools, increased attendance to 4,000,000 by 1881, by which time the grant had risen to £2,200,000.

Suspicion of the new boards brought together those of the rival denominations who thought more of their own religion than of the needs of the community: an alliance visible in the majority report of the Cross Commission (*q.v.*), which in 1888 recommended rate aid for the voluntary schools. Instruments to actualise their aspirations were provided in this year, when county councils were established. First used by the advocates of technical education, who empowered these councils to levy a penny rate, and further stimulated by the proceeds of a tax on beer and spirits, the county councils were approved in 1895 by the Bryce Commission as the proper new local authorities—a recommendation effected by the Education Act of 1902 (*q.v.*), which also empowered them to help voluntary schools from the rates.

With the infrastructures of primary and secondary education firmly built by 1902, a third or tertiary structure to accommodate those coming forward was needed. As *ad hoc* as the primary and secondary structures had been, the structure of the tertiary educational system was to be affected by the growth of the state grant in 1889. This was so small that even after the local colleges to whom it was given received their charters—Birmingham in

1900, Liverpool in 1903, Leeds in 1904, Sheffield in 1905 and Bristol in 1909—only other monies received for postulant teachers kept them afloat as universities. As with other things, their contacts with schools followed the model set by Oxford and Cambridge in 1858: a London Examining Board was set up in 1902, and a Northern Universities Joint Matriculation Board in 1903. Other institutions of tertiary education, such as technical and teacher training colleges, grew to maturity under the LEAs, but their relationship with the universities was the subject of a continuous dialogue. The universities came increasingly to rely for financial support on the University Grants Committee (*q.v.*). The growth of this committee and of its powers to ensure that universities are capable of meeting the national needs resulted in its being placed under the DES in 1964. This ensured for the first time that primary, secondary and tertiary education were at last articulated parts of a state system, excepting of course the public schools (*q.v.*), currently under scrutiny by yet another commission.

Articulation in the above context involves some notion of a machine, and it would be fair to regard the present English system as one designed to encourage, identify and nourish talent. But in doing so it has had to adopt discriminatory procedures. These were before 1965 critical at the age of 11; in the late 1960s they tended to be critical at the age of 18. Indeed, the pressure on institutions of tertiary education has been such that over the past few years degree courses have become available at most of the colleges of education in the country, whilst some 28 polytechnics, announced in May 1966, were confirmed on 7 April 1967. This means that the tertiary band of education is no longer the exclusive monopoly of the universities.

To mitigate the tyrannies inherent in local authorities that are too small or central authorities that are too remote, there has grown up a nexus of consultative bodies. These not only humanise the bureaucratic machine, but allow for interchange of opinion between the various levels of schools and colleges. Apart from the Central Advisory Council (established by the 1944 Act from the Consultative Committee, itself set up by the Education Act 1902, and going back to the Code Committee of the 1880s), there is the Schools Council (established in 1964, superseding the Secondary Schools Examinations Council established in 1917), and other councils for industry and commerce, as well as for the training and supply of teachers. There are also a number of professional organisations of teachers, the most powerful of which is the National Union of Teachers (established in 1870), all of whom have other means of access to the central authority.

This central authority, through its inspectorate, maintains its own intelligence service, and publishes an annual statistical report which is invaluable for any considerations made of either the past or the future of English education, for its latest report gives extrapolations of the school population up to 1990.

FURTHER READING
Schools
J. W. Adamson. *English Education 1789–1902*, Cambridge Univ. Press, 1930.
W. H. G. Armytage. *400 Years of English Education*, Cambridge Univ. Press, 1964.
J. S. Maclure. *Educational Documents, England and Wales, 1816–1963*, Chapman and Hall, 1965.
B. Simon. *Studies in the History of Education, 1780–1870*, Lawrence and Wishart, 1960. *Education and the Labour Movement, 1870–1920*, Lawrence and Wishart, 1965.
J. Simon. *Education and Society in Tudor England*, Cambridge Univ. Press, 1966
W. A. C. Stewart and W. P. McCann *The Education Innovators 1850–1880* Macmillan, 1967.

Other types of education
Quentin Bell. *Schools of Design*, Routledge and Kegan Paul, 1963.
W. M. Eager. *Making Men: the History of Boys' Clubs and Related Movements in Great Britain*, Univ. of London Press, 1953.

E. L. Edmonds. *The School Inspector,* Routledge and Kegan Paul, 1962.

T. Kelly. *A Select Bibliography of Adult Education in Great Britain,* Institute of Adult Education, 1962.

S. and V. Leff. *The School Health Service,* Lewis, London, 1959.

D. G. Pritchard. *Education and the Handicapped 1760–1960,* Routledge and Kegan Paul, 1963.

H. Rashdall, F. M. Powicke and A. B. Emden (eds.) *Universities of Europe in the Middle Ages,* Oxford Univ. Press, 1936.

Further bibliographical articles can be found in the *British Journal of Educational Studies.*

WHGA

HMC schools *See* **Headmasters' Conference schools**

Hockey Hockey, an 11-a-side game played entirely by amateurs about 75 years ago, has spread to many countries in the world. It has been taken up with enthusiasm in India and the players from that country and Pakistan produce some of the finest players and teams in the world. The game has had Olympic status for many years. It is played by both men's and women's teams, and is one of the few sports in which mixed teams compete, though only on a 'friendly' basis.

A hockey pitch measures 100 yards long and 55–60 yards wide with goals four yards wide at each end. (The markings on a pitch used by women players differ slightly from those on a men's pitch.) The object of the game is to score goals by propelling a white ball about the size of a cricket ball ($5\frac{1}{2}$–$5\frac{3}{4}$ oz.) into the opponents' goal by means of a stick weighing 12–28 oz., slightly curved and flat-faced at the bottom. A game consists of two halves, each of 35 minutes duration, and is controlled by two umpires each of whom is responsible for one half of the field and a complete side line. In Britain there are no leagues and all matches are played on a friendly basis. In schools little or no hockey is played before the secondary stage, though a game ('shinty') played in

many primary schools forms an excellent introduction to the basic skills of hockey. At the secondary education level hockey, along with netball, is a major winter game for girls. In recent years the game has also increased in popularity with boys.

Controlling bodies: Men's Hockey Association, R. J. W. Struthers, 26/29 Park Cres., London, W1. Women's Hockey Association, Mrs M. MacDonald, 45 Doughty St, London, WC1. Schoolboys' Hockey Subcommittee, D. J. Newton, Kennedy's Hse, Aldenham School, Elstree, Herts.

JE

Hogg, Quintin (1845–1903) Founder of the polytechnic movement in London, and during his working life a senior partner in a firm of sugar merchants, Quintin Hogg began his career in 1864 as a philanthropist by establishing a ragged school for boys in Charing Cross. After a period in a rather larger building, part of which he set aside for a youths' Christian Institute, he moved again in 1878 to Long Acre—leaving behind the ragged school, which was soon to be taken over by the School Board. In his new premises he was able to accommodate 500 students, and to them he made available not only technical courses but also opportunities for recreation at a ground at Mortlake, acquired in 1880.

In 1881 he leased the Royal Polytechnic Institution building in Regent Street, which had been erected in 1838 as a centre for scientific exhibitions but had later also provided technical instruction. Hogg enlarged the building, retaining the term 'polytechnic' for an institution that was now, under public management, to provide young people of both sexes from the lower middle class with opportunities for learning together with recreation and social activity. In a very short time the original 2,000 students increased to over 6,000. A day school was opened, providing professional, industrial and commercial courses; holiday tours were organised for students; an employment bureau was set up, its services not confined to Polytechnic students. From his own pocket Hogg contributed altogether £100,000 to the enterprise, to which in 1889 was added an annual grant from the redistribution of parochial charities in London; in the same year £35,000 was raised by public subscription. Towards the end of his life, as an alderman in the first London County Council, Hogg devoted himself to encouraging the establishment of other polytechnics.

Hogg, Rt Hon Quintin (b. 1907) Minister of Education, 1957; Minister for Science and Technology, 1959–64; Minister with special responsibility for higher education, 1963–4; Secretary of State for Education and Science, April–October 1964.

Hoggart, Professor Richard (b. 1918) Professor of English in Birmingham University since 1962, and director of the Centre for Contemporary Cultural Studies since 1964, Professor Hoggart wrote his highly influential *The Uses of Literacy* in 1957. He was a member of the Albemarle Committee on the Youth Services from 1958 to 1960 and of the Pilkington Committee on Broadcasting from 1960 to 1962.

Holland, Education in *See* **Netherlands, Education in the**

Holmes, Edmond (1850–1936) Chief Inspector of Elementary Schools, Holmes was the author of a confidential document (1911) concerned with the appointment of local inspectors. It contained very strong criticism of elementary teachers ('as a rule, uncultured and imperfectly educated'), and of local inspection ('on the whole a hindrance rather than an aid to educational progress'); and when it was mysteriously made public, it led to the resignation of the President of the Board of Education

(Mr Walter Runciman) and of R. L. Morant (*q.v.*), Permanent Secretary of the Board.

In the same year, Holmes published a condemnatory survey of the teaching methods of the time, *What Is and What Might Be*. He attacked the inactive role of the pupil and the generally repressive atmosphere of the schools.

Home and Colonial Infant School Society The Society was founded in 1836 to provide trained teachers for infant schools.

Home economics This is now the accepted term in education for what used to be known as domestic science. It consists of the study of those arts and applied sociological sciences relevant to home-making and management. The main elements in home economics include simple nutrition and the planning and preparation of family meals; the fabric of the home, including design, choice and maintenance of furniture, textiles and equipment; the study of physical factors influencing family life, and of the organisation and economic management of a home; and the study of the family within the community, with emphasis on the reciprocity of responsibilities.

See also **Home management (housecraft), Teaching of**

Home Economics, United Kingdom Federation for Education in The Federation consists of organisations engaged or interested in the teaching of home economics, and furthers interest and progress in the subject in the UK; it also secures that the UK is adequately represented in national and international organisations concerned with home economics.

Hon. Sec.: Miss A. P. Ramage, 36 Ravenscroft Ave, London, NW11.

Home Economics Education, National Council for The Council (formerly the National Council for

Domestic Studies) aims to promote the wider study of home economics. It arranges courses and conducts examinations, mainly in colleges of further education.

Sec.: Mrs. Mildred J. Purkis, 75 Ferme Park Rd, Crouch End, London, N8.

Home Economists of Great Britain, Association of A home economist has recognised specialist training in science, economics or the arts related to the home, making use of such training in professional work concerned with the everyday needs of home and family.

The Association was formed in 1953 because existing organisations which looked after the interests of people with a training in domestic science and related fields like nutrition and household science did not cater for home economists in business and industry. The Association now has just over 1,000 members and associate members. Full membership is open to those holding a degree, diploma or certificate resulting from a minimum two years' full-time training course in home economics at a recognised university, training or technical college.

The Association aims at promoting the interests of home economists engaged in industry, commerce and journalism. It also provides facilities for the free discussion and exchange of ideas on all matters relating to home economics; maintains an organisation through which the views of its members can be voiced both nationally and internationally; acts in an advisory capacity to would-be employers and employees in the field of home economics; encourages the greater use of professionally qualified home economists in industry, commerce and journalism; collates information on research relating directly or indirectly to home economics for the benefit of all home economists; studies and initiates projects, encourages training schemes and trains candidates suited to the career of home economics in industry, commerce, journalism and allied fields; affiliates with any organisation (national or international) whose objects have a direct or indirect bearing on home economics; obtains representation on such organisations or exchanges information with them.

Home economists are not store sales demonstrators. Although many home economists do demonstrate products in the course of their work, this is only one of the advisory functions they carry out. They work as consumer advisers in the gas, electricity and solid fuel industries, and for food manufacturers and food industry organisations, as well as engaging in recipe development work, preparing service publications, instructions, food for photography. They are food and home page writers on magazines and newspapers. They work in public relations and advertising. Domestic appliance and household equipment manufacturers employ home economists, as do some textile firms.

The specialised knowledge of home economists is found useful by voluntary organisations ranging from consumer groups to home safety committees and marriage guidance organisations. They are often able to help family service units with practical problems of home management and budgeting. They sit on industrial committees concerned with standards for consumer goods. In general they act as a stand-in for the consumer and as a bridge between consumer and supplier.

Sec.: 27 Andover Rd, Southsea, Hampshire.

Home Help Organisers, Institute of Following the National Health Act 1948, an Association of Home Help Organisers was formed with a view to helping local authority organisers with their problems. The number of organisers increased with the rapid expansion of the service, and the Association was dissolved and replaced by the Institute in 1954.

The Institute aims to increase the efficiency of the home help service, to give information and advice, to maintain contact with other organisations which may improve the service, and to establish and maintain a high standard of qualifications among its members. To encourage this last object, a training scheme has recently been developed by the Education Officer of the National Association of Local Government Officers in co-operation with the Institute. The training course can be taken by correspondence and a short residential course is held yearly. Sec.: 1 King Edward Rd, Maidstone, Kent.

Home management (housecraft), Teaching of This subject was originally taught as a set of distinct crafts (cookery, cleaning and sewing). Because of a continuing preoccupation with the craft aspects of the subject, many people regard it as the Cinderella of the curriculum: but the image is being changed by a more realistic use of time allocated, in terms of both quantity and range of work attempted. The pupil is now required to organise a variety of tasks, make comparisons and judgments, decide priorities in the deployment of time, money and energy. Attempts are made to relate the course as nearly as possible to everyday problems of living.

It follows from this that social trends must have a fundamental influence on the teaching of home management. For instance, one effect of the welfare state has been a general upgrading in standards of health and hygiene. Few teachers need to give the series of lessons based on simple personal hygiene that used to form the introductory theme of many courses. There is, however, a great need for improved teaching of nutrition, with the emphasis on simple, economic and nutritionally sound meals. Too few teachers use the many printed recipes available as an encouragement to an adventurous but critical approach to cooking. The various aspects of family

catering should be realistically related to a child's social background and not to pre-war middle-class standards.

Again it is important, now that the welfare state to a great extent supports the family, that pupils should know what kinds of help are available and how these may be obtained. (For a review of people's attitudes to the welfare state, see Richard and Hephzibah Hauser's *The Fraternal Society*[1]—their suggestions for displacing apathy and inertia by the stimulation of personal responsibility and concern for others could well be applied in housecraft teaching.)

The teaching of home economics is moving progressively outwards from the kitchen; more time is now spent considering the world beyond. Pupils often visit nurseries, child welfare centres, etc; more visitors come to the school, so forging links with the outer world. Sometimes this results in active social effort on the part of the pupils. Too often it does not progress beyond the question: 'What is in it for me?'

As W. S. Hargreaves has said in *Education for Family Living*,[2] 'A shift in the roles of husband and wife is occurring.' This means that if housecraft is educationally valid for girls, it is more than ever valid for boys. It would seem impossible to pursue effectively the avowed aim of studying family welfare without involving boys in the course. Many in the present generation of young men are successsfully sharing the tasks of home-making; but there are many others whose poor social development limits their ability to co-operate and to recognise and accept responsibility. Much could be done by the housecraft teacher to foster true working relationships. The need for this arises, not only from the nation's economic need for women's work outside the home, but also from a growing appreciation of the importance of the father's role in the family, and from acknowledgement of the woman's need for a fuller cultural and public life. Mental health for many women is directly dependent on their finding relief from the depression and loneliness that result from repetitive tasks performed within the isolation of the modern family.

The mechanisation of household work, together with the increasing degree of automation, calls for a more rapid shift of emphasis from separate craft skills: what must be fostered is the ability to select priorities and direct resources, so that more than one process may be carried on at a time, with understanding of the advantages and limitations of the machinery. Pupils need to be encouraged to consider how well-ordered work may save time and energy.

The present disproportionately high rates of pay for the young unskilled worker have made young people particularly vulnerable to advertising. Many systems are available offering deferred payments, and more calculation and forethought are needed if financial difficulties are to be avoided. Much is done by the housecraft teacher to train children to question the value of products and to understand the principles of simple budgeting, interest rates, etc. Earlier marriage, shortage of housing and inflated prices have also sharpened financial difficulties. Many senior groups in their housecraft lessons study the problems of finding and furnishing a home.

Personal relationships have been complicated by overcrowded living conditions and the confusions of a swiftly changing society. Patricia Vereker has written: 'Teachers have a serious supporting role to play in helping those in their care both to sort out their standards and values so that they may adjust themselves more effectively to the responsibilities of the adult world, and to enable them as parents of the next generation to establish the stable background necessary for home life.'[3] A teacher can scarcely avoid conveying certain standards and values, but does this justify the assumption that the home economics teacher is equipped to offer teaching on moral values and emotional problems? This is occasionally attempted in the informal atmosphere of group discussions. There is growing interest in, and concern about, the nature of this contribution.

Teaching method now relies less on demonstrations to a whole class, and more on assignment work. The main limiting factors are imposed by external examinations, though considerable progress has been made in the drafting of CSE syllabuses which encourage the tendency to develop individual work and techniques of investigation. Many teachers would be inclined to sacrifice time at present allocated to junior classes in order to develop more challenging courses for senior pupils.

Ancillary help for housecraft teachers is sometimes provided. One effect of this is that more profitable use can be made of class time formerly devoted to repetitive kitchen cleaning and maintenance.

So long as much of the actual practical work is carried out within the confines of the housecraft room, the scope of the work will be limited. Pupils can be given an opportunity to act out problems of family living through a period of work in a self-contained flat, but the value of this experience depends on the way it is organised. The trend now is to think in terms of an 'open plan' teaching room, designed to provide different types of accommodation for the increasing range of activities included in home economics teaching.

REFERENCES
1. Richard and Hephzibah Hauser. *The Fraternal Society*, Bodley Head, 1962.
2. W. S. Hargreaves. *Education for Family Living*, Basil Blackwell, Oxford, 1966.
3. Patricia Vereker. 'The Place of Personal Relationships in Home Economics Teaching', *Home Economics and Domestic Subjects Review*, November 1966.

See also **Housecraft teachers, Training of; Home economics**

RA

Home Office Children's Department This Government Department carries central responsibility for children deprived of a normal home life.

This definition covers: (1) children received into care by a local authority, because they have no parent or guardian, are abandoned or not properly provided for by their parents; (2) children and young persons committed to local authority care by a court as being in need of care and protection or as offenders against the law; (3) children placed privately with foster-parents for reward or placed for adoption, legal or *de facto*, by the local authority or by a voluntary organisation; (4) children being cared for by voluntary organisations in homes or foster-homes; (5) children and young persons in remand homes, Home Office approved schools or attending junior attendance centres.

The Department brings to the attention of local authority Children's Departments and other bodies concerned the statutory rules by which legislation affecting the welfare of children is to be enforced and interpreted, e.g. rules and orders governing the employment of children, the boarding out of children and young persons, the provision of accommodation for temporary reception of children who are homeless or not properly cared for, and the provision and conduct of residential nurseries. Homes and special residential schools for children and young persons must be registered with the Department and are subject to inspection by its officers.

The Department defines a *child* or *juvenile* as anyone under 14; a *young person* as between 14 and 17. These definitions do not match those of the Ministry of Social Security or the DES.

In 1964 the Department set up a National Bureau for Co-operation in Child Care in order to improve communication between statutory and voluntary services and different professional disciplines affecting children, to explore possibilities of more effective use of existing services and to recommend establishment of new ones where gaps are found, to encourage a preventive approach throughout the child care services, and to stimulate research.

The Department co-ordinates the training of child care officers and those concerned with the residential care of children, and issues a certificate granting professional status to those who have completed an approved course. It is advised in this connection by the Central Training Council in Child Care, and on its overall responsibilities by the Advisory Council on Child Care.
DLH

Home and school The many experiences of children in their school life, the relationships they form with their fellow-pupils and their teachers, their degree of participation and level of performance in school work and activities, the extent to which they benefit from the opportunities and facilities offered in the school—these clearly depend in large part upon the family background from which children come and the context of family life within which they live throughout their school course. The family is itself an educative group of the very greatest importance, and the links between home and school are of the most crucial kind for the personal life and the educational progress of the individual child. This has always been realised in educational theory, but during recent times much sociological and psychological research has been undertaken to explore and analyse the many factors involved. The more notable present-day findings are as follows:

(1) When various household conditions—such as overcrowding, the sharing of beds, the existence of a separate kitchen, bathroom, running hot water, etc.—are measured for members of all social classes (and classified as satisfactory or unsatisfactory according to certain criteria), it is found that they

undoubtedly have an influence upon the performance of children in the school. This influence, however, is various and complex. Among the working classes, children from homes which are unsatisfactory in these respects have lower test scores, and moreover these lower scores deteriorate significantly between the ages of eight and 11. But working-class children who come from satisfactory homes improve their performance during these later years of childhood. Among the middle classes, children from homes which are unsatisfactory actually improve their scores between the ages of eight and 11, somehow managing to overcome the earlier handicaps that these conditions provide.

(2) Housing in itself also has an important and similar influence. Poor housing is correlated with low performance, and again scores of working-class children progressively deteriorate with these background conditions, whereas scores of middle-class children show some improvement. One interesting point here is that when working-class families move from unsatisfactory houses rented from private landlords to accommodation on council house estates, the average school performance of their children improves; the chances, for example, that their children will go to grammar schools are increased. It is thought that this could be connected with the greater availability of grammar school places in areas which have large council house estates, but the improved housing conditions are clearly a significant factor.

(3) Conditions of home life appear also to be reflected in and reinforced by the attitudes of teachers. Children from poor home backgrounds are thought to be lazy, to lack powers of concentration and persistence of effort, and teachers tend to think that they will not be able to benefit from higher education. Children from satisfactory homes and family backgrounds are thought to possess better educational promise.

(4) One very important factor, however, is parental concern, interest and encouragement. When children enjoy parental support, noticeable differences are found in their performance at school. (*See* **Family size, Education and.**)

Though complex and requiring further analysis and explanation, all these findings bear out the common-sense persuasion that when a home provides security, comfort and good facilities; when it is situated in a pleasant neighbourhood and environment possessing good social and educational amenities; and when the parents have an affectionate and lively concern for the welfare and future of their children in school as well as out of it, and seek to achieve a good relationship between home and school—all these conditions maximise the extent to which a child can make use of the opportunities offered by his school and move happily towards his own educational advancement and personal fulfilment.

FURTHER READING
J. W. B. Douglas. *The Home and the School*, MacGibbon and Kee, 1964.

RF

Home and School Council Formed in the autumn of 1967 and representing a partnership between the Advisory Centre for Education, the Confederation for the Advancement of State Education (*q.v.*) and the National Federation of Parent-Teacher Associations, the Council aims to strengthen the role of parents in the educational pattern. It will seek to bring about the formation of PTAs and other parent groups in every school.

A pilot campaign, under a field officer appointed by the Council, is to be launched in Yorkshire, and on the basis of this effort the campaign will be extended to other parts of the country. The Council has urged all LEAs to implement the recommendation in the Plowden Report (*q.v.*) that among the managers or governors of any school there should always be a parent with a child attending the school.

See also **Parent-teacher movement**

Home study 'Home Study' used to conjure up a vision of the autodidact with his volumes of H. G. Wells, his encyclopaedia, or, more recently, his correspondence course. The means at his disposal are now technically more sophisticated. The correspondence course may be combined with a TV or radio series and may be supported by special texts, kits (e.g. for scientific experiments), tapes (e.g. for practising language pronunciation), or film loops for home projection. He may teach himself from gramophone records or from a programmed text. Educational technologists expect that individuals, sitting at their domestic consoles, will soon be able to 'retrieve information' and be in long-range communication with many of these teaching devices.

See also **Correspondence courses**
BG

Home tuition, Free *See* **School attendance**

Homework Homework is in almost universal use as a supplementary aid or method by teachers in all countries. It is the name given to set tasks, planned by the teacher and arising out of a lesson experience or sometimes leading to the next planned lesson, which the pupil is expected to complete outside the classroom. Homework in many countries is used by parents as an indication of the progress their child is making. Clearly extending the pupils' hours of learning, homework is an indirect admission that the curriculum cannot be completed within normal school hours.

Where the teacher is resourceful in making use of the special interests and backgrounds of pupils it can be an important aspect of teaching method. As in the case of all exercises, teachers should feel obliged to show real interest in all completed homework.
DJJ

Honduras, Education in Education is free, compulsory from seven to 15 years where places are available, and secular. About 40% of children of school age are enrolled. The university at Tegucigalpa, with faculties of law, medicine, pharmacy, engineering, economics and dentistry, has an enrolment of 2,572. There are higher education colleges at Tegucigalpa and San Pedro Sula, with facilities for studying nursing, journalism, public administration, business studies, auditing and accountancy. 1966 statistics: 4,120 primary schools (330,779 enrolments); 96 secondary and technical schools (26,527 enrolments).

The country's population was approximately 2¼ million in 1966.

Hong Kong, Education in Education is not compulsory. All schools are registered with the government education department and have to comply with the colony's regulations governing staff and buildings. Some schools are state-aided. The 1966 statistics give enrolments only: kindergartens 53,479; primary schools 636,455; secondary schools 195,802; post-secondary schools 41,306. Three teacher training colleges have 861 students. The University of Hong Kong has 2,146 students, and the Chinese University at Kowloon 1,823. The population of the colony was approximately 3¾ million in 1966.

Horological Institute Ltd, British Founded in 1858, with the object of promoting the science of horology and teaching its practice, the Institute is a scientific, technical and educational body also concerned with commercial ethics. It is the recognised examining body for the award of diplomas in horological subjects. An apprenticeship scheme is maintained for the use of members, and the library is the most

HOTEL KEEPING AND CATERING, NATIONAL DIPLOMA IN

comprehensive horological library in the world.

35 Northampton Sq., London, EC1.

HORSA Hut Operation for the Raising of the School Age—one of the means developed in 1947 to help to make available the extra 168,000 school places required when the school leaving age was raised from 14 to 15. Between 1947 and 1949, 6,838 HORSA classrooms equipped with special utility furniture were provided.

Horticultural Education Association The Association keeps in close touch with the industry, government departments, and public bodies concerned with educational policy and technical development in horticulture, and is consulted by these organisations as representing the professional worker. Membership is open to all professionally engaged in horticulture, including teachers in horticulture; associateship is open to anyone interested.

Gen. Sec.: J. H. Glazebrook, College of Horticulture, Pershore, Worcs.

Publication: *Scientific Horticulture* (annually).

Hospital play group *See* **Nursery assistants**

Hospital schools The first hospital schools in Britain were established by voluntary effort at the turn of the century to provide treatment and education mainly for crippled or tubercular children. Some of these (e.g. Chailey Heritage Craft Schools) still exist, but most hospital schools at the present time are established by LEAs in accommodation provided by regional hospital boards. A school can be established in any hospital, including psychiatric, where there is a sufficient number of children requiring treatment for more than a few weeks. Pupils are taught at the bedside, or in small groups, according to circumstances. Under section 56 of the Education Act 1944 full or part-time teachers can also

be provided for sick children in hospitals where there is no school.

Although the length of time spent by children in hospital is becoming shorter it is felt that education is essential for their mental health as well as to prevent falling off in their school work.

FURTHER READING

Association for Special Education. *Children in Hospital* (Conference Report), Liverpool, 1965.

Ministry of Health. *The Welfare of Children in Hospital*, HMSO, 1959.

See also **Special education**

MW

Hotel and Catering Institute Established in 1949 as the professional body for skilled members of the hotel and catering industry. The Institute aims at promoting technical education for the industry, imposing means for testing the qualifications of applicants for professional membership, encouraging ethical practices in the conduct of business and providing facilities for members to exchange ideas and information on matters of educational or professional interest.

Courses which lead to the following qualifications are sponsored by the Institute: General Catering Diploma, Housekeeping Certificate, Waiting Certificate, Final Waiting Certificate, Hotel Book-keeping and Reception Certificate, Intermediate Membership of the HCI, Final Membership of the HCI; and, in conjunction with the DES, the National Diploma in Hotelkeeping and Catering.

191 Trinity Rd, London, SW17.

Journal
The Hotel and Catering Institute Journal. Monthly.

Hotel Keeping and Catering, National Diploma in This is a qualification for managerial posts in the hotel and catering industry. The award of the diploma is administered by a joint committee of representatives of the Hotel and Catering Institute and the DES. Courses, which are held at establishments of further education, vary in length according to type, a full-time course lasting three years and a sandwich course (divided into periods in college and periods spent in gaining practical experience) lasting four years. The normal age for entry to a course is 17, and usually the entrant is required to have five subjects in GCE at O level. A still higher qualification for the industry can be obtained by taking a degree at certain universities (e.g. Strathclyde, Surrey) in hotel and catering management.

Hours of work in teaching The hours of work of the teacher are not necessarily confined to the time he spends in school. For most members of the profession extra work is involved in lesson preparations and the marking of pupils' work, much of which will be undertaken outside school hours. In addition, it is a feature of school life in the UK (though not in most other countries) that a whole range of 'extra-curricular' activities are undertaken in the form of sports, school societies and events, school journeys and other activities, all of which are organised voluntarily and without extra pay by teachers, and which invariably involve teachers in many further hours of work.

The length of class teaching duty will, however, be governed by the length of the school day and the number of sessions for which school is open each year. These are prescribed for all maintained schools by the Schools Regulations 1959 and are set down as follows:

'(1) On every day on which a school meets there shall be provided for the pupils—

(a) in a nursery school or nursery class, at least three hours of suitable activities;

(b) in a school or class mainly for pupils under eight years of age, at least three hours of secular instruction; and

(c) in a school or class mainly for pupils of eight years of age and over, at least four hours of secular instruction

divided into two sessions, one of which shall be in the morning and the other in the afternoon unless exceptional circumstances make this undesirable: Provided that—

(a) in a school which meets on six days in the week there may be on two of those days one session only of half the appropriate period of time prescribed by this paragraph; and

(b) it shall be sufficient to provide one-and-a-half hours of suitable activities for pupils attending a nursery school or nursery class for half a day only.

(2) For the purpose of this regulation, time occupied in marking the registers shall not be counted towards the required periods of activities or instruction, but there may be counted—

(a) in a voluntary school, the time required for the purposes of the inspection of religious instruction in accordance with subsection (5) of Section 77 of the Education Act 1944; and

(b) in any school, the necessary time for recreation, and any time occupied by the medical examination, inspection and treatment and dental treatment of pupils.

A school shall, apart from some unavoidable cause, meet for at least four hundred sessions in each year, from which may be deducted a number not exceeding twenty in respect of occasional school holidays granted during term.'

For those teachers who are engaged on a part-time basis there is no prescribed number of hours of teaching. These will vary with each appointment and the circumstances of the teacher and the school, although the general practice is for the part-time teacher to work for whole mornings or afternoons, rather than for individual lesson periods.

There has been a suggestion arising from the report of the Newsom Committee (CAC Report *Half our Future*) that an 'extended school-day' should be introduced in secondary schools which would involve teachers in duties in school outside the normal school hours. This suggestion would obviously involve a reconsideration of the traditional practice by which teachers voluntarily participate in out-of-school and other extra-curricular activities. While in some areas experiments on these lines are being carried out, no general decision on the Newsom suggestion has been taken as yet.

FJ

Housecraft ,Teaching of *See* **Home management (housecraft), Teaching of**

Housecraft teachers, Training of Housecraft as now taught is not concerned simply with the domestic arts; it deals with social policy, personal relationships and ethics as well. Home economics training is often offered as a main course in a college of education alongside the usual range of other subjects, instead of in the isolation of a relatively small specialist college. Some colleges run courses with a bias towards rural studies. All courses last three years. Degree courses (B.Sc. Household and Social Service) have been available for many years, but this is a qualification held by very few teachers because the emphasis in schools is on craft and teaching method rather than on scientific knowledge.

Social studies permeate the whole training and increasingly involve the student in the first-hand experience of working alongside social workers in other peoples' homes. It is hoped that students will gain insight into home backgrounds similar to those of their future pupils, while trying to apply their knowledge of home economics to the alleviation of some of the problems they will encounter. Within the craft sessions more time is spent than before in considering the application and presentation of the subject in school work. The study of scientific principles and their application to laundrywork, textiles, food chemistry, health and hygiene is directly linked with the practical content of the course. Interest in art as it applies to home furnishings, dress, embroidery and the appreciation of colour and good design is fostered throughout the course and often given specific training.

On the whole less time is given to the pursuit of craft skills and more is spent considering the principles of education and social studies. The course usually includes a period of supervised residential practice in the management of a home. Supervised practical teaching is also undertaken at intervals in a wide variety of secondary schools.

For further information: Central Register and Clearing House Ltd, 151 Gower St, London, WC1.

See also **Home management (Housecraft), Teaching of**

RA

Human Resources Centre *See* **Tavistock Institute of Human Relations**

Humane Society, Royal The aims of the RHS are to bestow awards for the preservation and restoration of life; to collect and circulate information relating to approved and effective methods for recovering persons apparently drowned or dead; to encourage knowledge of life saving, to investigate methods of life saving and resuscitation, and to reward such knowledge; to act as a record office holding particulars of resuscitation, the method used and medical data about the patient during restoration.

In 1965, 873 persons were rewarded for saving, attempting to save, or restoring life; 594 lives were saved, and there were 72 unsuccessful attempts to restore life.

Sec.: Lt-Col. R. W. G. Charlton, Watergate House, York Buildings, Adelphi, London, WC2.

Humanist Association, British

With a national individual membership and affiliated local groups throughout the country, the Association exists to promote humanist thought and action, through publications, courses and conferences, social projects and 'political' activity. There is an affiliated Humanist Teachers Association (*q.v.*). The BHA has an Education Committee which is primarily interested in moral and social education, and campaigns for a re-examination of the assumption that the public system of education in this country should have and can have a religious foundation.

President: Professor A. J. Ayer. Sec.: Miss Margaret Rogers, 13 Prince of Wales Terr., London, W8.

Humanist Federation, University

The UHF is a federal body of university humanist organisations, providing a central clearing house and literature and representing student humanists at national level. Membership is not confined to universities, in which there are thirty constituent groups, but is spreading also to other institutions of higher education. There is a category of individual membership open to students and university and college teachers. An annual conference is held in January, and various projects during the year. Humanists encourage a secular approach to university and college affairs, and are opposed to all compulsory religion and to unnecessary restrictions on individual liberty.

13 Prince of Wales Terrace, London, W8.

Humanist Teachers' Association

The Humanist Teachers' Association was formed in 1965 to give mutual support by discussion of and help with the particular problems humanist teachers have to face; to secure revision of the 1944 Education Act with regard to the teaching of religion in schools and the compulsory act of worship; and to consider ways of replacing religious indoctrination by a reasoned approach to the moral problems young people must face in modern life.

The Association supports the open approach to religious education and has produced two syllabuses of moral education. It has opposed the proposal to increase grants to denominational schools on the grounds that it is wrong to segregate children according to religious views, that the state should not be expected to pay for the inculcation of particular beliefs, and that the proposal could lead to the strengthening of the single school areas.

13 Prince of Wales Terrace, London, W8.

Hungary, Education in

Attendance at school is free and compulsory from six to 16 years. University education is subsidised by state and factory grants to students; there are four universities (at Budapest, Pecs, Szeged, and Debrecen), and six technical universities in these four cities and also at Miskolc and Veszprem. All non-state schools have to be licensed. 1965 statistics: 3,227 kindergartens (189,400 enrolments); 6,036 elementary schools (1,413,500 enrolments); 591 secondary schools (407,485 enrolments); 58 teacher training colleges; 92 higher education institutes (93,957 enrolments, of which 51,002 were full-time). The higher education institutes include a National School of Technology, a School of Agriculture, a School of Economics and an Academy of Economic and Technical Science. There are eight licensed RC schools, nine licensed Calvinist, two Lutheran, and two Jewish.

The country's population was approximately 10¼ million in 1965.

Huxley, Thomas (1825–95)

One of the most influential of the

mid-Victorian figures who pressed for a recognition of the importance of science in education, Huxley asserted (in *Science and Education*) that 'for the purpose of attaining real culture, an exclusively scientific education is at least as effectual as an exclusively literary education.'

Hygiene The teaching of hygiene which should, and more often than not does, begin in the home, normally forms part of the curriculum in most schools, though in primary schools much of the teaching is incidental or children copy the example set by teaching staff and welfare supervisors. The ever-increasing numbers of children using the school meals service has enabled teachers and supervisory staff to insist on personal cleanliness and correct eating habits among those taking school meals.

In secondary schools, the subject can be divided into two parts: personal and general hygiene.

The main aim of personal hygiene teaching is the development of hygiene consciousness in the child. Instruction is given under eight heads:

(1) Care of the feet, which demands both foot cleanliness and correctly fitting footwear. The importance of correct footwear is stressed in *The Health of the School Child* (HMSO, 1966), a report of the DES Chief Medical Officer. Guidance should also be given on the recognition and prevention of common foot troubles such as 'athlete's foot', verrucas, corns, callouses and bunions, as well as in the care of socks and footwear. (2) Selection and care of clothing. (3) Care of the skin and the need for regular washing, particularly when handling or consuming food. Under this head comes instruction in the prevention, recognition and treatment of common skin diseases such as scabies, ringworm and impetigo. (4) Dental hygiene. (5) Care of the hair—of particular importance now that long hair is fashionable. (6) Need for adequate sleep and relaxation— stress on this being very necessary, especially with the young adolescent and those preparing for examinations. (7) Uses and abuses of alcohol and tobacco. (8) Simple anatomy and physiology.

General hygiene is concerned with the need for hygiene in everyday life and the prevention of disease. It includes topics such as the handling and protection of food, infectious diseases, germs and germ carriers, and household and public sanitation.

The teaching of hygiene at secondary school level is most effectively carried out by teachers with specialist qualifications. These can be acquired by studying for the certificate and diploma examinations in general hygiene and school hygiene, arranged at local centres by the Royal Institute of Public Health and Hygiene. Successful candidates are entitled to apply for full or associate membership of the Institute.

Royal Institute of Public Health and Hygiene, 28 Portland Pl., London, W1.

See also **Health education**

JE

I

IAESTE (International Association for the Exchange of Students for Technical Experience) With 34 member countries, IAESTE arranges short periods of training, on a reciprocal basis, for technical students from affiliated universities and colleges. 178 Queens Ga., London, SW7.

Ice skating Figure skating, speed skating, ice-dancing and ice-hockey have all reached international status, largely owing to the construction of indoor ice-rinks in many large towns, which enable the sport to be carried on all the year round in pleasant conditions. Many schools have introduced ice skating into their PE curriculum and pupils attend local ice-rinks for expert instruction. The logical development of the growing interest in the sport must be the inauguration of national schools' championships and the formation of local ice-hockey leagues.

Iceland, Education in Education is free and compulsory from seven to 15 years. 1964 statistics: 234 primary schools (22,488 enrolments); 74 secondary schools (8,952 enrolments); 31 technical schools (2,451 enrolments); three teacher training colleges (423 enrolments); one university at Reykjavik (763 enrolments).

The country's population was approximately 192,000 in 1965.

Illiteracy A person is termed illiterate who can neither read nor write; a semi-literate is one who can read but cannot write. The amount of illiteracy in a country is not easy to establish as there are not adequate means of compelling members of a population to reveal evidence of illiteracy. Moreover the definition varies from country to country; some calculate the percentage of illiterates as being adults who cannot read or write, others take a narrower definition within an age range of 15 to 45. An additional complication is that frequently a person who can read is regarded as literate even though he cannot write. Among the developing nations there is a tendency to show a rapid decrease in the percentage of illiterates following educational programmes by changing the criteria formerly adopted. The definition used by UNESCO is as follows: 'ability both to read and write is used as the criterion of literacy; hence all semi-literates—persons who can read but not write—are included with illiterates'. The lower age level for measurement in most countries is 15 years.

It is estimated that there are 750 million illiterates in the world, most being engaged in agriculture. A country with a high percentage of illiterates is not necessarily one without schools: the fault may lie in the exclusiveness of the educational system, the schools being reserved for pupils whose families have money and position. In countries where illiteracy is spread evenly (e.g. the Sudan, where 95·6% are illiterate) the problem may give rise to less unrest than in a country where it exists in certain areas only (e.g. Italy, where according to the 1951 census 12·9% were illiterate). The first meeting of the International Consultative Liaison Committee for Literacy was summoned by UNESCO in June 1967, to advise the Director-General on action to be taken to eradicate illiteracy. Experimental projects, sponsored by UNESCO, are now under way in Algeria, Ecuador, Iran, Mali, Tanzania and Venezuela. India has embarked upon a crash programme to promote adult literacy among farmers as part of a plan to increase agricultural production. Cuba has a scheme by which teachers and high-school students instruct two or three pupils each, the belief being that an instructor is most effective where he has the fewest possible pupils.

Countries with a high percentage of illiterates (1967): *Asia:* Brunei 57·4, Bahrain 74·7, China 46·1, Indonesia 57·1, India 72·2, Iran 87·2, Iraq 82·7, Jordan 67·6, Kuwait 53·2, Malaya 53·0, Sabah 76·5, Sarawak 78·5, Singapore 50·2, Pakistan 81·2, Syria 64·6, Turkey 61·9, North Vietnam 35·5. *Europe:* Albania 28·5, Bulgaria 14·7, Greece 19·6, Portugal 38·1, Spain 13·3, Yugoslavia 19·7. *Africa:* Mauritius 38·4, Rodrigues 69·4, Morocco 86·2, Senegal 94·4, Seychelles 54·1, West Africa 73·1, Sudan 95·6, Swaziland 77·2, Tunisia 84·2, United Arab Republic 73·7. *America:* El Salvador 52·0, Honduras 55·0, Mexico 34·6, Nicaragua 50·4, Ecuador 69·4, Peru 39·9, Venezuela 34·2. *Oceania:* Christmas Island 36·6.

In the UK illiteracy is an individual but not a social problem, its causes being physical (e.g. dyslexia, *q.v.*), psychological (e.g. school phobia, *q.v.*) or cultural (canal boat children, gypsies, tinkers). Adult literacy classes are held in many areas.

See also **Adult illiteracy**

EP

Illiteracy, Adult *See* **Adult illiteracy**

In-service training of teachers This term is the name given to all courses for teachers with the aim of making them better teachers. It covers a large variety of needs and situations, and refers to a service provided in so many different ways that virtually the only common factor is that all the students are teachers. Until recently most had had their initial training in what were called teachers' training colleges. They are now called colleges of education. The description of what is provided for serving teachers needs a similar broadening to be truthful.

One useful classification is by the purpose to be served. First, and perhaps longest-standing, is the need to keep teachers up-to-date with the subjects they teach. In the course of a teaching career of 40 years great changes will have come about in almost every subject—much will have happened in history, been written in literature, discovered in science. A good teacher needs to keep abreast of developments, not only directly for his pupils' benefit, but for his own so that indirectly they may catch something of his sustained liveliness of mind. A second purpose is to enable teachers to take stock of new psychological knowledge about the growth of children and to re-assess their teaching methods in the light of this. The revolution in primary school mathematics and the new thought being given to religious education in the light of what is known about a child's progress towards conceptual thinking are examples of this. A third purpose is to enable teachers to make effective use of new techniques and technical devices such as the numerous mechanical aids to teaching from the film-strip to closed-circuit TV. These are all types of in-service training which all teachers really need at intervals during their teaching career.

Two other purposes may be mentioned which have a more limited application. The first is the need to bring women teachers up-to-date on their return to school work after a long period of absence for child-bearing and -rearing. The present common pattern of withdrawal from teaching in order to start a family after only two or three years' service makes it vitally important to provide some such re-introductory course if teachers are to have the confidence and the skill to return after a ten years' interval. The need is apparent; a beginning is slowly being made in meeting it. There is a rather similar need to provide courses for teachers who are about to undertake entirely or largely new duties. It may be that they are going to teach a new subject. The full-time courses provided for those who wish to teach Russian but have previously been teaching some other language—often classics—are an example. Teachers who are going to undertake special responsibility for a particular field such as the education of handicapped children, or who are likely to be promoted to headships, also require induction courses.

Another useful classification of in-service training is by the body which provides the training. The two longest established are the DES and the LEAs. About five or six thousand teachers each year attend short holiday courses organised by Her Majesty's Inspectors. A much larger number must attend the various local courses arranged by LEAs. The third principal agency is the complex of Area Training Organisations, the Institutes of Education under another name. These are normally university based. They are intended to be the principal means of providing in-service training, and they do in fact undertake a great deal of it already.

So far we have been concerned largely with that kind of in-service training which is given apart from the daily work of teaching by courses which last anything from a week to a year or for one evening a week for a consecutive number of weeks. But there is another equally valuable form of in-service training more closely associated with the actual problems that arise in the daily handling of work in the classroom. Most LEAs employ organisers or local inspectors, one of whose main duties is to help teachers with advice about their teaching, to disseminate new ideas both from outside the area and from one local school to another. Some authorities have specially appointed officers to supervise and help new teachers during the probationary year that all have to undergo. This form of tutorial in-service training is also one of the principal commitments of HMIs.

A recent development of in-service training has been the introduction of local teachers' centres or development centres, which may be described as co-operative workshops in which teachers work out practically together the precise ways in which they will incorporate new insights into what their pupils actually do in their classrooms. They are in a sense a hybrid between the short course or conference and tutorial help of the kind described in the last paragraph; they may well prove one of the most useful of all forms of in-service training. Skilled leadership is essential, but the essence of the programme lies in self-help—teachers learn best in teachers' centres in the experimental kind of way in which their pupils learn best in schools. It is the new methods in schools which have provided the impetus for the new methods in teacher training. This has been especially true in the field of mathematics and science. Between 1961 and 1964 about a quarter of all primary school teachers attended courses in mathematics. The burden of these courses has been the need for continuing local development work. Just as the conference house was the major contribution which many LEAs made to in-service training in the first dozen years after the war, it seems probable that the development centre will be their main contribution in the next dozen.

The longer forms of in-service training usually carry secondment on full salary from the LEA; it is customary for most authorities to pay the whole or part of the cost of a short course—about half the cost of a holiday course is probably the most common arrangement. While there is a requirement that all teachers should satisfactorily complete a period of initial training—for the present any form of university degree will do—there is no need for any teacher to undertake any form of in-service training and, for the most part, no financial inducement for him to do so. There is some support for the idea that more systematic provision is desirable.

DGOA

Ince Report (1945) *See* **Leaving school**

Incentive *See* **Positive reinforcement**

Incomplete sentences test A type of projection test (*q.v.*) in which the individual completes a number of sentences of which he is given only the beginning, e.g. 'I wish . . .', 'Nearly everybody . . .', 'People succeed who . . .'

Incorporated Association of Assistant Masters in Secondary Schools *See* **Assistant Masters Association**

India, Education in Education prior to 1947 was essentially the concern of the provincial governments and local bodies and the central government was somewhat indifferent to education and its financing. This attitude has now radically altered. Under the Constitution of India education is still mostly managed by the State governments, but the Union government has various responsibilities. A directive principle of the constitution enjoins on the Union to provide free and compulsory education to children up to 14 years of age. The Union is responsible for the maintenance of central universities

and institutions of national importance, the promotion of research, the co-ordination and maintenance of standards in higher education and research and the promotion of the Hindi language along with the other Indian languages. Economic and social planning is a concurrent responsibility of the Union and the States, and education is an integral part of this planning. The Union and State governments collaborate in the formulation, implementation and evolution of various education programmes. The Union government operates a broad-based system of grants-in-aid to the State governments for developing their educational programmes. The obligations of the Union government are discharged by the Ministry of Education through its various programme activities and through the agency of different bodies like the University Grants Commission.

The system of elementary education prior to 1947 was rather academic and book-centred. Since then a new pattern of basic education has emerged as a national system of elementary education. Its essential principles are productive activity, correlation of curriculum within physical and social environment, and contact with local community. Between 1950–1 and 1965–6 the number of children going to school rose from 19 million to about 52 million in Classes I to V and from 3 million to 11 million in Classes VI to VIII. The above-mentioned constitutional directive has yet to be fulfilled, but the current planning envisages substantial progress towards its fulfilment by 1981. Stagnation and wastage, the gap between the enrolment of boys and of girls, and the disparity between States are some of the major problems in this field, and various measures are contemplated to improve the quality of elementary education.

Since independence a serious effort has been made to introduce a national pattern of school classes covering 11 years—five years of lower primary, three years of upper primary and three years of higher secondary classes. As a result, significant changes have been made in the structure of education and great emphasis is being laid on the diversification of courses so as to make secondary education a terminal stage and to reduce the pressure on the universities. The impact of rapid expansion in primary education is reflected in secondary education and the enrolment rose from 1 million in 1950–1 to 5 million in 1965–6. Further expansion is expected, but the main effort will be concentrated on the reorientation and quality of education.

The expansion of education has meant a corresponding increase in the number of teachers and training facilities. The number of school-teachers increased from 750,000 in 1950–1 to about 2 million in 1965–6 and the number of trained teachers from 430,000 to 1·4 million over the same period. The training facilities have been strained to the utmost. Facilities for teacher training are being expanded, and in spite of best intentions much remains to be done to improve the quality, status and remuneration of the teaching profession at all stages of education.

As an integral part of the reorganisation of the educational structure, a system of a three-year degree course for the first degree in arts and science and a further two-year course for the post-graduate degree has been instituted. Enrolment at the university stage rose from 0·3 million in 1950–1 to 1·1 million in 1965–6. The University Grants Commission, which is the agency of the central government for higher education, has taken various steps to improve the quality of university education. But even greater effort is required to improve academic standards. While limited expansion is contemplated, in the coming years the main effort will be concentrated on consolidation and improvement.

The supply of trained manpower is an important factor in the economic and industrial development of the country and to meet its growing requirements technical and engineering education has received a high priority since independence. The number of engineering institutions at the diploma and degree level increased from 135 in 1950–1 to 434 in 1964–5 and enrolment from 10,122 to 67,299 over the same period. With the assistance of UNESCO, the Soviet Union, the United States, West Germany and the UK five higher technological institutions have been established—a fine example of international co-operation. Further expansion in facilities for technical education is contemplated.

During the years since independence there has been a remarkable expansion in educational facilities at all levels. This has meant an increasing outlay on education. Total educational expenditure increased from Rs1,444 million in 1950–1 to about Rs6,000 million in 1965–6. But this can hardly be regarded as adequate either for the expansion that has taken place or for the requirements of a modern educational system. The investment of inadequate resources, human and material, has produced a variety of stresses and strains in the educational system. The quality of education largely depends upon the teacher, the educational material that the teacher and the pupil can easily command, and the equality of opportunity for the boys and girls of all castes and classes. In all these respects a great deal remains to be done and it is not therefore surprising that the problem of educational and academic standards has proved intractable. The controversy about the language policy has distracted attention from the basic function of the Indian and foreign languages in education. Although literacy increased from 17 per cent in 1951 to 24 per cent in 1961, there remain 334 million illiterates.

There is an irresistible demand for education in India—a demand which can be justified both on grounds of social justice and economic development. Neither the expansion nor the measures for qualitative improvement can be considered adequate and much greater effort, ability and money will have to be invested in the educational system to meet the requirements of the age. If all the recommendations of the Education Commission, which recently examined all aspects of education, are implemented, a viable system of education may yet emerge within a reasonable period of time.

NSJ

Indonesia, Education in In January 1965 the country was declared to be free from illiteracy in age groups 13 to 45 years. Education is free and compulsory where school places are available, and it is hoped to extend compulsory education from the age of 7 to 14 to the whole of the country by 1969. There are 26 state universities and several private universities. 1964 statistics: 37,133 primary schools (enrolment 11,000,000); 6,875 secondary schools (enrolment 727,462); 79 higher education institutes (enrolment 279,624).

The country's population was approximately 98 million in 1964.

Industrial Council for Educational and Training Technology Founded in 1966, ICETT was formally established early in 1967 by the British Electrical and Allied Manufacturers Association (BEAMA), the British Radio Equipment Manufacturers Association (BREMA), the Electronic Engineering Association (EEA), and the Scientific Instrument Manufacturers Association (SIMA).

Its present structure is composed of: (1) A Council consisting of an elected chairman and two representatives from each member association—BEAMA, BREMA, EEA, and SIMA—which is

responsible for deciding financial and other major policy matters; negotiating on behalf of industry with ministries and other bodies at the highest level; and co-ordinating the working programme. (2) Six working groups: these are carrying out working programmes, e.g. on standardisation, teaching machines, language laboratories, tape recorders and video tape recorders and transfer media.

With further strengthening from film producing, book publishing, television and radio broadcasting, and material, equipment and systems facets of technology, a fully co-ordinated industry approach will be possible to discuss with users such as educationists, training officers, and instructors the overall system balance between fields such as books, films, broadcasting, and other new developments such as computerised teaching machine networks with student response facilities.

Industrial Design, Council of The Council was established in 1944 'to promote by all practicable means the improvement of design in the products of British industry'.

Members are drawn from industry, commerce, education, publicity, architecture and industrial design. The CoID receives an annual grant from government funds and earns a further substantial proportion of its total expenditure for its services to industry and commerce.

The Education Officer can help in encouraging design appreciation in schools. Information and material is supplied to schools, colleges of art and technology, training colleges and education authorities. Group visits to the Design Centre (*q.v.*) are arranged for schools and other organisations. The Education Officer also gives advice on careers and training in industrial design.

28 Haymarket, London, SW1. The Scottish Committee of the CoID is at the Scottish Design Centre, 46 West George St, Glasgow, C2.

Industrial education In industry and commerce there is a growing trend to regard educational schemes and training schemes as separate functions. The term 'educational schemes' is attributed to day-release for younger employees in non-vocational subjects, and opportunities for attendance at such centres as Outward Bound and Brathay Hall. Many companies support courses and summer schools organised by the National Association of Boys' and Mixed Clubs, and the YWCA for character training and broadening educational experience.

The Co-operative Movement has a long tradition of providing further education opportunities, and an increasing number of business concerns pay fees for employees' attendance at evening institutes for non-vocational courses.

'Training' in industry and commerce is concerned with vocational training, which varies in standard and practice from industry to industry and from firm to firm.

Craft apprenticeships Apprenticeship training is still the traditional entry to established trades. Until recently, apprenticeship training has remained unchanged both in length of training and in conditions of entry, but fortunately employers and trade unions are now becoming more flexible in their approach. Nevertheless a great deal needs to be done to gear craft training schemes to meet the needs of rapid technological change. The standards of training given can vary from learning on the job by assisting a skilled man, to a well-designed syllabus interspersing practical work with theoretical study. Many of the progressive companies take their training responsibilities seriously, and numbers of young men (fewer girls, unfortunately) have the opportunity of working for the Higher National Certificate and technical degrees at the company's expense. Sandwich courses are becoming more

popular, and offer exceptional training opportunities. Many firms are too small to have full-time training officers or training workshops, but the smaller firms who are linking up in group training schemes within their area are providing good training facilities. Day-release courses to supplement 'on the job' training are considered an essential part of any sound scheme. In remote areas where technical colleges are not accessible, block release of three to six months' duration is often arranged.

The Engineering Industries Group Apprenticeship scheme started in 1953, and consists of a confederation of local groups. Firms can, by paying a subscription, call on the services of a Group engineer to advise them on training programmes for their apprentices and link them up in interchange schemes with firms in their own locality.

Commercial apprenticeships These are relatively new in comparison with craft training, and more difficult to organise, but the day colleges are extending rapidly. A fairly recent development has been for large offices to set up their own training sections for secretarial and clerical training. Many companies arrange for staff to have specialised training in comptometer, accounting machine and computer operations. Financial organisations, such as banks and insurance companies, have provided excellent training schemes for many years.

In commerce there are many specialised professional courses—again a combination of 'on the job' training and recognised training courses at commercial colleges and institutes—which qualify men and women for diplomas in such fields as accountancy, law, estate management, architecture, draughtsmanship, etc.

Training in industry and commerce has now received a new impetus through the statutory requirements of the Industrial Training Act, which was implemented in March 1964. Its three main objectives are: to ensure an adequate supply of properly trained men and women at all levels in industry and commerce; to secure an improvement in the quality and efficiency of training; and to share the cost of training more evenly among firms.

As a result of the Act, training boards are being set up for every industry. These boards are responsible to the Central Training Council. Employers will be required to pay a training levy for all employees and, providing they can show evidence of time and expenditure spent on training of a required standard, they will receive a grant towards their training costs.

Training for management In addition to 'vocational' training in technical crafts and commercial professions, the postwar period has brought a significant change in the attitude and practice of employers towards supervisory and management training. The range of training is extensive, including regular and systematic courses for all levels of supervisors and managers, organised by the companies themselves; ad hoc courses organised from time to time for newly appointed supervisors; outside courses organised during working hours by technical colleges and management organisations; outside evening and weekend courses financed by employers; two- to five-day courses on staff management; three- to five-year courses at business colleges; three months specialised courses at the Administrative Staff College.

A big step forward in senior management training was taken in 1965 by the establishment of two business schools in London and Manchester.

For young people advice on industrial training is readily obtainable from careers masters and the Youth Employment Service (*q.v.*). For the more mature reader, a very useful guide is *A Conspectus of Management Courses* published by the British Institute of Management.

EMP

Industrial Psychology, National Institute of A non-profit-making independent scientific association founded in 1921, and governed by a council elected by its members, the Institute acts as a centre of information for its subject, maintains a reference library, publishes a members' *Bulletin* and a quarterly journal, *Occupational Psychology*, occasional papers and research reports, and provides introductory training courses. It undertakes research into general problems bearing on adjustment to working life. It maintains a vocational guidance clinic and advises organisations on virtually any kind of human problem.

14 Welbeck St, London, W1.

Industrial Retraining, Research Unit into Problems of Financed by the Social Science Research Council and the Ford Foundation of America, the unit is engaged on research into the adaptation of training methods for middle-aged workers who may, as a result of technological advances, need retraining for new jobs or work in new industries.

Administered by University College, London, the unit has its centre at 1 Silver St, Cambridge. Director: Dr Eunice Belbin.

Industrial and Scientific Film Association, British Set up in 1967 to serve the interests of all concerned with scientific, technical and industrial films in the UK, the Association (initially financed by the DES) acts as an advisory body as well as organising conferences and the showing of specialised films. It continues publication of the British National Film Catalogue.

Industrial Society The Society provides training, advice and information for its members on all aspects of industrial employment. Its services concern leadership, trade union/management relations, communication, physical

373

N

working conditions and the development of young employees. The Society is independent and self-financing; 20% of its revenue comes from subscriptions, the balance in payment for work done for its members. Its 3,000 members include industrial and commercial companies, nationalised industries, central and local government departments, employers' organisations and trade unions. The Society produces a magazine and books.

48 Bryanston Sq., London, W1.

Industrial Training, White Paper on (1962) Arguing that since the second world war the rate of economic expansion had been held back by the shortage of skilled manpower, the White Paper set out proposals for bringing about an increase in the supply of skilled labour and in its quality. Many firms, the White Paper pointed out, did not make adequate use of facilities for technical education. There had been increases in the numbers of apprentices recruited, but not enough to match future needs. Most unfilled vacancies called for some degree of skill: most of the adult unemployed were labourers.

A weakness in existing arrangements was that 'the amount and quality of industrial training' were 'left to the unco-ordinated decisions of a number of individual firms', who often lacked incentive to train people who might then pass on to other jobs. The benefits of training were being shared by all, the cost borne only by those firms that undertook it. The general intention of the government therefore was to strengthen and improve the existing partnership between industry, the government and the education authorities in the provision of industrial training, to the end that decisions on the scale of training might be better related to economic needs and technological developments; that the overall quality of industrial training might be improved, and minimum standards established; and that the cost might be more fairly spread.

The Minister of Labour was to be given statutory power to set up Boards responsible for all aspects of training in each industry. The Boards might be empowered to establish policy for training, standards and syllabuses, qualifications and tests for instructors and tests for trainees, and to pay grants to firms and to collect money from establishments in any industry by means of a levy.

See also **Industrial training boards**

Industrial Training Act (1964) This Act had three main objectives: to ensure an adequate supply of properly trained men and women at all levels of industry; to secure an improvement in the quality and efficiency of industrial training; and to share the cost of training more evenly between firms.

Industrial training boards were established for many separate industries, to supervise training and with the power to raise a levy. The levy was used to provide a grant to firms who established approved training schemes, as against the practice of some firms that did no training of their own, but recruited from other firms who did. The Act also established a Central Training Council (*q.v.*) to advise on the administration of the Act.

Industrial training boards These boards have been set up under the Industrial Training Act 1964, representing the employers, the employees, and the educational bodies. Their function is to ensure that the amount of training taking place in the various industries they represent is sufficient, and to ensure also that enough finance is raised, partly by levies on industrial firms, to maintain the level of training in both large and small industrial concerns. Many boards are being set up progressively to cover all aspects of industry.

Industrial Training Council (Central Training Council) The Council was set up under the Industrial Training Act 1964 to advise on the various provisions introduced by the Act.

Industrial Training and Education Group of the Gloucestershire and South Worcestershire Productivity Association The objects of this Group are to promote, advance and encourage training and education of those engaged or about to be engaged in industry and commerce and to strengthen the links between industry and educational establishments. The Education and Training Officer advises industry, further education establishments and schools; the Group is represented locally, regionally and internationally on various educational and vocational bodies. Each year a craftsmanship competition for secondary school children and apprentices is organised by the Association.

Sec.: A. Millar-Brown, Cheltenham Rd East, Gloucester.
Journal: *The Link*. Quarterly.

Industry, Confederation of British Set up in 1965 by amalgamation of the Federation of British Industries, British Employers' Confederation and the National Association of British Manufacturers, the Confederation has combined the responsibilities for the whole field of education and training as they relate to industry through its Education and Training Committee.

Particular aspects of joint interest and concern are reviewed by standing joint committees with schools, colleges and universities. In specific fields, standing panels have continued the work begun by the parent bodies—e.g. management education and training, Industrial Training Act, introduction to industry for teachers.

During 1966 a new publication was introduced—the *CBI Education and Training Bulletin*, which includes occasional supplements on matters of special current importance. Most of the *Bulletin* concentrates on developments under the Industrial Training Act and on developments in national education at the different levels with which industry is concerned.

The new Directorate of Education and Training covers the educational services, the vocational training services and an information service. It acts as a link with regional offices and member firms of the CBI, with government departments, and with educational authorities and institutions.

21 Tothill St, London, SW1.

Industry-based students *See* **Further education in England and Wales**

Industry and Commerce, National Advisory Council on Education for The Council was set up in 1948 on a recommendation of the Percy Committee on Higher Technological Education (*q.v.*). It is responsible for advising the Secretary of State for Education and Science on the whole range of national policy necessary for the development of education in relation to industry and commerce, including such aspects as the planning of new developments, the development of research and the methods of examination and certification of studies. After the publication of the Crowther Report (*q.v.*) a special committee of the NACEIC reported on the organisation of further education courses, with special reference to the day-time vocational education of students between the ages of 15 and 16. The chairman since 1956 has been Sir Harry Pilkington.

Ineducable children At one time children with less than IQ25 were thought of as ineducable and termed as 'idiots'. Between IQ25 and IQ55 they were termed as 'imbeciles' and, although still considered unsuitable for school education, could attend junior training centres (*q.v.*) or mental sub-normality hospitals with the appropriate units. Since the Mental Health Act of 1959, however, these harsh names have been dropped, and all children under IQ50 are classed as Severely Subnormal (SSN), 'a condition where the patient is so mentally retarded that he is incapable of leading an independent life or of guarding himself against serious exploitation.' IQ50, of course, is not meant to be taken as an arbitrary cut-off point between SSN and ESN children (*q.v.*), and there can be exceptions below or above this figure who may fit better in the other camp.

The causes of SSN states may lie with heredity, injury, infection during pregnancy, serious disease after birth, metabolic disorders of birth injury. There is also mongolism, the name given to a type of mental deficiency characterised by short growth, open mouth, flat facial features and a depressed nose bridge. Such children often have slanting eyes, and hence the original term 'mongol' for them. The cause of this state has been fairly recently discovered: mongol children have 47 rather than the normal 46 chromosomes in the body cell, and this development occurs very soon after conception.

FURTHER READING
H. C. Gunzburg. *The Social Rehabilitation of the Subnormal*, Baillière, Tindall and Cox, 1960.

NT

Infant schools The infant school, providing for children between five and seven years of age and with its own head teacher, has the longest tradition of any part of the primary section of the English educational system. Its roots and its development during the 19th and early 20th centuries are described in the Hadow Report 1933.[1] The Plowden Report refers to it as 'a distinctively English institution'[2] and its particular contribution to primary education (*q.v.*) is mentioned in the

handbook of suggestions of the Plowden Report, *Primary Education* (1959), thus: 'It is fortunate that when primary education was at last established as a separate phase in its own right, it had this cherished tradition of infant education to draw on; for here the nature and needs of children had become central to thinking and were accepted as the basis of educational practice.' This tradition of progressive practice has been maintained in spite of conditions and pressures which must have been daunting to many teachers: large classes; the parsimony associated with elementary education; the temptation to allow work to be geared, firstly to the annual examination (starting at seven years) incorporated in the Revised Code 1862, and later to the selective process for grammar school places (11-plus), rather than to the immediate needs of children below seven years.

The most marked features of forward thinking at the present time are concern about internal organisation, the form of the curriculum, and the use of school time.

The traditional form of internal organisation—classification primarily by chronological age—is being replaced in some schools by vertical grouping. This means that a school adopts by choice the classification enforced on very small, and especially rural, schools where children aged five, six and seven are necessarily placed in the same class. Thus, instead of one class for each of the three age groups, a school with a one-form entry would have three classes each comprising approximately equal numbers of five-, six- and seven-year-olds. Allocation to classes may take into account family and friendship relations so that a new entrant can be helped in the transition from home by the presence of an older brother, sister or near neighbour. Transfer between classes, should incompatibility arise between teacher and a child or between one child and others, is easily possible since there is no hierarchy of status among classes. Other advantages for infant school children are claimed to result from this form of organisation; hardly any research has been undertaken to establish these claims. The results of Mycock's work[3] suggest that some claims are not well-founded and that high quality in teachers is of crucial importance in the realisation of some potential advantages. The Plowden Committee reports possible disadvantages as well as advantages and does not recommend vertical grouping unreservedly, preferring to advise 'each head teacher, in consultation with her staff, to balance the gain and loss of classes containing more than one age group'.[4] It would be helpful to school staffs in making such decisions to have some firm evidence from research of the effects of different kinds of internal organisation in differing circumstances.

Concern with the form of the curriculum and with the use of school time is leading to reduction both in definition of boundaries between subject areas and in prescribed allocation of time to specific activities; the terms used to describe these developments are 'the integrated curriculum' and 'the free day'. The responsibility placed upon the individual teacher to ensure that material appropriate to all necessary areas of knowledge is available, and that time is being used in the best interests of the children and is used profitably by the children, is thus much heavier than that of the teacher provided with a detailed syllabus and a fixed timetable. Some assistance in carrying out the task is coming from such sources as the Nuffield projects in curriculum development for mathematics and science (*see* **Primary education**) as well as from research in the psychology of learning.

Should the Plowden Committee's recommendations on changes in primary school provision be implemented—the substitution of first schools

with an age range of five to eight years for the present infant schools—it would be necessary to examine the relevance of the above developments to internal organisation, curriculum and time-tabling for the extended age range. The tradition in infant schools of using available knowledge on the nature and needs of children to determine action would doubtless continue to influence practice.

FURTHER READING
L. Hollamby. *Young Children Living and Learning*, Longmans Green, 1962.
E. Mellor. *Education through Experience in the Infant School Years*, Blackwell, Oxford, 1950.
P. M. Pickard. *The Activity of Children*, Longmans Green, 1965.

REFERENCES
1. *Infant and Nursery Schools*, Chapter I.
2. *Children and their Primary Schools*, Section 261.
3. *British Journal of Education Psychology*, XXXVII, 1, 1967.
4. Sections 799–804.

JBC

Initial teaching alphabet (i.t.a.) An alphabet designed by Sir James Pitman for use in the initial stages of teaching reading. It is not intended to replace the traditional alphabet and would be rather unsuitable for this purpose. It consists of the lower case letters of the traditional alphabet, excluding the letters 'q' and 'x', plus 18 additional characters to represent phonemes commonly represented by groups of two or more letters in English, thus €€=ee, ⓦ=oo, ŋ=ng, æ=ay, etc. Capital letters are replaced by lower case characters printed in a larger size, so that there are actually fewer symbols in i.t.a. than in the traditional alphabet. The symbols are used very consistently in representing the phonemes of English but there are exceptions which are designed to aid transitions from i.t.a. to the traditional orthography (t.o.).

In large-scale experiments conducted by J. Downing of the London University Reading Research Unit children taught in i.t.a. classes learned to read

377

more quickly and read with greater comprehension than children in t.o. classes. They maintained a significant lead even after transition to t.o. and most subsequent experiments confirm these findings. It is argued that in these experiments factors other than the greater consistency of i.t.a. might account for the superior reading ability of children taught in i.t.a. classes, e.g. some form of 'Hawthorne effect' (*q.v.*). However, every attempt was made to control extraneous variables of this kind.

Most teachers who have used i.t.a. are convinced of its value, the theoretical arguments in favour of a consistent orthography are substantial and the experimental evidence to date tends to support the case for using such a medium for beginning reading.

FURTHER READING

H. Diack. *In Spite of the Alphabet: A Study of Teaching Reading*, Chatto and Windus, 1965.

J. Downing. *The Initial Teaching Alphabet*, Cassell, 1962. *The Initial Teaching Alphabet Reading Experiment*, Evans, 1964.

J. Downing and B. Jones. 'Some Problems of Evaluating the Initial Teaching Alphabet—A Second Experiment', *Educational Research*, VIII, 2, February 1966.

M. Harrison. *Instant Reading*, Pitman, 1964.

Sir James Pitman. *The Future Teaching of Reading*, 28th Educational Conference of the Educational Records Bureau, New York, 1963.

V. Southgate. 'Approaching Initial Teaching Alphabet Results with Caution', *Educational Research*, VII, 2, February, 1965.

W. D. Walls (ed.). *The i.t.a. Symposium*, National Foundation for Educational Research, 1967.

See also **Reading research; Reading, Teaching of**

JEM

Inner London Education Authority
In April 1965 the Inner London Education Authority (ILEA) took over responsibility for the education service formerly provided by the LCC. Its area is that of the 12 Inner London boroughs and the City, and more or less coincides with the former County of London.

A special committee of the Greater London Council, the ILEA is virtually autonomous but maintains close cooperation with other GLC services. Under the London Government Act 1963 it was required that this special arrangement for the Inner London education service should be reviewed by Parliament in 1970, but in 1965 the arrangement was made a permanent one.

Insight *See* **Gestalt psychology**

Inspection copies Publishers have adopted the inspection copy system to enable teachers to study a textbook in depth before deciding whether to select it for class use. Many publishers will send certain of their general non-net books on approval for a limited period; but these cannot, as is the case with non-net textbooks, be retained as free specimens if ordered in quantity.

Inspection and recognition Under certain conditions (laid down in DES Rules 16), certain schools and establishments of further education in the UK may be inspected and recognised as efficient by the Secretary of State for Education, though this will not make such schools and establishments eligible for the payment of grants. Recognition must be applied for. A first condition in the case of a school is that it must provide 'a progressive general education suitable at all stages for pupils of an age-range of normally not less than three years between the ages of two and nineteen'. In the case of an establishment of further education, courses must be provided which are 'educationally sound, suitable to the needs of students over the statutory school leaving age and have a content appropriate to their stated objectives.'

The requirements of the Education Acts 1944 to 1965, and of the Regulations made under them, must be complied with; a satisfactory level of efficiency is required similar to that demanded in the case of any school or establishment aided by grant. The number of pupils must be sufficient for economical and effective organisation. The teachers must be suitable and sufficient in number and qualifications, and no person may be employed as a teacher who in the opinion of the Secretary of State or any of his predecessors has been judged unsuitable on medical grounds or on grounds of misconduct or grave professional default. The premises must be adequate, suitable and properly equipped, and must be kept in a due state of repair, cleanliness and hygiene. There are a few other more particular conditions, and registers and records have to be kept and such information and returns made as from time to time the Secretary of State may require.

About 1,600 of the 4,000 independent schools in the UK are 'recognised as efficient'. Among those unrecognised are a number of highly regarded schools and other institutions that have never applied for recognition. All schools, however, must be registered with the DES, and all are liable to be visited by HM Inspectors. The Secretary of State has the power to strike off the register of independent schools any school that fails to remedy deficiencies discovered in it by an inspection.

In the autumn of 1967, new measures were announced to improve standards in independent schools that were registered but not recognised as efficient. Of these, 314 were boarding schools, and the standards required for recognition were to be applied to these schools by the DES over the next five years. Action will be taken under the Education Act 1944 against such schools as fail to meet the requirements.

Inspectorate, Her Majesty's Her Majesty's Inspectors of Schools work in two separate groups, one for England and the other for Wales, but these groups are closely associated and both report to the Secretary of State. In England the head of the Inspectorate is the Senior Chief Inspector; he is assisted by six Chief Inspectors, one of whom is his deputy. Each of the six is responsible for a broad sector of the educational field. A team of staff inspectors is responsible for individual subjects and phases of education. A group of senior inspectors have their base in the Department itself; the rest are deployed in the ten geographical divisions in England, each team being under a Divisional Inspector. The Welsh Inspectorate has a slightly different structure, with a Chief Inspector, Staff Inspector and Inspectors linking with the DES and the Education Office for Wales. Most Inspectors reside in the areas where the main part of their work is carried out.

The judgements that an Inspector makes inside a school or college are his own, as are his comments and advice; they are not necessarily those of the Secretary of State. Inspectors are concerned with schools of all types, maintained and independent, with colleges of further education (including technical, commercial and art colleges), with colleges of education, the youth service and adult education, but they have no direct relation with the universities.

Three kinds of inspection are carried out—general, specialist and district. General inspection involves responsibility for the overall work within a group of schools or colleges. Specialist inspection is concerned with a subject or phase of education over a much larger geographical area. Nearly all Inspectors operate in both fields, the aim being that they should become familiar with the work of schools and colleges as a whole and at the same time be particularly knowledgeable on one or other specialist topics. In district inspection, there is liaison with one or more LEAs, this providing close links with the DES. Each authority has at least two district HMIs, one for schools and one for further education.

In addition to its work of visiting and offering advice to schools, the Inspectorate provides a network through which information is passed to the DES. It represents the Department on many outside educational bodies. Inspectors are also seconded to work full-time with groups such as the Schools Council (*q.v.*) and the Architects and Building Branch of the DES.

Inspectors of Schools and Educational Organisers, National Association of NAISEO membership comprises nearly all officers on the educational advisory staffs of LEAs. Members' professional interests are served through NAISEO representation on the Soulbury Committee and by Association support in individual negotiations with employing authorities.

On the educational side the Association, alone or in collaboration, reports on topical questions; it is currently participating in a working party on problems of the teacher's probationary year. Educational subjects are discussed at three-day annual conferences and at local and special meetings.

Hon. Sec.: F. L. Boxall, 20 Riding Barn Hill, Wick, Bristol.

Institut Français du Royaume-Uni Founded in 1913, and run in conjunction with the Universities of Paris and Lille, the Institut provides lectures, concerts, exhibitions, films and evening classes, together with the use of a large library.

Queensbury Pl., London, SW7.

Institute of Community Studies An independent unit established under a deed of trust in 1954, the Institute conducts research in the social sciences. Its major reports have included studies of family life and the life of old people in East London, in the outer suburbs and in Lagos, Nigeria; a study of mental illness in the community; a survey of working-class children's experience of grammar school education; a study of university students; and an inquiry into the effects of streaming in primary schools. The studies are supported by grants from charitable trusts, and the general activities of the Institute by a grant from the Nuffield Foundation.

Directors: Michael Young and Peter Willmott, 18 Victoria Park Sq., Bethnal Green, London, E2.

Institutional management, Training for This training is designed to prepare students to take responsibility for the domestic management of an institution where large numbers of people live or work, e.g. in educational establishments of all types, hospitals, factories, offices and hotels. It includes large-scale cookery and catering, science applied to health, institutional administration, personnel management, bookkeeping, first aid, applied art and the maintenance of fabric and equipment.

A few domestic science colleges offer a selection of courses. Much of their work has been transferred to technical colleges and comes under the aegis of the Industrial Training Act.

Further information from: British Dietetic Association, 251 Brompton Rd, London, SW3; Institution Management Association Inc., Swinton Hse, 324 Grays Inn Rd, London, WC1; National Council for Domestic Studies, 75 Ferme Park Rd, Crouch End, London, N8; City and Guilds Institute, 76 Portland Pl., London, W1.

RA

Instrument and articles of government Every secondary school maintained by an LEA must have a body of governors. The composition of the governing body, the method of appointing governors, their period of office, and the regulation of their proceedings, are specified in a statutory instrument of government. The instrument is made by an order of the LEA for a county school: by the Secretary of State for a voluntary school. It is a requirement of the Education Act 1944 that the number of governors of a county school and the manner of their appointment shall be determined by the LEA; and, for a voluntary school, by the Secretary of State, after consultation with the LEA. The Act also requires that two-thirds of the governors of a voluntary aided or special agreement school shall be foundation governors, who represent the voluntary interests, and one-third shall be appointed by the LEAs; and that for a voluntary controlled school, one-third shall be foundation governors, and two-thirds be appointed by the LEA.

Arrangements may be made by the LEA for grouping schools under one governing body, but if any voluntary schools are to be involved in any such arrangement, the consent of their governors must be obtained.

The powers of the governing body are specified in the statutory articles of government of the school, which also regulate its conduct. The articles must, in particular, determine the functions to be exercised in relation to the school, by the LEA, the governors, and the head teacher.

For a county school, the articles of government are made by the LEA, and are subject to approval by the Secretary of State; for voluntary schools, they are made by an order of the Secretary of State.

For advice given by the Board of Education on the problems involved, see *Principles of Government in Maintained Secondary Schools*, a White Paper issued in 1944. For specimen instruments and articles for different types of school, see W. P. A. Alexander and F. Barraclough, *County and Voluntary Schools* (Councils and Education Press, London, 1963).

FB

Instrument and rules of management Every primary school maintained by an LEA must have a body of managers. The constitution of the managing body, the method of appointing managers, their period of office, and the regulation of their proceedings, are specified in a statutory instrument of management. The instrument for a county primary school is made by the LEA; for a voluntary primary school, by the Secretary of State. The number of managers of a school must not be less than six, which is also the number normally allowed for a single school.

In county council areas, the representative managers are those appointed by the LEA and the minor authority for the school area. If the school is a voluntary school, the managers appointed by the voluntary interests are designated foundation managers. The minor authority means the council of a non-county borough, or of an urban district, or of a rural parish, which appears to the LEA to be the area served by the school. In rural areas in which there is no parish council, the parish meeting is the minor authority. If a school serves the area of two or more minor authorities, they must act jointly in the appointment of the minor authority managers.

For schools for which the number of managers is six, the instrument of management must provide as follows: (a) for a county school, six representative managers (four LEA, two minor authority); (b) for a voluntary controlled school, two foundation managers, four representative managers (two LEA, two minor authority); (c) for a voluntary aided or special agreement school, four foundation managers, two representative managers (one LEA, one minor authority).

In a county borough area there is no minor authority, and the LEA appoint all the representative managers. In the area of the ILEA, the county pattern of appointment obtains, the minor

N*

authority being the council of the Inner London Borough concerned, or in the City, the Common Council.

The Education Act 1944 permits the grouping of schools under one management. That arrangement is commonly followed in county boroughs for county schools, and in the urban areas of counties, with usually a larger body of managers than six. Maintained primary schools must be conducted in accordance with statutory Rules of Management. These rules are made by the LEA for both county and voluntary schools; but, in the case of voluntary aided schools, the LEA must first consult the managers concerning the provisions to be included in the rules regarding the appointment by the managers of teachers to be employed for giving secular instruction, and for enabling the LEA to give directions as to the educational qualifications of the teachers to be so employed.

For specimen Instruments and Rules of Management for the different kinds of primary schools, see W. P. A. Alexander and F. Barraclough, *County and Voluntary Schools* (Councils and Education Press, London, 1963).

FB

Insurance, Qualification in Qualifications in insurance are normally awarded on the basis of examinations conducted by the Chartered Insurance Institute (20 Aldermanbury, London, EC2). These fall into three parts: the preliminary examination, from which entrants with suitable GCE A level results may be exempted; the Associateship examination, in three parts, which may be taken in any of the branches of insurance and should take three years; and the Fellowship Diploma examination, which is in three sections and normally requires two years' study.

Integrated day This is an arrangement of the school day by which the pattern is set by the flow of the children's interests rather than by a pre-determined timetable.

See also **Infant schools**

Intellectual Co-operation, International Council for *See* **UNESCO**

Intelligence, Distribution of Research into the intelligence level of the general population, by administering tests to large numbers of either adults or children, has established a principle that the distribution of human abilities conforms to a regular pattern. When the IQ scores from such tests are plotted, an approximately bell-shaped curve results.

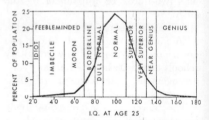

Distribution of IQs in the general population. (After Terman, *Measuring Intelligence*)

This curve is known as the normal or Gaussian distribution; one of its characteristics is that the IQs of about two-thirds of the sample fall near the average, or mean, between the range of 85 to 115. The curve evens out, with fewer and fewer scores appearing, as the extremities are reached. To obtain a perfect curve, a very large and unselected sample is needed for testing. If selection takes place (i.e. if the group tested are adults from a middle-class area, or are children from a grammar school) then the curve will be skewed and not symmetrical. The belief that the majority of people do not differ greatly from one another in their intelligence level was acted upon before research into intelligence provided confirmation of the belief. Mass entertainment, and most films, plays and books, are produced to appeal to this large audience whose intelligence lies within the normal range.

FURTHER READING

L. M. Terman and M. A. Merrill. *Measuring Intelligence*, Houghton Mifflin, New York, 1937.
P. E. Vernon. *Intelligence and Attainment Tests*, Univ. of London Press, 1960; *The Structure of Human Abilities*, Methuen, 1950; *The Measurement of Abilities*, Univ. of London Press, 1956.

EP

Intelligence quotient When mental tests are administered to very large numbers of children of certain ages it is possible to make an estimate of the standard of ability which characterises the various age groups, i.e. the nine-year-olds, the ten-year-olds and so on. A ten-year-old child who does as well in the test as the standard performance for the eleven-year-olds is said to have a mental age of eleven. The ratio of mental age to chronological age, expressed as a fraction (in this case, $\frac{11}{10}$), is multiplied by 100 to avoid the use of decimals, and the result is known as the intelligence quotient (usually written IQ). Thus the child cited above would have an IQ of 110 ($\frac{11}{10}$ x 100). This formula $\frac{MA}{CA}$ x 100 is generally employed as an index of an individual's brightness, and was first used in the Stanford-Binet tests of 1916, although W. Stern and F. Kuhlmann had mentioned earlier the need for some such concept in psychological testing.

Assuming that the child's environment (physical and emotional) remains stable, subsequent testing at later ages should produce the same quotient provided that the same test is used. On reliable tests, the average IQ is 100: one of 70 denotes an individual who is mentally defective and one of 130 a person of university standard. But there is a tendency for different tests to give varying results at the upper and lower reaches, i.e. although two tests would agree on an individual whose mental age was equal to his chronological age (IQ 100), an individual scoring an IQ of 130 on one test might show 150 on the other. So it is essential when comparing the IQs of different individuals to know whether they have been arrived at by the same test. To overcome the difficulties created when different tests are employed another method of expressing measured intelligence has been introduced known as *percentile* ranking. This is a method whereby the score obtained in a test is transformed into terms of the percentage of people taking the test. Thus a percentile of 50 indicates that the individual has an average score, percentiles higher than 50 indicate above-average performance and those below 50 an inferior performance. Percentiles can be converted into intelligence quotients by means of statistical tables, e.g. the percentile 75 is equivalent to an IQ of 110.

EP

Intelligence tests The term 'mental test' was first used in 1890 by an American psychologist, James McKeen Cattell, when administering individual tests to college students. The first group intelligence test was constructed in 1905 by two French psychologists, A. Binet (*q.v.*) and T. Simon, who produced the Binet-Simon Scale consisting of thirty problems arranged in ascending order of difficulty. This was adapted and revised, the most famous revision being that of L. M. Terman of Stanford University, USA, in 1916, known as the Stanford-Binet. In this test the term 'intelligence quotient' (*q.v.*), meaning the ratio between mental and chronological age, was first used. Later revisions of the test are still in use.

Research into the accuracy of tests has gone hand in hand with attempts to define and measure intelligence and special abilities and aptitudes. At first it was held that intelligence is an inherited quality which develops until maturity is reached in late adolescence, but which is incapable of being influenced by education or environment. Today the generally accepted theory is that an individual's intelligence develops as a result of the interaction between normal physical development and the stimulus provided by environment. If a child attends a school where the teaching secures his interest and both stimulates and satisfies his curiosity, making him eager to learn, and if his home background encourages his interests, it is known that his measured intelligence will improve. Because of this effect of environment on measured intelligence, intelligence tests are no longer regarded as reliable guides for estimating an individual's performance over a long period, but are fairly reliable as short-term predictors when there is less likelihood of environmental change.

Attempts have been made, chiefly by C. L. Burt and B. S. Burke, to estimate the genetic component in intelligence test scores, 75% to 80% being given as the likely contribution. These claims are disputed by P. E. Vernon and others (See *Further reading* for publications), whose researches show that the grasping of patterns and reasoning skills (needed for the solution of intelligence tests) are developed by the ethos of an individual's upbringing, whether it is restrictive or permissive, or favourable or unfavourable to the development of resourcefulness.

There are two schools of thought concerning the nature of intelligence today: (1) that propounded by C. Spearman and others, that there is a single factor of intelligence (labelled g); and (2) that propounded by E. L. Thorndike, L. L. Thurstone and others, that intelligence is not a single entity but is the combination of a number of distinct abilities. A good working definition of intelligence is given by P. E. Vernon, who calls it 'the name given to the overall efficiency and level of complexity of an individual's cognitive processes'. These cognitive processes depend on underlying mental structures which psychologists call by various names, e.g. bonds, connections, plans, associations or schemata. Some people are born with genes which are more favourable to the development of cognitive schemata than others, but these may not develop to the fullest possible extent unless stimulated by the emotional, physical and cultural environment of the individual which should provide interest and motivation. Psychologists at present accept it as unlikely that a test will be constructed to isolate and measure the hereditary factor in intelligence. D. C. Hebb faces the situation by differentiating between (1) intelligence A, the genetic potential which cannot be measured, and (2) intelligence B, which is revealed in thought and behaviour and is the result of environment interacting on intelligence A. Different tests produce different results when B is measured, so until tests become more accurate psychologists now speak of intelligence C, the result of attempting to measure B.

In the UK, intelligence tests are constructed chiefly by the National Foundation for Educational Research in England and Wales, at Upton Park, Slough, and by Moray House in Edinburgh. Because of the failure to agree on what constitutes intelligence, the term 'intelligence test' is slowly disappearing, being replaced by 'reasoning tests' in the UK and by 'classification and screening tests' in the USA.

Of the construction of reasoning tests for children the following description is taken from a booklet published by the National Foundation for Educational Research: 'The content of the test, the level of difficulty of each question and the distribution of score on the test as a whole are planned before the test is made. These questions are tried out in draft form in two or more schools to get a wide range of ability and the scripts are marked and analysed. Results of the test as a whole and results on each individual question are considered, weak questions are discarded or re-phrased, and the questions that have been found to be discriminating (i.e. when the question tends to be answered correctly more often by the children who do better on the test as a whole) are tried out again. This process is repeated until finally all the questions included in the test have proved to be discriminating, and the distribution of score on the test as a whole has proved to be close to what was planned. On the final try-out, evidence of the validity of the test is collected. Scores are correlated with scores on other tests of the same subject and with teachers' estimates of each pupil's attainment, and the test is sent out to experienced teachers for comment and criticism. If the test is found to be satisfactory, it is then printed and standardised'.

In the UK a mean of 100 is adopted for standardised tests, with a standard deviation of 15 (so that normal ability falls within the 85 to 115 range). The distribution of a standardised score is given below:

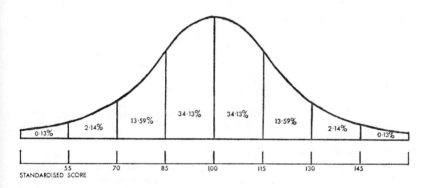

2.3% of the standardisation sample score 70 or below
13.6% score between 70 and 85
68.2% score between 85 and 115   (i.e. 100 ± 15)
13.6% score between 115 and 130
2.3% score 130 or above.

In the construction of the tests themselves the type of question has moved away from those which are marked according to the subjective judgment of the examiner (e.g. essay questions) towards those which can be answered correctly or incorrectly, ensuring uniformity of marking. Research has shown that test sophistication (*q.v.*) can have a bearing on scores.

Currently there has been a swing towards a belief in the multiple factor view of intelligence, based on the work by J. P. Guilford and others at the University of Southern California. Two American psychologists, J. W. Getzels and P. W. Jackson, are critical of the conventional objective tests in that these favour the performer who is conformist and of a non-creative turn of mind. Selecting for higher education and special training the non-creative and conformist individual may in the long run be to society's detriment. Work is being done to construct tests to measure divergent thinking, composed of questions for which there are no right answers but which nevertheless reveal creativity.

FURTHER READING
C. Spearman. *The Abilities of Man*, Macmillan, 1927.
D. C. Hebb. *The Organisation of Behaviour*, Wiley, New York, 1948.
. Piaget. *The Psychology of Intelligence*, Routledge, 1950.
L. M. Terman and M. A. Merrill. *Measuring Intelligence*, Harrap, 1937.
R. L. Thorndike. *Test and Measurement Techniques: Personnel Selection*, Chapman and Hall, 1949.
P. E. Vernon. *The Structure of Human Abilities*, Methuen, 1950. *Intelligence Testing*, Times Publishing Co., 1952. *Personality Tests and Assessments*, Methuen, 1953. *The Measurement of Abilities*, Univ. of London Press, 1956.

EP

Inter-Varsity Fellowship of Evangelical Unions Commonly known by the initials IVF, this body links the Christian Unions in all the universities, colleges of education, technical colleges and other colleges of higher education throughout the UK. These Christian Unions share a common doctrinal basis embodying the main elements of the orthodox Protestant confessions and rooted in the authority of the Bible and the centrality of the atoning death of the Son of God. Their principal aim is to be witnessing Christian societies within their universities and colleges and their principal activities are directed towards a better understanding of the Christian faith.

Each Christian Union is an autonomous, student-led body, but the IVF provides advisory services through its travelling secretaries, organises conferences and house parties, and publishes Christian books and a termly magazine. There are also specialist departments dealing with the needs of overseas students, and of theological students. The Graduates' Fellowship links Christian graduates in all walks of life, and has its own quarterly journal *The Christian Graduate*. The publishing department has produced in recent years an increasing number of works reflecting current evangelical scholarship, notably the New Bible

Dictionary and the Tyndale Commentaries on individual books of the Bible.

While the Christian Unions at Cambridge and Oxford and in some of the London Medical Schools can trace their history back to the 19th century, the Inter-Varsity Fellowship began to take shape at the first Inter-Varsity Conference in December 1919, and a number of university Christian Unions were formally brought together in the Inter-Varsity Fellowship in 1928. Internationally the Inter-Varsity Fellowship has co-operated with similar movements in other countries in a number of conferences since 1934, leading to the formation of the International Fellowship of Evangelical Students in 1947, a body of which the British Inter-Varsity Fellowship is a constituent member.

39 Bedford Sq., London, WC1.

Interdisciplinary enquiry (IDE) is the keystone of the new fourfold curriculum envisaged by teachers working with University of London Goldsmiths' College Curriculum Laboratory. These were experienced teachers from secondary schools attending pilot courses from 1965 onwards. Seeking to devise an education appropriate to young people growing up in a rapidly changing world, they argued that: (1) Much secondary education is totally unrelated to the interests and developmental needs of adolescents. (2) It does not give them experience of successfully identifying and exploring together problems which they recognise as important. (3) By its divisive and competitive nature it denies them the opportunity to gain confidence in themselves and each other. (4) Much schooling rewards only conventional thinking and accurate memorising, yet the sciences, physical and human, pure and applied, as well as the arts, all call for imaginative, flexible, perceptive behaviour, as do the ordinary problems of living our lives. (5) Hence education should be based on *enquiry*, interpreted broadly to include exploration (of materials and ideas), self-discovery and growth in perception of other people, and the creation and testing of hypotheses in both theoretical and practical studies. (6) Since most fundamental questions reach beyond subject barriers, an enquiry-based education must necessarily be largely *interdisciplinary*. (7) Owing to the increasing complexities of knowledge, education should stress acquiring the skills and interpretative concepts of the disciplines rather than subject matter, and this involves for part of the curriculum a co-operative interdisciplinary study, with specialist teachers acting as advisers and consultants.

IDE is thus sharply contrasted both with any attempt to diminish the importance of the disciplines as coherent intellectual or aesthetic systems, and with a merely integrated curriculum which denies to students the discovery of relationships and the satisfactions of collaborative exploration, only the teachers being creative. The task of students and teachers is seen as one of *collaborative learning*. In this situation, the class lesson is out of key and students spend most of their time working in small groups or individually.

The full IDE-based curriculum has four elements to meet different aspects of students' needs: (1) *IDE* undertaken in blocked periods (up to 50% of the time-table for younger secondary pupils); (2) *autonomous studies* with specialist teachers working separately; (3) *'remedial'* education, the coaching needed by all pupils at different times to counteract weaknesses or provide a groundwork for new advances; (4) *special interests*, pursued in mixed age-groups. This flexible planning is designed to meet the needs of children of all kinds and degrees of talent and achievement, and is seen as an important advance on both streaming and non-streaming in the opportunity it gives to students to group and re-group

according to their changing requirements, interests and likings.

Since 1965 IDE is increasingly being introduced in all kinds of secondary schools, secondary modern, comprehensive and grammar, on an experimental basis.

FURTHER READING

Ideas No. 1 and *Ideas No. 2*, (bulletins obtainable from Univ. of London Goldsmiths' College Curriculum Laboratory, 6 Dixon Rd, New Cross, London, SE14).
Charity James. 'The Schools and Social Change', *Forum*, October 1965. *Changing Perspectives in Secondary Education*, Pergamon Press, 1968.
Peter Mauger. 'The Extra Year', *New Education*, June 1966.
Pilot Course Reports, Univ. of London Goldsmiths' College.

CJ

Intermediate education Under the Welsh (Intermediate Education) Act 1889, intermediate education was defined as a 'course of education which does not consist chiefly of elementary instruction in reading, writing and arithmetic, but which includes instruction in Latin, Greek, the Welsh and English languages and literature, modern languages, mathematics, natural and applied science, &c.'

International Bureau of Education The Bureau, founded at Geneva in 1925, is an inter-governmental institution whose aim is to serve as a centre for educational information, documentation and research. Each year it convenes an International Conference on Public Education, since 1947 jointly with UNESCO, at which the annual reports from ministries of education on educational developments are presented and the Bureau's inquiries on current problems discussed prior to the adoption of recommendations.

The Bureau's publications (in French and English) are: *Bulletin of the International Bureau of Education, Educational Bibliography, International Educational Card Index Service, International*

Yearbook of Education and reports on comparative education.
Palais Wilson, Geneva.

International Copyright Union *See* **Berne Convention**

International Correspondence Schools Started as a public service over 70 years ago to help lessen the dangers of coal mining, International Correspondence Schools has played a prominent part in the development of education by correspondence, both in the UK and overseas. ICS offers a wide range of specially prepared home-study courses in general education, commercial and technical subjects (including preparation for the major examinations), as well as a number of leisure courses.

Through its associated companies — International Textbook Co. Ltd and International Educational Services — ICS is also concerned with the publication of a comprehensive list of technical books, and is the sole concessionaire in the UK and commonwealth for Berlitz language records.

Intertext House, Parkgate Rd, London, SW11.

International Office of Education (Geneva) *See* **Comparative education**

International Voluntary Service The aim of IVS (the British branch of Service Civil International) is, without regard to national frontiers, to give assistance in cases of natural catastrophe or of need, or with work that is publicly useful. In this way, through voluntary helpers, it aims to spread across the barriers that divide men a new spirit that will make war between the nations morally impossible. In Britain, IVS organises week-end workcamps (through local branches and groups) and international voluntary workcamps. It also recruits volunteers for service in short-term camps overseas or for longer periods in the developing countries.
91 High St, Harlesden, NW1.

Invalid Children's Aid Association Maintains four boarding special schools — two for boys with asthma and allied conditions, and two for children with communication difficulties caused by minimal brain damage or emotional disturbance. It also runs a day centre for the study and treatment of specific developmental dyslexia (word blindness). The Association administers a casework service in London and the home counties for families where the presence of an invalid child causes difficulties in relationships within the family or problems of a more practical nature. 'Invalid' is taken to cover physical handicaps, long-term illnesses such as heart disease or cancer, emotional disturbances and psychosomatic conditions.
Gen. Sec.: Miss Eileen Hilton, 4 Palace Gate, London, W8.

Iran, Education in In 1943 a law was passed to make possible the establishment of compulsory education by gradual stages, and in 1960 two-thirds of the child population was in school. The education system is highly centralised, the curriculum of primary and secondary schools being drawn up by the Ministry of Education. In state schools elementary education is free, but a small charge is made in secondary schools. 1966 statistics: 23,725 primary schools (2,181,633 enrolments); 3,540 secondary schools (493,735 enrolments); technical and vocational enrolments 15,160; teacher training enrolments 4,738; higher education enrolments 28,982. There are seven universities.

The country's population was approximately 26 million in 1966.

Iraq, Education in Education is free but not compulsory, the primary stage being six to 12 and the secondary 12 to

17 years. Arabic is the medium of instruction in most schools, but Kurdish is used in some primary schools in northern districts. There are two universities at Baghdad, one of that name and one the university of Al-Hikma. 1964/65 statistics: 4,430 primary schools (947,646 enrolments); 535 secondary schools (214,370 enrolments); 45 vocational training centres (10,303 enrolments); 29 teacher training colleges (6,867 enrolment); 45 technical colleges (8,011 enrolments); 38 higher education establishments (24,662 enrolments).

The population of the country was approximately 8¼ million in 1965.

Ireland, Northern, Education in Northern Ireland was set up in 1921 as an integral part of the UK but with its own parliament and government, autonomous in home affairs, including the education of a population now about 1½ million in two county borough and six county education areas.

The educational system has its foundations in the Education Act 1923 under which the LEAs were established and in which provision was made for LEA and voluntary management of schools. The 1947 Act, corresponding to the 1944 Act for England and Wales and the 1946 Act for Scotland, provides the framework of the present system which is closely related to that in England and Wales. *Growth of school population* From 1947/48 to 1965/66, the number of full-time school pupils increased by about 45% from 211,000 to 306,000 approximately. The factors contributory to this growth include the raising of the school leaving age to 15 in 1957, a higher birth rate and the increasing tendency for pupils to remain beyond the school leaving age in secondary intermediate (modern) and grammar schools. In the same period the number of teachers increased from about 6,600 to 12,250.

Primary schools In 1966 there were 1,400 primary schools (688 voluntary, 712 county), roughly half of the total being one-teacher or two-teacher rural schools. The policy of closing and amalgamating small, outworn, unhygienic schools on both educational and financial grounds has been intensified following publication of the White Paper *Educational Development in Northern Ireland* (1964).

About 40% of the pupils are in buildings provided or remodelled since 1948. In 1966 only about 5½% of the total primary school population aged 12 and over were still attending all-age (unreorganised) schools. Since 1948 the pupil-teacher ratio has been improved from 34.6:1 to 29.6:1, and the number of classes with over 40 pupils has been reduced from about 1,900 to about 700.

Secondary education The most important reform of the 1947 Act was the requirement for the provision of secondary education for all pupils over 11. A new type of secondary school was to be provided—secondary intermediate. By 1966 there were 143 such schools, and reorganisation is nearing completion. At a number of these schools extensions are already in hand for the planned raising of the school leaving age to 16 in 1972. The most marked development in secondary education has been in the scope and variety of courses introduced to meet the wide range of abilities, aptitudes and interests of pupils at these schools, some of which, for geographical and other reasons, have become comprehensive in character.

The system includes well-established voluntary grammar schools—59 out of a total of 81; 43 grammar schools (13 county and 30 voluntary) have preparatory departments. Since 1948 the number of pupils at grammar schools has more than doubled, the increase being particularly significant in the number taking GCE at A level.

An important contribution in secondary education has been made by technical intermediate schools (county intermediate schools in association with institutions of further education). These schools are being discontinued as similar courses are now available in many secondary intermediate schools.

In the White Paper of 1964 attention was drawn to disadvantages of the selective system and qualified encouragement was announced for experiments designed to dispense with selection. Since then a few comprehensive schools have been created or approved and a two-tier system is to come into operation in the Craigavon 'new city' area.

Further education There is a wide and varied range of full-time and part-time courses from evening classes in cookery at small remote centres to degree courses at the College of Technology, Belfast. In addition to three central institutions, the Belfast Colleges of Technology, Art and Domestic Science, there are about 27 institutions with 60 or so other centres. The work of these 27 institutions is now being co-ordinated at two levels—local and area.

Since 1948 full-time and day release enrolments have increased from 729 to 9,383 and from 958 to 9,585 respectively. In recent years there has been an encouraging expansion in National Certificate and City and Guilds of London Institute courses. A large increase in day release is expected as a result of the Industrial Training Act 1964.

Teachers There are three general training colleges—Stranmillis (1,200 students), St Mary's (400) and St Joseph's (300). Specialist teachers are trained in the Ulster College of Physical Education (women), the Belfast College of Domestic Science and the Belfast College of Art. The Department of Education of the Queen's University, Belfast, provides a one-year course for graduates. In recent years there has been a marked increase in the number of students attending colleges in Great Britain. Since 1948 the general colleges have provided a three-year course for primary and a four-year course for secondary teachers.

Higher education In 1965 the Report of the Committee on Higher Education under the chairmanship of the late Sir John Lockwood was published. As recommended in the Report, the general training colleges are to be designated 'colleges of education' to be associated with the proposed Institute of Education at Queen's University and to provide three-year courses as well as a course leading to the degree of BEd. A new university is to be established at Coleraine for 2,000/3,000 students by 1973 and with up to 1,000 extra places for student teachers in an education centre which will open in 1968. Magee University College, Londonderry, with about 350 students, is to become a constituent college of the new university. Queen's University with 4,700 students in 1965/66 is to be expanded for 7,000 students. A new central institution to be called the Ulster College is to be established in the Belfast area and will eventually include the Belfast College of Domestic Science, the Belfast College of Art, a new Regional College of Technology and other colleges catering for the whole of Northern Ireland.

Scholarships Grammar school, university and further education scholarships are on the English pattern, the grants for university scholarships being identical with those in England and Wales.

Grants For primary, secondary and special school buildings and improvements, the Ministry of Education makes grants of 65% to LEAs and voluntary managers. Voluntary managers of these schools receive a 65% grant from the Ministry of Education and LEAs for external and internal main tenance respectively. The cost of the salaries and superannuation of teachers in these schools is met in full from central and local government funds and there is an arrangement for these and other items of expenditure to be shared between the LEAs.

School meals service This service is run on the lines of the system in England and Wales. The government bears the whole cost of milk for pupils at all types of school and the net cost of the meals service at primary, secondary and special schools.

Youth Employment Service The Service is administered for the whole of Northern Ireland by the Northern Ireland Youth Employment Service Board which includes representatives of education committees and other bodies.

Youth welfare and physical recreation The youth service is administered under the Youth Welfare, Physical Training and Recreation Act 1962 by the Ministry of Education which is empowered to pay grants to voluntary organisations. A Youth and Sports Council acts in an advisory capacity.

WJD

Ireland (Republic of), Education in
Education in the Republic of Ireland was organised and has developed in three branches—primary, post-primary and university. Attendance at school is compulsory for children between six and 14.

Article 42 of the Constitution sets out the principles underlying education in Ireland. Emphasis is laid on the rights of the family as 'the primary and natural educator of the child' and on those of the state 'as guardian of the common good'.

All primary schools, called 'national schools' when provided and organised by the state, are managed by clergymen and are denominational in character. Post-primary education includes the independent, privately-owned secondary schools as well as the state-owned vocational and technical schools. The secondary schools may be described as denominational; they are owned by religious bodies or boards of governors or individuals.

There are two universities in the Republic; the National University of Ireland, which is organised on a federal basis with three constituent colleges and a recognised college, and the University of Dublin, comprising one constituent college, Trinity College. Both universities are self-governing institutions, but they receive aid from the state in the form of annual grants, including, from time to time, grants for capital.

The Ministry of Education (known in the Republic as the 'Department') controls the education provided in primary, secondary, vocational, reformatory and industrial schools. (Vocational schools are managed by local education committees but are in most matters subject to the sanction and control of the Ministry.)

Both primary and vocational schools are free of charge and open to all. The secondary schools have always charged fees and also exercised the right to accept or reject pupils. Increased state grants are now being offered to all such schools as are prepared to abolish fees.

Instruction in primary schools is usually confined to Irish, English, arithmetic, history and geography, but special emphasis is laid on the Irish language. Vocational education comprises continuation courses intended to supplement the education provided in primary schools, and technical courses which provide specialised training towards particular trades or professions. Pupils in secondary schools follow courses in a wide range of subjects leading to the Intermediate Certificate Examination, usually taken at 15-plus, and the Leaving Certificate Examination taken two years later. Both of these are state examinations.

Primary teachers, on completing their secondary school course, are trained for a period of two years at one of the recognised training colleges. Vocational teachers, other than those who are graduates, are trained in special colleges. Secondary teachers, to qualify for registration, must be university graduates who have taken a post-graduate diploma in education, or graduates of a college of art, of domestic science or of physical training.

The manager appoints the teacher in the primary schools and the state pays his entire salary. In secondary and vocational schools the appointment rests with the school authorities subject to the minister's sanction. The state pays the salary of vocational teachers in full, but in the case of secondary teachers the school pays the basic salary and the state the incremental portion (over 75%).

TJMcE

Irish National Teachers' Association This organisation secures legal protection for its 12,000 members, and negotiates salaries and sickness benefits. 35 Parnell Sq., Dublin, 1.

Publication: *The National Teacher* (monthly).

Isaacs, Susan (1885–1948) A psychologist and trained teacher, Susan Isaacs did her most famous work when she was principal of the Malting House School in Cambridge (1924–27). This was a private school with never more than twenty pupils from two to ten years old, almost all of whom were exceptionally intelligent. They were provided with a multitude of things to do with the emphasis very much on finding out how things worked—from practical biology to the workings of the school drainage system. The atmosphere was free but business-like, with more emphasis upon intellectual curiosity than self-expression.

From this experience Susan Isaacs wrote her two most famous books about children's intellectual and social growth. They were based upon a succession of minutely observed and recorded incidents concerning the children, duly interpreted and generally commented

on in the texts of her books. Particular importance was given to how children cope with their problems of aggression and sexual curiosity, and some of the conclusions are critical of Piaget (*q.v.*), since Susan Isaacs found that a number of her pupils seemed to be racing through stages of intellectual growth far more quickly than Piaget had suggested was possible.

FURTHER READING
Susan Isaacs. *The Intellectual Growth of Young Children*, Routledge and Kegan Paul, 1930. *The Social Development of Young Children*, Routledge and Kegan Paul, 1937.

NT

Isle of Man, Education in Education in the Isle of Man is governed by the Education Acts of 1949, 1955 and 1961, together with the Education (Young People's Welfare) Act of 1944. Copies of these can be obtained from the Government Treasurer, Government Office, Douglas, Isle of Man.

Israel, Education in
Historical background Under the British Mandatory Government, Jewish education in Palestine was to a large extent the responsibility of the Jewish Agency (the central representative body of the Zionist movement). In 1932 the Jewish Agency transferred its responsibilities in the field of education to the Vaad Leumi, the National Committee of the Jewish Community in Palestine. Both the Mandatory Government and the Jewish Agency supported Jewish education with financial grants to the extent of about 20% of the total budget, while the onus of finding the remaining 80% was borne by the Vaad Leumi, by local authorities and the parents of the pupils themselves. There was as yet no law of compulsory education, but, as far as the Jewish community was concerned, at least elementary education was universal.

Jewish schools were divided into three trends reflecting the various ideological divisions within the Zionist movement. These were the Labour trend, the General Zionist (middle-class) trend and the national-religious (Mizrahi) trend. The ultra-orthodox Agudat Israel organisation sponsored schools of its own which formed a fourth trend.

Government support was more lavish to the Arab population. The local authorities had only to erect the school buildings, while government provided the teachers, furniture, equipment and books. The number of Arab children attending school was comparatively high, second only to the mainly Christian state of the Lebanon.

In 1948 the newly established state of Israel took over the complete educational system from the Mandatory authorities. Hebrew was the main language of instruction and spoken universally both at home and at school. The demographic situation changed completely after the War of Independence in 1948. From a Jewish community of 650,000 in May 1948, through increased immigration following the establishment of the state, the figure rose to 1,400,000 by the end of 1951. (In 1967 the figure was over 2½ million.) In the course of the hostilities a substantial part of the Arab population fled to the neighbouring Arab states and out of 700,000 only 150,000 remained. This number has now grown through natural increase to some 300,000 while the unification of Jerusalem in 1967 and inclusion of the Gaza strip and West Bank of Jordan within the borders of Israel led to a considerable additional increase in the number of Arabs.

In 1949 the Compulsory Education Law was passed which made education free and compulsory for all children from the age of five to 14, without distinction of race, religion or sex. In 1953 a second law was enacted, the State Education Law, abolishing the trend system and aiming at the 'depoliticisation' of education. This law eliminated the undue influence of divergent ideologies. Henceforth, state schools were divided into state general schools, state religious schools, and the independent orthodox schools of Agudat Israel which are recognised under the law and assisted by government grants. The labour trend of mandatory times survives in the schools of the kibbutzim (collective agricultural settlements) which are run on free and progressive lines.

The enforcement of these two Education Laws has led to a centralisation of education, vesting responsibility in the Ministry of Education. This facilitates the enforcement of uniform standards on a population consisting mainly of immigrants with diverse cultural backgrounds, a population of which almost a third (733,000 —including 72,000 non-Jews—in 1966) attends school.

The educational structure One year of compulsory kindergarten attendance at the age of five is followed by eight years of primary school and four years of secondary school (1+8+4). At present there is a tendency to change this structure to 1+6+6 and there are already many secondary schools which accept pupils at the age of 12-plus. Secondary education is divided into academic (grammar), technical and agricultural. The pupils are guided into the school type for which they are most suited on the basis of the nationwide *Seker* (survey) examination at the age of 13-plus and their school records. At the end of the secondary course they take the *Bagrut* (Maturity) examination, roughly equivalent to the German *Reifeprüfung* or the British GCE A level. The fact that graduates of the four-year courses at the technical and agricultural schools have access to institutes of the calibre of the Technion (Israel Institute of Technology at Haifa) and the Weitzmann Institute of Rhovoth Faculty of Agriculture enhances the standing of these two types

393

of schools, which tend to be regarded as being of lesser prestige than the academic secondary schools.

Fees charged at secondary schools are graded according to the income of the parents. Children of the poorer strata of society are exempted.

The character of Israeli Jewish schools All Jewish schools include a strong Hebraic element in the curriculum, emphasised still more in the religious schools. The teaching of the Hebrew Bible forms part of the curriculum at all school levels, while the study of Jewish history and Rabbinics also forms a part of the syllabus. The curricula aim at a fusion of the Hebraic tradition and Western culture, despite obvious difficulties inherent in such an attempt. Speciali- sation is not as prominent as in the British system.

From an organisational aspect, in spite of the aim of centralisation, there is a tendency to encourage the muni- cipalities of towns and local councils of rural settlements to bear part of the responsibility for their children's education. Thus education departments have been established in town councils and municipalities, and even in smaller rural settlements there is an education officer who assumes the responsibility for local schools. This system leads to a certain amount of retention of freedom within a framework of co-operation and partnership with the central authority.

Arab education The policy of the Israeli Ministry of Education aims, in addition to the general education given in all schools, at fostering in the Arab schools: (1) the values inherent in their national-religious tradition, and (2) loyalty to the State of Israel. Hence, their curricula tend to emphasise the literary culture of the Arabs, including their religious diversification, Moslem, Christian or Druze. Hebrew is taught as a first foreign language already at primary-school level. The compulsory education act is enforced for girls as for boys, and this has wrought profound changes in the social structure of the Arab population in Israel, leading to gradual equalisation of the status of women with men in Arab society.

The problem of integration With the mass influx of immigrants from Middle Eastern and North African countries there has arisen the problem of smooth integration of the children of these communities (which now form 50% of the school population) into the Euro- pean-oriented educational system. This represents a challenging problem. To facilitate the absorption of these children into the existing system of education the following measures have been taken: (1) Adaptation of teaching methods to the special requirements of these children. (2) Free tuition at kindergarten from the age of four, where teachers 'make an effort to develop the children's powers of observation, to cultivate their voca- bularies and speaking ability, to advance logical thinking, to impart general knowledge and awaken a first understanding of number, space and direction'. (3) Curtailment of size of classes at primary schools. (4) Increase of hours of instruction (long school day). (5) Special advancement programme, including supervision of homework preparation by the children's own teachers. (6) Modification of secondary- school education to accommodate the special requirements of the children. Secondary education on 'comprehen- sive' lines, the creation of special two or three-year courses of post-primary education with a vocational bias. (7) Free boarding-school facilities for gifted children. (8) Free courses for youths serving in the army who have not completed their education at element- ary or secondary school level, as well as special courses for secondary-school graduates aiming at continuing their studies at one of Israel's universities.

FURTHER READING
Joseph S. Bentwich. *Education in Israel*, Routledge and Kegan Paul, 1965.

Educational Encyclopedia, Vol. 4 (in Hebrew), Ministry of Education and Culture and the Bialik Institute, Jerusalem, 1964.
Government Year Book 1967 (in Hebrew), Government Printing Office, Jerusalem.
Zvi E. Kurzweil. *Modern Trends in Jewish Education*, Barnes, New York, 1964.
Saul B. Robinsohn. 'Problems of Education in Israel', *Comparative Education Review*, VII, 2, New York, October 1963.

ZEK

I.t.a. *See* **Initial teaching alphabet**

ITA Educational Advisory Council *See* **Educational Advisory Council, Independent Television Authority**

ITA educational television School programmes have been shown on Independent Television since 1957, and regular series of adult education programmes were introduced in 1963.

School programmes ITV is a decentralised system of 15 mutually independent programme companies, each providing broadcasts for transmission by the Independent Television Authority, the government appointed body responsible for the service. One company operates at weekends only; the other 14 show school programmes, most of which are produced, for nation-wide 'net-working', by four large weekday companies, Thames Television, ATV Network, Granada and Yorkshire Television. But, in keeping with the decentralised regional pattern of ITV, additional programmes for local presentation are also produced by Scottish Television, Grampian Television, Tyne Tees Television and Harlech Television. There are at the time of writing (November 1968) seven weekly programme series for primary and nine for secondary schools, ranging from infants to sixth forms. Schools programmes represent 13–14% of weekly programme time and by November 1968 over 21,000 schools of all types had registered with the companies as 'intending viewers'.

Each year at Easter a booklet is distributed to all schools in the UK giving times and descriptions of series planned for the following school year; more detailed programme notes on individual series are also provided. Programmes are conceived as both supplementary and complementary to the work of the classroom teacher although this does not rule out the direct teaching approach where appropriate. All curriculum subjects are covered, especially science, geography, history, foreign languages, mathematics, English and social studies. Particular attention is given to the help that broadcasting can offer in areas of curriculum development, e.g. 'new' mathematics, primary French, sixth-form general studies.

Companies producing school programmes have advisory committees and education officers, as well as school liaison officers, who maintain contact with the educational world in their respective regions. Volunteer panels of viewing teachers comment on programmes to their regional company. On general educational policy, the ITA has the advice of an Educational Advisory Council assisted by two programme committees—the Schools Committee and the Adult Education Committee.

Adult education programmes These have been broadcast regularly by ITV since January 1963. Not being tied to institutional educational patterns, the adult education output cannot be as tidily described or defined as the school broadcasts can be. A nucleus of nationally networked programmes has been regularly transmitted on Sundays since 1963. On all other days of the week, adult education programmes may be seen in one or other of the 14 ITV regions. These are often produced by regional companies in consultation with LEAs and local universities.

During spring 1968 there were 24 different regular series being screened over the system as a whole. These included foreign languages, history, literature, music, psychology, sociology and local government. The vocational element is represented by programmes for farmers, doctors, teachers, etc. O level geography and physics series have been provided in conjunction with special correspondence courses.

Research has shown that a major part of the adult audience for educational television is made up of people who do not attend classes.

JW

Italian, Association of Teachers of The ATI was founded in 1966 by a group of teachers of the language to improve facilities for the teaching and study of Italian in Britain. There was a dearth of suitable text-books and annotated texts, and virtually no opportunities existed for pupils to study the language in Italy. The Association publishes a newsletter for the exchange of news and views of interest to teachers of Italian, and has set up sub-committees concerned with audio-visual material, text-books and examinations. A month's study course for pupils was held at the University of Perugia in the summer of 1967; a refresher course for teachers has been held, and others planned, and many members are playing an active part on examining boards.

Gen. Sec.: Denis J. Devereux, Sir John Leman Grammar School, Beccles, Suffolk.

Italian Institute The Institute provides lectures, concerts, films, exhibitions and discussion groups, and a library of books, newspapers and periodicals.

39 Belgrave Sq., London, SW1.

Italy, Education in Education is not compulsory from three to five years, but compulsory from six to 14. The elementary span is divided into primary (six to 11 years) and junior secondary (11 to 14 years). Senior secondary span provides specialisation in classical, scientific and technical education (which includes agriculture). 1965 statistics: 18,905 kindergartens (1,340,840 enrolments); 37,855 state primary schools (4,090,334 enrolments), 2,880 private primaries (336,684 enrolments); 5,231 junior secondary schools (1,610,900 enrolments); 1,999 senior secondary schools (990,917 enrolments); 30 universities and higher education establishments (281,423 enrolments). In the South Tirol, schools are classified according to the mother tongue of the pupils: 29,536 primary and junior secondary pupils and 9,150 senior secondary pupils were taught in German, 8,836 primary and junior secondary and 8,503 senior secondary were taught in Italian.

The country's population was approximately 53 million in 1966.

Ivory Coast, Education in In 1964/65 there were 1,857 primary schools (enrolment 425,251—330,551 in state schools, 94,700 in private schools); 79 secondary schools (enrolment 28,541 —20,229 state, 8,312 private); 10 technical schools (enrolment 2,704). The University of Abidjan had 1,938 students.

The country's population was approximately 4 million in 1966.

J

Jamaica, Education in Primary education from the age of six to 15 years is compulsory. In 1965 there were 739 government-aided primary schools with an enrolment of 323,527; 53 secondary (enrolment 25,494); eight post-secondary (enrolment 1,651)—consisting of six teacher training colleges, a school of agriculture and a college of science, arts and technology. The University of Jamaica, at Mona, has an enrolment of 3,038 and is open to students from all the islands of the West Indies.

Total population in 1966 was approximately 1¾ million.

See also **West Indies, Education in the**

James, William (1842–1910) American psychologist and philosopher and brother of the novelist, Henry James, William James was one of the founders of pragmatism (his own brand of this he named 'radical empiricism'). Rejecting metaphysical systems, he nevertheless allowed that a working hypothesis might be of a religious as well as a scientific character, since, as he held, it is not the truth of a belief that makes it work, but the fact that it works that makes it true. With Lange he propounded the theory that physiological changes produce emotions, rather than the reverse: that is to say, we do not take to our heels because we are afraid, but are afraid because we have taken to our heels. His most direct contribution to educational discussion lies in his *Talks to Teachers on Psychology*,

and to *Students on Some of Life's Ideals*, published in 1899.

Japan, Education in The modern history of Japan's educational system began in 1868, when a national policy intended to bring about the modernisation of the country was launched with the Five Articles of the Imperial Oath.

Before that date, each feudal clan under the Tokugawa Shogunate had two kinds of school—the *hanko* and the *gogaku*. Besides these (about 200 of each) there were some 30,000 private elementary schools called *terakoya*, one in nearly every village. The *hanko* was a high school, attaching special importance to Confucianism and the military arts. The *gogaku* and *terakoya* aimed chiefly at teaching the three Rs. There was no uniform length of course at any of the three kinds of school; very few girls were educated in them; and the numbers attending the schools fluctuated considerably.

Keio University, the oldest in Japan, was established in Edo (now Tokyo) in 1858, at first as a Dutch institute. The imperial university, Teikoku-daigaku (now Tokyo University), was founded in 1877, also as a development of a special institute.

In 1871, the year when clans were abolished and prefectures set up, the Department of Education was established; and in the following year the country's first centralised system of education came into being. The objectives, content and methods of education were radically changed, and

397

elementary schooling became compulsory. At first the minimum length of the elementary course was one year; but in 1880 two courses were introduced, lower and higher, each of four years' duration, and the former compulsory. Only a year later a new division was made into three courses, a lower (three years), a middle (three years) and a higher (two years), the lower again being compulsory. By the beginning of this century the compulsory system was complete.

An added impetus was given to the process by the Imperial Rescript on Education of 1890, which led to the rationalisation of the course of study through the elementary schools to higher institutions of education, and to the establishment of industrial and other special schools.

In 1907 compulsory education was extended to six years. Attendance rates increased from 47.36 in 1888 to 99.43 in 1925 (the figures for boys at these dates were 63 and 99.47; for girls, 30.21 and 99.38).

In the 1930s, against a background of international disturbance, Japan's educational system was steadily consolidated in terms of a nationalistic philosophy. In 1941 the elementary school was renamed *kokumin-gakko* (national school), and the higher grade (covering two years) was made compulsory in addition to the six-year first grade. This new compulsory system was not completely achieved, however, when war broke out in the Pacific and threw Japan's educational system into utter confusion.

After the war, in 1947, the Department of Education embarked on a drastic reform of every field of education, in conformity with advice given by the General HQ of the US Army. The Fundamental Law of Education required that Japan's education should be such as would lead her people to democratic practices and to a respect for human rights. The School Education Law initiated the 6–3–3 system,

a pattern of six years in the elementary school (the name 'national school' being abolished), three years in the new compulsory middle school and the remaining three years in the new higher school. The old higher school, the various kinds of professional school and the former normal school were also abolished. At the same time, a four-year university course and a new two- or three-year college course were established. Both public and private infant schools were put under the control of the School Education Law. (The first national infant school had been set up in 1872; and after the Infant School Act of 1926, the number of public and private infant schools increased considerably.)

Since these post-war reforms, education in Japan has made rapid progress. Today the attendance rate in the elementary school is higher than anywhere else in the world. The proportion of pupils entering the new higher school (70%), and the proportion of entrants to universities and colleges, are second only to those in the USA.

Recent developments have included the decision in 1962 to establish a new kind of five-year higher professional school. There has also been included in the curriculum of the elementary school and the new middle school a special course of moral education lessons to be given at least once a week—this following from warnings by leading Japanese thinkers that the system might be in danger of losing in quality what it gains in quantity.

The urgent need is felt in Japan, as elsewhere, for more to be done to match, educationally, the swift progress being made in the scientific and technological fields.

SK

Jaques-Dalcroze, Emile (1865–1950)
A Swiss composer born in Vienna, Jaques-Dalcroze was the originator of eurhythmics, a marriage of music and

physical movement. He taught at Dresden and also in Geneva, where he founded an institute, bearing his name.

Jespersen, Otto (1860–1943) Danish philologist, Professor of English Language and Literature at Copenhagen from 1893, Jespersen was the author of *A Modern English Grammar on Historical Principles*, produced between 1909 and 1931.

Jewish education in the UK Of an estimated 58,000 Jewish school children in the UK, five to 15 years old, 17% attend Jewish day schools, 15% state-aided, and the others independent schools—two of which are boarding schools for boys.

From five to 20 periods a week are devoted to Jewish studies. Most schools teach Hebrew, imparting at least the ability to read, scripture history, and Jewish observances. Others teach portions of the text of the Bible, particularly of the Pentateuch, and of the prayer-book. Some stress Hebrew as a living language and later Jewish history.

For children who do not attend Jewish day schools, Jewish religious education is provided out of school hours on Sunday mornings and midweek evenings. Attendance varies considerably. Some attend once a week for one year for as little as one hour per week, some five times a week for eight years or more for as much as ten hours per week. The whole system is voluntary. Girls attend as well as boys, but usually for a shorter period. Attendance drops severely at the age of 13. At any given time it is thought that half of the Jewish children in the UK are enrolled in Jewish day schools or in these part-time schools.

In London the largest administrative body is the London Board of Jewish Religious Education which controls some 80 part-time religious schools with 10,000 pupils. The Central Council for Jewish Religious Education inspects and advises schools outside London.

About 400 young men attend *yeshivot*, full-time colleges devoted to the study of the Talmud and works associated with it. Study at a *yeshiva* may lead to the title *rabbi* but it is more usually undertaken for its own sake. The largest *yeshiva* is in Gateshead, Co. Durham; others are in London, Manchester and Sunderland. Also in Gateshead is a training college for women teachers.

In London, Jews' College (founded 1855) trains ministers, rabbis, cantors and Jewish teachers; the Leo Baeck College trains rabbis for the reform and liberal communities.

FURTHER READING
I. Fishman and H. Levy. 'Jewish Education in Great Britain', *Jewish Life in Modern Britain*, Routledge and Kegan Paul, 1964.
V. D. Lipman. *Social History of the Jews in England, 1850–1950*, Watts, 1954.

HL

Jewish Lecture Committee of the Board of Deputies of British Jews, Central The Committee, formed in 1933 to improve inter-group understanding, provides speakers and material on Judaism, Jewish life and inter-group relations. It undertakes studies on religious education, education and inter-group and race relations, on problems of prejudices and on general education.

The Committee produces notes on Judaism, Jewish history, Anglo-Jewish life and community, illustrations for classroom use in religious education on Judaism and the Holy Land, and a film strip with commentary on 'The Synagogue'; enquiries on Judaism from lecturers and teachers are answered and visits are arranged to synagogues and the Jewish Museum in Woburn House.

Publications: Learning to Live with Our Neighbours and *Educational Techniques to Combat Prejudice and to Promote Inter-Group Understanding* (a report for the UNESCO Institute for Education).

Sec.: Myer Domnitz, MA, Fourth Floor, Woburn Hse, Upper Woburn Pl., London, WC1.

Jewish Religious Education, Central Council for The Council was established in 1946 as part of the post-war reconstruction of Jewish educational administration. It aims to promote Jewish religious education by inspecting full and part-time Hebrew schools in the UK outside London; by convening teachers' conferences; and by advising on methods and organisation. It fosters Jewish youth study groups, and arranges summer and winter schools for members. The Council runs two correspondence courses, for children in communities too small to have a school, on Hebrew (based on its publication *Hebrew for all*), and on basic Judaism.

Woburn Hse, Upper Woburn Pl., London, WC1.

Jewish Students, Education Aid Society for The Society grants interest-free loans to Jewish students wishing to enter the higher professions, carefully considering each application on its merit. The loans are intended to supplement grants or scholarships and are repayable in instalments when the student is qualified and has begun to earn.

10 Garrick Park, Holders Hill Rd, London, NW4.

Jewish Youth, Association for Formed in 1899 as the Jewish Athletic Association, this body serves to co-ordinate and encourage the work of Jewish youth clubs throughout the UK. A wide programme of activities is organised centrally, including training courses for leaders and senior members, specialist courses relating to Judaism and a substantial range of leisure time activities. There are approximately 120 affiliated clubs with an overall membership of about 25,000.

33 Henriques St, London, E1.

Joint Four Four separate and long-established professional associations of teachers in secondary schools have a joint executive committee to deal with matters of common interest. It is referred to as the Joint Four, and has local branches thoughout the country.

The four incorporated asssociations are for headmasters (IAHM), headmistresses (AHMI), assistant masters (IAAM), and assistant mistresses (AAMI). Before the Education Act 1944, when the term secondary school implied a grammer school, members of the associations were teachers in grammar schools, with some in public schools. The position is virtually the same now, though other types of secondary schools have emerged, e.g. secondary modern and secondary technical.

When the new complex of secondary schools replaces them all in the years ahead (comprehensive, junior high, middle schools, and sixth-form colleges) their staffs will comprise members of the associations mentioned, of the National Union of Teachers and of the National Association of Schoolmasters. It is too early to predict that professional unity will result, but important changes would appear to be inevitable. Meanwhile, each of the four secondary associations has separate representation on the Burnham Committee for the negotiation of teachers' salaries.

See also **Burnham Committees**

FB

Joint Negotiation Committee of Teachers and Authorities *See* **Consultation**

Jordan, Education in Education is free for a period of six years from the age of six/eight years, and is compulsory where places are available. 1965 statistics: 1,431 state schools, 239 private schools, 174 UNRRA schools for refugees (total enrolment 382,362); 16 trade schools (enrolment 2,230); three agricultural colleges (enrolment 297); seven teacher training colleges (enrolment 1,128); University of

Jordan (enrolment 1,680). The situation following the 1967 Arab-Israeli war remains obscure.

The population in 1965 was approximately 2 million.

Judo Judo, a modern sport of Olympic status, was derived from the one-time popular Japanese form of wrestling, ju jitsu, and is now quite widely practised in the UK in both boys' and girls' secondary schools. An excellent competitive sport, it is also a first-class method of self-defence, of particular value to girls in the adolescent and post-adolescent stages. Contrary to the opinion of some critics, it is an activity that can be practised over long periods by girls without destroying any of their femininity.

Though a general idea of judo techniques can be got from books, no-one can become proficient without personal instruction in a school or club from qualified teachers in the Black Belt grades. Progress in the sport is marked by the colour of the belt worn around the specially designed jacket. From the lowest grade upwards the colours are white, yellow, orange, green, blue and brown; these are known as the Kyu grades. After these come the Black Belt or Dan grades. Up to the Fifth Dan a black belt is worn; few people outside Japan get higher than Fifth Dan.

Practice and competition takes place on judo mats made of various substances from rubber to compressed straw in order to minimise the jar of falling (the art of falling safely is of paramount importance and is taught first).

British Judo Association, 26 Park Cres., London, W1.

FURTHER READING
BJA booklets on rules and examinations.
P. Butler. *Judo Complete*, Faber, 1963.
E. J. Harrison. *Judo for Beginners*, Foulsham, 1953.
S. Matsushita and W. Stepto. *Contest Judo*, Foulsham, 1961.
M. Sathaye. *Judo for Women*, W. and G. Foyle, 1964.
                                    JE

Junior Army Units *See* **Army Units, Junior**

Junior commercial school *See* **Technical school, Secondary**

Junior Leader Units *See* **Army Units, Junior**

Junior schools These provide for the education of pupils from seven to 11 years, and came into being in a small way after the Education Act 1918, but mainly following the recommendation of the Hadow Report 1926 (*q.v.*) that children over the age of 11 should be educated separately from those below that age. The elementary schools, which up to then provided for children aged seven to 14 (or five to 14), became junior schools (or junior and infant combined) once the older pupils were removed. By January 1965 all but a small residue of all-age schools (225 schools with 50,557 pupils on roll), mainly in the northern and north-western regions, had been reorganised. A contribution to the subsequent development of the junior school was the Hadow Report 1931 (*q.v.*) which advocated re-thinking of the curriculum and of the approach to education of the age-group in the light of the knowledge then available on child development and the psychology of learning; it also recommended a double- or triple-track organisation of classes in large schools, usually referred to as streaming (*see* **Primary schools**).

The curriculum restriction and the roles of the teacher as an instructor and the class as the unit of instruction, associated with the elementary tradition, tended to persist and much of the advice of the Hadow Report 1931 was repeated in the Ministry's report *Primary Education* (HMSO, 1959). The increasing competition to attain places in grammar schools, particularly after the Education Act 1944, tended to inhibit change since both teachers and parents feared, perhaps not unnaturally, that a curriculum much wider than that actually tested by the selection procedure, and methods less teacher-directed than usual, might prejudice children's chances for the much-coveted grammar school places. The experiments in re-organising secondary schools (e.g. as in Leicestershire) and the present plans for the provision of comprehensive schools on a national scale are expected to alleviate the pressures felt by junior schools.

JBC

Junior technical colleges *See* **Further education in England and Wales**

Junior technical school *See* **Technical school, Secondary**

Junior training centres These are establishments for severely subnormal (SSN) children set up by the local health authority. On the whole they concentrate on manual and physical training, such as fastening shoe-laces, and sense training involving the recognition of different colours, shapes

and sizes. There is also an emphasis upon kinaesthetic skills, and of course habit training for such things as washing hands, using cutlery, and later activities such as shopping or using public transport.

From being rather functional places, many progressive training centres are now experimenting far more on educational lines. Some Montessori ideas are now being used, and the growing realisation that severely subnormal is *not* the same as ineducable has led to far more imaginative time-tables, sometimes achieving goals that were once thought and stated to be impossible with such children. Training centres are currently staffed by supervisors who need not be trained teachers; but it is probable that, as things are now going, these places will become increasingly oriented towards education rather than medical control.

See also **Ineducable children**

FURTHER READING
H. C. Gunzburg. *The Social Rehabilitation of the Subnormal*, Baillière, Tindall and Cox, 1960. *Junior Training Centres*, National Association of Mental Health, 1965.

K

Kant, Immanuel (1724–1804) Main works relevant to education: *Groundwork of the Metaphysics of Morals* and *Education*.

According to Kant, rational nature is of supreme and absolute value, making all men equal as ends in themselves; they ought never to be treated by others merely as means. The duty of the individual rational agent is to will as his reason commands, not as any external authorities may command, or as his inclinations may prompt. This autonomous and free will is not lawless, for the moral law categorically commanded by reason is that a man should act in a way he can accept as valid for any other man. It is to be hoped that God will ultimately crown virtue with happiness, but duty for its own sake must remain the sole motive that is morally relevant.

The function of education is therefore to awaken in man a sense of his dignity as an autonomous rational agent, and to help him discipline his impulses so that they conform to his rational nature. Further to this, education should develop reason in its theoretical employments, cultivate taste, and attend to whatever else is instrumental to these ends.

See also **Philosophy of education**

RFD

Kay-Shuttleworth, Sir James (1804–77) As Dr James Kay, Kay-Shuttleworth was appointed the first secretary of the Select Committee of the Privy Council created in 1839 'to superintend the application of any sums voted by Parliament for the purpose of promoting Public Education.' In many important respects, he ranks as the effective founder of the system of popular education that came into being during the 19th century; many of its distinctive features—public inspection of schools, trained teachers, the pupil-teacher system — resulted from his work, and he was more than anyone else responsible for bringing about an acceptable combination of religious and secular education.

Trained as a physician, Kay worked in Manchester during the cholera epidemic of 1832 and wrote a pamphlet, *The Moral and Physical Condition of the Working Classes employed in the Cotton Manufacture in Manchester*, in which he drew attention to the squalid living conditions of the poor of that city. This led directly to measures of sanitary and educational reform.

He was later Assistant Poor Law Commissioner in East Anglia, Middlesex and Surrey.

Convinced that education was one of the most important counters to the wretched conditions in which so many poor people were living, he was critical of the monitorial system (*q.v.*) and came to believe that a system of pupil-teachers would produce more and better teachers. He experimented with such a system in the workhouse school at Norwood in London.

To Kay it seemed important that the pupil-teacher, after a period of apprenticeship under an experienced headmaster, should then proceed to a training college. Since there was no government support for such a scheme, he founded with E. C. Tufnell in 1840 a residential training college in Battersea, himself superintending the entire work of the college and giving lectures in educational theory and practice. Kay left the college in 1842, when, on his marriage, he took the name of Kay-Shuttleworth. The college, in financial difficulties, was put into the hands of the National Society (*q.v.*). Its example led to the creation of other training colleges by the Church.

The chief problem faced by Kay-Shuttleworth as secretary of the Committee of Council was the intricate and bitter inter-denominational struggle over the control of education. An early minute of the Committee, establishing a right of inspection of schools aided by public money, was objected to by the Church, but in 1840 Kay-Shuttleworth reached an agreement with the National Society by which the archbishop had the right to nominate inspectors of Church schools. His hope of securing a general provision of schools in industrial districts was set back when a Factory Bill with progressive educational clauses, introduced into the House by the Home Secretary, Sir James Graham, had to be abandoned when the nonconformists made unacceptable demands; it was replaced by a far more limited Bill which became law in 1844.

Two years later, in the Committee's minutes, Kay-Shuttleworth announced his teacher-training scheme, under which selected schools were recognised as suitable for the training of pupil-teachers. There was to be a five-year apprenticeship beginning at the age of 13, after which the pupil-teachers were to take an examination (the Queen's Scholarship), successful candidates being granted exhibitions to training colleges.

Ill-health obliged Kay-Shuttleworth to resign his post in 1849. He remained a radical and humane critic of edu-

cational provision in the mid-19th century, and was a thoroughgoing opponent of the Revised Code and the system of payment by results that it introduced. He wrote many pamphlets on educational and social questions, including a series of reports on the training of pauper children which appeared in 1841. 'To him, more than anyone else', wrote Sir Michael Sadler, 'we owe it that England is supplied with schools for the children of her people, and that this costly work has been accomplished without a breach between Church and State.'

EB

Keate, John (**1773–1852**) After 12 years as an assistant master, Keate, a fine classical scholar, was elected headmaster of Eton in 1809. At the time the school was remarkably ill-disciplined; it had only a tiny staff, and Keate himself in the upper school had charge of over 150 boys in one room. He set out to restore the school to order—a difficult task: before he succeeded, he endured occasional bombardment with rotten eggs, the screwing up of his desk and later its wholesale demolition, and the singing of choruses during lessons. His triumph was not brought about by gentleness; indeed in one day in June 1832 he flogged more than 80 boys, an incident of which he once said that his only regret was that he had not flogged more. He was, however, curiously popular, being cheered on one occasion after a spectacular flogging; and though by no means a progressive schoolmaster, he did encourage the setting up of school debating societies.

Keep Britain Tidy Group Formed in 1954 in an attempt to make Britain a cleaner, tidier and therefore more beautiful place in which to live, the Group hopes to achieve these aims through approach to people in all walks of life and particularly to children.

Keep Britain Tidy schools committees have been formed, each with its own boy or girl chairman, secretary and committee members. A wallet of badges is sent to each school committee when formed. The school committees do valuable work both in and out of school. Posters and leaflets are available.

27 Queen Anne's Ga., London, SW1.

Kempe Report A report covering the whole range of public finance, the Kempe Report appeared in 1914 and was pigeon-holed with the outbreak of war, but its recommendations on educational finance were leaned upon heavily by the drafters of the 1918 Education Act (*q.v.*). The Report established the principle of the percentage grant, and recommended in the case of elementary education that a block grant should be made on the basis of a standard expenditure of £3 per child, a standard local rate of 7d and a state contribution of two-fifths of the excess expenditure.

Kenya, Education in Less than 50% of the population is literate, and education is not compulsory. The government provides schools and aids independent schools. 1965 statistics: 5,078 primary schools (enrolment 1,010,889); 336 secondary schools (enrolment 47,976); 35 teacher training colleges (enrolment 5,061). There are also 12 technical and vocational schools and two technical colleges. The University College in Nairobi (1,000 students) is part of the University of East Africa. There are 5,000 students on higher education courses abroad. The country's population was approximately 9¼ million in 1965.

Kenyon-Slaney Clause A clause in the 1902 Education Act moved by Colonel Kenyon-Slaney, this laid down that religious teaching in a non-provided school must conform to the trust-deed.

Kindergarten *See* **Nursery school education** *and* **Nursery schools**

King George's Jubilee Trust Founded in 1935, the Trust exists to advance the physical, mental and spiritual welfare of the younger generation and especially of young persons between the ages of 14 and 20.

166 Piccadilly, London, W1.

Korea, North, Education in Primary education is free and compulsory for a seven-year period. 1964/5 statistics: 3,985 primary schools (enrolment 1,113,000); 3,217 middle schools (enrolment 704,000); 1,144 technical schools (enrolment 285,000); 464 higher technical schools (enrolment 156,000); 97 higher education institutions (enrolment 169,697). The University at Pyongyang has 16,303 students including 7,169 correspondent students. Total population: approximately 11½ million.

Korea, South, Education in Education is free and compulsory between six and 12 years. 1965 statistics: 5,125 primary schools (enrolment 4,914,345); 1,208 middle schools (enrolment 751,341); 389 academic high schools (enrolment 254,095); 312 vocational high schools (enrolment 172,436); 14 junior technical colleges (enrolment 7,623); 34 junior colleges (enrolment 15,536); 13 teacher training colleges (enrolment 5,920); 52 colleges and 18 universities (total enrolment 105,643); 37 graduate schools (enrolment 3,842). Total population: approximately 29 million.

O

L

Laban, Rudolf *See* **Dance in education**

Laboratories, School, Design and equipment of The design and equipment of school laboratories will of course vary with the nature and range of facility for which they have to provide: a range extending from the simple equipment of a working room for practical experiment and demonstration in the junior school, to the relatively sophisticated and specialised requirements of the sixth form. But despite the diversity of age and ability for which school laboratories cater, they have some common needs.

(1) A laboratory is a place for practical work and should supply sufficient working surface for each pupil, and free access to each working position without interference to others. (2) In most cases the laboratory must also provide for demonstration lessons, and there should be provision for sufficient space in front of the demonstration bench for the class to be seated occasionally as required. (3) Continuous and relevant provision must also be made for the safety of the pupils. Apparatus, materials and services available must be within the competence of the pupils. The teacher must have easy access to all working places, and be able to supervise work being done and, if necessary, interfere to prevent accident. (4) Finally there must be an adequate storage and preparation room adjoining the laboratory; sufficient display area and blackout; and draught-free ventilation.

The junior school laboratory Here the emphasis is on simplicity and adaptability. The pupils' working surfaces should consist of suitably solid tables which can be put together or arranged in any manner to suit the work in hand. Fixed benches should be provided against the walls, having sufficient depth to accommodate animal cages and aquaria. There should be wall benches provided with cold water, with one sink to twelve pupils. Benches should be of appropriate height, and the sinks deep enough to accommodate a plastic bucket. A fixed bench is desirable for the teacher, and this bench should be provided with a sink supplied with hot and cold water. An appropriate gas and electrical supply is needed for use with a film projector (the supply switch and gas tap in a lockable portion of the bench). In the use of apparatus, there should be the greatest possible improvisation.

Experiments in current electricity must be confined to those which can be performed with the use of torch or cycle lamp batteries as the source of supply. Wide use should be made of plastic containers, and measuring vessels and apparatus for weighing and measuring should be of a type easily handled (that is, of the kitchen type) and calibrated by the metric system.

Laboratories in secondary schools General considerations for the arrangement and equipment of laboratories in secondary

406

schools are clearly stated in the Ministry of Education Pamphlet No. 38 (*Science in Secondary Schools*), 1960. The increased provision for science subjects and the nature of the work in secondary schools emphasise the need for careful planning. Where several laboratories are provided they should be sited together. This arrangement offers several advantages: in the initial cost of providing services; in that more expensive items of apparatus may be moved from one laboratory to another without the expense of duplication; and in that an interchange of potentially dangerous material between laboratories can be made with greater safety.

At this stage there is an increased emphasis on the need for working space both at floor and bench level. The CSE examination has made a welcome provision for widening the scope of activity of science courses, and it is essential that this development should receive proper provision. Store and preparation rooms should be provided with an ample set of wood and metal vices, and craft tools necessary for apparatus-making should be available.

Ventilation in laboratories requires special consideration. All too often, increasing ventilation in summer produces draughts that affect bunsen flames.

All provision of services, storage room and materials should reflect the advice given in Education Pamphlet Number 53, *Safety at School*.

CRB

Laboratory assistants The laboratory assistant and the laboratory technician are in increasing demand across the whole spectrum of scientific work. The rapid expansion of technology and scientific development in industry, commerce, medicine, agriculture and in the Civil Service requires a corresponding supply of laboratory technicians and assistants; and the greater resources available in such fields as these compete against the more

limited resources of schools, colleges and universities for the supply of laboratory assistance.

Entry qualifications vary for training as a laboratory assistant. Passes in a science, mathematics and English at O Level GCE (or corresponding passes in CSE) are required by most employers. The trainee is encouraged to increase his qualifications by attending courses at a college of technology as part of his in-training in order to qualify for membership of relevant professional institutions. These courses lead to varying levels of qualification by way of examinations held under the auspices of several authorities, including the Institute of Science Technology; the City and Guilds of London Institute; the Animal Technicians' Association; and the Institute of Medical Laboratory Technology.

In schools the provision of skilled laboratory assistants makes possible the more efficient use of teaching staff. The duties of laboratory assistants in schools may include the preparation of routine demonstration apparatus; the preparation of bench reagents; the arrangement of laboratory stores, receiving and checking consignments; the maintenance of stock lists for requisition; the regular checking of potentially dangerous apparatus and materials; the preparation of distilled water; the arrangement of film and film strip apparatus; the maintenance of vivaria and aquaria; and the preparation of biological materials.

While the services of laboratory assistants are not at present available to most science teachers, it is probable that future grants will make such provision more general.

CRB

Labour Colleges, National Council of *See* **Labour education**

Labour education 'Labour education' may be regarded as a special sector of workers' education, which is in turn a special sector of adult education.

It is a term used more rarely in Britain than in North America, possibly because the existence here of a political Labour Party might make the term ambiguous; but the obvious alternative —'workers' education'—can be equally misleading in Britain, where the Workers' Educational Association (*q.v.*) is really a provider of liberal education to all interested adults.

The distinctive feature of labour education is its 'restricted market', for it caters for adults conscious of their functions as workers and particularly as organised workers, with the aim of helping them to assume more industrial, civic and social responsibility.

The stress is naturally upon such subjects as industrial relations, trade unionism, applied economics, co-operation, labour law and social security, but labour education usually goes beyond these fields in two directions. In the first place, the inadequate schooling of many of the students will necessitate that special training in the basic skills of study should form part of any labour education programme. Secondly, since the appetite for education 'grows with feeding', the curricula tend to broaden into more cultural themes, so as to educate 'the whole man as an individual and a citizen as well as a worker and a trade unionist' (*TUC Report*, September 1960).

If this is true, one may well dispute the wisdom of splitting adult education into such specialised categories and of segregating workers qua workers from other adult students. It can be argued that specialist study-groups of this kind lose much of their educational value through the one-sided narrowness of their discussions, cherished assumptions often passing unchallenged and even unexpressed. On the other hand, different forms of adult education need not be mutually exclusive and 'labour-education students' may also go to other adult classes. Furthermore, experience shows that courses specially directed at workers may succeed in recruiting people who would never otherwise be attracted to adult education, not least because of a widespread distrust and suspicion of the normal general adult education provision.

This suspicion goes back a long way and was certainly one of the symptoms of the growing consciousness of class divisions in Britain in the early 19th century. It can be seen in the attempts to found 'genuine working-class' adult education bodies—first by trying to take over the Mechanics' Institutes, then by Mutual Improvement Societies, Hampden Clubs, Owenite Halls of Science and Chartist Reading Rooms. Thomas Hodgskin summarised the distrust in the *Mechanics Magazine* of October 1823: 'The education of a free people . . . will always be directed more beneficially for them when it is in their own hands . . . Men had better be without education . . . than be educated by their rulers.'

This suspicion of 'Establishment-sponsored' adult education can be seen again in the early years of this century when considerable opposition was aroused by the foundation of Ruskin College, Oxford in 1899 and of the Workers' Educational Association in 1903, both aiming at providing workers with adult education of high quality but both being accused of being too much influenced by traditional attitudes. The Ruskin Students' Strike in 1909 led to the formation of a separate (and comparatively short-lived) Central Labour College with teaching on Marxist lines, and in 1921 the so-called National Council of Labour Colleges was set up as a rival to the Workers' Educational Trade Union Committees who were not committed to any one particular interpretation of the political and economic scene. Individual trade unions tended to sponsor one side or the other in this dispute and attempted to embroil the TUC, but it was not until during and after the second world war that trade unions began to consider seriously providing their own educational service.

In 1940 the Transport and General Workers' Union began its own correspondence courses and the TUC in 1944 resolved that it should itself provide 'facilities for training those who are to serve as officers and active members of the movement'. This decision began an expansion of work by the TUC at their Central College in Congress House—mostly one-week and two-week courses on specialised TU topics and staffed mainly by TUC officers—and in their residential summer school courses. Residential courses are now regularly provided by many individual unions (such as the TGWU, USDAW and the National Union of Agricultural Workers) whilst two unions (the Electrical Trades Union and the National Union of General Municipal Workers) run their own small residential college.

This mounting volume of labour education undertaken by the trade union movement itself might well suggest that 'labour education' is now synonymous with 'trade union education', particularly since the 1962 TUC decision to rationalise trade union education under the control of the General Council. This has entailed the winding-up of the Workers' Educational Trade Union Committee and the WEA District TU Advisory Committees, the Ruskin College correspondence courses and the National Council of Labour Colleges. The work of all these bodies has been taken over by the TUC General Council, acting with advice from newly-established Regional Educational Advisory Committees and backed by an 'educational levy' of 3d per affiliated member per annum (approximately £100,000 p.a.).

Much labour education is provided, too, by bodies other than trade unions. The university extra-mural departments and the university-WEA Joint Committees (in addition to their general evening and weekend courses) have substantially expanded their provision of day-release courses and cater weekly for hundreds of workers from mines and factories. Special types of labour education are being developed in some colleges of advanced technology, technical colleges and colleges of further education, including classes where shop-stewards and management trainees study together; and the long-term and short-term residential colleges now provide special facilities for individual students who wish to study more intensively.

The labour education scene in Britain is one of considerable overlapping and confusion but also of considerable variety and activity. It has been and still is one of the growing points in our adult education system. See also **Adult education**

PGHH

Labour Party and education Since the earliest days of socialism, popular movements in the UK have given education a high priority. Education was not only or mainly valued as a means for individual development but for its potential as a social force. It was seen as an instrument for the creation of a better society and the promotion of a system which offered the majority of the population a more dignified and less precarious existence. The Labour Party's educational policy aims to diminish educational inequalities and to improve the quality as well as the amount of educational provision. This is regarded as an essential part of its struggle towards a more equal and more civilised society.

The Labour Party maintains that social (and therefore political) values cannot be divorced from education policy. It is simply unrealistic to ignore the fact that education and society react on each other at every point. The structure of education must have profound effect on the social structure of any society as it will largely determine the degree of equality, justice, opportunity and social mobility in the community. In the same way, the kind of educational system which exists obviously affects the values of society. The social structure of a country determines the demand for education and the available pool of ability; it influences what is taught in the schools and the national attitude to education.

Every educational system, therefore, mirrors the needs and aspirations of the community which created it. The Labour Party recognises that as the needs of the community change, so the system must be changed in response to new demands and aspirations if the creation of new tensions is to be avoided.

It is important to see current and future Labour educational reforms against this background; in particular, the movement towards comprehensive education. Until recently the schools of the UK have been selective institutions, the educational system essentially geared to educating an élite, mainly middle-class in origin. The remainder were offered larger classes, sometimes inferior buildings and facilities, and were segregated in separate schools. Today, the pressure of democracy insists on full civil rights and their full incorporation in education as well as in other fields of human rights.

The Labour Party does not only advocate the improvement and expansion of the educational system, it wants injustices within the system to be rectified and to use the system positively to promote the underprivileged and disadvantaged in society so that equality of opportunity begins to exist. Only by distributing educational resources more equally can some of the more glaring abuses be rectified. This not only implies the introduction of comprehensive education, a five-year secondary education for all, and the integration of public schools into the state educational system; it means making the schools and quality of education received in underprivileged areas at least as good as those anywhere else. It means also broadening the intake of students into higher education, so that those who can benefit, rather than only those who can afford to, will be able to enter universities and colleges.

SW

Lacrosse Derived from a ball game played by North American Indians lacrosse was introduced into this country from Canada in 1867. It is played by fewer men than women in the UK.

Not so popular or widespread as hockey or football, it tends to be confined to the large cities and university towns. The relative scarcity of adult clubs, which makes it necessary for players to travel some distance to play the game, has not encouraged many schools within the state system to introduce lacrosse into the curriculum, for it has become almost axiomatic that whatever sporting activities are done in the school should be capable of being pursued *without undue difficulty* in the post-school stage.

All England Women's Lacrosse Association, 26 Park Cres., London, W1.

The English Lacrosse Union (for men), 3 Chessington Ave, Bexleyheath, Kent.

JE

Lancaster, Joseph (**1778–1838**) One of the chief English advocates (with Andrew Bell, *q.v.*) of the 'monitorial system'. He tried the system first in his school at Southwark, opened in 1801, being unable to afford the salaries of assistants.

See also **Lancasterian system**

Lancasterian system This takes its name from the application of assembly line techniques to teaching by Joseph Lancaster (1778–1838).

Beginning in 1798, by 1804 he had about 500 poor unruly pupils whom he taught by means of monitors. So well-organised were they that the cost of teaching seemed infinitesimal: he himself estimated that £300 a year would cover a school of 1,000, and he held open sessions four afternoons a week to demonstrate the system. Endorsed in the House of Commons, written up in the *Edinburgh Review*, copied all over the world, the Lancasterian system became the basis of the British and Foreign Schools Society (*q.v.*).

As described in his *Improvements in Education* (1803), it was based on monitors who, under a monitor-general, parcelled out the entire work of the school, not only in lessons but administration as well. Only name differentiates his idea from those of the Rev. Andrew Bell (1753–1832), founder of the Madras system (*q.v.*), who described his monitors as teachers, assistants or tutors. Lancaster certainly read Bell's *Experiment in Education* (1797) three years later and visited him in 1804. But his vanity and imprudence led fellow Quakers to organise themselves into a committee in 1808 which became the British and Foreign Schools Society. Lancaster became a lecturer at large, whereas Bell was recalled from Swanage to assume the superintendency of the rival Church of England educational body, the National Society (*q.v.*).

Lancaster's mission took him to North America in 1818. He established a school in Montreal. Before he died in 1833, a year after Bell, he had kindled interest in the monitorial system all over the world.

See also **Monitorial system**

WHGA

Lane, Homer (1875–1925) Undoubtedly one of the pioneers of progressive education, the American Homer Lane himself had an unsettled and in some ways tragic career, mingling brilliant successes with errors of judgement that constantly brought him into trouble. Without higher academic qualifications he became, through charm and ability, superintendent of a settlement for disturbed and delinquent adolescents near Detroit. There he introduced measures of self-government, including the establishment of a school court, that had remarkable success and quickly became well-known. Coming to England in 1913, he took charge of a similar organisation called the Little Commonwealth, and here he was able to develop his central idea that the best way to help a pupil, and especially a disturbed one, is to make him feel that the teacher is always genuinely 'on his side'. This might well involve the teacher having to put up with a certain amount of anti-social or aggressive behaviour without turning to punishment or general sanctions; but Homer Lane felt it was worth it, unless the position became quite intolerable, for the trust this would eventually win from someone who might have learned in the past to distrust all adults.

Lane was one of the first teachers working with disturbed children who advocated psycho-analysis as a method of understanding and treatment. Such ideas have become more popular since Lane first tried them. The very mistakes that so sadly terminated his educational career are instructive to the educationist.

FURTHER READING
David Wills. *Homer Lane: A Biography*, Allen and Unwin, 1964.

NT

Language laboratory This is a classroom fitted with electronic equipment which is used for group tuition in languages. In less-well equipped laboratories the fittings consist of berths or booths, one for each pupil, which insulate the students from classroom noise, and each pupil has a pair of headphones which enable him to listen to the teacher speaking or to a tape recorder or record player under the teacher's control.

In the better-equipped laboratories the headphones worn by the pupils are fitted with an attachment which supports a small microphone in front of the pupil's mouth, and the student has a tape recorder, usually with a dual track and dual record replay head, under his control. The teacher sits at a console which is so equipped as to enable him to hear the tape recordings of any pupil, and he can give instructions and correct a pupil's pronunciation— his words being heard only by the particular pupil concerned. In this more advanced type of laboratory, instruction is given to the pupils by speech prerecorded on the tape; through the headphones the pupil hears words and phrases spoken in the language being studied, and there is a pause to allow the pupil to repeat the words of the speaker two or three times. Later lessons contain question-and-answer exercises, and in some laboratories illustrations are flashed on a large screen which can be seen by all class members. These illustrations allow for exercises to test the vocabulary of the pupil, who has to describe the picture or answer questions about it. The pupil can rewind the tape he controls and listen to his responses, and the teacher at the console can also listen in.

The advantage of the language laboratory over traditional classroom instruction in languages is that it allows every pupil to participate continuously in the lesson, whereas the traditional method limits individual instruction to one pupil at a time. Pupils can listen to different lessons, and it is possible for a multi-lingual teacher to control a class of pupils learning different languages. Laboratories provide much more opportunity than traditional teaching methods for pupils to study the spoken rather than the written forms of the language.

A drawback to the method is that the intervention of the teacher from the console may not coincide with occasions when the pupil is most in need of correction, so that mispronunciation may be persisted in by the pupil even though he is imitating a native speaker on the tape recording.

Teaching by language laboratory overcomes the self-consciousness of some pupils who dislike attempting to speak in a foreign language in front of their fellows, and the privacy afforded by the booths and headphones aids concentration and assists in classroom control. Research has shown that language laboratories reduce the time needed for a pupil to reach a certain standard of proficiency and that examination success is increased.

Language laboratories are of course not confined to use in schools; commerce and industry and the services are also employing them for the training of personnel who need an additional language.

See also **Modern languages, Teaching of**

EP

Language Teaching, Centre for Information on The Centre has been established to collect and co-ordinate information about all aspects of modern languages and their teaching, and to make this information available to individuals and organisations professionally concerned in Great Britain. Two aspects receive special attention: the maintenance of the fullest information about relevant research and new developments in teaching techniques; and the provision of up-to-date and reliable information about available teaching materials.

It will be some time before the Centre, founded in 1967, is able to offer all the services that are desirable: but it is already developing a library service, sharing certain common resources with the British Council's English Teaching Information Centre (ETIC), which occupies adjoining accommodation. Notably these include a language teaching library, containing at present over 17,000 volumes, receiving and filing over 300 periodicals (including many published abroad) and housing a collection of documents and theses. Linguistic studies and a representative range of text-books and teaching materials relating to particular languages are being acquired as rapidly as possible. The library is primarily for reference, although some books may be borrowed on personal application, and working accommodation is available for those who wish to use the library for reference, study or research. The library is open to visitors without previous appointment. There is also a reference collection of audio-visual and recorded language teaching materials, with facilities for listening to and viewing tapes, records, film-strips, slides and other aids.

The Centre will produce specialised bibliographies, including lists of currently available teaching materials, courses and equipment, with a quarterly journal of abstracts of papers and articles concerned with research and teaching, and occasional surveys and reviews of special problems of language teaching. It maintains a register of current research.

In the first place, the Centre is concentrating on giving aid in the teaching of French, German, Spanish, Russian, Italian and English as a second language, within the UK. (Overseas aspects of the teaching of English as a second language are served by the adjoining English Teaching Information Centre.) Enquiries concerning other languages will be dealt with as far as resources permit, but may have to be referred elsewhere.

State Hse, 63 High Holborn, London, WCI.

Laos, Education in Education in Laos was disrupted by the civil war of 1953–63, and in consequence the illiteracy rate is high. At present students have to go to France for their university training, but a national university is planned at Sisa Vang Vong. 1966 statistics: 2,642 primary schools (enrolment 144,925); six colleges, four lycées and three technical (total enrolment 4,119). There are four teacher training colleges, a school of medicine and an institute of law and administration.

The population of the country was approximately $2\frac{1}{4}$ million in 1966.

LASMEC (Local Authorities School Meals Consortium) *See* **School meals service**

Late developer It is a mistake to expect any child to develop at an even rate; on the contrary, it is best to think of human growth in all spheres as a matter of plateaux and spurts. A 'late developer' may be a child who is at an apparent standstill for some time, but who can also be capable of quick progress in a comparatively short time. Unfortunately, this may be impeded if the parents have become over-anxious and demanding, with the result that the child may often 'stick' through sheer self-defence against all the pressure put upon him to crush his own individuality and 'be like other children'. Similarly, putting the child in a low stream in school may have the effect of discouraging the late developer from forging ahead, since by then he may have become used to the low standards expected of him. An educational psychologist is the most qualified person to diagnose whether or not a child is a late developer, and if he is, to suggest some of the possible reasons for this, or whether he is in fact genuinely of low potential.

FURTHER READING
A. Gesell. *The First Five Years of Life*, Harper and Row, New York, 1940.

NT

Lateral thinking A process of thought used in problem-solving in which the basic principles are (1) recognition of

o*

dominant or polarising ideas, (2) the search for different ways of looking at things, (3) a relaxation of the rigid control of traditional (vertical) thinking, and (4) the use of chance. The lateral thinker is not concerned with being right at every step in the problem-solving (as is the logical thinker) but only in reaching a solution. Thus lateral thinking does not achieve its results by the step-by-step logical method common to Western civilisation since Aristotle. Lateral thinking aids creativity and may be more common among those whose upbringing has been permissive rather than authoritarian, although its use can be developed by practice.

FURTHER READING

Edward de Bono. *The Use of Lateral Thinking,* Jonathan Cape, 1967.

Latin America, Education in The provision of education in Latin America is normally the responsibility of the central government, acting through a ministry of education which provides schools, lays down programmes of study, appoints and pays teachers, etc. In federal states, like Mexico and Brazil, these duties devolve on to provincial government, the central ministry limiting itself to coordination and equalisation. Municipal authorities may be expected to build and maintain schools. Private bodies, often Catholic, are sometimes free to open and maintain schools; sometimes, as in Mexico, only with the permission of government. Such schools usually charge fees and their pupils, mainly drawn from the middle classes, are prepared for entrance to universities.

The most common pattern is: a primary school of six years, followed by a variety of types of secondary school—such as agricultural, vocational, teacher training, college preparatory. In this last most common type, the subjects taught include Spanish (or Portuguese); mathematics; history; geography; a foreign language, usually English;

civics; art; general knowledge. The teaching is usually formal, verbal and bookish. Little attention is paid to science, classics, physical education or sport. The equipment is normally very poor, the classes over-large. Most secondary teachers work only part-time in any one school.

The reality of provision falls far short of the intentions. There is a chronic and disastrous shortage of teachers: their pay is scandalously low and many of them are badly trained. Schools are too small and too few. The problem of providing schools in the vast rural areas has not been solved. No one wants to teach in wretched conditions, among people suffering from ill-health and misery. Only in Argentina, Chile and Uruguay do standards equal those of southern Italy or Spain: i.e. literacy reaches 80%. In Mexico, nearly half the population is illiterate. In Bolivia, 70% are illiterate, in Haiti 90%.

Perhaps the most intractable problem is that of wastage: in the area as a whole only 20% of pupils complete their primary education and of every hundred enrolled in the first year of intermediate schools only 22 complete their studies. Out of every hundred children registered in the first year of the primary schools of Brazil, only 30 pass to the second year, 17 to the third, 10 to the fourth. The reasons are: poor buildings; bad teaching; the realisation by parents that what children are learning has no relevance to life and its problems. Taking into account the fact that more than half the rural teachers of Brazil themselves left school at 14, the reasons for this state of affairs are easy to understand.

There is very little vocational education. Only in the larger cities do technical schools exist, and they are often ill-equipped. Moreover, employers most often are themselves too ignorant to realise that it is more profitable to employ efficient rather than cheap labour. There is thus little incentive for parents to send their children to courses providing scientific and technological knowledge; there is no assurance that proficiency will lead to well-paid employment.

Since 1950 the demand for general secondary education, leading to the university, has grown fast: by nearly 12% a year during the last ten years. This is the result of the growing prosperity of the middle classes and of their rising ambitions: higher education is seen as the gateway to well-paid administrative and professional occupations.

There are about 130 universities in Latin America, of which 19 are in Brazil, 21 in Colombia, 30 in Mexico; and, altogether, some 750,000 students. The proportion to the population varies: from 1 in 1,650 in Argentina to 1 in 68 in Uruguay. The universities differ from those in Europe or in the USA, chiefly because they are usually collections of autonomous technological and professional schools, e.g. of medicine, law, engineering, etc. rather than communities of scholars promoting research and scholarship. Most of the professors are part-time teachers, pursuing their normal occupations as doctors, lawyers, engineers, etc. The majority of students, too, hold full-time posts, listening to lectures and learning textbooks by heart in their spare time. In medicine, however, and often in engineering, both highly respected and lucrative professions, standards are rigorous and high—the teaching compares well with that in any other country. It is normal for the students to share in the government of the universities. They tend to be very active politically and student-strikes are frequent.

The need for drastic reform is evident and it is accepted by all the republics, particularly Cuba, Mexico, Chile. Planning departments in the ministries support change and development, within the limits of financial restriction. Rural education grows fast: so does adult education. Teacher training colleges are being established

and expand: increase in the supply of trained teachers is everywhere seen as the condition for improvement. The present bottleneck is the secondary school, badly equipped, with poor workshops and laboratories, staffed by untrained, overworked, part-time teachers. The graduates from such schools are inadequately equipped to profit from higher education. Hence, schemes for the provision of general colleges or university preparatory colleges for the 17- and 18-year-olds. At the tertiary level a dozen or so universities are pointing the way to what should be done: for example, Los Andes in Colombia, Concepción in Chile, Brasília, Havana. The main drives sustaining reform and improvement are: urbanisation and its consequent problems; the pressure of left-wing political forces; the example and influence of the USA; the general realisation that there can be no economic development without appropriate schooling, that the only sound basis for general prosperity is good education.

JAL

Latin Teaching, Association for the Reform of *See* **Classics, Teaching of**

Law, Qualification in Two bodies control the training of members of the legal profession in England and Wales: the Law Society in the case of solicitors, and the Council of Legal Education in the case of barristers.

Solicitors Anyone wishing to be admitted as a solicitor must, under the Law Society's requirements, be of good character and have reached a requisite level of general education; except where exempted, must attend a recognised course of legal education; must serve under articles of clerkship for a certain period with a solicitor practising in England and Wales; and must pass both parts of the Law Society's qualifying examination, unless exempted from Part I of that examination. There are two different avenues to qualification for school leavers with acceptable GCE passes (which must include a pass in English at either level). The first is to go to a university where it is possible to read for a degree in law, and, after graduation and an interview conducted by solicitors appointed by the Law Society, to proceed with the Society's consent to enrolment as a law student. Exemption is granted from Part I of the Law Society's qualifying examination if at university a candidate has passed at an adequate level in the subjects covered by Part I. He may then either immediately enter into articles of clerkship for a period of two years and thereafter prepare for Part II and take it, or take Part II and then spend two years in articles.

The alternative approach to qualification for the 18-year-old is, having reached the required standard of general education at school and satisfied the Law Society that he is suitable for service as an articled clerk, to enrol as a law student and be articled to a solicitor for a period of at least five years. Before the first half of this five-year period has passed, he must have completed courses leading to Part I of the qualifying examination and have been successful in Part I. Thereafter he must put in a two-year period of service without preparing for or taking exams, followed by Part II of the qualifying examination.

There are various other approaches for older entrants, including graduates who have studied subjects other than the law at university.

About one in 20 of solicitors are women, who find it harder than men to become articled clerks (largely because firms are reluctant to take on someone who may well leave in order to be married).

Barristers Intending barristers must first enrol as a student in one of the four Inns of Court, which form the governing bodies of the profession. Applicants for enrolment must have GCE passes in five subjects, including English, two of them being at A level. Once admitted a student must 'keep terms' at his Inn of Court for a period covering eight terms (there are four terms in each legal year). He may do this at the same time that he is studying at a university. He must then pass the Bar examination, from some subjects in the first part of which he may be exempted if he has obtained a degree in law. The examination is in two parts. On passing, the candidate may be called to the Bar, but may have to undertake some practical training before practising.

FURTHER READING
Law, Choice of Careers Series, HMSO.
Becoming a Solicitor. Free from the Secretary, Education and Training, Law Society, The Law Society's Hall, 113 Chancery La., London, WC2.

Law of effect In 1930 a psychologist named Thorndike stated that behaviour which is followed by reward will be learned more readily than behaviour which is not rewarded, when the behaviour concerned may in fact tend to disappear. In human terms, the law of effect shows itself in our belief in the need for positive reinforcement (*q.v.*) as an essential aid to learning. However, Thorndike also believed that punishment prevents undesirable learning, though later he denied this as an absolute rule. The whole idea of negative reinforcement (*q.v.*) is still somewhat under question as an aid to learning.

FURTHER READING
R. S. Woodworth. *Contemporary Schools of Psychology*, Methuen, 1949.

NT

Law and the teacher The teacher is regarded in law as being *in loco parentis* to the pupils in his care, which implies a duty to take such care of them as 'a careful father would take of his children',[1] although one has to visualise a parent with a very large family.[2]

The test of the reasonably prudent parent must be applied not in relation to the parent in the home but the parent applying his mind to school life.[3]

The duty of care exists during the whole of the time the pupils are on the school premises or off the school premises on a school activity with the knowledge and consent of the school authorities. During such periods, the head teacher and staff of a school acting on behalf of the proprietor, who would either be the LEA or body of voluntary managers or governors, should have regard to the amount of supervision required to discharge that duty, taking into consideration the age of the pupils and the particular activity upon which they are engaged. During the times of class contact, the main problems which would arise in connection with the discharge of the duty of care would be in the practical classes and physical training periods. In these classes, it should be remembered that there are no detailed statutory safety regulations applying to the school, and general regard, therefore, should be paid to the safety aspect of any subject taught in the school. Emphasis should also be placed on the conducting of lessons in a recognised manner. If, in a practical class, either in a laboratory or gymnasium, the teacher can say 'In all that I did I followed the approved practice generally adopted throughout the land' he is in a position of considerable strength to answer a charge of negligence.[4]

The other times when the question of the discharge of the duty of care has to be considered are when the pupils are not in receipt of formal lessons but are on the premises with the knowledge and consent of the school authorities, i.e. before and after school, the recreation periods and the midday break. The question of supervision has to be considered on all these occasions, but except possibly in the case of children of very tender years, very close supervision would not be necessary. 'A balance must be struck between the meticulous supervision of children every moment at school and the desirable object of encouraging sturdy independence as they grow up.'[5] It has been held to be sufficient to show that the school premises are patrolled from time to time during these periods by responsible adults. It is the duty of the head teacher of the school in the discharge of his responsibility for the internal organisation, management and discipline, to devise, in consultation with his staff, a system of supervision suitable to the particular school. Teachers can be properly required by the head teacher to exercise this supervision, but it can also be exercised by ancillary assistants and the current trend is for more and more use to be made of ancillary assistants to relieve teachers of supervisory duties, particularly during the midday period. In a senior school, prefects can also be used under the general supervision of a responsible member of staff.

In the case of pupils participating in the midday meal, it is important to remember that Section 49 of the Education Act 1944 places upon the LEA the responsibility for maintaining a school meals service, and provides that no duties can be required of teachers other than the supervision of pupils. The effect of this is that although persons other than teachers can be employed to supervise the pupils participating in the school meal, there is power to require the teachers to undertake this duty. However, this is the only duty in connection with school meals that can be required of teachers, and any other tasks, such as the collecting of school meals monies, are done on a voluntary basis.

In general, the duties which can be properly required of the teachers are subject to the regulations made under the Education Act 1944 and, in particular, the Schools Regulations 1959 which provide that no duties can be required of the teacher other than those connected with the work of the school.

There is no definition in the Regulations of the term 'work of the school' and each case would depend upon its own facts. There would be no doubt, however, that all matters relating to the curriculum would be regarded as such, as would such matters as staff meetings. It follows, therefore, that the teachers can be properly required by their employers to attend staff meetings, even though they may be called outside the normal school session, i.e. on the last day of the vacation. Tasks connected, however, with hobby activities and parent–teacher meetings have not been so far regarded as part of the work of the school, neither has the supervision of bus queues forming up off the school premises, or the organisation of school crossing patrols. If teachers participate in these activities, they do so on a voluntary basis and could not be required by their employers to do so.

The individual teacher will be appointed by either a written agreement or minute of the employing authority, either to a specific school or to the service of the authority generally. The teacher enjoys considerable security of tenure and if at any time consideration is given to the question of the termination of his contract, he is entitled, under the National Conditions of Tenure which are adopted by almost every LEA, to a hearing before the managers or governors or the appropriate committee, at which he may be accompanied by a friend. There are also various statutory provisions relating to his conditions of service; for example, under the provisions of Section 30 of the Education Act 1944 he is entitled to freedom of conscience and, except in an aided school or in the case of a reserved teacher in a controlled or special agreement school, a teacher cannot be required to give religious instruction or be in any way penalised because of his religious beliefs. Under the provisions of Section 24 of the Education Act 1944, a woman may not be dismissed from a post by reason only of marriage. The schools regulations also provide that a teacher cannot be required to abstain outside school hours from any occupations which do not interfere with the due performance of his duties.

REFERENCES
1. Williams v. Eady, 1893, 10 TLR 41, CA per Lord Esher, MR.
2. Ricketts v. Erith Borough Council, 1943, 2 AER 629 per Tucker J.
3. Lyes v. Middx. The Guardian Law Report, 12 October 1962 per Edmund Davies J.
4. Meehan v. Derbyshire County Council, 1965, Nottingham Winter Assize per Sir J. Simon, Pres. Unreported.
5. Jefferey v. LCC, 1954, 119 JP per McNair J.

HP

Lawn tennis The modern game of lawn tennis was devised in 1874 by an Englishman, Major W. C. Wingfield, under the name of 'sphairistike', but this name was soon dropped and the sport became known as lawn tennis, distinguishing it from the old, indoor game of real (or royal) tennis.

The game is now played outdoors on grass or 'hard' courts (shale, asphalt, etc.) and indoors on a wood surface. A 'doubles' court measures 78 ft by 36 ft, and a 'singles' court 78 ft by 27 ft. In addition there must be a distance of 21 ft behind the service lines at each end to allow ample room for movement and a minimum distance of 12 ft from the side-lines to the next parallel court or surrounding netting.

At present players are divided into two classes, amateurs and professionals, though attempts are being made to have 'open' championships in which amateurs can play with or against professionals. In the UK the game is controlled by the Lawn Tennis Association with headquarters at Wimbledon (where the national championships are played each year), which runs an LTA Honorary Coaches Training Scheme. Details can be obtained from the Association.

Lawn tennis is played in almost every secondary school in the country, and many primary schools, mainly on hard courts which require little maintenance, and suffer less from inclement weather than grass courts. In all new secondary school building plans, provision is made for the laying down of one or more courts.

Lawn Tennis Association, Baron's Court, London, W14.

FURTHER READING
R. H. Applewhaite. *Lawn Tennis, Play the Game* Series, Educational Productions, 1956.
Lawn Tennis Association Handbook. Annual.
Main Headings and Brief Notes for the Elementary Certificate Course LTA Honorary Coaches Training Scheme, Lawn Tennis Association.

JE

Lawn Tennis Association, Girls' Schools' The Girls' Schools' Lawn Tennis Association has been in existence for 15 years and has over 750 member schools. Its purpose is to raise the standard of lawn tennis in girls' schools by holding teachers' courses, schoolgirl holiday courses and by publishing termly bulletins containing all sorts of tennis information. It is designed to be of use to both games' mistresses and schoolgirls.

All schools are linked with their county associations by a county liaison officer. The Association has a generous allocation of Wimbledon tickets, and affiliation allows a reduction in the entry fee to the schoolgirls' tournament, the Aberdare Cup.

Membership is open to all secondary schools.

Hon. Sec.: Miss M. E. Parker, St Michael's School, Limpsfield, Surrey.

Leadership Some people are often referred to as 'natural leaders', and it is true that assertive and self-confident individuals often seem to speak for the group they belong to at the time. But the individual who is a good leader in some circumstances may not suit at all

in other situations, where the changed needs of the group may call for a quite different type of leader. In fact, most people have the experience of being leaders in some groups at some time, when they are felt to be truly representative and understanding of the needs of the group and to have themselves the confidence and knowledge to succeed in the particular task at hand. For example, if a group of young men meet casually at a street corner and there is to be a fight, the most aggressive one may emerge as leader; but if the group decides to talk to girls, then the most engaging speaker may take the lead.

Leaders nearly always emerge informally by tacit agreement; there are of course elected leaders, or leaders imposed on groups without election, but if these are ever going to win genuine popular support, they will have to develop some of the qualities of an informal group leader. In other words, by getting to know members of the group, and becoming reasonably sensitive to their moods, needs and expectations, an established leader can also become a popular leader by not behaving in a distant manner and to a certain extent by embodying group values. He must also show that he is himself basically competent in the skills he is trying to foster in the group, and fairly consistent in the sort of behaviour he expects from others as well as from himself. He should also delegate his power on those occasions when it is suitable for someone within the group to emerge as a temporary leader in some specific task.

FURTHER READING:
W. J. H. Sprott. *Social Psychology*, Methuen, 1952.

NT

Learning There seem to be two basic methods of learning: firstly, where the individual gradually builds up, sometimes piecemeal, a skill or a store of knowledge, rather as the laws of association (*q.v.*) would suggest; and secondly where the individual discovers, sometimes suddenly, that he can organise the material in front of him into something meaningful (*see* **Gestalt psychology**). The first type of learning we may reserve for cumulative knowledge, as with learning lists of facts or associations, such as mathematical tables; whereas the second type is more concerned with problem-solving, or seeing the relationship between things. The teacher's job here is to ensure that his pupils have enough formal learning to be able to apply it to their own individual understanding of the wider aspects of a problem. The older and more intelligent a pupil, the more general understanding he should be capable of; but he will possibly learn very little unless he is adequately motivated to do so—either by positive reinforcement (*q.v.*) for his efforts, or by his own desire or even mild anxiety to do well. A pupil who is too anxious, however, may find this excessive anxiety an obstacle to really efficient learning.

Learning also happens much more quickly if the pupil really understands what he is doing and, for example, can remember it not in parrot fashion but in his own individual way. In many cases he may remember it even better if he has over-learned it, which means that he has continued to study the material even after he is really confident about it. It also helps occasionally if a student attempts to recite written material to himself as well as to re-read it, and in this way test himself. Some people prefer splitting a learning project, such as a long poem, into parts to be learned separately, while others find it easier to take it as a whole; there seems little to choose between the two methods. It is probably a mistake, however, to attempt to learn much material without short periods of rest, as this does not seem to allow the brain to digest the material

most successfully for its eventual retention (*q.v.*).

Of course, learning in a wider context takes place in different situations probably every day, and the rate of learning in a young child, long before he gets to school, is truly enormous. Here it is more difficult to chart any definite rules, although it is obvious that imitation, and learning through experience of doing something, are both immensely important. Once again, the most important things are still probably natural ability plus the desire to learn; though how far these are bound up with opportunity and encouragement is still not clear, and possibly never will be so long as there are things about human beings that remain beyond our understanding.

FURTHER READING

R. Borger and A. E. M. Seaborne. *The Psychology of Learning*, Penguin, 1966.

E. R. Hilgard. *Theories of Learning*, Methuen, 1958.

NT

Learning sets Alternatively referred to by psychologists as 'subordinate capabilities'. The pupil's ability to profit from a course of instruction depends primarily on the previous knowledge, skills, attitudes, etc., which he or she brings to the learning situation. These learning sets (or subordinate capabilities) can be identified only by asking, 'What must the learner be able to do *beforehand* in tackling each of the various component parts in the task hierarchy?' According to this theory, of which Gagne is the leading exponent, learning is a matter of transfer of training from a group of existing abilities to a new activity which incorporates them at a higher level. This higher level of mental activity is qualitatively different from the ones that precede it and make it possible; and its secret inheres in the combination of old learning sets to form new ones, not simply in being 'more difficult'.

Discovering the nature and extent of the pupil's learning sets is therefore the main purpose of the pre-test in programmed learning, as it is of course in all teaching.

See also **Programmed learning**

WKR

Leaving school In primitive societies the economic roles the young person has eventually to perform are displayed before him from the time he can toddle: he begins to learn them then, if only by playing at them. When the time comes for him to assume his full social responsibility there is no problem of transition. With his peer group, he has long known what will be expected of him.

The nearest approach to childish initiation into adult status we have in the west is Christian confirmation. The social importance of this has declined and in any case, theologically speaking, confirmation is not a social rite of passage but is acceptance into the family of the church and can occur at any age after about ten. What remains as the great mark of transition for those young people who do not go on to universities or equivalent institutions (the majority—only 15.6% of all leavers went on to full-time further education in 1963/64) is leaving school and going to work. The process of 'leaving school on Friday, going to work on Monday' was described by one report as 'walking over a precipice'. A 15-year-old girl summarised the traumatic experience at a school leavers' conference in these words; 'the first day at work I could have cried all the way home.'

In modern industrial and techno-logical society the world of work is completely different from the world of home and school. Home and school are child-oriented and have the child's scale. The world of industry and commerce is adult-oriented and has a scale grasped often by only a few in any enterprise. The topography is new, the chain of authority difficult to under-stand, confusion of counsel from workmates on the one side and em-

ployers on the other is common enough. There is sometimes a moral shock from the concepts and language of adults and through the revelation of business practices. Yet of course this work-world is the world the child has to enter to become adult. Here he finds the real challenge of life in his daily relations with others and in the disciplines the commercial or productive process and its materials impose on everyone alike. The school only counterfeits these: in relation to industry, school is the play world.

In the years before the second world war it was not generally recognised that the transition from school to work presented problems beyond finding jobs for the least educated. By the Labour Exchanges Act 1909 the Board of Trade was authorised to set up Juvenile Departments in Labour Ex-changes and by the Education (Choice of Employment) Act 1910, LEAs were empowered to set up special bureaux to help boys and girls to find employ-ment; but the social and psychological problems of transition were ignored. In the inter-war years of heavy unemploy-ment, children were lucky to get any job and were often told so.

Since the last war government departments, local authorities and voluntary societies have all recognised the obligations of society not simply to find jobs for school-leavers but to smooth the actual transition physically and psychologically, to keep a watch on the job-patterns of leavers and to promote their further education and general well-being. The success of the post-war policy of full employment made every worker, no matter how young, more valuable, and the ethos of the welfare state deepened social concern. The Albemarle Report on the Youth Service, 1960 (*q.v.*) spoke for public conscience when it pointed to the fact that so much could be done for the bright boy or girl—he or she could stay at school to 17 or 18, then go to training college or university for the next three years, sustained by grants, be given a home from home in union or hostel and be kept *in statu pupillari* until 21 or 22. On the other side, the early leavers, those therefore least equipped, were thrown into industry or commerce to fend for themselves at 15 or 16, without much hope of further help. Not only was there here a clear case of social neglect, but the cultural 'gap' in society was thereby made more divisive and a permanent sense of inferiority fostered in the 'failures'. Sociologists began to speak of the 80% and the 20%—the former those who left school at the earliest opportunity, the latter those who went on to further education.

But it is not only going to work for the first time which generates anxieties. These begin as school-leaving looms up. It is an insensitive child who does not ask—how can I find the right job? What qualifications do I have to have for the job I most want? How do I apply for it? Even in the years of full employment the openings for juvenile employment have been uneven: it was possible to leave school for unemployment. All social agencies have therefore been concerned with four kinds of services: (1) vocational guidance, (2) placement, (3) preparation for work, and (4) adjustment to industry.

The present machinery The statutory British authority for assisting boys and girls to find employment is the Youth Employment Service (*q.v.*). The Employment and Training Act 1948 brought it into being on the lines laid down in the Ince Report (1945). The Act made possible the continuation of the Service as one service locally under either Ministry of Labour control, or, where it elected to exercise its powers by a given date, of the LEA. Administration of the Service, no matter by what authority it was organised locally, was placed in the hands of a Central Youth Employment Executive staffed by officers of the Ministry of Labour,

the Ministry of Education and the Scottish Education Department, and constituting part of the structure of the Ministry of Labour. The Executive is advised by a National Youth Employment Council, and voluntary local Youth Employment Committees similarly advise local Youth Employment Bureaux. On 1 January 1965 there were 1,279 Youth Employment Officers employed by local authorities and 214 by the Ministry of Labour. Turnover is high—some 300 had left the Service in the previous two years. It is rather an elderly service—54% of YEOs are over 40.

The Ince Report not only devised the new machinery, it established the methods by which the leavers are at present helped—(1) a talk by the YEO on careers at least annually in each school for which he is responsible, often backed up with exhibitions; (2) an interview with each school leaver who wishes it in the last or penultimate term of his school life. (Normally the interview takes place at school with the headmaster or headmistress, and perhaps one other teacher, present. A parent is entitled to be present, but parents do not exercise this option in more than 50% of interviews.

The YES appears effective in placing one in three secondary modern leavers in their first places and one in five grammar school leavers. But as in fact it interviews just about every leaver its influence on placement will be higher than these ratios indicate. It carries on a follow-up system—called 'review of progress'—which produces some response from more than half the total of leavers. Mention should be made here of the excellent visual aids and careers guidance publications produced in abundance by the Central Youth Employment Executive and published by HMSO.

Non-statutory aid to school-leavers comes from three sources: (1) The school careers teacher; (2) school leavers' conferences run by churches, schools and voluntary organisations; (3) adjustment to industry courses, also run by voluntary organisations. The careers teacher (*q.v.*) usually has other teaching and administrative duties in the school and is not normally able therefore to give full-time attention to careers—sometimes he can only function after school-hours. His effectiveness will depend on his enthusiasm and the facilities granted to him by the school. He has been known to assert that, to render a service as effective as a YEO, he needs a telephone and a careers room for exhibits and interviews. Nevertheless, he can be particularly useful for grammar schools and public schools. Grammar schools sometimes complain that the YES is not a graduate service (almost half have some professional qualifications, just over a quarter are graduates) and therefore not able to understand the needs of grammar school leavers. The answer of the YES to this delicate problem has been the appointment of a senior type of officer, the Careers Advisory Officer, who works mostly with grammar and comprehensive schools.

School leavers' conferences, under a variety of names, take place locally under grass roots initiatives. The object of most of them is to bring leavers of both sexes together to visit factories, plants and stores, to meet and to listen to young employees, trade unionists, works managers, personnel managers, employers and others talking about job experience, opportunities and disciplines. Some succeed also in bringing the local clergy, teachers and parents to the consultations. They provide an introduction, for those still at school, to the world of work. They are available to only a fraction of leavers at present. Courses on adjustment to industry perform the same sort of service for those already at work.

The future In 1958, out of 269,805 leavers who started work only 93,212

or 34.4% became apprentices or learners. Of the total of 314,813 leavers in 1964 only 114,492 or 36.4% were so classified—not a very satisfactory result after nearly a decade of effort. It still is true that 36.3% of all leavers do not receive any form of training in their occupations: for Wales the figure is 46.0%; for Scotland 52.9%. The pattern of day release for further education shows the same slow progress. In 1965/66 only 32.6% of boys and 7.7% of girls at work in England and 30.8% of boys and 4.1% of girls at work in Wales got day release. Some industries—gas, electricity, water—reach almost 100% day release; engineering and public administration are very high indeed; the leather industry and distributive trades make the poorest showing.

Two developments could accelerate the rate of progress in the training of youth. The first is the Industrial Training Act 1964, which authorises the establishment of Industrial Training Boards to provide courses for those employees or intending employees for whom no training is at present available and to finance these by levies on employers who are failing or unable to provide training, and to make grants to assist training schemes. The second development is the report by a working party of the National Youth Employment Council, entitled *The Future Development of the Youth Employment Service*. It follows The Industrial Welfare Society (now The Industrial Society) report, *The Transition from School to Work*, in proposing the deepening and lengthening of the work of the YES in schools; the strengthening of its relations with the school staff and with parents; and the raising of professional standards. Administrative action has yet to follow to carry out the recommendations of the report. Both the YES and the Industrial Training Boards set up under the Industrial Act will have to move fast to cope with the situation which will be created by the raising of the school leaving age to 16 in the 1970s.

See also **School leaving age, Raising the; Youth Employment Service**

FURTHER READING

M. P. Carter. *Home, School and Work*, Pergamon, 1962. *Into Work*, Penguin, 1966.
Day Release (the report of a committee set up by the Minister of Education), HMSO, 1964.
Interim Report of the National Youth Employment Council on the Employment and Training of Young People, 1959–1961, HMSO, 1961.
Leslie Paul. *The Transition from School to Work* (a report made to the King George V Jubilee Trust and Industrial Welfare Society), Industrial Welfare Society, 1962.
Report of the National Youth Employment Council, HMSO, 1965.
Report on the Juvenile Employment Service (The Ince Report). HMSO, 1945.
Training for Skill (The Carr Report), HMSO, 1958.
T. Veness. *School Leavers, their Aspirations and Expectations*, Methuen, 1962.
The Work of the Youth Employment Service, 1962–1965, HMSO, 1965.
The Youth Service in England and Wales (The Albemarle Report), HMSO, 1960.

LP

Leavis, Frank Raymond (b. 1895) Editor of *Scrutiny* from 1932 to 1953, and one of the founders of this immensely influential critical review, Dr Leavis was a Fellow of Downing College, Cambridge, from 1936 to 1962; an honorary fellow from 1962 to 1964; and a University Reader in English from 1959 to 1962. In 1965 he was Visiting Professor at the University of York. He has written *Culture and Environment* (with Denys Thompson, 1933); *Revaluation: Tradition and Development in English Poetry* (1936); *Education and the University* (1945); *The Great Tradition: George Eliot, James and Conrad* (1948); *The Common Pursuit* (1952); *D. H. Lawrence: Novelist* (1955); *Anna Karenina and Other Essays* (1967).

Lebanon, Education in The state provides most of the primary education, but private schools cater in the main for secondary and higher education. In 1965 a school building programme was embarked upon, costing L£41 million for 629 schools. 1964 statistics: 1,048 state primary schools (enrolment 134,951); 225 state secondary schools (enrolment 21,608); 1,240 private primary schools (enrolment 175,650); 216 private secondary schools (enrolment 29,030). There are four universities in Beirut, one state and three subsidised: enrolments—State University of Lebanon 5,684; American University 3,245; Arab University 7,765; French University (St. Joseph's) 1,992. There are four state agricultural colleges, one state music college, one state hotel-keeping college, two teacher training colleges and a state reformatory for delinquent boys.

The population of the country was approximately 2¼ million in 1964.

Lecture At most universities and colleges, and in most subjects, the lecture is still the main vehicle of teaching, however much some people may share Dr Johnson's view that it became obsolete with the invention of printing. The Hale Committee on University Teaching Methods received a memorandum from the National Union of Students criticising many lecturers for presenting material already available in books and journals: but its own view was that the books are often not available or suited to the needs of students. It found the lecture justified as a way of introducing and opening up a subject, especially where the material is too complex to understand without oral explanation. 'It is also valued', the Committee wrote in its Report (1964), 'as a demonstration of technique and as a means of awakening a critical attitude on the part of the student.' And finally, the lecture provides a rare opportunity for the student to hear a distinguished or prophetic or eccentric personality thinking aloud, and this can be an inspiring experience.

Inevitably, however, most lecturers are less inspired and few of them have explicitly studied the art of lecturing, including the use of accompanying printed material. More important still, too little attention has been paid to the possibilities of dovetailing lectures and other modes of learning in smaller groups (perhaps activity groups) or privately.

BF

Left-handedness There is still argument about the cause of left-handedness. Some maintain that it is due to the superior development of the right hemisphere of the brain and can be inherited, whilst others put it down to quite different factors in early upbringing. Sir Cyril Burt (*q.v.*) has estimated that about 5% of the world's population is left-handed, and a puzzling fact is that the condition is more frequently found with boys than girls, and is very much more common amongst mentally defective children. A higher than average proportion of left-handedness has also been claimed amongst artists and designers.

At times in the past left-handedness has often been considered very undesirable, or as the words for it themselves suggest, 'gauche' or even 'sinister'; amongst Christians there was once an association between the left side and forms of witchcraft. Even now, left-handers may have difficulties in the sense that so many things, from telephone boxes to musical instruments, are designed for the right-hander. In schools, too, it is often unfortunately true that left-handed children are merely permitted rather than taught how best to write with their left hand, with the result that they often pick up bad habits that lead to painfully cramped and awkward handwriting. There is little reason why primary teachers should not now know the standard ways for helping left-handers, who otherwise may find all handwriting, with its left to right orientation, a considerable ordeal.

Very young children usually go through an ambidextrous phase, but should soon show signs of preferring to use one hand rather than the other for such things as cutting with scissors or throwing balls. If this clearly turns out to be the left hand, it would certainly be unwise to discourage them at this stage.

FURTHER READING:
Michael Barsley. *The Left-handed Book*, Souvenir Press, 1966.
Margaret Clark. *Teaching Left-handed Children*, Univ. of London Press, 1959.

NT

Legal rights and obligations of parents

School attendance It is the legal duty of parents, under the provisions of Section 36 of the Education Act 1944, to cause their children to receive 'efficient full-time education suitable to their age, ability and aptitude by either regular attendance at school or otherwise'. This duty is enforced upon the parents by the provisions of Section 37 of the Act which enables an LEA to serve notice upon those parents who are failing to perform their duty, giving them a period of up to 14 days in which they are to show that the children are receiving full-time education. If the parents do not comply with the notice, the LEA then has power to serve a school attendance order (*q.v.*), requiring the parents to send the child to a particular school. If the parents do not comply with the school attendance order, then they will be guilty of an offence and summary proceedings may be taken against them and they can be liable to a fine for the first offence of £1, £5 for the second offence and £10 for the third and subsequent offence, with the possibility of a month's imprisonment.

The Court also has power, under the provisions of Section 40, sub-section 3 of the Education Act 1944, to bring a child whose parents are the subject of non-attendance proceedings before the juvenile court as being in need of care and protection. Regular attendance within the meaning of the Section has been interpreted as attendance at the time when the school session begins, and persistent lateness after the close of the school register can be held to be failing to secure regular attendance.[1]

Choice of school Section 76 of the Education Act 1944 provides that an LEA in exercise of the powers under the Education Act shall have regard to the general principle that so far as is compatible with the provision of sufficient instruction and training and the avoidance of unreasonable public expenditure, pupils are to be educated in accordance with the wishes of their parents. This Section, however, only lays down a general principle and LEAs are not bound to comply with the wishes of parents and can have regard to other factors in the allocation of pupils to schools, in addition to the wishes of the parents. It would appear also that the wishes of the parents are restricted to matters relating to the curriculum of the school.[2]

In the main, however, parents are concerned with the particular school to which their children are to be sent and this might come into conflict with the limits of the catchment area of the particular school, as determined by the LEA. If parents take the view that the LEA is acting unreasonably in the allocation of schools for their children, they have the right to lay a complaint with the Secretary of State under the provisions of Section 68 of the Education Act 1944. The Secretary of State under this Section has, if he so determines, the power to give directions to the LEA. Authorities have powers to help parents with fees at an independent day school to meet religious preference if no maintained or direct grant school of that denomination is available.

Religion Section 25 of the Education Act 1944 gives parents the right to withdraw their children entirely from religious observance and instruction at school. They may also withdraw their children from maintained schools for the purpose of receiving denominational religious instruction, and from the denominational schools for the purpose of receiving religious instruction in accordance with the agreed (non-denominational) religious syllabus. Pupils, however, may not be withdrawn except at the beginning and end of a school session. Parents are also entitled to withdraw their children from school on any day exclusively set apart for religious observance by the religious body to which the parents belong.

Medical examination Parents can be required to submit their children to medical examination. LEAs have duties to ascertain whether children require special educational treatment and also to carry out periodical medical inspections. If a parent is not prepared voluntarily to permit a child to be examined, the Secretary of State has power under Section 69 of the Education Act 1944 to serve a notice on the parent requiring him to submit the child for examination, and if the parent does not, without reasonable excuse, comply with the notice, he is liable on summary conviction to a fine not exceeding £5.

Clothing If a child is unable to take advantage of the educational provisions in a school by reason of the inadequacy and unsuitability of his clothing, the LEA under regulations made under Section 5 of the Education (Miscellaneous Provisions) Act 1948 is empowered to provide the clothing free of charge or, as the case may be, to require the parent to make a contribution towards the provision of his clothing.

See also **Parental choice; School attendance**

REFERENCES

1. Hinckley v. Rankin 1961, 1 AER 692.
2. Wood and others v. Greater London Borough of Ealing, Times Law Report, 28 July 1966.

HP

Leicester Psychology and Mathematics Project An experimental scheme of mathematics for secondary schools prepared by Dr. R. Skemp, based on the unified psychological principles of concept formation and schematic learning. Pupils work in groups or individually from a text with teacher guidance. There are three sections: 'basic', 'traditional' for NUJMB Syllabus II, 'modern' for a special examination.

FURTHER READING
R. R. Skemp. *Understanding Mathematics*, Univ. of London Press, 1966.

Leicestershire Plan schools In 1957 the Leicestershire County Council introduced the Leicestershire Experiment in two school areas in the county (Oadby and Hinckley). The objective was to make possible the abolition of the 11-plus examination through the development of a system of comprehensive secondary schools making use of existing buildings, while at the same time avoiding the development of very large schools.

The main characteristics of this system are as follows: At the age of 11 all pupils from junior schools in the area proceed automatically to their local high school. At the age of 14, parents of pupils in high schools exercise their right to choose whether their child proceeds to the upper (grammar) school or not. If they choose the upper school for their child parents must give a guarantee that they will keep their child at school till he reaches the age of 16. If the parents do not wish their child to proceed to an upper school, he remains at the high school for a further year until reaching school leaving age. All examination work (GCE and CSE) is undertaken in the upper school.

Since 1957 the Leicestershire Experiment (now called the Leicestershire Plan) has gradually extended to many other areas in the county, and the objective is to reorganise all areas on this system. In 1965 the Leicestershire County Council took the decision to abolish parental choice of schools when the school leaving age is raised. When this is done all pupils will proceed automatically at the age of 14 to their local upper school.

BS

Lesotho, Education in 1964/5 statistics: in 1,111 schools and institutions there were 168,180 primary school children, 3,094 secondary, and 623 students at teacher training colleges; 220 Basuto students were studying at the University of Botswana, Lesotho and Swaziland at Roma, and 117 overseas.

The country's population was nearly one million in 1966.

Lesson period This is a unit in the time-table of a day's activity in school. In some countries, e.g. France, Russia, West and East Germany, all lessons are of the same length. In the UK there is greater variety. In general, lessons for younger children tend to be short, sometimes lasting only 15 or 20 minutes, while in secondary schools lessons are about 35, 40 or 45 minutes long. English teachers may plan their days to have seven, or eight, or even more lessons. Certain subjects are taught in double periods: it is common for laboratory work in the sciences to be time-tabled in this way.

In many English schools the unit of the lesson has disappeared: in infants' and junior schools the teacher may be given complete freedom to include as many lesson units of the length she thinks appropriate in any one day. In some secondary schools and also in some primary schools the teacher may have a session of the day, i.e. morning school or afternoon school, at his or her disposal for sustained work in a subject or field of study.

See also **Integrated day**

DJJ

Leverhulme Research Awards
Founded in 1933, the awards, including fellowships and grants, are made to senior workers prevented by routine duties or pressure of work from carrying out research. Except in special circumstances, the awards are limited to British-born subjects normally resident in the UK.

Room 904, 21–23 New Fetter La., London, EC4.

Lewis Report (1917): Report of the Departmental Committee on Juvenile Education in Relation to Employment after the War Terms of reference: to consider what steps should be taken to make provision for the education and instruction of children and young persons after the first world war, considering particularly the interests of those (1) who had been abnormally employed during the war; (2) who could not immediately find advantageous employment; (3) who required special training for employment. Chairman: J. Herbert Lewis, MP.

The Committee was part of the planning for reconstruction after the war. There had already been concern that the arrangements for half-time education for juveniles should be ended, and there was additional concern because the employment of juveniles had been disrupted by the war. The Committee recommended that the school leaving age be raised to 14, and that all half-time arrangements should be ended. These recommendations were implemented in the Education Act 1918.

Liberal Education, Association for
The Association was founded in 1961 to encourage the extension of liberal education in an increasingly specialised industrial society. It holds that formal education in the UK should not be confined by narrow or vocational curricula, and that it is the duty of teachers to revise subject-matter and teaching methods from time to time with this aim. Membership is open to all individually and to schools and colleges corporately.

The Association brings together, through regional groups, teachers and others concerned with liberal education, and conducts study groups.

Membership Sec.: Vivian Ramsbottom, Stuart Hse, Mill La., Cambridge.

Publication: *Liberal Education* (twice annually).

Liberal Party and education Since the Liberal Party believes both in liberty and equality it has always given an unusually high priority to education. This means, to be realistic, giving a lower priority to other things. At the general election of 1966 the Liberals were the only party who campaigned for a cut in military commitments east of Suez in order to provide more money for education. This readiness to divert resources, Liberals believe, is fundamental to any honest policy for educational reform and expansion.

Within the education system Liberals would give the top priority to the implementation of the Plowden Report (*q.v.*). Unless the standard of primary education for all children can be brought up to the level, not of the best, but of the good average, there will be many who cannot benefit from improvement or reform at the later stages. This means neither equality nor the liberty of each child to make the best of his own potentialities.

Liberals have long been convinced of the necessity of getting rid of the 11-plus, and the Party is committed to supporting a non-selective system of secondary education. But Liberals are not doctrinaire supporters of the 'all-through purpose-built comprehensive school.' Experiments with two-tier systems and sixth-form or junior colleges have warm Liberal support. Liberals recognise, too, that a reform of this kind must inevitably be spread over a number of years. They are opposed altogether to the 'abolition' of the public schools, holding this to be an infringement of essential freedom; but they would welcome some closer integration of the maintained and independent systems. This, they believe, would benefit the public schools by diversifying their social structure and benefit the nation by providing badly needed boarding places. The report of the Liberal working party suggested that the cost of such a reform might be shared between the public schools themselves and the central government, but should not fall on the LEAs.

In higher and further education the Liberal Party is opposed to a 'binary system' as an element in national policy. It believes that the distinction between 'vocational' and 'non-vocational' education is a false one, and would prefer to see an 'open' system with increasingly close links between universities and other institutions of higher education.

Most important of all, perhaps, is the Liberal Party's commitment to democratic regionalism, since this affects the whole organisation of education. For the provision of a modern well-equipped education service, the present pattern of 165 LEAs varying in size from Lancashire to Canterbury and with boundaries of medieval complexity makes no sense. Liberals believe that the great regions of England, together with Scotland and Wales, are the natural units to provide for the education of the people, with units much smaller than existing counties to supervise the day-to-day running of the schools. But both must be democratically controlled.

ADCP

Liberal studies Professional bodies, such as the Institution of Mechanical Engineers, have expressed dissatisfaction with the products of purely vocational training; examining bodies in further education, like the City and Guilds of London Institute, stipulate that candidates must pursue a course of general studies in addition to their specialised examination subjects; and in 1957 the Ministry of Education endorsed the view that it was the duty of educational institutions in this field to broaden the minds of their students as well as to improve their technical skills. There is, however, no agreement whether the desired 'liberal studies' should be tested by examination, or are even in principle assessable, whether they require a separate department in each college for their organisation, or even what their content ought to be.

A minority view holds that technical studies themselves can be adequately liberalised by enlarging their scope of reference. What underlies this view is resentment at the suggestion that technology is an essentially restricted study. A similar insistence produces the contention that any subject free of examination pressure is a liberal subject, so that carpentry could constitute the liberal study of a radio engineer.

The generally accepted view, however, is that liberal studies should not be even potentially vocational. As a result, students in technical colleges find themselves involved, willy-nilly, in courses in which they may see no advantage. Sometimes a choice of non-vocational studies can be offered, but time-tabling difficulties make the necessary amalgamation of classes difficult. To the problem of what sort of study deserves to be made universally obligatory, various answers are confidently given.

The aesthetic answer is to lay a foundation for the appreciation of art, drama, music, literature—everything that makes life desirable and enjoyable. Another view, which might be termed 'protective', holds that training should be given in moral judgment, personal relations, and critical examination of the mass media, while a more practical school advocates instruction in the use of money, trades unionism and citizenship. Probably the most popular answer is social studies. All four approaches can be mixed. Some syllabuses are planned as one- or even three-year courses; others develop spontaneously from the particular interests of each class.

Remembering the shortness of available time, it is clear that the value of such amorphous studies cannot lie in their content, but in what happens in the classroom when they are taught. This has been analysed by F. D. Flower in *Language and Education* (1966). These subjects stimulate discussion, and students become more articulate as a result. The value of liberal studies is thus defined as the provision of a context in which the student is encouraged to engage in communication at a level higher than that habitual to him, thus preparing himself for the non-technical responsibilities of the social role in which his technical training will cast him. In some technical colleges, however, a similar argument, but more personal and less social, is used to justify the choice of literature as the central liberal study.

See also **Further education; General studies**

FURTHER READING

C. A. Blackman *et al. Liberal Studies*, Books I, II and III, Cassell, 1962, 1964, 1966.
Sydney Bolt. *The Right Response*, Hutchinson Educational, 1966.
F. D. Flower. *Language and Education*, Longmans, Green, 1966.
Ministry of Education. *General Studies in Technical Colleges*, HMSO, 1962.
Liberal Education in Technical Colleges, Circular 333, HMSO, 1957.
National Institute of Adult Education. *Liberal Education in a Technical Age: A Survey of the Relationship of Vocational and Non-vocational Further Education and Training*, 1955.
Liberal Education, journal of the Association for Liberal Education.   SB

Liberia, Education in In 1964 there were 893 schools, with an enrolment of 85,861. Some were state schools, others mission schools supported by foreign missions and state-subsidised, private schools supported by endowments and subsidised by the state, and tribal schools controlled by tribal authorities. A four-year programme launched in 1967 aims to increase the number of primary pupils from approximately 64,000 to 80,000 by 1970, and secondary pupils from 8,400 to 13,500.

The population of the country was approximately one million in 1964.

Librarianship, Training for The mimimum educational qualifications for librarians are five passes in GCE including English language. Two passes must be at A level.

A full-time course at a school of librarianship, available at 11 centres of further education in the UK, lasts two years. Graduates may take a one-year special post-graduate course at schools of librarianship at University College, London, Sheffield University, or Queen's University, Belfast, where after passing the school's internal examinations and gaining a diploma, they are entitled to be placed on the Library Association register. At Belfast non-graduates may attend a two-year course leading to the University's diploma.

Library Association examinations are in two parts. Part I consists of (1) The library and the community; (2) government and control of libraries; (3) the organisation of knowledge; (4) bibliographical control and service. All four papers are taken at one sitting. Part II consists of three 'lists'. Candidates must take six papers, including one only from List A, which has three papers: (1) academic and legal deposit libraries; (2) special libraries and information bureaux; (3) public (municipal and county) libraries. List B consists of ten papers on particular aspects of library practice of certain kinds of library. List C gives a choice of over 40 papers on the bibliography and librarianship of different fields of knowledge.

Those who have passed the Library Association's examination and have three years' experience are placed on the register of Chartered Librarians, and are known as Associates of the Library Association. Associates of at least five years standing will be elected Fellows if they successfully complete a thesis on some aspect of librarianship.

Library Association, 7 Ridgmount St, Store St, London, WC1.

LMH

Libraries, Classroom *See* **Libraries, School**

Libraries, Friends of the National Founded in 1931 with the aim of giving to the great national libraries the sort of help that art galleries and museums receive from the National Art Collections Fund, this society promotes its work by direct contributions from its funds, by special appeals in special cases, and by encouraging (and acting as intermediary for) gifts and bequests. Membership acts as a recommendation for a reader's ticket in the British Museum and the National libraries of Scotland and Wales.

c/o The British Museum, London, WC1.

Libraries, Mobile *See* **Public library services to schools**

Libraries, School
History The development of school libraries has been something of a paradox. From a rare and feeble top growth in certain public and grammar schools, they have grown downwards to strike vigorous roots in infant schools during the last decade or so.

Official recognition came slowly. The Cross Report of 1888 (*q.v.*) recommended that school libraries be established. In the 1906 Building Regulations, the Board of Education spoke of the desirability of libraries in secondary schools. Not until 1914 were they considered essential. In 1930 the

Board's pamphlet on planning secondary schools described a room set apart for library use. Something more positive replaced mere encouragement in 1945 when the Statutory Rules and Orders No 345 required libraries to be provided in secondary schools. During the 1950s, awareness of the value of libraries in primary schools was shown in official publications, notably in *Primary Education*, the Ministry handbook of 1959, which stressed the usefulness of classroom libraries, giving the central collection lower priority.

In secondary schools Here libraries are usually single, centralised collections, although a few schools have quite large departmental libraries and rather more have small collections in subject bases such as laboratories. Some grammar schools have a junior library for the lower and middle schools.

The library is generally housed in a room measuring 1,500 sq. ft or less. This area might include a small workroom for the librarian. Stocks vary in size but often do not grow beyond 4,000 volumes since at this point replacement costs tend to absorb the library grant. Such schools have little chance of reaching even that most modest of targets, 10 volumes per pupil. Those schools which benefit from private funds or receive supplementary grants are more fortunate. LEAs either allocate a specified proportion of the capitation grant to the library or provide a block grant allowing the school to decide upon the library's share.

Although some schools prefer to classify their stock by the Cheltenham system, considering it better suited to academic requirements, most use the Dewey decimal classification since it is the one pupils are most likely to meet in other libraries. Also, schools which receive loans of books from public libraries (*see* **Public library services to schools**), which are usually classified by the Dewey system, find it easier to merge them into their own stocks if there is a common system.

Generally, standards of classification, cataloguing and recording of stock are low, but this is hardly surprising since most school libraries have to be run on a part-time basis. Losses of books are usually high for the same reason, and their cost probably offsets any economies made by parsimonious staffing.

The librarian is usually a teacher of English. He will probably take some of his classes in the library and may be given free periods in which to cope with administration. If not, he may have to work long after school hours and during vacations. A few larger authorities appoint professional librarians to all but the smallest secondary schools. Others provide non-teaching assistants who relieve the librarian of technical and supervisory work.

In some grammar schools sixth-formers only are allowed access to the library—which hardly makes it 'the centre of the intellectual life of the school', as described in the Ministry's *Building Bulletin No 2*. Such schools sometimes give pupils one or more visits to the library during their first year during which they learn how to use it. This insight is presumably meant to sustain them when they reach the sixth.

Happily, most schools try to give all pupils a chance to use the library, both for study and borrowing. This is not easy when, all too often, there is barely room to seat 40. Consequently, many children have to be content with a weekly 'browse and borrow' session. Quite a few schools are now exploiting their books more fully by making bulk loans to teachers for use in subject bases. These are the schools in which independent study is more common than class teaching. Their methods (individual assignments, projects and team-teaching) rely heavily on the use of library books by far more pupils than could be contained in any library room.

In primary schools Here one is likely to find a series of classroom libraries supplemented, in larger schools, by a central collection. This arrangement was often made necessary by the lack of a room in which to gather all the stock, but teachers were quick to appreciate its advantages. As learning by discovery supplanted rote learning of uncomprehended facts, teachers set out to create an environment in which books and materials could interact to arouse curiosity and make its satisfaction excitingly possible. In doing this they stopped buying sets of textbooks and, instead, bought library books, so that now it is not uncommon for larger primary schools to have stocks of 4,000 or more. These libraries are usually run co-operatively by the teachers and the children themselves.

Only schools with a fairly large central collection are likely to use a detailed classification such as the Dewey system. More common is a simple arrangement under very general headings. Children acquire a remarkable knowledge not only of the whereabouts of books but of their contents when they are using them continuously.

The future In both primary and secondary schools, libraries are now being built to house not only books but films, tapes, programmed material and the relevant machines; they are places in which all pupils will have opportunity to study.

RPAE

Libraries, University In August 1965 Britain's university libraries contained over 20 million volumes in collections varying in size between the London complex (4,122,000), Oxford (3,321,000) and Cambridge (4,017,000) and the newer universities each with collections of under 100,000. Apart from the three major units no British university library can compare quantitatively with its American or continental counterparts, and the lack of really adequate library provision is

432

currently an outstanding problem in higher education in the British Isles. The university libraries of Cambridge, Oxford and Trinity College, Dublin, are entitled, under the Copyright Act of 1911, to receive without charge one copy of each British publication. All university libraries in the UK rely almost entirely, except for some limited endowment income, on their university's internal allocation of funds received via the University Grants Committee. In 1965/66 total expenditure from this source was £6,306,565 (books £1,615,638, periodicals £878,170), or less than 5% of total university expenditure.

Because of the phenomenal increase in the output of scholarly publications, and because most libraries can acquire for themselves only a fraction of their needs, inter-library lending is a characteristic of university library activity—either by direct loans, through regional centres, or through the National Central Library (*q.v.*). The university libraries of Oxford and Cambridge do not, however, participate. The main organisation for this, and for all aspects of cooperation between university libraries, is the Standing Conference of National and University Librarians (SCONUL). Although their primary function is clearly to support teaching and research in their parent institutions, most university libraries lend extensively from their own bookstocks, via inter-library loan, to public and other libraries; most will allow non-university enquirers to have access to their collections for reference purposes. There is a SCONUL-operated scheme enabling undergraduates to make use of the libraries of universities other than their own during vacations.

Senior staff members are almost invariably university graduates, often with research experience, and frequently with a qualification in librarianship (there are courses for the academic post-graduate diploma in librarianship at University College, London, and at the University of Sheffield), and it is now normal for library staff grades to equate with academic grades. The university librarian is of professorial rank and is *ex officio* a member of senate or its equivalent. There is an increasing tendency for senior library staff to assume responsibility, as subject specialists, for particular sections of the library bookstock, and similarly more emphasis is now placed on active service to readers including instruction in the use of reference works, subject bibliographies, abstracts, indexes and catalogues. General library policy, finance and staff appointments are normally overseen by a library committee consisting of senior members of the university with, occasionally, lay representation.

Many university libraries are actively engaged in the mechanisation of routine processes including the use of computers for information storage and retrieval and for 'house-keeping' procedures, and research projects are being conducted into the adequacy and use of bookstocks and into undergraduate book provision. 1967 has seen the publication of the report of the Parry Committee (*see* **Parry Report**), probably the most comprehensive document yet produced on British university libraries. The report surveys the present position in detail and makes recommendations for future improvement and investigation. Librarians will await with interest some indication that its proposals are to be implemented.

Standing Conference of National and University Librarians (SCONUL)—Sec.: Dr R. J. Bates, Librarian, University College, Cardiff.

FURTHER READING

J. F. Foster and T. Craig (Eds). *Commonwealth Universities Yearbook*, Association of Commonwealth Universities.

W. L. Saunders (Ed.). *Librarianship in Britain Today*, Library Association, 1967.

University Grants Committee. *Report of the Committee on Libraries*, HMSO, 1967. *Returns from Universities and Colleges in Receipt of Treasury Grant*, HMSO, annual.

Journals
Journal of Documentation (quarterly), *ASLIB Proceedings* (monthly), *Library Association Record* (monthly), *Library World* (monthly), *Universities Quarterly*.

HF

Libraries in colleges of education

The aims, and consequently the composition, of college libraries, have expanded recently to reflect the developments in higher education suggested in various government or departmental reports and documents (see *Further reading* below). Most authorities concerned with teacher training would now expect college libraries not merely to service the academic and professional courses of the colleges, but to provide facilities for individual study by staff and students, and offer a spectrum of 'recreational' books to foster a permanent taste for reading. For the development of 'reading teachers' is one touchstone by which the success of a college may be judged. The example of a teacher rarely encountered without a book, eager and spontaneous in sharing his pleasure, will outweigh, with children, any amount of precept and exhortation from the dais.

Following publication in 1961 of the Ministry of Education pamphlet *Libraries in Training Colleges*, many colleges have appointed a tutor-librarian, or reading tutor—usually a teacher of high academic and sometimes professional librarianship qualifications—to be responsible for stocking and running the library, and for a lecture programme affording him contact with students and knowledge of their abilities and needs. As his duties include the close involvement of students with the library, the current tendency so to construct courses as to make students increasingly responsible for their own reading—to indicate avenues of enquiry, rather than to list 'set books'—helps to determine his function and guide the policy and work of the library.

College libraries naturally specialise in all aspects of education, and attempt to present a balanced and modern selection of reading for course work; a good fiction library is essential; a variety of periodicals is normally purchased, as much research work first finds publication in this form; some colleges have collections of gramophone records, tapes, and visual materials. The school practice library is an especially important concern of the librarian, and of the college education department. Like the main library it must be inviting, various, up-to-date, and generously stocked. Students may expect the widest practicable range of children's literature, and of specialist subject books for all levels of their school work. From these shelves, a student teaching retarded juniors, and another involved with intelligent adolescents keen to be introduced to adult fiction, will each find his needs met and his enthusiasm nourished.

The Bachelor of Education degree has presented college libraries with another problem. It may prove uneconomic to provide, in each college, highly specialist works needed by relatively few students. One suggested compromise is for member colleges of an institute each to specialise at this level in one area of study, and to give all BEd students within the institute access to their stock.

Adequate finance will be needed if college libraries are to keep pace with increasing student numbers, and with the developing range and academic content of courses. Nor must the educational principle be forgotten that reading is pleasure. The college library should not be a place where books are studied but never enjoyed.

FURTHER READING
Higher Education, Report of the Committee appointed by the Prime Minister under the Chairmanship of Lord Robbins, HMSO, 1963.
Library Practice for Colleges of Education, College Library Practice Sub-Committee, Library Association, 1966.

Libraries in Training Colleges, Ministry of Education, 1961.
Libraries in Training Colleges: Library Bookstock in Larger Colleges, DES, 1964.
M. B. Line. *The College Student and the Library*, Univ. of Southampton Institute of Education, 1965.
R. G. Ralph. *The Library in Education*, Phoenix, 1949.
E. Roe. *Teachers, Librarians and Children*, Crosby Lockwood, 1965.
The Second Annual Survey of Training College Libraries, Library Association, 1966.

Journals
Education for Teaching, Association of Teachers in Colleges and Departments of Education.
Education Libraries Bulletin, Univ. of London Institute of Education.
The L.A. Record, The Library Association.

NSA

Library Association The Association has the object of uniting all persons engaged or interested in library work, of holding examinations and acting as the professional body for librarians. It publishes *The Library Association Record* (monthly), together with other publications of interest to librarians and library-users, and also conducts examinations for a Certificate for Teacher-Librarians in collaboration with the School Library Association (*q.v.*).

Chaucer Hse, 7 Ridgmount St, Store St, London, WC1.

Libya, Education in Where school places are available, primary school education lasting six years is compulsory; three years preparatory and a further three years secondary are not compulsory. In Tripoli and Benghazi there are a number of schools for the children of non-Libyan communities with British, French, Italian, American and Dutch curricula. 1964–65 statistics: 747 primary schools (enrolment 170,188); 107 preparatory schools (enrolment 17,711); 18 secondary (enrolment 3,760); 16 teacher training colleges (enrolment 2,401); 11 technical colleges (enrolment 1,106); six higher education establishments (enrolment 1,949), and the University of Libya at

Benghazi (729 students). In 1964 the literacy rate was just over 25%.

The country's population was approximately $1\frac{1}{2}$ million in 1965.

Life-long integrated education This concept became part of UNESCO's official policy for education at the General Assembly in 1966. Its rationale is in part the same as that for adult education, except that it intrinsically involves a radical reform of the organisation, form and content of all other phases of education, and also implies a greater recognition of the educational functions of non-educational agencies. It is no longer desirable, for instance, to plan school and out-of-school forms of education as totally separate activities; and as a UNESCO paper explains, legislation governing education must be integrated with 'the organisation of . . . working . . . and leisure time, the laws relating to leave for study purposes . . . the trend and content of radio and television programmes'. It is not now desirable to divide life into three phases—preparation, work and retirement; on the contrary, education, work and leisure need to be elements continuing through life in changing proportions.

BG

Life Saving Society, Royal The aim of this Commonwealth society is to teach as many people as possible how to act individually to save a person in danger of drowning and how to carry out resuscitation, should this be necessary. The work is mainly directed to teaching children of school age. Classes are prepared by voluntary instructors for the graduated proficiency awards, the best known of which is the bronze medallion.

As a preliminary to life-saving instruction, the Society has water safety and safe swimming proficiency tests. For qualified life-savers the Society in the UK has a lifeguard corps, whose clubs arrange volunteer patrols at popular bathing places on beaches and inland waters. Resuscitation is included in the examination for all proficiency awards, and there are also separate resuscitation proficiency awards.

Headquarters: Desborough House, 14 Devonshire St, Portland Place, London, W1.

Life-saving and survival swimming Life-saving can be defined as the method of saving other swimmers from drowning; survival swimming is concerned with the techniques of saving one's own life when in danger on, or in, water. For personal safety it is vital that everyone should have a knowledge of both.

The Royal Life-Saving Society has for many years conducted examinations for their awards for life-saving. Classes for these awards are organised by most swimming clubs and many schools. Equally important is a knowledge of artificial respiration, which may be needed in the home or at work when someone's breathing has stopped after an electric shock. Two simple methods of restoring breathing, the prone pressure or Holger Nielson method, and the mouth-to-mouth, are described in the RLSS handbook.

In 1962 the Amateur Swimming Association launched a scheme for examinations in proficiency in personal survival, with bronze, silver and gold awards. The scheme has proved popular in schools and with adults.

Royal Life-Saving Society, 14 Devonshire St, London, W1.

Amateur Swimming Association, 64 Cannon St, London, EC4. Organiser of ASA Schemes for the Encouragement of Swimming: Miss L. V. Cook, 12 King's Ave, Woodford Green, Essex.

FURTHER READING
Illustrated Handbook of Life-Saving Instruction, Royal Life-Saving Society.
Survival Swimming, ASA, 1964.

JE

Linguistics *See* **Grammar, Teaching of**

Linguistique Appliquée, Association Internationale des Editeurs de An organisation set up to publish and distribute a series of books on linguistics written under the auspices of the Council of Europe. The Association has appointed the publishing firm of Harrap, a founder member, as sole distributor for the Commonwealth.

George G. Harrap and Co. Ltd, 182 High Holborn, London, WC1.

Linguists, Institute of A professional association for practising linguists, the Institute conducts qualifying examinations for entry to the profession. Its members follow a code of ethics.

The Institute is concerned with the rates of payment to members, whether as salaried members of organisations or as freelance interpreters, translators, teachers and so forth. It is also concerned with the standard of language teaching and professional training in the UK.

91 Newington Causeway, London, SE1.

Lip-reading This is a means of understanding used by the deaf and the partially deaf to replace or supplement hearing. Most of it can be done by guess work, according to the expression on the face, and through spotting a few key words. A lip-reader should therefore have a knowledge of the shape and movement of the lips in relation to sound: or, in other words, an understanding of phonetics. Particularly hard for lip-readers are homonyms, such as 'air' and 'heir'. If they attempt to work out every syllable that is spoken they may well become exhausted and behind with their 'translation'. When talking to a lip-reader, therefore, it is important not to go too fast and to pronounce each word clearly rather than loudly, and perhaps slightly exaggerate the positions of the mouth and the facial expressions one might anyway use. Women teachers of the deaf tend to use lipstick that will emphasise the line of the lips.

NT

Lists Lists of various kinds are published by the DES, usually giving information that can readily be set out in tables: e.g. List 172, *A Compendium of teacher training courses in England and Wales*.

Literacy Campaign, World *See* **UNESCO**

Literary institutes London, with its enormous numbers of potential adult students, has for many years provided opportunities for adult education which few if any other authorities could hope or expect to rival.

In 1913, it was decided to reorganise part-time education beyond school by housing separately the different kinds of education then provided in London's institutes—junior, vocational, recreational, and so on. Literary institutes were a distinctive feature of this scheme. They aimed to provide cultural studies at a high level (associating academic classes in the humanities with classes offering instruction in languages, music, art and drama), and to foster corporate and social activities. Owing to the war the first two literary institutes were not opened until 1919. Ten years later there were thirteen.

Today there are again only two, both in central London, the City Literary Institute (known as 'the City Lit') and the St Marylebone Literary Institute. This is because London's institutes were once again reorganised in 1957, largely to take account of the rising standards of cultural work in the general non-vocational institutes. As a result, London now has 35 adult education institutes with mixed non-vocational programmes, and two 'Lits' specialising in high-level work. The City Lit is one of the largest and best known centres for adult education in Britain, and today its annual enrolments exceed 25,000. It has a full-time academic staff of 10 and a part-time staff of more than 300.

BG

Literature, Royal Society of In 1823 the Royal Society of Literature was established under the patronage of King George IV and the Charter granted in 1825. Its purpose is to sustain all that is best in English letters. It administers a number of awards and medals, and also confers the honour Companion of Literature (CLit) upon men and women of conspicuous attainments in English literature.

Fellowship is conferred upon writers whose work is of a high literary standard. Members need not be authors of published works; it is enough that they should have a genuine interest in literature.

The Society holds lectures and poetry readings at its premises and publishes books of printed lectures.

1 Hyde Park Gdns, London, W2.

Literature, Teaching of *See* **Fiction, Teaching of**

Little Commonwealth *See* **Lane, Homer**

Local colleges *See* **Further education in England and Wales**

Local education authorities *See* **Administration, Educational**

Local Government, Royal Commission on *See* **Administration, Educational**

Local Government Examinations Board The Local Government Examinations Board was formed in 1946 to conduct promotion examinations for local government officers. It does this in two main classes, examining annually some seven thousand clerical staff and three thousand junior administrators

437

P

preparing for the Board's Diploma in Municipal Administration. The standard of this diploma is approximately that of a university pass degree. In 1958 the Board decided to expand its activities into the field of education and training. It is now concerned with the training of all manual employees, and individual local authorities and the regional organisations of the national joint industrial councils for local government administrative and manual staffs are encouraged and helped to provide induction courses for new entrants, courses for supervisors and foremen and refresher courses for examination candidates. Many of these are residential.

Alembic Hse, 93 Albert Embankment, London, SE1.

Local option *See* **Parental choice**

Locke, John (1632–1704) Main work on education: *Some Thoughts Concerning Education*.

Locke's fame as a philosopher rests largely on his *Essay Concerning Human Understanding*, yet his writings on education stand in almost total disconnection from that work. In the *Essay*, Locke presented an analysis of human knowledge which sought to exhibit all that we know as deriving solely from experience. The mind, he argued, has no innate ideas, but is at first a *tabula rasa* upon which two courses of experience, sensation and introspection, inscribe original and simple ideas. From these simple ideas all more complex ones are built up by such operations of the mind as comparing, relating and abstracting. Locke's educational writings, however, are concerned with the private education of gentlemen, for whom virtue is of the greatest importance and learning of the least: hence the disconnection.

For Locke, then, the aim of education is to produce gentlemen who are physically fit and hardy, who have achieved that self-control which consists in a submission of appetite and impulse to rational principle, and who have the breeding, wisdom and degree of learning necessary to set off their virtue and to be of use in managing their affairs, in being good company, and of service to their country. The learning of languages and grammar, the aquisition of basic skills and the study of scholarly subjects should all be governed by the criterion of their utility to a gentleman about his business, his social occasions and his recreation.

The principles Locke sets out for achieving these aims stress the importance of an early start, of habit and practice rather than of rule and precept, of observing children closely to see what is appropriate to their age and and what is stubborn wilfulness, and of procuring a ready submission to, and acceptance of, parental authority, without destroying a child's spirit. Children should be treated as rational creatures by giving them reasons that they can understand for what we require of them. Scholarly learning should never be made a burden, but rather should be as like play as possible, with doors being opened and fancy allowed to lead the way.

See also **Philosophy of education**

RFD

Logbooks Nothing better illustrates the close connection of the English educational system with navigational needs than the use of the term 'logbook' to describe the diary of events which every school must keep. The London School Board began the practice in 1871 by suggesting that heads should record events, especially punishments, and it was quickly taken up by other boards.

Logic blocks Blocks of different shapes, sizes, colours, and in some cases, materials. They are used for experience in sorting and classification, and as an introduction to work in sets (*q.v.*) and logic.

438

London allowance For the purposes of the Burnham Reports the 'London Area' comprises the City of London and the areas comprised in the Metropolitan Police District as defined in Section 76(1) of the London Government Act 1963, which includes Greater London, excluding the City of London; the urban districts of Chigwell and Waltham Holy Cross in Essex; the urban districts of Bushey, Cheshunt, Potters Bar, the rural district of Elstree and the parishes of Northaw in the rural district of Hatfield, and Aldenham in the rural district of Watford in the county of Hertfordshire; the borough of Epsom and Ewell and the urban districts of Banstead, Esher, Staines and Sunbury-on-Thames in Surrey.

At the present time the payment is £70 additional to the salary otherwise received for full-time service in the London area. Where, however, the teacher normally serves in the London area but is temporarily employed by his London area authority elsewhere, he is entitled to receive the allowance for the period concerned (*see also* **Arbitration**).

The London area for the purpose of additional salary means different things to different occupations. There is no common formula. The £85 allowance, arbitrated in 1968, arose out of the settlement recommended by the National Board for Prices and Incomes for the Civil Service and adopted by the government. This was for £125 for civil servants working in a 4-mile radius from Charing Cross, £75 if 4-16 miles from Charing Cross. Local government officers receive £5 more than teachers because of their longer working year.

Non-residential staff in approved schools and remand homes who are within the purview of the Joint Negotiating Committee and are employed at establishments within the London area receive the London allowance.

SEB

London Appreciation Society Founded in 1932, the Society is a rambling club with the purpose of enabling Londoners and others to visit places of historical interest with the assistance of competent guides and lecturers. A large number of teachers is among its members. Country members are entitled to advice on matters concerning London generally, and specifically in respect of visits they intend making to the capital.

Hon. Sec.: H. L. Bryant Peers, 8 Scarsdale Villas, Kensington, London, W8.

London Government Act 1963 *See* **Inner London Education Authority**

London Mathematical Society *See* **Mathematical Society, London**

London University London University is the most massive and diverse university in the country, and it has exerted great academic influence in England and throughout the Commonwealth. It was established in 1836 by royal charter not as a teaching but as an examining body, with power to confer degrees on students in any approved institutions. Thus it provided university standards and recognition for the two London colleges already in existence (University College, 1826, and King's College, 1829); and subsequently, through its external degrees, it became the academic midwife and godparent of virtually all English and many Commonwealth universities up to the middle of this century.

In London itself, the University grew steadily in size and scope, taking on teaching functions after 1898 and developing a federal constitution. Today it consists of 14 colleges, 13 medical schools and two postgraduate medical schools, and many other postgraduate and specialised institutions. Its total undergraduate and postgraduate population in 1966/67 was 29,590.

See also **Universities, English**

BF

439

Look-and-say A method of teaching reading that involves speed of recognition of, and response to, the printed symbols in English. *See* **Reading research**

Lowe, Robert (Viscount Sherbrooke) (1811–92) Vice-president of the committee of the Privy Council on education, 1859–64, Lowe was responsible for the adoption of the principle of payment by results—the tying of teachers' rewards to the tested results of their teaching. Designed to counter neglect of the three Rs, the system became an end in itself and had a stultifying effect on schools for over 20 years after Lowe's acceptance of it.

Lucas-Tooth Boys Training Fund The Fund trains young men to become qualified instructors in physical training (a three-year course is provided) and aims to inculcate powers of leadership and improve gymnastic performance of members. In addition, fitness classes for games players are provided.

Lucas-Tooth Gymnasium, 26 Magdalen St, Tooley St, London, SE1.

Luxembourg, Education in Education is compulsory between the ages of six and 15 years. In 1965–6 there were 431 primary schools (enrolment 34,058); seven secondary schools (enrolment 5,787); four technical and vocational schools (enrolment 4,049); two teacher training colleges (enrolment 255).The International University of Comparative Science has 200 students.

The population of the country was approximately 330,000 in 1964.

M

Macao, Education in In 1963–4 there were 141 primary schools (enrolment 49,179); 35 secondary schools (enrolment 8,625); 13 technical schools (enrolment 1,507). The Seminary of S. José had 72 pupils. Total population in 1964 was approximately 180,000.

MACE The Metropolitan Architectural Consortium for Education was established in 1966, its aims being to exchange ideas and experience in educational building, to develop new building techniques and to reap the advantages of bulk buying by encouraging the use of industrialised building systems and of rationalised purchasing procedures for standard components. Members are Barnet, Bexley, Brent, Brighton, Croydon, Ealing, East Sussex, Haringey, Havering, Hillingdon, Hounslow, Inner London, Kingston-upon-Thames, Merton, Newham (Surrey), Waltham Forest and the DES.

McMeeking Report (1959) *See* **Business education**

McMillan, Margaret (1860–1931) Born in the USA of a Scots family, Margaret McMillan began her adult life as a governess; she then joined her sister Rachel (1859–1917) in London, where both girls were drawn to social work and the Socialist movement. Her interest in schoolchildren began when in 1894 she was elected to the school board in Bradford. In 1899 she brought about the first known medical inspection of schoolchildren. Back in London

in 1908 with Rachel she set up a children's clinic at Bow, moving two years later to Deptford. The new clinic there was an instant and immense success, and in 1911 she secured a grant for dental treatment from the LCC, this being followed a year later by a grant for eye and ear treatment. She established camp schools for boys and girls and a nursery school; and during the first world war set up the first open-air nursery school. In 1930 she opened at Deptford the new building of the Rachel McMillan College (formerly the Rachel McMillan Training Centre).

Her works include a pamphlet for mothers on bad breathing habits among children; *Early Childhood,* which argued that only a healthy child can be successfully educated; a pamphlet, *The Ethical Aim of Education,* in which she urged that teachers should set out to evoke 'spontaneous attention' in the children they taught; and her major work, *Education through the Imagination.* In this last, she not only repeats and expands her view that preventible physical weaknesses make it impossible for many children to respond to education, but urges the study of the emotional and psychological needs of the pupil, which might help the teacher to release 'the creative power of the mind.'

Margaret McMillan was one of the first to point out powerfully and convincingly what in our own day has become a commonplace—that the home life of many children makes it difficult for them to respond to much that goes on in school, and especially to the subjects that nourish the emotions. In *The Nursery School* she urged that nursery schooling should not be regarded as something merely for the poor. There were strong general educational reasons for establishing nursery schools. The best of homes could not do what could be done in a good nursery school. 'The nursery school, if it is a *real* place of nurture, and not merely a place where babies are "minded" until they are five, will affect our whole educational system very powerfully and very rapidly.'

See also **Nursery school education**

McNair Report (1944): Report of a Committee to Consider the Supply, Recruitment and Training of Teachers and Youth Leaders Terms of reference: to investigate the sources of supply and methods of recruitment and training of teachers and youth leaders and to report what principles should guide the Board of Education in these matters in the future. Chairman: Sir Arnold McNair.

The Report considered that measures should be taken to raise the status of the teacher, and to draw recruits into teaching from a wider field. It also recommended that salaries should be increased, and that the Burnham Committee should be changed in constitution so that there should be a single committee for teachers in primary and secondary schools. It condemned the ban on married teachers. The government accepted the Report in principle and did raise the salaries, but the question of professional status has remained a difficulty ever since.

Madagascar, Education in Education is free and compulsory in primary schools for the six-to-14 age groups, but considerable use is made of private schools. In 1964/5 there were 3,486 primary schools (enrolment 454,584 in public schools, 178,445 in private); 262 secondary schools (enrolment 42,273 in public schools, 1,666 in private); 93 technical schools. The University of Tananarive, opened in 1964, has 2,313 students. There are four agricultural schools and one agricultural college in the republic.

The island's population was approximately six million in 1965.

'Madras' system The 'Madras' system, or, as it was called, the mutual or monitorial system, took its name from the employment of older children or 'monitors' as teachers by the Rev. Andrew Bell, an army chaplain at Madras. As described by him in *An Experiment in Education* (1797) it was first used in 1789. It was applied in 1798 at St Botolph's, Aldgate, and, on Bell's return to England, in his parish at Swanage. It both owed and gave something to the Lancasterian system (*q.v.*). Any differentiation between the two methods began to be increasingly exploited after 1805 for sectarian purposes, especially by the egregious Mrs Trimmer, while Lancaster's claims as 'inventor' of the monitorial system were championed by the nonconformists and Bell's by the Anglicans.

A system whereby the schoolmaster taught only the monitors and the monitors taught the children was also used in France at that time, and recommended by the Committee of Public Instruction. As the principle of the division of labour applied to education, it was widely hailed, and Jeremy Bentham wished it to be extended to all schools. Certainly it spread to public schools like Charterhouse and Edinburgh High School, and to many private schools as well.

WHGA

Magazines, National Association for School NASM is an organisation of schools and teachers formed to help schools to improve their magazines and, by organising conferences, exhibitions and lectures, to bring before the general public the creative work of young people in schools in the UK. Membership is open to individuals and organisations.

Sec.: Melville Hardiment, 68a Hammersmith Grove, London, W6. Journal: *Antiphon*.

Magazines, School It is symptomatic of the lack of interest in school magazines among educational authorities that the production of such magazines is the one activity of the educational process in our schools which is neither 'inspected' nor 'organised', and this may indeed be the reason why school periodicals and journals are so varied and individual. In one way or another, magazine publishing in our schools has been a part of school life for well over a hundred years. Among pioneers in this field are to be found two of the country's greatest schools—the Manchester Grammar School and the North London Collegiate School. The first-named pioneered *The Grammar School Magazine*, which in October 1845 was superseded by *MGS Miscellany*. *Ulula*, the present magazine of MGS, started life in 1873, to be followed in 1875 by *The Journal of the North London Collegiate School*. The latter seems to be the only school magazine extant which has been able to preserve a copy of every issue since its foundation.

Today there are as many as 15,000 magazines published annually or each term in our schools, with a total readership of some 4½ million children and old pupils. Some of these magazines are so well produced and contain such interesting reading that the editors are able to command national advertising rates, and to see their products on sale at the leading bookshops.

A close study of school magazines reveals a complete cross-section of the British way of life. The subject-matter in many of them is all-embracing, and room has been found for such extravaganzas as 'I married a jellied Eel', 'Dining out with Nkrumah', 'How to skin a snake' or 'Common Market: Is Europe really worth it?', as well as the interminable lists of examination passes and reports of house matches. Today, British school magazines lead the world in production and design: a development brought about largely through the work of the National Association for School Magazines (NASM), founded in 1963.

Any list of the best magazines must include *Atlantic College Magazine*, *Avenue* (Friends' School, Saffron Walden), *Burnt Mill* (Burnt Mill School, Harlow), *Camden* (Camden School for Girls), *Duffryn Leaves* (Duffryn High School, Newport), *Duncan House Magazine* (Duncan House School, Bristol), *Fullerian* (Watford Grammar School), *Gaytonian* (Harrow County School for Boys), *Image* (Merchant Taylors School, Crosby), *Journal of the North London Collegiate School*, *Lion* (Stockwell Manor School), *Phoenix* (Sir William Collins School, London), *Saga* (Bryanston School), *Salopian* (Shrewsbury School), *Sennockian* (Sevenoaks School), *St Christopher's* (St Christopher's, Letchworth), *Spark* (Spencer Park School), *Ulula* (Manchester Grammar School), *Verve* (Sevenoaks School), *Wheel* (St Birinus School, Didcot), *Willmott* (Willmott Grammar School, Sutton Coldfield).

FURTHER READING
Melville Hardiment (Ed.). *From Under the Desk*, Max Parrish, 1964.
Vanessa Redgrave (Ed.). *Pussies and Tigers*, National Association of School Magazines, 1963.

Journals:
Antiphon. Quarterly.
Sixth Form Opinion. Three times a year.

MHa

Main Committee *See* **Burnham Committees**

Main course Part of a teacher training course in which, to foster a student's personal education, one or two subjects are studied in depth.

Maintained schools These are schools that are maintained by LEAs, and they include county schools, voluntary aided schools, voluntary controlled schools and special agreement schools.

Maison Française d'Oxford Founded in 1946, and associated with the Universities of Oxford and Paris, the Maison is a cultural and social centre and organises exchanges between students and between teachers.

Westbury Lodge, Norham Rd, Oxford.

Major (building) works Major projects include all educational building work of a gross cost exceeding £20,000. Approval in principle is required from the Secretary of State and this is normally given by including the project in an annual building programme. Schedules of accommodation may be prepared in consultation with the DES, if experience in planning the particular project is limited, or reference may be made to DES publications, e.g. *New Schools—Preparing the Schedule of Accommodation*.

The Secretary of State's final approval is required for all major projects, and will be given if the project meets basic requirements, as set out in the DES's Building Code, i.e. if it provides accommodation adequate in amount and standard, and if it can be carried out within the DES cost limit, which is based either on cost per sq. ft or per place. Procedure for obtaining approval is laid down in the Code.

Unless the contract period exceeds two years, it must generally be let on the basis of a firm lump sum tender; and unless cost limits are exceeded by more than 1% the Minister's approval is not required before accepting a tender.

The layout and cost of playing fields are subject to DES approval, and should be planned to be ready for use when the school they serve is open.

MTH

Making Closely linked with IDE (interdisciplinary enquiry, *q.v.*) is the concept of *making*. This, together with *exploration*, is of fundamental importance in adaptive behaviour, and an education that sets a low value on it is seen as inimical to human growth. 'Making' is often interdisciplinary, but a more important function of the concept is that it bridges gaps that exist for many people between theory and practice, or between pure and applied studies. For it can refer to 'making' an enquiry, a scientific hypothesis, a machine, an opera, or a thumbpot. The criterion for 'making' is that what is made has its source in the students' invention or design, as opposed to 'doing', which is work done to an imposed pattern.

FURTHER READING
Charity James. *Live Now; Live Later*, Collins, 1968.
L. A. Smith (Ed.). *Ideas No. 2*, Goldsmiths' College Curriculum Laboratory, 1967.

CJ

Maladjusted Children, Association of Workers for The main aims of the Association are: to seek means by which maladjusted children may be educated and rehabilitated as useful members of society; to support schools and institutions for maladjusted children in evolving individual methods and techniques for carrying out their special functions; to promote research.

The Association acts as a channel for giving public expression to the views of its members, thus spreading its knowledge about enlightened methods of therapy and promoting a sympathetic and understanding attitude towards maladjusted children.

Other more specialised activity includes the provision of written and oral evidence to various professional bodies, the consideration of training schemes and conditions of staff, and the holding of conferences addressed by experts. The Association is also concerned with research and has completed an analysis of some significant features of schools for maladjusted children.

Hon. Sec.: Otto L. Shaw, Red Hill School, East Sutton, Nr Maidstone, Kent.

Maladjusted pupils 'Maladjusted pupils, that is to say pupils who show evidence of emotional instability or psychological disturbance and require special educational treatment in order to effect their personal, social or educational readjustment' were officially recognised as a category of handicapped children for the first time in 1945 (see the 1945 publication under *Further reading* below). This recognition of special emotional needs was due partly to the child guidance and progressive education movements during the 1930s, and partly to evidence of emotional disturbance revealed by wartime evacuation. The incidence is difficult to estimate since, with the expansion of services, the demand continually increases. Maladjustment may be revealed in aggressive antisocial or bizarre behaviour and also by excessive anxieties, solitary habits, nervous mannerisms and educational failure. In most cases maladjustment is associated with disturbed environment, especially unsatisfactory relationships within the home. In other cases, e.g. autistic, psychotic, or brain-injured children, constitutional abnormality may be a more important factor.

Maladjusted children are usually referred via an educational psychologist or school medical officer to a child guidance clinic, where the situation is investigated by a psychiatrist, psychiatric social worker and educational psychologist, in co-operation with the home and school. Sometimes the team includes lay psychotherapists and remedial teachers, who provide individual treatment, psychological or educational, for children while they continue to attend their normal schools. In such cases the psychiatric social worker maintains liaison with the home and the educational psychologist with the school. Where change of home and/or school is necessary, the maladjusted pupil may attend in a day special school or class, special boarding school, hostel or foster home. Some hospital provision is made for severely disturbed children.

Educational methods advocated have included: attitudes of total acceptance; opportunities to gain insight; creative expression in the arts; the sharing of responsibility; and skilled remedial teaching.

This form of special educational treatment is rapidly expanding but the shortage of skilled personnel is a major problem.

See also **Maladjusted Children, Association of Workers for**

FURTHER READING
Handicapped Pupils and School Health Regulations. HMSO, 1945.
Report of the Committee on Maladjusted Children, HMSO, 1955.

MW

Malawi, Education in The country has a high literacy rate. Schools are government-established or aided. 1965 statistics: 2,455 primary schools (enrolment 359,841); 38 secondary schools (enrolment 7,953); 11 teacher training colleges. The University of Malawi at Limbe, established in 1965, moves to Zomba in 1968.

The country's population was approximately 4 million in 1966.

Malaysia, Education in Free primary education is nominally compulsory in the Malayan states and is to be extended to the Borneo states. Schools are of three types—fully state-assisted, partially-assisted and private; and of four language categories—Malay, English, Chinese and Indian. There were in 1967 2,631 Malay schools (enrolment 673,862); 1,074 English schools (enrolment 552,190); 1,213 Chinese schools (enrolment 378,658); 704 Indian schools

445

(enrolment 76,691): a total of 5,621 schools with an enrolment of 1,681,401. In the secondary schools vocational training is given at four schools and technical education at three, these seven having an enrolment of 1,165 pupils. The technical college at Kuala Lumpur has an enrolment of 700 full-time and 92 part-time students, and the University of Malaya at Kuala Lumpur has 3,603 students.

The population of Malaysia in 1967 was approximately 10 million.

Mali, Education in In 1964/65 primary enrolment was 140,331, secondary school enrolment 24,318, technical and vocational enrolment 2,387. Students go abroad for higher education (1,249 in 1964).

In 1965 the country's population was approximately $4\frac{3}{4}$ million.

Malta, Education in Education is compulsory and is given in Roman Catholic State schools, instruction being in Maltese and English. In 1964/65 there were 113 primary schools with an enrolment of 45,547; six grammar schools (enrolment 3,775); 82 private schools (enrolment 1,737); nine technical colleges (enrolment 3,715); two teacher training colleges (enrolment 380); a polytechnic (enrolment 575); and the Royal University of Malta (enrolment 547).

The population of Malta was approximately 318,000 in 1966.

Malting House School *See* **Isaacs, Susan**

Management, Association of Teachers of The membership of this professional organisation is drawn from educational institutions, the public services, and industry and commerce.

Sec.: A. Henderson, University of Wales Institute of Science and Technology, 3rd Floor, Arlree Hse, Greyfriars Rd, Cardiff, CF1 3AE.

Management, United Kingdom Advisory Council on Education for Set up in 1961, the Council advises on management education in technical colleges at levels above those of a university first degree or its equivalent.

Management education At the present time management education is a growth industry. In the decade after the war it was carried out mainly in technical colleges and a few independent institutions, but the last ten years have seen a great increase in the amount of this education conducted in the universities, culminating in 1965 in the establishment of the London and Manchester Business Schools. Courses are now offered at most universities and technical colleges, while particular industries (e.g. iron and steel, electricity) and many major firms have also set up their own management education activities.

Three basic levels of courses can be distinguished: (1) post-experience courses for managers, often senior in rank, with considerable industrial experience. The courses may relate specifically to new management techniques or may, as with the Administrative Staff College, Henley, concern themselves with broadening the outlook of the specialist to make him better fitted to be a general manager. (2) Post-qualification courses. The National Scheme for the Diploma in Management Studies, which can be taken full-time or part-time at colleges of technology, is aimed at the qualified man in his late twenties who is beginning a career in management. Courses of study along the same lines, but in more depth, are now offered by universities for Master's degrees (based on the prototype of the Master of Business Administration Degree of the Harvard Business School). (3) Supervisory courses. The newly-established National Examination Board in Supervisory Studies regulates courses at technical colleges in supervision and related subjects.

The topics normally covered in a management education course are: basic disciplines of economics, sociology, psychology, industrial relations, law, mathematics, statistics. Functions of management: production (including factory organisation, production control, work study, industrial engineering); finance (including costing, estimating, budgeting, accounting); marketing (including market research, advertising, distribution); personnel (including manpower planning, selection, training, conditions of work, ergonomics, trade union negotiations). In addition there are rapidly developing a number of new integrative subjects that cut across traditional functional features of the field, e.g. operational research, systems analysis, organisation theory, business policy.

Although it relies on the traditional educational method of the lecture, management education has always been oriented to the development of participative methods. Thus the discussion of case studies in considerable detail was an early development. From this have stemmed other methods, such as role-playing, the critical incident technique, T-group training, business exercises, projects and investigations.

FURTHER READING
British Institute of Management. *A Conspectus of Management Courses* (7th ed.), BIM, 1968.
T. M. Mosson. *Management Education in Five European Countries*, Business Publications, 1965.
D. S. Pugh (ed.). *The Academic Teaching of Management*, Occasional Paper No. 4, The Association of Teachers of Management, Blackwell, Oxford, 1966.
DSP

Management Studies, Diploma in A national scheme for a Diploma in Management Studies was developed soon after the war, radically revised in 1961, and further modified in 1965 when a memorandum on the award was published by the committee which administers the Diploma in England, Wales and Northern Ireland. The aim of the Diploma course is to provide the student with a basic knowledge of the background to industry, to give him a broad understanding of management processes and to acquaint him with the tools and techniques of management. It is intended for those who combine the possession of a degree, final professional qualification or other qualifications broadly on this level, with practical experience in industry or commerce.

Managers, School *See* **Instrument and rules of management**

Manpower Research Unit Concerned to assess future distribution of manpower in the light of past trends and future developments (including the effects of automation and other technological changes), the Unit carries out general studies and also surveys of particular industries, occupations and developments.

Ministry of Labour, Almack Hse, 26-28 King St, London, SW1.

Mansbridge, Albert (1876-1952) In 1897, as a clerk employed by the Co-operative Wholesale Society, Mansbridge discussed in the *Co-operative News* his idea that an educational partnership should be brought about between the universities and the people. He developed this idea further in *University Extension* in July 1903, and with the support of a number of working men was made honorary secretary of the Association to Promote the Higher Education of Working Men. The first branch was established in Reading in 1904. A year later, the name was changed to the Workers' Educational Association (*q.v.*).

Marking For 'marking' read 'testing', 'examining', 'assessing' or 'evaluating' and the meaning is the same—or ought

447

to be. For most teachers, marking is a necessary but tedious chore, too often carried out mechanically. For most pupils marks have become a fetish, token rewards which are competed for eagerly.

Marking can be qualitative ('Good work', 'careless', 'Beta plus', etc.) or quantitative (7 out of 10, 56% etc.). While the qualitative assessment is readily translatable into numerical terms, there is a difference between the two methods, the latter being chiefly concerned to *measure* the pupil's performance, the former to *appraise* and *criticise* it. Thus at the primary school level it is customary to give numerical marks for subjects like arithmetic and qualitative ones for essay-writing. At the higher levels, as in degree examinations, qualitative assessments (e.g. First Class Honours) tend to take precedence.

Numerical marks are most reliable when awarded for memorised factual information or for questions calling for right-wrong answers, especially when objective-type tests are used. Qualitative marks are liable to be subjective unless they are adequately scaled. On the whole, teachers who are concerned to gauge the pupil's grasp of the subject-matter prefer numerical marks. Unfortunately, a numerical mark taken out of its immediate context is virtually meaningless: 56 out of 100 may represent a good pass mark for one teacher, failure in the eyes of another. The 56 takes on some semblance of meaning when it is accompanied by the class average or when it is placed in an order of merit. Even then, however, it is liable to be misleading to the teacher's colleagues, to the parents concerned, and not least to the pupil, unless the teacher-examiner has taken care to ensure that his *distribution* of marks is normal. In any normal distribution the majority of pupils will be in the middle of the range. In any homogeneous ability group, there is either something seriously wrong with the methods of teaching or with the system of marking if high marks are bunched at one end of the scale and low ones at the other.

Before assigning any sort of mark the teacher should be able to say precisely: (1) what it is he is testing; (2) why it needs testing; (3) what the mark stands for; and (4) for what purposes the mark is going to be used. Failing this there can be no way of interpreting his marks.

See also **Examinations**

WKR

Marriage Guidance Council, National The Council selects and trains education counsellors to run discussion groups with young people in schools and youth clubs. Counsellors work voluntarily, but all expenses are met by the local Marriage Guidance Council to which they are attached. (There are 116 such Councils.) Training of education counsellors is undertaken by the National Council, which is responsible for the maintenance of standards and receives a government grant. The Council also runs a summer school for teachers and youth leaders, and, in association with LEAs, organises training conferences for teachers concerned in group work with young people.

58 Queen Anne St, London, W1.

Married women teachers In Britain, before the second world war, any woman teacher who married had to leave the profession upon marriage. By the 1960s, however, the shortage of teachers had become so acute that married women teachers were the target of a special government drive to woo them back to the schools. A nationwide advertising campaign, promises to provide nursery schooling for the children of married women teachers, and special arrangements regarding the quota of teachers allocated to each local authority, were some of the measures designed to win back to the schools women who had trained as teachers but left the profession on assuming family or domestic responsibilities.

While there is no longer a ban on the married woman teacher continuing in employment after marriage (it was lifted in 1945) the teaching profession, like the rest of the community, has been affected by the phenomenon of earlier marriage and the trend to larger and younger families. This has given rise to what has become known, inelegantly, as the problem of 'wastage' in the teaching profession. In effect, this means that while the number of women students entering colleges of education for training as teachers has gone up dramatically in the post-war period, there has not been a comparable increase in the number of women teachers staying in the profession, since a very large proportion of the women trained marry at a very early stage in their career and leave when they start a family. It has been calculated that within five years, 60% of women teachers have left the profession for family and domestic reasons. What has not yet been established, however, is for how long these women are lost to the teaching profession. While a very substantial number of women do return to the profession when their children are old enough to permit this, it is too early to say for how long, on average, they will be lost to the profession or what proportion of women will ultimately return for what will become the second part of their professional career.

It is the expectation of the government and the LEAs, however, that a very substantial number of married women will resume their professional careers after a period of absence for family or domestic reasons, and the long-term forecasts of teacher supply now contain assumptions about the return of married women.

Indeed, official hopes of overcoming the teacher shortage depend to a considerable extent on the ability to attract large numbers of 'married women returners' back to the schools: hence the efforts of the government and local authorities in this direction.

The first concerted attempt to persuade married women teachers to return to teaching was made in 1961. Since then the annual recruitment of returning teachers has increased by more than a third, and in the same period the part-time teacher force, consisting very largely of married women, has more than doubled and at February 1966 stood at 36,200. In the twelve months up to February 1966 the number of qualified women teachers returning to the schools after a break in service of at least a year rose to a new high level of 7,200, a 12% increase on the level of 6,400 attained in the previous year. Of these, 3,400 returned to full-time service, and 3,800 to part-time service. Both primary and secondary schools benefit from their services.

Individual LEAs vary in willingness or ability to employ married women returners on a part-time basis, but by February 1966, 94 out of the 162 authorities employed part-time teachers to an extent equivalent to at least 5% of their total teaching strength, and there were only 28 authorities whose employment of part-time teachers represented less than 3% of total teaching strength.

In addition to the arrangements already mentioned, various steps are taken to assist 'married women returners' to resume their professional careers. Refresher courses, visits of observation and financial assistance in the period of re-training are among the measures which local authorities have introduced, and steps have also been taken to place the salaries and conditions of service of part-time teachers on a basis which stands in comparison with those of full-time teachers. The married woman teacher herself is expected to play as full a part as possible in the life of the school; her ability to do so may depend on the extent of her domestic commitments.

FJ

Martinique, Education in 1966 statistics: 244 primary schools (enrolment 89,218); 11 private schools (enrolment 2,591); three lycées (enrolment 5,390); one higher education institute (522 students). Total population: approximately 340,000.

Mary Macaulay Centre: Education for Living This voluntary movement in social education (formerly the Iona Adult Education Centre) was founded in 1944. It aims, by means of classes and lectures at the Centre and in schools, colleges and outside groups, to provide a greater understanding of the pattern of natural human development, especially in children, young people and family life. The qualities of manhood, womanhood, fatherhood, motherhood, marriage and the relationship between the sexes is studied to gain a greater understanding. The emphasis is upon prevention, through education, of personality disorders and unhappy relationships.

10–12 Exhibition Rd, London, SW7.

Publications: Mary Macaulay, *Understanding Ourselves* and other literature.

Mason, Charlotte (1842–1923) Founder in 1888 of the Parents' National Educational Union or PNEU (*q.v.*), Charlotte Mason was concerned with the problems of parents and governesses teaching children at home. At the time there were few private schools and much teaching, largely unguided, took place in the home. Charlotte Mason believed in the unique individuality of each child and his natural desire for learning. She believed that a child's potential qualities are most likely to be drawn out by a curriculum centring on good literature and in which the subjects are closely linked with one another—history and literature going side by side, for example. A deeply religious woman, Charlotte Mason was opposed to competition between children, believing that a child should vie against himself and not against others. Besides founding a Parents' Union School at Ambleside, she set up a training college for teachers (the Charlotte Mason College) which, until it was transferred to the LEA, trained teachers according to her methods and theories.

Mass media Generally taken to mean newspapers, TV, radio, pop music, films, advertisements, comics, magazines and paperback books aimed at a mass market. In the past, many of these mass media have been seen by their critics as cheapening and even corrupting in their effect, and teachers have often complained about excessive TV viewing or comic reading in their pupils. It is true that if young people spend most of their time with the least demanding of the mass media and nothing else, there will be little chance of their being stimulated to think for themselves; their interests will remain narrow and perhaps ultimately unsatisfying. But most of the horrific influences ascribed to the mass media have probably been exaggerated, although certain types of violence in comics or films may certainly undesirably stimulate someone who is already disturbed and aggressive. Most young people, and of course most teachers too, will inevitably spend some time with some of the mass media; and taken with some discrimination, there are things in these media that are contemporary, lively and entertaining. A teacher in school, therefore, who is concerned with the effect on his pupils of too much indiscriminate consumption of the mass media, may be better advised to show his pupils how to pick out the best rather than advise them to ignore these media altogether.

Since the original work in this field by F. R. Leavis and Denys Thompson, there has been much progress in techniques of discussing the mass media in schools, mostly in secondary or further education. There is however no reason to limit work of this kind to older children or, as often happens, to those in the lower forms of secondary schools, since there is value for everyone in such work, especially now that the mass media are playing larger parts in our lives than ever before.

FURTHER READING

F. R. Leavis and Denys Thompson. *Culture and Environment*, Chatto and Windus, 1948.

N. Tucker. *Understanding the Mass Media*, Cambridge Univ. Press, 1966.

NT

Maternal and Child Welfare, National Association for The Association publishes a textbook for schools, colleges and youth groups, *The Young Student's Book of Child Care;* also *Suggestions for Parentcraft Education in Schools and Colleges*, intended for teachers and group leaders. A book-list is available of works on aspects of child care and adolescence, written for children and young people, and on child care for expectant parents.

Tavistock Hse North, Tavistock Sq., London, WC1.

Mathematical Association Founded in 1871 as the Association for the Improvement of Geometrical Teaching, its scope has been widened to include all branches of elementary mathematics. The purpose of the Association is to form a strong combination of all persons interested in fostering good methods of teaching mathematics. It has a membership of over 6,000, drawn from universities, colleges and schools of all kinds.

A recognised authority in its own province, the Association exerts an important influence on methods of examination. It is represented on the Joint Mathematical Council, and has liaison with the Institute of Mathematics and its Applications, and with other mathematical societies. An annual conference is held, and members also meet at branches. A comprehensive library is available; and examinations are conducted for the Association's diploma.

Publications include the quarterly *Mathematical Gazette*, reports and other texts on teaching and content, covering traditional and modern topics and offering a strong lead to teachers at all levels.

Hon. Secs.: F. W. Kellaway, 87 Pixmore Way, Letchworth, Herts; Miss R. K. Tobias, 17 Ramsbury Drive, Earley, Reading, Berks.

Mathematical Colloquium, British The British Mathematical Colloquium is a meeting of mathematicians, from universities, colleges of advanced technology and other research institutions, held annually since 1947. Concerned primarily with mathematical research, it developed out of the London Mathematical Society but is now independent of this organisation.

Mathematical Society, London The Society was established in 1865 (royal charter 1965) 'for the promotion and extension of mathematical knowledge'. It fulfils this aim by providing monthly meetings at which distinguished mathematicians report on recent discoveries or give a survey of a particular field. Its *Proceedings* are exclusively devoted to research papers in mathematics; the *Journal*, in addition to shorter papers, also includes survey articles, book reviews, obituaries and other matters of interest to mathematicians. The Society takes part in several translation programmes of Russian mathematical journals and is one of the sponsors of *Mathematical Reviews*.

Since 1961 the Society has held biennial Instructional Conferences and it has close ties with the British Mathematical Colloquium.

Queen Mary College, London, E1.

Mathematics, Association of Teachers of An association of over 6,000 mathematics teachers, with the principal objectives of bringing together teachers of mathematics, whatever age-group or ability group they teach, to work for mutual understanding and a realisation of the unity of mathematical education; and of studying the process involved in learning mathematics, particularly through the evidence provided by children at work in the classroom. Members receive a free copy of each issue of *Mathematics Teaching* quarterly and other occasional publications.

Vine St, Chambers, Nelson, Lancs.

Mathematics, National Council of Teachers of An American organisation devoted to the development of mathematical education at all levels, having as affiliated groups most of the individual states' mathematics teachers' associations. Meetings of the NCTM, to which leaders in mathematics teaching and education are invited to speak, and where its major committees on such subjects as curriculum, instructional media, publications, and professional relations discuss their work in open session, are held annually.

Its publications include *The Arithmetic Teacher*, *The Mathematics Teacher* and *The Mathematics Student Journal;* all are available in the UK.

Mathematics, The new This is a *method* of learning mathematics (*q.v.*) as a practical activity covering a broad range of topics in counting; the number operations of addition, multiplication, etc.; the measurement of the physical quantities, such as length, weight, time and speed, and the properties of shapes and solids such as symmetry, space-filling, angles, etc.

The emphasis in the new mathematics is on acquiring mathematical concepts by carefully guided exploration of a selected aspect of the environment or structured apparatus,

e.g. Dienes (*q.v.*). Children are encouraged to formulate rules and methods of computation for themselves. Multiplication may be taken as an example. After suitable counting activities, attention is focussed on counting in equal groups, the operation being named as 'multiplication' and recorded by a suitable notation—$a \times b$. (Definition is applicable only to whole numbers.) Particular results are obtained in many different ways: e.g. by counting, weighing, the use of the abacus, Cuisenaire rods (*q.v.*) or number strips, the results being later systematised into 'tables' to save relearning. Children are given opportunities to recognise multiplication in a variety of real situations, and written work is largely a matter of recording results. Activities can now be introduced to illustrate the distributive law of multiplication (*see* **Arithmetic**), enabling the multiplication of numbers with two or more digits to be reduced to a number of simpler steps:

$$19 \times 6 = (10 + 9) \times 6$$
$$= 10 \times 6 + 9 \times 6 \text{ (Distributive Law)}$$
$$= 60 + 54 \qquad \text{(Using tables)}$$
$$= 114 \qquad \text{(Addition)}$$

Setting down the steps can gradually be modified until the most efficient and economical form is found. Recognition of the mathematical concepts of a problem, and confidence in their manipulation, are important aims.

The term 'new mathematics' may also refer to a more or less radical curriculum reform at the secondary stage in which the stress is on ideas and their modern applications (*see* **School Mathematics Project, Midlands Mathematical Experiment**). Such topics are:

1. *Sets and logic* (*q.v.*), which provide a precise language for the definition of most other mathematical ideas, and are necessary for a detailed understanding of a computer.

2. *Number.* Numeration systems using other bases than the common one

of ten—especially binary (base two) with its application to sorting, logical problems and computing. Modular or clock arithmetic is exemplified by a 12-hour clock. An interval of ten hours followed by six hours is recorded as four hours, or symbolically as

$$10 + 6 \equiv 4 \text{ (modulus 12)}.$$

Three successive intervals of five hours are recorded as three hours, or $3 \times 5 \equiv 3$ (modulus 12). Using a five- (or any prime number) hour clock, all the laws of arithmetic are obeyed. Studying such systems gives an insight into ordinary arithmetic and algebra.

3. *Algebra* (*q.v.*). An early introduction to the ideas of abstract algebra (*q.v.*) is suggested for those who will specialise in mathematics; such ideas also interest the non-specialist. Linear programming, a method of solving economic problems, may serve as an application of graphs of inequalities, such as 'x + y is less than 5', and the solution of simultaneous equations.

4. *Geometry* (*q.v.*). The tendency is to minimise the rigid scheme of theorems of Euclidean geometry and to make use of methods involving transformations of geometrical figures. Matrices and vectors are used to describe these transformations.

5. *Statistics*. A critical attitude can be fostered by analysing and comparing sets of data by measuring the average (arithmetical mean) and the spread or dispersion. The theory of probability forms the basis for making decisions on insufficient information.

New maths symbols

{ } 'set of'. Curly brackets enclose members of a set.

∈ 'is a member of a set'. Thus: Sir Laurence Olivier ∈ {Actor knights}, which means Sir Laurence Olivier is a member of the set of actor knights.

n (set) 'number of members in that set'. So: *n*(Beatles) =4.

⊂ 'is contained in'. Only used of sets, thus: {Dogs} ⊂ {Animals} which

means the set of dogs is contained in the set of animals.

∪ Union of two sets: {Labour Party} ∪ {Conservative Party} is a coalition of members from either or both parties.

∩ Intersection of two sets: {Blond-haired people} ∩ {Girls} = {Blondes}.

B' Complement of set *B*—containing all members *not* in *B*. Say *B* is the set of the Beatles. Then *B'* means everyone not a Beatle.

φ Empty set. It has no members: for example, the set of millionaire elephants = φ.

↔ 'matches'. So: 'Set of Beatles (four of them) matches set of Seasons (four of them)' or {Beatles}↔{Seasons}.

⇒ 'implies': as in 'he is my father⇒ I am his son'.

FURTHER READING

Trevor Fletcher (Ed.). *Some Lessons in Mathematics*, Cambridge Univ. Press, 1964.

Michael Holt. *What is the New Maths?*, Blond, 1967.

D. E. Mansfield and D. Thompson. *Mathematics: A New Approach*, Books 1–5, Chatto and Windus Educational, 1962–1966.

National Council of Teachers of Mathematics. *24th Yearbook: The Growth of Mathematical Ideas*, 1961.

Nuffield Mathematics Project. *I Do, and I Understand, Pictorial Representation, Beginnings, Mathematics Begins, Shape and Size, Computation and Structure, Desk Calculators, How to Build a Pond*, W. and R. Chambers and John Murray, 1967.

D. Paling and J. L. Fox, *Elementary Mathematics: A Modern Approach*, Oxford Univ. Press, 1965.

JCW

Mathematics, Teaching of (primary stage) Changes in teaching mathematics are based on modern theories of learning and vast increases in mathematical knowledge, both requiring new methods of instruction.

Mathematical and scientific concepts are formed by the sequence: experience —abstraction—generalisation—application. *Experience* is varied and unstructured at first (preliminary play), followed by structured activities increasingly rich in one concept, until there is abstraction of the common element of very different activities. Problems are posed and solved constructively with concrete materials. (This does not apply only to structural apparatus.) *Abstraction* or concept is labelled by a word or a symbol, which enables techniques of symbol manipulation to be devised and the relation of the concept to other concepts to be studied. *Generalisation*, or the *application* of the concept to solving problems in situations not previously experienced, is a natural extension and leads to the formation of higher concepts.

If these ideas are accepted, then the teaching method must change, and infant methods must be applied to the junior school curriculum, since concepts are slow in maturing. Consolidation by drill should take place only when the concept is reasonably stable.

Organisation and method Carefully designed activities are done in groups (preferably not more than two) embracing a wide range of examples within a topic. The aim is a minimum of direction, the child making his own discoveries, initially by trial and error. The teacher's role is to guide and encourage and above all *discuss* with the children, supplying appropriate terms at a receptive stage. The changeover from a formal to an activity method may be achieved by starting with a small group, which is split into pairs, while the rest of the class works on its own. The experiment is repeated with the rest of the class, group by group. The number of groups working during a lesson is gradually increased until the whole class is involved. The usual allocation is three periods a week for activities, and two periods for class lesson or discussion and computation practice. To reduce demands on apparatus groups, work is done on different topics.

Activities These are divided into four stages: (1) Discussion of the problem, method of solution, apparatus required —home-made if possible. (2) Collection of data and calculations. (3) Recording of the activity and results individually in a variety of ways either by verbal description ('functional' English) or by pictorial representation (tabulation, graphs, pictures, mappings, etc.). (4) Discussion of the completed problem should reveal understanding and suggest further questions and experiments. This stage is most important, as a sum in a book or a picture on the wall is not the final goal; each activity should raise further questions. The child should be trained to search for an underlying pattern or order which enables generalisation.

Content Mathematics has two aspects, cultural and utilitarian. That mathematics is an art has received tardy recognition in primary schools; but since it is an abstract logical science, full appreciation of its power and generality is only possible in late adolescence. Nevertheless, juniors can experience real mathematical insight while studying number and space. Provision of useful knowledge poses the problem: are children to be treated as potential specialists, or is the attempt to be made to convince every child that mathematics is interesting and relevant to his life?

(1) *Sets*. The foundations of mathematics are buried deep, but the most accessible part is the idea of a set. A set is a collection or class of objects or ideas. Infant activities include sorting and classifying a wide range of materials and attributes, e.g. red, cylindrical, plastic.

Relations between sets form the core of mathematics. Infants investigate such relations as longer, heavier, more, similar, greater than, before, vertical, equal, etc. (There is more inequality in real life than equality.)

A function or mapping is a special kind of relation. A very important function is the one-to-one correspondence, or pairwise matching of members of two sets, which is the basis of counting.

(2) *Number* is a *property* of a set (cardinality). While the concept of a number is being formed, structural apparatus may be introduced to supplement materials which form a concrete analogue of *operations* on numbers. Recording numbers requires a system of numeration, such as the Roman or Hindu-Arabic. Our system is denary (base ten) and positional (value of a digit based on position in relation to other digits). Dienes apparatus and abacus are useful for the formation of the concept of place notation and for understanding algorithms for computing. Methods of computation can be invented by children prior to the introduction of standardised 'efficient' procedures at a much later stage without endangering their 'selection'. Number bonds and multiplication tables are committed to memory when the need is seen to avoid tedious counting.

Attention should be given to simple properties of numbers, e.g. number patterns, primes, magic squares, modular arithmetic. The equivalence of subtraction to complementary addition, and as the inverse of addition, should be stressed, together with division as the inverse of multiplication. Eventually the child should appreciate the laws of arithmetic (*q.v.*). Using calculating devices requires good understanding of number operations and structure.

(3) *Measurement* is the comparison of physical entities, length, weight, time. A prerequisite is the conservation of scientific concepts, e.g. the volume of a liquid remains unchanged when poured into different containers, the length of a ruler is unchanged when moved. There is wide scope in this field for primary school activities.

(4) *Shapes* or geometry for juniors. Shapes are more readily apprehended than numbers, and make an immediate aesthetic appeal. We are aware of the shapes of a stained glass window before counting the pieces. A formal deductive system is out of place in a junior school, since appreciation of formal logic is not usually developed till adolescence. Coloured elastic bands on a lattice of nails in a board is an invaluable aid to exploring the relations between points, lines, shapes, area, etc. Some examples of topics are: (a) recognition and classification of shapes and solids; (b) symmetry—line symmetry by paper folding, mirror reflections, etc., rotational symmetry—fitting shapes into their outline; (c) tessellations or tiling; (d) area and volume; (e) transformations—translation or sliding, rotation, reflection; (f) direction and angle; (g) topology—unicursal figures, Möbius strip, etc.; (h) loci—circle, sphere, ellipse, parabola.

Infants deal more easily with three-dimensional shapes and this activity should be fostered at all stages.

(5) *Money* does not figure in any formal mathematical system nor in any scientific one. Familiarity is best gained by imitating commercial enterprises, using real coins.

FURTHER READING

Association of Teachers of Mathematics. *Notes on Mathematics for Primary Schools*, Cambridge Univ. Press, 1967.

Z. Dienes. *Building Up Mathematics*, Hutchinson Educational, 1967.

C. Gattegno. *Teaching Arithmetic by the Cuisenaire-Gattegno Method*, Educational Explorers, 1964.

HMSO. *Mathematics in Primary Schools*, 1965.

Primary Mathematics for Schools and Training Colleges, Association of Teachers in Colleges and Departments of Education, 1964.

L. G. W. Sealey. *The Creative Use of Mathematics in Junior Schools*, Blackwell, Oxford, 1965.

M. Wertheimer. *Productive Thinking*, Tavistock, 1961.

JCW

Mathematics, Teaching of (secondary stage) At this stage the average child is capable of reversible formal operations, i.e. he is able to deduce conclusions from abstract hypotheses, but visual and concrete aids should be used to clarify complex steps in reasoning. The ideas and methods of the primary stage are still applicable. If concepts are well formed and computational skill has been acquired, new ideas should be introduced as soon as possible to form higher concepts such as integers, functions, probability, group structure, etc. The subject matter may be developed more systematically, but its introduction should be contrived to appear naturally out of real problems connected with the child's own interests, or by reference to the historical situation. (Mathematics is indicative of man's evolving culture.)

The new movements in curriculum reform emphasise more explicitly the axiomatic basis of mathematics and awareness of the modes of reasoning. If the child can glimpse the essence of mathematical thinking, it should be easier to make him aware of the peculiar appeal of mathematics. The rigour of the proofs must be suited to the child's need and understanding. Intuition must be used but its pitfalls demonstrated, so that nothing has to be unlearned.

On the other hand, there is increasing need for mathematics as a tool of the sciences, both pure and applied (including social). Though the necessary techniques should be available when required, these subjects should not dictate the curriculum of mathematics as a self-contained discipline.

Content This is now controversial and several experiments are taking place, e.g. Nuffield, Midlands Mathematical Experiment (*q.v.*), Schools Mathematics Project. Only a broad outline is suggested here.

(1) *Sets and logic.* Set language is helpful in framing precise definitions. Its constant use in all branches of mathematics is essential so that a set algebra will crystallise from a wide variety of examples. The close connect-ion between sets and logic enables types of reasoning to be exposed, and in particular that of inference. Open sentences and their truth sets clearly explain what is meant by 'solving an equation'.

(2) *Function* or mapping is a very important concept, together with relations and their graphical representation. Applications are linear programming and solution of simultaneous equations.

(3) *Algebra* (*q.v.*). If general ideas are discussed as with sets and functions, the need for an algebraic notation should arise naturally. Dienes Algebraic Experience Material enables equations to be set up and solved with a variety of materials.

Abstract algebraic structures (*q.v.*), such as groups and fields, reveal clearly the rules of algebraic manipulations and minimise common mistakes. At the same time, unification is achieved by taking examples of similar structures from other areas of mathematics. By using Boolean algebra to represent logical statement, by switch circuits and binary arithmetic to represent a two-state system, the workings of a digital computer can be explained.

(4) *Number systems.* Natural numbers are acquired intuitively for counting. To solve equations new numbers are always needed. These may either be postulated as having the required properties or constructed, e.g. integers from ordered pairs of natural numbers.

(5) *Geometry.* The axiomatic system of Euclid has long been in disfavour, and alternative treatments are being tried, such as isometry transformations using matrices and vectors. Their novelty can stimulate an interest in traditional methods.

(6) *Statistics.* Investigations to test vague generalities made by pupils show the need for statistics. Data are presented in the most informative manner—by descriptive statistics: i.e.

mean, mode, median, variance; prediction and inference using simple ideas of probability and sampling; association of two variables indicated by scatter diagrams.

The aims of a mathematical education are to encourage a child to be motivated by his environment, recognise the mathematical elements of a problem, be flexible in the search for a solution and communicate his thinking in the best way possible.

FURTHER READING

T. Fletcher (Ed.). *Some Lessons in Mathematics*, Cambridge Univ. Press, 1964.
F. W. Land. *New Approaches to Mathematics Teaching*, Macmillan, 1963.
D. E. Mansfield and D. Thompson. *Mathematics: A New Approach*, Books 1–4, Chatto and Windus Educational, 1963.
Mathematical Association. *Mathematics in Secondary Modern Schools*, Bell, 1959.
D. Paling and J. L. Fox. *Elementary Mathematics*, Oxford Univ. Press, 1965.
W. W. Sawyer. *Vision in Elementary Mathematics*, Pelican, 1966.

JCW

Mathematics and Its Applications, Institute of Set up in 1964, the Institute exists to extend and diffuse the applications of mathematics in science, engineering, economics, &c., and to promote education in mathematics.

Maitland Hse, Warrior Sq., Southend-on-Sea, Essex.

Mathetics A term used in programmed learning. It involves the systematic application of reinforcement theory to the analysis of complex learning processes and the construction of programmes. In a mathetical sequence the unit is called an 'exercise' to distinguish it from the usual 'frame'; i.e. step size is determined not by breaking down the subject matter into minute items but in accordance with the learner's capability at a given moment. The strategy of an instructional sequence is varied so as to allow for discrimination, generalization and chaining, i.e. the sequencing of the learning process.

See also **Programmed learning**

Matriculation This was the name given to a School Certificate which contained credit passes in five subjects, including an English subject, one foreign language and either mathematics or a science. This certificate provided matriculation exemption for most universities. It therefore achieved such great prestige that gradually School Certificate lost some of its currency.

Mature State Scholarships Each year the DES offers a number of scholarships to students over 25 years old who were unable to take a university course at the normal age. Most of the candidates, since leaving school, will have attended adult education colleges or courses (*see* **Adults, Residential courses for**) arranged by university extramural departments and the Workers' Educational Association.

Mature students The phrase is a piece of jargon, not a compliment, and refers especially to students in long-term residential colleges, in courses for adults who have decided to take up or return to teaching after working in other jobs or rearing a family, enrolled at Birkbeck College in order to combine degree studies with a full-time job, or pursuing first-degree studies at other universities on 'mature' scholarships. A large proportion of students in further education generally are in fact over 21, but they are not normally classified as 'mature' on this account. Mature students are typically those who discover late in life that they are capable of study at a high academic level. There is no sign that their numbers have been abated by the mesh of selective and diagnostic devices used at the primary and secondary stages.

BG

Mauritania, Education in Most children receive little or no schooling. There are about 250 schools (enrolment 19,100 primary, 1,500 secondary). A few schools have been established for nomadic tribes.

The country's population was nearly one million in 1965.

Mauritius, Education in Primary education is free but not compulsory. 1965 statistics: 160 government primary schools (enrolment 89,374); 55 state-aided primary schools (enrolment 39,117); 116 unaided primary schools (enrolment 2,993) and seven grant-aided and 23 unaided secondary schools with primary sections (total primary enrolment 3,050); four government secondary schools (enrolment 2,367); 13 aided secondary schools (enrolment 5,568); 118 unaided secondary schools (enrolment 34,021); one agricultural college (enrolment 98); one teacher training college (enrolment 424); three vocational training centres (enrolment 134). Total population: approximately ¾ million.

Mayo, Charles (1792–1846) and Elizabeth (1793–1865) An Oxford don, Charles Mayo was given leave in 1819 to take up the post of English chaplain at the school founded by Pestalozzi (*q.v.*) at Yverdun. He spent three years there, in 1822 setting up a school on Pestalozzian lines at Epsom (moved to Cheam in 1826). The school flourished until Mayo's death in 1846. His sister, Elizabeth Mayo, taught there and wrote two books, *Lessons on Shells* and *Lessons on Objects*, which were firmly based on Pestalozzi's principle that learning should be rooted in objects and experiences; unfortunately the books were widely used, by teachers who failed to understand Pestalozzi's ideas, as school readers and as matter for rote learning. Miss Mayo was one of the first women to take part in teacher training, being appointed in 1834 to the position of supervisor of

teaching in the schools and the college of the Home and Colonial Society.

MCC Youth Cricket Association An advisory and co-ordinating body to County Youth Councils throughout the country, the Association is primarily concerned with the training of coaches and the award of coaching certificates.

Sec.: J. G. Dunbar, Lord's Cricket Ground, London, NW8.

MCT (Membership of the College of Technologists) *See* **Colleges of advanced technology**

Mechanics' institutes In 1800 Dr George Birkbeck, Professor of Natural Philosophy at Anderson's Institution, Glasgow, began a special course of lectures 'for persons engaged in the practical exercise of the mechanical arts'. So began the Mechanics' Institute movement, which aimed partly to satisfy the disinterested scientific curiosity of the craftsmen and partly to provide the better educated workmen that the new industries needed.

The classes continued after Birkbeck himself had moved to London where, with Francis Place, Henry Brougham and a number of prominent radicals, he was active in the foundation of the London Mechanics' Institute, formally inaugurated in 1823. This and similar institutions founded in Edinburgh in 1821 and in Glasgow in 1823 provided the starting point of a movement which expanded until, by 1851, there were in Great Britain some 700 mechanics' institutes and similar bodies (literary and scientific institutes, societies for the diffusion of useful knowledge, etc.), catering mostly for an upper-working-class and lower-middle-class clientele but sometimes more specifically for professional people.

Through lectures, classes and libraries the institutes provided an education which was at first heavily weighted in the direction of technology, but became more broadly cultural as time went on. Though the institutes were gradually absorbed into the main stream of the educational system, many becoming the nucleus of public libraries and technical colleges, the movement's stress on democratic control has exercised a continuing influence on adult education in the UK. Many of the institutes were started by workmen; some managed to be self-supporting; many more, even when financial support had to come from the outside, kept workmen in a majority on the management committee. The London Mechanics' Institute later adopted Birkbeck's name, and as Birkbeck College (*q.v.*) it is today a constituent college of the University of London.

See also **Working men's colleges**

BG

Medical Education, Association for the Study of The Association was set up in 1953 to exchange information and promote research into medical education.

53 Philpot St, London, E1.

Medical examination of school-children, Law on *See* **Legal rights and obligations of parents**

Medical Officers of Health, Society of Founded in 1856, the Society is a professional association with a membership of 2,500 and is primarily for medical and dental officers engaged or interested in the public health services or in the teaching of public health. It acts through regional branches and functional groups; for example, there are groups concerned with research, teaching, the school health service, maternity and child welfare, mental health and the dental services. Scientific meetings and courses are held throughout the year (many being open to qualified non-members) on all aspects of public health.

Journal: *Public Health*.

Sec.: Miss P. F. Cashman, Tavistock Hse South, Tavistock Sq., London, WC1.

Medical Officers of Schools Association The Association was founded in 1884 with the objects of promoting school hygiene and of holding meetings to consider all subjects connected with the special work of Medical Officers of Schools. Most of the ordinary members are resident or visiting medical officers of independent schools of both sexes, and of boarding or day pupil status. There are also a few associate members who are not doctors but headmasters or headmistresses, and honorary life members who are now retired, having served with distinction over a number of years.

The Association meets four times a year in London or the provinces, and meetings take the form of clinical meetings, conferences, the presentation of papers, or visits to educational establishments.

The Hon. Sec. is always ready to offer professional advice to members or non-members and to assist in negotiating terms and conditions of service for members within the framework of a model contract drawn up by the Association's Council. Hon. Sec.: Surgeon Capt. P. de Bec Turtle, Haileybury College, Hertford, Herts.

Publication: *School Medical Officers Handbook*.

Medicine, Qualification in The normal course of training for doctors lasts five years and must be undertaken at a medical school of one of the universities. Qualifications for admission differ somewhat from university to university, but are usually two or three passes in GCE A level with certain O level passes. The first two or three years of training (the time varies according to whether a student took his first-year subjects at school before beginning his course) are devoted to the study of the fundamental sciences involved in medicine, and are followed by work in the teaching hospitals. Those who qualify must spend another 18 months as a member of a hospital staff. All doctors must register with the General Medical Council, 44 Hallam St, London, W1.

FURTHER READING

Becoming a Doctor, British Medical Association, BMA Hse, Tavistock Sq., London, WC1.
Medicine and Surgery, *Choice of Careers* Series, HMSO.

Memory Memory can be divided into three phases: learning (*q.v.*), retention (*q.v.*) and finally remembering. It is necessary to make these distinctions, since faulty remembering may be due to poor learning, or for some reason a person may not be able to remember something that he has in fact retained in his brain, but is simply not accessible at a particular moment. For example, a person may be able to remember far more of his past if he revisits his childhood home than if he tries to remember things about it whilst elsewhere. In certain circumstances, such as examinations or moments of crisis, for some people memory becomes much better, or occasionally much worse.

Basically there are two sorts of memory: short-term and long-term. Short-term memory refers to the sort of information we keep normally for a few seconds, such as a string of numbers or a quite irrelevant thought or remark. Long-term memory is made up of material that we have learned or is of some other significance to us; but in many cases this is usually much less accurate and more distorted than we imagine. This distortion may involve simplifying the original memory, re-fitting it along the line of one's own interests or prejudices, or fusing one memory into another. This happens particularly with events or material that were originally rather puzzling or incomplete, and within the memory we seem to turn them into something more meaningful for us. Unpleasant memories are sometimes suppressed altogether, and although this may protect people from unhappy thoughts,

the process can have a bad effect on their overall mental life. Part of a psychiatrist's job may be to discover these memories with a patient and, by putting them into a more bearable context, to rid the patient of the anxiety and effort often caused by the unconscious process of repressing various thoughts and memories.

FURTHER READING

F. C. Bartlett. *Remembering*, Cambridge Univ. Press, 1932.
I. M. L. Hunter. *Memory, Facts and Fallacies*, Penguin, 1957.

NT

Mental age The mental age of a child is measured, by tests, against a scale established by discovering the attainment of the average child at the various chronological ages. Thus it is possible that a child's mental age may be higher or lower than his chronological age.

Mental Health, National Association for Founded in 1946 by the amalgamation of three voluntary mental welfare bodies: the Central Association for Mental Welfare, the Child Guidance Council and the National Council for Mental Hygiene. The Association is a voluntary organisation doing pioneer work, outside the NHS, to promote mental health and aid the mentally disordered. Its activities include the organisation of conferences for both professional and lay delegates; full-time training courses, approved by the Training Council for Teachers of the Mentally Handicapped, to qualify men and women who wish to specialise in the teaching and training of mentally subnormal children and adults. Homes and hostels are administered by the Association; and an advisory casework service is available to help anyone with a problem arising out of mental illness, subnormality or senility.

The Association publishes a number of books on mental health subjects and a quarterly magazine, *Mental Health*.
39 Queen Anne St, London, W1.
155/157 Woodhouse Lane, Leeds, 2.

Mental Health, World Federation of This organisation aims to promote mental health throughout the world in its broadest behavioural, medical, educational and social aspect. It has a consultant role with the UN Economic and Social Council, UNESCO, WHO and UNICEF. Membership is open to associations and societies in the medical, educational and behavioural fields, and associateship to individuals.

1 rue Gevray, Geneva.

Publications: books, reports, proceedings, etc.

Mental health services for the young The Mental Health Act 1959 allows for much greater provision in the services offered by the local authorities than in the past. The Act is intended to grant to all people, from childhood to old age, the type of social help and treatment which will prevent, cure or alleviate mental illness. Above all, it removes once and for all any idea of mental illness as a punishable sin. Its most important function is that it lays upon the local authorities the responsibility to see that, as far as possible, mentally ill people should be kept out of institutions and treated in the community as outpatients. To succeed with this, there must be the closest co-operation between the family doctor, the hospitals and the mental health department of the local authority. There must be a great deal of expansion in the present services available for help and protection of children and young people. This will require many new hostels, protected workshops, child guidance clinics, and many more mental welfare officers.

Child welfare clinics supervise the physical and mental development of children under five years old. To the child welfare clinic, an 'infant' is a baby under two years old. For the purposes of compulsory education he is a 'child' until he leaves school at 15, but if he is sent to an approved school he can be forced to stay on until 19, although he ceases to be a 'young person' at 17. The Home Office, which is responsible for the care of deprived and delinquent children, considers that a child is anyone under 14, a young person is aged between 14 and 17, and a juvenile is anyone under 17. These distinctions are important to know when seeking help for any child in trouble.

A most important service, provided mainly by LEAs, are the child guidance clinics, of which there are about 400 in the UK. These clinics help children who are emotionally or mentally disturbed. Children showing signs of psychological or emotional difficulties such as fears of going to school, nervous habits or 'tics', stealing, and so on, can be greatly helped if taken early enough to the clinic. The family doctor, or possibly the headmaster of the child's school, will know where to find the clinic. There is a Directory of Child Guidance Services which the local Citizen's Advice Bureau will have and which can be referred to.

It is the duty of the LEA to find out which children in the area need special education, and it has the right to examine any child over two years old who is thought to be in this category. Where possible, handicapped children are kept in ordinary schools, with a little extra help and sympathetic understanding from teachers and others concerned with their future development.

For severely mentally subnormal children who cannot benefit at all from ordinary schooling, training centres are provided by the local health authority, and although legally children can be made to attend these schools, the reality is that there are long waiting lists and more unhappiness is caused by being kept out than by being forced to enter.

As with all social services in Britain, great supportive help is offered by voluntary associations, and social workers may well be able to refer children with mental disorders to some voluntary service. A very helpful organisation is the National Society for Mentally Handicapped Children, and also the National Association for Mental Health (*q.v.*), which takes in the needs of people of all ages. The aim of the Association is to help mentally handicapped children and their families; to spread a more enlightened view about mental ill health in the community; and to provide practical services to doctors, social workers and local authorities who may seek them. Like all voluntary bodies, it depends on the support of helpers and sympathisers, and it works closely with the official education and health authorities.

The local authority children's department is increasingly important in our society, where family life seems to have lost some of its stability. It is the duty of the local authority to receive into its care any child under 17 in its area who is 'deprived of a normal home life'. It also looks after children under 18, if necessary, who are put in its care by juvenile courts. It supervises foster homes and helps with adoptions. Since 1963, a fairly new duty—and one which exemplifies the new attitude towards the need to prevent mental disturbance—is to help parents and their children to overcome difficulties which might lead to family breakdown. The well known and traditional organisations, such as the National Society for the Prevention of Cruelty to Children, carry on work which is vital even in our post-war society, but a great new field is opening up to the children's officer or the probation officer, to whom people are being encouraged to turn for advice and help with children showing signs of emotional disturbance and socially unacceptable behaviour.

Children who would otherwise be homeless after leaving the care of the children's officer at 17 can now ask the Children's Department to remain their 'guide and friend' until they are 21. Local authorities can (although not many do) provide hostels for young people who need a substitute family even though they go to work and seem to be living independent lives.

Mental health at all ages depends very largely on the sense of belonging to a family or a community which cares for its individual members whether they are 'well-behaved' or not. In fact, as most psychiatrists would agree, it is those who least inspire love and affection who are most in need of it.

SL

Mentally Handicapped, Training Council for Teachers of the Set up in 1964 by the Minister of Health 'to promote the provision of training for the staff (including hospital staff) of training centres for teachers of the mentally handicapped, and to approve courses of training.' The Council awards a diploma to students who have successfully completed an approved course. So far 17 courses have been approved, 12 in colleges of further education, and five run by the National Association of Mental Health. Further courses are planned.

Alexander Fleming Hse, Elephant and Castle, London, SE1.

Merit payment This is a recently introduced additional payment for teachers under the Burnham agreement enabling additional salary (at present £50) to be received in respect of prescribed qualifications or satisfactory completion of accepted courses. The general principle upon which this payment is based is that a graduate may secure the merit payment only if he or she has had training as a teacher either by following a full-time course in a department of education or at a college of education or has completed its part-time equivalent. If, however, such a course has already formed part of the teacher's qualifications for salary purposes, then there would be no entitlement to the merit payment. The other aspect of the general principle applies to non-graduates who undertake in-service training of not less than one year either at an advanced level or in respect of the teaching of handicapped children. Specific examples of the latter relate to diplomas for teaching the blind or the deaf, but there are others which are concerned with the wider field of special need and accordingly attract the merit payment.

Courses which satisfy the requirements in the general sense are mainly advanced courses either dealing with education widely or with a particular sector, for example, the junior school. Subject courses are not included. Thus, the teacher who may have qualified on two years of training and has subsequently taken a supplementary course for one year would not be entitled to receive the merit payment, but if instead he had satisfactorily completed one of the recognised advanced courses included in the programme of one-year courses issued by the DES each year, then such attainment would be rewarded by the merit payment.

SEB

Meritocracy A term invented by Dr Michael Young in his witty and disturbing satirical fable *The Rise of the Meritocracy* (1958) to point to the danger that a selective school system, and over-confidence in psychometry, might lead to a society in which human value would largely be determined by IQ. The basic tenet of Dr Young's imaginary society of the near-future was: 'IQ plus Effort equals Merit.'

Metalwork, Teaching of Most schools have general metalwork 'shops' containing equipment for forging, casting, turning, brazing, general benchwork and fitting, sheetmetal work, and art or beaten metalwork. The emphasis placed upon the different branches of metalwork varies according to the skills and interests of the teacher, and the requirements of external examinations. Since this wide range of equipment is available, teachers are expected to use it, and most syllabuses include sections dealing with all the kinds of work that are technically possible within the shop. This introduces the danger of a wide range of activities, with little depth.

Larger schools often have several specialist workshops equipped for light engineering, plumbing, and general metalwork. (The handicraft department in such schools will often have specialist provision for the various building trade activities such as bricklaying, carpentry, plastering and painting.) These schools pursue an indefinable compromise between general education and vocational training. A few schools have facilities for the practical study of metallurgy. The scale of provision for metalwork is, therefore, very diverse and courses differ accordingly.

The method problems of the teacher in the general metalwork room are quite considerable if he is to run an imaginative and interesting course, making the best use of his facilities. Filing is generally the only activity that can be carried on by all the boys at the same time. Too much filing can be heartbreaking to boys, and only the introduction of work in groups almost from the start makes it possible to provide the possibility of varied experience of interesting work. Wellorganised, progressive teachers divide their classes into four or five groups of boys, sometimes upon a sociometric basis, each group pursuing a different activity. This is not always easy to arrange but members of various groups usually help each other a great deal if encouraged to use their initiative, and the teaching load is not excessive.

The diversity of activities provided in metalwork often means that a boy is moved on to a new kind of work before he has become really familiar with the techniques of the previous one. Design work is difficult under such circumstances and there is probably more

463

working to prepared drawings, and jobs taken from books, than in woodwork. This is a pity, and a narrower range of activities in more depth, with design problems to solve, would be preferable.

Workshop equipment New workshops are almost invariably provided with the standard range of tools and machines recommended by the LEA specialist adviser. This scale of equipment is suitable for the kind of work normally undertaken. Schools are usually allowed to provide additional equipment of the type already provided, or special equipment for an experimental curriculum or syllabus, out of money available for running the school. Teachers able and willing to work out promising lines of work are unlikely to find their efforts frustrated by a parsimonious authority.

FURTHER READING
S. H. Glenister. *The Technique of Handicraft Teaching*, Harrap, 1953.
C. T. Page. *Engineering Among the Schools*, Institution of Mechanical Engineers, 1965.
R. Sandham, F. R. Willmore and C. Browne. *The Teaching of Metalwork*, Arnold, 1964.
Metalwork in Secondary Schools, HMSO, 1952.
A School Approach to Technology, Schools Council Curriculum Bulletin No. 2, HMSO, 1967.
See also **Handicraft**

FW

Meteorological Society, Royal This world-wide organisation for professional and amateur meteorologists provides assistance and two special lectures per year to educational authorities.
49 Cromwell Rd, London, SW7.
Publication: *Weather* (monthly), etc.

Meteorology in schools Weather study not only enriches work in a number of fields for pupils of all ages; it also provides a starting-point for practical training in scientific method, since pupils must learn to be observant and to record what they have seen,

knowing that at a later stage they will use their records and be required to make certain deductions from them.

There are three well-defined stages in weather study. With infants and lower juniors it is a matter of observing prevailing weather conditions and then recording them by the selection and exhibition of cards on a classroom weatherboard. These cards will say, for example, 'It is windy' or 'It is raining'. With older juniors, regular observations are made daily at 0900, 1200 and 1500 hours GMT. These include weather conditions which exist and have prevailed since the last observation: visibility; cloud types and amounts; wind speed and direction; air temperature; maximum and minimum temperatures; barometric pressure; the length of shadow cast by a vertical pole of standard height; and rainfall. At secondary level, all these observations are made together with hygrometric readings, sunshine recordings and soil and grass minimum temperatures. Older pupils study synoptic charts and the rudiments of air mass analysis.

The Meteorological Office's *Observers' Handbook* is an essential text.

SHF

Method Building, Consortium for Formed in 1963, this Consortium is one of several now in existence (*see* **CLASP**) which aim, by developing inter-related industrialised building methods, with as much interchangeability of components as possible, to achieve speed and economy in educational building. Members are Berkshire, Bristol, Cornwall, Devon, Oxfordshire, Plymouth, Somerset and Wiltshire.

Methodist Association of Youth Clubs The Methodist Association of Youth Clubs, founded in 1945, co-ordinates and guides the work of Methodist Youth Clubs and links their members in a fellowship which includes some overseas clubs. The clubs seek to serve the needs of young people without distinction and to introduce them to the Christian way of life. All the interests of young people are catered for and the importance of community service is emphasised. The Association consists of associate and full member clubs, the latter reaching certain standards which include a balanced programme and participation by members in club management.

A residential centre, Plas yr Antur at Fairbourne, Merioneth, is available for adventure courses. The 'London Weekend' each May involves over 10,000 club members and includes a congress, display, folk festival and service. There is a large-scale training programme for members and leaders, including courses for the Leaders' Certificate and Diploma and also Youth in Industry courses. Thirty-one district club secretaries organise the work in their respective areas, and district congresses, conferences, sporting events and holidays are arranged.

Methodist Youth Department, 2 Chester Hse, Pages La., Muswell Hill, London, N10.

Methodist Education Committee The Committee is reponsible for the work of the Methodist Church in the field of formal education. It has control of two colleges of education (Westminster College, Oxford, and Southlands College, Wimbledon), and 13 secondary boarding schools, seven being direct grant schools with a proportion of day pupils. The committee supervises 75 voluntary primary day schools, mostly in Lancashire. Five of these are joint Anglican/Methodist schools. The committee represents the Methodist Church in its dealings with the DES about educational matters.

Sec.: Rev. George R. Osborn, MA, 25 Marylebone Rd, London, NW1.

Metric system An international system of weights and measures using decimal multiples and submultiples of the metre and kilogram. The metre was intended to be one ten-millionth part of the arc from the N. Pole to the equator passing through Paris. It is now defined (1960) as 1,650,736.73 times a wavelength of light emitted by krypton.

The kilogram is the mass of a piece of platinum alloy kept in Paris. The unit of volume, the litre, is the volume occupied by a kilogram of water at 4°C, and was meant to be the same volume as one cubic decimetre.

1 metre = 39.37 inches; 1 kilogram = 2.205 pounds; 1 litre = 2.114 pints.

Mexico, Education in Primary education from nine to 15 years is free, compulsory and secular. The stages of education are: two years pre-primary, six years primary, three years secondary or vocational. 1965 statistics: 2,441 nursery schools (enrolment 314,505); 37,703 primary schools (enrolment 6,916,204); 3,608 post-primary schools (enrolment 913,649); 1,720 secondary schools (enrolment 74,550); 266 vocational schools (enrolment 97,180); 498 commercial colleges (enrolment 71,520); 236 normal academic institutions (enrolment 57,844); 427 professional colleges (enrolment 111,034); 461 specialist colleges (enrolment 81,521); 39 universities (of which the most important is the University of Mexico City) totalling 70,514 students. In 1943 a university was opened exclusively for women. All private schools must comply with government standards. Clergy cannot open schools.

The country's population was approximately 41 million in 1965.

Micro-projector *See* **Visual aids**

Middle schools movement Beginning in London (University College School 1828, KCS Wimbledon 1829), Birmingham, Sheffield, Leicester and Hull, day proprietary or joint stock schools for the middle classes took such effective shape that the headmaster of Shrewsbury prophesied they would ruin the public schools. He need not have worried, for the proprietary principle spread to public schools: Cheltenham (1841), Marlborough (1843), and Clifton (1863); assisted by the efforts of Catholics (Mount St Mary's, 1842) and nonconformists (Queens Taunton, 1843; Taunton School, 1847; Bishop's Stortford, 1868; the Leys, 1875) and Quakers (Ackworth, 1842). The movement altered the image of public schools from an upper-class preserve to a middle-class prerogative.

Anglicans were especially active. Even the National Society (*q.v.*) undertook in 1838 to establish 'middle' or 'commercial' schools, but as it was unable to start a fund until 1866 owing to the need to build training colleges, individual clergymen stepped in with some notable organisational efforts. Three deserve mention. The Woodard Corporation, destined to become by 1914 the largest governing body for secondary schools in the British Empire, began when Nathaniel Woodard founded a school for members of the upper-middle class in 1847 (later Hurstpierpoint College), and another for the 'poorest members of the middle class' (later Ardingly). 16 other foundations followed; 17 exist today.

The second organisation was the Middle Schools Corporation, founded by the Rev. W. Rogers, rector of St Botolph's, Bishopsgate, as a proprietary corporation to provide secular day schools. Among its foundations was the Central School, Finsbury.

The third and perhaps most significant organisation was the work of the Rev. J. L. Brereton who, as rector of West Buckland, established a middle-class 'county' school there in 1859 – a model for others at Cranleigh (1863), Framlingham (1865) and Barrow Castle (1883). He called them 'county' schools because he believed that education should be organised on a county basis. To provide these 'county' schools with a university outlet, he founded Cav-

endish College at Cambridge (discontinued in 1892).

WHGA

Midlands Mathematical Experiment An experimental syllabus for GCE O and A levels, using new topics such as sets, vectors, transformations, probability, to promote understanding and stimulate an interest in mathematics. Textbooks have been drafted for use in the schools taking part, and a feature is that they are used mainly as a basis for discussion. Some of these textbooks have been published; for further details write to the Secretary: R. H. Collins, BSc, Headmaster, Harold Malley School, Solihull, Warwicks.

Mill, James (1773–1836) A supporter of the educational projects of Jeremy Bentham (*q.v.*), Mill, like the other utilitarians, believed in a wide extension of state education. The education he gave his own son, John Stuart Mill (*q.v.*), starting with Greek when the boy was three years old, was so remote from the real nature and needs of a child that it led to breakdown. J. S. Mill described the experience in his *Autobiography*.

Mill, John Stuart (1806–73) The son of James Mill (*q.v.*), Mill received that extraordinary educational forcing at his father's hands which he describes in his *Autobiography* and which led in his late adolescence to a nervous breakdown. It had been an exclusively intellectual training, at the expense of the education of emotion and sensibility, and a belief in the value of poetry and art was a cornerstone of Mill's subsequent thinking about education.

Employed by the East India Company, he was a scholar, philosopher and critic, and originator of the term 'utilitarian'. In his *Essay on Liberty* (1869) he expressed concern at the increasing grip of the state on education; too much state control, he feared, would lead to uniformity. In his inaugural address as Rector of St Andrew's (1867) he outlined a view of the university as a clearing house of knowledge. Courses in the university should be liberal and not vocational; but, providing the general setting of a course was one of wide liberal study, any subject might provide its specialist core. Mill was an ardent believer in the intellectual equality of men and women.

Mills Music Limited Besides being the sponsors of the Canford Summer School of Music, Mills Music Limited have a catalogue of educational music which covers grades from the primary school to university. Included are operettas, action songs, music for choirs and school orchestras, string music, music for the piano and the classic guitar, the Michael Aaron piano tutor series and the Stephen Goodyear recorder tutor series. The programme *Threshold to Music* is being adopted by schools throughout the British Isles.

The Canford Summer School has been held every year since 1952 at Canford public school in Wimborne, Dorset. Here music students and non-professional musicians study famous works, in idyllic surroundings, under expert professional tuition.

20 Denmark St, London, WC2.

Ministry, Qualification for the To become a Minister of the Church in the UK it is necessary to have a university degree in a suitable subject and then go for training to a theological college, or be wholly trained in a Church college. The college course in the Church of England normally lasts two years, but this period may be modified for those who wish to make a late entry into the Ministry. Applications must be made to the Central Advisory Council of Training for the

Ministry, Church House, Westminster, London, SW1.

For the Roman Catholic Church, the relevant body is the Catholic Educational Council for England and Wales, 41 Cromwell Rd, London, SW7. Candidates for ordination as RC priests must make their intention known from the age of 13-plus, and are trained in a seminary after acquiring suitable passes at O or A level GCE. Within the nonconformist churches methods of qualification vary.

Minor authorities *See* **Instrument and rules of management**

Minor (building) works The DES Building Code 1962 includes a section on minor projects and information on the general principles, allocation and approval procedures concerning minor works. Minor capital projects may be undertaken to improve an existing school or to erect a limited amount of new building. Normally the limit of capital expenditure is not more than £20,000 at any one school. Larger projects may be undertaken within the minor works programme, but LEAs must obtain approval before planning begins. The Secretary of State's approval in principle must be obtained when a project is likely to exceed £25,000. When a new school is built piecemeal, it is essential to ensure that the balance of the cost limit covering the whole school will in fact be sufficient to complete the building in due course. Plans for improvements costing more than £5,000, and for an instalment when final approval for a new school is being sought, must be submitted to the Secretary of State.

There are two types of allocation: central, maintained by the DES, and local, distributed by LEAs. The uses of these allocations are listed in the Building Code. Most minor capital projects are subject to minor works allocation, but certain exceptions are listed. Approval procedure for minor projects carried out by LEAs is set out in Appendices 8–13 of the Building Code.

Many small village schools come under the category of minor works: three classrooms, a shared space (used as a hall), kitchen, boiler house and staffroom can be provided under the allowance.

DEC

Mirror writing This is writing that runs in an opposite direction from the normal, with the individual letters also reversed. It can best be read through its reflection in a mirror. Most infants will produce odd examples of mirror writing or the occasional reversal of single letters or numbers from time to time, and even adults—sometimes under the influence of drugs or alcohol, but otherwise in a mild state of mental abstraction—can surprise themselves by suddenly reversing a letter or word that they have written correctly countless times before. There is a far greater tendency for mirror writing amongst the left-handed or those with left-handed tendencies, and it is also fairly common with mentally defective children and adults.

So far its cause has remained something of a mystery, despite the interest in the subject arising, amongst other things, from the note-books of Leonardo da Vinci, all of which are in mirror writing. With children who find it hard to avoid reversals, some tracing of words and games such as 'I Spy' can help them to gain a left-right orientation.

NT

Missionary and Ecumenical Council of the Church Assembly Formed in 1964 by the fusion of the former Overseas Council with the Council for Ecumenical Co-operation, this organisation exists to provide a channel of communication between the Church Assembly and the missionary societies of the Church of England, the provinces and churches of the Anglican Communion, and the British and the World Councils of Churches.

Its main educational function is 'to stimulate in the Church of England a conviction of responsibility for the mission and unity of the Church at home and overseas'. It seeks to do this both by encouraging the activity of voluntary bodies operating in this field and by co-operating with them where necessary; and by putting out literature under its own imprint, where no one else is covering the same ground.

Examples are the *No Small Change* study course for Lent 1965, in which the Council co-operated with the missionary societies; and the ecumenical programme of study and action for use in spring 1967, *The People Next Door*, under the joint sponsorship of the British Council of Churches and the Conference of British Missionary Societies, in the preparation of which members of the Council's staff have taken a leading part.

Literature produced by the Council and designed to inform the church on matters of importance within its terms of reference includes *Christian Unity and the Anglican Communion* (2nd edition revised, 1966) by Canon David M. Paton and Rev. R. M. C. Jeffery and *An Anglican-Methodist Workbook* (1966) by Canon David M. Paton and Rev. Gordon Wakefield.

Church House, Deans Yard, London, SW1.

Sec.: Canon David M. Paton.

Mixed schools *See* **Co-education**

Mode 3 examinations This term describes one of the three ways, 'internal examinations externally moderated', in which examinations for the Certificate of Secondary Education (*q.v.*) may be conducted. Mode 1 is the familiar method of most external examinations. The examining body prescribes a syllabus on which the examination will be set. It sets the examination papers, which are expected to follow a pattern that soon becomes traditional; it marks the papers and decides which candidates have passed and which have failed. Mode 3 is as different as possible from this, while Mode 2 is in effect a compromise between Modes 1 and 3. Schools have a free choice between methods.

The original sponsors of CSE would probably claim that Mode 3 is the method which most nearly achieves two of their principal aims—the creation of a system which would measure and record what a pupil had actually mastered of what he had been taught; and of one in which teachers in a particular school would be free to decide what in their particular circumstances could most profitably be taught. To some extent differences between schools reflect differences of opinion on the relative educational value of different material—over the part that a study of probability should play in a mathematics syllabus, for example. More important, probably, are differences about what can effectively be taught in a particular place if the teaching is to be lively. History, geography and biology are all, for instance, subjects which are best taught to 15 and 16 year-olds if to a large extent they can be rooted in the school's own environment, or in one to which it has easy access. A combination of different environments and different interests and expertise in teachers will rapidly produce substantially different programmes of work in individual schools. What the pupils know, and therefore what they can be examined on, will differ from school to school. Mode 3, therefore, leaves each school free to devise its own syllabus with safeguards that the study will be of roughly comparable difficulty and intensity in all schools.

A standard type of examination question with a standard type of appropriate answer can have as deadening an effect on teaching and learning as a common syllabus. Mode 3, therefore, leaves the individual schools a fairly free hand to devise their own systems of examining the work that has been done, subject again to checks to secure that the testing will as far as possible be equally searching in all schools. It is expected that in most schools a good deal of attention will be paid to what is described as course work, that is to say to work done during the term and not during the examination period. This may well take the form of a group or individual project so that different members of the same form will have different fields of detailed knowledge as well as a broadly common fund of information. Mode 3 enables this to be taken into account. It seems clear that the especially enterprising teacher can make good use of his freedom from the stereotyped answers to external examination questions; what is not so clear is whether the average teacher will be able to pass on to his pupils the benefits of this freedom which he enjoys.

So far the majority of schools have preferred to use Mode 1; but the demand for Mode 3 is growing.

DGOA

Modern Humanities Research Association Founded at Cambridge in 1918, the MHRA aims to encourage and promote advanced study and research in the field of the modern humanities, especially modern European languages and literatures (including English). It is concerned with breaking down the barriers between scholars working in different disciplines and with maintaining the broader unity of humanistic scholarship in the face of increasing specialisation.

It is now an international organisation, with members in all parts of the world, and is an affiliated member

469

organisation of the International Federation for Modern Languages and Literatures sponsored by UNESCO.

Hon. Sec.: Dr J. C. Laidlaw, Trinity Hall, Cambridge.

Modern Language Association

Founded in 1893, the Association has as its objects to assist teachers and students of modern languages and to secure for these languages proper recognition of their value as educational and cultural instruments.

2 Manchester Sq., London, W1.

Modern Languages, Committee on Research and Development in

The first report of this committee, set up by the DES and the Scottish Education Department in 1964, appeared early in 1968. Referring back to the Annan Report of 1963 (*q.v.*), the report disclosed that, following the urgings of the Annan Committee, there had been an increase in the number of boys and girls taking Russian at A and O levels, but the numbers were still small compared with the number of those taking French and German. There had also been a fall in recruitment to the special one-year course for teachers wishing to add Russian to the subjects they taught. The main reason for this (put forward by the Association of Teachers of Russian, *q.v.*) was that teachers who underwent such training found on return to their schools that there was little opportunity to teach the subject. In fact, the committee commented, the conditions for expanding the teaching of Russian could not be more favourable, since audio-visual and other special teaching aids were now available.

There was an even more acute problem in the field of Chinese, a subject taught in only a few schools. The lack of pre-university teaching of the language meant that the six university departments of Chinese (which have altogether an annual intake of about 60 students) were obliged to provide both proficiency in the language and advanced academic studies, and for this the three-year honours degree course allowed insufficient time. The report recommended the setting up of a single Inter-Universities Chinese Language School to train first-year undergraduates and also to provide language teaching for scholars in other fields wishing to specialise in modern Chinese, as well as for others (for example, from the public service) needing the language. The scheme was discussed sympathetically by the heads of the university departments concerned and by the UGC, but there were both academic and financial problems yet to be solved.

The report stated that the committee was giving its full attention to the improvement of teaching materials for further education and post-A level studies. It had found that, despite official encouragement, many firms were unready to release employees for modern language training—even though it had been estimated that a student using modern methods could acquire an elementary knowledge (amounting to 500 words) of a European language, including Russian, after 50 hours of teaching, and could have a command of 1,500 words after 250 to 300 hours.

There had been successful experiments in primary school teaching of modern languages, but problems remained, especially that of ensuring a sufficient supply of language teachers for the schools. Nearly half the pupils in secondary schools were studying a modern language—a lower percentage than in some continental countries, but comparing favourably with others in Western Europe.

Modern languages, Teaching of

Until a century ago, modern languages were taught by the 'grammar translation' method traditionally employed in the teaching of the classical languages, i.e. the rules of the language's grammar and syntax were learned by rote, and then practised in exercises based on translation from the mother tongue into the target language.

There have been two main reactions against this method, historically almost exactly a century apart, and each based upon a new conception of the nature and function of language.

The first, based on the then new science of phonetics, held that languages consist not of letters and written words, but of sounds. Applied to teaching methods, the theory implied that the language to be taught was the spoken one, that mastery of it could only be attained by speaking it, and that the order of progress in learning would be listening, understanding, speaking, reading and finally writing. It was a short step from this belief to the assumption that the second language could and should be learned in the same way as the mother tongue, i.e. by unconscious assimilation, by imitation, by trial and error and without any translation from another language. This was the method frequently but loosely called the 'direct method'.

The movement towards a reform of teaching methods began in England about 1850 with the work of J. S. Blackie and C. Marcel (and later received the support of Sweet, Sayce, Widgery, MacGowan, and others); and in Germany about 1875 with the work of Count Pfeil, Perthes and Trautmann. The most famous teacher in the field was, however, Wilhelm Viëtor, whose pamphlet *Die Sprachunterricht muss umkehren* made history, though in fact it did little more than summarise in vigorous language the trends of the day.

In developments from the direct method, such as the oral and conversational methods, material to be taught was graded and systematised, whereas the direct method school has assumed that this was unnecessary, and that the teacher need only continue to speak the language in normal adult everyday use, until his class came to understand and master it. These methods enjoyed a wave of enthusiasm (and, in the hands of gifted teachers, of great success) during the '20s and early '30s. Their popularity declined owing to the tremendous demands they made on the teacher's linguistic competence, ingenuity and physical stamina, but they left a salutary effect on teaching methods in the increased importance attached to oral work, even by those unable to practise them fully.

The second revolution in modern language teaching dates from the second world war, but reached the classroom only in the late '50s and did not become an effective force until the '60s. Its sources included the work of the behaviourist psychologists, the fast growing science of linguistics, and the technological progress which rapidly improved the reproduction of sound in tape-recorders and developed twin-track models which made possible the early language laboratories or language teaching rooms. Political and social influences encouraged the progress of the new developments, and widespread public interest grew in crash courses for businessmen and courses for primary school pupils.

The linguistic sciences insist on the paramount importance of the spoken word, and hence concentrate on language as a means of communication, rather than on its literary forms. One of their contributions to foreign language learning has been to point out that a comparative analytical study of the mother tongue and of the target language highlights the learner's difficulties and shows where intense study is needed. Scientifically conducted vocabulary and structure frequency counts provide basic learning material. Scientific analysis of the contemporary spoken language picks out the target language's basic structures, which must be learned for simple communication and which can be practised by pattern drills in the classroom.

The contribution of applied linguistics was supplemented by that of the behaviourist psychologists who supported the principle of habit-formation by pattern drills. From all this sprang the audio-lingual courses, which are based on the assumption that foreign language learning is basically a mechanical process of habit-formation, that language skills are more effectively learned in the spoken form first, and that analogy, not analysis, is the best foundation for language learning. These courses emphasise over-learning by mimicry-memorisation and pattern-drill (the manipulative stage), but pay perhaps too little attention to the use of foreign languages in real communication—free, creative use of language.

New approaches were made possible by technological progress. The tape-recorder, though still not always quite perfect in the reproduction of sound, can present native voices in untiring drill material and continuous sequences. Twin-track machines can be used in such a way that the student can record his repetitions or answers on the second track and, by replaying, compare his attempts with the correct version on the master track, which is unaffected by his recording. A series of such machines, linked together and under remote control from a console, forms a language laboratory. Here each student can work individually, privately, and at his own pace; or he may be unobtrusively monitored by the teacher, whose help he can summon at all times if he wishes. The language laboratory can be used as a teaching machine by employing carefully programmed material, but is normally used to do work which is closely integrated with that done in the classroom. Its contribution to the perfecting of pronunciation and intonation is regarded as limited by some experts, but its validity as an instrument to practise structures is normally accepted.

Tape-recorders have also been linked with the use of film-strip in what are called audio-visual materials or courses. Here sound and pictures are closely linked and the language material is presented in global structures. These colourful and lively materials normally have sound linguistic foundations, but they have shortcomings. The sound is not always clear enough for a novice whose lack of experience in the language makes it difficult for him to supplement from the verbal context. The validity of the visual element in comprehension has also been questioned, and although the research which has been done is as yet limited and inconclusive, it seems to indicate that the teacher must undertake much greater responsibility for ensuring comprehension than was at first thought. Moreover, the materials need large-scale development and exploitation in the classroom before the level of creative communication is reached, and this is neglected by some teachers.

The post-war years have seen an unprecedented expansion in the field of language teaching. Well-planned, scientific research into material and techniques is being undertaken by groups like CREDIF in France and the Nuffield Foundation (q.v.) in England. Experiments such as the teaching of foreign languages in primary schools are being organised at national level. Language courses are being introduced on a wide scale into secondary modern and comprehensive schools so that the study of foreign languages is no longer the privilege of a grammar school élite. There are courses on radio and television, not only in conventional European languages but in non-Indo-European ones. Traditional university courses have been influenced towards the increased study of the contemporary spoken language, and prose translation is losing its stranglehold. Even more revolutionary changes have taken place in some of the newer universities, where language courses have been created so as to incorporate the linguistic research and technological aids referred to above.

See also **Annan Report; French in the primary school; Language laboratory; Language Teaching, Centre for Information on; Modern Languages, Committee on Research and Development in**

FURTHER READING
M. Gilbert. 'The origins of the Reform Movement in Modern Language Teaching in England', *Durham Research Review*, No. 4, 1953, and No. 5, 1954.

NC
GR

Modern Languages and Literatures, International Federation for *See* **Modern Humanities Research Association**

Modified Scheme For those teachers who elected to pay reduced contributions under the terms and conditions

Age of teacher at date of modification	*Yearly reduction of annual superannuation allowance for each year of contributory service after date of modifications*				
	Men			Women	
	£	s	d	£	s	d
20 or under	1	14	0	1	14	0
21 ,,	1	13	0	1	12	0
22 ,,	1	12	0	1	10	6
23 ,,	1	11	0	1	9	0
24 ,,	1	10	0	1	7	6
25 ,,	1	9	6	1	6	0
26 ,,	1	9	0	1	4	6
27 ,,	1	8	6	1	3	6
28 ,,	1	8	0	1	2	6
29 ,,	1	7	0	1	1	6
30 ,,	1	6	6	1	0	6
31 ,,	1	6	0		19	6
32 ,,	1	5	6		19	0
33 ,,	1	5	0		18	6
34 ,,	1	4	6		18	0
35 ,,	1	4	0		17	6
36 ,,	1	3	6		17	0
37 ,,	1	3	0		16	6
38 ,,	1	2	6		16	0
39 ,,	1	2	0		15	6
40 ,,	1	1	6		15	0
41 ,,	1	1	6		14	6
42 ,,	1	1	0		14	6
43 ,,	1	0	6		14	0
44 ,,	1	0	0		14	0
45 ,,		19	6		13	6
46 ,,		19	0		13	0
47 ,,		19	0		13	0
48 ,,		18	6		12	6
49 ,,		18	6		12	6
50 ,,		18	6		12	0

of the National Insurance (Modification of Teacher's Pension) Regulations 1948, and those who entered contributory service for the first time on or after 1 July 1948, the annual allowance will be reduced at age 65 in the case of a man (60 in the case of a woman) by reference to the period of service, years and days, performed after the material date (1 July 1948) during which reduced contributions were paid under the Teachers' (Superannuation) Acts. The scale of reduction will be according to the age of the teacher at the date reduced contributions commenced to be paid, as shown in the opposite table.

Thus in the case of a teacher aged 47 on the material date (1 July 1948), who had 25 years of service before that date and 15 years of service at reduced contributions after that date, the reduction of teacher's pension would be 19s × 15 = £14 5s 0d for a man, and 13s × 15 = £9 15s 0d for a woman. The amount of the reduction in teacher's pension in any particular case cannot exceed the original standard rate of National Insurance retirement pension of 26s per week, i.e. £67 15s 0d per annum. Parts of a year are counted proportionally.

For those teachers subject to the Modified Scheme on entry into teaching service and who have rendered 40 or more years of contributory service after the material date the teacher's pension will be reduced by the original standard rate of National Insurance pension, i.e. 26s per week or £67 15s 0d per annum. Where the teacher has rendered less than 40 years of contributory service the teacher's pension will be reduced by one-fortieth of 26s per week (£1 14s 0d per annum) in respect of every full year of contributory service.

SEB

Monitorial system Monitors preceded the system to which they gave their name (*see* **Lancasterian** and

Madras systems). In *Ludus Literarius* (1612) John Brinsley employed 'sub-doctors' in his school and advised the fullest co-operation of children in choosing them; Quaker schools in the 18th century employed them as part of a training in responsibility. In Arnold's time public schools monitors became prefects. They were also used at the same time in the University of Edinburgh by James Pillans during his long tenure of the chair of humanity and law.

WHGA

Montessori, Maria (1870–1952) The first woman ever to qualify as a doctor of medicine in Italy, Montessori became interested in education through working with defective children in Rome. Her theories, as applied to all children, soon made her an international figure and her influence upon nursery and infant education has been immense.

Basically, Montessori believed that children preferred work to play if only they were given the right sort of materials in the right environment. The purpose of this work, which involves a very wide range of materials, is to help the child to perfect his skills and explore his environment. Some of the materials, such as the number rods, would help prepare him for academic subjects, while others, such as diminutive brooms or dusters, would allow the child to explore the adult world on the child's own terms. Such play often involves a great deal of repetition, which Montessori saw as an essential characteristic of infant learning.

In a classroom run on Montessori lines, therefore, one could expect to see all furniture and fittings adapted for the use of children, and the teacher intervening only if the child were not concentrating or were disturbing the work of others. The whole idea of the 'prepared environment', otherwise, is for the child to grow quite independent of the adult, choosing his own work, so long as he knows how to use it, and getting on with it on his own rather than in a group. Reading and writing will start whenever the child shows an interest, and as so much of the classroom material is leading up to this, it is not surprising that literacy usually starts fairly soon.

Followers of Froebel (*q.v.*) have often found the system geared too much in the direction of work in these early stages, but Montessorians would probably reply that children regard work with things and materials *as* play, and that they often turn to 'make-believe' only because adults have suggested it, or because there is nothing better to do. By providing children with such a wide range of graded sensory material, Montessori hoped to give them something essentially satisfying, since it could not help but fulfil the needs of the child's growing intelligence and sensory skill. Indeed, Montessorians claim that the self-discipline children willingly impose upon themselves by following these things through is one of the most impressive aspects of the whole system.

Although in some ways the complete Montessori system may now seem a little rigid in places, there is no doubt that it has done a great deal in working toward a genuinely child-centred education. Whereas some of Froebel's ideas now seem a little sentimental, Montessori always built upon scientific observation and induction. Her emphasis, for example, upon concrete experience before going on to abstract mathematics, although revolutionary at the time, is now taken for granted, with so many of her other ideas, in nearly all progressive infant education.

FURTHER READING
Maria Montessori. *The Secret of Childhood*, Longmans Green, 1936.
E. M. Standing. *Maria Montessori*, Hollis and Carter, 1957.

NT

Montessori Society The Montessori Society in England works towards the further development of educational reform and the implementation and further interpretation of Dr Montessori's basic educational philosophy in the present age; and acts as a social link between those interested in these educational aspects.

Individual teaching is becoming established in both state and private schools. The Montessori Society aims to be at the forefront of further development in this field.

Diploma courses and various meetings are held in London. The *Montessori Bulletin* is published quarterly.

Hon. Membership Secretary, Eastleach Folly, Cirencester, Glos.

Montessori Training Organisation, Maria The training centre in England of the Association Montessori Internationale, the organisation conducts courses for adult students in child development and education according to Dr Montessori's principles. It is also responsible for several Montessori schools in the London area, and maintains and extends contact with educationists on an international level.

26 Lyndhurst Gdns, London, NW3.

Moral education Moral education comprises the complex of influences that promote the moral and social development of the child from the egocentricity of the baby to the responsible maturity appropriate to the adult. It is a process of nurturing development akin to any other learning process, differing from more specific tasks in the deep personal and social significance of the area involved rather than in the nature of the learning process.

Moral education involves social education, but extends beyond it in so far as it covers the way the individual deals with his own powers and potentialities as well as how he behaves in his relationships with other people and the community at large. Moral education is, in fact, as much concerned with

striving for personal wholeness as with generating a responsible attitude to others and an understanding of right and wrong behaviour. Much research remains to be done before it will be possible to describe in detail precisely what moral education involves, but the general strategy can be inferred from research in related areas.

The most constructive factor in moral education is a happy, purposeful, stimulating home life which encourages the child to explore his powers while offering loving guidance and setting appropriate limits to behaviour. After the start of schooling, one may assume, the socialisation process is most effective when sustained by a school that provides, for all children, warm and satisfying group and community life and relationships, and opportunities for sharing responsibilities with others and contributing to the life of the school in ways that are recognised and appreciated. These principles are well demonstrated in modern infant schools, where children learn from the activities of the school day how to be responsible for themselves and one another, and what the limits on personal behaviour have to be. Later on, at school, individualism and competitiveness may replace the early climate of co-operation, and the risk of individual children becoming isolated and possibly alienated is considerably increased. Isolation and alienation appear to hinder advance towards moral maturity.

Another important element would seem to be the development of a sense of self-esteem. A child who feels inadequate is unlikely to feel responsible. Delinquents, for example, are frequently low-attainers with a deep sense of personal inferiority. It would seem, therefore, to be an important task of moral education to foster the self-confidence of the child by assuring him of success as the reward of effort. To be in a position when the task is too hard, or too inappropriate, to make striving a rewarding experience is demoralising. For the successful, a manageable amount of failure can act as a stimulant to effort: but, for the persistently unsuccessful, the threat of yet more failure may undermine morale completely. An appropriate sense of status, and elbow room in which to grow, also seem to be important in developing social control.

In addition to the social and psychological conditions for fostering moral education we have also to consider its content. This falls under two headings: the non-specific and the specific. Under the first come, to a greater or less extent, all subjects. Mathematics and science can develop a sense of wonder as well as respect for truth. English literature can be used to promote understanding of human nature and of problems of inter-personal relationships. The arts have much to offer about human effort and dedication, as well as being a source of delight and personal involvement. The social studies tell the story of man's age-old striving to find truth and happiness, as well as presenting object lessons in evil purposes and their outcomes. To the extent that we personalise and socialise content—a current trend—all subjects are about the evolution of the human race and the challenges and responsibilities involved in that continuing process. So planned, all subjects help to provide perspective on the nature of man and the nature of the universe, without which the individual life may easily falter for lack of vision, dignity, and a sense of purposeful involvement.

The specific content of moral education is all that embraces the direct study of moral values and problems. This includes religious education, sex education, the study of human relationships, and the development of moral insight through the study and discussion of situational issues, including problems of personal behaviour.

Yet another important area of moral education is that of pastoral care. Any system of moral education will break down at its most vulnerable point if children and adolescents who feel the need for help with their personal problems, or show they do so by symptoms of stress, are not provided with adequate support, comfort and assistance. Moral breakdown that occurs at the secondary stage might well have been avoided if the underlying personal inadequacy or stress had been diagnosed and corrected at the primary stage; the upward trend of delinquency in the last year at school— evidence of social and moral immaturity at a stage too late to do much about it—might well be reduced or removed if really adequate pastoral care were available in the early years of secondary schooling. This links moral education with the establishment of counselling systems that are concerned particularly with the personal development of children and adolescents.

Relating moral education appropriately to the different stages of education is no great problem if the children themselves are taken as the starting-point, and not presuppositions about what children *should* be learning. Community structure appropriate to children and tasks itself develops opportunities for social education through involvement in group life. Content can be chosen on the basis of existing knowledge of the powers of children at different developmental ages. Abstract ideas in particular should be left until the secondary stage.

Two further aspects of moral education remain to be mentioned: example and service. The example of those in authority over children is plainly significant. Children will identify themselves with teachers they admire and will pick up the values they represent. Service within the school arises naturally in a community so planned that the children are encouraged to feel responsible for one another; opportunities for service beyond the school can both rescue the school from social isolation and extend the range of responsibility manifest in the school. It will be seen that present trends take us beyond the traditional concept of moral education as mainly a matter of inculcating ideas of right and wrong and reinforcing these ideas by conditioning. The modern approach is developmental and consequently more complex.

See also **Guidance and counselling**

FURTHER READING

Emile Durkheim. *Moral Education*, Free Press of Glencoe, USA, 1961.

Irven DeVore. *Primate Behaviour*, Holt, Rinehart and Winston, New York, 1965.

E. M. and M. Eppel. *Adolescents and Morality*, Routledge and Kegan Paul, 1966.

S. and E. Glueck. *Family Environment and Delinquency*, Routledge and Kegan Paul, 1962.

Ronald Goldman. *Religious Thinking from Childhood to Adolescence*, Routledge and Kegan Paul, 1964.

W. R. Niblett (ed.). *Moral Education in a Changing Society*, Faber and Faber, 1963.

R. S. Peters. *Ethics and Education*, Allen and Unwin, 1966.

Jean Piaget. *The Moral Judgment of the Child*, Routledge and Kegan Paul, 1932.

JH

Morant, Sir Robert (1863–1920) Educated at Winchester and Oxford, Morant as a young man was appointed tutor to the children of the Siamese ambassador, and later to the Siamese Crown Prince, and was responsible for reorganising the educational system of Siam. Forced to return home in 1893, he was appointed Assistant Director of the Education Department's Office of Special Inquiries and Reports.

Confronted with the muddle of educational administration at the time, he resolved to discredit the School Boards and so open the way for the passing of control over elementary and secondary education into the hands of the LEAs. The Cockerton Judgement (*q.v.*), which was the outcome of Morant's manoeuvres, by declaring that the use of funds by the London School Board to finance evening classes was illegal, made it necessary for the government to introduce an Act into Parliament that for the moment legalised the position of the School Boards until the passage of the 1902 Education Act (*q.v.*), which realised Morant's aims.

In 1904 Morant was made Permanent Secretary of the Board of Education (after a year as Acting Secretary), and he set about reshaping the Board. He established three branches—elementary, secondary and technical; reorganised and expanded the inspectorate; and set out the lines along which elementary and secondary education should develop. Limitations in his outlook made him see the secondary schools largely in academic terms: under his inspiration, they were geared to university entrance. His view of elementary education (and therefore the Board's approach to it) was less limited. With him, technical education was a blind spot, and the slow growth of provision for it was largely due to Morant's indifference.

During Morant's period at the Board, the first Act enabling LEAs to provide a school meals service (Education (Provision of Meals) Act 1906) was passed, together with an Act providing for school medical inspection and an Act (1907) which established the system of free places in secondary schools. Morant resigned from the Board in 1911 following a leak from a confidential document prepared by the Chief Inspector which contained an attack not only on elementary teachers ('as a rule, uncultured and imperfectly educated') but also on local inspectors and especially local Chief Inspectors ('the fountain heads of a vicious officialdom'). Morant later became Permanent Secretary at the Ministry of Health.

Moray House A college of education in Edinburgh with a student population of 1,700 which will increase in the near future to 2,500. It was established

477

Q*

in 1843 by the Free Church, two years after the opening of the first training college in Scotland which was founded at Glasgow by David Stow.

The Moray House intelligence and reasoning tests were formerly produced in Moray House by Sir Godfrey Thomson and his staff, Sir Godfrey being both head of the college and of the Edinburgh University Department of Education. In 1951 the posts of professor of education and principal of the college were split, and a separate trust fund was set up to administer the income derived from the tests. This is administered by a board of governors and the director of the Research Unit who is a member of the university staff. The principal of Moray House College of Education is a member of this board.

Morley College A London adult education centre best known for its work in the arts, particularly music, the College now has its own premises in Westminster Bridge Road; but until 1924 it was housed in the Old Vic Theatre, whose history it shares.

In 1880 Emma Cons took possession of the Royal Victoria Theatre, till then given over to the lowest kinds of entertainment, and reopened it as a centre for 'wholesome recreation'. Samuel Morley, the hosiery manufacturer, actively supported this venture. Within ten years the educational side of this work had grown from occasional lectures and choir practices in the theatre saloon into a new and separate foundation—the Morley Memorial College. From the beginning the College has been open to women as well as men (unlike the Working Men's Colleges), and its work, always of a high standard, has developed throughout this century. Its pre-eminence in music owes much to the tradition established by Gustav Holst, for a time its music director.

61 Westminster Bridge Rd, London, SE1.

FURTHER READING
D. Richards. *Off-spring of the Vic*, Routledge and Kegan Paul, 1958.

BG

Morocco, Education in Where places are available, education is compulsory between the ages of seven and 13. 1964–5 statistics: number of schools not available. Enrolments: primary 1,105,182; secondary 173,761; technical 19,900; teacher training 466; higher education 10,136. There are three universities, at Rabat, Marrakesh and Fez. An American university at Tangier is planned to open in 1968. Population: approximately $13\frac{1}{2}$ million.

Motivation Our most basic instincts can be traced to the need for our own survival and that of the species. However, there are many other strong motivations in human beings that cannot be traced directly to these instincts, and to explain these we must imagine certain drives or needs that may be learned from our own personal experience and the society we live in. Thus, if a child finds a certain activity rewarding, or offering positive reinforcement (*q.v.*), he may learn to look forward to it; but if it becomes associated with failure, pain or other negative reinforcements (*q.v.*), he may learn to avoid it as much as he can. Such children are often thought of as lazy and their school reports may contain phrases such as 'Could do better'. This, of course, is not an explanation for a child's failure to do his best; and, if there is the opportunity, the teacher or educational psychologist should try harder to understand the child's low motivation, and if possible do something about it, although this may not be at all easy.

NT

Motor ability There is probably no such thing as motor ability in a general sense, since a child may be unskilled in one particular performance but do well in others. For example, there does not seem to be a very high correlation between the abilities to throw, climb and jump. Obviously if a child is reasonably strong and can move quickly, he may have certain advantages in some physical tasks, but this ability is also very much influenced by his confidence, stamina and interest. With young children, there seems to be quite a high correlation between mental and motor ability, but this does not necessarily persist into adulthood.

Mountaineering Strictly speaking, mountaineering is the sport of climbing mountains; but the schools' concern is more with mountain walking and rock climbing.

Though the main mountaineering areas of the UK are situated in the Lake District, North Wales and Scotland, the sport of rock climbing is not confined to schools within easy reach of these areas, since the country abounds in rock outcrops on which the basic techniques of climbing can be learned, and the skills and practice needed for most difficult rock ascents.

As rock climbing *can* be dangerous, it is vital that expert progressive instruction is given to learners. This can be arranged by teachers either attending courses arranged by bodies such as the Central Council of Physical Recreation (*q.v.*) and then passing on the knowledge gained, or taking groups of pupils to training areas such as the Bowles Mountaineering Gymnasium, situated at an outcrop near Sevenoaks, Kent.

A recent development has been the setting up by LEAs, and even individual schools, of their own residential outdoor-pursuits training centres in suitable areas, to which groups of children go for short periods and take part in a wide variety of outdoor activities, including rock climbing, mountain walking, orienteering and even mountain rescue. A notable centre of this kind is the White Hall Centre, near Buxton,

Derbyshire, which takes parties from all over the UK. Courses are also arranged by the Youth Hostel Association at many of their hostels.

Central Council of Physical Recreation, 26 Park Cres., London, W1.

Mountaineering Association, 102a Westbourne Grove, London, W2.

Youth Hostels Association of England and Wales, Trevelyan House, 8 St Steven's Hill, St Albans, Herts.

See also **Rock climbing**

JE

Movement, Art of *See* **Dance in education**

MRST These letters (standing for 'Member of the Royal Society of Teachers') were used by teachers voluntarily registering with the Teachers' Registration Council set up in 1907. The aim of the Council was to raise teachers' status, but since membership, in the event, had little influence on either the Board of Education or the LEAs in their choice of candidates for promotion, the register contained the names only of a dwindling minority of teachers. Registration was abandoned in 1948.

See also **Teachers' Register**

Mulcaster, Richard (1530?-1611) The first headmaster of the Merchant Taylors' School from 1561 to 1586 (he may have taught Edmund Spenser), Mulcaster was made High Master of St Paul's in 1596. In many ways his views on education were well in advance of his age. He believed in the teaching of English, and that other languages should be postponed until that was well begun; he taught music and singing, and his pupils performed masques and interludes at Elizabeth's court. He stressed the importance of physical education and mathematics, and was a pioneer of the view that girls ought to be as well educated intellectually as boys. He was an advocate of the training of teachers, urged the need to raise the teacher's status, and gave early expression to the opinion that universal education was desirable.

Multilateral school An early attempt to create a comprehensive school, a multilateral (or many-sided) school divided the grammar, technical and secondary modern streams into separate compartments, and so was not truly comprehensive.

Multiple choice In questions of the true–false variety there are only two alternatives. In multiple-choice questions any number of alternatives may be presented: e.g. 'The smallest Scottish county is: Clackmannan, Bute, Kinross, Nairn, Kirkcudbrightshire, Banffshire, none of these.' In answering this type of question (characteristic of branching programmes as well as of many objective-type tests), the learner has to select from a given set of alternatives.

See also **Objective tests**

Municipal Administration, Diploma in *See* **Local Government Examinations Board**

Museum education Museum education has received more support in the USA than in Europe. More than 20 years ago Theodore Lowe pointed out[1] that support for museums would in future come more from the community than from the millionaire collector, and that education of this community should be the museums' prime object.

Never has the well-supported museum, well-displayed and well-staffed, been more needed. The art museum can supply the real food for art and art history; the natural history museum for the true understanding of botany, anthropology, geology, etc. and the science museum can provide illustrations not available to the average school-teacher of advances in physics, chemistry, etc. (e.g. the work done by the education department of the Science Museum, S. Kensington). Visual illiteracy—the want of visual memory and of ability to enjoy and experience through seeing—is fairly common today; the museum is the ideal place in which to stimulate seeing and learning through seeing.

A number of museums in the UK provide some form of loan education service.[2] Derby has a long-established organisation for loan to schools; others are provided by Newport, Leicester, the County of Oxford, Portsmouth, West Riding and Edinburgh. In London no national museum has such facilities. The GLC Geffrye Museum is the only children's museum with continuous opportunities for class work. The Natural History and the Victoria and Albert Museums provide facilities for junior classes to sketch in the galleries and to use a studio room for creative work. This encouragement of creative work is on the increase among the 40 or so museums in the UK where special educational appointments have been made. But the general poverty of the museums service does not encourage the type of adventurous work most needed. Too often the needs both of children and adults are met by the provision of guides who merely retail information, without being able to create a background for the work shown. Children in junior classes need well-directed activities; those in senior classes need stimulus to work for themselves; adults need an exciting introduction to something they will pursue further.

Museums and their localities should ideally be linked so that what is shown in the gallery relates to the wider world. Cathedrals, parish churches, great houses, ancient towns and villages, early factories, scenes of natural beauty and of geological and botanical interest, are part of the same world as the museum exhibit. It may be simpler for a teacher to use a labelled exhibit, but more than a label is needed to give it life. Museum teachers must be teachers first and experts second, not retailing information merely, but stimulating and answering queries.

Little outlay is needed to provide good museum teachers. The USA makes excellent use of volunteers—largely young graduate housewives who undergo a two-months training and practical course, and are devoted members of museum staffs. The alternatives in the UK would seem to be acceptance of volunteer staff or the deferring of massive development of museum education for another generation.

REFERENCES
1. *Education in the Art Museum*, Columbia Teachers' College, 1942.
2. See the list from the Museums Association, 42 Fitzroy Sq., London, WC1.

See also **Appendix 15**

HLo

Museum School Services Throughout Great Britain, Museum School Services offer help to teachers, student teachers and others engaged in educational work. These services cover the regular loan of museum material for use in the classroom or for exhibition purposes in the school or college, and talks in the galleries. Most of the services print catalogues of the material available for use in the area served.

Hon. Sec.: R. G. Payne, City Museum, Queens Rd, Bristol, 8.

Museums, Group for Educational Services in Affiliated to the Museums Association, the Group provides information and guidance to education authorities, teachers and others on school services in museums.

Sec.: G. I. McCabe, Group for Educational Services in Museums, Oxford City and County Museum, Fletcher's Hse, Woodstock, Oxford.

Publication: *Museum School Services* (handbook).

Museums and art galleries, Selected list of *See* **Appendix 15**

Music, Associated Board of the Royal Schools of The Board was established in 1889 by the Royal Academy of Music and the Royal College of Music, and joined in 1947 by the Royal Manchester College of Music and the Royal Scottish Academy of Music, Glasgow. It aims at improving the standard of musical education and offers in the British Isles and overseas a scheme of local graded examinations in keyboard and orchestral instruments, singing, general musicianship and theory of music, ranging from the beginning stages and leading up to diploma examinations of the Royal Schools.

Some of the Board's examinations in music are linked with the GCE examinations of some of the universities. The Board also confers by examination overseas the diploma of Licentiate of the Royal Schools of Music, which is equivalent to the LRAM or the ARCM. Examinations in speech and drama are held in the British Isles.

See also **Musical education**

Music, Examinations in Examination of ability on most solo instruments, piano duet and general musicianship, is available. Aural tests form part of these examinations, which are graded from near-beginner to near-diploma standard. Certain certificates issued by the Associated Board of the Royal Schools of Music (*q.v.*) are recognised parts of the GCE.

Trinity College of Music, the Guildhall School of Music and Drama and the London College of Music also conduct local examinations.

See also **Musical education**

Music, Standing Conference for Amateur The Standing Conference is a voluntary association which co-ordinates the work of national, regional, county and borough organisations concerned with school music and amateur music at all ages; it collects information, studies problems, advises, produces new ideas, and spreads the results through publications, bulletins to members and the holding of an annual residential conference.

The Standing Conference has initiated a number of experimental projects on a national scale, the most recent being summer schools for teachers of music to handicapped children, and the formation of the youth choral movement 'Sing for Pleasure'.

26 Bedford Sq., London, WC1.

Music Advisers' National Association The objects of the Association are to provide the means whereby those responsible for the development of musical education under a local authority may unite for the discussion of the most desirable policies to be pursued, and to provide advice and information upon such matters to other persons or bodies working in the educational field.

Membership is open to music advisers employed on a full-time basis by an LEA and whose work involves the supervision of teachers.

Hon. Sec.: Kenneth J. Eade, BMus, FTCL, LRAM, Education Office, Exchange Bldgs, Nottingham.

Music Association, Schools Founded in 1938 as a result of the success of the non-competitive schools music festival scheme, after the war the Association expanded to cover all aspects of music teaching in schools. It is supported by affiliated LEAs, schools festivals, private members, associate member schools and colleges, and industrial members, to whom it gives a free library service. The Association organises regional festivals for schools, courses for teachers, and orchestral courses for its two national orchestras, the British Youth Symphony Orchestra and the British Schools Orchestra, and runs an advisory and research sub-committee which publishes reports from time to time.

There are also regional committees.

With the British Standards Institution the Association has initiated the publication of specifications for musical instruments and audio aids supplied to schools.

Quarterly journal: *Music*.

4 Newman Rd, Bromley, Kent.

Music centres A report published in 1966 for the Standing Conference for Amateur Music by the National Conference of Social Service refers to 34 music centres in England and Wales, and describes six of them in some detail. Another section deals with the training of specially talented children.

Music, drama and dancing, Colleges of *See* **Appendix 4**

Music Masters' Association The Association's aim is to look after the interests of music masters in schools affiliated to the Headmasters' Conference and Incorporated Association of Preparatory Schools: recently the terms of the former have been extended to include those working in boys' boarding schools outside the HMC. Membership, which is voluntary, now stands at about 370. The Association meets twice a year: at New Year with the Incorporated Society of Musicians (ISM) and independently for one day in the summer term at a public school. Four newsletters a year are sent to members.

Hon. Sec.: Dr J. H. Alden, Cray Cottage, Bradfield, Reading, Berks.

Music Teachers' Association Founded in 1908, the MTA has the declared aims of fostering better musicianship; promoting progressive ideas on the teaching of music and furthering the cause of music in education; providing musical education and training; and giving opportunities to members and others to hear lectures, demonstrations and concerts.

These aims are pursued through a wide range of activities. Recently, for example, the MTA has held two important conferences on the economic outlook for the music teacher in private practice, resulting in a resolution to increase fees throughout the country. At the same time an examinations sub-committee has been meeting to draft proposals for an alternative syllabus in music at GCE O level. A similar sub-committee exists to deal with questions arising on examinations held by other bodies, such as the Associated Board of the Royal Schools of Music (*q.v.*) with which the MTA happily co-operates.

Advice to members on questions arising out of their professional work is readily available, either through the MTA office or, in the case of specialised inquiries, through the Association's journal *Music Teacher*.

During the winter, the MTA organises a series of lectures at headquarters and at its branches, covering topics of great interest to members, such as questions of technique and interpretation, teaching method and special demonstrations. Occasionally a British composer is invited to arrange a concert of items from his work.

The MTA's summer schools are known throughout this country and the Commonwealth for their high standards and thoroughness of approach. A course is run each August for young orchestral players between 12 and 18 years of age, at Downe House School, Newbury, Berks. Four youthful orchestras rehearse daily under expert supervision, and concerts are given at the end of the course.

A recent development is the organisation of short courses in London during the spring and autumn on features of music teaching needing concentrated attention.

106 Gloucester Pl., London, W1.

'Music and the Young' A report issued by the DES in 1967, based on information collected by H.M. Inspectorate, *Music and the Young* surveys work in music in schools, colleges and other educational institutions. Of the musical education provided by 97 out of the 144 county and county borough areas in England, the report said that it was 'fair, not altogether inadequate but undistinguished' or (in the case of 27 of these areas) 'inadequate'. The report found that 'interesting, lively and progressive work in music' was characteristic of the primary schools, but that the achievement of the secondary schools was more patchy. The musical adviser, employed by nearly all counties, was an important agent in the revolution in musical education that had occurred in the past 20 years. The general verdict of the report was that there appeared to be an upsurge of interest in music as part of general as well as specialised education.

Musical education Many educational writers including Plato, Milton, Pestalozzi, Froebel, Rousseau and Matthew Arnold have emphasised the importance of music in child development. Their ideas have often been adduced to support differing views on the purpose and scope of musical education. At different times and in different places the stress has been put on the theoretical bases of music, on more or less passive appreciation, music allied to movement and on music-making along lines themselves subject to shifting enthusiasms—percussion bands, bamboo pipes or recorders—with singing as one element of consistency.

Following the early examples of Cambridge (1463) and Oxford (*c.* 1500) in awarding musical degrees, several newer universities have founded faculties of music and shared in the administration of music examinations for the GCE at O and A levels. Performing ability is considered an essential part of GCE syllabuses, and for the assessment of this certain graded certificates of the Associated Board of the Royal Schools of Music (*q.v.*) are recognised.

In nursery and infant schools, music is approached as the continuation of ideal pre-school experience. (The BBC's *Listen With Mother* programme contributes with increasing success to the realisation of this ideal for each successive generation of infants.) Music may enliven any point of the day. Songs and nursery rhymes are sung and singing games played between other activities and as necessary adjuncts to story, dance and drama. Much depends upon the teacher's insight and ability. A clear, light singing voice, able to convey a sense of fun and characterisation, wins children's co-operation more readily than a highly-trained voice. As accompaniment, a good-quality Spanish guitar well played has more to commend it than any piano, on grounds of both immediacy and tonal quality. A child's ability to sing 'in tune' needs careful encouragement from the start, proceeding outwards from pitches closely related to those of his speaking voice and exploiting a natural wish to imitate the sounds of his environment. Although many children, no less musical than their fellows, acquire pitch perception only slowly, no hint of discouragement may be allowed to reach those whose singing is reluctant to leave one low note. Young children show delight in discovering the variety of sounds produced from wood, metal, water, strings, tubes, glasses, etc. They also enjoy bodily rhythm and engage enthusiastically and profitably in rhythmic clapping and stamping by imitation.

The ideas of Carl Orff (*q.v.*) have in recent years exerted an increasing influence on the teaching of music. Appropriate to most stages of children's music-making, Orff's *Schulwerk* is being more thoroughly investigated in junior and preparatory schools than elsewhere. Recent analysis of the processes basic to musical composition has enabled some teachers to provide their classes with guidance and stimulus to provoke from them remarkably fine original composition.

Throughout the primary school, children develop in their ability to enjoy group effort. In the junior school singing is still at the centre of musical experience. Nursery rhymes give place to the folk songs of Britain and other lands and to classical songs. Words are of basic importance in judging the suitability of this material. The teaching is usually the responsibility of each class teacher, though some schools have appointed a teacher with specialised responsibility to promote and co-ordinate musical activity.

Broadcasting has done much to energise music throughout the age-ranges. The BBC has developed several series of music programmes on sound radio, and more recently on television, designed to assist music teachers and to provide imaginative courses for schools where otherwise little music might be possible. These programmes emphasise the importance of guided listening, for at every stage children can be helped to enjoy hearing music well-suited to their comprehension, but not for so long that their concentration is exhausted. Most schools include a record-player and/or a tape-recorder as essential parts of their musical equipment, although no such aid can compare in value to a teacher who is himself a competent player and singer.

The junior school provides training in music-reading, often by means of pitch- and time-names. Progress in musical literacy is found to proceed faster and more surely when its choral application is backed by instrumental experience—on pipes, recorders, pitched percussion instruments or the more sophisticated orchestral instruments which many junior children begin to learn privately or in small groups under the tuition of one of the peripatetic teachers employed by many LEAs.

The cultivation of music varies enormously between one secondary school and another. Pupils bring from their primary schools a wide range of musical aptitude, interest and experience. In most secondary schools, up to three periods of music are arranged for each week of the first two or three years. The claims of specialisation and the problem of boys' changing voices are often considered adequate reasons for reducing this provision, or even for discontinuing class music altogether after the third year, except for those intending to take the subject in public examinations.

Much of the best music takes place as extra-curricular activity—choirs, instrumental groups, orchestra, school opera, music for morning prayers and at music society meetings.

The competence and enthusiasm of the full-time music staff are of fundamental importance, as is also the quality of peripatetic instrumental tuition. Adequate music rooms, schemes to enable young players first to borrow good quality instruments and then to buy them (by instalments, if necessary) and a school policy which values a high standard of musical achievement are other factors likely to contribute to musical virility in a secondary school.

The aims are to enable each pupil to leave school with sufficient eloquence to contribute to whatever musical environment catches his later interest, and with sufficient literacy to enable him to further his interest in that environment, together with an ability to relate an omnipresent popular musical culture to as wide a listening experience as possible.

FURTHER READING

Making Musicians, Report of a Committee to the Calouste Gulbenkian Foundation, 1965.

Standing Conference for Amateur Music. *The Training of Music Teachers*, National Council of Social Service. *Specimen*

Planning Notes on Musical Requirements in School Buildings and in Further Education Colleges (2 pamphlets), National Council of Social Service.

DB

Musical Education of the Under-Twelves This association promotes the use of music in the general education of young children, and the co-ordination of existing musical activities. Twice-yearly conferences cover all aspects of nursery, infant and junior music. Overseas members are welcomed.

Hon. Sec.: Miss K. M. Blocksidge, Banstead, Surrey.

Publication: *Bulletin* (twice yearly).

Musicians, Incorporated Society of Founded in 1882, the Society is a representative body for the musical profession, and candidates for membership must be 'solely engaged in the practice of music as a profession'. The main objects are to promote the art of music and to maintain the honour and interests of the profession. There are three specialist sections, each with its own committee: the solo-performers' section; the school music section (concerned with all matters relating to school music); and the private music teachers' section.

Conferences and other meetings are held at which professional matters are discussed. The Society publishes a *Handbook and Register of Members*, which is an invaluable professional directory, a periodical journal and many other occasional publications on professional matters.

Gen. Sec.: D. H. R. Brearley, PO Box 4LN, 48 Gloucester Pl., London, W1.

'Musicians, Making' The title of a report to the Calouste Gulbenkian Foundation on the training of professional musicians. Prepared by a committee under the chairmanship of Sir Gilmour Jenkins, the report was published in 1965.

N

NATE (National Association for the Teaching of English) The aim of NATE, working at local level (through branches and study groups) and at national level (through conferences, summer schools and large-scale studies and investigations), is to improve the quality of English teaching and to increase communication and discussion between teachers of English. It also publishes reports by its sub-committees, bulletins and other documents. It was one of the sponsors of the 1966 Dartmouth (US) seminar on the teaching of English. *Growth through English* by John Dixon (NATE, 1967) is the official report on the seminar, intended for professional readers; a parallel report by Professor Herbert Muller, addressed to the general public, is entitled *The Uses of English* (Henry Holt).

Hon. Sec: E. A. R. Jones, 197 Henley Rd, Caversham, Reading, Bucks.

National Academic Awards, Council for The Council was established by Royal Charter in 1964 on the recommendation of the Robbins Committee on Higher Education to provide more opportunities for students to take degree courses in the colleges of technology and the colleges of commerce and to cater especially for those with an interest in industry or commerce as a career. The Council's degrees are comparable in standard with those granted by universities. The Council awards the first degrees of BA and BSc, MA and MSc degrees for postgraduate courses of study and the research degrees of MPhil and PhD.

There are some 150 courses in a very wide range of subjects in science and technology, arts and business studies leading to the Council's degrees. Most courses are of the sandwich type and both honours and ordinary degrees are awarded.

Copies of the Council's publications, including the list of approved courses, may be obtained from the registrar and secretary.

24 Park Cres., London, W1.

National Book League The aim of the League is to encourage the 'full use and enjoyment of books'. It is a non-profit-making society supported by members' subscriptions, among whom are authors, teachers, publishers, booksellers, etc, also schools and libraries.

The largest proportion of the NBL's resources goes towards work in the educational field — exhibitions, book lists and information. The Education Department and the Book Information Bureau undertake to answer members' enquiries about books, and a list is available from the NBL of exhibitions in current circulation. These exhibitions can be hired by any organisation or school, but corporate and school members of the NBL pay at a reduced rate.

At the NBL headquarters in London there is a reference library of books about books, a members' restaurant and bar, and a permanent collection of children's books published during the previous twelve months.

7 Albemarle St, London, W1.

National Central Library The NCL acts as a central lending library (with a stock of over 350,000 volumes) from which libraries of all kinds, in the UK and abroad, can borrow. When it does not have a book, its function is to trace it to another library willing to lend it. It has built up a National Union Catalogue giving the location of some two million books in libraries in the UK.

The Library was created in 1916 as the Central Library for Students. One of its original functions, which still continues, was the supply of books to adult education classes. The Library became the centre of the national interloan system when it was re-organised in 1930. It lends books to serious readers through all types of library: university, public and specialised. No subjects are excluded, but current fiction is not dealt with.

Store St, London, WC1.

National Children's Home *See* **Children's Home, National**

National colleges *See* **Further education in England and Wales; Appendix 8**

National Economic Development Council, Educational activities of In consultation with government departments and educational and industrial organisations, the National Economic Development Council in 1967 set up a committee on management education training and development. The committee is reviewing the present and future needs of industry for management education and how far existing teaching institutions meet these needs. Currently the committee is looking into financial support of graduate students on post-graduate courses, and the improvement of marketing practices.

A number of the Economic Development Committees are looking at the problem of manpower in their industries and as part of their study are examining the facilities for training. In addition, where there is an industrial training board for the industry, the EDC maintains a constant working relationship with it.

The Economic Development Committee for Hosiery and Knitwear, Clothing and Wool Textiles is organising a summer school on management education for senior management in these industries. The Clothing EDC has set up a manpower working party which is considering ways to improve training in the industry following the Clothing Institute's survey of training needs.

The Economic Development Committee for the Distributive Trades has a training sub-committee to improve the standard of training in distribution. It has studied the training facilities available and has published a guide to the selection and training of sales staff in the smaller shop (*Grow Your Own Sales Staff—21 Golden Rules*). For large and medium-sized firms, the committee has published an introduction to management training, and is now engaged in drawing up a guide to the training of sales staff.

The Newspaper Printing and Publishing EDC has a working party on managerial development due to report in 1968, recommending some priorities for the industry's training board expected during the year.

National Education Union The Union was founded in 1869 by advocates of denominational teaching to oppose the Birmingham Education League (*q.v.*), which was pressing for a non-sectarian system of state education.

National Extension College An adult teaching and research unit set up in 1963 by the Advisory Centre for Education (*q.v.*), the College aims to provide educational facilities for students whose needs cannot be met by the existing educational system. To do this it uses a variety of techniques including correspondence courses, radio, television, programmed learning and short spells of residential tuition.

Most of the College's students are adults who find they need paper qualifications in middle life, so that most of its courses are for GCE subjects or London external degrees. But it also provides a number of courses designed to bring people up to date on new techniques or approaches which have been developed since they gained their basic qualifications. A growing part of the work of the College is to provide correspondence courses to schools who want to extend their range of teaching or are short of subject specialists (*see* **Correspondence courses in schools**).

The NEC is a non-profit-making body registered as a charity and governed by an educational trust. It derives its income from students' fees, grants from charitable foundations and grants from LEAs.

Shaftesbury Rd, Cambridge.

National Foundation for Educational Research in England and Wales *See* **Educational Research in England and Wales, National Foundation for**

National Insurance and the teacher The National Insurance Scheme is a comprehensive, and complicated, system of contributions for a range of benefits which relate to a wide sphere of human circumstances—sickness, unemployment, breakdown in health, maternity, widowhood, retirement, etc.

In general terms all employed persons, whether they are employed by others or by themselves, are required to pay contributions. There are also categories of non-employed persons from whom contributions, even if not legally required, are payable in order to avoid ineligibility to benefit. The payment of benefit is dependent upon the contribution record which varies according to the nature of the benefit required. In some cases, failure to comply with the contribution conditions disqualifies from benefit entitlement altogether, but in others the substandard contribution record may be sufficient to enable a sub-standard benefit to be paid. For example, the normal contribution conditions to qualify for the full retirement pension are (1) at least 156 contributions must be paid and (2) a yearly average of contributions paid or credited of not less than 50 must have been maintained from the date of entry into insurance up to the age of qualifying (60 in the case of a woman, 65 for a man). If, however, the contribution record is satisfactory except that a yearly average of less than 50 is established, then a reduced rate of pension is payable. However, should the yearly average be lower than 13 then the contributor has not satisfied the requirements and no retirement pension is therefore payable. This is perhaps one of the most straightforward complications in the scheme, but there are many others. Not only do rates of contribution vary from time to time but benefits also. A recent innovation has been the introduction of earnings related benefits (*q.v.*) for sickness and unemployment.

Unless a particular employment occupies less than eight hours per week, everyone is required to pay the weekly contribution which is usually deducted at source by the employer. Where entry into employment is delayed because of full-time schooling, no contributions are required and students over the age of 18 are permitted to create a gap in their record during full-time training. This gap, however, may adversely affect entitlement to benefit, and so a special concession is made enabling a student to make good the loss of contributions or any part of them during the six years following his first entry into the scheme.

It is obviously in the interests of any person seeking detailed information to secure the appropriate leaflet from the Ministry of Social Security or to seek an interview with the insurance officer.

Sick pay is usually provided by a teacher's employer under a local scheme, with the result that in normal circumstances the reduction in pay is limited to the sickness benefit receivable from National Insurance. The main interest of teachers centres upon eligibility to the retirement pension: the position is as follows.

Retirement pension When a teacher has retired from service and has reached minimum National Insurance retirement age (65 man, 60 woman), he or she will be eligible to receive the basic retirement pension, provided that his or her contribution record shows an annual average of at least 50 contributions during the whole of his or her insured life. If the yearly average falls below 50, then a reduced pension is payable.

About four months before the teacher reaches the minimum retirement age he or she should receive a form from the Ministry of Social Security for claiming the award of the pension. If the teacher will not have retired by the time the minimum retirement age is attained, he or she should still complete the claim form, but inform the Ministry that retirement is not contemplated at the present time. The contributions which he or she will continue to pay will then count towards additional pension. If a man remains in the teaching service after the age of 65 (or a woman after the age of 60) a higher rate of pension can be secured. For every subsequent twelve contributions pension will be increased by 1s per week. A man not only earns an increase on his own pension, but if his wife is 60 or over when he reaches the age of 65, her pension is eventually increased by 6d per week for every twelve contributions which he pays after the age of 65. If he dies before she does, any 6d increase earned for her pension is raised to 1s, which is added to her widow's retirement pension.

If a male teacher who has retired returns to teaching service, or undertakes some other form of insurable employment, he may arrange for his pension and his wife's pension to be suspended so that he may pay contributions and earn increases to both pensions.

Men (and women who are insured in their own right) who retire before reaching the minimum retiring age and who do not register as unemployed should continue to pay contributions at the Class 3 (non-employed) rate in order to safeguard their rights to a full pension.

SEB

National Playing Fields Association *See* **Playing Fields Association, National**

National Savings Committee The aim of the National Savings Committee in schools and colleges is to help and persuade young people to handle their money sensibly. With the co-operation of teachers, the Committee has established savings schemes in most schools, so giving children an early opportunity of learning the advantages of saving regularly.

The Committee also offers teachers a programme of studies and free money management booklets to help them to provide school leavers with timely information about budgeting and careful spending. Similar guidance on sound money management is also provided for students in colleges of education and further education.

Alexandra House, Kingsway, London, WC2.

National schools *See* **National Society**

National Society Formed in 1811 as the National Society for the Education of the Poor in the Principles of the Established Church, the Society inherited most of the schools established over the previous century by the SPCK. Within five years of its foundation the Society allowed its schools to put in their trust deeds a clause permitting dissenters' children to be withdrawn from religious lessons. In 1839 this clause became obligatory on all new trusts. By 1830 the Society had 3,670 day and Sunday schools, with one-third of a million pupils; in 1833, together with the British and Foreign Schools Society, it received a government grant.

The Society had its own teacher training system, from the model school established in 1812 at Baldwin's Gardens, to colleges like St Mark's, Chelsea, established in 1845.

'National' schools spread rapidly. By 1851 there were 17,015 schools with 955,865 pupils, as opposed to 1,500 'British' schools with 225,000 pupils. After the establishment of board schools (*see* **School boards**) the Society began to complain of pressure; subscriptions fell and fees had to be increased.

In 1934 the Society changed its name and its role, and became the 'National Society for the Promotion of Religious Education in accordance with the principles of the Church of England among all our subjects living in England and Wales, irrespective of age or degree'. Its role was to represent church opinion at government level, and to act as trustee for certain Church of England colleges.

Its functions were limited still further after 1948 when the Church of England Council for Education was established by the Church Assembly (which had been set up in 1919 'to deliberate on all matters concerning the Church of England and to make provision in respect thereof'). All five councils set up under the Church of England Council for Education have taken some of its work and responsibilities, so that today the Society is virtually a holding company of the Church.

FURTHER READING

C. K. Francis Brown. *The Church's Part in Education*, SPCK, 1942.

H. J. Burgess. *Enterprise in Education*, SPCK, 1958.

WHGA

National Trust Founded in 1895 by Miss Octavia Hill, Sir Robert Hunter and Canon Rawnsley to ensure the preservation of land of natural beauty and buildings of historic interest for public access and benefit. The Trust, which is incorporated by act of parliament, is independent of the state, and relies mainly on the voluntary support of its members. There is a special membership scheme for schools and youth groups. A panel of lecturers is available.

The Trust now owns some 180 historic buildings and over 400,000 acres of land in England and Wales, including coastland, mountain, common and nature reserves, villages, castles, country houses and collections of pictures, furniture and works of art.

42 Queen Anne's Gate, London, SW1.

National Union of Teachers *See* **Teachers, National Union of**

National Youth Orchestra *See* **Orchestra, National Youth**

Natural History Societies, Association of School The Association's aim is to link school natural history societies together by means of an annual exhibition, annual journal (*The Starfish*), newsletters, field courses, field meetings, etc. Advice is given on all natural history problems, including the identifying of specimens. Membership is open to all secondary schools interested in natural history, and not only to those with natural history societies.

The Association was founded in 1947 by David Stainer of King's School, Canterbury, at the suggestion of one of his boys. It is affiliated to the Council for Nature and other bodies.

Hon. Sec.: J. E. G. Morris, Strand School, Elm Park, Brixton Hill, London, SW2. Membership Sec.: Dr G. W. Shaw, Lancing College, Sussex.

Natural Science Society, School Founded in 1903 as the School Nature Study Union, the Society enables teachers, students and others interested in natural science to communicate and exchange ideas and advice. It is concerned with the development of natural science, including biology, natural history and the physical sciences in the primary, secondary and further stages of education.

Its activities include meetings for its members and for the public and a biennial exhibition. It publishes a journal three times per year and issues pamphlets on various aspects of science and on teaching methods.

Gen. Sec.: Miss Jenny Sellers, 2 Bramley Mansions, Berrylands Rd, Surbiton.

Naturalists' Association, British Young Founded in 1956, the Association aims to provide young people with means of furthering and maintaining their interest in natural history and other outdoor pursuits and of meeting others sharing these interests. Membership is open to children from eight upwards, and also to adults sympathetic to the organisation's aims and objects, as well as to clubs, schools and youth groups. Field centres at Scarborough, Yorks, ('Red House', Hackness and 'The Holt', Hutton Buscel) are used by secondary and primary schools and colleges of education. Activities include a merit award scheme; branches organised through the medium of Museum Clubs; the Association's *Bul-*

letin; identification of specimens; field courses and expeditions abroad; advice on careers, the keeping of pets, etc.; and an annual conference.

Hon. Gen. Sec.: D. H. Smith, FRES, 'Westland', Westfields, Kirbymoorside, York.

Nature, Council for The Council for Nature is the national representative body of the voluntary natural history movement in the UK, acting on behalf of naturalists and others to further the study and conservation of nature. The Council has 450 member natural history and conservation organisations, including 40 schools, colleges and youth organisations. A major part of the Council's function is to encourage among all a greater appreciation of wildlife; to this end it runs an information service, issuing information sheets on various aspects of conservation and publishing a monthly bulletin, *Habitat.* The Council is one of the sponsoring bodies of 'The Countryside in 1970' conferences.

Zoological Gardens, Regent's Pk, London, NW1.

Nature/nurture There is still some argument as to whether heredity is more important in shaping an individual than his environment might be—or, as it is often put, whether one's nature is more important than one's nurture. The answer is probably that, because each factor continuously influences and possibly stimulates the other throughout an individual's life, it is quite impossible to assess relative importance with any accuracy. It is true that some findings, involving identical twins living unknown to each other in different foster homes, seem to reveal a closer similarity in intelligence than one would expect through chance results; and it is also true that certain environments can be seen to produce fairly uniform poor results on intelligence tests, where one would expect more varied results. It is now thought that individuals may be born with different but still quite broad capacities for intelligence, but that it depends on their environment whether they will function to the top or the bottom of this capacity.

FURTHER READING
P. E. Vernon. *Intelligence and Attainment Tests*, Univ. of London Press, 1960.

NT

Nature study, Teaching of Nature study as a part of the curriculum of the primary school owes its place there more to historical accident than to deliberate planning. Its beginnings can be traced to the closing years of the 19th century when the bleak regimen of the Revised Code (*q.v.*) (which placed a heavy premium on the three Rs) was ending and Froebelian ideas about self-activity for pupils were coming to the fore. At that time it was felt that the natural interests of young children in plant and animal life could best be catered for by including a subject which was loosely called nature study. Accordingly, such activities as growing beans in jam-jars, collecting wild flowers and leaves, and keeping weather charts and pets in the classroom became increasingly popular. When supplemented by 'nature walks', these undoubtedly proved beneficial and were in keeping with the developmental approach recommended by psychologists.

Too often, unfortunately, teachers relied heavily on indifferent textbooks and lessons were simply a variant of reading. Behind the practice was a theory, best described as euphemistic, which affirmed that nature study served as a 'propaedeutic' (an introductory course) to the formal teaching of science. Below the age of 11 it was believed that most children were incapable of reaching the level of conceptual thought that was necessary for the understanding of scientific principles. In fact, the main reason for the adoption of the subject was that it was

cheap; no laboratories or equipment were needed. In practice, the propaedeutic theory has always been rendered nonsensical by the fact that more often than not nature study leads on to physics and chemistry, not to biology. Its content has always been a mixture of elementary botany, zoology and a smattering of climatology.

In urban schools, where opportunities for field studies are limited or non-existent, the subject is usually taught vicariously, often by teachers whose lack of interest in it is matched by their lack of knowledge. In rural areas, where opportunities are greater, the children's natural interests in the environment sometimes fail to live up to the hopes placed in them by the theorists. In an age dominated by scientific technology it is only natural that many children should be more attracted by space rockets and jet planes than by birds and beasts. Because of this, suggestions have been made for introducing physical science at a much earlier age than was formerly thought appropriate. In a word, the sociology of knowledge so far as nature study is concerned is changing.

Nevertheless, the original justification of nature study—i.e. that it appeals to the child's sense of wonder—remains valid. Clearly, if physics or astronomy is to be taught in the primary school, the teaching can be effective only if it takes notice of what Whitehead called 'the stage of romance.'

If this account of the rise and progress of nature study seems slightly jaundiced, it must at least be said that the proliferation of natural history societies, field studies associations, nature trails, etc., in the UK today owes a great deal to the teaching of this subject in the schools during the past fifty years.

WKR

Needlecraft, Teaching of Needlecraft is included in the curriculum at all ages and levels of ability, from primary schools to establishments for further education. Dressmaking, embroidery and, in some cases, tailoring and the making of soft furnishings are the traditional aspects of needlecraft courses.

At a time when the UK is known for the mass production of cheap clothing of good quality, teachers of needlecraft are seeking to present their subject in a new way. There is not the same attempt as in the past to justify the teaching of needlecraft as an economical means of clothing the family and furnishing the home, except in specialist fields such as hand tailoring and the making of some soft furnishings.

The aim is to produce finished articles in a relatively short time, at reasonable cost, and with such a finish that they will withstand constant use and the requirements of laundering and modern cleaning processes. The scope of the work is determined by the capabilities and experience of the student. Experience is given in the handling of a wide variety of high-quality and well-designed modern fabrics, the use of commercial patterns and of the modern sewing machine with its many possibilities.

There are many facets of needlecraft courses that do not involve plying the needle. A link is made with science in an attempt to give pupils some understanding of the qualities and limitations of fabrics, the finishing processes applied to them, and the cleaning processes and agents to which they may be subjected. Good grooming, deportment and personal hygiene (all connected and capable of contributing to the development of poise and self-confidence) are studied. In the understanding and adjustment of patterns, there is some correlation with mathematics. Despite the marked improvement in trade patterns and the reorganisation of their sizing, some examinations still call for dress design and pattern-cutting.

An appreciation of colour, texture and design (which later can help in the relating of style to fabric selected) is approached through the use of art and craft work, such as collage in various forms (individual and group), where practical needlework skill is not called upon in the first instance.

Most girls are interested in fashion and wish to be in line with present trends. This interest can be used as a stimulus to the attainment of the practical skill necessary for interpreting new styles in terms of home dressmaking; but pupils need to be helped to assess fashion trends and to apply them to their personal use. All this experience should have a direct bearing on the education of a girl as a future consumer.

The method of approach to the teaching of needlecraft depends on the ability and size of a class, the stage it has reached and the equipment available. The tendency to make a particular garment because by so doing it is possible to teach a whole class a set of processes is being replaced by systems of group teaching that use self-help methods, the pupil referring to a variety of teaching aids and specimens to complement the basic instruction. In this way pupils are encouraged to develop a greater sense of responsibility for their work; self-confidence grows, and boredom brought about by rigidity and repetition can be avoided.

Possibly as a reaction from the monotony of mass production methods, there is now a resurgence of interest in dressmaking and allied crafts (millinery, etc.).

RA

Negative reinforcement This means something which is basically unpleasant to a person, and which will make him want to learn how to avoid it in the future. Fear of pain, punishment or the teacher's displeasure are obvious examples, but these often seem to prove more effective in checking undesired behaviour than in teaching new desired behaviour, such as learning. Too much blame can lead to some children giving up altogether; and there have also been examples of punishment leading to increased bad behaviour, as in cases where an attention-seeking child might see punishment as a reward, since at last someone has noticed him. In fact, all that punishment may succeed in doing is temporarily to suppress undesired behaviour; the way to stop this altogether is to encourage the child to replace it with good behaviour. For this to happen successfully, the child will have to find good behaviour more satisfying than bad behaviour, which in turn will involve different levels of positive reinforcement (*q.v.*).

NT

Neighbourhood schools A neighbourhood school is intended to provide education for all the children of a particular age who live within a certain distance of it. This district is usually called the 'catchment area'. In the country, where population is sparse, a school's catchment area virtually defines itself without difficulty or formality. In towns several schools are often within reach. Rigid catchment areas are sometimes imposed for administrative convenience, but there is now influential support for them on social grounds. There is inevitable tension between those who hold this view and those who believe that parents ought to be able to choose a school.

There is a relation between the size of the catchment area and the age of the children for whom the school is intended. Primary schools have small catchment areas because young children ought not to have far to go to school, and because they ought not to go to big schools. They often serve socially homogeneous areas, such as part of a big housing estate. No problem arises. But they may be set on the edge of two contrasted areas, for instance between well maintained owner-occupied houses

and a slum clearance area. Ought there to be a compulsory catchment area to bring together the children from two localities which in other respects have little to do with each other? This is an extreme case, but problems of this kind are not uncommon, and have become more important with the need to integrate immigrants from other cultures.

A secondary school necessarily serves a much bigger catchment area than a primary school because older boys and girls have much more varied educational needs. Specialist teaching and equipment is necessary for all secondary pupils, but different pupils have different specialist needs. The less common of these needs can be economically and efficiently met only if the the pupils are drawn from an area too big to be called a neighbourhood. More frequently-required specialist subjects can satisfactorily be provided in a school serving a neighbourhood that is geographically compact, but which is almost certain to be large enough to be socially mixed.

Most day schools are inevitably neighbourhood schools in the limited sense that they take their character in part from the neighbourhood in which they are situated and from which their pupils come. But two different schools can serve the same neighbourhood and reflect quite different aspects of it. This is not enough for the advocates of neighbourhood schools, who want the school to be the only one to which the children of the neighbourhood may go so that it may be the means of social education in learning to live together irrespective of differences in sex, intelligence or social background. In some environments this is probably an attainable objective; in others, almost certainly doomed to fail.

DGOA

Neill, A. S. (b. 1883) After leaving Edinburgh University, A. S. Neill worked as an office boy, draper and journalist before becoming a teacher. Experience in Scottish state schools made him a rebel against conventional teaching, and in 1921 he was joint founder of the progressive International School at Hellerau, Dresden; the school was transferred three years later to Austria and then to England. As Summerhill, now at Leiston in Suffolk, it continues to be the best-known of the progressive schools, partly because of the stream of books that Neill has written about it and about his educational ideas. Neill's books include *A Dominie's Log* (1915), *A Dominie Dismissed* (1916), *A Dominie in Doubt* (1920), *A Dominie's Five, or Free School* (1924), *The Problem Child* (1926), *The Problem Parent* (1932), *That Dreadful School* (1937), *The Problem Teacher* (1939), and *Summerhill: A Compilation* (1962).

See also **Progressive education**

Nepal, Education in In 1964 there were 5,001 primary schools (enrolment 334,000); 645 secondary schools (enrolment 54,850); 31 higher education establishments (enrolment 6,372). About 100,000 students were in part-time vocational courses and nearly 2,000 adults attended literacy classes. There is a university at Kirtipur, Tribhubana.

The country's population in 1964 was approximately 10 million.

Netball Netball, a seven-a-side ball game for girls and women, usually played on an indoor wood or outdoor asphalt or hard-surface court, 100 ft x 50 ft, is probably the most popular of all games played by girls at both primary and secondary level. The object of the game is to score goals by dropping a ball (similar to a football) through a metal ring, from which a cylindrical net is suspended, fixed to a wooden or metal post at a height of 10 ft from the ground.

Played at speed, netball demands a high degree of fitness, skill in ball-handling, passing and shooting, and an ability both to mark and evade an opponent. Though the game is somewhat similar in nature to basketball there is little doubt that it will retain its position as a major game for girls and women.

The sport is organised at all levels by the All-England Netball Association which arranges competitions and rallies up to international standard and also sends teams to world tournaments held regularly in England and other countries.

All England Netball Association, 26 Park Cres., London, W1.

Journal: *Netball*, quarterly.

FURTHER READING
J. Baggallay. *Netball for Schools*, Pelham, 1966.
Hints to Coaches of Netball, AENA, 1966.
An Introduction to Netball in Junior Schools, AENA, 1965.
Netball, Know the Game Series, Educational Productions, 1966.
Official Rules of the All England Netball Association, incorporating *Hints to Umpires*.

JE

Netherlands, Education in Education is compulsory from the age of seven to 14 years, and denominational schools receive the same state aid as government schools. In 1965/66 there were 5,322 pre-primary schools (enrolment 457,130); 7,923 primary (enrolment 1,409,017); 2,238 secondary (enrolment 551,599); 1,964 technical and agricultural colleges (enrolment 552,929); 152 teacher training colleges (enrolment 39,748); and 12 higher education establishments (enrolment 64,432). Universities are at Amsterdam, Groningen, Leiden, Nijmegen (RC) and Utrecht. Five polytechnics have the equivalent of university status.

The country's population was approximately 12½ million in 1967.

New Lanark David Dale founded a cotton mill at New Lanark in 1783 in which, as was the fashion, he employed a number of workhouse children whom he taught to read and write after working hours. From 1800 his successor and son-in-law, Robert Owen, expanded this to include not only children but infants and adults. In a bold social experiment, Owen's New Institution for the Formation of Character was 'to ascertain whether, by replacing evil conditions by good, man might not be relieved from evil, and transformed into an intelligent, rational and good being'. His environmentalist theories so repelled his financial backers, especially William Allen, the Quaker, that Owen ultimately relinquished the New Lanark Schools to them and to the British and Foreign Schools Society in 1824, and himself entered wider spheres of public life.

But for eight years before that New Lanark was an educational Mecca for the world. It pioneered schooling for children from three to six, basing the curriculum on play and observation. Its schoolmaster, James Buchanan, opened the first infant school at Westminster in 1818.

WHGA

New Schools movement Begun in 1889 by a reformist group known as the Fellowship of the New Life (of which J. Ramsay MacDonald was secretary and the Fabian Society an offshoot) with the founding of Abbotsholme School under Dr Reddie as a boarding school for boys who worked together in a free adventurous community, organising as well as executing their various activities. The development of Abbotsholme School proceeded on a general surge of ethical idealism, manifest in a non-dogmatic religion virtually tailored for the school by Reddie himself. Three of his assistants went further: in 1893 J. H. Badley left to found Bedales as a co-educational boarding school and C. E. Rice left Bedales to found King Alfred School, Hampstead. In 1898 Dr Lietz opened a school at Ilsenberg in Germany. Another admirer of Abbotsholme was Edmond Desmoulins who founded the Ecole des Roches in France, whilst A. Devine's Clayesmore and Cecil Grant's school at Keswick, later at Harpenden, exhaled the same spirit.

Concomitantly, liberal child-centred ideas were being disseminated through the educational world by the work of G. Stanley Hall, John Dewey, James Sulley and J. J. Findlay, whilst increasing interest in engineering led F. W. Sanderson to reorganise Oundle School.

The New Schools movement was carried further by the New Ideals Group, formed in 1914. Among its members was Lord Lytton, who was responsible for Homer Lane's classic experiment in treating young delinquents through self-governing community therapy, and Caldwell Cook at the Perse School, Cambridge, a witness to the fact that such ideas were now influencing established schools. After the first world war, similar groups and schools in America and on the Continent were brought into closer touch through the New Education Fellowship, launched in 1921 at an international conference at Calais. *The New Era*, which became its journal, is a mine of information on its activities since then, all animated by what the Board of Education in 1935 described as 'the new humanism'.

FURTHER READING
Trevor Blewitt. *The Modern Schools Handbook*, Gollancz, 1934.
William Boyd. 'The Basic Faith of the New Education Fellowship', *Year Book of Education*, Evans Bros., 1957.
William Boyd and Wyatt Rawson. *The Story of the New Education*, Heinemann, 1965.
H. A. T. Child. *The Independent Progressive School*, Hutchinson, 1962.
L. B. Pekin. *Progressive Schools*, Woolf, 1934.
B. M. Ward. *Reddie of Abbotsholme*, Allen and Unwin, 1934.
See also **Progressive education**

WHGA

New Zealand, Education in New Zealand is a small nation of two and three-quarter million people living in an area about the same size as that of Great Britain. Except for a youthful and rapidly growing population of about 200,000 Maoris, the people are almost entirely of European, mainly British, descent. Present trends suggest that the country will have a population of about five million at the turn of the century.

From the beginning, two ideals have lain at the foundation of New Zealand's state. First, although still imperfectly accomplished, the ideal of racial harmony has exerted an immense, expanding and generally benevolent influence. A second, reinforced by geographic facts, has aimed at establishing a social order more truly egalitarian than that of its European homelands, and inspired a continuing effort to remove whatever obstacles, geographical, financial, social, or personal, that could have stood in the way of a better schooling for any child.

In state schools, primary and secondary, education is free from five to 19 years of age, and university education is also available at low cost to every person who gains the university entrance qualification and studies successfully as a full-time student. Schooling is compulsory until the age of 15, and almost 100% of those who begin at the age of five years complete at least 10 years of schooling. A high and increasing proportion of children stay at school beyond the minimum leaving age. By 1972 more than 90% are expected to proceed beyond this level, and the present proportion is already more than double that of the UK. One-eighth of all secondary pupils are in sixth forms; by 1980, this figure is expected to be more than one-seventh. The number of pupils who ultimately become university students is also relatively high, being equivalent to about 12% of an age-group. But this figure excludes students in teachers' colleges, technological institutes and special training schools. Thus, approximately 16% of all pupils

attend some institution of tertiary education after completing a secondary school course. Comprehensive provisions are also made for the further education of adults, technical or professional re-training, refresher courses and so on. All told, about 30% of the population is enrolled at an educational institution, and 12% of all government expenditure is allocated to these services.

In 1966 the dispersed and relatively sparse population of New Zealand (approximately 2¾ million in 1966) was served by 2,487 primary schools, 83 intermediate schools for 11- to 13-year-olds (non-selective and comparable with American junior high schools) and 373 five-year secondary schools, almost all comprehensive in emphasis. There are six publicly financed universities, five technological institutes and ten teachers' colleges. Approximately 11% of primary children, and 16% of secondary, attend private schools, mostly Roman Catholic. Generous provisions are also offered to assist with educational development in the islands of the Pacific, in SE Asia and elsewhere.

Since the nation is now alerted to the critical role of the education system in developing its intellectual resources, major programmes of expansion, reform and building are proceeding apace in the provisions for training teachers, technological education and at the university level. The respect and influence that New Zealand exerts in the world, however, may ultimately be determined more by the extent to which she can fulfil her aspirations as a bi-racial community. It is here, in the courtship of Europe and Polynesia, that a distinctive contribution of the New Zealand school system seems to be in the making.

JEW

Newcastle Report (1861) Terms of reference: to enquire into the state of popular education in England, and to consider and report what measures, if any, were required for the extension of sound and cheap elementary instruction to all classes.

This was the first really thorough enquiry into the education system, and the Report contained some far-reaching recommendations, although few were adopted at the time. One recommendation which was accepted was that the system of payments should be altered, and that schools should be financed partly through the rates and partly from direct grants. The rates contribution was to be determined by children's attainments, which were to be tested by examiners appointed by the county boards of education.

The Commission found that 120,305 children out of 2,535,462 were not receiving any form of education, and estimated that not more than a quarter of the children received a good education. They were against a compulsory school system managed centrally by the government because of the religious and political difficulties which might arise.

The Commission recommended that 10 or 11 was the age at which the education of 'the peasant boy' should end, and that it was against his interests to keep him at school until 14 or 15. They also condemned the abuse of religious controls: for instance where there was only one church school in an area which was forcing its doctrine on pupils of other denominations.

The majority of the Commission agreed with the provision of state aid for education, first introduced in 1839, while the minority thought that it would have been better if the government had not interfered.

The Commission found that trained teachers were better than untrained, but that they tended to be dissatisfied because 'their emoluments, though not too low, rise too soon to their highest level.'

Newman, Cardinal John Henry (1801–90) One of the Tractarians who

entered the Roman Catholic Church, Newman delivered lectures as Rector of Dublin University that were published under the title *The Idea of a University Reformed* (1873), his main argument being that the purpose of a university is to train the mind rather than to impart useful knowledge.

Newman Association Formed in 1942, the Association aims at bringing together Catholic graduates so that they might more effectively follow their vocations in the intellectual and cultural life of the Church in Britain. Its role is to break down the reluctance of the educated Catholic to bring his religious beliefs and practice within the framework of his professional and social life. Having contributed to the thinking and outlook which culminated in the reforming attitude of the second Vatican Council, the Association now takes its cue from the Council's pronouncements.

Members are grouped in about 50 local circles throughout the country, each deciding on its own programme of activities. In addition, there are specialised groups, linking together members of various circles and including a Psychology Group, a University Teachers Group, a Philosophy of Science Group (for those engaged in scientific teaching or research, or interested in the impact of science on the contemporary world) and a Legal Studies Group.

Hon. Sec.: 15 Carlisle St, Soho Sq., London, W1.

Newsom Report (1963) This was the Report of the Central Advisory Council for Education (England) which in March 1961 was asked by the Minister of Education, Lord Eccles, 'to consider the education between the ages of 13 and 16 of pupils of average or less than average ability who are or will be following full-time courses either at schools or in establishments of further education.' The Council was chaired by Mr (now Sir) John Newsom.

Under the title *Half Our Future* the Report recommended an immediate announcement that the school leaving age would be raised to 16 from 1965; the setting up of a working party to grapple with general social problems, including those of education, in slum areas; the extension of extra-curricular activities, and experiments in different types of extension of the school day; a survey of the need for residential courses; a revision of Agreed Syllabuses for RI; the giving of positive guidance to adolescent boys and girls on sexual behaviour; a final year programme in the schools that should be 'deliberately outgoing' and would provide 'an initiation into the adult world of work and leisure'; resistance by the schools to external pressures which would persuade them to extend public examinations to pupils for whom they are inappropriate, or which would extend the effect of such examinations for any pupils over an unduly large area of the school programme; speedier action to remedy the existing deficiencies of school buildings; an experimental building programme to try out various forms of school organisation and teaching methods; extended workshop and technical facilities, and the adequate provision of all secondary schools with modern audio-visual aids and facilities for using them.

The appearance of the Report was overshadowed by the publication, very shortly afterwards, of the Robbins Report (*q.v.*) on Higher Education, which attracted a greater share of public attention and discussion. Although the decision was made to raise the school leaving age to 16 in 1970/71, and many of the issues that concerned the Newsom Committee are the subject of discussion and experiment by those who are preparing for this moment of change when it finally takes place, following the 1967 decision to postpone it, many of the Newsom recommendations remain substantially unimplemented.

Newspapers and periodicals, Reduced rates for *See* **Periodicals and newspapers, Reduced rates for**

Nicaragua, Education in According to the constitution, primary and secondary education is compulsory and free. There were 2,235 primary schools in 1963/64, with 158,489 pupils aged seven to 12 years, and a teaching force of 4,186, of whom 42% possessed a degree or teacher's certificate. Secondary schools, which include technical and commercial schools, numbered 118 and had an enrolment of 19,473 students and 1,416 teachers. Two universities cater for 2,356 students. In 1967, a revision of the curriculum used in the primary and secondary schools was begun.

The population of the country in 1966 was approximately 1¾ million.

Niger, Education in Education is free, but the number of school places is insufficient for the needs of the country and as few as 6% of the children receive any education. In 1965/66 there were 538 primary schools (enrolment 61,948); 22 secondary schools (enrolment 2,978); three technical schools (enrolment 116). Students go to France or Senegal for higher education.

The country's population was approximately 4 million in 1965.

Nigeria, Education in 1964 statistics: 14,976 primary schools (enrolment 2,849,488); 1,327 secondary schools (enrolment 205,012); 35 technical schools (enrolment 7,702); 268 teacher training colleges (enrolment 32,008); five universities (enrolment 9,000). A sixth university is planned for Port Harcourt. Total population: approximately 56 million.

Norm A test score, or other measurement, of an individual or group has no meaning in itself; it must be referred to the standards or norms reached by some defined group of similar persons in order to be evaluated. Thus a man who measures 75 in. is tall because the normal average for English adult males is about 68 in., and only a tiny percentage measure 75 in. or over. Many tests for children are issued with age norms: thus a child obtaining a 10-year mental age on the Stanford-Binet intelligence test performs as well as the average 10-year-old.

Relative brightness or dullness was traditionally calculated from the ratio of mental to chronological age (the intelligence quotient). But most modern intelligence attainment tests now supply 'standard score' or 'deviation quotient' norms, based on the distribution of scores within the child's own age group. Such standard scores, with an average of 100, range from about 140 to 60, i.e. the scores obtained by the best and worst 0.4% of children. However, there is no necessity to refer scores to the total population of that age, and it is often difficult for the test constructor to obtain truly representative samples on which to base his norms.

Percentile norms are expressed in terms of the percentages of a specified group who score up to a given level. For instance, in a certain reading test a 13-year-old child scores 24 out of 40; it has been found that 80% of secondary modern pupils of his age score this much or less, and only 25% of grammar school pupils do so. Thus his score falls at the 80th and 25th percentiles respectively. Finally, a norm is not an ideal standard which a child or a class *should* attain; it is merely a statement of the standards actually found. Thus norms can easily become out of date when standards rise, as has occurred on most intelligence and educational tests since 1945.

See also **Intelligence quotient; Intelligence tests**

PEV

Normal distribution When measurements are made of some physical or mental characteristic among a large, representative group of people, and plotted according to the numbers obtaining each score, the resulting distribution often approximates to the symmetrical, bell-shaped curve known as the normal or Gaussian distribution. That is, the majority score near the centre or *mean*, and there are fewer towards each extreme. Algebraically it is the limiting form of the binomial distribution. Hence if we know the standard deviation (an index of the range or scatter of scores) we can determine from normal curve tables the proportion of cases obtaining any given score above or below the mean.

Though it is not true that most human attributes are so distributed, school marks and test scores often conform to it fairly closely when numbers are large, and this justifies the application of such statistical treatments as analysis of variance, correlations, etc. The normal distribution also plays an important part in studying the reliability of statistical data, for example, whether an obtained difference between boys and girls could be attributed to chance variations, or is statistically significant.

PEV

Northern Ireland Grammar School Certificate This is the qualification obtainable by children at grammar schools in Northern Ireland, roughly equivalent to the GCE O and A levels of the English GCE.

Norwood Report (1943): Report of the Committee of the Secondary Schools Examination Council on Curriculum and Examinations in Secondary Schools Terms of reference: to consider suggested changes in the secondary school curriculum and the question of the relevant school examinations. Chairman: Sir Cyril Norwood.

The Report recommended the abolition of the school certificate, to be replaced by the examining boards, assisted by panels of teachers. A school-leaving examination was recommended at 18 for university entrance and professional qualifications. The report also recommended part-time education up to 18 for those who left school earlier, and a six-month break between school and university, for public service of some kind.

See also **GCE**

Notes Notes have long been used, particularly by specialist teachers of history, geography and the sciences, as a form of class activity and so as part of a method of teaching. Notes and diagrams may be copied from the chalkboard by the whole class. Alternatively, skeletal outlines to be filled in by pupils may be used, either mimeographed or copied from the chalkboard, and subsequently marked by the teacher as an indication of the way in which various pupils have assimilated the lesson material. Note-making is considered as fulfilling two functions: it provides a record of a lesson event, and it helps to consolidate the lesson material within the pupils' memories.

DJJ

Nuffield Foundation The Foundation was created in 1943 with a benefaction from Lord Nuffield of shares in Morris Motors Ltd to the value of £10 millions. The annual income is now about £2½ million. This is shared between seven main fields of activity: medical research; research in biological and other sciences; social research and experiment; the advancement of education; the care of old people and research into the aging process; grants for projects in Commonwealth countries overseas; and a fellowships and scholarships programme.

Education has come to claim an increasing share of the Foundation's resources, and in recent years between a quarter and a third of the total grant budget has been devoted to it. Since 1962 the Foundation's main educational interest has been curriculum development; but, with the formation of the Schools Council (*q.v.*), it is likely that this will gradually diminish and attention will turn to new points in education.

The Foundation's various curriculum development schemes differ in points of detail, but share a fundamental objective and a common organisational pattern. Each arises from a growing concern among teachers that the whole teaching approach in classroom and laboratory should be reviewed in the light of recent advances in knowledge, current views on the nature of learning, and a new emphasis on the active part that the pupil should play in the learning process. There seems to be general agreement that the syllabus content needs bringing up to date in many school subjects, but that something more far-reaching should be attempted than a mere redrafting of syllabuses. So the schemes are designed to give teachers of outstanding ability the time and facilities to undertake a thorough reappraisal of aims and methods in a way not possible while they are teaching a full programme. Each scheme should not only provide a distillation of what lively teachers are already doing to revitalise the classroom presentation of their subject, but should also help to ensure by appropriate examinations that testing (as well as teaching) is directed towards the acquisition of a working understanding of a subject rather than the memorisation of formal knowledge about it.

The aim of those concerned in Nuffield projects is to develop this new approach by providing a full range of teaching resources for a particular age group of pupils in a special field of study. Materials are made available to teachers through normal channels, for use in any way they think fit. They do not consist of textbooks in the traditional

R

sense, but of integrated sets of teachers' guides, pupils' readers and work-books, visual aids and, where appropriate, tape recordings or laboratory apparatus. These materials are prepared by teams of teachers seconded from their schools for the necessary period. Early drafts and prototypes are submitted to extensive classroom trial in volunteer schools, and are revised before being made generally available. Each scheme is therefore essentially a co-operative activity, in which the Schools Council, the DES, LEAs, and individual teachers in many schools, collaborate with teams preparing initial materials to produce a final result likely to be widely useful.

Some of the programmes are based on appropriate university departments and are administered by them: in other cases the Foundation has acted directly as the sponsor, setting up *ad hoc* units to carry out the work.

The address of the Nuffield Foundation is Nuffield Lodge, Regents Pk, London, NW1.

The Science Teaching Project The main objective of this earliest of the curriculum development schemes (1962) is to promote an understanding of what science is, and how a practising scientist works. This has involved a much greater emphasis than in traditional courses on practical experimentation by pupils themselves, leading to first-hand scientific discovery. The content of the teaching has also been modified in the light of contemporary needs.

The work of the project covers the teaching of science in schools at all levels of age and ability. Courses in O level physics, chemistry and biology for pupils 11–16 were published in 1966. Other sections of the programme include junior science (for primary school pupils), a special introductory course in general science for 11 to 13-year-olds, and a programme for pupils of average and less than average ability

between the ages of 13 and 16. Plans are under way for the development of A level courses in physics, chemistry, physical sciences and biological sciences.

Publications include *Progress Report 1965 on the Nuffield Foundation Science Teaching Project* and *Science Teaching Project Newsletter*.

Professor K. W. Keohane, Mary Ward Hse, 5/7 Tavistock Pl., London, WC1.

Junior Mathematics Project This programme was begun in 1964. Its aim is to produce a course for children aged 5–13 designed to help them connect together many aspects of the world around them, to introduce them gradually to the process of abstract thinking, and to foster in them a critical, logical but also creative turn of mind.

A synthesis is being made of what is worth preserving in traditional work with various new ideas. These cover presentation as well as content, and emphasis is placed on the learning process. A concrete approach will be made to abstract concepts, and where possible children should be allowed to make their own discoveries. The work of the project is set against the present background of new thinking concerning mathematics itself. But there will be no novelty for its own sake: any topic or aspect of the subject introduced must be more intelligible and purposeful (and so easier to teach) than what it replaces.

The programme is being tested in a wide range of primary and secondary schools, in association with the Schools Council's Mathematics Pilot Scheme. The first testing of materials began in 1965, after a year of intensive in-service training for teachers in the pilot areas.

A bulletin is issued periodically to give schools outside the pilot scheme some idea of the progress being made and to provide a forum for the exchange of ideas. A short film, *I do—and I understand*, has been made with the help of British Petroleum, to show the organisation of a mathematics class in the spirit of the project.

Publications include *Nuffield Foundation Mathematics Project Bulletin* (from Fanfare Bureau, 516 Forest Rd, London, E17). The Schools Council's Curriculum Bulletin No. 1, *Mathematics in Primary Schools*, and the film *Maths Alive* (from the Educational Foundation for Visual Aids) are relevant to the work of this project.

Project Organiser: Dr G. Matthews, 12 Upper Belgrave St, London, SW1.

Language Teaching Materials Project This project is mainly concerned with the preparation of courses in French for pupils aged 8–13, and in German, Spanish and Russian for pupils aged 11–13. The aim is to develop carefully graded teaching materials for introductory audio-visual courses, using wherever possible new research findings and teaching techniques. The emphasis is on language as a means of communication, and the first stage of each case is purely oral; reading, writing and composition are introduced later in that order.

The French section's work began in 1963; draft materials are tested in association with the Schools Council's Primary French Pilot Scheme, and some stages are already published. In the Spanish and Russian sections, preparation, testing and publication were to be completed by December 1967, and, in the case of German, by 1968. The German section is based on the Language Teaching Centre at the University of York; the French, Spanish and Russian sections have their headquarters in Leeds.

The project also issues occasional papers of interest to teachers, and with the University of Leeds operates a modern language teaching library and information centre. A child language survey is designed to gather information on the linguistic performance and main centres of interest of English children aged 8–13. A parallel survey of French children is being conducted under the auspices of CREDIF (Centre de Recherche et d'Etude pour la Diffusion du Français), and it is hoped to make similar arrangements with research organisations in Spain and Germany.

Publications include *Audio-Visual French Courses for Primary Schools, Introduction to the Language Laboratory, Grammatical Analysis Code, French Readers for Primary Schools.*

A. Spicer, 5 Lyddon Terrace, The University, Leeds, 2.

Programme in Linguistics and English Teaching Under way in the Communication Research Centre of the Department of General Linguistics, University College, London, and directed by Professor M. A. K. Halliday, this programme is designed to help the teaching of the English language in schools, and is supported jointly by the Foundation and the Schools Council. Since it began, the Council has also undertaken a large-scale co-operative research programme entitled *Project English*, and the University College programme is part of this.

The team is producing work-papers on the use of a more effective description of the English language in the work of the schools, together with a descriptive manual of the English language as a work of reference for such improved teaching. It is hoped the project will help teachers to overcome the difficulties presented by traditional grammar, based largely on inappropriate categories derived from a prescriptive attitude to language teaching, together with inadequate understanding of the nature of language. No attempt will be made to tell teachers what to teach, but certain practices and approaches will be recommended as linguistically more desirable than others.

Research Director: Communication Research Centre, University College, London, WC1.

Cambridge School Classics Project Begun in 1966 under the auspices of the Faculty Board of Classics and the Department of Education, Cambridge University, this project is attempting to provide material and methods for teaching the early stages of a Latin course that aims at both reading fluency and a fuller knowledge of classical civilisation for those not pursuing the subject beyond O level or CSE. It will also keep in mind the needs of future classical specialists and those who may later study subjects to which classics are relevant.

On the linguistic side the problems of teaching Latin at the elementary stages are being examined in the light of current linguistic theory, and close links are maintained with the Department of Classics at Queen Mary College, where a full-scale linguistic investigation of Latin is being undertaken.

The second main objective of the project is to investigate and develop non-linguistic courses designed to convey in varied forms an understanding of the classical civilisation and culture suitable for pupils of a wide range of ability.

Project Director: D. J. Morton, 21 Silver St, Cambridge.

Society and the Young School Leaver The Foundation is collaborating with the Schools Council in a preliminary study of the form which future courses might take for the early school leaver, and the use they might make of visual and other techniques for involving the less academic pupils more closely in the study of questions likely to be important to them and relevant to their future lives. The aim is to undertake widespread discussion with interested teachers and to survey some of the work currently being done in the modern humanities and in social studies. Later a central curriculum development group might be assembled to put into effect the findings of this preliminary investigation.

Information from: Michael Schofield, Nuffield Lodge, Regent's Park, London, NW1.

Publications include *From School to Society: the Relevance of Education.*

Resources for Learning At a time of rapid changes in education and a shortage of teachers, it is generally agreed that the education service must make the best possible use of its skilled manpower and its available technology. This project is studying ways of organising work in schools so as to make the best use of teachers' skills and of new developments in methods and equipment. Questions being investigated include the points at which programmed learning, educational TV and other new media might make their best contribution to learning; the best arrangement of the school timetable for this purpose; the best way of deploying staff; the architectural, social and economic implications of any changes.

Begun in 1966, the project is devoting its first two years to a preliminary study, after which it is hoped (following research and small-scale experiment) to arrange an extensive series of trials in schools.

Co-ordinating Director: I. McMullen, Tavistock Hse South, Tavistock Sq., London, WC1.

See also **Schools Council for the Curriculum and Examinations**

Nuffield projects *See* **Nuffield Foundation**

Number Number is an abstract property of a set and is symbolised by a numeral depending on the system of numeration, e.g. Roman. Two sets have the same number if they can be completely matched pairwise.

Types of number

N. Counting or natural numbers are 1, 2, 3, 4, 5 · · ·

Z. Integers—positive and negative whole numbers: −2, −1, 0, +1, +2 · · ·

Q. Rationals—positive and negative fractions. Irrationals—numbers not expressible as rationals, e.g. $\sqrt{3}$, II.

R. Reals—rationals and irrationals. Represented by all points on a number line.

C. Complex—numbers of the form $a + ib$ where a, b are real and $i = \sqrt{-1}$.

JCW

Numeracy The ability to apply mathematical thinking to exploration of the environment and to communicate in an appropriate 'language'.

Numismatic Society, Royal The Royal Numismatic Society was founded in 1836, and assumed its present title in 1904, when it was granted a royal charter. The purpose of the Society is to promote the study of coinage of all periods.

Meetings, at which papers are read and discussed and rare coins or medals exhibited, are held monthly from October to June at the rooms of the Society of Antiquaries, Burlington Hse, London, W1.

The Society administers a fund for the distribution of books on coins to school libraries. An annual prize of 10 guineas is awarded for an essay on a numismatic subject (upper age limit of entrants, 21 years).

C/o Dept of Coins and Medals, British Museum, London, WC1.

Journal: *Numismatic Chronicle* (annual), available from Messrs Bernard Quaritch, 11 Grafton St, London, W1.

Nunn, Sir Percy (1870–1944) Nunn's father and grandfather were proprietors of a school in Bristol, later transferred to Weston-super-Mare, and at the age of 16 Nunn helped to teach there. On his father's death in 1890 he took over the school but, feeling that he was not sufficiently mature for the task, resigned the headship and taught in London. In 1905 he was made vice-principal of the London Day Training College, after 1913 combining this post with the chair of education in London University. When the college became the Institute of Education of London University, Nunn became its first director. His most important work was *Education, Its Data and First Principles* (1920). His basic belief was that the full flowering of individuality was the true end of education.

Nursery assistants The original nursery assistant in the nursery school was a girl who had just left school; she was known as a helper or probationer. She usually did this work for a year or two before beginning her own training as a teacher or nurse. The need for the immediate staffing of wartime day nurseries brought women of calling-up age into the service. They were known as CCRs (child care reservists), and a short course of three or four weeks was instituted for them; also a supplementary short course for suitably experienced CCRs, after taking which the CCR was known as a 'warden' and became an acting nursery teacher until a qualified teacher could be found. The term 'nursery assistant' now usually means 'nursery nurse', and it is she who is the usual adult helper of the nursery school teacher. Since September 1965 the nursery assistant has begun to be employed officially to help the infant school teacher too, since at that time National Nursery Examination Board regulations were extended from 0–5 years to 0–7 years.

NNEB training originated in 1946 and is based on a system of two-day release with provision for vocational and cultural aspects of work. The training is usually undertaken between 16 and 18 years of age, but provision is beginning to be made for some mature women too. The student must work in a nursery school or class, day or residential nursery, or (latterly) in an infant school recognised for training purposes.

There is no national standard for selection, and applications are submitted to the local authority, whose criteria are the right personality, a good school report and, for preference, one or two GCE O levels or CSE passes at Grade 1 or 2, or their equivalents.

Among a variety of posts open to the trained nursery assistant, there is the day and residential nursery and the comparatively new hospital play group.[1] The other main educational use of the nursery assistant is as an aide in a special school. Evidence in the Plowden Report (1967), para. 892, suggests that the use of the nursery nurse in the primary school is increasing rapidly.

REFERENCE
1. See the brochure *Play in Hospital*, the account of the findings of the UK National Committee of OMEP, 1966.

JHW

Nursery classes A nursery class is under the supervision of the head teacher of the primary school to which it is attached, and has up to 30 children between the ages of three and five, ordinarily in the charge of a qualified nursery school teacher with nursery assistants and/or National Nursery Examination Board students to help her (*see* **Nursery assistants**).

Some LEAs have preferred to provide nursery classes rather than small nursery schools, partly because this is more economical. Advantages of the nursery class are that the break at five years is avoided and five-year-olds and younger children can be brought to school together. To be successful, a nursery class needs a sympathetic head teacher and indoor and outdoor provision closely resembling that of the good nursery school.

JHW

Nursery Examination Board, National Established in 1945 for the purpose of holding examinations and granting certificates to girl students who have followed a specially designed course in a nursery approved under the Board's regulations.

90 Buckingham Palace Rd, London, SW1.

Nursery school buildings For reasons of safety and security, every nursery school should have a well defined boundary and firmly shutting gate. It is laid down (in the Ministry of Education Standards for School Premises Regulations, 1954 and 1959) that a 40-unit nursery school should be on a site of not less than one-quarter of an acre, with an additional eighth of an acre for every further 20 children. It is also stated that there should be 100 sq. ft of outdoor space for every child, 40 of which should be paved.

Undulating ground that has retained trees is to be preferred. Shrubs are an advantage as a windbreaker, and rough grass as well as a lawn is recommended. In addition to a cultivated garden, there should be earth that the children can dig for themselves, and a large sandpit with good drainage. Outdoor storage space for play equipment is necessary.

Playrooms should be light and have easy access to outdoor play space. They should also be near to cloakrooms, to facilitate the welcome of children and parents. A kitchen is usual and adds to homeliness.

JHW

Nursery school education 'Education must grow out of nurture as the flower from its root', according to Margaret McMillan; she and her sister Rachel are the prominent figures in the nursery school movement in Great Britain. But it can be said that Plato was a pioneer of the nursery school, and the thinking that inspired the pioneering of the McMillans echoed that of Comenius in the 17th century, Rousseau in the 18th and Pestalozzi, Froebel, Oberlin, Robert Owen, Maria

Montessori, John Dewey and Susan Isaacs since.

The forerunner of the nursery school, both in the UK and in the USA, was the free kindergarten, and the first of these in the UK is thought to have been the one Sir William Mather established in Salford in 1871. This was for poor children between the ages of two and seven, and it continued until 1880. Clearly, these free kindergartens were an attempt to help the underprivileged, and it was with the same intention that Rachel and Margaret McMillan opened their slum nursery school for two- to five-year-olds in Deptford in 1913: 80% of the children had rickets on admission, but within a year they were cured. From 1918 onwards, the first McMillan nursery school teachers were being trained, and it was one of these early students, Mabel Brydie, who founded the first Scottish nursery school in Dundee in 1919, rescuing young children from cellars where they 'lived and died only by gaslight'.

Official interest began alongside that of the pioneers when in 1908 a consultative committee of the Board of Education published its report *School Attendance of Children below the Age of Five*. From this it was evident that a large number of young children under five were then attending infant schools, where no proper provision could be made for them. School inspection began in 1907, and this called attention to the physical care that young children need. Accordingly, the Fisher Education Act 1918 gave permissive powers to LEAs to establish nursery schools and classes to promote healthy physical and mental development, and made grants available to them. The national economy of the early 1920s stood in the way of implementation, but the Nursery School Association (NSA) was founded in 1923, and was a most important stimulus to the movement. The economic depression of the 1930s was both a hindrance and a spur. For instance 1932 brought a ban on the opening of new nursery schools, but the Save the Children Fund (SCF) was working among the unemployed; and in 1934, through the joint efforts of the SCF and NSA, eight emergency nursery schools were opened in England and Wales. In 1923 there had been 24 nursery schools; at the outbreak of war in 1939 there were 114 nursery schools and numerous nursery classes in addition. The outbreak of war meant that city nursery schools were evacuated to the country, where temporarily they were residential nurseries. Some wartime nurseries were new nursery classes with extended hours, but still attached to primary schools and supervised by their head teachers.

The Butler Education Act 1944 gave great hope to the nursery school movement. It gave strong encouragement to LEAs to include nursery schools or classes in their development plans. Sites were reserved and some nursery school buildings were actually erected and are still being used for other purposes, mainly as primary schools. Many LEAs took over from the Ministry of Health the now redundant houses and prefabricated buildings that had formerly been wartime day nurseries, and though the 'prefabs' had been intended to last only ten years, many exist to this day, having been converted for educational use as money has gradually become available. There were high hopes of wide nursery school expansion. History, however, repeated itself, with an embarrassed national economy following war.

A further and still marked difficulty has been that bulges in the birth rate have inflated the school population and led to a shortage of teachers. In 1960 a Ministry of Education circular (the famous circular 8/60) had the effect of placing a total ban on new nursery school and class provision except as replacement (for example, if the lease of a site expired) so that although there have been a few excellent new nursery school buildings there has been virtually no expansion. However, within a few years the circular had had two addenda, as a result of which it became possible to open a nursery class where this would have the effect of bringing qualified married women back to teaching. The response, though very slight, may continue.

Demand for pre-school places so markedly exceeds supply that in the last decade there has been a mushroom growth of pre-school playgroups. In 1962 the National Association of Pre-School Playgroups (*q.v.*) was set up.

The Plowden Report recommends a large expansion of nursery education, starting in the Educational Priority Areas (EPAs) of the Report's designation (that is, with the underprivileged), and it suggests a start in the 1968–72 period. The Report devotes a considerable amount of space to evolving a plan whereby there could be expansion without, in the first instance, using more teachers but by using an increased number of nursery nurses instead. This is a concession to the present shortage of teachers. The Plowden Report states that, on a rough estimate, at least 15% of children should have a full-time nursery school education, but that because the EPAs have the most socially deprived 10% of the population, there should be provision for 50% of children to attend full-time, and all children in these areas between four and five years old should have the opportunity of part-time attendance.

Despite the large number of nursery schools in poor areas, there are a number of nursery schools for privileged children. The most famous of these is the Chelsea Nursery School, a fee-paying school founded in 1929. This is much used as a centre for observation, and has strong links with Susan Isaacs and the Child Development Department of London University.

From about 1950 onwards, it has increasingly been recognised as a principle that each child should be admitted to the nursery school gradually. It is usual in the first instance for the mother to come too, or (in the few cases where this is not possible) perhaps father or grandmother. Thus the child and the loved adult together are absorbed into an atmosphere centred in rich experience of people and of materials, where time is regulated only to meet the child's needs and where there is space and quietness to paint, to experiment with sand, water, clay, time to ask questions and be helped towards an answer. Here, as the children become ready for it, they can learn the give and take of playing together with bricks, boxes and tyres, to have the adventure of climbing in safe surroundings. Boys as well as girls can play with dolls, dress up and invent all kinds of play, for play for young children is a fundamental means of growing in personality.

From the beginning, play has been recognised as of great importance, but it is no longer interrupted by formal sense-training material, which has been seen to be unnecessary for normal children who are given a rich environment, helped to concentrate through absorbing interest and encouraged to use their senses to explore it, as they see the adults around them do. This leaves time to acquire a love of books, of which there is a lack even in some comparatively educated homes.

It is important that children should grow up among beautiful things, and the nursery school gives them opportunities for perception that few homes could equal. In recent years, the studies of Lewis, Bernstein and others have brought out clearly that concept-formation and the development of language are essentially interrelated as instruments of the power to reason. It has been shown that the socially underprivileged tend to be the intellectually impoverished because their language development has been stunted through lack of play and shortage of adults and other children to listen to for learning an acceptable pattern of speech. As the Plowden Report points out, not only can the nursery school help the child of less than average intellectual endowment through giving him the opportunity to develop his intelligence to the full, but the exceptionally gifted child can be helped too through being identified earlier.

Originally, it was necessary for the nursery school to provide breakfast, lunch and tea. Since the war, it has been necessary to provide lunch only, and even full-time four-year-olds do not always now require a daily rest in bed.

With more time than formerly to concentrate on mental health, it is possible even more than before for children, parents and staff together to enjoy the satisfying relationships of what is essentially a community school.

FURTHER READING
W. A. L. Blyth. *English Primary Education*, Vol. I, Routledge and Kegan Paul, 1965.
J. W. B. Douglas. *The Home and the School*, MacGibbon and Kee, 1964.
D. E. M. Gardner. *The Education of Young Children*, Methuen, 1956.
D. E. M. Gardner and Joan Cass. *The Role of the Teacher in the Infant and Nursery School*, Pergamon, 1965.
Lillian de Lissa. *Life in the Nursery School*, Longmans Green, 1949.
G. A. N. Lowndes. *Margaret McMillan, the Children's Champion*, Museum Press, 1960.
Dorothy E. May. *Children in the Nursery School*, Univ. of London Press, 1962.
Margaret McMillan. *The Nursery School*, Dent, 1919.
Nursery Infant Education (Report of Working Party), Evans for NUT, 1949.
Grace Owen (Ed.). *Nursery School Education*, Methuen, 1920.
Katherine H. Read. *The Nursery School: A Human Relationships Laboratory*, W. B. Saunders, revised ed. 1961.

JHW

Nursery school equipment The essential consideration is that equipment should be related to the child's needs. This means that chairs, tables, shelves, washbasins and toilets should all be of appropriate height and size and of good design. Furniture should be comfortable, light in weight, stackable and easily cleaned. Considerations of cleanliness and warmth are important in choosing floor materials. Rugs and curtains should be selected with a view to their aesthetic contribution.

Though space is of great importance, so too is a sense of security, and a large room needs dividing into smaller areas, easily changed in size and shape according to the child's varied needs during the day. This can be achieved by the use of light screens and/or movable shelves.

A long mirror is a useful stimulus to young children, so one should be provided at least in the bathroom, where narrow shelving will be needed for such items as beakers and combs. For reasons of hygiene, cloakroom and towel pegs should be at least 9 in. apart so that clothes and towels do not touch one another. It is necessary to have lockers or other storage arrangements for items such as wellingtons.

Since the children cannot read, their personal belongings, cloakroom and bathroom pegs, towels and blankets will be marked with recognisable symbols of some kind—necessary for reasons of hygiene, but important also as one of the ways through which a sense of personal identity and belonging in the community is acquired. Simple play equipment is far to be preferred to elaborate toys.

JHW

Nursery school teachers, Training of In the UK the training of nursery school teachers is basically the same as the training of other qualified teachers; entrance qualifications are exactly the same. Of about 150 general colleges of education at present, 22 offer a specialism in nursery infant teaching. This dual training for nursery and infant work is now universal. Students wishing to train for infants may take a nursery infant course, an infant course or an infant junior course. The colleges concerned are: London (Avery Hill, Froebel Educational Institute, Furzedown, Gipsy

Hill, Goldsmiths', Maria Grey, Philippa Fawcett, Rachel McMillan), Bradford (Margaret McMillan), Brighton, Bristol (College of St Matthias), Crewe (Cheshire College of Education), Chichester, Darlington, Derby, Hertfordshire (Wall Hall), Leicester, Ormskirk (Edge Hill), Swansea (Poulton-le-Fylde); together with day colleges at Birmingham (Bordesley) and Manchester (Long Millgate). It is to one of these colleges that intending nursery school teachers apply. The nursery infant student's course in education will lay particular emphasis on child development and the sociology of the family. On completion of her training, the nursery school teacher will be paid a Burnham Scale salary, just like any other qualified teacher. It is noteworthy that the Froebel colleges were offering a three-year course to their students, including nursery infant students, many years before the three-year course became general. It is at present usual for nursery school teachers to be women, but some within the field expect to see a few men teachers of young children in the years to come.

Because of the uneven distribution of nursery schools and classes during the present shortage, some nursery school teachers are teaching in infant schools although they would prefer to be in nursery schools. They are sometimes content to have reception (i.e. admission) classes, however, because here a knowledge of nursery school methods is essential. A knowledge of nursery school techniques is also a tremendous advantage to a teacher working in a modern infant school, for here there is probably an 'integrated day', i.e. one that follows the child's interests rather than a timetable, and there may be the vertical grouping (q.v.) to which the nursery school teacher is accustomed.

Nursery school teachers are valuable in special schools (q.v.) for which they often undergo further training. They can also be valued helpers in the youth service because of the emotional similarity between young children and adolescents. Experienced nursery school teachers are required as National Nursery Examination Board tutors. (NNEB tutors are required to train nursery nurses.)

JHW

Nursery schools Nursery schools are for children between two and five years, but since the war it has been much more usual to admit children at three and not before. In the UK there were in 1967 567 nursery schools (420 in England, 39 in Wales, 89 in Scotland, 19 in N. Ireland) catering for 30,000 children. The Plowden Report states (para. 293) that in 1965 about 7% of all children under five in England were receiving some form of education in a school or nursery class (though this is an unsatisfactory figure because children attending part-time are counted as full-time, including under-fives in reception classes). Even allowing for the fact that in the UK compulsory education begins at five and not at six or seven as in other European countries, rather fewer children have pre-school education in the UK than in France, Austria and Scandinavia.

Up to the time of printing, the nursery school for 40 full-time children has been the most usual unit in England, though there are some nursery schools for 45, 60 or 80 full-time children, and a few for rather more than 100 full-time children. The high cost of the traditional 40-children nursery school has been justified by the need to make it homely, though it should be emphasised that nursery schools have always been regarded as a supplement to the home, never a substitute for it. Traditionally, parents and teachers have worked together for the fulfilment of the child in this essentially family-centred form of education.

In 1953 a new development began with the experimental provision of some part-time places in nursery schools in London and Bristol. The number of LEAs making this provision increased rapidly, so that by January 1960 nearly 1,000 children, representing at least 11 LEAs, were attending a nursery school in the morning or the afternoon only and having lunch at home. This pattern is on the increase and the Plowden Report (*q.v.*) recommended it for the majority of children in the nursery school provision of the future. The pattern varies, but the characteristic arrangement is gradually becoming a mixture of full-time and part-time places within any one school. So far part-time places have been in the minority, but if this part of the Plowden Report is implemented, the situation will be reversed.

Since nursery schools provide excellent opportunities of observing the spontaneous behaviour of normal children in their formative years, the schools are increasingly visited by students taking initial and advanced courses of training connected with education and the medical and social services.

Most nursery schools are maintained through LEAs, but in January 1965 there were just over two hundred independent nursery schools in England, most of them unrecognised, but under the supervision of the DES (no figures are available for the rest of the UK). The unrecognised private nursery school can in many cases more correctly be termed a playgroup. On the other hand, the famous Chelsea Nursery School, opened in 1929, is the outstanding example of a pioneer private nursery school largely for the children of professional people.

JHW

Nursing, Qualification in A candidate for training as a nurse must be at least 18 years old in England, Wales or Northern Ireland (17½ in Scotland) and must normally have two passes in GCE, one being in English, together with a testimonial from school showing that a reasonable level has been reached in five other subjects; though some training hospitals are more exacting in their requirements. Alternatively a candidate may be accepted on the results of an entrance test, or after passing Part I of the General Nursing Council's Preliminary Examination at the end of a pre-nursing course.

A three-year course leads to the basic qualification, that of State Registered Nurse (SRN). The qualifying examinations are divided into the Preliminary Examination (Parts I and II) and the Final Examination. Part I may be taken after not less than six months' training, or after an approved course has been successfully followed before admission to a training school; or it may be taken together with Part II, that is when a year's training has been completed or at any time thereafter. The Final Examination may be taken, by a candidate who has passed the Preliminary Examination, at any time after the close of the prescribed period of training.

Qualification as a Registered Sick Children's Nurse (RSCN) follows a three-year course at a children's hospital; as a Registered Mental Nurse (RMN) or a Registered Nurse for the Mentally Subnormal (RNMS) after a course of the same length in a mental hospital or in the psychiatric unit of a general hospital.

The procedure in Northern Ireland is the same as for England and Wales. In Scotland, however, the equivalent to an SRN is a Registered General Nurse (RGN); and the RNMS there is known as a Registered Nurse for Mental Defectives (RNMD).

An allowance is paid during training, from which an amount is normally deducted for board.

Nursing Recruitment Service, 6 Cavendish Sq., London, W1. General Nursing Council for England and Wales, 23 Portland Pl., London, W1. General Nursing Council for Scotland, 5 Darnaway St, Edinburgh, 3.

Nursing Council for England and Wales, General The body responsible for the training and examining of nurses in England and Wales. A Register and Roll of Nurses is maintained by the Council, nurses being registered normally after three years' training or enrolled after two years' training.

PO Box IBA, 23 Portland Pl., London, W1.

Nursing and Midwives' Council for Northern Ireland, Joint This statutory body maintains a register and roll of nurses and midwives in Northern Ireland and controls their training.

Registrar: Miss M. E. Morrison, 5 Annadale Ave, Belfast, 7.

NUS *See* **Students, National Union of**

NUT *See* **Teachers, National Union of**

O

O level In 1951 O level (Ordinary Level, General Certificate of Education) replaced School Certificate. It was intended 'to provide a reasonable test in the subject for pupils who have taken it as part of a wide and general secondary course up to the age of at least 16' (first report of SSEC, 1947). At the same time, O level was made a subject examination (*q.v.*), candidates were forbidden to take the examination before the year in which they became 16 (abandoned in 1953), and gradually pass standard was raised until it equalled credit in School Certificate. In 1952, 147,556 candidates took O level papers; in 1964 the number was 442,228. This vast increase shows the complete failure of those who had hoped to abolish a school-leaving examination at 16.

O level has become an essential qualification for university matriculation and for entry to numerous careers and professions: not surprisingly, many schools have come to regard it as their chief objective. Inevitably a massive centralised examination tends to dominate the work of schools, and many teachers see nothing wrong in this. Nevertheless, such a system encourages learning of information rather than a capacity for individual thought and puts a premium on ease of examining. It also reduces the educational value of subjects like science, history and English.

However, the institution of CSE (*q.v.*) has at last encouraged serious thought about examining techniques, and the difficulty is realised of ensuring equality of standards between different examining boards. A gradual modification of GCE seems inevitable and its ultimate replacement by CSE a possibility: it could be argued that O level has outlived its usefulness. In any case, curriculum reform (*q.v.*) will lead to the reform of O level syllabuses.

See also **Examinations**

HD

Objective tests Objective tests are those which call for standardised marking by the examiners. A set of papers containing all objective test questions would not vary in scores when marked independently by a number of examiners. This insistence on standardised marking has influenced the construction of objective tests in recent years. In the early decades of the century, so-called objective tests frequently included essay questions. Research has shown that such questions were scored differently by examiners marking the same paper, and by the same examiners marking the same paper on different occasions. To eradicate these anomalies the trend has been towards many short questions, each of which makes a separate contribution to the whole assessment. Multiple choice exercises are the commonest form of objective test; these require the examinee to underline words, diagrams or pictures to indicate his response, or to insert a single word selected from a list of four or five. In the UK objective tests are constructed and standardised principally by two agencies, the National Foundation for Educational Research and Moray House.

See also **Examinations**

EP

Objectives A term used in programmed learning. The distinction between an 'aim' and an 'objective' involves more than a verbal quibble. Whereas the former tends to remain implicit, the latter is explicit in communicating the instructor's intention to the pupil. It tells the pupil what he or she is expected to do, what the minimum level of acceptance for his or her eventual performance is to be, and under what conditions it will be achieved. To be meaningful, any statement of objective must specify observable, preferably measurable, changes in the learner's behaviour at the end of the course.

See also **Programmed learning**

Occasional closures This is a term used in state schools by teachers and administrators to describe the handful of special holidays in the middle of terms which most schools grant. The special occasion may be some important local happening affecting the whole community, a school event, a religious festival or simply the desirability of a holiday. The distinguishing feature of occasional closures is that they are fixed by a particular school on its own authority, whereas terms and holidays are generally fixed by the LEA for all the primary or secondary schools in its area.

Office Studies, Certificate in An award supervised by the DES and administered by a National Committee, after examinations by eight regional examining bodies.

The course is intended for school-leavers of over 16 who leave school to enter clerical occupation with academic qualifications of less than four GCE O level passes. The course (available in many colleges of further education) lasts two years and assumes that employers will grant release from employment for study on one full day a week.

The examination takes place normally at the age of 18 and consists of two compulsory subjects (English and general studies; clerical duties) and two optional subjects chosen by the candidate. Although four subjects must be studied (certified by the technical college), a certificate is awarded to candidates passing in the two compulsory subjects and one optional subject.

See also **Business education**

WBR

Old People's Welfare Council, National The Council, started in 1940, is a focal point for information and advice on all aspects of the care of the elderly. It brings together in consultation representatives of approximately 1,600 old people's welfare committees throughout the UK, and also some 50 national voluntary societies, six government departments and individuals with special experience. Social, medical and other national interests are linked through this body, which also maintains contact with countries overseas. Pioneer work and an advisory service, a quarterly bulletin, national conferences, promotion of courses and other means are used to carry out the Council's aims and to ensure that those concerned in caring for the elderly are able to give help in the most effective manner.

Training forms an important part of the Council's work. Courses are arranged for those working with older people living in their homes, as well as training courses for potential wardens or matrons of residential homes and refresher courses for existing staff of these homes. A number of courses are arranged in conjunction with university adult education departments, technical colleges and further education centres. 26 Bedford Sq., London, WC1.

OMEP (Organisation Mondiale pour l'Education Pré-Scolaire) *See* **Early Childhood Education, World Organisation for**

O'Neill, Edward F. Pioneer teacher who, immediately following the first world war and for over 30 years afterwards, ran an elementary school at Prestolee, in Lancashire, on profoundly original lines, scrapping the conventional timetable, introducing 'self-activity' and self-government.

FURTHER READING
Edmond Holmes. *The Idiot Teacher*, Faber, 1952.

Only children There have been many generalisations made about the characters of only children, some of which contradict each other. Thus, some imagine such children to be inevitably sheltered and therefore timid and lacking in confidence, whilst others stress their precocious conversation and general arrogance towards other children. There is obviously no such thing as a 'typical' only child, and in general such children will be well or badly adjusted just as other children are, and depending on the type of relationship with the parents.

However, there are certain dangers in being an only child, and a wise parent would certainly be advised to guard against some of them. It is easy to 'spoil' an only child, either by giving him too much too easily, or else by continually reminding him that he is the total investment of all his parents' love and ambition, and that he is being kept under constant observation to make sure he is coming up to the high standards often expected of such a unique position. Instead, he should be treated as far as possible as other children are, and not turned into a premature adult companion to his parents. They should see that he always

has plenty of friends and social contacts outside the family. As he will have no brothers or sisters to quarrel with, the child may have difficulty in expressing his aggressive tendencies, and therefore the normal hurly-burly of childhood play and the occasional tantrum may be particularly important to him.

FURTHER READING
D. W. Winnicott. *The Child and the Family*, Tavistock Publications, 1957.   NT

Open air schools *See* **Delicate children**

Open plan 'Open plan' is a term used to describe schools in which traditional classrooms have been replaced by shared teaching areas, small quiet rooms and learning bays. This revolutionary development has been inspired by the desire of educationists to provide an environment which takes into account the physical, intellectual, social and emotional needs of young children while at the same time providing a learning situation which is informal and flexible.

Learning happens everywhere and in an open plan school no space is wasted. Corridors are divided into bays in which displays are mounted and apparatus and material left out for children to use; corners become libraries and kitchens, workshops and laboratories. If this method is to succeed, however, furniture and fittings have to be extremely flexible so that 'interest' or work areas can be created to meet the needs of small groups of children at any moment in the school day. These shared areas for play and exploration enable children of different age groups to associate freely, and the emotional tensions which sometimes characterise early school life are therefore more easily resolved. There is nothing to prevent an eight-year-old from playing with sand if he so wishes, or another, at six, from going swimming with children three years his senior.

This flexibility—which is often linked in open plan schools to family grouping (*q.v.*) and the integrated day (*q.v.*)—means that the dividing lines between nursery, infant and junior school become blurred and teachers are more able to appreciate a child as an individual (with specific needs and abilities). 'Year group' and 'class' are no longer of importance. But this fluidity also means that the traditional role of the teacher has to be re-examined. Teaching skills need to be shared, and part-time teachers, students, infant and junior helpers and auxiliaries to be welded into a team so that optimum use may be made of all the facilities available.

The concept of open plan education is not confined to primary schools, although it is within this age range that the greatest progress has been made. Secondary schools incorporating many of the ideas contained above—e.g. shared teaching areas, team teaching (*q.v.*), resource and display bays—are already being built. At both primary and secondary stages, however, the aim is the same; to provide a 'workshop' in which children can explore their environment and master skills so that they are more likely to become the adaptable, responsible and emotionally mature citizens of tomorrow.

FURTHER READING
Willem van der Eyken. 'Thinking in Concrete', *New Education*, May 1965.

HPl

Open University *See* **University of the Air**

Operant conditioning *See* **Programmed learning**

Operatic and Dramatic Association, National The Association, founded in 1899, consists of amateur operatic and dramatic societies and of individuals interested in their work. It is governed by a popularly elected Council divided into ten sections. It possesses a vast library of operatic and dramatic works and has intimate dealings, on behalf of members, with government departments, rights-holders, theatrical traders, railways, etc. It publishes a year book, and a NODA Bulletin three times a year for private circulation. An operatic summer school is run each August.

1 Crestfield St, London, WC1.

Operational Research, Institute for *See* **Tavistock Institute of Human Relations**

Orchestra, British Schools *See* **Music Association, Schools**

Orchestra, British Youth Symphony *See* **Music Association, Schools**

Orchestra, National Youth The National Youth Orchestra of Great Britain was founded in 1947 to further the musical education of the most talented and promising young musicians in the British Isles.

Children aged 11–16 who are not full-time students may apply for membership. Selection is by audition, and membership is for a minimum of two years. Those chosen meet for a week three times a year to work together as a full symphony orchestra; they also study individually and in sections under well-known teachers in order to achieve a really high standard of orchestral playing and musicianship. They are also able to study score-reading, conducting, orchestration, harmony, composition and improvisation. The all-round development of each child's personality is carefully studied and a high standard of discipline and dedication encouraged.

Orff, Carl (b. 1895) A German composer whose ideas on the musical education of schoolchildren are expressed in his and Gunild Keetman's

Schulwerk books (*Music for Children,* translated by Margaret Murray).

Work proceeds from a thorough investigation of rhythm to name-calling, slogans, proverbs, verse, by hand-clapping, stamping and finger-snapping. At all stages the work is creative, though it recognises that this requires the stimulus of imitation together with systematic training in aural and visual awareness and in muscular co-ordination. Several ranges of high-quality instruments have been developed, notably by Studio 49 of Munich—tambours and tambourines, untuned drums and timpani, cymbals and precision-tuned xylophones and glockenspiels with carefully designed beaters and removable bars. These latter enable purely rhythmic work to be transferred easily on to instruments with one, two, three or more notes. There is some emphasis on the pentatonic scale (a five-note scale containing no adjacent semitones, equivalent to the black notes of the piano), which is without the strong tonal polarity or 'pulls' of the major and minor scales, and which allows free melodic and harmonic invention to take place with small danger of harsh relationships.

All stages of the work are helped by use of tonic sol-fa. Musical memory is important; but the moment at which memory can no longer be relied upon to retain long or complex musical ideas is the point at which staff notation can be turned to as a friendly aid rather than as an incomprehensible tyrant. The piano does not blend well with the lightly-voiced instruments used, but the cello, water glasses, recorders and members of the harpsichord family can contribute usefully.

A training centre for teachers has been established at the Mozarteum Academy, Salzburg.

See also **Musical education**

DB

Orienteering Orienteering, which is basically cross-country or point-to-point racing on foot on compass bearings, was first devised in Sweden in 1919 by Major Killander, a youth and scout leader, as a means of reviving interest in athletic running. The sport became so popular that it spread to the whole of Scandinavia, to the rest of Europe, and more recently to the UK.

In competition, the participants run over a route chosen by the competitor, who has to find certain control markers or check points in a previously specified order. Before the start of a race, each competitor is supplied with a $2\frac{1}{2}$ in.-to-the-mile map of the competition area. On being given the start signal, he (or she) is allowed to examine a 'master map' which shows the control or check points; these points he marks on his own map. He is also provided with a route-card providing map references and other topographical details to assist him in recognising the check points. The winner is the one who traverses the prescribed course in the fastest time.

Apart from running ability, the sport demands a knowledge of map-reading and the accurate use of a compass. It is rapidly gaining popularity in this country in secondary schools and youth organisations, and a number of local associations have been formed.

Hon. Sec.: John Disley, Southern Orienteering Association, 38 Broom Close, Teddington, Middlesex.

JE

Ornithology, British Trust for With the general aim of promoting research into bird life, the Trust invites members to take part in varied field investigations, with emphasis on conservation problems e.g. counting common birds, making nest records, bird-ringing (by special permit only after considerable training and practice) and regular censuses of heronries and of other species.

The resources of a large library are available to members through the post. Meetings are arranged with local societies all over the country, and courses are organised on migration and field studies. The minimum age of membership is 15. Schools may be affiliated as corporate members and take part in the Trust's projects, but there are no services specially for teaching purposes. Members receive *Bird Study* (incorporating *Bird Migration*) and the news sheet *BTO News*.

Sec.: D. R. Wilson, Beech Grove, Tring, Herts.

Ornithologists' Club, Young Run by the Royal Society for the Protection of Birds for boys and girls up to the age of 18, the Club's activities include courses, meetings, projects and field work.

The Lodge, Sandy, Beds.

Journal: *Bird Life*. (Quarterly).

Outward Bound Trust The Trust provides training courses at Aberdovey, Eskdale, Burghead, Ullswater and Ashburton to equip boys to face hazards and emergencies on the mountains and at sea. Modified courses with the same purpose are provided for girls. Applicants (boys between $14\frac{1}{2}$ and $19\frac{1}{2}$ years of age, girls between 16 and 20) must be sponsored by education authorities, employers, youth organisations or similar bodies, who may be able to give financial assistance. Courses last for 26 days. The Trust now has facilities for training 4,000 boys and 500 girls each year.

123 Victoria St, London, SW1.

Over-achievement This term usually refers to academic performance that is far better than one could predict from the results of an intelligence test. At the time when IQ tests were considered to measure an individual's full potential, over-achievement in this sense was thought of as a logical impossibility, and could be explained only by postulating errors in the original intelligence test. This was sometimes the truth; but the real explanation probably was that the intelligence test, however well administered, could not measure all intellectual factors that influence performance, such as creativity and the various aspects of personality and motivation that can make a child a good learner, despite an IQ score that may not not look over-impressive. Another factor in so-called over-achievers may be a high level of individual anxiety or pressure from home; but on the whole teachers faced with this situation should consider the total picture very carefully and possibly consult an educational psychologist before advising the child to take things more easily. Whatever we may think, such children may be far happier working at the level they have set themselves, and given less work to do could become even more anxious. They can, however, be given different kinds of work to do, some of which may have a relaxing effect, like painting or acting.

NT

Overhead projector *See* **Visual aids**

Overseas Aid and Development, Voluntary Committee on The committee co-ordinates the work of eight major organisations concerned with overseas development—the Catholic Institute for International Relations, Christian Aid, Freedom From Hunger Campaign, Overseas Development Institute, Oxfam, Save the Children Fund, United Nations Association, War on Want—and provides liaison with the Ministry of Overseas Development. One of its principal objectives is 'the improvement of public knowledge in Britain about the world problems of hunger, disease and ignorance and about the work being undertaken to deal with them'. Its education unit provides a service of information, advice, reading lists, literature, and teaching aids for students and teachers concerned with any aspect of these problems. It also provides material for adult education.

69 Victoria St, London, SW1.

Overseas qualifications for teaching *See* **Qualified teachers**

Overseas students, Scholarships for For overseas students in the UK, scholarships are available from a number of sources. These include the students' own governments; the British government, which annually makes up to 240 awards for post-graduate or similar studies; the British Council, which awards over 500 scholarships a year to students from all over the world wishing to engage in advanced studies or research, and also offers bursaries for shorter periods; UNESCO (details are to be found in its publication, *Study Abroad*); and various other award-making bodies, including some firms and educational foundations.

FURTHER READING
Study Abroad, UNESCO, Paris.
Higher Education in the UK, Longmans, Green for the British Council.
United Kingdom Post-Graduate Awards, Association of Commonwealth Universities, London.

Overseas Visual Aids Centre Sponsored by the British government and the Nuffield Foundation, the Centre exists to give advice and help on all aspects of audio-visual aids to teachers, community development workers and others from overseas. A library and various publications are available together with permanent displays, and training courses and facilities for viewing material are arranged.

Tavistock Hse South, Tavistock Sq., London, WC1.

Owen, Robert (1771–1858) *See* **New Lanark**

Oxbridge Thackeray coined the names 'Oxbridge' and 'Camford' to lump together the Universities of Oxford and Cambridge. They share, indeed, many distinctions and not a few disabilities. They are the oldest and, but for London, the largest, most opulent, most beautiful, and most eminent of British universities. They have also been the most cumbrous (except perhaps again for London), the most awkwardly independent, the most conservative, and the most retentive of monopoly, privilege and social snobbery.

The complex and often intertwined histories of Oxford and Cambridge fall into four periods. The first period, from their origins in the 13th century to the mid-16th century, saw the gradual rise of these two medieval universities as pre-eminent centres of learning in theology, philosophy and the arts, endowed with a growing number of residential halls and colleges, at odds with their localities and using royal and ecclesiastical support to gain a large measure of juridical independence.

The second period, one of renascent intellectual liberation complicated by the dislocations of the Reformation, saw the effective rise of the colleges to power. Elizabeth's Act of 1571 remodelled the universities and elevated the heads of the colleges. But by the 18th century the intellectual life of the country shifted to the metropolis, and Oxford and Cambridge became provincial seats of ignorance, indolence and genteel dissolution, relieved by small pockets of academic brilliance, like mathematics at Cambridge.

The 19th century, which saw at long last the creation of other universities, gradually re-established the pre-eminence of Oxford and Cambridge. Examinations were introduced and the curricula were refashioned, religious tests were abolished and places were thrown open to competition, women were admitted, and the general administration of the universities was restructured.

Today, Oxford and Cambridge are in the process of trying to redefine their roles in relation to a national system of higher education. The pressure of numbers and the need to do away with categories of privileged entrants, the changing social assumptions of the faculty and the diminishing autonomy of the college vis-à-vis the university, the enormous growth of the science faculties and laboratories, the numbers of women in the university, and above all, perhaps, the balance between research and teaching—these questions permeated the life of the universities after the first world war and have dominated it since the second. Major changes and reforms have been mooted, new colleges have been founded, other universities have achieved comparable distinction, and all the time there has been an inescapable pressure towards full participation in the national machinery of university affairs. The Franks Report of 1966 (*q.v.*) is both a statement and symptom of the situation.

BF

Oxford, Act of Parliament on (1854) This Act was part of the implementation of the recommendations of a succession of commissions, who wanted to see the universities opened to a wider range of students and fellows.

Oxford and Cambridge, Reports of the Royal Commissions on the Universities of (1852/3) Terms of reference: to enquire into the discipline, studies and revenues of these Universities and their Colleges. Chairman: Rt Rev. Dr Samuel Hinds, Bishop of Norwich.

The Report led to the Oxford University Act 1854 and the Cambridge University Act 1852. Oxford was less welcoming than Cambridge to the idea of reform and a broader membership.

P

Painter-Etchers and Engravers, Royal Society of The Society, founded 1884, promotes an annual exhibition of prints and engravings ranging from the traditional to the most modern. Allied to this Society is the Print Collectors' Club. Two or three lectures and/or demonstrations are given annually.

RWS Galleries, 26 Conduit St, London, W1.

Painters in Water Colours, Royal Society of The primary object of the Society (founded 1804) is the exhibition of members' work in two shows a year: spring and autumn. There are only 50 full members, including the leading water colour painters in the UK.

Allied to the RWS is the Old Water Colour Society's Club. Members are collectors and connoisseurs who meet twice a year during the RWS exhibitions. For over 40 years the Club has published annually, for private circulation to members, an illustrated volume dealing with water colour painters and painting.

RWS Galleries, 26 Conduit St, London, W1.

Pakistan, Education in Bengali and Urdu are the national languages, but English remains the official language until 1972. In 1961 it was estimated that 19.2% of the population over five years of age was literate, and a long-term programme of education expansion aims to provide school places for three out of every five children.

Schools are organised in four stages: primary, 5 to 10 years; lower secondary, 10 to 12 years; secondary, 12 to 14 years, and higher secondary, 14 to 16 years. Teacher training is in three categories, specialising in teaching for either primary, lower secondary or secondary schools. In 1963 there were 58,294 primary schools (enrolment 6,051,675); 7,421 secondary (enrolment 2,062,057); 16 teacher training colleges and 93 teacher training schools (enrolment 15,866); technical, art, medical, science, law and engineering colleges numbered 330 (enrolment 224,115); and 10 universities had an enrolment of 17,742.

The population of the country was approximately 97 million in 1965.

EP

Panama, Education in Education is compulsory between the ages of 7 and 15. 1965 statistics: 99 infant schools (enrolment 4,825); 1,580 primary schools (enrolment 203,429); 190 secondary schools (enrolment 54,906); University of Panama 6,954; Catholic University of Santa Maria la Antigua 233.

The country's population was approximately 1¼ million in 1965.

Paperbacks Blanket assessments of paperbacks have in the past condemned them as unsuitable for children, dismissing them as concerned with 'sex, sadism and violence'. Much of the suspicion and hostility has now evaporated: the range of subjects covered by paperbacks and their low cost mean that children of all ages, interests and abilities have a rich store of reading matter to select from, which they are able to buy out of pocket-money. Reluctant readers are cajoled by a bargain price, a colourful cover and an article that looks much less forbidding than a hardback.

For younger children, Puffins still reign supreme: a superb collection of the best children's books, backed by a thriving Puffin Club and an extensive programme of help to schools.

New challengers have entered children's paperback publishing: for example, Faber Paper-Covered Editions, New English Library, Armada (Collins), Dragon Books (Atlantic Book Publishing Co.), Junior Pacemakers (Burke), Dancing Bear (Sphere), Summit and Zebra (Evans Bros), Collie (Transworld), Merlin (Hamlyn). Knight Books (Brockhampton Press) offer a wide variety from classics to Enid Blyton; Topliners (Pan/Macmillan) are aimed directly at the teenage market.

Among the 25,000 titles in print are many, fiction and non-fiction, suitable for older boys and girls. A judicious sifting of adult titles provides a vast supply for sixth-formers (and often for younger teenagers) and helps in the difficult task of bridging the gap between children's books and adult reading.

Text-books and prescribed examination texts are increasingly appearing in paperback form; university and college students are particularly well catered for, although prices of technical and scholarly paperbacks tend to be high. In addition to their regular trade information, some leading publishers of paperbacks issue special educational lists.

Various methods have been tried to make paperbacks easily available to children in schools: a shelf in the library, form or subject collections, a bookshop (*see* **Book agencies**), a visiting book-van.

Scholastic Publications (64 Bury Walk, London, SW3) organises paperback book clubs for all age-groups from five to 19. Suitable paperbacks, professionally selected, are offered for direct purchase by pupils through a scheme designed to encourage the habit of book-buying and the building of personal libraries at minimum expenditure.

Publishers' addresses and details of available titles are contained in *Paperbacks in Print* (J. Whitaker and Sons, 13 Bedford Sq., London, WC1).

GBo

Paraguay, Education in The system provides free compulsory education at the primary stage from seven to 14 years, and non-compulsory free education afterwards. In 1965 there were 2,632 primary schools, with an enrolment of 365,000; and 244 secondary schools, with an enrolment of 33,252 in art, technical, commercial and vocational training. Teachers numbered 4,039 in 1965. There are two universities with 5,560 students. Expenditure on education rose from 316,829,000 guaranies in 1955 to 802,584,000 guaranies in 1965.

The population of the country was approximately two million in 1966.

Parental choice The opportunities for parents to choose the school to which they wish to send their child — if it is a county or voluntary school maintained by an LEA — and the limitations restricting their choice in practice, derive from two provisions of the Education Act 1944. The first of these provisions (Section 36 of the Act) makes it the duty of the parent of every child of compulsory school age to cause him or her to receive full-time education suitable to his or her age, ability, and aptitude. In practice, that means that a primary school child should attend a primary school appropriate to his or her age; similarly for a secondary school child —

with the reservations imposed by the LEA as to selection, where a selective system of secondary education exists — and, again, similarly, for a handicapped child who has been ascertained by the LEA, in fulfilment of their duties, as needing education in a special school for the handicap from which he or she suffers.

The second provision of the Act mentioned, which both offers and limits parental choice of school, is the frequently misquoted Section 76 of the Act, which reads as follows, the words in italics being the ones that are often overlooked by parents: 'In the exercise and performance of all powers and duties conferred and imposed on them by this Act the Minister and local education authorities *shall have regard* to the general principle that, *so far as is compatible with the provision of efficient instruction and training and the avoidance of unreasonable public expenditure,* pupils are to be educated in accordance with the wishes of their parents'. The first words in italics mean no more than that the LEA, so far as the issue concerns them, must take the general principle of parents' wishes into account, and weigh them with the other considerations of the Section, also in italics. The Minister (now Secretary of State) is involved because, in the event of an unresolved dispute on the subject between a parent and the LEA, it is his duty, if the matter is referred to him, to adjudicate on it.

To illustrate first the practical problems of the LEA, to which the words in italics of S.76 refer, it is a duty of the LEA to avoid the provision of superfluous school accommodation, as that would involve unreasonable public expenditure. So, to begin with, parents may usually be limited, in their choice of school for their children, to the nearest available school, because another school which they would prefer is fully required to serve the children of its own neighbourhood. As for the phrase: '*the provision of efficient instruction and training*', this prevents parents from choosing a school for their children at a distance from their home if the time and journey involved for their child would be excessive for his age.

In the light of the two practical limitations on parental choice mentioned, any LEA will consider — and so will the Secretary of State if the matter is referred to him — the individual requests of parents for the admission of their child to a school, other than the nearest available, on various grounds: (1) that they prefer another school to the one in their neighbourhood, and there is room for their child without detriment to the children living in the vicinity of that school; (2) that they wish their child to attend a denominational school and the journeys to and from it are not unreasonable; (3) that they already have one child attending the school of their choice for their other child; (4) that they prefer a single sex school, or a co-educational school, for their child; (5) that they have removed house but wish their child to continue at the school where he or she was before they removed; (6) that for valid medical reasons, they wish their child to attend a certain school, where accommodation is available and to and from which the journey is reasonable.

All such individual preferences will be considered by the LEA, but, as the Act says, in the light of the avoidance of unreasonable public expenditure and the provision of efficient instruction and training.

A different type of parental choice arises when a parent does not wish to send his child to a school maintained by the LEA, but to an independent fee-paying school. The LEA have power to agree to such a request and to give financial assistance, according to the parents' means; but the LEA are under no obligation to do so if the schools they maintain or assist can enable them to comply with their duty under the Act. Broadly speaking, if a parent prefers to contract out of the public system of education, he may do so, but at his own expense and without financial assistance from the rates. Just as citizens who prefer the better facilities of the Times Book Club to those of the public library must pay the library rate, and receive no assistance from the rates towards their subscription to the Book Club, so they must pay the education rate, without remission, whether they use or contract out of the public system of education.

For further information on choice of schools, see *Manual of Guidance No. 1*, issued by the DES (HMSO, London).

See also **School attendance; Zoning**

FB

Parent-teacher movement There was a tendency in the UK in the late 19th century for teachers to work behind closed doors and for parents to show only a passive interest in the work of the school. On the Continent and in North America, however, the value of parent-teacher co-operation was becoming apparent: for in 1866, a national organisation to further this co-operation was formed in Holland, and in 1897 the National Congress of Parents and Teachers came into being in Washington DC.

In the UK, although many individual associations existed, it was not until 1929 that sufficient groups banded together to form the Home and School Council of Great Britain.

The past: Home and School Council of Great Britain Founded in 1929 at a time when rapid advances were being made in the understanding of children and their fundamental needs, the Council's purpose was to provide an opportunity for both parents and teachers to study the new developments in child psychology which related to the upbringing and the education of the child as a whole.

By 1939 some hundreds of PTAs had affiliated to the Council, which by then had contact with similar bodies in other countries.

In the early 1950s, the Home and School Council ceased to exist partly owing to the difficulty of obtaining adequate financial support, but mainly through the conviction, then widely held by teachers and professional bodies, that over-organisation and an attempt to make home-school co-operation conform to a single pattern would be a grave error 'since it could destroy sympathy for the movement among teachers, and might tend to hamper spontaneous development suitable to local conditions.'

The present: England—National Federation of Parent-Teacher Associations After the second world war many PTAs existed as single units but derived benefit from joining together in areas of dense population and in county areas as regional federations (e.g. Greater London, Nottinghamshire, Cheshire and West Midlands). In 1954 the Birmingham Federation felt the need for a national organisation and arranged a meeting of various regional representatives. From the discussions that followed the National Federation of PTAs came into existence on 9 June 1956.

The national body exists to promote the formation of new associations and to act as a 'clearing house' for ideas and suggestions. It also publishes twice yearly its own magazine *The Parent-Teacher*.

Representatives from the NUT, the NAS, the Joint Four and the NAHT attend Executive Committee meetings of the National Federation.

Scotland—Council of PTAs of Scotland There have been PTAs in Scotland for over 30 years. The Education Acts of 1945/46 stimulated the movement throughout Scotland and at a conference held in Glasgow on 15 May 1948 delegates unanimously established the Council of Parent-Teacher Associations of Scotland.

The future At the Conference of the World Federation of Educational Associations in 1927 the following resolution was adopted:

'The WFEA recommends, since the child receives its education in home, school and community, the promotion of co-operation between home and school, and their joint efforts to secure in the community such conditions as will supplement the best instruction given by the parent and teachers for the development of the whole child in all three of these relationships.'

This resolution is the justification for the existence forty years later of PTAs throughout the country.

With the momentum gained from the publication in 1967 of the Plowden Report, *Children and their Primary Schools*, which stressed the positive correlation between the degree of home and school harmony and the scholastic achievement of the pupils, the future for parent-teacher co-operation has never seemed so bright.

See also **Home and school**

FURTHER READING
Children and their Primary Schools (Plowden Report), HMSO, 1967.
The Parent-Teacher, VI, 1, Spring 1967.
Parent-Teacher Co-operation (Reports of National Teachers Association given at the World Confederation of Organisations of the Teaching Profession Assembly of Delegates), August 1953.
Statement of Executive Policy on Parent-Teacher Co-operation, National Union of Teachers, November 1946.

JAJ

Parents' National Educational Union This is an association through which members' children may be enrolled in a school conducted by correspondence. This is of particular interest to parents living overseas where no local education is available.

The aim of the school is to give children a wide and balanced curriculum. Programmes covering a wide syllabus are provided for a whole term's work, using wherever possible books of literary value with living ideas.

PNEU work is based upon the educational principles of Charlotte Mason, to be found in her book *An Essay Towards the Philosophy of Education.*

Murray Hse, Vandon St, London, SW1.

See also **Mason, Charlotte**

Parish Schools Bill 1820 Introduced into the House of Commons by Lord Brougham (*q.v.*), who pointed out that at the time only one in 16 of the population was receiving any education whatever, this Bill was opposed by the Church of England and the nonconformists and was withdrawn.

Parity of esteem A much-quoted phrase from the Ministry of Education's 1947 publication, *The New Secondary Education*, in which it was stated that: 'The modern school will be given parity of conditions with other types of secondary school; parity of esteem it must secure by its own efforts.' For a discussion of this statement, see Professor William Taylor's *The Secondary Modern School* (London, 1963), pp. 42–55, where he concludes that 'given the existing distribution of status and rewards, the occupational implications of secondary education will always set a limit on the extent to which a school can secure parity of esteem on its own terms rather than those dictated by society'.

See also **Secondary modern schools**

Parks Commission, National The Commission is a public body set up under the National Parks and Access to the Countryside Act 1949. Members are appointed by the Minister of Housing and Local Government. They are concerned with the preservation of landscape beauty and the use of the countryside for open-air recreation in England and Wales. Advice is also given to planning authorities on proposals affecting coast, countryside, open-air recreation and the development of information services to further the public enjoyment of the National Parks. The total area of the ten National Parks is 5,258 sq. miles.

1 Cambridge Ga., Regent's Park, London, NW1.

Parliamentary Group for World Government *See* **World Government, Parliamentary Group for**

Parochial Schools Bill 1807 The first attempt to bring about the provision of popular education by the state, this Bill was introduced into the Commons by Samuel Whitbread and would have set up parochial schools in England and Wales. It met with strong opposition and was rejected.

Parry Report (1967): Report of the Committee on Libraries The work of a body appointed by the Universities Grants Committee in 1963, under the chairmanship of Dr Thomas Parry, Principal of the University College of Wales, Aberystwyth, to consider the most effective and economical way of supplying books and periodicals to universities, CATs and central institutions. The committee was also required to report on the possibility of shared facilities between universities and colleges and other library systems. The main recommendations of the report were that a British National Library be set up as a centre of inter-library lending and as the apex of the country's library system, and that the British Museum should, when its new library building is completed, assume this central role; and that a voucher system should be established to ensure that students made proper use of their book grants. A survey showed that of the £35 allowed to each student for the purchase of books, only an average of between £10 and £11 was so spent.

See also **Libraries, University**

Part pension, Allocation of Under the Teachers (Superannuation) Act 1937, provision is made whereby a teacher, subject to proof of physical fitness, may allocate part of pension for the benefit of wife or husband, or a dependant of the teacher in the event of his or her dying before the beneficiary.

A teacher may make an allocation in favour of one person only and that person must be either the wife or husband or a dependant of the teacher. In this context, 'dependant' is taken to mean a person not necessarily a relative who is wholly or partially dependent upon the teacher for support.

The amount of the benefit depends upon the sum allocated and the ages of the teacher and the beneficiary. An actuarial calculation shows the amount of benefit which would be payable on the death of the teacher.

The scheme may be taken up by a teacher on reaching the age of 60 (not before, although application to allocate may be made about four months before the age of 60 is attained), whether or not he or she intends to retire at that time. The allocation would therefore be either as a 'retiring teacher' or a 'continuing teacher'. If allocation is made as a continuing teacher, then the beneficiary is covered from the date of the acceptance by the Secretary of State of the allocation declaration. In both cases, the teacher may choose either Option A or Option B. Under Option A the benefit is a pension payable to the wife or husband or dependant of the teacher after the death of the teacher. Option B is applicable only to a wife or husband and the benefit consists of two parts, viz. (1) an annuity payable to the teacher from the date of commencement of the annual superannuation allowance while the wife or husband of the teacher is alive and ceasing on the death of the wife or husband and (2) a pension of double the amount of this annuity payable to the widow or widower on the death of the teacher.

An application to participate in the allocation scheme should be made before retirement to the pensions branch of the DES. There is provision on Form 14 Pen. for a teacher to state that he or she wishes to consider making an allocation of part pension. On receiving the application the DES will send the teacher an explanatory booklet containing the statutory rules, option tables, some typical examples and the necessary forms for completion.

It should be noted that once an allocation declaration has been lodged with the Secretary of State, it may not be cancelled. In the case of a continuing teacher, an amendment may be made at the date of actual retirement if the teacher wishes to improve the allocation in the light of longer service and/or increased salary.

SEB

Part-time salaries Since May 1968 teachers in regular part-time service have been paid a proportion of the annual salary that would be appropriate if they were employed full-time. The proportion corresponds to the proportion of the school week that the LEA deems the teacher to be normally employed (lunch breaks being excluded).

Allowances and additional payments prescribed in the Burnham Report for designated posts of responsibility are normally payable only to full-time teachers. Where, however, an LEA is satisfied that it is unable to fill a post with a suitable full-time teacher, it may temporarily appoint teachers in regular part-time service to fill the post and pay such teachers a proportion of the prescribed allowance or additional payment. The proportion of the allowance or additional payment paid in any particular case is determined by reference to the proportion of full-time that the teacher spends undertaking the duties of the post and must not exceed the proportion of annual salary payable under the above paragraph.

SEB

Part-time superannuation Part-time teachers in primary and secondary schools engaged on a regular basis, i.e. those who are under a contract to work the same number of hours or periods each week (excluding those paid at an hourly rate or by capitation fees), are able to make their service pensionable. Like the full-time scheme a superannuation contribution of 6% of gross salary is required. A condition of entry into the scheme is that teachers must have done at least one year's full-time pensionable service. The scheme also applies to 'relief' (supply) teachers in primary and secondary schools, whether they work for full days or only parts of days, but for these teachers the condition stipulating that one year's pensionable service must have been completed will be waived. Entry into the scheme is voluntary and the option may be taken up at any time. Once a teacher has elected to participate and after his/her application has been accepted by the Secretary of State, he/she will not be permitted to withdraw. Until the teacher is granted superannuation allowances, or attains the age of 70, whichever is the earlier, all regular part-time service or relief service in primary and secondary schools will be treated as pensionable and superannuation contributions will be payable in respect of it.

The scheme does not provide for any retrospection and, generally speaking, retired teachers in receipt of pension are not able to participate.

The employer is responsible for calculating the amount of service to be recorded for pension purposes. The actual amount of reckonable service is determined by the following formula:

$$\frac{\text{actual salary paid}}{\text{full-time annual salary rate}} \times 365 \text{ days}$$

SEB

Part-time teaching 'Part-time teachers are now being employed over the greater part of the country on a scale large enough for their value to the schools to be rightly appreciated and more and more schools are learning how to make the best use of them': Department of Education statement, August 1966.

The employment of teachers on a part-time basis has indeed increased considerably in recent years, mainly as a result of the pressing need to alleviate the teacher shortage by employing married women teachers who have been persuaded to return to the profession after a period of absence due to family commitments. There has always been an element of part-time teaching in the UK, but so far as the schools are concerned it was until quite recently largely confined to the secondary schools and to the employment of specialist teachers of such subjects as music, commercial subjects, domestic science and religious education. The main change which has come about is the extension of the practice of part-time teaching to general class teaching and to the primary schools.

This change has been forced upon LEAs and schools by the continuing shortage of teachers and the realisation that one of the principal factors in the shortage is the 'wastage' due to women teachers marrying and leaving the profession after a few years to take up family and other domestic responsibilities. If such women are to be attracted back to the hard-pressed schools, it is argued officially, then it has to be recognised that many will be available, at least in the early stages of their resumed career, only on a part-time basis.

It is not always easy to fit a part-time teacher into a school staffing pattern, especially in the primary school where the tradition is for each member of staff to be in charge of a particular class for the bulk of the week and the whole range of the curriculum, and for specialist teaching to be undertaken on only a limited basis, and mainly in the last year or two of the junior school. (In secondary schools the practice is

different with each class being taught for much of the week by different subject specialists; there has, therefore, been no marked change in the pattern of school organisation so far as the employment of part-time teachers is concerned, and irrespective of the teacher shortage the practice would almost certainly have grown with the increasing complexity of the secondary school curriculum.)

Apart from the problems of time-tabling, some head-teachers and staff members have been reluctant to accept the idea of the part-timer out of an understandable suspicion that such members of staff would not accept their fair share of such aspects of school work as extra-curricular activities, lunch hour duties, and school/parent relationships. While in some cases this suspicion has doubtless proved well-founded, there is no evidence that this is generally the case, and more often one hears of head-teachers who are deeply grateful for the contribution made by part-time members of staff. In any event such is the overall staffing position in the schools, and the long-term trend in supply and growth of child population, that it seems inevitable that part-time teaching will be a feature of school organisation in many schools for the foreseeable future. The extent to which it has become established already is shown by the latest statistics, which reveal that by February 1966 the part-time teacher force stood at 36,200, and out of a total of 162 LEAs 94 employed part-time teachers to an equivalent of at least 5% of their total teaching strength and 10 authorities employed them to the extent of 10% of their teaching strength.

There is no fixed basis for the employment of the part-time teacher. The number of days or hours he or she will work depends on the needs of the school and the teacher's personal circumstances. Some part-time teachers teach for, say, the first two or three days of the week; others might teach every morning or every afternoon, while others again might teach for an agreed number of periods, or be on call for particular occasions. Because of the rapid growth of part-time teaching, however, there has been a demand for salary payments, pensions and conditions of service for such teachers to be put on a more regular footing, and negotiations have recently taken place to this end.

So far as salaries are concerned, the Burnham Committee has agreed that part-time teachers engaged on a regular contract, i.e. teachers who are under contract to work the same number of hours or periods each week, or who undertake a regular pattern of work, shall receive a fraction of the appropriate annual salary based upon the hours of part-time employment expressed as a fraction of the school week determined by the LEA, excluding the lunch-time break. The Committee has also agreed that allowances for additional responsibility should normally be paid only to full-time teachers, but it has been recognised that part-time teachers might occasionally need to be appointed temporarily to special posts pending the appointment of a suitable full-time teacher. Where such allowance is paid it will be on the same proportionate basis. Part-time teachers who are not engaged on a regular contract will not be covered by the mandatory provisions of the Burnham Report, but there will be a recommendation relating to their position in an Appendix to the Report.

Provision has also been made recently for the introduction of superannuation in respect of part-time teachers. The scheme is voluntary and will apply to those teachers who have previously rendered at least one year's full-time service. The amount of pensionable service credited to a part-time teacher depends on the proportion of the full annual salary paid. Thus, if a teacher received two-fifths of annual salary, he would be credited with two-fifths times

365 days (146 days) of pensionable service.

While salary and pension arrangements for part-time teachers have been the subject of national negotiation, conditions of service are still likely to vary from one LEA to another, but even here the DES has been able to report considerable progress and growing uniformity of approach. In 1966 the Department stated: 'More than four-fifths of all authorities now encourage part-time teachers to fulfil regular engagements and there seem to be very few authorities who still retain the view, once quite common, that part-time teachers are to be regarded as no more than temporary stop-gaps. Authorities' increasing willingness to treat part-time teachers as regular members of the staff is reflected in the security of tenure they offer to those who wish to give regular service. About a third of the Authorities give regular part-time teachers the same, or virtually the same, terms of notice as those for full-time staff; and a similar proportion give notice of at least one month. Many of these, together with some of those who formerly prescribed shorter terms of notice, or do not prescribe any formal terms at all, indicate that they would expect in practice to give generous notice at the termination of a part-time teacher's appointment; and several authorities say that the occasion for doing so has rarely or never arisen.

'About two Authorities out of three allow part-time teachers paid sick leave, sometimes on certain conditions as to the amount of service given in a week (e.g. the equivalent of at least two days a week) or as to the duration of the teacher's engagement (e.g. after service of at least one term). Almost as many Authorities allow part-time teachers special leave on the same conditions as those which apply to full-time teachers. A quarter of the Authorities allow part-time teachers paid maternity leave, usually on similar conditions to those applying to the grant of sick pay. Many Authorities indicate, however, that this question has not yet arisen and a number of these imply that application for paid maternity leave would be sympathetically considered.'

See also **Teacher estimates and teacher shortage; Married women teachers**

FJ

Partially sighted children At the beginning of this century Dr Kerr—ophthalmologist to the London School Board—discovered many children with defective vision either failing badly in ordinary schools or being unnecessarily taught Braille in schools for the blind. As a result the first 'sight-saving' class was established in Camberwell. Similar classes followed in America, Germany, France as well as other parts of the UK. As a result of the Report of a Committee of Enquiry in 1934[1] it was recommended that partially sighted children should be educated separately from the blind and with more emphasis on normality. This was not put into effect until after 1945 when partial sight was officially recognised as a separate handicap with the definition: pupils who by reason of defective vision cannot follow the regime of ordinary schools without detriment to their sight or their educational development but can be educated by methods involving the use of sight.[2]

The incidence of partial sight requiring treatment in special schools or classes is less than 1 in 3,000. The maximum number of pupils in a class is 15. The curriculum of the special classes is as normal as possible, including specialist teaching. There is less stress on 'sight-saving' than formerly because it has been found that the use of the eye is unlikely to damage it further.[3] Caution is still exercised in physical education, particularly for children with myopia, in view of the danger of detachment of the retina by violent and jerky movements. Children are helped by special equipment such as spectacles, powerful lenses, adjustable desks, and by good even lighting without glare. Books are selected for the clarity of their print and some are specially printed in larger type. The pupils are regularly examined by an ophthalmologist.

There is no special qualification for teachers of partially sighted children, but some have taken a general qualification in the education of handicapped children. The Association for the Education and Welfare of the Partially Sighted is a professional body which holds conferences and publishes a newsletter.

REFERENCES

1. Board of Education. *Committee of Enquiry into Problems Relating to Partially Sighted Children*, HMSO, 1934.
2. *Handicapped Pupils and Special School Regulations*, HMSO, 1962.
3. I. Mann and A. Pirie. *The Science of Seeing*, Pelican, 1946.

MW

Payment by results *See* **Codes of Grants**

Payne, Joseph (1808–76) Payne became the first professor of education in England, a post established by the College of Preceptors following a vigorous campaign conducted by Payne for the development of educational method. Born of poor parents, he received only an elementary education, earning his living as a youth by teaching and writing for the press. A small class he taught in south London grew into the Denmark Hill Grammar School. From 1871 onwards Payne devoted himself especially to improvements in the training and status of teachers and to support for the Women's Educational Union.

Pearson-Bravais method *See* **Correlation**

Peer groups These are basically groups made up of equals of roughly the same age. Such informal groups often have strong codes of behaviour, and children identifying strongly with their peer groups, whether at home or at school, may be far more affected by what they feel their contemporaries think of them than by anything the teacher has to say. For this reason, the teacher should at least be aware of the pressures and conventions of such groupings, and choose his ground carefully if he wishes to modify some of these attitudes.

Pelham Committee This Committee, whose first chairman was Lord Pelham, reports on scales of salaries for the teaching staff of colleges of education. In the sense that its deliberations do not come within the terms of the Remuneration of Teachers Act, it is not a Burnham Committee. On the other hand, the Secretary of State receives the report from the chairman to approve and to confirm payment of salaries for the purposes of Regulation 18 of the Training of Teachers (Local Education Authorities) Regulations 1959. As in other salaries negotiating committees, it consists of two panels— the authorities' and governors' panel, and the teaching staff panel. The latter is represented entirely by 12 members of the Association of Teachers in Colleges and Departments of Education. The former panel is made up as follows: County Councils Association (two), Association of Municipal Corporations (two), Association of Education Committees (two), ILEA (two), Welsh Joint Education Committee, Local Authorities Sub-Committee (one), Council of the Church Training Colleges (three), Methodist Education Committee (two), Catholic Education Council (two), British and Foreign School Society (two).

Pelham Scales Scales of salaries for the teaching staff of colleges of education are as follows:

Assistant lecturers £1,120 × £50(4) to £1,320.

Lecturers £1,480 × £50(12) to £2,080. *Senior lecturers* £2,080 × £60(2) × £65(4) to £2,460.

Principal lecturers £2,460 × £80(3) × £85(1) to £2,785. Where a principal lecturer has special responsibility for the overall supervision of the work of four or more staff in a major subject or group of related subjects, or has substantial responsibilities other than the supervision of staff which the authority or governing body think justify the payment of an allowance, the LEA or governing body of a voluntary training college may pay an allowance to him or her of not less than £125 per annum and not more than £640 per annum over and above the scale salary.

Deputy principals A senior lecturer or principal lecturer shall be designated deputy principal in each college where there are 241 or more students. There are provisions in the relevant report for deputy principals to be appointed or to be continued in their appointments in cases where there are fewer than 241 students. An allowance shall be paid to a deputy principal over and above the scale salary which is applicable to him or her as senior lecturer or principal lecturer. The amount of such an allowance shall be:

Group	No. of students	£
2	241– 350	215
3	351– 500	300
4	501– 650	385
5	651– 800	470
6	801– 950	555
7	951–1,150	640
8	1,151–1,350	725

Principals—

Group	No. of students	Salary (£)
	Under 18	By agreement with the Secretary of State
1	181–240	$2,950 \times 100(3)$ to 3,250
2	241–350	$3,160 \times 100(3)$ to 3,460
3	351–500	$3,370 \times 100(3)$ to 3,670
4	501–650	$3,585 \times 100(3)$ to 3,885
5	651–800	$3,800 \times 100(3)$ to 4,100
6	801–950	$4,010 \times 100(3)$ to 4,310
7	951–1,150	$4,225 \times 125(3)$ to 4,600
8	1,151–1,350	$4,440 \times 125(3)$ to 4,815
	Over 1,350	By agreement with the Secretary of State

Provision is made empowering the LEA or the governing body in a particular case to pay a higher scale or higher maximum. This power will be exercised in agreement with the Secretary of State. Provision is also made for an annual review of salaries of principals and the allowance for deputy principals.

The London allowance at the level of £85 applies to principals as well as to other members of staff.

SEB

Pension contributions for service abroad and certain other service

If the employment of a teacher in contributory service is discontinued for a period not exceeding five years, or not exceeding such longer interval as the Secretary of State may in a particular case direct, and the teacher is employed during that period: (1) in full-time service as a teacher in any part of Her Majesty's dominions outside the UK; or (2) as a teacher in any school in a foreign country which is shown to the satisfaction of the Secretary of State to be a school in which it is expedient to facilitate the employment of British teachers; or (3) in an educational service outside the UK in employment which to a substantial extent involves the control or supervision of teachers; or (4) in some other employment, not exceeding five years, in respect of which the Secretary of State is satisfied that the employment provides experience of value to teachers; or (5) as a teacher in any school maintained within the UK by the government of any part of Her Majesty's dominions outside the UK— but not exceeding one year in any other case, a teacher may with the consent of the Secretary of State pay, at such times as may be required by way of contributions for pension benefits under the Act, an amount equal to the teacher's and employers' contributions on the salary which, in the opinion of the Secretary of State,

the teacher would have received had he or she remained in contributory service; the interval in service for which contributions have been paid will be treated as pensionable accordingly.

The one year of absence from contributory service provision will benefit teachers who leave contributory service for a year and enter a university for tuition or research work or who leave the profession temporarily for recuperative purposes. Under this provision they will be able to pay $14\frac{1}{2}\%$ of their salary and receive ultimate pension benefits as if no absence had occurred.

Where a teacher, not having previously been employed in contributory service, takes up service in any school outside the UK, Isle of Man or the Channel Islands which is shown to the satisfaction of the Secretary of State to be one in which it is expedient to facilitate the employment of teachers from the UK, he may, with the consent of the Secretary of State, pay the full teacher's and employers' contributions on the amount of salary which he would have received had he been employed in contributory service, up to a maximum of five years of such service, or not exceeding such longer period as the Secretary of State may direct in the particular case. If the teacher does not return to normal contributory service within two years of completing the period of service abroad for which contributions have been paid, the teacher's contributions will be refunded, but not the amount paid in respect of the employers' contributions, and the period of service abroad will not count for pension.

In every case where service abroad is contemplated, and the teacher is anxious to safeguard his pension benefits, he should write to the Secretary of State to make the necessary arrangements before leaving contributory service.

SEB

Pensions, Teacher's, How to claim
The pension claim must be made on
Form 14 Pen., obtainable from the
DES. The completed form should be
sent to the LEA at least four months
prior to retirement, or at age 60,
whichever is the later. The LEA will
then complete its section of the form
and send it to the DES.

Any communication to the Department on superannuation matters should
be addressed to the Secretary, Department of Education and Science
(Pensions Branch), Honeypot Lane,
Stanmore, Middlesex, stating at the
head of the document the reference
number and full Christian names and
surname of the teacher concerned. In
the case of a married woman the
maiden name should also be given.
Correspondence in respect of the payment of pension, etc., after award,
should be addressed to: HM Paymaster-
General (Teachers Pensions), High
Street, Crawley, Sussex.

Pensions increase Pensions in the
teaching profession and in the public
services are mostly contributory, and
benefits are usually calculated in
respect of a terminal average salary. In
most cases the period used to find this
average is the final three years. Thus,
in inflationary times, a retiring public
servant has the advantage of securing
a pension benefit related to current
salary levels, but after his retirement
he is not in the same bargaining
position as employed persons are to
secure improvements in income. On
the other hand, a pension is an income
no less subject to the deterioration
which economic conditions may
produce. There is thus an obvious need
for subsequent improvements to be
made in the pension originally received.
Since the payment of occupational
pensions in the public services comes
very largely from central sources, the
responsibility for making improvements
no longer rests with the separate
employing bodies but with the government. For this reason any decision to
improve an existing pension level
applies throughout the public services
under the same act of parliament.

Basically the principle is that the
government should be expected to
behave in the same way as any other
good employer in this respect. That is
to say, money should be found out of
current expenditure to bolster up a
pension whenever the inroads of
inflation make it desirable to do so.
Naturally the pensioner feels that this
should be done more frequently and
that the resulting pension should
match the one currently awarded for
similar length of service and status. In
this event pressure has to be exerted
upon the government to act. For this
purpose a Public Service Pensioners'
Council has been formed whose chief
function is to look after the pension
interests of retired public servants and
to make representations to the government whenever it thinks fit.

Since the war inflation has been
continuous, with the result that the
government of the day has passed
Pensions Increase Acts in 1944–47,
1952, 1956, 1959, 1962 and 1965.

SEB

Percentiles *See* **Intelligence quotient**

**Percy Report (1945): Report of the
Special Committee on Higher
Technological Education** Terms of
reference: Having regard to the
requirements of industry, to consider
the needs of higher technical education
in England and Wales and the respective contributions to be made by
universities and technical colleges; and
to make recommendations on how to
maintain appropriate collaboration between universities and technical colleges
in this field. Chairman: Lord Eustace
Percy.

The Committee found serious shortcomings in the training of technologists,
and recommended that a carefully
selected number of colleges should be

S

redesignated as colleges of technology with the power to build up full-time degree courses, while remaining under the wing of the LEA.

See also **Colleges of Advanced Technology**

Performance tests These are tests that attempt to measure concrete rather than abstract intelligence. Usually the individual is asked to *do* something rather than use his verbal skill in writing or answering questions. Thus performance tests may range from assessing the reaction times of potential bus drivers to requiring those being tested to fit puzzles together or copy complex designs. The attraction of performance tests has often been that they seem to eliminate the bias that goes with verbal testing and springs from different cultural levels of verbal skill. But it is now thought that, even so, this cultural bias will still play its part, since many performance tests are easier for the individual who has been brought up with good experience of creative play. For many non-verbal tests, too, it is still evident that individuals will verbalise to themselves when trying to solve them, and that verbal facility can once again help in finding the correct answer.

FURTHER READING
P. E. Vernon. *The Structure of Human Abilities*, Methuen, 1950.

NT

Periodicals and newspapers, Reduced rates for About 40 magazines and newspapers offer students reduced subscription rates. 1967: *The Times* and *Morning Star* are available at half-price; *Punch* is on offer at £4.8s. p.a. instead of £5.5s.; *The Economist* at £3.12s. instead of £6; and *The Spectator's* concession is from £3.15s. to £3.3s. The biggest concession comes from *Architect and Building News*, which can be obtained for £1.10s. p.a. as against the normal subscription of £4.10s. The National Union of Students publishes a booklet listing concessions available to its members, which includes not only periodicals, but insurance, travel and the retail trades.

Permit system The Association of Publishers' Educational Representatives (APER) was directly responsible for the introduction of the permit system of school visiting by bona fide representatives which is now generally in use throughout the UK. A few LEAs, while not issuing permits, allow visiting for the purpose of displaying books at the discretion of the head teacher.

Permits are usually obtained by the representative, but some authorities require the application to be made by the group secretary of the Publishers' Association. The APER impresses upon its members that they should never visit schools in a permit-granting area without first obtaining a permit.

FURTHER READING
School Books Must Cost More. Educational Group, Publishers' Association, 1951.
Enquiry into Expenditure by Local Authorities in Class Books, National Book League, 1952.

Persian Gulf states, Education in Bahrain enrolments in 1965 were: primary schools 19,595 boys, 8,981 girls; intermediate schools 3,644 boys, 4,790 girls; secondary schools 2,473 boys, 1,465 girls; teacher training college 26. Total population in 1965: approximately 180,000.

Qatar enrolments in 1965: 50 boys' primary schools (6,982); 28 girls' primary schools (3,874). The population in 1966 was approximately 70,000.

Trucial States (seven states in all): 13 boys' schools in four of the states, six girls' schools in two of the states. No enrolment figures are available. Trade schools and apprentice training schools are run by industrial organisations. The combined population of the States was approximately 111,000 in 1966.

Personality tests Roughly speaking, there are two quite different types of personality test: objective and projective. Objective tests are usually made up of fixed questionnaires where, if the individual answers honestly, it will be possible to assess for example how neurotic, introverted or extraverted he may be. This is done roughly by matching his results with those of previously tested neurotic or extravert groups, and seeing where his responses and the pattern they form stand in relation to them. Such comparisons may be very useful at times; but any fixed questionnaire is inevitably something of a blunt instrument for really fine measurement of personality.

Projective tests, on the other hand, invite the individual to give his first impressions or to make up stories about word-associations, pictures, or even ink-blots (*see* **Rorschach tests**). It is thought that by this method the individual may unconsciously project his own needs, fears and ideas onto the material he is asked to describe or embellish. Although this undoubtedly happens, once again it is difficult for the examiner both to measure this accurately and also to prevent his own subjective impressions from playing too important a part in his assessment.

Psychologists who administer these tests are divided as to which type gives the best results. Despite a voluminous literature on the subject, there is still not one test that everyone agrees gives a thoroughly reliable and all-round picture of the personality.

FURTHER READING
P. E. Vernon. *Personality Tests and Assessments*, Methuen, 1953. *Personality Assessment; a Critical Survey*, Methuen, 1964.
NT

Peru, Education in Primary education between the ages of six and 12 is free and compulsory. Secondary education is optional; pupils can stay three years and then, for a further two, may follow letters or science studies which cover commercial, technical, agri- cultural and cattle husbandry courses. Higher education is available for those entering the professions. In 1967 there were 2,412,000 pupils in primary schools, 402,300 in secondary schools, and 95,700 in technical education. Students training to be teachers numbered 23,600, and there were 63,700 in universities. There are 20 universities, of which seven are private. That of San Marcos, founded in 1551 at Lima, is the oldest.

The population of the country was approximately 12 million in 1966.

Pestalozzi, Heinrich (1746–1827)
Born in Zurich, Pestalozzi was brought up by his mother after his father died when the boy was five years old; and in this experience was rooted his view, central to his educational outlook, of the importance in early education of mother and home. Strongly influenced by the writings of Rousseau (*q.v.*), Pestalozzi abandoned ideas of entering the ministry and later the law, and became a farmer (not a successful one). An industrial school for 20 orphans, which he set up and in which work and learning were to be combined, was a financial failure. He turned to writing, the work that made the most powerful impact being a novel of village life, *Leonard and Gertrude*, in which he described a form of home instruction where learning was based on immediate observation by the children (e.g. they began arithmetic by counting the panes in a window). His work attracted great attention, and the importance attached to it by the philosopher Fichte made it influential in the development of German educational ideas.

In 1798, Pestalozzi was briefly given charge of a school of orphans in Stanz, in Switzerland, and afterwards, his ideas sharpened by the experience, was appointed head of a teachers' training college at Burgdorf. In 1805 he set up the Institute of Yverdon, a magnet for teachers and pupils from many European countries. Quarrels broke out among his supporters, and the school was closed in 1825. His most important book, *How Gertrude Teaches her Children* (1801), was based on his experience at Burgdorf.

Essentially, Pestalozzi believed with Rousseau that the primary concern of education is with the individual, and that a true method of education must be based on a firm understanding of the way in which generally children develop. Like Rousseau, he believed that the life and operation of a school should resemble those of a family, but unlike Rousseau he did not feel that the success of the home or the school called for exceptional parents or teachers or for ideal circumstances. And, though he shared Rousseau's concern for individuality, he recognised that a child depends a great deal on his social role for the full development of his powers.

In Pestalozzi's approach to method is found the first modern statement of a view of learning now widely followed: that it must begin in experience (Pestalozzi's word was *Anschauung*) and lead on to ideas, and that it must always be within a child's grasp. There must be progress from the near at hand to the distant, from the simple to the increasingly complex.

Pestalozzi Children's Village Trust
The Trust is building a village for deprived children irrespective of nationality, race or creed at Sedlescombe, Battle, Sussex, similar to the international Children's Village at Trogen, Switzerland. The village at Sedlescombe, opened in 1959, is designed for 300 children living in national family groups and receiving their education in an international school, thus learning in a practical way tolerance and international understanding. Its first inhabitants are refugees from displaced persons' camps, deprived British children, Tibetan refugees and children from India, Jordan, Thailand and Nigeria.

Philately Philately is used in many schools throughout Britain as a visual aid in the teaching of history and geography. Simple historical events, such as the discovery of America, the battles of the American Civil War, the rise and fall of Nazi Germany, the discovery of Canada and the mutiny on the *Bounty*, are all recorded on stamps and can be used to illustrate lessons. The range is very great, and basic geographical facts, the character of a region's industries and natural history, man's conquest of space, and the world's art, can all be approached and illustrated from postage stamps. Apart from this direct use of philately in the classroom, teachers are also employing it as a means of 'leisure learning'.

The Stamp Collecting Promotion Council (6 Broadway Mansions, Brighton Rd, Worthing, Sussex) was formed in 1960 to promote stamp-collecting among the young and also to provide facilities in the educational field. It makes postal exhibitions of stamps and a range of film strips available on loan, free of charge, to educational authorities and school stamp clubs. It provides information on ways of starting a school stamp club, and can also supply wall charts on Africa, the Commonwealth, animals, birds, communications and Europe.

A new Council venture is a travelling van that goes on tour to schools, libraries and museums with a permanent exhibition of stamps produced by the GPO, the United Nations, the Crown Agents for Overseas Territories and the Inter-Governmental Philatelic Corporation of New York. Altogether, the issues of 85 postal administrations are featured.

OWN

Philippines, Education in the 1965 statistics: 307 kindergartens (enrolment 30,445); 24,165 primary schools (enrolment 5,578,140); 2,062 secondary schools (enrolment 1,037,109); 501

further education colleges (enrolment 44,499); 600 vocational colleges (enrolment 69,327). There are 27 universities.

The population of the islands was approximately 32 million in 1966.

Philological Society The Society was founded in 1842 to investigate and promote the study and knowledge of the structure, affinities and history of languages.

University College, Gower St, London, WC1.

Philosophical Society of England Established in 1913, the Society aims to spread a knowledge of practical philosophy among the general public by teaching and research and through its publications, *The Philosopher* and *Views and Comments*. There are centres in London, Manchester, Edinburgh, Glasgow and the USA. Associateship (APhS) is awarded by examination, but exemption from this is sometimes granted by the Society's Council if a candidate has studied some branch of philosophy in his professional training. Fellowship (FPhS) is awarded to associates who submit an original thesis of acceptable standard, or publish a work of philosophical value.

Gen. Sec.: Dr L. Eaton, Stone Mount, 233 Chester Rd, Hartford, Cheshire.

Philosophy of education To attempt a precise definition, either of philosophy in general or of the philosophy of education in particular, could serve no useful purpose, other than that of orthodoxy, for the boundaries of any active discipline must inevitably be in varying degrees uncertain. A certain rough adumbration of central concerns is, however, both possible and desirable, for philosophy does constitute a distinctive discipline with its own methods of inquiry and forms of argument.

First, then, the philosophy of education can no more be separated from general philosophy than can educational psychology from general psychology, or the sociology of education from general sociology. But neither is there a simple identity between the two, for not every branch of general philosophy is of equal relevance to education, while the philosophy of education includes among its concerns concepts which may be of no more than peripheral interest in general philosophy. The distinctiveness of the philosophy of education lies in its criteria of relevance, for it is philosophy organised by its concern with those general aims and principles which are, or ought to be, at the centre of educational endeavour.

Two distinct tendencies may be discerned in the history of the philosophy of education, though the distinction is one of relative emphasis only. On the one hand there is a tendency towards the construction of large systems, often embracing not only education but also social institutions and arrangements generally, and giving a distinctive account of human knowledge and of human nature. This system-building tendency is well exemplified in the philosophies of Plato, Aristotle, Kant and Dewey, who proceed to their main educational proposals from very general considerations to do with man, knowledge and society.

The second tendency, by contrast, is towards a more detailed, piecemeal and analytic approach, and though this too has its representatives in the history of philosophy, it is perhaps at the present time that it has gained its most marked ascendency, at least in English-speaking countries. This approach to the philosophy of education is, no less than the other, centrally concerned with general aims and principles, but it is so less in a profoundly revisionary spirit than in a spirit of more modest inquiry aiming at clarifying the meaning of particular concepts and probing the justification for particular value-judgments. This conception of philosophy is more that of the under-labourer, employed, as Locke put it, 'in clearing the ground a little, and removing some of the rubbish that lies in the way of knowledge'.

It may be surmised that such differences of tendency as these are not unrelated to the historical and social circumstances in which philosophers find themselves. When philosophy springs from a deep dissatisfaction with existing social institutions and arrangements, or from a conviction of the falsity of widely current estimates of knowledge and of man, then its outcome must be an attempt at the large-scale revision of existing values and concepts. Such was the case with Plato and with Dewey, for example. But when philosophers feel that widely shared values and the current advancement of knowledge are fundamentally sound, then their attention will more naturally be taken up with those perplexities and misunderstandings which are constantly arising and confusing the issue. At the present time, this contrast in tendency can be seen between the Existentialist preoccupations of Central European philosophy and the less anguished problems of British and American analytical philosophy.

To turn to a more specific account of the philosophy of education, however, one will first of all note a concern with varying concepts of education itself, that is to say, with the different sets of values which are or have been put forward as formulating the main aims of education. Some philosophers, such as Plato and Aristotle, have put forward theoretical studies as being properly pre-eminent in value, while others, such as Locke and Kant, have set moral character and a good will above everything else. Important issues are raised here not only over how to justify the worthwhileness or relative priority of different forms of understanding, but also over the way in which one form may distort the others. Art, morals and history are perhaps those most apt to be distorted, or even submerged, by other forms of understanding, or by cherished doctrines. Sometimes the philosopher may see his role as that of showing how certain proposed aims are misconceived, at least in the way in which they have been presented. Examples of such 'aims' might be those of mental health, growth and development, for these notions do not by themselves indicate the positive directions in which education should go.

Another side to the question of aims concerns the issue of general education and specialisation, or slightly differently, of liberal education and vocational training. But whatever the aims of education may be thought to be, institutional arrangements will have to be made for their pursuit, which will involve some consideration of education in a political setting. Concepts of philosophical interest here, with their related problems of justification, are those of liberty, authority, equality, justice and democracy. So far, then, it may be seen that the areas of general philosophy especially relevant in the philosophy of education will be those of ethics, epistemology and social philosophy.

When one turns from aims to principles of procedure in education, the philosophy of mind is the most relevant background from which to work. Concepts of interest here are, on the cognitive side, those of thinking, imagination, creativity, intelligence, experience and understanding, and of activity, behaviour, play, purpose and interest on the conative side. Concepts specifically related to teaching and learning have also to be considered, such as those of training, instruction, discovery, conditioning, indoctrination, teaching, learning and concept-formation. The emotions, in relation both to cognition and to action, need examination. There is also an important function for the philosophy of mind in examining the presuppositions of psychology in its contribution to education, for it may be that in some of its phases psychology is confused in what it is trying to do, or that it is unconsciously assuming a certain concept of man which is quite inadequate and which certainly cannot be regarded simply as a given.

A further aspect of the philosopher's interest in educational principles arises from the fact that such principles are often organised into a comprehensive picture of the model educational situation. The role and validity of these models needs to be examined. Some of the things which have been said in the past about principles of education, however, are not of much interest to a philosopher, not because they are not right or sensible, but because they lack any kind of reasoned philosophical backing. There is a certain tradition of prophetic pronouncement which has not been without influence in the history of education, but which is perhaps of more interest to the historian of educational ideas than to the philosopher. This would be largely true of the writings of such educators as Pestalozzi and Montessori.

A third area in which the philosopher is interested is the more specific one of particular curriculum subjects and their rules of method. Here the various 'philosophies of', such as the philosophy of history, of religion, of mathematics and of science, moral philosophy and aesthetics are especially relevant. The issues here will be particular ones arising from puzzlement over some feature in one or another of these forms of understanding, such as the nature of a historical 'fact', the criteria of religious truth, the nature of unobservables in science, or the principles of art criticism. Another kind of issue is that of the extent to which the nature of a subject must determine how it is to be studied. This is the problem of 'the logical and the psychological'.

FURTHER READING
R. D. Archambault (ed.). *Philosophical Analysis and Education*, Routledge and Kegan Paul, 1965.

W. K. Frankena. *Three Historical Philosophies of Education*, Scott, Foresman, Chicago, Ill., 1965.
T. H. B. Hollins (ed.). *Aims in Education*, Manchester Univ. Press, Manchester, 1964.
D. J. O'Connor. *Introduction to the Philosophy of Education*, Routledge and Kegan Paul, 1957.
R. S. Peters. *Ethics and Education*, George Allen and Unwin, 1966.
R. S. Peters (ed.). *The Concept of Education*, Routledge and Kegan Paul, 1967.
L. A. Reid. *Philosophy and Education*, Heinemann, 1962.
I. Scheffler. *The Language of Education*, Blackwell, Oxford, 1960.
I. Scheffler (ed.). *Philosophy and Education*, Allyn and Bacon, Boston, Mass., 2nd ed. 1966.
B. O. Smith and R. H. Ennis (eds.). *Language and Concepts in Education*, Rand McNally, Chicago, Ill., 1961.

Periodicals
British Journal of Educational Studies. Twice yearly. London.
Educational Theory. Quarterly. New Brunswick, NJ.
Harvard Educational Review. Quarterly. Cambridge, Mass.
Studies in Philosophy and Education. Quarterly. Edwardsville, Ill.
See also individual philosophers

RFD

'Phonic' A word used to describe a method of teaching children to read which concentrates on the introduction of related sound-symbols in English.

Physical education
Historical background Probably the first to realise the values of what we now call physical education were the Spartans and the Athenians. The Spartan system was designed, primarily, to condition a man for military service; but that of Athens was much more balanced, having aims defined by Aristotle as 'health, strength and beauty'.

The Romans, too, were aware of the value of strenuous exercise both as recreation and as a form of military training. It is claimed that they were responsible for the introduction into Britain of primitive forms of football and boxing.

With the decline of Mediterranean power and influence, interest in PE was lost for some centuries. The first signs of reawakening interest came in the late 14th century, when an Italian, Da Feltre, ran a school in which physical activities such as riding, fencing, running, archery and daily exercises took their place alongside academic studies. In the 17th century, Locke in his treatise *Thoughts Concerning Education* stressed the physical as one of his three divisions of education—the others being the moral and intellectual aspects; while Rousseau emphasised the importance of the intimate relation between mind and body.

The great revival of interest, however, really began in Germany and Sweden in the 19th century. In the early 1800s, a practical teacher, Guts Muths, wrote *Gymnastics for the Young*, while a Prussian named Jahn opened the first outdoor gymnasium and also invented the horizontal bar. Between 1810 and 1858, another German, Spiess (who spent some time as a teacher in Froebel's school in Switzerland), was intimately concerned with the development of PE in schools. He produced a practical manual and ran courses for teachers. Perhaps his greatest contribution was his insistence that his teachers should have academic status as well as a knowledge of physical training. (The need for this was not appreciated in the UK until about 1934.)

In 1805, P. H. Ling, a teacher of languages and fencing at Lund University, Sweden, began to work out a system of gymnastics based on the anatomical needs of the body; and Nachtigal, of Copenhagen University, was responsible for making Denmark the first country in Europe to give physical training instruction as part of the normal curriculum.

In 1822, a Swiss army officer, C. H. Clias, was appointed to introduce gymnastics into the British army, the navy, and Charterhouse School; but the experiment came to an end in 1825 when Clias fell ill.

It was not until after 1860 that there was real progress in PE in schools. In 1870, the Education Act referred to 'drill' and suggested the employment of army drill instructors. In 1885, the Dartford Women's Physical Training College was opened and, significantly, the term 'drill' was replaced by 'physical exercise'. In 1904 the first official syllabus of physical training for schools was published.

In 1905, the army abandoned the German system of gymnastics and introduced Swedish gymnastics. Four years later, the Board of Education did the same, producing a syllabus based on the Swedish system. A new syllabus in 1919 stressed for the first time the recreative side of PE, though by modern standards the work was unbelievably dull and static. This syllabus remained in use until 1933.

1933–53 During the 14 years from 1919 to 1943, the germ of 'recreation' spread rapidly. In 1900 Professor L. P. Jacks published *The Education of the Whole Man* which stressed the indivisibility of academic and physical education. A further step forward was taken with the publication in 1933 of a new *Syllabus of Physical Training for Schools*. This swept aside the static work of the 1919 syllabus and offered, instead, freedom and movement. There was a weakness here, for to many teachers, movement and yet more movement became the be-all and the end-all of PE; they failed to distinguish between movement for its own sake and purposeful movement. However, as time went on the pendulum came to the end of its violent swing, and a balanced outlook began to prevail in most schools.

In the mid-30s, a new system, evolved by Neils Bukh of Denmark and called 'primary gymnastics', began to creep into PE schemes for secondary schools. In this system, rhythm and rhythmic movements played a

540

prominent part along with passive exercises, with the inevitable result that many teachers forgot everything but rhythm.

Thus in 1939 this country was in the rather curious position of having primary school PE based still on a Swedish system, while secondary school work was largely Danish in origin.

Post-war developments and present trends
Post-war developments in PE can be divided into two clearly defined parts: those in infant and junior schools, and those in secondary schools. In infant and junior schools, these developments might well be described as the age of apparatus and of self-expression in physical movement; while secondary school developments might be summarised as wider aspects of physical and social experience.

During the war years, much experimentation had been going on in primary PE. Those concerned with formulating policy came to the conclusion that any PE scheme for primary schools should be based on the natural play and physical interests of young children, and not on what adults considered they ought to be doing; that the children's experience of physical movement should be broadened and not confined to the somewhat formalised movements of the Swedish system; and that '"movement" is not simply an affair of muscles and strong joints but part and parcel of personality.'

It was realised that running, jumping, throwing, climbing, swinging and experimentation in physical movement were essential features of the growing-up process. To cater for the first five of these activities, many and varied pieces of apparatus were provided—some fixed in school playgrounds, others portable for use in school halls and playrooms. Formal teaching, necessary when using the old syllabus, largely gave way to individual coaching and encouragement. Early fears that this new apparatus might be highly dangerous proved groundless since 'caution and tendency to careful exploration are evident in children at all ages within the primary range.'[1]

The use of music as a motivation for physical experience has also spread considerably; and, with girls in particular, excellent results have been achieved. In many parts of the country this kind of work is also being done with boys, though there are conflicting views as to its suitability. In general, with an enthusiastic, skilled and dedicated teacher, this type of training can produce first-class results.

Another interesting development has been the lowering of the age at which swimming is introduced into schools. Today, when many primary schools are using shallow learner-pools, swimming is actually being taught to children under seven years of age, and children of all ages are being given instruction in survival swimming or 'drownproofing'.

In secondary schools, the narrow syllabus of formal gymnastics, together with two or three major games such as football, rugby and cricket, has given way to a much wider conception of PE. It has been realised more and more that PE should not be simply a means of physical development but a preparation for a full adult life. The outlook has also been affected by the prospect of a growth of automation and the increased leisure that will result. Thus new outdoor activities, such as rock climbing, orienteering (moving across country on compass bearings), canoeing, dinghy-sailing, adventure physical training, basic ski-training, archery, golf, riding, rowing, sub-aqua swimming and even gliding, have found their way into the curriculum.

In the gymnasia and sports halls now being built in many schools, formal gymnastics have given way to judo, weight training, basketball, volley ball, trampolining, fencing, badminton and circuit training.

Another important aspect of this wider conception of PE is that it has increased not only the range of activities but also the number of potential expert participants. Under the narrow conception of major games, many boys and girls were classed as 'poor at games', when in fact they were poor only at the few games provided. A poor football player might have turned out to be an international fencer had he been introduced at school to fencing, and given basic instruction. With increasing publicly-provided, reasonably cheap sports facilities, there is scope for further expansion; and in the near future, sports and recreations such as water-skiing and go-cart racing might well become commonplace in schools.

See also **Gymnasia; Games, Organised; Health education**

REFERENCE

1. *Moving and Growing: Physical Education in the Primary School*, HMSO, Part I, 1952.

FURTHER READING

HMSO. *Moving and Growing: Physical Education in the Primary School*, Part I, 1952. *Planning the Programme: Physical Education in the Primary School*, Part II, 1952.

P. C. McIntosh. *Physical Education in England since 1800*, Bell, 1952.

P. C. McIntosh, J. G. Dixon, A. D. Munrow and R. F. Willetts. *Landmarks in the History of Physical Education*, Routledge and Kegan Paul, 1957.

M. W. Randall. *Modern Ideas on Physical Education*, Bell, 1967.

JE

Physical Education Association of Great Britain and Northern Ireland
A non-governmental body founded in 1899 as the Ling Physical Education Association, the Association exists to encourage and facilitate the scientific study of the physical health of the community through physical and health education and recreation. Among its objects is to educate and instruct specialist teachers in physical and health education and recreation in current theory and practice, both in the UK and overseas. It conducts research, issues publications, arranges meetings and discussions, provides an information and advisory service together with a lecture service, and maintains a reference library which includes a comprehensive collection of relevant British and foreign periodicals.

Ling Hse, 10 Nottingham Pl., London, W1.

Physical education equipment
Before the second world war PE equipment was mainly limited to small items such as balls, skittles and mats in primary schools, and portable gymnastic apparatus such as vaulting boxes, bucks and horses, mats and benches in secondary schools.

Towards the end of the war, heaving, swinging and climbing apparatus was introduced with excellent effect into primary schools, on the grounds that the fundamental desires of children to throw, climb and swing were not being satisfied. Fears that such equipment would lead to a great increase in the accident rate were not justified; this was due to the sensible attitude of teachers who refrained from transmitting their own fears to the children, and to the children's own instinct of self-preservation.

With broadening concepts of PE, new apparatus such as the trampoline, weight training equipment and even climbing walls (for basic mountaineering training) was introduced into secondary schools. The tendency, however, has been to take more activities out of doors; standard equipment in many schools now includes items such as canoes, sailing dinghies, tents, archery and climbing apparatus.

JE

Physical education training colleges There are eight PE colleges for women and one for men in England and Scotland (*see* Appendix). These colleges provide three-year courses for teachers of phsyical training. Various other general colleges of education provide main courses in PE for men and women, and some provide a special one-year supplementary course for teachers who have completed two years of general training. At the University of Birmingham, PE may be offered as one half of the BA honours degree in combined subjects. At Leeds University a diploma in PE is offered by the Institute of Education after a one-year course, but this is open only to qualified teachers who must normally have had not less than five years' teaching experience. The University of Manchester accepts PE as part of the post-graduate studies on education.

Physical Recreation, Central Council of Formed in 1935, and sponsored by the Physical Education Association of Great Britain and Northern Ireland and the British Association of Organisers and Lecturers in Physical Education, the Council is a national voluntary organisation, in receipt of grant-aid from the DES and the Ministry of Education for Northern Ireland. Its aim is to promote and improve the physical health of the community through physical recreation. Two-thirds of the 300 members represent national bodies concerned with the development of some branch of physical recreation.

The CCPR offers administrative, technical and advisory services, gives practical assistance in the organisation of conferences, training courses, displays, lectures and film shows, and arranges national and regional conferences. It organises a training programme in which the main emphasis is on courses for those willing to train as coaches or instructors. Most local courses are held in evenings or at weekends; national courses are usually residential.

A distinctive and increasingly important part of the CCPR's work is carried on at National Recreation Centres, which combine residential accommodation with first-class facilities for a wide range of physical activities. In addition to serving the general public, these centres can be booked by sports bodies, youth organisations, colleges of education, for conferences, training courses and other events. The four centres so far established are at Bisham Abbey, Berks; Lilleshall Hall, Shropshire; Plas y Brenin, Caernarvonshire; and Crystal Palace, London (the largest multi-sports centre in the country, with a floodlit stadium seating 12,000, an Olympic swimming pool, and a large sports hall). It is hoped that a National Sailing Centre will be opened at Cowes, Isle of Wight, and a National Recreation Centre for Wales at Cardiff.

An information service supplies schools, sports clubs, youth clubs, etc. with full details of the CCPR's activities.

26 Park Cres., London, W1.

See also **Crystal Palace National Recreation Centre**

Physically handicapped pupils These were defined in 1945 as 'pupils not suffering solely from a defect of sight and hearing who by reason of disease or crippling defect cannot, without detriment to their health or educational development, be satisfactorily educated under the normal regime of ordinary schools.'[1] This category is a very varied one including various crippling conditions resulting from poliomyelitis, cerebral palsy, spina bifida, muscular dystrophy and congenital deformities, as well as heart disease and haemophilia.

Little was done for the education of crippled children until the end of the 19th century. Even after elementary education became compulsory, physically handicapped children were usually exempted because of transport difficulties. It was by the efforts of the Charity Organisation Society, the Invalid Children's Aid Association and various university settlements that schools were established, especially the first day schools in London and Liverpool and the famous Chailey Heritage Craft School (established 1903). Provision is now adequate to meet the needs as the number of physically handicapped children is falling.

Since 1945 there has been growing interest in the education of cerebral-palsied children, including spastic and athetoid children. Since this condition is due to brain injury, the children may have multiple disability including defects of speech, vision and hearing, abnormalities of perception and limited general intelligence. A voluntary body, the Spastics Society, has raised funds to finance research and improve facilities for education and training.

In schools for physically handicapped children, the maximum size of class is 20. Many day schools admit children under official school age. Medical and surgical care, nursing and physiotherapy are important features of the special educational treatment. Special equipment is devised to aid physical control, mobility and manipulation. The curriculum is not different from that in normal schools, except in cases of dual handicap. At one time vocational training (e.g. in tailoring and bootmaking) was prevalent. This has been abandoned in favour of general education, both practical and academic, but pupils leaving special schools can proceed to vocational training covering a wider range of occupations.

Hospitals providing prolonged medical or orthopaedic treatment for children usually have a school established in the hospital premises by the local education authorities. Tuition can also be provided for any child who is in a general or children's hospital even for a few weeks.

Teachers may have additional training for work with physically handicapped children or a general training in the education of handicapped children. Such training is not yet compulsory.

See also **Delicate children; Spastic children**

REFERENCE
1. *The Welfare of Children in Hospital*, HMSO, 1959.
FURTHER READING
HMSO. *The Health of the School Child*, 1962–3, 1964.
R. Illingworth. *Recent Advances in Cerebral Palsy*, Churchill, 1958.

MW

Physics, Teaching of Contemporary physics teaching is beginning to assume a shape and style different from that of a decade ago. For generations physics courses have been based on mechanics, magnetism and electricity, heat, light and sound—areas of physics which appeared to be relatively self-contained and coherent and seemed fundamental to the subject as a whole. The increasing importance of theoretical and practical physics of the atom, the electron and kinetic theory, together with the breadth of phenomena and understanding which a study of wave motion can embrace, have caused a regrouping of subject matter more in line with mid-20th century knowledge. An example of an up-to-date physics course is that of the Nuffield Science Teaching Project which is based on these and other topics, together with the energy and mechanics which will always be fundamental to a sound understanding of physics at any level. For 50 years it has been claimed that a large fraction of the time studying physics in school should be spent on practical work by pupils themselves. Many time-tables include for each form a single theory period and two practical periods per week to allow plenty of pupil experiment. Much of the practical has been routine, repetitive work checking the validity of laws and the values of constants, every boy carrying out the same experiment and often writing a stereotyped account for homework. New courses retain much practical work, but this is less formal and confined than it used to be.

Apparatus has been carefully designed so that a boy can ask of it questions that require a thoughtful contribution from him and yet will produce results that are meaningful in terms of the subject. He notes his results in a clear, concise and pertinent form as they are taken, rather than forcing them into a standard format later.

For the most able pupils, today's physics teaching is designed to match the interests of boys and girls to the theoretical structures of the subject. Induction from observations precedes theorising and mathematical deductions. Areas of study are chosen to illuminate and exemplify developments in the thinking of physicists, and experiments and methods of treatment are determined substantially by the interests and abilities of the boys and girls. New courses in all science subjects are proliferating throughout the world. The major contribution which workers in physics have made here is in this matching of subject to boys' interest. The large number of pieces of apparatus required to keep every boy experimenting, and the sophistication of some of the specialised demonstration equipment, make today's physics teaching expensive and require the services of skilled technicians and storemen if the teacher's skills are to be used to the full.

For less able pupils, many teachers are developing their own schemes, less confined by the logic of theoretical physics and even more closely related to boys' and girls' interests. Household electricity, a motor-car gear-box, or a camera can be the starting-point for a study taking what it needs from electricity, mechanics or optics. The range of activities and abilities which can be covered by such an approach is wide— from model-making to a highly theoretical treatment. It may be a means of drawing pupils' attention to the interest and opportunities existing in technology, a field which does not yet have much influence on the teaching of physics in most of our schools.

FURTHER READING
Association for Science Education. *Science and Education: Physics for Grammar Schools, An Expansion and Teachers' Guide to Physics for Grammar Schools*, John Murray, 1961.
Nuffield Science Teachers' Project. *Fifteen Physics Tests*, Longmans/Penguin, 1966–7.

See also **Nuffield Foundation; Science, Teaching of**

PER

Piaget, Jean (b. 1896) Unquestionably one of the great pioneers in psychological investigation and theory, Piaget has revolutionised our understanding of intellectual growth in young children. Working in the Universities of Paris and Geneva, and devising ingenious experimental situations for children, including his own, Piaget has been able to build up a picture of the child's world that is still largely uncontradicted. For example, it is now believed that the young child will see everything as necessarily revolving around himself: if he wants an object, he often feels it therefore becomes his as of right, and that the event of his going to bed will in itself cause night to fall. Gradually, however, he will learn to explore his environment and organise his experiences into coherent patterns. Piaget makes the point most strongly that this sort of organisation has to be learned through constant exploration and play, and that if a child is deprived of fairly wide sensory and motor experience in his first years, then his development may be seriously retarded.

Many of children's judgements and perceptions at the infant stage are based on what a child sees from his own viewpoint, and often on the immediately visible aspects of the situation such as apparent height and width, rather than on any simple logic. Thus, many children under seven will imagine taller people to be older than shorter people, or that seven matches spread out on a table will be more numerous than seven matches put close together in a small group, because in each case they *look* bigger. Ideas on time, space, weight and length are similarly subjective. By about the age of seven, however, children seem to become less ego-centric and can think quite logically for themselves when faced with simple concrete problems which they are allowed to solve largely for themselves. Genuine abstract thought, though, does not really develop until a child is anything from 11 to 14 years old, and formal education before this time, based on abstract reasoning and suppositions, will probably be wasted. Even though some young people may be able to reproduce, for example, certain quite abstract geometric concepts while still in their 'concrete' stage, it is improbable that many of them will have really understood what they are doing, unless they have worked out those concepts by concrete methods. In fact Piaget stresses that before moving on to abstract thought, it is most important that children should have worked through most of the stages of concrete reasoning in order to build up a proper foundation.

It is impossible to summarise briefly the many other contributions Piaget has made to our understanding of children's use of language, and their basic intellectual development. He has sometimes been criticised for basing too many of his findings on children functioning in a laboratory rather than in a classroom; while others find the questions he has put to children, in an effort to probe their understanding, somewhat too leading in tone. Yet it is remarkable how many of Piaget's findings have since been confirmed by other psychologists. His main conclusions, particularly that children learn by continuous interaction with their environment, and that they go through a succession of intellectual stages that should be respected by the teacher, have had a strong indirect effect upon activity and discovery methods now used in schools.

FURTHER READING

J. H. Flavell. *The Developmental Psychology of Jean Piaget*, Van Nostrand, Princeton, NJ, 1963.
Nathan Isaacs. *The Growth of Understanding in the Young Child*, Educational Supply Association, 1961.

NT

Pilgrim Trust Founded in 1930 by the late Edward Stephen Harkness of New York, the Trust exists to help preserve the national heritage of the UK, and to promote the future well-being of the country and its people. Since the last war it has devoted the main part of its resources to proposals for the encouragement of learning and the arts and for the preservation of ancient buildings, historical records and the countryside.

Millbank Hse, 2 Great Peter St, London, SW1.

Pilkington Committee (1966), Report of *See* **Agriculture, Qualifications in**

Planetarium, London Schools *See* **Astronomy in schools**

Plato (428–347 BC) Plato's main works relating to education are the *Republic, Laws, Meno* and *Protagoras*.

Socrates had been convinced that the excellence of the good man lay in his knowledge, yet neither the Athenian public nor the professional teachers, called the Sophists, seemed on examination to possess such knowledge. Where, then, was this knowledge to be found?

Plato argued that besides the world of sense-perception there must exist a second order of reality consisting of unchanging Forms, such as Justice, Equality, Beauty, and the Good. Knowledge, as opposed to shifting opinion, is possible of the Forms alone, but to gain such knowledge is a task within the capacity of only a very few. These few, as authorities on the Good, should rule in the ideal city-state, frame its laws, control its size, wealth and outside contacts, and above all supervise its educational system.

First, they should select and rigorously train those few who are by nature fitted to rule. Their character should be formed by literature, music and physical education, then they should be led, through a study of mathematics, to turn towards the Forms and ultimately to the vision of the Good itself.

In the *Laws*, it is clearer that for the majority Plato thought it sufficient to be imbued with true doctrine. To attain this end of unquestioning acceptance, every important environmental influence should be used and controlled. Games, stories, the arts and popular religion all ought to be censored, shaped or invented to obtain the desired result of a self-perpetuating, unchanging, harmonious society.

See also **Philosophy of education**

RFD

Play centres Whereas playgrounds in parks or blocks of flats are supervised by a caretaker or attendant, perhaps responsible to the Housing or Parks Committee, play centres are run by the LEA, and are looked after by an approved supervisor with one or two assistants. Functioning mainly in school buildings after school hours or during the holidays, play centres usually offer a fairly wide range of activity to children who are already attending their own school or nursery. There are also some play parks, under the supervision of an approved play leader, open for all children up to the age of 15, and although these too are not designed for the under-fives, they can sometimes be accepted. Adventure playgrounds (*q.v.*), such as those organised by the Save the Children Fund, are yet another variation.

FURTHER READING
Lady Allen of Hurtwood. *Design for Play*, The Housing Centre Trust, 1962.

Play groups Pre-school play groups originally were privately organised by the many parents who were generally unable to find nursery class places for their children, but who still felt that some experience of social play is necessary before beginning full-time schooling. There is now a National Association of Pre-school Playgroups (*q.v.*), and altogether about 20,000 children are making use of these groups at present. The Association also runs courses for potential supervisors, and has always made it clear that playgroups are a stop-gap rather than a replacement for proper nursery education, when it is available.

Playground duty Supervision of children in a school playground is performed by teachers as a duty additional to their normal teaching duties. It is usually shared among the members of a school staff on a rota basis and normally covers the period immediately before school commences, and the mid-morning and mid-afternoon breaks; it might also cover the lunch hour, depending on the general arrangements made for supervision of school meals, but rarely applies to the period after school hours. The number of teachers on 'playground duty' at any one time will depend on the size of the school and location of its playground space and will be determined by the head-teacher.

The reason for this element of supervision over and above the normal supervision for which a teacher is responsible in the classroom arises from the special relationship between a school's staff and its pupils. The teacher is said to be *in loco parentis* to his pupils. This relationship means that at all times when the teacher has charge of children, he or she is under a duty to exercise that standard of care which would be expected of a careful and prudent parent in like circumstances. In the event of any injury to a pupil, which could be attributed to a lapse in this standard of care, the teacher might incur some legal liability in respect of that injury. In addition, as employers are held in law to be vicariously responsible for the negligent acts of their employees committed in the course of their employment, the LEA or governors or managers of the school could also be held to be legally liable for the injuries to pupils arising from the negligent acts of staff.

It follows, therefore, that a reasonable system and standard of supervision is a necessity in the schools of this country, although the system must be adapted to meet the needs and requirements of the particular school and its pupils. The periods when children are at play in the school playground are obviously a time when they are at risk, and when an element of supervision is necessary. The responsibility of the teacher or teachers on duty at this time is to exercise that 'standard of care which would be expected of a careful and prudent parent in like circumstances.' Since the number of teachers on duty at any one time will be limited, the degree of supervision exercised is inevitably less rigorous than in the individual classroom.

See also **Extraneous duties; Accidents in schools**

FJ

Playing fields At one time many schools had neither playing fields on their sites nor even access to any in local parks and recreation grounds. Today, children from old schools still lacking their own facilities are often taken considerable distances by special transport to the outer suburbs of large cities, where extensive and well-equipped playing fields have been laid out for their use. It is obligatory for all new schools to be provided with such fields on the site, to certain fixed scales as laid down in the DES publication *Building Bulletin 28: Playing Fields and Hard Surface Areas* (1965).

It is present-day government policy not to provide fields as such for infants'

schools; a 'hard' area is compulsory, but the space can be used in a flexible manner, and the tendency is now to devote part of the stipulated area for conventional PE purposes and part for such things as 'adventure' and 'activity' areas, designed to provide 'a varied and stimulating environment in surroundings very different from the expanses of brick and concrete in which the children so often live'.

In junior schools, provision must be made for playing fields, ranging from half an acre for schools of up to 50 children to three acres for the largest school.

In secondary schools, the building regulations now permit 'the provision of a hard porous surface of up to one-half the grass area'. This, ideally, should be quick-drying, hard-wearing, non-slip, suitable for use in times of snow and frost, not too expensive to contruct and maintain, suitable for minor and major ball games and reasonably soft to fall down on. No complete answer has yet been found that fulfils all these conditions, but much experimental work is being done. It is visualised that, in the future, these and other school playing facilities will be used by children and other local organisations at weekends and holidays when the schools are not occupied.

Where school playing areas are grass only, the minimum areas must be: for two-form-entry, boys, $7\frac{1}{2}$ acres; for three-form-entry, mixed, 10 acres; and for three-form-entry, girls, $8\frac{1}{2}$ acres.

The National Playing Fields Association gives advice and technical assistance to schools, youth and adult organisations. Its booklet *That Playing Field You Want* (1965) gives sources of financial assistance.

National Playing Fields Association, 57b Catherine Pl., London, SW1.

JE

Playing Fields Association, National The Association aims to ensure that facilities for active recreation are available to every member of the community.

Supported by its affiliated county and city associations, the NPFA operates in three main ways. First, it offers financial help. Since its formation in 1925, almost £2m., all raised voluntarily, has been given or lent to local authorities, sports clubs and voluntary organisations, providing some 13,000 different facilities. In 1965, the total money allocated in grants and loans (£120,643) was almost 50% higher than the 1964 figure.

Secondly, it gives advice. The NPFA operates a free technical advisory service, undertakes original research in association with other sports bodies, and publishes a wide range of technical booklets.

Thirdly, it persuades. It urges local authorities to provide sufficient facilities for sport, to grant rating relief to sports clubs, to start play leadership schemes, and to allow public use of school fields, and so on. The Association also vigorously opposes plans to erect buildings on public open spaces.

An annual conference is held in London.

Playfield House, 57b Catherine Place, London, SW10.

Playing Fields Officers, Association of Membership of this professional body is drawn from England, Scotland, Wales and Northern Ireland. Technical papers based on the collective experience of members are circulated to members.

Gen. Sec.: A. Jordan, Brooksby Agricultural College, Brooksby, Melton Mowbray, Leics.

Playing Fields Society, London The objects of the Society are to encourage and develop outdoor physical recreation in the Greater London area by providing playing fields for the benefit of clubs and schools in this area.

The Society was founded in 1890 and by the generosity of many organi-

sations and private individuals, including members of the royal family, was enabled to buy and equip several playing fields in the London area. It now holds four large grounds—at Boston Manor (near Brentford), Raynes Park, Walthamstow, and Fairlop Oak (near Ilford), totalling 150 acres in all. It was granted a royal charter in 1925.

45 Denison Hse, Vauxhall Bridge Rd, London, SW1.

Plowden Report (1967): 'Children and their Primary Schools' The Central Advisory Council for Education (England) was asked in 1963 by the Minister, Sir Edward Boyle, to 'consider primary education in all its aspects, and the transition to secondary education.' Under its chairman, Lady Plowden, the Council reported in 1967.

Among its 197 recommendations and conclusions, some of the most important urged that there should be greater and more effectual contact between home and school; that educational priority areas should be designated in which the schools should be favoured by 'positive discrimination'; that in such areas measures should be taken to improve the ratio of teachers to children to a point at which no class exceeded 30; that teachers in these areas should be paid additions to their salaries; that approximately £5,000 should be allocated for minor works in each school in priority areas; that in these areas especially, but ultimately in all areas, community schools (q.v.) should be developed; that various steps should be taken to improve the education of children of immigrants; that there should be a large expansion of nursery education; that as soon as there was nursery provision for all children whose parents wished it, for a year before starting school, the normal time by which a child should go to school should be the September term following his fifth birthday; that in the interim children should begin full-time attendance at school twice a year, those reaching the age of five between 1 February and 31 August in the September following, and those reaching five between 1 September and 31 January in the following April; that there should be a three-year course in a first (at present the infant) school, and that this should be followed by a four-year course in a middle (at present the junior) school; that there should be flexibility both in entry to school and in transfer between the first and middle stages, allowing for individual differences; that the most suitable organisation of primary education was in separate first and middle schools, with some exceptions in rural areas and for some voluntary schools; that children should make at least one visit to their new school in the term before they entered it, and that parents should receive leaflets from the authorities explaining the choice of secondary schools available and the courses provided in them; that the most satisfactory size for new reorganised first schools should be taken to be 240 children, and for middle schools 300 to 450; that there should be more freedom in the interpretation of the law on the Act of Worship, and that further inquiry should be made into the aspects of religious faith that can be presented to young children; and that corporal punishment should be forbidden.

Recommendations were also made on school-staffing, on the deployment of staff, on the training of primary school teachers (into which the Council believed there should be a full inquiry), on the training of nursery assistants and teachers' aides, and on the independent primary schools (the DES, it was suggested, should reconsider the terms 'recognised' and 'registered' and try to devise more informative ones). On primary school buildings and equipment, the Report recommended that the government should make additional money available for a building programme of minor works over seven years, starting in 1971, at an annual cost of £7–10 million, the aim being to rid primary schools of their worst deficiencies.

See also **Primary education**

FURTHER READING
Children and their Primary Schools, 2 vols, HMSO, 1967.

Poetry, Teaching of Poetry, in the form of songs, rhymes, spells and incantations, is an important part of most children's lives, informing and intensifying their games and their lore. But at about 16, many adolescents leave school with a marked distaste for it; it serves none of their needs and is not merely irrelevant but a bore. The reasons for this are many and complex. One source of trouble is that pupils are told too much *about* poetry—definitions of figures of speech, details of the poet's biography, and sonnet rhyme-schemes. Again, too much of the poetry that they meet derives from experiences that they cannot comprehend, let alone enter into and feel. Furthermore, it is enclosed within a 'poetry lesson', and turned by hook or by crook into 'work'.

There are, however, signs of change. Teachers are recognising more and more that learning and involvement are active, and that an active re-creation of the poem is one of the most congenial ways in which to possess it. Similarly, the experiences and situations from which the poem emerges are crucial to any degree of understanding; so poems are finding their way into the classroom that speak of conditions and states of feeling and of mind in which pupils can see themselves. The range of poetry is also being enlarged, to embrace not only official poetry by recognised poets but also folk-songs and ballads, English, American and Australian, both rural and industrial. The BBC is doing excellent work in this field, especially in its *Listening and Writing* programmes, and is helping us to recognise the close personal relationship between the act of taking others' poems and making them our own, and of making poems out of our own selves and our own world.

Few teachers will claim that the poems their pupils write are works of art: this is not the point. The delight and satisfaction are found in the making, in the recording of a valued experience, in fixing it in words: such activities are important as experience at a personal level; the quality of what is made is a secondary matter, although many pupils surprise by the vivacity and felicity of what they make.

FURTHER READING

M. L. Hourd. *The Education of the Poetic Spirit*, Heinemann, 1949.

M. L. Hourd and G. E. Cooper. *Coming into their Own: A Study of the Idiom of Young Children Revealed in their Verse-Writing*, Heinemann, 1959.

GS

Poetry Book Society Ltd Non-profit-making and financially assisted by the Arts Council of Great Britain, the Society provides its members with a book of new English poetry every quarter, chosen by selectors appointed annually. The subscription costs no more than the total published price of the books received. A quarterly *Bulletin* is published, with contributions from the authors of books chosen and recommended, together with a special poetry supplement at Christmas and an annual checklist of books of new verse. Many schools are in membership.

4 St James's Sq., London, SW1.

Poetry Society The Society is an association of members dedicated to the encouragement of the writing and speaking of poetry and its appreciation as a living art. It is a registered educational charity, open to all poetry-lovers, which conducts nearly 20,000 examinations in speech annually, leading up to the Gold Medal, the highest award in the country. The Board of Examiners is headed by Sir John Gielgud and Dame Sybil Thorndike, supported by 25 highly qualified teachers of speech and drama.

21 Earls Court Sq., London, SW5.

Poland, Education in In Poland the primary and secondary schools, as well as teacher training colleges, come under the Ministry of Education; the universities, technical and agricultural colleges and schools of economics come under the jurisdiction of the Ministry of Higher Education, while medical schools are the concern of the Ministry of Health and Social Welfare. Fine art colleges are under the Ministry of Culture and Art, military colleges under the Ministry of National Defence, and physical education colleges under the Central Committee for Physical Culture and Tourism.

Children over three years of age may attend nursery schools which are run both by the state and by community organisations. In 1964/65 28.1% of urban children aged three to six and 16.1% of rural children were in nursery schools (a total of 580,000). Compulsory primary education over an eight-year period was introduced in 1966, the normal age range being seven to 15 years; but if a young person begins employment without completing his eight-year period he is obliged to attend an evening school for workers and, for him, compulsory education continues until 17 years. The secondary school system is wide-ranging, including general, vocational, technical and agricultural studies, all of which can lead on to graduate status. The state system also provides for working people to continue their education on part-time basis up to graduate level. In 1966/67 primary schools totalled 25,564 with an enrolment of 5,527,050 pupils; secondary schools, 866 with an enrolment of 322,706; and students in the country's 76 colleges of higher education (including eight universities) numbered 273,227.

The population of the country was approximately 31½ million in 1965.

Polish Cultural Institute Founded to promote cultural exchanges between Great Britain and Poland.

16 Devonshire St, London, W1.

Polytechnics The term *polytechnic* first came into general use towards the end of the 19th and beginning of the 20th century when certain charitable bodies founded institutes in the London area, in the wake of the general development of Mechanics' Institutes (*q.v.*). During the first quarter of the 20th century expansion of the work of the London polytechnics and the effect of inflation, together with a growing realisation of the importance of the work of these colleges for economic, social and political reasons, caused an increasing amount of financial assistance to be given by the local authority concerned and the London polytechnics became 'aided' institutions deriving an ever-growing proportion of their financial income from the public purse. Nearly all technical and other further education colleges founded outside the London area were wholly dependent on finance derived from the local authority concerned and were thus 'maintained' institutions. The London polytechnics, however, have to this day preserved their aided status and thereby a significant measure of financial and governmental independence, although virtually the whole of their income, apart from the relatively small proportion from students' fees, now derives from the local authority concerned.

During the period 1919 to 1939 the bulk of the growth of further education took place by means of evening classes, although there were notable exceptions in London and elsewhere where a significant number of full-time courses at university level were developed. Most of this full-time university work was made possible by the University of London external degree system. In a very small number of cases local arrangements were made for internal degrees of neighbouring universities.

The social and technological demands of society after 1945 resulted in a growing recognition of the importance of part-time day release and of full-time or sandwich courses, especially for qualifications at or near degree level. The technical colleges generally made a large and socially important contribution to the provision of higher education for ex-service men and women after the second world war, but the facilities and staff resources built up in the colleges came to be less effectively used during the 1950s. In order to rationalise the provision of courses and to use scarce resources more effectively, the government introduced in 1956 a classification of colleges into four categories, namely colleges of advanced technology, regional colleges, area colleges and local colleges[1]. There was, however, considerable overlap in the terms of reference of, for instance, CATs and regional colleges as well as between other groups within the new classification.

The establishment of the National Council for Technological Awards in 1955 provided an opportunity for the larger and more developed colleges, mainly, though not wholly, CATs and regional colleges, to provide qualifications of honours degree standard in science and technology which rapidly gained national recognition.

The Robbins Report (*q.v.*) on Higher Education[2] recommended that the then CATs should become technological universities with full university rights and privileges and this recommendation was implemented by the then government almost immediately. The Robbins Committee also recommended that 'some ten' regional and other colleges or combinations of colleges should attain independent university status during the period

1963 to 1980. The Committee recommended that until these colleges attained university status and in respect of other further education colleges who would remain outside the university ambit, a Council for National Academic Awards be set up to enable such colleges to provide courses leading to honours and ordinary degrees without the inhibiting features of the London University external degree system.

The Council for National Academic Awards was set up by Royal Charter during 1964, but the government of the day decided that further universities should not be created and that no regional or other college should be allowed to attain university status either in its own right or by association with neighbouring universities for at least ten years. The government's philosophy concerning continuance of a binary or dual system of higher education was explained by the Secretary of State for Education and Science in a speech at Woolwich Polytechnic in 1965[3].

It was clear, however, that the larger regional colleges in particular required a more positive policy framework than that provided by the negative decision not to allow any of them to progress towards university independence. The then Joint Minister of State at the DES established an informal advisory group to discuss the future of the higher education system in the public sector. As a result the government published a White Paper in 1965[4]. This White Paper outlined proposals for the establishment of about thirty polytechnics based largely on the regional colleges, including in some cases amalgamations or mergers of existing colleges some miles apart and of certain colleges of art and commerce. It was also envisaged that a limited number of specialist institutions would be created in respect of certain not wholly defined colleges providing specialist higher education which could not,

or would not, become parts of polytechnics.

After receiving comments on this White Paper from national representative bodies concerned with higher education and various Regional Councils, the Secretary of State published an Administrative Memorandum in 1967[5], which set out in some detail the organisational, governmental and academic provisions he expected to be made for the proposed polytechnics and a list of thirty such polytechnics which he proposed to designate, subject to the receipt of adequate proposals on government and academic organisation in respect of them. Proposals were to be submitted by the LEAs concerned for the approval of the Secretary of State. Final designations were expected to be announced in the academic year 1968/69 with a view to the naming of the polytechnics coming into formal existence by September 1969.

The method of government envisaged for these new polytechnics is based on a continuance of policy control by elected LEAs. Apart from major decisions of policy and finance, however, which are by statute reserved to such LEAs, it is intended that the day-to-day decisions and the implementation of the policy agreed by the LEA shall be carried out by strong governing bodies upon which elected LEA members will be in a small minority. The remainder of the governing body will consist of members of the academic staff of the polytechnic, representatives of both sides of industry, of professional bodies and of certain individuals with a particular contribution to make in the public sector of higher education. The proposals also involve the creation of strong academic boards for the polytechnics which will recommend to the governing body the academic policy for the institution.

The polytechnics are to be concerned with higher education for full-time (including sandwich) as well as part-time students. For this purpose higher education has been defined as comprising those courses devised for students normally aged 18 years and over and possessing at least five passes at GCE O level. This definition has clearly been adopted in order to include within it colleges of education for the training of teachers. Most of the courses likely to be found in polytechnics will have higher minimum academic qualifications.

It is clear that the broad policy intention of the government is to concentrate full-time and, so far as reasonably practicable part-time, higher education in the polytechnics on grounds of general economy and the use of scarce resources in buildings and manpower. The system of government consisting of academic boards and governing body in the manner defined is clearly similar to that of Senate and Council of the modern universities. The principal difference lies in the fact that the major policy decisions about capital investment and finance will be subject to the agreement of LEAs concerned, consisting of elected members. In terms of courses to be provided the principal characteristic of the new style polytechnics, which can be reasonably looked on as emerging state universities, will be the provision of a proportion of part-time courses of higher education, greater bias towards applied courses in science, technology and the social sciences than is customary in most universities, and continuing and developing strong links with industry, commerce and the public services, as well as research programmes and higher-degree courses of an applied and industry-orientated nature.

The number of students for whom the new style polytechnics are likely to provide higher education is considerable. Precise statistics cannot be available at the present time because the latest published figures are in respect of November 1966. The amalgamations of certain colleges and the inclusion of selected colleges of art and commerce in proposed polytechnics also makes it impossible to obtain a precise estimate. Nevertheless, it can be said that in November 1965 the universities in England and Wales had some 140,000 first-degree, higher-degree and diploma students. At the same time the public sector, excluding colleges of art, had over 21,000 students on such courses. Of these nearly 13,000 were in the then 25 regional colleges. Since then there has been a considerable upsurge in the number of CNAA degree students at the colleges which will in almost all cases become polytechnics, and it is reasonable to estimate that in 1969 one-fifth to one-sixth of all undergraduate and postgraduate students in England and Wales will be in the polytechnics. In addition, of course, the polytechnics will provide for substantial numbers of students on Higher National Diploma and similar full-time and sandwich courses, and for many thousands of part-time students on regular courses and on short advanced courses of the refresher and up-dating type.

See also **Further education,** etc. and **Technical education**

REFERENCES
1. Ministry of Education. *The Organisation of Technical Colleges*, Circular 305, HMSO, 1956.
2. Committee on Higher Education. *Higher Education*, Cmnd 2154, HMSO, 1963.
3. Department of Education and Science. *The Role in Higher Education of Regional and Other Technical Colleges Engaged in Advanced Work*, Administrative Memorandum 7/65 (including Secretary of State's Woolwich speech).
4. Department of Education and Science. *A Plan for Polytechnics and Other Colleges*, Cmnd 3006, HMSO, 1966.
5. Department of Education and Science, *Polytechnics*, Administrative Memorandum 8/67.

AJR

Pony Club The objects of this organisation are to encourage young people to ride and to provide instruction both in horsemastership and the care of their animals, thus promoting sportsmanship, citizenship and loyalty and cultivating strength of character and self-discipline.

There are 274 branches in the British Isles, administered by a District Commissioner assisted by a local committee. Membership is open to boys and girls under 21 years of age and is divided into two sections: ordinary members under 17 and associates 17 to 21 years.

The main activity within the branches is the Working Rally at which some form of instruction is given, either mounted or dismounted. Visits to places of interest, such as studs, kennels, etc., inter-branch competitions and special shows are organised. Most branches hold a summer camp.

Efficiency certificates are awarded by the Pony Club as an encouragement to members to improve their standard of riding and horsemastership.

National Equestrian Centre, Stoneleigh, Kenilworth, Warwickshire.

Pony trekking A relatively new form of outdoor recreation that has grown rapidly in popularity with young people over recent years. It combines basic instruction in horse riding and horse management with healthy outdoor recreation, usually in picturesque locations such as the Scottish Highlands, the Lake District, North Wales, Dartmoor, Exmoor and the Pennines. Courses or holidays at comfortable centres in areas such as these are normally open to those over sixteen years of age with or without any experience of riding.

The first two or three days of the week or fortnight are spent in learning such basic techniques as saddling, mounting, stopping and grooming the ponies provided. Once these fundamentals are mastered, gradually lengthening rides are made along unfrequented lanes and hill tracks. The course often concludes with a two-day trek, including an over-night stay under canvas in relatively wild or open moorland country.

A number of local authorities already provide facilities for pony trekking at their own out-door pursuits centres. Many private centres throughout the country run courses at reasonable cost.

The Central Council for Physical Recreation has popularised this admirable form of recreation, organising courses during the spring and summer months at several centres in the British Isles. Particulars of these can be obtained from their headquarters, 26–29 Park Cres., London, W1.

JE

Pool of ability The Crowther Report 1959 (*q.v.*), finding that length of education is related more closely to parents' occupation and size of family than to ability, concluded that many children of high promise were not benefiting fully from their education. 'It may well be', the Report commented, 'that there is a pool of ability that imposes an upper limit on what can be done by education at any given time. But if so it is sufficiently clear that the limit has not been reached and will not even be approached without much more in the way of inducement and opportunity'.

Portugal, Education in Education is free and compulsory from the age of six to 11 years, and the upper limit is to be extended to 13 years in 1970. About 70% of the total population of 9¼ million (1965) is literate. In 1964/65 there were 17,120 public primary schools (enrolment 850,105); 795 private primary schools (enrolment 44,090); 446 secondary and grammar schools (enrolment 144,657); 436 technical and profession-training colleges (enrolment 153,870); and seven colleges of music (enrolment 176). There are three universities at Lisbon, Coimbra and Oporto (enrolment 21,007); a technical university at

Lisbon (enrolment 4,600); and military and naval colleges and art schools at Lisbon and Oporto (enrolment 2,031).

Positive reinforcement Knowledge of success in a given task, and of the pleasures and rewards that can follow this success, are basically what is meant by positive reinforcement. It seems to work most effectively if it comes soon after the child has succeeded, in the sense that it will immediately 'reinforce' his memory of the method that won him success, and also give him the confidence to want to go on and try something else. However it may be a mistake to reward too liberally with praise, for example, each time a pupil succeeds, since although this might work with anxious insecure pupils, it can obviously lead with the more confident to complacency and a desire to rest on one's laurels. Perhaps the best formula is to give pupils fairly prompt knowledge of their results, which for many should be sufficient reward if their answers are mostly correct, and then to set them another challenge which should, however, always be within their capacity. In this way, with success breeding success, even the slowest pupil should be able to have a sense of achievement, providing the tasks he is set have been carefully chosen and presented to him. Traditional incentives to learn used by teachers, such as marks, competition between pupils, and form positions, may have a positive effect upon abler pupils but too often serve to depress the less able, who may in this way become habituated to the idea of failure.

See also **Negative reinforcement**

NT

Pottery Pottery has attained a high level of invention, imagination and creative design in schools. The basic materials of pottery are earthenware and stoneware clays. Earthenware clays of the red and buff varieties are best for schools with kiln temperatures limited to 1,100°C. Stoneware clays are only suited to schools with kilns capable of reaching temperatures 1,200°C-1,300°C. Clays can be kept plastic in airtight polythene bags or sheet. The most common methods of pottery making are: coiledware; pinchware; tiles; slabware; pressedware; wheelthrownware; mosaic; ceramic jewellery; slipcast forms; modelling.

The methods of applying decoration to pottery in schools are varied. Liquid clay slip of various colours and of the consistency of cream can be applied, prior to firing, by dipping, trailing or pouring. By sgraffito the slip can be drawn through to reveal the clay body underneath. Underglaze colours can be applied by painting after bisque firing to pottery and then glazed. On-glaze colours are mixed with an oil medium and applied to the glazed article and fired at approximately 750°C. Other methods of decoration are sprigging, impressed and incised decoration. The final process, except for on-glaze decoration, is one in which the porous bisque earthenware is covered with a glaze by dipping or pouring. It is then fired in the kiln to form a glass and renders the porous ware impervious to water. Stoneware glazes in schools are usually of three types; ash, slip (engobe), and feldspathic. All require a kiln temperature between 1,200°C-1,300°C, and they produce glazes of great beauty and subtlety under oxidation or reduction firing.

FURTHER READING
Bernard Leach. *The Potter's Book*, Faber and Faber, 2nd ed., 1960.
Daniel Rhodes. *Clay and Glazes for the Potter*, Greenberg, 1958.
Ernest Röttger. *Creative Clay Craft*, Batsford, latest ed. 1967.
Catalogues from W. Podmore and Sons Ltd, Shelton, Stoke-on-Trent, Staffs.

DJM

Pre-school Playgroups, National Association of Founded in 1961 to meet the needs of 2–5-year-olds deprived of nursery education by the continuing shortage of places, the Association receives a three-year grant from the DES for a national adviser. Its Code of Standards urges members to seek expert advice where qualified staff are not available. The Association stresses participation by parents, and is concerned with family welfare and education for parenthood.

Toynbee Hall, Commercial St, London, E1.

Monthly journal: *Contact*.

Preceptors, College of Founded in 1846 and incorporated by Royal Charter in 1849, to advance the interests of education and to promote sound learning, with authority to hold examinations for teachers and to make appropriate awards.

The College operates in the sphere of higher professional education for teachers by holding examinations for the qualifications of Associate, Licentiate and Fellow; by providing personal study courses leading to these qualifications; and by arranging short term residential and non-residential courses on curriculum development and management studies related to the role of head of a school.

Publications include an international digest of educational literature; *Education Today;* and the annual reference book *Teachers' Guide*.

2 and 3 Bloomsbury Sq., London, WC1.

Prefects Like the monitorial (*q.v.*) or pupil-teacher (*q.v.*) systems, the prefect system is an expedient hallowed by tradition. Whether they acted as policemen, form captains, reporters, takers of roll calls, deputies for masters or indeed informers, the custom of boys being appointed, or elected, to look after their fellows is as old as the very institution of a school.

Fellows 'more advanced than the rest in age and sense' were appointed at Merton College from 1270 to secure attendance at chapel. To secure the speaking of Latin, scholars 'of good behaviour and more advanced than the rest in age, discretion and learning' were appointed at Winchester from 1382. Praepostors were similarly so appointed at Eton from 1443. By the 16th century such officers became known in some schools as monitors.

They were certainly needed in the days when schools were understaffed, and often were more amenable than 'ushers' (as assistant masters were called).

Aware that when boys were left to form an independent society of their own, they exercised an influence over each other far greater than that exercised over them by the masters, Dr. Thomas Arnold (*q.v.*) resisted the temptation to cut the power of the sixth form (as reformers wished) and instead firmly maintained that praepostors should have the power of chastising those who resisted their authority. A. P. Stanley in his *Life and Correspondence of Dr Arnold* writes that 'there was no obloquy which he would not undergo in the protection of a boy, who had by due exercise of this discipline made himself obnoxious to the school, the parents, or the public.' He himself said 'When I have confidence in the Sixth, there is no post in England which I would exchange for this; but if they do not support me, I must go'.

So much were prefects identified with the public schools that at those founded in the 19th century, like Wellington and Marlborough, their headmasters made them the basis of discipline. Such prefects as appeared before the Clarendon Commission (*q.v.*) approved of the system.

As progressive schools got under way, prefects tended to become elective officers, magistrates and part of the machinery for humanising what might otherwise have been a bad atmosphere. A closer analogy with shop stewards could no doubt be pressed in the case of particular schools.

FURTHER READING
A. P. Stanley. *Life and Correspondence of Dr Arnold*, London, 1890.
Rupert Wilkinson. *The Prefects*, Oxford Univ. Press, 1964.

WHGA

Preparatory schools The word preparatory, in general terms, covers those schools in the independent system which prepare boys or girls for some form of secondary education, in most cases for entry into the public schools. They take children aged about seven or eight and keep them usually until their 14th year. Some of these schools have a junior department which would accept children at the age of five, others would expect to pass them on to a local grammar or direct grant school when they are 11, while others again are junior departments of some public school. Most of the schools are charitable trusts, some are owned by limited companies and a rapidly diminishing number are still in private ownership.

Usually they are single-sex schools, especially those that cater only for boarders; co-education is found chiefly among the large day schools in urban areas and then, as a rule, only up to the age of 11.

The average size of the preparatory schools is about 100 for those that provide boarding education only; day schools or mixed day and boarding schools tend to be rather larger. The staff ratio, as one might expect, is higher than is possible in the maintained system, the size of classes varying between about 14 and 20.

For their first two years, from the age of eight to 10, children follow a curriculum not dissimilar to that used in the local primary schools, with English and its ancillary subjects such as history, geography and scripture taking most of the time, together with mathematics and oral French, music, drawing and handwork. The next three years are spent on the Common Entrance examination syllabus, with a start being made in science and perhaps in Latin. This part of the course is completed by the brighter children in two years, and they can then spend their last three or four terms preparing to take entrance scholarships to the public schools. The scholarship examinations are of course competitive, whereas the Common Entrance is merely a qualifying examination with the standard varying from school to school. Promotion is nearly always by stage, not age. By the age of $12\frac{1}{2}$ a child of average ability could pass the Common Entrance into most public schools; a year later the brighter children will have reached GCE O level standard in some subjects.

To start a child off at a preparatory school does not mean that parents are committed to eight or ten years of fee-paying in the independent system, and transfer to the maintained system is always possible at 11 or at 13. So long as the public schools insisted on Latin as a compulsory subject in the Common Entrance, transfers in the other direction were not so easy; children wishing to go to a public school usually had to leave their primary schools about the age of 10 and spend two or three years at a preparatory school concentrating largely on those subjects which they would not have started in the maintained system. But this obstacle is rapidly being removed and transference between the two systems is being greatly facilitated.

The next few years are also likely to see a considerable swing in the direction of co-education, partly because more and more parents seem to prefer this for its own sake and partly because for parents with more than one child to educate simultaneously, expenses can be appreciably reduced by sending them to the same school.

It would indeed be a poor preparatory school that did not provide its pupils with full scope to indulge in as wide a variety of hobbies as possible, and many teachers would feel that in training children how to use their leisure they were providing them with help every bit as valuable as anything they can offer in the classroom.

Nearly all schools include religious instruction; this is usually on the broadest basis of the Church of England or Roman Catholic or some other denomination, though few exclude children of other denominations. Attendance at school prayers, either at assembly or in the school chapel or local parish church, is in most cases compulsory.

Although anything from a third to a half of the children in preparatory schools come from homes where the fathers were not educated in the independent system, the fact remains that entry is still confined to those whose parents can afford to pay the fees—in many cases with help from LEAs or other outside sources. There are probably few headmasters or headmistresses who would not like to see the doors open to a far wider section of the community.

See also **Private sector in England and Wales; Public schools**

FURTHER READING
Curriculum for the Preparatory Schools, Warren and Sons, Winchester, Hampshire.
P. L. Masters. *Preparatory Schools Today*, A. and C. Black, 1966.
Prospect (the report of a Curriculum Committee; chairman D. S. Piper), Joseph Smith, Bakewell, Derbyshire, 1965.
Journal
The Preparatory Schools Review. Three times a year. Plan Publications.

RAH

Preparatory Schools, Incorporated Association of An association of preparatory school headmasters (and their partners) whose schools have been recognised as efficient by the DES, and which contain not fewer than 35 boys under fifteen years of age. The Association was founded in 1892, and incorporated in 1923. It now represents over 500 schools in Great Britain, Ireland and overseas. There is a council of 26 members, with a chairman elected annually.

138 Church St, Kensington, London, W8.

Preparatory Schools, Society of Assistants Teaching in The Society was founded in 1953 by the Rev. John Williams. Activities include bi-annual conferences and an annual art competition. Separate subject groups for teachers of English, French, mathematics, science, classics, history, music and PE each publish termly broadsheets and arrange group meetings. Services to members include an appointments scheme, a BUPA group scheme, advice on careers and conditions of service, a discount service and special insurance rates. Close contact is maintained with headmasters and teachers in HMC and maintained schools.

Hon. Sec.: J. B. Maflin, The Pound, Blatchington, Seaford, Sussex.
Publication: *News and Views*. Termly.

Previous employment relevant to teacher's pension *See* **Buying-in of previous employment of value to teaching for pension purposes**

Primary education in England and Wales Since the head of each primary school in England and Wales enjoys much autonomy, there are differences between schools in both the approach to and the emphases in practice. Primary education is here described in terms of those elements of practice which are most widely accepted by educationists (these include people working outside as well as in schools) as leading to the provision of a good education in the first stage of the school system.

Primary education continues, complements or compensates for education received in the pre-school years. Attention is paid to the meaning and present knowledge of the growth, development and consequent needs of children, both before and after the statutory ages defining the primary stage. Teachers (and this word is used throughout to include heads as well as assistants), by keeping in touch with current thinking and research in the fields of psychology, human biology and sociology, have information to aid them in assessing the educational needs of the individuals within a class as well as of the class group as a whole; each child is seen as having particular needs since the circumstances for each are unique and each is also a member of the school social groups. Thus, both the approach to and the content of the work in the classroom are based on the available knowledge about child development and learning, and about ongoing interactions in the class and between home and school environments.

Probably the most decisive tenet derived from this knowledge is the importance of ensuring that the child shall be, insofar as his experience and abilities allow, the agent of his own education. In the early years, this belief leads to the provision of long spans of time, and ample, varied and carefully chosen materials and equipment, for the kind of activity normally, if unfortunately, described as 'play'. It consists, in fact, of physical, intellectual and social experimentation; of creation, and sometimes destruction and re-creation; of practice in, and mastery of, skills and behaviours with specific materials and situations, some of which are designed to prepare for further stages of learning.

In the later primary years, the same belief in the importance of the learner's active participation in his own education leads to opportunities being given, at one time for choice among suggested topics of study, at others for the development of explicit personal interests; for experimentation in teacher-designed situations, with encouragement to the following through of interesting observations and to the designing of other experiments; for acquisition of knowledge by use of the many possible aids, including the actual environment and books, and the checking of observation by book reference. The same approach is evident in provision for creative experience whether it be in language, physical and dramatic movement, music, or the variety of artistic media within the increasing manipulative scope of the children. Just as the word 'play' gives an overall description of approach with younger primary children, so does 'discovery' for the older ones. Both terms indicate the mainspring in the learning situation, and both can easily be misunderstood. Neither is intended to suggest, for example, that there is no place for the teacher, on occasions, to instruct an individual, a group or the class, only that this will not be the prevailing means of education.

The range of content in primary education is nowhere laid down. There is, however, considerable similarity between schools in the particular fields of knowledge introduced. Decisions are based on the teachers' assessment of social needs and of the constitution of a general and liberal education, and on this there is some consensus of opinion. There is no disagreement, and parental and public expectations demand, that skill in reading should be attained. There has been controversy over the years as to the most efficient way of helping children in this attainment and, while much assistance has come from surveys and research, the whole process of learning to read is as yet imperfectly understood. The use of an initial teaching alphabet (q.v.), which is an aid and not a method, is still at an experimental stage and its claims are not fully tested. Certainly, beginners and slow learners have achieved reading skill when it has been used with a variety of methods, and have found little or no difficulty in transferring to ordinary print. At the start of primary schooling, learning to read is an integral part of classroom activity and only as readiness for specific skills is shown is it separated out for systematic study, which is required by the majority of children to the age of about seven to eight years and, for a minority, beyond this age.

The other areas of study can be grouped as follows: language (communication, writing, literature, a second language); mathematics and science (biological, physical); environmental studies (natural, geographical, historical aspects); expressive arts (dance, drama, music, poetry, art and craft). In addition, there is physical education. The only legally required subject is religious education, from which children may be withdrawn at their parents' request (*Education Act* 1944, Section 25). Variations between schools, all of which might be judged to be providing sound primary education, lie both in the weighting between and within groups and in the content of any particular section. Some schools, for example, do not teach a second language; some, while not omitting any of the expressive arts, develop one further than the others. These variations may reflect staff interests and qualifications as well as judgments on the value of certain aspects to the children in a given locality and, sometimes, to individuals in the school. Variations in content again reflect particularities of staff, children and locality.

Responsibility for selection of worthwhile material is the teacher's. Assistance in defining profitable topics and practices, and methods of evaluation, in mathematics and science is being provided from the curriculum development projects of the Nuffield teams; the research work and the inspiration of the Geneva school are helping teachers to plan in terms of developing conceptual thinking in several aspects of study, including religious education. In the early primary years, there is little differentiation into subject areas, nor is the day restricted by a time-table, apart from the allocation for use of such community spaces as the hall. Differentiation appears with increasing age of the children but, since most primary classes spend all or the major part of the day with one teacher, rigid subject division and strict time-tabling are not required, nor are they considered desirable in the interests of good education. In one matter, primary schools are required to show conformity: the day must be divided into two sessions and secular instruction must be provided for at least three hours for pupils mainly under eight years of age and for four hours for those aged eight and over (School Regulations, 1959).

No statement of the objectives of primary education exists except in very general terms, e.g. 'all round development of the individual'. Sections 502 and 503 in *Children and their Primary Schools* (Plowden Report 1967) suggest some more specific forms for evaluating a school's practices. In a national survey of the state of primary education, carried out by HMIs for the Plowden Committee, the following rather general and subjective criteria were used to assess present quality: standard of work, personal relationships, awareness of current thinking, recognition of children's educational needs, a balanced curriculum, absence of disciplinary problems. These criteria incorporate most of the elements already described as relevant to an account of primary education.

One element not so far mentioned is personal relationships; it is regarded as a highly important factor in primary schools. At the entry of a child to school, it is of obvious importance that the relationship between child, mother and teacher shall be such as to ease the transition from home, the teacher being initially in the position of a mother-substitute. (*See* **Reception class.**) Because of the organisation of primary schools mainly in classes each with its own teacher, there is opportunity for the establishment of relationships which are conducive to children's successful development socially, intellectually and emotionally. Respect among children and adults for each other, ability of children to work with their peers, and trust in an adult who is helpful in setting and maintaining standards of behaviour —these are the main characteristics looked for in a good relationship.

It is important to stress that primary education as described here cannot be found in every school. On their criteria, the survey by HMIs showed that 33% of the primary school population are in schools 'which are quite clearly good' and just over 5% in schools which are clearly poor. For the remainder, some but not all of the features here described are present, with the distribution 'quite markedly "skewed" towards good quality.' (*Plowden Report*, Sections 270–5).

Developments in primary education appear likely to take place in an extension of curriculum study on the pattern of the Nuffield projects (*q.v.*). Teachers would then be helped, in other areas of the curriculum, to define objectives more clearly, to plan the most beneficial experience for pupils at different stages, to understand how best to help them to structure that experience, and to evaluate progress effectively. Allied to the general approach, in terms of educational needs of children and of their most appropriate ways of learning, studies of this kind could provide teachers with information on which to base their selection of content and which at present they lack. The current examination of organisation, both of the primary stage as such and of within-school arrangements, may lead to changes—e.g. entry to secondary schools at twelve, with a break between 'first' and 'middle' schools at eight; team teaching (*Plowden Report*, Sections 406, 761–8)—which would necessitate some rethinking while not altering the basic nature of primary education today.

See also **Infant schools; Junior schools; Plowden Report**

FURTHER READING

W. A. L. Blyth. *English Primary Education: A Sociological Description*, Vols I and II, Routledge and Kegan Paul, London, 1965.

R. Dottrens. *The Primary School Curriculum*, HMSO, London, 1962.

D. E. M. Gardner. *Experiment and Tradition in Primary Schools*, Methuen, London, 1966.

S. Marshall. *An Experiment in Education*, University Press, Cambridge, 1963.

A. D. C. Petersen (Ed.). *Techniques of Teaching*, Vol. I: 'Primary Education', Pergamon Press, Oxford, 1965.

JBC

Primary School Report (1931): Report of the Consultative Committee of the Board of Education Terms of reference: to enquire into and report on the courses of study suitable for children up to the age of 11 in elementary schools (other than children in infants' departments), with special reference to the needs of children in rural areas. Chairman: Sir W. H. Hadow.

The Report confirmed the recommendation that the division between primary and secondary education should be at 11, and that between infants and juniors at seven. It also stated that there were such broad differences in the abilities of children of the same chronological age that there should be some form of streaming. It recommended that 'the curriculum of the primary school is to be thought of in terms of activity and experience, rather than of knowledge to be acquired and facts to be stored.' It also recommended a maximum of 40 for the size of a primary school class.

Primary schools The possible upper age limits for children whose education takes place in primary schools are legally defined in three Parliamentary Acts: the Education Act 1944 calls primary education that which is full-time and 'suitable to the requirements of junior pupils' (Section 8) and defines a junior pupil as 'a child who has not attained the age of 12 years' (Section 114); the Education (Miscellaneous Provisions) Act 1948 allows the terminal age to be as early as, but no earlier than, 10 years 6 months for pupils 'whom it is expedient to educate together with senior pupils', i.e. in secondary schools (Section 3); the Education Act 1964 allows proposals to be put before the Secretary of State for the adoption of age limits below 10 years 6 months and above 12 years, but such proposals can be made only for new schools which would be in the nature of experimental establishments. The present plans for changes in secondary school organisation—raising the leaving age to 16 years and organising schools on comprehensive lines—include permission for LEAs to make 12 or 13 years the age for transfer to the secondary stage, but they would be required to justify such a change 'by reference to some clear practical advantage' (Circular 13/66). Thus, in general, primary schools provide for children not yet 12 years of age, with some rather loosely defined exceptions.

All schools admitting children below the statutory ages for the commencement of secondary education are, therefore, primary schools and the title of a school indicates the approximate age-range for which it provides, viz. nursery schools (q.v.) two to five years; infant schools (q.v.) with a nursery class or classes, three to seven years (without such classes, five to seven years); junior schools (q.v.), seven to 11 years; combined infant and junior departments, five to 11 years or, should nursery classes be provided, three to 11 years. The age of compulsory attendance—when a child 'has attained the age of five years' (Education Act 1944, Section 35)—serves as a dividing age between nursery and infant pupils; beyond this, there is no legal basis for these divisions of the primary stage; they are an outcome of historical processes and have now become largely fixed by custom and local circumstances.

Depending on the local provision, and disregarding transfer between schools due to parental mobility, the pattern of a child's primary schooling can therefore be: only one primary school and no transfer (in combined departments); or with one transfer (infant to junior); or with two transfers (nursery to infant and infant to junior). Each pattern can be argued as advantageous and disadvantageous to the pupil; the only evidence at present available in favour of any one pattern is that good progress in reading at the junior stage appears to be associated with being educated in a separate infant school, i.e. the pattern with at least one transfer.

The Plowden Report argues the case for revision of the age limits, divisions and naming of types of schools for younger pupils: 'first school' to provide a three-year course from the September following a child's fifth birthday, this being preceded by part-time nursery experience where parents desire it; and 'middle school' to provide a four-year course with 'a median age range from 8 years 6 months to 12 years 6 months'. While the proposed ages of transfer can be justified in terms of known norms of development and achievement, the proposed names of schools could result in blurring the idea of progressive stages in the educational system—primary, secondary, further—as established in the Education Act 1944, Section 7. The pattern of schooling for nearly all children within the present primary age limits would therefore include one transfer at about $8\frac{1}{2}$ years, with the possibility of a prior one between the nursery establishment and the first school.

Primary schools—and from this point the term excludes nursery schools—are normally co-educational, only 2% being single-sex in January 1967 (Statistics of Education, Part One, 1967); the number of single-sex schools has been declining steadily in recent years. The size of primary schools can vary from less than 25 to over 800, determining factors being location (urban, rural), status (county, voluntary), composition in terms of age range (infant, junior or the two combined), and any peculiarities of the district served (e.g. new housing estate, demolition area). At present, the general situation is that (1) the majority of infant schools are in urban areas and have between 100 and 300 on roll, with a very few being larger than 400; (2) the majority of junior schools are also in urban areas and have between 200 and 400 on roll, with a very few over 600; (3) the majority of infant and junior combined schools have between 26 and 200 on roll, those with less than 100 being mainly in rural areas; the overall proportion of this type of provision has increased slightly in recent years. The Plowden Committee deprecates the combination in one school of their proposed first two stages, except in rural areas and for voluntary schools. The sizes of school recommended as satisfactory are close to the majority picture given above for the comparable establishments: first schools, 240 children; middle schools, 300–450 children. The Committee further recommends that study should be made of educational characteristics and economic data in relation to school size, for their recommendations are considered proposals rather than proven necessities (*Plowden Report*, Chapter 13).

The internal organisation of a primary school, i.e. the formation of classes, is partly a function of overall size and, where size permits choice, largely the outcome of head teacher policy. The one-teacher school—probably rural and with an age-range of five to eleven—is the only kind of establishment where no choice is available. In schools larger than this, the most common criterion used in forming classes is chronological age. Thus, in a two-teacher school, a division into

younger and older primary pupils is likely, although the precise age of division could vary from year to year according to the proportion of children in the different age-groups, and adjustments could be made for individual cases on another criterion, e.g. achievement. In one-form-entry schools whether infant, junior or combined departments, one class per age-group is the traditional pattern of organisation. With more than one-form-entry, the traditional pattern tends to differ between the infant and junior age-groups, the infant schools adhering more closely throughout to division by chronological age. At the junior stage, a criterion of achievement—in one or more areas, most frequently in reading, or ability assessed by testing or by subjective judgment—may be used in addition to that of chronological age. Some infant schools may use such additional criteria for classifying their older pupils.

With the implementation of the re-organisation of the educational system as recommended by the Hadow Report 1926 (*Education of the Adolescent*) *q.v.*, large urban junior schools appeared whose internal organisation was influenced by the recommendation of the Hadow Report 1931 (*The Primary School*) *q.v.*, that classification into two or three classes for each year of chronological age be according to 'natural gifts and abilities' or children's 'capacity'. This recommendation was subsequently accepted as giving official approval to internal organisation by streaming. In recent years, the use of the criterion of chronological age at the infant stage and of achievement or ability at the junior stage has been questioned. Thus each stage has produced its experimental form of internal organisation: vertical grouping in infant schools (*q.v.*) and non-streaming in junior schools (*see* **Streaming**).

* The staffing of primary schools is normally by men and women who have gained a teaching qualification after a

course in a college of education. A small proportion, approximately 4%, of the teaching force are graduates, with or without a subsequent professional course. There are also some unqualified teachers, the proportion varying between authorities; the Plowden Committee quotes figures for 1965 of 35% in two areas and of 'well above 20 in three other areas' (Section 885). While the national average is certainly very much lower than this, there seems little doubt that the proportion of unqualified teachers has risen above the figure of 6% given in a 1962 survey (*The State of Our Schools*, NUT).

Shortage of qualified teachers is more acute in infant than in other types of primary school and is connected with the fact that almost 100% of infant school teachers are women; in January 1967 there were 117 men teaching in infant schools out of a total of over 35,000. In combined infant and junior schools the proportion of women teachers was 73% and in junior schools 60%.

In the national situation of marriage and child-bearing occurring at a younger age than formerly and for a higher proportion of the nation's women, the full staffing of primary schools in the traditional proportions of qualified men and women has become impossible. Expedients to overcome the difficulty, apart from employing more unqualified people, include appeals to qualified married women to return to the profession as soon as domestic commitments permit; an increase in the number of part-time posts which may be more acceptable to married women than full-time; encouragement to colleges of education to accept a higher proportion of male students than formerly; provision of courses whereby older men and women may become qualified.

The size of classes in primary schools is affected, not only by the size of the available teaching force, but also by the financial resources allocated for buildings and by historical factors, the most important being the legacy of the elementary school where large classes were assumed to be appropriate to the teaching of the mass of the nation's children. Thus the present statutory maximum class size for primary schools is larger than for secondary schools: 40 and 30 respectively. In view of contemporary purposes and practices in primary education (*q.v.*), the assumption underlying these figures is no longer tenable. In January 1967, 14·8% of primary pupils were in classes over 40. Although the reduction of class size below this figure is universally considered a desirable aim, its achievement is obviously not immediately attainable.

The traditional pattern of teaching in primary schools is for one teacher to be responsible for all the work of one class for a whole school year; he or she is a general practitioner as compared with the specialist of the secondary school. In practice, there has always been a small amount of specialisation, particularly for the junior age groups and particularly in music, and sometimes in art and physical education; the introduction of a second language into the curriculum may also require specialisation. No evidence exists of the amount of specialist teaching in primary schools as a whole nor of its distribution; it seems likely that its occurrence results from the particular combination of circumstances—e.g. staff qualifications and interest, school curriculum, head teacher policy—in an individual school. The Plowden Committee examined possible teaching patterns, including team teaching, and concluded that 'the class, with its own teacher, should remain the basic unit of school organisation, particularly for the younger children', with a recommendation that, nevertheless, 'children should have access to more than one teacher, and teachers should work in close association' (*Plowden Report*, Sections 761–77).

565

T

Developments in primary schools in the immediate future appear likely to occur in experiments in internal organisation and possibly in teaching patterns. Should the reorganisation recommended by the Plowden Committee be fully implemented at a later date, primary schools would disappear in name and the establishments replacing them would have a more closely defined age-range which would apply on a national basis.

See also **Infant schools; Junior schools; Plowden Report; Reception class**

FURTHER READING

W. A. L. Blyth. *English Primary Education: A Sociological Description*, Vols. I and II, Routledge and Kegan Paul, 1965.

R. Dottrens. *The Primary School Curriculum*, HMSO, 1962.

J. W. B. Douglas. *The Home and the School*, MacGibbon and Kee, 1964.

D. E. M. Gardner. *Experiment and Tradition in Primary Schools*, Methuen, 1966.

S. Marshall. *An Experiment in Education*, Cambridge Univ. Press, 1963.

A. D. C. Peterson (ed.). *Techniques of Teaching*, Vol. I: *Primary Education*, Pergamon, 1965.

JBC

Principal teachers These are appointments in approved schools but are in the process of being replaced by senior assistants (*q.v.*). In the case of existing occupants the allowance paid in addition to the salary as a teacher is as follows:

Group	Certified accom.	Allowance (£)
2	18 to 51	125
3	52 to 102	140
4	103 to 171	160
5	172 to 257	175
6	258 to 360	200

Principles of education Principles of education are prescriptions, essentially of a general kind, as to the right procedure to adopt in educating. To give some historical examples, a principle of Plato's was to censor the stories, poems and music heard by the young in order to obtain the best possible moral influence on them;

Froebel made it a principle always to encourage self-activity in the child; a leading principle of Dewey's was to arrange lifelike problematic situations as the main means of educating. Examples of educational principles in more recent vogue are to organise children into groups, to start from existing interests, to learn by discovery, to give opportunities for creative work and to allow as much freedom and personal responsibility as possible. (By contrast with this, rules of method for introducing fractions, for instance, or making Roman history more vivid or for teaching modern languages directly, are too specific to count as educational principles.)

Principles of education are logically very complex, as indeed at another level are rules of method. This complexity becomes apparent when one inquires into their justification. On the one hand, they presuppose the acceptability of various value-judgments, and ultimately of those values formulated as 'aims' (*see* **Aims of education**), hence the frequent coupling of 'aims and principles', while on the other hand they assume the truth of many empirical statements of varying degrees of generality. They are thus vulnerable to attack from two directions. For example, Plato's principle mentioned above presupposes both the value of unshakable moral convictions and the truth of such empirical statements as that very few are capable of seeing for themselves what is right, that the majority are nevertheless susceptible of being trained by a suitable environmental control, and that a heavy dose of selected literature and music will in fact produce unshakable convictions. Against this might be launched either a critique of Plato's values, or an empirical refutation, based on research, of his factual assumptions.

This makes it clear that there are at least two distinct senses in which one might speak of 'educational theory'. First, 'an' educational theory would be a set of principles of the kind just discussed and often organised in such a way as to present a comprehensive picture of the model educational situation. In this sense one speaks of 'Froebel's theory', or the 'child-centred theory'. Secondly, the phrase 'educational theory' could be used to refer to the theoretical contributions of the various empirical disciplines which bear upon education, such as psychology and sociology. This might include matter on the psychology of perception, learning theory, social structure and social processes, individual differences, child development and so on. It deserves notice, however, that 'an' educational theory cannot be inferred from such empirical matter as this alone, but requires also the assumption of certain educational values as criteria of relevance and as warrants for issuing in practical recommendation.

FURTHER READING

R. D. Archambault (Ed.). *Philosophical Analysis and Education*, Routledge and Kegan Paul, 1965.

S. J. Curtis and M. E. A. Boultwood. *A Short History of Educational Ideas*, Univ. Tutorial Press, 4th ed. 1965.

K. Price. *Education and Philosophical Thought*, Allyn and Bacon, Boston, 1962.

B. O. Smith, W. O. Stanley and J. H. Shores. *Fundamentals of Curriculum Development*, Harcourt, Brace, New York, revised ed. 1957.

J. W. Tibble (Ed.). *The Study of Education*, Routledge and Kegan Paul, 1966.

RFD

Printing crafts in schools Printing crafts are part of the activities of the art department in many schools. They range from primary exploration of texture and simple repeat patterns, through pictorial and decorative work, to the consideration of illustration related to type-setting and the development of a sense of design and layout even among those pupils who have no ability to draw but can put together and print type.

The simplest methods may begin with only an ink roller which when rolled over a sheet of paper placed on simple objects such as card shapes, string or wire mesh will print on the paper the image of the objects underneath. Alternatively the shapes or objects themselves may be inked, placed between two clean sheets of paper and pressure applied with a roller or press to obtain prints on the two sheets. If leaves are used in this way accurate study prints may be made for nature note books. When card shapes, perhaps letter forms, are cut out and stuck to a base sheet a printing block is formed which will print a number of similar copies.

Lino-cut printing can develop from this simple process. A design is cut in the surface of a piece of lino which is then inked with a roller. A sheet of paper is laid on this inked surface and rubbed with a clean roller or a spoon to take a print. Several colours may be overprinted from further blocks if a system of registration is used to ensure accurate placing of the blocks.

Lino-cut printing offers far greater possibilities if a small press is available. Much can be done with a simple screw press and many schools have acquired Albion or Columbian flatbed presses which, by taking much of the physical effort out of the process of printing, encourage far more ambitious work, complicated overprinting with thin layers of transparent inks, and simpler, more accurate registration of overprints. Examinations for CSE and GCE at O and A levels include wide opportunities for work in this field. The wider scope of the CSE syllabus is especially welcome to teachers able to offer printing facilities for lino-cuts if type is also available. Projects may include designing and printing paper bags, book jackets, record covers and so on.

The printing of geometrically shaped blocks to standard nets of mathematical models takes this two-dimensional craft into three dimensions while relating the studies in art and mathematics departments. This worthwhile relationship can be developed and/or printed constructions may be exploited within the art department alone.

Where a school has facilities for printing with type, there is the possibility of using type with lino-cuts in the production of simple book projects involving pupils in group effort. ditions Eare best limited to copies for those involved; larger productions for sale require greater labour but bring little educational gain, and perhaps even add an unwelcome commercial aspect to the project.

Any school which has a press and some type will be in a position to print its own tickets, programmes and so on. Where this can be absorbed as project work, designed and carried out by pupils, this can be very satisfying. The inherent danger is that school printing may become a cheap alternative to the printing trade, and the educational value of this experience can be overwhelmed by the amount of work called for. 'Printed in the school' should never be an apology for inferior work. Unless a school is properly geared to vocational training it should not attempt to teach what the printing industry prefers to teach apprentices itself. But an awareness of what is good or bad about the printing we see every day is something to be encouraged by all schools, with or without presses.

See also **Silk screen printing**

FURTHER READING

Fred Gettings. *You Are an Artist*, Paul Hamlyn, 1965.

John Ryder. *Printing for Pleasure*, Phoenix House, 1957.

Michael Rothenstein. *Lino Cuts, Wood Cuts and Other Methods of Print Making*, Studio, 1962.

Harvey Weiss. *The Young Printmaker*, Nicholas Kaye, 1961.

EJH

Prison, Adult education in Education is today regarded as an essential part of prison training. The aim is to provide some stimulus to counteract the mental stagnation of prison life, to give the prisoners something to talk and think about. Until the 1920s almost the only instruction available was in classes for the illiterate. In 1923, at the suggestion of the Adult Education Committee of the Board of Education, a more comprehensive system was adopted. The scheme developed rapidly. Since the second world war, though attention has still to be given to the problems of illiteracy, particular emphasis has been laid on training in the use of English, both written and spoken. Classes in handicrafts and in the creative arts are also given prominence. Full- and part-time tutors (whose work is often supplemented by voluntary workers) are appointed through the LEAs, but the work is the responsibility of the Prison Department of the Home Office.

BG

Private sector in England and Wales Nearly half a million boys and girls attend independent schools, that is to say schools that are neither maintained by LEAs (state schools) nor receive a grant from the government. They form about 6% of the whole school population, rather less (about 5%) of all pupils of compulsory school age, considerably more (about 10%) of the under-fives who go to school and many more of the sixth-formers (about 15% of those aged 17).

There are two categories of independent schools—'registered' and 'recognised as efficient'. Nobody may run a school which is not 'registered'; but anybody has a right to register one, and can be stopped from running it only if it can be proved to be really bad. The owner has a right of appeal to the courts, so that a school must be bad indeed before action will be taken. Registration, then, tells a parent nothing about a school, good or bad, except that it has a right to exist. Some registered schools are excellent, some the reverse. A 'recognised as efficient' school is one that has applied of its own accord to the DES to be placed on the official list of schools which are found on inspection to provide a satisfactory education for boys and girls of a particular age. A parent, therefore, knows something on impartial, expert testimony about the state of such a school, at least when it was last inspected. This may have been some years ago. The smaller the school, the more rapidly it is liable to change. From the school's point of view the great advantage of recognition is that it makes it a good deal easier to recruit qualified teachers. There are slightly more registered than recognised schools but $2\frac{1}{2}$ times as many pupils in recognised as in registered schools. This is partly because the recognised schools are to a much larger extent schools for young children; indeed, up to the age of seven there are more pupils in registered than in recognised schools, and for the under-fives the proportion is roughly three to one. The fact that these are small local schools, well known in the locality, means that parents have something to go on in choosing a school, although the absence of an external educational assessment is a handicap. From the age of eight onwards there are more pupils in recognised than in registered schools, and from 15 onwards the proportion is about four to one.

Independent schools are concentrated to a disproportionate extent in southern England and especially in Kent, Surrey and Sussex. In these three counties nearly 15% of all schoolchildren attend independent schools. It is not that the state schools are worse in southern England than elsewhere. On the contrary they have a higher proportion of boys and girls staying on at school to 17 and 18 than the Midlands and the North.

Probably the most common educational reason why parents choose independent schools is the fact that they are more likely to find small classes there. The contrast is especially marked in primary schools, where the ratio of teachers to pupils in registered schools is about one to 14 compared to twice that figure in maintained schools. Recognised schools are even better off. The advantage in this respect of the private sector holds good also of secondary schools, though not to quite the same extent. The independent schools make a much greater use of part-time teachers than the maintained schools do, and are more inclined to employ professionally untrained teachers.

The independent schools are for the most part single-sex schools after the age of seven, whereas the state school system is virtually entirely co-educational up to the age of 11, and increasingly so beyond it. This is another factor which leads parents to choose one type of school in preference to the other.

It is a mistake to think of independent schools as being for the most part boarding schools. Fewer than a third of their pupils are in fact boarders. Even among the boys in recognised efficient secondary schools only a little over a half are boarders. But boarding schools, on the other hand, are to an overwhelming extent independent schools. Three-quarters of all boarders in England and Wales attend independent schools. It is certain that a number of parents choose to pay fees because they want a boarding school education for their children rather than because they want an independent school. Parents are no more inclined to use independent schools for their sons than for their daughters; but they are much more likely to send them to a boarding school. About two-thirds of all the boarders in independent schools are boys. (*See* **Boarding school education.**)

Often the matter of cost settles which system a parent will use. The whole cost of education at independent schools normally falls on parents, though in a relatively small number of instances some small proportion may be covered by endowments, plus of course their share in taxes and rates for the state system. It is not that the private sector is profit-making while the state sector is not, but that the necessary cost of running a school is high. Most recognised secondary schools are in fact run by non-profit-making bodies, and those independent schools which are officially profit-making probably seldom to-day yield their proprietors much more than a reasonably well paid opportunity to perform a useful service which they enjoy. On the whole, independent school fees have had to be increased once every two or three years since the war to keep pace with increasing costs. In the year 1967 the average fee charged by public schools for boys was rather more than £500 per annum, while in public schools for girls the figure was rather more than £450 per annum.

An awkward matter for parents who wish to transfer their children at some stage from the public to the private sector or vice versa is that the state system is based on a break for boys at 11, whereas the greater part of the independent system for boys places the break two years later. Although by the time they reach the sixth form boys brought up on either system will have covered identical ground in an identical range of subjects, the development of the various individual subjects varies between the two systems so that transfer is difficult. There is much less difference between independent and state girls' schools.

DGOA

Probation service Probation Officers are professional social workers attached to law courts. While the training of officers is in the hands of the Probation and After-care Department of the Home Office, the service is organised on a local basis. Appointment and supervision of officers is by a Probation Committee representing all the magistrates' courts in a district (known as a Probation Area) and composed of Justices of the Peace. A Principal Probation Officer is in charge of each Area. The services are financed jointly by the local authorities concerned and by the Home Office, whose inspectors may examine them at any time.

A probation officer's work falls into four main categories:

(1) Making enquiries as to the home circumstances, work history, family relationships, income and social background of an offender when required to do so by magistrates. It is common for a convicted person to be remanded either on bail or in custody while such a report is made, before an appropriate sentence is determined.

(2) Supervising those offenders placed on probation by magistrates' courts or higher courts of law.

(3) Undertaking matrimonial conciliation work arising from domestic proceedings in the magistrates' courts.

(4) Supervising young people from approved schools, detention centres or borstals, and adults from prisons, for the statutory period of after-care following their release.

Since 1967, some probation officers have been appointed as Prison Welfare Officers, working inside the institutions to prepare inmates for discharge or parole.

The probation order is shown by statistics of reconviction to be the most successful penal method in Britain. It is made only if the offender concerned agrees voluntarily to accept supervision by an officer. The probationer is made aware that failure on his part to comply with the terms of the order (e.g. to report to the officer for interview when requested, or to inform him of change of address) may result in his return to court for the award of an alternative sentence for the original offence. Thus the probation officer has a powerful sanction should his client fail to respond as required. Probation orders are usually applied for one, two or three years. Every part of the offender's life may be subjected to scrutiny by the officer while an order lasts. For this reason, probation is not always acceptable to the man closely involved in criminal activities, who may prefer a short term of imprisonment after which he is free of such interference. Contrary to popular belief, probation orders are made in respect of people of all ages, not only juveniles, and applied not infrequently to offenders who have a history of institutional confinement behind them.

Both in preparing reports for the courts and in their work of befriending and advising clients on probation, officers depend heavily on the cooperation and goodwill of other social workers. In the case of juveniles, consultation with teachers is particularly valued if professional confidence is effectively recognised on both sides.

FURTHER READING

M. Monger. *Casework in Probation*, Butterworth, 1964.
P. Parsloe. *The Work of the Probation and After-care Officer*, Routledge and Kegan Paul, 1967.

DLH

Probationary year According to the government's Schools Regulations 1959, the intial period of service of a teacher as a qualified teacher 'shall be a probationary period of one year, during which he may be required to satisfy the Secretary of State of his practical proficiency as a teacher.'

The purpose of the probationary year is to make sure that the newly qualified teacher can make the transition from the period of supervision and tutelage in a college of education to the exercise of direct personal responsiblity that is required of every teacher.

The probationary period applies to all qualified teachers employed in maintained schools in England and Wales and starts from the moment a teacher first takes up a full-time appointment. (It does not, however, have to follow immediately upon the successful completion of the training course). It cannot be served in another country; if a person goes abroad before completing the probationary period he will still be subject to probation on returning to England or Wales. While the period of probation is normally one year, the Secretary of State for Education has power to dispense with, shorten or extend it. The power to dispense with or to shorten probation would only be applied exceptionally to teachers coming into service in maintained schools with long experience as teachers outside the maintained school system, and not necessarily even then.

The outcome of the probationary period is determined, so far as a teacher trained at a college of education or university department of education is concerned, by the LEA employing him. For any other teacher, such as an unqualified graduate or a teacher from overseas, a favourable decision is taken by the Secretary of State after receiving the advice of the LEA and of one of Her Majesty's Inspectors. Under both procedures, if a teacher is deemed not to have satisfactorily completed the probationary period, a recommendation has to be made to the DES about that teacher's future. The Schools Regulations state that 'if at the end of the probationary period the Minister determines a teacher to be unsuitable for further employment as a qualified teacher, he shall not be so employed'. Failure in this sense, however, involves only a very small proportion of teachers.

LEAs employ different means to assess the teacher's performance. The views of the head-teacher are almost certain to be taken into account, and in addition the authority's own inspectors may visit the school and the teacher. It must not be assumed that the decision will be derived from one or more formal 'inspections'. These may or may not occur but the LEA will make its assessment on the performance of the teacher as a whole during the probationary period. There is no prescribed method of doing this.

Satisfactory completion of the probationary period has no effect on a teacher's salary. So long as he is employed as a qualified teacher he will receive the appropriate salary as determined by the Burnham Report. Increments on pay are given according to the time served as a teacher, and do not depend on the successful completion of probation.

FJ

Product-moment method *See* **Correlation**

Programme, Extrinsic (*and see* **Teaching machines**) Computer-aided instruction goes further than branching programming in catering for individual differences. The student's performance is continuously monitored by the machine, which adapts the pace and level of difficulty to suit the individual's needs. The control is 'extrinsic' in the sense that the necessary adjustments are not written into the programme itself as happens in a branching programme (*q.v.*).

Programme, Intrinsic *see* **Branching programme** *and* **Programmed learning**

Programme, Linear A technique of programming originally associated with the principles laid down by Skinner's Operant Conditioning psychology, in which the learner is presented with a fixed sequence of small steps. Essentially, each step consists of a bit of information accompanied by a question which the learner has to answer before carrying on to the next one. The term 'linear' is appropriate in so far as the progression is straightforward and the same for all.

See also **Programmed learning**

WKR

Programmed Instruction, Register of First issued in 1965, this register is now being revised and developed by the British Association for Commercial and Industrial Education (BACIE) with the aid of a grant from the Ministry of Labour.

Programmed learning From small beginnings in the 1920s, programmed learning has since 1950 developed into an international educational movement, and may best be defined as an attempt to devise a systematic technology of instruction. In all its forms it sees the process of instruction as a dialogue between a single tutor and a single student. One of the chief advantages claimed for it, indeed, is that it makes allowance for individual differences — unlike the mass media. Another is that it enables the student to learn on his or her own in the absence of an instructor, and to that extent may be regarded as the first stage in a development which will lead to fully automated teaching. In the USA it is customary to refer to it as programmed instruction, but, if only because programming de-emphasises the importance of the part played by the 'flesh-and-blood teacher', the term programmed learning seems more appropriate.

While the pioneering efforts of Sidney Pressey (usually credited with the invention of the first 'teaching machine') cannot be ignored, the movement got off the ground only after the publication of B. F. Skinner's article *The Science of Learning and the Art of Teaching* in the *Harvard Education Review*, 1954 (*see* **Skinner, B. F.**). Skinner's behaviourist psychology, known as Operant Conditioning, was based on experimental work with animals, chiefly pigeons and rats, and achieved spectacular results in shaping their behaviour by means of schedules of reinforcement. A pigeon pecking at a key was said to emit an operant response. By reinforcing ('rewarding') the response with food, the chances of its repeating the same response were increased. In this way, by pre-selecting a series of responses, the animal's terminal behaviour could be built up gradually, each move being rigorously controlled by the experimenter. Skinner's contention was that much the same techniques could be applied to human learning. In effect, a linear programme, as developed by him, serves as a schedule of reinforcement. The terminal behaviour is first defined; the subject matter, process or skill is analysed and broken down into its elements, and the material is then presented in a logical sequence of small steps. At each step, the learner is given just enough information and guidance ('prompts', *q.v.*) to ensure that normally the response he or she makes will be the one desired. The satisfaction derived from continuously giving the correct answer is held to be an adequate reinforcement. The learner receives immediate confirmation of the results of his or her responses, works at his or her own rate and checks his or her own progress.

Leaving aside the many objections raised against Skinner's learning theory, extensive experience with linear programmes in schools, in industry and in the armed forces suggests the following conclusions:

(1) Normally, a linear programme is a fixed sequence, i.e. all pupils receive the same information and follow the same set of instructions. (True, skip sequences can be introduced, but this is at best a clumsy makeshift and one not often resorted to in published programmes.)

(2) While the target of 90% success with 90% of the population is rarely reached, post-test scores show a distribution which is usually more homogeneous than the distribution of marks in examinations based on conventional methods of teaching. Average and below-average pupils tend to do as well as, and sometimes better than, the abler ones. The long 'tail' of failures or near-failures is reduced, if it does not disappear altogether.

(3) At the same time, Skinner's original belief that the same programme served equally well for the bright and the dull pupils has been shown to be false. The evidence indicates fairly conclusively that, to be fully effective, a linear programme needs to be specially designed and prepared for a particular age and ability group.

(4) In general, it is safe to say that a linear programme loses little or nothing in being presented in the form of a text. Housing it in a machine slows down the rate of progress and in practice has nothing to recommend it, except possibly in the case of very young pupils. As regards cheating, the research evidence is, to say the least, equivocal.

(5) Linear programmes can be tolerably effective at all ages and ability levels. This is not to say that they are so, but simply that it has been established that learners from pre-school to postgraduate stages find the small-step approach acceptable.

(6) In the present state of the art, linear programmes tend to be most successful when taken in small doses. They are less effective, and may be worse than useless, in the absence of sympathetic monitoring and assistance by the teacher.

(7) The great majority of programmes produced so far belong to the linear type.

(8) Most of them deal with mathematical, scientific or technical subjects. How far this repertoire can be explained in terms of supply and demand, and how far by limitations in the technique itself, remains arguable. In theory, the assumption that any subject that can be taught can be programmed is almost certainly valid, but it does not follow that all subjects lend themselves equally well, if at all, to systematic analysis or to small-step treatment.

While it would be misleading to suggest that Skinner's insistence on the need for small steps has been rejected

T*

by second generation programmers, there has undoubtedly been a shift of emphasis, and many of the alleged 'principles' of linear programming have come to seem slightly doctrinaire. Gilbert's *mathetics* (*q.v.*), Mager's highlighting of the need for clearly specified *objectives* (*q.v.*), and Gagne's focusing of attention on *learning sets* (*q.v.*) exemplify this shift. Dissatisfied with the theoretical model of the Skinnerian school, and the lockstep practice it imposed (i.e. the arrangement by which all pupils cover the same ground at the same rate), the new school of programmers is addressing itself to the problems of instruction from new angles. The stress on logical, frame-by-frame presentation of *information* has to some extent given way to a more open-ended approach which envisages the learning process more in terms of guided *inquiry*. According to Mager, indeed, motivation increases as a function of the degree of control, or apparent control, which the learner is allowed to exercise over the learning experience; in other words, once the learner has been given the objectives the programmer may not have to do much else.

An alternative method, devised and perfected by Norman Crowder, goes by the name of branching programming (*q.v.*), though its originator prefers to call it intrinsic programming. In his view, a low error rate cannot be taken as the sole guarantee, still less the sole criterion, of successful learning. The most carefully prepared fixed sequence, he argues, cannot hope to cater for individual differences. Not only do pupils learn at different rates, they also follow different routes. In the first instance, therefore, all the teacher can do is to present a unit of information and see how each individual responds. The individual's response serves as a signal which indicates what the next move ought to be for him or her. Hence, incorrect responses must be allowed for: they provide the pointers

enabling the teacher to plot the right course for each individual. The surest way to reduce errors is to explain the nature of them to the learner as and when they occur. Accordingly, all the remedial material is built into a branching programme. The learner is presented with a paragraph or so of information and, having read it, is asked a multiple-choice question (*q.v.*) to test his comprehension. If the response is correct he carries straight on to the next step, as in a linear programme. If it is a near miss, he may be guided to the correct answer at a second or third attempt, failing which he may be transferred to a sub-sequence which explains the point to him in elementary terms. Whatever it is, the learner's response is treated on its merits.

Branching programmes may take the form of a scrambled book ('tutor-text') in which the remedial material appears on separate pages, but seem to be most effective when installed in a teaching machine of the auto-tutor or Grundy-tutor type. It is claimed, with some justification, that these programmes represent a more flexible strategy than the one adopted in linear programming. It seems likely, however, that branching programming will prove most effective only when computer-assisted instruction becomes widely available. So-called adaptive teaching machines have immense possibilities not only in monitoring the student's performance but also in enabling the programme to be continuously revised and improved while actually in use. At the moment, sophisticated installations of this kind are prohibitively expensive, and the main efforts are addressed to the writing and testing of programmes. In the future, however, instrumentation is certain to play a more prominent part than it has done hitherto, in which case teaching machines (*q.v.*) will become standard equipment.

WKR

Programmed Learning, Association for Representing all those interested in programmed learning, the Association has group members (including education authorities, some government departments, teaching machine manufacturers, publishers, etc.) and individual members. Apart from a year book, it supplies members with a newsletter (four times a year) and the journal *Programmed Instruction* (at half-price), and organises an annual conference and week-end courses. 27 Torrington Sq., London, WC1.

Progressive education This is the description usually given to educational practices developed in a small number of independent schools founded at various dates since 1893 and representing a minority movement in the private school world. The first of these schools, Abbotsholme, was a boys' boarding school; but Bedales, founded shortly after as a similar school, soon admitted girls and the King Alfred School in Hampstead (1898) was from the beginning a co-educational day school.

This diversity between boarding and day, single-sex and mixed schools is typical of the movement. The innovation of co-education, in boarding or day schools, made the greatest mark. A number of LEA day schools are co-educational but among private boarding schools co-education has in general remained a feature peculiar to the progressive school. In their attitude to religion the progressive schools also differ among themselves. Abbotsholme was from the first an orthodox school while Bedales was more broadly based; the founders of the King Alfred School instituted no religious practices or instruction. These patterns were variously followed by some later schools, but Summerhill, Dartington and Monkton Wylde remain the only schools in the movement which, like the King Alfred School, have no organised religious observance. All the schools are characterised, however, by tolerance of diverse religious beliefs and freedom from religious indoctrination.

The early progressive schools instituted practices not accepted in orthodox private schools of the time and many of their innovations remain in today's progressive schools. Among the first to break away from the traditional emphasis on the classics, the progressive schools broadened the academic curriculum to include history, modern languages and science, and gave a high status to the teaching of art, music and crafts. Manual labour for the benefit of the community, both indoors and outdoors, became an integral part of school life, and no cult of athleticism was developed. The schools opposed all forms of pre-military training, were free from jingoism and tolerant and pacific in outlook. Simplicity of living was a keynote, but it was a simplicity designed to promote good health; comfortable dress and planned diet and the new methods of physical education from Scandinavia were used to this end. Above all they set out to adapt their ways to the individual needs of the boys and girls who came to them, rather than to impose on them the accepted educational patterns of the time.

Progressive schools rapidly increased in number after the first world war, and by 1934 they numbered 21. By this date, however, concepts in educational thinking had been immeasurably widened as a result of work in the new field of psychology. Psychologists had begun to develop new techniques of mental measurement and to arrive at new definitions of individual difference, while the study of child development and its relation to the fields of depth psychology had thrown new light on children's behaviour. The older progressive schools drew new inspiration from these findings while the new ones thought in psychological terms from the start. Thus progressive education has come to be closely connected with psychological thinking.

Informed conclusions of educational psychologists about individual differences in intelligence and maturation confirmed that the emphasis of the early progressive schools on the study of individual needs was correct. Objective measurements of potential and progress are now the ordinary practice in progressive schools. By their use schools free themselves as far as possible from the danger of unrealistic academic pressures and standards, without losing awareness of the need for challenge and stimulus for the academically able. Again, schools in which the readiness to experiment with curriculum and teaching methods was present from their origin found entrance easy to an experimental world based more firmly on objective criteria.

But it is in their adaptation of school regimes, both in and out of the classroom, to current knowledge of the psychology of the whole child that progressive schools have continued to be most clearly differentiated from other schools. They have accepted the idea of the emotional life of children having a pattern of development which is a vital part of growth and which if neglected hampers all development, and it is attention to this pattern of development that underlies their academic and social life. In the classrooms they act on the belief that readiness and ability to learn has an emotional factor at least as important as the factor of intelligence or chronological age. They do not consider the stimulus of competition or the fear of punishment as sound ways of motivating learning, and some dispense with these practices altogether.

The value of play as a foundation for proper development is stressed for younger children, as is the adolescent's need for time to himself as a protection against the dangers of modern academic pressure. Creative activities of all kinds are seen as an aid to emotional growth and as an essential means of self-expression, and more than usual weight is given to artistic education which remains an integral part of the schools' curricula.

The attitude of the schools towards deviant behaviour is to recognise it as a developmental or psychological problem, to be understood, rather than as an undesirable trait to be eliminated by punishment. Punishment, indeed, in some of the schools is noticeably absent in any form. There is in all the schools a greater permissiveness as regards behaviour than is usual, but it is a permissiveness which has the positive aim of training for self-knowledge and self-discipline.

Thus the climate of progressive schools is one of freedom, and control depends upon the good relationships of staff and pupils. Authoritarianism is not seen as a necessary component of these relationships, and a high degree of informality between old and young encourages an ease of communication with adults which is a desired objective. Most of the schools have some form of pupil participation in government and regard this as an essential part particularly of adolescent training and well-being; in some of the schools this participation extends to the choice and planning of subjects to be studied.

In the last twenty years, some of the practices of progressive education have been adopted by other schools, both public and private. But generally progressive education still belongs as a system to those schools which accept the title of progressive schools and are committed consistently in their whole life and organisation to its fundamental principles.

FURTHER READING

H. A. T. Child (Ed.). *The Independent Progressive School*, Hutchinson, 1962.

LAC
HATC

Project A major purpose which may cut across subject-barriers in the curriculum. It demands co-operation by a number of teachers and needs the support of resource materials, visits, interviews, etc. It may result in the preparation of a report or booklet and the holding of an exhibition of the work accomplished.

Project work Influenced by the work of Dewey and Froebel, many junior schools after the first world war tried setting their pupils projects, which might be anything from organising a pageant to producing a magazine, but would always give reason to hope that they would engage the pupils' interests and initiative. Such projects might be given to individuals or to small groups, and although they did not generally take up the whole school day, unlike the Dalton Plan (*q.v.*), they would certainly lead to a flexible timetable and the abandonment of too many lessons following one another in strict routine and aiming solely at the acquisition of useful facts. The advantages of projects were many: they might cut across subject barriers (for example, a project on stamp collecting might involve both history and geography). In Belgium, Professor Décroly encouraged school projects around what he termed mankind's principal needs: food, protection, shelter and work.

The teacher's part in all this was to supervise, give information and guidance when asked, and always to be around to breathe new life into a project, or if necessary to abandon any that might have gone on rather too long or turned out to be ill-chosen. Project method is now a fundamental part of English infant and junior education, both for groups and for individuals, and there are signs that many secondary schools are now beginning to adopt these methods, especially under the stimulus of new examinations such as the Certificate of Secondary Education.

NT

Projection tests These are used in the assessment of personality, the best known being Rorschach Inkblots (*see* **Rorschach tests**), the Thematic Apperception Test, the Incomplete Sentence Test and the Word Association Test (*qq.v.*). The tests' aim to to reveal how the individual views his environment, e.g. whether friendly or threatening, his role in it and his attitude towards it, whether welcoming or withdrawing. The essence of a projection test lies in its unstructured situation; the individual projects his own attitudes and needs and thus reveals personality traits.

See also **Personality tests**

Projector (Film-strip-, Micro-, Movie-, Overhead-, Slide-, etc.) *See* **Visual aids** *and* **Film in education**

Prompt This is a term borrowed from the stage, now widely used in programmed learning. In linear programmes a prompt usually, but not necessarily, takes the form of a verbal hint, its purpose being to help the learner to make the desired response without actually telling him or her what it is. The verbal context serves to narrow the question down so that the answer can be seen more easily, e.g. 'The higher the temperature the faster the molecules move. The lower the temperature the —— they move.'

See also **Programmed learning; Fading**

Protestant Schools in Ireland, Incorporated Society for Promoting The Society was founded in 1733 by royal charter and reconstituted in 1894 under the Educational Endowments (Ireland) Act 1885. In the 18th century it provided primary education in its famous charter schools. On the establishment of a state-aided primary schools system in 1831, state grants to the Society ceased, the number of its primary schools decreased and it became more interested in intermediate or secondary education.

The Society now has seven secondary schools in which pupils are prepared for the examinations of the Department of Education, for university matriculation and for the examinations in religious knowledge sponsored by the Board of Education of the Church of Ireland. Mountjoy School, Dublin, and Kilkenny College, founded in 1538, are boarding and day schools for boys. The Collegiate School, Celbridge and Rochelle School, Cork are boarding and day schools for girls. Sligo Grammar School and Bandon Grammar School, founded in 1641, are co-educational boarding and day schools and Cork Grammar School is a co-educational day school. The Society holds endowments in trust for needy pupils and grants scholarships and allowances worth over £10,000 a year.

79 Merrion Sq., Dublin, 2.

Psychiatric Social Workers, Association of A professional organisation for social workers qualified to work in the field of psychological medicine. Formed in 1930 with 17 members, it now has about 1,100. Since 1961 the Association has kept a register of fully qualified members who are entitled to use the letters AAPSW after their names.

The aims of the Association are: to ensure that standards of qualification and professional work are maintained; to improve technical and professional knowledge through meetings, lectures, seminars and refresher courses and the encouragement of research; the publication of a journal, books, papers and reports; to contribute to the development of social work in general.

Training for psychiatric social work is in the hands of the universities and invariably involves post-graduate work. But information and advice concerning training may be obtained from the Association.

The Association runs a trainee scheme in which people wishing to proceed to post-graduate professional training may gain practical experience in the psychiatric field under the supervision of a senior psychiatric social worker.

Oxford House, Mape St, London, E2.

Psychologist, Educational An educational psychologist is usually a teacher with a degree in psychology, who has gone on to further training at an approved centre. He may work either in the school psychological service, where he will spend his time in and out of schools, or he will work in the child guidance service, as part of the normal psychiatric team. In fact many educational psychologists work for both services at once, when they are combined together as part of the education system.

The educational psychologist's job is often thought of merely in terms of administering countless intelligence tests, but of course there is far more to it than this. When he is required to assess a behaviour or learning problem there are many other techniques at his disposal, from tests in attainment to tests in personality. Moreover, the important part of the assessment lies often in the quality of subsequent interpretation by the educational psychologist and whether that interpretation leaves the teacher or parent feeling even more helpless than before or with some constructive ideas or proposals to work on. The educational psychologist may often have to persuade the teacher to look on the problem rather differently, and perhaps with more understanding; in these cases the psychologist may find it easier if he has already organised courses or discussion groups for groups of teachers in order to work towards such ends. Very often he will play a part in assessing educationally subnormal children, and in providing other special classes or groups for children who need them. In his advisory capacity he may be consulted on almost any matter from problems of placement to the use of new teaching methods. He himself may conduct research projects and advise schools how to use the ever-growing network of social welfare and services, which can be very confusing—especially to a new head-teacher. So far as an individual pupil is concerned the educational psychologist may himself treat him or may offer some sort of remedial teaching or therapy.

If he is centred upon a child guidance clinic, the educational psychologist, as well as carrying out his normal work of assessment, can be a valuable link with the schools, keeping both sides informed as to the progress of the various child patients concerned. He may see parents, either in the clinic or at school, if it is a question of assessing a family situation or offering advice.

Sir Cyril Burt (*q.v.*) was the first educational psychologist to be appointed by an LEA and since 1944 there has been a steady if slow growth in the service.

FURTHER READING
Isabella Maclean. *Child Guidance and the School*, Methuen, 1966.
Report of the Committee on Maladjusted Children, HMSO, 1955.

NT

Psychologists, Association of Educational Membership is open to educational psychologists employed by LEAs and those who have contributed to the subject.

Gen. Sec.: P. C. Love, Trelake, 32 Lower Hill, Barton Rd, Exeter, Devon.

Publication: *Newsletter* (three times annually).

Psychology, Educational Educational psychology is largely a 20th-century science, although it has important roots in the 19th century. Philosophers from Plato onwards have discussed childhood and learning, and there was a flourishing 19th-century school of philosophical psychology, often resulting in worthy books that were described at the time as 'everything that is dull and unreadable'. But the first genuinely scientific

study of the child was probably Charles Darwin's *Biographical Sketch of an Infant*, written in 1877 from a strictly biological viewpoint and based on observation of development and behaviour. This approach, although desirable in its objectivity, tended to treat children as organisms genetically structured to adjust to their environment, and it was left to Darwin's half-cousin Francis Galton (*q.v.*), with his meticulous if occasionally eccentric measurements, to treat children as individuals and bring out their essential differences as well as to emphasise their common biological and behavioural norms.

His work was continued by James Sully, Professor of Mind and Logic at University College, London, who opened in 1896 a psychological laboratory where teachers were encouraged to bring their more difficult pupils for examination. Sully was also the first president of the British Child Study Association, founded in 1894 and devoted to the study of 'the normal as well as the abnormal' with particular emphasis on the study of the effects of environment upon the child as a possible explanation for his apparent abnormalities.

This early stress on sociological explanation, possibly due to educational psychology's early biological bias over such questions as 'adjustment', was particularly important since compulsory education in the UK had brought to light many defective children who had difficulty in coping with school and often needed some form of special education. In some cases, particularly where delinquency, maladjustment or backwardness were concerned, this led to disputes in diagnosis between doctors, who tended then to see defective children in terms of organic defect, and psychologists who insisted that on occasions there were social or emotional rather than medical reasons for abnormalities. In order to discover these reasons, where they existed, Sully recommended that psychological specialists should develop 'sympathetic insight' into their patients, as well as have a full understanding of the diagnostic techniques at their disposal. School inspectors attended some of Sully's courses, and a group attached to the London County Council were instrumental in getting Cyril Burt (*q.v.*) appointed as the first educational psychologist working for a local authority.

The science having slowly gained official approval, the application of educational psychology went on to have a fundamental influence both on education and its administration. It was not difficult to demonstrate at the time how unfair and haphazard selective examinations then in use so often were, and Burt's *Mental and Scholastic Tests* (1921) did a great deal to popularise testing on a more scientific basis. Today selection, with its overtones of 11-plus, is less popular in educational circles, but it must be remembered that standardised tests were a fairer means of selecting than any other in use at the time, if selection was going to rate place anyway. Properly constructed tests of attainment or intelligence can also be used in many different contexts far removed from selection, and perhaps it is unfair that educational psychologists have sometimes been blamed as the 'witch-doctors' behind selective examinations that were in fact the instrument of educational rather than psychological policy. Nevertheless, it is also probably true that for a time educational psychology became more interested in scientific measurement than in individual variation, and so may have missed some of the inevitable weaknesses and inconsistencies in large-scale selective procedures that have now become so evident.

In another field, again rather unfairly, educational psychology became associated with excessive freedom. It is true that some educational psychologists became very interested in psycho-analysis and theories of the unconscious, and may well have advocated less punitive and more understanding approaches to children, and especially to those who might be maladjusted. But neither they nor most of the founders of progressive education ever put forward the exaggerated ideas attributed to them by those who still hankered after clear-cut moral judgements and 'no-nonsense' techniques of treatment for problems that tended in fact to respond far better to a more understanding approach.

So far as the school curriculum was concerned, the work of Piaget (*q.v.*) had an important effect in underwriting some of the educational theories of Montessori and the Froebelians, since it gave scientific justification for the importance of imagination and play in school. More detailed knowledge of child development, as taught in universities and training colleges, also led to the abandonment of many formal methods which may have suited teachers but had little positive effects upon their pupils. Thus class teaching began to be replaced by group work with pupils working at their own speed. The teaching of reading began to use far better-constructed methods and textbooks, and backward pupils could now be split up more accurately into those who were genuinely dull, those with some specific difficulty, and those who were simply not responding to school. In particular, Professor F. Schonell (*q.v.*) pioneered these new reading and diagnostic techniques. More educational research was being carried out, and in 1945 the National Foundation for Educational Research (*q.v.*) was founded as a co-ordinating body. Scotland, however, had its own Council for Educational Research dating from 1928.

Today, educational psychology is less bound up than it used to be with theories of intelligence and mental testing, but the statistical basis to much psychology and social investigation is still important, and some understanding along these lines is essential for any teacher who wants to understand contemporary research. In another field, educational psychology continues to provide the theoretical understanding for all learning processes, and the explanation for some of the failures to learn. There have been new insights into the effect of environment upon personality and intelligence, both in and outside the classroom. Programmed learning, streaming, reward and punishment are all topics that come within the sphere of educational psychology, and there is in addition a growing need to explain the ramifications of special education, social welfare, and some of the techniques of the educational psychologist to teachers who otherwise become confused by the welter of problems in some of their schools, and the provisions for some of these at their disposal.

The main focus for educational psychology, however, is still the same: the emotional, intellectual, physical and social development of children, and the techniques and understanding the teacher may need in facing up to this in all its various forms—usually, but not always, in the classroom.

FURTHER READING
J. C. Flugel. *A Hundred Years of Psychology*, Duckworth, 1951.
L. S. Hearnshaw. *A Short History of British Psychology*, Methuen, 1964.
Gertrude Keir. *A History of Child Guidance*, British *Journal of Educational Psychology*, XXII, 1952.

NT

Psychotherapist Children who need psychiatric help may get this either from a child psychiatrist (*q.v.*) or from a psychotherapist. The latter is some-one, not a doctor of medicine, who has had long special training in giving therapy to disturbed children, generally either in child guidance clinics or else in maladjusted schools.

Public Libraries Act (1919) *See* **Board of Education**

Public Libraries Act (1964) *See* **Public library services to schools**

Public Libraries and Museums Act (1850) This enabled the local authorities to provide public libraries and museums. Only 80 authorities had established them by 1877, but many were started by the mechanics' institutes and subsequently taken over by the local authorities.

Public library services to schools
The amount of help a school may expect from a public library depends upon whether it is in an area served by a county, county borough or municipal library system. Whereas a county library is likely to be subsidised by an LEA, the municipal library will not be. Thus it will be able to give no service or a very limited one. It is impossible to generalise about county borough libraries, but it is safe to say that very few receive any subsidy. The majority of them leave school services to the county library, giving occasional help to individual schools.

County library services
   Loans to schools. The most common form these take is the general bulk loan, the size and nature of which will approximate to the needs of the recipient school. Book collections thus loaned are sometimes static, but are usually partially or wholly changed each term. This type of loan is not intended to meet specific needs but, in some areas, a degree of content control by teachers is made possible by allowing teachers and children to select books at the school from a display van which may carry up to 3,000 volumes. This method works particularly well when one van is devoted to a particular kind of school, say primary or secondary, thus giving a wide range of books. In many cases collections are made up at a county or regional HQ, especially in

the case of secondary school loans where large numbers are involved.

In densely populated areas with HQs easily reached from schools, it is sometimes possible for teachers to select books from the library shelves. These are then packed and despatched. This sort of selection is probably the best for a more purposeful type of loan: one made in response to a request by a teacher, department or school. Such loans are often met from a special, heavily duplicated stock. More commonly, they are made up by library staff upon whose knowledge of subjects and teaching methods their quality depends.

A more unusual form of loan is that of books listed by a school and specially bought by the library for issue on a semi-permanent basis. New schools which have not yet built up their libraries find these loans especially valuable, as do those engaged in curriculum experiment involving transitory needs.

A few authorities operate a centralised buying system, with the county library receiving a proportion of the capitation grants of the schools in the area and acting as a buying agent. The library processes the books, loans them permanently to the schools and, in some cases, maintains them. This system cuts costs and relieves the schools of the chore of processing and maintaining stock, but can lead to excessive central control of content. Such schemes are sometimes run in conjunction with a large selection library.

Mobile libraries. In rural areas, many people are served by mobile libraries which, of necessity, often call while children are at school. To give them an opportunity to select their own books, some mobile libraries call at village schools.

Exhibition services. At many county library HQs and some regional ones, large exhibition stocks are kept. Teachers visit these when listing books for purchase by their schools. These stocks are also drawn upon for local and school exhibitions.

Bibliographic services. County libraries usually issue occasional booklists on particular subjects, and also regular general ones. The latter are sometimes published in periodicals issued to schools by LEAs. Frequently, subject bibliographies are provided for an individual school or teacher.

Advisory services. Many county libraries will give advice on the technical administration of libraries and, if asked, on their design in new schools. Actual help in classifying and cataloguing is sometimes given—a useful service to schools reorganising their libraries. In a few cases the library authority actually provides school librarians.

Visits to libraries. To encourage children to use public libraries, visits to local branches are arranged. In some areas groups or classes make regular study visits, often to use local history collections.

Municipal library services

Loans. These can rarely be made on a regular basis, but some library systems lend small collections to meet special subject requests.

Visits. Many towns have a long tradition of visits by classes, mainly to foster library use but sometimes to supplement the resources of school libraries. Children are also helped to pursue private studies in the libraries and, in a few areas where home conditions are bad, homework facilities are provided.

Bibliographic services. Numbers of fine booklists and library magazines are produced and these are highly valued by local schools.

Future developments. The Public Libraries Act 1964 gave control to the DES. It is to be hoped that one result of this will be the extension of good county-library-type services to schools in all areas.

See also **Libraries, School**

RPAE

Public schools The term 'public school' is notoriously hard to define. It is used here to denote about 200 independent schools taking pupils, mainly boarders, from 13 to 18. All these schools are single-sex: approximately 120 boys', 80 girls'. Almost all of them are in England, and most in the south of England. About 15,000 children enter these schools each year; this is little over 2% of the age group. Yet the predecessors of the present 2% compose 20% of those now at British universities, and they hold one in three of the top jobs in business and two in three of the top jobs in the professions.

No other country has a system like this. The continent has its independent boarding schools; though quite numerous, they are mainly confessional and carry no particular social cachet. Most English-speaking countries also have their independent boarding schools; these often have the prestige of the English public schools upon which they were originally modelled, but they are too few (except perhaps in Australia) to make a significant impact upon society. Nowhere, in fact, is there a system anything like so closely knit or so influential as in England.

The typical English public school is a mid-19th century Church of England Foundation, in a small country town. The school is unendowed, and the fees of £500-£600 per annum allow for no luxuries. The relatively small margin by which the fees exceed those of state-run boarding schools is devoted largely to staff salaries; the staff in a public school are slightly more numerous and rather better qualified than in a maintained grammar school. Half the fee-paying fathers were themselves at a public school, the other half not; half of them are professional people, the other half in business. The 400 or so pupils cover an intelligence range a good deal wider than that of a grammar school, yet parental support is so strong and the teaching so good that almost all the pupils stay on into the sixth form and half, on leaving, will go on to some form of further education.

Even so short a description of the type reveals that the obvious standard of comparison is with the English grammar school. Not only are the traditions and the functions of the two kinds of school similar, but their historical origins are almost inseparable. About a third of boys' public schools are in fact grammar schools founded between the 14th and 17th centuries which somehow succeeded in attracting pupils from a wider area and thus became 'public' as opposed to 'local'. Their tradition was one of Christian humanism, whether in origin medieval-monastic, as at William of Wykeham's Winchester, or Renaissance-secular, as at Colet's St Paul's. Their aspirations derive from Christianity and Stoicism: they go back to St Paul and Plato (more rarely to Jesus and Socrates), with Pelagius contributing an important ingredient in his doctrine of salvation through effort. *Orando laborando* is the characteristic school motto of public and grammar schools alike.

There is however in the ethos of the public schools another strand which is unlike that of the grammar schools, an aristocratic, amateur emphasis. It shows itself in the admiration of versatility, in a preference for pure over applied science, in a dislike of the application of scientific method to human affairs. Historically this can be seen as part of that cult of the gentleman which to foreigners seems characteristic of all Englishmen.

These two emphases—middle-class and aristocratic, Puritan and Cavalier, Whig and Tory—are partly in tension in the public schools. But the tension seems to the insider to give them not only their flavour but also an unusual resilience and adaptability to change. One can illustrate this adaptability by considering some of the changes that have come over these schools during the last half century.

At the beginning of this period a large number of public schoolboys were still going out to proconsular jobs in the Empire. The country needed such young men, and the young men needed certain qualities: the schools supplied these qualities by proven methods. The intellect was developed by a traditional syllabus, based on the classics, the character by more recent inventions such as Thomas Arnold's prefectorial system and the cadet force. Half a century later the picture has changed markedly. The country now needs industrial managers, and young managers need different qualities: the schools have adapted themselves accordingly. The syllabus is now biased towards science, discipline is kept less by authority than by consultation, the cadet force is usually voluntary; corporal punishment is on its way out; co-education is on its way in.

But this is not all. For 40 years now headmasters of public schools have been lamenting the fact that the fee-barrier compels their schools to be one-class institutions. During the second world war they persuaded the government to set up a committee to try and find ways of enabling clever boys from poor homes to come to their schools. In 1944 the Fleming Report (q.v.) was published, recommending a scholarship system such that '25% in the first instance' of the places in public schools should go to such boys. The Report was never implemented, mainly because it was left to LEAs, who had other more important claims on their money. But the schools have gone on pressing—and the pressure now comes not only from headmasters but from staffs and pupils.

In 1966 the present Public Schools Commission (q.v.) was set up under the chairmanship of Sir John Newsom. Its job is to 'integrate' the public schools. It has recommended that some 38,000

boys and girls wanting boarding school education be admitted to public boarding schools annually, their fees being paid by the government or LEAs.

Of course there is opposition to this sort of change. The extreme right is against any change which may curtail freedom or lower standards: the extreme left is against spending any public money to bolster up separatist institutions. But the central view is strong, and commands the support not only of all headmasters but (officially at least) of both political parties. It holds that these schools are good schools with something special to offer; but that for that very reason it is wrong in principle for *all* the places in them to be confined to the well-to-do; and that a one-class education is a bad thing not only for those who are shut out but for those who are shut in. Its proponents look to the reforms that have come over Oxford and Cambridge since the war, and believe that, if recruitment to the public schools can be changed similarly, the wheat in them will be winnowed from the chaff and they will be able to go on doing their traditional job with a clear conscience.

JCD

Public Schools Act 1868 Following the Report of the Clarendon Commission (q.v.), this Act required each public school to draw up a constitution for the approval of the commissioners or to accept one drawn up by them; laid down the character and constitution of new governing bodies; and empowered the governors to determine the number of pupils, the amount of fees and the nature of the curriculum, and to appoint the headmaster.

Public Schools Appointment Bureau Established in 1942, the Bureau is a country-wide careers advisory service with branches in Edinburgh, Leicester and York, for schools whose headmasters are members of the Headmasters' Conference (*q.v.*) or which belong to the Association of Governing Bodies of Public Schools. The Bureau advises individual boys on the choice of a career and places them in employment. It supplies careers masters with comprehensive careers information by means of its publications, which are available to non-member schools.

The Bureau was the first organisation in the country to introduce careers conventions for careers masters and practical careers courses for boys, and it is now developing an industrial projects scheme for schools in conjunction with a number of large firms. 17 Queen St, Mayfair, London, W1.

Public Schools Bursars' Association Full membership of the association is open to bursars of schools included in the Association of Governing Bodies of Public Schools or in the Association of Governing Bodies of Girls' Public Schools. Bursars in other schools may apply for associate membership, provided certain conditions are fulfilled.

The object of the Association is to promote administrative efficiency in public schools and to assist members by sharing information on matters of common interest. The Association holds an annual conference, publishes an annual report and issues bulletins periodically to its members.

The first meeting of the Association was held in 1932 and was attended by representatives of 47 schools. There are now 421 members and associate members representing 469 schools.

Sec.: D. M. Sherwood, Badminton School, Westbury-on-Trym, Bristol.

Public Schools Commission Set up in 1965, under the chairmanship of Sir John Newsom, the Commission has as its main function to advise on the best way of integrating the public schools with the state system of education.

Announcing the setting up of the Commission, the Secretary of State said the government intended that public schools should make the greatest possible contribution to the country's educational needs, and that this should be done in a way that reduced the socially divisive influence they now exert. This meant that public schools should become progressively open to boys and girls irrespective of their parents' income; that they should move towards a wider range of academic attainment, so that they could play an increasing part in the national movement towards comprehensive education; and that they should help to meet the unsatisfied need for boarding education among wider sections of the population.

In the autumn of 1967 it was announced that the Commission was to extend its review to include the direct grant grammar schools in England and Wales and the grant-aided schools in Scotland. These new terms of reference would take effect when the Commission turned its attention to the day independent schools, which would form the basis of a second report.

The chief recommendation of the Commission's first report, published in July 1968, was that each year some 38,000 boys and girls in need of boarding school education should be admitted to the public boarding schools, their fees being paid by the Government or by local authorities. This would mean, by the Commission's calculation, that within seven years half the children in any such school would have been admitted on grounds of need, and thus the 'socially divisive' character of the schools would have been overcome. This recommendation was widely criticised on the grounds that most children with 'boarding need' would be maladjusted, and that admission to public schools would be a most unsatisfactory way of meeting their problems.

See also **Private sector in England and Wales**

Publishers' Association, Educational Group of the *See* **Educational Group of the Publishers' Association**

Publishers' Educational Representatives, Association of Formed in 1898 to further the work of school book representatives. Members comply with a strict code of conduct which confines their activities to the introduction of books that will ultimately be ordered on school requisition, and debars them from direct selling and the taking of orders. The Association introduced the 'permit system' whereby members are authorised by LEAs to call on schools.

Hon. Secretary: T. R. Wood, 23 Lynton Gardens, Harrogate, Yorks.

See also **Educational publishing**

Publishers' Educational Representatives, Scottish Association of Instituted in 1911 to take united action upon matters affecting the professional interests of its members and those of the firms whom they represent. Membership is open to accredited representatives of educational book publishing firms regularly visiting schools in Scotland and not engaged in the sale by subscription or similar means of the products of such firms.

Hon. Sec.: J. M. Watson, 5 March Rd, Edinburgh, 4.

Puerto Rico, Education in Education is compulsory between the ages of six and 16. 1965–6 enrolments: state schools 640,544; accredited private schools 67,808; state junior college 1,352; Catholic college 302; University of Puerto Rico 26,886; Catholic University 4,256; Inter-American University 6,115. Number of teachers 19,947.

The population of the island was approximately 2½ million in 1965.

Punctuation, Teaching of Despite Bernard Shaw, the apostrophe is still with us; and it is still useful as a means of achieving clear statement. Defenders of the apostrophe and semi-colon, and of all the devices for pointing and clarifying, may nevertheless welcome the more relaxed attitude of many teachers to punctuation. As in other matters, the aptitudes and motivations of the individual child are factors that we ignore at our peril and at the price of much wasted effort. The policy of many effective teachers is to keep the teaching of rules to an absolute minimum and to allow the pupil to grow in skill according to his own rhythms. When the teacher plays it sensitively, by ear, he recognises the point at which an explicit formulation of a rule or convention will be most useful, i.e. most useable by the pupil.

Mistakes in the past have been to overvalue the virtues of neatness and precise conformity to arbitrary rules, to teach rules which were too complicated and premature for the pupil (and sometimes only half understood by the teacher), and to turn the act of writing into a condition of anxiety about typographical conventions. Given the congenial motive and an individually felt sense of standards, pupils will in due course use and respect such conventions, but teaching which begins and ends with such matters is subject to the law of diminishing returns.

GS

Punishment *See* **Negative reinforcement**

Punishment books *See* **Corporal punishment**

Pupil-teacher centres Diocesan 'central schools' for providing a brief introduction to the monitorial system were established by the Church of England as early as the 1830s. This practice was even more marked when the school boards were set up after 1870; in their central classes specially selected teachers could teach the pupil-teachers. This practice spread after 1880 when the code was altered: no longer was such instruction to be given only by the certificated teachers in the school where the pupil-teacher served. A few years later the Cross Commission (q.v.), both minority and majority, endorsed the improvement of pupil-teachers' general secondary education. In 1898 a departmental committee report on the system recommended that to complete their education all intending teachers should pass through a secondary school, and deplored the 'cramming' that went on at the centres.

By 1902 all urban areas had centres; 12,000 of the total of 32,000 pupil-teachers were attending them. In the following year new pupil-teacher regulations made it impossible for them to become apprentice teachers until the age of 16–17, and suggested the establishment by LEAs of a system of scholarships for intending teachers to secondary schools. As a result many of the pupil-teacher centres, and the most effective, became secondary schools. In 1907 bursaries were instituted at secondary schools for children of 16 or over to enable them to prepare for college.

A shortage of teachers after the first world war led to the reopening of pupil-teacher centres, and, after the second world war, to emergency training colleges.

See also **Teacher education in England and Wales**

WHGA

Pupil-teachers An 'apprenticeship' system of teacher training which replaced the monitorial system (q.v.). Kay-Shuttleworth (q.v.) began the system in the poor law schools at Norwood in 1838 and, on becoming secretary of the Committee of Council in 1839, started a private training college at Battersea with eight pupil-teachers from Norwood. In 1846 his minutes enabled selected boys and girls from 13 to 18 to be indentured to teachers who would train them.

The name 'pupil-teacher' comes from the fact that they received 7½

hours instruction every week in addition to spending 5½ hours a day in some form of teaching. Examined annually, they had the opportunity of competing for Queen's Scholarships tenable at a training college. If unsuccessful they were eligible to be considered for civil service clerkships (withdrawn in 1852). The training colleges obtained a per capita grant for every pupil-teacher, and the teachers, when successful, obtained a proficiency grant.

Pupil-teachers proved a great success. In 1852 Matthew Arnold described them as 'the sinews of English primary instruction'. In the first year there were 200 and in 1859, 15,224. But they suffered from the Revised Code (q.v.), as the head teacher had less opportunity to train them and no fee. Originally he had received £5 for one pupil-teacher, £9 for two and £3 for each additional one; now an agreement was made between the pupil-teacher and the managers. As a result, numbers fell by a third and the standard of admission to training colleges fell too.

The system was progressively modified. Board schools, with their separate classrooms, were not such convenient training centres as the old 'hall' type schools. Moreover, some boards developed pupil-teacher centres (q.v.). The minority report of the Cross Commission, 1888 (q.v.) criticised their preparation, and in 1900 the period of their apprenticeship was reduced from five to two years by raising the age at which they could be indentured. As secondary schools became more diffused after 1902, the system waned.

The waning process was recognised when the King's Scholarship—the king-pin of the system since 1846— was abolished in 1907 and in its place a preliminary examination for the elementary school teacher's certificate was established. At the same time an alternative to the pupil-teacher system was put forward whereby intending teachers with two (later three) years of secondary school education could claim a bursary for a year and then take the preliminary examination to college, or, if they wished, continue as pupil-teachers. These bursaries were, in turn, abolished in 1921 when the Burnham Committee recognised that the proper route to the teaching profession lay through the secondary school.

See also **Teacher education in England and Wales**

WHGA

Puppetry A new look is apparent in school puppetry. More and more schools are eschewing the grey pudding of paper pulp or the tedium of paper layer heads. There are fewer lengthy battles with slow-yielding wood and tangled strings. Nowadays the accent is on the accumulation and use of 'junk'—egg boxes, ice cream cups, cheese boxes, plastic bottles and foam sponge; string, wool, fur fabric; buttons, beads and bottle tops, and so on.

While the glove puppet is preferred by small children, there is a welcome appearance of simple rod puppets: i.e. picnic plates stuck on laths. With the older age groups there is still a leaning towards the marionette; but, as always, too little time is given, and too little skill is acquired, for development in this direction.

There has recently been a growing tendency to experiment. Teachers are becoming aware of the possibilities of rod puppets; starting with the simple stick, it is comparatively easy to elaborate. The puppet may have jointed arms and legs, a head that turns—and, for those determined to be more particular, moving eyes and mouths. However, it is far better to avoid complications unless they really add something to the production.

Increasingly, puppetry is progressing from a purely craft subject to a proper part of drama. Improvisation is invaluable, since it is important that children should feel free in the puppet stage, as they cannot be if they are tied to a script. The withdrawn child often loses all trace of shyness in the concealment of the stage, and teachers are frequently surprised at the encouraging effects of puppetry on such children.

It is important that the production of puppet plays should be approached in the right manner. Not only should a script be dispensed with, but the imagination should be encouraged to flow. Fantasy rather than reality is the essence of puppet theatre; it is a mistake for children to be encouraged to imitate the live actor.

Experiment is essential—improvisation with materials, situations and dialogue. Use of the shadow screen is an aid to experiment: an old picture frame with a piece of white sheeting stretched across it, a pair of wooden feet being added so that it will stand on a table. Light must fall on the back of the screen, either daylight or artificial light. Cut-out shapes provide the shadows, but grasses, feathers, coloured cellophane can be used, with coloured lighting for special effects.

British puppetry societies Educational Puppetry Association, 23a Southampton Place, London, WC1. British Puppet and Model Theatre Guild, 90 The Minories, London, EC3. British Section of UNIMA (Union internationale de la marionnette), c/o Educational Puppetry Association. UNIMA is the only international organisation, with members in over fifty countries.

FURTHER READING

Hans Baumann. *Caspar and his Friends. Ten Puppet Plays*, Dent, 1967.

Helen Binyon. *Puppetry Today*, Studio Vista, 1966.

A. P. Philpott. *Let's Look at Puppets*, Muller, 1966. *Modern Puppetry*, Michael Joseph, 1966.

S. and P. Robinson. *Exploring Puppetry*, Mills and Boon, 1967.

Wall, White and Philpott (Eds.). *The Puppet Book*, Faber, 3rd ed., 1965.

John Wright. *Your Puppetry*, Sylvan Press, 1951.

Eight Plays for Hand Puppets, Garnet Miller, 1968.

VP

Q

Quakers and education In 1695 Quakers decided 'that, where Friends can, they would get such schools and schoolmasters for their children, as may bring them up in the fear of the Lord and love of His truth, that so they may not only learn to be scholars, but Christians also. . . .' No schools survive from that time. In England, the Society of Friends now runs nine schools, primarily boarding, the first founded in 1702. Six are co-educational, two are for boys and one for girls. They are maintained by a total in the UK of little over 20,000 Friends. Together they hold 3,000 pupils between 11 and 18, but only 750 are members of the Society; more than half of all Quaker children of suitable age attend state schools by parental choice. Similarly, of some 1,500 teachers who are Quakers, from nursery school to university level, few choose to teach in Quaker schools. These choices are influenced less by financial considerations than by a desire to opt out of what these teachers and parents consider a privileged opportunity or a lessening of family ties.

But schools and individual Friends agree that personal development should not be sacrificed to academic development, and today the schools are not comprehensive in the technical sense but are places where pupils learn to live comprehensively. The tone is set by the fundamental Quaker principle that God can speak directly to each person, to children as to adults. Each is a community of teachers and scholars trying to live and work together in friendship, but under discipline. The historical equality of men and women in the Society of Friends is seen in the pioneering work in co-education, its current value being to meet the sexual problems of adolescence as they occur with the understanding of 50 years' experience.

Quaker influence on the educational system is at least as wide as its direct practice. Quakers founded the oldest hall of residence outside Oxbridge and the 19th century adult school movement. Problems of delinquency have led individuals to serve in, and groups to found or to manage, approved schools and schools for the maladjusted. Teaching is long established in the developing countries and African Friends are a bigger group than in any other continent.

Indirectly, interest can be seen both in penal reform and in the development of an enlightened approach to mental sickness, the one free from sentiment, the other from the still existing shackles of ignorance and prejudice.

The original belief in the value of education has never faltered. In 1964 the Society declared that 'true education . . . should be continued throughout life and that its privileges should be shared by all. . . .' Friends were urged 'to approach new theories with discernment. . . . Christianity is not a notion but a way.' So the spiritual foundations of Quakerism are also the source of its concern with education which has a beginning, but no end.

See also **Friends' Education Council**
IG

Qualified teacher status In England, Wales and Northern Ireland qualified teacher status is determined by the Secretary of State for Education and Science. This situation is regarded as unsatisfactory by the National Union of Teachers and other teachers' organisations who have sought to secure self-government for the teaching profession by the establishment of a Teachers Registration Council, which would control conditions of entry. In the meantime the influence of teachers' organisations is limited to the part they play in the National Advisory Council for the Training and Supply of Teachers (at the time of writing this body is suspended), which gives advice to the Secretary of State on entry and training requirements for teaching. (In Scotland the position is somewhat different in that there is now a General Teaching Council, with a majority of teachers, which has certain advisory functions regarding conditions of entry to the profession and which maintains a register of qualified teachers).

Under the existing Regulations, a person may achieve qualified teacher status by satisfying one of the following criteria.

(1) By satisfactory completion of a course at a recognised college of education. Until 1960 the normal general course was of two years, although certain specialist colleges already had three-year courses. Today, all normal courses are of three years' duration. Area training organisations are, however, empowered to admit students to shortened courses of two years' duration, and very exceptionally of one year's duration, on the recommendation of a particular college of education.

(2) The possession of certain other qualifications, listed in an appendix to Ministry of Education circular 6/59, concerning in the main music, drama, technological, technical and handicraft subjects. They are limited in application and the categories are slowly being reduced.

(3) Graduation: A graduate of a university of the UK is entitled to the status of qualified teacher, if he is so employed, by virtue of his degree alone, no matter what the contents of the degree or its relevance to the subjects taught. Many graduates, of course, take a one year's course of professional training for teaching. A former Minister of Education, Lord Eccles, issued a warning that at some time in the future a professional training would be necessary for all graduates before they could be recognised as qualified teachers.

(4) The possession of certain other qualifications that are listed in an appendix to the Burnham Report, consisting in the main of professional qualifications which are recognised as equivalent to a first degree of a university.

Scotland The General Teaching Council for Scotland, set up under the Teaching Council (Scotland) Act 1965, advises the Secretary of State on the conditions of admission to the teaching profession; registration by the Council, following a course of training at a college of education, is necessary to qualify any teacher who means to teach in a school maintained or given aid from public funds. This arrangement replaces the former one in which certification was awarded by the Secretary of State.

The situation in Scotland differs from that in England and Wales in that all men teachers and all secondary school teachers must either be graduates or hold some qualification that is the equivalent to a degree; and they must also have taken a course of teacher training (such training is not given by Scottish university departments of education). A primary school teacher must have been awarded the Teacher's Certificate (Primary Education); a woman may acquire this after a three-year course in a college of education, but it may also be awarded to graduates after a one-year course. The secondary school qualification is the Teacher's Certificate (Secondary Education).

Equivalents to a degree include approved diplomas from colleges of commerce, art or music, and there are some differences of qualification in the case of PE, domestic science and handiwork.

FJ

Qualified teachers The normal avenue to recognition as a qualified teacher is the successful completion of a three-year course of training at a college of education. These colleges, formerly 'training colleges', are established specifically for the purpose of training teachers, and it is usual for them to specialise in one or two branches of the service. For example, a college may be entirely devoted to the training of infant school teachers or secondary school teachers, but it is not unusual to find courses offered particularly at the primary level so that students may train either for infants or juniors at one college.

Although three years training is the normal period, special concessions are sometimes made when students over 25 enter training, and if their previous experience and qualifications satisfy the college authorities they may be allowed to complete their training course in two years. For the normal student, however, entry cannot take place before the age of 18 (unless the student is 18 during the first term of the course), and so qualified status is achieved about the age of 21. At present university graduates are automatically accepted as qualified teachers, although they are urged to follow their degree course with a course of teacher training at a department of education or at a college of education. Such students complete their teacher training course in one year.

There are a number of qualifications in special subjects, particularly art, handicraft, music, needlecraft and domestic subjects, science, speech and drama, technology, where on completion the appropriate award offered by the college at which the student has trained may satisfy the Secretary of State for recognition for qualified status. For example, a London University Diploma in Fine Art or the Graduate Diploma of the London School of Music would satisfy the requirements at present. In some circumstances the combination of qualifications taken separately would not provide qualified status.

The DES issues a circular (6/59) which gives full details of qualifications obtained not only in the UK but overseas which at the present time are acceptable alternatives to the normal method of training. It should be noted, however, that this document also indicates that certain qualifications which may have been acceptable in the past are no longer accepted and so reference to precise details is strongly advised.

SEB

Qualifying service Qualifying service is of various forms. It is not pensionable but it may be used towards the minimum period required to satisfy eligibility for a pension. Teaching service for which contributions have been withdrawn is qualifying service. Teaching service which is rendered under a contract of not less than half-time service is recognised as full-time qualifying service. There are other forms of qualifying service, e.g. some teaching rendered abroad. In such cases a teacher who wishes this service to be recorded as qualifying must write immediately to the DES.

Quinquennial grant system Government grants to universities towards their recurrent expenditure, or running costs, are made on a quinquennial basis, and have been since

1889. The system has run into difficulties, and the House of Commons *Fifth Report of the Estimates Committee for 1964-5* recommended that the DES and the Treasury should undertake an urgent review of the system and effect changes early in the next quinquennium of 1967-72. Universities, although autonomous bodies, are now so dependent on public funds that, apart from an annual subvention of well over £30 m. from local authorities, more than 85% of the rest of university receipts come from the Exchequer; and while Exchequer grants were £32 m. in 1955-6, they had exceeded £200 m. in 1967-8. Of the latter sum, separate non-recurrent grants were made towards capital expenditure, but over £150 m. was for recurrent expenditure for the year, and it is the latter kind of grant that is settled on a quinquennial basis.

In other words, universities, unlike public bodies which budget from year to year, budget for their running costs for a five-year period. Their budgets are examined by the University Grants Committee (*q.v.*), which, though subsidiary to the DES, has a majority of academic members. Once the global recurrent grant for the whole of the universities for a quinquennium has been agreed by the Treasury, the UGC decides the allocations to the individual universities, who are at liberty to apply them as they see fit towards their running costs, and their accounts are now subject to government audit.

The quinquennial system was devised to facilitate academic planning for five years ahead, and as an aid to the preservation of the academic freedom of universities. But in a rapidly developing period, it is extremely difficult for any organisation to budget for as far ahead as five years, particularly when it is necessary to convince the Exchequer of the correctness of the financial demands. And although, in a time of price inflation, the government supplements the quinquennial grant to meet unforeseen increases in academic salaries and in rates payable on university premises, and to meet some other rises in running costs in the grant-period which are held to be necessary by reference to an elaborate index of university costs, the university financial shoe tends to pinch towards the end of a quinquennium. Moreover, uncertainty prevails about the period ahead until the next quinquennial grant is announced.

The government announced in 1967 that it did not propose to alter the arrangements for the financing of universities by means of capital and recurrent grants allocated by the University Grants Committee. However, the aid from the exchequer is subject to the approval of the Estimates by Parliament; and, beginning in the year 1968, it has been made a condition of grant — as unanimously recommended by the Public Accounts Committee — that the books and records of the University Grants Committee shall be open to inspection by the Comptroller and Auditor General in respect of the expenditure of grants.

See also **University Grants Committee**

FB

Quintilian (Marcus Fabius Quintilianus, *c.* AD 35-100) Spanish-born Roman rhetorician, Quintilian was the author of *Institutio Oratoria*, devoted partly to expounding the principles of rhetoric, also giving an account of Roman education.

Quota system for teachers The quota system for teachers in England and Wales is, in effect, a form of rationing maintained by the DES with the aim of ensuring that in a period of continuing teacher shortage, each local authority will have an opportunity to secure a fair share of the available teachers. Under the terms of the salary agreements negotiated on the Burnham Committee it is not permissible for any individual LEA to pay salaries in excess of the nationally agreed scales, and consequently those particularly hard-pressed authorities which find it more difficult to attract teachers than other authorities are not permitted to tempt teachers to their schools by salary inducements, even if they are willing to offer them. They are, therefore, dependent on the quota—which in essence says that any authority can employ only up to a particular annually stated level—to help them maintain their staffing ratios. While it is true that some authorities are worse hit than others, despite the existence of the quota, the general feeling is that they would suffer even more were it not for the quota arrangements.

Although the present quota arrangements are of fairly recent origin, and the introduction of a single, nationally determined basic salary scale is a post-war phenomenon, measures affecting the distribution of teachers have been a feature of the educational scene for a much longer time.

Before the second world war, staffing establishments for each LEA were approved and reviewed annually by the Board of Education under a Code introduced in 1926. This arrangement applied only to elementary schools; and, although it controlled the distribution of teachers, it existed not because they were in short supply but as a means of ensuring control of educational expenditure. Individual staffing establishments were abandoned at the outbreak of war, but in 1941 each LEA was assigned a quota of newly trained teachers who were required to spend at least a year in the service of their first employer. This scheme ended in 1946 since it was considered inappropriate for teachers returning from HM Forces, or for those qualifying through the emergency training scheme, many of whom had family responsibilities.

By 1948 the schools needed an increasing number of infant teachers, and arrangements were then introduced to control the distribution of women teachers. By 1955, when the pressure of numbers had shifted to the junior and secondary schools, the National Advisory Council on the Training and Supply of Teachers recommended that this scheme should be replaced by one covering all teachers in primary and secondary schools. Early in 1956 the women teachers' scheme was discontinued and LEAs were allowed complete freedom in the number of appointments they made. The better placed authorities were asked to exercise restraint in recruiting and to make maximum use of married women teachers and of teachers over pensionable age. During the year, however, evidence of increasing maldistribution accumulated and many hard-pressed areas asked the Minister to take steps to safeguard their staffing standards.

In October 1956 the Minister held a conference of representatives of local authority and teachers' associations which conducted a full examination of the problem. The conference reached general agreement that positive steps would have to be taken to improve the distribution of teachers, and that the Ministry should issue guidance about the staffing policies local authorities should adopt and what staffing standards would be appropriate. Following these recommendations, and after further consultation, the Minister issued a circular amplifying the advice previously given to LEAs and introducing a new method of tackling maldistribution. This set each LEA a precise objective (a 'quota') by which to shape staffing policies, expressed in terms of the total number of teachers who should be employed in their primary and secondary schools in January 1958.

At the 1956 conference, prospects for the supply of teachers seemed promising. Consequently the need for close control over the distribution of teachers was thought to be only a temporary expedient and was accepted on that basis. In the event these expectations were disappointed, and persistent staffing difficulties have made it necessary to prolong the quota arrangements from year to year until the present time. During the scheme's existence modifications have been made in its scope and in the method of calculating individual quotas, in the light of experience and in response to changing circumstances.

The main aim of the quota scheme has been to enable LEAs to secure a fair share of the total number of teachers available year by year for the schools. When the scheme started there were wide variations between the staffing standards of different authorities. Movement towards the scheme's objective has deliberately been gradual, and progress in this direction has been achieved mainly by requiring the well placed authorities to mark time or to move forward only slowly, thus increasing the opportunities for the less fortunate authorities to improve their standards. The outcome has been that the gap between the staffing standards of the best and worst placed authorities is now appreciably less than it was in 1956, and the staffing standards of the great majority of authorities now fall within quite a narrow range of variation.

The current arrangements cover all full-time qualified teachers, but exclude temporary and occasional teachers and all part-time teachers. Married women returning to teaching after a break in service, and married women graduates entering teaching for the first time some years after taking their degree, do not count against the quota in the first two years of their return or entry. In calculating quotas for each LEA, account is taken of the latest information available about staffing standards, both national and local, of forecasts of each authority's population by age groups, and of estimates of the number of full-time qualified teachers expected to be available.

LEAs are notified at the beginning of each year of the number of teachers covered by the quota whom they should aim to be employing in their primary and secondary schools by January of the following year. This enables them to adjust recruitment to match retirements and resignations as they occur during the year. Authorities are never expected to terminate any teacher's appointment in order to conform to their quotas. Progress is reported to the Minister periodically, which enables excesses over the quota, or likely excesses, to be discussed with the LEA concerned. Most authorities which find it easy to attract teachers have readily exercised restraint to ensure the effective operation of the system and, when intervention has become necessary, little difficulty has been experienced in persuading the authorities in question to modify their staffing policies for the common good.

There are limits to what the quota scheme can achieve. The distribution of teachers under the scheme is related to the area of each LEA as a whole. The scheme cannot, therefore, solve particular local difficulties; some authorities have devised their own methods of dealing with these problems. Again, the scheme does not regulate the staffing of individual schools and cannot ensure that teachers with the right qualifications, training or experience, will be forthcoming to fill particular vacancies as they arise. Nor can any system of distribution operated by the Minister extend beyond the schools maintained by LEAs. The Minister did, however, enlist the help of the independent schools in limiting their calls during 1962–63 on the supply of teachers available that year, which was much reduced as a consequence of extending the training college course to three years in 1960.

It is not legally binding on LEAs to comply with the quota. The DES circulars are, however, in the nature of a very strong recommendation. As the majority of students come out of training in September, the LEAs' peak position for staffing is in October. After that date there is, of course, a certain wastage by reason of retirement, marriage, death, transfer to other posts, etc. Local authorities, therefore, have to make their calculations of staffing requirements having regard to these factors, and it would be impossible for them to make an entirely exact assessment. They are expected, however, to get as near to their quota figure as possible. Experience shows that if an authority is one or two over the quota, the DES takes no action, but that when it is much over this, then the Department will bring pressure to bear on the authorities concerned.

Among LEAs there are mixed views about the operation of the quota; the principal teachers' organisation also has strong misgivings about it, considering that the operation of such a system is a limitation on the freedom of teachers in their choice of employment. It seems certain, however, that such a system will continue so long as a serious teacher shortage exists, and so long as LEAs are prevented from offering salary and other inducements to attract teachers to their areas.

See also **Teacher estimates and teacher shortage**

FJ

R

Race Relations, Institute of
Founded as an independent body in 1958, the Institute aims at promoting the study of relations between racial groups and making available information concerning race relations. It sponsors research projects; runs a library and information service; and organises conferences, lectures and discussions. The IRR publishes books (including paperbacks) and pamphlets, the *IRR Newsletter* covering Britain and overseas (monthly), *Race* (quarterly) and IRR *Special Series* (theses and reports). It also provides reading lists and advice on speakers.

36 Jermyn St, London, SW1.

Race Relations in Britain, Survey of A five-year research project launched in 1963 with a grant from the Nuffield Foundation, the Survey published its first main study in 1967: John Rex and Robert Moore, *Race, Community and Conflict, a Study of Sparkbrook*.

Director: E. J. B. Rose, 33 Sackville St, London, W1.

Radio Society of Great Britain The Radio Society of Great Britain, founded in 1913, exists to assist, encourage and protect the interests of radio amateurs living in the UK. It achieves these aims firstly through its monthly publication *Radio Communication*, in which are articles of a technical nature, announcements concerning meetings of its affiliated societies, and details of contests which the society promotes. Secondly, it looks after the interests not only of its own members but of all amateurs in the UK, through its liaison with the GPO Radio Engineering Services, its representation at the International Amateur Radio Union and at other international conferences.

35 Doughty St, London, WC1.

Radioactivity, Teaching of Studied as a branch of modern physics, this is the phenomenon of spontaneous disintegration of elements by the emission of sub-atomic particles. Radioactivity has now become part of the syllabus for many of the GCE Boards, both at O and A levels; it is also included in the Nuffield Science Scheme and in most CSE syllabuses.

Although radioactive substances can be very dangerous, they are of the type that gives no warning; radiation cannot be felt and the damage caused probably has no immediate effect. Large amounts of radiation can lead to cancer and leukaemia. The use of radioactive substances makes it inevitable that those concerned will be exposed to radiation in addition to that they receive from the natural background. In addition to the dose they will receive from sources external to the body, there is the further risk that they may also be irradiated by radio-nuclides inadvertently taken into the body by inhalation, ingestion or directly through a wound.

Owing to the potentially dangerous nature of radioactive substances upon the health and safety of those who work with them, certain regulations have been brought into force which all teachers must comply with, and approval must be obtained from the Secretary of State for Education before any such work can be undertaken.

For basic work in schools, application is made on Form IRN and a science teacher is deemed qualified for the work. For more advanced work application is made on Form IRN, but teachers involved must first have undergone a recognised course on handling radioactive materials. Approval is also required before using apparatus capable of producing X-rays, except in the case of TV sets used for normal viewing, application being on Form IRX. This does not apply if the apparatus is operated at a voltage below five kilovolts.

If the work done in establishments of further education and colleges of education is at school level, the same regulations apply as for schools. In all other cases the college concerned must inform the Secretary of State that it is working under the regulations of the Code of Practice for the Protection of Persons Exposed to Ionising Radiations. Copies of the Code may be obtained from HMSO or through any bookseller.

All forms are available from the DES (Architects and Building Branch), Curzon St, London, W1. Administrative Memorandum 1/65, also available from the Department, sets out full details of the amounts of material that can be kept, the manner in which they must be stored, and the records that must be kept of the receipt, removal and disposal of radioactive substances to comply with the Radioactive Substances Act. On approval, establishments will also be informed of the safety precautions necessary, and the nearest hospital that will deal with radioactive accidents.

A booklet, *Radioactive Substances Act 1960—An explanatory memorandum to persons keeping or using radioactive materials*, can be obtained from HMSO or through any bookseller. Establishments proposing to use radioactive substances in excess of the quantities specified in the Exemption Order must apply for registration and, if necessary, authorisation on Forms RSA1 and RSA3, obtainable from the Ministry of Housing and Local Government, Whitehall, London, SW1.

NLR

Radiovision *See* **BBC educational broadcasting**

Ragged school movement The pioneer of the ragged schools—schools for children who were utterly destitute, with bad or poor parents or no parents at all—was John Pounds, a cobbler, who opened such a school in Portsmouth in 1818. The movement to provide ragged schools grew from that date onwards, coming under the guidance of Lord Shaftesbury in 1843 (a Ragged School Union was founded a year later) and continuing until the passing of the Education Act 1870. The schools were run by persons paid by individual philanthropists or charitable organisations, or by philanthropists themselves. At the peak of the movement, in the late 1860s, there were over 600 of these schools, a third of them day schools, another third Sunday schools, and the rest evening schools, with a total average attendance of over 25,000 children of all ages.

Raikes, Robert (1735–1811) A Gloucester publisher who was appalled by the ignorance of the prisoners in the local gaols, Raikes opened his first Sunday School in 1780 and five years later formed the Society for the Support and Encouragement of Sunday Schools in the Different Counties of England. He employed teachers and established a monitorial system for the teaching and practice of reading. Raikes was more dissatisfied with the limitations of Sunday education, and secured higher standards of teaching, than most other pioneers of the Sunday School movement.

U

Ranfurly Library Service Operated by unpaid volunteers, the Service distributes new and second-hand books (given to it free) to schools, libraries and individuals in developing countries. It has already delivered over two million books to 61 countries.

18 Carlton Hse Terrace, London, SW1.

Rank order coefficients *See* **Correlation**

Rapid reading The sum of human knowledge constantly increases; government and management grow more complex. These conditions favour the production of printed information which academics, scientists, administrators and businessmen must assimilate. To enable them to cope with the increase, research into the reading process has provided techniques which enable the speed of reading to be advanced without loss of comprehension. C. Poulton reported in the *British Journal of Educational Psychology* in 1961[1] that the average reading speed of students at rapid reading classes started at between 160 and 280 words per minute, and ended, after tuition, at between 340 and 500 words per minute. Tested again after 13 weeks, the students had retained a gain in speed of 93%; after six or more months the figure had dropped to 61% retention.

The method used to teach rapid reading aims to increase the number of words seen in the eye's 'span of recognition'. When eyes are reading a line of print they make a series of short jerky movements, stopping briefly after every one or two words. The words seen during this pause or 'fixation' seldom number more than two or three. The average reader has a fixation on a word of average size or two small words, and takes two fixations to see a very long word. But as meaning is chiefly conveyed not in single words but in phrases it is possible to increase the number of words within the span of recognition when a fixation occurs. Faults which hinder the development of rapid reading techniques are: (a) using a finger or pencil to mark the line being read; this tends to focus the eye on the word being pointed to by the marker instead of on a number of words or a phrase; (b) vocalisation, the mouthing of words as the eye sees them on the line, and sub-vocalisation, speaking the word in the mind; and (c) regression along the line of print already encountered in order to look again at a word. It has proved difficult to eradicate this last habit; even good readers make regressions.

Tests have shown that 70% comprehension can be achieved when reading at such high speeds as 500 words per minute. A greater degree of comprehension is only attained by reducing the speed of reading. But as writers have a tendency to repeat their salient points, a 70% comprehension figure is considered adequate. In the UK, some technical colleges have introduced rapid reading courses into their syllabuses, and a number of professional associations organise rapid reading courses for their managerial and executive personnel.

REFERENCE
1. *British Journal of Educational Psychology*, XXXI, 2, June 1961.

FURTHER READING
Edward Fry. *Teaching Faster Reading*, Cambridge Univ. Press, 1963. *Reading Faster: A Drill Book*, Cambridge Univ. Press, 1963.

EP

Read, Sir Herbert (b. 1893–1968) Poet and critic whose book *Education through Art* has had considerable influence on current ideas about the teaching of art in schools.

Readers, Backward Three groups of backward readers may be distinguished:

(1) Children who are moderately backward as a result mainly of environmental factors — homes limited in

cultural and verbal experience; inefficiencies in schooling (large classes, frequent changes of teacher, premature teaching); poor health resulting in absences. The children in this group usually respond to a 'reading drive' in school and regular remedial teaching in groups by interesting methods.

(2) Those whose backwardness is associated with some form of emotional disturbance resulting usually from unsettled family relationships. Some may need child guidance treatment, some a more therapeutically conceived remedial teaching in school.

(3) Those whose backwardness appears to have an organic or constitutional rather than environmental basis. They often come from good homes, and are often of good intelligence and competent in subjects or activities which do not require reading. Emotional difficulties when present are often reactions to their failure. The uncertain concept of dyslexia (*q.v.*) is applied to many of this group. Progress can be slow in spite of their eagerness to learn. Sometimes remedial teaching is very successful, though difficulty may still be experienced in acquiring fluency or in reading aloud.

Since the war, the amount of backwardness in reading has been reduced; but in some of the poorer areas of large towns there is still a problem with children of the first group. Children of the other two groups crop up in any kind of school.

See also **Reading research**

RG

'Reading, Progress in' A report published by the DES in December 1966, *Progress in Reading*, claimed that there had been a notable improvement in standards of reading in the schools since the end of the war. In 1964 the average standard of 11-year-olds was equivalent to that of children aged 12 years 5 months in 1948. The standard reached or exceeded by half the children of 1948 was reached or exceeded by three-quarters of the total number of school children in 1964.

Reading, Teaching of Reading was formerly taught by the alphabetic method (memorising the names of letters); then by the phonic method (learning the sounds of letters). Both methods isolated sound from meaning and were of limited value in a largely non-phonetic language. The whole-word methods (learning the names of objects or actions) were followed by the sentence methods where sound was linked with meaning, e.g. 'Peter brought this train'. It is now generally accepted that motivation through meaning and interest is important, but that usually, at some later stage, sounds need systematic introduction.

Reading is affected by the standard of literacy in the home; where a child at home has little verbal stimulus, the school attempts to compensate. Interesting activities lead to conversation and to the essential oral development on which reading is based; things made or collected are talked about and labelled: drawings and paintings are captioned by the teacher and the captions are read by the child; books are made by the teacher, recording the children's interests in their own words. There is usually a book corner with attractive, easily accessible books, used by the teacher not only as story books to be read aloud, but also as objects of interest and conversation. Together, this introduction of attractive books and the use of captions in situations meaningful and interesting to the child prepare the way for more systematic learning. Some teachers introduce pre-reading materials, e.g. matching games and other activities which encourage left-to-right eye movements. At the appropriate time, i.e. when a group of children seem at a point of sufficient maturation, the teacher introduces the group to a systematic reading scheme. Different published schemes have different strengths, and many teachers use a combination of schemes. Children who pass quickly through the early stages of a scheme are encouraged to read supplementary readers and to draw from the wide selection in the book corner.

Books are used in as many meaningful situations as possible: e.g. a book about shells in conjunction with a collection of shells; a book about ships together with the model of a ship made by a child. Children are encouraged to use books as sources of information. This aspect of learning is developed in the junior school, where less formal reading is done except with the more backward children, and where children are given further experience of the use of books as a means of information and reference as well as of imaginative pleasure. The provision of class library corners, the publication of increasing numbers of books suitable for this age range, and the use of 'finding out' activity methods, all help to strengthen this development.

The difficulties of some children in the early stages have led to the introduction of the Initial Teaching Alphabet (*q.v.*).

The developments of the last decades treat reading as an integrated part of language development, rather than as an isolated skill to be drilled out of context. Though some drills and systematic instruction may be necessary, these are introduced at a stage when the need and purpose of the skill have become apparent.

JF

Reading Association, International
See **Reading research**

Reading Association, United Kingdom *See* **Reading research**

Reading readiness In 1931 an experiment in the USA suggested that the best time to teach reading to children was when they had attained a mental age of 6½ years. This led to the concept of 'reading readiness' and the belief that it might be positively bad for children to be faced with reading in school before they were really equipped to tackle it. Although it may be possible to drill words into less mature children, this was thought not to produce genuine reading but rather a process often described as 'barking at print', where a child might be working entirely from memory rather than any sort of phonic analysis, and might understand little of what he was reading so fluently. There was always the risk, too, that such children would be put off reading by having had it thrust down their throats before they were ready for it.

Although the broad truth of the notion of reading readiness is still largely recognised today, it is often attacked on various grounds. Whereas it may be perfectly correct to give a culturally deprived child a great deal of stimulation from pictures, stories, vocabulary games and from talking about common experiences before getting on to reading about such things, there is no point in *not* teaching another child of the same age to read if he has gone through the stage of discussion at home and is eager and able to begin. In each case the aim is the same—not to make the individual child feel anxious by starting reading too early, or in the other case by starting it too late.

When preparing a child before organised reading lessons begin, the teacher should certainly introduce simple word-recognition and odd reading games at an early stage since, as the Scottish Council in Education has said, 'Reading readiness is largely reading achievement in its early stages'. In other words, the onset of reading readiness should and can be speeded up before pupils become too old, and no teacher should simply sit back on the grounds that 'reading is caught, not taught' and wait for the right stage somehow to arrive. On the other hand, few would wish to return to the days when beginning infant school meant intensive reading from the first day onwards.

FURTHER READING
F. J. Schonell. *The Psychology and Teaching of Reading*, Oliver and Boyd, Edinburgh, 1961.

NT

Reading research The 1960s have seen a renaissance of interest in the subject of reading—although, naturally, it has always been a topic of concern for the primary-school teacher. This increased interest has probably to a large extent been stimulated by two important research projects.

One has been conducted by Dr Joyce Morris at the National Foundation for National Research in England and Wales. She published[1] in 1959 the results of a survey of the reading attainments of over 8,000 children aged seven to 11 in a random sample of 60 primary schools in Kent, and she extended the area of her work to show that the problems found in Kent were representative of schools throughout the country. Briefly, Dr Morris found that at the age of seven, 19% of children entering the junior course were non-readers, and a further 26% had 'not sufficient mastery of reading mechanics to enable them to make progress on their own.'[2] She concluded that 'a continuation of the kind of teaching associated with the infant school was required by nearly half the children at the time of transfer.' Her investigation of the reading attainments of older children led Dr Morris to propose that teachers in the later years of the junior school and in the secondary school require a knowledge of methods of teaching the skill of reading. The extent to which such knowledge existed seemed doubtful.

Dr Morris has continued her research, and at the end of 1966 she published a new book[3] containing evidence of grave concern to British educators and parents. She related children's reading attainments to individual differences in the children's abilities, their home backgrounds and their school conditions. The results of her research show unmistakably that 'a good deal of reading backwardness can be attributed to school conditions.'[2] The main problem revealed was 'a marked tendency for late beginners, who need the most encouragement in their subsequent schooling to become effective readers, to receive the least.' This seems to be because 'juniors who are backward in reading are . . . under-privileged with regard to their teachers', chiefly because of the latter's lack of understanding and knowledge of the basic needs of children who are still in the beginning stages of learning to read.

It seems clear that future improvements in reading standards will depend to a very important degree on the improvements that can be made in the pre-service and in-service training of teachers in the special knowledge required to help children to learn to read and to maintain and polish their reading skills. Further discussion of this need for improved training and some suggestions have been provided recently in two papers by Dr Mary Austin[4] and William Latham.[5]

The other stimulating reading research project is the one conducted between 1960 and 1966 on the Initial Teaching Alphabet (*q.v.*). This research dealt with the basic raw material of reading and writing— what the science of linguistics terms the 'writing-system' of a language: i.e. the system of printed or written characters used to represent the system of sounds which is the spoken language. This investigation revealed another serious problem which should be of great concern to anyone devoted to improving literacy in English—the handicap of our conventional writing-system, the traditional orthography (t.o.) of English.

In 1961, Dr John Downing began an experiment which involved some

5,000 children in 150 schools. Half the pupils were in an experimental group which learned to read and write with a new simplified and regularised writing-system called the Initial Teaching Alphabet (i.t.a.)—devised by Sir James Pitman—while the other half were in a control group which learned with the more complex and irregular t.o. writing-system. The children's personal, home and school backgrounds were matched and they were taught with the same reading books, the only difference being that the experimental group's *Janet and John* series and many other books (see National Book League's list[6]) were printed in i.t.a. while the books used by the control group were in t.o.

The conclusion reached as a result of the i.t.a. experiment—a conclusion of major significance for the teaching of literacy in English—is that t.o. is a serious handicap to teachers and pupils in beginners' classes. The complexity and irregularity of t.o. cut the t.o. pupils' (t.o.) reading vocabulary to less than half of the (i.t.a.) reading vocabulary of the i.t.a. pupils—as based on parallel tests administered at the end of the first year and in the middle of the second year. Similarly, t.o. frustrated the development of written vocabulary in creative writing activities. Thus t.o. has been shown to be a seriously restricting factor in the early reading and writing activities of the infant school.

However, i.t.a. has a problem. It is not used in *all* books, and therefore i.t.a. pupils must transfer their i.t.a. reading and writing skills to reading and writing in t.o. When presented with t.o. tests at the end of the second year, i.t.a. pupils cannot read t.o. as well as they can read i.t.a. However, if time is allowed for adjustment, by the end of the third year they have picked up their steady line of progress and actually have an advantage of about five or six months of reading age (in t.o.) over pupils who have not used i.t.a. books.

A comprehensive report of the results of the i.t.a. experiments and a full discussion of their implications in educational theory and their relations to the psychological basis of the reading process have been published by Dr Downing.[7] The report of his first i.t.a. experiment has been reviewed by an international panel of independent experts in education and psychology, and this review has been published by the National Foundation for Educational Research.[8]

The i.t.a. experiment also confirmed Dr Morris's conclusion that teachers in the junior school need to be well informed about the teaching of reading, and Dr Downing has supported Dr Morris's plea for efforts to improve teachers' knowledge in this field.

An optimistic sign for such future improvement is to be found in new organised attempts to bring it about. Two new organisations are making good progress in this direction: the United Kingdom Reading Association (UKRA) and the International Reading Association (IRA).

United Kingdom Reading Association: Sec.: John Merritt, University of Durham Institute of Education, Old Shire Hall, Durham. Journal: *Reading*.

International Reading Association: Sec.: Dr Ralph Steiger, Tyre Avenue at Main Street, Newark, Delaware 19711, USA. Journals: *The Reading Teacher* and *Reading Research Quarterly*.

REFERENCES

1. J. M. Morris. *Reading in the Primary School*, 1959.
2. J. M. Morris. 'How Far can Reading Backwardness be Attributed to School Conditions?', *First International Reading Symposium* (Ed. J. A. Downing), 1966.
3. J. M. Morris. *Standards and Progress in Reading*, 1966.
4. M. C. Austin. 'Training Teachers to Teach Reading', *Second International Reading Symposium* (Ed. J. A. Downing), 1967.
5. W. Latham. 'Are Today's Teachers Adequately Trained for the Teaching of Reading?', *Third International Reading Symposium* (Ed. J. A. Downing), 1968.

6. National Book League. *I.t.a. Books for the Teacher and the Child*, 1965.
7. J. A. Downing. *Evaluating the Initial Teaching Alphabet*, 1967.
8. National Foundation for Educational Research. *The I.t.a. Symposium*, 1967.

FURTHER READING
J. A. Downing. *Evaluating the Initial Teaching Alphabet*, Cassell, 1967.
J. A. Downing (Ed.). *First International Reading Symposium*, Cassell, 1966. *Second International Reading Symposium*, Cassell, 1967. *Third International Reading Symposium*, Cassell, 1968.
H. P. Smith and E. V. Dechant. *Psychology in Teaching Reading*, Prentice-Hall, Englewood Cliffs, NJ, 1961.
M. D. Vernon. *Backwardness in Reading*, Cambridge Univ. Press, 1957.
Journals:
British Journal of Educational Psychology (three times a year).
Educational Research (three times a year).

JAD

Reading schemes Reading schemes are designed to help teachers to teach reading to classes or groups of children. Most include a graded series of children's books planned to teach reading from the very earliest stages to full fluency. The books are written on a basis of a controlled vocabulary, words being introduced gradually with a high rate of repetition and carry-over from book to book. Between 1,000 and 2,000 words are taught in this way, helped by the use of auxiliary apparatus and reading games.

In the UK there is freedom of choice of books and methods of teaching. Experiment is encouraged. In *The Teaching of Reading* (Publication 113 of UNESCO and the International Bureau of Education) it is shown that of 45 countries seven allow freedom of method. Only five have complete freedom of choice of books in schools.

In the UK a combination of three teaching methods is used—the sentence', 'word' and 'phonetic' methods. The 'sentence' method is the most widely used in the world, and it has much in common with the 'word' method. In these, children begin with words and/or sentences to do with their activities, needs and interests, without specifically learning their constituent parts or structure. 'Phonetic' methods stress the sounds of letters and combinations from the beginning. It appears that most teachers slightly delay the teaching of sounds because English is not a purely phonetic language.

Reading schemes reflect current teaching trends, and now that the emphasis has shifted from drills and exercises towards child study, reading is generally treated as one aspect of a language/arts programme, and meaningful reading is emphasised. The work done before the war by the Beacon Readers has been followed up by a number of other series which further emphasise the *use* of language and the importance of attitudes to learning. Typical of the aims of currently popular reading schemes are the following:

Janet and John. 'To produce effective, lasting results, a reading scheme must be engineered with the precision of a highly complicated piece of machinery, it must be comprehensive enough to meet every possible requirement of teachers, and yet to the child it must be as compellingly attractive as a favourite toy.'

Ladybird Key Words Reading Scheme. 'The essential harmony of the teacher/child relationship is achieved more easily when the chosen reading scheme has a strong attraction for the child and when it ensures rapid success. This necessitates a carefully planned psychological approach throughout the text which should include eye-appeal, self-identification, and a scientific control of vocabulary.'

Happy Venture. 'For success in the classroom, a reading scheme must be evenly graded, realistic in content, attractively presented to the child, wide in scope at each level, well supported by a good variety of auxiliary material, durably and economically made'.

Auxiliary books and apparatus In most reading schemes a number of auxiliary reading aids is provided. Items in popular use include workbooks for reading, writing, drawing, tracing and colouring; comprehension cards for practice in reading, understanding and writing; wall pictures for promoting the free use of language and for introducing word and sentence cards linked with each picture; flash cards, large and small, for word drills and word games; and picture-sentence and picture-word matching cards for desk use.

FURTHER READING

Publishers offer a wide variety of reading schemes (including teachers' books) to suit the methods chosen by teachers. Some of the reading schemes and graded readers available are:

Janet and John (Nisbet); *Ladybird Key Words* (Wills and Hepworth); *Happy Venture* (Oliver and Boyd); *Gay Way* (Macmillan); *Pilot* (E. J. Arnold); *Mckee* (Nelson); *Happy Trio* (Wheaton); *Queensway* (Evans); *Vanguard* (McDougall); *Mike and Mandy* (Nelson); *Adventures in Reading and Writing* and *More Adventures* (University of London Press); *Griffin* (E. J. Arnold); *Royal Road* (Chatto and Windus); *Words in Colour* (Educational Explorers); *Beacon Readers* (Ginn); *Oxford Colour Reading Books* (Oxford University Press); *Ready to Read* (Methuen); *Colour Story Reading* (Nelson); *Time for Reading* (Ginn). Many of these reading schemes are also published in the initial teaching alphabet (i.t.a.) which is described elsewhere in this book.

WM

Reading tests There are now many reading tests, usually measuring a pupil's ability to read sentences or a series of individual words. From his performance on these tests, it is possible to assess a child's reading age by comparing the number of words or sentences he gets right with the average score for a child his age. Thus, if a child of seven can read the amount of words or sentences normally achieved by an average child one year older, he will have a reading age of eight years. Reading tests are also useful for spotting the different types of reading mistake that occur, and for assessing the

progress a child might have made after intense remedial help with his reading.

FURTHER READING

F. J. and F. E. Schonell. *Diagnostic and Attainment Testing*, Oliver and Boyd, Edinburgh, 1950.

Reading tutor *See* **Libraries in colleges of education**

Reception class A term sometimes used for the class into which children are received on their first admission to school. Its special designation reflects a recognition of the importance to children of the transition from home to school, and of the need to help them to accept the new situation so that they can take full advantage of the opportunities which school has to offer. It is therefore the aim of a head teacher to make this class a small community, to place it in the care of an experienced teacher who fully understands the needs of children in the new situation, and to equip the classroom in a way which will assist a smooth transition. Hindrances to achievement of these aims may arise from the actual numbers which have to be admitted and from the present difficulty of staffing infant schools at all adequately (*see* **Primary schools**).

Although entry to school is legally compulsory on reaching the age of five years, local conditions differ to the extent that in some areas children may be accepted into the reception class for the term preceding their fifth birthday if their parents so desire. In other areas children may have to wait for admission until the term after their fifth birthday. Since it is normal and usually necessary to admit children at the beginning of each of the three terms of the school year, the length of a child's stay in a reception class may be one, two or three terms. If numbers for admission in the second or third term are large, promotion of some previous admissions is essential if the reception class is to remain a reasonable size; the likely criteria for such promotion are chronological age and success in adaptation to the school situation. This practice cannot be considered satisfactory for the children, the reception class teacher or the school as a whole. The termly disturbance of class composition, which may affect all or most classes in the school, militates against the cultivation of the kind of personal relationship which good infant education requires, and against a sense of stability in the school community.

Some infant schools have overcome the problem by substituting vertical grouping (*see* **Infant schools**) for the traditional classification by chronological age, thus eliminating entirely the need for a reception class. The Plowden Committee, while admitting that vertical grouping gave this and some other advantages, does not recommend its introduction without reservation (*Plowden Report*, Sections 799–804). It prefers to eliminate termly admissions by recommending that children enter school only in the September following their fifth birthday; the age range of new entrants would therefore be from five years to five years eleven months, but it has to be remembered that this recommendation is inseparable from a requirement that nursery provision be available for the year before compulsory entry for all children whose parents desire it. As an interim measure, the Committee recommends two admission dates, September and April (*Plowden Report*, Sections 357–9, 399–400). Should these recommendations be implemented, there would still be a place for the reception class in the first schools, and it could be expected to serve more adequately the purposes of such a class.

JBC

Reckonable service *See* **Contributory service**

Recognised as efficient *See* **Inspection and recognition**

Record Association, British Founded in 1932 as a national organisation to co-ordinate and encourage the work of the many individuals, authorities, institutions and societies interested in the conservation and use of records, the Association has secured the establishment of the National Register of Archives and has caused a postgraduate course in archive administration to be instituted at University College, London, as well as a course in document repair at the London School of Printing and Graphic Arts. It has set up a Records Preservation section, with the aims of saving records that are in danger of loss or destruction through ignorance and neglect and of ensuring that such records find suitable permanent homes.

The Master's Court, The Charterhouse, London, EC1.

Recorded Sound, British Institute of Britain, unlike most other Western countries, had no national record collection until, in 1955, the British Institute of Recorded Sound launched its first appeal for records old and new, asking the public to give their unwanted 78s and LPs and to offer private recordings to be copied for preservation. The Institute's policy is to preserve recordings of every kind— including everyday sounds doomed to disappear with changing times. With slender resources, the Institute has collected almost 100,000 recordings, including broadcasts which the BBC has permitted it to record, and the nucleus of a national collection now exists. A reference library of books, periodicals and record catalogues has been formed, and is used on an increasing scale for research and as a source of information on all aspects of recorded sound. With the help of grants and support by members of the public enrolled as Friends of the Institute, it is hoped eventually to secure better facilities for storing the collection and library and making them available for use.

29 Exhibition Rd, London, SW7.

Recreation Centres, National *See* **Physical Recreation, Central Council of**

Recreative Evening Schools Association *See* **Continuation schools**

Red Cross Society, British The aims of the Society are the promotion of health, the prevention of disease and the relief of suffering throughout the world.

This humanitarian movement, conceived by Henri Dunant, a Swiss, after he had seen the horrific aftermath of the Battle of Solferino in 1859, has grown into the world-wide organisation, the International Red Cross, which makes no discrimination as to race, class, creed or politics. The British Red Cross is a member society.

Its activities fall under three main headings—first aid, nursing, welfare. Among the services it runs are: picture libraries in hospitals; outpatients' canteens; first aid posts; nursing help for the district nurse and for hospitals; holidays and clubs for old people and for handicapped of all ages; language cards; escorts for invalids.

It trains its own members in all aspects of its work and runs short first aid and nursing courses for members of the public, believing that there should be someone in every home with some knowledge of these subjects. In addition a number of other courses are arranged for organisations or schools requiring the Society's certificates.

An integral part of the Society is the the British Junior Red Cross, of which there are over 85,000 members with the aims of protecting life and health, rendering service to the sick and suffering, and promoting international friendship and understanding. Through their training in such subjects as first aid,

nursing, mothercraft, health and hygiene and accident prevention, they learn to become useful members of the Society and to help those less fortunate than themselves—in particular the old and lonely, physically handicapped children and the deaf and blind.

14 Grosvenor Cres., London, SW1.

Refunded pension contributions, Repayment of If a teacher to whom contributions have been repaid is subsequently re-employed in contributory service, he or she may, at any time while so employed, repay the gross amount previously refunded with compound interest at the rate of $3\frac{1}{2}\%$, and have the period represented by those contributions reinstated as pensionable.

Regional Advisory Councils for Further Education *See* **Further Education, Regional Advisory Councils for**

Regional colleges *See* **Further education in England and Wales; Appendix 9**

Regression *See* **Defence mechanism**

Regulations, Statutory Although Education and other Acts define at great length the powers and duties of the Minister, LEAs, and third parties (e.g. parents, and managers and governors of schools), they do not deal in detail with many matters that Parliament still wishes to be legally enforced.

For such matters the Acts empower or require the Minister to prescribe the details in regulations made by him. Scores of regulations are made by statutory instrument, all having the force of law. Examples are: standards for school premises; school regulations; further education regulations; training of teachers regulations; provision of milk and meals regulations; regulations for scholarships and other benefits. The

Minister has to lay the regulations before Parliament and they may be annulled by either House within a specified period of days. Parliament is therefore spared some details during the passage of a bill, and the Minister is allowed to make administrative law without the three readings in each House required of a bill. The Acts also empower or require the Minister to make statutory orders or to give statutory directions with respect to other matters specified in the Acts.

In addition, the DES issues circulars to LEAs and others involved, for their guidance or direction on matters of national policy under the Minister's control. The DES also issues administrative memoranda on matters of detail. Some of the many circulars and administrative memoranda are ephemeral; an index of the ones current at the beginning of each year is published by HMSO.

See also **Education and Science, Department of**

FURTHER READING

G. Taylor and J. B. Saunders. *The New Law of Education*, Butterworth, 1965.

FB

Reinforcement (*and see* **Feedback**) A psychological term widely and loosely used in programmed learning. Behaviour is modified whenever a response produces a consequent stimulus event, such as a reward, which strengthens or confirms that response. To be effective, the reinforcing stimulus must immediately follow the response to be learned—hence the insistence on the need for immediate 'knowledge of results'. Positive reinforcement may take the form of food or financial gain or, less tangibly, of praise and status-seeking. Negative reinforcement may be broadly equated with any unpleasant situation.

WKR

Relief of Schoolchildren Order (1905) *See* **School medical service**

Religion in schools In England and Wales it is a legal obligation, laid down by the Education Act, 1944 that every county and voluntary school shall begin the day 'with collective worship' and shall provide 'religious instruction' for its pupils. Religion is the only subject mentioned in the Act which must, by statute, be provided. There are safeguards to protect parents and teachers. No child shall be compelled to attend worship or RI if it is contrary to his or her parents' wishes. Teachers in these schools are not obliged to attend religious assemblies nor to teach the subject of religion. Most religious surveys reveal that no more than 10% of the adult population attend a place of worship with regularity, yet a national opinion poll, taken in 1965, showed strong support for the continuation of religion in schools. Ninety per cent of all those polled wished the arrangements under the Education Act 1944 to continue. Despite poor attendances at churches, 79% of these adults also thought that Britain was a Christian country.

The Act itself nowhere lays down that the religion taught shall be Christianity. RI, however, must be taught according to an 'agreed syllabus', that is a syllabus agreed upon locally by three parties—representatives of teachers, the LEA and churches. Roman Catholic representation is not included, since they stand outside the county and voluntary system of education. The churches invited to be represented are the historic Protestant denominations, and do not include the smaller sects.

The result of this system is not that there are as many syllabuses as there are LEAs, but that many committees agree to adopt another authority's syllabus. The syllabuses most popular are from Cambridgeshire, the West Riding and Surrey. There are about thirty syllabuses in use in England and Wales, many of them borrowing from each other. While the law lays down that a syllabus 'shall not include any catechism or formulary which is distinctive of any particular religious denomination', all syllabuses are unmistakably Christian and mainly involve the study of the Bible.

Outwardly the law, with a generous measure of public support, upholds the system, but within the teaching profession much criticism of syllabuses has been made in the 60s. This was supported by varied research carried out, for example, by a Sheffield group. Loukes and Goldman (see *Further reading*) and other investigations appear to point in the same direction. If knowledge of the Bible is the criterion of success, then religious education in schools is open to much criticism. New syllabuses, based upon children's real experience, are being advocated; the first to appear is the new West Riding syllabus, issued in 1966.

In 1965 seven leading researchers and writers in the field of religious education submitted an open letter to LEAs. This dealt with problems relating to teachers, children and the teaching of the subject. Several recommendations were made, among them the reform of syllabuses from Bible-centred content to content more in accord with children's needs and interests, stimulation of teachers in more modern methods of teaching, and the appointment of advisers in religious education to help teachers to be more effective. A final recommendation calls for the aims of teaching to be educationally sounder and more in accord with the times, namely 'the active encouragement of teachers to help their pupils towards critical choice, and to see the aim of religious education in terms of personal search, rather than the imparting of a body of fact.' This recommendation has become known as 'the open-ended aim of religious education' in opposition to outdated aims of indoctrination and instruction. Many educators prefer the term 'religious education' to 'religious instruction', since it has a broader meaning and implication.

The mid-60s has brought considerable re-thinking and discussion to the subject of religion in schools. An important document was published by a group of Christians and humanists (see *Further reading*: Alves *et al.*). Some of the proposals are similar to the recommendations of the Open Letter, and although there are differences the tone and outlook of the document by the Christians and humanists are remarkably similar to the Open Letter group.

The key to change lies in the hands of teachers. In primary schools where the class-teaching structure is normal, teachers cover the whole range of subjects and religion is one of the subjects normally taken, unless a teacher invokes the Act's conscience clause. In secondary schools, religion is frequently taught by specialist teachers. There is a shortage of teachers academically well qualified for teaching religion in secondary schools, but existing specialists mainly support the open-ended approach with adolescents. In an age of enquiry, many find it impossible to do anything else when examining such questions as the authority of the Bible. The situation is different in primary schools where many teachers, although dissatisfied, seem content to tell stories, with unquestioning acceptance of the authority of the Bible, of miracles for instance, and involving primitive theological ideas.

The issues with adolescents are clearer because many of them do not hesitate to query, but concern is felt that in primary schools children will believe literally most of what they are told and that here religious education comes very close to indoctrination. Evidence can be seen that before the end of primary schooling children are beginning to separate their experiences into two worlds, one a religious world of God, Jesus, Bible and miracle, where anything can happen; the other a world of science and technology, of cause and effect, where God is invisible and inactive. Informed teachers see as their task the keeping of the two world views together, so that everyday experience can be looked at within a religious frame of reference. The open-ended approach makes this possible, enabling teacher and taught to explore religion and retain intellectual integrity.

FURTHER READING

R. Acland, R. Batten, E. Cox, J. Daines, R. Goldman, H. Loukes and V. Madge. *An Open Letter to LEA Religious Education Advisory Committees*, published privately, Reading University, 1965.
C. Alves, H. J. Blackham *et al. Religious and Moral Education: Some Proposals for County Schools*, published privately, Borough Road College, 1965.
M. Argyle. *Religious Behaviour*, Routledge and Kegan Paul, 1958.
R. Goldman. 'Do we want our Children Taught about God?', *New Society*, 139, 27 May 1965. *Religious Thinking from Childhood to Adolescence*, Routledge and Kegan Paul, 1965. *Readiness for Religion*, Routledge and Kegan Paul, 1965.
H. Loukes. *Teenage Religion*, SCM Press, 1961.
University of Sheffield. *Religious Education in Secondary Schools*, Nelson, 1961.
Education Act 1944, sections 25–32, Chapter 31, HMSO.

RJG

Religious assemblies All county and voluntary schools in England and Wales must by law[1] begin the school day 'with collective worship on the part of all pupils in attendance at the school.' The tradition of school worship was established long before the law required it. The religious clauses of the Education Act 1944 make it clear that withdrawal of pupils and teachers is an important right not only for parents who wish their children to worship according to specific tradition, but also for those who for various reasons do not wish their children to participate in religious assemblies at all.

The law insists that school assemblies shall not 'be distinctive of any particular religious denomination.' This is often misinterpreted as the need to hold all assemblies on an undenominational basis. More accurately interpreted it means that a balance and mixture of various traditions should be observed; Anglican, Presbyterian or Quaker worship, for example, may form the liturgical or devotional structure of assemblies, but one type should not predominate over a period of time. As with religious teaching (*see* **Religion in schools**) the Act does not even specify which religion should be the form of worship. By law it is possible, in a school where a majority of the children may be from Indian homes, for the school assembly to take the form of a Hindu celebration.

By custom many head teachers conduct daily assembly, but a growing practice is for other teachers to do this in turn, and for pupils themselves to take part. The most progressive schools often have a school orchestra playing the music, pupils presenting a play or situation and other pupils presiding or participating. The move is away from an adult-imposed tradition of formal worship which may have little reference to the daily life of the pupils.

The anomaly has been pointed out[2] that worship imposed upon unwilling and sceptical adolescents can only lead to unfortunate results. A suggestion is made that at least from the official school-leaving age, those remaining at school should decide for themselves whether or not to attend assemblies.

REFERENCES
1. *Education Act, 1944*, HMSO, chapter 31, section 25.
2. C. Alves, H. J. Blackham *et al. Religious and Moral Education: Some proposals for County Schools* (private publication), Borough Road College, Isleworth, 1965.

RJG

Religious Education in Accordance with the Principles of the Church of England, National Society for Promoting Established in 1811, the Society was incorporated in 1817, and granted its supplemental charter in 1934. In promoting religious education the Society makes grants for the improvement of church schools, and provides free legal advice on administrative problems to managers, governors and trustees of church schools.

As trustee to a number of church training colleges and schools, the Society is directly concerned with the training of teachers and children, and it works closely with the School Council of the Church of England Board of Education (*q.v.*). The Society is a charity dependent upon gifts and legacies.

69 Great Peter St, London, SW1.

Religious Teaching Certificates *See* Catholic colleges of education

Remand homes salaries
Superintendents The salary scale, within the salary ranges for both superintendents and deputy superintendents, is comprised of five annual increments of £45.

Superintendents and deputy superintendents who are qualified teachers and who hold university degrees or other recognised qualifications and extra training provided for in the 'Scales of Salaries for Teachers in Primary and Secondary Schools, England and Wales, 1965' are paid the appropriate amounts in addition to their salary.

Teachers Qualified teachers, unqualified teachers and temporary teachers employed as such in remand homes are paid in accordance with the salary scales as set out in the Burnham Report, together with an addition which is carried beyond the maximum of the scale as follows: qualified teachers £215, unqualified teachers and temporary teachers £155.

Senior assistants The allowance paid in addition to the salary as a teacher is as follows:

Approved max. no. of beds	Allowance
Up to 29	£100
30 to 49	£120
50 and over	£135

SEB

Remedial classes These provide remedial teaching to overcome a child's retardation in a basic subject, e.g. reading or arithmetic, so that he or she can benefit from the normal curriculum provided for his or her age and ability. They have, therefore, a short-term aim of helping the child to catch up, and should be distinguished from a special class or stream for slow learning children who need a more continuous form of special teaching.

Remedial groups may be organised within a school so that children are drawn from their own classes for regular periods of remedial teaching. Sometimes remedial classes are held in a child guidance clinic or in a conveniently placed remedial centre. Sometimes, children attend a remedial class for a continuous period and then return to their normal class. Remedial group teaching within the school is to be preferred in order to make liaison easier between the remedial and the ordinary class teacher.

See also **Backwardness; Retardation**

RG

Remedial teaching This form of teaching is given to pupils who for various reasons have failed to learn to a level that might be expected of them, e.g. children of average ability who have difficulty in the 3 Rs. Remedial teaching can be distinguished from special education by its short-term aims. It should also be distinguished from coaching which is extra tuition. The following principles can be suggested.

(1) Remedial teaching should be based on an assessment of the nature and, if possible, the causes, of the failure. For example, in reading, it is necessary to discover what skills have not been acquired. In arithmetic, basic

arithmetical concepts may not be understood. In both subjects there may be gaps or confusion in the child's knowledge. Assessment of the child's strengths and weaknesses in mental abilities, emotional attitudes to him or herself and to learning and his or her background experiences at home and school often provide clues to the causes of the difficulty and, more important, pointers to the selection of methods and approaches in teaching him or her.

(2) Provisional aims and plans should be formulated, though these are frequently modified as new insights are obtained in the course of remedial teaching.

(3) Good teacher–pupil relationships are essential.

(4) Remedial work should be well-motivated to overcome feelings of failure. Often, initial success has to be engineered.

Some children require little more than good individual teaching in an encouraging, non-critical atmosphere. Some, particularly those whose failure is associated with emotional reactions, need a more informal, indirect approach to teaching. Great ingenuity is needed to arouse their will to learn and promote their personal maturity before more systematic work can be attempted. Others are impeded by special difficulties — weaknesses in auditory or visual discrimination, persistent laterality difficulties showing in reversal tendencies in reading and writing, inexplicable difficulties in acquiring basic number concepts, difficulties in coordination which affect writing and spelling.

Remedial teaching should attempt to remedy such difficulties by specific training and experience, but should also promote progress by using skills and abilities in which a child is relatively more successful. (Thus, a child with auditory difficulties may make progress in reading using visual — look and say — methods though he or she

also needs help to use phonic cues in reading.) Successful achievements in other school work, e.g. practical and creative work or hobbies and interests, can be used to motivate remedial work and to compensate for feelings of failure.

Remedial teaching requires study of the individual child's difficulties leading to a prescription for teaching; but there is no mystique about it. Observant, sympathetic teachers who understand their children and know the subject thoroughly can do it well. But further training is an advantage especially for remedial teaching in a clinic, or for work as an advisory remedial teacher. The DES programme of courses of further training lists appropriate one-year courses.

See also **Backwardness; Retardation**
RG

Remuneration of Teachers Act 1963 This Act gave the Minister the power, where he had rejected a Burnham award, to make a single salary award in its place.

Reports, School The traditional school report, with its equally traditional vocabulary of approval or criticism, is still with us: but dissatisfaction with it, as a fundamentally stilted document belonging to a period of primitive communication between school and parent, is growing.

It seems likely that in most schools the report is still a termly document which records a child's marks and position in class in each subject during term and in examinations, with a brief comment from each subject master (where the problem of commenting does not defeat him), with at the foot of the report a summary statement on the child's general progress and conduct by his form-master, housemaster or headmaster. The problem of saying, in a very short space, something about a child's work that will be meaningful and helpful to his parents, and of composing many such comments within a very short space of time, has taxed the skill of teachers throughout the years; the retreat to such clichés as 'fair', 'satisfactory' or 'could do better' is common enough. One of the trends of our time, resulting partly from a new recognition of the importance of a fuller relationship between home and school, is the increase in research into means of improving communication between a child's teachers and his parents; and it seems probable that as a result of this the school report as we know it, though it may survive as a record or a formal summary, will cease to be regarded as a satisfactory major means of informing a parent of his child's progress.

Of course, there have long been schools that have attempted to make the report a profounder and more helpful communication than it commonly is; but these have most often been small, well-staffed schools catering for parents who expect as a matter of course to be told as much as possible about their children's work and welfare at school. There have been experiments, also, in which children have reported on themselves (see for example A. W. Rowe, *The Education of the Average Child*), and even in which children have reported on the school and the teachers (see Kneebone's *I Worked in a Secondary Modern School* and E. R. Braithwaite's *To Sir with Love*).

EB

Requisition dates The dates stipulated by the LEAs by which requisitions for books and materials must be received at the Education Office. Most authorities stagger dates for ordering, but the major part of the capitation allowance is usually dispensed during the January–April period.

Research into Higher Education, Society for A registered charity and also a company limited by guarantee and not having a share capital, the Society was set up in 1964 to encourage and co-ordinate research into all forms of higher education. It seeks to make research findings more generally available and to promote their more effective use. Its activities include the organisation of conferences, study groups, seminars and other meetings at national, regional and local level; the holding of an annual conference at which recent research findings are presented and discussed; the maintenance of a register of research in progress; the issue of a quarterly series of abstracts of the more important literature; the publishing of bibliographies, reports, review monographs and a monthly bulletin; the collection of unpublished research material; and collaboration with other national bodies interested in such research and with overseas organisations. A grant is received from the DES.

There are two types of membership, individual and corporate. Corporate membership entitles the organisation to receive a limited number of copies of the Society's publications and to send any of its members to the Society's functions.

2 Woburn Sq., London, WC1.

Reserved teachers A reserved teacher is one who is appointed to a voluntary or special agreement school by the managers or governors of that school, and not by the LEA, on his undertaking to give religious instruction.

See also **Controlled schools**

Residential Child Care Association Founded in 1949 by members of the first Home Office Training Courses for Houseparents, the Association has now developed into a nation-wide professional body with nearly 2,000 members. Its aims include the creation and maintenance of a high standard of training and work in child care; the promotion of a wide knowledge of recent developments in the field; and the provision of opportunities for the exchange of knowledge and experience between individual members and organisations.

RCCA is the UK section of an international organisation set up by UNESCO in 1949, the Fédération Internationale des Communautés d'Enfants.

Gen. Sec.: George Forrest, Earlsfield Hse, Swaffield Rd, London, SW18.

Publications: *The Child in Care* (monthly), *The Annual Review*.

Residental courses *See* **Adults, Residential courses for**

'Resources for Learning' (project) *See* **Nuffield Foundation**

Responsibility allowances As their name implies, these are payments made in respect of additional responsibility which may be undertaken. Such payments are quite distinct from any extra pay due for additional training or extra qualifications. The normal pattern of allowances for extra responsibility is that a school will have a deputy head (unless it is very small), making the deputy head the next highest paid to the head teacher of the school. In addition to this there are provisions for such appointments as second masters or second mistresses, heads of departments and graded posts. The opportunity for making such appointments varies according to the size of the school and in some cases according to the way in which an LEA exercises the discretion available to it under the Burnham Report. For example, in a mixed school in Group 7 or above, the LEA may designate a teacher of the opposite sex to that of the deputy head teacher as second master or second mistress, as the case may be. The teacher so designated shall receive an additional payment, the amount of which shall be determined by the LEA and appropriately related to the deputy head teacher for the school.

If a new deputy head teacher of the same sex as the teacher who has been designated second master or second mistress is appointed to the school or the department, the existing second master or second mistress may continue to be so designated and receive the appropriate additional payment while he or she remains in the post, but no other teacher may be designated second master or second mistress while that payment is being made.

Details regarding heads of departments and graded posts are given in separate articles (*q.v.*). There are, however, arrangements whereby teachers not attached to the staff of a particular school but considered by the employing LEA as having duties and responsibilities equivalent to a head of department or a teacher in a graded post could, at discretion, receive the appropriate payment for the additional responsibility. Again, there are opportunities for allowances to meet special circumstances, and an example of this would be that if a post-holder is absent for a prolonged period, then a teacher who undertakes duties during a temporaray period could receive the allowance for the period concerned. SEB

Responsible bodies This term has been used for a number of years in the official Further Education (Grant) Regulations to cover those organisations 'responsible for the provision of liberal education for adults' which are eligible for a direct grant from the DES in respect of the courses which they provide. This definition excludes the LEAs, but includes the university extra-mural departments and the Workers' Educational Association (*qq.v.*). The other RBs are the Seafarers' Education Service, the University of Wales Council of Music and the Welsh Executive Committee of the Young Men's Christian Association.

Scotland In Scotland there is no equivalent to the English and Welsh 'responsible body'. This is because the only bodies responsible in Scottish law for providing primary, secondary and further education are the LEAs. No money is made available to any other organisation. Scottish universities have extra-mural departments, but they carry out their functions as agents of the LEA. The difference is not merely administrative. In practice Scotland has not had to suffer the rather uneasy division of subject by providing body, some concerned with theory, others with practice, that can confuse everyone in the South but the theorist. LEA and extra-mural classes can be in practical craft work or in liberal studies or a combination of them, as seems appropriate.

Retail Trades Education Council
The objects of the RTEC include the encouragement and promotion of education and training for those engaged in the retail trade; the provision of a medium for the exchange of information on retail education and training; the securing wherever possible of an integrated educational policy among kindred bodies, and of co-ordination in the field of education and training between the trade, Industrial Training Boards, appropriate government departments and educational organisations and establishments. Research is promoted and conducted and advice given to careers advisers and those contemplating a career in the retail trade; and the Council also acts as an endorsing authority for the Retail Trades Junior Certificate and the Certificate in Retailing.

56 Russell Sq., London, WC1.

Retardation Refers to slowness or lag in development. Thus mental retardation is sometimes used as synonymous with mental handicap or subnormality. In education, the term is used with the specific meaning of a discrepancy between educational age (or attainment) and *mental* age, whereas the similar term 'backwardness' involves a comparison of educational age and *chronological* age. The concept is useful. Thus,

a child may be backward (i.e. achieves less well than his or her age group) but he or she may not be retarded (i.e. he or she is achieving as well as his or her abilities would lead one to expect). Another child may be backward *and* retarded, e.g. he or she is an obviously intelligent child who is under-achieving. In both cases, we should, as with all pupils, work for improvement. In the latter case, we ought to leave no stone unturned to get to the root of the failure. The concept has value if it draws attention to the fact that backward classes commonly contain some intelligent retarded children whose abilities merit more demanding academic work. The concept has recently fallen somewhat out of favour, one reason being the difficulty of defining or measuring the discrepancy between achievement and potentiality.

See also **Backwardness; Remedial classes; Remedial teaching**

RG

Retention Perfect memory is an impossibility, and however carefully something may be learnt much of it will soon be forgotten unless steps are taken to re-learn it at increasing intervals of time. It is a good idea to learn something just before going to sleep, as this seems to give the brain an opportunity to consolidate what it has learned. If, however, one period of learning is followed by another, and if the material to be learned is rather similar, then it is quite likely that the two memories will become confused.

See also **Memory**

Retired teachers, Re-employment of
Full-time teaching service If a retired teacher takes a full-time teaching post in a state school, or in an independent school which comes under one or other of the schemes of superannuation for independent schools, at a rate of salary not less than his former highest rate, his pension will cease for the duration

of the re-employment. If, however, it is less, then he will receive so much of his pension as will bring up his new rate of salary to his former highest rate. If the teacher is under 70 years of age and has not completed 45 years of contributory and/or recognised service, superannuation contributions will be payable. If he completes at least 12 months' service before final retirement, then his pension and lump sum will be re-assessed on current salary. Any fresh pension which may be granted, however, will not be less than his original pension. If the teacher does not complete at least 12 months' additional service, or if his service does not result in the award of a higher rate of pension or lump sum, then the contributions which he has paid in respect of the additional service will be refunded to him.

If a pensioner is over the age of 70 the same rule applies so far as the reduction of his pension is concerned, but superannuation contributions are not payable and his pension and lump sum will not be re-assessed in respect of the service rendered after the age of 70.

Part-time teaching service If a teacher takes a part-time teaching post his pension will not be affected provided that his part-time salary and pension together, in any one quarter of the year, do not exceed the quarterly current rate of salary payable in respect of the highest post he held when he was employed in full-time contributory teaching service. If his part-time salary and pension together did exceed this notional rate of salary, then his pension would be reduced by the amount of the excess. (Where the pensioner has allocated part of his pension, the notional salary is taken as reduced by the amount of pension surrendered.) Under this rule, supply service is reckoned as part-time service.

Other employment If a teacher after retirement takes a post other than one in the teaching service, then the above rules would not apply unless the salary received came wholly or in part from public funds. Employment with a purely private concern would have no effect upon the teacher's pension irrespective of the amount of earnings.

Informing Paymaster-General of re-employment The Paymaster-General should be notified by letter of any employment in grant-aided service, whether of a contributory or non-contributory nature and full particulars, including the amount earned during each quarter, should be inserted on the pension form containing the declaration. If the pensioner is re-employed in grant-aided school service, then all pension forms should be returned direct to the Paymaster-General at the Teachers' Pensions Department, High Street, Crawley, Sussex.

SEB

Retired teachers and income tax
A teacher's pension is reckoned as 'earned income' for the purposes of assessing income tax and is therefore subject to the two-ninths earned income allowance. The lump sum is tax-free and should not be included in the income tax return.

Persons over the age of 65 are allowed to treat the whole of their income, whether earned or unearned, as earned income, where the total income does not exceed £900. Where a single person over the age of 65 has a total income not exceeding £390, no tax is payable. The figure for a married couple, where either husband or wife is over 65, is £625.

On retirement, income tax matters concerning a teacher's pension are dealt with by HM Inspector of Taxes, Public Departments (3), Ty Glas Rd, Llanishen, Cardiff, and any enquiries relating thereto should be addressed to that office, quoting the tax reference. If the teacher feels that a personal interview would be helpful in settling a tax problem, the inspector at Cardiff will arrange an appointment for the teacher with his local office.

In the year of retirement, income tax is assessed on salary to the date of retirement and the amount of pension due from that date to the following 5 April.

Any alteration in the teacher's financial circumstances should be notified to the Cardiff office immediately, so that any adjustment necessary to the teacher's income tax position can be made.

Where a teacher pensioner undertakes part-time teaching or other work, then the income tax payable in respect of the part-time earnings will be dealt with by the inspector of taxes for the district in which the teacher is employed, whilst tax due on the pension will continue to be dealt with by Cardiff.

SEB

Retirement, Preparation for It is now normal, where it used to be exceptional, to live into old age; it is also customary, where it used to be rare, for people to stop work, regardless of their state of health or mind, when they reach pensionable age. This combination confronts a steadily increasing number of people with problems arising from reduced income and status, more leisure than is always welcome, changed personal relationships, unstable or deteriorating mental and physical health.

Some of the more progressive industrial concerns and adult education agencies, and certain specially constituted retirement councils, are promoting conferences, courses, group discussions and other encounters to encourage men and women approaching retirement to estimate their own spiritual, financial and other resources, and to plan the best, happiest and most profitable use of them. Education in budgeting, health and the purposeful enjoyment of leisure customarily form part of the diet of such discussions, but there is much to be learned about how to make them most effective. There is a central clearing-house through which experience of such pre-retirement preparation is pooled: the Pre-Retirement Association, which provides an advisory service to firms wishing to do more than issue gold watches and handshakes, and to others seeking through education to help people turn old age into a positive phase of life with its own special virtues and opportunities.

BG

Retirement benefits, Calculation of A teacher's pension and lump sum are calculated with reference to the whole period of contributory service, years and days, and the average salary for the last three years of that service. The maximum service allowed for calculating retirement benefits is 45 years and not more than 40 years rendered before the age of 60 can be taken into account. Each year of service earns a pension of one-eightieth of the average salary and, so far as the lump sum is concerned, each year of service to 30 September 1956 earns one-thirtieth of the average salary and each year thereafter earns three-eightieths.

Examples:

Pension. Total contributory service 30 years. Average of last 3 years' salary £1,600. Annual pension:

$$\frac{30 \times £1,600}{80} = £600$$

Lump sum. Forty years' contributory service, 30 of which were rendered prior to 1 October 1956. Average of last three years' salary £1,600. The lump sum is calculated in two parts: the service prior to 1 October 1956 is based on one-thirtieth; the service after that date is based on three-eightieths. Lump sum:

$$\frac{30 \times £1,600}{30} + \frac{3 \times 10 \times £1,600}{80}$$

$$= £1,600 + £600 = £2,200$$

SEB

616

Retirement pension, Reclaim of contributions for Where a teacher leaves contributory service before becoming qualified for an annual superannuation allowance or short-service gratuity, the superannuation contributions which have been deducted from the teacher's salary may be reclaimed with compound interest at 3%, less deductions for income tax and National Insurance graduated contributions. Applications for refund of contributions cannot be made until after the teacher has been out of contributory service for a continuous period of three months.

Where the number of years of service has not been sufficient to enable the teacher to qualify for retiring allowance at age 70, the contributions are, on attaining that age, reclaimable with compound interest at 3%.

Retiring pension, Qualification for To qualify for a retiring pension one of the following conditions of service must be satisfied:

(1) The normal service minimum to qualify for a pension is 30 years; of this period at least 10 years must be contributory. All recognised full-time teaching is contributory service.

(2) In the case of a married woman teacher the 30 years' requirement will be reduced by the number of completed years, not exceeding 10 in all, during which she is absent from pensionable or qualifying service while married. Absence as a widow or as a divorced woman can form part of the 10 years' absence. Thus, 10 years of pensionable service, 10 years of qualifying service and 10 years of absence while married qualifies the teacher for pension at age 60.

(3) A late age entrant into pensionable service can qualify for pension by completing a period of pensionable service amounting to two-thirds of the period between the date of entering into such service and the date of attaining the age of 65, subject to a minimum period of 10 years. A teacher entering the profession at age 50 or over will qualify for a pension after 10 years of contributory service.

(4) Where a teacher makes a return to service after an interval in service, he can qualify by completing a period of pensionable service amounting to two-thirds of the period (not being less than 10 years) between the date of re-entering into service and the date of attaining the age of 65. Any pensionable service rendered before the date of re-entry does not count towards this qualifying period, but if qualification is established, the earlier service is taken into account in the calculation of pension.

The provisions outlined in (3) and (4) above are of assistance to teachers in technical schools and colleges who have spent a number of years in industry or commerce gaining practical experience before entering teaching service, and those teachers who have an interval in service shortly after commencing teaching.

Except in the case of breakdown, no pension or lump sum is payable before the teacher reaches his 60th birthday.

From 1 October 1956 pensionable service is generally speaking full-time service as a teacher, lecturer or educational organiser under an LEA, or in schools and establishments grant-aided by the DES, between the ages of 18 and 70, or up to the completion of 45 years if that occurs before the age of 70.
SEB

Revised Code *See* **Codes of Grants**

Rhodes Trust Founded in 1902, the Trust endows Rhodes Scholarships at Oxford University for men from the British Commonwealth, South Africa and the USA.

Rhodes Hse, Oxford.

Rhodesia, Education in 1965 statistics: *African education*—3,228 primary schools (enrolment 638,370); 75 secondary schools (enrolment 11,495); 42

teacher training colleges (enrolment 2,819); 16 technical and vocational schools (enrolment 832). Nearly all African children receive the minimum of five years schooling. *Non-African education*—184 primary schools (enrolment 32,302); 33 secondary and technical schools (enrolment 18,416); one teacher training college (enrolment 420); 42 private schools and colleges (enrolment 8,865). The multiracial University College of Rhodesia and Nyasaland has 814 students. Population: Africans 4,210,000; Europeans 225,000; others 22,000; total approximately 4,457,000.

RI *See* **Religion in schools**

Richardson, Marion *See* **Art in education**

Riding Riding was at one time regarded as a sport for the more wealthy section of the community, and almost automatically required the ownership of one or two horses or ponies. To-day, however, with the enormous growth in the number of riding schools, the provision of beginners' courses by bodies such as the Central Council of Physical Recreation, and the formation of pony clubs throughout the country, the activity is enjoyed by people of all ages, many of whom develop into first-class riders and ultimately take part in competitions such as show jumping at the highest level.

The activity has been introduced into many schools and colleges as part of their PE schemes, often with the help of riding schools that make mid-week provision for riding instruction on a group or class basis at reduced costs. This is particularly the case in the Greater London area, where the demand is so great that it is now difficult to find riding schools with vacancies for additional numbers.

JE

Robbins Report (1963): Report of the Committee on Higher Education Chairman: Lord Robbins. Terms of Reference: To review the pattern of full-time higher education in Great Britain and in the light of national needs and resources to advise the government on what principles its long-term development should be based; in particular, to advise, in the light of these principles, whether there should be any changes in the pattern of full-time higher education, whether any new types of institution are desirable and whether any modification should be made in the present arrangements for planning and coordinating the development of the various types of institution.

The Report expressed its alarm at the increasing number of capable and qualified students who were unable to obtain admission to university education, and recommended that places should be available in full-time higher education for about 390,000 students in 1973–4, and about 560,000 in 1980–1.

It also recommended that steps be taken to reduce the relative attraction of Oxford and Cambridge; that the work of the Universities Central Council on Admission (*q.v.*) should cover applicants to all universities and the CATs; that steps should be taken to avoid overloading of syllabuses of first-degree courses, and to broaden the courses for a higher proportion of students; that there should be consultation between universities to establish uniformity of standards; that the teacher training colleges should be renamed Colleges of Education, and the colleges in each university's Institure of Education and the University Department of Education should be formed into a School of Education; that to the three-year courses for teachers should be added (for suitable students) four-year courses leading both to a degree and to professional qualification, and that the aim should be by the 1970s to achieve a big increase in the number of students taking four-year courses; that opportunities should be provided for trained teachers to complete their degree qualifications by part-time study; that the colleges of education should have independent governing bodies and should be financed by ear-marked grants made through the universities to schools of education by a new Grants Commission; that the Grants Commission should be responsible for advising the government on the needs of all institutions of higher education; that there should be a major effort to encourage an increase in technological as well as scientific research; that CATs should be designated as technological universities, with powers to award both first and higher degrees; that the links between universities and government research departments and industry should be strengthened; that many existing universities should be expanded to 8,000 or 10,000 places each, and six new universities should be established at once, the majority of these and of institutions chosen for the granting of university status being in or near large centres of population; that there should be encouragement of those who wish to embark on or resume higher education later in life; that a large part of vacations should be spent on work related to students' fields of study, and grants assessed accordingly; that there should be a Minister of Arts and Science responsible for the Grants Commission, the Research Councils and other autonomous state-supported activities administered on similar principles; and that the responsibility for other institutions of higher education should remain with the Minister of Education and, in the main, with the LEAs.

Rock climbing Rock climbing has been accepted for some years as an eminently suitable sport or recreation for inclusion in the ever-widening PE schemes of many secondary schools and colleges. Mountains or mountainous country are not essential for its pursuit; nor, if properly taught, is the sport more dangerous than any other activity with an element of risk. Many of the basic techniques (which should always be taught by experienced rock climbers) can be acquired in a school gymnasium using improvised apparatus, or on commercially produced artificial 'walls'. In some of the newest gymnasia, such 'walls', providing 'climbs' of varying degrees of difficulty, are being built as an integral part of the structure.

In most regions of the country there are rock outcrops where climbing can be learned and practised, and at many such locations there have been established climbing schools, suitable both for beginners and climbers with experience. Such outcrops are to be found for example, in the Tunbridge Wells area of Kent where (as elsewhere) the Central Council of Physical Recreation (26–29 Park Cres., London, W1) organises courses of instruction. Many local authorities also organise courses at their own outdoor pursuits centres, as do the Youth Hostels Associations (*q.v.*) at a number of their own centres.

Some rock-climbing is now being done on stretches of cliffs around the coast, but in general, owing to the additional danger from water, such locations are not suitable for school climbing clubs.

See also **Mountaineering**

JE

Role playing *See* **Social sciences, Teaching of**

Roman Catholic education, *etc. See* **Catholic education,** *etc.*

Roman Studies, Society for the Promotion of Formed in 1910 'to deal with the archaeology, art and history of Italy and the Roman Empire down to about the year AD 700', the Society publishes an annual journal, maintains with the Hellenic Society a joint library and collection of lantern slides, and holds meetings four times a year in London. Besides individuals, membership includes libraries, schools and other institutions.

31–34 Gordon Sq., London, WC1.

Romania, Education in Education is free and compulsory for an eight-year period. In 1965/66 there were 7,627 kindergartens (enrolment 353,721); 15,521 elementary schools (enrolment 3,347,076); 349 technical schools (enrolment 68,409); 441 schools for apprentices (enrolment 182,391); and 183 colleges of higher education (enrolment 130,614). Teacher training colleges, 24 in all, had 12,703 students, and the five universities at Bucharest, Jassy, Cluj, Timisoara and Craiova had an enrolment of 6,566.

The population of the country in 1966 was approximately 19 million.

Rorschach tests These take their name from a Swiss psychiatrist who was interested in the reactions of patients in a mental home when asked to give their comments on a variety of large ink blots making plain or multi-coloured designs on paper cards. These same ink blots have since been reproduced and used by psychologists on a wide cross-section of the normal population, and from this a scheme of personality has been devised. Many different interpretations of patients' reactions are possible: for example, it is thought significant if some of the blots are seen as frightening, or if the individual interprets the blots in separate parts or as one whole. Rorschach tests are thought by many to be effective in the diagnosing of certain mental states or diseases, but there is less general agreement as to their reliability with normal individuals. As with so many personality tests (*q.v.*), the material produced by the individual is often full of interest, but impossible

to diagnose beyond question of doubt or error.

FURTHER READING
Theodora Alcock. *The Rorschach in Practice*, Tavistock, 1963.

NT

RoSPA *See* **Accidents, Royal Society for the Prevention of**

Rounders This is a popular game for boys and girls in primary schools, girls at the secondary stage, and with mixed teams in youth clubs. A team consists of nine players. Rounders is played on a pitch, roughly diamond-shaped, marked out on asphalt or grass. Four posts are needed for pitch corners, a stick not more than 18 in. long, and a ball similar to a cricket ball.

Since 1945 the National Rounders Association has been responsible for the rules of the game. It also arranges tests for prospective umpires and coaches.

Hon. Secretary: Miss B. A. Furlong, 81 King Harold Rd, Colchester, Essex.

FURTHER READING
The Rules of the Game of Rounders, PE Association of Great Britain and Northern Ireland, 1966.
Rounders (*Know the Game* series), Educational Productions, 1957.
The Coaching of the Game of Rounders, NRA.
Hints to Umpires, NRA can be obtained from Miss E. Driver, 21 Hale End Rd, London, E17.

JE

Rousseau, Jean Jacques (1712-78) Main works on education: *Emile* and *The New Héloise*.

Rousseau was appalled at the corruption and acquisitiveness of social life, but instead of accepting these evils as the inevitable consequences of original sin, he regarded them as wholly avoidable distortions of a natural tendency to justice and sympathy which we all originally share. He held that democratic social order needs to be introduced which will express these tendencies, and a form of education to be adopted which will preserve them from corruption.

Such an education would begin with a study of child development, for in treating children simply as miniature adults we ignore the distinctive stages through which our faculties ought naturally to develop. First, in childhood, would come the perfecting of sense through activity, with no book but the world and with natural consequences acting as the guide to behaviour; in childhood, utility would be the touchstone of all learning about the world. In adolescence reason would awaken, and the child could emerge from a rural setting and by degrees begin to enter social life, with religion and morality being taught by an appeal to natural reason alone. Rousseau maintained that it was always better to delay in teaching than to risk error by instilling prejudices or having to appeal to authority, though he considered these methods appropriate enough in the education of women.

RFD

Rowing Long regarded as an expensive sport and confined, educationally, to a few public schools situated near rivers and to some universities, rowing has been growing in popularity in state schools over the last few years. This has been due largely to the provision of boats (which can cost £400 or more) by LEAs to be used communally by a number of schools, and the opening of sailing and boating centres on rivers, lakes and reservoirs.

The Amateur Rowing Association, the controlling body of the sport in the UK, estimates that at present there are some 10,000 schoolchildren taking part in rowing, and the number is increasing rapidly. The number of girls and women taking up the sport is also growing. There are nearly 500 rowing clubs in the UK.

Races are organised at regattas for 'eights' (eight oarsmen, and a cox who steers the boat), coxed and coxless 'fours', coxed and coxless 'pairs', double sculls and single sculls. A racing oarsman either rows (which means he uses only one oar or blade) or sculls, which means that he uses two blades.

Amateur Rowing Association, 36 Park Cres., London, W1.

For the under-18s: A. C. Scott, Council for Youth Rowing, St Davids, Duseley Lodge, Old Windsor, Berks.

JE

Royal Air Force, Education in the The RAF Education Branch is composed of officers, most of whom are university graduates and trained teachers, and a small number of civilians. Almost half the officers are employed on instructional duties in the RAF College, schools of flying and technical training and other training establishments. A small number is engaged on staff duties in the Directorate of RAF Educational Services at the Air Force Department HQ and at the HQs of RAF Commands and other formations, whilst the remainder are employed in implementing the general educational scheme on stations at home and overseas.

At the RAF College, professional training is given to cadets of the General Duties, Engineer, Equipment and Secretarial Branches and of the RAF Regiment. In addition, basic training courses are held for engineer officers, or there are courses in advanced and guided weapons technology. Technicians and craft apprentices are trained in schools of technical training, and adult airmen and airwomen are trained in a number of trade training establishments. The span and depth of the educational content of syllabuses, for which Education Officers are responsible, depend on the purpose of these courses: these range from basic studies for airmen at mechanic level to an honours degree in engineering for officers undergoing technological training. The subjects taught include mathematics, physics, mechanical, electrical and aeronautical engineering, electronics, war studies and the humanities. A substantial element of instructional technique is included in the courses at the RAF School of Education, which also has a responsibility for educational research.

The objects of the general education scheme are to assist officers and airmen to meet the service's educational requirements for promotion and to provide individuals with the opportunity, by means of libraries, leisure-time activities and cultural pursuits, of becoming well-informed and effective members of an all-regular force. Also under the scheme students are prepared for GCE and the examinations of professional institutions. Most of the teaching is done by Education Officers, assisted by part-time civilian teachers and by members of other branches of the RAF; university and other civilian lecturers are employed when necessary. Officers and airmen attend the classes and courses at civilian educational institutes and correspondence courses are available through the Forces Correspondence Course Scheme and other sources.

Station Education Officers are responsible for the organisation and co-ordination of programmes of continuation trade training. The advancement of a tradesman's knowledge and skill by means of practical and theoretical instruction continues progressively throughout his career; with the appropriate educational studies, he is fitted for successive promotions.

Children's education abroad is on an inter-service basis. Educational facilities and opportunities are provided which are comparable to those given by LEAs in the UK. There are RAF schools in the Near, Middle and Far East, in Malta, North Africa, Ghana and in Fontainebleau, Naples and Oslo. The administration and control of these schools is the responsibility of the RAF Education Branch.

GWEN

Royal Anthropological Institute of Great Britain and Ireland *See* **Anthropological Institute of Great Britain and Ireland, Royal**

Royal Commonwealth Society *See* **Commonwealth Society, Royal**

Royal Geographical Society *See* **Geographical Society, Royal**

Royal Humane Society *See* **Humane Society, Royal**

Royal Life Saving Society *See* **Life Saving Society, Royal**

Royal Navy, Education in Education in the Royal Navy has three main functions. First, and perhaps most important, it is part of the professional and technical training of all officers and men. As a further contribution to the training of officers and men as disciplined sailors and effective leaders, it ensures that they are well-informed citizens, well able to communicate with their seniors and juniors and possessing an understanding of their fellow men. Thirdly, facilities are provided for the development of cultural interests, and for the acquisition by individuals of qualifications for their own purposes— primarily in preparation for the inevitable return to civil life.

The RN and the navies of the old Commonwealth countries are alone among the world's navies in having a uniformed body of education officers— 650 in the RN, now known as the Instructor Branch. There have been Instructor Officers in RN ships from the 16th century onwards and their activities have always been an integral part of naval training. The earliest definition of the Instructor Officer's task (1702) was that he should 'employ his time on board in instructing the volunteers in writing, arithmetic and the study of navigation and in whatsoever may contribute to render them artists in that science.' Navigation and seamanship were the technologies of that age; the technologies of today are much broader in their range but the Instructor Officer's part, in laying the foundations of literacy and numeracy as the basis of technological studies, has undergone relatively little alteration.

Most of the formal training of individual officers and men is now carried out ashore, leaving ships free to undertake team training and to perform their operational task. Training courses are designed for all branches and all levels of ability, but all contain an essential element of education. This varies from the three-year engineering degree course for the technical officer, to a three-year Ordinary National Certificate course for the skilled Artificer rating or a short course in basic English and arithmetic for the unskilled rating entry. Whatever the course, an attempt is made to link the final standard achieved with a nationally recognised qualification. The standard qualification for ratings' advancement within the RN for many years, the Higher Educational Test, was linked recently with the Associated Examining Board's GCE. In 1966, ratings in the RN obtained a total of 3,600 subject passes at O level in this examination.

Although the great majority of Instructor Officers serve ashore in training establishments, they also serve in all major ships and are responsible there for providing an education service to meet all individual demands. The policy is to ensure that all men of ability are given opportunities and every encouragement to develop their educational background to the full. Considerable use is made of correspondence courses and programmed learning material in the development of which the RN has done much pioneer work.

The whole of the RN's educational effort is directed from the Ministry of Defence, through Command Instructor Officers, by the Head of the Instructor Branch, who holds the unique rank of Instructor Rear Admiral.

See also **Forces, Teaching in the**

AJB

Royal Numismatic Society *See* **Numismatic Society, Royal**

Royal Schools of Music, Associated Board of the *See* **Music, Associated Board of the Royal Schools of**

Royal Society of Arts *See* **Arts, Royal Society of**

Royal Society for the Prevention of Accidents *See* **Accidents, Royal Society for the Prevention of**

Royal Society for the Prevention of Cruelty to Animals *See* **Animals, Royal Society for the Prevention of Cruelty to**

RSPCA *See* **Animals, Royal Society for the Prevention of Cruelty to**

Rugby football Alleged to have originated at Rugby School in 1823 when William Webb Ellis 'picked up a ball and ran with it,' rugby football spread to other schools and beyond them, and many clubs were formed and organised by the Rugby Union. A dispute over the legalisation of payment for players who had lost time from work led to the formation, by a number of clubs mainly in the north of England, of the Rugby League. Though the rules of the game were common once to the two organisations, changes have taken place over the years: the chief differences are that in League football, professional players are permitted and a side has 13; whereas in Rugby Union all players are amateurs and there are 15 in a team. Most schools play according to Union rules.

Over the past 30 years there has been a great increase in the number of schools playing the game—largely a result of the provision of better ground facilities and of the widening of the scope of the PE programme, together with the efforts of the RFU in providing coaching courses, coaching films, audio-visual aids and excellent training manuals. Recently a professional coaching organiser has been appointed to promote the development of school rugby.

Rugby Football Union, Whitton Rd, Twickenham, Middlesex.

Schools RFU, 12 Kennersdene, Tynemouth, Northumberland.

FURTHER READING
RFU. *Coaching Rugby Football. Training for Rugby Football.*

JE

Rugby Football Union, English Schools' The ESRFU functions as two groups catering for pupils up to 15 and 19 years of age respectively. The 15 Group was founded in 1904 and was drawn mainly from rugby-minded towns in the Midlands and South West. The first match, against the Welsh Schools' Rugby Union, took place at Cardiff Arms Park on 12 March 1904.

The 19 Group was formed in 1948 and draws its members from all types of school in all parts of England.

The expansion of the ESRFU and of rugby have gone hand in hand, and today every part of the country is affiliated through its schools' County Union. Home and away matches against the Welsh take place annually and, with an increasing interest taken by the RFU, a home match takes place at Twickenham in March on the Wednesday following the Calcutta Cup Match.

The standard of play in both groups is high, and many players have gone on to win senior international honours. As a whole, the Union now represents over 1,400 schools and, by arranging trials at county and regional levels, encourages the playing of rugby football in all schools as an essential part of a boy's education.

Hon. Sec., 12 Kennersdene, Tynemouth.

Ruleg system A technique used in programmed learning. According to this system all statements can be classified in two categories: rules and examples. In general a 'rule' is a definition, a mathematical formula, a scientific law or an axiom, i.e. an abstract concept from which particular instances — 'examples' — can be obtained. Thus the algebraic equation 'x plus $y = y$ plus x' states the general 'rule'; while the statement '4 plus 3 = 3 plus 4' provides a particular 'example'.

Under the Ruleg system, all the pertinent rules are first written down and then arranged in a logical sequence, with relevant illustrative examples, to form a flow chart (*q.v*).

See also **Programmed learning**

Rural Industries Bureau Sponsored by the Development Commission to assist rural industries in England and Wales, the Bureau provides advice and consultancy on technical and managerial problems. Priority is given to small firms with employment potential or firms which contribute to export. The Bureau also gives instruction in basic skills which cannot be obtained elsewhere.

Apprenticeship training schemes are in operation in thatching, saddlery, and the utilisation of minor forest produce. Full information on local opportunities for apprentices can be obtained from county Rural Industries Organisers, who can not only advise on the prospects but, being constantly in touch with the workshops in their area, are able to assist with the selection of suitable employers.

35 Camp Rd, Wimbledon Common, London, SW19.

Rural Life at Home and Overseas, Institute of Founded in 1949, the Institute aims to bring together on a Christian basis peoples of any race or occupation and to further their education in the understanding of rural life. Its purpose is to strive for a greater acceptance of Christian values in the economic and social development of rural communities throughout the world. The Institute implements its aims by giving advice on rural problems, acting as an information bureau, organising conferences and lectures and publishing a quarterly review, *Rural Life*. Other publications of community development subjects are issued from time to time, and a small library is maintained. Financial support is solicited for selected community development projects overseas.

27 Northumberland Rd, New Barnet, Herts.

Rural Music Schools Association
The Association co-ordinates the policy and assists the work of rural music schools, supervises them where necessary, and establishes new schools and music centres.

The objects of the 13 centres are to encourage the pursuit of music as a leisure-time occupation among people of all ages and classes; and to provide skilled teaching in instrumental and choral music at fees which will exclude no one. Day and weekend courses and musical events, for teachers and for amateurs, are held throughout the year at the Association's residential headquarters. Visitors may use practice-rooms and the music library.

Publication: *Making Music*.
Little Benslow Hills, Hitchin, Herts.

Rural studies In pre-war years little more than school gardening in secondary schools, this subject adopted an applied scientific approach and became known as 'rural science'. During the past decade, school gardens have altered in design to provide a wide range of features, offering a child a multiplicity of situations and experiences; they have ceased to be merely areas provided for pure garden crafts. The child's experience has been broadened by the inclusion of livestock, ranging from small animals kept in vivaria to larger animals such as poultry, pigs and goats. The environment has been enriched further through rural craft work and by extending studies beyond the school boundaries into farms and local industries, and to natural features such as ponds, rivers, woods and parks.

Thus the subject has developed into a method of educating through motivation arising from the child's experience in real-life situations. The more obvious benefits are the learning of unified science and crafts. But, once within a real-life situation, children are urged to communicate and to achieve greater fluency in speaking, writing and in mathematical skills, the search for fluency arising from a natural need stimulated by interest. Children find physical and aesthetic satisfaction in dealing with life and natural materials, and begin to appreciate the uniqueness and interdependence of life, the ways in which man can manipulate his environment to his advantage and the responsibilities that arise from so doing.

The use of rural studies in primary schools has recently shown a marked increase, partly as a result of the wide acceptance of the view that the young child learns best through doing and creating in response to diverse and numerous experiences. Many primary schools succeed with a rural studies approach without teaching gardens. As a wide exploration of the child's environment, rural studies at this level leads to discoveries in the areas of science, natural history, geography and history, and these in turn create a need for skill in language and mathematics. At both infant and primary stages, opportunity for growing plants and keeping animals enriches such discovery enormously.

At secondary level, some schools have extensive garden environments, with plants and animals in great variety, and including areas for studies of weather and soil. There may be provision for craft work, using natural local materials. There is likely to be an overflow from the school estate into the surrounding environment. Because of its wide spectrum, rural studies is a particularly suitable means of stimulating children of all ability ranges. It may be offered as a subject for CSE, and at GCE 'O' level it offers an enlightened means of preparing pupils for biology, rural biology, agricultural science or general science. Cases are on record of pupils achieving 'A' level in biological subjects through a rural studies course. As a course of general education, it stimulates interest and improves the academic skills of candidates for examination in other subjects. For non-examination pupils, a rural studies department provides realistic situations for developing character and for learning—virtues so often in the past lacking in courses for such pupils.

With the recent development of rural studies, teachers of the subject have drawn together to exchange ideas and experiences. This has resulted in the formation of the National Rural Studies Association (*q.v.*).

RFM

Rural Studies Association, National

A professional association for teachers interested in rural studies in schools. Membership can be individual or through one of 37 affiliated county associations.

The Association holds a conference each September and has set up standing committees for research and policy in relation to primary and secondary schools. It represents the ideas and interests of rural studies teachers to the DES or other bodies, and takes its part in putting the point of view of teachers interested in the inter-relationship of education and the countryside.

Information: S. McB. Carson, Rural Studies Office, Offley Place, Great Offley, nr. Hitchin, Herts.

Ruskin College, Oxford *See* **Labour education**

Russell, Bertrand (b. 1872) Main works on education: *On Education* and *Education and the Social Order*.

Russell argues that the influence of church and state on public education should be strongly resisted, and that individuality should be fostered. In this development of individuality the personal qualities commended are vitality, courage (together with the absence of irrational fears), a sensitiveness to or love of others, and intelligence (comprising such intellectual virtues as curiosity, concentration, open-mindedness and exactness).

Since human nature is malleable, once these aims are accepted it is a matter for psychology to determine the most efficient way of developing them. Russell had in mind early Behaviourism and Freudian psychology in particular.

Russell, Charles (1866–1917) devoted his life to boys' welfare at a time when adolescence and its problems were largely ignored or misunderstood. In 1913 he was appointed Chief Inspector of Reformatory and Industrial Schools.

Through the leadership of a boys' club from 1892 Russell obtained unrivalled knowledge of Manchester working-class boys and their families. His pursuit of their welfare, based on Christian principles, included recreation, further education, employment, and the aftercare of young offenders.

From 1905 he wrote sketches for the *Manchester Guardian* which described Manchester boys as he knew them. The sketches were collected in book form under the title *Manchester Boys*. His other books included *Working Lads' Clubs* and *Young Gaol Birds*.

Russian, Association of Teachers of The aims of the ATR are to exchange information and experience concerning methods of teaching Russian; to exchange information concerning textbooks and teaching aids and, where necessary, to compile new ones; to provide information for education authorities, heads of schools and heads of departments interested in initiating the teaching of Russian; to review existing examinations and to suggest improvements; to encourage the establishment of Russian with a regular place in secondary curricula; and to press for more frequent and widespread interchange of teachers, students and materials with the USSR. Local groups cater for members on a regional basis. An annual conference is held, usually between Christmas and the New Year. Membership, or associate membership, is open to all interested in the teaching of Russian.

33 Victoria Rd, Horley, Surrey.

'Russian, The Teaching of' (Annan Report) *See* **Annan Report (1963): 'The Teaching of Russian'**

Rwanda, Education in 1965 statistics: 352,406 children in primary schools, 7,800 in secondary schools, 85 students at the National University. A few students study in Belgium or the Congo. Total population: approximately 3 million.

S

S level S (special) level papers are intended for high-flying candidates in the A level examinations of the GCE; they are more searching than the basic A level papers, and call for a wider spread of knowledge and a more original critical quality. They may be offered in any subject, except practical ones, by a candidate who is also offering the basic A level paper in that subject. No pass is awarded but, provided a candidate has reached a sufficiently high grade in his A level paper, performance at S level is considered by universities and other institutions of higher education when awarding places, and by local authorities when awarding scholarships. The purpose of the papers, in fact, is wholly that of providing extra evidence of a candidate's quality.

Sabbatical year As commonly understood, the sabbatical year is a year's vacation allowed to a university teacher once in seven years and used by him generally to study an aspect of his subject in greater detail or to bring himself up-to-date on new developments in his field, probably by travel abroad.

In practice, however, this facility is by no means universally enjoyed in British universities. A recent survey by the Association of University Teachers revealed that out of 43 institutions replying to a questionnaire, only eight had any definite and regular system for sabbatical or study leave, and in only one of these could such leave be claimed as a right. In a much larger number of cases, namely 38, the granting of such leave was either a recognised practice or was given as an act of grace. In about half the cases where such leave is granted this is done at irregular intervals. In three institutions the leave usually takes the form of one year in seven, and in another three institutions one term in seven.

In other spheres of education, and especially in the state school system, the sabbatical year is an opportunity long sought after by teachers but as yet denied to them, at least in the form enjoyed by university teachers. As long ago as 1944 the McNair Report (*Teachers and Youth Leaders*) declared: 'There has been much talk for many years about sabbatical terms for teachers, but nothing systematic has been done to establish or authorise them.' While doubting whether all teachers, or perhaps even most teachers, wholly lose their freshness after ten or twenty years of continuous teaching, it nevertheless felt that 'teaching, with its constant pre-occupation with the young, probably makes greater demands on resources and personality than any other type of occupation; and the danger, after a period, of failing to work at maximum capacity is very real.'

The McNair Committee refrained from making any specific recommendation for the introduction of systematic arrangements for sabbatical terms for schoolteachers, but it did say that 'when circumstances make it practicable every teacher who makes suitable proposals for the use of the period should be allowed a sabbatical term on full pay after five years' continuous teaching, and that, where the circumstances and proposals of the teacher warrant, the period should not be limited to one term.'

More than twenty years after publication of the McNair Report, that proposal remains largely a dead letter. Only two or three LEAs in England and Wales make any provision for a sabbatical term for their teachers, and even these provide them on a limited basis.

On the other hand, there has been a substantial increase in the provision of opportunities for further training for teachers and though, strictly speaking, these do not have quite the same purpose as the sabbatical year or term, they do in some respects offer the teacher an opportunity to bring himself up-to-date with developments in his particular subject, or in teaching techniques.

Briefly, the opportunities for further training consist of:

(1) Special 'advanced courses' and 'supplementary courses' lasting one year (or exceptionally, one term), together with their part-time equivalent. These are provided on a national basis, mainly in university departments or in institutes of education, and are intended for serving teachers with normally not less than five years of teaching experience. The teachers undertaking the courses are seconded by their employing authority on full pay.

(2) Short courses of various kinds provided by many different bodies including the DES, institutes of education and extra-mural departments of universities, LEAs and professional associations.

FJ

Sadler, Sir Michael (1861–1943) A member of the Bryce Commission (*see* **Bryce Report**), Sadler was appointed

in 1894 Director of the Education Department's Office of Special Inquiries and Reports. It was he who appointed Robert (later Sir Robert) Morant (*q.v.*) as Assistant Director. Clashes of opinion between Sadler and Morant, when the latter had become Permanent Secretary of the Board of Education, led to Sadler's resignation. He was employed thereafter by a number of LEAs to survey the educational needs of their areas, following the instructions of the Education Act 1902. This he did brilliantly. He was later made Professor of the History and Administration of Education at Manchester, and ended his career as Vice-Chancellor of the University of Leeds.

Safeguarding A noteworthy feature of the Burnham Report is the salary safeguards which it provides in certain circumstances. For example, the holder of a graded post need have no fears about his position if a triennial review were to place his school in a lower group than at previous reviews. His entitlement to the allowance for a graded post continues so long as he remains on the staff of the school or the school department. Naturally, however, this is a personal safeguard, and if a teacher in that position leaves for an alternative appointment, then the school adopts the 'lower score' which the school justifies and so in that event there is no vacancy to be filled.

Such a positive provision has not existed in relation to a school which has been reorganised, but recently a change has affected this situation. Until the Burnham Report of 1967, a head teacher, a deputy head teacher and indeed others holding special posts have relied upon the goodwill of the local authority to exercise discretion in safeguarding their position. A head of department, for example, did not have the same safeguard as a graded post holder. The local authority could safeguard either the salary of a head or his deputy, or, better still, the prospective salary which might have been secured had reorganisation or closure not occurred. In many cases, safeguards were given for limited periods of time. A great tussle was fought over this issue in the 1967 negotiations and later still in the arbitration court, over the salary prospects of a teacher if reorganisation or closure occurred. The teachers advocated that every teacher should be fully safeguarded, i.e. continue to receive salary for the post he had, adjusted to current rates every time a new Burnham Report is issued. They were prepared to deny this advantage to any teacher who unreasonably refused an offer of a suitable alternative post. The management panel of the Burnham Committee were prepared to do this only for the over-50s. The outcome was a victory for teachers, for the arbitrators determined as follows:

'A teacher whose post is lost or whose remuneration is diminished as a result of reorganisation or closure of a school but who continues in the teaching service of the Local Education Authority shall be safeguarded in respect of both the salary he enjoyed at the date of reorganisation or closure and any further benefit which he would have enjoyed if he had continued in occupation of that post under the provisions of the present or subsequent Burnham Reports, provided that if a teacher so safeguarded unreasonably refuses an offer of an appointment by the Authority the safeguarding shall cease.'

In fact, when this principle was incorporated in the current Burnham Report, it was recognised that such consideration would be unfair if it were not applied retrospectively. Thus, any teacher in the past whose post is lost or whose salary is diminished as a result of reorganisation or closure of a school is entitled to be safeguarded in his salary as from 1 July 1967, provided that in the interval he has not un-

reasonably refused an alternative offer of employment from the local authority. As far as is known, this position is unique among the safeguarding provisions in respect of salaries.

SEB

Sail Training Association Founded in 1955 with the Duke of Edinburgh as Patron, the Association aims to provide opportunity for adventure and character-development for young men between the ages of 16 and 21. Fourteen-day cruises take place between March and December, costing each participant about £40 (local authorities may make grants covering some or all of this fee). The Association's two specially built schooners enter the annual international Tall Ships Races, in which crews consist at least 50% of trainees. The two schooners accommodate a total of over a thousand young people annually on cruises, some being reserved for girls only.

Market Chambers, Petersfield, Hants.

Sailing Sailing, or yachting, at one time almost a prerogative of the more wealthy sections of the community, is now widely enjoyed, and is extremely popular in many schools throughout the country, whether they are close to the sea or make use of lakes, rivers, reservoirs and flooded, disused gravel pits. Many LEAs are now establishing special sailing centres for schools in their areas.

This change has been brought about by two main factors: the work done by the Central Council of Physical Recreation in popularising the sport by running instructional and building courses at the national recreation centres and at specially selected sites situated inland and on the coast; and the introduction of 'do-it-yourself' kits by a number of commercial firms, which enable an individual or school to purchase, at reasonable cost, prefabricated parts of small yachts or sailing dinghies and assemble them at home, or at school under the guidance of the master responsible for woodwork. Most of these specially designed craft, which have hulls made from marine bonded plywood, are light in weight, easy to handle, cheap and easy to maintain by young people, and very seaworthy.

Much information on types of boats and equipment suitable for schools can be obtained at the *Daily Express* Boat Show, held in London in January each year.

Sailing clubs are to be found in most large towns and a Schools' Sailing Association has been formed which runs an annual national championship. Details of the various sailing organisations and of vacation courses and recommended publications can be obtained from the CCPR, 26–29 Park Crescent, London W1, or from its regional offices.

JE

St John Ambulance Brigade The St John Ambulance Brigade, founded in 1887, is the uniformed Foundation of the Order of St John, familiar to people throughout the world, and consists wholly of voluntarily trained first aiders—men, women, boys and girls—numbering 250,000 in England, Wales, Northern Ireland and the Commonwealth.

The services of the Brigade can be commanded by anyone, and members give over four million hours' voluntary service every year; this covers a wide field of activities, including first aid at places where crowds gather and there is a likelihood of accident or sudden illness. They care for the aged, handicapped and lonely, and supplement ambulance services. They also provide speedily mobilised groups in time of disaster. Escort duties of sick and injured persons are undertaken by land, sea and air with a specially trained reserve of air escorts to and from anywhere abroad.

8 Grosvenor Cres., London, SW1.

Sample study *See* **Geography, Teaching of**

Sampson, George (1882–1950) Educationist and man of letters, and at one time Inspector of Schools for the LCC, Sampson might be described as the father of the modern liberal approach to the teaching of English. It was he who coined the phrase 'every teacher is a teacher of English'. His most important book was *English for the English* (1921).

Samuelson Report (1882–4; Royal Commission) Terms of reference: to enquire into the instruction of industrial workers of certain foreign countries in technical and other subjects for the purpose of comparison with that of corresponding classes in this country; and to study the influence of such instruction on manufacturing and other industries at home and abroad.

Some of the recommendations of this report were implemented in the Technical Instruction Act 1889, which followed the Local Government Act 1888. Further grants were made available in 1890.

The report affirmed that Britain was still ahead in the industrial world, but drew attention to the systematic instruction in drawing given especially in France, Belgium and Italy, and to the general diffusion of elementary education in Switzerland and Germany.

The Commission recommended an increase in science and art teaching in training colleges, the modernisation of the curricula of endowed schools, and that LEAs should be empowered to set up technical and secondary schools. The Commission also called for more support for young workers in works schools, and for more support for the City and Guilds of London Institute.

Sanderson, Frederick William (1857–1922) H. G. Wells's 'great schoolmaster', Sanderson took a first-class degree at Durham in 1877, was elected a fellow of the university, and, after a period of coaching and lecturing at Cambridge, was appointed assistant master at Dulwich College in 1855. There he was instructed to expand the teaching of chemistry and to introduce physics, which he did; but he also introduced, on a scale and in an experimental spirit new to public schools, a course in engineering, which embraced applied mechanics and physics, workshop practice with actual working engines, and mechanical drawing.

In 1892 he was appointed head of Oundle. At the time the school was in a poor way, and its numbers had fallen to fewer than 100. He was specifically required to re-organise the school and its teaching and to introduce new subjects; he did so well that by the time of his death the numbers had risen to 500. He believed that many boys, lacking the interest to do well in classics, would respond to 'real work' in science (but it had to be of genuine use). He set up science and engineering sections, adding laboratories and workshops, a machine shop, a foundry and a farm. The work resembled exactly that of ordinary engineering shops, except that the boys were given opportunities to experience the whole range of skills involved. Sanderson believed that schools normally laid too great a stress on individual effort, and too little on co-operation. Every boy in the Oundle workshops was made responsible for his own task, but was required to co-operate with his fellow-workers. So well equipped and efficient were these workshops that in the first world war they were converted into munition shops.

Sanderson applied his principles to other subjects, especially English, history and geography. He was a pioneer in the creative use of the school library, dividing the boys in each form into groups, with each group set to study a single aspect of a topic and then to combine the results of their researches. With Edward Thring of Uppingham (*q.v.*), Sanderson was one of the first schoolmasters to act on a large and successful scale on the belief that every boy's interest can be aroused, if only one can find out where his interest lies. 'Education,' he said, 'must be fitted to the boy, not the boy to education.' He also strongly believed in breaking down the barriers between a school and the world outside it.

FURTHER READING
H. G. Wells. *The Story of a Great Headmaster: Sanderson of Oundle*, Constable, 1924.

'Sandwich' courses *See* **Further education in England and Wales**

Saudi Arabia, Education in Elementary and secondary education is free but not compulsory, and available to girls as well as boys. There are two universities: a secular university at Riyadh (enrolment 1,319), and a religious university at Medina (enrolment 512). 1965 statistics: 1,072 primary schools (enrolment 174,514); 62 intermediate schools (enrolment 11,734); six secondary (enrolment 2,484); 16 vocational (enrolment 3,878); and 30 teacher training colleges.

The population of the country was almost six million in 1965.

Save the Children Fund An independent voluntary organisation of nearly 50 years standing, professionally staffed, the Fund exists to promote the welfare of needy children irrespective of nationality or religion. It operates in 28 countries through over 1,100 field workers, including doctors, nurses, welfare workers and administrators. In the UK its homes, clubs and playgroups meet needs not fully covered by the government.

The ultimate aims of the SCF are to create conditions in which children can grow to a healthy maturity, and to train local workers to take over the responsibility themselves. These world-wide operations cost £5,000 a day sub-scribed at home and abroad, and bring food and care to 120,000 children a day.

The Fund distributes information about its work regularly to over 7,000 UK schools, colleges and universities, from whom it receives extensive financial support. It is a member of the Voluntary Committee on Overseas Aid and Development (*q.v.*) and takes part in the work of the Committee's Education Unit.

29 Queen Anne's Ga., London, SW1.

Scandinavia, Education in Den-mark, Norway and Sweden present different facets of a distinctive and homogeneous culture. All three belong to the same racial group, share the same religious denomination (Luth-eranism), and are constitutional monarchies. At the same time, the differences exhibited in their education-al systems provide an interesting comparative study. Broadly speaking, Sweden tends to be the most radical member of the group, Denmark the most conservative, with Norway holding a balance between innovation and tradition. Alternatively, the differences may be seen as stemming from opposing views about the function of the state: in Denmark the farming community has always disliked governmental inter-ference and insisted on the rights and duties of the individual and the family; in Norway the preference is for policy-making at the local authority level; in Sweden overall state planning is favoured.

During the past 20 years Sweden has been actively engaged in reorgani-sing its system on comprehensive lines. The aim of the 1950 Education Act was to bridge the gap between the social classes and to abolish differential treatment of pupils in separate schools. In effect, this has been done by extend-ing the old Folk School so as to offer a common nine-year course (7–16). To begin with, all pupils take a common core of subjects, though limited options are allowed in the later stages. In-dependent schools are permitted, but must be so organised as to conform with state-maintained schools. Beyond the compulsory school-attendance age of 16, secondary education may be continued either for two years in some kind of vocational-continuation school or for three years in the gymnasium. The latter offers a wide range of courses classed as academic (classical, modern, general) or technical and commercial. The academic courses enjoy the highest prestige and are the most popular.

Possibly the best proof that these reforms have succeeded in raising standards of attainment and in esta-blishing greater educational opportu-nity is provided by the fact that the numbers of candidates sitting for the leaving certificate (Student's exami-nation) have trebled since 1950, as has the proportion of successful candidates. This has been accompanied by a notable expansion of all forms of higher education. Sweden has five univer-sities: Uppsala, Lund, Stockholm, Göteborg and a new foundation at Umeå.

At the further education level, the Folk High School represents a uniquely Scandinavian institution. Initiated by Bishop Grundtvig and Christen Kold in Denmark during the first half of the 19th century, the Folk High School has always aimed at the disinterested development of the learner's persona-lity, stressing spiritual values and the responsibilities of the individual and the family group. Most of the courses are residential, intended mainly for students between the ages of 14 and 18. In the past they have flourished in rural areas. Now that the school leaving age has been raised to 16 in Sweden (15 in Norway, still 14 in Denmark), it seems likely that their clientele may change and that their future role will take on more of the character of adult education.

In Denmark the school has always had a limited function, restricted to formal instruction. Even under the 1958 Education Act, which sought to convert the Folk School into a common school (7–14), the choice between academic and non-academic courses is largely left to the parents. Beyond the minimum school leaving age (14) pupils may be assigned either to a two- or three-year general or technical course, or to a three-year *realskole* course leading to the Students' examination. The intention is to raise the school leaving age in the near future. Denmark has two universities (Copenhagen and Aarhus).

As might be expected in a mountainous, thinly populated country, the administrative arrangements in Norway are flexible, but may in general be described as midway between the Swedish and Danish systems. At present there is a common eight-year school (7–15), which provides general education for all pupils and forms the basis for further studies. There are two universities (Oslo and Bergen).

If only for economic reasons, the Scandinavian countries are not always in step with each other in carrying out educational reforms, but certain common features emerge, among them the adoption of the common school principle, the abolition of selection and streaming, and the retention of a belief in general studies. WKR

Schism Act (1714) *See* **Dissenting schools**

Scholarship, Closed Any scholarship, to school or university which is open only to candidates of a particular kind (for example, those whose fathers belong to a certain profession, or candidates drawn from a particular area).

Scholarships and other benefits Various scholarships and other benefits are awarded to pupils and students by LEAs in England and Wales. In 1964–5 the total cost of the awards was over £63 million, and the true cost to public funds was considerably greater (see below).

In secondary schools maintained by LEAs, grants are made to meet the cost of school uniforms and membership of school societies for children whose parents are poor. Maintenance allowances are also given to parents of limited means, to encourage them to allow their children to stay at secondary school beyond the statutory school leaving age in order to complete their main course, or to stay on in the sixth form. These allowances are intended to offset, to a limited extent, the wages that a child could earn by leaving school as soon as possible. The amount of an allowance and the income test applied to parents are decided by the individual LEA concerned, the maximum allowance usually being about £120 a year. In 1964–5 the total expenditure of LEAs on maintenance allowances was just over £1 million.

In the same year LEAs also paid over £10 million to meet, or to assist parents to meet, the fees of children at fee-charging schools. The expenditure was mainly on account of children attending direct grant grammar schools, used by LEAs to supplement their own provision. Few pupils are assisted by LEAs to attend public schools: because they are so much more expensive than their own maintained schools; because the selection of pupils for such assistance would be difficult and invidious; and because it is generally held by LEAs that parents who prefer to contract out of the publicly maintained educational system should do so at their own expense.

The largest item of LEA expenditure on awards is for university students, and in 1964–5 was £30 million for 92,000 students in England and Wales. Both figures will increase very substantially under the continuing expansion of university provision. The amount of an award to a student is determined by a national scale of assessment of parents' income; but a small minority of mature students are assessed on their own means. The fees charged by universities are, however, only a fraction of the true costs, so that even students of rich parents, whose LEA award has a minimum value of £50 a year, receive, in fact, an award worth several hundred pounds.

The device of undercharging for university fees effects no saving to public funds, as the exchequer makes direct grants towards universities' expenditure. In 1964-5 these amounted to £150 million in England and Wales, the bulk being attributable to the provision of premises, equipment and the education of undergraduates. The Robbins Committee considered that university fees should be more realistic, but believing that university expansion might not proceed as quickly if that change were made, thereby revealing a truer cost of awards to rich and poor students alike, decided that the time was not opportune to make such a change.

In 1964-5 LEAs in England and Wales also made awards tenable at other further education establishments as follows: 19,000 awards for students taking degree and comparable courses; and 50,000 awards to students taking other courses. The cost of these awards was £15 million, again only a fraction of the true cost. In 1964-5 there were also some 61,500 students training as teachers in colleges of education in England and Wales. Grants made to them by LEAs totalled over £9 million, which again was only a fraction of the true cost to public funds. Here, too, the large-scale expansion of teacher training will greatly increase the figures mentioned.

The Secretary of State makes awards to post-graduate students in universities; these amounted to nearly £5 million in 1964-5. He also gives grants to graduates training as teachers in university departments of education.

The statutory regulations for scholarships and other benefits, and for university and other awards, are set out in *The New Law of Education*, by Taylor and Saunders.

FURTHER READING
G. Taylor and J. B. Saunders. *The New Law of Education*, Butterworth, 1965.

FB

Schonell, Professor Sir Fred (b. 1900) Born in Australia, where he has been Vice-Chancellor of the University of Queensland since 1960, Professor Schonell was engaged in full-time research in educational psychology from 1928 to 1931; was lecturer in educational psychology, Goldsmiths' College, London, 1931–42; honorary secretary of the British Psychology Society (Education Section), 1931–37; Professor of Education, University College of Swansea, 1942, and Professor of Education, Head of the Department of Education and Head of the Remedial Education Centre, 1946–50. He was the first recipient, in 1962, of the Mackie Medal for outstanding work in education in Australia. His works include *Essentials in Teaching and Testing Spelling* (1932); *Backwardness in the Basic Subjects* (1942); *The Psychology and Teaching of Reading* (1945); *Diagnostic and Attainment Testing* (1949); *The Subnormal Child at Home* (1959) and *Failure in School* (1962).

School attendance The duty of causing a child of compulsory school age to receive full-time education suitable to his or her age, ability and aptitude, either by regular attendance at school or otherwise, is laid upon the parent of every child, and the term 'parent' includes a guardian and every person who has the actual custody of the child.

Compulsory school age The limits of compulsory school age are at present five to 15 years (16 for a handicapped child at a special school), and it is intended to make the latter age 16, beginning with the school year in August 1972. The time of attaining any age is deemed to be the beginning of the day before the anniversary of the birthday, but two points should be noted.

(1) An LEA is not obliged to admit a child to school until the beginning of the school term after he or she has reached the age of five, and, where such a rule is applied, the child is not deemed to be of compulsory school age during the term prior to his or her admission to school.

(2) In the case of children of compulsory school age, the law allows them to leave school only at a certain time, *viz.*, children who reach the age of 15 during the months of September to the following January, at the end of the school term before the Easter holidays, and children who reach the age of 15 during the months of February to August, at the end of the school term before the midsummer holidays of that year. Until the allowed leaving date, the children concerned remain of compulsory school age.

Full-time education Schools maintained by an LEA are normally required by law to divide a school day into two sessions, morning and afternoon, and to arrange at least 400 sessions in the school year, beginning in August, from which they may be allowed to deduct up to 20 sessions for occasional holidays granted during term. And again, normally, at least three hours secular instruction must be given on every school day to children under eight years of age, and at least four hours to children aged eight and over. Independent schools have to satisfy the Secretary of State about their arrangements for full-time education of their pupils; and parents whose children are educated otherwise than at school, e.g. at home, have to satisfy their LEA about their arrangements (*see* **School attendance orders**).

If a child is so severely handicapped that he or she cannot attend school, arrangements may be made, such as the provision of free home tuition by the LEA, for the child to receive less than full-time education, with the approval of the Secretary of State.

Regular attendance at school If a child of compulsory school age who is registered as a pupil at a school does not attend regularly, the parent is guilty of an offence under the Education Acts; and if the LEA consider it necessary to prosecute in order to enforce the parent's duty, they must do so. For a first offence a fine not exceeding £1 may be imposed, a fine not exceeding £5 for a second offence, and for a third or subsequent offence a fine not exceeding £10 or imprisonment for up to one month, or both. In addition to, or instead of, such proceedings before the magistrates, the child may be brought before a juvenile court, which may make an order, including an order committing the child to the care of a fit person, to secure the child's regular attendance at school.

A child is not deemed to have failed to attend school regularly in any of the following circumstances: (1) if he or she was prevented from attending by sickness or any unavoidable cause; (2) on any day exclusively set apart for religious observance by the religious body to which his or her parent belongs; (3) if the parent proves that the school is not within walking distance of home, measured by the nearest available route (two miles for a child under eight, three miles if aged eight or over) and that the LEA have not made suitable arrangements for the child's transport to and from school or for boarding accommodation for him or her at or near the school or for enabling him or her to become a pupil at a school nearer to his or her home; (4) that the child was absent from school by leave given on behalf of the managers, governors, or proprietor, of the school. Leave may be given, for instance, for a pupil to be absent for up to two weeks in a calendar year to go with his or her parent on the latter's annual holiday.

A child who is a boarder at a school is deemed to have failed to attend school regularly if he or she is absent without leave during term when he or she was not prevented from being present by sickness or any unavoidable cause. In the case of children with no fixed abode, e.g. canal boat children, the parent is not guilty of an offence, in this connection, if he proves that his child has attended a school at which he or she was a registered pupil, as regularly as the nature of the trade or business of the parent permits; and that, if his child is six years of age or above, he or she has made at least 200 attendances at school during the previous 12 months.

School welfare officers LEAs used to employ school attendance officers to persuade and press parents to send their children regularly to school, and failing that, to appear for them in proceedings against the parent. Although that work is still part of the duties of school welfare officers, they are now mainly engaged on general welfare activities of schools and children.

FB

School attendance committees School boards, created by the Elementary Education Act 1870, had power to make by-laws to enforce school attendance. But in many places, notably rural areas, school boards were not appointed, the provision of voluntary schools being deemed adequate without the need to establish board schools. In such places, no attendance by-laws were made, as there was no power to do so until 1876. The Elementary Education Act 1876 attempted to deal with the problem by creating school attendance committees in those areas. In boroughs, the committees were to be appointed by the borough councils; elsewhere by the board of guardians. But because many school attendance committees failed to exercise their powers, particularly in rural areas, the law was amended in 1880 requiring them to make school attendance by-laws.

The Education Act 1902, which created LEAs, and abolished school boards, also abolished school attendance committees.

See also **School boards**

FB

School attendance officers *See* **School attendance**

School attendance orders If an LEA consider that the parent of a child of compulsory school age in their area is failing to cause his child to receive efficient full-time education suitable to his or her age, ability, and aptitude, either by regular attendance at school, or otherwise, it may be necessary for the LEA to make a school attendance order and serve it upon the parent. Circumstances in which that may happen are: (1) the child has not become a registered pupil at a school, and appears to be receiving inadequate education, or none at all; (2) although the child is attending a school, the LEA consider that the education he is receiving is not suitable or efficient for him, by reason of some ascertained handicap or other cause.

In such circumstances, if the matter is not otherwise settled to the satisfaction of the LEA, the LEA must first serve a notice on the parent requiring him to satisfy them within a period specified in the notice and not less than 14 days from the service of the notice, that the child is receiving efficient full-time education suitable to him or her. If the parent refuses to do so within the period mentioned, or is unable to satisfy them, and if the LEA consider that it is expedient that the child should attend school, or some other school, as the case may be, they must serve a statutory school attendance

v*

order on the parent requiring him to cause his child to become a registered pupil at a school to be named in the order. The procedure to be followed in the making and service of the order is prescribed in the Education Acts, in such a way as to give the parent an opportunity of considering his position, and of making any representations he desires, if need be to the Secretary of State, who has the final decision as to the school to be named in the order, if the parent disputes the case.

If, after a school attendance order has been made, the parent considers that circumstances have changed, he may apply to the LEA for an amendment or revocation of the order. If the LEA refuse his request, the parent may appeal to the Secretary of State for a direction on the issue.

Failure on the part of a parent to comply with the requirements of a school attendance order in force constitutes an offence under the Education Acts, with the possibility of exactly the same consequences as those described in the article **School attendance** (*q.v.*), in the case of the failure of a parent to send his child regularly to school. The courts, if they acquit the parent, may direct that the school attendance order shall cease to be in force. Otherwise, the order continues in force so long as the child remains of compulsory school age, subject to any amendment of it that may be made by the LEA, or unless it is revoked by the LEA.

In the case of a vagrant child of compulsory school age, i.e. a child whom a person habitually wandering from place to place takes with him, and for whom the school attendance order procedure would be useless, the LEA of the area in which the child is at any time, may bring him or her before a juvenile court, and unless it appears to the court that the child is receiving efficient full-time education suitable to his or her age, ability, and aptitude, the court may make an order to remedy the position, including committing the child to the care of a fit person.

FURTHER READING
George Taylor and John B. Saunders. *The New Law of Education*, Butterworth, 6th ed. 1965.

FB

School bases The idea of the school base was popularised by J. Howard Whitehouse in his book *The School Base* (1943). The main proposal is that schools of varying types (e.g. grammar, modern and technical) should be situated together on the same base, sharing a number of facilities such as playing fields, and operating both as differentiated schools, and to some extent as a unity. The division of pupils between the different types of school was to take place according to the normal methods of selection, but placement of the schools on one base would, it was thought, provide the opportunity for close social and to some extent academic relationships to be built up between the schools.

School bases of this type were established by some LEAs following the second world war, in particular by Bolton, where all the schools were organised by this method in the early 1960s, and Durham. Following Circular 10/65, however, these schools began to be more integrally unified on comprehensive lines.

BS

School boards Modelled on American precedents, school boards were created by the Education Act 1870 to 'fill the gaps' in the existing system of voluntary schools. Where these gaps had not been, or could not be, filled by the end of 1870, a school board was to be set up.

These new *ad hoc* local authorities were to be elected for a period of three years, and were endowed with powers to establish and maintain elementary schools by levying rates, charging fees and receiving government grants. They could, if they wished, make bye-laws compelling children between the ages of five and 12 to attend school, and for that purpose could appoint school attendance officers, and remit fees in the case of poor children. They could also allow their schools to offer religious instruction, but only within the context of the Cowper-Temple clause (*q.v.*). To these boards women could be, and were, elected. From the opening of the first at St. Austell, Cornwall in 1872, board schools grew rapidly. In 1880 there were 3,433 as opposed to 14,181 voluntary schools.

Though in large towns, especially London where they could attract members of the calibre of T. H. Huxley, school boards were innovatory and efficient, the reverse was often true in rural areas. In 1889 the Technical Instruction Act recommended that the county and county borough councils (established in the previous year) should be empowered to levy up to a penny rate to provide technical and manual instruction. Charges of inefficiency were less damaging than accusations of godlessness, especially when coming from the Roman and Anglican churches. The newly-formed education committees of the county and county borough councils resented school boards levying a rate which others had to collect. The Bryce Commission on Secondary Education (1894–5) claimed that the higher grade schools (*q.v.*) established by them should be removed from their control. After the Cockerton Judgement (1900) which virtually effected this, the Education Act 1902 replaced over 2,500 school boards by 300 education committees, of which 120 were those of counties or county boroughs.

See also **Morant, Sir Robert**

WHGA

School broadcasting *See* **BBC educational broadcasting; ITV educational television**

School Broadcasting Council for the UK *See* **BBC educational broadcasting**

School Building Consortiums *See* **CLASP, CLAW, MACE, SCOLA, SEAC**

School buildings in Britain It is only in the last 20 years, largely as a result of the 1944 Act and the burst of school building after the war, that educationists have really begun to demand from their architects buildings that are formed around the educational process. More recently, educationists have seen that a beautiful building of today can in itself form part of that process.

In 1840 the first government publication on school building was still able to suggest for schools that 'a barn furnishes no bad model, and a good one may be easily converted into a schoolroom'. This was at a time when intellectual thought in the sciences, arts, engineering and politics was bursting with new ideas and largely shaping the modern world. The reason for the poverty of the quoted definition was that education had generally been left to the churches, who were disinclined to encourage the ordinary man to know more than they thought was good for him. Building requirements were therefore correspondingly simple. The 1870 Act at last made a break with the churches (this being inevitable, with Darwin strongly in the air) and school design began its long development towards its proper aim.

The earliest schools had no special structures of their own and used churches and other ecclesiastical buildings. Gradually adjacent buildings were provided by the Church, usually in association with cathedrals and collegiate churches in England rather than monasteries as in Scotland. The first English school was probably at Canterbury (AD 598) followed by Dunwich, Rochester, York and Winchester grammar schools. The first secular teaching in Scotland was probably in the monastery at Whithorn (founded 397). Many schools were founded in this way long before the Conquest, but the first school to be founded as a separate entity was Winchester College in 1382. Intended to provide suitable scholars for New College, Oxford, this was the prototype for the English public school. Lancing College, founded nearly 500 years later, was little different in concept or building. The first independent grammar school in Wales was founded about 1407 at Oswestry.

During the middle ages a number of grammar schools were founded by guilds (Louth, Stratford, Boston), though still firmly under the direction of the Church. There were charity schools for choristers (Durham, Reading, Coventry, Westminster) and schools kept by the priests of endowed chantries (City of London, Chipping Camden, St Paul's), as well as schools of hospitals (Ewelme, St John's Hospital, Coventry). The Reformation closed the vast majority of schools since they were under the control of the Church. Subsequently, Edward VI re-opened and founded a number of new schools. Only the larger and more important survived, and it was not till the very end of the 17th century that the Protestant Church began promoting parish schools for elementary education. Unlike the Catholic schools of the past, these did not have buildings with a strong ecclesiastical character but were much more domestic in design. Many were makeshifts, using existing houses, but were distinguished essays in the palladian style (The Latin School, Warminster; The Bluecoat School, Frome; The Free School, Watford; The Charity School, Denham). All look like comfortable country houses of the period. In Scotland the Dollar Academy (1821), a privately endowed school designed by Playfair, is a distinguished example of the later Grecian style. Towards the end of the

18th century it was felt that the child's place was in the factory rather than the school and Sunday Schools, using less time, became popular. This resulted, however, in such a drop in educational standards throughout Britain that both the Anglicans and nonconformists started new societies to set up monitorial schools. In 1833 the government decided to assist these societies financially, and in 1839 formed the Committee of Council on Education to supervise expenditure. Their published minutes show plans for various sizes of schools, complete with specifications for building. For the most part they are simple one- or two-room affairs, with separate play yards for girls and boys and a small house for the master. Substantially built, many are still in use; others are converted to country cottages — for which use they are equally well suited. Designed in the Gothic style then fashionable, they are important in that they were the first serious attempt to set standards for school buildings.

During the latter half of the 19th century the large single classroom was gradually dropped in favour of the corridor and multiple classroom plan. This made assembly of the whole school difficult, and eventually the large single classroom was restored in the form of a central hall. The forerunner of this plan type was the three-storey Ben Jonson School, London, designed by Roger Smith. Although excellent for discipline (then still the most important factor in education), this design was later felt to be bad for physical health since there was no cross ventilation and plenty of cross infection. But mental health aids such as trees, grass, flowers, vistas, sunshine, and fresh air, were still thought unimportant. Early 20th century schools had better ventilation, but the playground remained asphalt — sensible and hardwearing, with no trees to clog drains with leaves or endanger climbers.

Schools ceased to look like churches, grand houses, or prisons for minor offenders, and began to reflect civic pride and to look like town halls.

The revolutionary social ideas behind early modern architecture gave architects, revolutionaries or not, the clue they needed. Efficiency in planning for the fundamental purpose of the building became more important than external ornamentation. Landscaping, sunshine and the excitement of living had all found their expression in the new concrete and glass buildings. After mass housing and factories had been tackled, schools were the next obvious problem to be examined. (Curiously, churches, private houses, prisons and civic halls have only lately begun to feel the fresh draught of new thought.) The new schools were designed on one floor, each classroom being given the maximum light and sunshine. Natural materials were used for their intrinsic qualities: beech furniture, cork floors, exposed brick and stone walls. Landscaping was very important, and for the first time seated pupils were allowed to look out of the windows. Good teaching was taking over from good discipline. Two well-known schools of this period are Walter Gropius' and Maxwell Fry's Village College at Impington and Dennis Clarke-Hall's Richmond High School.

The war put a temporary stop to the new train of thought; and when it re-emerged, reinforced by the 1944 Act, the enormous demand for new schools, especially primary schools, gave ample opportunity for experiment and development. C. H. Aslin, county architect for Hertfordshire, gathered around him some of the brightest young architects in the country, including David Medd (later to head the Ministry of Education school building section), Bruce Martin and Oliver Cox. Together with the Ministry of Education (later the DES) they not only developed prefabricated systems to speed building, but designed new sanitary fittings, floor coverings, heating systems, windows, furniture and colour schemes, involving the examination of every facet of educational building. Never before had a building type received such detailed attention, and the effect was a fundamental influence on British architecture at the time. Many of the new ideas in construction and design have been adopted in other buildings, reversing the trend of the previous centuries. Honesty was the key note, (for instance, all service pipes were left exposed and painted bright colours as in a ship). But these schools were still unsophisticated in design, examples of straightforward thinking rather than formal masterpieces. It was left to the next generation of architects to re-think in monumental terms what had been discovered. It is interesting to find that the first example of 'New Brutalism' was a school at Hunstanton by Alyson and Peter Smithson. Here the revolution is complete, in that the building itself was treated as a form of visual education. By its treatment of light, space and form it made a totally new experience for the child.

There are now two streams of thought, one embodied in the Ministry of Education designs, true descendants of the original research in Hertfordshire, and illustrated in a mass of useful *Building Bulletins* published by HMSO. The other stream, less 'pure' but visually more stimulating, has recently begun to influence university building (*See* **University buildings and planning**).

Both these streams of thought seem to have reached their zenith. The next step will follow from the acceptance of the computer and teaching machine. This will await another rapprochement between educationist and architect. The implications are enormous and a radically different form of school will emerge. However, it seems more likely that this form of school will start in the underdeveloped countries, where the teacher shortage is most acute and where British architects as a whole have usually found more scope for new ideas.

JBP

School Care Service This organisation was set up by the London County Council in 1907 to advise and help families in difficulties and to authorise such things as free meals, clothing and footwear. Each school in London should now have access to a Care Committee of voluntary workers, who are recruited, trained and advised by professional social workers known as School Care Organisers. A care committee worker may visit a house for many reasons: there may be a suspicion of parental cruelty, neglect or moral danger, or it may be a case of assisting a family to pay for a school journey or some other aspect of school life that would otherwise be inaccessible to impoverished parents. All care committees work in close co-operation both with the head-teacher and with all the other specialised services concerning children.

Springing from a voluntary committee set up in London in 1887, the School Care Service is unique and its history is worth noting. It originated in Islington, where a headmaster, finding his children to be in a condition 'so wretched that education was a farce', established a fund from which he provided them with boots, took them for an annual outing to the seaside and provided them with food four days a week. (On two of those days it was soup, on the third boiled suet pudding and on the fourth 'large sandwiches'.) By 1904 there were 170 voluntary committees providing school meals for very poor children. In 1907, following the passing of the Education (Provision of Meals) Act the previous year, the LCC made use of these volunteers to administer the new meals service.

There are now over 2,000 care committee workers who attend school medical inspections to inform doctors about the backgrounds of poor children; advise mothers on the carrying out of doctors' instructions; help with applications for maintenance grants and tax rebates; help with clothing and with the cost of school journeys; recommend cases for free school dinners; and generally advise parents who are in difficulties.

School Conditions, NUT National Survey of In 1962 the National Union of Teachers conducted a National Survey of Schools in which over 22,000 schools participated. The findings of the survey, published in a report entitled *The State of Our Schools*, provided what is almost certainly the most comprehensive picture of conditions in maintained schools in England and Wales yet issued.

The survey dealt with the age an state of school buildings, the provision of equipment, and the standard on staffing in maintained primary and secondary schools. The information when published attracted nation-wide publicity and caused something of a scandal, for the picture to emerge was one of obsolescence, dilapidation and insanitariness on an extensive scale in the schools, and serious shortcomings and high turnover in staffing. Any suggestion that the report might have over-stated the situation was dispelled when, two years later, the DES published the *School Building Survey 1962*. This contained statistics relating to a survey carried out shortly after the NUT's survey and, while confined to building conditions, the picture it revealed substantially confirmed that painted by the NUT's report.

The survey was carried out for the NUT by Research Services Ltd under the supervision of Dr Mark Abrams. A questionnaire was sent out to every maintained primary and secondary school and every direct grant school in England and Wales. Slightly more than 22,000 questionnaires were completed and returned, and these were analysed by Research Services. In order to save time it was decided to collect from the completed forms a sample of 3,000 and to use these as the basis for the report. This was done by first dividing all 22,000 forms into three main groups: (a) maintained schools; (b) direct grant schools; and (c) special schools. The number from the latter two types of school was small, and the real sampling problem came with the maintained schools. This was handled as follows:

First they were all divided into seven types of maintained schools: primary, secondary modern, grammar, technical, bilateral and multilateral, comprehensive and other secondary schools. Next, each of the seven types of maintained schools was sorted into five geographical areas: LCC, South, Midland, North and Wales. Forms from each of the known LCC areas were sorted into two types of LEA—counties and county boroughs. These gave 63 groups of forms, and from each of these 63 groups there was selected a random sample (using a varying sampling fraction) so that the final sample of 3,051 forms reflected the composition of all 30,108 schools shown in the Ministry statistics for 1961.

From the findings of the questionnaire the following are among the more significant points that emerged when the first part of the report, dealing with primary and secondary modern schools, was published in January 1963.

Primary schools 55% had buildings dating back to the 19th century.

At 21% of schools, the classes exceeded the maximum of 40 children per class; in approximately 10% the average class was nearer 50.

60% had no separate dining room. 40% had no separate room for the head-teacher or the staff.

39% had only 'fair to poor' heating. 17% had no hot water. Only 50% had a playing field and no more than 56% had an assembly hall.

Of 15 'specialist rooms' named in the questionnaire, at least six do not exist in nearly all primary schools. These included the gymnasium, the library and the school office.

43% had lavatories outside the main building only.

Secondary modern schools 20% were still having to make do with 19th-century buildings.

59% required additional specialist teachers for the education of backward children, and 43% needed additional specialists in mathematics. 36% needed specialists in English and 29% needed specialists in science.

16% had no playing field.

25% had inadequate supplies of books and 32% had inadequate library equipment.

In August 1963 a further report was published on grammar, comprehensive and special schools, and the following are the most significant points emerging from that report.

Grammar schools Three in ten grammar schools had some buildings that dated from the 19th century or earlier.

There was a great need for additional specialist teachers in certain subjects, especially mathematics and science. Twenty-eight additional specialists per hundred schools were required for maths, and 24 additional specialists per hundred schools were required for teaching science. One fifth of the schools had no specialist in religious education.

Respondents were asked to relate the number of pupils to the available number of classrooms (on the basis of 30 pupils to each classroom). Using this defination, 55% of the schools suffered from overcrowding.

About one-fifth of grammar schools were without stage facilities, a separate dining room and a gymnasium, and almost half had no medical inspection room.

24% of the schools were dissatisfied with their supplies of textbooks, and 13% with the reference books available.

Comprehensive schools Almost three-quarters of these schools were mixed, but 15% were for boys only and 11% for girls only. Nearly two-thirds were housed in entirely post-war buildings, and over half had at least 1,000 pupils.

There was a great need for additional specialist teachers, particularly in mathematics and science and the education of the backward child. Fifty-nine additional specialists per hundred schools were required in science teaching; 68 per hundred schools in maths teaching and 63 per hundred schools for teaching backward children.

On the basis of 30 enrolled pupils to a classroom, about 40% of the schools suffered from overcrowding.

42% of the schools said they did not have enough textbooks, and 37% said they needed more reference books for staff.

Special schools In these schools there was an acute shortage of teachers trained to teach the educationally backward child. Fifty-two additional specialists per hundred schools are required.

The statistics in the report were supplemented by a study based on the usual comments by head-teachers in reply to three non-statistical questions put in the survey questionnaire. This study was written by Mr Tyrrell Burgess, a former director of the Advisory Centre for Education at Cambridge, and the following quotation from his report is typical of what he had to say:

'Continuing shortage and makeshift (even when there is no actual squalor) was the picture that emerged from the comments examined. This was true of staff, buildings, books and equipment. Many head-teachers appeared angry, resigned, bewildered, bitter or hopeless. They did not expect things to improve. On the contrary, they expected the staffing position to deteriorate. All over the country, day after day and year after year, there are heads and assistant teachers who know they are forced to do a less than adequate job and who see no prospect of change.'

One headmaster summed up a general feeling:

'We mourn the death of a resourceful and imaginative inspector who was the only person I have met with the vision and enthusiasm to get something done. For far too long the prevailing result has been that of "make do and mend". The children of this school are receiving what is called a secondary education, in spite of and not by virtue of the facilities provided. For too many pupils the tragedy is "too little and too late".'

After publication the report continued to make its impact, and as late as 1967 it was quoted in evidence by the Plowden Committee report on the primary schools.

FJ

School dental officer Separate dental inspections are held in all state schools, and the school dental officer is responsible for making the recommendations for necessary treatment. A physically handicapped or disabled child must also be seen by the school doctor to ensure that he or she is fit to have a dental operation or anaesthetic.

When the school medical service was introduced in 1907, the existing dental problems were very great. It was found that up to 75% of children had hopelessly decayed teeth by the time they were 14. The local authorities began to organise a school dental service by contract with private dentists or by establishing school dental clinics, and through the dental hospitals. At first it was possible to provide dental care only for elementary school-children, and just before World War I it was found that the school dental service was coping with not more than 10% of the needs of only half the school population. After World War I it was considered that three times as many dentists were required to care adequately for school-children. The 1944 Education Act ensured that secondary-school children should have at least the same facilities as primary pupils. By 1948 nearly all the LEAs were employing senior dental officers. However, after the introduction of the National Health Service in 1948, there was a great shortage of dentists employed in local government since working in their own practices was made more remunerative.

The Dentists Act 1956 made the profession, for the first time, self-governing and independent of the medical profession. To overcome the staff shortage it was decided to introduce a new class of ancillary workers; they can work in the national and local authority health services, or with general dental practitioners. Their functions are limited, but they work at a high standard under the supervision of the busy dental officers. The dental auxiliary also has the important role of teaching children about dental hygiene. This can make a major contribution to the reduction of dental caries.

SL

School fees In 15th-century medieval grammar schools fees for day-boys were 1d, and for boarders 8d, a week. The great surge of endowments between 1460 and 1660 was often accompanied by specific exclusion of fees as such, or in the form of cock-penny, victor-penny or potation-penny (gratuities offered to the schoolmaster by parents) for those 'on the foundation'.

The increase of fee-payers not on the foundation enabled some schools to reduce their 'free' pupils, thereby transforming themselves from local day grammar schools into non-local boarding schools. It has been suggested that since the annual stipend of £10 allowed to grammar school masters remained statutory until the time of George III, grammar schools had to take boarders to compensate for the fall in the value of money.

Voluntary societies charged fees or school pence, and in the second elementary education bill ever to be submitted to Parliament (*see* **Parish Schools Bill, 1820**), Brougham proposed that parochial schools, in addition to enjoying the fruit of a rate of 4d in the £, should charge a fee of 1d a week. The Wesleyans indeed had to prevent their masters charging too much in 1854. In 1861 between a quarter and three-fifths of the cost of voluntary schools was contributed by school pence. Fees were higher in 'British' schools (established by the British and Foreign Schools Society) than in National Schools, and they were on a sliding scale, according to the parents' social position; managers made special terms in special cases. The whole weekly cost per pupil in 'British' schools was 8d for a 44-week year. In most schools the fee was less than 3d a week. According to an act of 1844 children in factory schools were not to be charged more than 2d a week. The Newcastle Commission (1861) recognised that if fees were raised, schools would attract children of a higher class, for whom the government grant was not intended.

School boards also charged fees, though theirs were 15% less than those charged by the voluntary schools in 1885. Clause 25 of the 1870 Act made provision for the fees of poor children at voluntary schools to be paid.

In 1891 fees in schools charging less than 10s a year were abolished; they were lowered in schools charging above 10s and prohibited in all elementary schools to be built in the future. G. A. N. Lowndes attributes to this the mushrooming of school savings schemes, citing the fact that in 1937 there were 22,000 such school-based groups (*The Silent Social Revolution*, 1937). All fees in maintained grammar schools were abolished as from 1 April 1945.

The burden of mounting fees at public schools was cushioned by the institution of educational policies by insurance companies. Indeed some insurance companies in the 1920s came into the field as backers of new public schools. As waiting lists at these schools grew longer, covenants, trusts and specially created charities—to say nothing of employers offering school fees in order to obtain high-value employees—have all made the question of fees far more sophisticated than it appears from the bald list appended to such schools in, say, *Whitaker's Almanack.*

WHGA

School finance The administration of public education in the UK, apart from the universities, is mainly the responsibility of LEAs, but a number of functions are carried out by the DES. The 146 LEAs maintain some 30,000 primary and secondary schools, 700 technical colleges and over 100 teacher training colleges. In addition, they provide a wide range of educational services for children at school, for young people and for adults. About 84% of public educational expenditure in the UK is thus made by the LEAs.

The financing of public education presents a rather different picture, and a substantial proportion of the expenditure of LEAs on education derives from grants received from central government. Present methods of transferring funds from central authorities to LEAs do not, however, permit precise estimates of the relative importance of central and local financing of education.

Between 1918 and 1959, LEAs' expenditure on education was supported by central government by means of a percentage grant. The precise details of this percentage grant varied from time to time, but in essence the central government met a fixed percentage of all LEA expenditures on education. In 1953, 65% of LEA expenditure on education was financed by the central government. The system was flexible in that it was possible to encourage progress in particular sectors by paying

a preferential grant, as was done in 1952–9 for advanced technical education. By 1958, this device was being severely criticised for encouraging wasteful expenditure by the LEAs, who contributed only about 35% of any item of expenditure, and as permitting too much central control of the details of educational administration. It was therefore abandoned by the government in 1959 in favour of the 'block grant' system.

Under this system a substantially larger part of the grant aid from the central authorities to LEAs is in the form of general assistance for local authority expenditure (including certain health services, fire services and town planning). The amount of this grant is fixed in advance for a short period of years and is distributed among LEAs, not according to expenditure but by reference to certain objective factors (school population, number of old people, density of population, population trends, etc.).

Since April 1959, therefore, there has been no central government grant relative to, or even identified with, educational expenditure. However, the educational element is the major part of the total field covered by the grant (amounting to as much as 85%) and the number of pupils in school is a very important factor determining its distribution.

In addition to their support of LEA expenditure the central authorities maintain a number of national non-university institutions such as the College of Aeronautics, the Royal College of Art and the Colleges for Agricultural Engineering, Food Technology, Rubber Technology, etc. as well as providing a capitation grant for students in some independent secondary schools. The DES also sponsors and finances educational research, and assists a number of national bodies for general services of value to education. However, in 1962–63 direct expenditure on goods and services by the DES represented only about 5% of all public educational expenditure.

The situation is vastly different in many other countries. The proportion of public educational expenditure under direct control of the central authorities is about 85% in France, 73% in the Netherlands, 90% in Portugal and 60% in Austria. On the other hand, it is only 30% in the USSR, 7% in Canada, 7% in the USA and 1% in Western Germany.

In addition to financing by public authorities, schools receive funds for current and capital purposes from a variety of other sources, school fees, endowments, grants from profit-making and non-profit-making enterprises, special taxes on enterprises, ownership of land and other property, etc. With the rapid expansion of education in recent years there has been considerable interest in exploring the possibility of increasing the contribution made by some of these sources of funds. It is, however, a field where reliable statistical information is sadly lacking and current discussion is characterised more by its heat than its light.

See also **Grants, General**

FURTHER READING
W. H. Burston. 'The Incidence of Taxation and of State Provision for Education: United Kingdom', *Yearbook of Education*, Evans, 1956.
A. T. Peacock and J. Wiseman. 'The Finance of State Education in the UK', *Yearbook of Education*, Evans, 1956.
OECD. *Financing of Education for Economic Growth*, Paris, 1966. (See especially 'Methods of Control of Educational Expenditure in the UK' by J. Embling.)
GLW

School health service *See* **Ancillary services**

School health visitor Each school nurse (or health visitor) is assigned to a group of schools. She prepares for and assists at medical inspections, and at each school she carries out a yearly health survey to discover any child who appears to need a medical examination, and who is therefore referred for future examination by the school doctor.

A health visitor has important responsibilities, including other health surveys and home visiting. She can help to control the spread of infectious diseases and test children for eye defects. She is the main link between home, school and clinic. Her work often takes her to the school, and she can more easily become well-known to the children and the staff. In secondary schools adolescent girls often consult her, and she can do much to help and advise them in their special difficulties.

There has been a slow but steady increase in the number of nurses. Postwar regulations require school nurses to hold the health visitor's qualifications unless they work only in a school clinic, or in other special capacities. This facilitates the interchange of staff, secures continuity in the care of the children, and unifies the school, child welfare and health services.

Health visitors should make as much time as possible available for health education and social service; others may do the more routine jobs such as cleanliness inspections and attendance at minor ailments clinics. Health visitors should attend medical examinations, where there are excellent opportunities of carrying out health education among parents and discussing cases with doctors and teachers. They can help particularly in discussing with teachers the general problems arising from defects found in children, and in child guidance, and giving group health education. Health visitors can best be organised by combining the home visiting of the local health and education authorities; home visits then become the essential bond between home and school, and health visitors the most qualified to make them.

See also **Health education; School medical service**

SL

School Journey Association of London A non-profit-making association of serving teachers for the encouragement and arrangement of school journeys of all kinds. Membership is open to primary and secondary schools, colleges and public and private schools catering for pupils and students below the age of 18.

Tours are arranged to most European countries. A booklet of inspected and approved holiday accommodation is issued to member schools. Film evenings, adult meetings and competitions for schoolchildren are regularly held.

23 Southampton Pl., London, WC1.

Publications: A termly newsletter; pamphlets on all aspects of school journeys.

School journeys The annual school journey, either within the UK or abroad—or, in larger schools, a whole range of journeys, of varying ambition and at different times of the year—is now a feature of the life of an increasing number of schools. At home most LEAs maintain establishments catering for school parties ranging from camping sites to country houses and offering activities that include walking, climbing, boating, flying, riding, farming and general cultural pursuits. The Crystal Palace Recreation Centre (q.v.) provides facilities, through LEAs, for children to play games and to swim and ski. Some of the more progressive LEAs make it possible for children to spend at least one period during their school life away from home and school in a stimulatingly new environment of their choice. Some schools themselves arrange for exchanges between their pupils and others of a similar background either at home or abroad.

As for foreign journeys, there are authorities that charter liners in which pupils may cruise to the Mediterranean or even beyond (see **Educational cruises**). For most school journeys abroad, however, a school must make use of the services of one of the scores of travel agencies, specialising in such travel, that have been set up within recent years. Most of these are reputable firms: advice in the choice of an agency may always be sought from the Central Bureau for Educational Visits and Exchanges (q.v.) or from the other associations mentioned below. Most European countries and many others are on the agency lists, and itineraries exist to suit most demands.

After a choice of journey has been made, passports must be obtained. For parties of 50 pupils or fewer, all British subjects and under the age of 18, a collective passport is to be recommended: it is easy to handle and cheap, costing £3 and being obtainable from local branch passport offices. Once it is acquired, foreign money may be obtained from a bank and, where necessary, a visa from the appropriate consulate. As for staff passports, it should be remembered that any married woman teacher who normally travels with her husband on a joint passport must obtain her own separate passport if she is going on a school journey without him.

Special allowances for persons in charge of pupils travelling abroad for educational purposes may be claimed on Form T through UK branches of banks.

Some LEAs provide a general comprehensive insurance policy to cover their pupils and employees only while on journeys. It is essential, however, to check that such policies, when held, provide sufficient cover and that such activities as ski-ing, mountaineering, flying or boating are not excluded where they will form part of a journey. These policies do not cover former pupils of a school or pupils who officially leave school whilst on a journey. Nor do they include people who may join the party but are not employees of the authority. For such travellers, separate and adequate cover for personal accident and liability, expenses, baggage and money can be obtained from an insurance company for a few shillings.

Taking a party of schoolchildren abroad needs very methodical preparation. The party leader, or one of the leaders—often a language teacher—should have some experience of foreign travel. Written permission must be obtained from parents for each child travelling with the party, and this should embody a clause indemnifying the leaders of the party and the authority from unreasonable responsibility. Every parent and child should be supplied with a list of suitable clothing. The leader should make sure that every parent has the address or addresses of the place where the party will be staying—together, if possible, with a telephone number so that swift contact can be made in an emergency. He should insist that every child always carries both his home and holiday address with him; and he must exactly assess the complete cost of the journey for each child, including passport, insurance, any extras such as guides' fees and the expense of incidental trips not included in the overall programme, plus a small 'floater' for unforeseen emergencies.

National organisations catering for school journeys are the School Travel Organisation (165 Kensington High St, London, W8) and the School Journey Association of London (23 Southampton Pl., London, WC1). The latter is a voluntary association of teachers that organises, and helps to organise, all kinds of school journey; membership is not confined to teachers working in London. Booklets are published on the organisation of school journeys at home and abroad.

PCJL

School leaving age, Raising the
The intended raising of the school leaving age to 16 in the 1970s marks a further stage along the road, mapped out in the Education Act 1944, leading to secondary education for all. It will mean retaining in school for a fifth year of secondary education some 60% more of the age group than now stay on voluntarily. Some of these pupils will actively resent the new requirement; many others will have little desire for extended education; and the majority of those affected will have at best only an average aptitude for work of this kind traditional to English secondary schools. The decision will take effect in a period of great social and economic change when personal development in adolescence proceeds at a rapid rate. Thus the schools face a difficult situation, which is not made easier by prospects of staff shortage, lack of suitable accommodation and a general climate of financial stringency.

Criticism of the traditional school curriculum is not confined to the pupils. Historically, British society was divided into a small, well-educated élite, who held power and staffed the liberal professions, and the masses who worked in unskilled and semi-skilled callings which demanded only a basic grounding in literacy and numeracy. During recent decades industrial development, scientific discovery, technological innovation, improved communications, changes in the balance of world power and the emergence of a mass culture have dealt a mortal blow to the concept of 'the two nations'. Teachers and others interested in education have become increasingly restive about the basic assumptions of the tripartite system, the excessive formalism of much secondary school work and the undue emphasis traditionally placed on inert factual knowledge and on theoretical concepts divorced from practical experience. In part this anxiety is due to a growing realisation of the impossibility that any human being could ever master the sheer volume of accumulating knowledge. However, it also recognises the nation's insatiable demand for skill (particularly in the technical and human relations fields) and embraces a growing awareness of the necessity for ordinary citizens to increase their capacity for thinking productively and wisely about the nature of the world and of human experience.

During the same decades the findings of behavioural science have helped to modify concepts of human nature and of the learning situation. Early in the century the human being was regarded as an organism responding to stimuli rather than as one initiating encounters with his environment. It is now recognised that biological drives (instincts) play only a small part in human motivation, and that the individual uses values and purposes as organising elements in life situations. In school, as elsewhere, much behaviour is now being explained in terms of the pupil's attempts to understand his experience and to manipulate his environment in accordance with his wishes.

The pupil's self-picture is recognised as a major factor affecting his approach to school work, and links can be discerned between this on the one hand and his early childhood experiences and/or school experiences on the other. Studies of both motivation and scholastic attainment stress the importance of early upbringing. At the same time, the school's expectations (as perceived by the pupil and by the peer groups to which he belongs) have also been shown to influence the direction and amount of adolescent learning.

When learning was conceived of as building connections to elicit specific responses, educational objectives could be formulated in specific and detailed terms. As evidence accumulates that human beings can learn more general behaviour, greater stress is being laid on teaching for the understanding of principles basic to many situations. It is also becoming more widely recognised that such understanding involves both intellectual and emotional growth:

that is, both comprehension and appreciation.

The developments summarised above imply modern projections of twin conceptions of the purposes of public education which have been present throughout its development in England and Wales. First, education is to be thought of as a basic human right, given regardless of whether in each individual case there will be any return. It includes a school's duty to foster and respond to human aspirations, that the young may have life more abundantly. It is an extension of the duty traditionally recognised by the parent to provide for his children and by the rich man to help the poor. Secondly, education is a form of national investment providing for an adequate supply of the brains and skills needed to sustain national well-being. This conception recognises society's duty to maintain and, where possible, to enlarge the pool of talent. It affirms that a nation can control its own development and that education plays a major part in this, both by promoting necessary change and by harmonising the effects of other interacting forces.

At present a tension exists in educational circles between those who, in assessing educational programmes, wish to use product criteria and those who favour process criteria. Product criteria depend for their definition upon a set of goals towards which education is directed. In the past these have tended to be expressed either in ultimate terms (such as 'to develop good citizens') or as a series of specific isolated targets (as is often found in syllabuses for public examinations). In its modern connotation, however, the notion refers to the sequential aspects of pupil growth, with goals expressed in operational terms and in varying degrees of proximity. However, the more ultimate of these are really goals of society. Thus, having formulated their sequences, those who support this view generally wish to concentrate attention in school on the outcomes of particular teaching-learning experiences, using evidence accumulated immediately after completion of the teaching programmes concerned.

Process criteria include those aspects of teacher and pupil behaviour which are believed to be worthwhile in their own right. They are most often described in terms of either teacher behaviour (e.g. good rapport, effective but not harsh discipline, individualised instruction) or pupil behaviour (e.g affection for the teacher, interest in school-work, high level of aspiration). The interaction between teacher and pupil appears to be the dominant aspect of the whole process of learning. It is widely believed that a greater sense of commitment would emerge in educational settings which pupils could perceive as being less authoritarian and impersonal than many schools appear to them to be to-day. Yet such commitment would not necessarily be followed by higher scholastic attainments, for process criteria deal with means whilst product criteria emphasise educational ends.

In recent years, also, assumptions about the limitations set to pupils' capacities by their low-measured intelligence have been challenged by studies of creativity, and it is now asserted that in solving problems a thinker uses both a-rational and rational processes. In the act of creation a thinker must be open to both new stimuli from without and acceptance of impulse from within. Thus it is being argued that premature censorship of ideas, whether by the pupil himself or by his teacher, inhibits creative thinking. Encouragement of creative activity involves the teacher in providing not only discipline and criticism but also opportunities for pupils to stretch their imagination and to discuss divergent, even fantastic, ideas.

The changes referred to above have influenced the work of the Schools Council, whose major functions include organising and supporting research and development work in preparation for raising the school leaving age. The Council recognises that extended courses must take account of the pupils' own evaluations of what is relevant. Such evaluations provide points of departure for study, and at least half the task is that of finding starting points. Yet more is at stake than this, and the Council asserts that the schools must also carry the pupils forward, so that what is learned has relevance to at least the next stage in the pupils' development. For the pupils will be left prisoners of their own experience if the teacher cannot find a way of so enlarging their vision that they come to see value for themselves in gaining some understanding of man's total experience, and with this some capacity for contributing to its further enlargement.

The Newsom Committee, upon whose report (q.v.) the decision to raise the school leaving age was based, argued that the secondary education of pupils who are average and below-average in general ability should be practical, realistic, vocational and should permit an element of choice. The Schools Council interpreted the Committee's objectives in terms of a range of powers of body and mind skills, knowledge and forms of expression to be cultivated, rather than as a corpus of factual knowledge to be taught within strict subject boundaries. Opinion generally supports this emphasis, but is divided as to the form of curriculum which will best ensure that such pupils master the essentials of all disciplines basic to life in the modern world.

Agreement about objectives is greatest in respect of science, mathematics and language teaching, and for these subjects national efforts in curriculum development are well under way. The Nuffield Foundation, which plays a major role in such work, has arranged for small teams of hand-picked teachers to devote themselves full-time to the preparation of new and reorganised teaching materials for attaining the agreed objectives. Extensive field trials, again using outstanding classroom practitioners, provide feedback evidence on which to base successive revisions of the programmes. Following publication, the main body of teachers will study and experiment with the new materials during in-service training courses.

In respect of the humanities, great difficulty is being experienced in translating ultimate objectives into operational goals. Moreover, since it is primarily upon these studies that discussion centres as to the relative validity of product and process criteria, it is to be expected that national efforts in this field, organised along the lines described above, will take some years to mature. Meanwhile, groups which have adopted particular viewpoints are experimenting with related teaching materials, and the Schools Council advocates widespread local activity, thought, discussion, experiment and the like, out of which it hopes broad agreement will eventually take shape.

For this and other reasons local teachers' centres (*see* **Development centres**) are being established in many parts of the country under full—or part-time—leaders. There is widespread support among teachers for curricula based on so-called 'studies in depth' and 'discovery' methods, and many local experiments are in progress. Aside from their ostensible aim, experiments serve also to develop local thinking on many of the general issues discussed above.

On any realistic view, the issues are unlikely to be resolved completely by the date finally chosen for the raising of the school leaving age. Yet if the best is made of the opportunities presented by the decision, the level of the platform will be raised upon which the next generation of teachers, parents and public can build. In this sense curriculum development should be a continuing exercise in which studies of objectives, content, teaching method and techniques of assessment follow one another in cycle and each lead to feedback of new evidence for the next cycle. The need for such an approach to study of the content of education was never greater than it is today.

WGAR

School leaving certificates The transformation of the British educational scene by the Butler Act 1944 (*q.v.*) brought in its train a reformation of the examination system upon which the School Certificate and Higher School Certificate had so far been based. After a series of reports of the Secondary School Examinations Council the Ministry introduced in 1951 new examinations, on an open subject basis in place of the minimum attainments in a group of obligatory subjects previously demanded. The new examinations, collectively the General Certificate of Education (*q.v.*), with their two levels of attainment, ordinary and advanced, have formed the basis for selection for further education ever since 1951. With the minimum age of entry at first at 16 the examinations were clearly intended for pupils at selective grammar and technical schools.

The Butler Act intended that pupils at non-selective secondary schools— the eleven-plus 'failures', of course, constituting about 60% of all scholars —should receive a non-academic type of education which freed them from examination pressures and provided the staff with opportunities for creative educational experiment. Nevertheless, the demand grew from modern school pupils, their parents and employers for a school leaving certificate which measured attainments and was based on examinations.

Under this pressure a confusion of practices grew up in modern schools: by 1958 fifth-form pupils were sitting a variety of examinations—GCE, College of Preceptors, Royal Society of Arts, London Chamber of Commerce, Union of Lancashire and Cheshire Institutes, and new regional examining boards. Indeed, by that year it appeared that almost every fifth-form modern school pupil was sitting some external examination: by 1960 some were taking more than one. The demands of these external examining bodies were everywhere narrowing the syllabuses. The situation could not continue. A sub-committee of the Secondary Schools Examinations Council reported in 1960 in favour of a new Certificate of Secondary Education of national standing but organised on a regional basis, effectively under the control of teachers, and co-ordinated by a central body which had power to initiate research. It was stipulated that the examinations should be designed for a lower level of ability than GCE and should not impose their own patterns on curricula, but faithfully reflect the work the schools themselves have initiated.

The Minister of Education approved these recommendations in 1962 and a further recommendation, from the Seventh Report of the Secondary Schools Examination Council 1963, linked the CSE examinations with the GCE so that 'a sixteen-year-old pupil whose ability in the subject is such that he might reasonably have secured a pass in the ordinary level of the GCE examination, had he applied himself to a course of study leading to that examination, may reasonably expect to secure Grade I in the CSE examination . . .' This ponderous official language only partially obscures the fact that a common standard for both examinations was being proposed. The first examinations for CSE were offered in May 1965 by some nine of the 14 CSE boards established on the initiative of the Ministry and co-ordinated by the Schools Council: some 66,000 candidates sat. In 1966 the figure of candidates was 141,000 from 14 boards.

Research appears to indicate that there is a need to keep GCE and CSE separate even though they maintain standards in common. They do cater for different levels of ability. According to figures taken from a sample of 10 comprehensive schools in 1961, the total GCE passes per candidate was 2.8: only 15 % of pupils secured passes in four or more subjects. On the whole it does look as though GCE is by present standards suitable for only about one in five of non-selective school pupils. The CSE is bound to retain its place while that situation obtains. Eventually perhaps CSE will come to relate to GCE O level as O level relates already to A. It is ironical to note that the pattern of educational diversity which the Butler Act expected to establish particularly for modern schools is giving way in the field of examinations to uniformity of standards.

See also **Examinations**

FURTHER READING
The Certificate of Secondary Education (Fourth Report of the Secondary Schools Examinations Council), HMSO, 1961.
Examining at 16+ (Report of the Joint GCE/CSE Committee of the Schools Council), HMSO, 1966.
Secondary School Examinations other than GCE (Report of a Committee appointed by the Secondary Schools Examination Council), HMSO, 1958.
Statistics of Education Part III, HMSO, 1965.
LP

School Library Association Membership of the SLA is open to individual school librarians and anyone interested. Corporate membership is open to schools and other organisations, and local branches are set up for the exchange of views and opinions. In collaboration with the Library Association, the SLA awards, on the results of an examination, a Joint Certificate in School Librarianship to recognised teachers of not less than three years experience. Publications include pamphlets and book lists and *The*

School Librarian and School Library Review, published three times a year and free to members.

Premier Hse, 150 Southampton Row, London, WC1.

School Management Studies, Diploma in

Syllabuses for this new diploma have been prepared by the Academic Board of the College of Preceptors for the first examination held in August 1968. The examination for the diploma consists of four papers and a 10,000-word thesis of university final-degree level.

The decision to create this diploma follows from recent ministerial statements on the need for the head of a school, and members of the staff responsible for the school's administration, to develop an expertise like that of business executives.

School Mathematics Project

The Project, directed by Professor Brian Thwaites, is designed to integrate modern ideas into a syllabus for GCE O and A levels. A number of schools are collaborating in writing suitable textbooks. Set language is employed consistently, and methods of 'proof' made explicit. Geometrical transformations are studied first, leading to an algebra of matrices and group structure.

Further particulars from the Director, Southampton University.

School Meals Equipment Consortium, Local Authorities'

Formed in 1961 for the purpose of re-designing heavy kitchen equipment used in the school meals service, the consortium consists of the 23 LEAs in Lancashire and Cheshire.

School Meals Organisers of the Institutional Management Association, National Association of

The Institutional Management Association itself, founded in 1938, is the profes-

sional association for those working in large-scale catering and in domestic administration. The National Association of School Meals Organisers was founded in 1965 to maintain the professional standing of its members and to ensure a flow of professional knowledge and information among them.

School meals service

The school meals service as we know it today is the culmination of sporadic efforts to provide food for young children, from as early as 1864, by interested parties ranging from individuals and voluntary, philanthropic and political associations, the larger boroughs and rural authorities to the Board of Education, their concern being mainly to provide free meals for the destitute and undernourished.

In 1906 the Education (Provision of Meals) Act empowered LEAs to provide meals free to needy elementary school children, the cost to be rate-borne. During the first world war the Act of 1914 made funds available to LEAs in grant form with some indication of the quality of the meal to be provided and that it should be taken under supervision. In 1924 publicity was directed towards popularising milk in schools. During the 1930s an increasing awareness of malnutrition in children resulted in the 1934 circular which authorised free milk and meals on medical grounds. Few schools had purpose-built kitchens or dining halls. However, some authorities achieved early success in establishing meals services, those of note being Kent, Cheshire and East Sussex. Throughout the country there were many instances of the 'canteen' initiated by teachers to meet pressures of local need. It was common practice for meals to be provided in grammar schools for pupils travelling from a distance, the cost to the pupil being determined by the overheads required to be met. Most schools had kitchens and many had dining halls provided.

Throughout this period two problems had evaded solution: the selection of deserving children identified as destitute or malnourished and the insurance of the nutritional value of the meal. Over and above these difficulties was the overall problem of unsatisfactory conditions, e.g. unsuitable premises, poor and limited equipment and inadequate supervision.

With the outbreak of war in 1939, involving the movement of children from evacuation areas, the problem of providing food for the overnight invasion of reception areas entailed using hired premises, increasing the output from existing kitchens and conveying meals to dining centres from central kitchens and emergency feeding depots which were brought into use. This surge of additional responsibility with special requirements made necessary the setting up of meals departments by LEAs and also the appointment of School Meals Organisers as required by the Board of Education. Specialist inspectors for the school meals service were appointed by the Board. A Board circular in 1940 had recognised school meals as part of the war economy.

In 1941 a circular on nutrition[1] and the availability of increased funds, furniture, equipment and utensils and unrationed foods was followed by *Circular 1571*[2], the 'bible' of the service, which set out the average daily nutritional requirement (i.e. 20–25 g. protein, 30 g. fat and 1,000 calories per meal), and included the valuable advice that 'Economy should be studied . . . by avoiding waste, by skilled buying and by good cooking'. This set the standard; and since that date, the school meals service has aimed to produce the best type of home-cooked meal. Meals were still free to needy children, and the charge made to cover cost of food varied over the years only as follows: 1941—5d, 1950—6d, 1951—7d, 1953—9d, 1956—10d, 1957—1s, 1968—1s 6d.

The realisation that school meals had come to stay was confirmed by the 1944 Education Act. Reappraisal of kitchen and dining facilities resulted in new schools being built with kitchens and dining areas, though later these areas were planned for dual usage. Over the years many schools have had meals facilities replaced or improved. However, progress has been hampered by the competing need to provide, from the same fund, additional meal production and dining area to meet the steadily increasing demand for meals.

The actual service of the meal varies considerably, but in general has taken the form of cafeteria, monitor or family service. The cafeteria system is usually adopted in very confined conditions where social training must take second place to speed. Tables may be laid, the children collecting the first course of the meal on entering the room, returning later to collect the second and disposing of first course dirties en route. In some instances cutlery, and both courses of the meal, are collected at the same time. Queueing is an unhappy feature of this service as is also the impersonal nature of a system that requires children to fill up spaces in order of entry. Monitor service, where selected children collect the food on plates for the rest (a type of service more usually found in primary schools) can be socially instructive and a rewarding occasion to child and adult alike. Indeed, to be a monitor is considered a privilege. The family service, imitating the traditional family meal, is a valuable exercise in sharing, consideration for others, and natural social intercourse. However, the spirit of any type of service can be enhanced by teachers sharing the meal with the children, particularly at the same table.

By the very nature of the service, its supervision has fallen to the lot of the teachers, whose response has been generous. Dinner duty, however, could become onerous, and it quickly became apparent that additional help was required. Some relief was given by the appointment of supervisory assistants to a scale related to numbers and conditions laid down by the Ministry of Education.

The School Meals Organisers have liaised between the schools and the LEAs, advising the appropriate committee of their Councils on matters relating to the operation of the service, and heads of schools on the organisation and general conduct of the meal, as well as the setting of standards in all aspects of the production of the meal.

There have been significant changes in all aspects of the service. The meal has greatly improved in variety, cooking-craft and appealing presentation. While the traditional character of the meal is being retained, international dishes are commonly served, and an ever-widening horizon of food presented, with an increasing range of sauces and lengthening list of salad items and a firm policy of encouraging the consumption of fresh and raw foods.

For a long time improvement in kitchen equipment design lagged behind that in the domestic market, and eventually the Local Education Authorities' School Meals Consortium (Lasmec) developed a modula design in stainless steel specially for the school meals service. Lasmec[3] is now being installed in kitchens throughout the country. Staff recruitment has been eased by the incorporation of work-study methods and motion-study planning in kitchens, while the quality has improved by the attraction of in-service training. The setting up of formal training schemes by LEAs was encouraged by the DES and many have been developed with DES approval. The 'bible' circular was replaced in 1965 by the report *Nutritional Standard of the School Dinner*[4], which made available an increased amount of protein foods and wider range of other foods, thus confirming what had already largely become common practice.

The structure of communications between the DES and LEAs was changed with the appointment of advisory personnel, with the general inspectors becoming responsible for the meals service in the schools. School meals personnel come within the scope of the recently formed Hotel and Catering Industry Training Board.

Comprehensive schools have brought special problems in the serving of meals. One way of resolving these has been by establishing a reception and preparation kitchen, from which prepared food is distributed to smaller kitchens for finishing and serving to one or more houses. Another solution has been to build independent kitchens to serve one or two houses. A better organisation may yet emerge, since the position is still fluid. Sixth-form units will present a challenge. A complete breakaway from normal types of service is envisaged. One method advocated is to give a choice of snack meals eaten at small tables. Others include a two-course meal with choice of dishes, with cheese, fruit and beverages as optional additions—or several small sittings with a more conventional meal. The introduction of these types of meal will affect staffing hours and scales; more labour-saving devices will be required, more flexible equipment with revised kitchen planning.

Lasmec will undoubtedly be followed by other forms of specially designed equipment. Great flexibility will be required in the design of buildings, equipment and utensils as well as in the personal approach to the new types of service.

Convenience foods may well become more generally used, with deep freezers becoming a standard requirement. While microwave or regethermic cooking may well be out of reach of the schools, the forced air convection oven might have possibilities with its specially designed loading trolleys, interchangeable shelf and freezer storage units. This could possibly represent a solution to staffing problems.

The more varied the type of meal required, the wider the range of menu, the more flexible the equipment, so the better trained must be the school meals staff. As hours of work grow longer the strain on goodwill will increase and it will become increasingly important to ensure that the good feeling between school meals staff, teachers and pupils is conserved and fostered. The entire tone of the future school catering service may well hinge on this relationship.

REFERENCES
1. *The Nutrition of School Children*, Circular 1567, 1941.
2. *School Meals*, Circular 1571, 1941.
3. *Report of Working Party*, Local Authorities School Meals Equipment Consortium, County Hall, Preston, 1965.
4. *The Nutritional Standard of the School Dinner*, 1965.

FURTHER READING
The Milk in Schools Scheme, Circular 1565, HMSO, 1941.
The Provision of Meals and Milk for School Children in War-time, Circular 1520, HMSO, 1940.
The Provision of Meals for Children Attending Public Elementary Schools, Circular 1443, HMSO, 1935.
The Provision of Milk for School Children, Circular 1437, HMSO, 1934.
The School Health Services in War-time, Circular 1490, HMSO, 1939.

MCMB

School medical officer The school medical officer is responsible in the first instance to the Principal School Medical Officer (who is also the Borough's Medical Officer of Health). Any problems which arise are discussed with the MOH or his deputy. The School Health Service in Inner London is administered by the Principal School Medical Officers in each Borough area. The ILEA also has a medical adviser, with staff at County Hall, to co-ordinate the service throughout the area.

Before the passing of the Education Act 1907, the visiting school doctor was sometimes the Medical Officer of Health, who had of course many responsibilities other than that of the school-children's health. Today each school physician is assigned to a number of schools, and the MOH arranges when and how frequently each school should be visited. The school physician usually does other welfare work for the local health department, including maternal and pre-school child welfare clinics.

At an inspection the school doctor will have before him the main school medical record of each child who is to be seen. This is intended to furnish a continuous record of events of medical importance in the child's life from the time of birth to the time of school-leaving. A summary of infant welfare records is included in the main school records. The card follows the child from school to school. When the school doctor finds that a child requires treatment, he can make the necessary recommendation. Treatment is provided either by the council clinics or by arrangement with the hospital authorities, or the child may be referred to the family doctor. The school doctor has other responsibilities, such as seeing that documents are kept up to date, that equipment and accommodation in the medical room are adequate (e.g. that there are facilities for vision testing, weighing and measuring). He is also responsible for seeing that the toilet and washing facilities for the children, the lighting and ventilation in the school are satisfactory. Any deficiency is referred to the MOH. The school doctor has to maintain a good relationship with the head teacher and the staff, in order to achieve full co-operation for promoting the welfare of the children in the school.

SL

School medical service The school medical service has the important task of holding the balance between the two worlds of school and home. Health education linked with measures for maintaining physical and mental well-being throughout the school years is the key to healthy maturity.

How the service grew Officially, the school medical service began with the Education Act 1907, when LEAs were entrusted with the duty of arranging medical inspections of school-children and generally supervising their health. The creation of the school medical service was an important step forward, but its origins can be traced back at least 100 years to the reforms urged by such as Chadwick, Dr Southwood Smith and the Earl of Shaftesbury for the improvement of the living and health standards of the people. Reforms in the factory system led to changes in education and to a school medical service. The Education Act 1870 provided for schools wherever they were needed, but many children were found to be physically unfit even for ordinary schooling and special schools were introduced for blind and deaf children, and the mentally defective or physically handicapped. A further stimulus to the development of the service came with the sudden need for fit young men to serve in the Boer War; only about one in three were found fit enough to be soldiers. It was then realised that hundreds of thousands of recruits would have reached the required standard of health if they had had better treatment when young. At the dawn of the 20th century, children in school were examined periodically, particular attention being paid to eyes, teeth and general health. However, the work of controlling the spread of infectious diseases was enough to swamp the other requirements. The first school nurse appointed in London in 1901 was soon given the nickname of 'the ringworm nurse'.

Many children were coming to school suffering from constant underfeeding; school meals were left to be provided mainly by voluntary bodies and local authorities. Generally, the main concern was to ensure that only those most in need would receive free or aided meals. The government of 1905 passed the Relief of the School-Children Order, which permitted Boards of Guardians to help needy children without also forcing their fathers to enter or be set to work in the workhouse. The Education (Provision of Meals) Act was passed in 1906, but school meals were increased at first by only 5%.

The Education Act 1907 made local authorities responsible for arranging the medical inspection of all children entering elementary schools, and subsequently at intervals as agreed with the Board of Education. Medical inspection became part of the law of the land, but treatment was still conditional. The Board of Education established a medical department whose first chief officer was Sir George Newman. The school meals service was expanded and one-third of a pint of milk a day free for every school-child was introduced in 1946. (It ceased to be provided for secondary school children in 1968).

Treatment through the school medical service was provided for cleanliness, infection from vermin, ringworm, scabies, impetigo, minor ailments, defects of vision, speech defects and defective hearing. Many LEAs provided a chiropody service for schoolchildren to deal with the many cases of corns and other foot defects. This was to improve posture and help remedial work (including games, dancing, swimming and physical culture) generally.

How the school medical service works Today, routine medical inspections are carried out on primary school entrants, on eight-year-olds, secondary-school entrants and school-leavers. The aim of these inspections is to ensure that the child will receive the maximum benefit from the school years, and to make it possible for teachers and parents to co-operate together with the health staff to encourage full development of each child.

This approach is much broader than the inspections of 1905, which took account mainly of physical defects in chest, teeth and ears. Today the main emphasis in routine medical inspection is early detection of defects, but now doctors are watching for signs of stress not only in the physical examination but in the teacher's report of the child's social adaptation in the school environment, as well as observing the child's behaviour for early signs of emotional immaturity and instability. The modern approach of promoting the welfare of school-children requires not only teamwork between the school doctor and those participating in the actual medical inspection, but also a liaison between the school doctor and the family doctor, between the school team and the welfare, housing and health departments of the local authority.

To make this possible, it has been suggested that selective school medical inspection should be more widely introduced, so that the minority of children with specific disabilities can receive closer attention. Those with a real or threatened handicap are entered on a specific register by the school doctor. Teachers may bring forward pupils they are concerned about for assessment at any time in their school career. When the first medical examination is conducted during the child's first term at school, if the head teacher and parent are present, an initial assessment can be made. Children with a clear health check are then seen only at primary and secondary school entrance and at school-leaving examinations. The others are seen more frequently as required. A child with a permanent handicap may already be receiving treatment at a hospital, and the school health service can act as liaison, helping the teacher and parents in the management of the child in school. Children with several disabilities, such as recurrent bronchitis and carious teeth, can be entered so that the doctor and

teacher can help the parent to follow through the necessary treatments. Children with minor neurotic symptoms, e.g. bed-wetting, nail-biting, etc, can be helped through these passing difficulties by sympathetic support from the school. More seriously disturbed children can be sent for child guidance, but not before the school doctor has consulted with the family doctor to understand the whole family situation. Children from difficult home backgrounds—low-income families with many children, broken or unstable marriages—may be reviewed more frequently so that outside specialist help can be readily called in where necessary.

Health education Health education in school can reinforce the work of medical inspection. Classes in both primary and secondary schools can be addressed regularly by school doctor and nurse. Young children can begin to learn how the body works and how they can maintain or increase its efficiency. Older children are usually taught human biology by the teaching staff. The school doctor and nurse, however, can teach about common diseases, accidents and vulnerable groups in society. Children can learn how to avoid many of the prevalent diseases of an advanced industrial society, and can participate in discussions on how to promote the security of the community. This teaching by doctor or nurse should fit in with the rest of the school syllabus so that the knowledge of good health and the community in which we live is part of every school-child's basic education.

SL

School phobia A phobia is an intense and irrational fear of something, and can be mild or extremely powerful. It may have an unconscious origin, such as fear of spiders, or else be linked with a traumatic experience, as with someone who has nearly drowned and has since developed an intense fear of water.

Some children have such a phobia about school and, far from malingering or needing a firm hand, may get into such a state of fear and panic about school that their enforced presence there may become impossible. What often puzzles teachers of these children is that before such an outburst the child may have been working quite well at school and even enjoyed it. On investigation, it usually transpires that such children are not so much frightened of school as terrified of leaving home, owing perhaps to maternal over-protection or other neurotic states in the home that may suddenly become too much for the child to deal with. Such a child may become totally dependent upon being with his parents, or else he may have terrifying fantasies about what may be happening at home once he is away from it, and feels that he must keep returning to confirm that everything there is all right. Treatment for school phobia usually involves investigating the whole family situation in an effort to relieve some of the tensions and anxieties there, though some psychologists have tried to condition school-phobic children into accepting the idea of school without an outbreak of fear.

FURTHER READING
J. H. Khan and J. P. Nursten. *Unwillingly to School*, Pergamon, 1964.

NT

School Secretaries' Association

The Association's aim is to enable secretaries in schools, training colleges and university departments to meet together, usually once a term, and exchange ideas in connection with their work.

Mrs. Z. Williams, Lewes Grammar School for Girls, Lewes, Sussex.

School welfare officers *See* School attendance

School year

The school year with its three terms derives from the university year, and this with its long summer vacation was influenced by the agricultural year and the need for a long pause during the busiest working season. The long summer break in the school year is now determined largely by the need to arrange that as far as possible parents' holidays will fall outside school terms, and that sufficient time is left between the final school examinations and the beginning of university and college terms to allow applications which depend on the examination results to be properly considered.

There are usually about 39 working weeks in the school year. The first, or autumn, term and the summer term are traditionally longer than the spring term, which has been kept relatively short because there is more illness and lower attendance at this time. Recently, however, the external examinations taken at the end of school life have begun earlier than formerly and schools have tended to shorten the summer term so that the time after the examinations is reduced. This 'lame duck' period is difficult to organise and often largely wasted. For obvious reasons the school's own internal examinations usually take place about the same time as the external ones, and it is on the results of these that changes in forms and sets are made to take effect at the beginning of the following term.

It is clear that pupils and staff are both over-tired by the end of a long term. This has led a growing number of schools to experiment with a four-term year. This usually involves starting the summer holiday as soon as examinations are over and fitting in two terms before Christmas. Other schools reach something of the same result, though less satisfactorily, by taking at least a week for two of the three half-terms.

The fact that secondary schools are open for not much more than half the days in the year, while most adults have to work on about two-thirds of them, often causes comment. Various suggestions have been made for securing more intensive use of expensive buildings and equipment by some form of staggered holidays for pupils and teachers, but this has not come about partly because teachers are in much shorter supply than buildings, and partly because any such scheme would cut across the unity of the school community. The total length of the school year is probably about as much as is good for most children, and about as long as most teachers can contrive to be near their best; but it does not follow that the present arrangement of terms and holidays is right.

DGOA

Schoolkeeping A schoolkeeper is responsible for the fabric and contents of a school building, and in carrying out his duties is usually supported by a divisional office, an area architect (for building repairs), a supplies department (for goods and services), and an engineering department (for heating and ventilation and for electrical and other equipment).

The first duty of any schoolkeeper on being appointed to a school is to make himself thoroughly conversant with the premises. He must, for example, establish the compass bearing of every exterior wall; this will help to prevent the inaccurate fitting of light switches, blackboards and other items by visiting workmen who have been given vague directions.

Much of the success of the schoolkeeper's work depends on his cleaning staff, and these must be carefully chosen and properly instructed. The cleaning of school premises is usually based on a unit of one hour's sweeping and dusting for a certain number of square feet per week. High-level cleaning is done by the schoolkeeper himself, or by his assistants in larger schools.

A specimen day's work for the schoolkeeper will begin with the opening of the premises at about 6 a.m., when cleaning staff are admitted and the heating system attended to (a temperature of 60° within the building must be obtained before 9 a.m.). The schoolkeeper must, among other duties, visit each cleaner, sweep playgrounds and empty litter bins, check that door mats are bedded into floor wells, take the post to the head-teacher, watch continually for broken fixtures that may threaten the safety of children, accept delivery of goods. Toilets have to be hosed and cleaned several times a day, boilers stoked, light fittings checked, rooms prepared for evening classes where they are held in a school, all visitors to the premises noted in a daily diary, all furniture replaced that has been moved. At the end of the working day the schoolkeeper must securely lock all ground-floor doors and windows.

Most education authorities allow the schoolkeeper a certain number of hours of assistance on a casual basis for furniture moving, for help with heating during very cold weather, and with the patrolling of premises where a building is used for busy evening institutes.

EH

Schoolmasters, National Association of Established in 1922 after the NUT had adopted a policy of 'equal pay for equal work', the Association grew steadily until the Second World War, when its membership was seriously reduced; but there are now just under 40,000 members (all practising schoolmasters), making it the second largest organisation of teachers in the country. In 1961 its members staged a one-day strike in support of its campaign for official recognition, and the NAS was granted representation on the Burnham Committee.

The NAS exists to safeguard and promote the interests of schoolmasters

W

and schoolboys, demanding that school-masters' claims should be negotiated separately from those of schoolmistresses so that a rate of salary is obtained that will ensure an adequate supply of well-trained men and will recognise their greater social and economic responsi-bilities. It aims also to secure represen-tation on public and private com-mittees concerned with educational matters and so to afford the govern-ment, the DES and the LEAs the advice and experience of associated schoolmasters. The NAS is also en-deavouring to secure the establishment of a teachers' general council. Its activities include vigorous pressure for a royal commission to investigate the problems facing a rapidly expanding education service, financed by inade-quate resources; and campaigns to direct the attention of MPs and the public to the serious deficiencies of the service and to the widespread use of unqualified persons as teachers, and to ensure that plans for secondary school reorganisation are evolved in full consultation with teachers' organisa-tions and are likely to produce im-proved opportunities for pupils and to safeguard the interests of the teachers involved. The Association has criticised the DES's approach to the recruitment of part-time returners to teaching, and has called attention to the serious danger of projecting a wrong image of professional teachers. Publications in-clude many reports (e.g. on ancillary assistance in schools and the longer school day).

Swan Court, Waterhouse St, Hemel Hempstead, Herts.

Schoolmasters, Society of A chari-table organisation for the assistance of necessitous masters of public schools, grammar schools and preparatory schools, their widows and orphans.

Sec.: Mrs. H. E. Closs, 308 Galpins Rd, Thornton Heath, Surrey, CR4 6EH.

Schoolmistresses' and Gover-nesses' Benevolent Institution The Institution was founded in 1843. Because many governesses were ill-equipped for their work, a teacher training college was established from which many of the pioneers of girls' education received diplomas. Queen's College became independent in 1853, and the Institution continued to assist governesses in financial difficulties.

In 1952 schoolmistresses in private schools were admitted and, in 1967, the words 'Schoolmistresses' and' were added to the name. Today the Institu-tion helps in many ways over 400 women private teachers in the UK and overseas.

39 Buckingham Ga., London, SW1.

Schools' Athletic Association *See* **Athletics**

Schools Council for the Curriculum and Examinations This body was set up in 1964 to keep under review the curricula, teaching methods and exami-nations in primary and secondary schools, including aspects of school organisation so far as they affect the curriculum. There are three Curri-culum Steering Committees, covering the age ranges of 2–13, 11–16 and over 14, and a Welsh Committee. Other committees include a General Purposes Committee, a Co-ordinating Commit-tee, a CSE Committee to act as a central co-ordinating committee for the admini-stration of the CSE examinations, and a GCE committee which performs the same function for the GCE exami-nations. There are also ten separate subject committees; mathematics, science, modern languages, English, Welsh, history, geography, religious instruction, classics and technical and engineering studies.

38 Belgrave Sq., London, SW1.

See also **Curriculum reform; Ex-aminations**

Schools (Scotland) Code (1956) The conduct of all public and grant-aided schools is governed by regulations made by the Secretary of State. The Code deals with such matters as the size of classes, permitted accommodation, classrooms, registration, qualifications of teachers, pupils, records, education to be provided, and approved schemes of work.

See also **Scotland, Education in**

Science, British Association for the Advancement of Founded in 1831, and open to all, the Association aims to promote a more general interest in science and an understanding of its concepts, language, methods and applications. In pursuit of this aim it now reaches an audience of approximately 250,000 annually, including very many young people. Its activities include an annual meeting, held in a different city each year, which lasts eight days and is the largest scientific gathering of its kind in the country and the only one which members of the public can attend on equal terms with scientists; local programmes of lectures and films arranged by two branch and 19 area committees in Great Britain and Northern Ireland; hundreds of lectures arranged each year for schools, in addition to special 'Junior British Association Meetings' and 'Science Fairs'; a central lecture service; a visual aids service. Publications include the monthly *Advancement of Science*.

3 Sanctuary Buildings, 20 Great Smith St, London, SW1.

Science, Teaching of The emphasis in 20th century school science teaching in the UK has been on experiment by boys and girls themselves. Laboratories and apparatus have been provided in secondary schools, and a wide range of class experiments has been developed to stimulate an interest in, and an understanding of, science. The experimental approach has reached a peak in the work of the Nuffield Science

Teaching Project. Demonstration apparatus has also been available but has not been as fully developed as in some European countries, notably in Germany.

The growth of science education outside the universities began about a hundred years ago in a few public or private schools. They were preoccupied, in the main, with classics and mathematics (both subjects claiming superiority as being suitable for 'training the mind'), but began to include science as an optional extra—not without some misgivings. At Rugby in 1849 and Cheltenham in 1854 systematic instruction in 'natural philosophy' was introduced. Rugby's purpose-built laboratory and science lecture theatre were opened in 1860, and the growth of science education had begun. But England had to wait 20 or 30 years, for Tyndall, Huxley and Herbert Spencer who became vigorous advocates of the inclusion of science teaching in school, before worthwhile expansion took place.

Early developments in elementary schools were even less fortunate. Many promising schemes, as at King's Sombourne, Hampshire, were allowed to die following Lowe's Revised Code of 1862 which provided for teachers to be paid by results—and the results of science teaching did not qualify! Payment by results for the teaching of science in the evenings to older pupils under the auspices of the Department of Science and Art, although encouraging science teaching, did nothing to increase its quality. The emphasis was on rote learning and routine testing of factual knowledge. This often led to a rigidity and lack of genuine understanding which compares unfavourably with the freedom and flexibility to explore experimentally and intellectually which is now considered to be essential to a creative education in science.

H. E. Armstrong at the beginning of this century deplored the inadequacies of students entering his university Chemistry Department and urged schools to adopt an approach based on experiment, questioning and discovery. His 'heuristic method' (*q.v.*), in which pupils made reference to materials and apparatus rather than to an authoritative textbook or schoolmaster, has influenced teaching to the present day. It is often claimed that his method was impossibly slow and inconclusive, but it certainly worked at Christ's Hospital under Armstrong's direction. Criticisms are often based on a misunderstanding of his recommendations. Today's thinking about science teaching reflects Armstrong's ideas more accurately than the second-hand, garbled versions sometimes attributed to him. Of all men he has had most influence on British science education.

In secondary schools the science teacher shares with his colleagues in other subjects a great freedom of choice over syllabus and teaching method. In practice, however, the most able children usually follow a syllabus and a teaching scheme determined largely by one of the eight examining boards for GCE (*q.v.*). At O level there is considerable range of subjects: physics, chemistry, biology, physics with chemistry, general science and some other science-based papers usually designed with the non-specialist in mind. This wide choice allows schools to vary their curriculum in the years before O level and yet still to insist that their pupils study some science. This most do, although the shortage of good science teachers in girls' schools often leads girls to drop science at an earlier age than boys. Of entrants to sixth forms about 50% of boys and 20% of girls study mathematics and science subjects to A level GCE, and even in the arts sixth most pupils have an opportunity to study science, often biased towards history and philosophy, in their minority time.

Schools teaching for the CSE (*q.v.*) offer even more freedom to the teacher,

and an increasing number are determining the content, the teaching and the assessment of their own personal course. The flexibility of the CSE requirements allows teachers to adapt their teaching not only to changes in science itself but also to the responses of their own particular pupils in their own particular circumstances. For below-average pupils there is even less external control over their courses, and these vary widely from school to school and from teacher to teacher.

Guidance concerning science teaching and curricula has long been available from the publications of the Science Masters' Association and the Association of Women Science Teachers (amalgamated in 1963 to form the Association for Science Education). Universities through their institutes of education, the Ministry of Education (now the DES) and independent bodies, including some commercial firms, have also offered training and advice. Recently, however, there has been a powerful drive towards curriculum reform in science. In 1957 the SMA began considering changes needed to bring courses up to date, and the Scottish Education Department published reports on the teaching of science which had an immediate effect in schools and on examinations.

Still more recently the Nuffield Foundation and the Schools Council (*q.v.*) have initiated and financed research and development into the science teacher's task. The Nuffield Science Teaching Project has involved many teachers in the development of detailed teaching schemes, beginning with the traditional subject groupings of physics, chemistry and biology for GCE and extending to courses for the average and below-average child, and the sixth-former. Teachers have developed particularly interesting schemes for the primary school, where the traditional formal nature study is being transformed into an experimental 'discovery' activity and extended to include non-living aspects of the child's world.

The voluntary, part-time committees of the Association for Science Education have produced a series of booklets *Science and Education* relating to the activities of the most able quarter of the boys and girls in secondary schools. They were concerned with bringing the content of science teaching up-to-date and recommended syllabuses including atomic physics at O level, organic chemistry, energetics and new experimental projects in biology. The ASE work was a useful preliminary to the Nuffield Foundation's projects, which have not only included much 20th-century science but have suggested a teaching pattern in which the early years of the secondary school involve extensive informal pupil experiment. The child is set to solve a problem rather than to verify laws or follow a series of instructions. In the two years before O level this slowly changes to a more rigorous and quantitative approach in which the pupil sees great theories develop. For further information concerning the teaching of particular branches of science, reference should be made to the appropriate entries in this encyclopaedia.

The policy statement of the ASE entitled *School Science and General Education* in the series *Science and Education* includes a clear and concise statement of the aims of contemporary science teaching: 'Science should be recognised—and taught—as a major human activity which explores the realm of human experience, maps it methodically but also imaginatively and, by disciplined speculation, creates a coherent system of knowledge. As a human quest for Truth—and it is much more subjectively human than is often realised—science is concerned with basic human values and is, indeed, an active humanity'.

The ASE holds strongly that science should be a 'core' subject in grammar schools and suggests six 40-minute periods a week for years 1 and 2 and nine periods for years 3, 4 and 5. It is still an exceptional school which allows so much time; four and six periods respectively is more common and there are many schools with less.

General science has received little attention in recent reports and published teaching schemes. It reached its peak just before the second world war but is still considered to be of value, particularly for less able pupils. General science is often taught in the first one or two years of the secondary course, sometimes by a topic method where areas of study embracing several branches of science are integrated, as in the study of air, water or soil. Attempts are now being made to integrate sixth-form physics and chemistry at a conceptual level by approaching the physical sciences via the electron, the atom, the wave and the study of energy and energy changes.

The quality of science teaching will depend on the number and the quality of the staff, provision of laboratories and apparatus and on the time allotted to it. Grammar schools have, in the past, been staffed almost entirely by well-qualified graduates, and the most able children in all types of secondary schools are usually taught by a graduate, although often there are few applicants for vacant posts. In the lower streams of comprehensive and secondary modern schools the staffing situation is much less satisfactory and many vacancies remain unfilled or are filled by men and women not well qualified to teach science. If applicants are of poor quality or non-existent then a specialist in another subject is sometimes appointed in order to keep the overall pupil-teacher ratio down. The consequent reduction in science teaching time decreases its effectiveness.

Laboratories are provided in nearly all maintained secondary schools. The DES recommends that elementary laboratories of 960 sq ft be built in all new schools; and for the public and private schools a more generous provision has been recommended by the Industrial Fund Committee which from 1955 to 1963 distributed £3,200,000, donated by industry, in an effort to raise the standards of laboratory provision outside the public sector. The provision of apparatus and equipment for use in laboratories varies greatly from school to school. In 1958 an SMA report recorded a variation of from 1s 1d to £3 8s 10d per pupil per annum in the sample of schools it questioned. It suggested that 10s per head per annum is the absolute minimum allowance for materials on which a science department can function effectively. (*See* **Laboratories, School, Design and equipment of**).

Britain's troubles in finding good science teachers and providing the conditions in which they can work best are not unique. They can be found in almost every country in the world. Britain has, however, the advantages of a substantial number of well-qualified teachers, many of whom are forward-looking and inventive. Armed with new courses, new ideas, new inspirations, science teachers' centres and a freedom to experiment, Britain's science teaching shows every sign of the continuous creative change which will be needed to match the rapid developments of science itself.

FURTHER READING

Association for Science Education. *Science and Education* (seven booklets), John Murray, 1961.

Department of Education and Science. *Science in Secondary Schools* (Pamphlet No. 38), HMSO, 1960.

Nuffield Science Teachers' Project. *Physics, Chemistry and Biology Texts*, Longmans/Penguin, 1966.

PER

Science and Art Department *See* **Board of Education**

Science Education, Association for
Formed in 1963 from the Science Masters' Association and the Associa-

tion of Women Science Teachers, and now with a membership of over 11,000, the Association exists to improve the teaching of science; to provide an authoritative medium through which opinions of science teachers may be expressed in educational matters; and to afford a means of communication among those concerned with science teaching and with education in general. It promotes its objects through national and branch activities; the publication of a journal (*The School Science Review*, appearing three times a year) and other literature; the maintenance of an administrative and information centre; the interchange of information with scientific and industrial organisations employing scientists and technologists; co-operation with other bodies, including the DES and examining boards. Some success has been achieved in influencing examination syllabuses in accordance with the Association's views on the kind of science suited to the school stage of education.

52 Bateman St, Cambridge.

Science Equipment, Consortium of LEAs for the Provision of Founded in 1963 after a meeting of chairmen of the Education Committees of London and the Home Counties, which was held to examine and assess existing science apparatus used in schools, to devise new equipment and stimulate new ideas, the Consortium includes the following members: Barking, Barnet, Bedfordshire, Berkshire, Bexley, Brent, Brighton, Bromley, Buckinghamshire, Cornwall, Croydon, Eastbourne, Enfield, East Sussex, Essex, the GLC, Harrow, Haringey, Hastings, Havering, Hertfordshire, Hillingdon, Hounslow, Kingston-upon-Thames, Merton, Newham, Redbridge, Richmond-upon-Thames, Southend-on-Sea, Surrey, Sutton, Waltham Forest, West Sussex.

Science Masters' Association *See* **Science, Teaching of**

Science in the primary school In a scientific age it is appropriate that scientific experience should be part of the educational environment of all children from the time they start school.

The early scientific experience fostered during the primary stage grows as the children explore a rich environment that provides ample stimulus to curiosity and the means to satisfy this curiosity by extended observation and experiment. 'Children are especially alert to any experience or finding that challenges their previous belief';[1] this is close to the spirit of the scientist.

Through their guided explorations, encouraged but not interfered with, or forcibly directed, by the adult, children become increasingly aware of the workings and relationships of the animate and inanimate world around them, and build up concepts based on understanding. As they interpret their findings in the light of previous experiences, the development of concepts may proceed by stages of wrong assumptions and partial truths which will be recognised and corrected by the children as further experience, discussion, argument and reading bring new evidence.

In this way the scientific attitude becomes well established as a procedure that each child uses to solve *his own* problems—the only problems that will enable him to think constructively and make his own judgements. This 'concurrent organic growth, carried forward year by year, towards science both as ordered knowledge and as method'[2] leads naturally into scientific method and should establish a flexibility of outlook consistent with the ever growing and changing scientific knowledge of today.

A syllabus stipulating facts to be covered is quite inappropriate at the primary stage, though the teachers must, of course, know the possible lines of development of any area of experi-ence that forms the starting point of their study. They must have this knowledge in order that adequate provision may be available for the variety of exploration that will follow when the children explore those areas which have most stimulated their imagination and curiosity. The facts required for these studies rarely fall beyond the inevitable topics of biology, physics, chemistry, astronomy and geology: but their combinations may vary considerably, as will also the extent of their content, both with the subject under discussion and the ability of the child involved.

Apparatus and equipment should be available at all times, and simple and direct so that children may devise and carry out their own experiments and make appropriate observations of a direct nature.

After children have built up a mass of fragmentary information is the natural time to begin to organise it. To provide adult generalisations before this serves only to inhibit; it does not help the development of thought or growth of scientific understanding.

Imaginative use of the school environment for expeditions, field work and interest tables is essential; a classroom that is a workshop is more valuable than a laboratory that separates science from the rest of the curriculum. The world of a primary child is not divided: his learning must also be integrated.

Books of great variety, always available, visual and other aids, used as appropriate by individuals, groups or the whole class, supplement and extend experience.

REFERENCES
1. Nathan Isaacs. *Early Scientific Trends in Children*, NFF.
2. *Ibid.*

FURTHER READING
Association for Science Education booklets available from John Murray, 50 Albemarle St, London, W1: *Children Learning through Science*; *List of Books* (marked for suitability for teachers, infants, juniors,

lower secondary); *List of Teaching Aids* (comprehensive list of addresses for pamphlets, cards, posters, specimens, films, filmstrips, etc.); *Materials and Equipment.*

National Froebel Foundation. *Children Learning through Scientific Interests* (co-operative survey of work done by teachers in ordinary classroom situations), 1966.

School Natural Science Society provides a journal and leaflets on many topics to aid teachers of junior and lower secondary children. Leaflets Secretary: M. J. Wooton, 19a King's Gdns, Cranham, Upminster, Essex.

GEA

Science Teachers, Association of Women *See* Science, Teaching of

Science Technology, Institute of

The Institute was formed to advance the knowledge of science laboratory techniques and to promote the professional standing of science laboratory technicians. To this end, it examines at two levels in conjunction with the City and Guilds of London Institute. For technicians who work in narrow, specialised fields, the Institute offers a specialised diploma examination.

There are 26 branches in various parts of the country which hold regular meetings, including lectures by prominent scientists, the reading of members' papers and discussions. Membership is open to all science laboratory technicians, the grade of membership depending upon the qualification and experience of the applicant.

Gen. Sec.: Mrs V. D. Lenton, AIST, 106 Hampstead Rd, London, NW1.

Publications: *Journal* (quarterly); *Bulletin* (monthly); *The Care, Handling and Disposal of Dangerous Chemicals* by P. J. Gaston; and a careers pamphlet.

Science and Technology Act (1965) *See* Scientific Policy, Council for

Science and Technology, National Lending Library for

This library, opened in November 1965, provides a postal loan service to organisations, including industrial companies, learned societies and educational establishments. Individuals can borrow through the public library system. It has a stock of about 500,000 volumes and 22,000 current periodicals. Its gross annual expenditure is in the region of £450,000, but part of its initial stock was drawn from the library of the Science Museum in London.

Director: D. J. Urquhart, Boston Spa, Yorks.

'Science and Technology, Statistics of'

Published jointly by the DES and the Ministry of Technology in 1967, this report forms a one-volume source of all the relevant statistics on science and technology at all levels of education. It showed that expenditure on research and development in the UK, amounting in 1961–2 to £657,700,000, had risen three years later to £771,400,000, the main growth being in universities and technical colleges (from £32,400,000 to £55,900,000). The number of first-degree graduates qualifying in engineering, technology and science in British universities rose between 1960 and 1965 from 10,000 to 13,000, of whom nearly 30% took up post-graduate studies and only 14% went into schools, colleges or institutions of teacher training. In the same five-year period, the annual supply of qualified scientists and engineers increased from 16,770 to 21,680, and the number of mathematicians from 880 to 1,657. It was estimated that in January 1966 there was an active and qualified manpower in science and technology of 327,000; of these, 147,000 were scientists and 180,000 were engineers and technologists. This was 67,700 more than in 1961.

In recent years, the report found, the proportion of first-degree graduates entering schools, colleges and teacher training had decreased, but the proportion of science graduates to all graduate teachers had remained fairly stable. Between 1962 and 1964 the number of science graduates in maintained schools in England and Wales rose from 15,340 (27·6% of all graduate teachers) to 16,448 (28·4%).

Scientific and Industrial Research, Department of The DSIR originated in 1919 after the Haldane Committee on the Machinery of Government recommended that departments should have research and intelligence branches. It was dissolved under the Science and Technology Act 1965, and its functions were redistributed; responsibilities for civil science went to the Secretary of State for Education and Science and to the Ministry of Technology.

Scientific Management in the Home, Council of The Council came into being to prepare a British contribution to the domestic section of the International Scientific Management Congress held in Amsterdam in 1932. The second world war interrupted its rapidly expanding activities, but in 1946 it was re-convened. It undertakes and promotes appropriate research and investigation, makes known the results and endeavours to help housewives to improve the standards of domestic practices.

It is a voluntary body, consisting of representatives from women's organisations, observer members from government departments and a few individual members with special qualifications.

Public lectures are arranged annually and reports of these, together with results of research, are on sale to the public.

26 Bedford Sq., London, WC1.

Scientific Policy, Council for The Council exists to advise the Secretary of State for Education and Science on matters concerning scientific research. It was set up under the Science and Technology Act 1965, and its present chairman is Sir Harrie Massey, FRS, Quain Professor of Physics at University College, London. Current studies being undertaken by the CSP include a range of enquiries into the mechanisms of scientific growth. These will include the relationship with the educational system, the availability of qualified manpower, the measurement of increased costs due to the growing complexity of scientific technique, the improvement of the scientific environment, and our international scientific relations.

Scientific Workers, Association of Founded in 1918, the Association is a registered trade union affiliated to the TUC. Membership is open to natural and social scientists, engineers and technicians. Through a standing Science and Education Committee, the Association works to improve the supply of science teachers and the position of scientific and technical education at university, technical college and school level. Affiliations include the WEA and the Council for Educational Advance. The *AScW Journal* is issued bi-monthly.

15 Half Moon St, London, W1.

SCOLA (Second Consortium of Local Authorities) The original consortium of local authorities, CLASP (*q.v.*), formed to use a special method of building, was set up in 1957. Its success was followed in 1961 by the setting up of SCOLA, a group with the same aims as CLASP, though they are not concerned as CLASP has been to cut down the cost of precautions against mining subsidence. Members of SCOLA are Cheshire, Dorset, Gloucestershire, Hampshire, Leeds, Shropshire, West Sussex, Worcestershire, Leicestershire, Sheffield, Northumberland, and the DES.

SCONUL (Standing Conference of National and University Librarians) *See* **Libraries, University**

Scotland, Association of Directors of Education in Formed in 1920, the Association has a membership confined to directors of education and their deputies and assistants: it at present stands at 102. Representatives serve on over 100 statutory and voluntary bodies active in education, industry and the social services.

An important part of the work of the Association is the discussion of and commenting upon proposals, legislative or otherwise, relating to education. In this it works closely with the Scottish Education Department and other government departments. There are two conferences each year.

Gen. Sec.: Thomas Henderson, MA, BSc (Econ), Midlothian Education Department, 9 Drumsheugh Gdns, Edinburgh 3.

Scotland, Education in

History The aim of providing a comprehensive system of education from which none would be excluded has a long history in Scotland. It lay behind a provision of the Reformed Church, in 1560, that every town should have a school, every parish a schoolmaster. Knox laid it down as a principle that boys who were 'apt to letters and to learning' not only had the right but also the moral obligation to pursue their studies. This was an ambition beyond the power of the Reformers to carry out, and even an Act of the Scottish Parliament, passed in 1696 and requiring that a school building be provided in every parish, together with a schoolmaster's salary, was only slowly carried into effect.

The date when the burden of organising education passed from the churches and other voluntary agencies to the state was 1872: the Education (Scotland) Act of that year led to the setting up of nearly 1,000 school boards, empowered to levy rates for the maintenance of existing schools and the provision of new ones, to ensure universal attendance, and to enforce the Code of the Scottish Education Department, which distributed the Parliamentary grant. School was made compulsory

between the ages of five and 13, but exemption granted to children able to show that they could read and write and had an adequate mastery of elementary arithmetic. For those over 13, the school boards were given the power to provide evening schools. To this, six years later, was added the power to maintain Higher Class schools.

The school leaving age was raised to 14 in two steps. By the first of these, embodied in the Education (Scotland) Act 1883, the age was raised for any child whose grasp of reading, writing and elementary arithmetic failed to satisfy one of HM Inspectors of Schools. The second step, the raising of the leaving age for all children, came in 1901, with the Education (Scotland) Act of that year.

Secondary education committees were set up in 1892 to distribute grants allocated for the first time in that year.

Under the Education (Scotland) Act 1908, local authorities were empowered to provide for the medical examination of school-children; for the conveyance to school of children living at a distance, or their boarding near the school if necessary; and for the prosecution of neglectful parents. School boards were required to provide further education in continuation classes for those over 14. Ten years later, under the 1918 Act, the school boards themselves, no longer competent to deal with the expanding system, were replaced by 33 county and 5 urban authorities, supported by school management committees who kept alive local interest in education. Bursaries were provided for the secondary education of the needy, voluntary schools came under the management of the education authorities, and schemes were drawn up in each area for the provision of primary and secondary education. Under the same Act, local authorities were given the power to provide nursery schools and a library service for children and adults.

The next step came with the abolition, under the Local Government (Scotland) Act 1929, of ad hoc education authorities, and the transfer of administration to the county councils and the town councils of Aberdeen, Dundee, Edinburgh and Glasgow. An Act of 1936, which would have raised the school leaving age to 15 at the end of 1939, was not carried into effect owing to the outbreak of war, and Scotland had, with England and Wales, to wait for this development until 1947.

The pace of reform had been so much quicker than in England and Wales that the Education (Scotland) Act of 1945 was less dramatic, and introduced smaller changes, than the English Act of the year before: the effect was to tidy up rather than to innovate.

The present system The early aim of comprehensive education in Scotland provided the framework for a national system long before England had anything of the sort, and it established that respect for 'sound learning' which has always been a feature of Scottish education. The Scots, almost from the start, were shrewd enough to see education in terms of economic investment. The early burgh and parish schools were freely open to all, and to this day Scottish schools remain relatively free from social class distinctions. At the same time, there has always been, and there remains, a strong disposition to favour the 'lad o' pairts', and also a marked tendency to make formal, academic attainment the first priority. The myth of Scottish superiority in educational matters, which may have been justified during the 19th century (when the English provision was second-rate by comparison), dies hard, but it is no accident that the Scottish system, unlike the English, has frequently served as a model in countries throughout the English-speaking world.

Central authority is vested in the Secretary of State for Scotland, whose overall responsibilities include those normally exercised by a Minister of Education. The administrative work involved in implementing the policies embodied in the Education Act (Scotland) 1945, and later legislation, is carried out by the Scottish Education Department. Compared with its English counterpart, at any rate until recent years, the latter has always maintained close control through its regulations and memoranda over the curricula and methods used in schools. While it would be wrong to infer that the Department is in any way authoritarian, its affinities (possibly due to the 'auld alliance') have always been with the French system rather than with the English—a distinction borne out by the old Board of Education's publication entitled *A Handbook of Suggestions for the Consideration of Teachers.*

Local administration is in the hands of the Counties and the four cities (Edinburgh, Glasgow, Dundee, Aberdeen). Broadly speaking, the organisation of schools is much the same as in England, though there are significant differences, among which are the following:

(1) Religious instruction and a daily act of corporate worship are not compulsory.

(2) All public schools, with the exception of those maintained by the Roman Catholics, are undenominational.

(3) The age of transfer from the primary to the secondary stage is normally 12, not 11 as in England.

(4) The proportion of the age-group allocated to a five-year academic course is roughly 35%, against 20% in England.

Primary schools cover the ages 5-12, with no division into infants and junior schools. Secondary schools have hitherto been classified as senior secondary (offering a five-year course leading to the leaving certificate examination) and junior secondary (offering a three-year course). However, unlike

England's grammar and secondary modern schools, these types are by no means always housed in separate buildings, and secondary schools accommodating both academic and non-academic pupils have always been common, especially in the counties. Following the Secretary of State's Circular 600, the secondary schools are at present undergoing reorganisation on comprehensive lines, a reorganisation which is likely to be effected more smoothly than in England if only because the Scottish tradition has always been to some extent in keeping with the 'comprehensive principle'. Moreover, the independent sector is insignificant; virtually all schools in Scotland are public schools in the sense that they are open to all free of charge. One issue which has to be resolved, however, concerns the charging of (usually modest) fees in some state-maintained schools.

Until recently, senior secondary pupils took a broad-based examination, the Scottish Leaving Certificate, before going on to the university. As a result there has been no division into arts and science 6th forms as happened in the English grammar school. Latterly, an O grade and A grade examination structure has been adopted more or less on the English pattern, but the old 'highers' are retained, with the result that some candidates may sit for examinations at 15, 16 and 17. The numbers staying on for a sixth year are steadily increasing, but as yet there is nothing like the sixth-form 'explosion' which has taken place in England since 1944.

The proportion of academic pupils gaining a university place has always been, and remains, slightly higher than in England. The four ancient universities (Glasgow, St Andrews, Aberdeen and Edinburgh) offer four-year courses leading to the first degrees of MA and BSc, either of the ordinary or honours type. The Scottish ordinary degree, in which the undergraduate studies a range of different disciplines, continues to be popular, and was commended in the Robbins Report. New universities have been founded: Strathclyde (formerly the Royal College of Science and Technology, Glasgow); Dundee (formerly incorporated with St Andrews); Stirling (an entirely new foundation); and Heriot-Watt, Edinburgh.

In common with those of other countries, the Scottish system of education is being forced to come to terms with the demands made on it by an advanced industrial society. Canny in the face of innovation, fiercely proud of its traditions and achievements, it believes in hastening slowly. From 1696, when the Scottish Parliament passed its Act for Settling Schools, to the setting up of a General Teaching Council in 1965, its temper and its progress have been essentially democratic.

FURTHER READING
Board of Education. *A Handbook of Suggestions for the Consideration of Teachers*, 1937.
G. S. Osborne. *Scottish and English Schools*, Longmans, Green, 1966.
Scottish Education Department. *Education in Scotland* (annual report), HMSO, Edinburgh.

EB and WKR

Scotland, Educational Institute of
This Institute, representing more than 30,000 members, is the major body formulating teacher opinion in Scotland. Its main aims are to promote sound learning, serve the best interests of children, and improve the conditions of service of Scottish teachers. The Institute also safeguards the professional rights and interests of individual teachers and includes within its membership majorities of all categories of teacher.

Founded in 1847 and incorporated by Royal Charter in 1851, the Institute has played a vital part in furthering the progress of Scottish education.

In 1966 the Institute's negotiators played a major part in securing a revision of Scottish teachers' salaries and have now submitted proposals for a new salaries revision. The Institute operates through a number of committees: Education, Salaries, Finance, Parliamentary, Benevolence, etc. The Education Committee has recently prepared a number of major policy documents including a memorandum on fee-paying schools, evidence to the Royal Commission on Public Schools, a statement on comprehensive education, and a survey, entitled *Towards 1970*, of the challenges facing teachers when the school leaving age is raised.

Gen. Sec.: Gilbert S. Bryden, 46 Moray Pl., Edinburgh 3.

Scotland, Further education in *See* **Further education in Scotland**

Scotland, General Teaching Council for The setting up of the Council was recommended in 1963 in the report of the Committee on the Teaching Profession in Scotland, under the chairmanship of Lord Wheatley.

Constituted in 1966 as provided by the Teaching Council (Scotland) Act of the previous year, the Council is required to keep under review and advise the Secretary of State on the standard of education, training and fitness to teach of entrants to the profession; to make recommendations on the supply of teachers (but not on matters of salary or conditions of service); and to maintain a register of qualified teachers. The Council undertakes duties concerning colleges of education, and is responsible, through its Investigating and Disciplinary Committee, for deciding on the removal from the register of teachers convicted of an offence or guilty of misconduct in a professional respect. Such decisions are subject to appeal to the Court of Session.

The Council has 44 members, 25 of them being certificated teachers from schools, further education centres and colleges of education.

Registrar: George D. Gray, MA, 140 Princes St, Edinburgh 2.

Scottish Central Film Library This is the central distribution agency through which educational films are supplied to Scottish schools. The Library is under the control of the Scottish Film Council (*q.v.*).

Started by the Council in 1938, with the aid of a grant of £5,000 from the Carnegie UK Trust, the Scottish Central Film Library has developed into the largest single source in the UK for the supply of educational, documentary and industrial films.

The Library stock at 1 April 1967 consisted of 6,000 titles, including 1,500 Central Office of Information subjects.

16-17 Woodside Terrace, Glasgow, C3.

Scottish Certificate of Education The Certificate examination is normally taken at the end of senior secondary courses of four or five years. Students may attempt as many of a wide range of subjects as they can at one of two levels. The first, lower level approximates to that of the English GCE O level. The second, higher level, which is usually taken one year after the lower, is accepted as slightly lower than that of the English A level GCE. Teachers' estimates, as well as written performance in the examination, are taken into account, as in the English CSE examinations.

The examinations were conducted by the Scottish Education Department until 1965, when they became the responsibility of the Scottish Certificate of Education Examinations Board.

Scottish Community Drama Association Formed in 1926, the SCDA is an association of clubs and individuals whose aim is to encourage drama in Scotland and to organise festivals of community drama. A staff of professional advisers is employed whose services are available for lectures, demonstrations, courses, classes, tutorial rehearsals and to give advice on both the theatrical and technical sides of 'theatre'. Fees for the services of advisers are supplied on application to the national organiser.

Activities include not only annual one-act and three-act play festivals, but also play-writing competitions, a summer course at Stratford-upon-Avon and an annual residential summer school, usually held in Aberdeen. Membership is open to all individuals, clubs and societies interested in drama. The Association issues a bulletin three times a year, and provides libraries in Edinburgh, Glasgow, Aberdeen, Inverness and Kirkcaldy.

19 Melville St, Edinburgh, 3.

Scottish Council of Physical Recreation

The Council's aim is to provide opportunities for people of all ages to increase their knowledge of games, sports and a variety of leisure-time activities, or to learn new ones.

The membership of the Council at present comprises some 145 national organisations including governing bodies of sport, professional physical education organisations, the armed forces, and many other comprehensive organisations concerned with sport, medicine and health, voluntary work, etc. In addition the Council has close links with government departments, education and other local authorities, colleges and universities, industry, tourist and other agencies.

The Council administers the two Scottish National Recreation Centres —at Glenmore Lodge, Inverness-shire, and Inverclyde, Largs—where courses offering tuition in a variety of games, sports and outdoor activities are available. The Council provides a central source of information on all aspects of sports development, including an advisory service to local authorities on the provision of sports facilities. School groups regularly attend the two National Recreation Centres.

4 Queensferry St, Edinburgh, 2.

Publications: *Annual Report*; brochures on courses at the National Recreation Centres; an annual brochure (jointly with the Scottish Tourist Board) on sports holidays in Scotland.

Scottish Council for Research in Education

The Council was set up to encourage and organise research work into education in Scotland. It also receives suggestions for research, approves schemes and allocates finance for them, and publishes the results.

The main projects being undertaken at the moment by the Council are a study of bilingualism in Scotland, a survey of the attainments of primary school children in English and arithmetic, a study of the age of transfer between primary and secondary education, an enquiry into the retention of learning by pupils of school-leaving age, and a survey of attainments in mathematics at different levels of the secondary school. The Council is also following up a large group of young people leaving school after completing five or six years of secondary education, and standardising the Wechsler Intelligence Scale for Scottish Children. There is a historical and experimental study of handwriting in progress, and a bibliography of Scottish education is being prepared. Histories of education in Scottish counties are being prepared for publication.

President: D. M. McIntosh, 46 Moray Pl., Edinburgh, 3.

Scottish Education Department

The government body responsible for the administration of education in Scotland, with a function equivalent to that of the DES of England and Wales.

St Andrews Hse, Edinburgh; Dover Hse, Whitehall, London, SW1.

Scottish Educational Film Association The Association promotes use of educational film, television, tape recording and other audio-visual aids. Membership is general.

16–17 Woodside Terr., Glasgow, C3. Publication: *AV News* (thrice annually).

Scottish Film Council The Council's principal aim is to encourage the use of film as an educational, instructional and cultural medium. It performs in Scotland the functions carried out in England and Wales by the British Film Institute (*q.v.*).

The Council is a co-ordinating body to which are linked all other non-commercial film organisations in Scotland. The Council itself is responsible for the operation of the Scottish Central Film Library (*q.v.*), the SFC Industrial Panel (*q.v.*), the SFC Repertory Season, the Scottish Amateur Film Festival (an open international event first held in 1938) and for organising courses in film study, film production and film projection.

16–17 Woodside Terrace, Glasgow, C3.

Scottish Film Council Industrial Panel The Industrial Panel of the Scottish Film Council was formed in 1938. Its main objects are to promote the use of films in industry for training, research, publicity and prestige purposes.

Nearly a hundred Scottish industrial organisations and firms are members of the Panel.

16–17 Woodside Terrace, Glasgow, C3.

Scottish Higher Leaving Certificate This was the title used between 1951 and 1961 for the higher level of the present Scottish Certificate of Education; it was changed when the Certificate examination was opened to students from further education bodies and individual candidates sponsored

by the education authorities; until 1961 it was open only to pupils in senior secondary schools.

Scottish Institute of Adult Education A voluntary body, the Scottish Institute has the purpose of encouraging adult education in Scotland. Supported by subscriptions from individual members and affiliated bodies (including the Scottish universities, the LEAs, a number of central institutions and many voluntary organisations), the Institute conducts its work largely through district conferences and an annual national conference.

Education Offices, Alloa, Scotland. Publication: *Scottish Adult Education* (three times a year).

Scottish Leaving Certificate This was the title used between 1951 and 1961 for the present Scottish Certificate of Education; it was changed when the Certificate was opened to students from further education bodies and individual candidates sponsored by the education authorities.

Scottish Secondary Teachers' Association The aims of the Association are to advance education in Scotland, with particular regard to secondary education, and to safeguard and promote the interests of members. The Association was formed in 1944. The outstanding feature of the constitution of the Association is its insistence upon equality of representation of the three main categories of secondary teachers—honours graduates, ordinary graduates, and teachers of practical and aesthetic subjects—in all the organs of the Association including Congress, the supreme governing body. The Association's publications have contributed to educational research; the most recent publication (1967) examines the possibility of reorganising the school year into four terms.

15 Dundas St, Edinburgh, 3.

Scottish Student Drama Festival
See **Students, Scottish Union of**

Scottish Technical Education Consultative Council The Council aims to promote vocational further education and to secure the widest possible measure of consultation on it between employers, employees and those responsible for its provision. Of the 19 Council members, seven are from industry (including three from the Scottish TUC) and seven represent educational interests.

Sec.: Mrs. E. C. G. Craghill, York Buildings, Queen St, Edinburgh, 2. Publication: *Link-up* (quarterly).

Scottish Youth Hostels Association The Scottish YHA shares the aims of the YHA of England and Wales (*q.v.*). It has 90 hostels situated in the main tourist areas. Each is in the charge of a warden, and members look after themselves and play their part in the general housekeeping, under the warden's direction.

National Office: 7 Glebe Cres., Stirling.

Scout Association Founded by Baden-Powell in 1907, the Association aims to encourage the physical and spiritual development of young people throughout the world by means of a scheme of progressive training based on the Scout law and promise under adult leadership. It is not a religious movement, although its members have an obligation to follow the religion of their choice. The training, which is made enjoyable and attractive, is based largely on outdoor activities, with service to the community playing a large part; it is designed to encourage young people to take a constructive role in society. Age range, with suitable training for three separate groups, is from eight to 20 years of age.

25 Buckingham Palace Rd, London, SW1.

Screen education The use of film and television as teaching *aids* is well established. The study of film and television in themselves, as important means of communication and powerful cultural forces, has developed more slowly. Yet these media play a large part in the lives of most children and adults, and film, after only 70 years, has become a major art form worthy of study at the highest level. The Newsom Report on the education of average and below-average 13–16-year-olds (*Half Our Future*, 1963) described the mass media as 'the most significant environmental factor that teachers have to take into account' and continued: 'We need to train children to look critically and to discriminate between what is good and bad in what they see. . . . Just as we have traditionally thought it important to broaden children's response to and experience of literature and music, so we must now offer a comparative education in the important and powerful visual media.' This kind of teaching—education *in* rather than *by* film and television—is known as screen education.

The main qualification required of the screen education teacher is a respect for film and television as media in their own right and a belief that they are capable of conveying worthwhile and enjoyable experiences. Film and television should not be regarded merely as a means of leading young people to literary classics or the live theatre. Moreover, although many films and television programmes are very poor, young people often get some sort of enjoyment from them and outright condemnation may destroy the sympathetic relationship between pupil and teacher which is essential for the teaching of discrimination, i.e. the ability to distinguish between good and bad. The aim should rather be to increase awareness and response and thus develop young people's tastes so that they can enjoy, and appreciate to the full, good films and television programmes of all kinds.

If young people are to enjoy the best, they must have ample experience of it—a teaching method which has traditionally, and rightly, been used by teachers of literature, music, etc. The method can easily be used with films, many of which are available for school use in 16-mm. versions. It is wise to start with good examples of the kinds of film with which the class is familiar. Finance can be a problem, but enough money must be provided if film is to be studied seriously in school. The voluntary film society, financed by members, is not a satisfactory alternative. Providing experience of good television is more difficult. Schools programmes are only marginally suitable for classroom study, which should be primarily concerned with young people's main television experience, i.e. evening programmes. Only limited success can be achieved by attempts to influence their choice of such programmes. Thus 16-mm. tele-recordings are needed in large numbers; these are slowly becoming available.

Films and tele-recordings should not merely be shown but also studied. Discussion is perhaps the most valuable method; it is, moreover, a method which can be used even when no suitable film or television study material is available in school. Full appreciation and awareness come about only when young people begin to think about what they have seen. This is unlikely to happen unless they are stimulated and, if the right questions are asked, free discussion is the best method of providing this stimulation. Ideas develop in the give and take of classroom discussion.

Classroom analysis of films and tele-recordings provides an opportunity for that careful training in looking and listening which is one of the foundations of discrimination. Study material can also be used to teach the elements of movie 'language', though the importance of this knowledge should not be over-emphasised; it is not an end in itself but merely a means to greater appreciation. Despite superficial differences, the 'languages' of film and television are essentially the same— selection, juxtaposition through editing, use of camera angles and lighting, choice of sound, etc. For the teacher, the most important difference between the two media is in content; much more fiction is seen on television than in the cinema.

Classroom study of films and television programmes may well be more fruitful if a comparative approach is adopted. Inferior examples may be studied along with similar but more worthwhile material. Different film treatments of the same theme may be compared—young people, personal relationships, war, race, etc. A variety of television programmes concerned with similar subjects may be studied— crime or medical series, pop music, topical programmes, etc.

Practical experience is an essential part of any school course in art, music or drama. Similarly, a screen education course cannot be regarded as complete unless it affords some opportunity to participate in the making of films. There is a wide variety of opinion among teachers about the aims and methods of film-making with young people, and about its appropriate place in a screen education course— if indeed it is part of an organised course at all.

Society for Education in Film and Television (SEFT), 70, Old Compton St, London, W1. A voluntary organisation of practising teachers. Publishes *Screen Education Yearbook*, and six times a year the magazine *Screen Education*.

Education Department, British Film Institute (BFI), 70, Old Compton St, London, W1. Provides advice, study materials, lecture service, etc. and publishes occasional pamphlets.

See also **Film in education**

677

FURTHER READING

Film and Television in Education for Teaching, BFI/ATCDE, 1963.

P. Harcourt and P. Theobald (eds). *Film Making in Schools and Colleges*, BFI, 1966.

A. P. Higgins. *Talking about Television*, BFI, 1966.

A. W. Hodgkinson. *Screen Education*, UNESCO, 1964.

J. Kitses. *Talking about the Cinema*, BFI, 1966.

J. M. L. Peters. *Teaching about the Film*, UNESCO, 1961.

A. Richardson, R. C. Vannoey and D. Waters. *A Handbook for Screen Education*, SEFT, 1961.

P. Whannel and P. Harcourt (eds). *Film Teaching*, BFI, 1966.

APH

Scribes and Illuminators, Society of Formed to re-establish a tradition of craftmanship in calligraphy, lettering and illumination, the Society draws its members from those engaged professionally in the production of manuscripts as works of art. Many members teach lettering and calligraphy, privately or in art schools.

Art Workers Guild, 6 Queen Sq., Bloomsbury, London, WC1.

Scripture Union *See* **Bible Societies**

Sea Cadet Corps A voluntary youth organisation for boys between 12 and 18, the Corps sets out through its discipline and training at sea to help those who are considering a seafaring career. It is not a pre-service organisation and no cadet is obliged to become a sailor. The Corps is nevertheless recognised by the Navy as providing pre-entry training for boys who later join the RN or one of its Reserves.

Grand Bldgs, Trafalgar Sq., London, WC2.

SEAC The South Eastern Architects' Collaboration, formed in 1963, has as its aim the sharing of professional and technical resources in the development of inter-related systems of building, to be directly applied to the educational programme buildings of each member.

The members are Essex, Hertfordshire, Kent, West Suffolk, Ministry of Public Building and Works, and the DES.

Seafarers' Education Service *See* **Responsible bodies**

Secondary education, Selection for Until the 20th century secondary education in most countries existed only for the children of the rich, leisured classes, who would become the leaders, priests and lawyers of the next generation. It was based on the classical tradition and was given, mostly in boarding schools, by teachers who were university graduates but had no training in teaching.

Elementary or primary education was provided for the masses, first by the churches and then by the state, and was confined mainly to the three Rs and moral instruction. Teachers were themselves mostly products of the elementary system, not graduates, but trained on the job or at training colleges. There was scarcely any bridge between the two systems apart from a few scholarships for the exceptionally clever poor children. Selection then was chiefly by wealth and social status, though a small number could be admitted on the basis of achievement. With the rise of the middle classes and the need for better educated skilled workers in the late 19th century, there was an enormous expansion of subsidised secondary education which charged modest fees to most parents, but admitted an increasing number of children free on the results of an examination—in England and Wales special places, scholarships and later the 11-plus.

With the greater demand for education and the spread of democratic ideas, the restriction of secondary education to an élite minority became unacceptable, and various alternative forms of post-primary education were initiated in European countries for those who did not wish, or were not able, to cope with the strenuous five-to eight-year academic secondary school course. Thus in Britain the Education Act 1944 aimed to provide secondary education for all and enjoined the LEAs to maintain schools appropriate to the age, ability and aptitude of their pupils. In practice this chiefly became selection of the most able 20% of 11-year-olds to the grammar schools (though the figure varied from under 10% in some LEAs to over 50% in others). A few were allocated to technical schools at 11 or 13, while most of the remainder went to secondary modern schools. In addition the private or fee-paying sector continued to cater for many middle-class children, and schools of highest repute, such as the public schools, admitted on the basis of the common entrance examination at 13.

Thus in Britain after the 1944 Act there was still, in the eyes of politicians and the public, a cleavage between advanced secondary education, leading to the universities and to non-manual jobs, for the few, and an inferior education for the majority. Actually a very small percentage of clever modern pupils were transferred to grammar schools; with the rise of colleges of further education, many more now carry on to 'A' level work and even to university.

At the time of writing various forms of secondary reorganisation are being worked out in Britain, mostly designed to abolish selection, by sending all pupils to common or comprehensive schools from 11 till 14, 16 or 18. In such schools there is still differentiation of the more from the less able, since the classes are streamed by ability, or to some extent by parental choice of type and length of course. But as the streams are not segregated in different schools, transfer is easier—at least in theory.

Other European countries are coping with the same social and educational problems in their own ways, and though all of them retain differentiated schools at some stage, the majority now have a common core curriculum till 14 or 15. Even in France the dual system has at last been breached. The Communist countries have gone furthest in denying that pupils vary widely in their capacities and desires for advanced secondary education; and yet in the USSR promotion to fifth and to eighth grades depends on passing examinations, and there is very rigorous selection for education beyond 17 years. The USA has always aimed at universal, free education and its common high school is indeed, in contrast to British comprehensive schools, unstreamed. But it still practises concealed selection, partly through retardation of the weaker, and acceleration of the brighter, primary pupils, and partly through self-selection and guidance of only the more promising and well-motivated students into college preparatory or other advanced secondary courses.

Formal selection by examinations or tests is most rigorously practised now in developing nations, such as those of the British Commonwealth where secondary education (still largely in the British mould) cannot be provided for more than 1%–3% of the population, though since independence and with improved primary schooling the demand has enormously increased.

In England and Wales, then, the controversies over selection arise because the pressures for social mobility clash both with the vested interests of tradition, and with the presumed requirements of educational efficiency. It is argued that the clever and keen can and should be educated to a higher level and at a more rapid pace than the dull and uninterested, and that the former will be held back, and the latter demoralised, if all ranges are taught together. Obviously this is true of education beyond the normal school-leaving age, but the experience of other countries—not only the USA and USSR—shows that common education can be carried to a much later stage than is generally believed possible in Britain, especially when teachers are trained to give more individualised and flexible tuition within their classes. England and Wales in fact succeeds in exaggerating differences in educability by its practice of streaming and selection; for a wider range of attainment, e.g. in arithmetic, is found here at 13 years than in any other comparable country. Selection also helps to maintain a diversity of schools to suit different needs, which is educationally healthy (the university-oriented grammar school curriculum is certainly not suited to everybody). But it has other disadvantages.

Children's abilities and interests naturally change as they grow older, hence a sharp division or segregation at one age, especially the rather early age of 11, is inevitably unfair to a minority who develop more rapidly later. Considering the unpredictability of human beings, the accuracy of current selection procedures is remarkably high. However, this is to some extent spurious since those who fail now naturally have less opportunity to catch up with the successful later. It follows too that a bigger proportion of the child population could be educated to a higher level, and the nation can ill-afford this wastage. There is also the complaint that children from middle-class families get a larger share (though not in fact a larger total) of grammar school places than working-class children. But it is difficult to see the force of this, since parents of any social class who are themselves intelligent and well-educated naturally give more educational support and encouragement to their children.

A very real defect is that a competitive selection examination inevitably stimulates coaching by the schools and parents, and distorts progressive primary teaching. This has been mitigated in recent years by placing more emphasis on junior school reports than on test results, but it can permeate the

work of the whole junior school and lead to undesirable streaming in the larger schools, even on entry. If a seven- to eight-year-old is treated as a failure from the start he naturally stays a failure. The supposedly harmful effects of the 11-plus in producing strain and worry among children are often exaggerated, and nowadays where examinations still exist they are usually conducted more informally. While it can reasonably be argued that everyone has to face both selection and disappointment at some stage in his life, most would now agree that $10\frac{1}{2}$ years (let alone $7\frac{1}{2}$) is too early for a child's educational future to be decided. It is preferable to differentiate gradually over the ensuing years by letting children, along with their parents and teachers, discover what level of education and type of specialisation they are best suited to.

See also **Scotland, Education in; Selection, Borderline cases in; Selection procedures for secondary education; Selection tests; Comprehensive schools; Ireland, Northern, Education in; Thorne scheme**

FURTHER READING

J. W. B. Douglas. *The Home and the School*, McGibbon and Kee, 1964.
P. E. Vernon (ed.). *Secondary School Selection*, Methuen, 1957.
A. Yates and D. A. Pidgeon. *Admission to Grammar Schools*, Newnes, 1957.

PEV

Secondary intermediate schools *See* **Ireland, Northern, Education in**

Secondary modern schools In 1965 secondary modern schools in England and Wales, lineal successors to senior elementary schools, provided secondary education for over one and a half million boys and girls in over 3,000 schools. With fewer than 100,000 pupils over the age of 11 years still in all-age schools, the reorganisation recommended by the Hadow Report (1925) was virtually complete.

In the early decades of the century a secondary school was one established and maintained by the LEA, available without fees to a limited number of able pupils selected by a fiercely competitive examination from local elementary schools and to others on payment of fees in whole or in part. The curriculum of this early secondary school approximated to that of the older grammar schools, but with greater stress on mathematics and science and less on the classics. By the 30s these new secondary schools had come to be called grammar schools and were indistinguishable from them. Those children who were not selected for free places either moved at 11 to the local senior elementary school if there was one, or remained at the school which they had attended as five-year-olds. Secondary modern schools thus inherited the children, the buildings and the traditions of the Victorian elementary school.

But the 1944 Act used the term 'secondary' to indicate not a type of school but that stage of education which followed primary and preceded further education, and which pupils entered at about the age of 11. To distinguish the ex-elementary schools from the existing secondary grammar schools they were to be called 'modern schools', the term 'modern' appearing for the first time in educational usage in the Hadow Report, presumably to suggest schools with a curriculum appropriate to the modern age. Not surprisingly, overseas educationists have sometimes expected to find secondary modern schools places where the most modern buildings, curriculum and methods of teaching could be observed.

During the late 40s, some secondary modern schools were experimenting with social studies, general science, rural surveys and projects. But by the middle 50s these activities were largely abandoned, together with the term 'modern', and 'county secondary school' became the customary appella-tion to distinguish the non-selective schools from the selective grammar or technical schools. Thus the local secondary school of pre-war days is now the esteemed grammar school, the pre-war senior elementary is now the county secondary school. Much confusion has arisen from this change in terminology.

At its best the secondary modern school of the late 40s was a fine school, as envisaged in the Hadow Report. Most successful in a rural setting, it taught rural crafts, initiated rural surveys, drew on the locality for local studies in history, geography and biology, and was a genuine focus for the local community. Not infrequently the school resembled a miniature farm with pigs, poultry, bees, rabbits, possibly sheep or a cow. The care of these animals with the outdoor work in field and garden gave clear meaning and purpose to work in the class-rooms.

But most post-war secondary modern schools were not country schools, and the attempt during the 50s to find a curriculum which had purpose and reality for boys and girls living in industrial, urban and suburban areas led to the introduction for older pupils of a variety of courses with some vocational relevance, in addition to the general course. Commercial studies, light and heavy engineering, catering and needle trades, pre-nursing and child care courses began to appear on the timetable. It became difficult to distinguish some secondary modern from technical schools.

Meanwhile, by the provision of extended courses, schools had begun to provide for the growing number of boys and girls prepared to remain at school beyond the minimum statutory leaving age of 15 and who did not necessarily want a course of study linked with any particular vocation. Already by the early 50s a full four-year course was becoming the rule for the ablest pupils in the most favoured areas.

The announcement in 1953 of the College of Preceptors' new examination to be taken at the end of a four-year secondary course seems to have triggered off the widespread drive for a school-leaving examination for secondary modern pupils. Particularly in London, the south-east and the south, numbers remaining at secondary modern schools for a full fourth year and for part of a fifth year began quite dramatically to rise.

Extended courses led naturally on to GCE courses at 'O' level; semi-technical courses similarly led on to examinations set by the RSA or City and Guilds of London or other examinations originally intended for those who had already left school. In some areas, e.g. south-west Hertfordshire and Southend, local teachers had begun to experiment with local examinations. If there were fees to be paid, parents willingly paid them. Meanwhile, despite pressure, the Minister refused to recognise for grant any fees for examinations other than those conducted by the eight, and, with the addition of the Associated Board, the nine national examining boards for the award of the GCE.

By the mid-50s it was clear that the terms 'secondary modern' or 'county secondary' referred to schools growing ever more diverse in curriculum and organisation. There was the large suburban school in good buildings with children from middle-class families who were prepared to support the school by encouraging their children to stay on for a five-year course, by providing a school uniform, by attending school functions, by co-operating over homework. Many secondary modern schools of this type were virtually indistinguishable from grammar schools. Other schools, notably boys' schools in industrial areas, were hardly to be recognised from technical schools in the excellence of their workshops and laboratories, and the degree of collaboration with the local technical college. In new towns the new non-selective schools with superb buildings and equipment were clearly moving towards the comprehensive pattern.

It was in the downtown areas that secondary modern schools seemed least changed. There the school buildings and the school yards were often, externally at least, as dismal as the surrounding housing. Home conditions for many of the children were bad; the shortage of teachers and lack of well-qualified teachers were acute. Where most was needed of a school least could be given, in spite of the devotion and tenacity of many of the staff.

And in all areas there were secondary modern schools where the work was simply dull, conventional and unimaginative, pointless and irrelevant to both teachers and taught.

The report of the Newsom Committee (q.v.) based on a stratified national sample of secondary modern schools confirmed the experience of those who knew the schools at first hand. This humane document focussed attention on the needs of the least able children, the so-called Newsom children. In many areas remedial departments and special classes had already been established. The extension of graded posts to secondary modern schools had made it possible for specially trained and experienced teachers to be given responsibility for remedial departments. Where this was done effectively, the improvement in children's ability to read was one measure of their general advance.

For the abler children in secondary modern schools the ever more intense drive for a school leaving certificate of some kind led to the setting up of the Beloe sub-committee, and marked the change in the middle 50s from a secondary school deliberately left free from external examination and encouraged to experiment with curricula and teaching techniques, to a school more exam-ridden than any other secondary school. On the recommendations of the Beloe sub-committee, the Minister finally approved the establishment of a regionally organised CSE to be under the control of practising teachers who would, it was hoped, determine both the appropriate subject syllabuses and examining techniques for the pupils they taught.

The drive for success in the GCE 'O' level had already produced the phenomenon of children who, five years after their failure to be selected for an academic course, were equalling or surpassing those who had been selected at 11-plus. The increasingly obvious errors in selection led more and more teachers and parents to doubt the validity as well as the justice of selection. As evidence began to accumulate, an increasing number of teachers began to lose confidence in the prognostic value of standardised tests. Studies of the variability in human growth became more widely known; the fatalistic and deterministic attitude to children's abilities and attainments began to change. Failure in the 11-plus, with consequent relegation to a secondary modern school, had led many children to believe themselves incapable of success in any area of school life. Generations of teachers had come to regard children in secondary modern schools as second-class citizens, incapable of understanding or living effectively in the contemporary world. There was in most secondary modern teachers a benevolent paternalism but not a real or deep belief in the educability of their pupils. But the results of local and national examinations began to undermine teachers' belief in the infallibility of tests.

In the late 40s teachers in secondary modern schools had been urged to develop their own curricula, to devise their own syllabuses and to work out new techniques of teaching. There was plenty of exhortation, but very little practical help. The introduction of Mode 3 in the CSE has taken place under more promising conditions. Not only has there been nearly 25 years of in-service training available through Institutes of Education, LEAs and Ministry courses, but books, visual aids, technical innovations pour out in bewildering profusion. Experiment in curricula, teaching techniques and methods of assessment are not only encouraged by the Schools Council but supported by a stream of publications. In particular, working papers such as *Raising the School Leaving Age* and the series of Examination Bulletins make available to teachers the technical knowhow and practical stimulus to experiment, both absent in the 40s. It will be ironic if teachers become possessed of the essential techniques of curriculum construction and of evaluation, but fail to maintain their independence and rights as teachers to plan learning experiences for their pupils.

As society in England becomes more orientated to middle-class attitudes and values, a type of secondary school with its roots in the Victorian elementary school for children of the labouring poor seems an anachronism in the more egalitarian society of the second half of the 20th century. But secondary modern schools where they still exist are still schools for children of manual workers, the skilled, semi-skilled and unskilled. As neighbourhood schools they reflect the social attitudes of the local community and just as clearly the differing social attitudes of the regions, which in this small tightly-packed island remain remarkably distinct.

See also **Hadow Report (1926); CSE**

FURTHER READING

Central Advisory Council for Education. *Half our Future* (Newsom Report), 1963.

Department of Education and Science. *The New Secondary Education*, HMSO, Pamphlet No. 9, 1947.

H. C. Dent. *Secondary Modern Schools*, Routledge and Kegan Paul, 1958.

R. M. T. Kneebone. *I Work in a Secondary Modern School*, Routledge and Kegan Paul, 1957.

H. Loukes. *Secondary Modern*, Oxford Univ. Press, 1956.

A. W. Rowe. *The Education of the Average Child*, Harrap, 1959.

JAMD

Secondary Teachers, Ireland, Association of The ASTI was formed in 1909 by a small group of teachers who combined because of the plight in which teachers then found themselves—with no minimum salary, no minimum incremental salary, no superannuation scheme, no system of registration, no security of tenure. It has now achieved the status of a register of secondary teachers. It has contracts of employment with most school bodies; an appeal authority against abrupt or unjust dismissal; a superannuation scheme and a scheme of conciliation and arbitration. Non-sectarian and non-political, it continues to press the claims of teachers to more equitable salaries.

11 Hume St, Dublin, 2.

Secretarial training The type of training necessary to qualify as a secretary is fairly well defined. It comprises instruction in shorthand, typewriting, transcription training, audiotyping, office practice and production, secretarial duties, the communications aspect of English; it may also include book-keeping, elementary statistics, business calculations, economic geography, economics, office machines and such social subjects as deportment, speech, social conventions, fashion, make-up, etc.

The distinction between the shorthand/audio-typist, the secretary, and the PA (personal assistant) is not, however, so clearly made. Many shorthand-typists call themselves secretaries. A secretary should have all the basic skills and knowledge at a higher level but in addition act as a social secretary, a personal consultant to the executive for whom she works, an office controller and, in addition, is quite often an executive with responsibility in her own right. A PA is no more than this,

except that where ultimate responsibility lies with the executive who employs the secretary, it lies to some defined extent on the PA.

The opportunities for secretarial work are very wide-ranging and varied and continue to grow. There are, in addition, specialised areas of secretarial work, e.g. medical secretaries, bi-lingual secretaries, etc.

Courses of training vary in length from three or four months up to two years. The syllabus is narrow or wide in proportion to the length of the course. Courses are offered in most technical colleges, colleges of commerce, and state secondary schools (including comprehensive schools). They are also offered by a number of independent schools and colleges, and by the training units of some large firms; employment opportunities are provided by Youth Employment Offices and by many agencies and bureaux engaged in this work.

Fees vary but are much lower (if anything is charged at all) in state education. Independent schools maintain themselves in the field by highly specific vocational training and by adapting the most up-to-date techniques of instruction in order to bring students up to a higher level of skill and knowledge in a shorter time. A good independent school may charge £60—£90 a term.

Generally accepted standards of attainment are 80—120 words a minute in shorthand, 40—60 words a minute in typewriting and 20 plus words a minute in transcription together with other qualifying examinations in these and the other subjects of the curriculum.

Appropriate examinations are run by a number of independent bodies, e.g. the Royal Society of Arts, Pitman Examinations Institute, London Chamber of Commerce, Union of Lancashire and Cheshire Institutes, Union of Educational Institutions, the Scottish Council for Higher Administrative and

Professional Examinations. Of these the Royal Society of Arts is nationally and internationally known, their total of single-subject examinations in the field being approximately half a million per annum. Group certificates are also awarded. The RSA awards Secretarial and Commercial Certificates, the London Chamber of Commerce a Private Secretary's Diploma, and Pitman Examinations Institute Higher Secretarial Group Certificates.

Students most likely to succeed are those with alert minds, a good background of general education particularly in English, pleasant manner and social address, effective speech and balanced temperament with high physical and nervous stamina. Salaries paid range from £500 to £1,250 or even more per annum for élite secretaries. A five-day week of 40 hours is now the common requirement. Fringe benefits are usually secured.

Teacher training for business education is conducted in several training colleges. Particulars may be obtained from the Department of Education and Science, or in Scotland from the Scottish Education Department.

A professional association for secretaries is the Institute of Qualified Private Secretaries Ltd (27 Henberton Rd, London, SW9).

One outcome of the Industrial Training Act 1964 has been to focus attention much more sharply on training for office work. The Commercial and Clerical Training Committee of the Central Training Council reported on this topic in *Training for Commerce and the Office* (HMSO).

BWC

Secretary of State for Education and Science The Secretary of State for Education and Science is a member of the government and political head of the Department of Education and Science (*q.v.*). To assist him in discharging his wide responsibilities concerned with schools, further education, teachers and kindred subjects in England and Wales, universities in Great Britain, civil science, the arts and sport, the Secretary of State has three Ministers of State and a Parliamentary Under-Secretary.

The Education Act 1944 made it the duty of the Minister of Education to promote the education of the people of England and Wales and the progressive development of institutions devoted to that purpose, and to secure the effective execution by local authorities, under his supervision, of the national policy for providing a varied and comprehensive educational service in every area. Since 1 April 1964 these duties have been those of the Secretary of State.

Two central Advisory Councils (one for England and one for Wales) advise the Secretary of State on matters connected with educational theory and practice, usually on subjects specifically referred to them. Discussions are held on important matters at national level with representative bodies such as local authority associations, teachers' associations and bodies representing religious interests. There are also three National Councils concerned with specific aspects of the education service, further education, the training and supply of teachers, and art education.

The Secretary of State exercises his responsibility in relation to universities through the University Grants Committee (*q.v.*).

Secular Society, National Founded in 1866 by Charles Bradlaugh, parliamentarian and radical leader, the NSS is devoted to the secularisation of society and the concentration of all man's energies on this world. During the last hundred years the NSS has advocated and campaigned for reforms in all spheres of social activity. These have included free, compulsory and secular education, birth control, the rational use of Sunday and freedom of speech and publication. In recent times it has been chiefly concerned with amendment of the 1944 Education Act, and the acceptance of the following recommendations:

(1) To abolish collective worship and RI in county schools.

(2) To introduce a syllabus of social morality and citizenship for all students.

(3) To offer comparative religion and philosophy to senior students.

(4) To remove all subsidies from denominational schools.

(5) To integrate the public schools into the maintained system and to abolish compulsory chapel.

The NSS recently published *Religion and Ethics in Schools — the Case for Secular Education* by David Tribe.

13 Borough High St, London, SE1.

Seebohm Committee *See* **Children's Officers, Association of**

Séguin, Edouard (1812-80) French pioneer in the education of idiots who taught that such education was possible only if the body and the senses were trained as part of the whole personality.

Selection, Borderline cases in In selecting children for grammar school places it is unsatisfactory to rely merely on the combined results of intelligence and attainment tests or examinations. For obviously there is nothing to choose in ability between those who score at or just above the minimum total for admission, and those who score just below this minimum. Indeed if a parallel set of tests were sat next day, many of those above and below the borderline would change places. Hence most authorities recognise a 'border zone' of doubtful candidates. When the total places amount to some 20% of the age group, the top 15% may be admitted automatically, the bottom 75% excluded; the intermediate 10% come up for individual scrutiny by panels of teachers and an education officer. Cases of discrepancy, where the junior head's judgment conflicts with the test findings, may also be included in this group.

The additional evidence most frequently consulted is the child's primary school record and head's assessment. His or her essay may be marked, or specimens of work submitted by the junior school. Information on health and home background may be taken into account in exceptional cases. Sometimes additional tests are given; thus the whole top 25% may take a Part 2 examination, set and marked at the grammar school of choice. In one or two areas a War Office selection board procedure, suitably modified for children, has been tried and found useful.

It should be realised that all these procedures assume that the subjective judgments of the panel are more accurate than the objective findings of the selection tests or examinations. This is likely to be true in some cases, false in others. The point is, though, that the system appears more humane, and it reassures parents and junior and secondary teachers that the fairest possible consideration has been given before a vital decision is taken.

See also **Selection procedures, etc.**
PEV

Selection procedures for secondary education Each LEA responsible for selection to grammar schools decides its own procedure. But there is considerable uniformity, as shown by the surveys carried out by the National Foundation for Educational Research in England and Wales. (No account can be taken here of what happens where selection has been or is being completely eliminated.)

Early in the calendar year almost all LEAs assess those pupils who will reach the age of 11 the following September. Many also allow some under-age candidates to enter. In 1956 nearly 90% of LEAs employed a standardised 'intelligence test' (now better named as a 'test of verbal reasoning'); virtually all included either standardised tests or 'home-made' examinations in English and arithmetic. A majority of areas added an English essay, which may be marked only for borderline candidates, and most claim to make use of junior school records or heads' assessments for additional information (*cf.* **Selection, Borderline cases in**). The interviewing of pupils is generally condemned and has been abolished in almost all areas.

Since it has been shown that junior heads' rating of their own pupils can give as accurate predictions of future secondary school work as any battery of tests, several LEAs have abandoned formal tests or examinations while retaining selection. The schools may use tests internally to guide their assessments. Unfortunately this does not solve the problem of equating standards of judgment between schools, though rough corrections can be made through education officers' and secondary heads' knowledge of the standards of different schools. Also age differences are not justly catered for. Hence some LEAs retain an external test or tests, mainly for standardising the assessments.

PEV

Selection tests Standardised objective tests have been adopted more and more widely by LEAs for 11-plus selection examinations because of the difficulties of marking very large numbers of more conventional papers in a short time with reliability.

The verbal reasoning or 'intelligence' test usually contains 100 short multiple-choice items, to be answered in 45 minutes. Arithmetic consists of a section of 'mechanical' sums and a section of problems; in recent years alternative versions reflecting the newer approach to number teaching have become available. Some English tests are also multiple-choice, but since these were found to discourage the teaching of English writing in junior schools, alternatives have appeared where the pupil is required to write a word or a phrase as his answer. These too can be marked rapidly and with almost complete consistency between different markers.

All these tests are constructed and tried out beforehand so as to yield scores (or so-called quotients) which average 100 and range from 70 to 140; a correction for age differences among the candidates is incorporated. Often these scores are totalled and a cut-off is set to admit as many pupils as there are places available. Thus with a 20% entry, the requisite total is about 335 (cf. **Selection, Borderline cases in**). Separate totals are generally adopted for the two sexes since girls tend to score higher in English and verbal reasoning at this age. New versions of tests are published annually; sales are restricted to education officers, so that they can be kept confidential.

PEV

Semantics The study of the meaning of meaning (e.g. what did he *really* mean when he said, 'Nice weather we're having'?) enjoyed considerable popularity in the 40s and 50s but recently less has been heard of it. In secondary schools, especially in sixth-form work, the teacher is rightly concerned to sharpen his pupils' attentiveness to the distinctions between ostensible and covert meaning, especially in the study of social communication and literature.

Seminars These are regular meetings of ten or so students in groups for the purposes of discussing with a tutor, and further elucidating, data or ideas previously presented by another teacher, lecturer or professor. Successful seminars usually demand written preparation from the student members in turn.

Senegal, Education in Education is officially compulsory between the ages of six and 14, but shortage of school places means that only about half of the children in this age range are in schools. Mission schools are still widely used in addition to state schools. In 1965 there were 255 elementary schools (enrolment 206,300 including 26,000 at 67 mission schools); in secondary and higher education the enrolment was 38,000 (including 3,400 at five mission colleges, 7,000 at three technical schools). The University at Dakar had 2,447 students in 1965.

In 1965 the country's population was approximately 3½ million.

Senior assistants These are posts of responsibility which apply to approved schools coming next in the hierarchy after heads and deputy heads. The allowances paid in addition to the salary as a teacher or instructor are as follows:

Group	Certified accom.	Allowance (£)
(1)*	(Up to 17)	(135)
2	18 to 51	160
3	52 to 102	180
4	103 to 171	205
5	172 to 257	220
6	258 to 360	240

*Where an appointment is made.

Service abroad, Pension for *See* **Pension contributions for service abroad and certain other service**

Sets Sets are collections of distinct things which are called members or elements. Sets can be described by (1) listing the members of a set in any order in curly brackets e.g. {cup, saucer, spoon}; (2) description: e.g. $P = \{n|n \text{ is prime}\}$, read as P is the set of numbers n such that n is a prime. Each number considered must have the property to be included in the set.

Venn diagrams are used to depict sets.

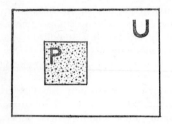

Outer enclosure (*U* for Universal Set) contains all numbers. Inner enclosure, labelled *P*, contains all the prime numbers.

Operations on sets
(1) Complement, A': the set whose members are not members of set A.

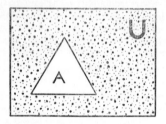

(2) Intersection, A∩B: the set whose members are common to sets A and B.

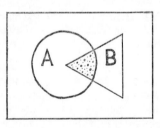

(3) Union, A∪B: the set whose members are in sets A or B or both.

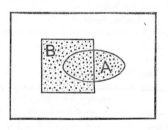

JCW

Setting This is a device used in time-tabling activities in a large school. By this means children may be organised in 'sets' instead of forms and classes. These 'sets', engaged in the same subject at the same time-table period, include pupils of comparable attainment entirely irrespective of the classes or forms in which they are otherwise accommodated.

Severely subnormal children *See* **Ineducable children**

Sex education Sex education, which commenced with the limited objective of acquainting young people with the facts of reproduction, has extended of late years to include all aspects of sex in the life of the individual and society. Its aim is to promote—along with knowledge of the sex function—an understanding of the emotions, challenges and responsibilities that are bound up with relationships between the sexes. Sex education embraces personal development, fostering emotional maturity, and preparation for family life.

So seen, sex education not only has its own particular content but touches many other subjects as well. English and history provide insight into human relationships. Moral issues associated with sex arise naturally in religious education and civics. The so-called facts of life, as well as much information about family life among animals, fit into lessons in hygiene, anatomy and physiology, and biology. Domestic science or homecraft offers opportunities for teaching child care and home-making, including an elementary understanding of their psychological aspects. Yet another source of modern sex education in school, youth club and college is the self-generating content of group discussion. And yet another, the personal counselling systems now being organised in some schools and colleges. (*See* **Counselling.**)

Since sex education is a developing sector of the curriculum, it is not surprising that wide differences in treatment may be observed between countries, and between schools. Although variation is considerable, trends may be observed which indicate the lines on which sex education is likely to stabilise. Four main areas can be differentiated:

(1) Information about the facts of life.

(2) Direct consideration of sex as an aspect of personal life and responsibility.

(3) Supplementary insight into human emotions and relationships arising from subject teaching.

(4) The provision of group discussion and individual guidance concerning problems of personal sexuality and of relationships with the other sex.

Who shall provide sex education is at least as important as what is taught. This raises the question of the criteria on which to select those who are to participate in the more personal aspects of sex education. Essentials seem to be emotional maturity, a warm personality, ease in relationships with young people, and ability to handle group discussion. Parents—who are solely responsible for the start of sex education, and are, of course, very important throughout—may themselves need guidance and encouragement in order to provide their children with that part of sex education which is the home's especial task. This applies particularly to meeting the young child's questions with simple and frank answers within the range of the child's understanding. Formerly, the point of view was widely held that sex education should be left entirely to the parents. The modern view is that parents and schools should act as a team, each sustaining the other in the developing programme of sex education. During the adolescent phase particularly, most parents appreciate the contribution to sex education that can be provided by schools, colleges and youth clubs.

At one time, there was felt to be no need for the school to participate in sex education before the secondary stage. The earlier maturation of boys and girls has caused a modification of this viewpoint. The *average* age of puberty for girls, in technologically advanced societies, is now around 13 years and, for boys, about a year later. This means that many boys and girls will reach puberty before leaving the primary school. It is extremely important that girls shall be prepared for menstruation, and boys for nocturnal emissions, before they occur. Research shows that many parents are loath to do this and a number of primary schools are providing courses on the facts of reproduction with opportunities for asking questions. As children are today interested in sex at an early age, the educational choice is to provide accurate information or to leave the children to gather what they can where they can—a likely source of misinformation, anxiety and dubious values.

One question arising at the secondary and tertiary stages of education, and in club work, is how far sex education shall be provided by internal resources and how far by visiting specialists. Some schools now have on the staff selected and trained pupil counsellors who can run courses and discussion groups, and provide individual guidance when called for. More commonly, the direct approach to sex education is dealt with periodically by visitors, who may be doctors, health workers, the education counsellors trained by the Marriage Guidance Council (*q.v.*), or equivalent skilled personnel. Courses are sometimes offered on only one occasion during secondary schooling, but this provision is tending to expand to two or three spaced courses.

At the first stage, at 12 or 13 years, the main purpose is to clear away any ignorance about 'the facts of life', and to relieve personal anxieties about what normal sexual development en-

tails. The second course, at 14 or 15, deals with boy-girl relationships, especially the emotional aspects, and with relationships with adults, particularly parents. The final course, at 16 or 17, is mainly directed to helping young people gain clearer insight about themselves, their personal problems, and what marriage and parenthood involve.

Even where the school has good internal resources for dealing with its own sex education, visiting specialists may be brought in from time to time as adolescents seem to appreciate a chance to discuss their problems with well-informed visitors, just because they are not regular members of the school community. Films and books are, of course, also used. Sex education in the training of teachers is of the same kind as at the third secondary stage—personal clarification. It should be noted that college students are not sufficiently mature to be trained *as* sex educators although good sex education at college paves the way for this.

A certain amount of controversy exists about the limits that should be put on the content of sex education. Content has expanded steadily over the past few decades wherever sex education has been seriously undertaken. At one time venereal disease, prostitution, abortion and homosexuality were usually omitted; now they are usually included. But doubts are still felt in some quarters concerning the dissemination of information about contraceptives, owing to the fear that knowledge may increase promiscuity. The contrary argument is that ignorance will certainly increase the incidence of illegitimate babies and forced marriages. This controversy is perhaps more academic than real since, where trust exists, and discussion is encouraged, young people seek detailed information about methods of contraception. And where trust does not exist and discussion is not encouraged, any attempt at sex education will be treated with suspicion, if not rejection, by the young people themselves.

By giving most of the space available to describing what is being attempted in sex education, a false picture may have been given of the overall position. Unfortunately the evidence is that provision still falls far short of need. Some schools, like some countries, have as yet barely made a start in sex education.

FURTHER READING
For very young children
Cyril Bibby and Ian T. Morrison. *The Human Body*, Puffin, 1955.
Sten Hegeler. *Peter and Caroline*, Tavistock and Methuen, 1966.

For young adolescents (13 plus)
National Marriage Guidance Council. *The Approach to Womanhood* (pamphlet). *Boys' Questions Answered* (pamphlet).
P. Reynold. *Mother and Child*, Longmans, 1963.
Marjorie Richards. *For Girls*, Basil Blackwell, 1963.
Llewelyn Richards. *For Boys*, Basil Blackwell, 1963.

For the older adolescent (16 plus)
Alan Dale. *An Introduction to Social Biology*, Heinemann Medical Books, 1964.
Rose Hacker. *The Opposite Sex*, Pan Piper, 1963.
Alan Ingleby. *Towards Maturity*, Robert Hale, 1966.

For teachers and parents
Albert G. Chanter. *Sex Education in the Primary School*, Macmillan, 1966.
Dr Julia Dawkins. *A Text-book of Sex Education*, Basil Blackwell, 1967.
James Pike. *Teenagers and Parents*, Gollancz, 1965.

JH

Seychelles, Education in the 1965 statistics: 23 kindergartens (enrolment 517); 33 primary schools (enrolment 7,341); 12 secondary schools (enrolment 1,260); one vocational school, one continuation centre, one teacher training college (enrolments not available). Total population: approximately 47,424.

Ship Adoption Society, British Formed in 1936 to link schools with merchant ships primarily for education purposes, the Society, with power-

ful help of friends in shipping and education, has given great impetus to the teaching of geography and kindred subjects.

During the second world war, the Society's work was maintained and membership increased. Schools concentrated on sending war comforts to their adopted ships, and from such small beginnings stemmed the Merchant Navy Comforts Service. In 1939, in conjunction with Seafarers' Education Service and under the title of The Sea War Library Service, the Society helped to supply books free of charge to all merchant ships of the British and allied fleets. Large numbers of allied ships became members and, after the war, some allied countries successfully started their own Ship Adoption Societies. Although there are over 750 ship and personal links, there is also a very lengthy waiting list of school members.

HQ: 'Wellington', Temple Stairs, Victoria Embankment, London, WC2.

Short, Rt Hon Edward (b. 1912) Appointed Secretary of State for Education and Science, 1968.

Short-service gratuity Where a teacher has permanently broken down in health, after completing three years of service and before completing 10 years, a short-service gratuity is payable of an amount not exceeding one-twelfth of the average salary in respect of each year of recognised and/or contributory service. The six months condition in regard to disablement allowance benefits is also applicable to the award of a short-service gratuity. The form required in this connection is the same as that for disablement allowance benefit.

Shropshire Mathematics Experiment The original purpose of this experiment was to test the suitability of a syllabus for secondary schools containing some elements of modern mathematics. The syllabus is fully integrated to show the use of the new language in a traditional context. The syllabus is itself now evolving and will shortly incorporate many more new developments.

Initially the call for some enquiry into the content and teaching methods in mathematics came from the teachers themselves, and was encouraged and given practical support by the Shropshire Education Committee. Thirty-six schools agreed to participate in the experiment and teachers involved met weekly to discuss the progress of the work and to revise the draft texts, where necessary, in the light of their classroom experience. Penguin Books published the subsidised trial edition of the text and now publish the final drafts, together with a Parents' and Teachers' Handbook.

FURTHER READING
R. S. Heritage. 'The Shropshire Mathematics Experiment', *The Mathematical Gazette*, May 1965. *Learning Mathematics*, Penguin Books, 1967.

Sick leave A period of sick leave will be treated as contributory service for pension purposes. Sick leave, however, cannot be treated as contributory unless (a) the teacher's employer approves it, and if required, furnishes the Secretary of State with satisfactory evidence; (b) the teacher has been continuously absent on sick leave for more than 12 months, with the exception of absence due to pulmonary tuberculosis when the period of sick leave will be extended to 18 months; (c) a medical certificate has been given which shows that the teacher has become permanently incapable through infirmity of mind or body of serving efficiently as a teacher in contributory service; (d) unless the teacher is entitled to allowances equivalent to at least half pay, disregarding any deduction or refund provided for by the terms of his employment.

LEAs have arrangements for making up pay during periods of absence, but this does not include benefit under the National Insurance Scheme. Although there may be local variations, the position generally is that nationally teachers are granted periods of absence on full pay which increase up to a maximum according to the length of service. However, as all employers come within the terms of the National Insurance Scheme, periods of absence in excess of three days usually attract sickness benefit under that scheme, with the result that the LEA deducts the benefit receivable from the teacher's pay. Where, however, a teacher has exhausted entitlement to full pay, then a period of half pay follows, but during this period it is not usual to deduct the benefit receivable from the National Insurance Scheme.

It should be noted that the only people who have some option under the National Insurance arrangements are married women who may, if they so choose, pay the industrial injuries contribution weekly only. If they limit their contribution in this way they are still subject to the deduction in pay from the LEA, but they are not eligible to receive benefit from the National Insurance Scheme and so to that extent their pay is reduced. Such reductions also include the earnings related benefits (*q.v.*) with the result that, according to the salary received, up to £10 2s. could be deducted weekly from the pay of a married woman who has elected to pay only the industrial injuries contribution apart from the compulsory graduated contribution.

SEB

Sierra Leone, Education in 1965 statistics: 828 primary schools (enrolment 135,000); 51 secondary schools (enrolment 13,550); seven teacher training colleges (enrolment 700). There are two university colleges.

The country's population was approximately 2¼ million in 1965.

Silk screen printing Most schools have a fabric printing room or a part of the art department which is used for this craft. As well as batik, tie dyeing and lino block printing, silk screen printing is now widely used as a craft.

Silk screening is a stencil method of printing whereby dye, or colour, in a fairly fluid state, is forced through silk (or organdie) mesh with a squeegee, on to material or paper or whatever is being treated. It is an ideal subject for school use, as it requires very little equipment, a large table for printing, covered with rubber or another waterproof material, strong simple frames which are easily built, gas ring and saucepans for mixing the dyes and plenty of space for drying the fabrics.

Children of all ranges of ability can achieve successful results using this method as it lends itself equally well to very simple printing in single colours for table mats, scarves, toys, etc., or for more complicated repeat patterns in several colours for fabric lengths. The children are usually organised into groups, according to experience and ability, with several working on one project at once. It is a great advantage for them to have the co-operation of the needlework department to help make up the work produced.

Screen printing is also a very efficient method of printing posters and programmes for school events.

FURTHER READING
Will Clemence. *Screen Process Printing*, Blandford Press, 1959.
Tony Kinsey. *Introducing Screen Printing*, Batsford, 1967.
Nora Proud. *Introducing Textile Printing*, Batsford, 1968.
Joy Wilcox. *Printed Rag Toys*, Batsford, 1967.

EM

Simplified Spelling Society For more than a hundred years the greatest authorities on language, from A. J. Ellis and Henry Sweet to Gilbert Murray and Daniel Jones, have advocated the reform of our spelling.

The Simplified Spelling Society was founded in 1908 by a group of scholars under the chairmanship of Professor W. W. Skeat, author of *Principles of English Etymology* and the *Etymological English Dictionary*. After appropriate research—much of it by Professor Walter Ripman and William Archer—the Society published its recommendations in *New Spelling*: the fifth edition was produced in 1940 by a committee of experts under the chairmanship of Professor Gilbert Murray, and the sixth edition of 1948 was revised by Professor Daniel Jones (now president of the Society) and Professor Harold Orton.

Members believe that experiments in Britain and America have fully proved the case for spelling reform, and that reform will not only satisfy eminent scholars but will also result in better education for children of all levels of ability. The Society's chief work now is to publicise the facts about spelling and to spread a knowledge of the advantages that reform would bring.

48 Dumpton Park Dr., Broadstairs, Kent.

Simultaneous system *See* **Teacher education in England and Wales**

Singapore, Education in In the Republic of Singapore, every child is entitled to six years free primary education in the language medium of instruction of his parents' choice. Pupils of Malay descent are also provided with free education up to university level. Although attendance is not compulsory, in the city of Singapore 98% of the school age group are in school. In 1966 the number of primary and secondary school pupils numbered 502,987, of whom 292,652 were in English-medium schools, 172,224 in Chinese-medium schools, 36,351 in Malay-medium schools and

1,760 in Tamil-medium schools. Of this total of 502,987, 370,889 were receiving primary education; 115,432 were receiving secondary education; and 16,656 were following technical, vocational and commercial courses. State schools numbered 257, state-aided 269 and independent 75.

An unusual feature of the Singapore system is the integrated school; there are 76 such schools accommodating 115,906 pupils, and in them pupils of two or three language streams study in the same building under a single administration. The Republic has one teacher training college of 6,000 students, of whom 4,827 are full-time and the remainder on in-service and 'national language' courses. A second training college is planned under the 1966–70 Five Year Development Plan.

Singapore University with 3,012 students has faculties in arts, science, social science, pharmacy, dentistry, law, medicine and education. The Nanyang University in Singapore, with 1,851 students, has arts, science and commerce departments; and Singapore Polytechnic, with 2,642 students, provides diploma courses in engineering, architecture and building, accountancy, and rubber and plastics technology. The Ngee Ann College is a private institution for higher education with seven departments and an enrolment of 852 in 1966.

The Singapore Adult Education Board provides courses at school certificate and higher school certificate level, and literacy and language courses in the four official languages. In 1967 the Hai Sing Institute, a vocational training school for women, opened with an enrolment of 200, offering courses in secretarial practice, stenography and clerical work, retail selling and tailoring.

The total population of the Republic was nearly two million in 1966.

Sir Ernest Cassel Educational Trust Founded by Sir Ernest Cassel in 1919, the Trust is devoted to aiding adult education and modern language research abroad and making Edwina Mountbatten Awards to Commonwealth students taking higher education courses in the UK. Hardship in the final stages of their courses must be proved by these students to satisfy the requirements of the trustees.

Sec.: Professor David Hardman, 21 Hassocks Rd, Hurstpierpoint, Sussex.

SISTERS As part of a programme of expansion in higher education, the Robbins Report (*q.v.*) recommended the setting up of five new Special Institutions for Scientific and Technological Research (SISTERS), each with 4,000 students. This recommendation has not been implemented.

Sixth form This is the name customarily given to that part of a secondary school which is concerned with work undertaken after O Level GCE, usually in preparation for A level. Most pupils stay two years in the sixth; a few stay three; some only one. The sixth is normally organised in separate lower and upper forms. Because of the nature of its work it was until recently virtually confined to maintained and direct grant grammar schools and independent schools. The possession of a sixth form was, and largely still is, their common distinguishing feature as against modern schools. The changes brought about by the introduction of comprehensive schools are described at the end of this article.

The curriculum of most sixth forms has undergone little change for well over a generation. Its main mark is specialisation, the study in relative depth of three subjects instead of the seven to nine subjects which have been taken up to O level. These three subjects occupy between two-thirds and three-quarters of the working time of most sixth-form pupils and a higher proportion of their serious study, since out of the balance has to come physical education and, where this is provided, the practice of a craft or an art. The subjects studied are not only reduced in number; they are concentrated in compass. The most common group is made up of mathematics, physics and chemistry. On the arts side there is no single grouping which is as prominent since the main subjects—English, history, geography, French, German and Latin—are found in varying combinations. It is, however, the exception for one of them to be found in a group with mathematics or a science. The most common exception, and one of long standing, is biology with two arts subjects for girls; while recently mathematics is beginning to occur fairly frequently in combination with two arts subjects.

The lopsidedness of sixth-form studies is characteristically, and almost exclusively, English. It is open to serious objection, but no solution has been found which would not jeopardise the self-directed intensity of effort which is one of the virtues of good sixth-form work. During these two years, boys and girls are learning to work on their own in private study or experimental work in the advanced school laboratory. Too broad a curriculum at the age of 17 is likely to go against the grain of perhaps the majority of clever boys and girls. The introduction of general courses outside the specialist work has had distinct but limited success (*see* **General studies**).

The biggest single influence on the sixth-form curriculum, however, has been and still is the requirements of university departments. This directly determines for many pupils not only the standards to be achieved but also the range of subjects. It indirectly decides the curriculum pattern of work for other pupils, since there is only a limited freedom of manoeuvre in making a school time-table.

There has been one marked change since the war in the near-disappearance from grammar schools of the special one-year courses which were designed to meet the needs of girls who were going to teachers' training colleges, as colleges of education were then called, or to become nurses. For some years the pressure to select girls with A level passes has been growing, and this has now led in the majority of schools to a common curriculum for university and college of education candidates.

The revolutionary changes since the second world war have been not in the curriculum, but in the size and composition of sixth forms. In the leading independent and direct grant schools it had long been the custom for the great majority of pupils to enter the sixth form, but in the maintained grammar schools the proportion soon after the end of the war was only a quarter. There has been a marked levelling-up, and the proportion over the whole country is now about half. This has been largely the result of two converging influences. On the one hand parents have wanted their children to stay longer at school, partly because of the differential advantage that this gives in terms of employment. On the other hand occupations, such as accountancy and engineering, which used to recruit largely at 16, now find that they can maintain the quality of their recruits only if they take them in at 18 with A level behind them. In consequence, the character of the sixth form itself is changing. It used to be largely made up of boys and girls who were preparing for some form of full-time higher education. To-day it contains a large group who are going straight into employment, though normally of a kind which expects or provides further study. Another consequence of the increasing proportion of pupils who enter the sixth form is that it has become much more widely representative of all social classes than it used to be.

The introduction of comprehensive schools has brought a new set of sixth-form problems. These schools normally have a relatively small number of sixth-form pupils who are doing just what they would have done in a grammar school sixth form, and doing it probably just as well. These academic sixth-formers are probably as high a proportion of all the school's pupils of 'grammar school ability' as in any other school, but inevitably they are a much smaller fraction of the comprehensive school's whole intake. Their total number may be uneconomically low, just as most pre-war sixth form numbers were, but they are without the same potential for growth. Furthermore, whereas before the war highly qualified teachers were easy to recruit, they are now so scarce that it is difficult to justify their being employed in situations where there are not sufficient pupils of high academic calibre to make up economically sized teaching groups.

If a wider definition of sixth form is adopted so that all pupils in their sixth or subsequent year of secondary education are reckoned sixth-formers, then there is a whole new and still largely unexplored field of work opening in comprehensive schools. There are everywhere considerable numbers of such pupils who at present are either attempting to secure one A level pass, to get one or two additional O levels or to take more subjects in the CSE. Many have a programme of largely technical work in commerce or some form of craft. It is clear that the right permanent patterns of work have not yet been found for them, though interesting experiments abound. There is an equally serious problem in finding time to bring such diverse elements as university candidates and non-academic sixth-formers into a genuine working partnership.

DGOA

Sixth-form college This term has been used in the UK to describe a proposed separate educational institution for young people above the age of compulsory school education and below the age for university entrance (i.e., between 15 or 16 and 18). It came into educational discussion in the early 1960s when it was put forward as part of the educational development plan for the borough of Croydon through the advocacy of the then Chief Education Officer, Wearing King.

Two factors led to its attractiveness from an administrator's point of view. First there was and still is a marked trend for more and more young people voluntarily to continue in full-time education after the period of compulsory attendance; and secondly there would still not be enough of these, nor enough specialised staff to deal with a large range of specialised studies, for every general secondary school to grow its own upper secondary school or sixth form. It therefore seemed sensible to concentrate resources in a few well-staffed and well-equipped places.

More important, however, was the increasing realisation that young people of this age are often disenchanted with schools (and their rules, necessarily made for younger children) and feel themselves to be young adults rather than boys and girls. Strong objection has been made by headmasters and headmistresses of academic secondary schools already having a sixth form. They maintain that this is important in running their schools and that many of their teaching staff would not wish to be in schools that offered them no opportunity of teaching in an upper school. Nevertheless the idea has proved attractive to a number of LEAs. These were all asked during 1966/67 to submit plans for the reorganisation of their secondary education and by March 1967 25 authorities had included such sixth-form colleges in their schemes, with 33 colleges in all.

The sixth-form college has sometimes been thought of as a place for the 'academic' young person following the comprehensive secondary school up to the age of 15 or 16. The term 'junior college' has sometimes been used to described an institution for all young people of these ages staying on in full-time education (this is not a happy use of the term for it echoes the American junior college which receives students later, at the age of university entry). But increasingly the conception of the sixth-form college under that name has been of an institution for all who wish to stay on in formal full-time education between these ages. Some education authorities have preferred to bring into a school with an existing sixth form those who wish to stay on from schools without one, but this proposal is to be distinguished from the sixth-form college proper, whose essential idea is of an intermediate institution between school and the institutions of higher education.

HLE

Size of schools There is a gradual and proper increase in the size of school a child goes to as he grows older. If he starts in a nursery school before the age of five he is unlikely to have more than 50 other children with him, and quite likely not to have more than half that number. If his next school is a separate infants' school it is likely to have between 100 and 200 children or perhaps between 200 and 300. Nearly four-fifths of all infants' schools are of this size. If he goes to a combined primary school, taking all children from five to 11, he is likely to be in a smaller school—half of such schools have fewer than a hundred pupils. Junior schools, for children from seven to 11, tend to be much bigger than combined schools and rather bigger than infants'. Even so, only about one-seventh have more than 400 pupils.

There is no compelling educational reason why any primary school should have more than one class for each year of school life. There is no difference between what one child and another has to learn at this stage. Each has to cover the same ground; all of it is necessary. The class, then, can be a self-contained unit: and, on the whole, the class teacher can be responsible for all the work of her pupils. Two factors only have made for larger schools. First, schools need halls as well as classrooms, and it is uneconomic to provide big enough halls for very small schools. Secondly, it has been widely held that children make better progress if they are taught only with other children of roughly the same ability (*see* **Streaming**). This is impossible unless there is more than one class per year. But this educational reason for larger primary schools is less commonly believed than a short time ago. On the other hand the introduction of new subjects into the upper part of junior schools—French, for instance—will make some specialisation among teachers necessary, and this may involve rather bigger primary schools than one-class-thick. But they can still be small.

Secondary schools are necessarily bigger than primary schools because different boys and girls need to learn different subjects, and because the teachers can no longer be competent to teach everything in the school curriculum. History, for instance, needs to be taught by somebody who has made a special study of history, but a one-form-thick secondary school would not give him enough to do. Secondary schools are bigger to-day than they were a few years ago for two reasons. First, boys and girls stay longer at school. A school which takes in a hundred new pupils each year may well find its total numbers up by over 50 simply for this reason. The raising of the minimum school leaving age by a year may well add another hundred, 150 all told, to its original size. The second reason why secondary schools are bigger to-day and still growing is the trend towards comprehensive education. This means that more different subjects have to be taught, and this in turn means that the number of pupils per year must be increased so that the additional specialist equipment and specialist teachers may be economically, and not extravagantly, used. The trend towards comprehensive co-educational schools accentuates this need for large numbers, since boys and girls have different needs in craft subjects.

There is a wide range of size in all types of secondary schools. It is reasonable, however, to think of a modern school as a school of between 400 and 500 pupils, of a grammar school as having about 600 pupils and a comprehensive school as about 1,200 to 1,500 strong—some are bigger. Experiments are being tried to keep this size down by limiting the age range in one way or another—by providing separate sixth form colleges (*q.v.*), by raising the age of transfer from primary schools or by dividing the schools horizontally halfway through the secondary course.

DGOA

Ski-ing Until recent years, ski-ing was regarded as a sport for those who could afford to visit winter-sports resorts in Switzerland, Italy and Austria. There were no facilities in the UK available to the general public, much less to young people in schools.

Today the situation has changed. The change has been brought about largely by the increase in school travel abroad; by the development of facilities in the UK—mainly in Scotland, which to schools north of Lancashire and Yorkshire has brought the sport within a relatively short travelling distance; by the training courses run in the UK and abroad by the Central Council of Physical Recreation (*q.v.*), which has introduced the sport to many teachers and provided a nucleus of enthusiasts capable of giving basic instruction; and by the provision of artificial ski-training slopes at various centres in the country. The provision of artificial slopes is increasing, and it

may well be possible soon for children from all schools to receive basic training at a convenient local centre during their normal PE period, much as they now attend swimming baths. Even with present limited facilities, many schools include ski-ing among their wider PE activities.

Central Council of Physical Recreation, 26-29 Park Cres., London, W1.

Ski Club of Great Britain, 118 Eaton Sq., London, SW1.

Scottish Ski Club, 147 Bath St, Glasgow, C2.

JE

Skinner, B. F. (b. 1904) A professor of psychology at Harvard, Skinner set out from 1953 to remedy 'the built-in inefficiency of the ordinary classroom', and was probably more influential than any other pioneer of programmed learning in drawing attention to the need to break the study of a subject down into a number of linear steps to encourage the learner following from each step.

See also **Programmed learning**

Sleep-learning Predicted by H. Gernsback in his novel *Ralph 124 C 41+* and featuring in Aldous Huxley's *Brave New World*, sleep-learning or hypnopaedia is in the state of experimental exploration. Its theory rests upon the findings that the human brain is capable of absorbing and registering information during the initial stages of sleep. Soviet, US, British and Czechoslovak psychologists and physiologists largely agree that it is possible to utilise the initial stages of sleep to memorise verbal information. Latent knowledge acquired this way may support daytime learning.

Transfer of training, in which preliminary learning during the hypnopaedic training session prepares the mind for relearning of the same material and learning of fresh but related material in the classroom, accords with Ebbinghaus's basic principles of *original learning* and *relearning*. Night lessons are presented at the periods of 'falling asleep' and 'emerging from sleep', and require timing and programming. Sleep-learning does not replace daytime study but the *distributed learning* (i.e. learning periods interspersed with rest periods) it provides may help to speed up the learning process.

The variables involved in sleep-learning are complex, and the educational possibilities of the process have not yet been evaluated. Material that is learned by rote is the most suitable content of sleep-lessons. Vocabulary of foreign language courses, essential facts in science or arts subjects may be memorised to various levels of efficiency. O-level audio-aids have been produced in the UK that are also suitable for the requirements of the sleep-learning method.

In the present state of knowledge caution is still necessary and professional advice recommended before sleep-learning is practised.

FURTHER READING
A. L. Bliznitchenko. *The Presentation and Consolidation of Information During Natural Sleep* (USSR Academy of Sciences, Kiev, 1966), Sleep-Learning Association, London, 1968.
F. Rubin. *Current Research in Hypnopaedia*, Macdonald, 1968.

FR

Sleep-learning Association An organisation founded in 1964 for the initiation of research into hypnopaedia and with the aim of establishing the technique as a supplementary aid to education. The Association is equipped to undertake joint ventures with educational institutions.

14 Belsize Cres., London, NW3.

Publication: *Journal of the Sleep-learning Association* (quarterly).

Slides *See* **Visual aids** *and* **Film in education**

Slow learning children *See* **Educationally subnormal children**

Sloyd A method of handicraft training first worked out by Uno Cygnaeus, a Finn, and made known outside Scandinavia at the end of the 19th century through the courses for foreign teachers run by a Swede, Otto Salomon, 'sloyd' was intended to provide a core activity and experience for the whole of education. It influenced the character of woodwork teaching in a number of British schools with a progressive outlook, and was an element in that general attack on the over-academic curriculum that led to the requirement of the 1918 Education Act that practical work should be part of the curriculum of all elementary schools.

Smoking amongst schoolchildren For obvious reasons it is impossible to give an exact estimate of the number of schoolchildren who smoke. It is certain, however, that regular smoking out of school hours is common practice; that illicit smoking takes place inside many secondary schools; that many new entrants to secondary schools have already acquired the smoking habit—and even the smoker's cough; and that chain smoking has been known in a five-year old.

Smoking is not only a socially acceptable habit, but is also one that is socially encouraged. Clearly, children whose parents smoke are more likely to smoke themselves. The habit spreads readily among friends. Apart from this spread from person to person, there is a constant pressure to smoke (to which children like the rest of the population are vulnerable) through advertisements.

Lung cancer, strokes, heart-attacks, pneumonia, bronchitis and stomach ulcers are all increased by the smoking of tobacco. The danger is clear, and an attack has been launched on the habit of smoking among children. Mobile vans have been taken to schools by health education teams, but questionnaires given to children before such visits, and again one year afterwards, have shown that sporadic efforts of this kind fail to influence attitudes to smoking.

It seems that any really effective attack must start from the observation that it is far easier for someone to abstain from smoking altogether than to abandon the habit once it has been acquired. It is therefore important that systematic and persistent approaches be made to children, from the primary school onwards, to dissuade them from ever smoking their first cigarette. In the junior school, anti-smoking propoganda should be simple and direct. In the secondary school it should be linked to an understanding of the stresses that smoking imposes on health, and of the dangers that are peculiar to an affluent society. The reasons for smoking, the problems of tension and anxiety, and the social role of the habit should be discussed and related to the general problems of an advanced industrial community. Above all, teachers, doctors, youth workers and parents should help to set new standards by never smoking in front of young people.

SL

Soccer *See* **Association football**

Social Biology Council, British The Council was set up in 1914 to promote and encourage the teaching of human biology as a cultural and practical subject, and to preserve and strengthen the family as the basic social unit.

69 Eccleston Sq., London, SW1.

Social class and education Since the second world war, much sociological study has been concentrated upon the relationship between social class and education. This, undoubtedly, has been because of the moral and political insistence (deeply and generally felt) upon observing the principles of social justice in the creation and maintenance of the welfare state. For a century or more the provision of educational opportunity (*q.v.*) for all children in society had gradually come to be regarded as an essential social service. But since the war the emphasis has been placed upon the achievement of equality of opportunity.

Equality itself has long been maintained as a principle of social justice. This has not meant that all men are in fact equal (which is clearly untrue) but only that all men, as persons and citizens, have a right to equal consideration in the treatment of their claims. This is especially so because individuals are usually not responsible for, or to blame for, many of the differences of their nature (whether they are strong or puny, intelligent or mentally defective, born into wealthy or into destitute families, etc.). But equal consideration does not necessarily imply equal treatment. It would be unjust and absurd to educate a mentally defective and a highly intelligent child in the same way. Equality, therefore, does not mean equal and uniform treatment. What it means essentially is that the treatment of the claims upon society of individuals should not be arbitrary, but that it should, after equal and impartial consideration of relevant factors, be appropriate and equal for all individuals who share a like condition.

The principle of equality in education, as in social justice generally, has thus come to be emphasised in the form of 'equality of opportunity'. Children should have equal opportunity to demonstrate their intelligence, aptitudes, potentialities (which might otherwise be distorted or hidden by social differences) so that they can then enjoy the most appropriate educational provisions.

However, this is far easier said than done because of the subtlety and intractability of many social differences. And the most conspicuous focus of these differences is the marked division in society between social classes. Those members of the community who perform the more demanding roles and occupations; who have to exercise power, authority, responsibility; who enjoy considerable material possessions and high incomes; who have received a high level of education and training (together with an experience of all the traditions which such a background entails) are quite conspicuously marked off, both in social intercourse and in their own consciousness, from, for example, relatively unskilled workers who possess no authority and little responsibility, who are relatively poor and insecure, and whose families have a social and educational background quite lacking in distinction. And they clearly enjoy far greater educational opportunities. The gradations of class and status in modern society are, of course, not as simple as this two-fold picture suggests, but though more complex the distinctions of class are still sharp and telling in human relationships.

Class differences in educational opportunity are not just a matter of unequal economic resources. It is not only that some have the money to pay for private education whilst others do not. Social classes are the embodiment of very distinctive styles of life, values, patterns of expectations and attitudes, habits of mind and behaviour, which differentiate people in a stratified way throughout society and are very difficult to eliminate. Thus, even when educational opportunity is provided 'equally' by the administrative apparatus of the state—by means of a systematic provision of schools, grants, etc., according to the merit shown in formal examinations—children still benefit unequally from it, and make unequal use of it, because of the strongly continuing power of these class differences. Even in the most basic qualities of mind—the forming of concepts, ideas, attitudes, and the vocabularies in which these are couched

—children are equipped differently from the very beginning of their lives by their class background.

Middle-class children grow up with the expectation of a long-continuing pattern of education as a normal element of childhood, youth and growth towards adulthood and their preparation for a certain level of life and work, whereas working-class children lack this. Middle-class homes usually enjoy, also, an articulate background of information and discussion, and a wide range of experience of many aspects of life and society, whereas many working-class homes are localised, limited, and have appropriate sentiments, values and loyalties. Differences of this kind lead to fundamental differences in the mind, personality and approach to life of individuals, and this must affect their attitudes and approaches to education. Middle-class parents, too, will know more about the educational system. They will be more knowledgeable in trying to ensure that their children get the best they possibly can from it. They will encourage their children and try to equip them for educational advancement and fulfilment by giving them help and good conditions of study at home, visits abroad, etc. Working-class parents, on the other hand, are often groping tentatively in a situation they do not fully know or understand.

Social class therefore remains a very telling factor in the allocation of educational opportunity. It remains a powerful determinant both because the more privileged classes can still buy a private education for their children which is different from and still considered superior to that provided by the state, and because the many qualitative differences in class background make for inequalities even within the public system of education whose organisational and financial structure seeks to embody an equality of provision according to equality of opportunity. The problematical and

701

X*

perplexing thing here is that the continued differences of educational opportunity in a society whose ostensible aim is equality of opportunity serve to perpetuate, if not to sharpen and intensify, the differences of class and status. It is in fact more difficult to change society in accordance with our desired ends than is commonly thought, and this problem is likely to exercise us for some time hence.

FURTHER READING

B. Bernstein. 'Social Class and Linguistic Development', *Education, Economy and Society*, Free Press of Glencoe, New York, 1961.

J. W. B. Douglas. *The Home and the School*, MacGibbon and Kee, 1964.

J. E. Floud, A. H. Halsey and F. M. Martin. *Social Class and Educational Opportunity*, Heinemann, 1956.

D. V. Glass (Ed.). *Social Mobility in Britain*, Routledge and Kegan Paul, 1954.

A. H. Halsey et al. *Education, Economy and Society*, Free Press of Glencoe, New York, 1961.

RF

Social Democratic Teachers, International Union of *See* **Socialist Educational Association**

Social Research, Centre for Applied *See* **Tavistock Institute of Human Relations**

Social Science Research Council Set up in 1965, the Social Science Research Council awards grants for post-graduate research into ten subjects, including economics, economic history, human geography, sociology, and town and country planning.

Social Sciences, Association for the Teaching of The Association exists to promote and encourage the teaching of the social sciences at all levels of education. Teachers and student teachers describe and assess methods of teaching appropriate to various age groups; this interchange of ideas takes place by correspondence, through the *Bulletin* published by the Association and at day, week-end and other resi-

dential conferences. Work schemes and other materials are being produced and made available to members. At present most meetings are London-based, but branches are developing in other parts of the country. Membership is open to individuals, schools, colleges and other organisations, and to student teachers.

Hon. Sec.: 69 Cuckoo Hill Rd, Pinner, Middlesex.

Social sciences, Teaching of The social sciences are still largely non-school subjects, but there are vigorous movements to discover an interpretation of these disciplines meaningful both for teachers in training and for pupils at school.

At degree level, both internally and in the regional technical colleges, the social sciences are taught to increasing numbers of undergraduates; the academic approach to sociology, economics, anthropology and political science is modified in the more applied courses of social administration. Industrial applications are developed in business administration degrees, while case-work skills are taught chiefly in diploma courses. Post-graduates are given specific help in developing methods for teaching some of these subjects in secondary and further education and for counselling on educational and social problems of schoolchildren (*See* **Guidance and counselling**).

Colleges of education teach the social sciences in three contexts. The sociology of education (*q.v.*) provides part of the professional background of the teacher, exploring the relationship of child, family and school and the extent and significance of social mobility. The disciplines are also taught as 'main' or academic courses, whereas the subjects tend to overlap when developed in 'method' courses; experience with in-service courses for teachers is extending such developments to work with immigrant children. Finally the social sciences are taking a substantial part in the BEd degrees that involve teachers in a fourth year at college.

Colleges of further education are meeting a growing demand for courses in economics and sociology to GCE A level and for similar options in the National Diploma in Business Studies (*q.v.*). When offered as part of day release liberal studies (*q.v.*) the teaching may be modified to encourage discussion work on 'social problems'.

Within the secondary system, economics, constitution and some sociology are taught to GCE O and A level, with CSE the main growth point. Teachers are offered an opportunity to devise unique or Mode III (*q.v.*) courses, several being nearly ready to enter candidates. Where the approach to the secondary pupil is inter-disciplinary, there is some rethinking of the traditional subject boundaries; this happens within particular schools as teachers jointly adapt to new areas of study. In environmental or local studies, historians and geographers are involved as well as available social scientists. Many teachers are shifting the focus of their courses outside the school—towards industry, commerce and community service; here the social scientist can help to systematise the classroom work, adapting and presenting information to put the studies into a wider social perspective and thus re-vitalising some courses in civics. This work is not confined to leavers and gains something where it is part of the studies of those taking public examinations.

Publishers are responding to the demand thus created, while teachers are working out adaptations of existing teaching methods. 'Role playing' gives experience in mock social situations where students take the role of customer and assistant, social survey interviewer or supervisor dealing with a regular latecomer; the important part of the exercise lies in the critical assessment of the relationships revealed. Younger pupils can act out their 'stereotypes' of foremen or personnel officers. 'Case studies' give life to generalisations as when considering the expansion of a particular firm; completing unfinished studies can reveal the students' awareness of social institutions. Many reading lists and study schemes are published by teachers' organisations and examining boards.

FURTHER READING
Annual Report, Universities Central Council for Admissions, London.
Compendium of University Entrance Requirements, Association of Commonwealth Universities, London.
Compendium of Advanced Courses in Technical Colleges, Technological Education, London.
Courses in Colleges and Departments of Education, Methuen, 1967.
W. Philip and R. Priest. *Social Science and Social Studies in Secondary Schools*, Longmans, 1965.

PSN

Social Service (Inc.), National Council of The central voluntary agency for the co-ordination and promotion of social services in town and country by developing co-operation among voluntary service agencies and between them and statutory authorities, the Council provides the secretariat for consultative groups of national social service agencies (e.g. National Old People's Welfare Council, National Federation of Community Associations). It is the headquarters of the Citizens' Advice Bureaux, etc., and has local counterparts in Rural Community Councils in the counties, and Councils of Social Service in large towns.

Journals: *Social Service Quarterly, The Village, The Amateur Historian*.

26 Bedford Sq., London, WC1.

Social Work, Council for Training in Established by the Health Visiting and Social Work (Training) Act 1962, the Council's main task is to promote training in such social work as is required in the health and welfare services.

The Council seeks to secure suitable facilities for training; it approves courses, and seeks to attract trainees. It is empowered to provide courses for further training, and to undertake, or assist others, in research.

In 1966 there were 21 two-year courses in colleges of further education in the UK; also six emergency one-year courses, designed for existing staff, aged over 35 and with five years' experience, from local authority health and welfare services. The Council awards a certificate in social work to those successfully completing its courses.

Clifton Hse, Euston Rd, London, NW1.

Social Work Training, National Institute for The object of the Institute, set up in 1961, is to advance training, research and experiment in social work.

5 Tavistock Pl., London, WC1.

Socialist Educational Association The SEA exists to foster a socialist approach to educational issues and to promote a socialist educational system in Britain. These aims are pursued through the Association's journal, *Socialism and Education*, and in pamphlets, including *Guide to Comprehensive Education*, *The Public Schools* and *Examining at 16 Plus*.

SEA is affiliated to the Labour Party, at the annual conference of which it puts forward resolutions on educational matters. It also organises public meetings. A growing number of branches throughout the country initiate policy discussion and help to foster the Association's aims at local government level.

Internationally SEA is a member of the International Union of Social Democratic Teachers, and sends a delegation to the Union's annual conference. Membership is open to all who are eligible for membership of the Labour Party. Practising, retired and trainee teachers, lecturers in univer-

sities and colleges of education, members of local education committees, school governors and managers, educational administrators and Members of Parliament may become full members; associate membership is open to parents and all others who share the aims of SEA.

Gen. Sec.: R. G. Wallace, 11 Bessborough Gdns, London, SW1.

Society for Promoting Christian Knowledge *See* **Christian Knowledge, Society for Promoting**

'Society and the Young School Leaver' (project) *See* **Nuffield Foundation**

Sociological Association, British Set up in 1951, the Association has as its object to promote interest in sociology, to advance its study and application in the UK and to bring about contacts between workers in all relevant fields of enquiry.

Skepper Hse, 13 Endsleigh St, London, WC1.

Sociology of education Much care must be exercised when defining 'specialisms' within sociology if claims which are too pretentious are to be avoided. The appearance in prospectuses of titles such as Industrial Sociology, Political Sociology, the Sociology of Religion, the Sociology of Education, and the like, suggests that there are several different *kinds* of sociology, each with its own expertise. But there is danger in this notion. First of all—there is only *one* sociology, and any 'specialism' is, at best, only the concentration of this sociological analysis upon one specific sector of social life. But even *this* idea of specialisation has to be qualified very carefully, because—secondly—the basic assumption which is the distinguishing point of departure of sociology as a subject is that no one part of a society can be fully known and understood in isolation from all the others. A society is a system of interdependent elements of social organisation, and any one part can only be properly understood within the context of the whole. No specialism in sociology, therefore, can possibly be a study of one aspect of society alone.

'Specialisms' emerge for various reasons. Problems arise in particular areas of social organisation (e.g. the 'educational system'), detailed knowledge is desired, policies have to be formulated, so that some sociologists come to concern themselves more with this one sector of society than with others. Career pressures, too, sometimes impel sociologists (and this, of course, applies to scholars of all subjects) to concentrate their powers upon one particular area of study, and, sometimes, to inflate it into an 'academic specialism'. Also, sociologists are faced with their individual limitations and the vastness of their subject. A society is a very complex entity indeed, and it is difficult to establish knowledge about it. Sociological analysis and knowledge relies upon the cumulative contributions of many students. Meanwhile, each individual has to 'break in' to the complexity of society in some way which he feels most promising, and he tends to do this in accordance with his chief personal interest (perhaps in religion, or education, or economic organisation), or because of some strong theoretical persuasion—e.g. that economic factors, or educational, or moral, or military factors, are particularly important for explaining the set of problems with which he is concerned.

Concern about the definition of 'the sociology of education' is necessary because specialisation tends also to go to very considerable lengths even within each special field itself. One specialism can become so dominant as to appear to characterise the entire field. For example, since the second world war there has been an intense concern over the educational injustices attendant upon class privilege. As a result, studies of social stratification and educational opportunity have dominated the sociology of education, so much so that an untutored person might well think them synonymous. Education has been thought of almost exclusively as a kind of machinery for social allocation and social mobility (movement between social classes). But, of course, both education itself and the sociology of education have many important dimensions other than these.

Given these preliminary grounds for caution, we can define the sociology of education simply as follows. Sociology is the scientific study of social systems: the study of all forms of human association known to us—their nature, functions, and interconnections in various types of society. It provides an analysis of society which insists upon the interdependence of all elements of social structure (family, law, government, morality, social stratification, religion, education, economic system, etc.) in society as a whole. The sociology of education is the application of this sociological analysis in order to achieve a full knowledge of the nature of education in particular, and its place within the entirety of society.

Some distinctive and important points follow immediately upon the adoption of this sociological perspective. Firstly, education—whatever form its institutional procedures takes—is thought of broadly in terms of the social functions which it fulfils. In any society, education seeks to ensure the preservation and improvement of the social order. It consists of the transmission of those skills, knowledge, beliefs and values which are thought to be important in society, from one generation to the next. In doing this, it provides the basis for the individual's life within the community with due emphasis upon the individual's duty to the community.

Secondly, it is clear from this that education in any society must always have certain basic components, possess certain characteristics, make certain provisions. For example, education must always be:

(1) *Vocational:* providing instruction and training in all the tasks and skills (at all levels) of the social order.

(2) Centrally concerned with *selection* (of individuals for various kinds of education) and *allocation* and *recruitment* (of individuals to those tasks in society for which they appear best fitted and best trained).

(3) *Moral* and *cultural:* seeking to establish the allegiance of the young to those values, ideals, ends of endeavour, which are thought to be of crucial importance.

(4) *Differential* and *specialist:* providing education and instruction of different levels appropriate both to different levels of ability and to different ends (e.g. a nurse, a school-teacher, a judge). No educational system can be equal and uniform for all.

(5) *General:* providing a basis of knowledge and judgment for life in society, for citizenship, and for personal enquiry and fulfilment as a whole, in addition to a training in special skills.

(6) Concerned with *study and research* if society's achievements and heritage of knowledge and skills are to be preserved, appreciated, understood, and possibly improved.

Thirdly, it is at once clear that education in society goes far beyond what we ordinarily think of as 'educational institutions' proper. Education is not one particular aspect of society provided by one specific set of institutions (the 'educational system'). It is an implicit and an explicit element of *every* institution in society. Education interpenetrates the entire social order. The family, for example, is an educative group of the greatest importance, inculcating certain habits of feeling, thinking, and behaving in children,

before, during and after their experience in school. Industrial firms train apprentices in certain skills and demand certain values, regulations and backgrounds of knowledge. Social classes with their differing 'styles of life' have important educative influences. Similarly, trade unions, professional associations, political parties, military organisations, religions, all have their powerful educational influence in society. The educational aspects of all the forms of mass-communication—press, radio, TV—are so obvious, so widespread, and of such tremendous power, as scarcely to need mention.

These functions of education in society can, of course, be fulfilled in many ways, on the basis of very different criteria, and with very different institutional frameworks. Much is now known about the history of education in many societies, and social anthropology has provided many good descriptive accounts of education in the simpler, non-literate societies. The grounds for detailed comparative study are therefore already quite substantial, and a systematic coverage of analysis and certain broad generalisations are already established.

A fourth point worth mentioning, though without elaboration, is that it is also clear at once that for the individual as well as for society, education is something going far beyond educational institutions as such. Education is not something provided only by the 'educational system' during a limited, and very early, period of life. Nor is it only one aspect of personal experience and behaviour. Every aspect of a person's social experience and behaviour, and at all ages, has its educational impact and influence. A person's life is a long sequence of aging attended by a sequence of social situations (the nature of which will depend upon the society in which he lives), each bringing its own demands, promises and constraints. 'Learning to live' is therefore a lifetime's business, and does not cease until death. The so-called 'socialisation' of the individual is not something over and done with by school leaving age.

The sociology of education, in its full dimensions, is therefore not a study only of educational institutions proper, but also of the educational aspects of all elements of society, and of all relevant aspects of the experience and behaviour of individuals within it. Again, it can be seen that, strictly speaking, it is part of sociological analysis as a whole.

In primitive societies, for example, there are no special educational institutions as such. Education is an aspect of all the other elements of social structure: family and kinship relationships, age-sets, occupational groupings, procedures of custom, law, government, and of religion and its ritual practices, etc. Educational institutions proper emerge in societies which are larger in scale and more complex in organisation. For example in the large societies resting upon settled agriculture, temple schools emerged. The need for written records, careful calculation, careful contracts of transactions, gave rise to the new skills of literacy and numeracy and clerks and administrators had to be trained for these tasks in society. The knowledge available of widely differing educational systems is, of course, very detailed indeed, but the emphasis in modern scholarship is to concentrate upon the distinctive characteristics of modern industrial societies. Strictly speaking, 'educational systems'—systems of specialised educational institutions serving the entire population of society—are a distinctive outcome of modern industrialisation.

Scientific knowledge and its application in industrial technology, and the growing specialisation of industrial techniques, have made necessary a working population capable of literacy and skilled work. Without a modicum of knowledge and skill, industrial society as we now know it simply could not function. The same complex techniques with their attendant complexity of social organisation also force other dilemmas upon society which the educational system has to try to resolve. For example, both specialist and general education are necessary if society is to function efficiently and if individuals are to live meaningful and satisfying lives within it. Also both scientific and wider cultural elements of education are desirable. Carefully devised syllabuses attempt to achieve all these ends, but with great difficulty. But also—with greater literacy, articulation, education, economic power and political representation—the 'working classes' of industrial societies have increasingly demanded equality of rights, and, in particular, equality of educational opportunity for their children. This has given rise to great issues of social justice in education, and to a continual reform of educational institutions: from elementary education for the masses and grammar schools for the few, to primary and secondary education for all; from tripartite selection at 11-plus to comprehensive secondary education; from universities for the privileged élite to the extension of grants seeking to open university education to all who deserve it, and so on.

When studying education in contemporary industrial societies, the sociologist of education has therefore to devote a good deal of attention to the 'educational system' itself, because qualitatively new problems have arisen within this new organisation itself, and also with regard to its relationships with other institutions—the state, the economy, etc. The educational system itself has become extremely complicated. Much study is required fully to understand the public sector of education, the differing aspects of the private sector in education, the nature of the different kinds of schools, colleges, universities and other educational establishments, and the relationships between them all. Also government officials, educational administrators, school-teachers and others are involved in complicated professional relationships with each other, all of which are attended by economic problems, career problems and the like. All this requires much study in addition to, though still within the context of, the wider aspects of education in society which, of course, still exist, and still have their importance.

It is impossible to indicate adequately the wide range of work which has been undertaken in the sociology of education during the past twenty years or so. Among aspects so far studied are social class and educational opportunity (Floud, Halsey, Banks— see *Further reading* for these and other writers mentioned below), tripartism versus the comprehensive school (Pedley), class influences upon vocabulary development and concept formation, and the consequences for educational opportunity (Bernstein, *q.v.*; J. W. B. Douglas), education and its relation to specific areas of social organisation and behaviour (e.g. Cotgrove, Williams, Himmelweit, Whyte, Thrasher), the school as a social group and the functions of teachers in society (Oeser, Floud, Wilson, Tropp).

The sociology of education is of considerable importance for its practical implications as well as for its academic interest. Educational policies are continually being formulated to meet supposed social and individual needs, and it is a matter of urgency that these should rest upon the most reliable knowledge possible. Also, it is perfectly clear that education is one of the most important agencies in social creativity. In trying to change and improve our societies, it is not enough simply to institute new administrative frameworks and procedures. Individuals must appreciate their worth and support them in their lives and actions, and for this education is required. The sociology of education has already made a substantial contribution, and has changed many perspectives of thought; but, if properly conceived and thoroughly developed, it can be a subject of the greatest importance in contributing to the solution of the problems of modern scientific and technological society, and ensuring that, in the teeth of all these impersonal complexities, all that is best for the life and fulfilment of the individual will be preserved and furthered.

FURTHER READING

Olive Banks. *Parity and Prestige in English Secondary Education*, Routledge and Kegan Paul, 1955.

Basil Bernstein. 'Social Class and Linguistic Development', *Education, Economy and Society: A Reader in the Sociology of Education* (Eds Jean Floud, A. H. Halsey and C. A. Anderson), Free Press of Glencoe, New York, 1962.

F. J. Brown. *Educational Sociology*, Prentice-Hall, London and New York, 1947.

S. T. Cotgrove. *Technical Education and Social Change*, Allen and Unwin, 1958.

J. W. B. Douglas. *The Home and the School*, MacGibbon and Kee, 1964.

Jean Floud. 'Trend Report on the Sociology of Education', *Current Sociology*, VII, 3, 1958. 'Teaching in an Affluent Society', *British Journal of Sociology*, XIII, 1, 1962.

Jean Floud and A. H. Halsey. *The Sociology of Education*, International Sociological Association, Oxford, 1958.

Jean Floud, A. H. Halsey and C. A. Anderson (Eds). *Education, Economy and Society: A Reader in the Sociology of Education*, Free Press of Glencoe, New York, 1962.

Elizabeth Fraser. *Home Environment and the School*, University of London Press, 1959.

Hilde T. Himmelweit. *Television and the Child*, Oxford University Press, 1958.

O. A. Oeser. *Teacher, Pupil and Task*. Tavistock Publications, 1955.

A. K. Ottaway. *Education and Society*, Routledge and Kegan Paul, 1953.

E. G. Payne. *Principles of Educational Sociology*, New York Univ. Press, New York, 1928.

Robin Pedley. *Comprehensive Education: A New Approach*, Gollancz, 1956.

Jean Piaget. *Language and Thought of the Child*, Routledge and Kegan Paul, 1926.

F. Thrasher. *The Gang. A Study of 1,313 Groups in Chicago*, Univ. of Chicago Press, 1936.

Asher Tropp. *The School Teachers*, Heinemann, 1957.
W. F. Whyte. *Street Corner Society*, Univ. of Chicago Press, 1955.
Gertrude Williams. *Recruitment to Skilled Trades*, Routledge and Kegan Paul, 1958.
Bryan Wilson. 'The Teacher's Role', *British Journal of Sociology*, XIII, 4, 1962.
Newsom Report, Plowden Report, Robbins Report, etc.

RF

Sociometry Exactly as the term implies, sociometry is concerned with the *measurement* of *social* relationships, but two aspects of this definition should perhaps be distinguished.

First, sociometry concerns itself with the detailed measurement (following upon close and meticulous observation) of the number, kinds and patterns of social relationships which are manifested among the members of small groups—factory work-groups, school classes, etc. In this sense, sociometry measures patterns of *group relationships*.

However, some research of a sociometric nature concentrates upon the preferences experienced, expressed and exercised by individuals in their group behaviour. This emphasis is rather more upon individual psychological aspects of the behaviour than upon the number and pattern of the relationships as such. It seeks the understanding of group relationships through an understanding of the preferences of individuals rather than an understanding of their experience by establishing a knowledge of their group relationships.

Both aspects are clearly of use, are not in conflict, and can be conjoined in research.

Sociometric studies can illuminate, for example, the group processes whereby leadership emerges; what kinds of leadership are found in what kinds of group; what qualities leaders in various groups appear to possess; how 'authority' and 'submission', 'conflict' and 'co-operation' come to be experienced, established and maintained in group relationships.

The scholar most influential in establishing sociometry was J. L. Moreno. He was interested in the kinds and degrees of attraction and repulsion between individuals in small groups, and wished to measure these as exactly as possible. According to him: 'Sociometry deals with the mathematical study of psychological properties of populations, the experimental technique of and the results obtained by application of quantitative methods'.

Sociometric techniques have since been developed and employed in a variety of studies. The following are a few examples.

FURTHER READING
A. Bjerstedt. *Interpretations of Sociometric Choice Status*, Munksgaard, Copenhagen, 1956.
H. M. Jennings. *Leadership and Isolation*, Longmans Green, 1950.
J. L. Moreno. *Who Shall Survive?*, Beacon House, New York, 1953.
M. L. Northway. *A Primer of Sociometry*, Univ. of Toronto Press, Toronto, 1952.
Journal:
Sociometry. Quarterly. American Sociological Association, Washington, DC.

RF

Socratic method A teaching method by which progress and understanding proceed by sustained and directed questioning, use being made of the correct element or part in each answer.

Somali Republic, Education in Elementary education is free where places are available. 1964/5 statistics: 233 elementary schools (enrolment 26,980); 26 intermediate schools (enrolment 5,961); eight secondary schools (enrolment 1,128); six teacher training colleges (enrolment 359). University Institute of Somalia at Mogadishu (723 students). Total population: approximately 2½ million.

Sonnenberg Association of England and Wales The SAEW is an association for understanding among peoples throughout the world. It is non-denominational and non-sectarian, and membership is open to all. Formed in 1955, it is affiliated to the International Sonnenberg Association (administrative offices in Brunswick), the International House (conference centre) being at Sonnenberg (Harz Mountains). Bi-lingual conferences are held at Sonnenberg, most of which have some aspect of education as their main theme. The SAEW holds its own international conference once every two years at Culham, and various meetings are arranged throughout the year. The motto of the association is: talk together; overcome prejudices; understand one another; act responsibly.

Hon. Sec.: Dr Walter Roy, 16 Honeygate, Luton, Beds.

Soulbury Committee The Committee, whose first chairman was Lord Soulbury, responsible for producing the salary scales and service conditions of inspectors, organisers and advisory officers of LEAs. The Committee produced its first report in 1947 and there have been seven further reports since then. It is similar to the Joint Negotiating Committee for Youth Leaders in that it is not mandatory and its provisions include service conditions as well as salary scales.

Like other negotiating committees, it consists of two panels with representatives on the following basis: (1) The Authorities' Panel representing County Councils Association (two), Association of Municipal Corporations (two), Association of Education Committees (two), Welsh Joint Education Committee(one) and the Hon. Secretaries of the Authorities' Panel of the Burnham Primary and Secondary Committee, ex-officio (two); (2) The Officers' Panel representing NUT (four), National Association of Inspectors and Educational Organisers (four), British Association of Organisers and Lecturers in Physical Education (two), Association of Educational Psychologists (one), National Association of LEA Youth Service Officers (one), Institutional Manage-

ment Association (one) and the Leader and Hon. Secretary of the Teachers' Panel of the Burnham Primary and Secondary Committee, ex-officio (one).

The Committee considers the salaries and service conditions of the following categories of officers: (1) General inspectors and general organisers of schools, (2) educational psychologists, (3) organisers and organising inspectors of special subjects, e.g. domestic science, handicrafts, music and PE, (4) youth service officers, (5) organisers of school meals, and makes recommendations of appropriate salary scales. The scales are not applicable to officers who are employed for only part of their time upon duties which are the concern of officers in the categories referred to above.

Soulbury Scales Salary scales and service conditions of Inspectors, Organisers and Advisory Officers of LEAs are as follows:

General Inspectors and General Organisers. Grade I £1,690 x £40(6) x £45(3) to £2,065; Grade II £2,065 x £45 x £50(7) to £2,460; Grade III £2,460 x £75(4) x £85(2) to £2,930.

Educational Psychologists. Grade I £1,630 x £35(5) x £40(3) to £1,925; Grade II £1,925 x £45 x £50(7) to £2,320; Grade III £2,320 x £75(3) x £85(3) to £2,800.

Organisers and Organising Inspectors of Special Subjects. Grade I £1,630 x £35 (5) x £40(3) to £1,925; Grade II £1,925 x £45 x £50(7) to £2,320; Grade III £2,320 x £75(4) to £2,620.

Youth Service Officers. Grade I £1,275 x £35(9) x £40 to £1,630; Grade II £1,630 x £35(5) x £40(3) to £1,925; Grade III £1,925 x £45 x £50(7) to £2,320; Grade IV £2,320 x £75(4) to £2,620.

Organisers of School Meals. Grade I £1,090 x £35(3) x £40(4) to £1,355; Grade II £1,355 x £35 x £40(6) to £1,630; Grade III £1,630 x £35(4) x £40(5) to £1,970; Grade IV £1,970 x £45(8) to £2,330.

London Allowance. The addition is at the rate of £85 per annum for the 'London Area' comprised as follows— the London Boroughs of Barking, Barnet, Bexley, Brent, Bromley, Croydon, Ealing, Enfield, Haringey, Harrow, Havering, Hillingdon, Hounslow, Kingston, Merton, Newham, Redbridge, Richmond, Sutton, Waltham Forest.

In the larger LEAs, the duties and responsibilities involved in the case of any particular officer may, in the opinion of the authority, warrant a higher scale of salary than the highest scale provided under the Report. Where in the case of a particular officer or group of officers, the authority is of the opinion that the Grade III scale (Grade IV in the case of Youth Service Officers and Organisers of School Meals) is not adequate having regard to the duties and responsibilities involved, it may pay such higher scale as it deems appropriate. An LEA may also in its discretion pay an Organiser or Organising Inspector of a Special Subject or an Educational Psychologist on the scales for General Inspectors and General Organisers.

SEB

Soulbury Scales *See* **Soulbury Committee**

South Africa, Education in Education and politics are inextricable in South Africa: the educational structure avowedly subserves the political ideology of Apartheid or separate development. Thus English and Afrikaans-speaking whites (19% of the total population of the Republic in 1961) are educated separately and, among non-whites, Coloureds (9%), Asians (3%) and Africans (68%)— and even different African tribal groups —are educated apart from one another, this on the assumption that the products must be prepared, not for living in the total context of South Africa, but for a separate and different role there, i.e. 'to serve their own communities'.

Education began in South Africa under the aegis of the church and, for non-whites, out of missionary zeal. Secular primary and secondary education for all races then developed under the jurisdiction of the provincial governments; differences were those of degree (inferior for non-whites), but not of kind, until 1953 when the Bantu Education Act was passed, based on the recommendations of the Eiselen Commission of 1951. This Act placed Bantu education (in South Africa, Africans are called 'Bantu') under the central government: that is, not under the Department of Education but under the Department of Coloured Affairs, and Indian (or Asiatic) education was transferred to the Department of Indian Affairs. Thus the provincial governments are now responsible only for the primary and secondary education of white children, but under directives from the central government. Private schools have continued, in the English-speaking white sector particularly, partly as a reflection of traditional practice in England, but also as a reaction against increased state interference: many parents have seen standards in English declining with the ascendancy of Afrikaans since the Nationalist government came to power in 1948. The state now controls over 90% of all white education, and there has been a steady increase in the number of children whose medium of instruction is Afrikaans. Separation in the medium of instruction persists, although the urban complexes contain children of both white groups living side by side.

White education Primary education for whites is divided into sub-standards and five standards, secondary education into five standards. Education for whites is compulsory from the age of seven to 16 (or until the completion of eight years exclusive of sub-standards) but may begin earlier. The onus is on parents to send their children to school and to prove their racial origin for the purpose of entry. Education in state schools is free for whites, and in the primary school textbooks and stationery are provided. Primary education is co-educational, secondary education both single-sexed and co-educational. Pre-school education is fee-paying and attendance is optional. In 1959 activity methods were introduced into white primary schools in South Africa and 'social studies', embracing man's environment and his activities in that environment, replaced geography and history and stressed self-discovery and initiative—this chiming with progressive trends in other parts of the western world. Owing to various pressures, however, social studies was discontinued in 1964 and history and geography re-instated, along with a renewed emphasis on class teaching. Recently, new syllabuses for the different 'subjects' of the primary school have been drafted in all provinces, and specific methods have even been laid down that teachers are expected to follow.

South Africa, stressing separation in all else, has had largely comprehensive white secondary education, with courses divided into academic, commercial and domestic science curricula and culminating in different certification based on different examinations. The school leaving examinations are 'group' exams: it is not possible to accumulate single subjects as can be done at English GCE O and A levels. At one and the same examination the candidate must achieve a certain standard in his six subjects in order to matriculate. The passes are graded, and a certain pass is required for entry to a university.

Higher education is not provincially controlled. The universities grew out of colleges. The Afrikaans-medium universities have always restricted their intake to whites, and of the English-medium universities, Rhodes University remains, as it has always been, for whites only, while Fort Hare has become exclusively non-white and Natal University accepts white and non-white students, but in parallel classes. The Universities of Cape Town and of the Witwatersrand (Johannesburg) were always academically integrated (though never for sports and social activities). Student bodies there have been traditionally active in the attempt to extend integration. The University Councils were always autonomous though receiving a considerable portion of their funds from the state, and they continued after 1948 to cling to academic non-segregation. But in 1959 it became a criminal offence to register at an 'open' university without prior consent from the Minister. Fort Hare was turned into a Xhosa tribal college and the government established two non-white colleges and one Indian college.

Colleges of education train white teachers for three years. University institutes of education, with responsibilities for colleges of education, do not as yet exist, and there is in fact a history of hostility between university faculties of education offering postgraduate diplomas in education and degrees in education, and the colleges which train teachers.

Adult education was always in the past particularly valuable in raising standards of literacy among non-whites, but the Bantu Education Act of 1953 reverberated in this sector too: it became illegal to operate an unregistered school. Control of this area became the responsibility of the Department of Bantu Education. University students and white housewives who ran such schools in their homes were subjected to scrutiny by the Department though it in no way subsidised them.

Bantu education 'There is no place for (the Bantu) above the levels of certain forms of labour'. This being the hypothesis behind the Bantu Education Act, it is now literally impossible for a non-white student to emerge at the end of his academic career with the same qualifications as his white counterpart.

After the passage of the Act, the church bodies controlling subsidised schools were given the choice of relinquishing their control or their government subsidy—with the result that African education is now overwhelmingly under the control of the Department of Bantu Affairs. Education is optional for Africans, and the government has acted on the advice of the Eiselen Commission that 'the Bantu should play a direct part in finding a certain proportion of the funds for their own education'. The way to expansion was to be financed through increased taxation of the poorest sector of the community. The per capita expenditure on education by the state is £75 for white children, £30 for coloured and Asian children, and for African children dropped from £9 in 1953-4 to just over £6 in 1962-3.

The schools are inadequate and overcrowded; the teacher/pupil ratio imposes double- and sometimes triple-session teaching (i.e. half schooling for the child, but a double teaching load for the teacher). Between 1954 and 1963, the number of children at school doubled, but the number of teachers increased by only one-third. The salary scales and content of Bantu education are unattractive to teachers: children are to be trained to 'serve their communities' rather than educated; fewer than half of the African teachers in 1965 were getting more than £1 per working day (their white counterparts were receiving three times as much). The content of Bantu education is as follows: up to standard six—or the end of primary education (with the aim that this should be extended up to matriculation), all education is in the vernacular and there is early specialisation, with stress on the teaching of subjects like gardening. At all levels teaching staff have to be 'politically reliable'.

There is a deliberate and declared withholding from Africans of the scientific and technological expertise necessary to control a modern industrialised economy: this is the guarantee of white supremacy. The four secondary schools in Johannesburg's African townships, for example, are quite unable to prepare students for genuine university work in science. If an African managed to emerge fitted for further study abroad, the only way he could leave the country for this purpose would be by taking an exit permit. Such an African is not given a passport, but is deprived of citizenship and the right to return to South Africa.

FURTHER READING

F. E. Auerbach. *The Power of Prejudice in South African Education: An Enquiry into History Text-books and Syllabuses in the Transvaal High Schools of South Africa,* A. A. Balkema, 1965.

Behr and MacMillan. *Education in South Africa,* J. L. van Schaik, Pretoria, 1966.

Brian Bunting. *Education in Apartheid: A South African Education Fund Pamphlet,* Christian Action.

Muriel Horrell. *A Decade of Bantu Education,* South African Institute of Race Relations, Johannesburg, 1964.

Report of the Commission on Native Education (headed by Dr. W. W. M. Eiselen), 1951.

1961 Educational Panel First Report: Education for South Africa, Witwatersrand Univ. Press, Johannesburg, 1963.

1961 Educational Panel Second Report: Education and the South African Economy, Witwatersrand Univ. Press, 1966.

LL

Spain, Education in Before 21 December 1965 state education was free, but compulsory attendance could not be enforced because of lack of schools. As part of the Economic and Social Development Plan 1964–67, attendance was made compulsory on that date and the school leaving age was raised from 12 to 14 (the age of entry remaining at six years). A continuing school building programme including the provision of flats and houses for teachers had made this advance possible.

Illiteracy is a problem in Spain, 9.6% being illiterate over the age of 10 years in 1965; this was reduced to 5.2% in 1967. There are 12 universities in Spain itself and one in the Canary Islands, all under state control except the Catholic foundation at Pamplona. University undergraduates numbered 13,105 in 1965/66. Primary pupils (six to 10 years) numbered 2,599,644 in 1964/65; secondary (11 to 14 years) 1,788,100.

Total population was approximately $31\frac{1}{2}$ million in 1965.

Spain, Institute of Founded in 1946, the Institute offers courses in the Spanish language and in Spanish culture, and the use of a library.

102 Eaton Sq., London, SW1.

Spanish and Portuguese, Association of Teachers of Amongst the Association's activities is the organisation of school competitions (throughout the UK) in lectures, verse, prose and drama.

Hon. Sec.: Miss F. M. Brunt, 17 Duke's Ave, Canon's Pk, Edgware, Middx.

Publication: *Vida Hispanica* (three times annually).

Spastic children Spasticity is a form of cerebral palsy (paralysis due to brain injury) in which the limb muscles remain in a state of spasm. Other forms of cerebral palsy are athetosis (with writhing involuntary movements) and ataxia (muscular unco-ordination). The word 'spastic' is popularly used to cover all these conditions.

Spastic children are educated either in hospitals or schools for physically handicapped children, or in special schools established by the Spastics Society (12 Park Cres., London, W1).

See also **Physically handicapped pupils**

MW

Spastics, Scottish Council for the Care of Founded in 1946, the Council provides three residential schools for children disabled by cerebral palsy. Two of these schools, Westerlea in Edinburgh and Corseford in Renfrewshire, each cater for 45 children who are classified as educable and receive primary and secondary education. The third school, in Lanark, is classified as an occupational training centre and is for 80 children who are severely physically handicapped and mentally backward. The cost of running these residential schools is met by grants from the Scottish Education Department and fees paid by sponsoring local authorities. The school curriculum includes therapeutic treatment.

Gen. Sec.: 22 Corstorphine Rd, Edinburgh, 12.

Spastics Society When the Society was formed in 1952, cerebral palsy was a condition that had suffered centuries of neglect, and all over Britain there were men, women and children with no hope of the treatment and training that might help them towards a more normal life. Swift action was essential, and in the first 15 years of its life the Society concentrated on building more than a hundred schools and centres. Many of these were pioneer projects in the field of education and training. For example, the Meldreth School, opened near Cambridge in 1966 for spastic pupils with severe mental and physical handicaps, is believed to be the first school of its kind in the world. The Thomas Delarue School in Tonbridge, Kent, is the first grammar school in Britain for spastics of normal intelligence; and the Oakwood Centre in Kelvedon, Essex, is a pioneer development providing further education, together with cultural and social studies, for young adult spastics with normal intelligence but severe physical handicaps.

The Society has six schools, an educational assessment centre and two further education centres. These are run on a national basis. There are also educational facilities at many of the Society's local centres throughout England and Wales.

After-school work training is provided on a national basis at three centres, and one of these—Sherrards at Old Welwyn, Herts—was the first training establishment in the world exclusively concerned with the industrial training of spastics. Another residential training centre will open shortly in Lancaster.

The Spastics Society has guaranteed £600,000 to maintain a Department at the University of London to give special training to teachers of spastic and other handicapped children. It has also opened Castle Priory College in Wallingford, Berks, which provides courses for the staff of the Society and other organisations, with residential training for houseparents.

12 Park Cres., London, W1.

SPCK *See* **Christian Knowledge, Society for Promoting**

Special agreement schools By special agreement, LEAs are able to undertake to contribute between a half and three-quarters of the cost of a new voluntary secondary school. In such a school, two-thirds of the governors are appointed by the voluntary body and the rest by the LEA.

Special classes These are a means of providing special education within ordinary schools for pupils who are very backward or handicapped. Ideally, a special class should, like special school classes, have smaller numbers (maximum 20) and should have a curriculum

and methods designed to meet the needs of backward pupils. The class should be in the charge of a teacher experienced in the problems presented; eventually it is hoped that special class teachers will be trained and qualified and paid extra accordingly. (Eventually also it is to be hoped that special class teachers in different schools can be linked together in some way to overcome the isolation they sometimes feel).

Special classes are not substitutes for special schools but desirable alternatives, a way of offering special education in ordinary schools, as the 1944 Act envisaged. A very large number are needed for children with milder mental and educational handicaps. Classes are being increasingly provided for maladjusted children as an alternative to special school placement. Partially sighted children are in many areas accommodated in special classes owing to their small numbers. Since 1947 there has been a continued trend to provide units in ordinary schools for partially hearing pupils so that they have the benefit of verbal and social contact with normal children.

One of the problems of special classes is age range. In the junior school, for example, it seems inadvisable to have pupils from 7 to 11 in one class and, equally, 11- and 15-year olds in the same class at the secondary stage. Another problem is ensuring continuity, so that a child who needs special education in the ordinary school can move from one special class to another as he grows older. This applies particularly in the 11-plus transition.

See also **Backwardness; Maladjusted pupils; Special education**

RG

Special education Special education as understood in Britain is education adapted to the needs of pupils who are handicapped by a disability of body or mind. By the Education Act 1944 it is the duty of each LEA to provide for these pupils. The recognised categories of handicap are: blind, partially sighted, deaf, partially hearing, delicate (including diabetic), educationally subnormal, epileptic, maladjusted, physically handicapped and speech defective.

Special educational treatment is not confined to special schools: it can be given in ordinary schools, special classes, boarding homes and hostels, hospitals, speech, hearing and child guidance clinics, or in children's and teachers' own homes. LEAs may also pay for the education and maintenance of handicapped pupils in independent schools, provided that these are recognised as suitable by the DES.

History Little public provision for the education of handicapped children was made before the end of the 19th century, but private enterprise and charitable organisations had been active for more than a century earlier. Provision for children with sensory loss (blindness and deafness) was in advance of that for the mentally and physically handicapped. Recognition of emotional handicap (maladjustment) followed much later.

The first school for the deaf was opened in Paris in 1760. In the same year, Thomas Braidwood of Edinburgh admitted a deaf boy to his private school and eventually taught him to speak. Paris also opened the first school for blind children in 1784. England's first school for the blind was established in Liverpool in 1791.

Early in the 19th century interest in mental deficiency was stimulated by Itard's attempt to educate 'the Wild Boy of Aveyron' at the Paris school for the deaf. This experience inspired the work of Edouard Seguin who in 1846 published his treatise on the education of idiots. Seguin in turn influenced Maria Montessori, whose apparatus for teaching mentally defective children is still widely used in modified form. Throughout the 19th century there were spasmodic attempts to educate

mentally defective children, usually severely subnormal, since those now described as educationally subnormal did not attract attention in a largely illiterate population.

Official provision for handicapped children did not become possible until the Education Act 1870, which introduced universal elementary education, and thereby drew attention to the many children unable to profit from instruction given in ordinary elementary schools. The London School Board very quickly made special provision for the deaf and blind (1874), but it took a little time to discover the needs of slow learners. In this, Germany had shown the way with the establishment of *Hilfsschulen* from 1876 onwards. These schools were immediately successful and were used as models when the London School Board decided to establish special schools for 'defective' children in 1892.

Leicester had opened a special class earlier in 1892, and other authorities soon followed. From 1889 onwards, a series of Royal Commissions and departmental committees collected evidence on various aspects of handicap. Legislation when it did come was at first permissive only, but the education of blind and deaf children was made compulsory in 1893. The Education Act 1899 mentioned defective and epileptic children; provision for feeble-minded children was not statutory until 1914; and the physically handicapped had to wait until 1919. The Education Act 1921 established statutory provision for five categories: blind, deaf, mentally defective, physically defective and epileptic. The implementation of this Act was slow despite the setting up in 1924 of a joint departmental committee (Wood Committee) on mental deficiency. Its report in 1929 coincided with a period of depression which prevented progress up to the time of World War II. The recommendations of the Wood Committee did however influence those parts of the 1944 Act which concerned special education.

During the 30s, interest in emotionally disturbed children grew. Child guidance clinics were established, first by voluntary societies and then by hospitals and education authorities. The first to receive recognition for grant purposes was in Birmingham in 1935. Meanwhile LEAs took advantage of the fact that by the provisions of the Education Act 1921 children could be boarded out in the interests of their health. During the war the experience of evacuation drew public attention to the social and emotional problems of children. As a result, special educational treatment for maladjusted children was officially recognised in the Education Act 1944.

This Act made other important changes in the administration of special education. Special education was seen as part of the LEAs' duty to provide for all children in accordance with their age, ability and aptitude. The Act did not name the different handicaps: these were described in subsequent 'regulations'—an arrangement which permits more frequent revision. The Act also allowed special education to be provided 'wholly or partly in substitution for the education given in ordinary school' and 'otherwise than at school'. This opened the door to the home teacher. The ten categories named in the current regulations are comprehensive, though severely subnormal children and children committed to approved schools by a juvenile court are still educated outside the education system.

Administrative procedures Children over the age of two may be examined with a view to deciding whether they are in need of special education, and in some cases, especially with blind, deaf and physically handicapped children, education begins before the children reach compulsory school age. Parents may ask for the examination, but where the handicap is less obvious, health visitors, family doctors and later teachers may be the first to observe any deviation from normal development. The children are then referred to the school medical officer who will arrange examination by a specialist. The result of this examination, together with other relevant information, is communicated to the LEA with a recommendation as to the form of special education required. Special forms have been devised for this purpose—Form 2 HP for mentally handicapped and Form 4 HP for physically handicapped children—though their use is not obligatory. A child considered unsuitable for education in school by reason of severe subnormality is referred on Form 2 HP to the public health authority responsible for the care and training of severely subnormal children.

The statutory school-leaving age for children who attend special schools is 16, i.e. one year older than the minimum leaving age. Some handicapped children are, however, permitted to leave earlier if they seem likely to make their way in the world. Others—usually children of higher academic ability—may stay on at school up to the end of their 19th year or even longer with special permission. Some handicapped children receive further education financed by the LEA, or vocational training financed by the Ministry of Labour. All pupils leaving special schools are entitled to use the Youth Employment Service, and some LEAs appoint a specialist YEO to meet the needs of handicapped schoolleavers. Apart from vocational guidance and, in some cases, further education, the after-care of handicapped school-leavers passes to the health and welfare departments of the local authority, though most special schools try to further the interests of their former pupils by means of clubs, evening classes and informal social contacts. It is often felt that LEAs should be empowered to provide after-care for a transitional period immediately after the handicapped pupil leaves school. Handicapped young workers whose homes cannot give them adequate support may need hostel placement. Some hostels have already been established by the health and welfare departments of local authorities and also by independent bodies.

The nature of special educational treatment Varying according to the handicap, its essential feature is that the pupil's individual needs should be met. This is made possible by a more generous staffing ratio than in ordinary schools and by the provision of medical consultation and non-teaching staff such as nurses, therapists and attendants. The DES lays down the maximum size of class for each handicap. Blind and deaf children have to be taught by special methods, but with other handicaps the special educational treatment is more likely to depend on physical care, individual therapy and psychological attitudes than on teaching methods or curricula. The underlying assumption behind all special education is that the child's educational needs cannot be met without full attention to his physical, social and emotional growth.

Teacher training for special education Since the earliest official provision of special education in England and Wales it has been the practice of most LEAs to recruit experienced teachers from ordinary schools and to pay them an extra allowance for teaching handicapped children. Additional training is desirable but has been slow to develop. It is not yet compulsory, except for teachers of blind and deaf children who in 1908 set up their own examining bodies. Training for other handicaps is by means of one-year advanced or supplementary courses provided by institutes of education. A list of these courses, intended for trained teachers with some previous experience, is published annually by the DES. Most LEAs will second teachers on full salary to take these courses, and teachers who gain this extra qualification are entitled to a small additional payment.

FURTHER READING
HMSO. *Education of the Handicapped Pupil 1945–1955*, 1956. *The Handicapped Pupils and Special School Regulations*, HMSO, 1959. *Special Educational Treatment*, Pamphlet No. 5, 1946.
J. M. G. Itard. *The Wild Boy of Aveyron*, Century, New York, 1932.
D. G. Pritchard. *Education and the Handicapped*, Routledge and Kegan Paul, 1963.

MW

Special Education, Association for This body exists to further the education and welfare of handicapped children. It was established in 1903 as the Special Schools Association. Its membership, mainly teachers but also drawn from other professions working with handicapped children, is spread over 37 branches covering most of Great Britain. Its journal *Special Education* is published quarterly, in collaboration with the Spastics Society. A *Newsletter* is also distributed to members three times a year. National conferences are held annually, and local and regional conferences are frequently organised.

Sec.: L. J. McDonald, 19 Hamilton Rd, Wallasey, Cheshire.

Special Education, College of A charitable organisation founded in 1965 by the Guild of Teachers of Backward Children, the College aims to improve the educational treatment of handicapped children in ordinary and special schools. It takes the view that since the present large numbers of backward pupils cannot be catered for by the relatively few specially trained teachers, it is imperative not only that more teachers be encouraged into this field, but that teachers in ordinary school classes should be better equipped with information that will help them to deal with such children in the normal course of classroom work. To provide this service, an advisory and information centre for teachers has been opened, with voluntary teams of advisers and study panels to assist in dealing with queries.

The College hopes, as a result of a public appeal for funds, to expand the centre's activities, undertake wide-scale studies, finance publications, operate a lending library, organise special lectures, seminars and correspondence courses for teachers, and to move from its temporary premises to a suitably equipped building that would become a national centre for special education.

3 Lower James St, London, W1.

Special schools *See* **Special education**

Specialisation The term is ambiguous. As normally understood, it means concentration of study in a single subject or field to the exclusion of others. Thus the Ministry of Education's 1961–2 statistics define a specialist as a pupil opting for one of three groups of subjects: science group—biology, physics, chemistry, mathematics, etc; arts group—English, history, languages etc; other subjects—art, music, general studies, religious instruction, etc.

Concern over the alleged evils of premature specialisation at the sixth-form level has been voiced in recent years, and critics have not been slow to point out that the problem is a peculiarly English one, affecting the grammar school much more than it does academic secondary schools in other countries. It is urged that this is where the 'great divide' between the Two Cultures begins and that the bifurcation at 15–16 into arts and science 'sides' commits pupils to a narrow intellectual horizon. Against this, it is argued that (1) without study in depth, rigorous scholarship is impossible and (2) that an advanced industrial society increasingly demands specialists of all kinds.

Because of the explosion of modern knowledge it is no longer possible to master even the basic principles of the various disciplines, as used to be the case during the era of the *artes liberales*—hence specialisation is inevitable. On the other hand, the proponents of general education insist on the need for a broad-based curriculum. The controversy stems from the different emphases placed on general and special aims. Thus the Harvard Committee advocates a threefold approach, using social studies as a link between arts and science, in order to foster 'the recognition of competence in any sphere', while Sir Eric Ashby suggests that 'the path to culture in the modern world is through a man's specialism'. The pros and cons so hotly discussed in the 20th century are much the same as those which arose in the 19th over Herbert's doctrine of 'many-sided interest' vis-à-vis Kerschensteiner's claim that 'vocational training leads to moral training'.

These rival claims are not incompatible. If anything, opinion is hardening in favour of courses which seek to make the best of both worlds, e.g. combinations of arts and science subjects, or, better still, courses covering related *fields*, as distinct from compartmented subjects. In the sense which Whitehead had in mind when he said that 'education should turn out people who know something well and can do something well', specialisation is clearly desirable. Moreover, there is no denying that in the educated society only the qualified person achieves status, so that if only because of the pressure of examination requirements it seems likely that specialisation in one form or another will increase rather than diminish in the future.

FURTHER READING
Harvard Committee. *General Education in a Free Society*, Harvard Univ. Press, Cambridge, Mass., 1945.
W. Kenneth Richmond. *Culture and General Education*, Methuen, 1963.

WKR

Speech defects Children do not all learn to speak at the same time, and it has been claimed that Einstein could not speak properly until he was four years old. Some speech delays can be a sign of deafness or partial hearing but apart from this it has been suggested that parents of such children are often emotionally unstable, restrictive or over-protective, and that this in itself seems enough in some cases to inhibit speech for a considerable time. But very delayed speech, together with pronounced backwardness in other fields of development, usually indicates a mentally retarded child.

Indistinct speech, such as lisping, usually disappears without treatment, although if a serious lisp persists beyond the fourth birthday it may be wise to consult a speech therapist (*q.v.*) before schooling begins. Stuttering, however, which again often occurs naturally with young children as a passing phase, may often be made worse by the actions of dominating or over-protective parents if they tend to fluster their child and make him more anxious about his speech. It has been claimed that stuttering is also part of a general motor retardation and can be due to heredity, but there is still a fundamental lack of knowledge about the cause of this speech defect, and the courses it can take in different individuals.

FURTHER READING
R. M. Williams. *Speech Difficulties in Childhood*, Harrap, 1962.

NT

Speech and Drama, Society of Teachers of Formed to protect the professional interests of those engaged in the teaching of speech and drama, and to promote the advancement of knowledge, study and practice of speech and dramatic art in every form. Membership is open to qualified specialist teachers. The Society conducts an active campaign to secure the proper status of spoken English in edu-cation, to ensure that those who teach this subject are properly qualified, and to encourage the use of good speech as a means of communication and of interpretation. The Society is represented in all English-speaking countries, and its services are available to any individual or organisation requiring advice or assistance.

Journal: *Speech and Drama*.

St Bride Institute, Bride Lane, London, EC4.

Speech therapist A speech therapist is a specialist trained to help with speech defects. Methods of tackling these tend to differ; but one of the common factors is always to relax and build up the confidence of the patient and, in the case of children, to reassure the parents and try to relieve any excessive tension in the home caused by the defect.

Speech training Speech and language training are today considered of vital importance in all branches of education and at all levels. The subject forms an integral part of schools' curricula, is studied and practised in the training of teachers in colleges of education, while courses in communication in industry, commerce and technology frequently appear in further education programmes. In addition, the status of speech is being raised by the setting of oral tests in English as part of some of the normal school examinations.

Oral communication is closely bound up with the everyday needs of life, in work, social relationships and cultural activities. In educating people to take their place happily and successfully in a democratic community, a basic need is to develop an ability to speak well and to communicate honestly, intelligibly, freely and acceptably.

Speech is not an end in itself, but is a means to a more complete existence for the individual and the community in which he lives. Speech education is the responsibility of all teachers and lecturers concerned with training, even though a qualified speech specialist may be available. The 'subject' may be taught in its own right, but should be extended into all forms of oral work in all subjects.

There have been changes in attitudes and methods of teaching speech, and most teachers will have a highly individual approach, but it is generally accepted that there should be encouragement by personal discovery rather than by imitative methods which superimpose the teacher's personality. In schools, the work of the teacher is to provide situations closely related to the pupils' real or imagined experience which challenge them to use language well.

In planning a programme, it is the fundamental attributes of good speaking that must be considered. These may be summarised as first having something to say, next the ability to arrange one's thoughts before uttering them, then the imagination to choose suitable language, and finally the ability to speak clearly, intelligibly and agreeably, with sensitivity towards the listener.

Speech is inseparable from the speaker. It is first a bodily activity, a product of the muscular and nervous system; it is an intellectual activity, for it demands clear thinking and the power to reason; finally it is both an imaginative and emotional activity. The expression of the emotions, feelings and desires is a deep-seated inner necessity, and the opportunity to use speech freely and expressively gives enrichment and satisfaction.

A variety of methods of speech training are adopted. Some teachers believe that the most powerful incentives to speech and language development in schools occur in movement and drama lessons and similar activities which capture the children's imagination. With older pupils, it is considered by some to be desirable to make a more specialised study of speech, of both the artistic and technical aspects.

No matter what method may be pursued, the intention of all educationists should be to develop the child's or student's ability to express himself coherently, fluently, and concisely, in correct and pleasing English. There will always be diversity of accents, and many teachers consider that no standard of acceptability should be set to which all must conform, but that the accent best suited to the needs of the speaker and the situation may be allowed, provided it can be understood and accepted by all who may use English as a first language.

MC

Spelling The English language contains some 40 sounds and there are roughly 2,000 ways of writing these, using the 26 letters of the conventional alphabet. It is not surprising, therefore, that spelling reform has had many advocates down the centuries. The first known spelling reformer was a monk named Orm, who lived about 1200 AD, and the list of his successors includes Sir Thomas Smith, Secretary of State to Queen Elizabeth; Richard Mulcaster, tutor to Edmund Spenser; Jonathan Swift; Sir Robert Bridges; Bernard Shaw and Sir James Pitman. Unfortunately, the reformers have not been able to agree among themselves how conventional spelling should be amended. Some have been concerned to preserve certain anomalies in order to indicate the language from which a word was derived; others have aimed to show the length of vowels by doubling or not doubling consonants or by using accents. In consequence, it has been the printers and not the reformers who have had most influence on common usage.

An impetus to reform came from two sources in the 19th century: (1) the introduction of a shorthand system by Isaac Pitman which, being based on phonetic principles, emphasised the anomalies of conventional spelling; and (2) the Education Act 1870, which led to the discovery that the teaching of English spelling in all its complexity took up far too much of the curriculum. Two societies, the Society for Pure English and the Simplified Spelling Society (*q.v.*), both advocated reform at the beginning of the 20th century, the latter having more influence and remaining in existence until the present day. The sixth section of its manifesto, *New Spelling*, was published in 1948.

George Bernard Shaw took an extreme line in proposing that the existing alphabet should not be amended but should be replaced by one of his own invention, containing 40 or more new letters. Shaw died before perfecting his system, but he left money to further his aims. The first book to be printed in the Shavian alphabet, *Androcles and the Lion*, appeared in 1962. In it, 40 letters were used and eight digraphs (these being groups of letters representing single sounds). Sir James Pitman, grandson of the inventor of Pitman's shorthand, supported Shaw's efforts but also produced an alphabet of his own, originally called the Augmented Roman Alphabet but now known as the Initial Teaching Alphabet (*q.v.*), or i.t.a.

See also **Reading research**

EP

Spencer, Herbert (1820–1903)
Author of *Education: Intellectual, Moral and Physical* (1861), Spencer was the most categorical advocate of scientific education of his time, and his work was widely influential. He held that science was of greater importance than any other school subject whatever, as a preparation for life, as an introduction to the duties of a citizen (through the social sciences) and as an intellectual discipline. Many of his statements about education seem today over-stated and over-confident, but in the battle to establish the importance of science in the curriculum his vehemence played a vital part.

Spens Report (1938): Report of the Consultative Committee of the Board of Education on Secondary Education with Special Reference to Grammar Schools and Technical High Schools Terms of reference: to consider and report upon the organisation and interrelation of schools other than those administered under the Elementary Code which provide education for pupils beyond the age of 11-plus; particular consideration was to be given to the framework and content of the education of pupils who did not remain at school beyond the age of about 15. Chairman: Will Spens.

The Report rejected the idea of the comprehensive school, mainly on grounds relating to the size and to the intellectual composition of the annual intake, but approved of the 'multilateral idea' in separated schools. It recommended the raising of the school leaving age to 16, and that grammar school places should be made available for about 15% of the population. It did not agree with the idea of the sixth-form college.

Spoken English, Diploma in *See* **English language schools**

Sports, National Council for School Founded in 1948, the Council co-ordinates and advises on the work of a number of national school sports associations.

64 Winchester Rd, Andover, Hants.

Sports Medicine, Institute of Founded in 1963 by the British Association of Sport and Medicine, the Physical Education Association of Great Britain and Northern Ireland and the British Olympic Association, the Institute exists to study and promote all aspects of medical and allied disciplines in relation to sport, PE and recreation. It has set up a clearing house for information on all aspects of physiology, psychology, pathology, kinesiology, ergonomics, physics and allied sciences related to sport. Information is disseminated by written publication, lectures, demonstrations and other appropriate means. Facilities are arranged for the study and treatment of breakdowns in fitness in sportsmen.

Ling Hse, 10 Nottingham Pl., London, W1.

Squash A highly energetic ball game, invaluable for those seeking strenuous exercise in a limited time. It is played in an enclosed, wooden-floored court, 32 ft long by 21 ft wide and not less than 15 ft high. In essence the game resembles fives, except that a light circular-headed racket is used and the ball, approximately $1\frac{3}{4}$ in. in diameter, is made of low-inflated black rubber.

In the world of education, particularly from the upper secondary level onwards, the game is of great value because of its high-pressure activity level, for at this stage the student preparing for examinations is often reluctant to devote the amount of time to recreation demanded by major team games.

In recent years the game has grown enormously in popularity in schools and colleges as everywhere. Expansion is prevented only by lack of courts and the high cost of building them. There have been developments, however, in the production of portable squash courts, which can be assembled and dismantled in, say, a hall or gymnasium, in a matter of minutes. This could well lead to a very large growth of the game in the educational field.

JE

Stamp Collecting Promotion Council *See* **Philately**

Standard Book Numbering Growing use of computers in the book trade led in 1967 to the introduction by the Publishers Association of the Standard Book Numbering scheme. Numbers first appeared in lists and later in books themselves. Usually the number (the SBN) is printed on the verso of the title page (the page which normally gives the printing history), the jacket and on the cover of a paperback, sometimes on the binding of a hard-cover book. An SBN always consists of nine digits, is in three parts separated by spaces, and is usually printed as follows:

SBN: 8436 1072 7

The first part is the publisher prefix; it can be anything from two to seven digits and always identifies the publisher. The larger the publisher, the smaller the number of digits used to identify him. The second part of the number identifies the title or the particular volume or edition. This section can also be of varying length. The final digit is the check digit which is a device that guards against a computer accepting a wrong number and thus supplying the wrong book.

For the customer, say a school teacher, book numbering means giving the number in the publisher's list as well as the title and author when ordering. This may seem an additional chore but it will ensure greater accuracy of ordering and as the use of computers increases both by those ordering educational books and those supplying them it will be possible, by arrangement, to order by number alone. The next stage, being experimented with already, will be the exchange of computer tapes. One tape fed straight into the supplier's computer is the order, the other is the supplier's invoice. This will speed up invoicing procedures and the physical looking out of books against an order (all books being stored in number order); the result better, faster service, an objective which must be wanted by everyone whether a book user or supplier.

Standard deviation *See* **Normal distribution**

Standard score *See* **Norm**

Standardised tests *See* **Objective tests; Selection procedures for secondary education**

Standards First introduced by the Revised Code (*q.v.*) to replace the four age groups, the six standards became normative patterns for schools earning government grants.

They represented the six years of school life: Standard I (ages 6–7) replaced group I (3–7) and covered the reading of monosyllables, recognising and writing figures up to 20 and adding and subtracting figures up to 10. Standard II (7–8), Standard III (8–9) and Standard IV (9–10) covered mastery of the three Rs. Requirements for Standard V (10–11) and Standard VI (11–12) rose slowly and with the 'specific' subjects allowed in the 1871 Code provided a basis for 'secondary' education that was to develop into 'higher grade schools' (*q.v.*), especially after Standard VII was introduced by the Code of 1882.

This undoubtedly affected the Cross Commission's recommendation in 1888 (*Final Report*, 170) that 'scholarships' to secondary schools should be awarded at the age of 11.

WHGA

Standards Institution, British The British Standards Institution (BSI) is the national standards body of the UK, responsible for the preparation, by agreement among producers, users and other interests concerned, of industrial standards, including specifications, test methods, codes of practice, definitions and symbols; it is the UK member of the international standards bodies preparing agreed recommendations on these matters. It is also concerned with promoting the use of standards to increase the efficiency of the national economy.

Originating in 1901 as the Engineering Standards Committee, BSI was granted a Royal Charter in 1929 and the present name was adopted in 1931.

Today its activities cover nearly every field of industry, commerce and technology and there are about 5,000 current British Standards, over 400 being published each year, increasingly on the basis of the metric system.

British Standards, providing fundamental data for industrial practice, are an essential part of scientific and technical education; BSI speakers assist in lectures and courses on standards and their use.

2 Park St, London, W1.

Standards for School Premises Regulations, 1959 These regulations prescribe the minimum standards to which the premises of schools maintained by LEAs are to conform, and came into force in their present form on 27 May 1959.

The regulations form an appendix to the DES's Building Code. They are split into parts; the first defines the terminology, and others lay down standards for different types of educational buildings, i.e. primary schools, secondary schools, nursery and nursery classes, special schools and boarding accommodation. The Standards are concerned with:

(1) Appropriate area of sites and amounts of paved areas for certain numbers of pupils; (2) playing field accommodation; (3) teaching accommodation (minimum areas and appropriate numbers of teaching spaces); (4) storage of teaching apparatus, equipment and materials; (5) storage of pupils' outdoor clothing; (6) sanitary accommodation for pupils; (7) washing accommodation for pupils: (8) staff rooms; (9) cloakroom, sanitary accommodation for adults; (10) facilities for medical inspection and treatment; (11) storage facilities for school stocks, maintenance equipment, furniture and fuel; (12) accommodation for meals; (13) additional items for nursery schools—garden playing space, playroom accommodation; (14) additional

items for boarding accommodation—dormitories and cubicles, dayroom space and sick rooms.

There is also a section dealing with general requirements for schools and boarding accommodation. This section includes regulations concerning structural loadings, protection against weather, precautions for health and safety, lighting, ventilation and heating, acoustics, water supply, gas and electricity power, washing and sanitary accommodation, and drainage and sewage disposal.

All school projects have to be submitted to the Minister who will approve any project which meets the minimum requirements prescribed in the regulations; he will also approve any project which provides higher standards, so long as the limit of cost applicable to the project is not exceeded.

See also **Minor (building) works; Major (building) works**

DEC

Stanford-Binet tests *See* **Intelligence quotient; Binet, Alfred; Intelligence tests**

State Education, Confederation for the Advancement of (CASE) CASE's aims, agreed in 1962, are to secure increase and improvement of educational facilities and opportunities; to ensure that the appropriate sections of the 1944 Education Act are implemented (this is regarded as a minimum aim); to make constructive suggestions, at both local and national level, as to ways in which improvement may be brought about; to inform the public fully of the issues in order that any increased expenditure required to improve education should be generally accepted. The Confederation recognises that improvement may indeed involve the further expenditure of public money, and believes that the improvement of education in any single area should not be restricted by the funds available in that area; rather, the primary responsibility for financing education should be seen to lie with the central government, and standards should be as uniformly high as possible throughout the country.

The more particular objects are to facilitate the exchange of information among Associations for the Advancement of State Education and interested individuals; to encourage and assist in the formation of such associations; and, having published such opinions as are held by a substantial majority of member Associations, to organise concerted action.

The first Association was formed in Cambridge in 1961 by parents who were dissatisfied with conditions in a local state school. There has since been a very large growth of Associations throughout the country.

Hon. Gen. Sec.: Mrs. Diana Lamb, 9 Addison Rd, Great Ayton, Middlesbrough, Yorkshire.

State scholarships State scholarships to the universities were first offered in 1911, when the Board of Education made grants to students wishing to become teachers. Like LEA scholarships, State scholarships were originally awarded on the basis of high performance in the Higher School Certificate examination; but in 1948, as a result of a recommendation by a working party appointed in that year, the procedure was changed to one in which scholarships were awarded on the basis of promising attainment in GCE A and S level papers. State scholarships were also awarded to mature students of 25 or over.

Following the recommendations of the Anderson Committee (which reported in 1961), these scholarships were replaced by open entry scholarships offered by the universities.

Statistics, Teaching of *See* **Mathematics, Teaching of**

Y

Statute of Charitable Uses (1601)
This Act gave protection to the various charities which had been set up, mainly by Protestant organisations, to provide free grammar school education for most of the boys of England. The Act protected these funds from abuse, and enabled the Chancellor to appoint a commission to inquire into their use, where they were suspected of being misapplied.

Steiner, Rudolf (1861–1925) Austrian social philosopher who founded anthroposophy, a mystical system originated by Steiner in reaction to the Theosophical Society. Turning its back on the eastern inspiration of the theosophists, the system rests on the belief that playacting, art and myth-making are essential human experiences, that these have been denied to men by the materialist character of modern life, and that they can be restored through a special system of education, in which mythology bulks large and art and eurhythmics play an important part. There are Rudolf Steiner schools throughout England and elsewhere. Steiner wrote *The Philosophy of Freedom* (1894).
See also **Steiner's Waldorf Educational Method**

Steiner's Waldorf educational method This method has been practised in England for over 40 years. It is co-educational, from ages six to 18, following a pre-school kindergarten.
Children are grouped according to their natural, rather than their mental age, as the teacher cultivates feeling and will, not only intelligence. By harmonising all three, strong forces of character can be developed for after-school life. In the upper school there is specialised examination preparation for university entrance, or for GCE in as many subjects as are considered appropriate or necessary. By deferring specialisation as long as possible, each child receives a broad education in the humanities and sciences, as well as languages, music, arts and crafts. The education is Christian in outlook, but non-denominational.
Schools which are members of Steiner Schools Fellowship are to be distinguished from the homes and schools, also based on Rudolf Steiner's work, which are concerned essentially with maladjusted, delinquent and handicapped children.
Sec., Steiner Schools Fellowship Ltd, Wynstones, Whaddon, Gloucester.

Stern's apparatus With her structural materials, Catherine Stern endeavours to put the number system into such a form that children may develop an understanding of its structure and the fundamental arithmetic operations in a concrete situation.
The apparatus is made up of a number of parts, the most commonly used being:
(1) *Blocks*—analogues of the numbers 1 to 10: coloured lengths of wood of $\frac{3}{4}$ in. square cross-section and multiples of $\frac{3}{4}$ in. long, from $\frac{3}{4}$ in. to $7\frac{1}{2}$ in. and scored at $\frac{3}{4}$ in. intervals.
(2) *Counting board*—containing recesses into which children can fit blocks of the appropriate size. A number marker can be fitted to the board so that each recess has the correct numeral at its head.
(3) *Pattern boards*—ten boards containing recesses made to receive cubes the size of a block.
(4) *Number cases*—ten hollow squares, each one the same colour as the largest block that will fit along an interior side used to build up number bonds, e.g. $5 = 4 + 1 = 3 + 2 = 2 + 3 = 1 + 4$.
(5) *Number track*—A hardwood strip, in jointed sections, with a trough down the centre to receive the blocks and marked down one side with the natural number sequence 1 to 100.

FURTHER READING
Catherine Stern. *Children Discover Arithmetic*, Harrap, 1966.

WD

Streaming Streaming is a form of internal school organisation, where the classes making up the school are arranged according to some criterion of ability, aptitude or intelligence or a combination of these factors. The children in the school are placed in streams according to some measurement or assessment of such factors. The criteria, which are usually applied to all the children in the school whose ages fall within certain limits (most often the calendar year which accords with the school year), vary from teachers' assessments of ability and aptitude to a series of objective tests involving some type of measurement of intelligence and attainment.

The criteria that are applied depend on the stage a child has reached in his educational development and the type of school he is attending. For example, many children who transfer at the age of seven-plus from a separate infants' school to a separate junior school would be classified according to their reading ability or an assessment made by the teachers, or more often the headteacher, of the infants' school. The streamed classes in the junior school would then be organised initially by grouping all the most able readers in an A stream, the average readers in a B stream, and the slower readers in a C stream, where the numbers allowed for a three-stream intake. In the transfer of children from junior to secondary school, more elaborate criteria are used in which, during the last 30 years, intelligence tests have played a large part. The streaming, which becomes more intense at the secondary stage, is related to many differing factors in any given local authority area. In any area, the main limitations rest on the amount, variety and balance of secondary education available: that is, on the pattern of grammar schools, secondary modern schools, secondary technical schools and comprehensive schools. Theoretically, comprehensive reorganisation should lead to a minimising of this concern at the secondary stage with the varying abilities of children and individual differences between them.

At present, most secondary schools are streamed, although experiments in non-streaming are under way in some places. Some girls' grammar schools have applied only limited streaming, and some boys' grammar schools are streamed only in the upper school; but it appears that very few secondary modern schools have been unstreamed.

Historical If schools are considered to be primarily institutions of intellectual education, where differences in intellect are of fundamental concern, then the organisation of schools will clearly reflect such a view. And on that view, the practice of streaming is squarely based. But today many teachers consider their task as being to promote the all-round development of the child, which means being concerned with a child's emotional, cultural and social development as well as with his intellectual powers. This wider sense of the teacher's task is one of the reasons for the present movement away from streaming.

The practice of streaming has rested largely on the refinement of testing techniques, which were able to claim greater predictive power than traditional examinations; on the increase in the size of schools as urban populations and suburban areas have grown (streaming rarely being found in village schools, which are usually small); on the priority given to the education of the most able and on the economic limitations that have led naturally to a restrictionist selective policy of secondary education.

In the Hadow Report of 1926 (*q.v.*), which has secondary schooling for all in its sights, there is to be found the first major statement of the argument for selective treatment of children in school. In the second Hadow Report on the primary school in 1931 (*q.v.*), streaming is strongly recommended as a means of ensuring that the various types of secondary school are adequately supplied with selected and non-selected children. But by 1945, after a world war had stirred the nation to reconsider its educational programmes, the report *The Nation's Schools, Ministry of Education Pamphlet No. 1* questioned the desirability of grading classes on a streaming principle. In 1959 *Primary Education*, a report produced by Her Majesty's Inspectorate, made tentative suggestions as to the skills involved in teaching children in classes of mixed ability (i.e. unstreamed classes). In 1967 the Plowden Report (*q.v.*) stated: 'We welcome unstreaming in the infant school and we hope that it will continue to spread through the age groups of the junior school'. One educational journal, *Forum*, has concerned itself during the decade 1957–67 with the problems of curriculum organisation in flexible non-streamed schools.

Research Various researches on aspects of streaming and non-streaming have been conducted by the National Foundation for Educational Research and by individuals working on theses for higher degrees, and research is continuing in many places.

The results, as is often the case with educational research, seem somewhat inconclusive. No-one has yet been bold enough to inquire into the organising ability of teachers in relation to homogeneous groupings of children on the one hand, and heterogeneous groupings on the other. In the research findings, teachers' attitudes to streaming or non-streaming feature prominently; but questions of teaching skill, and how adequate they are in one form of class organisation or the other, are rarely mentioned. The main conclusions of research appear to be that non-streaming is socially desirable and is more likely to bring about the all-round personal development of child-

ren; that, where one has a democratic school-based educational system such as is found in the UK, socio-economic and neighbourhood variables loom large and make it difficult to match schools for research purposes; and that the attitude of the teacher is all-important, the enthusiast for non-streaming being most likely to make an educational success of it.

As a recent piece of American research concluded: 'Ability grouping is inherently neither good nor bad. It is neutral. Its value depends upon the way in which it is used. . . . Grouping arrangements by themselves serve little educational purpose. Real differences in academic growth result from what is taught and learned in the classroom.' (Goldberg and Passow, see *Further reading*.)

In the final analysis, as the research in the Plowden Report stresses, streaming and non-streaming rest on opposing educational philosophies. One favours the creation of an intellectual élite and, it follows, an educationally depressed minority (since much research seems to show that streaming is a self-confirming device, children tending to remain in the streams in which they are originally placed); the other philosophy, which would lead to non-streaming, is concerned to mobilise and realise the talents of all.

FURTHER READING

Children and Their Primary Schools (*Plowden Report*), Vol. I: 'Report' (esp. Chap. 20 'How Primary Schools Are Organised'); Vol. II: 'Research and Surveys' (esp. Appendix II 'The Organisation of Junior Schools and the Effects of Streaming'), Central Advisory Council for Education, HMSO, 1967.

J. W. B. Douglas. *The Home and the School*, MacGibbon and Kee, 1964.

M. L. Goldberg and A. H. Passow. *The Effects of Ability Grouping*, Teachers' College Press, Columbia Univ., New York, 1966.

Brian Jackson. *Streaming: An Educational System in Miniature*, Routledge and Kegan Paul, 1964.

B. Simon (Ed.). *Non-Streaming in the Junior School*, PSW (Educational) Publications, Leicester, 1964.

Alfred Yates (Ed.). *Grouping in Education* (Report of UNESCO Hamburg Conference), John Wiley, New York, 1966.

Periodical
Forum, Vols. I–X, Leicester.

EL

Student Christian Movement *See* **Christian Education Movement**

Student grants *See* **Students, Grants for**

Student representation University, technical college and education college students' demands for more say in the running of their institutions had been gradually growing in volume throughout the 1960s and reached their point of greatest clarity in 1966 during the formulation of a Royal Charter for the new University of Surrey, a test case for such charters. Students demanded that their rights should be recognised in three respects:

(1) Union autonomy: the students' union should have the right to decide how to administer its funds.

(2) Discipline: a student suspended by the university should be allowed to call witnesses in his defence, should be heard by a committee composed of students as well as staff, and should have a right of appeal to a further committee on which the students should be represented.

(3) The students should be represented on the policy-making committees of the university, and in particular on its governing body.

The Surrey Charter conceded the bulk of these points; but in the older universities, whose charters already existed, the struggle continued. By the end of 1967, according to a survey by the NUS, out of 27 universities or university colleges among those responding (including some technical colleges), 21 gave a right to a disciplinary hearing, 19 allowed a student to present witnesses, and 11 had an appeals machinery. Representation on

university committees showed a more mixed picture, a steadily increasing number of universities and colleges according students representation on committees concerned with health, welfare and living conditions of students, but only a small minority allowing such representation on academic committees. Of 174 constituent unions of the NUS who replied to another NUS questionnaire, only 23 said they had student representatives on the academic committee or governing body.

However, the original philosophy behind the concept of university authorities being *in loco parentis* was dead or dying by the mid-1960s even at Oxford, where a college dean was reported as saying that the spikes on the college walls should be removed because they constituted a danger to student health, and at Cambridge, where, more significantly, Sir Eric Ashby, Master of Clare College, said in 1965 that a student 'must have the confidence which comes from participation in community living: that is what he gets from belonging, as a coequal, to a society of chancellor, masters and scholars'.

Most university authorities are not merely reconciled to, but actually anxious for, student representation in university affairs except on purely academic matters—that is, matters which concern the content of undergraduate courses; but the relations between dons and students have been embittered by student demonstrations, some of them violent, some merely obstructive, some concerned with internal matters, some with international politics. The classic example was at the London School of Economics in 1967, where what began as a purely political protest over the appointment of a new school director ended with a 'sit-in' by students on the question of student rights at the School.

The student revolts on the Continent in the spring of 1968 led to a wave of similar, if milder, outbreaks in England—though some of these (as at the Universities of Essex and Manchester) had their origin in disciplinary action taken after student demonstrations against visiting political speakers or scientists working for the chemical warfare establishment at Porton. The student rebellion at the Hornsey College of Art in May and June 1968 was caused largely by dissatisfaction with the organisation and quality of the courses in colleges of art.

Meanwhile, many university authorities regard student demands for representation as self-limiting. They argue that wider acquaintance with necessary but boring committee work will make students disenchanted with the consolations of student power.

NB

Student travellers, Reduction in fares for A student identity card is not a passport for cheap travel. The railway administrations and airline companies offer a range of international fare reductions for children, but there are virtually none for student travellers. The 'student fare' advertised by the airlines is a basic 25% discount off the normal fares but it is so hedged around with restrictions (e.g. only for students travelling between home address and place of study, specific age limits, etc.) —as is the recently introduced 'youth fare' for persons under 22 years of age (a return journey has to be booked)— that it is by no means universally applicable to students' actual requirements. In most cases students can pay less by booking 'night flights' or 'tourist returns'.

Some railway administrations (notably the French, Spanish and German) allow reduced fares for students travelling to attend universities or study courses but again there are a number of 'ifs and buts' and mere possession of student identification is insufficient.

Shipping companies, especially in the Mediterranean area, are rather more generous: nearly all Greek and Israeli companies and the nationally owned Turkish and Yugoslav companies give specific published discounts against evidence of student status, as do the Soviet Baltic State Line. Norwegian students travel cheaply on the North Sea crossings of Bergen and Olsen Lines; all students travelling to a continental university can claim a reduction in the Zeeland companies' channel ferry. Student certificates are required in all these cases.

A consequence of the situation has been that many organisations in the field of student affairs arrange their own charter flights and group travel schemes (groups of 10 or more juveniles or students can travel by rail at anything up to 50% reduction), but these by their nature tend to be geared to the specific requirements of the organisation concerned rather than to individual requirements. Such organisations are the British Universities Students Travel Association (157 Victoria St, London, SW1), the United Nations Student Association (93 Albert Embankment, London, SW1), the British Universities Society of Arts (32 Shaftesbury Ave, London, W1). Another result has been that individuals and small firms (some, as in any business, of dubious reliability) organise cheap travel for students which is cheap either because it is uncomfortable (e.g. long-distance coaches or mini-buses) or because only minimum facilities are included (e.g. a tour with meals excluded from the price).

The happiest result of this lack of facilities for penurious students (who are, after all, probably the keenest travellers in the world), has been that the national unions of students of many countries have banded together to offer a co-ordinated international student travel programme for individual students. The programme is currently operative only in Europe and the Near East, but in the UK the 358,000 student members of the National Union of Students (3 Endsleigh St, London, WC1) not only have the services of the largest student travel bureau in the country but are also able to use those of all the other national unions. This means a massive coverage of Europe by nearly 1,000 student chartered flights, many more student train-groups and a number of ship travel schemes. (The only disadvantage of this co-operation is that for economic reasons it is essential that all traffic is two-way, which is why for example there are no charter flights from Britain to Iceland or Morocco.)

International transportation firms may one day offer more inducements to an ever-expanding section of their market which, at the moment, they largely ignore.

Students, Grants for Under regulations made by the DES, local authorities are now obliged to make grants to students who have the requisite qualifications for higher education courses and have obtained places in recognised universities or colleges. The maximum standard grant made by LEAs covers payment of approved fees, which include tuition fees, lecture, laboratory and course fees, etc., and an annual grant for maintenance. The approved fees are paid direct to the college by the local authority, but the maintenance grant is paid to the student.

In 1968, the maximum maintenance allowances for awards for first-degree and comparable courses were: Oxbridge and London universities and further education establishments in the London area, £395 per annum for students living in halls of residence or lodgings and £290 if living at home; for other universities, £360 in residence and £290 at home. Smaller additional grants were made for study abroad, instruments for medical and dental students, etc.

At colleges of education, where the terms are longer, resident students receiving free board and lodging were awarded £163 maintenance (maximum) and £290 if living at home with parents.

Parents of students are expected to contribute according to their joint income towards the approved fees and maintenance grants and to provide most of the cost of maintenance during college vacations. The means tests allow for certain deductions from the gross income for other dependents, mortgages, insurance payments and the like (but not income tax), and contributions are levied on the remaining balance of income. The scale ranges from an annual parental contribution of £20 when the balance of parental income is £900, to £30 in the case of an income of £1,000 and £230 for an income of £3,000; but a minimum grant of £50 is payable irrespective of income.

The number of LEA grants taken up by students rose from 22,727 in 1956 to 95,801 in 1966.

See also **Scholarships, etc.**

FURTHER READING
National Union of Students. *Grants Handbook*, 1968.

EP

Students, National Union of Founded in 1922, the NUS now has 310,000 members in over 620 affiliated colleges.

Services to students include: travel agency, student insurance brokerage, entertainments booking agency, international summer schools, vacation work bureaux, annual drama festival. The NUS also advises individual students on problems concerning grants, discipline and welfare; and assists local unions in the development of facilities and with college negotiations.

Through its wide range of publications, press and parliamentary liaisons and meetings with government, the NUS puts forward student views on all aspects of education; and maintains relations with student organisations throughout the world, bilaterally and through the International Student Conference.

3 Endsleigh St, London, WC1.

731

Students, Scottish Union of The independent national union representing students in the universities and colleges of Scotland both nationally and internationally. It was founded in 1888 as the Federation of Scottish University Student Representative Councils, and in 1945 incorporated the colleges.

The SUS makes representation to government bodies on student grants, welfare and all aspects of education, and carries out research to support its submissions. It cooperates closely with the Scottish Education Department, the Educational Institute of Scotland and other educational bodies. It organises educational travel and exchange visits and publishes a careers magazine, *The Scottish Graduate*, a termly features magazine, and other publications of practical and educational interest to students. Other activities include participation in voluntary service, all forms of insurance for students, organisation of cultural events such as the Scottish Student Drama Festival and of seminars and conferences of general and educational interest.

Internationally the SUS is a member of the International Student Conference, based in Leiden, Netherlands.

30 Lothian St, Edinburgh, 8.

Sub-aqua swimming For boys and girls who can swim well, are in the late secondary school stage, have taken one of the awards of the Royal Life-Saving Society, and are not interested in competitive swimming, interest and experience can be increased (as is being done in many schools) by the introduction of sub-aqua swimming to the PE curriculum.

For the introduction of this activity, however, it is absolutely essential that trained and competent instructors should be available. This can be achieved by a member of staff attending the courses run throughout the country by branches of the British Sub-Aqua Club. Particulars of these branches and courses can be obtained from the general branch, 25 Orchard Rd, Kingston-upon-Thames, Surrey.

The first stages of training involve the use of the basic and relatively inexpensive equipment—fins, mask and snorkel (a breathing tube enabling the swimmer to breathe freely whilst swimming face downwards on the surface of the water). When the techniques of using this equipment have been mastered and tested the swimmer can go on to training in the use of the aqualung, an ingenious piece of equipment which, by means of a demand-valve, makes it possible to obtain compressed air from a cylinder carried on the back at the same pressure as the surrounding water, thus making breathing easy at any depth.

FURTHER READING
British Sub-Aqua Club Diving Manual.
G. F. Brookes. *Underwater Swimming, Know the Game* Series, Educational Productions, 1962.
Edmund Burke. *The Underwater Handbook*, Muller, 1962.
K. McDonald and P. Smith. *Spearfishing in Great Britain*, Stanley Paul, 1963.

JE

Subject examinations Those in which a candidate is assessed on his performance in each subject separately, as in GCE. In contrast, a School Certificate could only be obtained when a candidate had passed in five subjects, including one from each of three groups. A GCE is awarded to a candidate who has a pass in one subject at any level. Paradoxically, the demands of universities and professional bodies for passes in specified subjects have done much to destroy the conception of GCE as a subject examination.

Subordinate capabilities *See* **Learning sets**

Sudan, Education in Education is free but not compulsory in primary schools (seven to 11), intermediate schools (11 to 15) and secondary schools (15 upwards). There are many private schools in addition to state institutions. Enrolment figures for 1964/5 were: kindergartens (private) 2,210; primary schools—government 466,873, private 11,500; intermediate schools—government 41,081, private 27,283; secondary schools—government 15,955, private 9,217; government further education and technical colleges 907; vocational colleges 230; teacher training colleges 2,210. Khartoum University has an enrolment of about 2,100 students.

The population of the country was approximately 13½ million in 1965.

Supervisory Studies, National Examination Board in *See* **Management education**

Supply teaching A supply teacher is a teacher who is sent on a short-term basis to a school which has a temporary staffing difficulty. If a member of the regular staff is absent owing to illness or some other unforeseeable emergency, then the head-teacher will normally seek a replacement from the LEA's 'supply staff' to meet the situation. Foreseen staff absences of limited duration, owing for example to a member's attendance at a short training course or conference, might also be covered in the same way. The supply teacher is usually but not always an experienced teacher who may receive extra payment for undertaking such work.

The status of supply teachers may vary from one part of the country to another. In some LEAs there is what is known as 'the permanent supply staff'; this is made up of well qualified and experienced teachers who are fitted to cope with the somewhat difficult assignment of taking over another teacher's class or work at short notice. These supply teachers usually work full time in the employment of the LEA and are likely to be used to cover the somewhat longer and foreseeable absences of other teachers.

Other supply teachers are employed on a day-to-day basis and may be on call when needed by the LEA. The supply teacher is not to be confused with the temporary (*q.v.*) or occasional teacher.

FJ

Surinam, Education in Education is free and compulsory between the ages of six and 13. 1965 statistics: 399 schools including kindergartens (enrolment 104,672); two teacher training colleges; one technical, one medical, one law school (enrolments not available). Total population: approximately 350,000.

Surveying, Qualification in The chief professional body in the UK is the Royal Institution of Chartered Surveyors; it is the only body that examines in all branches of surveying. There are two major approaches to qualification. For the first, a candidate must possess two or three GCE A levels (including mathematics) and must combine four or five years employment of an approved nature in a surveyor's office with part-time study at a technical college or by correspondence for the professional examinations. For the second approach, a two- or three-year full-time course at a college recognised by the RICS is followed by a combination of approved experience in an office and preparation for the final professional examinations. A degree in estate management will exempt a candidate from examinations but must be accompanied by two years' approved practical training.

Royal Institution of Chartered Surveyors, 12 Great George St, London, SW1; 7 Manor Pl., Edinburgh.

Swann Report: 'Interim Report of the Working Group on Manpower Parameters for Scientific Growth' (October 1966) The Swann Committee reported that the best qualified graduates tend to remain in the universities and not to enter industry or the schools. The Committee recommended new forms of postgraduate training of a less academic kind involving closer links between universities and industry. It also wished to see the development of more attractive opportunities in schoolteaching and the educational use of highly qualified science and engineering staff in government establishments.

Swaziland, Education in 1965 statistics: in 364 schools and colleges there were 49,464 primary school children, 2,854 secondary, 106 technical and vocational, and 159 students at teacher training college.

The country's population was nearly 400,000 in 1966.

Swimming Over the last 20 years the general pattern of swimming instruction in schools has undergone a considerable change. At one time, owing to a shortage of swimming bath accommodation, few children received school-organised coaching in swimming techniques before the secondary school stage. Even if instruction was given to top-primary children, teaching by class methods was difficult because the water in the average municipal swimming bath was too deep for the children, even at the shallow end.

This state of affairs was changed completely by the advent of shallow 'learner pools' small enough to ensure close contact between teacher and pupil during instruction, in which the first emphasis was on water-confidence and not on swimming stroke techniques. In addition, the excellent work of the English Schools Swimming Association in promoting and encouraging the building of relatively cheap swimming pools in individual schools has not only led to a great increase in the numbers receiving instruction but has also made instruction available even to children in the infant stage.

The increase in the number of children proficient in swimming has also played a part in widening the PE curriculum at the secondary school stage, for the ability to swim is compulsory in activities such as sailing, rowing and canoeing.

Amateur Swimming Association, 64 Cannon St, London EC4.

English Schools Swimming Association; S. Hartley, 106 Bocking La., Sheffield 8.

FURTHER READING
ASA Diving Manual, ASA, 1964.
ASA Handbook. Published annually in April.
J. Edmundson. *The Pan Book of Swimming and Water Sports*, Pan, 1965.
H. Littlewood. *Learning to Swim*, Bell, 1964.
Swimming and Diving. Official ESSA coaching book.
Swimming Instruction, ASA, 1964.

JE

Swimming Association, English Schools The Association, which is not normally able to answer general inquiries about swimming, publishes an annual handbook, giving names and addresses of local association secretaries, dates of galas and suggested standards, and also is responsible for *Swimming and Diving* (Heinemann), the coaching handbook of the ESSA.

Gen. Sec.: E. H. Burden, 190 Nether St, West Finchley, London, N3.

Swimming baths, School Ideally, children should be taught to swim while at primary school, so that when they begin secondary education they have enough confidence and basic proficiency to enable them to concentrate on the more interesting aspects of swimming. Unfortunately, it is seldom possible to provide the range of facilities that would permit this progression of increasing skills, since most school swimming baths are used primarily for teaching the fundamentals of swimming. In a conflict between a bath's various uses, priority should be given to the provision of adequate teaching facilities; it is preferable that limited resources should be used to teach all children to swim proficiently rather than to train a few to become experts.

More comprehensive facilities may be provided where the LEA is willing to contribute to the education committee's resources and to provide a swimming bath for joint use by school and public.

In instructional swimming baths the water and air have to be maintained at higher temperature than in a bath used by more advanced, competitive swimmers. If a bath is used outside school hours by local organisations, the ventilation, heating and filtration plant must be able to cope with the extra load. It should also be capable of easy maintenance by the school caretaking staff.

Changing rooms should be so flexible that they may be used by varying numbers of boys and girls, without wasting time at the change-over between teaching periods. The relationship of swimming bath, changing rooms and laundry facilities to the rest of the school is important. The children should be able to move from one to the other in the correct sequence along the easiest and shortest routes. If the bath is used by the public it should be so sited that access is convenient and direct and does not involve passing through other parts of the school.

FURTHER READING

Swimming Bath Costs (Ministry of Housing and Local Govt Ref. SfB (95) UDC 725.74).

Indoor Swimming Bath Spaces, Fixtures and Equipment (Architects' Journal Information Sheets Ref. SfB (85) dated 21–25 October 1964).

JCP

Switzerland, Education in The great variety in Swiss schooling is due to the fact that Switzerland is a confederation of 22 cantons. The federal constitution imposes on the cantons the duty of providing a sufficient education, but leaves them to decide the form. The Conference of the Cantonal Educational Directory acts as a co-ordinating body.

The general principles are: (1) compulsory education is free; (2) no child is compelled to attend classes for religious instruction; (3) private schools must be open to inspection by the authorities.

Children join the elementary school at the age of six or seven, and all children born in the same year are taught together. For those who remain in the elementary school the course lasts seven, eight or nine years. The practice varies in the different cantons, but somewhere between the fourth and sixth years the majority of pupils transfer to a secondary school or, at a higher academic level, to a 'gymnasium'.

Secondary schools aim to provide sufficient schooling for children in the middle range of intelligence who do not expect to go on to the university. Following the secondary school course there are often vocational schools for artisans, technicians and mechanics, and craft schools for decorators, painters and photographers. At Lausanne and Lucerne there are hotel schools, and at Geneva and Zurich there are restaurant schools.

The gymnasium is the high school at which the curriculum is based on the requirements of the Maturity examination, which is the entrance requirement for the universities.

In the field of higher education, degree courses are available at the Federal Institute of Technology and the School of Economics and Public Administration as well as at the seven universities.

Syria, Education in 1966 statistics: 4,647 primary schools (enrolments 688,165), 581 secondary schools (enrolments 46,796); vocational schools had 7,583 students and teacher training colleges 5,198. There are two universities at Damascus and one at Aleppo (total enrolment 34,092 students). Total population was approximately $5\frac{1}{2}$ million in 1966.

T

Table tennis A game similar to table tennis was in existence as long ago as 1880, and in 1902 a Ping Pong Association was formed; but the game lost its popularity until just after the first world war. Table tennis has since developed enormously and is played to an exceedingly high level of skill all over the world, with a regular world championship competition. A curious feature of the game is that no distinction is made between amateurs and professionals.

At top-class level this is essentially a young person's game because of the speed at which it is played; indeed, the youngest international (probably in any sport in the world) was Joy Foster, who in 1958 won the Jamaican singles and mixed doubles championship at the age of eight.

With the present wider concepts of PE in schools, table tennis is recognised as a game worthy of inclusion in the curriculum both for its skill and its recreational quality.

Table Tennis Association, 26 Park Cres., London, W1.

JE

Talmud The Talmud is a collection of Rabbinic law and discussion comprising the *Mishnah*, a succinct statement of Rabbinic law compiled c. 200 AD, and two wide-ranging elaborations thereof, the Palestinian or Jerusalem Talmud, c. 400 AD, and the Babylonian Talmud, c. 550 AD.

Talmud Torah This is a Hebrew term meaning either the study of the Torah (*q.v.*) or an elementary Jewish school devoted to the study of basic Jewish religious texts.

Tanzania, Education in There are not enough schools to provide universal primary education. All schools are either government-established or wholly or partially maintained by the state or local authorities. 1964 statistics: Tanganyika: 3,639 primary schools (enrolment 633,678); 68 secondary schools (enrolment 19,907); 3 vocational and technical schools (enrolment 2,955); 21 teacher training colleges (enrolment 2,261). There were 700 students at the University College of Dar es Salaam, part of the University of East Africa. Higher education is pursued by a number of students in the UK, USA, Canada, India, Pakistan and other East African territories; the total number of overseas students was 1,300.

Zanzibar: 76 primary schools (enrolment 20,551); 10 secondary schools (enrolment 1,510); 4 vocational schools (enrolment 182); 2 teacher training colleges (enrolment 105).

Population in 1964 (approximate): Tanganyika 10 million, Zanzibar 300,000.

See also **Africa, East, Education in**

Taunton Report (1868) (Royal Commission) Terms of reference: to enquire into the education given in schools not included under the Newcastle and Clarendon Reports, and also to consider and report what measures, if any, were required for the improvement of such education, considering especially endowments which were or might be applicable.

The report covered all the schools between the elementary ones of the Newcastle Report, and the nine public schools of the Clarendon Report. The grammar schools were re-classified into non-classical and grammar. The Commission then considered how schools could be arranged to fit in with the wishes of the parents, and with their social background, and classified them as first, second and third grade, where pupils would stay until 18 or 19, 16 and 14 respectively.

The Report made many recommendations concerning the chaotic administration of the time, and suggested that the boards of governors should join together into boards of education, and administrate on a local basis, together with the official district commissioners who were appointed by the charity commissioners.

The Commission also criticised the state of education for girls.

Tavistock Institute of Human Relations The Tavistock Institute studies human relations in conditions of well-being, conflict or breakdown, in the family, the work group and the larger organisation. It provides postgraduate training in its main spheres of work and gives priority to supervised practical work and to courses in theory and technique related to such practice.

The Institute was incorporated in 1947 as a company limited by guarantee and not for profit, and is at present organised in five units: the Human Resources Centre; the Centre for Applied Social Research; the Institute for Operational Research; the Committee on Family Psychiatry and Community Mental Health; and the Family Discussion Bureau.

The two last-named units work in conjunction with the Tavistock Clinic, a unit of the National Health Service, and together with the Clinic offer full-time and part-time courses of training in family psychiatry and community mental health for psychiatrists, clinical and educational psychologists, child psychotherapists (non-medical), social caseworkers, caseworkers specialising in marital work, general practitioners, public health officers and teachers. A prospectus giving details of these courses is published annually.

Tavistock Centre, Belsize Lane, London, NW3.

'Tax on Knowledge' Act (1819) This Act established a tax on all cheap newspapers except those which contained matters of devotion, piety or charity and was an attempt by the government to squash the radical and the critical press of the time. The tax was reduced after extensive protests in 1836 and abolished finally in 1855.

Teach-in An American term, strictly indicating an event in which experts, holders of opposing views and inquirers contribute to a running discussion the main aim of which is that a topic of great current interest should be thoroughly sifted. The edge that a real teach-in has over a normal debate or conference might be said to lie in the urgency with which all concerned set out both to become more informed about a topic and to carry its discussion purposefully forward.

Teacher education in England and Wales The need for a system of teacher training in England and Wales became apparent around 1840. The limitations of the 'monitorial system', developed by Bell and Lancaster earlier in the century, were by then very plain; the 'simultaneous system' of class teaching had been popularised by David Stow and a technique of training for it was first devised at the Glasgow Normal Seminary.

In England at this time there existed a number of short courses of training provided by the National Society and the British and Foreign Society in London and 35 provincial centres. Many of these were the embryos of the training colleges which developed between 1839 and 1846. The Committee of the Privy Council on Education 1839, with Dr J. P. Kay as its first secretary, had proposed a national training college (an outburst of sectarian protest buried this proposal); Kay (Kay-Shuttleworth) started a normal school at Battersea, largely at his own expense. Battersea, with the model of the Glasgow Seminary and the continental normal schools behind it, was a pioneer institution. Complementary to it and feeding it was Kay-Shuttleworth's 'pupil-teacher' training scheme, whereby bright children from the elementary schools became apprentices at 14 to experienced teachers, continuing their own education and undergoing practical training concurrently.

For the rest of the century the expanding elementary system depended on the pupil-teachers as the chief means of meeting its staffing problems: the majority of them became certificated teachers by taking the examinations conducted (until the 1920s) by the Education Department (later Board of Education). By 1900 the meagreness of the academic education which had to cover the whole range of the elementary curriculum and the formality and sterility of the professional training had become apparent.

The training colleges, of which Battersea was the main prototype, took over the dual function of the pupil-teacher system: it was indeed the only solution at that time and until, in 1902, the earlier academic education of teachers could be entrusted to the secondary schools. Apart from this the characteristic of Battersea and later colleges was an emphasis on the formation of character, achieved through the development of a sense of vocation, the appeal to Christian charity as a motive, spartan conditions of life, constant activity from 5 am to 9 or 10 pm, close supervision, and a model school where instruction in 'the system' was supervised by a 'master of method'.

St Mark's College, founded about the same time as Battersea by the National Society, represented a variant model in some respects. Its first principal, Derwent Coleridge, admitted 'social advancement' as a proper motive (in this he was much before his time), and in fact it was a complaint about St Mark's that many of its students did not enter or stay in elementary school service but went into higher-class schools, entered the Church, or took up other occupations. Coleridge did not approve of the 'bald utilities and white-washed parallelograms' provided by most training colleges; he thought the goal to be aimed at should be, as far as possible, that provided by the older universities and their ideal of a liberal education. The emphasis at St Mark's was therefore on literary studies, including Latin, and professional training was of secondary importance. The conflict between the academic and professional sides of the college's work constitutes a problem that has not to this day been successfully solved.

The period of college-founding between 1839 and 1846 was followed by a period of stabilisation, with academic standards set by the national certificate examinations, professional standards by the criticism and demonstration lessons which established models for imitation, and social and moral standards by the cloistered and gregarious life, the strict discipline, and emphasis on religious observance. Any chance of broadening and deepening the education provided by the colleges was cut off sharply by the effects of the Revised Code 1861 (*q.v.*). The impact on both the quantity and quality of teacher education was disastrous. The numbers of pupil teachers fell by over 4,000 in five years and the numbers of students in the colleges diminished, too; and although later revisions of the Code mitigated some of the evils, it was not until the last decade of the century that signs of renewed progress appeared.

In the decades before and after the turn of the century, a number of steps were taken which had a decisive effect on the quality of teacher education in England and Wales. The first of these came in 1890 when the Education Department drew up regulations for the administration of day training colleges in association with university institutions, and by 1899 seventeen of these colleges had been set up. It was by now apparent that some ex-pupil-teachers and residential college students were well capable of reaching degree standard; the existence of the London external degree had indeed enabled some of them to take concurrently a degree course and a course of professional training. The facilities were extended and standardised in day-training-college concurrent three-year courses. The stresses and strains in such a course and the rivalry for students' time and attention between the academic departments and the training departments of the universities led to a change in 1911 to a four-year consecutive course, a year of professional training following a mainly academic degree course. This is still the pattern in the initial training courses for graduates provided by the university departments of education, which developed from the day training colleges; the London Day Training College became an Institute of Education in 1932.

At an international conference on education in 1884, Professor Meiklejohn had deplored the lack of interest of the English universities in the professional education of teachers. 'There is, in no university in England, a single person whose duty it is to guide a teacher in his daily practice. So far as the English universities are concerned, education is still in its amateur and empiric stage'. Chairs in education had been established at Edinburgh and St Andrew's in 1876. At the 1884 conference, R. H. Quick had said, 'I say boldly that what English schoolmasters now stand in need of is *theory*; and further, that the universities have special advantages for meeting this need'. He, with Oscar Browning, pioneered the setting up of the Cambridge Syndicate in 1879 to arrange lectures and grant certificates in the theory and practice of education.

The acceptance of this function by the universities in general, old and new, after 1890 laid the foundations for the development of the study of education in a form and to a standard appropriate to a university subject. R. H. Quick's *Essays on Educational Reformers* (1868) foreshadowed the remarkable spate of studies in educational history published by the Cambridge University Press between 1897 and 1920. J. W. Adamson, Michael Sadler, F. A. Cavanagh, W. H. Woodward, R. L. Archer, Foster Watson and Frank Smith were among the scholars who developed this field; the study of English educational institutions and of the work of the great educators gradually became a normal part of the syllabus in departments and colleges of education. A more recent development has been the methodical study of comparative education, and several universities have established chairs in this subject.

The other main contribution to the developing study of education came from the field of psychology. Alexander Bain (*Education as a Science*, 1879) and James Sully (*Teachers' Handbook of Psychology*, 1886) were pioneers in relating psychology, then in process of transition to its modern more 'scientific' form, to education. Sully was the first to introduce systematic instruction in child psychology into courses for teachers; and from 1895, when Bain's and Sully's books were first introduced as texts into the third-year syllabus of the teachers' certificate examination, child study and other branches of educational psychology were gradually introduced into the department and college courses in principles of education. C. H. Judd, writing in 1914 (*The Training of Teachers in England, Scotland and Germany*), repeated the earlier plaint of Quick and Meiklejohn about the neglect of theory in the English training college courses. He attributed this to the influence of the pupil-teacher tradition on the colleges with its emphasis on an apprenticeship in practical teaching. As we have seen, 'theory' in this tradition was meagrely represented by instruction in class and school management. By 1924, L. G. E. Jones (*The Training of Teachers in England and Wales*) was noting the development of a more scientific kind of training, based on the study of psychology, though he also noted that the quality of staff and students was not yet high enough to avoid the pitfalls of 'potted psychology' and 'assurance begotten of little knowledge'.

In the years between the world wars, the 'scientific' aspects of educational psychology were developed in the work of Cyril Burt, Charles Spearman and Godfrey Thomson. Percy Nunn's *Education, its Data and First Principles* (1920) was an application of William McDougall's then fashionable 'hormic' psychology to the field of education and provided academic support for the basic principles of 'progressive education'. During these same years, modern applications of the ideas and practices of Pestalozzi and Froebel had transformed infant education in the country; this may be attributed largely to the efforts of the Froebel Society (founded in 1874) and the three-year colleges and courses it sponsored where 'progressive' theory and practice in the kindergarten schools attached to them were very closely integrated. Other influences in the same direction came

from the Montessori Society and the schools using Montessori methods, Margaret McMillan's work at Deptford and her book *Education through the Imagination* (1913), and the coming together of progressive educators from many countries to found the New Education Fellowship, Calais, in 1921.

By 1940 the training colleges had moved far from their 19th-century tradition of rigidity and cultural poverty; they had become largely 'progressive' in both theory and practice. In addition to the study of education, each student read one or two main or special subjects in depth and for his or her own personal and cultural benefit. In short the whole course, apart from school practice and the curriculum work needed for practical purposes, had moved very near to the pattern of a university general or combined studies degree.

What had made this possible in the first place had been the decision foreshadowed by the Departmental Committee's Report of 1898 which 'looked forward with confidence to the use of Secondary Schools as the best means of overcoming that narrowness of intellectual and professional outlook which has long been felt to be one of the weakest points of the profession'. The Education Act 1902 made this development possible. The pupil teacher centres, which received their first grant in 1902, came increasingly to be associated with the expanding system of secondary schools; and in 1906 a bursary and student teacher system was established which by 1910 was supplying as many teachers as the pupil teacher system. With the grammar schools taking responsibility for the basic academic education of teachers, the colleges were freed for the development of deeper study both in education and in selected academic subjects.

The closer approximation of university and college courses was aided by an administrative change in the late

1920s. The Board of Education handed over its supervision and control of syllabuses and examinations for the teacher's certificate to regional joint boards or syndicates, each centred in a university department of education, and provided the services for the colleges in the area. Here in embryonic form were the institutes or schools of education which came into being after 1946, implementing the recommendation of the McNair Committee's report. This proposed two patterns of association of area training organisations with universities; the universities, with one exception, either chose the pattern of closer association to begin with, or changed to it after trial of the other. The institutes, since their inception after the war, have not only acted as area training organisations for the initial training courses; they have developed in-service courses, both full-time and part-time, long and short, for practising teachers on a much larger scale than existed before.

In the period since the end of World War II, efforts to improve the quality of teacher education have had to compete with the urgent need to expand the number of students in training. The first crisis arose from the post-war bulge in the birth rate and this was met by the emergency training scheme which provided one-year courses for older students in temporary buildings. It was then thought that after the bulge the birth rate would return to its pre-war level, and on this expectation government approval was given for an extension of the general colleges' two-year course to three. The first students embarked on these courses in 1960. But by then it had become clear, first that the population expansion was not immediately going to level off, and secondly that a change to an earlier age of marriage and child bearing would result in a high rate of fall-out of young women soon after they had entered the profession.

The teacher shortage was most acute in the primary schools, and a change in the balance of training was effected whereby 80% of the college population would in future be prepared for primary work. At the same time plans were made for a permanent expansion of the numbers of teachers in training through a variety of measures: new buildings in existing colleges, new colleges, use of improvised buildings, annexes and outposts, crowding, and reorganisation of time and space. In the event the 22,000 teachers in training of 1950 had become 84,000 in 1967.

The stresses, strains and challenges involved in this expansion have been extreme. In the process the image of the training college (now college of education) has been transformed. In 1958, 98 out of 140 colleges had fewer than 250 students; in 1967, of 160 colleges only 18 had fewer than 250, and 13 had 750 or more. In the same period the number of colleges admitting men and women rose from 15 to 100. In these conditions, the changes in social and educational climate, which had begun in many colleges in the pre-war period, were further stimulated and extended.

The Committee on Higher Education, reporting in 1963, re-emphasised the McNair Report's plea that the universities should assume fuller responsibility for the education of teachers. The Robbins Report recommendation that bachelor of education degrees be made available for some college students has been adopted now by all the universities with institutes of education; in most cases degree syllabuses have been approved and the first students registered. The Robbins Committee's other main recommendation that the colleges be brought fully within the university orbit financially and administratively was not accepted by the government. The cleavage between the two sides of the dual system of higher education runs through the heart of every college of education; it continues to have to serve two masters, very different in their outlook and ways of operating. Some bridges across the gulf are blue-printed in the recommendation of a working party on the government of colleges; these have now been accepted by the government.

The story is not yet finished: but it can be said that teacher education in England and Wales is now at long last in sight of the goal envisaged for it one hundred years ago by a handful of pioneers and visionaries.

FURTHER READING

George Z. F. Bereday and J. A. Lauwerys (Eds.). 'The Education and Training of Teachers', *Year Book of Education 1963*, Evans, 1963.
M. V. C. Jeffreys. *Revolution in Teacher Training*, Pitman, 1961.
R. W. Rich. *The Training of Teachers in England and Wales during the 19th Century*, Cambridge University Press, 1933. *The Teacher in a Planned Society*, University of London Press, 1950.
J. W. Tibble (Ed.). *The Study of Education*, Routledge and Kegan Paul, 1966.
Asher Tropp. *The School Teachers*, Heinemann, 1957.
Report of the Committee on Higher Education (Robbins Report), HMSO, 1963.
The Supply, Recruitment and Training of Teachers and Youth Leaders (McNair Report), HMSO, 1944.
Education for Teaching (Journal of the Association of Teachers in Colleges and Departments of Education). Thrice yearly from 1942.

JWT

Teacher estimates and teacher shortage The most important practical problem in education is teacher supply. Official forecasts of supply and demand for teachers have seriously under-estimated the size of the problem at different times during the past 15 years, in spite of the assiduous attention of the National Advisory Council on the Training and Supply of Teachers (*q.v.*).

Demand for teachers is governed by the birth-rate, and estimates of births have been wide and low of the mark. In 1939, live births in England and Wales were 614,000. The post-war bulge brought the figure to 881,000 in 1947, followed by a decline to 668,000 in 1955. Contrary to forecasts, the figure had since increased to over 850,000 a year by 1966—the result of new trends in the affluent society; earlier marriage, closer spacing of families, and an increase in the size of completed families.

Taking account of these factors, recent forecasts predict a steady and continuing increase in the number of births, rising to nearly one million a year by 1981. It remains to be seen whether the assumptions on which these forecasts are based will remain entirely valid. Nevertheless, forecasting births as far ahead as 1981 and beyond is necessary in estimating the demand for teachers; and the National Advisory Council in their *Ninth Report* (1965), have used these figures.

On that basis, it is estimated that the number of children in the maintained primary and secondary schools of England and Wales, now just over 7 million, will increase to 10 million by 1981. In the shorter term, for which the estimates are obviously more reliable, the number of school children in 1972 is given as 8.7 million, including an additional 350,000 on the raising of the leaving age to 16 in 1972–3, and 9.5 million in 1976.

Accepting these figures, the National Council have estimated the demand for teachers to ensure that school classes shall not exceed 30 in a second-ary school, or 40 in a primary school—limits prescribed in statutory regu-lations, first made in 1945, with an escape clause allowing larger classes until the shortage of teachers and school accommodation could be over-come. It has been necessary to rely heavily on the escape clause so far, and this will continue for several more years. In estimating the demand for teachers, it must be remembered that many school classes will remain well below the limits mentioned (for ex-ample, in village schools, in secondary school sixth forms, and in practical classes) and that, except in the smallest schools, head teachers are not in full-time charge of a class; and that children do not come to primary or secondary schools in precise packages of 30 or 40.

Allowing for all these factors, the National Council estimate the demand for teachers, compared with the demand in 1963, as follows:

	1963	1968	1972	1978	1981
Demand for teachers (ooos)	334	358	420	461	491

Also, advocating that as soon as practicable the maximum size of a primary school class be reduced to 30, the National Council give a further estimate of the demand for teachers as 545,000 in 1978 and 562,000 in 1981.

On the subject of teacher supply, past estimates have been belied by the new and pervasive tendency of young women teachers to marry, start families and leave the service soon after beginning to teach; although supply has been greatly enlarged, so has wastage. Later, increasing numbers of married women teachers return to full or part-time teaching (which has become a permanent feature of supply arrangements and will develop still further); by this time, however, the number of pupils in schools has increased substantially. In part mitigation of this problem, arrangements have been made to increase the proportion of men teachers from 30% to 36% of the total, and to recommend an increase to 40%.

To cope with the main problem of teacher supply, colleges of education have already been built or extended to increase the annual intake of students from 14,000 in 1957–8 to 29,000 in 1965, and the figure is to be increased to 40,000 in the early 70s. With recruitment from other sources, e.g. universities and married women returners, it is estimated that the number of qualified teachers in service will rise from the figure of 280,000 in 1963 to 440,000 by 1976 and 540,000 in 1981. Referring to the figures given earlier, it is estimated that the shortage of 54,000 teachers in 1963 will be reduced to 21,000 by 1976 and overtaken before 1981 on current policies for staffing, thereby providing for a reduction below 40 of the maximum number in a primary school class.

All the figures quoted refer only to the maintained primary and secondary schools in England and Wales, which, however, constitute 80% of the problem of teacher supply and demand. If all other educational establishments in England and Wales are included— universities, technical colleges, colleges of education, direct grant and independent schools, and special schools —their demands of 83,000 teachers in 1963 are estimated to increase to about 150,000 by 1981.

The massive expansion of universities, colleges of education, and other higher education establishments, under the recommendations of the Robbins Report (q.v.), accepted by the government, are expected to cope with the demands of all professions and industries for recruits from the higher education system. But to meet the demands of all educational establishments for teachers will involve about half the total annual output from the whole higher education system being recruited for teaching service of one kind or another. Whether or not it is possible to achieve that has not so far been examined. On the other hand, the rapid development of new teaching aids and techniques may affect the current pattern of school organisation and proportionately reduce the rate of demand for qualified teachers. And although the idea of employing unqualified auxiliaries has, understandably, not yet been welcomed by the teaching profession, the future position may be different.

See also **Married women teachers**

FB

Teacher-pupil relations Classroom climates have changed a great deal since the harsh days of Dickens' Mr Gradgrind. At all levels and in all subjects methods of teaching are less authoritarian. The repressive discipline which prevailed in 19th-century schools, and the corporal punishment that went with it, have given way to a more permissive atmosphere. The growth of extra-curricular activities has helped to reduce the social distance between teacher and pupils, at any rate outside the classroom. Inside it, too, it is easier than before for the teacher to assume the role of guide, philosopher and friend.

There are many reasons for the change. Not the least important is the long-term effect of the increased provision and rising standards of education, which tend to make both pupils and parents less amenable to authoritarian treatment. Another factor is the secular trend towards earlier physical maturity, which means that methods once thought appropriate for 10- to 11-year olds have had to be revised. The emergence of an adolescent culture—the 'teenage revolt', as it is sometimes called—reflects the same trend. Again, the pervasive influence of the mass media is to promote, however superficially, a certain sophistication, and to that extent has eroded any oracular role the teacher may have had.

While the more informal relationships in school life and work are best understood as part of a wider social change, the influence of child-centred theory and practice, stemming from the writings of John Dewey (*q.v.*), Jean Piaget (*q.v.*) and others, should not be minimised. This school of thought has a long history, dating back to Comenius (*q.v.*) and Rousseau (*q.v.*). The advocacy of so-called activity methods, first mooted in England in the Hadow Committee's 1931 Report *The Primary School*, has in the long run been vindicated. As yet research findings which actually prove that 'progressive' methods are more effective than the traditional ones are hard to come by, though there is some supportive evidence in the Plowden Report. In the USA the widely publicised Lippitt, White and Young experiment investigated three different classroom climates—authoritarian, laissez-faire and democratic—and concluded that the latter was superior in all respects. How far these findings are applicable in British schools, where social and cultural conditions are different, remains questionable.

At the moment sociologists and psychologists are carrying out investigations into the social structure of schools, including the close analysis of pupils' responses in various types of learning situations. Sociometry (*q.v.*) and group dynamics are two studies which represent attempts to apply the techniques of social science to problems of school organisation. As the school unit, particularly at the secondary stage, becomes progressively larger the danger is that individual differences may be lost sight of in a depersonalised, institutional atmosphere. If he is to retain the 'human touch', the modern teacher must know something about the techniques of social science, otherwise the problems of maintaining morale and pupil-teacher contact are likely to be left to chance.

WKR

Teacher representatives *See* **Consultation**

Teachers, National Union of The National Union of Teachers is one of the biggest professional organisations of teachers in the world. Its membership is confined to England and Wales but very friendly relations are maintained with the Union's sister organisations in Scotland and Northern Ireland and the Union plays a leading part in the World Confederation of Organisations of the Teaching Profession.

With 287,713 teacher and student members in 1967, it has nearly three times as many members as all the other teacher organisations in the country combined.

Apart from its size, the NUT differs from the other teachers' organisations in that it is the only one open to all qualified teachers irrespective of sex, status and qualifications and the type of school or college in which the teacher serves. It has members throughout the education service, including higher and further education. The NUT strongly supports the concept of one professional organisation for all teachers and has consistently sought to promote professional unity. As a practical step towards this goal, the NUT has entered into partnership schemes with a number of other professional organisations: The Association of Teachers in Technical Institutions, the Association of Teachers of Domestic Subjects, the British Association of Organisers and Lecturers in Physical Education, the Association of Educational Psychologists, the National Association of Youth Service Officers, the Youth Service Association, and the British Association of Art Therapists. Its partnership agreements provide reciprocal membership and wide co-operation.

Foundation The NUT celebrates its centenary in 1970. Before its foundation in 1870 a number of separate teachers' associations existed in different parts of England and Wales, each small in size and possessing little influence. In most cases these associations were connected with a religious denomination or a broad religious interest. There was no organisation which united the teachers in elementary schools, as such, into one body. In 1870, however, the growing interest in popular education, the passage of the Education Act 1870, and the general discontent of the teachers with their conditions, especially payment by results, convinced their leaders that the time was ripe for union.

Three associations in London—the Church, British and Wesleyan Teachers' Organisations—summoned the first conference of representatives from the various teachers' associations in the country. Delegates from twenty-six associations, representing some 400 individual members, meeting at King's College, London, passed a resolution declaring the National Union of Elementary Teachers formed. The word 'Elementary' was dropped from its title in 1888.

Aims The early aims of the Union, stated in the first document it issued, were to unite public elementary teachers throughout the kingdom, by means of local associations, so that they might express their opinions when occasion required and take united action in matters affecting their interests. Among the issues to which the Union first turned its attentions were the revision of the new code, the working of the 1870 Education Act, the establishment of a pension scheme, the opening up of higher educational posts to elementary teachers, and the raising of professional dignity by means of a public register of duly qualified teachers (*See* **Teachers' Register**).

While some of the aims of the founders are past history, the present objects retain something of the early flavour and also indicate the range of the NUT's present activities. They include the improvement of education in England and Wales and the establishment of a national system of education, 'co-ordinated and complete'; the securing for all state-aided schools of financial assistance from public sources, together with 'suitable conditions'; to advise the government, the Ministry and the LEAs; to secure the effective representation of educational interests in Parliament; to secure the recognition of the teaching profession as a diploma-granting authority; to watch over the administration and working of the various Education Acts and other Acts of Parliament connected with education, together with Regulations made under those Acts and Memoranda and Circulars issued by the Ministers concerned, to endeavour to amend them where educationally desirable, and to secure the removal of difficulties, abuses and obsolete regulations that are detrimental to progress; to maintain a high standard of qualifications, to raise the status of the profession and to ensure that all posts in the educational service are open to members; to extend protection to teachers where necessary; to watch the administration of the Superannuation Acts and Pension Regulations, and to endeavour to have them amended where necessary; and to establish, or join with other bodies in establishing, charitable trusts of an educational nature and to subscribe to such trusts as already exist.

The NUT has a long record of achievement in its struggle to raise the status of, and win better conditions for, the teaching profession, and to secure more and better education for the nation's children. Sir George Kekewich, a former Secretary of the Board of Education, said of the NUT: 'They have always fearlessly attacked all absurdities of our educational system, have never cringed before officialism, have stood for progress—never for apathy or reaction—have constantly and consistently used their powerful influence for the good of the child as well as of the teacher, and have been the mightiest lever of educational reform.'

Parliamentary activities The NUT has always seen its role as a broad one. While it provides a wide range of services and benefits for its members, and has created ancillary organisations to provide yet more benefits, it has always devoted much of its effort to securing greater opportunities for children and promoting educational reform, frequently conducting campaigns (such as the highly successful one against the importation of 'horror comics') which put the interests of children first. The NUT lobby in Parliament has long been one of the strongest; it was probably at its height in the period leading up to the passage of the 1944 Education Act, but ever since the war the NUT has campaigned vigorously on educational issues, organising lobbies of MPs, seeking to amend legislation, and exerting pressure directly on Ministers and the DES. Since 1895 there has been a succession of eminent NUT MPs. In the present Parliament (1968) there are more than 30 MPs who are members of the NUT. Nevertheless, the NUT has always maintained its non-party political character, and has confined its political action exclusively to securing educational developments and the advancement of the teaching profession.

Staff The NUT has grown enormously since its early days, and today nearly 300 people are employed at Hamilton House, the headquarters in Bloomsbury. Many of these employees are engaged in the work of the ancillary bodies, which were established after the NUT had been founded and whose activities are described below.

The NUT staff consists of the officials, clerical and technical staff who work in the departments at Hamilton House, and the regional officials who serve in 12 electoral regions into which England and Wales are divided. Those regional offices represent a unique feature of the NUT's services to its members; the Union is the only teachers' organisation with full-time officials working outside London, and they handle much of the case-work on teachers' problems and negotiate with the LEAs. The departments at Hamilton House deal with education, legal services, salaries and superannuation, membership and organisation, finance, publicity and public relations, and international relations. There is also a large library and information bureau, the facilities of which are available free to members.

The NUT's general secretary, Sir Ronald Gould, is also President of the World Confederation of Organisations of the Teaching Profession. The World Confederation is one of the three international bodies in which the Union plays a leading part; the other bodies are the International Federation of Teachers' Associations and the International Federation of Secondary Teachers. The NUT's general secretary is also the leader of the teachers' panel of the Burnham Primary and Secondary School Committee. The Union has a majority on the teachers' panel.

The NUT is represented on over a hundred other bodies and institutions. It maintains frequent and direct day-to-day contact with the DES on matters affecting teachers, and is regularly consulted by the Department on draft circulars and on developments in educational policy. Similarly, the NUT is frequently in touch with the local authority organisations and individual LEAs on matters affecting teachers and the education service.

Ancillary bodies In 1962 the Teachers' Provident Society (founded 1878) and the Teachers' Assurance Company Limited (founded 1936) merged to form the Teachers' Assurance, and between them they promote facilities for sick pay, life assurance, annuities and endowments, house purchase and advances on mortgages. The total invested funds of the TA exceeded £23 million in 1967. The most recent development in this field has been the establishment of the Teachers' Building Society, which aims to give house purchase facilities to teachers on very favourable terms. The Society met with an immediate response from teachers and the public, and within a year of its establishment had amassed funds from investors of over £4 million.

The Orphanage and Orphan Fund founded in 1878 for the benefit of teachers' children developed into the Benevolent and Orphan Fund, which in 1967 changed its name to the Teachers' Benevolent Fund. The purpose of the Fund is to help teachers in sickness and distress and to give aid to the widows and orphans and dependants of deceased teachers. It also runs homes for sick and elderly teachers. The annual expenditure of the Fund exceeded £200,000 in 1967, and in spite of the creation of the welfare state, demands on the Fund have increased year by year. The Fund obtains its income from the voluntary donations of teachers and by appeals and special fund-raising activities.

The Schoolmaster Publishing Company is responsible for publication of the Union's weekly journal *The Teacher*, first published in 1872 as *The Schoolmaster*. The journal is obtainable through newsagents and is published on Fridays; copies are also distributed direct to schools. *The Teacher* contains the *Educational Appointments Gazette*, which is sponsored jointly by the Schoolmaster Publishing Company and the Council for Education Press, the publishing company of the Association of Education Committees. The Company also publishes a variety of books and pamphlets (as does the NUT itself), and *Youth Review*, the journal of all those engaged professionally in youth work.

FJ

Teachers' Assurance *See* **Teachers, National Union of**

Teachers' Benevolent Fund *See* **Teachers, National Union of**

Teachers' Building Society *See* **Teachers, National Union of**

Teachers in Colleges and Departments of Education, Association of
The ATCDE is the professional association of men and women engaged in the training of teachers in colleges, university departments and institutes of education in England and Wales. Its objects are the improvement of the

education and training of teachers, the protection of the professional interests of its members, the furtherance of their educational interests and the promotion of research in education.

The Association was founded in 1943 to replace the former Training College Association and the Council of Principals. The present membership is nearly 5,000. The Association is active in the discussion and formation of national policies on the supply and education of teachers.

The journal of the Association, *Education for Teaching*, is published three times a year and is available to non-members. Together with the British Psychological Society the ATCDE is responsible for the publication three times a year of *The British Journal of Educational Psychology*. Other publications include *The Handbook on Training for Teaching*.

151 Gower St, London, WC1.

Teachers' Family Benefits Scheme
As the name implies, the Teachers' Family Benefits Scheme is intended to provide cover for a teacher's wife and children against his death in service or as a pensioner. The contributions are paid into a fund controlled by a board of management.

A man entering teaching for the first time pays 2% of his salary for the benefits; relief from income tax is likely to apply. For men whose teaching begins after 31 March 1969 membership of the scheme will be compulsory. Those who enter pensionable teaching service before then may take part if they wish, but only if they apply for membership within a stipulated period, normally three months from the date of appointment. Those who elect to join cannot afterwards withdraw; those who do not apply for membership within the time limit cannot join later unless they subsequently marry or re-marry.

Where a teaching appointment is taken up either before or after 31

March 1969, thereby constituting re-entry to teaching, then participants must buy in the whole of the past service if less than 10 years, or at least 10 years if more than that time had been served as a teacher. The buying in of past service adds to the cost, but there are various methods of meeting the cost.

There is a separate scheme enabling teachers to provide for dependants other than widows and children of a marriage. Both men and women teachers can apply, and subject to certain age limitations they may do so at any time.

A widow's pension is one-third of the pension the teacher was receiving when he died. If death occurs in service after ten years or more as a teacher, the widow's pension will be one-third of the pension which would have been due if a breakdown in health rather than death had caused the teacher to cease his career (*See* **Breakdown pensions**). The minimum widow's pension, however, is £125 per annum, provided the qualifying period of ten years is established. Considerably more than £125 can be secured if the pension or salary position justifies it.

Short-service widow's pension Eligibility occurs after three years of service provided there is a child of the marriage but the benefits are lower. If on death a teacher had rendered at least three years' service and a child's pension was payable, his wife would also receive a short-service widow's pension. This would normally cease with the child's pension (unless the wife was then 50 or over) or on re-marriage.

If he had rendered at least three years' service and his wife was 50 or over at the time of his death she would receive a pension for life or until re-marriage, whether or not a child's pension was payable. Similarly she would receive a pension if she was under 50 on her husband's death but a child's pension would continue until she was 50 or over.

In either case the rate of pension would depend upon the number of completed years of service as follows: for three completed years, £63 a year, for four years £71, for five years £80, for six years £89, for seven years £98, for eight years £107 and for nine years £116 a year. A widow's pension is paid in addition to any children's pension.

Children's pension Provided a teacher has at least three years' service and is also survived by his wife, pensions for children are payable at these annual rates: for one child £65, for two children £120, for three children £175 and for four or more children £230.

If a wife should not survive the teacher, or if she should die while any of the children were still eligible for pension, the annual pensions would be: for one child £95, for two children £180, for three children £265 and for four or more children £355.

A legally adopted child of the teacher would qualify. A step child or illegitimate child, or an adopted child of the teacher's wife, would qualify if mainly dependent on the teacher before his retirement and at the date of his death.

A child will continue to be eligible so long as he is under 16. If he is receiving full-time education or being trained full-time for a trade or profession, pension will continue to be paid in full after 16 if his pay while in training does not exceed £115 a year; but, unless a teacher had covered at least ten years of service, payment would cease at 19. If pay during training were more than £115 a year the pension would be reduced by the amount of the excess, but not so as to affect any pensions payable for the benefit of other children.

A daughter's pension will in any case cease on her marriage.

An incapacitated child, that is to say a child who is mentally or physically incapable of earning a livelihood, and who is not wholly or mainly supported out of central or local government funds, will continue to be eligible for pension during his period of incapacity, irrespective of his age. When he reaches 16 the rate of his pension will be increased to £210 a year if there is a surviving widow or £325 a year if there is not. This pension will be paid in addition to that for other surviving children.

SEB

Teachers' General Certificate (Scotland) This is one of the three main kinds of certificate issued by the Secretary of State to teachers in Scotland. It qualifies the holder to teach primary school subjects, and may be followed by a further course to gain additional qualifications.

Teachers' General Council The argument that teachers should be able, through a general council, to have control over their own professional affairs is strongly urged by the seven main teachers' associations in England and Wales. The argument has been resisted by the Secretary of State for Education, mainly on the grounds that the setting up of such a body, controlling entry to the profession, would be out of place in a time of teacher shortage.

Teachers' Guild Benevolent Fund Established in 1898, this is a very small trust fund from which grants can be made 'for the relief of deserving men or women teachers in distress through temporary and unforeseen causes'.

Applications should be addressed to the Clerk to the Trustees at Gordon Hse, 29 Gordon Sq., London, WC1.

Teachers Overseas, National Council for the Supply of Established in 1960, the Council brings together representatives of teachers' organisations, LEAs, recruiting bodies and interested government departments in order to keep under review the progress of recruitment to teaching posts overseas; generally to assist the recruitment of teachers for service in the developing countries overseas and their resettlement on return; and to stimulate in the UK interest in service overseas in the developing countries and to promote a climate of opinion in which periods of service overseas are recognised as an asset in subsequent employment.

The Council is not concerned with posts in university institutions overseas except in relation to teachers in schools, technical colleges and colleges of education in the UK who wish to take such posts, and teachers in such posts who wish to serve in schools, technical colleges and colleges of education on return to the UK.

Teachers' Provident Society *See* **Teachers, National Union of**

Teachers' Register At present there is no precise definition of what constitutes the 'teaching profession'. In maintained primary and secondary schools in England and Wales, the large majority of those who teach have recognised qualifications and are accorded the status of 'qualified teacher' by the DES. In colleges, universities, and the whole range of other educational institutions, however, those who undertake teaching functions are likely to possess a variety of qualifications, and while many of these institutions may lay down or insist upon recognised teaching qualifications, in others the qualification of the teacher relates to the subject matter of his teaching or professional qualifications. Indeed, in institutions of further education and university faculties and schools the teachers are very often qualified members of other professions.

In Scotland the situation is different. With effect from April 1968 the Teachers' (Education, Training and Registration) (Scotland) Regulations 1967 prescribed that only those teachers registered with the General Teaching Council for Scotland (*q.v.*)

would have the right to hold permanent posts in education authority schools and to claim admission to the teachers' superannuation scheme. The Regulations prescribe the education and training conditions to be fulfilled by candidates before being recommended for teacher registration with the General Teaching Council. Recommendations are made by the governing bodies of colleges of education.

In effect, the establishment of the General Teaching Council means that in Scotland control of entry to the teaching profession is now vested in the hands of teachers, for the Council is a body elected by the teachers themselves; but in England and Wales, while teachers have sought comparable powers for nearly a century, they as yet lack them. Determination of qualified teacher status and hence of entry to the profession, in so far as there is any formal method of entry, is still vested in other hands. Attempts to establish a General Teachers' Council have failed in recent years because of the unwillingness of the government to hand over its powers to a body controlled by teachers. Even the Teachers' Register, which did exist for a long period, is now of only historical interest.

The idea of an official Register of Teachers was pressed in the latter part of the 19th century, and many attempts were made to secure legislation with a view to establishing a Register. It was not until the Board of Education Act of 1899, however, following the recommendations of a Royal Commission, that the Board of Education was empowered to establish a consultative committee of the Board and assigned to it the duty of framing regulations for a Register of Teachers. The first Register had two columns, one consisting of the names of teachers serving in elementary schools and the other of names of teachers serving in secondary schools and other educational institutions. There was, however, opposition to this on the ground that such a system of registration was based upon a class distinction of service in a particular type of school. A further Act in 1907 authorised the establishment of a Teachers' Registration Council with the duty of forming and keeping a Register of Teachers, the names to be established in one column and in alphabetical order. Even then it took some five years to devise a constitution for the proposed Council, but in February 1912 a Privy Council Order was issued establishing a Teachers' Registration Council on a representative basis and including in its membership teachers of every type nominated by universities and various organisations of teachers.

As at first constituted the Council was composed of four groups of teachers (11 in a group), each group representing a distinct type of professional interest, viz. elementary, secondary, specialist and university, with an independent chairman elected by the Council from outside its own personnel. The individual appointments to each group were made on the nomination of existing teachers' national organisations. As the number of registered teachers grew, a movement to elect members of the Council by the direct vote of the registered teachers themselves became apparent. It culminated in the adoption of a scheme whereby the four groups were to be continued as at first determined, but the individual members of each group were to be elected by the direct vote of the registered teachers whose interests they were to represent. Safeguards were also provided to ensure the election of men and women and heads and assistants. This scheme was adopted by the Council and implemented by the issue of another order in Council in 1926.

The object of the Register was to provide a list of persons eligible to teach in educational institutions, private and public, and to prevent those who were not on the Register from teaching. The Register was compiled by the Teachers' Registration Council and by 1929 the Council succeeded in obtaining the recognition of all registered teachers as members of the Royal Society of Teachers. Teachers who fulfilled the conditions laid down by the Council were admitted to registration and thereby became full members of the Royal Society of Teachers and were entitled to use for professional purposes the designation MRST. There was a single and final payment of a registration fee, which in 1931 was £3.

By 1931 98,548 teachers had been registered but in the 17 years between 1931 and 1948 only 9,246 new teachers were registered.

The inter-war years saw a decline in the influence that the Teachers' Registration Council may have had initially, for individual teachers looked more and more to their professional organisations. Eventually the Council ceased to make any contribution towards the improvement and control of teachers' qualifications, with the final result that its existence was terminated by Order in Council in 1949 and its Register was taken over by the Ministry of Education. The Register is still maintained by the DES for the declining number of teachers who were originally entered upon it. A number of causes have been advanced for the failure of the Teachers' Register, among them the following: (1) The Register and the Registration Council failed largely because registration was not compulsory and no powers were vested in the Council. (2) There were no clearly recognised qualifications for teachers, except in elementary schools, in which there were certificated teachers, uncertificated teachers and supplementary teachers. In secondary schools there were two main categories— graduate and non-graduate. In private or independent schools there were no uniform requirements. (3) The Board of Education also kept a Register of Teachers serving in grant-aided schools and institutions, in some of which the Board laid down the qualifications required of the teachers. (4) There were three Burnham Committees which dealt with the salaries of teachers. These three committees tended to divide rather than unite teachers in grant-aided institutions, in spite of the attempts which were made to unify the various teachers' organisations, whose main activities were centred on the three salary-negotiating committees. (5) The Board of Education was the government's centre of power and had responsibilities, including financial responsibilities, for (i) grant-aided schools and other educational institutions, (ii) the training and qualification of teachers, (iii) teachers' salaries, and its decisions had more influence on the lives and activities of teachers and their organisations than had any of the activities of the Teachers' Registration Council.

The above account perhaps understates the influence which teachers in England and Wales exert on standards of entry to their profession. While lacking a Registration Council governed by themselves and exerting control of entry to the teaching profession, the teachers do exert influence on entry standards in a variety of ways. Until recently their chief source of influence was through the work of the National Advisory Council for the Training and Supply of Teachers. The teacher organisations had representations on this body which advised the Minister on matters relating to the training of teachers and the supply of teachers. For example, it recommended the Minister to accept a lengthening of the basic training course from two to three years. The operations of this body were suspended by the Secretary of State for Education and Science in 1965 on the grounds that he felt a less unwieldy body was required, but in principle the Secretary of State has acknowledged the need for a new body to be set up and this is likely to be established shortly. If it retains the same functions as its predecessor, then the new body will give teachers a voice in matters relating to training and thereby of entry to the profession. One other way in which the teachers exert an influence is by their participation in the governing bodies of the various training institutions.

The efforts of teachers in England and Wales to secure a General Teaching Council have in the past been rejected by the Secretary of State for Education and Science largely on the grounds that the establishment of such a body might, at a time of teacher shortage, lead to the adoption of an obdurate attitude on the exclusion from schools of unqualified persons. However, with the setting up in 1968 of a working party of representatives of LEAs, teachers' organisations and the DES, responsible for studying the whole question of the employment of unqualified persons, this particular problem may be resolved; and there would then appear to be no major reason why the Secretary of State should refuse teachers in England and Wales registration machinery comparable to that already existing in Scotland.

FJ

Teachers' Registration Council *See* **Qualified teacher status**

Teachers Superannuation Act (1918) This Act provided for a compulsory pension scheme in all state-aided schools, financed partly by the teacher and partly by the government. This put the smaller public schools in a difficult position, and brought about their closer co-operation with the state system.

Teachers in Technical Institutions, Association of Founded in 1904 as the professional organisation of teachers in the public sector of further and higher education, the Association has as its aims and objects: to protect and promote its members' interests; to advance further and higher education, especially professional and vocational; to promote exchange of ideas about education; to bring its members' views before the authorities concerned with education and before the public; to aid its members in professional matters; and to maintain standards of professional conduct.

The ATTI campaigns for a salary scale appropriate to its members' responsibilities and the key position of their work in the country's economy; it also works for improvement in teachers' superannuation and pensions, and for a national agreement on conditions of service for further-education teachers. The other main aspect of its work is publication of policy statements on the development of education. It has recently been particularly concerned with working out a policy for the development of higher education within regional and area colleges of technology.

The Association has the right of direct access to the Secretary of State, and is recognised as the salary-negotiating body for technical teachers, being represented on the Burnham Main and Further Education Committees.

Publication: *The Technical Journal*.

Gen. Sec.: Edward L. Britton, Hamilton Hse, Mabledon Pl., London, WC1.

Teaching machines (*see also* **Programmed learning**) Any device which facilitates learning, from the primitive abacus to the latest computer-based installation, may be classified as a 'teaching machine'. In current usage, however, the term refers to a variety of exposure devices for displaying pro-grammed material which have been marketed during the past ten years. Discounting Pressey's prototype, which was more in the nature of a test-scoring mechanism, three main types may be distinguished.

(1) The first self-announced teaching machines were simple, non-electrical boxes housing linear programmes of the Skinner type. The various frames were displayed one at a time at a 'window' beneath which was an open space in which the learner wrote his or her constructed response (*q.v.*). In the original models the box was locked to prevent cheating and the programme could only be wound on — never backwards! In practice it has been found that machines of this type are cumbersome and that most linear programmes can be presented just as effectively in the form of a text. Pressey himself has criticised them as 'about as hampering as a scanning device which requires one to look at a picture only one square inch at a time' — a criticism not without force.

(2) A second stage of development is represented by machines of the auto-tutor and Grundy tutor type, which display branching programmes. The programme is on film, and the learner responds to the material on the screen by pressing one of the buttons. If his or her response is the one desired he or she is told 'You are correct' and is immediately presented with the next unit of information in the main sequence. If his or her response is incorrect, the nature of the error is explained and he or she is asked to think again.

As a vehicle of communication, machines of this type have several advantages: their storage capacity is considerable — compared, that is, with a 'scrambled book'; they are easy to operate; they control the learning situation more efficiently than a 'scrambled book' can hope to do; and there is some evidence that the satisfaction of operating a machine enhances motivation.

Even so, now that the first flurry of publicity has died down, it has to be said that teaching machines got off in the late '50s and early '60s to what now looks suspiciously like a false start. At that time it was thought by many people that the age of auto-instruction was being ushered in overnight. For various reasons, the main one being that the impossible always takes a little longer, this initial flush of enthusiasm was short-lived; which is not altogether regrettable, since the indifferent success (or partial failure, according to the viewpoint) of the first rudimentary models has at least provided a breathing space in which programmers can get down to the basic problems of refining their techniques. The problems of instrumentation have been temporarily referred back to the drawing board. In a way, therefore, the fact that the first so-called teaching machines were little better than page-turners, with a decidedly limited usefulness, was a blessing in disguise.

(3) The stage is now set for a new advance, with instrumentation coming into its own and in a big way. Computer-assisted instruction, already widespread in the USA, offers tremendous advantages. Essentially, the equipment consists of a series of storage units, a data processing or computing unit, a transmission control unit, a temporary storage unit, and individual student terminals — printer keyboards.

From the instructor's point of view one of the main advantages is that he can write and revise his course while the students are actually taking it. Flexibility is built into the system and much of the hard grind of programme-writing is removed. The computerised programme can accommodate a vastly wider range of contingencies than can be bargained for in any of the branching techniques developed so far. It can discriminate between fine shades of meaning in the students' responses and instantly adjust the next item for display to suit the individual's needs.

In a sense, then, computer-assisted instruction approaches the ideal of genuinely 'adaptive programming'. Each student's performance is continuously monitored and the feedback of information is used to control his or her progress. Not only do the storage units house the course material (up to as many as two million items per disc pack), but they also record and analyse individual and class performances, besides acting as book-keepers and registrars. Each student is free to sign on and off as he or she pleases. Where several are at work, not necessarily on the same course, the traffic of messages is handled by the transmission control unit; and because the interchange is virtually instantaneous each student feels that the system is operating for his or her own special benefit.

As things are, however, the third phase in the development of teaching machines still leaves us in a learning situation largely restricted to verbal, written instructions and verbal, written responses. We are still at the silent stage of the industry. With the advent of synchronised audio-visual adjuncts to computer-assisted instruction we are nevertheless within sight of the all-talking, all-colour, all-everything stage — a stage which will culminate in a multi-media communication system. Such a system will be capable of responding to the student's behaviour as sensitively as he or she does to it; capable, too, of adapting itself to changes of pace and the host of variables that go to make up the sum of individual differences.

WKR

Teaching methods Until fairly recently, long-established teaching methods absorbed a disproportionate share of professional interest among those working in the service of education. Teaching methods played a most important part in the initial training for new entrants and were also necessarily of critical value to teachers in schools. Many parents, too, have for years been interested in teaching methods, since their knowledge of what was taking place in school helped them to encourage their children in further work at home; this has generally been true of parents of children in Continental and American schools. Methodology was studied in relation to the age of pupils being taught, their cultural background, the aim of a particular lesson or course of lessons, the physical resources of the school and its neighbourhood, the special interests of the individual teachers, the demands of the subject matter, and the body of established relevant experience. In many countries, and in some cases in the UK, serious efforts have been made to establish common methods for certain special teaching situations.

Early developments in teaching methods were based on the need to organise class-teaching (*q.v.*) as efficiently as possible. Many teachers acquired what were called 'tricks of the trade': how to phrase and distribute oral questions; how to select individual answers and how to treat the right or wrong responses; how to apply a Socratic method (*q.v.*); how to use the teacher's voice or skill in the use of chalkboard (*q.v.*) for illustration or for progressive summary of the whole lesson material; how to plan pupils' activity or participation then, or later in their lives, in the ideas taught in the lesson and in their application to real situations.

When confronted by very large classes, teachers were readily convinced that their interest was always in the development of individual pupils, and were generally easily persuaded to organise 'group' methods (*q.v.*) and 'individual' methods. Teachers also received information about new theories of learning; the acceptance of new theories led to the evolution of new methods. This process is by no means ended: family grouping (*q.v.*) and programmed learning (*q.v.*) are ex-

amples of new methods of teaching becoming increasingly popular.

Teaching methods have varied with the main purposes of particular lessons, e.g. communicating data, developing skills, inculcating attitudes and fostering values. In communicating data or information teachers have sought first to create an interest, and then to present by oral, visual and mimetic exercises such quantity of data as seemed memorable and useful to the particular pupils. Passivity in a class of interested children is frequently avoided by dividing the lesson period (*q.v.*) into a number of contrasting but integrating activities. It has frequently been thought desirable for children to make notes (*q.v.*) and to invent or copy sketches, diagrams or illustrations. This method of teaching is almost invariably accompanied for older pupils by further exercises completed as homework (*q.v.*) and, at reasonable intervals of time, revision-tests or examinations to check retention of data.

An essential feature of teaching a skill is the demonstration of the operation of the whole skill or the exhibition of the products of the use of the skill. Many teachers also find it necessary to present examples of important stages of achievement. Motor development, body image, muscular control, visual activity and physical co-ordination all tend to underlie the successful growth of a physical skill. In physical education, for example, it is often desirable to demonstrate efficiently the final performance being aimed at and then to break the complex movement up into component parts. In large scale PE, as in skills in military drill, reiteration to the point of near-automatic response leads to the kind of success looked for. In school, however, the dullness of constant repetition would destroy interest. This method is, therefore, used only in a highly qualified sense, and has recently been much influenced by the understanding of movement. Practical subjects in the

755

curriculum (including particularly craft skills in woodwork, metal work, and home economics, resting on interest in achievement on the part of pupils) are examples of this kind of teaching.

It is almost impossible to describe any single method adopted for the purpose of inculcating values or encouraging attitudes. Some success necessarily belongs to the personal example of the teacher and to the whole ethos of the school community of which the teacher is a part. The fundamental view of the curriculum held by a group of teachers in a school or by the profession as a whole may well be a means, if not strictly speaking a method, of avoiding prejudice of any kind. Similarly, the interests of teachers or of a whole school staff may indirectly contribute to the preservation of cultural standards in a community. Aesthetic interests and some related skills, such as dance and drama, are in many cases fostered so well in schools that the whole community ultimately benefits.

The school has been easily recognised as an educational society in the traditional English setting. Uniforms, school games, academic and other distinctions, former pupils' associations, and school social-service programmes have all served to identify the school to the outside community and to the pupils themselves. The problems of organising schools are increasing in complexity, and the methods by which such organisation may lead to desirable educational ends is currently under most active discussion.

It is in the confrontation of classes of children of roughly the same age or of similar educational achievement or of comparable estimated capacity that teachers have begun afresh to examine methods with increasing care. The attempt to conserve the responsibility of the teacher for the progress of the individual pupil in the class has also focussed attention on methodology. The present awareness of new audio-visual and electronic aids in support

of the printed book has also increased the current interest in methodology.

In early 20th-century teaching. an assumption regularly made by those who trained teachers was that there was an intrinsic validity in a scheme of dividing the lesson into a series of steps sometimes called the Herbartian steps (*q.v.*). An early familiarity with child psychology led to these steps being modified in each lesson unit into introduction, development and conclusion. Special emphasis was laid on declaring an aim for each lesson, both within itself and in relation to a course of such lessons. At this time, for example, a PE lesson, planned always to exercise a whole class at a time and with minimum gymnastic apparatus, had to begin with some introductory activity and then in turn provide exercises for trunk, arms, balance, lateral and abdominal muscles: such a lesson had to conclude with a general opportunity for movement.

The dependence of the learner on the teacher for exposition was challenged by supporters of the Dalton plan (*q.v.*) and by developmental psychologists whose work, initially the study of young children, led to a complete reform of the formal ritualistic processes that had characterised infants' education. Indeed the reform of almost all methods of teaching has followed from pioneer work with young children. Interest in the ways in which children develop diverted attention from the teacher's view of the learning process to that of the learner. The teacher's view of the value of methods had led to the application of theories of progression which the teacher had to weave into his lessons. The developmental approach led on the other hand to education and method being centred on the child. The starting point of learning was the child as he was—at any stage of education—and not the will or professional purposefulness of the teacher.

Progress in understanding the role of methodology in a teaching-learning situation was not arrested at this point. Compromise between individual interest and class teaching led first to the 'topic' method (*q.v.*) by which the interest of groups of learners and of their teacher could be brought together. This was followed in turn by the use of projects (*q.v.*). There grew a great enthusiasm for 'learning-by-doing' and the 'activity' method (*q.v.*) became popular. Groups or classes could be 'active' in studying a 'topic', but teachers and pupils alike felt freer when engaged in an activity. At first activity was probably too narrowly interpreted as physical activity. Soon, however, the realisation that discovery was effected by activity took teachers to a new appraisal of the 'heuristic' approach (*q.v.*). This is a necessary basis for understanding modern 'discovery' methods. When teachers adopt these methods a situation is created in reaction to which children learn without their ultimate discovery being completely controlled by the teacher.

Much of the progress in the teaching of new or modern physics, chemistry and biology depends upon a carefully planned use of discovery methods. A characteristic feature of science teaching in British schools has been demonstration by teachers and practical experimental work completed by pupils in laboratories. In some countries a 'cabinet' method has been used which has offered interesting demonstrations but has always given pupils the chance of experimenting. The new developments in Britain, associated with the pioneering interest and support of the Nuffield Educational Foundation, have led to an increase in laboratory facilities with the use of additional equipment and an increase in the use of curiosity or discovery techniques on the part of pupils.

No account of teaching methods would be complete without reference to the primary school teacher as, in the main, a general practitioner with responsibility for the progress of a whole class, and to the secondary school teacher as, in most countries, a specialist. This difference has important bearings on teaching methods: the primary school teacher may be for a whole year with the same class of children of one age while the secondary specialist may be teaching a subject to classes of different ages every day in a classroom specially equipped for his subject. A current development should be noted, however. This is described as Interdisciplinary Enquiry (*q.v.*) and if generally adopted might call for more general teaching in some parts at least of secondary schools.

Older pupils and students are taught by methods designed to foster their independence of judgment and originality of thought. These methods include discussion techniques (*q.v.*), tutorials (*q.v.*) and seminars (*q.v.*). A comparable development in schools may well be that of team-teaching (*q.v.*).

For nearly a century many students have been taught by correspondence, and institutions offering this service have developed special methods. More recently great strides have been made in teaching by TV. Some of the methods used were originally practised by radio teachers: in Australia, for example, much teaching is done by radio. Almost any age of pupil or student may be taught by TV or, indeed, by radio: there is, therefore, amongst educational broadcasters a great interest in selecting the most valuable method for each transmission.

From time to time the use of special teaching aids leads mistakenly to the assumption that a completely new method is in use. For example the use of audio-visual materials in modern language teaching has somewhat mistakenly led to references to the audio-visual method. In the same way the use of the initial teaching alphabet (i.t.a— *q.v.*) has frequently been spoken of as a method for teaching reading comparable with phonic (*q.v.*), look-and-say (*q.v.*) and whole-sentence (*q.v.*) methods.

Nevertheless, great developments in methods have been taking place. Some of these are connected with new electrical and electronic devices like tape-recorders and language-laboratories; some are the results of organisational developments in schools which result in further changes like 'setting' (q.v.). It is no longer possible, for example, to claim that the classics are still taught as they have been for nearly 600 years. Indeed, the second half of the 20th century has seen more developments in methodology of teaching than ever took place previously.

FURTHER READING

John Blackie. *Inside the Primary School*, HMSO, 1967.

W. H. Burston and C. W. Green (Eds.). *Handbook for History Teachers*, Methuen for Univ. of London Institute of Education, 1962.

HMSO. *Primary Education*, 1959.

J. H. Panton. *Modern Teaching Practice and Technique*, Longmans Green, 1945.

A. Pinsent. *The Principles of Teaching Method: With Special Reference to Secondary Education*, Harrap, 1962.

Bernard Rainbow (Ed.). *Handbook for Music Teachers*, Bks I and II, Novello for Univ. of London Institute of Education, 1964.

Schools Council. *Extended Series of Working Papers*, 1965-8.

J. Lloyd Trump and Dorsey Baynham. *Focus on Change: Guide to Better Schools*, Rand McNally, Chicago, Ill., 1961.

DJJ

Teaching practice The term refers to the apprenticeship served by students during their course of training before they become certificated teachers. Broadly speaking, there are two types of teacher training course in the UK. One, provided by the colleges of education, lasts for three years and is classed as a 'concurrent' course in which the students' general education and professional studies run parallel with periods of supervised practice teaching in the schools. The other, provided for graduates in departments of education in universities in England and Wales (but *not* in Scotland), is an 'end-on' one-year course and normally follows the first degree award. In 'concurrent' courses, periods of school practice are spread over the three years: in 'end-on' courses they tend to be concentrated in blocks either of one whole term or six-week periods.

As the Robbins Report commented, very little is known about the correct admixture of theory and practice in such courses. The arrangements vary from institution to institution and are largely dependent upon the number of schools available in the catchment area. Many colleges of education have their own demonstration school in which students observe experienced teachers in action and discuss the various methods used. The general policy is to place the student in the classroom initially as an observer, then as a practitioner under the supervision of the teacher in charge of the class, and finally to leave him in full control. The student is supervised and advised by a college/university tutor.

While the arrangements often leave something to be desired, it is probably true to say that the majority of students find this on-the-job experience more directly helpful than the theoretical studies of principles and method which bulk so large in most courses for prospective teachers. In some European countries, considerably less time is devoted to teaching practice than in the UK: on the other hand, more use is made of the internship system in which students who are not yet qualified serve their apprenticeship under a master teacher and receive a salary. With a chronic shortage of teachers, which promises to be permanent, and with solutions such as team teaching (q.v.) finding increasing favour, it may well be that some similar system will have to be devised in the UK.

WKR

Teaching profession, History of the In primitive societies the initiation of the young is left to the family or to purely informal agencies. Even in ancient Greece a rudimentary division of labour allowed of only a semblance of institutional, formal schooling. Boys received instruction in music from the *kitharistes*, athletic training from the *paidotribes*, and were chaperoned by a slave, the *paidagogos*, who was in no sense a teacher. From the 6th century BC onwards the *grammatistes* (who taught reading, writing and something akin to arithmetic) becomes increasingly prominent—the prototype of the teacher as we now know him. The Athenian dislike of banausic activities, however, carried with it a profound distrust of professionalism in any shape or form—a distrust exemplified in Socrates' famous quarrel with the Sophists (who professed to provide advanced vocational training for young men).

The Romans' more practical genius favoured the development of something like a professional class, the *grammaticus*, who taught both Greek and Latin, but it is only at the stage of higher professional training, as exemplified in Quintilian's *Institutes of Oratory*, that this development becomes at all clear.

With the onset of Christianity, which was (and is) nothing if not a great teaching religion, the work of formal instruction was largely taken over by the priest; and throughout the medieval period *the* educational institution was the church. The bishop's licence was the sole qualification for teaching. The rise of the universities (Bologna 1185, Paris c. 1200), represents the first move in the direction of autonomous secular scholarship, a move which was reinforced during Renaissance times, when the key figures were the classical humanists rather than the clerics. Vittorino da Feltre (1378–1446), often called the first modern schoolmaster, was one such figure. Significantly the first treatises on English education, e.g. Elyot's *Book of the Governor* and Ascham's *Scholemaster*, date from this period. Significantly, too, most of these treatises conceived of teaching in terms

of a relationship between a tutor and an individual pupil, the latter almost invariably being thought of as a member of the aristocracy—a conception which continued to hold good as late as Locke's *Thoughts concerning Education* (1693) and even Rousseau's *Emile* (1762).

Any concept of popular education, first adumbrated by Reformation thinkers—Luther, Calvin, Comenius and John Knox among others—remained virtually in a state of arrested development until the industrial revolution rendered its implementation both practicable and necessary. The early monitorial schools of Bell (*q.v.*) and Lancaster (*q.v.*) saw the beginnings of something like an apprenticeship system of teacher training, older pupils helping with the instruction of the younger ones in the rudiments of reading, writing and arithmetic.

In the meantime, the possession of a university degree was regarded as an adequate preparation for teaching in grammar schools. In elementary schools, where the overriding aim was the removal of national illiteracy, standards of training remained decidedly makeshift until the second half of the 19th century. Scotland led the way and for a long time provided the only source of certificated teachers in the country. John Wood's Edinburgh Sessional School (founded 1812) and David Stow's Glasgow Normal School (1816) both grew out of Sunday schools and became in effect the first teacher training colleges in Britain. Thanks to their example, Dr Kay, first Secretary of the Committee of Privy Council on Education, established the Battersea Training College (1840), forerunner of the present colleges of education.

Not until 1890, however, did the universities enter the field of teacher training. By 1900 16 university 'day training colleges' (now university departments of education) were in existence, but only 1,355 graduates were taking the course. To this day, indeed, training for graduates tends to be looked upon as desirable rather than essential in England—though in Scotland the regulations require it.

The binary system, developed during the 19th century, may be regarded as a reflection of the 'two nations' mentality. There are, in fact, two distinct types of course for prospective teachers: (1) 'concurrent', i.e. courses in which general education and professional, pedagogical studies are taken side by side; (2) 'end-on', i.e. professional, pedagogical studies following a university degree course. The former qualifies for certificated work in primary and non-academic secondary schools, the latter for grammar school work. Each has arguments in its favour, but, as the Robbins Report commented, the most judicious admixture of the two types has yet to be found. Since the McNair Report 1943 no serious attempt to evaluate methods of teacher education and training has been made, though considerable organisational changes have been effected in the post-war years. The setting up of area training organisations based on university institutes of education has to some extent cross-fertilised the two methods, and the recently established college of education courses leading to the BEd degree will, it is hoped, lead to further equalisation of professional competence. Teachers' professional organisations, however, continue to reflect the old social class distinction between 'school teacher' and 'schoolmaster', with the National Union of Teachers (founded 1870) representing the interests of the majority. As regards status and salaries, teaching has always compared unfavourably with the recognised professions. Historically, its evolution has taken place in three stages: (1) the stage of craftsmanship—'chalk and talk'; (2) the stage of technique—in which a variety of audio-visual aids is introduced; and (3) the stage of technology—in which the role of the 'flesh and blood' teacher is largely taken over by technologies of instruction as foreshadowed, e.g. in programmed learning (*q.v.*). Stage 1 lasted from earliest times until the late 19th century—and needless to say still persists. Stage 2 is nearing completion. Stage 3 has barely begun. As the explosion of knowledge continues, however, it is evident that something has to be done to increase the teacher's productivity, i.e. to step up his powers of mediating ideas and information. The days of the all-purpose teacher facing a class of 30–40 children in an 'egg-crate' type of school building are clearly numbered.

FURTHER READING
George Z. F. Bereday and Joseph A. Lauwerys (Eds). *Year Book of Education 1963: The Education and Training of Teachers*, Evans Bros.

WKR

Team-teaching This involves the use of a team of teachers. In its simplest form a 'master-teacher' presents his material to a large number, probably hundreds, of pupils in the presence of a number of teachers. In turn these teachers pursue the material offered in further tutorials or seminars with their own classes. In some cases the master-teacher may broadcast on closed-circuit TV.

Technical College Resources, Committee on the Effective Use of Set up by the DES, the Committee is a sub-committee of the National Advisory Council on Education for Industry and Commerce. Its terms of reference are to suggest ways of making the most effective use of available resources and those likely to become available in technical colleges of further education.

Technical colleges, Junior *See* **Further education in England and Wales**

Technical drawing The importance of technical drawing in secondary education has changed enormously in the past 20 years. Where previously it was considered only as a by-product of the craft lesson, it is now thought to be an essential area of study for children of all abilities living in our present technological society, whether it is vocationally directed or not. It is an important aspect of any technical education, but is equally valid in any programme of environmental studies, upon which many secondary schools are now basing their curricula. All examination boards offer technical drawing as a subject at A level and O level—usually with alternative papers for building or engineering, etc., and it also usually comprises one complete paper in the handicraft A and O level papers. It is also featured in CSE exams and naturally therefore it is studied in colleges of education, technical colleges and universities, where it forms part of engineering and architectural studies.

Technical drawing is essentially a means of communication and offers scope for technical expression in the most succinct and unambiguous way possible. Its purpose is to represent three-dimensional objects two-dimensionally by means of freehand and mechanical drawing using a system of conventions recognised by the British Standards Institute. This requires draughting technique, knowledge and practical application of plane and solid geometry, and a certain awareness of industrial processes. For these reasons it is an important field of study in any curriculum aimed at the removal of subject barriers. On the mathematical side, for instance, it is possible to deal at an early stage with curves not usually met until much later, such as conics, spirals, cycloids, etc. Other developments might include studies such as harmonic motion, force and vector diagrams and bending moments, etc. The range of subject-material is so wide that it is possible for a student to become personally involved in the practical implications of his work. At the simplest level, it is possible for a student to solve problems graphically that would have proved very difficult using any other method.

In the planning of any three-dimensional project, the detailing must be carefully worked out through a series of drawings first. Such design solutions, therefore, are reached as the result of a systematic analysis of the problem, collecting and recording of relevant data through sketching, personal selection of facts for the ultimate solution, and finally the selection of the assembly and detail drawings to portray the solution adequately. It is this complete intellectual involvement, coupled with the practical element, that makes the subject so fundamental to secondary education today.

MHi and GAH

Technical education Technical education as we know it has its origins in the 19th century. Prior to this period few examples can be found of schools giving their pupils training which would be relevant to any scientific or technical occupation which they might follow after leaving school.

The industrial revolution brought about changes which led to a need for training manual workers in technical skills, and for the more enterprising of their numbers to gain an understanding of the process involved in the new industries. Technical education or training therefore evolved as a provision for the poorer or working classes and hence on a part-time basis, and with a practical or vocational basis rather than as a part of a liberal education. As a result it acquired an image of inferiority in quality, social esteem and educational value—an image not easy to eradicate.

Some recognition that there was a need for technical training came during the 1830s with, for instance, the provision of a small government grant for a Normal School of Design. From 1841 onwards grants were also made to a number of design schools in certain provincial industrial centres. But technical instruction did not figure otherwise in the curricula of existing schools nor at the universities.

Following Birkbeck's successful lectures for artisans in Glasgow and later in London, mechanics institutes (*q.v.*) were set up in many parts of the country to provide instruction in science and the applications of mathematics for artisans and other workers. Unfortunately, as time went on many of these became middle-class centres devoted to liberal rather than technical education, and a period of general decline in their influence ensued.

A number of engineering institutes were set up during the 19th century (e.g. civil engineering in 1818) to provide an index of professional standards—to be reached by degree or private study together with practical or industrial experience.

But in spite of the establishment of these institutes and of the British Association for the Advancement of Science, the Royal Institute of Chemistry, the Society of Arts, the School of Mines and other independent bodies during the first half of the century, progress was slow chiefly because of the lack of any widespread elementary education in the country.

Following the Great Exhibition of 1851 the government established a Department of Science and Art—initially at the Board of Trade and later in the Department of Education. Funds from the Exhibition and elsewhere were also used to establish scientific and technical centres, particularly in South Kensington. The Department of Science and Art administered grants to encourage the teaching of art and science particularly in evening classes, and an examination framework was built up from 1859 onwards.

The London City and Guilds Institute was established in 1880, taking over and expanding many of the technical examination systems and founding the first English technical college at Finsbury. A Royal Commission under the Duke of Devonshire sat from 1870 to 1875 and issued eight reports relating to science in training colleges and elementary schools, to the universities, and to science research by the government. The later part of the 19th century showed an increasing tempo of activity as universal elementary education followed the 1870 Education Act. A Royal Commission on Technical Instruction in 1881 was followed in 1889 by the Technical Instruction Act leading to the establishment of technical colleges. The 1889 Act empowered local authorities to levy a local rate to finance courses in technical instruction—first at craft apprentice level and later at more advanced levels. Further revenues from customs and excise duties ('whisky' money) were also made available for technical education after 1890. This period also saw the establishment of many of the famous polytechnics in London.

The 1902 Education Act co-ordinated most forms of education under local authorities and in particular made the authorities responsible for secondary education which came to include some technical schools, admission to which was usually at age 13 years. Technical education however continued to be essentially part-time evening instruction combined with industrial experience. During the 1920s as a result of co-operation between the Board of Education and the Engineering institutes there emerged a higher-level system of examinations—the Ordinary and Higher National Certificates and Diplomas; these 'Nationals' were identified with particular professions, particularly engineering—mechanical, electrical, civil, etc. Assessment was based not only on theoretical examinations but also on practical studies. Thus professional qualifications for technological careers became possible by part-time—or full-time—study at technical colleges, allied to practical training.

Technical colleges, of course, also provided for a variety of recreational and other pursuits, but after the second world war there was a rapid expansion in technical education at all levels. A committee was set up under Lord Percy in 1944 to report on the needs of higher technological education. This recommended a small number of technical colleges developing courses of university-level, regional advisory councils and a National Council of Technology, and an award (to be made by the National Council) of degree level in technology.

The Council came into being in 1948 (National Advisory Council on Education in Industry and Commerce) but not the degree-level award, although students following Higher National Diplomas and Certificates increased appreciably in numbers. In 1955 the NACEIC submitted further proposals for a national award, and the government established a National Council for Technological Awards under Lord Hives with power to confer a Diploma in Technology. Courses for these were prepared by certain colleges and approved by boards of studies of the Council. In 1957 eight colleges were designated Colleges of Advanced Technology (q.v.)—two further colleges were added later. The colleges (CATs) became independent of their LEAs, developed degree and postgraduate level work and gradually shed all work below degree, Dip Tech and HND level. Some regional colleges continued to offer a limited amount of work at this level.

It is worth noting that whilst universities had always enjoyed considerable autonomy, technical colleges were financed and administered by local authorities and their students took examinations set by outside bodies following syllabuses often determined by those bodies (London University, the Engineering Institutes, etc.) The emergence of the CATs thus brought a new degree of academic and administrative freedom into technical education. The development of more advanced work in the selected colleges followed a distinctive pattern different from that of the universities in that, for instance, high-level courses contained a significant practical content usually in the form of practical periods for students in industry. This pattern of 'part college–part industry' known as the 'sandwich' pattern has persisted as the level of the courses has been raised to degree standard.

Following the publication of the Robbins Report, the government accepted a recommendation that the then CATs should be raised to university status, and these colleges have now all received their charters as independent universities. This has meant that the Diploma in Technology (q.v.) has disappeared, being replaced by internal degrees given by the former colleges now operating as universities in their own right, and by CNAA degrees (see below) in the other (regional) colleges. A higher-level award—known as Membership of the College of Technologists, corresponding to the university PhD—has also disappeared since the new universities award their own higher degrees.

The structure of technical education has been rationalised to some extent, in that below the colleges of advanced technology are colleges designated as regional colleges which include a certain amount of degree work in their syllabuses; below these, area colleges; and finally local colleges. More recently, some of the regional colleges have been designated as polytechnics (q.v.) by the government and these colleges are being allowed to award degrees under the aegis of a new organisation known as the Council for National Academic

Awards (CNAA). This again is a non-university body which deals with, in this case, the award of degrees—rather like the former National Council for Technological Awards which supervised the award of the Diploma in Technology. Thus there has emerged a binary system of higher education in which students may go to university and take university degrees or go to a polytechnic and take a degree awarded by the CNAA.

Technical education is still the centre of conflict and strains; the raising of the school leaving age in 1972/3 will take some of the lower-level courses away from the local and area colleges, the polytechnics and technological universities are taking the higher-level work away, and the work in between is still governed largely by outside bodies like the engineering institutes and so on.

See also **Further education,** *etc.;* **Technology, Diploma in**

FURTHER READING
M. Argles. *South Kensington to Robbins,* Longmans Green, 1964.
W. H. G. Armytage. *A Social History of Engineering; Heavens Below,* Routledge and Kegan Paul, 1961.
H. C. Barnard. *A History of English Education from* 1760, Univ. of London Press, 1961.
S. F. Cotgrove. *Technical Education and Social Change,* Allen and Unwin, 1958.
P. F. R. Venables. *Sandwich Courses for Training Technologists and Technicians,* Max Parrish, 1959.

Government Reports
Higher Technological Education (Percy Report), HMSO, 1945.
Technical Education, HMSO, 1956.
15–18 (*Crowther Report*), Ministry of Education Central Advisory Council for Education, HMSO, 1959.
Higher Education (Robbins Report), HMSO, 1963.

Journals
Technical Education Abstracts, National Foundation for Educational Research.
Vocational Aspects, Association of Teachers in Technical Institutions.

KA

Technical education, White Paper on (1956) Stimulated partly by evidence of the enormous Russian advances in technology and technical education, the White Paper proposed an all-round expansion of technical education, the creation of Colleges of Advanced Technology and an increase in sandwich courses.

Technical Education in Schools, Association for This association brings together teachers and others who believe that in our technological society the technological element, together with literary and scientific elements, should permeate the whole secondary curriculum, and that the curriculum should emphasise innovation and investigation rather than imitation and instruction.

The Association was formed at a conference on curriculum research in applied science and technology held at Sheffield in 1964, and replaced the Association of Heads of Secondary Technical Schools. Each term it holds one-day conferences in Sheffield or Manchester and in the north-east. Plans are in hand to hold additional meetings in the midlands and in London. A *Bulletin* is published twice a year.

Secretary: W. S. Brace, Elgin Secondary Technical School, Carr Hill, Gateshead, 9.

Technical Education and Training for Overseas Countries, Council for Established by the government in 1962, the Council aims to intensify British assistance, non-governmental as well as governmental, in the field of technical education and training for overseas countries. Mainly advisory to the British government, and particularly to the Ministry of Overseas Development, the Council is also concerned with recruiting staff for technical, commercial and management education and training overseas.

Eland Hse, Stag Pl., Victoria, London, SW1.

Technical Education in Wales, Report of the Central Advisory Council for Education (Wales) (1961) Terms of reference: 'In the light of contemporary changes in the industrial pattern of Wales, to consider what educational provisions should be made to serve the best interests of industry and those employed in it.' The Council proposed the setting up of a national craft apprenticeship scheme that should be supervised by the Ministry of Education and should work through various representative bodies. It also proposed the establishment of apprentice training centres to which apprentices would be admitted, normally at the age of 16, for a full-time course of practical training lasting three years. The Council's proposals, which it pointed out would not make sense if applied only to Wales, were not acted upon. In 1962 came the government's White Paper on Industrial Training (*q.v.*).

Technical Experience, International Association for the Exchange of Students for *See* **IAESTE**

Technical high school *See* **Technical school, Secondary**

Technical Institutions, Association of The Association's aims are to promote the efficient organisation and management of technical institutions, to facilitate concordant action among their governing bodies and to further the development of technical education.

39 Beak St, London, W1.

Publications: *Year Book*; papers read at twice-yearly conferences.

Technical Institutions, Association of Principals of Membership is open to principals of technical institutions in the UK or overseas.

Gen. Sec.: R. C. Helmore, St Albans College of Further Education, 29 Hatfield Rd, St Albans, Herts.

Technical Instruction Act 1889 A permissive Act, this empowered local authorities to provide schools for technical instruction, to make grants to institutes providing technical education, and to set up technical scholarships and exhibitions.

See also **Whisky money**

Technical intermediate schools *See* **Ireland, Northern, Education in**

Technical school, Secondary Few schools have had such a chequered career as the secondary technical schools of England and Wales. First established after the Education Act of 1870 by certain energetic school boards with the assistance of grants from the Science and Art Department, they were squeezed out of existence by the Cockerton Judgment of 1900 (*q.v.*), resuscitated by the Board of Education Regulations of 1913, received an official stamp of approval in the Spens and Norwood Reports, acquired an air of respectability following the Education Act 1944, and finally were given a death sentence by the DES Circular 10/65.

Until 1948 the junior technical, junior commercial and trade schools, the precursors of the secondary technical school, had normally been housed in and regarded as a department of technical colleges or institutes with the head teacher under the control of the principal. Their accommodation was as unsuitable as their location. At one stage, they were forbidden to teach a foreign language. They recruited their pupils at 13-plus for a two- or a three-year course from those who had failed to secure entry to a grammar school, and frequently parents had to sign an undertaking that their children would definitely follow the occupation for which they were to be trained. There were four categories which prepared pupils to enter either (1) specific industries or groups of industries; (2) specific occupations; (3) domestic occupations; or (4) commerce.

In spite of every conceivable handicap, the number of junior technical, commercial and trade schools increased steadily and by 1929 there were 108 in existence with 18,000 pupils, of whom 4,600 were girls. In 1936, there were 194 of them: 97 were junior technical schools (13,972 boys), 37 were junior technical trade schools (3,278 boys), 10 were junior housewifery schools (495 girls), 50 were junior commercial schools (6,100, mainly girls). Two years afterwards, there were 248 junior technical, junior commercial, trade and art schools with 30,457 pupils on roll. The full range of two or three year courses offered was: engineering, building and building trades, constructive industries, general industrial, nautical, book production, boot and shoe manufacture, cabinet making, carriage building, motor and aero metalwork, chefs and waiters, hairdressing, meat trades, music trades, photo-engraving and photography, rubber trades, silver-smithing and jewellery, tailoring, dressmaking, vest-making, millinery, corset-making, lingerie, embroidery, upholstery, domestic service, cooks, nursemaids, laundry-work, home management, commercial. The majority of these highly specialised courses were provided in the Greater London area.

The Spens Report (1938) recommended the establishment of a new type of secondary school—a technical high school—as an alternative to the traditional grammar school. The Norwood Report (1940) reinforced the case for separate secondary technical schools.

The Board of Education in its 1943 White Paper on Educational Reconstruction officially approved the Spens Committee's advocacy of a new alternative to the traditional grammar school. 'Too many of the nation's abler children', it said, 'are attracted into a type of education which prepares primarily for the university and for administrative and clerical professions: too few find their way into schools from which the design and craftsmanship of industry are recruited'.

Only some 40% of LEAs ultimately established them although they did provide technical *instruction* in all types of secondary school, particularly in bi-lateral and multi-lateral organisations. It has always been the case that more technical instruction has been provided in other schools than technical schools.

The number of separately established secondary technical schools was highest in 1948, when there were 319 in existence with 71,698 pupils. The greatest number in them at any time was in 1957, when they had 102,715 pupils on roll in 290 schools. The latest available statistics show that in 1966 there were 150 schools in existence with a total of 73,644 pupils.

The secondary technical school was, strictly speaking, a product of the Education Act 1944. Recruiting at 11-plus, some schools provided five-, and some seven-year courses. Only the latter justified the title 'technical high school', offering courses comparable with grammar schools. The curriculum usually included: RI, mathematics, English, science, French/German, history, geography, art, music, physical education, domestic science and commerce for girls, technical drawing and crafts for boys. The vocational flavour was introduced in the middle school after a three-year course of a general character. All pupils then took a common course in the basic subjects for approximately two-thirds of the week, the bias course selected by or for the pupils taking up the remaining one-third of the time-table. These courses consisted of groups of subjects broadly related to a specific vocational (or academic) interest. Schools with advanced courses in the sixth form offered additionally an *à la carte* menu to meet the needs of individual pupils. There was greater freedom of choice of subjects in the sixth forms of technical high schools than in the grammar schools.

Where established, the new technical schools for both boys and girls were an outstanding success. Yet they rarely acquired the parity of social esteem which the Spens Committee had hoped they would ultimately achieve. The tri-partite and bi-partite systems prevented rather than encouraged parity whilst the new technical schools were undoubtedly handicapped in their struggle for parity by their predecessors, the trade schools and the junior technical and commercial schools. They were often looked upon with suspicion by grammar schools which regarded them as rivals for the financial resources which local education authorities had available for the education of their most promising children.

Many competent educationists argued that it was impossible to ascertain accurately at the age of 11 which pupils would profit most from a secondary technical course or from a grammar school course and that a bi-lateral or multi-lateral organisation was best. In practice, administrators normally allowed, after a pupil's success in the 11-plus examination, a free choice of entry to a grammar school or to a secondary technical school and discovered inevitably that, with few exceptions, the grammar school course was more attractive to the parents, if not to the pupils.

There were unexpected developments in the period 1950–60. The success of the technical high schools in combining both advanced academic and advanced technical courses led to the introduction of courses with a vocational bias into grammar schools. As a consequence, the post-1944 grammar schools tended to become grammar-technical schools whilst at the same time the technical high schools tended to become technical-grammar schools. The main reasons for this were: (1) The requirements of public external examinations and the entrance requirements of the universities forced sixth-form courses in the technical high schools to become almost identical with those in the grammar schools. (2) There was resolute and continuous opposition from the Secondary School Examinations Council to the approval of certain technical subjects for the A level GCE examinations. (3) The universities and colleges of technology made it quite clear that they preferred future entrants to devote their time in the sixth form to additional mathematics, applied mathematics, and physics rather than to engineering workshop theory and practice and to engineering and geometrical drawing. (4) The climate of opinion regarding the pattern the future system of secondary education should take altered radically between 1950 and 1960, when it became generally recognised that the Spens and Norwood Reports had done a grave disservice to secondary education since each had stressed the differences between the various types of secondary schools and not the essential unity of their educational purpose.

The secondary technical school has no future. It will become in the years ahead only a part of the history of secondary education in this country. Yet the amount of instruction in technical subjects is likely to increase year by year in the new comprehensive schools since this instruction is a fundamental part of all types of secondary education. The vexed question of parity of esteem between the secondary technical school and the grammar school will have disappeared for ever. The problem of parity of esteem for teachers taking technical subjects in all types of secondary schools in the future will still remain.

FURTHER READING

Curriculum and Examinations in Secondary Schools (*Norwood Report*), HMSO, 1943.

Reese Edwards. *The Secondary Technical School*, Univ. of London Press, 1960.

The Junior Technical School, Board of Education Pamphlet No. 83, HMSO, 1930.

The Nation's Schools: Their Plan and Purpose, HMSO, 1945.

The New Secondary Education, Ministry of Education Pamphlet No. 9, HMSO, 1947.
The Organisation of Secondary Schools, DES Circular 10/65, HMSO, 1965.
Report of the Consultative Committee on Secondary Education with Special Reference to Grammar Schools and Technical High Schools (Spens Report), HMSO, 1938.
The Secondary Technical School, Association of Teachers in Technical Institutions Memorandum, 1955.
'Secondary Technical Schools' (7 articles), *Times Educational Supplement*, 23 June 1961.
Testing for the Technical Secondary School, Association of Teachers in Technical Institutions Report, 1945.
RE

Technical Staffs, Universities' Committee on *See* **Vice-Chancellors and Principals of the Universities of the UK, Committee of**

Technological Awards, National Council for *See* **Polytechnics**

Technological Education, Regional Advisory Council for (London and Home Counties) The Council, formed in 1947, exists primarily to ascertain the needs of industry and commerce for technical and commercial education in the region, and to advise member education authorities so that they can make the necessary provision for courses in polytechnics, colleges and establishments of further education. It enables LEAs and industry and commerce to be fully aware of the facilities in all parts of the region, and to be informed of new developments. It provides a channel for a joint approach by education authorities and industry and commerce to the DES, other government departments and national bodies generally.

The Council is financed by contributions from 35 LEAs extending from mid-Hertfordshire in the north to the south coast, from Buckinghamshire and Surrey in the west to Essex and Kent in the east. This area has a population of 13 million people, including the Greater London area with its population of 8 million.

Tavistock Hse South, Tavistock Sq., London, WC1.

Technologists, College of *See* **Technical education**

Technology, Diploma in This diploma was a short-lived but historically significant award (*see* **Technical education**). Part of its significance however is not peculiar to technical education in that it was the first degree-level award to be made by a government-appointed body and in this sense was the forerunner of the degrees now being awarded by the National Council for Academic Awards.

During and after the second world war there was a major demand for more and better trained technologists, and the Percy Committee (*q.v.*)—set up in 1944 to consider these needs—made a number of recommendations which included the concentration of university-level courses in technology in selected colleges, the setting up of regional councils and a national council for technology, and the institution of a national degree-level award in technology.

The National Advisory Council on Education in Industry and Commerce came into existence in 1948 but the degree-level award was deferred. There was considerable argument as to what such an award should be called and by whom it should be conferred. However, after further recommendations from the NACEIC the government set up a National Council for Technological Awards in 1955 under the chairmanship of Lord Hives. This Council was empowered to award a Diploma in Technology.

A White Paper in 1956 recommended a five-year plan to build up a number of colleges (colleges of advanced technology) to provide advanced technological education. These colleges were to operate on a national rather than a regional basis, to be financed by the government, and were to concentrate on courses for degrees, usually London external degrees, for the Diploma in Technology and for postgraduate work.

They had 4,700 students in 1956/57; this number had grown to 10,300 by 1962/63 when approximately 80% of these students were studying for the Diploma in Technology. In other words the diploma was becoming the main activity of these colleges rather than the external degrees as in the earlier years.

Other colleges (the regional colleges) were also able to provide courses leading to a Diploma in Technology, but the number of these was much smaller and the majority of courses approved by the National Council for Technological Awards were in the CATs. Courses for the Diploma in Technology were drawn up by the colleges and submitted to the boards of studies of the National Council, the colleges conducting the examinations and assessments with the help of external examiners. The administrative arrangements and the introduction of the diploma, therefore, provided the colleges with a greater degree of autonomy than had been possible in the past—when they had been subject to financial and administrative control by their LEAs and the syllabuses of degree and other courses had been laid down by outside organisations. By January 1963 the Council had awarded over 2,000 Diplomas in Technology, and a postgraduate award of PhD level known as Membership of the College of Technologists had also been introduced.

The Diploma in Technology differed from a traditional degree course in that it had a large practical content; in fact the courses were built up on what has come to be known as the 'sandwich principle' in which students spend part of their time in college and the other part in industry. These are full-time courses as opposed to the part-time provision in many earlier technical college courses. Different forms of the so-called sandwich courses arose, some in which the students spent a six-month period in industry followed by six

months in college; this pattern was repeated during the four-year diploma course. In others a 'thicker' sandwich principle operated in which the student spent, say, two years in college, one year in industry and then another year in college.

Each of these patterns has its own advantages and disadvantages—for instance, the frequent interruptions of a college course by short periods in industry do not help in the development of student membership of college life; again, the arrangements which have to be made for a number of short periods in industry provide administrative problems for the college. However, it is claimed that, following industrial placements, students develop a more mature attitude towards their studies. Again, two categories of students approached these diploma courses: first, those who were sponsored by industry, known as 'industry-based' students, and secondly, those coming into the college *ab initio*, who had to be provided with industrial placements, the latter being known as 'college-based' students.

Another feature of these diploma courses which to some extent distinguished them from traditional degree courses is the inclusion of what are usually termed 'liberal studies' courses. These involved courses in English, modern languages, social studies, and so on, and were designed to help students avoid too narrow an outlook on their studies and to help them see their work in the context of present-day society.

The development of the Diploma in Technology has been closely allied with the evolution of the colleges of advanced technology, and following the government acceptance of the Robbins Report recommendation that these colleges should achieve university status the Diploma in Technology has come to an end, being replaced by internal degrees of the new (technological) universities and superseded by degrees of the National Council for Academic Awards in the regional colleges. The degree courses of the new universities retain the sandwich pattern in many cases and are therefore of four rather than three years' duration. However, by following the slightly longer terms (inherited from their technical college days) they are able to include at least as many weeks of university study as in the conventional three-year courses of the traditional universities.

See also **Further education; Technical education**

FURTHER READING
M. Argles. *South Kensington to Robbins*, Longmans, 1964.
M. Jahoda. *The Education of Technologists*, Tavistock, 1963.
P. F. R. Venables. *Sandwich Courses for Training Technologists and Technicians*, Max Parrish, 1959.
UNESCO. *Higher Education*.
Government Reports:
Higher Technological Education (Percy Report), HMSO, 1945.
Technical Education, HMSO, 1956.
Higher Education (Robbins Report), HMSO, 1963.
Reports, National Council for Technological Awards.

KA

Television, Educational *See* **BBC educational broadcasting; ITA educational television**

Television drama for children The most obvious aspect of drama on TV for children is the lack of it. What there is may be divided into three sections: (1) TV versions of 'classic' novels, pioneered by the BBC, but designed basically for family entertainment; (2) drama series which are 'shadow' versions of series that children, in any case, view later in the evening, e.g. Rediffusion's *Orlando*; (3) a very restricted amount of good drama which in the last few years has come from Southern Television with its adaptation of T. H. White's *The Master*, and an original series, *The New Forest Rustlers*.

Very little money, time, talent or creative thought has been given to this area of TV, and no concept of drama as a creative link between children and TV seems to have been employed.

In the past years three programmes, however, did use experimental means to attempt to work towards creative children's programming: ATV's *Wonderworld* with Marjorie Sigley, and Rediffusion's *Write a Play* and *Stage One* with Gwyneth Surdivall. *Write a Play* encouraged a prolific production of original play-writing by children, and both *Stage One* and *Wonderworld* used improvisations with children creatively and constructively. *Stage One* won the 1966 International Prix Jeunesse.

The fact remains that drama does not occupy as much air time as magazine programmes and quiz shows, and the general state of children's TV, to date, remains deplorable.

FURTHER READING
Ted Willis (ed.). *Five Plays from Write a Play*, Blond Educational, 1967.

MS

Television Service of the University of Manchester Institute of Science and Technology The Television Service is a designated centre of high activity in audio-visual aids specialising at present in television. It is professionally equipped and staffed technically and academically to produce television programmes of broadcast quality, films and other educational communications.

The department provides a central service to both the sponsoring institutions and in addition is charged with research into the value and most advantageous use of television in university teaching and research. It is also expected to provide training facilities and originate material for inter-university exchange.

Temporary allowance Where a teacher holding a post of deputy head teacher, head of department, second master or second mistress in a mixed school, or a graded post, is absent for a prolonged period, a temporary (acting) allowance may be granted, at the discretion of the LEA, to the teacher who undertakes the duties of the post during such absence. This is providing that the rate of such allowance is not in excess of the allowance or additional payment which would be payable to the teacher if appointed to the post.

A teacher may resume teaching service in a maintained school after returning from a period of service overseas on (1) secondment under arrangements approved by the National Council for the Supply of Teachers Overseas; (2) secondment to schools conducted by the Ministry of Defence for the education of children of members of HM Forces; or (3) such other service as may be approved for this purpose by the Burnham Committee. In these cases a temporary allowance may be granted to the teacher for a period not exceeding two years from the date on which teaching service is resumed. The allowance will be as much as may be necessary to ensure that the total rate of remuneration paid to the teacher during that period shall not be less than the corresponding remuneration which would have been payable if the teacher had continued to serve in the post held by him or her immediately prior to secondment.

Such a temporary allowance will normally be payable by the LEA by which the teacher was seconded and only for as long as the teaching service in respect of which it is paid continues to be in a school maintained by that LEA. If, however, a teacher who would otherwise have been eligible to receive a temporary allowance either resumes teaching in or transfers to a school maintained by an LEA other than the one by which he or she was seconded, the temporary allowance may then be paid or continued by that other LEA. This is providing the other LEA is satisfied that there were good reasons

for the teacher not resuming or not continuing teaching service in the school by whose LEA the teacher was seconded.

SEB

Temporary teachers The temporary teacher is an unqualified person whose terms of employment as a teacher are prescribed by the Schools Regulations 1959. Such a person is not to be confused with a qualified teacher engaged in temporary employment.

Regulation 17 of the DES's Schools Regulations 1959 states:

'(1) A person who is not a qualified teacher may, with the approval of the Minister, be employed as a temporary assistant teacher if he is 18 years of age and has passed one of the examinations specified in Part I of the Schedule to the Training of Teachers (Local Education Authorities) Regulations 1959, or possesses some other qualification approved by the Minister.

(2) Such employment shall not be for a period exceeding two years unless the Minister approves of employment for a longer period.'

In amplification of this Regulation a departmental circular issued in 1959 stated:

'(1) The Minister will continue to approve the employment of temporary teachers under the provision of Regulation 17 of the Schools Regulations 1959.

(2) The initial period for which approval is given shall be not more than two years. Extension of this period will be granted only if one of the following conditions applies:

(a) The employing authority is unable to find a qualified teacher to fill the post;

(b) the teacher has applied for, or intends immediately to apply for, admission to a course of teacher training leading to the status of qualified teacher;

(c) the teacher is actively pursuing a course of study which will lead to qualified teacher status within a reasonable period;

(d) the teacher, having failed to complete a course of teacher training satisfactorily, has an opportunity to retrieve failure.'

In practice, the majority of people who are employed in this category are young men and women who are awaiting entry to a college of education to take a course of teacher training. According to the latest official statistics, there were 3,738 temporary teachers employed in primary and secondary schools in England and Wales at 31 March 1964.

FJ

Ten-pin bowling Nine-pin bowling originated in Europe hundreds of years ago and has since been played extensively in England mainly as an outdoor game. The nine-pin game became popular in America, but about 1845 the game was banned by the Connecticut and New Haven state legislatures. To evade the ban, a tenth pin (or skittle) was added and ten-pin bowling was born.

In the last few years, the game has been introduced commercially into Britain and bowling alleys have been set up in many towns throughout the country. At the present time it is enjoying considerable popularity, but whether or not this will be maintained or will wane (as did roller skating in the early 1900s) remains to be seen.

Ten-pin bowling demands a high degree of skill, gives fairly concentrated physical exercise, and appeals to adolescents both from a physical and social viewpoint. Though it remains unlikely that any school in the near or distant future will be provided with a ten-pin bowling alley on site as part of the normal PE facilities, attempts may be made at the improvisation of such facilities. Certain LEAs have recognised the game as one worthy of inclusion within the PE curriculum and have made arrangements to hire local facilities for the use of selected schools within their area.

FURTHER READING
Strike (Top Rank Manual of Ten Pin Bowling), Rank, 1965.
Ten Pin Bowling, Know the Game Series, Educational Productions, 1965.

JE

Tennis *See* **Lawn tennis**

Test sophistication An individual with previous experience of taking intelligence or verbal reasoning tests will have an advantage over one who is taking his first test, in that the type of question will be familiar and there will be a gain in self-confidence. Research in the USA and Britain has shown that both these factors influence performance: e.g. E. A. Peel reported[1] on a study of British schoolchildren to whom two forms of a verbal intelligence test were administered within a few weeks of one another. The scores of the second test showed an increase of between two and five IQ points. Even more startling was the result of an earlier investigation by A. G. Rodger[2], in which six different group intelligence tests were given to children at fortnightly intervals. There was a mean rise in IQ from 101.9 on the first test to 109.8 on the sixth.

This test-taking skill, or *test sophistication*, is a problem which is dealt with in various ways. Some local authorities administer practice tests in the weeks prior to the 11-plus selection tests, so that all the children taking part have a measure of test sophistication. When certain tests are being standardised an estimate is made of the effect of test sophistication, and a deduction of a certain number of points is recommended when alternative forms of the test are administered within a few weeks of one another. A parallel problem is that of 'test-wiseness' which operates, for example, in questions of the true/false variety, statements which include the words 'always' or 'never' tending to be false, and those with 'usually' and 'seldom' tending to be true. Examinees with test-wiseness are thus able to use it as a substitute for knowledge.

REFERENCES

1. *British Journal of Educational Psychology*, XXI, 2, June 1951.
2. *British Journal of Educational Psychology*, VI, 3, November 1936.

EP

Test-wiseness *See* **Test sophistication**

Tetrachoric 'r' *See* **Correlation**

Thailand, Education in Education is compulsory from seven to 14 years and is free in local and municipal schools. Literacy was 53.7% in 1947 but an expanding educational system has raised it to 70.8% in 1960 for those over the age of 10 years. In 1964 there were 58 kindergartens (enrolment 13,083); 24,148 local schools (enrolment 3,702,002); 455 municipal schools (enrolment 230,472); 444 secondary schools (enrolment 159,136); 2,908 private schools (enrolment 837,236); 201 vocational schools (enrolment 44,839). There are seven universities; Chulalongkorn, Thammasat, Medical Science, Agriculture and Fine Arts at Bangkok, the University of the North East at Khon Kan, and one at Chiengmai.

The population of the country was approximately 32 million in 1965.

Thematic apperception test (TAT) A projection test (*q.v.*) in which the individual being tested is shown a number of pictures and is invited to make up stories about them. Details in the pictures, attitudes of characters towards each other, expressions on their faces, are deliberately ambiguous, and this permits different people to interpret the pictures differently. Responses are analysed and may reveal recurring themes such as conflict with older people, suggesting poor relationships with parents or authority. One of the best known is the Murray TAT.

FURTHER READING

H. A. Murray. *Explorations in Personality*, Oxford Univ. Press, New York, 1938.

Theosophical Society An international, non-sectarian body founded in 1875, the Society exists to make available the teachings known in the West as Theosophy and the Perennial Philosophy, and in the East as Brahma Vidya and Divine Wisdom. The only condition of membership is sympathy with the Society's three objects: to form a nucleus of the universal brotherhood of humanity, without distinction of race, creed, sex, caste or colour; to encourage the study of comparative religion, philosophy and science; and to investigate unexplained laws of nature and the powers latent in man.

50 Gloucester Pl., London, W1.

Thomson Foundation Founded in 1963, the Foundation provides educational and vocational training facilities in the emergent countries, particularly those within the Commonwealth.

Thomson Hse, 200 Grays Inn Rd, London, WC1.

Thorne scheme A system of selection for secondary education named after the district of the West Riding of Yorkshire where it was first tried. Based on the observation that the proportion of grammar school places awarded to any primary school varies little from year to year, the system allocates a quota of selective places to each school, usually based on results in the previous three years, with various checks to ensure the accuracy of the allocations. Noting that the system achieves its object of freeing the primary school curriculum from distortion by external tests, the Plowden Report 1967 urged authorities continuing to use selection procedures to study the scheme.

See also **Secondary education, Selection for**

Thring, Edward (1821-87) Headmaster of Uppingham from 1853 to 1887, Thring was a pioneer of optional subjects—the afternoons were given to drawing, carpentry, etc.; believed in small classes, and in the need to educate every pupil and not merely the clever ones; and set out to improve the aesthetic environment of the school by hanging pictures in classrooms and introducing pleasant furniture.

Timetables, School Physically, the school timetable takes many forms: from the simple handwritten pattern of squares sellotaped to the headmistress's wall in a small primary school, to the elaborate patchwork of coloured cards, many feet long by many feet wide, that might be found in a large comprehensive. The techniques of creating a timetable can be taught, but even then they remain difficult in all but the simplest cases, since what has to be juggled with is not only a complex of variables—accommodation, staff, subjects—but also many factors of an even more sensitive kind: such as the need to consider the susceptibilities of staff, their vanities perhaps, and even the need to keep one teacher physically remote from another. It is not unknown for a new timetable to preoccupy a headmaster or his deputy (or perhaps a mathematician, where it is felt special skills ought to be brought to bear) for half a term. Many have thought that the whole process is, in the modern context, absurdly slow and time-wasting. Why not feed all the problems into a computer and get it to provide the answer (and perhaps a more reliable one than even the head of the maths department can be sure of achieving) within a matter of seconds?

Other, and more radical questions, lie behind this one; for we are clearly moving into a period when the whole organisation of the school day, as it is commonly arranged at present, is likely to come under sharp scrutiny.

Indeed, of course, the best means of shaping the school day has always been under dispute. Is there a best time for certain subjects? How long should a period be? Are certain subjects, laid side by side, hostile to one another? And the whole conventional concept of the timetable, of course, has been criticised from time to time. Should it be allowed to impose its rigid pattern on the teaching in a school, so that, however promising the point that a lesson may have reached, it must be abandoned when the bell or the clock insists; or should a timetable be left so loose and flexible that the flow of interests as they arise may be followed (*see* **Integrated day**)?

But the questions that are beginning to be asked, and will certainly be asked more urgently in the near future, are of a more probing kind even than these. They spring partly from the condition of teacher shortage that is not only universal but is plainly here to stay. Since we shall never have enough teachers, and certainly not enough good ones, is it sensible to continue to arrange timetables as at present, in which teacher is methodically matched with subject and class? Do not the new teaching methods—including that complex that comes under the head of 'programmed learning', as well as radio and television—coupled with the teacher shortage, suggest that we should seek to devise such uses of the new aids that we are no longer bound by the equation of teachers, subjects and classes? (The argument here has been initiated most forcefully by a BBC pamphlet, *School Broadcasting and the Shortage of Teachers*). This argument flows easily into another, which holds that the new methods may in some cases be superior to the old ones, that an aid may not only in itself provide a better form of teaching but may make good teaching available to very large groups of children. Finally there come into the discussion the question of the physical shape of schools, together with revolutionary new ideas (most strongly explored in the USA) as to the pattern of a teaching programme.

These last two (and indeed, all of these factors) tend to be closely related. Uncertainty that the individual teacher facing his class is as fundamental to teaching and learning as has usually been thought brings with it doubt as to the arrangement of a school building as a honeycomb of fixed classrooms. Do we not, on the whole, teach children to be taught, rather than to learn? If that is so, in order to reverse the process we need to provide far more opportunity for individual work (for which the conventional classroom is unsuitable), for discussions in small groups (which require an intimate setting), for the study of books and recordings and the use of radio and television (which call for libraries and listening rooms) and for large-scale demonstrations and lectures (which would need their own kind of accommodation). A new pattern of school building assumes a new sort of timetable, and vice versa. Moveable partitions may replace fixed walls.

It seems most likely that, under one assault or another, or many together, the common school timetable as we now know it will before too long have become a museum piece. But the actual problems of matching accommodation, resources, and the complicated pattern of learning will remain with us, however unlike present-day timetables those of the year 2,000 turn out to be.

FURTHER READING
John Vaizey. *Education for Tomorrow*, Penguin, 1962.
School Broadcasting and the Shortage of Teachers, School Broadcasting Council for the UK/BBC, 1965.

EB

Timor, Education in In 1963–4 there were 180 primary schools (enrolment 16,946); two secondary schools (enrolment 481); one technical school (enrolment 18). Population in 1964 was approximately 600,000.

Toc H Toc H is an international movement, basically Christian but open to all irrespective of race, creed or background, seeking to bridge the barriers that separate man from man and man from God, encourage moral thought, combat prejudice, discover the needs and problems of neighbours and respond with friendly help.

Founded in 1920 in London by a Church of England chaplain, the Rev. P. B. Clayton, with headquarters at Talbot House (named after Gilbert Talbot, son of the Bishop of Wincester, who fell in the first world war), the movement took its name from the signallers' method of pronouncing the initials of Talbot House.

Men and women meet regularly in branches or centres wherever possible, various youth groups engage in regular community service, contact is maintained with many schools and a regular programme of work and study projects arranged for boys and girls of 15 upwards.

15 Trinity Sq., London, EC3.

Togo, Education in 1964/5 statistics: 754 primary schools (enrolment 149,657); 43 secondary schools (enrolment 10,336); 17 technical schools (enrolment 875).

The country's population was approximately $1\frac{1}{2}$ million in 1964.

Topic Normally an integral part of a subject syllabus, a topic affords opportunity for pupils to engage in investigation. It serves to illumine an area of human knowledge and rests on special interests aroused in pupils by the teacher.

Torah A Hebrew word meaning literally *teaching*—in a narrow sense the Pentateuch; in a wider sense, all Jewish teaching derived from, or associated with, the Pentateuch.

Town planning, Qualification in Candidates for the intermediate

775

examination of the Town Planning Institute must be at least 18 years of age, have employment in the profession (i.e. in a local planning authority office or with a private consultant), have five passes (two at least at A level) in GCE in approved subjects (including English, mathematics and either history or geography or a language other than English), and must become students of the Institute. Alternatively, after qualifying as an architect, civil engineer or surveyor, or gaining a degree in economics, geography or sociology, a candidate may be exempted from the intermediate examination of the TPI and either take the Institute's final examination or undertake postgraduate courses (normally two years in duration full-time, or three years part-time) at a university or technical college awarding a degree or diploma in town planning that is recognised for exemption from the Institute's final examination. There are also four-year or five-year undergraduate courses that lead to a degree or diploma in town planning and so to exemption from the examinations of the TPI.

Town Planning Institute, 26 Portland Pl., London, W1.

Trade schools Since Elizabethan times, apprenticeship has been supplemented by trade schools, usually of as ephemeral a character as the trades for which they trained. By the 19th century they were supplementing the work of elementary schools in Manchester and Liverpool (Mechanics' Institute Schools) and London (Birkbeck Schools). After the Great Exhibition of 1851 the RSA canvassed the possibility of establishing proper trade schools in various industrial towns, and these discussions led to the Department of Science and Art (a government department established in 1856) financing several which later developed into organised 'science schools'.

One of the earliest institutions to bear the name 'trade school' was the Diocesan School at Bristol, which was converted by Canon Moseley into a trade school. This provided an advanced course for all elementary schools in Bristol at a fee of 9d a week. Opened in 1856, charging fees of 15s a quarter, it found difficulty in paying its way. Further trade schools at Worcester and Wandsworth followed, but they tended to revert to elementary schools, as pupils preferred to attend mechanics' institutes in the evenings rather than trade schools by day.

Another type of trade school began in 1874 at the Artisans' Institute under Henry Solly (see **Working men's clubs and institutes**) but their most fluent advocate was C. T. Millis, headmaster of the Borough Polytechnic Day School, whose paper to Section L of the British Association at Leicester in 1907 provided justification for the 20th century variant of the trade (or junior technical) schools, which aimed at providing boys and girls from 13 to 16 with the education formerly provided by the higher grade schools (*q.v.*). They began in 1905, and Michael Sadler examined the aims and courses of 16 of them in *Continuation Schools in England and Elsewhere* (Manchester, 1908). They numbered 194 by 1934, with 22,158 on the register. Today trades change so rapidly that a basic education in science is an indispensable preliminary to any formal training in them.

WHGA

Trade union education *See* **Labour education**

Trades Union Congress Education Committee The TUC Education Committee is a standing sub-committee of the TUC General Council and is served by an Education Department at TUC headquarters. The Committee has two main functions: first, to advise on TUC policy regarding public education and related questions; and secondly, to provide a service of trade union education to unions affiliated to the TUC. The views of the TUC on questions of public education policy are put in evidence to governmental and public inquiries and in discussion and correspondence with ministers and government departments. The service of trade union education provided by the TUC comprises short residential courses at the TUC Training College, postal courses, annual residential summer schools and youth schools, and district and local week-end, day-release and evening courses. The TUC Educational Trust provides a number of one-year scholarships and bursaries for courses of full-time study at certain adult residential colleges and for the one-year course in trade union studies at the London School of Economics.

Congress Hse, Gt Russell St, London, WC1.

Training Officers, Institution of

The Institution was founded in 1964 with the aim of providing a professional organisation for training officers in industry and commerce. It holds conferences and evening discourses on aspects of training and associated education and, through its Education and Training Committee, carries out investigations into training methods both at home and abroad.

The Institution has five classes of members: Fellows and Members, who form the corporate body, and Honorary Fellows, Associates and Graduates, who are non-corporate members. Though most of its membership is drawn from training officers in the UK, an increasing number of applications for election to the Institution is being received from overseas.

By the spring of 1967, 11 branches of the Institution had been established, and others were in the process of formation.

Sec.: S. Medforth, OBE, Hon. MA, MscTech., LLB, 55 Station Road, Beaconsfield, Bucks.

Journal: *The Training Officer.* Every two months.

Training and Supply of Teachers, National Advisory Council on the

Terms of reference: to review national policy on (1) the training and conditions of qualifications of teachers; and (2) the supply and distribution of teachers in ways best calculated to meet the needs of schools and other educational establishments.

The Council is composed of representatives of all the teaching and training organisations. At the time of writing the Council is suspended.

Trampolining Until recent years, trampolining was regarded as a circus or variety activity for professional acrobats; but this has changed, and trampolining is now a sport pursued in most secondary and many junior schools. The trampoline is rapidly becoming a standard item of equipment, alongside the vaulting horse, box and buck. Basically it is a horizontal nylon web 'bed', 12 ft x 6 ft, attached by elastic cables inside a tubular steel frame standing 3 ft from the ground. The performer stands in the centre of the 'bed' and gains height by controlled jumping, assisted by the spring provided by the elastic cables; this enables the performer to carry out a wide range of often spectacular gymnastic movements. These complicated and highly skilled movements are built up gradually from a series of relatively simple basic jumps which the beginner must master thoroughly; if this is done the element of danger becomes almost negligible. Every learner is taught to stand by when others are performing on the equipment.

Championships are arranged, from school to international level.

British Trampoline Federation, c/o Polytechnic, 309 Regent St, London, W1.

English Schools Trampoline Association, c/o J. Wickersham, Ramsden School, Gillmans Rd, Orpington, Kent.

FURTHER READING
J. Edmundson and J. G. Garstang. *Activities on PE Apparatus*, Oldbourne, 1962.
L. Griswold. *Trampoline Tumbling*, W. H. Allen, 1948.
N. Loken. *How to Improve your Trampolining*, Bailey Bros. and Swinfen, 1954.
Trampolining, *Know the Game* Series, Educational Productions, 1964.

JE

Transfer of skills The idea that learning a logical language such as Latin will necessarily help someone to think logically in other spheres of thought is still popular with certain educationists. It is now generally thought, however, that this sort of transfer of skills from one subject to another will occur only if the learner can understand the learning *principles* he is using in each case. Thus, merely learning a poem will not help in learning irregular verbs unless the learner has worked out the best principles for memorising anything, and can apply these to his new task. The more intelligent the child, and the more insight he has into the essence of his own reasoning, the more he will be able to see the possibilities for transfer. With very dull children, however, who may find the intellectual effort necessary for this sort of generalising particularly difficult, it may be best to teach each new task as something quite separate and specific, even though it may be fairly similar to something that the class has recently tried.

NT

Transport to and from school *See* **Walking distance from school; School attendance**

Trend Report (1962): Organisation of Civil Science Terms of reference: to consider whether any changes were desirable in the existing functions of various agencies, for which the Minister for Science and Industrial Research was responsible, concerned with the formulation of civil scientific policy and the conduct of civil scientific research; whether any new agencies should be created for these purposes; what arrangements should be made for determining, with appropriate scientific advice, the relative importance in the national interest of claims on the Exchequer for the promotion of civil scientific research in the various fields concerned; whether any changes were needed in the existing procedure whereby the agencies concerned were financed and required to account for their expenditure. Chairman: Sir Burke Trend.

The Report recommended that the Department of Science and Industrial Research should be broken up into three new research councils: the Industrial Research and Development Authority, the Science Research Council and the Natural Resources Research Council. It also recommended that the Department should be given further powers, staff and money.

'Trend', The A phrase used to describe the growing tendency for children to stay at school beyond the statutory leaving age. *See also* **School leaving age, Raising the**

Trial and error learning If someone, for example, wishes to drive a car and does not recognise any of the controls on the dashboard, he may have to find the self-starter through a process of trial and error, which may, for example, involve turning on the windscreen-wiper before he hits upon the correct solution. If he is keen to drive, however, and receives strong positive reinforcement (*q.v.*) on making the right response, and if he can begin to see a general pattern emerging from his right responses to each situation, then his learning may progress quite quickly.

There may however be fluctuations in growth of skill in a trial-and-error learner, particularly in the case of physical skills such as playing golf or learning to type. It will always remain most important for him to know immediately when he has done the right thing or the wrong thing, so that this knowledge of results may enable him to practise right responses and immediately avoid wrong ones before they become a habit with him.

NT

Trinidad and Tobago, Education in
Education is free and compulsory between the ages of six and 15 years. There are a number of private schools, some of which are state-aided. In 1964 there were 91 state and 366 state-aided primary and intermediate schools (enrolment 200,016); 20 state and 16 state-aided secondary (enrolment 17,425); 130 primary and 67 secondary private schools (enrolment 23,465). There are three teacher training colleges, a technical college at San Fernando, a technical institute at Port of Spain and a vocational centre at Point Fortin, all state establishments. The university of the West Indies (which is jointly controlled since the dissolution of the West Indian Federation) has its faculties of arts and science, engineering and agriculture at St Augustine, Trinidad.

In 1965 the total population of the islands was nearly one million.

See also **West Indies, Education in the**

Tripartite system A term used to describe the characteristic post-war division of the secondary school system in England and Wales into three parts: grammar, secondary modern and technical. As there is roughly only one technical school to every six grammar schools and every 17 secondary modern schools the system would better be described as essentially a bipartite one.

Tripos The main university degree examinations have various names. At Cambridge the undergraduate examination is called the Tripos (after the three-legged stool on which the medi-

eval oral examiner sat). It is in two parts: the first normally at the end of the second year and the second part at the end of the third year. This makes it possible for an undergraduate to transfer to a different subject for his third year; and it is this that enables a particularly successful student to win a Double-First.

Truancy Many children may play truant on one or two isolated occasions, but the persistent truant often comes from a bad home, or else may suffer from lax and inconsistent home discipline that might even abet him in his truancy. Bad attendance may lead to slow progress and few friends at school, which in turn may become a disincentive for him to attend at all. There is a very strong connection between persistent truancy and lying, stealing and eventual delinquency (*q.v.*), resulting in what Burt describes as 'the first step on the downward stairs to crime'. As such, persistent truancy must be seen as a behaviour disorder, rather than as laziness or mischief. Although it is primarily the responsibility and the fault of the home, teachers can help by following up all cases of truancy promptly, before it becomes a habit, and also by trying to discover ways in which school may become particularly attractive for such children.

FURTHER READING
C. Burt. *The Young Delinquent*, University of London Press, 1925.

NT

Trusts, Educational *See* **Charities, Educational**

Tunisia, Education in Primary education is free. 1966–7 statistics: 1,941 primary schools (enrolment 777,686); 60 secondary schools (enrolment 70,836); 66 technical and vocational schools (enrolment 29,769); five teacher training colleges (enrolment not available). The University of Tunis has 6,830 students. Population: approximately 4½ million.

Turkey, Education in Education is compulsory from seven to 14 years and free in state schools. The primary stage is from seven to 12 years; while secondary education is in two stages, from 12 to 14 and from 15 to 17 years. In the second of these stages, provision is made for specialist and vocational training; i.e. for higher education, for agricultural technicians, skilled workers or business administrators.

Total population in 1965 was 31½ million. In 1964/65 there were 3,814,133 pupils in 29,070 primary schools; 565,548 in 1,761 secondary and vocational schools; 42,295 in 73 teacher training colleges; and 52,768 in the seven universities. The universities are at Istanbul (two, one of which specialises in technology), Ankara (two, or which one is the new Middle East Technical University), Izmir, Erzurum and Trabzon. Under the First Five-Year Development Plan, 1963–67, investment in education was fixed at 4,227 million liras for the period.

Tutor-librarian *See* **Libraries in colleges of education**

Tutor-text *See* **Programmed learning**

Tutorial Ideally, this is a meeting between a tutor and a single student to discuss some work prepared and submitted by the student. Modifications exist whereby the tutor meets for similar purposes a very small group of students. A tutorial system, now used in many colleges of education, arranges for a tutor to have a measure of pastoral interest in, and academic concern for, a group of students who may collectively or individually meet the tutor from time to time, usually at agreed intervals.

Tutorial system The tutorial system of teaching began in the colleges of Oxford and Cambridge, where attendance at university lectures, at any rate in arts subjects, remains optional. This pattern has been adopted by the new universities, in contrast to the system of more or less compulsory attendance at many hours of lectures which, until recently, dominated the civic universities.

The weekly tutorial or supervision brings together a tutor and two students, and their discussion is normally based upon the students' essays. Thus the tutorial is a demanding intellectual exercise which depends for its success on intensive reading, and on a capacity to commit thoughts to paper and to re-examine them critically in discussion. While the tutorial (and the seminar of eight or so students) can well be the main teaching method in arts subjects, it is likely to be subservient to the lecture or the laboratory-period in the sciences.

Two cultures, The 'The Two Cultures' was the title of C. P. Snow's Rede Lecture delivered at Cambridge in 1959. It has since become almost a catch-phrase in the discussion of modern educational problems. Snow's argument was that specialisation in modern society and education has gone so far that those who become expert in any one specialism are incapable of understanding, even of communicating intelligibly with, those who are expert in others. He emphasised that there were many divisions of specialisation, but still maintained that broadly this problem could be seen most conspicuously in the division between the sciences on the one hand and the arts and humanities on the other. The man educated and trained within the 'culture' of rigorous scientific procedure and terminology, and the man educated within the 'culture' of artistic, literary and philosophical discourse, were poles apart. Neither could understand the language, concerns, or basis of judgment of the other.

The élite in modern society who ought to be concerned with human problems in their entirety, taking into account all dimensions of them, was therefore split into 'two cultures' totally out of touch with each other. Snow believed that this was not only unfortunate, but also exceedingly dangerous in that all the many dimensions of modern human dilemmas would not satisfactorily be taken into account. Those responsible for governing us would either be expertly informed in science but lack all those kinds of knowledge and qualities of reflection necessary for the taking of sound decisions, or would be well-informed about human values and all the arts of reflection, deliberation and judgment, but incapable of seeing where and how scientific knowledge was relevant, of understanding it, and of incorporating it properly into the business of decision-taking. Only by altering our education radically, he thought, could we bring the 'two cultures' together and produce an élite possessing a well-balanced basis of knowledge and judgment. This was not entirely possible. The range of modern specialisation was so great that no-one could possibly encompass all knowledge. Still, at least a good deal could be done.

In a later lecture ('The Two Cultures: A Second Look') Snow suggested that the development of certain 'mid-way' subjects—such as sociology, psychology, social history, etc. (which necessitated and cultivated a knowledge of both scientific methods and humanistic insights, values, and judgments)—might do something to bridge the two cultures, but he again pleaded that new approaches in education were essential if the worst dangers of the problem were to be avoided.

Many critics have argued that Snow has too starkly over-emphasised the division between the 'two cultures' and the difficulty of bridging them. However, the problem appears to be of such importance as to warrant exaggeration. The enormous growth of the discussion about it indicates how crucial it is thought to be in societies all over the world which are grappling with the complex problems of industrial civilisation.

See also **Specialisation**

FURTHER READING

C. P. Snow. *The Two Cultures and A Second Look*, Cambridge Univ. Press, 1964 (contains both lectures).

RF

Two-tier comprehensive schools The first example of a two-tier system of comprehensive schools was that introduced by the Leicestershire County Council in 1957. Since then, two-tier systems have been developed in both rural and urban areas in different parts of the country. The term has come to mean systems of comprehensive schools where pupils pass from a lower to an upper school at the age of 13 or 14; it refers to the post-11 phase of education only. The term is not generally used to include systems with a break at 16, involving comprehensive schools from 11 to 16 followed by a sixth-form college or a junior college, although the principle is similar.

See also **Leicestershire Plan schools**

BS

U

UCCA *See* **Universities Central Council on Admissions**

Uganda, Education in The majority of schools are state-aided or sponsored. 1965 statistics: 2,580 primary schools (enrolment 569,219); 86 junior secondary schools (enrolment 9,237); 66 senior secondary schools (enrolment 17,323); 32 teacher training colleges (enrolment 3,883); 53 technical and vocational schools (enrolment 3,219). Ugandan students at University College of East Africa at Makerere (Kampala) numbered 477, at Nairobi 148, and at Dar es Salaam 31. There were 2,166 students on higher education courses abroad. Ugandan policy is one of integration, but most schools are uni-racial (i.e. have predominance of European, African or Asian children).

The country's population was approximately 7¾ million in 1966.

Ulpan This is an Israeli institution which provides a crash course in modern spoken Hebrew directed chiefly to new immigrants.

Ulverscroft Large Print Books This is a series of works largely of popular fiction, designed for the partially sighted who no longer find it possible to read from a normal print size. Advice and assistance is given to the publisher by librarians, welfare officials and committee members of institutions for the blind.

F. A. Thorpe (Publishing) Ltd., Station Rd, Glenfield, Leicester.

Unattached teachers Where a teacher is unattached to the staff of any particular school but is required by the LEA to teach in more than one school, he is placed upon the unattached staff. The appointment may be a full-time one or the teacher may have a contract which enables duties to be performed at irregular intervals as the employing LEA requires. The payment of salary would be no different from the teacher's entitlement if he were full-time and attached to the staff of a particular school or, in the event of part-time working, the appropriate fraction of the full-time salary.

Where the LEA consider that the duties and responsibilities of an unattached teacher should be regarded as equivalent to those of a head of department or of a teacher in a graded post, an allowance corresponding to the appropriate post under the Burnham Report is payable at the discretion of the LEA.

In some LEAs appointments may be made to what is usually known as 'the supply staff' of one or more teachers paid on the scales applicable to head teachers of schools or departments in Groups 0, 1 or 2, where the LEA may require a teacher to fill temporarily vacant head teacher posts in primary and secondary schools. Such appointments must of course be on a permanent basis as far as the teacher and the LEA are concerned, although the duties may vary from time to time. Thus a teacher may be required to perform the duties of a head teacher in those schools which are too small to have a permanent deputy head appointment, but there may be occasions where the absence of any head teacher vacancies requires the teacher to perform the normal teaching duties of a classroom teacher.

SEB

Under-achievement This is a term generally used to describe academic performance well below the expectations raised by the results of an intelligence test. In some cases the IQ score may be lower on the second testing, but in other circumstances it will probably be that personality factors which cannot be adequately measured by an IQ test (such as low level of aspiration, maladjustment, or poor motivation) are serving to depress the child's actual performance. In this sense, the knowledge that a child is under-achieving can be a valuable diagnostic tool for the teacher or educational psychologist, and can lead to paying more attention to the child's motivation and personal adjustment in school, as well as any problems in his life at home.

Underwood Report (1955): Report of the Committee on Maladjusted Children Terms of reference: to enquire into and report upon the medical, educational and social problems relatings to maladjusted children, with reference to their treatment within the educational system. Chairman: J. E. Underwood.

The Committee recommended a very large expansion in the facilities available for treating maladjusted children: that there should be a comprehensive child guidance service available for the area of every LEA, involving a school psychological service, school health service and child guidance clinics, all of which should work in close co-operation. Local authorities should plan on the assumption that a child guidance team (consisting of the equivalent of one full-time psychiatrist, two educational psychologists and three psychiatric social workers) can adequately serve 45,000 schoolchildren. The Report also emphasised that teachers must be made aware of the facilities which are available.

See also **Child guidance**

UNESCO UNESCO (United Nations Educational, Scientific and Cultural Organisation) is one of a dozen specialised agencies which, though largely autonomous bodies of independent membership, have been brought by negotiated agreement within the general ambit of the Economic and Social Council (ECOSOC) of the United Nations. It is thus closely associated with other world functional organisations like the World Health, Food and Agriculture, and International Labour Organisations, and with the World Bank for Reconstruction and Development.

Creation and aims The distinctively ethical purpose of UNESCO is emphasised in its constitution, the Preamble to which opens: 'Since wars begin in the minds of men, it is in the minds of men that the defences of peace must be constructed.' Article I goes on more explicitly to state: 'The purpose of the Organisation is to contribute to peace and security by promoting collaboration among the nations through education, science, and culture in order to further universal respect for justice, for the rule of law, and for the human rights and fundamental freedoms which are affirmed for the peoples of the world, without distinction of race, sex, language, or religion, by the Charter of the United Nations.'

UNESCO's aims are to promote among all peoples of the world mutual knowledge and understanding, educational and cultural progress, and the increase and diffusion of knowledge.

UNESCO must be viewed not as working alone or independently but in association with many other bodies, governmental, non-governmental, and voluntary, and as acting sometimes as a framework, sometimes as a stimulus, in far-reaching efforts in international collaboration. From its foundation at the end of the second world war UNESCO sought to revive, strengthen or create, and associate with its work, bodies that had a world view, and often long traditions of internationalism.

UNESCO's inter-governmental field had to some extent been prepared by the International Council for Intellectual Co-operation (ICIC) appointed by the League of Nations in 1921, and the foundation of the International Bureau of Education in 1925. The immediate forerunner and architect of UNESCO, however, was the Conference of Allied Ministers of Education (CAME), first called together by the President of the Board of Education (now Lord Butler) in 1942. Reinforced in 1944 by the Fulbright Delegation from the USA, and concerned primarily with problems of restoring the deliberately destroyed educational systems of the occupied countries of Europe, the expanded CAME went on to consider a permanent organisation of wider aims. Prompted by a resolution of the Charter Assembly of the UN at San Francisco in June 1945, CAME submitted a draft constitution to delegates from 44 nations, invited to a conference in London by the British and French governments in November 1945.

This conference revised and approved the constitution of UNESCO, appointed a preparatory commission, and decreed that the Organisation should come into existence as soon as 20 nations had deposited instruments of acceptance. In November 1946 the first General Conference of UNESCO took place in Paris where it had been decided to establish the permanent headquarters.

Structure and budget The organisation of UNESCO includes the General Conference, the Executive Board, and the Secretariat.

The General Conference of delegates appointed by all member states, and meeting at first annually but since 1952 every two years, discusses and approves the programme and budget. Membership has increased from 20 to 120 states, half of which have attained independent nationhood since 1946. Since 1958 they have met in the new UNESCO Building in the Place de Fontenoy, described as the most international in Paris by reason of its design, construction and purpose.

The Executive Board, now increased to 30 members, are elected by the General Conference, half at each biennial session, for a term of four years.

The Secretariat, among whom there is an international balance of personnel, is headed by a Director-General appointed by the Conference on recommendation of the Board for a term of six years. The first DG, Julian Huxley, at his own request served for two years, and has been followed by Torres Bodet, Luther Evans, Vittorino Veronese and, from 1961, René Maheu.

As provided in UNESCO's constitution, most member states have set up national commissions to promote interest and strengthen participation. Some 400 international non-governmental bodies have consultative status in varying degrees in matters within their competence.

UNESCO's regular budget is contributed by all member states on a percentage basis, which currently shows, for example, that the USA contributes 30%, the USSR 14%, and the UK approximately 7%, while the contribution from one of the underdeveloped countries may be as low as .04%. From a mere $7 million in 1947 the budget has increased to some $60 million in 1967. But to add to this relatively modest amount, UNESCO has from the start attracted much voluntary contribution from public and private sources, and has engaged in important work largely financed through other channels, notable examples of which are: educational provision for Palestine refugees under the UN Relief and Works Agency (UNRWA), and training of primary school teachers under the UN Children's Fund (UNICEF).

Moreover, extra-budgetary funds at UNESCO's disposal have been progressively and substantially increased since 1950 by its share of the UN Expanded Programme of Technical Assistance (EPTA), and since 1958 by the UN Special Fund upon which UNESCO can draw to assist projects in underdeveloped countries to set up technical institutions, university science departments, and training institutions for secondary school teachers. Since 1962 these two funds have been merged in a UN Development Programme which in 1967 provided for UNESCO an extra-budgetary $60 million—approximately equal to its regular budget.

From time to time UNESCO-sponsored appeals have elicited munificent donations from governmental and private sources. Recent examples are the restoration of Florentine art treasures, and the strikingly imaginative and costly preservation of the Nubian monuments and the temples of Abu Simbel.

Activities The criticisms levelled against UNESCO in its earlier phase are no longer valid. They were chiefly based on the piecemeal and impractical diffuseness of its programme. On the other hand, the delegates at the first General Conference were determined to emphasise UNESCO's world role and initiate projects of some kind in all its main fields. The programme divisions they instituted are still current, namely, education, natural sciences, social sciences, cultural activities—philosophy and humanistic studies, arts and letters, libraries and museums —and mass communication. They initiated large-scale projects not only for reconstruction, but also for fundamental education, international understanding, and international scientific co-operation.

A second phase may be dated from 1954 when the General Conference trimmed its far-flung programme and differentiated UNESCO's special activities to meet specific problems in member states from its general activities or permanent functions. This helped to clear the way for the considered selection of long-term major projects, three of which were launched in 1956: Primary Education in Latin America, Arid Lands Research, and Mutual Appreciation of Eastern and Western Cultural Values. From the same time dates the Associated Schools Project in Education for International Understanding and Co-operation.

Confronted by the 'education explosion' it had helped to bring about, UNESCO in 1960 decided to make education its prime objective.

Conferences were convened between ministers concerned with education and with economic development in countries in Africa, Asia, the Middle East, and Latin America to work out long-term plans for universal primary education and increased access to secondary schools and universities. To assist these developments UNESCO in 1963 set up an Institute for Educational Planning and from 1964 gave priority to special measures for the promotion and teaching of science and the training of scientists and technologists.

To sustain these long-term efforts to underpin economic development with educational advance, more immediate steps were called for to combat widespread adult illiteracy. In 1963 the UN General Assembly unanimously adopted the principle of a World Literacy Campaign, and called upon UNESCO and the other agencies to prepare plans. UNESCO's experimental programme convinced the World Congress of Ministers of Education at Teheran in 1965 that, to be effective, literacy should be integrated with economic development in projects for 'functional literacy', i.e. literacy linked with vocational training and the promotion of skills in agriculture and industry. It is in keeping with this new phase that the UK National Commission for UNESCO was transferred in 1965 from the Ministry of Education to the Ministry of Overseas Development.

At all times UNESCO has concerned itself with the improvement of the school curriculum, both in content and method; with the revision and provision of text-books; with the more adequate training and supply of teachers; and with research into new techniques and instructional aids.

FURTHER READING
Among UNESCO's 4,000 or more publications are the unique *Scientific and Cultural History of Mankind*, *Study Abroad*, which gives students up-to-date information about opportunities in 120 countries, and the *Source Book for Science Teaching*, which has sold half a million copies in 22 languages.

Of a dozen UNESCO periodicals, the monthly illustrated *UNESCO Courier*, widely circulated in eight languages, is designed to keep the general reader abreast of developments.
HRK

UNESCO, United Kingdom National Commission for The Commission was established in 1946 to advise the government on all aspects of UNESCO's activities, to present its aims and operations to the people of the UK, and to act as a liaison body between UNESCO, the government and national and specialist organisations with interests in UNESCO's work.

The National Commission is composed of 23 members of UNESCO's fields of activity, closely acquainted with one or another, who serve on a voluntary basis under the chairmanship of the Minister of Overseas Development. It is assisted by four Programme Advisory Committees covering education, the natural sciences, the social sciences and culture, by a Public Relations Committee and by a Development Sub-Committee which advises on UNESCO's activities in the light of the needs of the developing countries.

Eland House, Stag Pl., London, SW1.

UNICEF (United Nations Children's Fund) Set up in 1946 to meet the emergency needs of children, especially in countries devastated by war, UNICEF in 1950 enlarged its concern to include the long-range needs of children and young people in under-developed countries. The Fund receives voluntary contributions from governments and individuals for its work in the fields of child and maternal welfare, control of disease, the development of social services for children and the improvement of education, vocational training and nutrition.

In association with UNESCO, UNICEF is devoting a rapidly increasing proportion of its resources to the extension of education in the developing countries. In 1967 nearly one-quarter of UNICEF's allocations were devoted to this end. Assistance in expanding education is being provided in 67 countries. This assistance is primarily in the form of training teachers and supplying educational equipment for schools, colleges, etc. Special emphasis is laid on training teachers in such matters as health, education, nutrition and food production, and the development of practical skills, particularly in relation to rural conditions.

C/o United Nations Office, 14–15 Stratford Pl., London, W1.

Uniform, School The original purpose of school uniform was to identify publicly the pupils of a particular school. The grammar schools followed the original lead of the public schools, and in their lists of requirements sometimes rivalled the public schools themselves. Now secondary modern schools, comprehensives and primary schools have widely taken to uniform.

Among all the arguments for and against its adoption, one thing is certain: most parents and teachers favour it and so do most children, at least up to fifth- or sixth-form level. It is argued that it has an equalising effect on children coming from varying backgrounds (provided it is not so expensive that parents who need a school uniform grant find the grant does not cover all the items required). Teachers tend to believe that the wearing of uniform gives the children a standard of smartness and a sense of being under school discipline whenever the uniform is worn.

The major case against uniform is that it is snobbish and out of date. It is argued that the differences between clothes worn by rich and poor children are less than they were and are diminishing. Ranges of good, cheap clothing have never been more extensive. Parents who oppose the wearing of uniform believe that teachers tend to like it because the spectacle of ranks of children dressed identically gives an illusion of a unit working towards a common goal.

The trend towards the wearing of special clothing for school is certainly growing. But criticisms are widespread. Too much effort has to go into keeping it clean and ironing it. Mothers want tunics, skirts and trousers, blouses, shirts or sweaters to be fully washable by machine, drip-dry and non-iron, and to be made of material that does not quickly become threadbare. They want tunics for growing girls to be unbelted, unpleated, and cut on lines that do not draw attention to figure problems. For summer they favour any basic princess-line dress in school colours. They are against white and pale-coloured shirts, blouses, socks and football gear—and against shirt collars and ties. They would prefer brushed cotton sweaters that wash easily for both sexes. They do not want blazers for everyday wear (Consumer Council research showed that there was no really durable blazer cloth and that coloured blazer cloths were, though often more expensive, even less long-lasting than navy). Instead, they would welcome anoraks or strong zip-fronted tweed jackets. Buttons, press-studs, hooks and eyes—anything needing an extra sewing process that adds to the cost of manufacture and also requires attention from time to time—should, they feel, have no place on school uniform.

Indeed, being a set of working clothes, school uniform should (whilst being reasonably smart) be durable enough to stand up to the hard wear of a school day, and should be composed of items widely available at sensible cost. Every school that expects children to wear uniform should see that sample patterns of many items are available for home dressmakers and knitters. Samples of approved materials and a note of their prices should be provided to parents. A cheap, practical style that can be adapted at little cost for indoor wear by pre-'teens of both sexes is a smock-and-overall that completely covers the child's own clothes. It can be cheap to produce, easy to wash and as warm or as cool as the clothes underneath it.

A radical approach to changes in traditional uniform needs strong-minded head teachers prepared to pioneer for ease, comfort and practicality—sometimes in the teeth of opposition from tradition-biased parents and children. Parents have to pay a high price for exclusive colours and styles. Standardisation is the only way in which costs can be brought down. Whether school colours are brilliant or confined to 'school navy-blue' can have no effect on academic standards. The individuality of a school can very well be expressed by means of a badge.

FURTHER READING
About Buying School Uniform, Consumer Council, 3 Cornwall Terrace, London, NW1.

YM

United Arab Republic, Education in (The UAR formerly consisted of Egypt and Syria, but Syria withdrew in 1961.) Education is free and compulsory in primary schools between the ages of six and 12 years, and free but not compulsory in secondary schools. In 1964/5 there were 7,698 primary schools (enrolment 3,294,832); 1,171 intermediate schools (enrolment 515,825); 362 secondary (enrolment 265,498); 71 teacher training colleges (enrolment 41,259); six universities (enrolment 140,346). Universities: Cairo University, Ain Shams at Cairo, American University at Cairo, Alexandria University, Asyut University, and the Mosque and University of Al-Azhar at Cairo, the seat of Koranic learning, founded in AD 972, which admitted women students for the first time in 1962.

The population of the country was approximately 30 million in 1965.

United Nations Information Centre, London The UN Information Centre in London is one of over 50 such centres established by UNO throughout the world, and is staffed by members of the UN Secretariat. It maintains a reference library, open to students among others, and a photograph library covering the activities of the UN and its specialised agencies. Graphic materials including posters, photographic wall-sheets and organisational charts are distributed, on request and on a limited scale, to educational institutions in the area serviced by the centre.

14–15 Stratford Pl., London, W1.

United Nations Student Association Aiming to create an informed body of

student opinion actively interested in international affairs and organisations, the Association has 10,000 members drawn from a hundred universities, colleges of education, technical and other colleges throughout Britain. Each branch has its own programme, which includes teach-ins, study groups, surveys, fund-raising projects, the welcoming of overseas students as part of UNSA's 'We are no Strangers' Project, and the recruitment of volunteers for both short and long term service in Britain and abroad.

UNSA also organises international seminars, each with participants from some 30 countries and held under the auspices of the International Student Movement for the UN (ISMUN), of which UK-UNSA is one of the 40 members. Contact with other UNSAs is frequent, through joint projects and seminars and through the travel programme which offers charter flights to the USA, East and West Africa, India and Pakistan—the UNSAs of these countries arranging hospitality and programmes.

UK-UNSA was one of the three UNSAs—the others being those of Denmark and Nigeria—to win a UNESCO award for their research projects. The UK project seeks to evaluate the extent of education for international understanding in schools.

93 Albert Embankment, London, SE1.

United Society for the Propagation of the Gospel The Society exists to further Christian work overseas by encouraging support in England, Wales and Ireland. It selects, trains and sends missionaries to serve as requested by the bishops of over 60 Anglican dioceses, and in addition promotes a fund which supports the Church of South India. It makes grants to these dioceses for missionaries' salaries and for such other objects as its funds allow.

The Society was formed in 1965 by the merger of the Society for the Propagation of the Gospel (1701) and the Universities' Mission to Central Africa (1857), and has throughout its history accumulated responsibilities for education in many countries. Most, though not all, of the newly independent nations decide at some stage to nationalise Church schools. This means that fewer schools receive direct financial support from the Society, though there is a continuing need to recruit teachers.

In December 1966 the Society had on its list of missionaries 41 lay men and 83 women teaching abroad, as well as many clergy. They serve in the West Indies, Tanzania, Ghana, Rhodesia, Zambia, and Malawi, South Africa, Madagascar, India, Pakistan, Japan, and North Queensland. They range from university teachers and chaplains to primary teachers, but the majority are required for secondary education. 15 Tufton St, London, SW1.

Universities, Civic Ever since the 16th century there have been sporadic proposals to found universities outside Oxford and Cambridge, but except for Durham, which was established in 1557 and dissolved in 1660, it was not until the 19th century that a series of universities managed to establish themselves in the main civic centres of the country. The needs of the medical and other professions in the first half of the century, augmented by a growing demand for scientific and technological education on the one hand and for literary and extension courses on the other, led to the foundation of colleges in the main cities of England.

The first to be founded were the London colleges (the 'godless' University College, 1826; the Anglican King's College, 1829), and then the University of London itself was created in 1836 as an examining and degree-awarding institution.

In 1837 a collegiate university was founded at Durham ('to serve God and thwart Mammon'), which linked itself with colleges of physical science and medicine in Newcastle in 1852 and again in 1870.

In the century after 1850, there followed the emergence in England of 12 university colleges, teaching and researching at university level but following the syllabuses of and being examined by London (except for Manchester, Leeds and Liverpool, which during the 1880s formed themselves into the independent federal Victoria University). Their charters of independence were only granted after long apprentice years. The following list gives the dates of foundation and of their charters of independence; and also the size of their undergraduate and postgraduate population in 1966/67:

Manchester (1851; 1880; 7,160), Birmingham (1876; 1900; 6,135), Liverpool (1881; 1903; 5,792), Leeds (1874; 1904; 7,160), Sheffield (1879; 1905; 5,109), Bristol (1876; 1909; 5,103), Reading (1892; 1926; 3,303), Nottingham (1881; 1948; 5,293), Southampton (1902; 1952; 3,480), Hull (1925; 1954; 3,301), Exeter (1893; 1955; 2,700) and Leicester (1918; 1957; 2,583).

The civic universities, sometimes called 'modern' or 'redbrick', were not particularly 'civic' in their foundations. Many of them owed their foundation to the enlightenment of an individual benefactor: John Owens at Manchester, Mark Firth at Sheffield, Sir Josiah Mason at Birmingham, H. R. Hartley at Southampton; others to the determination of small groups of public men, as at Leeds, Bristol and Liverpool; or to the development of the Oxford and Cambridge extension schemes, as at Reading and Nottingham. These various local efforts were not, for a long time, supported by national funds— in 1889, for the first time the government shared out £15,000 between ten colleges and Leicester and Hull were not taken into the UGC grant list until 1945.

Today, however, these 'civic' universities are in all respects national institutions. They draw their students, not from the locality or the region, but from the whole country. However, as they have developed, local laymen continue to take a considerable hand in shaping the government of these universities. Academically the civic universities were strongly influenced by German concepts of research and teaching, and thus they established themselves on departmental lines. Many of their subject departments have today attained great research and academic eminence, as well as considerable size, power and independence.

BF

Universities, Collegiate There are seven English collegiate universities: Oxford (with 32 colleges and postgraduate societies), Cambridge (with 26 colleges and collegiate societies), Durham (with 10 colleges), York (with two colleges, and six more projected), Canterbury (with two colleges and two more projected), and Lancaster (with three colleges and a number more projected). The status of these colleges varies a good deal from one university to another, some being large and virtually autonomous bodies (like Trinity at Cambridge, Balliol at Oxford), and others being integral parts of the university, more akin to academic halls of residence.

Universities, English There are today 33 universities in England, i.e. independent degree-awarding institutions of higher education in receipt of government grants from the University Grants Committee (*q.v.*). They are very varied in character: ancient and new, large and small, collegiate, federal and unitary. Yet they tend to share many common assumptions, for instance about academic autonomy, about the relationship between teaching and research, about academic standards, and about the structure of the undergraduate degree course.

Kinds of universities The English universities may be classified into six groups:

(1) Oxford and Cambridge, the two 'senior' collegiate universities founded in the Middle Ages; (2) London, founded in 1836 and today the largest university, a federation of colleges and schools; (3) the older and larger civic universities, such as Manchester, Leeds and Bristol, founded in the latter half of the 19th century; (4) the smaller civic universities founded as university colleges in this century, such as Reading, Nottingham and Exeter; (5) the 'new' universities founded since the second world war: first Keele, and then the group of seven (e.g. Sussex, York, Lancaster) which were the first English universities to be created by government decision as autonomous universities; and (6) the technological universities, which have been created during the past few years out of the former colleges of advanced technology.

Government of universities Except for Oxford and Cambridge, London, and the older Scottish foundations which were constituted by Acts of Parliament, the universities derive their power from the crown. They are governed and administered in accordance with their charters and statutes, which lay down the universities' functions and duties (e.g. to teach and examine) and which can be modified only by the Privy Council. Oxford and Cambridge are unique in being governed wholly by academics (graded into professors, readers and lecturers), who exercise their ultimate power through Congregation or Regent House. But being also, for the most part, members of colleges, the dons often have divided allegiances, with the result that change is all too often modest and slow. The civic and new universities are governed by a partnership of academics and lay people sitting in court and council; but effectively the academic life of the universities is in the hands of the senate, usually composed of senior academics and occasionally of students, and of the boards of faculties (groups

790

of related subjects) which in civic universities have considerable power and independence, being responsible for admitting, teaching and examining students and for research.

The UGC The universities are autonomous institutions, and until this century many of them were financially independent of the state. In 1919 the Board of Education handed over its administration of university grants to the University Grants Committee (UGC), an independent body composed of academics working under the aegis of the Treasury. In 1919 it disposed of nearly £1 million, a sum which had doubled by 1938/39, when the total of full-time students was 50,000. By 1965/66, the student population had risen to nearly 170,000, and the annual recurrent grant to almost £117 million; and a further £266 million had been provided since 1947 for capital expenditure. The UGC has proved a notable success in many ways; its block grants for quinquennial periods have given the universities great freedom to plan their own development, and the academic membership of the UGC endorsed the universities' claim to a very large measure of self-government. Nonetheless, in 1964 the UGC was transferred to the new DES, and in 1967 the government decided that the universities' accounts should be opened to the scrutiny of the parliamentary Select Committee on Public Accounts. Undoubtedly the size of the UGC's budget, which now provides over 70% of the universities' recurrent income, must justify this development.

Academic life The universities exist to extend knowledge through research and to pass it on through teaching, and a university don or faculty member will divide his time between these two activities. Undergraduates, who attend the university for three years, opt either to study in a single field or a mixture of subjects, for an honours or a pass degree; between 40% and 45% opt

for the arts and social sciences, the same for science and technology, and about 12% for medicine and dentistry. Some 15% of them stay on to take postgraduate and professional courses or to do research.

The mode of study varies considerably from one university and subject to another: from discussions in tutorials of two or seminars of eight to twelve, based on programmes of intensive reading, to lectures in large numbers; together with laboratory and workshop periods for scientists and applied scientists. Because of these variations, though the ratio of faculty to students is much the same (about 1 to 9), the amount of teaching a student receives may vary from 4 to 28 hours per week.

An appreciable proportion of the undergraduates' time is taken up with revising for and sitting examinations, on the results of which they move from one stage to the next and, finally, are awarded their degree.

Today the research departments of universities are very large and costly, and the PhD degree (established in 1919) represents the main peak of academic study. Over 70% of postgraduates are in the fields of science, technology and medicine, though many more would stay on to study arts and particularly social sciences if funds were available. Research moneys come from industrial and trust sources, and government grants are provided through the Science, Medical, Agricultural and Social Science Research Councils.

Extra-mural responsibilities The universities have a long extra-mural tradition, stemming from the evening classes of the mechanics' institutes, the literary and philosophical societies and the extension movement of the 19th century. Today the universities' extra-mural departments provide a great range of academic, professional and refresher courses, most of them on a sessional, but some on a three-year basis, and a number of them in the form of short-term residential courses.

Since 1944, the universities have also been responsible, through their institutes of education, for collaborating with the colleges of education and for supervising their syllabuses and examinations; and now they have created the BEd degree for college students staying on for a fourth year.

Questions and reports The years since the last war have witnessed major changes in the universities, which have naturally aroused considerable discussion and which have been the occasion of, and have even been occasioned by, national enquiries. The main areas of change and development, and the main controversies, are:

Size and numbers. The population expansion plus the increased numbers staying on into sixth forms led to a great increase in the number and size of universities, a policy hastened by the Robbins Report (1963). But the proportion of the age-group in universities is still small by European and North American standards, and it is socially unrepresentative. How fast and how large should (and can) British universities grow?

Standards and wastage. The British university course is very short and its standard is very high; at the same time the wastage rate is comparatively low (about 14%). All of these conditions might alter if the universities were to take in a much larger proportion of the age-group. The present wastage rate conceals wide variations (from about 5% to 35%), and is a matter of growing concern since it is equivalent to the population of a large university annually.

Oxbridge. The dominance, opulence and independence of Oxford and Cambridge create their problems in a national system, problems particularly of prestige and monopoly of talent. Some have argued that they should

become graduate universities. Internally, they suffer from a lack of equilibrium as between university, colleges, faculties and research laboratories, and from cumbrous systems of government—these problems were considered by the Franks (*q.v.*) and Bridges Committees.

Syllabuses and teaching methods. The 'new' universities have created syllabuses permitting broader interdisciplinary study, and it remains to be seen whether the older institutions are led to modify their specialist syllabuses. Increasing attention is also being paid to teaching methods, which until the Hale Report (1964) have been all too little studied. Developments are also likely to flow from the report of the Brynmor Jones Committee on the use of film and especially TV in universities.

The binary structure. A major controversy has surrounded the government's decision to develop a 'binary' structure of higher education, in contrast to the Robbins Committee's concept of a flexible system graduated up to the universities. The 'binary' system envisages an alternative system of degree-level institutions, mostly polytechnics, based on local authorities and receiving their degrees through the non-university Committee for National Academic Awards (CNAA).

Student participation. The changing character of teenage culture has affected the traditional attitude of students towards the universities. Students are becoming more powerfully organised and wish to participate in the government of universities and in the discussion of policy. In a few 'new' universities, students already have seats on the senate and serve on joint committees.

Planning and co-ordination. Finally, all these and kindred problems raise the question how far the universities have developed individually the planning and cost-accounting skills appropriate to large and costly institutions—traditionally they have resisted the economist's concepts of 'efficiency'. Also they need to develop the machinery for collective planning and for co-ordination, tasks which the Committee of Vice-Chancellors and Principals has hitherto not undertaken. Lastly, how far is the UGC, in its present form, capable of mediating successfully between the government and the universities in a time of increasing financial scrutiny by parliament?

See also **University entrance; University Grants Committee; Appendix 1; etc.**

BF

Universities, Federal In the two federal Universities of London and Wales, academic and financial matters involving the whole university are managed from the centre, by a senate or academic board and by a court or council respectively. For the rest, the 14 non-medical and 15 medical schools and colleges of London, and the seven colleges of Wales, are virtually independent, each with its own board of governors, council and senate.

Universities, New Of all possible titles for groups of universities, 'new' is the least helpful and attractive, and fortunately it is bound to be the shortest-lived. For a time the title referred to a distinctive group of seven universities started between 1958 and 1962. But in 1965 the ten English Colleges of Advanced Technology were placed on the UGC grant list and also became 'new' technological universities, and so the label lost whatever homogeneity it may briefly have enjoyed.

In fact, the first of the 'new' universities had already been created ten years before 1958 with the founding of the University College of North Staffordshire at Keele. A premonition of what would have to come, rather than an act of national planning, Keele owed its foundation to the pioneering zeal of its first Principal, Lord Lindsay.

It was, and remains, something of an anomaly: it was given the power of awarding its own BA from the first, but the standard of its undergraduate degree and the award of its post-graduate degree were guaranteed by the Universities of Birmingham, Manchester and Oxford; it has a four-year undergraduate course, with a first 'foundation' year, followed by a measure of interdisciplinary study; and finally it is wholly residential. Keele was a bold academic gesture; but by the time it was chartered as the University of Keele thirteen years later, it had become clear that the creation of a very small and wholly residential four-year university was no solution to the problems facing the universities in the post-war years.

The immediate problem was of one numbers. The higher birth-rate, the increasing numbers of boys and girls staying on into sixth forms, and the extension of local authority grants combined to produce an unprecedented pressure on university places. By 1956 the UGC (*q.v.*) had accepted the idea of creating new institutions; a year later the government agreed to the founding of a university college at Brighton; within five years the vice-chancellors of seven new universities had been appointed: Sussex (1959), York (1961), East Anglia (1961, at Norwich), Essex (1962, at Colchester), Kent (1962, at Canterbury), Warwick (1963, at Coventry), and Lancaster (1962). Within ten years, some of them were already universities of the first rank.

These seven universities were intended by the UGC to be new in four ways. To begin with they were unique in England for being the product of an act of national academic planning. Then they were to grow rapidly, aiming at not less than 3,000 full-time students as a minimum target within ten years—some of the new vice-chancellors have spoken in terms of 10,000, 15,000, even 20,000 as their

793

final targets. Thirdly, they were to be fully independent chartered universities from the start, guided initially by independent academic planning boards. And fourthly they were to be experimental.

Thus Sussex at once announced its fundamental break with the hallowed concept of the single subject department and degree and set up Schools of Studies, each of them a pattern of related disciplines. In their various ways the other universities have also welcomed the unprecedented opportunity to devise their academic and social lives from scratch and to experiment, e.g. with patterns or clusters of subjects, as at Essex and East Anglia, or with common interdisciplinary first-year courses, as at Warwick and Sussex, or with new forms of collegiate life, as at York and Kent and Lancaster. All these universities have now established postgraduate and research studies on an appropriate scale, though the majority of them have been unexpectedly reluctant to start professional studies. For all these reasons, these universities have attracted excellent faculties and students in large numbers.

Finally, the new universities are distinctive in their settings, being located (if partly for economic reasons) in spacious sites outside lesser-sized towns; and they are being built by the country's leading architects and planners.

BF

Universities, Northern Irish *See* **Ireland, Northern, Education in**

Universities, Provincial *See* **Universities, Civic**

Universities, Redbrick An alternative, and architecturally somewhat derogatory, name for 'provincial' or 'civic' universities, coined by Bruce Truscot in his *Red Brick University* (1943).
See also **Universities, Civic**

Universities, Scottish The Scottish university system began on an appreciable scale in the 15th century, with the foundation of universities at St Andrews in 1410 (undergraduate and postgraduate numbers in 1966/67: 1,799), at Glasgow in 1451—it was reconstituted in 1577 (7,231), and at Aberdeen in 1494 (4,042). To these episcopal foundations was added, in 1582, the civic University of Edinburgh (8,193). These four ancient foundations, whose cheap lodgings and absence of religious tests made them attractive to students from south of the border, established the broad undergraduate curriculum, with its emphasis on philosophy, which persists to the present as the ordinary degree, the first honours degree of MA taking an additional fourth year. These four universities were reconstituted under Acts of Parliament in 1858 and 1889, which bound them to act in collaboration.

Four more Scottish universities have been created in this century. Strathclyde (4,578) was founded in 1796 in Glasgow as a centre of scientific and practical study; in 1913, as the Royal Technical College, it was affiliated with the University of Glasgow, and received its own charter in 1964. Heriot-Watt (1,124) grew into a similar institution in the 19th century and was affiliated to the University of Edinburgh in 1933; it gained its independence as a technological university in 1966. Queen's College at Dundee (2,167), which was founded in 1881 and subsequently affiliated to St Andrews, gained its independence in 1967. And lastly, Scotland has its own 'new' university, at Stirling, created in 1964.
See also **Appendix 1**

BF

Universities Central Council on Admissions (UCCA) The UCCA was set up by the universities of the UK in 1961. The UCCA office receives applications for admission to first degree courses at nearly all the universities and university colleges in the UK; decisions on such applications are made by the universities themselves and transmitted through the UCCA office.

The Council, which consists of representatives of all participating universities, publishes annual reports and statistics about university admissions. Its activities are financed by the universities.

Chairman: Dr Geoffrey Templeman, Vice-Chancellor, University of Kent, Canterbury, Kent. Sec.: L. R. Kay, 29 Tavistock Sq., London, WC1.

Universities Council for Adult Education *See* **Adult Education, Universities Council for**

University of the Air This phrase was given currency in Britain in a speech which Mr Harold Wilson gave in Glasgow in 1963. In February 1966 the government produced a slim, somewhat confused White Paper which sketched out the objectives of the University of the Air more fully. In September 1967 a working party was set up, charged to turn the idea into a reality—a fully chartered university with its own vice-chancellor, offering degrees to people reaching the required standards regardless of their previous qualifications, acquired through the accumulation of credit if necessary. The students would be inspired and paced by special TV and radio programmes, taught through correspondence courses and assisted by occasional encounters with tutors. The essence of the scheme is manifestly sensible—to use mass communications to help meet the unprecedented demand for education; but it was (and still is) received sceptically by many in the educational world.

The Open University, as it is now officially called, is expected to start in January 1971, and the first students to enrol at the end of 1970; foundation courses, mainly provided through the BBC and correspondence, are planned for its main degree lines.

BG

University Appointments Boards Most universities have appointments boards to provide a co-ordinating link between professional and business employers and the graduates of the universities.

University buildings and planning During the ten years between 1957 and 1967, 10 new universities and two very considerable enlargements have been planned in the UK and are all now under construction. Throughout the whole of this time there has also been a good deal of building at the established universities and many of the best known buildings in the UK— the engineering building at Leicester by Stirling & Gowan or Harvey Court at Cambridge by Sir Leslie Martin & Colin St John Wilson, for example— were designed for existing universities.

The new universities are the most recent instalment in a long history of university expansion and are to some extent also a reaction to, and a criticism of, the past. This is true of their academic programmes as well as their architectural projects. The architects of these new institutions set out to solve a number of problems, most of which had no satisfactory solution in the universities created during the latter part of the 19th century and the first half of the 20th. The principal among these problems was how to create a probably continually—but unpredictably—increasing organisation that would have coherence between those parts used for teaching and those for living, and where activities could be close enough to each other to allow as much interaction as possible between them. This idea runs parallel with academic and social notions about the need to break down specialisations and to make the university into a community and not just a nine-to-five place.

There were no very good precedents for such designs. The planning of the American university and college campuses had assumed a very loose organisation of isolated pavilions. This did not seem to suit the idea of maximum interaction. The pre-war university buildings in the UK, on the other hand, were laid out on rather rigid plans which hardly allowed for change and increase. It was obvious however from the report on 'Higher Education' under the chairmanship of Lord Robbins published in October 1963, and the discussion which followed it, that there would be a considerable increase in student numbers but that the actual rate would be hard to forecast since so much depended on political decisions.

The architects therefore turned to current ideas in town planning to see whether any of these would be applicable to university design. A university is, after all, not unlike a small town. A good many of these ideas had to do with movement patterns and the relation of buildings to these routes; there was an attempt to relate buildings, cars and pedestrians, and this principle took many forms.

The first new university to be designed, the University of Sussex on the slopes beyond Brighton, for example, places individual pavilions among the trees, with lawns and paths stretching between them. It depends for its success on a deliberate balance between landscape and building which is not very different from that of the traditional English country house. In terms of movement it attempts to produce pedestrian areas, partly defined by the buildings, and to keep cars and their associated roads and parking to the periphery. Each pavilion caters for a particular use and is intended to expand away from the precinct it encloses. As it does so it bridges across the peripheral service road. There is a sense of coherence early in the develop-

ment and, through the emphasis on landscape, a feeling of permanence and stability. Sir Basil Spence, the architect to the University, has said: 'I think we owe it to the students that they should go away with the experience that they have been at a university where there is a consistent feeling of enclosure, and a consistent feeling of having been cosseted in the architectural sense'.

The ideas put forward for Lancaster, the last of the first group of seven new universities to be planned, stemmed from different principles even though the aims were frequently similar; as at Sussex, for instance, completeness was sought at each stage, and an ability to adapt to change. The principle adopted, however, came from the belief that some structuring device—some intellectually graspable system of ordering—was necessary. The architects, Peter Shepheard and Gabriel Epstein, used the device of an urban street, acting as a pedestrian spine extendable at both ends. Buildings occur on both sides of this street and are planned around courtyards. The buildings are serviced by two roads, one on each side of the spine running parallel with it, and these have short culs-de-sac at right angles forming inlets between groups of buildings. The two parallel roads are linked by two connecting roads which go under the pedestrian spine. There is thus vertical segregation at two crucial points, horizontal segregation elsewhere.

Very similar ideas of using a linear organisation capable of being extended both sideways and at each end occur in the plans for the University of Bath by Robert Matthew, Johnson-Marshall; the University of Essex by Architects' Co-Partnership; the University of Surrey by Building Design Partnership; and, in a greatly modified form adapted to the falling ground outside Norwich, in those for the University of East Anglia by Denys Lasdun & Partners, where stepped terraces of students' rooms enclose a land harbour backed by the central functions of the university and a long belt of academic buildings.

The second new university to be designed and built, that at York, also by Robert Matthew, Johnson-Marshall, uses a somewhat different principle. It makes clusters on the site, each consisting of buildings for both student living and teaching, and connects these by covered ways. Each cluster is able to be a self-contained stage in the building programme. York has also adopted for its construction a variant of the prefabricated system known as CLASP (*q.v.*), first used for schools in the Nottingham area.

Though other universities use different constructional methods, all have considered the serious implications of a large building programme and its continuation over a period of years. There is thus an attempt to find a system using repetitive elements. This has technical as well as visual effects. University buildings of the 1950s and '60s have become much more matter of fact than their predecessors and have been thought of very much more as gradually evolving enclosures within the changing context of the university as a whole. Occasionally, no doubt, this preoccupation with the idea of future variability may have caused some loss in the quality of the environment as we now see it. The experiment was, however, it would seem, worthwhile, for this is a problem that needs study and trial not only in university buildings but equally in many other fields of design.

FURTHER READING

Michael Brawne (Ed.). *University Planning and Design*, Lund Humphries, 1967.
David Daiches (Ed.). *The Idea of a University: An Experiment in Sussex*, André Deutsch, 1964.
Richard P. Dober. *Campus Planning*, Reinhold Books, New York, 1964.
A. Sloman. *A University in the Making* (Reith Lectures 1963), BBC, 1963.
Architectural Design; Architectural Review (monthlies), London.

MB

University entrance British university policy is different from that of the USA and from those of most European countries. The entry is highly selective (only just over 7% of the age group goes to fulltime courses of higher education compared with 30% in the USA); and in the UK a distinction is made, as in other European countries it generally is not, between universities and other institutions of higher education.

Competition for entry to British universities is therefore heavy, not only because of the comparatively small number of places available, but also because of the universities' prestige among sixth-formers and parents compared with that of other institutions. To qualify for entry does not ensure a place. Thus of 90,952 candidates who applied for entry in October 1966 through the universities' clearing house (Universities' Central Council on Admissions, *q.v.*), only 44,526, or just under half the number of applications, were accepted for the following year.

The Robbins Report on Higher Education (October 1963) proposed that 'the number of places for entrants should be assumed to rise at the same rate as the number of qualified entrants.' By 1966 the university student population had increased to 187,000 from 113,000 in 1961–2, and by 1967 the programme of expansion in higher education as a whole was already ahead of the Robbins schedule.

However, the Robbins Report had suggested that its estimates of future demand for places were modest, and in fact in 1967 it was generally admitted the Report's projections were out of date, the demand having risen faster than had been foreseen in 1963.

This situation explains the wide difference between the general university entrance requirement on the one hand, and the course requirement on the other. The general requirement merely qualifies for a place; the course requirement, which is invariably more

AA*

exacting and is laid down by the relevant subject department, must also be met if a place is to be won.

The general requirement, theoretically, aims to ensure that a candidate has the all-round academic standard needed to take a university course, whereas the course requirement tests his fitness to cope with the particular subject for which he is aiming.

The general requirement varies between universities, but the basic pattern is five passes in the GCE, of which two must be at A level, or four such passes, of which three must be at A level. Some universities ask that one of the passes shall be in English (notably the five universities which use the Joint Matriculation Board); others (notably London) believe, paradoxically, that evidence of general literacy can better be discovered by the schools themselves than by a set examination. Oxford and Cambridge ask for passes to include two foreign languages, a maths or science subject, and a 'Use of English' paper. The technological universities (formerly colleges of advanced technology) give candidates the choice of taking either the General Certificate or an Ordinary National Certificate or Diploma. City University, for example, allows ONC or OND to be offered 'in a relevant subject to an approved standard'; Brunel University, however, lists no general requirement but arranges the qualifications required subject by subject.

The course requirements differ from the general ones in three important ways. First, individual departments specify particular subjects to be passed in the GCE, either at O or A level or both. For example, to read English Language and Literature at Hull a candidate must be sure to have passed English, and preferably Latin as well, at A level, with French at O level plus Latin if it has not been passed at A. To study the same subject at Newcastle, he is asked only to get O level Latin or Greek; Southampton requires A level

English and prefers an A in Latin or another foreign language as well. Oxford and Cambridge again differ in having no course requirements; instead the colleges make the decision.

Secondly, individual departments often ask for three A levels rather than the two needed for the general requirement. Commonly the aspiring physicist or chemist will need three As in science or maths. In such cases any claim that the 'general' requirement is a guarantee of all-round academic ability must go by the board. The intense specialisation to which the British schoolboy is subjected, in extreme cases from the age of 14, is the result. The cause has already been suggested: a restricted entry, together with a comparatively low failure rate among those who do manage to get to university (the national drop-out average is about 14%), and the shortest first-degree courses in the world (generally only three years: in other countries, between four and seven). The Robbins Report declared that the British system was among the most efficient in the world, and so it is, but at some cost to the schools. Fresh decade-by-decade accretions to science syllabuses have also helped to make for early specialisation.

Thirdly, individual departments ask for more than the simple 'pass' which is enough to qualify for entry under the general requirement: they also want a grade. The grade required varies according to the popularity of the subject and the university chosen. By the middle 1960s the popular swing away from the sciences among sixth-formers and towards the humanities and social studies meant that the grade asked for by science faculties was generally lower than that asked for in the arts. A D or, exceptionally, an E might do for candidates in technology where a C and even a B might be the minimum for a student of French or English. In March 1967 the Universities' Central Council on Admissions reported that there had actually been a shortfall of candidates in pure science totalling 1,100 and in technology of 500.

The tendency among science candidates towards greater specialisation than arts candidates, and yet towards lower entrance standards in the subjects in which they have been specialising, has given cause for much concern. But arts faculties have no grounds for complacency. There is reason for alarm over their students' ignorance of the methods and philosophy of science (thus a frequently-yawning gap in understanding between the man in Whitehall and the man in the big research department), and there is a growing feeling that what is tested by, say, O level English literature papers (and, many would say, A level too) has little to do with academic flair or even native wisdom.

By 1967 two moves were afoot to improve things. First, the Schools Council had some two years earlier produced a working paper for discussion by schools and universities proposing a new shape for the general entrance requirement. This, like some of the Robbins proposals, would bring Britain nearer Europe by requiring, or at least encouraging, a wider spread of subjects at A level, and would divide A level papers into 'majors' and 'minors', with a suggestion that at least one of the 'minors' could be from the other side of the arts-science barrier. In the spring of 1968 it was announced that a joint working party would be set up by the universities and the Schools Council to examine the changes proposed and to devise curricular experiments. The Standing Conference on University Entrance expressed some doubt about a second proposal in Schools' Council working paper, which might reinforce specialisation by increasing the effort given to A levels. Instead, the Conference was anxious that consideration should be given to broadening the sixth form curriculum to four or five subjects, equal in weight, and spreading across the arts and science; though it was admitted that such a scheme would create staffing and timetable problems and would reduce the content of each subject to below present A level standard, and this in turn would affect the standard of university courses.

The second move was an experiment, proposed by the Universities' Standing Conference on University Entrance, to use standardised intelligence tests to give the university selectors another yardstick. A pilot scheme was introduced at the end of 1967. It was recognised that the standardised tests are by themselves a very crude measure of academic potential, but used in conjunction with conventional examinations, interviews and reports they could enlarge the context of choice.

Application for a university place must be made through the Universities' Central Council on Admissions on a form provided by the UCCA (GPO Box 28, Cheltenham, Gloucestershire). The form ask for six choices of university in order of preference, though no guidance is available on the respective popularity of courses or institutions. By an absurdity of timing, the form is generally filled in during the November or December of the year before the candidate expects to go to university, so the universities generally do not know what A levels he has passed: he has not even taken them yet. The system was designed to put an end to the free-for-all which built up during the late 1950s, when there was no clearing house for applications and candidates often applied to as many as 19 universities at once. The system works well but still gives some headaches to selectors, who find it necessary to offer provisional places to many candidates whose A level chances are uncertain. The practice of interviewing candidates varies between departments, some interviewing only those who have put that university as a first choice, others, if they are small, trying to interview all candidates; a few are asking for sixth-form course-work, a useful addition to schools' reports. Meanwhile, an accurate way of prognosticating a candidate's performance when he does get to university has yet to be found.

See also **Dainton Report; Robbins Report**

FURTHER READING

Association of Commonwealth Universities. *A Compendium of University Entrance Requirements*, The Country Press, Bradford.

Klaus Boehm. *University Choice*, Pelican, 1966.

W. D. Furneaux. *The Chosen Few*, Oxford Univ. Press, 1961.

Higher Education (Robbins Report), HMSO, 1963.

UCCA. Annual Reports. *How to Apply for a University Place. Statistical Supplement* (annually).

University and College Entrance: The Basic Facts, National Union of Teachers.

'Where' Supplement No. 7: From School to University, Advisory Centre for Education, Cambridge, 1967.

Which University? Cornmarket Press.

NB

University Entrance, Standing Conference on *See* **Vice-Chancellors and Principals of the Universities of the UK, Committee of**

University extra-mural work The universities play a very important part in British adult education, as opposed to other European countries where the universities commonly concentrate almost exclusively on research and internal teaching. Except for the most recent foundations, each British university has an extra-mural department which takes responsibility for providing adult education of a university character in a specific geographical area.

The University of Cambridge first formally accepted this responsibility in 1873, following pioneer courses given in the late 1860s by James Stuart of Trinity College. By the end of the century Oxford, London and most of the other universities had followed suit and were offering a considerable range of certificate courses in the arts and sciences—mostly short courses but sometimes linked together to provide for continuous study. In the early years of the present century this 'extension' work dwindled to very small proportions, but the universities found a new field of activity in the provision of education for working-class students in collaboration with the Workers' Educational Association, founded in 1903 (*q.v.*). The main instrument of this work was the tutorial class meeting weekly during three successive winters.

Extension work and tutorial class teaching still continue, but since the 1930s have been supplemented by a wide variety of other courses, long and short, residential and non-residential, the subjects reflecting the whole range of internal university provision. The teaching is undertaken by a small number of full-time tutors, with part-time assistance from the internal staff and other specialists.

BG

University Grants Committee The University Grants Committee, which has no parallel anywhere abroad, has been described as 'an eminently successful example of administrative ingenuity' and could probably have been conceived only by the British. Its function is to ensure that Parliament is able to vote more than £200 million a year for the universities without being able to direct how this large sum should be spent. The Committee puts the universities' financial needs to the government and is told how much they are to be allowed; it is a link (or, as some prefer to say, a buffer) between the policies of the politicians on one hand and those of the academics on the other, and the way in which it allocates the money granted to the universities is never questioned by the government.

The 21 men whose business it is thus to see that scholarship gets state support without losing freedom from state control—that the piper, in effect, can play his own tune—are chosen by the Secretary of State for Education and Science, but they are not civil servants, though the secretariat is. Thirteen of them are active academics, two from another branch of education, and three from industry—the aim being to avoid any hint of bureaucratic control. The other three on the Committee are the full-time salaried chairman and his two part-time salaried deputies.

Members of the Committee usually serve for five years, but their term of office can be extended. The Secretary of State can vary or extend the Committee's composition at will.

Since the majority of the Committee are practising academics devoting only about one-fifth of their time to UGC business, for which they meet regularly once a month, the Committee is constantly in touch with the universities. Apart from informal contacts, the Committee makes a grand visitation to all the universities every five years to discuss their needs for recurrent finance over the following quinquennium. It then analyses the estimates the universities have given it both of their continuing needs and of what they would like to spend on new developments, and submits the details to the government under those two heads, together with a further category of 'special needs', for instance where a government research grant has come to an end but the university concerned thinks the work should go on. This quinquennial submission to the government is preceded by very detailed conversations with the universities, which invariably know exactly what the UGC's submission will contain and in what respect it will differ from their own demands. In view of the composition of the Committee these conversations can be relied on to be both frank and gentlemanly.

When the UGC comes to discuss the financial needs of the universities with the government, the discussion is carried on in terms of the universities' needs as a whole and not in terms of the needs of individual universities.

The next stage is the government's vote. This is in the form of a block grant; no strings are attached. But when, as may be expected to be the case, the government's vote is less than the UGC's submission, the UGC can redistribute the sum according to what it considers individual universities' needs. The allocation generally takes place in the last few months of the fourth year of a quinquennium to give the universities time for forward planning. But in 1967 the universities were in the position of having known for some time what their provisional allocation for the first year of the 1967–72 quinquennium would be, but not what they would get for the rest of the quinquennium—a situation which made for some alarm and annoyance among the academics, particularly since the provisional allocation was very much less than they had hoped for.

Capital expenditure does not come under the quinquennial grant, and the money for it is earmarked, except for a small ration for minor works (projects costing less than £20,000). But again, the UGC does not discuss individual buildings with the Department.

Despite its ingenuity, the UGC system had for many years been under attack by the Public Accounts Committee. In 1966 the PAC took evidence 'to see whether the proper demand of Parliament for assurance that public funds are spent by the universities with due regard to economy and efficiency can be reconciled with the proper demand of the universities that academic freedom be preserved.' It reported the following January. It pointed out that the universities were 'the sole major exception' to the rule under which the Comptroller and Auditor General has access to the books of public spenders; that 70% of the universities' recurrent and 90% of their capital expenditure came from public funds; that the C and AG saw the hospitals' books without interfering with the freedom of doctors, and that he could in any case neither prevent government interference nor compel it. The PAC's report was accepted and from 1 August 1967 the C and AG was allowed to see the books.

There were assurances on all sides that the DES had no intention of interfering with academic freedom. But it was already clear from the activities of the UGC that academic freedom cannot be more than a comparative term. The Committee has become increasingly powerful during the past few years; it has increased its size and the number of its sub-committees, its staff has doubled, and such developments 'will go a long way', as it told the PAC, 'to "professionalise" the activities of the Committee and to increase its influence and authority with the universities and with the government.'

Though recurrent grants are not earmarked, the universities get 'the fullest possible guidance' from the UGC in the light both of government policy and of the UGC's own yardsticks, and 'the universities are aware that unwise developments are likely to prejudice their claims in the next quinquennium'. The UGC is thus the judge between rival claims for money. Further, in 1965 it profoundly irritated many dons by asking all of them for an account of how they divided their 'effort' (later amended to 'time') between teaching and research; and two years later it added to its unpopularity by peremptorily (it was said) changing the procedure for allocating funds for furniture and equipment and thus leaving universities short.

However, the universities have a large stock of patience with the UGC, for they know that 'judgment by peers' is preferable to interference by politicians.

See also **Quinquennial grant system**

FURTHER READING
Parliament and the Control of University Expenditure (special report of the Committee of Public Accounts), HMSO, 1967.

NB

University of London Act (1898) This Act, under which the University of London received its permanent charter, was one of a series of moves to confer charters on, and increase the status of, many universities, including Birmingham, Liverpool, Leeds, Sheffield and Bristol. The main force behind it was R. B. Haldane, one of the founders of the London School of Economics and later President of Birkbeck College.

University Professors and Lecturers, International Association of Founded in London in 1944 by the merging of the International University Conferences (founded 1934) and the Association of Professors and Lecturers of the Allied Countries in Great Britain (1942), the IAUPL has consultative status with UNESCO.

The Association aims to develop academic fraternity, protect independence and freedom of teaching and research, further interests of university teachers and consider academic problems. It organises international university conferences on academic subjects and international seminars on university teachers' status.

Secretary-General: Prof. A. Hacquaert, Rozier 6, Ghent, Belgium.

Journal: *Communication*. Five times annually.

University Teachers, Association of This professional organisation negotiates salaries, conditions of service, superannuation, income tax allowances and trading concessions. It provides legal advice and assistance, public liability insurance, and a Benevolent Fund.

Bremar Hse, Sale Pl., London, W2.

Publications: *British Universities Annual*; *AUT Bulletin* (quarterly).

University of Wales Though universities were proposed for Wales in the 15th century, the first Welsh degree-giving college, St David's College at Lampeter, was not chartered until the 19th century; and then, as an Anglican foundation, it was not linked to the federal University of Wales when this was established in 1893. The University was composed of the colleges of Aberystwyth (opened 1872, chartered 1889; undergraduate and postgraduate numbers in 1966/67, 2,161), Cardiff (opened 1883, chartered 1884; 3,212), and Bangor (1884; 2,146). A new charter of 1920 set up a fourth college at Swansea (2,962), and gave all four colleges more independence. But proposals to give the colleges full autonomy were rejected in 1964 in favour of continuing the federation under a rotating vice-chancellorship with its administrative headquarters at Cardiff. In 1961 Cardiff assumed sponsorship for Lampeter (263).

See also **Appendix 1**

BF

University of Wales Council of Music *See* **Responsible bodies**

Unstreaming *See* **Streaming**

Unsuitable for education in school *See* **Educationally subnormal children**

Upper schools *See* **Leicestershire Plan schools**

Upper Volta, Education in There are both private and state schools. In 1965/66 there were 557 primary schools (enrolment 89,694); 166 country schools (enrolment 7,276); 31 secondary schools (enrolment 6,632); 60 technical schools (enrolment 1,010); one teacher training college (28 students).

The country's population was approximately 5 million in 1966.

Uruguay, Education in Primary education is compulsory, and primary and secondary education are free. Literacy was 90% in 1963, evening classes being provided for adult illiterates who represent the largest section. In 1964 there were 2,362 primary schools (enrolment 270,985); 205 secondary (enrolment 71,175). At Montevideo the College of Arts and Trades has an enrolment of 26,909, and 43 technical schools throughout the country have an enrolment of 15,000. The University of the Republic at Montevideo has an enrolment of about 16,200 students. Religious organisations maintain a school of domestic science, one school for the blind and two for the deaf and dumb.

The population of the country was approximately $2\frac{1}{2}$ million in 1965.

US mathematical projects

Madison Project, Syracuse University Main features are the early introduction of fundamental concepts, creativity and discovery.

Cambridge Conference on School Mathematics, reported in *Goals for School Mathematics* (1963) and prepared by professional mathematicians. Topics are tried out experimentally in schools and published as reports, e.g. probability, function concept, vector geometry. Details from ESI, Box 415, Waterton, Mass.

School Mathematics Study Group aims to provide courses for grades 4 to 12. Yale University Press, 92A Yale Sta., New Haven, Conn.

UICSM, University of Illinois, for grades 9 to 12 and an arithmetic project for lower grades. Published courses aiming at consistency and precision, with awareness and verbalisation.

College Entrance Examinations Board Responsible for many innovations in college curricula such as abstract algebra, vectors, nature of proof.

JCW

USA, Education in the It has become a conventional over-simplification to describe the American system as 'highly decentralised'. True, each of the 51 states organises its own system and appeals to the Tenth Amendment (which established the principle that any powers and responsibilities *not* specified in the Constitution are reserved to the several states) whenever its autonomy seems in any way threatened by the Federal government. The latter, however, has enacted legislation from time to time affecting education on a nation-wide basis—e.g. the Morrill Act 1862 (which appropriated lands for the setting up of agricultural and mechanical colleges) and the Smith-Hughes Act 1917 (which subsidised vocational-technical teaching).

For many years the question of whether or not federal aid should be increased was hotly disputed, the fear being that acceptance would jeopardise state autonomy, but during the Johnson administration various measures (including 'Operation Headstart'—aimed at reducing inequalities in educational opportunity) have pointed the way to a compromise solution. In general, however, a grassroots philosophy still prevails, i.e. the common belief is that education is best provided for by local community efforts. This grassroots philosophy originated during the pioneering days at the frontier when the 'little red school-house' was the outward and visible sign of New World democracy in action. To this day, the school district with its elected school board remains the administrative unit throughout most of the USA (though in New England the 'township' is the unit, and in the south the county). As recently as 1950 there were 90,000 school districts administering some 153,000 schools: Minnesota alone had

over 7,000. These have subsequently been drastically reduced in number by a process of consolidation in the interests of greater efficiency—but belief in the need for local community participation at all levels remains unshaken.

As a result, the Federal Office of Education has no powers comparable with those exercised by a ministry: it functions rather in a fact-finding and advisory capacity. In most states there is a State Board of Education which is in effect a legislative body empowered to formulate policies, fix the school-leaving age, lay down codes, approve courses of study, etc, in some cases from the kindergarten to the university. The Board's members may be elected, appointed or *ex officio*. The work of enforcing regulations and implementing the Board's policy is left to the State Department of Education, headed by an official known either as the State Superintendent of Schools or the Commissioner of Education. In many states he, too, is elected for terms of office varying from one to five years.

Up to 1940 the ratio of state aid to local community support was 3:7. In 1966 the ratio was roughly 5:5. Moreover, the contribution from federal sources is now massively greater than it was before World War II.

Broadly speaking, types of school are uniform throughout the USA. Most systems follow a 6:3:3 pattern—six years of elementary ('grade') school, followed by three years of junior high and three years of senior high school. In some areas, mainly rural, the old 8:4 pattern—eight years elementary followed by four years at high school—is retained. The high school is 'fully comprehensive' in the sense that it admits all pupils regardless of social class, creed or ability. Unlike European secondary schools, it is in no way subservient to university entrance requirements, and pays as much attention to the mass of average and below-average pupils as it does to those taking the so-called 'college preparatory' course.

Instead of taking a leaving certificate examination of the A level or baccalaureat type, pupils 'graduate' on completing the twelfth grade by a process of continuous assessment. Certain core studies, including English, mathematics, American history, general science and health education, are common to all courses, and in addition there is, at any rate in the larger high schools, a wide variety of optional subjects.

As regards standards of scholastic attainment, it may be conceded that the average twelfth-grader is anything from eighteen months to two years 'behind' the English sixth-former, but most American educationists do not regard this as a disadvantage, maintaining that any losses on the academic side are more than compensated for by social gains. More particularly since the sputnik scare, however, opinion has hardened in favour of stepping up standards of attainment by means of 'acceleration courses' and in some subjects—mathematics and biology are two of the most obvious—spectacular advances have been made. In the past decade, American academics have co-operated with high school teachers in hammering out detailed curricular reforms.

Even so, it is unlikely that the American high school will ever resort to the kind of selection and streaming that is thought necessary in most European academic secondary schools. Something like 40% of high school pupils now proceed to some kind of full-time higher education, and the proportion is increasing. Those not taking a four-year degree course may attend a two-year junior college. The majority, however, go on either to a liberal arts college, or to an independent university, or to a state university, state college or state teachers' college. At the undergraduate stage, styles of teaching and assessment resemble those in use in the high school. Here again, standards tend to be lower than those expected in the UK, but as numbers increase the centre of gravity has shifted to the post-graduate schools—and it is here, if anywhere, that cross-country comparisons can best be made.

In short, the American system of education gives the lie to assertions that 'more means worse' and vindicates the belief that the ideals of quality and equality are in no way incompatible.

FURTHER READING
E. J. King. *Society, Schools and Progress in the USA*, Pergamon, 1965.
W. Kenneth Richmond. *Education in the USA*, Redman, 1956.

WKR

Use of English paper This paper, set at A level, was introduced as a result of general disquiet at the low level of literacy displayed by many undergraduates. Its aim was to promote greater fluency, elegance and precision of written expression: an unexceptionable and, indeed, worthy aim. Its introduction resulted in a proliferation of 'Use of English' textbooks and specimen papers, most of which exemplified a narrow preoccupation with mechanical 'skills' such as précis-writing and comprehension at a fairly literal level. Some of the examinations, too, demonstrated a very limited notion of what literacy at 18-plus is all about. If there was a general mistaken assumption to be found in such a situation, it was that competence in communication is merely a matter of routine and explicitly learnable skills, rather than a function of the personality, a living thing not to be acquired through exercises but rather to be nurtured in conversation, discussion, an increase in self-awareness and an adequate motive for the rigorous task of achieving articulate precision.

The results of the examination have been very mixed. At their best, lessons in the 'Use of English' are characterised by freely exploratory discussion conducted in a liberally Socratic way, with recourse to literature as and when appropriate. At their worst, they are the least desirable of the old-fashioned O level English language courses elaborated to a point of extreme boredom.

The need for such a paper is debatable; but the recognition of some malaise certainly points to our need to rethink the whole ethos of the upper forms of secondary schools in terms of conversation, discussion and talk.

GS

USSR, Education in the Education in the USSR is free, comprehensive, co-educational, secular, politically oriented, totally state-run and subject to a high degree of central control, with substantially uniform curricula and schemes of work throughout the country. The principal types of institution are as follows:

Pre-school institutions Crèches, for infants under three, and kindergartens, for children between three and seven, are not part of the normal system. They are voluntary, and may make a charge for maintenance. Nevertheless, they are attended by a large minority (about 40%) and are growing in number and importance.

The eight-year school This is the basic unit of the educational system, providing for the entire length of compulsory schooling (ages 7–15). It is divided into two departments: elementary (classes I–IV) and incomplete secondary (classes V–VIII). This, however, is an internal convenience; there is a change from general to specialist teaching, but no selection or reallocation of pupils. Except for a few repeating the year's work, the whole class moves on as a group. The school is unstreamed throughout, the same course being followed by all children; this includes a substantial amount of science and one foreign language, usually English. Except for places where the 'shift'

system survives, lessons are held only in the mornings; the afternoons are free for hobbies, sport or 'study circles', so that abler pupils can add to their curriculum if they wish.

Secondary schools The parting of the ways comes at 15. Some leave and go to work; the majority, however, continue with some kind of secondary course. These are of three main types:

The Secondary Polytechnic School offers a two-year course leading to the school leaving certificate (*attestat zrelosti* or 'attestation of maturity') which entitles the holder to apply for a university or college place. The course is largely academic; polytechnic education—the theoretical and practical study of agricultural and industrial production—was emphasised during the Khrushchev period but has become less important since 1964. Schools of this type are often organised together with eight-year schools to form ten-year schools.

The Secondary Specialised School or Tekhnikum gives a three- or four-year course leading to the Attestation of Maturity and a qualification in a semi-professional occupation. Ten-year school graduates can take a shortened course.

Vocational Technical Schools train skilled workers. About 15% of the time is devoted to general studies, the rest to trade training. Courses last from one to three years, depending on the trade.

Secondary polytechnic and some *tekhnikum* courses are also available through evening, shift or correspondence study.

Alongside the ordinary system, there are special schools for the handicapped, for army and navy cadets, and for children with special talents, especially in music and ballet. Boarding schools follow exactly the same programme as day schools.

Higher education This is provided in universities and equivalent specialised institutions. Courses vary from four to six years, rather longer for the part-time students who make up half the total number. The USSR has one of the highest numbers of students in relation to population in the world; competition for entry, however, remains keen.

Although it is not formally part of the system, mention must be made of the youth movement—the Octobrists (for children under 10), Pioneers (10–15) and Komsomol (15–27). Not only do these organisations provide for leisure activities of all kinds, but they play a central role in the maintenance of school discipline and in social, moral and political education. They are thus an important adjunct to the school system, especially in those fields which are considered fundamental tasks of the Soviet school.

See also **Communist education**

FURTHER READING

George Z. F. Bereday, William W. Brickman and Gerald H. Read (eds). *The Changing Soviet School*, Constable, 1960.

Nicholas De Witt. *Education and Professional Employment in the USSR*, National Science Foundation, Washington, DC, 1961.

Nigel Grant. *Soviet Education*, University of London Press, 1965.

E. J. King (ed.). *Communist Education*, Methuen, 1963.

S. G. Shapovalenko (ed.). *Polytechnical Education in the USSR*, UNESCO, 1963.

NG

V

Vagrant children *See* **School attendance orders**

Venezuela, Education in Education is free and compulsory from the age of seven to the completion of the primary stage. Illiteracy is being slowly reduced; in 1965 just under 20% of the population over the age of 10 years was illiterate. The government controls the opening of independent educational establishments; two private universities at Caracas were approved by the government in 1953. There are now seven universities, the largest being the Central University of Venezuela at Caracas with 24,000 students. A Workers' University was opened in the same city in 1947. In 1966 there were 10,837 kindergartens and primary schools, with an enrolment of 1,421,959; 539 secondary schools, with an enrolment of 173,436; 117 normal schools, with an enrolment of 17,337; 232 technical schools, with an enrolment of 82,100; two pedagogical institutes, with an enrolment of 2,641; seven universities, with an enrolment of 38,731.

The country's population was approximately 8¾ million in 1965.

Verbal reasoning, Tests of *See* **Selection procedures for secondary education**

Verminous pupils LEAs have powers under the provisions of Section 54 of the Education Act 1944 to authorise a medical officer to examine the pupils and their clothes when the medical officer is of the opinion that such an examination is necessary in the interests of cleanliness. Further, if a medical officer has cause to suspect that a pupil or his or her clothing is infested with vermin or in a foul condition, he can order an examination of the pupil.

If a pupil or his or her clothing is found, by a person authorised by an LEA to examine pupils, to be infested with vermin or in a foul condition, any officer of the authority can serve upon the parent of the pupil a notice requiring him to cause the pupil or his or her clothing to be cleansed. If the parent does not comply with the notice after 24 hours, the medical officer can direct that the pupil should be cleansed under arrangements made by the LEA. An order by the medical officer will be sufficient to enable an officer of the authority to take a pupil to suitable premises, keep him or her there and clean his or her person or clothes.

If a medical officer suspects that a pupil or his or her clothes are verminous and he cannot immediately make an examination or arrange for the cleansing of the pupil and his or her clothes, he can direct that the pupil be excluded from school until an examination or a cleansing can be carried out. The head teacher should only exclude a pupil on the advice of a person authorised by the LEA who has examined the pupil or on the directions of the school medical officer. The period of exclusion of the pupil in these circumstances should not normally be more than three days.

If, after a pupil has been cleansed under the provisions of this Section, he or she is again found to be infected with vermin or in a foul condition and it is proved that this is due to the neglect of the parent, the parent will be liable to a fine on summary conviction.

See also **Legal rights and obligations of parents**

HP

Vertical grouping *See* **Family grouping**

Vice-Chancellors and Principals of the Universities of the UK, Committee of Membership of the Committee includes the vice-chancellors and principals of all the UK universities and additional members from the federal universities of London and Wales. Its functions are to keep under review the full range of university interests and to speak on behalf of the universities in general in their relations with other fields of education, with industry and with government. The Committee has a substructure of divisions each concerned with a particular sphere of its activities. Two delegate bodies, the Standing Conference on University Entrance and the Universities' Committee on Technical Staffs, which were established by the universities on the recommendation of the Vice-Chancellors' Committee, are serviced by the Committee's secretariat which is within the office of the Association of Commonwealth Universities.

36 Gordon Sq., London, WC1.

Victoria League for Commonwealth Friendship *See* **Commonwealth Friendship, Victoria League for**

Vietnam, North, Education in Education is compulsory for a 10-year period where places are available. 1966 statistics: 6,240 general schools (enrolment 3,100,000); 34 secondary

vocational schools (enrolment 49,600); eight higher education colleges (enrolment 15,900). The University of Hanoi has an enrolment of 1,075 students. Total population: approximately 16 million.

Vietnam, South, Education in 1964/5 statistics: 5,788 primary schools (enrolment 1,603,484); 587 secondary schools (enrolment 330,677); three higher education colleges (enrolment 23,662); three universities (enrolment 24,122). Total population: approximately $14\frac{1}{4}$ million.

Village colleges In theory, the village college co-ordinates under one roof all forms of education for a whole group of villages, together with social and recreational facilities. The college idea is usually associated with Cambridgeshire, for it was put forward in 1924 by Henry Morris, Secretary for Education for that county. He envisaged that each college should include a nursery and primary school, a secondary school, rooms for adult classes, a branch of the county library, a village hall and facilities for indoor and outdoor recreation. This plan was accepted and the first village college opened at Sawston in 1930.

There are now twelve colleges in Cambridgeshire. They come close to Morris's idea, for though nursery and primary schools are not usually in the college building, the newer welfare clinics are, and the colleges have certainly brought a valuable stimulus to declining rural areas. Similar schemes have now been developed in other places, notably Leicestershire, Cumberland and Monmouthshire.

BG

Virgil Society The Virgil Society, founded in 1943 with the late Mr T. S. Eliot, the late Monsignor Ronald Knox and Mr Robert Speaight amongst its sponsors, exists to unite all those who cherish the central educational tradition of Western Europe. Of that tradition Virgil is the symbol. Membership is open to all in sympathy, whether they know Latin or not. Hon. Sec.: H. MacL. Currie, Queen Mary College, London, E1. Hon. Treas.: Dr J. G. Landels, The University, Whiteknights Park, Reading.

Visual aids This is a term used to cover a variety of methods of illustration. Television has become well established in recent years. The older medium, film, continues to be one of the most popular aids (*see* **Film in education**).

There are other aids which also use projector and screen. The episcope projects an image of any object which can be placed on a platform in the machine—diagrams, maps, photographs, etc. and three-dimensional objects such as models, biological specimens and even scientific experiments. Thus objects which could otherwise be seen by only a few pupils at a time can be seen simultaneously by larger numbers. The advantage of the episcope is that material need not be specially prepared; but because light is reflected from the object (rather than transmitted through a slide), good black-out is essential.

The diascope projects an image from a $3\frac{1}{4}$ in. x $3\frac{1}{4}$ in. (or similar) slide. Nowadays it is not so widely used as the miniature diascope, i.e. the slide or film-strip projector (see **Film in education**). The epidiascope is a combination of episcope and diascope.

The micro-projector combines the virtues of microscope and diascope by projecting a greatly enlarged image (up to x 6000) from a 2 in. x 2 in. slide or small living specimen. In the overhead projector, light is directed from below through a 10 in. square glass table and reflected by a mirror above to produce, in daylight, an image on a screen behind the operator. It can be used merely as a more convenient form of the traditional chalkboard, the operator writing on a roll of clear acetate sheet which passes over the glass table. Its full value is not realised, however, unless material is carefully prepared in advance—e.g. colour slides (made from photographic negatives, photo-copied material, etc.), perspex working models, etc. Slides may be superimposed (e.g. to build up a diagram gradually), and the operator can make additions to the slide during use, the marks being easily erased afterwards. The white 'chalkboard' (*q.v.*) (felt-tip pen replaces chalk) can also serve as a screen.

Of the non-projected aids, the best modern 'blackboard' is neither black nor board; even 'chalkboard' is not a completely accurate term. A flexible material, usually green, which can be moved on rollers, gives excellent results. Words, symbols etc. cut from flannel or similar material, or paper cut-outs mounted on flannel, will adhere to a piece of the same material stretched over a board. This 'flannelgraph' can be used to build up or modify a display during the course of a lesson. Modern versions of the flannelgraph may be made of plastic, nylon, pegboard or magnetic board.

Wallcharts and models complete the list of visual aids.

National Committee for Audiovisual Aids in Education, 33 Queen Anne St, London, W1.

Monthly magazine: *Visual Education*.

FURTHER READING
N. J. Atkinson. *Modern Teaching Aids*, MacLaren, 1966.
C. W. H. Erickson. *Fundamentals of Teaching with Audiovisual Technology*, Macmillan, New York, 1965.

APH

Visual Aids, Educational Foundation for Set up in 1948 by the Ministry of Education in consultation with the LEAs, the Foundation has special responsibilities for the distribution, production and cataloguing of classroom films and filmstrips, the supply of equipment and the provision of technical advisory and maintenance services. The EFVA *Catalogue of Visual Aids: Films and Filmstrips Parts 1–8* gives details of films and filmstrips from producers of material for classroom use; all are available from the EFVA Film Library, Brooklands House, Weybridge, Surrey.

33 Queen Anne St, London, W1.

See also **Audio-Visual Aids in Education, National Committee for**

Visual Aids Groups, Central Committee of Teachers' *See* **Audio-Visual Aids in Education, National Committee for**

Visual Education National Information Service for Schools A service provided by the National Committee for Audio-Visual Aids in Education (*q.v.*), VENISS offers members, for their annual subscription, copies of the *Wallchart Catalogue*, the *Visual Education Year Book*, the monthly *Visual Education*, pamphlets, catalogues, leaflets and lists.

33 Queen Anne St, London, W1.

Volleyball For many years a most popular indoor and outdoor court game in America and on the continent of Europe, volleyball has only relatively recently begun to grow in favour in Great Britain. It has also been accepted for inclusion as a major game in the Olympic Games.

The game, played between teams of six-a-side on a court with maximum dimensions of 50 ft × 30 ft, is not only in itself a fast, excellent sport, but is valuable as a training activity for most major sports in that it helps to develop both speed and stamina.

In essence, the game consists of 'volleying' an inflated ball somewhat similar to but smaller than a football, over a net eight ft high, with the object of making it touch the ground in the opposing team's half of the court and at the same time preventing it touching the ground in one's own half of the court.

Though the game, with modifications, has been played sporadically in schools in this country for some years, it is only recently that a Schools Volleyball Association has been formed as a section of the Amateur Volleyball Association. This has speeded the development of the game; it is likely that within a few years it will rival basketball in popularity, though there is ample room for the inclusion of both games in the school curriculum.

Amateur Volleyball Association of Great Britain and Northern Ireland: Hon. Sec.: R. Pankhurst, Southgate Technical College, High St, London, N14.

FURTHER READING
D. W. Anthony. *Volleyball, Do It This Way* Series, Murray, 1964.
R. E. Laveaga. *Volleyball, How to Improve Your Sport* Series, Bailey Bros. and Swinfen, 1964.
P. Wardale. *Volleyball*, Faber, 1964.

JE

Voluntary Aided Secondary Schools, Association of Formed in December 1967 by the amalgamation of the National Association of Governing Bodies of Aided Grammar Schools and the Association of Governing Bodies of Greater London Aided Secondary Schools, the Association has the following aims: (1) to help, advise and encourage co-operation between the governing bodies of aided grammar schools and other aided secondary schools in England and Wales in carrying out their duties and obligations; (2) to promote public understanding and support of the role of such schools in the education system of England and Wales; (3) to collect and disseminate information of interest to such schools; (4) to assist the schools in negotiations with the DES, LEAs and other bodies.

The Association has an Executive Committee (Chairman: Keith Gammon, MBE) and an Inner London Council (Chairman: Anthony Jones) which deals specially with matters relating to the ILEA area.

Sec.: F. W. G. Ridgewell, 20 Reddons Rd, Beckenham, Kent.

Voluntary Service Overseas An independent organisation, founded in 1958, to link young people with those of their generation in the developing territories of the world. From a small beginning — 18 boys were sent out in the first year — VSO has expanded so that in 1966-7 there were some 950 graduate teachers, agriculturists, doctors, medical auxiliaries, and other trained and qualified people, and some 450 school-leavers and ex-apprentices from industry, serving in the developing countries overseas.

More than 2,800 volunteers have so far served in 65 different territories, from Fiji to the Falkland Islands, and from Togo to Thailand. Some 70% are engaged in teaching, whether in universities, training colleges, secondary schools (boarding and day), technical institutes or trade schools. The remainder are engaged in agricultural work, forestry, fish culture, medical duties of all kinds, work in homes for the disabled, in leprosariums, in youth clubs or among refugees.

3 Hanover St, London, W1.

See also **International Voluntary Service**

Voluntary Societies' Committee on Service Overseas (British Volunteer Programme) Formed in 1962, the Committee co-ordinates the programme under which graduates and other trained volunteers are sent overseas to work in developing countries. The volunteers are sponsored by International Voluntary Service (*q.v.*), the United Nations Association, Voluntary Service Overseas (*q.v.*) and the Catholic Institute for International Relations.

26 Bedford Sq., London, W1.

W

Wales, Education in Although the pattern of education in Wales (including Monmouthshire) broadly resembles that of England, some distinctive features, more indelible than regional variations, emphasise that 'Cymro' and 'Sais' often think on different wavelengths. A sense of apartness from England, born of history and national temper, pervades the education service in Wales, which is sometimes overlooked by the metropolitan intellect. Unlike Scotland and Northern Ireland, Wales does not enjoy Education Acts and statutory regulations of its own. Legislative sanctions may be shared, but practice diverges. Governmental and physical boundaries are missing; but Offa's Dyke exists, so to say, in the minds of men, in the habits and traditions of the Celtic people.

Specific administrative machinery ensures that the educational needs of Wales are properly considered. A separate Welsh Department was established in 1907 for 'the better administration of primary, secondary and technical education in Wales and Monmouthshire.' The Principality now has a Secretary for Welsh Education who heads the Education Office for Wales, located in Cardiff. A Central Advisory Council for Education (Wales), which advises the Secretary of State on Welsh problems, has submitted nine reports since 1949, ranging from the future of secondary education and the place of the arts and of science, to technical education. The latest report on primary education (*see* **Gittins Report on Primary Education in Wales**) constitutes the Welsh version of Plowden. HMIs in Wales, Welsh-speaking almost to a man, together with a Chief Inspector, maintain cordial relations with their English colleagues but discharge an entirely separate commission.

A unique institution, the Welsh Joint Education Committee, guarantees that Welsh views on education will be expressed and that, where possible, a common Welsh policy emerges through this advisory and co-ordinating body. Its 115 members are drawn from the LEAs (87) and different educational interests (28) among which teachers predominate. It provides a forum for the 17 LEAs to discuss affairs of mutual concern. Certain enterprises beyond the resources of all but the largest authorities are undertaken on a co-operative basis, such as the residential school for the deaf, the schools museum service, the Welsh national youth orchestra and the publication of Welsh books. Some degree of uniformity in administration is also achieved, for example, in devising standard scales of payment for part-time teachers in further education. Its representatives are appointed to national committees or working parties and the DES consults with the WJEC as one of the organs of LEA opinion. The Joint Committee acts as the examining body for the GCE and CSE examinations in Wales. Even the Schools Council for Curriculum Research and Development, which began work in 1964, hived

813

off a Welsh committee to initiate and superintend kindred activities.

This considerable administrative apparatus serves a nation and not a mere region. The preservation of its language and cultural heritage is the joint task of home and school. With the exception of a few anglicised areas like Newport, Welsh is taught in all primary schools, in accordance with the official bilingual policy of the Welsh Office. Especially in the north and and west, English is taught as a second language, where the mother tongue is Welsh. At its lowest, in the non-Welsh regions, this policy 'forces an unwanted language down unwilling throats': at its best, it perpetuates a living language, essential to a full understanding of Welsh culture. If another foreign language—French—is taught in a primary school, Welsh children have to acquire three vocabularies. In the secondary school, Welsh may become optional when formal examinations loom, but the study of Welsh *mores* continues. Welsh history forms a necessary part of the general history syllabus.

Growing social mobility and the mass media have tended to reinforce other influences inimical to the use of the Welsh language. The Welsh-speaking now number only 25% of the population. A concentration of linguistic resources is being tried. In some primary schools, most subjects of the curriculum are taught through the medium of Welsh. A few all-Welsh secondary schools are under way. The university and colleges of education organise courses of instruction exclusively conducted in Welsh. The BBC helps with school broadcasts in Welsh. Welshmen fear that if the spirit of Wales is not fostered 'the Welsh nation will become only derivative and second-rate, an imitator of something inferior to her own true life'.

Customarily in Wales, a higher proportion of pupils has entered grammar schools, percentages of 40 and 50 being not uncommon. A Welsh child had a two-to-one chance of admission over his English neighbour. The Welsh Intermediate Education Act 1889 gave the Principality a head start before the Act of 1902 ushered in the state secondary school. In addition, Welsh parents, driven by economic circumstances, believed strongly in education and showed a willingness to make sacrifices for their children. The change to comprehensive schools has not diminished this pre-eminence. Anglesey stands alone with all pupils in comprehensive schools. On average, twice as many children in Wales attend such schools as in England: a third of Welsh LEAs rank very high.

Wales can fairly claim to be the home of adult education, which originated in their Sunday Schools of the 19th century. The residential Coleg Harlech, the extra-mural departments of the university and a constellation of voluntary bodies, vigorously uphold a movement which no longer draws its strength from the 'knowledge is power' affirmation of earlier days. The federal university, comprising four constituent colleges at Aberystwyth, Bangor, Cardiff and Swansea, was itself founded by the pennies of the people. It has been the university of everyman, as against the aristocratic endowment of Oxbridge and the civic beginnings of Redbrick. Even before the Robbins expansion, more Welsh students, proportionately, attended college than in England.

The design of technical and further education in Wales is changing. Earlier LEAs tended to expand their buildings and advanced courses in isolation to meet the demands of industry. The WJEC tried with little success to rationalise the provision of technical facilities which could be over-costly if staffing and equipment were duplicated in adjacent areas. New centralised procedures for the recognition of courses, the application of the Pilkington formula and the logic of the binary system have at last rationalised re-sources. A polytechnic is imminent at Treforest, Glamorgan, and North Wales authorities have been prompted to discuss similar possibilities. The former CAT at Cardiff now belongs to the University as the Institute of Science and Technology. The industrial train-ing boards stimulate principals to organise integrated courses at all levels. In art the Newport and Cardiff colleges, following their designation by the Summerson Council, alone func-tion as centres for Diploma in Art and Design students.

In shortage conditions, England depends more than ever on Welsh-trained teachers who can be exported. Fortunately, Welsh colleges of education train more students than Wales is able to absorb under the quota system. The pupil-teacher ratio in Wales is far superior. As county boroughs, Merthyr and Swansea top the combined league table, while Radnor and Cardigan lead the English and Welsh counties.

Though the structure of the educa-tional system is common to both countries, the schools in Wales, in some respects, possess different identities. A school *eisteddfod* on St David's Day—always celebrated by a half holiday—and the exhortation to 'wear a leek on this day in your cap but always in your heart' shows a sincerity that never belonged to the Empire Day pro-gramme of old. When the occasion is enhanced by the choral and dramatic talent which sings penillion to the harp accompaniment or recites verses from the Mabinogion, one is left in no doubt of the strength of the national sentiment that the educational system endeavours to foster and preserve.

Wales participates vigorously in the curriculum revolution. Two major researches into 'compensatory educa-tion' and 'attitudes and motivation in the learning of Welsh' are afoot at Swansea, while Cartrefle College of Education, Wrexham, is exploring the role of environmental studies. Teaching materials for Welsh as a first language, and the problems of science and mathe-matics taught in Welsh, may also be investigated soon.

The White Paper *Local Government in Wales*, published in July 1967, re-commends a plan of reorganisation whereby five new counties—Gwynedd, Powys, Dyfed, Glamorgan and Gwent —and three county boroughs (Cardiff, Swansea and Newport), would replace the 17 LEAs currently operating. A change in the existing pattern of administration seems essential if Wales is to discharge its responsibilities effectively.

FURTHER READING
Bilingualism in the Schools of Wales, Ministry of Education, 1962.
Curriculum and Community in Wales, Ministry of Education, 1952.
Education in Wales 1847–1947, Ministry of Education, 1948.
Pioneers of Welsh Education, Faculty of Education, Univ. College of Swansea, 1965.
The Place of Welsh and English in the Schools of Wales, Ministry of Education, 1953.
Science in Education in Wales Today, Depart-ment of Education and Science, 1965.

LJD

Wales, Education Office for With its centre in Cardiff, the Education Office for Wales is part of the DES (*q.v.*).

Wales, National Association of Teachers of (Undeb Cenedlaethol Athrawon Cymru—UCAC) The only professional body created specifically for teachers in Wales. It embraces teachers in all educational establish-ments, from nursery schools to the university. It has legal, insurance and house purchase departments, a sick scheme and provident fund and publishes not only periodicals for its members but also Welsh language textbooks. UCAC fights for better conditions for all teachers and cam-paigns for a unified system of education which pays regard to the national and cultural needs of Wales as well as to developing modern techniques for the improvement of teaching at all levels.

11 Gordon Rd, Cardiff.

Wales, Primary education in See **Gittins Report on Primary Education in Wales (1968)**

Wales, University of See **University of Wales**

Walking distance from school It is a defence to proceedings against a parent for non-attendance of his child at school if the school at which the child is a registered pupil is not within walking distance from the child's home and no suitable arrangements have been made by the LEA for transport to and from school or for boarding accommodation at or near the school. Walking distance in this context is, under the provisions of Section 39(5) of the Education Act 1944, stipulated in the case of a child under eight as two miles, and in the case of any other children three miles, measured by the nearest available route. In determining the nearest available route, distance, not safety, is the test.[1] Also, the nearest route need not necessarily be along a road; any footpath, public or private way could be used.

Under the provisions of Section 55 of the Education Act 1944, the LEA has a duty to make arrangements for the provision of transport or otherwise as it considers necessary, or as the Secretary of State may direct, to facilitate the attendance of pupils at schools, and the LEA may pay the whole or part of the travelling expenses of pupils for whom transport arrangements are not made under the provisions of this section. The arrangements, however, must be suitable, and if a child lives more than three miles from his or her school, the LEA must provide for his or her transport for the full distance.[2]

REFERENCES
1. Shaxted v. Ward, 1954, 1 AER 336.
2. Surrey County Council v. Ministry of Education, 1 AER 705.

HP

WEA See **Workers' Educational Association**

Weight training There is a clear distinction between 'weight training' and 'weight lifting'. The latter is an internationally recognised sport in which the aim is to lift, by recognised methods, greater and greater poundages. Competitors are divided into 'weights' similar to those used in boxing. Little weight lifting as such is done in schools. Weight training, on the other hand, is now practised in many secondary schools as an aid to physical fitness and as a method of intensive training for a wide range of sports. It is essentially a means of exercising the body, using weights to add increased resistance to the physical movements being performed.

It has been proved conclusively that a muscle will increase in bulk to a greater extent and far more quickly than by normal exercises if it is 'overloaded'; i.e. if it has to work against ever-increasing resistance. This resistance is supplied by weight training apparatus, such as steel bars to which are attached circular weights of known poundages, steel 'shoes' (for leg exercises) to which weights can also be fixed, and various items of fixed apparatus designed to give controlled resistance.

Whilst weight training can be satisfying in itself, through rapid development of muscular physique and use as a 'high pressure' activity by students preparing for examinations and adults leading busy commercial lives, its main attraction is as a method for improving physical performance in almost every modern sport and particularly athletic field events (jumping and throwing), rowing, boxing, tennis and swimming. The old theory that weight training led to athletes becoming 'muscle-bound' (i.e. stiff in joint movement) has been proved to be completely fallacious.

FURTHER READING
D. G. Johnson and O. Heidenstam. *Modern Body Building*, Faber, 1955.
A. Murray. *Modern Weight Training*, Kaye and Ward, 1963.
J. Murray and P. V. Karpovitch. *Weight Training in Athletics*, Prentice-Hall, 1956.
E. Taylor. *Training with Weights*, Murray, 1962.

JE

Welsh Intermediate Education Act (1889) *See* **Aberdare Report**

Welsh Joint Education Committee This Committee co-ordinates certain of the functions of the Welsh education authorities, provides GCE and CSE examinations and examinations for part-time pupils in technical institutions, and acts as a Regional Advisory Council for further education in Wales.

Sec.: D. Andrew Davies, 30 Cathedral Rd, Cardiff.

Welsh Secondary Schools Association Membership of this professional association is open to headmasters and headmistresses of all secondary schools in Wales and Monmouthshire.

Gen. Sec.: H. J. Davies, Ynysawdre Comprehensive School, Tondw, Bridgend, Glamorgan.

Publication: *Welsh Secondary Schools Review* (twice annually).

West Indies, Education in the It is almost impossible to understand the position of education in the West Indies of today without reference to their history, and also to the isolation of the islands owing to the considerable stretches of sea between them. History brought two clear main divisions, namely the white 'plantocracy' of privilege and the masses of dark-skinned slaves. Although some planters treated their slaves with humanity, the slaves had no rights of their own.

With the dawn of emancipation philanthropists and missionary bodies showed considerable energy in providing forms of education for the masses; in most cases government departments of education evolved slowly. However, whether sponsored by philanthropists, missionaries or state officials, the educational models were taken from the patterns then existing in metropolitan countries. One result was extreme respect for the formal and academic, a legacy that is dying very slowly.

Generally speaking, as late as the second world war the chances of a high school education in the British West Indies were for the relatively few, and to a large extent dependent upon ability to pay fees. Elementary schools for the masses were totally insufficient in number, vastly overcrowded and lacking the necessary staff; those available were mostly unqualified and underpaid. It is, therefore, not surprising that strict discipline was necessary to maintain some order and that much of the learning was by rote.

With the end of the war, enlightened men in the metropolitan lands and among West Indians themselves made increasing efforts to modernise education in the West Indies and to tackle the teacher problem. Moreover, with the demands for whole or partial self-government educational reform became a matter of urgency. It made necessary the abolition of an elementary system for the masses and a secondary one, with notable exceptions, for a somewhat privileged élite. There was also a realisation that without provision for technical training, islands creating a diversified economy would not have available a labour force with the necessary skills. Teacher training was expanded, and from teacher colleges—particularly in Jamaica, Trinidad and Barbados—there began a flow of teachers with a knowledge of the history, geography, flora and fauna of the West Indies (previously teachers tended to know all about the metropolitan countries and nothing about the West Indies).

During the past few years there has been a marked educational advance in the larger islands, with imaginative planning to provide sound primary and secondary education for all, a move away from the purely academic and the establishment and development of technical and agricultural institutions geared to West Indian needs. Owing to their size and lack of adequate funds, the smaller and poorer islands have moved educationally at a rather slower pace. Nevertheless, gains, real if not spectacular, are being made. These islands have benefited greatly from the excellent work of the Extra-Mural Department of the University of the West Indies, work that necessarily had to start at a somewhat lower level than normal for such departments though in the last few years it has been possible to reach levels that might previously have been thought remote.

Most of the above refers to those islands which were once under British rule. The Netherlands Antilles, an integral part of the Kingdom of the Netherlands, has a sound educational system, following, with variations to meet local needs, the metropolitan system, and with opportunities for university and higher technological education in the Netherlands. The French West Indies are a special case, in that islands like Martinique and Guadeloupe are Departments of France, equal to any other Department in that country. The education is intimately related to the system prevailing in any other French Department, including the famous lycée. As with the Netherlands Antilles, university and higher training in skills is available in the metropolitan country.

The overall situation of education today in the West Indies is promising. There remains the problem of matching the expanding number of schools with a sufficient number of trained teachers from the islands, and in some small islands the question of how to find the necessary money to provide more teachers and more schools. One encouraging aspect is that there is noticeable movement from teacher-centred to child-centred education, and this is proceeding almost side-by-side with the introduction of modern ideas about discipline and more informality in the early stages of education.

HWH

West Indies British Crown Colonies, Education in These Colonies are the British Virgin Islands, Cayman Islands, Montserrat, and Turks and Caicos Islands. In 1964 primary schools numbered as follows: British Virgin Islands 16 (enrolments 1,960), Cayman Islands 17 (enrolments 1,460), Montserrat 15 (enrolments 3,000), Turks and Caicos Islands 13 (enrolments including secondary 1,500). Secondary schools: British Virgin Islands 8 (enrolments including technical 550), Cayman Islands 3 (enrolments 430), Montserrat 1, Turks and Caicos Islands 1. The University of the West Indies, Jamaica, takes students from these islands.

The population of the Colonies in 1965 was approximately as follows: British Virgin Islands 7,300, Cayman Islands 7,600, Montserrat 12,100, Turks and Caicos Islands 5,700.

West Indies States Associated with Britain, Education in These states are Antigua, Dominica, Grenada, St Kitts-Nevis-Anguilla, St Lucia, St Vincent. In 1963–4 primary schools numbered as follows: Antigua 50 (enrolments 11,100), Dominica 51 (enrolments 15,400), Grenada 56 (enrolments 28,000), St Kitts-Nevis-Anguilla 44 including combined primary and secondary (enrolments 16,300), St Lucia 58 (enrolments 23,400), St Vincent 56 (enrolments 24,600). Secondary schools: Antigua 47 (enrolments

6,100), Dominica 4 (enrolments 1,600) Grenada 9 (enrolments 2,300), St Kitts-Nevis-Anguilla 5 (enrolments 1,500), St Lucia 3 (enrolments 1,000), St Vincent 9 (enrolments 1,900). Technical schools: Dominica 3, St Kitts-Nevis-Anguilla 2. Teacher training colleges: Grenada 1, St Lucia 1, St Vincent 4. The University of the West Indies, Jamaica, takes students from these states.

The population of the islands in 1965 was approximately as follows: Antigua 62,000; St Kitts-Nevis-Anguilla 60,000; Dominica 66,000; Grenada 98,000; St Lucia 103,000; St Vincent 87,000.

Wheatley Report (1963) *See* **Scotland, General Teaching Council for**

'Whisky Money' Act (1890) A tax levied on spirits was credited to county councils, who were free to allocate the money as they thought fit. The original scheme was that this money should be used partly for police superannuation, and partly for the purchase of publicans' licences in order to buy up redundant public houses. But this proposal was challenged by Sir William Mather and A. H. D. Acland, who wanted to see the proceeds devoted to the support of technical education in England and Wales. The counties were given a free hand, and within the next five years 93 out of the 129 borough councils were spending their entire 'whisky money' on technical education.

Whitehead, Alfred North (1861–1947) Main work on education: *Aims of Education.*

For Whitehead, the educated man has general culture and expertise in some specialism. His general culture is intellectual, aesthetic and moral. Learning should not just be the storing of inert ideas, or a sharpening of supposed faculties, but should be an active assimilation of general ideas.

These ideas should be tested, applied to life and inter-related as much as possible, to give an understanding of the present. To achieve this, not too much should be taught, but it should be taught thoroughly. There is a characteristic rhythm in learning: from initial romance to precision and finally to generalisation.

RFD

Whole-sentence method A method of reading which demands that children learning to read shall proceed by recognising a whole sentence at a time and so comprehending its sense.

See also **Reading research**

Wilderspin, Samuel (c. 1792–1866) A Londoner who at the age of 22 became master of the Spitalfields Infant School, Wilderspin was influenced by the ideas of Pestalozzi (*q.v.*), though he was never eager to acknowledge his indebtedness. He was responsible for the foundation of the short-lived Infant School Society. His writings include *On the Importance of Educating the Infant Children of the Poor* (1824), which contained harrowing accounts of the condition of these children, and *Early Discipline* (1832), in which, among other themes, he explored the idea that parents might be regenerated through their children. In his teaching Wilderspin aimed at the education of the whole being, with games, music and the use of the playground playing a large part.

Winnetka Plan The plan takes its name from a village on the north shore of Lake Michigan, Illinois, USA, now a residential suburb of Chicago some 17 miles away. Here in the 1920s the pioneer work was done in the municipal schools under the leadership of Carlton W. Washbourne, superintendent of schools. The plan aims to give each pupil the basic skills not through class teaching but by a system which allows him to develop at his own pace, and self-instructive exercises are therefore an essential part of the method. The rate of progress of the individual is judged by diagnostic tests. The plan recognises that the individual must also operate as one of a group, and it makes provision for group activities aimed at creating a social consciousness in the child, but the main emphasis of the plan is on individual progress.

Winnicott, D. W. (b. 1896) At one time it was considered that a child under three years old could not have emotional or even psychological problems; and this might explain why some of the early training regimes for babies were so rigid and even punitive in their total effect. Dr Winnicott, a paediatrician and also a psychoanalyst, by concentrating on the emotional needs of babies and their mothers, has done a great deal to change attitudes in this field, emphasising the mother's instinctive feelings for her child rather than rules and regulations on baby care. Thus, breast feeding is seen as an important psychological link between mother and child, as well as having nutritional advantages, and early toilet training is deferred in recognition of the damage it can cause if pressed too rigorously. Many childish complaints may have their root in emotional disruption or neglect which might best be helped by family consultation rather than by drugs or medicine. Dr Winnicott has also helped to promote greater interest in children's art, fantasy and dreams, in place of the tendency to discuss them as childish baubles of no real significance.

Winnicott's writings, which also deal with adult needs and disorders, do not always make easy reading, but their total effect—especially in the field of paediatrics—has been very great indeed.

FURTHER READING
D. W. Winnicott. *The Child, the Family, and the Outside World*, Penguin, 1964. *The Child and the Family*, Tavistock, 1957.

NT

Winston Churchill Memorial Trust Inspired by the example of Sir Winston Churchill, and by the belief that his adventurous life and travels did much to make him the man he was, the Trust makes annual awards of travelling fellowships within selected occupations and fields of activity covering a wide area of national life. The categories are varied from year to year. In 1968, for example, fellowships were awarded to men and women working in hospital nursing, educational broadcasting, the conservation of wild life, animal welfare and the veterinary service, the fishing industry, personnel management, on the shop floor in the steel industry, in yacht, pleasure craft and marina design and construction, exploration and archaeology, and the arts. A travelling fellowship is not normally awarded solely for formal study. Applicants are required to show a sense of purpose in travelling, and to explain how the experience gained would benefit the community.

37 Charles St, London, W1.

Wolfenden Report (1960): Sport and the Community Terms of reference: to examine the factors affecting the development of games, sports and outdoor activities in the UK and to make recommendations to the Central Council of Physical Recreation as to any practical measures which should be taken by statutory or voluntary bodies in order that these activities might play their full part in promoting the general welfare of the community. Chairman: Sir John Wolfenden.

The Committee recommended that there should be a much clearer link between the youth service, statutory and voluntary, on the one hand, and the bodies responsible for games, sports and outdoor activities on the other. More time should be found for training courses for youth leaders. The Committee recommended that many more facilities for sport should be introduced or expanded, and more coaching schemes be made available. It asked for a sports development council of six to ten persons to be established, with a direct grant of about £5 million, which the Council would be free to distribute.

Wolfson Foundation Founded in 1955, the Foundation exists to promote education and health in the UK and Commonwealth, with particular reference to scientific and technological education, building facilities for higher education, youth activities, medical research, cancer research, and the medical, surgical and nursing services.

Universal Hse, 256 Tottenham Court Rd, London, W1.

Women, Higher education for The post-school education of women in the UK dates in its modern form from the latter half of the 19th century and precedes the development of secondary education for girls, which was given great impetus by the need to provide well-educated girls for the newly founded colleges.

Cambridge University Among the first pioneers anxious to establish university education for women, Emily Davies, founder of Girton College, Cambridge, stands out. Miss Davies was supported in her general principles by influential and academic men in and outside the universities, but she disagreed with many of them, notably Henry Sidgwick of Cambridge, as to whether women should actually take the same examinations as men or whether special examinations should be designed for them. She felt passionately that they should take the same examinations.

In this she disagreed with Miss Anne Clough, who had founded the North of England Council for promoting the higher education of women, with Mrs Josephine Butler as president and herself as secretary. Its aims were to improve and extend the education of upper and middle-class women. The Council played an important part in the opening of the provincial universities to women, but the immediate objective was to admit women to an examination higher than the existing university local examinations. In the meantime Miss Davies was working to get women accepted for the Cambridge Littlego or Previous examination.

It was suggested that a new college at Cambridge might be linked with similar colleges at Oxford, Cambridge and London, and that the joint institutions might become a university for women. Miss Davies was very much opposed to this idea, and in the end got her way, so that the new college was linked with the University of Cambridge. The first five students lived in a small house at Hitchin, Herts., opened in 1869. These five had been carefully selected from 21 who took the entrance examination. In the first Littlego examination, all five students were successful in classics, and finally two of the students passed the Tripos examination in classics and one in mathematics. In the same year Hitchin was incorporated as Girton College and moved to Girton, outside Cambridge.

Meanwhile Miss Clough started a series of lectures for women in Cambridge, and eventually took charge of a house for women students. Merton Hall, as it was called, was a huge success, and in 1879 it moved to Newnham where, in 1880, it was incorporated as Newnham College. Here the pace was gentler than at Girton and there was no assumption that all students must take the Tripos examination on the same terms as men.

After her retirement as Mistress of Girton, Miss Davies threw herself into the fight to get women students admitted to the degrees earned by their examination results. Her case was strengthened when a Girton student, Charlotte Scott, although officially unplaced in the Maths Tripos, was equal to the eighth wrangler. Still further support came when Agnata Ramsay was the only candidate placed in the first division of the first class of the Classical Tripos, but it was not until after the second world war that women in Cambridge were finally admitted on equal terms with the men as full members of the university.

Other universities At Oxford, which conceded degrees to women in 1920, women's education developed on much the same lines as at Cambridge. Two colleges were opened for women in 1878–9, Lady Margaret Hall on a religious foundation, and Somerville on undenominational lines. Two further colleges, and a home students' association, later St Anne's College, soon followed.

Following the success of individual undergraduates, women in both universities were admitted as examiners and candidates for university fellowships and colleges.

In the meantime, in London, Mrs Reid had founded Bedford College for Women in 1849. The idea of the college took shape after the development of Queen's College, Harley Street, originally planned to educate and examine governesses. Mrs Reid organised courses and lectures for young women in her house and followed this up by helping to buy a house in Bedford Square for a non-sectarian college for women. This was a bold and imaginative venture, but Bedford had to wait until 1878 for its students to be admitted to London University degrees. Westfield College, Hampstead, was founded in 1882 for the higher education of women on Christian principles. Royal Holloway College, Egham, followed as the result of the initiative of Thomas Holloway, a wealthy pill manufacturer. In the 1960s all three London women's colleges began to admit men undergraduates.

The large co-educational colleges in London, University College, King's from the 1840s, and the London School of Economics from the 1890s, admitted women equally with men. The Imperial College of Science now admits women equally with men but gets far fewer applications from women, who remain very much a minority. Scottish, Welsh and English provincial universities freely admitted women to all their courses for higher education, and the post-war universities did so automatically. In some of the new universities, men and women are admitted in the same halls of residence. Men still outnumber women in British universities; the ratio is about four to one.

In the USA, women were accepted at the universities and many women's colleges were especially founded at an earlier date than those in England; Commonwealth countries, still developing their educational system, admit men and women equally, though in practice more men than women go on to higher education.

Colleges of education University education of women concerns, of course, only a minority, and many other kinds of education have developed. Whereas the women's university colleges belong to the same middle-class tradition of the North London Collegiate School and the high schools, the colleges of education (formerly training colleges) have grown out of the working-class elementary school tradition. Early training colleges were mostly for pupil teachers educated in elementary schools and were founded to provide a teaching force for the grant-aided primary schools. The number of women applying to colleges of education grew from about 6,000 before 1939 to an annual admission of 30,000 in the mid-60s.

There were a few training colleges for men, but colleges were predominantly staffed by women for women; although in church colleges clergymen often held office as principal. The mid-60s saw the development of a policy of increasing the number of men training for teaching, and also male recruitment to the staffs of women's colleges. Many single-sex colleges changed to co-educational colleges.

In addition to general colleges of education, as training colleges originally founded to provide teachers for elementary schools, but which now supply teachers for the whole field of primary and secondary education, there are specialist training colleges for domestic science subjects and physical education. These two specialisms have been popular forms of higher education for women.

Other forms of higher education Other kinds of higher education for women include the whole field of secretarial training and the medical auxiliary services. Women's training courses in physiotherapy, radiography, ortho-optics and occupational therapy provide a satisfactory form of education for able and practical but not essentially academic women. The medical profession itself has been open in theory to women since the latter years of the 19th century, but in the mid-6os it became extremely difficult for women to gain admission to medical schools; they have to reach a higher standard than men before they are accepted. Nursing training is a long established form of further education while working.

A few women take engineering or other technical courses through the technical colleges and the City and Guilds examination, and large numbers of women take the increasingly professional diploma courses at colleges of art.

A small number of women are able to make up some of the gaps in their secondary education by courses at colleges like Hillcroft, where work is not geared to examination requirements.

However, the vast majority of women still do not experience any of these forms of post-school education;

their education comes through local associations, churches, women's institutes, the National Council of Women, business and professional clubs, university extension courses, evening institutes and day classes.

In the mid-6os, with the great demand for trained women, a new pattern of education emerged. Many women take a preliminary course of training, practise their skill or profession for a few years, then withdraw to start a family and look after the early education of their children. After some form of retraining they return, but not necessarily to the same work. The development of part-time day courses for women in technical colleges all over the country is filling a need created by the existence of many middle-aged women now ready to start work again, but whose early education is no longer entirely relevant. Teaching draws heavily on the reserves of married women. Initial training courses for mature women (and men), in addition to postgraduate and refresher courses, are developing both in special colleges such as Sidney Webb College (ILEA) and within the traditional colleges.

MM

Women, National Council of *See* **Adult education, Women in**

Women's Clubs, National Association of *See* **Adult education, Women in**

Women's Co-operative Guilds *See* **Adult education, Women in**

Women's Employment Federation A registered charity, the Federation was founded in 1933 to give advice on training and employment to girls and women. Its founders were a group of women interested in all aspects of women's education and training.

The advisory department gives personal consultations by appointment, arranges conferences and publishes literature. Lectures to schools, organisations and colleges can be arranged. A loan fund lends money free of interest for training that will lead to useful and progressive work.

251 Brompton Rd, London, SW3.

Women's Institutes, National Federation of The NFWI consists of 61 county and island federations to which 8,914 Women's Institutes are affiliated. The first Women's Institute in Britain was founded in 1915, and the objects of the movement are to improve and develop conditions of rural life and to make provision for the fuller education of countrywomen in a wide range of subjects, including citizenship, international understanding, music, drama, art and practical skills. Courses catering for all interests are provided at Denman College, the WI short-term residential college. Members with special interests are catered for locally by crafts and produce guilds, art groups, drama groups, choirs, etc. The National Federation publishes a wide range of leaflets, and a monthly magazine, *Home and Country*.

39 Eccleston St, London, SW1.

Women's Royal Voluntary Service The WVS—made 'Royal' in 1966—was formed in 1938 to recruit women for work connected with air raid precautions, but the scope of its activities has since been considerably widened and adapted to suit changing needs.

The WRVS works closely with government departments and local authorities. Work is carried out through 1,541 centres and falls into three main groups: help to local authorities in emergencies such as flood, fire or accident; special training courses for women on emergency welfare; a wide variety of welfare work for members of the community with special needs, including children and old people. This includes 9,000,000 Meals on Wheels delivered annually, welfare work for hospital patients and staff, the housebound and homeless, refugees and repatriates, prisoners and their families, and members of HM Services overseas and at home.

The WRVS has no educational aims as such, but plays a small part in the field of adult education by training volunteers for work in various aspects of social welfare.

17 Old Park La., London, W1.

Women's Voluntary Service *See* **Women's Royal Voluntary Service**

Wood Committee (1924) *See* **Special education**

Woodard Schools *See* **Middle schools movement**

Woodwork, Teaching of The most important problems facing woodwork teachers arise from the intrinsic difficulty of working wood accurately by hand methods. The problem is exacerbated by the common bias towards cabinet-making. Handicraftsmen in wood have traditionally taken a number of years of full-time apprenticeship to become proficient, but schoolboys have only a few woodwork lessons each week. Seen in this way the problem is truly formidable, and it is obvious that the situation has built-in factors which are highly conducive to failure. Some radical changes are called for if handicraft is to become a truly creative activity for most boys.

Teachers organise woodwork courses in different ways, but most syllabuses begin with a basic course designed to teach the fundamental skills of woodwork and the basic constructions used by joiners and cabinet-makers. This course is sometimes extremely formal and may last one, two or even more years. It may consist of a series of joints, or a number of useful articles incorporating joints, or a combination of both. The old controversy about the relative superiority of these different ways of running the basic course is somewhat pointless since their essential similarities far outweigh their differences. There is little scope, as a rule, for individual choice, pupil initiative, or an introduction to concepts of design. The 'models' are small and few of the 'useful articles' are in fact worth possessing. Boys are quickly involved in tasks needing fine work and the making of good joints. This seems somewhat unreasonable. Successful early work ought not to be dependent upon critical standards of accuracy. The difficult constructions used by the joiner and the cabinet-maker may be mastered during the course, as tool skills are gradually developed, but beginners should be expected to find them too difficult.

Some teachers are developing a different approach which is more imaginative, takes greater account of boys' interests, and gives better opportunities to introduce the consideration of design right from the start. Simple constructions using ready-planed timber, plywood and block-board, nails, glue, screws and dowels replace some of the former basic exercises. Ideas for suitable pieces of work may sometimes originate from the teacher, but they are related to boys' interests wherever possible. The boys themselves are encouraged to contribute their own suggestions for individual or group projects. Most boys try to make rabbit hutches or soap-box cars on perambulator wheels, and many other things in their spare time at weekends and during the holidays. They use great ingenuity at home in working out functional designs that are within the limits imposed by their levels of skill, the materials at hand, and the makeshift facilities that are available. This is first-class design experience, and pupils should be encouraged to pursue such spontaneous activities in the school workshops where they can receive the kind of help and guidance that is needed

if they are to improve their skills and raise the level of their creative efforts.

The role of the teacher is changed by this kind of scheme. He becomes a valued consultant and collaborator instead of a formal instructor and shop foreman. The calls made upon his professional skill are more complex since he has to handle a wide variety of problems created by the boys' own ideas. He must provide a working environment that is a rich and stimulating source of ideas for the boys. The teacher will, in fact, have substituted a clear concept of a flexible and dynamic educational method for the equally clear but rigid and stereotyped basic course of training.

The introduction of this way of working at the beginning, or very early in the course, does not preclude the systematic teaching of fundamental skills. Most projects will require boys to measure, saw, plane, and use chisels. These skills may be demonstrated to all the class and individual help given in the usual way. There is no need for all the boys to be simultaneously sawing similar pieces of wood or making identical objects. There are very few really basic tool skills of woodwork, but they must be taught well and thoroughly mastered. The applications of these skills in specific joints and constructions can be dealt with as the need arises.

The most progressive GCE and CSE examinations are designed to measure design ability and creativity, as well as craft skill. A flexible course based upon the kind of approach briefly described above is far better preparation for such an examination than the traditional scheme of work. In these days of Mode 3 examinations and individual school syllabuses for GCE, a course containing long periods of joint practice and test-piece construction can no longer be justified by the demands of an external examination.

See also **Handicraft**

FURTHER READING
S. H. Glenister. *The Technique of Handicraft Teaching*, Harrap, 1953.

FW

Word association test A type of projection test (*q.v.*) in which a series of words, unconnected with each other, are read out or shown to the examinee, e.g. wealthy, rapid, feeble, wicked. These are stimulus words and the examinee is asked to respond by saying the first word that comes into his mind. In some test situations the reaction time is noted to see how quickly the individual responds.

Word blindness *See* **Dyslexia**

Work experience schemes A number of LEAs, together with firms in their areas, have devised schemes whereby boys and girls about to leave school are given short experiences of industrial, commercial or professional work. Views vary as to the effectiveness of such schemes, and some critics regard the experience as too artificial to be really useful; but thought is being given to the part they might play in the 'outward-looking' curriculum that should accompany the raising of the school leaving age when it comes.

Workers' Education Centre Holding classes open to immigrants from all parts of the world, the WEC aims to help students to acquire a working knowledge of the English language and to understand the customs and manners of the English people. Courses are offered in the English language, geography, arithmetic and first-aid. Classes are held on Saturday and Sunday evenings, with a special class for ladies only on Thursdays.

Sec.: E. Akin Olulode, Toynbee Hall, 28 Commerical St, London, E1.

Workers' Educational Association A non-sectarian and non-party political federation of almost 3,000 educational and workers' organisations, the WEA was founded in 1903 to stimulate and satisfy the demand of workers for education and to further the advancement of education, to the end that all children, adolescents and adults might have full opportunities of the education needed for their complete individual and social development.

The WEA is a countrywide movement based on local branches, of which there are more than 800, grouped for administrative purposes in 21 districts. These branches organise approximately 7,000 classes, with an enrolment of some 120,000 students. Subjects are chosen by the students themselves, and courses vary in length from 6 to 24 weekly meetings, while single lectures, one-day and week-end schools are also arranged on subjects of current interest.

Each district, except those in Scotland and Northern Ireland, is recognised by the DES as a responsible body for the provision of educational facilities, in respect of which it receives grant under the Department's regulations. LEAs make grants towards the administrative expenses of the districts.

Temple House, 27 Portman Sq., London, W1.

See also **Adult education; Mansbridge, Sir Albert**

Workers' Music Association The Association aims to provide opportunities for people to develop their musical tastes and improve the level of their musical understanding as a result of their own activities and experiences.

236 Westbourne Park Rd, London, W11.

Working men's clubs and institutes The Working Men's Club and Institute Union was founded in 1862, largely owing to the efforts of the Rev. Henry Solly, a Unitarian minister at Lancaster. Solly resigned his ministry at Lancaster to become full-time secretary to the Union, which aimed at promoting clubs for working men by circularising mechanics' institutes and provincial newspapers, promoting public meetings and assisting other clubs to become self-supporting and self-governing. Solly hoped these clubs would be more recreational than mechanics' institutes, and healthier than public houses.

By 1867, 350 clubs had been founded. As places where friendly and provident societies could hold meetings, they helped raise the level of social intercourse. The Union has a convalescent home, accommodating 600, at Pegwell Bay, Isle of Thanet; in 1904 its *Club and Institute Journal* circulated to 992 clubs (with 380,000 members). Of these 48 were temperance clubs, 200 were political and the rest social, band, trade or friendly societies. 3,500 club members served on public bodies, from parliament to parish councils. There were only five clubs in Ireland and Scotland, few in Wales.

Of the 2,000 other clubs outside the WMCIU, 800 were members of the National Association of Conservative Clubs, and 900 were not members either because they could not reach the standard of admittance, or preferred local federations like the Yorkshire Liberal Club, or the London Federation.

Solly resigned the secretaryship in 1872 in order to devote himself to the Artisan Institute, St Martin's La., London.

WHGA

Working men's colleges A passionate belief in education as the solution to all social problems characterised most of the working-class movements of the 19th century. The early years of the century saw the foundation of mechanics' institutes (*q.v.*). But to F. D. Maurice and other radical thinkers the mechanics' institutes seemed not to meet the needs of the working class: they believed that education should be liberal and not technical, and that the development of social life was as important as academic study. These were the aims of the London Working Men's College, set up in 1854 with Maurice as its first principal, but owing something to an earlier 'People's College' launched at Sheffield in 1842. The idea quickly spread to the provinces.

The colleges ultimately achieved only a limited success, but are important in the history of adult education because of the clear distinction they made between technical and liberal studies. The London Working Men's College still bears that name, though it now admits women into membership. Outside London, the only one to survive to the present day is Vaughan College at Leicester, which is now Leicester University's extra-mural centre.

BG

World Citizenship, Council for Education in Aim is to encourage in UK schools the study of international affairs in general, and of the UN and its related agencies in particular. It offers its member schools a variety of services, including: the provision of speakers for meetings during school time and for extra-curricular activities on subjects of international concern; organisation of inter-school conferences, or co-operation with schools and LEAs in the organisation of such meetings; provision of a library of visual aids, exhibitions, film strips, etc; opportunities for schools to participate in the UNESCO gift coupon scheme; and the organisation of visits abroad for young people, holiday and educational. The Council also advises teachers about suitable materials, new books and publications, etc.

CEWC was established in 1939 and is composed of representatives of all the principal educational associations in the UK. It operates as an autonomous part of UNA, but concerns itself only with educational matters and does not express an opinion on matters of international controversy.

CEWC is especially famous for the annual Christmas holiday lectures —

now in their 24th year — which bring to London for four days some 3,000 senior grammar school pupils from all parts of the UK. In recent years the lectures have also been attended by pupils from American high schools who have flown to London for the occasion.

93 Albert Embankment, London, SE1.

World Education Fellowship Founded as the New Education Fellowship in 1921, and perhaps the oldest international educational organisation in the world, the WEF is a non-governmental organisation with 21 national sections and UNESCO consultative status. It aims to bring about changes in education to meet the changing needs of successive generations; to develop the potentialities of the individual child, together with a sense of purpose and responsibility, thus providing through education a lasting basis for international understanding. Present activities include the development of the themes and conclusion of the 1966 international conference on new educational thinking on personal fulfilment, the roots of morality, new perspectives on human destiny, and the use and abuse of automation.

Journal: *The New Era.*

Gen. Sec.: Miss Y. Moyse, 55 Upper Stone St, Tunbridge Wells, Kent.

See also **Progressive education**

World Government, Parliamentary Group for The Education Advisory Committee of the Group, founded in 1959, acts as the agent in the field of education for the World Security Trust, which is a registered charity. The aim of the Committee is to encourage a dual perspective in education—world as well as national—so that opportunity is given in the curriculum for balancing national loyalty with a measure of conscious loyalty to the human race as a whole, in all its diversity. All those responsible for drawing up syllabuses, especially those of history and social science, are encouraged to ask themselves whether their educational material helps understanding of the movement towards the present stage of world history, with its transcendence of nationalism and the growth of supra-national organs of government; whether it conduces to understanding of the pressing problems of today that are world-wide, such as the food and population problem; and whether it is wide enough in its imaginative range to satisfy the educational need to promote the capacity to feel, think and act 'as members of one another' in the world community.

The Committee works through a series of sub-committees and working parties. It is closely linked with the group of sponsors, under the chairmanship of Mr Lionel Elvin, which since 1966 has organised summer schools on problems of world order. It also has sub-committees on adult education, further education, teacher training colleges and secondary education, and on audio-visual media. The latter has received an award from the Leverhulme Trust for a survey of audio-visual material useful in the teaching of world community.

House of Commons, London, SW1.

World Health Organisation, UK Committee for Set up in 1955, the Committee exists to make known the work of WHO and to supply information about it. A reference library is being organised, and a panel of speakers set up whose names can be given to groups wishing to hear about WHO.

c/o London School of Hygiene and Tropical Medicine, Keppel St (Gower St,) London, WC1.

World University Service World University Service was founded in 1921 under the name of 'European Student Relief' with the purpose of assisting the many students made destitute in a war-ravaged Europe. Today, International WUS, with 60 national committees, has a programme of $2½ million per annum in Africa, Asia and Latin America. The work includes scholarship programmes, hostel and health centre projects, community development, the provision of books, printing equipment and laboratory apparatus. In addition to raising funds for this programme, the UK Committee has a programme of assistance for overseas students in the UK and has initiated research on topics of importance to British staff and students. In 1961 two conferences of experts on student mental health were held and reports published. In 1967 WUS held a similar conference on staff-student relations. WUS has recently published a report of this conference in collaboration with the Society for Research into Higher Education.

59 Gloucester Pl., London, W1.

Worship, Collective An act of non-denominational worship must, by provision of the Education Act 1944, begin the school day in every state-aided school; but parents who wish to do so may withdraw their children.

See also **Religion in schools**

Writing Despite the growing attention now paid to oral English (*q.v.*), many teachers still regard writing as the most important part of English. The historical reasons for this include the potent influence of public examinations and the utilitarian notion that pupils must learn to write in order to be efficient clerks and typists.

The assumptions that lie behind much written work are, however, now moving in a more liberal direction. A handy, if arbitrary, distinction can be made between functional writing and autonomous writing. The field of functional writing embraces such forms as business letters, reports and public notices; the primary purpose of such writing is to transmit information or instructions; the key factors of purpose and public (or reader) are receiving greater attention. Pupils in school are engaged in functional writing in many lessons besides those actually devoted to English, but the English teacher helps specifically by attending to such matters as tone, style, organisation, usage and spelling.

The second field, that of autonomous writing, belongs almost exclusively to work in English. Examples of autonomous writing are poems and stories, which the pupil writes in part because of his 'satisfaction that it was as it was and not otherwise' (D. W. Harding). It is in finding a larger and sometimes a central place for such writing that English teaching has changed most decisively in the last 20 years. Many teachers now assume that the writing of essays is neither appropriate to the needs or skills of many younger children nor the only possible mode that writing can follow. For many years, the centre of written English was the essay, which was divided, arbitrarily, into such categories as descriptive, reflective, argumentative, etc, and the priority accorded to the essay was due largely to the influence of public examination at 16 and 18, duly rendered respectable by an appeal to such marginal writers as Lamb and Hazlitt. Yet, as a mode, it is obviously more suited to the mature reflections and logical disciplines of the intellectual adult's mind than to the experiential needs and life-style of the adolescent. It has accordingly been partly, or totally, displaced by the writing of poetry, fiction and autobiography, which tends to be more concrete, more specific, more closely derived from the experience of the writer than do the urbane generalities of the essayist.

The term commonly applied to such work is 'creative writing', and activities such as writing stories and poems have been criticised because they often appear both to tolerate error too permissively and to fail to ensure any marked improvement in the mastery of the skills of writing. Such criticisms are indeed almost invited by a term commonly used for such work—'free writing'—in which the pupil merely responds to a given stimulus such as a picture or a poem in a way which is not predetermined by the teacher, and to which the teacher rarely responds by attending to errors of punctuation, grammar or spelling.

In the event, however, the conflict between 'creative writing' and 'discipline' is more apparent than real, for in the best teaching—which allows and encourages autonomous writing—the teacher modifies and corrects the pupil's work in such a way as to point him towards socially effective norms, both in the field of usage and of spelling. The available evidence suggests that children who read much and write extensively, under the guidance and instruction of a teacher who cares for standards, fare better in the mastery of skills than children who are restricted to a piecemeal diet of text-book exercises.

In many primary schools, children are expected to engage in widely varying modes of writing: reports of first-hand observation, short stories, poems, records, etc; they compile class- or school-newspapers; and they produce 'books' on geographical, historical and scientific topics. Such work yields a rich harvest both of competence and of joyful involvement. Many secondary schools continue this good work, refining and sharpening the pupils' control of language both in its vocabulary and in its structures; and they extend the range of discourse so as to embrace comparatively impersonal and abstract disciplines as well as writing of a personal kind.

FURTHER READING
A. B. Clegg (Ed.) *The Excitement of Writing*, Chatto and Windus, 1964.
B. Ford (Ed.). *Young Writers, Young Readers*, Hutchinson, 1960.
P. Gurrey. *The Teaching of Written English*, Longmans Green, 1954.

GS

Writing, Free A term most closely associated with Miss Dora Pym, formerly lecturer in the Department of Education at the University of Bristol, and best explained, as she herself explained it, by reference to its origin. Asked by a group of students to assist them with essay-writing, of which they felt both afraid and incapable, she found that the conventional method of causing students to write (that is, by giving them an essay title) produced painful and inhibited results. She therefore presented them with a miscellaneous collection of objects—they included a small ebony elephant, a carrot and a safety-pin—and required them to choose one object each and write whatever came into their heads. The writing was now much more free; and became happier still, and even more successful, when she experimented with other stimuli—various sounds and noises, music, blindfold touching of objects, smells.

Miss Pym's deduction was that her students' sense of incapacity arose from the rooting of the work required from them in a form of words, rather than in a sensual experience. 'The simple, though varied, sense starting points tapped sources, individual, authentic and vital'. Moreover, the requirement that they write had always come from outside, and had not sprung from any desire or need of their own. The use of sensual stimuli awoke in students both a wish to write and a sense that they were doing something necessary and not merely obligatory.

As devised by Miss Pym, this use of non-verbal means of stimulating students to write was put to test for several years as part of the Wiltshire 11–plus selection examinations. Since that time (1947–51) the technique has been widely employed and refined.

FURTHER READING
Dora Pym. *Free Writing* (University of Bristol Institute of Education Publication Number 10), University of London Press, 1956.

Y

Yehudi Menuhin School This boarding school, which was opened in London in September 1963 and removed to Surrey in September 1964, provides about thirty children between the ages of eight and 15 with general education under a resident headmaster, and with special music training under visiting specialist teachers in an integrated programme. The high standards maintained, particularly on the musical side, are due to the influence of Yehudi Menuhin and fellow-musicians who share his approach to musical education.

Stoke D'Abernon, Surrey.

Yemen, Education in No current educational statistics are available.

Yeshiva (pl. **yeshivot**) This is a school of higher Jewish learning devoted mainly to the intensive study of the Talmud (*q.v.*).

YMCA *See* **Christian Associations Inc., National Council of Young Men's**

Young Enterprise Open to all young persons between the ages of 16 and the early 20s, this organisation (formed in 1962) aims to provide young people with a basic knowledge of the organisation, methods and economics of business, thus helping them in their choice of career and providing for better understanding within industry of the problems involved at every level.

At the Young Enterprises Centres, young people form and run miniature companies under the advice of local businessmen, and learn what is involved by actually doing the job themselves. Each Young Enterprise company operates on one evening a week between September and June. At present the Young Enterprise programme is operating in limited areas only. It is hoped that Centres will be opened in the next few years to provide facilities in most of the larger towns.

Standard Hse, 16–22 Epworth St, London, EC2.

Youth clubs Established for the underprivileged young people of the 19th century, youth clubs have been transformed into leisure-time centres for the affluent generation of the 20th. They may be sponsored by voluntary agencies or by LEAs, and range from the one-night-a-week club in a village to the large youth centre of 1,000 members in the middle of a large city. Many clubs are still led by voluntary leaders; but larger centres are staffed by professional workers who have taken specialised training in youth leadership. Youth clubs are normally open to all young people between the ages of 14 and 21, although some clubs are organised for single-sex groups.

Most clubs are governed by management committees drawn from local people of good standing; but great emphasis is laid on the democratic participation of the members themselves, who are allowed a good deal of self-determination. Commonly there is a members' committee, together with ad hoc groups with some responsibility for developing programmes, raising money and maintaining premises. Clubs are normally open in the evenings, though full-time activity at weekends is becoming more and more common. Facilities usually take the form of a coffee bar, games room, girls' room, showers, a quiet lounge, an outdoor games area, and there is often a floodlit court for netball or football. Clubs also organise many activities outside their own walls — holidays, camps, excursions, participation in the Duke of Edinburgh's Award Scheme, and so on.

Most youth clubs have moved away from stereotyped and rigidly planned programmes and allow spontaneous activities to arise and change in accordance with fashion and the interests of the members. The gregariousness of the younger generation is recognised, together with their need to explore a wide variety of experiences. The club leader acts as a source of ideas and his role is to try to help members to interact in pursuit of valuable social and personal objectives. All youth clubs are voluntary, in the sense that members may join or leave at will, and therefore a major aim is to make premises and activities colourful, attractive and up-to-date.

A useful pamphlet is *Looking at Youth Clubs* by E. L. Sewell (National Association of Youth Clubs, 30 Devonshire St, London, W1.)

See also **Youth service**

HH

Youth Clubs, National Association of The National Association of Youth Clubs was established over 60 years ago under the auspices of the National Council of Women. Its founders were concerned about the moral and social welfare of young people in large cities, and out of it grew the National Council of Girls' Clubs which began to sponsor mixed clubs during the war and is today a major agency in the promotion and servicing of mixed youth clubs through its county associations and divisions in England, Scotland and Wales.

In 1966 the Association had 234,508 members in 3,244 clubs which were led by 14,441 leaders. In addition to the services provided by both county and city associations to affiliated groups, the Association sponsors training for part-time voluntary leaders, senior members and young people in industry. It has a publications service and provides visual aids and programme materials. Conference centres are established in Hampshire, Wales and London. The Association receives grants from the DES and from trusts for its training programme and experimental projects amongst the younger generation.

30 Devonshire St, London, W1.

Youth Employment Executive, Central *See* **Leaving school**

Youth Employment Officers, Institute of The Institute is the professional body for the Youth Employment Service, and most officers are members. It aims to promote the advancement of the principles and practice of vocational guidance; to improve the professional knowledge of persons engaged in, or training for, the Youth Employment Service; to develop the interchange of information and questions generally linked with employment and unemployment; to safeguard the interests of Youth Employment Officers and to act as spokesman of the Youth Employment Service to both statutory and voluntary bodies; to concern itself with the interests of young people particularly in respect of their further education, training and employment.

Hon. Sec.: C. P. Walton, County Education Office, Castle St, Worcs.

Publications: *Youth Employment* (four-monthly journal). Pamphlets currently available include *Advising Young People as a Career, Preparation of Young People for Employment, First Survey of Recent Research Relevant to a Careers Service for Young People.*

Youth Employment Service A service for young people at the stage of transition from school to work. It is available to all up to the age of 18, or beyond that age if still at school. It provides information about employment and careers, gives vocational guidance, helps to find suitable employment and keeps in touch with young people during the early part of their careers in case any further help or advice is needed. It also assists employers to find suitable young workers.

There are YE offices throughout the country; addresses are given in the telephone directory, or may be obtained from any employment exchange. The Service is administed on behalf of the Minister of Labour by the Ministry of Labour Central Youth Employment Executive. There is a Regional Representative of the Executive in each of the Ministry's regional offices.

Youth hostelling The Youth Hostels Association of England and Wales (Trevelyan House, St Albans, Hertfordshire) is a voluntary organisation run by members for members and provides hostels to enable anyone, especially young people, to explore the countryside at a low cost. In Great Britain and Ireland there are over 400 hostels: in Europe there are nearly 3,000 more. The movement has become almost universal and covers nearly every country in the world.

Membership of the YHA is open to all over five years of age, but members under 12 years of age must be accompanied by an adult. It is understood that while hostelling members must travel on foot, on horseback, by cycle or canoe, other forms of transport may be used to reach the holiday area.

Annual membership costs 5s (five to 16 years), 12s 6d (16 to 21 years) and £1 for those over 21 years of age. When staying at a hostel the present charges do not exceed 5s per night; meals cost 4s for a three-course supper, 3s for breakfast and 2s for a packed lunch, though there are also facilities for members to provide and cook their own meals.

Of special interest to schools are organised adventure holidays including pony trekking, sailing, gliding, underwater swimming and winter sports, and spring tours abroad.

Personal enrolment may be made at, or further information obtained from, the following YHA offices: 29 John Adam St, London, WC2; 93a Scotland Rd, Liverpool 3; 16 Queen St, Manchester 2; 203 Gibraltar St, Shalesmoor, Sheffield; 374a Shirley Rd, Southampton; 92 Aston St, Birmingham 4. Scotland: National Office, 7 Glebe Cres., Stirling.

Publications: *Youth Hostels for School Journey Parties, Youth Hostels for Field Studies.*

JE

Youth Hostels Association (England and Wales) The YHA was founded in 1930 'to help all, especially young people of limited means, to a greater knowledge, love and care of the countryside, particularly by providing hostels or other simple accommodation for them in their travels; and thus to promote their health, rest and education'. The YHA had in 1967 some 260 hostels and nearly 220,000 members. It is linked through the International Youth Hostel Federation with similar associations in 40 countries. Hostel buildings vary from cottage to castle, but all provide simple accommodation for people touring on foot or bicycle, including dormitories, washing facilities, a common room and a kitchen where members cook their own food. Many hostels also supply cooked meals prepared by the warden in charge.

Members share simple domestic duties.

By prior arrangement, school parties can use most hostels during term without joining the YHA; 20 hostels have special field study facilities. 'Adventure holidays' with tuition, such as pony trekking, sailing and canoeing, and conducted tours abroad are arranged. There are also special tours abroad for schools and youth groups where the party supplies its own leader, but everything else is arranged by the YHA. Membership is open to all over five years of age.

National Office: Trevelyan Hse., St Albans, Herts.

Youth Hostels Association of Northern Ireland The Association has 15 hostels providing over 500 beds in districts such as the Mourne Mountains, the Antrim Coast, the Sperrin Mountains and the Fermanagh Lakes. No meals are provided but the hostels are equipped with ample cooking facilities for members.

Bryson Hse., 28 Bedford St, Belfast, 2.

Youth leader scales The salary scale for a qualified youth leader is £895 × £50(9) × £55(1) to £1,400. This scale assumes an entry age of about 23 and new entrants are paid at a suitable level having regard to age and previous experience.

Additions for longer training and/or higher qualifications Where the employing authority considers that a qualified youth leader has had longer training and/or a standard of qualification substantially higher than the minimum requirements, they may pay an addition to the scale at the rate of £100 per annum. In an exceptional case where the authority or voluntary organisation considers £100 to be inadequate for the particular qualifications and/or length of training of an individual leader, a payment in excess of £100 may be made.

Posts of responsibility There shall be additions, at the discretion of the employing authority, of £115 to £475 for posts carrying greater responsibility, for example, youth leaders in charge of large clubs where another youth leader is engaged full-time, and youth leaders in charge of large clubs where a substantial amount of part-time leadership has to be co-ordinated and supervised. The employing authority has discretion to make a payment in excess of £475 in very exceptional cases where they consider that the responsibilities involved justify higher payment.

Unqualified youth leaders The scale for unqualified youth leaders is £690 × £30(1) × £35(5) to £895. Unqualified youth leaders are not eligible to receive the above-mentioned additions.

London addition The addition payable here is the same as that payable under the Primary and Secondary Schools Report.

Remuneration for residential duties by emoluments Remuneration for residential duties by emoluments or otherwise is a matter for determination apart from the provisions of these scales.

Incremental date Increments accrue on 1 April of each year, subject to six months' service provided that in the case of a youth leader transferring from service under a Burnham or allied report with a 'uniform incremental date' of 1 April, such 'uniform incremental date' shall be continued in the case of that leader.

Transfer from unqualified scale to qualified scale Where an unqualified youth leader becomes recognised for the purposes of a Burnham or allied report as a qualified youth leader, he shall be placed on the qualified scale in accordance with the provisions under the heading *New appointments* below, except that any part of his experience which is deemed to be part of the qualifications for the purposes of the report shall not be taken into account for the purposes of the paragraph below.

New appointments Youth leaders appointed as such on or after 1 April 1965 shall be placed at the minimum of the appropriate scale, unless the employing authority or voluntary organisation consider that, having regard to the age, qualifications and previous experience of the youth leader, a higher commencing salary is appropriate, in which case such higher commencing salary should apply.

SEB

Youth Leaders, National College for the Training of Established as part of the Government's plans to carry out the recommendation of the Albemarle Committee that the number of full-time youth leaders should be increased from 700 to 1,300 within five years. In 1963 it was decided to extend the life of the college until at least 1971.

The college offers a one-year course for men and women who wish to train as qualified full-time youth leaders. The course is designed to foster the knowledge, skill and understanding which the professional youth worker needs in order to help young people to enlarge their opportunities and take the fullest possible responsibility for their social life and leisure activities in clubs, centres, etc.

The College's Diploma in Youth Work is awarded on satisfactory completion of the course, and the status of qualified leader is acquired, subject to a period of probation, on taking up approved work with young people.

Humberstone Drive, Leicester.

See also **Albermarle Report; Youth service**

Youth Leaders and Community Centre Wardens, Joint Negotiating Committee for This Committee consists of representatives from associations of employers—known as the Employers' Panel—and representatives from associations having members in the services covered—known as the Staff Panel. On the employers' side, the associa-

tions and the number of representatives are: County Councils Association (three), Association of Municipal Corporations (three), Association of Education Committees (two), Welsh Joint Education Committee (one), ILEA (one), Standing Conference of National Voluntary Youth Organisations (two) and National Federation of Community Associations (one). The Staff Panel consists of representatives from the following bodies: Youth Service Association (six), NUT (two), National and Local Government Officers' Association (two), Association of Teachers in Technical Institutions (two), Community Service Association (two). The employers' side has two secretaries, one of whom is drawn from the membership of the panel. The staff side has one secretary who is additional to the membership of the Committee.

The work of this Committee is not merely concerned with negotiation of salaries, as is the case with the Burnham Committee, but adds to its responsibilities those of defining the qualifications which will entitle the holder to qualified status and the conditions of service—sick pay, superannuation and holidays—for those who come within the terms of the Report. These conditions of service, as well as the salary scales provided in the Reports of the Committee, are not mandatory, but as with any other National Committee which has been set up specifically for a similar purpose, it is expected that employers will honour the provisions.

The Joint Negotiating Committee for Youth Leaders was formed following the recommendations of the Albemarle Committee on the Youth Service on 28 February 1961. In 1965 the scope of the Committee was extended to include community centre wardens.

The Report applies to (1) persons (qualified or otherwise) employed full-time by LEAs as youth leaders or community centre wardens and (2) persons (qualified or otherwise) employed full-time as youth leaders or community centre wardens by voluntary organisations receiving grants from LEAs or from the DES.

A person who makes up full-time service by combining service partly in a post under the Report and partly in a capacity to which the provisions of the Burnham Reports apply should be paid wholly under the Report if half or more of his time is devoted to this service; otherwise, he should be paid wholly under the provisions of the appropriate Burnham Report.

SEB

Youth Officers *See* **Youth service**

Youth Organisations, Standing Conference of National Voluntary
The Conference acts as a forum and mouthpiece for the non-political voluntary youth organisations.

26 Bedford Sq., London, WC1.

Publication: *Bulletin* (four times yearly).

Youth Service Youth Service is the name given to the partnership existing in this country between statutory and voluntary agencies for providing leisure-time activities and facilities for young people between the ages of 14 and 21. The Youth Service began about 100 years ago as a voluntary service provided by organisations like the YMCA, and led to the development of such uniformed organisations as the Boys' Brigade and the Boy Scouts. The Youth Service programme is under the general direction of the DES, from which it receives grants. The work of national voluntary youth organisations is co-ordinated through the Standing Conference of National Voluntary Youth Organisations within the National Council of Social Service.

Under the 1944 Education Act, each LEA is charged with the responsibility of providing social and leisure-time facilities for the young. The usual practice is for each authority to appoint a Youth Officer who helps to promote the work of voluntary agencies. Local authorities themselves provide youth clubs, youth centres and training programmes for voluntary youth workers, and may help those active in the youth field by the securing of premises and personnel, by cash grants and by the provision or loan of equipment.

In 1960 a Government Committee on the Youth Service in England and Wales made recommendations about the future of the service (the Albemarle Report, *q.v.*), and a Youth Service Development Council was set up with special responsibility for initiating new and experimental work among those unattached to any form of youth organisation. A National College for the Training of Youth Leaders was also established. Colleges of education and other institutions offer professional training for youth leaders. Youth work is recognised as a profession by the DES, and a joint negotiating committee, working within the framework of the NUT, formulates the conditions of service and salary.

About 40% of the nation's young are members of some form of youth group. Much educational and social experiment is directed to attracting the 60% who remain unattached. A capital building programme of between four and five million pounds is envisaged. Closer links are being forged between secondary schools and youth services. The needs of youth groups are served by many ancillary organisations, such as the Central Council for Physical Recreation, the Youth Hostels Association, the Society for Education in Film and Television.

A useful history of the development of the Youth Service is given in *Young People in Society* by W. Evans (Basil Blackwell and Mott, Oxford).

See also **Youth clubs; Youth Leaders, National College for the Training of**

HH

Youth Service Development Council *See* **Albemarle Report (1960)**

Youth Service Information Centre
The Youth Service Information Centre is a clearing-house for information on youth work of all kinds, and for material which sets youth work in the wider educational and social context. It was established in April 1964 by the governors of the National College for the Training of Youth Leaders at the request of the DES.

As well as answering individual enquiries and operating a loan service of copies of its many documents, the Centre publishes a monthly information Digest with abstracts from a wide range of sources. The Centre's other publications, which have periodic revisions and supplements, are the *Annotated Youth Work Book List*, the guide *Youth Work Training Films* and *Youth Work Project Summaries*, concise accounts of experimental approaches; *Youth Service Guide to Conference and Holiday Centres; A Survey of Young People's Counselling Services;* and the compendium *Youth Work Training Aids*. The Centre also identifies projects requiring research and maintains lists of research and experimental projects and of relevant articles, reports and surveys.

The National College for the Train-ing of Youth Leaders, Humberstone Drive, Leicester.

Youth Work, Diploma in *See* **Youth Leaders, National College for the Training of**

Yugoslavia, Education in Education is free and compulsory from six to 14. National minorities living in the country have their own elementary and secondary schools; the Albanian and Magyar minorities are much the largest and possess many teacher training colleges. There are seven universities. In 1964/65 there were 14,317 primary schools, with an enrolment of 2,972,225; 370 secondary schools, with an enrolment of 161,630; 1,259 technical schools, with an enrolment of 380,655; 90 teacher training establishments, with an enrolment of 28,942; 266 universities and higher education colleges, with an enrolment of 170,499. There are also 737 schools for adults, with an enrolment of 58,981.

The country's population in 1964 was approximately 19¼ million.

YWCA *See* **Christian Association of Great Britain, Young Women's**

Z

Zambia, Education in There are both state and private schools. 1966 statistics: 2,099 primary schools (enrolment 484,868); 107 secondary schools (enrolment 24,005); 13 teacher training colleges (enrolment 1,603). The University of Zambia at Lusaka has 312 students. Agricultural research for Central Africa is carried on at Mount Makulu, and veterinary research at Mazabuka Research Station.

The country's population was nearly 4 million in 1966.

Zoning Zones, or catchment areas, are allocated to schools in areas where otherwise some schools might be too full and others under-used. LEAs are required to give full public notice of their intention to zone, and the scheme does not normally affect children already in schools. Although under zoning some children may have to attend schools which are not the nearest to their homes, LEAs are expected to take account of denominational preferences, exceptional cases and any dangers from traffic that might arise. Zoning should be adopted only where necessary, and abandoned once the need is past.

APPENDIX

Appendix

All items hereunder cover the United Kingdom of Great Britain and Northern Ireland

1. Universities
2. Colleges of education
3. Agricultural colleges
4. Colleges of music, drama and dancing
5. Colleges of arts and crafts
6. Art colleges with courses leading to the Diploma in Art and Design
7. Schools of architecture
8. National colleges
9. Regional colleges
10. Adult education
11. Examining bodies
12. Members of the Educational Group of the Publishers' Association
13. Members of the Educational Equipment Association
14. Educational journals
15. Selected museums and art galleries

1. UNIVERSITIES

England

University of Aston in Birmingham (1966[1]; formerly College of Advanced Technology, Birmingham), Gosta Green, Birmingham, 4.

University of Bath (1966; formerly Bristol College of Science and Technology), Ashley Down, Bristol, 7; and Claverton, Bath. School of Education; Centre for Adult Studies, Northgate House, High St, Bath.

University of Birmingham (1900), PO Box 363, Birmingham, 15. School of Education; Department of Education; Department of Extra-Mural Studies, PO Box 363, Birmingham, 15.

University of Bradford (1966; formerly Bradford Institute of Technology), Richmond Rd, Bradford, 7.

University of Bristol (1909), Senate House, Bristol, 2. Institute of Education; Department of Education, Helen Wodehouse Building, 35 Berkeley Sq., Bristol, 8. Department of Extra-Mural Studies, 20a Berkeley Sq., Bristol, 8.

Brunel University (1966; formerly Brunel College), Kingston La., Uxbridge, Middx.

University of Cambridge (13th century). *Men's colleges*: Christ's (1505); Churchill (1960); Clare (1326); Clare Hall (1965, graduates only); Corpus Christi (1352); Darwin (1964, graduates only); Downing (1800); Emmanuel (1584); Fitzwilliam (1869); Gonville and Caius (1348); Jesus (1496); King's (1441); Magdalene (1542); Pembroke (1347); Peterhouse (1284); Queen's (1448); St Catharine's (1473); St Edmund's House (1964); St John's (1511); Selwyn (1882); Sidney Sussex (1596); Trinity (1546); Trinity Hall (1350); University (1964, graduates only).
Women's colleges: Girton (1869); Lucy Cavendish (1964, graduates only); New Hall (1954); Newnham (1871).

Institute of Education, 2 Brookside, Cambridge. Department of Education, 17 Brookside, Cambridge. Board of Extra-Mural Studies, Stuart House, Mill Lane, Cambridge.

City University (1966; formerly Northampton College of Advanced Technology, London), St John St, London, EC1.

University of Durham (1832), Old Shire Hall, Durham. *Colleges in Durham*: University; Hatfield; Grey; Van Mildert; St Chad's; St John's; St Mary's; St Aidan's; Bede; St Hild's; Neville's Cross; St Cuthbert's Society; The Graduate Society.

Institute of Education; Department of Education, 46–49 Old Elvet, Durham. Department of Extra-Mural Studies, 32 Old Elvet, Durham.

University of East Anglia (1964), Earlham Hall, Norwich.

University of Essex (1961), Wivenhoe Park, Colchester, Essex.

University of Exeter (1955), The Queen's Dr., Exeter. Institute of Education, University of Exeter, Gandy St, Exeter. Department of Education, 'Thornlea', New North Rd, Exeter. Extra-Mural Department, University of Exeter, Gandy St, Exeter.

University of Hull (1954), Hull. Institute of Education; Department of Education, 173 Cottingham Rd, Hull. Department of Extra-Mural Studies, Dept of Adult Education, 195/197 Cottingham Rd, Hull.

University of Keele (1962), Keele, Staffs. Institute of Education; Department of Education; Department of Extra-Mural Studies: address as University.

University of Kent at Canterbury (1964), The University, Canterbury, Kent.

University of Lancaster (1964), Bailrigg, Lancaster. Department of Higher Education: address as University.

University of Leeds (1904), Leeds, 2. Institute of Education; Department of Education; Department of Extra-Mural Studies, 33 Hyde Terrace, Leeds, 2.

University of Leicester (1957), University Rd, Leicester. School of Education, University Rd, Leicester. Department of Adult Education, 104 Regent Rd, Leicester.

University of Liverpool (1903), Brownlow Hill, Liverpool, 3. School and Institute of Education, 19–23 Abercromby Sq.,

---

[1] Date of foundation of university.

Liverpool, 7. Department of Extra-Mural Studies, 9 Abercromby Sq., Liverpool, 7.

University of London (1836), Senate House, London, WC1. *Schools of the University General:* Bedford College (1849), Regent's Park, NW1; Birkbeck College (1823), Malet St, WC1; Imperial College of Science and Technology (1907), South Kensington, SW7; King's College (1829), Strand, WC2; London School of Economics and Political Science (1895), Houghton St, Aldwych, WC2; Queen Elizabeth College (1908), 61–67 Campden Hill Rd, W8; Queen Mary College (1915), Mile End Rd, E1; Royal Holloway College (1886), Englefield Green, Surrey; Royal Veterinary College (1791), Royal College St, NW1; School of Oriental and African Studies (1916), University of London, WC1; School of Pharmacy (1841), 29–39 Brunswick Sq., WC1; University College (1826), Gower St, WC1; Westfield College (1882), Kidderpore Ave, Hampstead, NW3; Wye College (1893), Wye, Nr Ashford, Kent.

Undergraduate medical schools: Charing Cross Hospital Medical School (1818), Chandos Pl., Charing Cross, WC2; Guy's Hospital Medical School (1724), St Thomas's St, SE1; King's College Hospital Medical School (1831), Denmark Hill, SE5; London Hospital Medical College (1740), Turner St, E1; Middlesex Hospital Medical School (1835), Mortimer St, W1; Royal Dental Hospital of London, School of Dental Surgery (1858), 32 Leicester Sq., WC2; Royal Free Hospital School of Medicine (1874), 8 Hunter St, Brunswick Sq., WC1; St Bartholomew's Hospital Medical College (12th century), West Smithfield, EC1; St George's Hospital Medical School (1756), Hyde Park Corner, SW1; St Mary's Hospital Medical School (1854), Norfolk Pl., Paddington, W2; St Thomas's Hospital Medical School (16th century), Albert Embankment, SE1; University College Hospital Medical School (1828), University St, WC1; Westminster Medical School (1834), Horseferry Rd, Westminster, SW1.

Institute of Education, Malet St, WC1. Departments of Education, Institute of Education, Malet St, WC1 and King's College, Strand, WC2. Department of Extra-Mural Studies, 7 Ridgmount St, WC1.

Loughborough University of Technology (1966; formerly Loughborough College of Technology), Loughborough, Leics.

University of Manchester (1880), Oxford Rd, Manchester, 13. School of Education; Department of Education; Department of Audiology and Education of the Deaf; Department of Physical Education; Department of Adult Education; Department of Extra-Mural Studies: address as University. Institute of Science and Technology, Sackville St, Manchester, 1.

University of Newcastle-upon-Tyne (1963), The University, Newcastle-upon-Tyne, 1. Institute of Education; Department of Education; Department of Adult Education, Joseph Cowen House, St Thomas' St, Newcastle-upon-Tyne, 1.

University of Nottingham (1948), University Pk, Nottingham. University of Nottingham School of Agriculture, Sutton Bonington, Notts. Institute of Education; Department of Education: address as University. Department of Extra-Mural Studies; Dept of Adult Education, 14/22 Shakespeare St, Nottingham.

University of Oxford (13th century). *Men's colleges:* All Souls (1438); Balliol (1262); Brasenose (1509); Christ Church (1546); Corpus Christi (1517); Exeter (1314); Hertford (1874); Iffley (1965, graduates only); Jesus (1571); Keble (1868); Lincoln (1427); Magdalen (1458); Merton (1264); New (1379); Nuffield (1937, graduates only); Oriel (1326); Pembroke (1624); Queen's (1340); St Antony's (1950, graduates only); St Catherine's (1962); St Cross (1960, graduates only); St Edmund Hall (1269); St John's (1555); St Peter's (1929); Trinity (1554); University (1249); Wadham (1612); Worcester (1714).

Women's colleges: Lady Margaret Hall (1878); St Anne's (1879); St Hilda's (1893); St Hugh's (1886); Somerville (1879); Wolfson (1965, graduates only). *Permanent private halls:* Campion Hall (1896); Greyfriars (1910); Mansfield College (1885); Regent's Park College (1810); St Benet's Hall (1897).

Institute of Education; Department of Education, 15 Norham Gdns, Oxford. Department of Extra-Mural Studies, Rewley House, Wellington Sq., Oxford.

University of Reading (1926), Reading. Institute of Education; Department of Education; Joint Committee for Tutorial Classes: address as University.

University of Salford (1967; formerly The Royal College of Advanced Technology), Salford, 5, Lancs.

University of Sheffield (1905), The University, Sheffield, 10. Institute of Education; Department of Education; Department of Extra-Mural Studies: address as University.

University of Southampton (1952), The University, Highfield, Southampton.

Institute of Education; Department of Education; Department of Extra-Mural Studies: address as University.

University of Surrey (1966; formerly Battersea College of Technology), Battersea Park Rd, London, SW11.

University of Sussex (1961), Falmer, Brighton. School of Educational Studies: address as University.

University of Warwick (1965), Coventry, Warks.

University of York (1963), Heslington, York. Department of Education: address as University.

Wales

University of Wales (1893). School of Education, University Registry, Cathays Pk, Cardiff. I University College of Wales (1872), Aberystwyth. (Department of Education: address as I University College. Department of Extra-Mural Studies, 12 Marine Terr., Aberystwyth.) II University College of North Wales (1884), Bangor. (Department of Education; Department of Extra-Mural Studies: address as II University College.) III University College of South Wales and Monmouthshire (1884), Cathays Pk, Cardiff. (Department of Education: address as III University College. Department of Extra-Mural Studies, 40 Park Pl., Cardiff.) St David's College, Lampeter (1822). IV University College of Swansea (1920), Singleton Pk, Swansea. (Department of Education: address as IV University College. Department of Extra-Mural Studies, Berwick House, 6 Uplands Terr.,

Swansea.) V Welsh National School of Medicine (1931), 34 Newport Rd, Cardiff. University of Wales Institute of Science and Technology (designate), Cathays Pk, Cardiff.

Scotland

University of Aberdeen (1494), Aberdeen. Department of Education; Department of Extra-Mural Studies, Taylor Building, King's College, Old Aberdeen.

University of Dundee (1967), Dundee. Department of Education: address as University.

University of Edinburgh (1583), Edinburgh. Department of Education, 48–50 Pleasance, Edinburgh, 8. Department of Adult Education and Extra-Mural Studies, 11 Buccleuch Pl., Edinburgh, 8.

University of Glasgow (1451), Glasgow, 2. Department of Education; Department of Extra-Mural Studies: address as University.

Heriot-Watt University (1966; formerly Heriot-Watt College), Chambers St, Edinburgh, 1.

University of St Andrews (1410), St Andrews, Fife.

University of Stirling (1964), Stirling.

University of Strathclyde (1964), George St, Glasgow, C1.

Northern Ireland

Queen's University, Belfast (1908), University Rd, Belfast. Department of Education; Department of Extra-Mural Studies: address as University.

New University of Ulster, Coleraine, Co. Londonderry.

2. COLLEGES OF EDUCATION

ATO—Area Training Organisation
C of E—Church of England
corr.—correspondent
LEA—Local education authority
M—for men

Prot.—Protestant
RC—Roman Catholic
und.—undenominational
vol.—voluntary
W—for women

England

Bedfordshire
Bedford College of Education, 14 The Crescent, Bedford; LEA; und.; W; primary; resident and day; corr. Director of Education, Shire Hall, Bedford; ATO Cambridge.

Bedford College of Physical Education, Lansdowne Rd, Bedford; LEA; W; three-year course; ATO Cambridge.

Putteridge Bury College of Education, Luton; LEA; und.; M/W; infant and primary; day only; ATO Cambridge.

Berkshire
Bulmershe College of Education, Woodlands Ave, Woodley, Reading; LEA; und.; M/W; primary and secondary; two-year course for mature students; corr. Director of Education, Shire Hall, Reading; ATO Reading.

Culham C of E College, Abingdon; vol. C of E; M/W; primary and secondary; ATO Oxford.

Easthampstead Park College of Education, nr Wokingham; LEA; und.; W; infant, junior and junior/secondary; corr. Director of Education, Shire Hall, Reading; ATO Reading.

Buckinghamshire

North Buckinghamshire College, Bletchley; LEA; und.; M/W; primary and secondary; corr. Chief Education Officer, County Office, Aylesbury; ATO Oxford.

Newland Park College of Education, Chalfont St Giles; LEA; und.; married W day; M resident and day; infant, primary and secondary; corr. Chief Education Officer, County Offices, Aylesbury; ATO Reading.

Cambridgeshire

Homerton College, Cambridge; vol.; und.; W; primary and secondary; fourth year for selected students leading to BEd; postgraduate training; ATO Cambridge.

Cheshire

Cheshire College of Education, Alsager, Cheshire; LEA; M/W; primary and secondary and BEd; one-year supplementary course in mathematics; one-year supplementary course in handicrafts; one-year course of initial professional training for mature craftsmen and one-term courses in the education of the dull child and in primary mathematics; day students taken; corr. Director of Education, Education Department, County Hall, Chester; ATO Keele.

Cheshire College of Education, Crewe Rd, Crewe; LEA; und.; W; secondary, junior, infant and nursery; supplementary course in English; resident and day; corr. Director of Education, County Hall, Chester; ATO Keele.

Chester College, Chester; vol.; C of E; M/W; junior-secondary; ATO Liverpool.

Derbyshire

Thornbridge Hall College of Education, Ashford-in-the-Water, nr Bakewell; LEA; und.; W; primary; mature day; corr. Director of Education, PO Box 67, Leopold St, Sheffield, 1; ATO Sheffield.

Bishop Lonsdale College of Education, Western Rd, Mickleover, Derby; vol.; C of E; M/W; nursery, infant, infant/junior, junior/secondary; specialist physical education for women; supplementary English; resident and day; ATO Nottingham.

Matlock College of Education, Matlock; LEA; und.; M/W; infant, primary and secondary; supplementary for teachers of backward children; resident and day; corr. Director of Education, Derbyshire; ATO Nottingham.

Devonshire

St Luke's College, Exeter; C of E; wing courses in physical education and science; specialist courses in mathematics; supplementary courses in mathematics and English; postgraduate; men for the main courses; women students admitted to postgraduate and supplementary courses; junior and secondary; ATO Exeter.

Rolle College, Exmouth; LEA; und.; W; infant, junior, junior/secondary, secondary; four-year BEd course; three-year general course; optional course in youth leadership for selected students; two-year shortened course for mature students; one-year professional training for teaching after successfully completing two-year course in (a) music, or (b) dance and drama, or (c) art at Darlington College of Arts; one-year professional training for teaching for qualified musicians; corr. Chief Education Officer, County Education Office, County Hall, Exeter; ATO Exeter.

Dorset

Weymouth College of Education, Dorchester Rd, Weymouth; LEA; und.; M/W; infant, junior and secondary; three-year course; two-year course for mature students; corr. County Education Officer, County Hall, Dorchester; ATO Southampton.

County Durham

Darlington College of Education, Vane Terr, Darlington; vol.; und.; W; nursery, infant, junior, junior secondary; resident W; day M/W over 21; ATO Durham.

College of the Venerable Bede, Durham; vol.; C of E; M; general; secondary and junior; one-year supplementary course in science; one-term supplementary courses in film and television and in audio-visual aids; three-year degree courses; postgraduate training in education course; courses for BEd (registration at end of first year); three-year certificate course; shortened one- and two-year courses for mature students; youth work courses; annexe at South Shields for older men and women as day students; ATO Durham.

Neville's Cross College, Durham; LEA: und.; M/W; general training, with additional specialist course for physical education; Licensed Hall of Residence of Durham University for degree and postgraduate training in the University; corr. Director of Education, Shire Hall, Durham.

St Hild's College, Durham; vol.; C of E: W; four-year degree and postgraduate certificate University course; four-year BEd course; three-year certificate course: ATO Durham.

Sunderland College of Education, Langham Tower, Ryhope Rd, Sunderland; LEA; und.; M/W; four-year BEd course; three-year general course; one-year supplementary course in history; one-term course in history; corr. Director of Education, 15 John St, Sunderland; ATO Durham.

Essex
Brentwood College of Education, Sawyer's Hall La., Brentwood; LEA; und.; M/W; outposts at Chelmsford, Harold Wood and Southend; day only; infant, junior, junior-secondary; corr. Chief Education Officer. Education Department, County Hall, Chelmsford; ATO Cambridge.

St Osyth's College, Marine Pde, Clacton-on-Sea; LEA; und.; M/W; infant, junior and junior-secondary; specialist courses in housecraft and needlework; corr. Chief Education Officer, Education Department, County Hall, Chelmsford; ATO Cambridge.

Saffron Walden College, South Rd, Saffron Walden; vol.; und.; W; infant, infant/junior, junior and junior-secondary; day students taken; ATO Cambridge.

Gloucestershire
College of S. Matthias, Fishponds, Bristol; vol.; C of E; M/W; nursery, primary and rural; day students taken; ATO Bristol.

Redland College, Bristol; LEA; und.; M/W; secondary, junior and infant; corr. Chief Education Officer, Council House, College Grn, Bristol, 1; ATO Bristol.

West of England College of Art, Queens Rd, Bristol, 8; LEA; M/W; art teachers' diploma; corr. Chief Education Officer, Council House, College Grn, Bristol, 1; ATO Bristol.

St Mary's College, The Park, Cheltenham; vol.; C of E; infant, junior, junior-secondary; secondary (PE and science only); supplementary course in divinity, science; needlework one term only; ATO Bristol.

St Paul's College, Cheltenham; vol.; C of E; M; initial training course; secondary and junior/secondary courses for specialist teachers in secondary schools in handicraft, physical education and science; supplementary courses in religious education and science; ATO Bristol.

Gloucestershire Training College, Oxstalls La, Gloucester; LEA; und.; W; teacher training in home economics (secondary) and general subjects (infant/junior/secondary); BEd agreed in principle by University of Bristol, arrangements proceeding; institutional management diploma course; course for BSc (domestic science) in conjunction with Bristol University; postgraduate course for teacher training (domestic science); corr. Chief Education Officer, Shire Hall, Gloucester; ATO Bristol.

Hampshire
Bournemouth and Poole College of Art, Lansdowne, Bournemouth; LEA; M/W; art teacher's diploma; supplementary art and crafts; corr. Chief Education Officer, Town Hall, Bournemouth; ATO Southampton.

City of Portsmouth College of Education, Locksway Rd, Milton, Portsmouth; LEA; und.; M/W; general course for primary and secondary teaching, two-year course for mature students; within general course, BEd courses; selected students will undertake a course in youth leadership; for serving teachers supplementary course in history and one-term course in biology, and day release courses in biology, chemistry and physics, with reference to Nuffield and other modern developments concerning GCE studies; day students accepted in all courses; corr. Chief Educational Officer, Education Department, 17–18 Western Pde, Portsmouth; ATO Southampton.

College of Education, The Avenue, Southampton; vol.; RC; W; infant, junior and secondary general course; two-year (shortened) course for mature students (M/W); resident and day; ATO Southampton.

King Alfred's College, Winchester; vol.; C of E; M/W; special provision for science, woodwork and metalwork; one-year courses for those who have passed the first examination and section one of the second examination for the City and Guilds of London Institute's Handicraft Teacher's Certificate, or have the Full Technological Certificate and five years' industrial experience; resident and day; ATO Southampton.

Herefordshire
Hereford College of Education, College Rd, Hereford; LEA; und.; W; primary (infants and junior), junior/secondary youth work endorsement possible; one- two- and three-year courses for mature students; day students taken; corr. Director of Education, County Offices, Bath St, Hereford; ATO Birmingham.

Hertfordshire
Trent Park College, Cockfosters, nr Barnet; LEA; und.; M/W; three-year course in general subjects, with advanced level

work for selected students; shortened courses in music, drama and art; supplementary course in handicrafts; one-year professional course for qualified musicians; combined courses for approved students with (a) Guildhall School of Music and Drama, (b) Addlestone Art of Movement Studio; resident and day; corr. Chief Education Officer, London Borough of Enfield, Education Department, Church St, Edmonton, London, N9; ATO London.

Hockerill College, Bishop's Stortford; vol.; C of E; W; infant, junior, junior-secondary; mature students M/W; ATO Cambridge.

Balls Park College, Hertford; LEA; und.; W; infant, infant-junior, junior, junior-secondary and secondary; two-year shortened course for mature students M/W; day or resident; ATO Cambridge.

Wall Hall College, Aldenham, Watford; LEA; und.; W; three-year course, nursery, infant, junior and junior-secondary; two-year course for mature students M/W; ATO Cambridge.

Kent

Stockwell College of Education, The Old Palace, Bromley; LEA; und.; M/W; primary and secondary; specialist and supplementary course in secondary and primary mathematics; day and resident; corr. Clerk to the Joint Education Committee, Springfield, Maidstone, Kent; ATO London.

Christ Church College, Canterbury; vol.; C of E; M/W; infant, junior, infant/junior, junior-secondary and secondary; ATO London.

Dartford College of Physical Education, Oakfield La., Dartford, Kent; LEA; corr. Education Officer, County Hall, Westminster, SE1; ATO London.

Nonington College of Physical Education, Nonington, Dover; LEA; advanced three-year specialist course; art and science of movement; ATO London.

Coloma College, West Wickham; vol.; RC; W; three-year course, infant, infant-junior, junior, junior-secondary, shortened courses for mature students; resident and day; ATO London.

Lancashire

Bolton College of Education (Technical), Chadwick St, Bolton; LEA; und.; M/W; one-year course of professional training; four-term sandwich course and one-term course for teachers serving in technical colleges; one-year supplementary course in science and mathematics and also in the teaching of general and liberal studies; one-term courses in programmed learning; short courses for technical teachers; resident and day; corr. Chief Education Officer, Nelson Sq., Bolton; ATO Manchester.

Chorley College of Education, Union St, Chorley; LEA; und.; M/W; infant, junior, secondary; mature students, day only; corr. Chief Education Officer, County Hall, Preston; ATO Lancaster.

St. Martin's College of Education, Lancaster; C of E; M/W; infant-junior, junior-secondary, secondary; one-year post-graduate course; day students taken; ATO Lancaster.

Christ's College of Education, Woolton Rd, Liverpool, 16; RC; M/W; secondary, junior-secondary, junior, infant-junior and infant; resident and day; ATO Liverpool.

City of Liverpool C. F. Mott Training College, The Hazels, Prescot; LEA; und.; M/W; secondary modern, junior and infants; postgraduate course mature students; corr. Director of Education, Education Offices, 14 Sir Thomas St, Liverpool, 1; ATO Liverpool.

City of Liverpool F. L. Calder College of Education for Domestic Science, Dowsefield La., Liverpool, 18; LEA; und.; W; three-year teacher training courses in domestic science and in needlecraft and textiles; four-year BEd course for domestic science teaching; one-year course in advanced studies for diplomas in teaching of home management and family affairs and in education with special reference to food and nutrition; corr. Director of Education, Education Officer, 14 Sir Thomas St, Liverpool, 1; ATO Liverpool.

Ethel Wormald College, 70 Mt Pleasant, Liverpool 3; LEA; und.; M/W; infant and junior; day only; January entry; corr. Director of Education, 14 Sir Thomas St, Liverpool 1; ATO Liverpool.

I. M. Marsh College of Physical Education, Barkhill Rd, Liverpool, 17; LEA; three-year certificate course; four-year BEd course; ATO Liverpool.

Kirkby Fields College of Education, Kirkby, nr Liverpool; LEA; und.; W; primary, junior-secondary; BEd course; corr. Director of Education, Education Offices, 14 Sir Thomas St, Liverpool, 1; ATO Liverpool.

Notre Dame College of Education, Mount Pleasant, Liverpool, 3; vol.; RC; W; infant, infant-junior, junior, junior-secondary, secondary; three-year course; day students taken; ATO Liverpool.

St. Katharine's College, Stand Park Rd, Liverpool, 16; vol.; C of E; M/W; primary and secondary; resident and day; ATO Liverpool.

Liverpool Regional College of Art, Hope St, Liverpool; LEA; M/W; art teachers' diploma course; Diploma in Art and Design in Fine Art, Graphic Design and Fashion and Textiles; college diploma in industrial design, typographical design and commercial design; ATO Liverpool.

De La Salle College of Education, Middleton, Manchester; vol.; RC; M; primary and secondary; three-year course; two-year compressed course for specially qualified students; part-time in-service course for teachers of the sciences; deferred supplementary course in science for serving teachers; one-year course for specialist teachers of woodwork/metalwork who possess the appropriate full technological certificates; two specialist courses within the three-year courses for teachers of science and teachers of woodwork and metalwork; resident and day; ATO Manchester.

Didsbury College of Education, Wilmslow Rd, Manchester, 20; LEA; und.; M/W; general; one-year postgraduate course in education; four-year BEd course; resident and day; corr. Chief Education Officer, PO Box 480, Manchester, 3; ATO Manchester.

Elizabeth Gaskell College of Education, Hathersage Rd, Manchester, 13; LEA; und.; W; four-year BEd courses; three-year courses for teachers of home economics, needlework and general subjects; infant, infant-junior, junior, junior-secondary; three-year course for Diploma of the Institutional Management Association; two-year courses for Certificate of IMA and one-year IMA abridged course; three-year course in speech therapy; resident and day; corr. Chief Education Officer, PO Box 480, Manchester, 3; ATO Manchester.

Manchester College of Education, Long Millgate, Manchester, 3; LEA; und.; M/W; day students only; three-year general course; one-year course of professional training for students holding musical qualifications; supplementary course for teachers of handicapped children; part-time (evenings) Froebel Trainer's Diploma course; one-term courses for teachers of slow-learning children attending ordinary schools; part-time training (evenings); corr. Chief Education Officer, PO Box 480, Manchester, 3; ATO Manchester.

Mather College of Education, Whitworth St, Manchester, 1; LEA; und.; M/W; day only; primary; corr. Chief Education Officer, PO Box 480, Manchester, 3; ATO Manchester.

Manchester College of Art and Design, All Saints, Manchester, 15; LEA; und.; M/W; one-year course for the Art Teachers' Certificate; corr. Chief Education Officer, PO Box 480, Manchester, 3; ATO Manchester.

Sedgley Park College of Education, Prestwich, Manchester; vol.; RC; W; general and BEd; day students taken; ATO Manchester.

Edge Hill College of Education, St Helens Rd, Ormskirk; LEA; und.; M/W; primary and secondary; social work (main subject: three-year); one-year courses for teachers of slow-learning children attending ordinary schools; one-term courses for teachers of immigrant children; careers guidance teachers, teachers of Newsom children; one-term courses in Urban Studies in the North-West, New Thinking in English, and school social work; residential and day; corr. Chief Education Officer, County Hall, Preston; ATO Liverpool.

Poulton-le-Fylde College of Education, Breck Rd, Poulton-le-Fylde, nr Blackpool, Lancs; LEA; und.; M/W; primary; day students taken; corr. Chief Education Officer, County Hall, Preston; ATO Lancaster.

Padgate College of Education, Fearnhead, Warrington; LEA; und.; M/W; infant, junior and secondary; one-term course for teachers of mathematics in primary schools; corr. Chief Education Officer, County Hall, Preston; ATO Manchester.

Leicestershire

City of Leicester College of Education, Scraptoft, Leicester; LEA; und.; M/W; infant-nursery, primary and secondary; corr. Director of Education, City Education Department, Newarke St, Leicester; ATO Leicester.

Leicester College of Domestic Science, Knighton Fields, Leicester; LEA; und.; W; three years' teacher training in domestic subjects; institutional management courses; corr. Director of Education, City Education Dept, Newarke St, Leicester; ATO Leicester.

Leicester College of Art and Design, The Newarke, Leicester; LEA; M/W; Art Teachers' Diploma; corr. Director of Education, City Education Dept, Newarke St, Leicester; ATO Leicester.

Loughborough College of Education, Loughborough; LEA; und.; M (secondary); W (primary); creative design; corr. Director of Education, Education Department, Grey Friars, Leicester; ATO Nottingham.

Lincolnshire

Kesteven College of Education, Stoke Rochford, nr Grantham; LEA; und.;

M/W; infants, junior, junior-secondary, secondary; day and residential; corr. Director of Education, County Offices, Sleaford; ATO Nottingham.

Bishop Grosseteste College, Lincoln; vol.; C of E; W; local men as day students; primary and secondary; ATO Nottingham.

London

Avery Hill College of Education, Eltham, London, SE9; LEA; und.; M/W; nursery, primary and secondary; postgraduate training; PE wing, W, specialist course; supplementary course in mathematics; one-year course for teachers of handicapped children; day students taken; corr. Education Officer, County Hall, London, SE1; ATO London.

Battersea College of Education: Home economics at 58 Clapham Common, North Side, London, SW4; training for primary school teachers at the Manresa Annexe, Holybourne Ave, Roehampton La., London, SW15; ILEA; und.; M/W; corr. Education Officer, County Hall, London, SE1; ATO London.

Cavendish Square Graduate College, 11 Cavendish Sq., London, W1; vol.; RC and other equally; W; one-year postgraduate course; secondary and primary; University of London postgraduate certificate in education; resident and day; ATO London.

College of S. Mark and S. John, King's Rd, Chelsea, London, SW10; vol.; C of E; M; some W, non-resident, admitted to certain courses; Teacher's Certificate, BA and BSc (general) degree; BEd, postgraduate; supplementary courses in chemistry, English, history; one-year post-diploma course for music students for the Teachers' Certificate; junior-secondary, secondary; day; ATO London.

Digby Stuart College of the Sacred Heart, Roehampton, London, SW15; vol.; RC; W; secondary, junior-secondary, junior, infants, infant-junior, housecraft; ATO London.

Froebel Institute College of Education, Grove House, Roehampton La., London, SW15; vol.; und.; M/W; primary (including nursery); ATO London.

Furzedown College of Education, Welham Rd, London, SW17; LEA; und.; M/W; nursery, primary and secondary; supplementary science course; resident and day; corr. Education Officer, County Hall, London, SE1; ATO London.

Garnett College, Downshire House, Roehampton La., London, SW15; LEA; und.; M/W; technical and general subjects (one-year course); four-term

'sandwich' course and one-term course for serving teachers in further education; Diploma in Further Education; corr. Education Officer, County Hall, London, SE1; ATO London.

Goldsmiths' College, University of London (Dept of Arts, Science and Education), New Cross, London, SE14; vol.; und.; M/W; nursery, infant, junior, secondary-junior, secondary; four-year course BA(Hons), BMus, BA or BSc (general) degree including one-year professional training; one-year course for graduates; supplementary courses; ATO London.

Goldsmiths' College School of Art, University of London, New Cross, London, SE14; vol.; und.; M/W; one-year professional course for the Art Teachers' Certificate; full-time art course; ATO London.

Maria Assumpta College, 23 Kensington Sq., London, W8; vol.; RC; W; three-year course for the Teachers' Certificate; infant, infant-junior, junior, junior-secondary; resident and day; ATO London.

Philippa Fawcett College of Education, 94–100 Leigham Court Rd, London, SW16; LEA; und.; M/W; primary (nursery, infant and junior), junior-secondary, secondary; corr. Education Officer, County Hall, Westminster Bridge, London, SE1; ATO London.

Rachel McMillan College of Education, Creek Rd, Deptford, London, SE8; LEA; und.; W; nursery, infant and junior; four-year course for mature students; resident and day; corr. Education Officer, County Hall, SE1; ATO London.

St Gabriel's College, Cormont Rd, Camberwell, London, SE5; vol.; C of E; W; general; ATO London.

Sidney Webb College, 9–12 Barrett St, London, W1; LEA; und.; M/W; general–primary; domestic science; day only; ATO London.

Southlands College of Education, 65 Wimbledon Parkside, London, SW19; vol.; Methodist; M/W; secondary and primary; day annexe for married women at Croydon; ATO London.

Whitelands College, West Hill, Putney, London, SW15; vol.; C of E; M/W; three-year infant, infant-junior, junior-secondary, secondary (shortage subjects only); two-year shortened supplementary course; one-year postgraduate course; supplementary divinity; annexe for mature students; four-year course for overseas graduates; ATO London.

Middlesex (postal district)

Hornsey College of Art, Crouch End Hill, London, N8; LEA; M/W; Art Teacher's

Certificate; full-time art course; corr. Head of Department of Teacher Training, Page Green School, Broad La., Tottenham, London, N15. ATO London.

Borough Road College, Isleworth; vol.; und.; M/W; Teacher's Certificate course (three years); combined degree and certificate course for London general BSc, general BA and BEd (four years); supplementary courses in mathematics and divinity; various advanced specialist courses including PE; ATO London.

College of All Saints, London, N17; vol.; C of E; M/W; three-year general and home economics course; infant, infant-junior, junior-secondary, secondary; day students taken; ATO London.

Maria Grey College, 300 St Margaret's Rd, Twickenham; LEA; und.; W; Advanced Diploma course in the education of children in the junior school; supplementary course in the education of handicapped children; three-year primary course, one-year postgraduate courses for primary and secondary (men admitted to some one-year courses); corr. Chief Education Officer, London Borough of Hounslow, 88 Lampton Rd, Hounslow, Middlesex; ATO London.

St Mary's College, Strawberry Hill, Twickenham; vol.; RC; M/W; Teachers' Certificate; Postgraduate Certificate; four-year concurrent BA and BSc; supplementary in the teaching of handicapped children; one-term courses in mathematics; wing PE (men); ATO London.

Norfolk
Keswick Hall, Church of England College of Education, Norwich, NOR 93B; vol.; C of E; M/W; secondary, junior and infant; postgraduate course; annexe for mature students; ATO Cambridge.

Northumberland
Alnwick College, The Castle, Alnwick; LEA; und.; W; infant and junior and junior-secondary; M/W; for two-year mature course, infant, junior, junior-secondary and secondary; corr. Director of Education, County Hall, Newcastle upon Tyne, 1 (enquiries about admission of students should be addressed direct to the principal and not to the correspondent); ATO Newcastle upon Tyne.

Kenton Lodge College of Education, Kenton Rd, Newcastle upon Tyne, 3; LEA; und.; W; nursery-infant, primary and secondary; day students taken; corr. G. Squires, Education Office, Civic Centre, Barras Bridge, Newcastle upon Tyne, 1; ATO Newcastle upon Tyne.

Newcastle upon Tyne College of Education, 50 Northumberland Rd, Newcastle upon Tyne, 1; LEA; M/W; infant, junior and secondary; day college for mature students; corr. Director of Education, City Education Offices, Civic Centre, Barras Bridge, Newcastle upon Tyne, 1; ATO Newcastle upon Tyne.

Northern Counties College of Education, Coach La., Newcastle upon Tyne, 7; Joint Education Committee; M/W; general course for teachers (infant, primary and secondary) and specialist home economics studies course for teachers; BEd; day and resident; corr. Secretary to the Governors, City Education Offices, Civic Centre, Newcastle upon Tyne, 1; ATO Newcastle upon Tyne.

Northumberland College of Education, Ponteland, Newcastle upon Tyne; LEA; und.; M/W; infant and junior, junior-secondary, French and mathematics; BEd courses; ATO Newcastle upon Tyne.

St Mary's College of the Sacred Heart, Fenham, Newcastle upon Tyne, 4; vol.; RC; W; primary and secondary; postgraduate course; ATO Newcastle upon Tyne.

Nottinghamshire
Mary Ward College of Education, Keyworth, Nottingham; RC; W; infant, primary and secondary; Teacher's Certificate course (three years); wing course in home economics; resident and day.

Nottingham College of Education, Clifton, Nottingham; LEA; und.; M/W; infant, junior, secondary; specialist science, mathematics and music courses; corr. Director of Education, Exchange Buildings, Smithy Row, Nottingham; ATO Nottingham.

Eaton Hall College of Education, Retford; LEA; und.; M/W; primary and secondary; handicraft course for men; corr. Director of Education, County Hall, West Bridgford, Nottingham; ATO, Nottingham.

Oxfordshire
The Lady Spencer Churchill College, Wheatley; LEA; und.; W; primary, 450 students; corr. F. J. North, MA, Chief Education Officer, County Offices, Aylesbury; ATO Oxford.

Westminster College, North Hinksey, Oxford; vol.; Methodist; M/W; three-year for junior and secondary; one-year postgraduate (taking the Oxford University Diploma in Education); supplementary courses in religious education, mathematics and music; ATO Oxford.

Shropshire
Radbrook College, Shrewsbury; LEA; und.; M/W; three-year home management social science course; three-year home economics-rural course; three-year RDE teachers' course; three-year Institutional Management Diploma course; two-year Institutional Management Certificate course; National Council for Home Economics Education Certificate in Home Economics; corr. Chief Education Officer, County Buildings, Shrewsbury; ATO Birmingham.

Somerset
Bath College of Education (Home Economics), Sion Hill Pl., Bath; LEA; und.; W; three-year teacher-training course in home economics or in needlework and design; one- and two-year shortened courses for mature students; one-year Advanced Certificate course for experienced teachers; day students taken; corr. Director of Education, Guildhall, Bath; ATO Bristol.
Newton Park College (City of Bath), Newton St Loe, Bath; LEA; und.; M/W; mature day students; general; infant, junior and secondary; one-year course for students with qualification in agriculture, horticulture, or dairying; one-year course for students with degrees or diplomas in music; supplementary English course; corr. Director of Education, Guildhall, Bath; ATO Bristol.

Staffordshire
Madeley College of Education (County of Stafford Training College), Madeley, nr Crewe, Cheshire; Annexe, Nelson Hall, nr Stafford; LEA; und.; M/W; primary and secondary; home economics (housecraft) courses; physical education specialist training for men; specially timed course for married women at Nelson Hall Annexe; corr. Director of Education, County Education Offices, Stafford (all correspondence about admission of students should be addressed to the Principal at the college); ATO Keele.
West Midlands College of Education, Gorway, Walsall, Staffs; LEA; und.; M/W; infant, infant-junior, junior and junior-secondary; three-year course of initial training and shortened two-year course for mature students; four-year BEd degree course; resident and day; ATO University of Birmingham.
Wolverhampton Teachers' College for Day Students, Walsall St, Wolverhampton; LEA; M/W; infant and junior; mature students; corr. Director of Education, Education Offices, North St, Wolverhampton; ATO Birmingham.

Wolverhampton Technical Teachers' College, Compton Road West, Wolverhampton; LEA; und.; M/W; one-year (pre-service and in service); four-term (in-service) sandwich; one-term (in-service, agriculture and horticulture only); one-year course and two-year part-time day release (in-service) courses of professional training for teaching in further education; corr. Director of Education, North St, Wolverhampton; ATO Birmingham.

Surrey
Shoreditch College, Cooper's Hill, Englefield Green, Egham; LEA; und.; M; general course centred on study and practice of handicraft; secondary; specialist and supplementary courses; day students admitted; corr. Education Officer, County Hall, London, SE1; ATO London.
Gipsy Hill College, Kenry House, Kingston Hill, Kingston upon Thames; LEA; M/W; nursery, infant, junior and secondary (up to 13 plus); day students admitted; corr. Chief Education Officer, County Hall, Kingston upon Thames; ATO London.

Sussex
Bognor Regis College of Education, Upper Bognor Rd, Bognor Regis; LEA; und.; M/W; secondary-junior, junior-infant; day students admitted; corr. Dr. C. W. W. Read, County Hall, Chichester; ATO Southampton.
Brighton College of Art, Grand Pde, Brighton; LEA; M/W; teacher training, fine art, architecture, graphic design, interior design, dress design, etc; ATO Sussex.
Brighton College of Education, Falmer, Brighton; LEA; und.; M/W; further education/secondary; secondary; junior-secondary; infant-junior; nursery-infant; two-year shortened course for older students; one-term supplementary course in English for secondary school teachers; mathematics for primary school teachers; corr. Director of Education, 54 Old Steine, Brighton; ATO Sussex.
Bishop Otter College, Chichester; vol.; C of E; M/W; secondary modern, intermediate, junior, infant and nursery schools; special main (wing) course in physical education for women; supplementary courses in divinity and mathematics; older day students accepted for three- and two-year courses; ATO Reading (proposed Sussex).
Chelsea College of Physical Education, Carlisle Rd, Eastbourne; LEA; three-year course; also three-year course in

advanced dance; four-year course leading to BEd; one-year supplementary course; one-year course for women graduates wishing to prepare to teach some PE as well as degree course subject; youth leadership course for selected students; ATO Sussex.

Eastbourne College of Education, Darley Rd, Eastbourne; LEA; und.; W; M/W day students accepted; primary and secondary; one-year course for teachers and intending teachers of handicapped children; corr. Chief Education Officer, Education Office, Grove Rd, Eastbourne; ATO Sussex.

Seaford College of Education, Seaford; LEA; und.; W; secondary range, specialist home economics; corr. Chief Education Officer, County Hall, Lewes; ATO Sussex.

Warwickshire

Birmingham College of Art and Design, New Corporation St, Birmingham, 4; LEA; M/W; Diploma in Art Education (awarded by Birmingham University); art teacher training course; supplementary course in art and crafts; ATO Birmingham.

Bordesley College of Education, Camp Hill, Birmingham, 11; LEA; und.; W; three-year general teachers' course (nursery, infant and junior); corr. Chief Education Officer, Council House, Margaret St, Birmingham; ATO Birmingham.

City of Birmingham College of Education, Westbourne Rd, Birmingham, 15; LEA; und.; M/W; infant, junior and secondary; one-year paedagogic course for students of music, supplementary course in health education, supplementary course for teachers of handicapped children; corr. Chief Education Officer, Council House, Margaret St, Birmingham; ATO Birmingham.

St Peter's College, Saltley, Birmingham, 8; vol.; C of E; M; junior, junior-secondary, secondary; three-year course for Certificate in Education; one-year postgraduate course; one-year supplementary courses in mathematics, handicrafts; one-year course in handicraft teaching for holders of Full Technological Certificate of London City and Guilds; day students admitted; ATO Birmingham.

Westhill College of Education, Selly Oak, Birmingham; vol.; Free Church; M/W; junior, infant, secondary (specialist religious knowledge only); supplementary course in religious education; certificate in youth service; day students taken; ATO Birmingham.

Coventry College of Education, Canley, Coventry; LEA; und.; M/W; special

advanced course in physical education (women); supplementary courses for mathematics (M/W) and physical education (women); supplementary and part-time course for teachers of handicapped children (M/W); Certificate and BEd degree of the University of Warwick; corr. Director of Education, Council Offices, Earl St (South Side), Coventry; ATO Birmingham.

St Paul's College of Education, Newbold Revel, Stretton-under-Fosse, Rugby; vol.; RC; W; general; ATO Birmingham.

Anstey College of Physical Education, Sutton Coldfield; LEA; corr. Director of Education, County Education Office, Stafford.

Westmorland

Charlotte Mason College, Ambleside; LEA; und.; W; general; infant-junior, junior-secondary; special course in regional studies; day students admitted; ATO Manchester.

Wiltshire

College of Sarum St Michael, 65 The Close, Salisbury; vol.; C of E; W; general course; shortened course for mature students; ATO Bristol.

Worcestershire

Shenstone College, Burcot La., Bromsgrove; LEA; und.; M/W; infant and junior, junior and secondary, secondary; corr. County Education Officer, Worcester; ATO Birmingham.

Dudley College of Education, Castle View, Dudley; LEA; und.; M/W; infant, infant-junior, junior-secondary, secondary; three-year courses and specialist secondary courses in science, boys' handicrafts, economics, commerce; one-term course for teachers of pupils of average and below average ability; day students admitted; corr. H. W. C. Eisel, Education Offices, Dudley; ATO Birmingham.

Worcester College of Education, Henwick Gro., Worcester; LEA; und.; M/W; primary and secondary; three-year specialist courses in science, rural studies, domestic science (optional rural bias); supplementary courses in English, mathematics, science, rural studies; one-year professional course for students with degree or diploma qualifications in agriculture or horticulture; one-term courses in physics (for specialist teachers); creative dance in junior school; corr. Director of Education, 5 and 6 Barbourne Ter., Worcester; ATO Birmingham.

Summerfield, nr Kidderminster, Worcs; LEA; und.; W; infant, infant-junior,

junior; day students admitted; corr. County Education Officer, Education Office, Castle St, Worcester; ATO Birmingham.

Yorkshire

Wentworth Castle College of Education, Stanborough, nr Barnsley; LEA; und.; W; general; primary; corr. H. A. Redburn, Education Department, Town Hall, Barnsley; ATO Sheffield.

Bingley College of Education, Lady La., Bingley; LEA; und.; M/W; infant-junior, junior-secondary, secondary; one-term course for returners and graduate late entrants to teaching; one-term supplementary course in mathematics for primary teachers; general; day students taken; corr. Education Officer, County Hall, Wakefield; ATO Leeds.

Margaret McMillan Memorial College of Education, Trinity Rd, Bradford, 5; LEA; und.; W (resident and day); M (day only); nursery, infant and junior, junior-secondary; corr. Director of Education, Town Hall, Bradford, 1; ATO Leeds.

Doncaster College of Education, High Melton Hall, Doncaster; LEA; und.; W only, except for supplementary mathematics course; primary and secondary; corr. Chief Education Officer, Education Office, Whitaker St, Doncaster; ATO Sheffield.

Huddersfield College of Education (Technical), Holly Bank Rd, Lindley, Huddersfield; LEA; und.; M/W; training courses for teachers in colleges of further education; corr. Chief Education Officer, Education Offices, Ramsden St, Huddersfield; ATO Leeds.

Oastler College, Buxton Rd, Huddersfield, Yorks; LEA; und.; M/W; modern languages, English, art and craft, biology, maths, environmental studies, religious studies; day students admitted; places offered to mature students, four-year part-time course for married women; corr. Chief Education Officer, Education Office, Civic Centre, Huddersfield; ATO Leeds.

Ilkley College of Education, Wells Rd, Ilkley; LEA; und.; W; home economics, junior-secondary and youth leaderteacher courses; corr. Chief Education Officer, County Hall, Wakefield; ATO Leeds.

Endsleigh College of Education, Kingston upon Hull; vol.; RC; W; infant, primary and secondary; three-year general course; three-year specialist course for secondary school PE; four-year course leading to BEd degree; resident and day; ATO Hull.

Kingston upon Hull College of Education,

Cottingham Rd, Kingston upon Hull; LEA; und.; M/W; infant-junior, junior-secondary, secondary; corr. Chief Education Officer, Guildhall, Kingston upon Hull; ATO Hull.

All Saints College, Troy, Horsforth, Leeds, 2; RC; M; three-year general course; fourth year of study for selected students leading to BEd; ATO Leeds (in association with Trinity College).

Carnegie College of Physical Education, Beckett Park, Leeds; LEA; one-year course for graduates and serving teachers; three-year course for intending teachers organised jointly by College and City of Leeds College of Education; one-year special course of advanced study for experienced teachers; ATO Leeds.

City of Leeds College of Art Teacher Training Department, 3 Hyde Terr., Leeds, 2; LEA; M/W; University of Leeds Institute of Education Art Teacher's Certificate; supplementary courses; refresher courses; ATO Leeds.

City of Leeds College of Education, Beckett Pk, Leeds, 6; LEA; und.; M/W; three-year general teachers' course; three-year course for specialist teachers of physical education (jointly with Carnegie College) and science; one-year postgraduate course; special one-year course for handicraft and education of backward children; one-term supplementary courses in physics (Nuffield) and education (Newsom); fourth year of study for selected students leading to BEd; corr. Chief Education Officer, Education Department, Leeds, 1; ATO Leeds.

The James Graham College (formerly the Leeds Day Training College), Lawns House, Chapel La., Farnley, Leeds, 12; LEA; und.; M/W; junior secondary and infants; day only; corr. Chief Education Officer, Education Department, Calverley St, Leeds, 1; ATO Leeds.

Trinity College, Troy, Horsforth, Leeds, 2; RC; W; fourth year of study for selected students leading to BEd; ATO Leeds (in association with All Saints College).

Yorkshire College of Education and Home Economics, Calverley St, Leeds, 1; LEA; und.; W; home economics, secondary; fourth year of study for selected students leading to BEd; corr. Chief Education Officer, Education Offices, Calverley St, Leeds, 1; ATO Leeds.

Middlesbrough College of Education, Borough Rd, Middlesbrough, Yorks; LEA; und.; M/W; junior-secondary, junior, infant; opportunities for BEd; ATO Durham.

Ripon College of Education, Ripon; vol.; C of E; W; general; fourth year of study for selected students leading to BEd; day students taken; ATO Leeds.

North Riding College of Education, Filey Rd, Scarborough; LEA; und.; W and mature men; infants and juniors; fourth year of study for selected students leading to BEd; corr. Secretary for Education, County Hall, Northallerton; ATO Leeds.

Lady Mabel College of Physical Education, Wentworth Woodhouse, Rotherham; LEA; W; junior-secondary (general) course; annexe at Castleford for part-time training of married women, infant-junior, secondary; residential and day; ATO Sheffield.

City of Sheffield College of Education, Collegiate Cres., Sheffield, 10; LEA; und.; M/W; infant, primary and secondary; supplementary courses in geography, mathematics and the teaching of mentally handicapped children; handicraft wing; one-term postgraduate course, one-term course in the teaching of sciences (biology) and one-term course in handicraft; corr. Director of Education, Education Office, Leopold St, Sheffield, 1; ATO Sheffield.

Totley Hall College of Education, Totley, Sheffield; LEA; und.; W; three-year specialist course in home economics; three-year course for primary teachers; ATO Sheffield.

Swinton Day Training College, Swinton, nr Mexborough; LEA; und.; M/W; secondary, junior and infant; corr. Education Officer, Education Department, Bond St, Wakefield; ATO Sheffield.

Bretton Hall College of Education, West Bretton, nr Wakefield; LEA; und.; M/W; secondary, junior and infant; combined junior-infant; three-year course for teachers of music, art and craft, including needlecraft and dress, speech and drama, English, science, mathematics, religion and worship; one-year professional training in teaching in music, drama and certain other subjects for those holding suitable degrees or diplomas in appropriate fields; one-year supplementary course in English for serving teachers; fourth year for selected students leading to BEd; corr. Chief Education Officer, Education Offices, Bond St, Wakefield; ATO Leeds.

Scawsby College of Education, Scawsby, nr Doncaster; LEA; und.; M/W; secondary, junior and infant; corr. Education Officer, Education Department, Bond St, Wakefield; ATO Sheffield.

St John's College, York; vol.; C of E; M/W; three-year general teacher's course for primary and secondary; English, history, divinity; geography, art and craft and music; three-year courses for specialist teachers of PE, science (physics, chemistry and biology), rural science and handicraft; one-year course for suitably qualified candidates in rural science; suitably qualified students can proceed to fourth year of study for BEd; ATO Leeds.

Wales
Caernarvonshire

Normal College, Bangor; LEA; und.; M/W; infant, primary and secondary; three-year course for domestic science students; day students taken; ATO Wales.

St Mary's College, Bangor; vol.; Church in Wales; W; infant-nursery, junior, secondary; day students taken; ATO Wales.

Carmarthenshire

Trinity College, Carmarthen; vol.; Church in Wales; M/W; three-year course for Teacher's Certificate; one-term supplementary course in mathematics; four-year course for BEd (Wales); day students taken, and mature students for approved shortened courses; ATO Wales.

Denbighshire

Cartrefle College of Education, Wrexham; LEA; und.; W; infant-junior, junior-secondary; corr. Director of Education, Education Offices, Ruthin; ATO Wales.

Glamorgan

Glamorgan College of Education, Buttrills Rd, Barry; LEA; und.; M/W; primary and secondary; PE wing course for women; one-year supplementary course in teaching handicapped children; oral Welsh course (termly); corr. Director of Education, County Hall, Cathays Pk, Cardiff; ATO Wales.

City of Cardiff College of Education, Cyncoed, Cardiff; LEA; M/W; infant, junior, secondary, PE wing (men only); supplementary PE (men); one-year professional course for qualified teachers of music; resident and day; corr. Director of Education, City Hall, Cardiff; ATO Wales.

College of Art, The Friary, Cardiff; LEA; M/W; Art Teacher's Diploma; supplementary course in art and crafts; ATO Wales.

College of Domestic Arts, Llandaff, Cardiff; LEA; und.; W; secondary; home economics; three-year teacher training course; three-year course for Diploma in Institutional Management; ATO Wales.

Swansea College of Education, Townhill Rd, Sketty, Swansea; LEA; und.; M/W; general (main commerce, main social studies with youth leadership, subsidiary youth leadership); corr. Director of Education, The Guildhall, Swansea; ATO Wales.

Monmouthshire

Caerleon College of Education, Caerleon; LEA; und.; M/W; two-year and three-year general course for infants, junior and secondary; one-year supplementary course for teachers of ESN children; corr. Director of Education, County Hall, Newport; ATO Wales.

Scotland

Aberdeen College of Education, St Andrew St, Aberdeen; M/W; all categories of training except PE and further education.

College of Domestic Science, Queen's Rd, Aberdeen; Diploma courses for intending teachers, dieticians and institutional managers; IMA Certificate courses in institutional housekeeping and catering; and for matron-housekeepers.

Dundee College of Education, Park Pl., Dundee; M/W; all categories except specialisation in PE, homecraft and further education.

Dunfermline College of Physical Education, Cramond, Edinburgh, 4; three-year course.

Craiglockhart College of Education, 219 Colinton Rd, Edinburgh, 11; RC; W; ordinary and postgraduate courses except PE and further education.

Edinburgh College of Domestic Science, 5 Atholl Cres., Edinburgh, 3; W; domestic science.

Moray House College of Education, Holyrood Rd, Edinburgh, 8; M/W; all categories except PE.

Glasgow and West of Scotland College of Domestic Science (Incorporated), 1 Park Dr., Glasgow, C3.

Jordanhill College of Education, Jordanhill, Glasgow, W3; M/W; all categories of training except PE for women.

Notre Dame College of Education, Courthill, Bearsden, Glasgow; RC; W; infant, primary, secondary; music and art.

Callender Park College of Education, Falkirk, Stirlingshire; W; three-year course for the Teacher's Certificate (Primary Education).

Craigie College of Education, Ayr; W; three-year course for teaching qualification (Primary Education); in-service and vacation courses; day students and in residence in approved lodgings.

Northern Ireland

College of Domestic Science, Garnerville Rd, Belfast, 4; LEA; und.; W; domestic science teacher training; IMA diploma courses.

St Mary's College of Education, Belfast, 12; vol.; RC; W; three-year course—Primary School Certificate; four-year course—Secondary Intermediate School Certificate; one-year postgraduate course.

St Joseph's College of Education, Trench House, Belfast, 11; vol.; RC; M; three-year course—Primary School Certificate; four-year course—Secondary Intermediate School Certificate; one-year postgraduate course.

Stranmillis College, Stranmillis Rd, Belfast, 9; government training college; M/W; combined university college course (four years); postgraduate course (one year); primary school course (three years); secondary school course.

3. AGRICULTURAL COLLEGES

Harper Adams Agricultural College, Newport, Salop.

Royal Agricultural College, Cirencester, Glos.

Seale-Hayne Agricultural College, Newton Abbot, Devon.

Shuttleworth Agricultural College, Old Warden Pk, Biggleswade, Beds.

Studley College (Agricultural and Horticultural College for Women), Studley, Warks.

Edinburgh and East of Scotland College of Agriculture, Edinburgh School of Agriculture, West Mains Rd, Edinburgh, 9.

School of Agriculture, Aberdeen, North of Scotland College of Agriculture and Department of Agriculture, Aberdeen University, 41B Union St, Aberdeen.

West of Scotland Agricultural College, 6 Blythswood Sq., Glasgow, C2; and Auchincruive, nr Ayr.

4. COLLEGES OF MUSIC, DRAMA AND DANCING

Birmingham School of Music, 27 Dale End, Birmingham, 4.

Central School of Speech and Drama, Embassy Theatre, London, NW3.

City of Cardiff College of Music and Drama, The Castle, Cardiff.

Dartington College of Arts (covering music, dance, drama and the visual arts), Totnes, S Devon.

Guildhall School of Music and Drama, John Carpenter St, Victoria Embankment, London, EC4.

Laban Art of Movement Centre, Woburn Hill, Addlestone, Surrey.

Liverpool Matthay School of Music, 25 Islington, Liverpool, 3.

London Academy of Music and Dramatic Art, Tower House, Cromwell Rd, London, SW5.

London College of Music, Great Marlborough St, London, W1.

Northern School of Music, 99 Oxford Rd, Manchester, 1.

Rose Bruford Training College of Speech and Drama, Lamorbey Park, Sidcup, Kent.

Royal Academy of Dancing Teachers' Training Course, 6 Addison Rd, London, W14. *RAD offices:* 15 Holland Park Gdns, London, W14.

Royal Academy of Dramatic Art, 62 Gower St, London, WC1.

Royal Academy of Music, Marylebone Rd, London, NW1.

Royal College of Music, Prince Consort Rd, London, SW7.

Royal College of Organists, Kensington Gore, London, SW7.

Royal Manchester College of Music, Devas St, Oxford Rd, Manchester, 15.

Royal School of Church Music, Addington Palace, Croydon, Surrey.

The Royal Scottish Academy of Music, St George's Pl, Glasgow, C2.

Tonic Sol-fa College of Music, Curwen Memorial Building, 9 Queensborough Terr., London, W2.

Trinity College of Music, 11 and 13 Mandeville Pl, London, W1.

Webber-Douglas Academy of Dramatic Art Ltd, 30–36 Clareville St, London, SW7.

5. COLLEGES OF ARTS AND CRAFTS

(*See also* Colleges of Education)

Byam Shaw School of Drawing and Painting Ltd, 70 Campden St, London, W8.

College of Handicraft, Long Riston, Hull.

Duncan of Jordanstone College of Art, Perth Rd, Dundee.

Edinburgh College of Art, Lauriston Pl, Edinburgh, 3.

Glasgow School of Art, 167 Renfrew St, Glasgow, C3.

Royal Academy Schools of Painting and Sculpture, Burlington Gdns, London, W1.

6. ART COLLEGES WITH COURSES LEADING TO THE DIPLOMA IN ART AND DESIGN

Bath Academy of Art, Corsham Court, Corsham, Wilts.

College of Art and Design, New Corporation St, Birmingham, 4.

College of Art, Grand Pde, Brighton.

Camberwell School of Arts and Crafts, Peckham Rd, London, SE5.

Canterbury College of Art, St Peters St, Canterbury.

Cardiff College of Art, The Friary, Cardiff.

Chelsea School of Art, Manresa Rd, Chelsea, London, SW3.

City of Coventry College of Art, Cope St, Coventry.

Exeter College of Art, Gandy St, Exeter.

Gloucestershire College of Art, Pittville, Cheltenham, Glos.

Goldsmiths' College School of Art, University of London, Lewisham Way, London, SE14.

High Wycombe College of Technology and Art, Queen Alexandra Rd, High Wycombe, Bucks.

Hornsey College of Art, Crouch End Hill, Crouch End, London, N8.

Kingston College of Art, Knights Pk, Kingston upon Thames.

Kingston upon Hull Regional College of Art, Anlaby Rd, Kingston upon Hull.

Leeds College of Art, Vernon St, Leeds, 2.

Leicester College of Art and Design, The Newarke, Leicester.

Liverpool Regional College of Art, Hope St, Liverpool, 1.

Central School of Art and Design, Southampton Row, London, WC1.

London College of Printing, Elephant and Castle, London, SE1.

Loughborough College of Art, Ashby Rd, Loughborough.

Maidstone College of Art, Faith St, Maidstone, Kent.

Manchester College of Art and Design, All Saints, Manchester, 15.

College of Art and Industrial Design, Clayton Rd, Jesmond, Newcastle upon Tyne, 2.

Newport College of Art, Clarence Pl, Newport, Mon.

Nottingham College of Art and Design, Waverley St, Nottingham.

Portsmouth College of Art and Design, Hyde Park Rd, Portsmouth.

Ravensbourne College of Art and Design, Bromley, Kent.

Saint Martin's School of Art, 109 Charing Cross Rd, London, WC2.

Sheffield College of Art, Brincliffe, Psalter La, Sheffield, 11.

Stoke-on-Trent College of Art, Stoke-on-Trent.

Sunderland College of Art, Backhouse Pk, Ryhope Rd, Sunderland.

West of England College of Art, Clanage Rd, Bower Ashton, Bristol, 8.

Wimbledon School of Art, Merton Hall Rd, London, SW19.

Winchester Art School, Park Ave, Winchester.

Wolverhampton College of Art, St Peter's Close, Lichfield St, Wolverhampton.

7. SCHOOLS OF ARCHITECTURE

The Architects Registration Council of the UK (68 Portland Pl., London, WC1) exists to maintain and publish a Register of Architects, to maintain correct standards of professional conduct, and to award scholarships and maintenance grants to students in need. Qualification for admission to the Register is a pass in one of the examinations in architecture recognised under the Architects (Registration) Acts.

The entire system of architectural education in the UK is controlled by the Royal Institute of British Architects (66 Portland Pl., London, W1) through its Board of Architectural Education. The schools listed below are recognised by the RIBA and are visited regularly by the RIBA Visiting Board to ensure that they meet the minimum standards for exemption.

University schools

(Subject to exceptions noted below, courses are full-time for five years, leading to a degree or diploma.)

Bath: University of Technology.

Belfast: Queen's University.

Bristol: University Dept of Architecture. School of Architecture and Building Technology, King's Weston Hse, Bristol.

Cambridge: University School of Architecture.

Cardiff: The Welsh School of Architecture. Institute of Science and Technology.

Edinburgh: University of Edinburgh, Dept of Architecture.

Glasgow: University of Strathclyde School of Architecture.

Liverpool: University of Liverpool School of Architecture.

London: Bartlett School of Architecture, University College London.

Manchester: University of Manchester School of Architecture.

Newcastle upon Tyne: University School of Architecture.

Nottingham: University Dept of Architecture and Civic Planning.

Sheffield: University Dept of Architecture.

Non-university schools

(5-yr full-time courses leading to a diploma)

Aberdeen: Scott Sutherland School of Architecture, Robert Gordon's Institute of Technology.

Birmingham: School of Architecture, College of Arts and Crafts, New Corporation St.

Brighton: School of Architecture, Brighton College of Art, 62 Grand Pde.

Canterbury: School of Architecture, Canterbury College of Art, St. Peter's St.

Dundee: School of Architecture and Town Planning, Duncan of Jordanstone College of Art, Perth Rd.

Edinburgh: School of Architecture, Edinburgh College of Art, Lauriston Place.

Glasgow: School of Architecture, Glasgow School of Art, 167 Renfrew St, (5-yr part-time course leading to the Certificate of the School).

Hull: School of Architecture, Regional College of Art, Anlaby Rd.

Kingston upon Thames: School of Architecture and Civic Design, Kingston College of Art, Knight's Pk.

Leeds: School of Architecture, Leeds College of Art, 43A Woodhouse La.

Leicester: Faculty of Architecture, Leicester College of Art and Design, 1 Newarke St.

London: Architectural Association School of Architecture, 36 Bedford Sq., WC1. Department of Architecture, Brixton School of Building, Ferndale Rd, SW4. Polytechnic School of Architecture and Advanced Building Technology, Regent St, W1. Dept. of Architecture, Surveying, Building and Interior Design, Northern Polytechnic, Holloway, N7. Dept. of Architecture, Hammersmith College of Art and Building, Lime Grove, W12.

Manchester: School of Architecture, Manchester College of Art and Design, Cavendish St (6-yr composite course).

Oxford: School of Architecture, College of Technology, Headington Rd.

Portsmouth: School of Architecture, Portsmouth College of Technology, High St.

8. NATIONAL COLLEGES

College of Aeronautics, Cranfield, Beds.

National College of Agricultural Engineering, Silsoe, Beds.

College of Air Training, Hamble, Southampton.

Royal College of Art, Kensington Gore, London, SW7.

Advanced School of Automobile Engineering, Cranfield, Bedford.

National College of Food Technology, University of Reading, Reading, Berks.

National College for Heating, Ventilating, Refrigeration and Fan Engineering, Borough Polytechnic, Borough Rd, London, SE1.

National Leathersellers College, Tower Bridge Rd, Bermondsey, London, SE1.

National College of Rubber Technology, Northern Polytechnic, Holloway Rd, London, N7.

9. REGIONAL COLLEGES

Barking Regional College of Technology (formerly South-East Essex College of Technology), Longbridge Rd, Dagenham, Essex.

Borough Polytechnic, Borough Rd, London, SE1.

Brighton College of Technology, Moolsecoomb, Brighton.

Brixton School of Building, Ferndale Rd, London, SW4.

Glamorgan College of Technology, Llantwit Rd, Treforest, Pontypridd.

Hatfield College of Technology, Hatfield, Herts.

Huddersfield College of Technology, Queensgate, Huddersfield.

Kingston College of Technology, Penrhyn Rd, Kingston-upon-Thames, Surrey.

Lanchester College of Technology, Coventry, Priory St, Coventry.

Leeds College of Technology, Calverley St, Leeds, 1.

Leicester College of Technology, Leicester.

City of Liverpool College of Building, Clarence St, Liverpool, 3.

Liverpool Regional College of Technology, Byron St, Liverpool, 3.

North Staffordshire College of Technology, College Rd, Stoke-on-Trent.

Northern Polytechnic, Holloway Rd, London, N7.

Nottingham Regional College of Technology, Burton St, Nottingham.

Plymouth College of Technology, Tavistock Rd, Plymouth.

Polytechnic, 309 Regent St, London, W1.

Portsmouth College of Technology, Hampshire Terrace, Portsmouth, Hants.

Rugby College of Engineering Technology, Eastlands, Rugby.

Rutherford College of Technology, Ellison Pl., Newcastle upon Tyne, 1.

Sir John Cass College, Jewry St, London, EC3.

Sunderland Technical College, Chester Rd, Sunderland, Co. Durham.

West Ham College of Technology, Romford Rd, Stratford, London, E15.

Woolwich Polytechnic, Wellington St, Woolwich, London, SE18.

10. ADULT EDUCATION

University departments of extra-mural studies and adult education

England

Oxford: Delegacy for Extra-Mural Studies, Rewley House, Wellington Square, Oxford.

Cambridge: Board of Extra-Mural Studies, Stuart House, Mill Lane, Cambridge.

London: Department of Extra-Mural Studies, University of London, 7 Ridgmount St, WC1.

Durham: Delegacy for Extra-Mural Studies, 32 Old Elvet, Durham.

Birmingham: Department of Extra-Mural Studies, PO Box 363, The University, Birmingham, 15.

Bristol: Department of Extra-Mural Studies, The University, Bristol.

Exeter: Department of Extra-Mural Studies, The University, Exeter.

Hull: Department of Adult Education, The University, Hull.

Keele: Department of Extra-Mural Studies, The University, Keele, Staffs.

Leeds: Department of Adult Education and Extra-Mural Studies, The University, Leeds, 2.

Leicester: Department of Adult Education, The University, Leicester.

Liverpool: Department of Extra-Mural Studies, 9 Abercromby Sq., Liverpool.

Manchester: Department of Extra-Mural Studies, The University, Manchester, 13.

Newcastle: Department of Adult Education, The University, Newcastle upon Tyne.

Nottingham: Department of Adult Education, 14–22 Shakespeare St, Nottingham.

Reading: The University, Reading.

Sheffield: Department of Extra-Mural Studies, The University, Sheffield.

Southampton: Department of Extra-Mural Studies, University of Southampton.

Wales

University Extension Board, University Registry, Cathays Pk, Cardiff.

Aberystwyth: University College, Aberystwyth.

Bangor: University College, Bangor.

Cardiff: University College, Cardiff, Department of Extra-Mural Studies, 38–40 Park Pl., Cathays Pk, Cardiff.

Swansea: University College, Swansea.

Scotland

Edinburgh: Department of Adult Education and Extra-Mural Studies, The University, Edinburgh.

Glasgow: Department of Extra-Mural Education, 57–9 Oakfield Ave, Glasgow, W2.

St Andrews: Department of Extra-Mural Education, The University, St Andrews.

Aberdeen: Department of Extra-Mural Studies, The University, Aberdeen.

Northern Ireland

Belfast: Queen's University, Department of Extra-Mural Studies and Adult Education.

Educational centres (Residential Colleges for adult education offering courses of one year or longer)

England

Co-operative College, Stanford Hall, Loughborough, Leics. (M/W).

Fircroft College, Selly Oak, Birmingham, 29 (M).

Hillcroft Residential College for Women, Surbiton, Surrey.

Plater College, Boars Hill, Oxford (M/W).

Ruskin College, Oxford (M/W).

Woodbrooke, 1046 Bristol Rd, Selly Oak, Birmingham, 29. Quaker foundation for Religious, Social and International Studies (M/W). Shorter courses also available.

Wales

Coleg Harlech, Harlech, Merioneth (M/W).

Scotland

Newbattle Abbey College, Dalkeith, Midlothian (M/W).

Residential colleges offering shorter courses

Attingham Park, nr Shrewsbury (Shropshire Adult College).

Avoncroft Residential Centre for Short Courses, Stoke Prior, nr Bromsgrove, Worcs.

Belstead House, nr Ipswich, Suffolk.

Braziers Park, Ipsden, Oxon.

Borton Manor, Neston, Wirral, Cheshire.

Debden House, Debden Green, Loughton, Essex (Newnham Education Committee).

Denman College, Marcham, Abingdon, Berks (NFWI).

Dillington House, nr Ilminster, Somerset.

Dunford House, Midhurst, Sussex (YMCA Adult Education and Training Centre).

Granley Hall, nr Ripon, Yorks.

Holly Royde College (of Manchester University Extra-Mural Dept), 56–62 Palatine Rd, West Didsbury, Manchester, 20.

Kingsgate College, Broadstairs, Kent (YMCA College for Adults).

Knuston Hall, Irchester, Wellingborough, Northants.

Missenden Abbey, Great Missenden, Bucks.

Moor Park College, Farnham, Surrey.

Offley Place, nr Hitchin, Herts.

Pendrell Hall College, Codsall Wood, nr Wolverhampton (LEA).

Roffey Park Institute, Horsham, Sussex.

University College, Cambridge (10 places reserved each term for YMCA students from industry and commerce; two months general cultural course).

Urchfont Manor, Devizes, Wilts.

Wansfell College, Theydon Bois, Epping.

Wedgwood Memorial College, Barlaston, nr Stoke-on-Trent.

Westham House, Barford, nr Warwick.

Principal university settlements and adult education centres

Birmingham: Birmingham Settlement, 318 Summer Lane, Birmingham, 19 and 610 Kingstanding Rd, Birmingham, 22.

Boston: Department of Adult Education, University of Nottingham, Pilgrim College.

Bradford: University Adult Education Centre, 10 Mornington Villas, Manningham Lane, Bradford, 8 (Dept of Adult Education and Extra-Mural Studies, University of Leeds).

Bristol: The Folk House, 40 Park St; Headquarters, 43 Ducie Rd, Barton Hill.

Dundee: Grey Lodge Settlement, Wellington St.

Edinburgh: Edinburgh University Settlement, Cameron House, Prestonfield; Adult Education Centre, Kirk o'Field College, Morton House, Blackfriars St, Edinburgh, 1.

Leeds: Swarthmore Educational Centre, 3–5 Woodhouse Sq., Leeds, 3.

Leicester: Vaughan College.

Liverpool: Nile Street Centre; Victoria Settlement, 294 Netherfield Rd N, Liverpool, 5.

London: Bedford Institute Association, 128A Hoxton St, N1 (Friends' centres at Barking, Bethnal Green, Clerkenwell, Hoxton, Walthamstow); Bermondsey Settlement, Scott Lidgett Cres., SE16; Bernhard Baron St George's Jewish Settlement, Henriques St, E1; Blackfriars Settlement (formerly Women's University Settlement) 44 Nelson Sq., SE1; Cambridge House, 131–139 Camberwell Rd, SE5; City Literary Institute, Stukeley St, WC2.

Dockland Settlements: Isle of Dogs, E14; Rotherhithe, SE16; Stratford, E15; also at Bristol; Devonport; Dagenham Rock and Hainault, Essex; Rossshire (School of Adventure); Herne Bay, Kent (Holiday Home); Gen. Sec.: R. W. Logan-Hunt, 164 Romford Rd, Stratford, E15.

Goldsmiths' College, New Cross, SE14; Mansfield House, Fairbairn Hall, E13; Morley College, 61 Westminster Bridge Rd, SE1; Oxford House in Bethnal Green, Inc., Mape St, E2; Poplar House Presbyterian Settlement and Training Centre, 56–58 East India Dock Rd, E14; Robert Browning Settlement, Browning St, Walworth, SE17; Roland House (Scout Centre), 29 Stepney Green, E1; St Margaret's House Settlement, 21 Old Ford Rd, Bethnal Green, E2; Toynbee Hall, The Universities' Settlement in East London, 28 Commercial St, Whitechapel, E1; Working Men's College, Crowndale Rd, NW1.

Loughborough: Quest House, Loughborough Technical College, Radmoor.

Manchester: Round House, 20 Every St, Ancoats, Manchester, 4.

Middlesbrough: Middlesbrough Settlement Community Centre, 132 Newport Rd; Middlesbrough University Adult Education Centre, 37 Harrow Rd, Linthorpe (Department of Adult Education and Extra-Mural Studies, University of Leeds).

Spennymoor, Co. Durham; Spennymoor Settlement, 58 King St.

Wilmslow, Ches.: The Wilmslow Guild, 1 Bourne St.

York: York Educational Settlement, Holgate Hill.

11. EXAMINING BODIES

General Certificate of Education

Associated Examining Board for the General Certificate of Education: Sec. B. C. Lucia, BSc, Wellington House, Station Rd, Aldershot, Hants.

Cambridge Local Examinations Syndicate: Sec. T. S. Wyatt, MA, MLitt, Syndicate Buildings, 17 Harvey Rd, Cambridge.

Joint Matriculation Board (The Universities of Manchester, Liverpool, Leeds, Sheffield and Birmingham): Sec. R. Christopher, BA, MEd, Manchester, 15.

University Entrance and School Examinations Council, University of London: Sec. G. Bruce, MA, Senate House, London, WC1.

Oxford and Cambridge Schools Examination Board: Secs. A. E. E. McKenzie, MA, 10 Trumpington St, Cambridge; and J. M. Todd, MA, Elsfield Way, Oxford.

Oxford Local Examinations: Sec. J. R. Cummings, Delegacy of Local Examinations, Summertown, Oxford.

Southern Universities' Joint Board for School Examinations (Universities of Bristol, Exeter, Reading, Southampton and Surrey): The Secretary, 22 Berkeley Sq, Bristol, 8.

Welsh Joint Education Committee: Sec. D. Andrew Davies, BA, 30 Cathedral Rd, Cardiff.

Certificate of Secondary Education: Regional Examining Boards

South Western Examinations Board (Cornwall, Devonshire, Gloucestershire, Somerset, Wiltshire, Bath, Bristol, Exeter, Gloucester, Plymouth): Sec. H. L. M. Household, BSc(Econ), 23–29 Marsh St, Bristol, 1.

Southern Regional Examinations Board (Berkshire, Buckinghamshire, Dorset, Hampshire, Isle of Wight, Oxfordshire, West Sussex, Bournemouth, Oxford, Portsmouth, Reading, Southampton, Guernsey, Jersey, Service Children Overseas): Sec. D. C. Spencer, DFM, MA, 53 London Rd, Southampton.

South-East Regional Examinations Board (Kent, Surrey, East Sussex, Bexley, Bromley, Kingston upon Thames, Merton, Richmond upon Thames, Sutton, Brighton, Canterbury, Eastbourne, Hastings): Sec. P. N. Anderson, BA, Beloe House, 2 and 4 Mount Ephraim Rd, Tunbridge Wells, Kent.

Metropolitan Regional Examinations Board (Inner London Education Authority, Croydon, Newham): Sec. D. H. Board, MA, 23–24 Henrietta St, London, WC2.

Middlesex Regional Examining Board (Barnet, Finchley, Friern Barnet and Hendon), Brent, Ealing, Enfield, Haringey, Harrow, Hillingdon, Hounslow, Richmond upon Thames (Twickenham)): Sec. W. J. Leake, BA, The Old Court House, High St, Wealdstone, Harrow, Middlesex.

East Anglian Examinations Board: Northern Sub Region—Bedfordshire, Cambridgeshire and Isle of Ely, East Suffolk, Huntingdon and Peterborough, Norfolk, West Suffolk, Great Yarmouth, Ipswich, Luton, Norwich. Southern Sub Region—Essex, Hertfordshire, Southend, Greater London Boroughs of Barking, Barnet (part), Havering, Redbridge, Waltham Forest: Sec. A. Johnson, MSc, 'The Lindens', Lexden Rd, Colchester, Essex.

West Midlands Examinations Board (Herefordshire, Shropshire, Staffordshire, Warwickshire, Worcestershire, Birmingham, Burton-on-Trent, Coventry, Dudley, Warley, Solihull, Stoke-on-Trent, Walsall, West Bromwich, Wolverhampton, Worcester): Sec. J. Aspinwall, FCIS, Norfolk House, Smallbrook, Ringway, Birmingham, 5.

East Midlands Regional Examinations Board (Derbyshire, Leicestershire, Lincolnshire (Holland), Lincolnshire (Kesteven), Northamptonshire, Nottinghamshire, Rutland, Derby, Grimsby, Leicester, Lincoln, Northampton, Nottingham): Sec. W. C. Watterson, BSc, Robins Wood House, Robins Wood Rd, Aspley, Nottingham.

North Western Secondary Schools Examinations Board (Cheshire, Isle of Man, Lancashire, Barrow-in-Furness, Birkenhead, Blackburn, Blackpool, Bootle, Burnley, Bury, Chester, Liverpool, St Helens, Southport, Stockport, Wallasey, Warrington, Wigan): Sec. I. K. Jackson, BSc, PhD, Africa House, 54 Whitworth St, Manchester, 1.

Associated Lancashire Schools Examining Board (Bolton, Manchester, Oldham, Preston, Rochdale, Salford): Sec. P. Lawrence, BA, MA(Econ), 77 Whitworth St, Manchester, 1.

West Yorkshire and Lindsey Regional Examining Board (Lincolnshire (Lindsey), Yorkshire (West Riding), Barnsley, Doncaster, Rotherham, Sheffield): Sec. R. G. Capes, MA, LlB, Barrister-at-Law, Scarsdale House, 136 Derbyshire La., Sheffield, 8.

Yorkshire Regional Examinations Board (East Riding, North Riding, Bradford, Dewsbury, Halifax, Huddersfield, Hull, Leeds, Wakefield, York): Sec. J. Pare, MA, 7–9 Cambridge Rd, Harrogate, Yorks.

North Regional Examinations Board (Cumberland, Durham, Northumberland, Westmorland, Carlisle, Darlington, Gateshead, Middlesbrough, Newcastle upon Tyne, South Shields, Sunderland, Tynemouth, West Hartlepool): Sec. J. A. Winterbottom, BA, Neville Hall, Westgate Rd, Newcastle upon Tyne, 1.

Welsh Joint Education Committee (Wales, Monmouthshire): Sec. D. Andrew Davies, BA, 30 Cathedral Rd, Cardiff.

Technical education

City and Guilds of London Institute, 76 Portland Pl, London, W1.

Art School, 122–124 Kennington Park Rd, London, SE11.

Regional Examining Unions

East Midland Educational Union: Sec. W. C. Watterson, BSc, Robins Wood House, Robins Wood Rd, Apsley, Nottingham.

Northern Counties Technical Examinations Council: Sec. A. T. Morrison, 5 Grosvenor Villas, Grosvenor Rd, Newcastle upon Tyne, 2.

Union of Educational Institutions: Sec. J. Aspinwall, FCIS, Norfolk House, Smallbrook, Ringway, Birmingham, 5.

Union of Lancashire and Cheshire Institutes: Sec. I. K. Jackson, BSc, PhD, Africa House, 54 Whitworth St, Manchester, 1.

Yorkshire Council for Further Education: Sec. A. Fieldsend, BA, Bowling Green Terr., Jack La., Leeds, 11.

Other bodies

College of Preceptors: Sec. J. Vincent

Chapman, FCP, 2 and 3 Bloomsbury Sq, London, WC1.

London Chamber of Commerce (Incorporated): Principal, R. K. Brown, Commercial Education Dept, 69 Cannon St, London, EC4.

Royal Society of Arts: Sec. G. E. Mercer, BA, John Adam St, Adelphi, London, WC2. Principal, Examinations Department, F. A. Wheeler, 18 Adam St, Adelphi, London. WC2.

Various professional bodies covered individually in this book conduct their own examinations.

Scotland

Scottish Certificate of Education Examination Board: Director, 140 Causewayside, Edinburgh, 9.

Scottish Universities Entrance Board (Preliminary Examination): Sec. C. W. Michie, CMG, OBE, MA, Kinburn House, St Andrews, Fife.

Scottish Association for National Certificates and Diplomas: Sec. J. F. Walker, BSc, FRIC, FEIS, 38 Queen St, Glasgow, C1.

12. MEMBERS OF THE EDUCATIONAL GROUP OF THE PUBLISHERS' ASSOCIATION

George Allen & Unwin Ltd, 40 Museum St, London, WC1.

Allman & Son (Publishers) Ltd, 50 Grafton Way, Fitzroy Sq., London, W1.

E. J. Arnold & Son Ltd, Butterley St, Leeds, 10.

Edward Arnold (Publishers) Ltd, 41 and 43 Maddox St, London, W1, PO Box 482.

Athlone Press of the University of London, 2 Gower St, London, WC1.

Barrie & Rockcliff (Barrie Books Ltd), 2 Clement's Inn, London, WC2.

G. Bell & Sons Ltd, York House, Portugal St, London, WC2.

A. & C. Black Ltd, 4, 5 and 6 Soho Sq., London, W1.

Blackie & Son Ltd, Bishopbriggs, Glasgow.

Basil Blackwell & Mott Ltd, 49 Broad St, Oxford.

Blond Educational Ltd, 56 Doughty St, London, WC1 and Iliffe House, Iliffe Ave, Oadby, Leicester.

Cambridge University Press, 200 Euston Rd, London, NW1.

Cassell & Co Ltd, 35 Red Lion Sq., London, WC1.

W. & R. Chambers Ltd, 6 Dean St, London, W1 and 11 Thistle St, Edinburgh.

Chatto & Windus Ltd, 42 William IV St, London, WC2.

Chatto & Windus (Educational) Ltd, 40–42 William IV St, London, WC2.

Collet's Holdings Ltd, Denington Estate, Wellingborough, Northants.

Collier-Macmillan Ltd, 10 South Audley St, London, W1.

Wm. Collins, Sons & Co Ltd, 144 Cathedral St, Glasgow, C4; and 14 St James's Pl, London, SW1.

Davis & Moughton Ltd, Ludgate House, 23-25 Waterloo Pl, Leamington Spa.

J. M. Dent & Sons Ltd, Aldine House, Bedford St, London, WC2.

Dryad Ltd, Northgates, Leicester; and 22 Bloomsbury St, London, WC1.

Gerald Duckworth & Co Ltd, 3 Henrietta St, London, WC2.

Educational Explorers Ltd, 40 Silver St, Reading, Berks.

Educational Productions Ltd, East Ardsley, Wakefield, Yorks; and 17 Denbigh St, London, SW1.

The Educational Supply Association Ltd, Pinnacles, Harlow, Essex.

The English Universities Press Ltd, St Paul's House, Warwick La, London, EC4.

Evans Bros Ltd, Montague House, Russell Sq., London, WC1.

Faber & Faber Ltd, 24 Russell Sq., London, WC1.

Robert Gibson & Sons Glasgow Ltd, 2 West Regent St, Glasgow, C2.

George Gill & Sons Ltd, 67-68 Chandos Pl, London, WC2.

Ginn & Co Ltd, 18 Bedford Row, London, WC1.

Grant Educational Co, 91-95 Union St, Glasgow, C1.

Hachette, 4 Regent Pl, London, W1.

Hamilton (Hamish) Ltd, 90 Great Russell St, London, WC1.

George G. Harrap & Co Ltd, 182 High Holborn, London, WC1.

Rupert Hart-Davis Educational Publications Ltd, 1-3 Upper James St, London, W1.

Heinemann Educational Books Ltd, 48 Charles St, London, W1.

Holmes McDougall Ltd, 30 Royal Terr, Edinburgh; Glasgow Branch, W. & R. Holmes (Books), 98-100 Holm St, Glasgow, C2.

Hulton Educational Publications Ltd, Alan House, 55-59 Saffron Hill, London, EC1.

Hutchinson Educational Ltd, 178-202 Great Portland St, London, W1.

Iliffe Books Ltd, 42 Russell Sq., London, WC1. *Sales Dept* Dorset House, Stamford St, London, SE1.

W. & A. K. Johnston & G. W. Bacon Ltd, Edina Works, Easter Rd, Edinburgh; and 30 Museum St, London, WC1.

Longmans, Green & Co Ltd, 48 Grosvenor St, London, W1.

McGraw-Hill Publishing Co Ltd, McGraw-Hill House, Shoppenhangers Rd, Maidenhead, Berks.

Macmillan & Co Ltd, 3, 4, 5 Little Essex St, London, WC2.

The Medici Society Ltd, 34-42 Pentonville Rd, London, N1.

Methuen & Co Ltd, 11 New Fetter La, London, EC4.

Mills & Boon Ltd, 50 Grafton Way, Fitzroy Sq., London, W1.

Frederick Muller Ltd, Ludgate House, 110 Fleet St, London, EC4.

John Murray (Publishers) Ltd, 50 Albemarle St, London, W1.

Thomas Nelson & Sons Ltd, 36 Park St, Park La, London, W1; and Lincoln Way, Windmill Rd, Sunbury-on-Thames, Middx.

Newnes Educational Publishing Co Ltd, Tower House, Southampton St, London, WC2.

James Nisbet & Co Ltd, Digswell Pl, Welwyn, Herts.

Novello & Co Ltd, Borough Green, Sevenoaks, Kent; and 27-28 Soho Sq., London, W1.

Oliver & Boyd Ltd, Tweeddale Court, Edinburgh, 1; and 39a Welbeck St, London, W1.

The Oxford University Press, Education Dept, Walton St, Oxford.

Penguin Books Ltd, Education Dept, Morton Rd, West Drayton, Middx.

Pergamon Press Ltd, Headington Hill Hall, Oxford; and 4-5 Fitzroy Sq., London, W1.

George Philip & Son Ltd, 98 Victoria Rd, London, NW10.

Philograph Publications, 69-79 Fulham High St, London, SW6.

Sir Isaac Pitman & Sons Ltd, 39 Parker St, London, WC2.

Prentice-Hall International Inc, Pegasus House, Golden La, London, EC1.

The Religious Education Press Ltd, Headington Hill Hall, Oxford.

Rivingtons (Publishers) Ltd, Montague House, Russell Sq., London, WC1.

Routledge & Kegan Paul Ltd, 68 Carter La, London, EC4.

Schofield & Sims Ltd, 35 St John's Rd, Huddersfield.

Student Christian Movement Press Ltd, 56-58 Bloomsbury St, London, WC1.

University of London Press Ltd, St Paul's House, Warwick La., London, EC4.

University Tutorial Press Ltd, 9-10 Great Sutton St, London, EC1.

Ward Lock Educational Co Ltd, Warwick House, 116 Baker St, London, W1.

Frederick Warne & Co Ltd, Bedford Court, Bedford St, Strand, London, WC2.

C. A. Watts & Co Ltd, 39 Parker St, London, WC2.

A. Wheaton & Co Ltd (a member of the Pergamon Group), Headington Hill Hall, Oxford.

13. MEMBERS OF THE EDUCATIONAL EQUIPMENT ASSOCIATION

Paul & Marjorie Abbatt Ltd, 94 Wimpole St, London, W1.

Addo Ltd, Addo House, 85 Great North Rd, Hatfield, Herts.

ADM Business Systems Ltd, ADM House, Northfield Av., London, W5.

Adventure Playthings Ltd, Queensway, Glenrothes, Fife.

George Anson & Co Ltd, Solway House, Southwark St, London, SE1.

E. J. Arnold & Son Ltd, Butterley St, Leeds, 10, Yorks.

Associated Adhesives Ltd, Distributive Div., 8th Avenue Works, Manor Park, London, E12.

Bible Lands Society, HighWycombe, Bucks.

Block & Anderson Ltd, Banda House, Cambridge Gro., Hammersmith, London, W6.

G. Blunt & Sons Ltd, North Acton Rd, London, NW10.

Bogod Machine Co Ltd (Bernina Sewing Machines), 50-52 Great Sutton St, London, EC1.

Boosey & Hawkes Music Publishers Ltd, 295 Regent St, London, W1.

Boosey & Hawkes (Sales) Ltd, Sonorous Works, Deansbrooke Rd, Edgware Middx.

Bristol Tutor Group, Mark La., Bristol, 1.

British Olivetti Ltd, 30 Berkeley Sq., London, W1.

British Pens Ltd (incorporating the Cumberland Pencil Co Ltd), 'Pedigree' Works, Bearwood Rd, Smethwick, 41.

British Sugar Bureau, Suite 11, 140 Park La., London, W1.

Brookwick Ward & Co, 8 Shepherds Bush Rd, London, W6.

A. Brown & Sons Ltd, Perth St West, Hull, Yorks.

Challenge (School) Products, 211-221 City Rd, Fenton, Stoke-on-Trent.

F. Chambers & Co Ltd, The Pencil Works, Stapleford, Nottingham.

Charles and Son Ltd, Woodbridge House, 1 Woodbridge St, Clerkenwell Grn, London, EC1.

Clarke & Smith Mfg Co Ltd, Melbourne Works, Melbourne Rd, Wallington, Surrey.

Colour-Factor Ltd (Mathematics), 72 London St, Reading, Berks.

Common Ground (1951) Ltd, 44 Fulham Rd, London, SW3.

Community Playthings, *See* Adventure Playthings.

John Compton Organ Co Ltd, Chase Rd, North Acton, London, NW10.

Cosmic Crayon Co Ltd, Ampthill Rd, Bedford.

Councils & Education Press Ltd, 10 Queen Anne St, London, W1.

Cuisenaire Co Ltd, The, 40 Silver St, Reading, Berks.

J. Curwen & Sons Ltd, 29 Maiden La., London, WC2.

G. Cussons Ltd, The Technical Works, Lower Broughton, Manchester, 7.

Dancer & Hearne Ltd, Penn Street, Nr Amersham, Bucks.

Dargue Bros Ltd, New Simplon Works, Halifax, Yorks.

Decca Radio & Television, 15 Ingate Pl., Queenstown Rd, London, SW8.

Diamine Ltd, Diamine Works, Tariff St, Liverpool, 5.

Dryad Handicrafts, Northgates, Leicester; and 22 Bloomsbury St, London, WC1.

Dunn & Wilson, Ltd, Bellevue Bindery, Falkirk, Scotland.

Eagle Pencil Co, 25 Ashley Rd, Tottenham, London, N17.

Educational & Municipal Equipment Ltd, Watersheddings Factory, Kilburn St, Oldham, Lancs.

Educational and Municipal Equipment (Scotland) Ltd, Blackaddie Rd, Sanquhar, Dumfries.

Educational Productions Ltd, East Ardsley, Wakefield, Yorks.

Educational Supply Association Ltd, School Materials Division, Pinnacles, Harlow, Essex.

E.S.A. Kingfisher (Furniture Sales Division), Esavian Works, Stevenage; Fenner Rd, Gt Yarmouth; Charles St, West Bromwich, Staffs; 121 Avenue St, Bridgeton, Glasgow, SE.

E.M.I. Records (The Gramophone Co Ltd), E.M.I. House, 20 Manchester Sq., London, W1.

Elington Industries Ltd, Nutsey La., Totton, Southampton.

Elite Optics Ltd, 354 Caerphilly Rd, Cardiff.

Ellams Duplicator Co Ltd, Walton Rd, Bushey Hall Rd, Watford, Herts.

Elliott-Automation Computers Ltd, Elstree Way, Borehamwood, Herts.

B. Elliott (Machinery) Ltd, Victoria Rd, London, NW10.

Encyclopaedia Britannica International Ltd, Dorland House, 18-20 Lower Regent St, London, SW1.

Essex Distributors (Colchester) Ltd, Chichester Canvas Works, Quarry La., Chichester, Sussex.

Esterbrook Pen Co Ltd, Moland St, Birmingham, 4.

Fitchett & Woollacott Ltd, Popham Street Works, Nottingham.

Fordigraph Educational Aids—Ofrex Ltd, Ofrex House, Stephen St, London, W1.

Galliard Ltd, 148 Charing Cross Rd, London, WC2.

James Galt & Co Ltd, ('Early Stages' Division), Brookfield Rd, Cheadle, Cheshire.

General Engineers Supply Co (1937), 555-7 High Rd, Leytonstone, London, E11.

G. B. Educational Equipment Ltd, Fresh Wharf Estate, Barking, Essex.

Joseph Gillott & Sons Ltd, Victoria Works, Birmingham Rd, Dudley, Staffs.

Globe Book Services Ltd, Brunel Rd, Basingstoke, Hants.

Goodsell Ltd, New England House, Brighton, 1, Sussex.

Gordon-Laycock Electronics Ltd, Birch House, Chipperfield, Herts.

Granada Educational Service, Sharston Rd, Wythenshawe, Manchester 22.

Grange Fibre Co Ltd, 13 Welford Rd, Leicester.

Grant Educational Co Ltd, 91-95 Union St, Glasgow, C1.

Granwood-Stonewood Ltd, Riddings, Derby.

Green Brothers (Geebro) Ltd, Hailsham. Sussex.

Griffin & George Ltd, Ealing Rd, Alperton, Wembley, Middx; Science Teaching Equipment Division, Frederick St, Birmingham.

Gymnastic Equipment Eng Co, Hampden Works, Clober Rd, Milngavie, Glasgow.

Geo. M. Hammer & Co Ltd, Crown Works, Hermitage Rd, Harringay, London, N4.

Harbutt's Plasticine Ltd, Bathampton, Bath, Som.

L. & C. Hardtmuth (Gt Britain) Ltd, Ashley Rd, Tottenham, London, N17.

Philip Harris Ltd, 63 Ludgate Hill, Birmingham, 3.

Helix (Universal) Co Ltd, Engine La., Lye, Stourbridge, Worcs.

Esmond Hellerman Ltd, Hellerman House, Sunbury Trading Estate, Windmill Rd, Sunbury on Thames, Middx.

G. D. Holder, White Lion Rd, Amersham, Bucks.

Thomas Hope & Sankey Hudson Ltd, Hope Mills, Pollard St, Manchester, 4.

Hostess Tubular Equipment Ltd, Vulcan Rd, Bilston, Staffs.

A. & F. Howland (Wycombe) Ltd, Eaton Avenue Works, High Wycombe.

Hulton Educational Publications Ltd, Alan House, 55-59 Saffron Hill, London, EC1.

Hunt and Broadhurst Ltd, Botley Rd, Oxford.

International Tutor Machines, Ashford Rd, Ashford, Middx.

Inveresk Paper Products (Cresco) Ltd, 214 Oxford St, London, W1.

Invicta Plastics Ltd, (Educational Aids Division), Oadby, Leicester.

Izal Limited, Thorncliffe, nr Sheffield.

S. C. Johnson & Son Ltd, Frimley Green, Camberley, Surrey.

Samuel Jones & Co Ltd, Butterfly House, Dingwall Rd, Croydon, Surrey.

Jupiter Recordings Ltd, 140 Kensington Church St, London, W8.

John T. Keep & Sons Ltd, Victor Paint Works, 15 Theobalds Rd, London, WC1.

Longmans Green & Co Ltd, 48 Grosvenor St, London, W1.

Kimberly-Clark Ltd, Larkfield, Maidstone, Kent.

Leeds Music Ltd, MCA House, 139 Piccadilly, London, W1.

Leighton Baldwin Cox & Co Ltd, Grovebury Rd, Leighton Buzzard, Beds.

Lines Educational Service Ltd (Lines Bros Group), Lavant, Chichester, Sussex.

London Showrooms, Triang House, Edgware Rd, London, W1.

Lion Ink Ltd, Century Works, Booth St, Walkden, Manchester.

Macmillan & Co Ltd, Little Essex St, London, WC2.

Magneta (B.V.C.) Ltd, Parsons Green La., Fulham, London, SW6.

Mann Egerton (Manufacturers) Ltd, Cromer Road Works, Norwich.

Mapograph Co Ltd, 440 High Rd, Chiswick, London, W4.

Margros division of Eagle Pencil Company London, N17 and Monument Way West, Woking.

E. Marshall Smith (School Utilities) Ltd, 5-9 Church La., Romford, Essex.

Mills Music Ltd, 20 Denmark St, London, WC2.

Minnesota Mining and Manufacturing Co, 3M House, Wigmore St, London, W1.

Mitre Sports, 56 Fitzwilliam St, Huddersfield.

Monitor Language Laboratories (Scrivener S. L. T. Ltd), 43-45 Queen's Rd, Bristol, 8.

Robert Morley and Co Ltd, 4 Belmont Hill, London, SE13.

Morol Ltd, Gresham Rd, Staines, Middx.

Morris Laboratory Instruments (Sales) Ltd, 96-98 High St, London, SW15.

Muldivo Ltd, 28-42 Banner St, London, EC1.

Necchi (Great Britain) Ltd, Diana House, 33-34 Chiswell St, London, EC1.

Thomas Nelson & Sons Ltd, 36 Park St, Park La., London, W1.

Nottingham Handcraft Co, Melton Rd, West Bridgford, Nottingham.

Parker-Knoll Contracts, The Courtyard, Frogmoor, High Wycombe, Bucks.

P.B. Educational Supplies Ltd (Educational Division of the Royal Sovereign Group of Companies), 83 Copers Cope Rd, Beckenham, Kent.

Perforated Front Projection Screen Co Ltd, 43-49 Higham St, Walthamstow, London, E17.

E. S. Perry Ltd, Osmiroid Works, Gosport, Hants.

Philip & Tacey Ltd (Philograph Publications Ltd), 69-79 Fulham High St, London, SW6.

Pictorial Charts Educational Trust, 132 Uxbridge Rd, West Ealing, London, W13.

Platignum Pen Co Ltd, Six Hills Way, Stevenage, Herts.

Progress Floor Treatments Ltd, Cressex Estate, High Wycombe, Bucks.

Pye T. V. T. Ltd, PO Box 41, Coldham's La., Cambridge.

Pyser-Britex (Swift) Ltd, Fircroft Way, Edenbridge, Kent.

Radio Rentals, Seymour Mews House, Wigmore St, London, W1.

Rank Organisation, The, Audio Visual Division, Woodger Rd, Shepherds Bush, London, W12.

R.C.A. Great Britain Ltd, Sunbury-on-Thames, Middx.

Reeves & Sons Ltd, Lincoln Rd, Enfield, Middx.

Remploy Ltd, Remploy House, 415 Edgware Rd, Cricklewood, London, NW2.

Reynolds & Branson Ltd, North West Rd, Leeds, 6.

Roneo Ltd, Roneo House, Lansdowne Rd, Croydon, Surrey.

George Rowney & Co Ltd, PO Box 10, Bracknell, Berks.

Royal Sovereign-Staedtler Ltd, 83 Copers Cope Rd, Beckenham, Kent.

Russell Bookcrafts, Hitchin, Herts.

Russell Kirby Ltd, Birchill Rd, Kirkby Industrial Estate, Nr Liverpool.

Sanders Papworth Music Co Ltd, 32 Alfreton Rd, Nottingham.

Scholaquip Industries Ltd, Manor La., Holmes Chapel, Ches.

The Schoolmaster Publishing Co Ltd, Hamilton House, Hastings St, London, WC1.

Seamer Products (Sculptorcraft) Ltd, 23-27 Eastbourne St, Hull, E. Yorks.

Singer Sewing Machine Co Ltd, Educational Dept, Singer Building, 1 City Rd, London. EC1.

Solarbo Ltd, Commerce Way, Lancing, Sussex.

Scientific Teaching Apparatus Ltd, Colquhoun House, 27-37 Broadwick St, London, W1.

South West Optical Instruments Ltd, Hoopers Pools, Southwick, Nr Trowbridge, Wilts.

Science Research Associates Ltd, Reading Rd, Henley-on-Thames.

Spencers of Enfield, Crown House, Southbury Rd, Enfield, Middx.

The Stephens Group (Henry C. Stephens Ltd); Drayton Park, London, N5.

Stephenson Arcade Ltd, Chesterfield, Derbys.

Taskmaster Ltd, (formerly H. C. P. (Products) Ltd), 165-7 Clarendon Pk Rd, Leicester.

Henry Taylor & Sons, 188-192 Hoe St, Walthamstow, London, E17.

H. Tempest Ltd, The Colour Laboratory, St Ives, Cornwall.

British Thornton Ltd, PO Box 3, Wythenshawe, Manchester, 22.

Time-Life International Ltd, Time & Life Building, New Bond St, London, W1.

Transart Ltd, Visual Education Division, Cambridge St, Godmanchester, Huntingdon.

Tutor-Tape Co Ltd, 2 Replingham Rd, London, SW18.

United Technical Supplies Ltd, 29 Tottenham Court Rd, London, W1.

Universal Edition (London) Ltd, (Alfred A. Kalmus, Ltd) 2-3 Fareham St, Dean St, London, W1.

USI Great Britain Ltd, Grosvenor House, 125 High St, Croydon, Surrey, CR9 IPP.

Venus Pen & Pencil Co Ltd, 169-171 Lower Clapton Rd, Clapton, E5.

Viking-Husqvarna Ltd, Viking House, 5-11 Worship St, London, EC2.

Visigraph Ltd, Rawberry St. Bromyard, Hertfordshire.

Wake & Dean Ltd, Avon Bldgs, Lower Bristol Rd, Bath, Som.

Westland Engineers Ltd, Yeovil, Som.

R. W. Whittle Ltd, P. V. Works, Monton, Eccles, Manchester.

Wholesale Libraries Ltd, Shire Works, Great Glen, Leics.

Wills & Hepworth Ltd, Derby Sq., Loughborough.

Wilson & Garden Ltd, Newtown St, Kilsyth, nr Glasgow.

Winsor & Newton Ltd, Wealdstone, Harrow, Middx.

Woodberry Bros & Haines Ltd, Springfield Rd, Highbridge, Som.

Woodfield & Stanley Ltd, Wakefield Rd, Moldgreen, Huddersfield.

14. EDUCATIONAL JOURNALS

AAM (Journal of the Association of Assistant Mistresses in Secondary Schools): Three times a year. Gordon Hse, 29 Gordon Sq., London, WC1.

Adult Education: Bi-monthly. National Institute of Adult Education, 35 Queen Anne St, London, W1.

Adult Education: Quarterly. Adult Education Association of the USA, 1225 19th St, NW, Washington, DC 20036.

AMA (Journal of the Incorporated Association of Assistant Masters in Secondary Schools): Eight times a year. 29 Gordon Sq., London, WC1.

Approved Schools Gazette: Monthly. Editor, Essex Home School, Chelmsford.

Art and Craft Education: Six times a year. Evans Bros, Montague Hse, Russell Sq., London, WC1.

Athene: Twice a year. Society for Education through Art, Morley College, 61 Westminster Bridge Rd, London, SE1.

Bacie Journal: Quarterly; members only. 16 Park Cres., Regent's Park, London, W1.

British Esperantist: Monthly. 140 Holland Park Ave, London, W11.

British Journal of Educational Psychology: February, June and November. Editor, Institute of Education, The University, Sheffield, 10

British Journal of Educational Studies: Twice a year. 24 Russell Sq., London, WC1.

British Journal of Sociology: Quarterly. Routledge and Kegan Paul Ltd, 68-74 Carter La., London; EC4.

Bulletin of Hispanic Studies: Quarterly. The University, Liverpool, 7.

Bulletin of Mechanical Education: Quarterly. Pergamon Press Ltd, Headington Hill Hall, Oxford.

Bulletin of Physical Education: Quarterly. Editor, Dept of Physical Education. The University, Liverpool, 7.

The Catholic Teacher: Three times a year. 23 Robin Hood Cres., Hall Green, Birmingham, 28.

Catholic Teachers Journal: Six times a year. St Mary's College, Strawberry Hill, Twickenham, Middx.

Child Education: Monthly. Montague Hse, Russell Sq., London, WC1.

The Commercial Teacher: Quarterly. 59 Arundel Dr West, Saltdean, Brighton, Sussex.

Comparative Education: Three times a year. Pergamon Press Ltd, Headington Hill Hall, Oxford.

Conference (Journal of the Headmasters' Conference): Three times a year. c/o The Master, Wellington College, Crowthorne, Berks.

DCTA (Journal of the Devon County Teachers Association): Three times a year. 18 Hill Cres., Pine Park, Honiton, Devon.

Education: Weekly. 10 Queen Anne St, London, W1.

Education for Teaching: Three times a year. Association of Teachers in Colleges and Departments of Education, 151 Gower St, London, WC1.

Education Today: Six times a year. 2 and 3 Bloomsbury Sq., London, WC1.

Education Today and Tomorrow: Five times a year. 16 King St, Covent Garden, London, WC2.

Educational Research (Journal of the National Foundation for Educational Research in England and Wales): Three times a year. The Mere, Upton Pk, Slough.

Educational Review: Three times a year. Education Dept, The University, Edgbaston, Birmingham, 15.

Educator: Six times a year. 48 Masons Hill, Bromley, Kent.

English Language Teaching (English as a Foreign or Second Language): Three times a year. Oxford University Press, Ely Hse, 37 Dover St, London, W1.

The Esperantist Teacher: Quarterly. 2 Hazel Grove, Hartwood Park, Chorley, Lancs.

Essex Education: Six times a year. Education Dept, County Hall, Chelmsford, Essex.

Focus on Education (Journal of the Conservative and Unionist Teachers' Association): Twice yearly. 32 Smith Sq., London, SW1.

Forum (for the discussion of new trends in education): Three times a year. 86 Headland Rd, Evington, Leicester.

Forward Trends (in the treatment of the backward child): Quarterly. 7 Albemarle St, London, W1.

Greece and Rome: Oxford University Press, Oxford.

Head Teachers Review: Quarterly. 29a The Broadway, Crawley, Sussex.

Health Education Journal: Quarterly. Central Council for Health Education, Tavistock Hse North, Tavistock Sq., London, WC1.

Higher Education Journal: Three times a year. Hamilton Hse, Mabledon Pl., London, WC1.

Historical Journal: Three times a year. Cambridge University Press, Bentley Hse, 200 Euston Rd, London, NW1.

Home Economics and Domestic Subjects Review: Monthly. 92a Kensington High St, London, W8.

Home Study: Quarterly. National Extension College, 8 Shaftesbury Rd, Cambridge.

Housecraft (Journal of the Association of Teachers of Domestic Science): Monthly. 10 Queen Anne St, London, W1.

The Humanist: Monthly. 40 Drury La., London, WC2.

Independent School: Three times a year. Max Ga., Burgh Hill, Etchingham, Sussex.

Institutional Management (Journal of the Institutional Management Association): Monthly. Swinton Hse, 324 Gray's Inn Rd, London, WC1.

International Journal of Educational Sciences: Quarterly. Pergamon Press Ltd, Headington Hill Hall, Oxford.

International Journal of Electrical Engineering Education: Quarterly. Pergamon Press Ltd, Headington Hill Hall, Oxford.

Journal of Biological Education: Four times a year. Institute of Biology and Academic Press, Berkeley Sq., London, W1.

Journal of the Institute of Education of the University of Newcastle upon Tyne: Five times a year. Institute of Education, St Thomas' St, Newcastle upon Tyne, 1.

Journal of the Institute of Mathematics and its Applications: Quarterly. Academic Press, Berkeley Sq. Hse, Berkeley Sq., London, W1.

Kent Education Gazette: Monthly. Kent Education Committee, Springfield, Maidstone, Kent.

Linguist: Monthly. 20 Grosvenor Pl., London, SW1.

London Linguist (Journal of the London Associations of Language Teachers): Editor, 5 North Side, London, SW4.

London Schoolmaster (Journal of the London Schoolmasters' Association): Monthly, except August. London Schoolmasters' Association, Flat 3, 8 Adamson Rd, London, NW3.

Mathematical Gazette: Quarterly. G. Bell and Sons Ltd, York Hse, Portugal St, London, WC2.

Mathematical Pie: Once a term. Mathematical Pie Ltd, 100 Burman Rd, Shirley, Solihull.

Mathematics Teaching: Quarterly. Vine St Chambers, Nelson, Lancs.

Minerva: Quarterly. Ilford Hse, 135 Oxford St, London, W1.

Modern Language Review: Quarterly. Shakespeare Institute, University of Birmingham, Birmingham, 15.

Modern Languages (Journal of the Modern Languages Association): Quarterly. 2 Manchester Sq., London, W1.

Music in Education: Bi-monthly. 27–8 Soho Sq., London, W1.

National Institute Economic Review: Quarterly. National Institute of Economic and Social Research, 2 Dean Trench St, Smith Sq., London, SW1.

New Era in Home and School: Ten times a year. 32 Earls Rd, Tunbridge Wells, Kent.

New Schoolmaster: Monthly, except August. National Association of Schoolmasters, Swan Court, Waterhouse St, Hemel Hempstead, Herts.

Oxford Magazine: Weekly during term. 1a Littlegate St, Oxford.

Parents' Review: Monthly. Murray Hse, Vandon St, London, SW1.

The Parent-Teacher: Twice a year. National Federation of Parent-Teacher Associations, 127 Herbert Gdns, London, NW10.

Physical Education: Three times a year. Ling Hse, 10 Nottingham Pl., London W1.

Pictorial Education: Monthly. Evans Bros, Montague Hse, Russell Sq., London, WC1.

Pitman's Business Education: Monthly. Sir Isaac Pitman and Sons Ltd, Pitman Hse, Parker St, London, WC2.

Pitman's Office Training: Weekly. Sir Isaac Pitman and Sons Ltd, Pitman Hse, Parker St, London, WC2.

Practical Education: Monthly. 3 Bitterne Way, Bitterne, Southampton.

Preparatory Schools Review: Three times a year. 212 Shaftesbury Ave, London, WC2.

Programmed Learning (Journal of the Association for Programmed Learning). Four times a year. 27 Torrington Sq., London, WC1.

Quarterly Journal of Mathematics: Quarterly. Clarendon Press, Oxford.

Quarterly Journal of Mechanics and Applied Mathematics: Quarterly. Clarendon Press, Oxford.

Review of English Studies: Quarterly. Clarendon Press, Oxford.

Review of Incorporated Association of Head Masters: Three times a year. 29 Gordon Sq., London, WC1.

School and College: Monthly. 18—20 York Bldgs, Adelphi, London, WC2.

School Buildings Equipment and Supplies: Quarterly. Darby Hse, 98 Kingston Rd, London, SW19.

School Government Chronicle: Monthly. Darby Hse, 98 Kingston Rd, London, SW19.

The School Librarian: Three times a year. School Library Association, Premier Hse, 150 Southampton Row, London, WC1.

School Science Review: Three times a year. 80 High St, Harrow-on-the-Hill, Middx.

Science Club: Six times a year. 60 Paddington St, London, W1.

Science Club Junior: Six times a year. 60 Paddington St, London, W1.

Science Teacher: Seven times a year. 60 Paddington St, London, W1.

Scottish Adult Education: Three times a year. Education Offices, Alloa, Scotland.

Scottish Educational Journal: Weekly. 46 Moray Pl, Edinburgh 3.

Scottish Educational Studies: Annually.

SSTA Magazine (Journal of the Scottish Secondary Teachers' Association): Three times a year. 15 Dundas St, Edinburgh, 3.

The Scottish Schoolmaster: Bi-monthly. 10 Atholl Cres., Edinburgh, 3.

Screen Education: Five times a year. 1 Nightingale Rd, Clapton, London, E5.

Seafarer: Quarterly. Seafarers' Education Service, Mansbridge Hse, 207 Balham High Rd, London, SW17.

Socialism and Education (Journal of the Socialist Educational Association): Termly. 38 Lidiard Rd, London, SW18.

Soviet Studies: Quarterly. The University, Glasgow, W2.

The Sower: Quarterly. 17—23 Denbigh Rd, London, W1.

Special Education (Journal of the Associaton for Special Education and Educational Journal of the Spastics Society): Quarterly. 12 Park Cres., London, W1.

Speech and Drama: Twice a year. St Bride Institute, Bride La., Fleet St, London, EC4.

Sport and Recreation: Quarterly. 26–29 Park Cres., London, W1.

Student News: Monthly. National Union of Students, 3 Endsleigh St, London, WC1.

Teacher Education: Three times a year. Institute of Education, University of London, Malet St, London, WC1.

The Teacher (Journal of the NUT): Weekly. Hamilton Hse, Hastings St, London, WC1.

Teacher in Commerce: Quarterly. 101 Greenbank Rd, Edinburgh, 10.

Teacher in Wales: Fortnightly. Caxton Press, Oswestry, Shropshire.

Teacher of the Blind: Quarterly. College of Teachers of the Blind, c/o Liverpool School for the Blind, Liverpool, 15.

Teacher of the Deaf: Six times a year. Oak Lodge, 103 Nightingale La., London, SW12.

Teachers World: Primary Education and *Teachers World: Secondary Education:* Weekly. Evans Bros Ltd, Montague Hse, Russell Sq., London, WC1.

Teaching Arithmetic: Three times a year. Pergamon Press Ltd, Headington Hill Hall, Oxford.

Technical Education and Industrial Training: Monthly. Montague Hse, Russell Sq., London, WC1.

Technical Journal: Monthly. Association of Teachers in Technical Institutions, Hamilton Hse, Mabledon, Pl., London, WC1.

Times Educational Supplement: Weekly. Printing Hse Sq., London, EC4.

Times Review of Industry and Technology: Monthly. Printing Hse Sq., London, EC4.

Topic Termly. Mathematical Pie Ltd, 100 Burman Rd, Shirley, Solihull.

Trends in Education (Journal of the DES): Quarterly. HMSO, Atlantic Hse, Holborn Viaduct, London, EC1.

UTU News (Journal of the Ulster Teachers' Union): Monthly. Imperial Bldgs, 72 High St, Belfast, 1.

Universities Quarterly: Quarterly. Turnstile Press, 10 Great Turnstile, London, WC1.

Use of English: Quarterly. Chatto and Windus, 42 William IV St, London, WC2.

Visual Education: Monthly. 33 Queen Anne St, London, W1.

Vocational Aspect of Secondary and Further Education: Three times a year. Pergamon Press Ltd, Headington Hill Hall, Oxford.

WEA News (Bulletin for students of the Workers' Educational Association). Twice a year. Temple Hse, 27 Portman Sq., London, W1.

Where: Six times a year. 57 Russell St, Cambridge.

World: Termly. Council for Education in World Citizenship, 93 Albert Embankment, London, SE1.

Yr Athro: Ten times a year. Undeb Cymru Fydd, 24 Ffordd y Mor, Aberystwyth.

15. SELECTED MUSEUMS AND ART GALLERIES

National museums

British Museum, Great Russell St, London, WC1.

Victoria and Albert Museum, Cromwell Rd, London, SW7.

Royal Scottish Museum, Chambers St, Edinburgh, 1.

National Museum of Wales, Cathays Pk, Cardiff.

Ulster Museum, Stranmillis, Northern Ireland.

Agriculture

Agricultural Museum, Wye College, Wye, Kent.

Rothamsted Experimental Agricultural Institute, Harpenden, Herts.

Reading University Dept. of Agriculture Museum, Reading, Berks.

Cambridge Agricultural Institute, Cambridge

The Curtis Museum, High St, Alton, Hants.

West Yorkshire Folk Museum, Shibden Hall, Halifax, Yorks.

The arts

National Gallery, Trafalgar Sq., London, WC2.

National Portrait Gallery, Trafalgar Square, London, WC2.

Tate Gallery, Millbank, London, SW1.

Victoria and Albert Museum, Cromwell Rd, London, SW7.

Wallace Collection, Hereford Hse, Manchester Sq., London, W1.

Sir John Soane's Museum, 13 Lincoln's Inn Fields, London, WC2.

Dulwich College Picture Gallery, College Rd, London, SE21.

The Queen's Gallery, Buckingham Palace, Buckingham Palace Rd, London, SW1.

Courtauld Institute Galleries, Woburn Sq., London, WC1.

National Gallery of Scotland, The Mound, Edinburgh, 1.

Scottish National Portrait Gallery, Queen St, Edinburgh, 2.

Scottish National Gallery of Modern Art, Royal Botanic Gdns, Edinburgh.
City of Glasgow Art Gallery, Kelvingrove, Glasgow.
National Museum of Wales, Cathays Pk, Cardiff.
Fitzwilliam Museum, Trumpington St, Cambridge.
Ashmolean Museum, Oxford.
Museum of Eastern Art, Broad St, Oxford.
Bowes Museum, Barnard Castle, County Durham.
Walker Art Gallery, William Brown St, Liverpool.
City Art Gallery and Museum, Cartwright Hall, Bradford, Yorks.
Whitworth Art Gallery, Oxford Rd, Manchester.
Birmingham Art Gallery, Congreve St, Birmingham, 3.
Barber Institute of Fine Arts, The University, Birmingham, 15.
Norwich Castle Museum, Norwich.
Graves Art Gallery, Sheffield, 1.
City Art Gallery, Leeds.
City Art Gallery, Mosley St, Manchester.

Children's museums

Bethnal Green Museum, London, E2 (especially for dolls and dolls' houses).
Tollcross Museum, Tollcross Pk, Glasgow.
The Toy Museum (National Toy Collection), The Grange, Rottingdean, Brighton.
Museum of Childhood, High Street, Edinburgh.
Museum of Childhood and Costume, Blithfield Hall, nr Rugeley, Staffs.

Costume

Victoria and Albert Museum, Cromwell Rd, London, SW7.
Bethnal Green Museum, Cambridge Heath Rd, London, E2.
London Museum, Kensington Palace, Kensington Gdns, London.
Gallery of English Costume, Platt Hall, Rusholme, Manchester, 14.
Museum of Costume, Assembly Rooms, Bath.
Canongate Tolbooth, Edinburgh, 8.
Castle Howard Costume Gallery, Castle Howard, Yorks.

Furniture

Geffrye Museum, Kingsland Rd, London, E2.
Iveagh Bequest, Kenwood, London, NW3.
Old House, High Town, Hereford.
Georgian House, Great George St, Bristol.
Ham House, Petersham, Surrey.
Temple Newsam, nr Leeds.
The Pavilion, Brighton.

Geography

British Museum (Ethnographical Department), Great Russell St, London, WC1.

Imperial Institute, South Kensington, London, SW7.
Horniman Museum, London Rd, London, SE23.
Royal Geographical Society Museum, 1 Kensington Gore, London, W8.
Pitt Rivers Museum, Parks Rd, Oxford.
Cambridge University Museum of Archaeology and Ethnology, Downing St, Cambridge.
Pitt Rivers Museum, Farnham, Blandford, Dorset.

Medical

Wellcome Historical Medical Museum, Wellcome Bldgs, Euston Rd, London, NW1.
British Dental Association Museum, 63–64 Wimpole St, London, W1.
Gordon Medical Museum, St Thomas St, London, SE1.
University Medical School Museum, Hospitals Centre, Birmingham, 15.
Museum of the School of Hygiene, 126 Mt Pleasant, Liverpool.

Music and drama

British Piano Museum, 368 High St, Brentford, Middx.
Royal College of Music, Donaldson Museum, Prince Consort Rd, South Kensington London, SW7.
Geffrye Museum, Kingsland Rd, London, E2.
British Theatre Museum, Leighton Hse, 12 Holland Park Rd, Kensington, London, W14.
Royal Shakespeare Theatre Picture Gallery, Stratford-upon-Avon, Warks.

Natural history and geology

British Museum (Natural History), Cromwell Rd, London, SW7.
Royal Botanic Gardens, Kew, London.
Zoological Gardens, Regent's Pk, London, and in other big cities.
Geological Museum, Exhibition Rd, London, SW7.
Oxford University Museum, Parks Rd, Oxford.
Botanic Gardens, Oxford.
Cambridge University Museum of Zoology, Downing St, Cambridge.
University Botanic Gardens, Cambridge.
Birmingham City Museum, Department of Natural History, Congreve St, Birmingham, 3.
Cannon Hill Museum, Pershore Rd, Birmingham.
Geological Departmental Museum, The University, Edgbaston, Birmingham, 15.
Hancock Museum, Barras Bdge, Newcastle-upon-Tyne, 2.
Zoological Museum (British Museum, Natural History Department), Akeman St, Tring, Herts.

Marine Biological Station, Aquarium and and Fish Hatchery, Port Erin, Isle of Man.

Royal Scottish Museum (Natural History Department), Chambers St, Edinburgh, 1.

Robertson Museum and Aquarium, Marine Station, Keppel Pier, Mullport, Scotland.

National Museum of Wales, Cathays Pk, Cardiff.

Prehistory, early civilisation and ethnography

British Museum, Great Russell St, London, WC1.

Horniman Museum, London Rd, Forest Hill, London, SE23.

Pitt Rivers Museum, Parks Rd, Oxford.

Ashmolean Museum, Beaumont St, Oxford.

Fitzwilliam Museum, Trumpington St, Cambridge.

Birmingham City Museum, Congreve St, Birmingham, 3.

Bath Roman Museum, Abbey Churchyard, Bath.

Reading Municipal Museum, Blagrave St, Reading.

Avebury Manor, Avebury, Wilts.

Wells Museum, Cathedral Green, Wells, Somerset.

Yorkshire Museum, Museum St, York.

Roman Site and Museum, Corbridge, Northumberland.

Viroconium Museum, Wroxeter, Salop.

Verulamium Museum and Roman City, St Albans, Herts.

Museum of the Glastonbury Antiquarian Society, Glastonbury, Somerset.

National Museum of Antiquities of Scotland, Queen St, Edinburgh, 2.

City of Glasgow Corporation Museum, Kelvingrove, Glasgow.

National Museum of Welsh Antiquities, University College of North Wales, College Rd, Bangor.

Legionary Museum, Caerlon, Wales.

Science

Science Museum, Exhibition Rd, South Kensington, London, SW7.

Wellcome Historical Medical Museum, 183 Euston Rd, London, NW1.

Museum of the History of Science, Broad St, Oxford.

Whipple Museum of the History of Science, 14 Corn Exchange St, Cambridge.

Science and Engineering Museum, Exhibition Pk, Great North Rd, Newcastle.

Birmingham City Museum, Dept. of Science and Industry, Newhall St, Birmingham, 3.

Anatomical Museum, University New Bldgs, Teviot Row, Edinburgh, 8.

Social and domestic history

Victoria and Albert Museum, Cromwell Rd, South Kensington, London, SW7.

London Museum, Kensington Palace, London, W8.

Guildhall Museum, King St, Cheapside, London, EC2.

Public Record Office and Museum, Chancery La., London, WC2.

Cambridge and County Folk Museum, Cambridge.

Stranger's Hall Folk Museum, Charing Cross, Norwich.

York Castle Museum, Tower St, York.

Kent County Museum, Chillington Manor House, Maidstone, Kent.

Manx Village Folk Museum, Cregneash, Isle of Man.

National Museum of Antiquities of Scotland, Queen St, Edinburgh, 2.

Folk Museum, Kingussie, Inverness.

Welsh Folk Museum, St Fagan's, Glam.

List of Contributors

RENE ADAMS, University of London Teachers' Certificate. Lecturer, Leicester College of Domestic Science. Formerly Lecturer, Borthwick Emergency Training College. RA

G. E. ALLEN, MSc. Principal, Natural Science Department, Froebel Institute College of Education, London. Formerly Lecturer, Weymouth Training College. Author (with L. Morris) of *Water*. GEA

PROFESSOR W. H. G. ARMYTAGE, MA. Professor of Education, University of Sheffield. Author of *Heavens Below; Civic Universities; The German Influence on English Education; The French Influence on English Education; Four Hundred Years of English Education; Social History of Engineering; The Rise of the Technocrats*. WHGA

N. S. ASBRIDGE, MA. Senior Tutor-Librarian, Bingley College of Education, Yorks. Formerly Tutor-Librarian, Kingston upon Hull Regional College of Arts and Crafts. NSA

PROFESSOR K. AUSTWICK, MSc, PhD. Professor and Head of School of Education, Bath University. Formerly Lecturer and Senior Lecturer, Sheffield University; Deputy Director, Institute of Education, Reading University. Editor of *Teaching Machines and Programming*. KA

D. G. O. AYERST, CBE, MA. Former HM Inspector of Schools (Staff Inspector); Assessor to the Central Advisory Council for Education (England) for the Reports on *Early Leaving, 15 to 18* (Crowther), *Half our Future* (Newsom). Also formerly Headmaster, King Edward VII

School, Lytham, Lancs. Author of *Understanding Schools*. DGOA

NICHOLAS BAGNALL, BA. Education Correspondent, *Sunday Telegraph*. Editor, *The Teacher*, 1961–5. NB

DR. S. E. BARNES, MA, BSc, PhD. Senior Official, National Union of Teachers; Technical Adviser, Teachers' Panel of the Burnham (Main) Committee and the Officers' Panel of the Committee on Salary Scales and Service Conditions of Inspectors, Organisers and Advisory Officers of Local Education Authorities; Leader and Secretary, Teachers' Panel of the Burnham Committee for the Teaching Staff of Farm Institutes and for Teachers of Agricultural (including Horticultural) Subjects; Secretary, Staff Side, Joint Negotiating Committee for Salaries and Service Conditions for the Staffs of Approved Schools and Remand Homes; Secretary, Staff Panel, Joint Negotiating Committee for Youth Leaders and Community Centre Wardens; Member, Board of Management and Investment Committee, the Teachers' Family Benefits Scheme. Hon. Secretary, Public Service Pensioners' Council; Member, National Insurance Tribunal. SEB

FRANK BARRACLOUGH, CBE, MA. Consultant to Sir William Alexander, Secretary of the Association of Education Committees. Formerly Secretary for Education, North Riding of Yorkshire. Author (with Sir William Alexander) of *County and Voluntary Schools*. FB

871

GEOFFREY BEAGHEN, ATD. Director, Foundation Course in Art, Thurrock Technical College, Grays, Essex. Formerly Head of Art Department, Crown Woods School, London; Chief Examiner, LCC Pilot Scheme for CSE Art Examination; Member, Council and Executive, Society for Education through Art. GB

INSTRUCTOR REAR ADMIRAL A. J. BELLAMY, OBE, MA. Director, Naval Education Service, Ministry of Defence. Dean, RN Engineering College, Plymouth, 1956–60; Director (Personnel), Naval Education Service, 1960–3; Director of Studies, HMS Collingwood, 1963–5. AJB

J. BENJAMIN. Community Play Scheme organiser, London Borough of Camden. Formerly Project Leader, Grimsby Adventure Playground Association, 1955–9; Member, National Executive Committee, Youth Service Association; Course Tutor, Child Care and Social Studies Department, North Western Polytechnic. Author of *In Search of Adventure.* JB

M. C. M. BINKS, MBE, Teacher's Diploma, Domestic Subjects. Chief School Meals Organiser, Somerset County Council. Formerly School Meals Organiser, Durham and Gloucestershire. MCMB

PROFESSOR BERNARD R. BLISHEN, MA. Professor of Sociology and Dean of Graduate Studies, Trent University, Peterborough, Ontario. Formerly Research Director, Royal Commission on Health Services. Joint Editor, *Canadian Society.* BRB

EDWARD BLISHEN. Author and broadcaster. Formerly Teacher-Librarian, Archway Secondary School, Islington. Author of *Roaring Boys; Education Today* (with Brian Groombridge); *Town Story.* Editor of *The Oxford Book of Poetry for Children; Come Reading; Miscellany* (1–5). EB

SYDNEY BOLT, MA. Senior Lecturer in charge of Liberal Studies, Cambridgeshire College of Arts and Technology. Author of *The Right Response; Poetry of the 1920s; Twentieth Century Love Poetry.* SB

GEORGE BOTT, BA, Dip Ed. Senior English Master and Librarian, Cockermouth Grammar School, Cumberland; Book Editor, Scholastic Publications, London. Author of *George Orwell: Selected Writings; Shakespeare: Man and Boy; Read and Relate.* GBo

DEREK BOWSKILL, TC, RBTC. Head of the Department of Drama, Film and Television, Eastbourne College of Education. Formerly County Drama Adviser, Devon. DBo

DR R. D. BRAMWELL, MA, PhD. Principal, Newcastle upon Tyne College of Education. Author of *Elementary School Work, 1900–1925.* RDB

MICHAEL BRAWNE, MArch (MIT), AA Dip, ARIBA. Architect in private practice in London (Michael Brawne and Associates); Member of teaching staff, University of Cambridge School of Architecture. Director, AA/RIBA seminar on University Planning, University of Sussex, 1964. Author of *The New Museum*; Editor, *University Planning and Design.* MB

DR S. A. BRIDGES, MA (Glasgow), BSc, MA (London), PhD. Principal Lecturer in Education, Brentwood College of Education, Essex. Formerly Principal, Gombe Training College and Okene Training College, Northern Nigeria. SAB

DEREK BRYAN, MA, OBE. Visiting Lecturer in Chinese, Holborn College of Law, Languages and Commerce. Member of HM Foreign Service in China, 1933–51; First Secretary (Chinese Affairs), HM Embassy, Nanking and Peking, 1946–51. Author of *The Land and People of China.* DBr

C. R. BURROWS, Cert Ed. Headmaster, Rushey Mead Boys' School, Leicester. Formerly Deputy Headmaster, Moat Boys' (Intermediate) School, Leicester. CRB

DONALD BURROWS, FRCO, ARCM. Principal Lecturer in Music, Christ Church College, Canterbury. Formerly Music Master, Stansted County Secondary School, Essex; Senior Lecturer in Music, Padgate College, Lancs. DB

NADINE K. CAMMISH, BA, Cert Ed, Advanced Dip Ed. Lecturer in Modern Languages, Department of Education, University of Hull. NC

B. W. CANNING, BA, FRSA, FSCT. Principal, Secretarial and Training Division, Sir Isaac Pitman and Sons Ltd. Author of *Shorthand Teaching Technique; Principles of Teaching Applied to Shorthand*, etc. BWC

H. A. T. CHILD, BA. Until 1968 Joint Principal Dartington Hall School, Totnes, Devon. Formerly Senior Educational Psychologist, LCC. Editor of *The Independent Progressive School*. HATC

LOIS CHILD, MA. Until 1968 Joint Principal, Dartington Hall School, Totnes, Devon. Formerly part-time Lecturer in Education, Southlands Training College, Wimbledon. LAC

DAVID E. CLARK, Dip Arch, ARIBA. Assistant Group Leader, Notts County Architects Department. DEC

MAISIE COBBY, LCSM, LUD. Lecturer, Adjudicator and Examiner. Formerly Senior Inspector, Speech and Drama, LCC; Professor, Guildhall School of Music and Drama; Drama Adviser, Essex County Council. Author of *We Play and Grow*; co-author of *The Playmakers; Speaking Together; Adventures in Group Speaking*. MC

DR JEANETTE B. COLTHAM, MA, PhD. Senior Lecturer in Education, Department of Education, University of Manchester. JBC

J. C. DANCY, MA. Master, Marlborough College. Formerly Headmaster, Lancing College. Author of *The Public Schools and the Future*. JCD

PROFESSOR HARRY DAVIES, MA. Professor of Education and Director of the Institute of Education, Notting-ham University. Formerly Headmaster, Northallerton Grammar School; Headmaster, High Pavement School, Nottingham. Author of *The Boys' Grammar School; Culture and the Grammar School*. HD

COLONEL T. J. H. DAVIES, MA. Chief Inspector/Colonel (Research), DA Education's Inspectorate. TJHD

W. DAVIES, BSc. Lecturer in Mathematics, Middlesbrough College of Education. WD

JOAN A. M. DAVIS, BA, MA. Until 1967 Senior Lecturer in the Curriculum of the Secondary Modern School, Institute of Education, University of London. Formerly Headmistress, Sincil Bank Girls' Secondary School, Lincoln. JAMD

R. F. DEARDEN, BA. Lecturer in the Philosophy of Education, Institute of Education, University of London. Author of *The Philosophy of Primary Education*. RFD

ALEC DICKSON, MA, CBE. Hon. Director, Community Service Volunteers. Founder, Voluntary Service Overseas; Chief, UNESCO Fundamental Education Mission, Iraq, 1955–6; Founder-Principal, Man O' War Bay Training Scheme, Nigeria/ Cameroons, 1950–4. Author of *Count us in: A Community Service Handbook; School in the Round* (both with Mora Dickson). AD

W. J. DICKSON, BSc. Director of Education, County Armagh, Northern Ireland. WJD

DR JOHN DOWNING, PhD, BA. Senior Lecturer in Educational Psychology, Institute of Education, University of London; Visiting Professor of Educational Psychology, University of California, Berkeley, 1967–8. Author of *Evaluating the Initial Teaching Alphabet; The Initial Teaching Alphabet Explained and Illustrated; The International Reading Symposia*. JAD

L. J. DREW, MA, MEd. Director of Education, Swansea. Formerly Director of Education, Aberdeen;

Deputy Director of Education, Sheffield. LJD

DR CHARLES DUDDINGTON, MA, PhD, FLS, MIBiol. Senior Lecturer in Botany, The Polytechnic, Regent Street, London. Author of *Practical Microscopy; The Living World; Algae and other Seaweeds*. CD

ANTHONY DUNK, MSc, FGS. Senior Lecturer in Geology, College of St. Mark and St. John, London. Head of Geology Department, Queen Mary's Grammar School, Walsall. ADu

JOSEPH EDMUNDSON, MC, Dip PE. Organiser of Physical Education and Social Activities, The Polytechnic, Regent Street, London. Formerly Organiser of Physical Education, Middlesex County Council; Commandant, Mediterranean PT School. Author of *Technique in Physical Education; PE Teachers' Handbook for Primary Schools; PE Teachers' Handbook for Secondary Schools, etc*. JE

REESE EDWARDS, MA, MSc, MEd. Formerly Director of Education, Wigan. Author of *The Secondary Technical School; The Classification of Pupils for Secondary Education; Vocational and Occupational Guidance*. RE

R. P. A. EDWARDS, ALA. School Libraries Adviser, Leicestershire Education Authority. Formerly Librarian in charge of work with young people, Shoreditch, London. Author of *Words Your Children Use*. RPAE

H. L. ELVIN, MA. Director, Institute of Education, University of London. Director, Department of Education, UNESCO, 1950–6. Professor of Education with special reference to Education in Tropical Areas, Institute of Education, University of London, 1956–8. Author of *Education and Contemporary Society*. HLE

J. FAIRBAIRN. Principal Lecturer in Education, St John's College, York. Formerly Headmaster, Long Hembrough Primary School, Oxfordshire. JF

H. FAIRHURST, MA. Librarian, University of York. Formerly Deputy Librarian, University College of Rhodesia and Nyasaland. HF

S. H. FISHER. Deputy Editor, *Teachers World*. Formerly headmaster of LEA schools in Norfolk and Lincolnshire; head of a department in a college of education. Author of *Jam Jar Science; Changing Units and Decimal Currency —A Preliminary Survey*. SHF

PROFESSOR RONALD FLETCHER, BA, PhD. Professor of Sociology and Head of Department of Sociology, University of York. Formerly Lecturer in Sociology, University of London: Bedford and Birkbeck Colleges. Author of *Instinct in Man; Issues in Education; The Family and Marriage in Britain; Human Needs and Social Order; The Making of Sociology*. RF

PROFESSOR BORIS FORD, MA. Professor of Education and Dean of the School of Educational Studies, University of Sussex. Director, Bureau of Current Affairs, 1946–51; Information Officer, Technical Assistance Board, UN, 1951–3; Head of Schools Broadcasting, Associated Rediffusion, 1957–8; Education Secretary, Cambridge University Press, 1958–60; Professor of Education and Director of the Institute of Education, University of Sheffield, 1960–3. Edited *Young Writers: Young Readers; Pelican Guide to English Literature*. BF

K. E. FOSTER, ARIBA. Principal Architect, Department of Education and Science. LCC Architects' Department, 1954–61. KEF

STANLEY FOSTER, Director, University of London Press Limited; Chairman, Educational Group, Publishers' Association. SF

D. E. M. GARDNER, MA, National Froebel Union Higher Certificate and Diploma in the Training of Teachers. Formerly Head of the Department of Child Development, Institute of Education, University of London. Lecturer in Education, Bishop Otter College, Chichester, 1930–6; Head of the Department of Primary Education, City of Leeds Training College, 1936–42; Supervisor of Schools, Bolton, Lancs, 1942–3. Author of *The Children's Play Centre; The Role of the Teacher in the Infant and Nursery School, etc.* DEMG

C. J. GILL, CB, MA, BSc. Gulbenkian Lecturer in Education, University of Keele. Formerly HM Inspector of Schools; Chief Inspector with responsibility for teacher training. CJG

DR R. J. GOLDMAN, BA, BD, MA (Chicago), MA (Birmingham), PhD, NFF Teachers' Certificate, FPsSoc. Principal, Didsbury College of Education, Manchester. Formerly Senior Lecturer in Educational Psychology, University of Reading. Author of *Religious Thinking from Childhood to Adolescence; Readiness for Religion.* Editor of *Breakthrough: Autobiographies of Disadvantaged Children.* RJG

W. A. GRANDAGE. Driving School owner. RAC Registered Driving Instructor; MOT Approved Driving Instructor; Member, Institute of Advanced Motorists. WAG

NIGEL GRANT, MA, MEd. Lecturer in Education, University of Edinburgh. Formerly Lecturer in Education, Jordanhill College of Education, Glasgow. Author of *Soviet Education; Society, Schools and Progress in Eastern Europe.* NG

IVAN GRAY, MA, Dip Ed. Headmaster, Ackworth School, Pontefract, Yorks. Headmaster, Friends' School, Lisburn, Northern Ireland, 1952–61. IG

BRIAN GROOMBRIDGE, MA. Education Officer, Independent Television Authority. Formerly Deputy Secretary, National Institute of Adult Education. Author of *Education and Retirement; Education Today* (with Edward Blishen); *The Londoner and his Library.* BG

RONALD GULLIFORD, BA, Dip Ed Psych. Senior Lecturer and Tutor to the Diploma in Social Education, School of Education, University of Birmingham. Formerly Educational Psychologist, Bolton Education Committee; Lecturer, Centre for Child Study, University of Birmingham. Author of *The Education of Slow Learning Children* (with A. E. Tansley). RG

MELVILLE HARDIMENT, MBSocA. Head of Department of Social Education, The Robert Montefiore Secondary School, London. Author of *The Indestructibles; From Under the Desk.* MHa

R. A. HARRISON, MA. Headmaster, Marlborough House School, Hawkhurst, Kent, 1930–7. Until 1968 Treasurer and Secretary, Incorporated Association of Preparatory Schools. RAH

L. M. HARROD, FLA. Senior Lecturer (in charge of Course for Overseas Librarians), School of Librarianship, North Western Polytechnic, London. Formerly Director, National Library, Singapore; Chief Librarian and Curator, Islington Public Libraries, London. Author of *Librarians' Glossary . . . and Reference Book; Libraries of Greater London; Lending Library Methods.* LMH

M. T. HASKEW. Architect, Nottinghamshire County Council. MTH

ERNEST W. HAWLEY, MBICSc. Supervisor of Schoolkeepers and Cleaners, ILEA. Formerly Head of Schoolkeeping Department, London College of Printing. EH

HAROLD HAYWOOD. Director of Education and Training, National Association of Youth Clubs. Formerly Youth Tutor, Westhill College of Education. Author of *Young People Talking; The One Night a Week Club.* HH

DR JAMES HEMMING, BA, PhD. Educational psychologist. Author of *Democracy in School Life; Sixth Form Citizens; The Teaching of Social Studies in*

Secondary Schools; Problems of Adolescent Girls; Individual Morality. JH

GEOFFREY HERBERT, BA. Head of Economics Department, Northampton Grammar School. GH

J. HEYWOOD. Lecturer in Higher Education, University of Lancaster. JHey

G. A. HICKS, MCollH, Tech. Cert of the City and Guilds (Machine shop engineering). Principal Lecturer and Head of the Handicraft Department, University of London Goldsmiths' College. Assistant Examiner, Oxford GCE O level, Engineering Drawing; Chief Examiner, London GCE O Level Handicraft. Author of *Modern Technical Drawing* (2 vols). GAH

A. P. HIGGINS, BA. Headmaster, St Bernadette's Catholic School, Nottingham. Former Chairman, Society for Education in Film and Television. Author of *Talking about Television.* APH

PROFESSOR DENYS HINTON, AA Dip, FRIBA. Professor of Architecture, University of Aston in Birmingham. DH

MICHAEL HIRST, Diploma in Mathematics and its Teaching, Teachers' Certificate. Head of Department, Linwood Boys' School, Leicester. Author of *Technical Drawing.* MHi

E. J. HODGES, NDD (Sculpt), ATD. Art Department, Elliott School, Putney, London. EJH

DEREK J. HOLROYDE, BA. Director of Television, University of Leeds. Producer and Senior Producer, BBC North American and Overseas Service, 1949–53; BBC Representative, India and Pakistan, 1953–7; Producer and Executive Producer, BBC Television, 1958–65. Member, Government Advisory Committee on the University of the Air; UK Inter-Universities Working Party on Television Co-operation. DJH

PHILIP G. H. HOPKINS, BA, BSc (Econ). Warden and Principal, Fircroft College, Selly Oak, Birmingham. Formerly Lecturer, Southampton University Extra-mural Department;

Consultant in Workers' Education, International Labour Organisation and Ministry of Overseas Development. Author of *Manual on Workers' Education.* PGHH

D. L. HOWARD, BSc (Econ), JP. Lecturer in Sociology, Brighton College of Education. Formerly Assistant Education Secretary, National Marriage Guidance Council; Education Organiser, HM Borstal, Dover. Author of *The English Prisons; The Life of Britain; British Life and Institutions.* DLH

DR H. W. HOWES, CMG, OBE, MA, MSc, PhD, KSG. Author, examiner in English, lecturer. Formerly Director of Education in Gibraltar, British Honduras, Ceylon; UNESCO Adviser on Education with Caribbean Commission. Author of *Sacrament and Rite; Blackboard and Easel—Talks to Teachers; Survey of West Indian Education; Presenting Modern Britain; We go to Spain.* HWH

CHARITY JAMES, MA. Director, University of London Goldsmiths' College Curriculum Laboratory. Staff Officer in charge of ATS Education, 1941–5. Author of *Live Now, Live Later: A Policy for Secondary Schools.* CJ

MARK JAMES, MA. Head of Lower School, The Gordano School, Portishead, Somerset. Formerly Careers Master, Withywood School, Bristol. JMJ

WALTER JAMES, BA. Lecturer in Adult Education, Department of Adult Education, University of Nottingham. WJ

FRED JARVIS, MA, Social Science Certificate of Distinction, MIPR. Head of Publicity and Public Relations Department, National Union of Teachers. President, National Union of Students, 1952–4. Editor of *Youth Review, NUT Newsletter, NUT Guide to Careers for Young People,* etc. FJ

D. J. JOHNSTON, BA, FCP. Adviser to Teachers, Institute of Education, University of London. Author of

School Teaching as a Career; Who Dares to Teach. DJJ

JACK A. JONES, ACP. Editor, *The Parent-Teacher*; Officer, Executive Committee, National Federation of Parent-Teacher Associations; Deputy Headmaster, Istead Rise Junior School, Northfleet, Kent. Formerly Publicity Officer, National Federation of PTAs. JAJ

DR N. S. JUNANKAR, BA, BLitt, DPhil, FRSA. Formerly Deputy Educational Adviser, Indian Ministry of Education; Education Adviser, Indian High Commission, London; Professor of Logic and Philosophy, S.L.D. Arts College, Ahmedabad. Author of *A New Pattern of Education for India.* NSJ

ANTHONY KAMM, MA. Editor-in-Chief, Brockhampton Press; Chairman, Children's Book Group of the Publishers' Association. Author (with Boswell Taylor) of *Books and the Teacher.* AK

JAMES KENYON. Sales Director and Associate Editor, Blond Educational Ltd. JK

H. RAYMOND KING, CBE, DCM, MA. Chairman, English New Education Fellowship; Chairman, Editorial Board of *Forum*. Headmaster, Wandsworth School, London, 1932–63. Chairman, UK National Commission for UNESCO Text-Books Subcommittee, 1948–60; Adviser to Education Section, 1960–5. HRK

PROFESSOR SUMIE KOBAYASHI, PhD. Emeritus Professor and Lecturer, Keio University, Tokyo, Japan. Author of *An Encyclopaedia of Education; An Introduction to Educational Theory.* SK

PROFESSOR Z. E. KURZWEIL, DPhil, BA. Head of Department of General Studies and Teacher Training, Technion-Israel Institute of Technology, Haifa, Israel. Formerly Inspector, Central Council of Jewish Education, London. Author of *Modern Trends in Jewish Education; Anxiety and Education; Education in a*

Technological Society (in Hebrew); *In Defence of the Child* (in Hebrew). ZEK

DR ROYSTON LAMBERT, BA, MA, PhD. Fellow of King's College, Cambridge; Director, Research Unit into Boarding Education. Since 1968 principal, Dartington Hall School, Totnes, Devon Author of *Sir John Simon and English Administration; Nutrition in Britain, 1950–60; The State and Boarding Education; The Hothouse Society: Boarding Schools by Boarders.* RL

PROFESSOR J. A. LAUWERYS, DSc, DLitt, FRIC. Professor of Comparative Education, Institute of Education, University of London. Joint Editor, *World Year Book of Education.* Author of *Roots of Science; Morals, Democracy and Education.* JAL

DR SONYA LEFF, MB, BS, DCH, DPH. Medical Officer, London Borough of Camden. SL

HAROLD LEVY, MA. Inspector, Central Council for Jewish Religious Education. HL

PROFESSOR L. J. LEWIS, BSc, Dip Ed. Professor of Education and Head of the Department of Education in Tropical Areas, Institute of Education, University of London. Formerly Professor of Education and Director of the Institute of Education, University College, Ghana; Overseas Editor, Oxford University Press. Author of *Educational Policy and Practice in British Tropical Areas; Educational and Political Independence in Africa; The Management of Education* (with Loveridge); *Society, Schools and Progress in Nigeria.* LJL

LEONIE LICHTENSTEIN, BA. Lecturer, English Department, St Gabriel's College of Education, London. Formerly Tutor, English Department, Witwatersrand University, South Africa; Lecturer in English and Drama, Teachers' College, Bulawayo, Rhodesia. LL

P. C. J. LIKEMAN. Headmaster, County Secondary School, Olney, Bucks. PCJL

ERIC LINFIELD, MA. Senior Lecturer in Education, Newton Park College, Bath. Formerly Headmaster, Redlands Junior School, Fareham, Hants. EL

JOHN ANTHONY LLEWELLYN, BSc, FSS. Principal Lecturer in Computer Science, Constantine College of Technology, Middlesbrough. Member of the Council of the British Computer Society. JALl

I. L. M. LONG, MA. Lecturer in Geography, Institute of Education, University of London. Chief Examiner in Geography, University of London O Level Examination Board, 1961–5. Author of *Teaching Geography* (with B. S. Roberson). ILML

HELEN LOWENTHAL. Educational Adviser, National Trust. Museum Lecturer, Victoria and Albert Museum, 1952–66. HLo

T. J. MCELLIGOTT, MA, NUI, HDip Ed. Senior French Master, Mountjoy School, Dublin. Formerly Assistant Headmaster, Headfort House School, Kells, Co. Meath. Author of *French Essays for Schools; Education in Ireland.* TJM

DONALD MCLEAN. Education Correspondent, *Sydney Morning Herald,* Australia. Formerly School Principal; Lecturer in Child Welfare; Editor of Publications Department of Education, Sydney. Author of *No Man is an Island; Education of the Personality; Nature's Second Sun; The World Turned Upside Down; The Roaring Days.* DMcL

PHILIPPA MACLIESH, MA. Assistant Secretary, Society of Authors. PM

EDWIN MASON, MA. Director of Courses, Curriculum Laboratory, University of London Goldsmiths' College. Formerly Deputy Headmaster, Peckham Manor School, London. EM

ANGUS MAUDE, MP, MA. Formerly Chairman, Conservative Party Committee on Education. Author of *The English Middle Classes; Professional People; Good Learning.* AM

T. W. MELLUISH, MA. Senior Classics Master and Deputy Headmaster, Bec School, London, 1927–65. Honorary Secretary, The Classical Association, 1948–68; President, The Association for the Reform of Latin Teaching, 1965–8. Joint author of *Teach Yourself Greek; Catullus Selections.* TWM

D. J. MERRIMAN, Teachers' Dip. Head of Art Department, King Edward VII Upper School, Coalville, Leicestershire. DJM

JOHN E. MERRITT, BA, Dip Ed Psych, ABPsS. Lecturer in Education, Institute of Education, University of Durham. Formerly Senior Educational Psychologist, Kingston upon Hull. JEM

MARGARET MILES, BA, London Teachers' Certificate. Headmistress, Mayfield School, London. Formerly Headmistress, Pate's Grammar School, Cheltenham; Lecturer in Education, University of Bristol. Author of *And Gladly Teach; Comprehensive Schooling.* MM

YVONNE MILLWOOD. Information Officer, Consumer Council. Author of *About Buying School Uniform; About Buying Toys,* etc. YM

RICHARD F. MORGAN. General Secretary, National Rural Studies Association; Lecturer in Rural Studies, Chorley College of Education, Chorley, Lancs. Author of *Environmental Biology.* RFM

ALAN MORTON, MA. Principal, Danes's School of English, Hove, Sussex. Formerly British Council Representative, Mauritius. AMo

JOYCE MPANGA, BA, MSc (Ed). Lecturer in Education, Makerere University College, Uganda, until 1967. JM

ELIZABETH MUGRIDGE. Teacher, Fulham and South Kensington Institute and Beckenham Art Centre. EMu

D. E. MUMFORD, MA. Principal, Cambridgeshire College of Arts and Technology, Cambridge. Formerly

Assistant Education Officer, Shropshire. DEM

WILLIAM MURRAY. Headmaster, Westlands School, Cheltenham. Formerly Remedial Advisory Teacher, Devonshire. Author of *Key Words to Literacy* (with J. McNally); *The Ladybird Key Words Reading Scheme*. WM

WING COMMANDER G. W. E. NEWBY. RAF Educational Service, Ministry of Defence. GWEN

O. W. NEWPORT. Editor, Philatelic Magazine; Philatelic Correspondent, *Daily Telegraph* and *Sunday Telegraph*. OWN

P. S. NOBLE, BSc (Econ), Dip VG. Economics Teacher, Rickmansworth Grammar School; Hon. Sec., Association for the teaching of the Social Sciences. Formerly Head of Economics and Careers, Heriots Wood Grammar School, Stanmore; Assistant Youth Employment Officer, Middlesex. Author of *The Entrepreneur and the Market*. PSN

EDWIN PACKER, Dip Econ Pol and Social Studies. Head of Publications Section, Advisory Centre for Education, Cambridge. Author of *Social Work*. EP

LESLIE PAUL, MA, FRSL. Lecturer in Ethics and Social Studies, Queens College, Birmingham; Lecturer in Theology, University of Birmingham. Leverhulme Research Fellow, 1957–9; Research Fellow, King George Jubilee Trust and Industrial Welfare Society, 1960–1; Research Director, Church of England, 1961–4. Member, Albemarle Committee. Author of *Annihilation of Man; Angry Young Man; Reasons and Perceptions; Transition from School to Work; Deployment and Payment of the Clergy; Alternatives to Christian Belief*. LP

ELIZABETH M. PEPPERELL, OBE, Dip Soc (Sc), Mary MacArthur Scholar (1938). Assistant Director, The Industrial Society. Chief Personnel Officer, Carreras Ltd, 1940–51. Author of *Office Work—Selection and Training; School to Work—Guide to Supervisors; What they expect from Work; Using Secretarial Services*. EMP

A. D. C. PETERSON, MA. Director, Department and Institute of Education, Oxford. Formerly Headmaster, Adams Grammar School; Headmaster, Dover College; Deputy Director, Psychological Warfare, SEAC; Director, General Information Services, Malaya. Author of *The Far East; 100 Years of Education; The Future of Education*. ADCP

VIOLET PHILPOTT. Professional puppeteer. Instructor in Puppetry, ILEA. Member, Council of Educational Puppetry Association and Committee of the British Section of the Union International des Marionettes (UNIMA). VP

HUGH PIERCE, BA. Solicitor, National Union of Teachers. HP

HENRY PLUCKROSE. Headteacher, New Barbican Primary School, London. Formerly Deputy Head, Eveline Lowe School, London. Author of *Creative Art and Craft*. HPl

J. C. POULTON, Poly Dip ARIBA, Dip TP. Deputy Group Leader, Nottinghamshire County Council Architects' Department. JCP

JOHN B. PRIZEMAN, AADipl, ARIBA. Architect. Formerly Tutor, Architectural Association School of Architecture. Planned Trinidad City. Author of *Kitchens*. JBP

DEREK S. PUGH, MA, MSc, FSS, ABPsS. Reader in Organisational Behaviour, London Graduate School of Business Studies. Formerly Senior Research Fellow, Industrial Administration Research Unit, University of Aston in Birmingham. Joint author of *Writers on Organisations; Exercises in Business Decisions*. DSP

NEILL L. RANSOM. Head of Physics Department, Box Hill School, Mickleham, Surrey. NLR

P. RICHARDS-JONES, FRAS, MInst Nav, Master Mariner. Director of the Planetarium, Head of Astronomy and Nautical Studies, Wandsworth

School, London. Formerly Marine Superintendent, Walford Lines Ltd. PR-J

GEOFFREY RICHARDSON, BA, Dip Ed, MA. Senior Lecturer in Education, University of Hull. Lecturer in Education, University of Leicester, 1955–65. GR

DR A. J. RICHMOND, BSc, PhD, MIMechE. Principal, Lanchester College of Technology, Coventry. Senior Lecturer, Battersea Polytechnic, 1946–55; Head of Department of Mechanical Engineering, Welsh College of Advanced Technology, Cardiff, 1955–8. Author of *Applied Thermodynamics: Problems for Engineers* (with W. J. Peck); *Problems in Heat Engines*. AJR

P. E. RICHMOND, MA, BSc, AInstP. Lecturer in Education, Department of Education, Southampton University. Formerly Senior Science Master, Hayes County Grammar School, Middlesex. PER

W. KENNETH RICHMOND, MA, MEd. Senior Lecturer in Education, Glasgow University. Visiting Professor of Education, University of Texas, 1966. BBC Education Officer (Midlands), 1945–51. Author of *Readings in Education—A Sequence; The Teaching Revolution; Teachers and Machines; Culture and General Education; Education in the USA*. WKR

JOHN ROBINSON, MA. Further Education Liaison Officer, BBC. Formerly Area Further Education Organiser, East Sussex. Edited *Educational Television and Radio in Britain; New Media and Methods in Industrial Training*. JRo

F. RUBIN, BA, BSc, Dip Psych. Research Officer and Scientific Adviser, Sleep-Learning Association. Former adviser on personnel selection, Hungarian Armed Forces. Author of *Current Research in Hypnopaedia*. FR

DR W. G. A. RUDD, BA, MA (Ed), PhD. Senior Lecturer in Curriculum Development and Leader of the North West Regional Curriculum Development Project, University of Manchester. Lecturer in Education, St Lukes College, Exeter, 1954–7; Organising Tutor, School of Education, University of Manchester, 1958–65. WGAR

JOAN M. RUSSELL, FLG. Principal Lecturer and Head of the Dance Department, Worcester College of Education. Author of *Modern Dance in Education; Creative Dance in the Primary School*. JMR

K. V. RUSSELL, MEd, FBSC. Senior Lecturer in Education, City of Leicester College of Education; Secretary, Inter-Professional Committee Enquiring into Drug Abuse amongst Young People in Leicester City and County. Formerly Deputy Headmaster, Fir Tree County Infants, School, West Bromwich. Author of *Learning to Give* (with Dr J. D. Tooke). KR

DR W. BONNEY RUST, PhD, BSc (Econ), ACIS. Principal, West London College. Author of *Examinations: Pass or Failure?* WBR

MICHAEL SEGAL, BSc (Econ). Freelance television and film producer. Television Producer, Rediffusion Television, 1962–4; Head of Children's Programmes, Rediffusion Television, 1964–6. MS

ALD. C. H. SHEILL, KSG. General Secretary, Catholic Teachers Federation of England and Wales; Treasurer, World Union of Catholic Teachers. CHS

PROFESSOR BRIAN SIMON, MA. Professor of Education, University of Leicester. Author of *Intelligence Testing and the Comprehensive School; The Common Secondary School; Studies in the History of Education, 1780–1870; Education and the Labour Movement, 1870–1920*. BS

BARONESS MARY SMIRNOFF, Associate of ISTD, AIChor. Ballet Teacher, Ballet Rambert School, Mercury Theatre, London. MSm

L. A. SMITH, BSc (Econ). Director of Consultative Services, Curriculum

Laboratory, University of London Goldsmiths' College. Formerly Headmaster, Mark House Secondary School. LAS

R. IRVINE SMITH, MA. Lecturer in Education, University of York; Hon. Secretary, General Studies Association. Editor of *Man and Societies; Examples of Experimental Courses in the Humanities*. RIS

FRANCES STEVENS, BA, PhD. Senior Lecturer, University of Leeds Institute of Education. Formerly Senior English Lecturer, Exhale Training College; Headmistress, Alderman Newton's Girls' School, Leicester. Author of *The Living Tradition: A Study of the Social and Educational Assumptions of the Grammar School*. FS

J. C. STONE, Dip Arch, ARIBA. Principal Assistant Architect, Essex County Council. Formerly Architect, Nottinghamshire County Council. JCS

GEOFFREY SUMMERFIELD. Lecturer in English and Education, University of York. Member of Secondary English Subcommittee, Schools Council. Author of *Topics in English; Voices; Creative English*. Co-editor of *Selected Poetry and Prose of John Clare*. GS

H. T. SWAIN, FRIBA, AA Dip. County Architect, Nottinghamshire County Council. HS

L. SYSON, DLC, MCollH. Head of Technical Studies, Sandbach School, Cheshire. Author of *British Watermills*. LS

A. L. TIBAWI, BA, PhD, DLit. Lecturer, Institute of Education, University of London. Formerly Chief Education Officer, Mandatory Palestine. Author of *British Interests in Palestine, 1800–1901: A Study of Educational and Religious Institutions; American Interests in Syria, 1800–1901: A Study of Educational, Literary and Religious Work; Russian Cultural Penetration of Syria and Palestine in the Nineteenth Century; Lectures on the History of the Arabs and Islam*, 2 vols (in Arabic). ALT

PROFESSOR J. W. TIBBLE, MA, MEd. Academic Secretary, Universities Council for the Education of Teachers. Formerly Professor of Education and Director of School of Education, University of Leicester. Author of *John Clare: A Life* (with Anne Tibble). Edited *The Poems of John Clare; The Study of Education*. JWT

NICHOLAS TUCKER, MA, PGCE, ABPsS. Educational Psychologist, ILEA. Formerly part-time Lecturer in Education, University of York. Author of *Understanding the Mass Media*. NT

PROFESSOR P. E. VERNON, MA, PhD, DSc. Professor of Educational Psychology, University of Calgary, Alberta, Canada. Formerly Professor of Psychology, Institute of Education, University of London. Author of *The Measurement of Abilities; Personnel Selection in the British Forces* (with J. B. Parry); *The Structure of Human Abilities; Personality Tests and Assessments; Intelligence and Attainment Tests; Personality Assessment: A Critical Survey*. PEV

J. C. WALTERS, BSc. Head of Mathematics Department, Middlesbrough College of Education. JCW

JACK WALTON, MA. Senior Staff Tutor, Institute of Education, Exeter University. Formerly Headmaster, Beaminster School, Dorset; Headmaster, Kingsway Secondary Modern School, Notts; Head of History Department, Great Barr Comprehensive School, Birmingham. JWa

JOHN E. WATSON, MA. Assistant Director, New Zealand Council for Educational Research. Author of *Intermediate Schooling in New Zealand; Horizons of Unknown Power—Some Issues of Maori Schooling*. JEW

JOSEPH WELTMAN, MA. Head of Programme Services, Independent Television Authority. Formerly Education Officer, ITA; Head of Schools Broadcasting, Granada TV; Programme Producer, BBC. JW

J. HELEN WHEELER, University of London Teachers' Certificate, Advanced Certificate in Child Development. Senior Lecturer in Education, Cheshire College of Education, Crewe. JHW

KEITH S. WHEELER, BSc, Cert Ed. Senior Lecturer in Geography, City of Leicester College of Education. Editor of *Geographical Fieldwork: a Handbook*. KSW

G. L. WILLIAMS, MA. Deputy Director, Unit for Economic and Statistical Studies on Higher Education, London School of Economics and Political Science. Formerly Principal Administrator, Organisation for Economic Co-operation and Development, Paris. GLW

DR IOLOWYN WILLIAMS, BSc, PhD, ARIC. Lecturer in Education, University College of Swansea, University of Wales. IWW

J. D. WILLIAMS, BSc. Officer in charge of the Section for Mathematical and Conceptual Studies, National Foundation for Educational Research. Author of *Mathematics Reform in the Primary School*. JDW

SHIRLEY WILLIAMS, MA. Minister of State, Department of Education and Science. Parliamentary Private Secretary, Minister of Health, 1964–6; Parliamentary Secretary, Ministry of Labour, 1966–7. SW

S. J. WILLIS, BSc (Agric). Director of Studies, Shuttleworth College, Biggleswade, Beds. Formerly Assistant Lecturer in Agricultural Science, Hertfordshire Institute of Agriculture. Author of *Weed Control in Farm and Garden*. SJW

DR MARY D. WILSON, BA, Dip Ed, PhD, LRAM. Staff Inspector for Special Education, ILEA. Senior Educational Psychologist, Borough of Ealing, 1949–56. Author of *Education of Brain Injured Children*. MW

K. L. WOODLAND, BA. Former Chairman, Chess Education Society. KLW

FRANK WORTHINGTON, DLC, Dip Ed, MEd. Head of the Education Department, City of Bath College of Education. Formerly Senior Lecturer in Handicraft, College of St Mark and St John, Chelsea. FW

ADVERTISEMENT SECTION

INDEX TO ADVERTISERS

	Page
Angus & Robertson	xvii
E. J. Arnold	xiv
Basil Blackwell & Mott Ltd.	xxiii
Anthony Blond Ltd.	xxii
Blond Educational Ltd.	viii
Jonathan Cape Publishers Ltd.	vii
Careers Research Advisory Committee	xii
Cornmarket Press Ltd.	iii
André Deutsch Ltd.	xv
Education Committees Year Book	vii
Encyclopaedia Britannica Ltd.	xiii
European Schoolbooks Ltd.	v
Evans Brothers Ltd.	x
Faber and Faber Ltd.	xvii
Ginn and Co. Ltd.	ix
Hachette	xx
L. Haig & Co. Ltd.	v
Hutchinson Publishers Ltd.	xvi
Macdonald Educational Ltd.	xxi
Methuen & Co. Ltd.	vi
Timothy Morgan Ltd.	iv
John Murray & Son Ltd.	xxi
M. Myers Ltd.	ix
New Science Publications Ltd.	xix
Pelham Books Ltd.	vi
Pitman & Co. Ltd.	x
Routledge & Kegan Paul Ltd.	xi
Rupert Hart Davis Ltd.	xvii
Sweet & Maxwell Ltd.	iv
The Teacher	xiii
John Wiley & Son Ltd.	xv

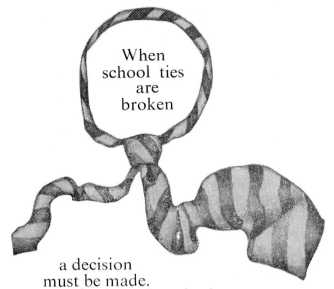

When
school ties
are
broken

a decision
must be made.
A career or further education?
In either case Cornmarket have a directory for you.

Careers for School Leavers

contains expert advice on all aspects of career planning and a survey of training requirements in the major professions. Details are given of opportunities offered by nearly 400 commercial, industrial and government organisations, trade associations and professional bodies. *Paperback and hardback editions*

Directory of Further Education

The first complete listing of technical colleges and their daytime courses. From accountancy to zoology, City and Guilds certificates to CNAA degrees, the directory lists more than 30,000 courses at 802 colleges in the United Kingdom. *Paperback and hardback editions*

Which University

lists every first degree course in every university in the United Kingdom, together with notes on accommodation, welfare, sport and amenities of university towns. *Paperback and hardback editions*

Directory of Postgraduate Courses and Opportunities

contains details of all longer term degree, diploma and certificate studies except medicine and dentistry. The directory lists the departments of universities and colleges engaged in postgraduate work and describes the major regulations in higher degrees in each university. *Paperback edition for undergraduates; hardback edition for general sale.*

Paperback editions 18s   hardback editions 42s

For further information please contact Nigel Cumming
Cornmarket Press Limited 42/43 Conduit Street London WIR ONL
Telephone 01-734 8282

BLOND EDUCATIONAL

Publications include—

PRIMARY

Assignment Cards
ALL AROUND YOU: AUTUMN
Maurice Jones
ALL OVER THE WORLD
Donald H. Gale

English
ALIVE ALIVE-O!
I. P. Jones and S. F. Jex
ALL TOGETHER! David J. Aitken
MAKE-A-PLAY BOOKS
David Oakden

Mathematics
THE DECIMAL STORY
Donald H. Gale

Science
JAM JAR SCIENCE S. H. Fisher

SECONDARY

English
ACTIVE ANTHOLOGIES
A. W. Rowe
DISCOVERY WITH BOOKS
A. Percival
EMERGENCY WARD 10 READERS
ENGLISH THROUGH
EXPERIENCE
A. W. Rowe and Peter Emmens
FIVE PLAYS FROM WRITE A
PLAY
GO READERS Martin Calman
JIM STARLING READERS
E. W. Hildick
READ, ACT, TALK, WRITE
C. E. Stuart-Jervis
SIMON AND DOROTHY
READERS Peter Emmens
SPACE AGE READERS S. S. Segal

Geography
GEOGRAPHICAL FIELDWORK
K. S. Wheeler and M. Harding

History
HISTORY ALIVE Peter Moss
MACHINES, MONEY AND MEN
D. P. Titley
TODAY IS HISTORY:
THE UNITED NATIONS
Katharine Savage
STRIKE OR BARGAIN?
David Williams
FROM OMDURMAN TO VE
DAY A. M. Gollin
A STATE OF WAR
Katharine Savage

PROTEST Michael O'Connor
CRIME AND SOCIETY
Ben Whitaker
I SWEAR AND VOW
Eric J. Trimmer
THE MONARCHY Roger Lockyer
THE PRESS Brian Inglis
THE WAGE PACKET P. Hanson
RUSSIA Brian Hammond
LAND OF THE FREE: THE USA
Meredith Hooper
LATIN AMERICA Simon Collier
MANCHESTER N. J. Frangopulo
GLASGOW J. R. Kellett
WORLD RELIGIONS F. G. Herod
TOWN STORY Edward Blishen

Mathematics
DECIMALS THROUGH
EXPERIENCE Michael Holt
HOUSEMATHS J. M. Jody
MATHEMATICS THROUGH
EXPERIENCE
Michael Holt and D. T. E. Marjoram
SPORTSMATHS J. M. Jody

Music
CLASSICAL SONGS FOR
CHILDREN
Countess of Harewood
and Ronald Duncan

Religious Instruction
THE CHRISTIAN ADVENTURE
H. G. Moses
OPERATION THINK
Donald Tytler

Science
LEARNING FOR LIVING
Ann Salway and Howell G. Moses
SCIENCE THROUGH
EXPERIENCE L. G. Humphrys

Technical
DESIGN IN METALWORK
R. L. Andrews and G. S. Dobbs
PROJECTS IN METALWORK
C. Gorham
TECHNICAL DRAWING M. Hirst

Inspection copies may be obtained
from
BLOND EDUCATIONAL
Iliffe House · Oadby · Leicester
56 Doughty Street · London WC1

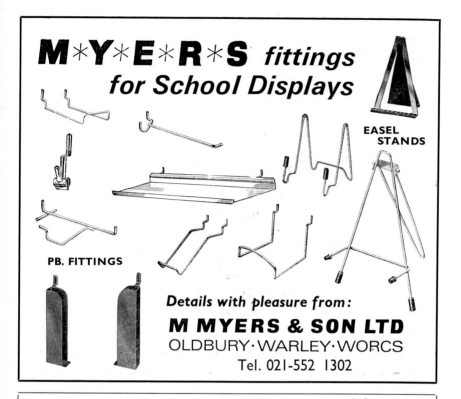

Routledge & Kegan Paul

are long-established as publishers for universities. The resources and experience of this academic publishing house are now being directed, additionally, to the publication of a wide range of exciting books for secondary schools and other institutions of further education.

The following titles form the basis of just one of the new series in this rapidly expanding programme. We would be pleased to supply inspection copies of textbooks and descriptive catalogues in any of the major school subjects to lecturers and secondary school teachers.

Outlines for the Intending Student

Conceived primarily as guidebooks for sixth formers and other intending students, the *Outline Books* provide clear and detailed surveys of the scope and content of the major university subjects. Written by experts, they offer authoritative and stimulating source material for discussion in liberal and general studies course and are also recommended for career guidance.

Political Studies
Edited by PROFESSOR H. VICTOR WISEMAN   21s   *Paper* 12s 6d

Law
Edited by PROFESSOR R. H. GRAVESON   25s   *Paper* 13s 6d

The Social Sciences
Edited by PROFESSOR DAVID C. MARSH   20s   *Paper* 10s 6d

Psychology
Edited by PROFESSOR JOHN COHEN   25s   *Paper* 12s 6d

Philosophy
Edited by PROFESSOR R. J. HIRST   25s   *Paper* 13s

Teachers of General and Liberal Studies
are invited to write for inspection copies
68 Carter Lane, London EC4

CRAC

The Careers Research and Advisory Centre

The Careers Research and Advisory Centre is an independent educational charity. Its wide range of publications and services include the following:

GUIDES TO DEGREE COURSES IN THE UK - 44 booklets each containing about 40 pages analysing the content and variation between degree courses DESTINATION BUSINESS - a description of the routes to full professional qualification in business THE CBI YEARBOOK OF EDUCATION AND TRAINING OPPORTUNITIES - 'a comprehensive guide showing the relationship between A-levels degrees and occupations MIDDLE SCHOOL CHOICE - a guide for pupils choosing their O-levels UPPER SCHOOL CHOICE - a guide for pupils choosing their A-levels BEYOND A DEGREE - introductory guide lines for the undergraduate approaching the problem of choosing a career and for the sixth former showing the possible career implications of Beyond a Degree subjects.

CRAC publishes more than sixty books and booklets each year. A full list will be sent on application. In addition CRAC runs Seminars and Study Courses for teachers, employers and other professional advisers on careers.

The Careers Research and Advisory Centre

Bateman Street Cambridge

CB2 1LZ

Hutchinson Educational

This imprint within the Hutchinson Group now includes a School
Book division, a Scientific and Technical division, and the Hutchinson
University Library. It offers a wide range of educational
books for Secondary Schools, Technical Institutions and Universities.

School Book Division

Among the particularly successful books published are the anthologies,
Here Today and **Billy the Kid** ; school editions of **The Diary of Anne Frank** and
The Day of the Triffids ; J. C. Mathews, **A Modern Chemistry Course** ; the
Advanced Geographies and the **New Visual Geographies ;** the **Portraits and
Documents** series for historians ; and Margaret Coulthard's
French books at O and A level.

Scientific and Technical Division

Among the many outstanding titles are to be found Barnaby's **Basic
Naval Architecture** ; Blaxter's **The Energy Metabolism of Ruminants** ; Titcomb's
Fundamentals of Engineering Science ; Abercrombie's **The Anatomy of
Judgement** ; Bishop's **An Outline of Crystal Morphology** ; and Hillier and
Pittuck's **Fundamentals of Motor Vehicle Technology**.

Hutchinson University Library

The library now consists of over 160 titles, arranged in 18 sections, each
section edited by an eminent scholar. There are particularly strong lists of
titles in Biology, Economics, English, Geography, History and Philosophy.
Many of the titles are now available as attractive student paperbacks.

For further information, catalogues, specialised lists etc., write to

Hutchinson Educational Ltd.,

178-202, Great Portland Street, London, W.1.

Rupert Hart-Davis
Educational Publications

French for Primary Schools
FRERE JACQUES

Commissioned by the French Government and developed by BELC (Bureau d'Etude de la Langue et Civilisation Française) this course was perfected by more than four years of experiment and validation in British schools.

Vocabulary, grammatical concepts, the rate of progression, the nature of the audio-visual element and the reading and writing materials were subjected to an exhaustive process of testing and modification before they were accepted in their final form.

The components of the course are a simple and flexible range of visual, audio and pupils' materials. Learning the spoken language precedes learning the written language. The pupil learns first to listen and to speak and then, towards the end of the first year, he begins to learn to read and write.

English for Foreign Students
ENGLISH FAST

An audio-lingual course in four levels. Each level consists of a student's book and a set of tapes which can be used either in a language laboratory or the classroom. These materials give students aural and oral practice in the structures of spoken English from the initial to an advanced stage. The course is an essential complement to the work covered by main course books.

Details and sample material will be sent on application.

Send also for our catalogues of books for the classroom and school library.

Rupert Hart-Davis Educational Publications
3 Upper James Street Golden Square London W1
Telephone 01-734 8080
One of the Granada Publishing Group